THE ROUTLEDGE HANDBOOK OF PARLIAMENTARY ADMINISTRATIONS

The Routledge Handbook of Parliamentary Administrations brings together an international, multidisciplinary group of contributors providing a systematic and comprehensive analysis of parliamentary administrations.

Including chapters on the administrations of national parliaments in every member state of the European Union, in most of the EU candidate countries and in key liberal democracies around the world, this book represents a uniquely broad-ranging resource. Each national system is treated in a consistent manner, with authors providing relevant facts, figures and critical analysis according to a common framework. Additionally, it provides coverage of transnational parliamentary administrations in different regions around the globe and includes a number of cross-cutting chapters, addressing key issues of relevance for a better understanding of parliamentary administrations such as the potential for politicisation, professionalisation, digitalisation or Europeanisation with the comparative analysis of different national experiences. This handbook will enable readers to better comprehend the role and influence of parliamentary administrations and in doing so will enhance our understanding of their importance for the effective functioning of representative democracy more generally.

The Routledge Handbook of Parliamentary Administrations constitutes a unique tool and prime reference for any researcher, scholar or practitioner working in the area of parliamentary and legislative studies, governance, democracy, public policy and administration, as well as more widely to European studies, general political science and comparative politics.

Thomas Christiansen is a Professor of Political Science and European Integration at LUISS University, Italy.

Elena Griglio is a Senior Parliamentary Official of the Italian Senate and teaches Comparative Public Law at LUISS University, Italy.

Nicola Lupo is a Professor of Public Law and Director of the Center for Parliamentary Studies (CESP) at LUISS University, Italy.

"Parliamentary administrations assure that legislatures' formal authority translates into de facto power. The editors provide unique insights on parliamentary administrations worldwide. Historical trajectories, institutional capabilities and current challenges are systematically compared. An overdue Public Administration complement to Parliamentary Studies."

Michael W. Bauer, *European University Institute, Florence, Italy.*

"A major contribution to an overlooked, but key element of the political system. This volume breaks new ground in the range of questions it addresses and the systematic analysis it undertakes. An impressive feature is that it extends beyond the 'usual suspects' in making its selection of cases."

Hussein Kassim, *University of East Anglia, United Kingdom.*

"This handbook highlights the central importance of administrative resources within democratic legislatures through a broad array of case studies and a careful selection of comparative thematic chapters. The volume provides a new and invaluable resource for comparative research on the quality, capacity and evolution of administrative organization in legislatures."

Amie Kreppel, *Professor and Jean Monnet Chair, University of Florida, USA.*

THE ROUTLEDGE HANDBOOK OF PARLIAMENTARY ADMINISTRATIONS

Edited by Thomas Christiansen, Elena Griglio and Nicola Lupo

LONDON AND NEW YORK

Cover image: © Getty Images

First published 2023
by Routledge
4 Park Square, Milton Park, Abingdon, Oxon OX14 4RN

and by Routledge
605 Third Avenue, New York, NY 10158

Routledge is an imprint of the Taylor & Francis Group, an informa business

© 2023 selection and editorial matter, Thomas Christiansen, Elena Griglio and Nicola Lupo; individual chapters, the contributors

The right of Thomas Christiansen, Elena Griglio and Nicola Lupo to be identified as the authors of the editorial material, and of the authors for their individual chapters, has been asserted in accordance with sections 77 and 78 of the Copyright, Designs and Patents Act 1988.

All rights reserved. No part of this book may be reprinted or reproduced or utilised in any form or by any electronic, mechanical, or other means, now known or hereafter invented, including photocopying and recording, or in any information storage or retrieval system, without permission in writing from the publishers.

Trademark notice: Product or corporate names may be trademarks or registered trademarks, and are used only for identification and explanation without intent to infringe.

British Library Cataloguing-in-Publication Data
A catalogue record for this book is available from the British Library

ISBN: 978-1-032-02024-2 (hbk)
ISBN: 978-1-032-02027-3 (pbk)
ISBN: 978-1-003-18152-1 (ebk)

DOI: 10.4324/9781003181521

Typeset in Bembo
by KnowledgeWorks Global Ltd.

CONTENTS

List of Figures	*xi*
List of Tables	*xiv*
Notes on Editors	*xvi*
Notes on Contributors	*xviii*
Foreword by Lord Philip Norton	*xxiii*
Preface	*xxv*
List of Abbreviations	*xxvii*

1 Introduction: A Global Perspective on the Role of Parliamentary Administrations *Thomas Christiansen, Elena Griglio and Nicola Lupo*	1

PART I
Cross-cutting Analyses of Parliamentary Administrations — 17

2 A Distinct Role for Parliamentary Administrations in Presidential and Parliamentary Systems? *Cristina Fasone*	19
3 The Internal Administrative Structure and the Relationship with the Speaker *Luigi Gianniti and Rosella Di Cesare*	38
4 The Administration of Bicameral Parliaments *Elena Griglio and Nicola Lupo*	52
5 The Europeanization of Parliamentary Administrations *Anna-Lena Högenauer*	75

6 Parliamentary Diplomacy 88
Jonathan Murphy

7 Parliamentary Administration Facing the Digital Challenge 105
Fotios Fitsilis and Olivier Costa

8 Parliamentary Administrations and the Provision of Scientific Expertise 121
Giovanni Rizzoni

PART II
Administrations of National Parliaments 135

PART II.I
In the EU 137

9 Austria's Parliamentary Administration 139
Christoph Konrath, Johannes Pollak and Peter Slominski

10 Belgium's Parliamentary Administration 152
Pieter Dirck G. Caboor and Patricia Popelier

11 Bulgaria's Parliamentary Administration 163
Martin Belov

12 Croatia's Parliamentary Administration 176
Jelena Špiljak

13 Cyprus' Parliamentary Administration 187
Natia Karayianni

14 Czechia's Parliamentary Administration 199
Petr Kaniok

15 Denmark's Parliamentary Administration 211
Helene Helboe Pedersen

16 Estonia's Parliamentary Administration 222
Leif Kalev, Ott Lumi and Tõnis Saarts

17 Finland's Parliamentary Administration 233
Tapio Raunio

18	France's Parliamentary Administration *Angela Tacea*	243
19	Germany's Parliamentary Administration *Felix Arndt, Anna-Lena Högenauer and Claus Koggel*	255
20	Greece's Parliamentary Administration *Fotios Fitsilis*	268
21	Hungary's Parliamentary Administration *Zsolt Szabo*	281
22	Ireland's Parliamentary Administration *Mellissa English and Tara Murphy*	291
23	Italy's Parliamentary Administration *Luigi Gianniti and Nicola Lupo*	306
24	Latvia's Parliamentary Administration *Daunis Auers and Visvaldis Valtenbergs*	320
25	Lithuania's Parliamentary Administration *Modestas Gelbūda*	331
26	Luxembourg's Parliamentary Administration *Astrid Spreitzer*	344
27	Malta's Parliamentary Administration *Mark Harwood*	355
28	The Netherlands' Parliamentary Administration *Afke Groen*	365
29	Poland's Parliamentary Administration *Maciej Serowaniec*	378
30	Portugal's Parliamentary Administration *Ana Vargas, Bruno Dias Pinheiro and Teresa Fonseca*	391
31	Romania's Parliamentary Administration *Alexandra Alina Iancu*	403

32 Slovakia's Parliamentary Administration 413
    Natália Švecová

33 Slovenia's Parliamentary Administration 425
    Alenka Krašovec

34 Spain's Parliamentary Administration 435
    Mario Kölling and Ignacio Molina

35 Sweden's Parliamentary Administration 447
    Ingvar Mattson and Thomas Larue

PART II.II
In the Wider Europe **461**

36 Albania's Parliamentary Administration 463
    Afrim Krasniqi

37 Bosnia and Herzegovina's Parliamentary Administration 476
    Damir Kapidžić and Lejla Tafro-Sefić

38 Iceland's Parliamentary Administration 487
    Þorsteinn Magnússon

39 Montenegro's Parliamentary Administration 499
    Dražen Malović and Mirko Mijanović

40 North Macedonia's Parliamentary Administration 511
    Vlora Rechica

41 Norway's Parliamentary Administration 522
    Hilmar Rommetvedt

42 Serbia's Parliamentary Administration 534
    Davor Jančić

43 Switzerland's Parliamentary Administration 547
    Andreas Ladner

44 Turkey's Parliamentary Administration 557
    Damla Cihangir-Tetik and Selin Türkeş-Kılıç

45	United Kingdom's Parliamentary Administration *Alexandra Meakin, Ben Yong and Cristina Leston-Bandeira*	570

PART II.III
Worldwide — **581**

46	Argentina's Parliamentary Administration *María Paula Bertino*	583
47	Australia's Parliamentary Administration *Valerie Barrett*	597
48	Brazil's Parliamentary Administration *Fabiano Santos and Fernando Saboia Vieira*	611
49	Canada's Parliamentary Administration *Jonathan Malloy*	624
50	India's Parliamentary Administration *Milind Thakar*	635
51	Israel's Parliamentary Administration *Susan Hattis Rolef*	644
52	Japan's Parliamentary Administration *Karol Żakowski*	656
53	Korea's Parliamentary Administration *Youngah Guahk*	666
54	Mexico's Parliamentary Administration *Fernando Nieto-Morales*	678
55	South Africa's Parliamentary Administration *Timothy Paul Layman*	689
56	Tunisia's Parliamentary Administration *Faten Sliti*	699
57	The United States Congressional Administration *B. Guy Peters*	713

PART III
The Transnational Dimension of Parliamentary Administration 723

58 European Parliament's Administration 725
   Francis Jacobs and Alfredo De Feo

59 Global and Regional Perspectives on Transnational Parliamentary
   Administrations 738
   Davor Jančić

Index 752

FIGURES

5.1	The number of EU experts in national parliaments (2021)	78
8.1	Web portal of the House of Commons Library	128
8.2	Web portal of the Italian Chamber of Deputies research service	129
8.3	2030 agenda Sustainable Development Goals	129
9.1	Budget development 2010–2020	142
9.2	Staff 2010–2020	142
10.1	Political component of the House of Representatives	154
10.2	Administrative component of the House of Representatives	156
12.1	Organizational chart of the Croatian Parliament	178
15.1	Organizational chart of the parliament administration	213
15.2	The resources of Folketing's administration 2007–2019	214
15.3	Academic staff and procedures for recruitment	214
16.1	Structure of the Chancellery of Riigikogu	225
18.1	The organization of the General Secretariat of the Assemblée nationale and of the Presidency	245
18.2	The General Secretariat of the Questure	246
18.3	The organization of the administrative structures of the Sénat	247
18.4	Organization of the common services	248
19.1	The administration of the Bundestag	257
19.2	Organizational structure of the Bundesrat	259
20.1	Evolution of budget size and number of personnel, from 2004 to 2021, in Greece	270
22.1	The Oireachtas' organizational chart	294
24.1	Structure of the *Saeima* Administration	322
24.2	*Saeima* Administration employees 2006–2020	323
24.3	Annual *Saeima* budget 2006–2020 (millions, EUR)	323
25.1	Organizational structure chart of the Seimas administration (Lithuania)	335
26.1	Size of parliamentary administration in the Luxembourg chamber of deputies, 2001–2021 (n, FTE)	345
26.2	Total expenditures and staff costs, 2001–2019 (in million)	345

Figures

26.3	Organisational chart of the parliamentary administration in the Luxembourg chamber of deputies (2021)	346
26.4	Number of staff per service and percentage of staff attributed to political support work and specialized support services, 2021	347
27.1	The Maltese parliament's governance structure	357
28.1	Evolution of the budget for scrutiny and legislation of the Dutch House of Representatives and the Senate (2002–2021)	366
28.2	Percentage of total budget earmarked for apparatus, research, and party groups in the Dutch House of Representatives (2007–2021)	367
28.3	Organogram of the Dutch House of Representatives (2021)	369
28.4	Division of staff members across three main administrative branches of the administration of the Dutch House of Representation (2021–2022)	370
29.1	Organizational chart of the Chancellery of the Sejm	379
29.2	Organizational chart of the Chancellery of the Senate	380
30.1	Graph of development of staff size of the *Assembleia da República*	392
30.2	Organizational chart of the *Assembleia do República*	395
31.1	The budget of the Romanian Chamber of Deputies – Camera Deputaţilor	407
32.1	Average number of employees of the National Council of the Slovak Republic	414
32.2	Evolution of the size of the parliamentary administration in Slovakia	416
33.1	Organizational chart of the Državni zbor in 2021	427
34.1	Evolution of the budget of the Cortes Generales (2004–2019) in euros	441
35.1	Annual workforce (line/left scale) and budget (millions SEK – stacks/right scale) of the Riksdag Administration	448
35.2	Riksdag Administration	449
35.3	Number of interpellations (dotted line) and no. of plenary hours (stacks)	450
35.4	Number of private members motions (line/right axis), Government bills (light grey) and committee reports (dark grey)	451
35.5	Number of total inquiry assignments to the Research Services of the Riksdag (and source of the assignments)	453
37.1	Organization chart of the Secretariat of the PABiH	480
39.1	Number of employees 2006–2021 in the Parliamentary Service of Montenegro	501
40.1	The progression of the assembly staff size over the years, North Macedonia	516
40.2	Sector for support of the Council of the Assembly TV Channel	517
41.1	Organizational chart of the Norwegian Storting's administration (2019)	524
41.2	MPs and staff resources in the Storting (1971–2020)	529
41.3	Parliamentary questioning by type of questions (1945–2021)	530
41.4	Number of private members' bills and proposal submitted (1984–2021)	530
41.5	Per cent of committee recommendations with dissenting remarks (1945–2013)	531
44.1	Organizational chart of the administrative structure of the GNAT	562
45.1	House of Commons—governance structure	573
45.2	House of Lord—governance structure	574
47.1	Parliamentary departments staffing growth: 2004–05 to 2019–20	600
47.2	Parliamentary departments funding growth: 2004–05 to 2020–21	601
47.3	Parliament of Australia: governance and senior executive structure	605
50.1	Lok Sabha and Rajya Sabha secretariat organization chart	637
51.1	Knesset administration chart (2021)	645
52.1	Organizational structure of the Shūgiin Secretariat	657

52.2	Organizational structure of the Sangiin Secretariat	658
52.3	Number of staff of the Shūgiin and the Sangiin Secretariats	659
53.1	Korean Assembly bills statistics	673
54.1	Organizational chart of the administration of the Mexican Chamber of Deputies	681
54.2	Organizational chart of the administration of the Mexican Senate	682
54.3	Annual budget of the Mexican Congress (2011–2021). NB. Vertical lines mark the beginning/end of legislative terms	686
55.1	The current macro structure of the Parliamentary Administration of South Africa	692
55.2	Parliamentary staffing and funding over a ten year period (Parliament Republic of South Africa, Annual Report, 2011 – 2020)	693
58.1	Ratios EP managers and all staff related to MEPs (in %)	729
58.2	Gender equality in the EP 2021	730

TABLES

2.1	Forms of government vis-à-vis budgetary autonomy, parliamentary staff's size, status, and system of recruitment	24
3.1	Organization of parliaments and presence of the SG	42
3.2	Types of SG appointment procedures	44
4.1	Overview of administrative arrangements in bicameral parliaments	56
5.1	Committees responsible for EU affairs scrutiny	79
5.2	Staff support for sectoral committees	80
5.3	The role of staff in EU affairs scrutiny	82
13.1	Services of the House of Representatives	190
13.2	Comparative view of the personnel of the House	191
14.1	Number of staffs in Senát and in Poslanecká sněmovna	202
14.2	Staff training in SC	203
14.3	Overview of SC main activities	204
14.4	Overview of citizens' requests for information between 2005 and 2020	205
15.1	List of parliamentary networks	218
16.1	General trends in personnel	226
21.1	Budget and number of employees (2010–2021)	283
22.1	Staffing levels in the Service	293
24.1	Number of studies carried out by the Analytical Service 2017–2022	324
25.1	Structure of employees	332
25.2	Employment dynamics at the parliamentary administration	333
25.3	The annual budgets from 2001 to 2021	333
25.4	Comparison of the legislative activities in different parliamentary terms of the Seimas	338
25.5	The standing committee secretariats activity report for 2021	339
29.1	The expenditures of the Chancellery of the Sejm and Chancellery of the Senate (2000–2020, in thousand PLN)	384
29.2	Number of employees in the Chancellery of the Sejm and Chancellery of the Senate (2000–2020)	388
30.1	Dimension of the parliamentary staff	392
32.1	Selected aspects of employment statistics	415

33.1	Number of employees in the Državni zbor administration (1992–2020)	427
33.2	Number of people employed in PPGs (1992–2020)	432
34.1	Human resources of Congress and Senat (2020)	439
34.2	Evolution of staff assigned to political groups and individual members 2000 and 2020	440
36.1	The number of employees of the Assembly 2002–2021	465
36.2	Parliamentary services (in %)	466
36.3	The administrative structure of the assembly in the years 2018–2021	467
36.4	Budget assembly (2010–2020)	471
37.1	Number of staff in the Secretariat	478
38.1	The main functions of the Secretariat's organizational units	489
38.2	The highest level of management by gender 2000–2020	490
38.3	The size and gender composition of the Althingi staff 2000–2020	490
38.4	The Althingi's staff turnover rate in 2005–2020	491
41.1	The standing committees of the Norwegian Storting	528
41.2	Parties, MPs and administrative personnel in the Norwegian Storting (selected years)	529
42.1	The Legislation Sector within the National Assembly of Serbia	537
42.2	Serbian National Assembly delegations to international parliamentary institutions	541
44.1	Total number of the staff member of the GNAT (NTV-MSNBC, 2000; Pakdil, 2009; The Journal of the Committee on Planning and Budget, 2019; 2020)	562
44.2	Total number of the staff member of the GNAT and their units by December 2020	563
44.3	Number of inter-parliamentary friendship groups of the GNAT	566
45.1	Departments within the parliamentary administration	576
47.1	Main functions of the chamber departments	601
47.2	Main functions of the Department of Parliamentary Services	602
47.3	Governance and oversight mechanisms in the Australian Parliament	603
50.1	The Lok Sabha's senior officers	638
51.1	Number of positions in the Knesset (excluding Knesset Guard) 2000–2019	651
51.2	Number of positions in the Knesset Guard 2003–2019	651
56.1	Evolution of the organization of the Tunisian administration	703
57.1	Congressional staff members (1979–2015)	714
57.2	Staffing in the US congress, 2015	715
57.3	Congressional Staff Members 1979–2015	719
57.4	Annual Maximum Pay for Selected Staff in House Member's Offices, 2001–2019	720
58.1	Functional distribution of EP staff and contractual agents 2019	728

EDITORS

Thomas Christiansen is a Professor of Political Science and European Integration at LUISS University, Rome. He previously held positions at Maastricht University, at the European Institute of Public Administration, at Aberystwyth University of Wales and at Essex University. He is Executive Editor of the Journal of European Integration and co-editor (with Sophie Vanhoonacker) of the "European Administration Governance" book series at Palgrave Macmillan. He has published widely on different aspects of European Union politics. He recently co-authored, with Emil Kirchner and Uwe Wissenbach, the European Union and China (London: Palgrave, 2019) and co-edited, with Diane Fromage, Brexit and Democracy – The Role of Parliaments in the United Kingdom and the European Union (London: Palgrave, 2019). The Contestation of Expertise in the European Union (London: Palgrave), co-edited with Johan Adriaensen and Vigjilenca Abazi, The Making of European Security Policy, co-edited with Roberta Haar, Sabina Lange and Sophie Vanhoonacker (London: Routledge) and Security Relations between the European Union and its Asian Partners, co-edited with Emil Kirchner and Tan See Seng (London: Palgrave), were published in 2021.

Elena Griglio is a Senior Parliamentary Official of the Italian Senate. She teaches Comparative Public Law and Security Law and Constitutional Protection at LUISS University, Rome. PhD in Public Law, University of Turin, she has been postdoc Fellow in Public Comparative Law at the Luiss University and Visiting Fellow at the European University Institute – School of Transnational Governance. In 2020, she obtained the national scientific qualification as second-level professor in the Sector 12/E2 "Comparative Law". She recently authored the monograph "Parliamentary oversight of the executives. Tools and procedures in Europe", Oxford, Hart Publishing, 2020.

Nicola Lupo is a Professor of Public Law and Director of the Center for Parliamentary Studies (CESP), LUISS University, Rome. He holds a PhD from the University of Florence. He has been parliamentary advisor to the Chamber of Deputies, research assistant at the Italian Constitutional Court and advisor to the Minister of Economy and Finance. Currently, he coordinates the Italian Prime Minister's "Unit for the rationalisation and improvement of regulation", for the purpose of implementing the National Recovery and

Resilience Plan (NRRP). He has held a Jean Monnet Chair in parliamentary democracy in Europe and is visiting professor at Nicolaus Copernicus University, Law and Administration Faculty, Torun (Poland). His publications include a handbook on the Italian Parliament (*Corso di diritto parlamentare*, III ed., Il mulino, 2018, with Luigi Gianniti) and a book on the Italian Constitution (*The Constitution of Italy. A Contextual Analysis*, Hart, 2022, with Marta Cartabia).

CONTRIBUTORS

Felix Arndt is the ECPRD Correspondent and Head of Research Section WD 8 (Environment, Nature Conservation, Nuclear Safety, Education and Research) at the German Bundestag.

Daunis Auers is a Professor at the Department of Politics, University of Latvia.

Valerie Barrett is a former senior executive in the Australian Parliamentary Service and former Visiting Fellow at the Australian National University.

Martin Belov is a Professor in Constitutional and Comparative Constitutional Law at the University of Sofia "St. Kliment Ohridski", Bulgaria.

María Paula Bertino is a Political Science PhD for the National University of General San Martin (UNSAM) and a tenured professor in the University of Buenos Aires, Argentina.

Pieter Dirck G. Caboor is the Deputy Director for Legal Affairs at the Belgian Federal House of Representatives, Brussels.

Damla Cihangir-Tetik is an Assistant Professor at Faculty of Political Sciences, Department of Political Science and International Relations of Istanbul University, Turkey.

Olivier Costa is a CNRS Research Professor at the CEVIPOF (Sciences Po, Paris), and Director of European Political and Governance Studies at the College of Europe (Bruges).

Alfredo De Feo is a Professor at the Collegio Europeo in Parma, Italy, and Fellow at the Robert Schuman Centre for Advanced Studies (RSCAS) at the European University Institute, Florence, Italy.

Bruno Dias Pinheiro is a Permanent Member of the COSAC Secretariat and former Permanent Representative of the Portuguese Parliament to the EU institutions.

Rosella Di Cesare is an Advisor at the Senate of the Italian Republic, Rome, Italy.

Contributors

Mellissa English is the Chief Parliamentary Legal Adviser to the House of the Oireachtas, Dublin, Ireland.

Cristina Fasone is an Associate Professor of Comparative Public Law, Department of Political Science, Luiss University, Rome, Italy.

Fotios Fitsilis works for the Scientific Service of the Hellenic Parliament, Athens, Greece.

Teresa Fonseca is the Contents Coordinator of the Communication Office of the Portuguese Parliament, Lisbon, Portugal.

Modestas Gelbūda is the Secretary General at the Seimas administration and, in a part-time capacity, Professor at ISM University of Management and Economics in Lithuania.

Luigi Gianniti is a Professor of Parliamentary Law at the University of Roma Tre and Director of the Research Service of the Senate of the Italian Republic, Rome, Italy.

Afke Groen is a Researcher at the Hans van Mierlo Foundation, The Hague, the Netherlands.

Youngah Guahk is a Lecturer in Asian Affairs at Luiss University, Rome, Italy.

Mark Harwood is an Associate Professor and Director at the Institute for European Studies of the University of Malta, Tal-Qroqq, Malta.

Anna-Lena Högenauer is a Deputy Head of Institute of Political Science at the University of Luxembourg.

Alexandra Alina Iancu is an Associate Professor at the University of Bucharest, Faculty of Political Science.

Francis Jacobs is an Adjunct Senior Research Fellow at University College Dublin, Ireland, and a Visiting Professor at the Collegio Europeo in Parma, Italy.

Davor Jančić is a Senior Lecturer at the Department of Law, Queen Mary University of London, United Kingdom.

Leif Kalev is a Professor of State and Citizenship Theory, Tallinn University, Estonia.

Petr Kaniok is an Associate Professor at the Department of International Relations of Masaryk University, Brno, Czech Republic.

Damir Kapidžić is an Associate Professor of Political Science at the University of Sarajevo, Bosnia and Herzegovina.

Natia Karayianni is a Clerk to Parliamentary Committees at the Cyprus House of Representatives, Nicosia.

Claus Koggel is the Head of the Parliamentary Relations Division of the German Bundesrat.

Contributors

Mario Kölling is an Assistant Professor at the Department of Political Science at the Spanish National Distance Education University (UNED), Madrid, Spain.

Christoph Konrath is the Head of the department Research and Support in Parliamentary Matters in the Austrian Parliamentary Administration, Vienna, Austria.

Afrim Krasniqi is a Professor and Director of Institute of History (IH) and Institute for Political Studies (ISP), Tirana, Albania.

Alenka Krašovec is a Professor of Political Science at the Faculty of Social Sciences, University of Ljubljana, Slovenia.

Andreas Ladner is a Professor of Political Science at the Swiss Graduate School of Public Administration (IDHEAP) at the University of Lausanne, Switzerland.

Thomas Larue is the Director of the Riksdag's Evaluation and Research Secretariat (ERS), Stockholm, Sweden.

Timothy Paul Layman is a Manager of Policy Analysis and Evaluation at the Legislative Sector Support (LSS), Parliament of the Republic of South Africa.

Cristina Leston-Bandeira is a Professor of Politics at the University of Leeds, United Kingdom.

Ott Lumi is a PhD candidate in Government and Politics, Tallinn University, Estonia.

Þorsteinn Magnússon is a Deputy Secretary General of Althingi Parliament House, Reykjavík, Iceland.

Jonathan Malloy is the Honourable Dick and Ruth Bell Chair in Canadian Parliamentary Democracy and Professor in the Department of Political Science at Carleton University, Canada.

Dražen Malović is the Head of the Department of Legal, Personnel and Administrative Affairs.

Ingvar Mattson is a Secretary General of the Riksdag of Sweden, Stockholm.

Alexandra Meakin is a lecturer in Politics at the University of Leeds.

Mirko Mijanovič is the Head of the HR Bureau in the Parliamentary Service of Montenegro, Podgoriça.

Ignacio Molina is a Senior Analyst at the Elcano Royal Institute and Lecturer at the Department of Politics and International Relations at the Universidad Autónoma de Madrid, Spain.

Contributors

Jonathan Murphy is the Head of Programme for INTER PARES at the International Institute for Democracy and Electoral Assistance (International IDEA), Stockholm, Sweden.

Tara Murphy is a Legal Adviser to the Houses of the Oireachtas, Dublin, Ireland.

Fernando Nieto-Morales is an Associate Professor of Public Administration at the Centre for International Studies of El Colegio de México, Mexico.

Helene Helboe Pedersen is a Professor of Political Science at Aarhus University, Denmark.

B. Guy Peters is a Maurice Falk Professor of American Government at the University of Pittsburgh, United States.

Johannes Pollak is a Professor of Political Science at and Rector of Webster Vienna Private University, Senior Fellow at the Austrian Institute for Advanced Studies (on leave) and Chairman of the Board at the Institute of European Politics (IEP), Berlin.

Patricia Popelier is a Professor at the Law Faculty and Director of the Research Group of Government and Law at the University of Antwerp, Belgium.

Tapio Raunio is a Professor of Political Science at the Faculty of Management and Business, Tampere University, Finland.

Vlora Rechica is a Researcher and Head of the Centre for Parliamentary Support and Democratization at the Institute for Democracy "Societas Civilis" Skopje (IDSCS), North Macedonia.

Giovanni Rizzoni is the Head of the Research Department at the Italian Chamber of Deputies, Rome, Italy.

Susan Hattis Rolef is a Retired senior researcher in the Knesset's Research and Information Center, Jerusalem, Israel.

Hilmar Rommetvedt is a Research Professor at NORCE Norwegian Research Centre, and Adjunct Professor at the University of Stavanger, Norway, retired.

Tõnis Saarts is an Associate Professor of Comparative Politics at the School of Governance, Law and Society of Tallinn University, Estonia.

Fernando Saboia Vieira is a Political Scientist and Former Staff Member of the Brazilian Chamber of Deputies, Brasilia, Brazil.

Fabiano Santos is an Associate Professor of Political Science at Institute of Social and Political Studies at the State University of Rio de Janeiro (IESP-UERJ), Brazil.

Contributors

Maciej Serowaniec is an Associate Professor at the Department of Constitutional Law of Nicolaus Copernicus University, Torun, Poland.

Faten Sliti is a Director of International Cooperation Department of Assemblée des Représentants du Peuple, Tunis, Tunisia.

Peter Slominski is an Assistant Professor at the Department of Political Science/Centre for European Integration Research, University of Vienna, Austria.

Jelena Špiljak is the Head of Secretariat of the European Affairs Committee of the Croatian Parliament, Zagreb, Croatia.

Astrid Spreitzer is a PhD candidate at the University of Luxembourg and research associate at the Chair on parliamentary studies of the Luxembourgish Chamber of Deputies.

Natália Švecová is a Director of the Parliamentary Institute and Chancellery of the National Council of the Slovak Republic, Bratislava.

Zsolt Szabo is an Associate Professor of Constitutional Law at the Károli Gáspár University of the Reformed Church and a Senior Research Fellow at Ludovika University of Public Service (Budapest), Budapest, Hungary.

Angela Tacea is an FWO (Research Foundation Flanders) postdoctoral fellow at the Vrije Universiteit Brussel, Belgium.

Lejla Tafro-Sefić is the Head of the Information and Documentation Department at the Secretariat of the Parliamentary Assembly of Bosnia and Herzegovina.

Milind Thakar is a Professor of International Relations at the University of Indianapolis, United States.

Selin Türkeş-Kılıç is an Associate Professor at the Department of Political Science and International Relations and EUDIOC Jean Monnet Module Coordinator at Yeditepe University, Turkey.

Visvaldis Valtenbergs is an Associate Professor at the University of Latvia.

Ana Vargas is the Adviser to the Communication office at the Portuguese Parliament, Lisbon, Portugal.

Ben Yong is an Associate Professor in Public Law and Human Rights at the University of Durham, United Kingdom.

Karol Zakowski is an Associate Professor at the Department of Asian Studies, Faculty of International and Political Studies, University of Lodz, Poland.

FOREWORD

Legislatures are core national institutions. From an institutional perspective, they are powerful bodies. Executives need them to legitimize their policies, translating political wishes into binding measures, and to approve budgets. Achieving their assent may not always be difficult politically, but it may be time-consuming and onerous, especially with highly institutionalized bodies. But they are also typically much more than law-effecting bodies. They are multi-functional and functionally adaptable bodies. Even in non-democratic regimes, legislatures can have a number of consequences for the system, including serving as a safety valve for popular feelings or ensuring the views of constituents and expressed to those in power.

Though scholarship on legislatures is a poor relative of the studies undertaken of executive power, there is now a solid library on legislatures, especially individual legislatures. Truly comparative studies are rarer. Scholarship is extending beyond purely the formal functions to encompass a wider array of consequences that legislatures have for their political systems. Empirical and sometimes highly quantitative analyses have been undertaken of legislative behaviour. However, the focus has been on the public and formal, primarily what goes in the chamber and committee rooms. Such behaviour is observable and measurable. It occurs within a clear and structured institutional framework. There are rules, agenda and presiding officers.

What has not matched this scholarship has been examination of what happens away from the public arena. There are two major dimensions to this activity that merit attention.

One is what members do outside the chamber and committee rooms. Parliamentarians are not discrete entities that simply come into the legislature to speak and vote. They spend time within the legislature in both informal and formal space. The former comprises areas where members can mix with one another and exchange views, lobby and gossip; the activity is not publicly visible and has no structured agenda or presiding officers. Private space is where members meet on an organized basis – for instance, a parliamentary group – with an agenda and presiding officers, but gather behind closed doors. Only now is this behaviour starting to garner scholarly attention.

The other dimension is the administrative support provided within legislatures. In fulfilling their various tasks, members need support, be it administration or research. This encompasses what members do in the chamber and in committee. There are clerks and other administrators who not only maintain records of what is said and done but also provide guidance on the rules and procedures. Members are rarely experts and there not be much institutional memory among them. Members also typically need information and research briefings and analyses. These can be provided to members individually, the support coming from staff in their offices, as well as from a central research body serving all members, such as a library or dedicated research division. Committees also require administrative and often research support and may thus have their own staff. Then there are the administrators required to keep a legislature running as a building or buildings as well as to ensure members have the physical and technical resources necessary to sustain their work. As the demands on legislators grow, so the greater the need for administrative support. The emergence of the Internet and the digital age also creates challenges in enabling members to communicate with citizens as well as providing opportunities for the institution to disseminate and to receive information.

How legislatures are administered is fundamental to understanding how a legislature operates and the consequences it has. Structures and processes are not neutral in their effect. Examining how they are administered, and how that administration differs from one parliament to another, is crucial to explaining how well parliaments fulfil their various functions. Yet what has been remarkable has been how little has been written about parliamentary administrations. This handbook helps fill a massive gap. It does so through a commendable range of scholarship, both in terms of individual legislatures and through comparative analysis. Simply by revealing how particular legislatures are administered is a major contribution to knowledge, but the volume also has a utilitarian purpose. It provides a handbook for reform, enabling legislators to look at practice in other legislatures, especially those in the same system of government (presidential, parliamentary), and see how they may adapt their administrative arrangements to meet their needs more effectively. It facilitates parliaments learning from one another.

The editors and authors have done a sterling service. Once having read this volume, one may well wonder why such an exercise has not been undertaken before. A debt of gratitude is owed to all contributors for filling a massive gap in the literature.

Philip Norton
[Lord Norton of Louth]
Professor of Government, University of Hull

PREFACE

This publication is a good (and positive) example of unintended consequences. When we started work on this project, we did not set out to edit a "Handbook on Parliamentary Administrations". Rather, with each of us having done prior work on different aspects of the manner in which parliaments are being administered, we agreed to collaborate on a joint publication that would bring together recent scholarship on the issue. In our view, this question of administrative support for parliamentary work – which some may consider as niche – is fundamental to the functioning of modern representative democracies. At a time in which parliaments, and even liberal democracy itself, are facing an increasing number of threats, scholarly work is needed to improve our understanding of the bureaucratic "underbelly" that in various ways has allowed parliaments to play such a central role in democratic systems.

Our initial focus was on developments in the European Union, involving the study of both its national parliaments and the European Parliament. After many conversations among ourselves, exchanges with other scholars, the organisation of several (online) workshops, the acceptance of our proposal, the submission of academic papers and the completion of the usual peer review process, we published a special issue of the *Journal of Legislative Studies* in 2021.[1] Mission accomplished!

Or was it? In the context of this collaboration, we realized that there is actually a significant gap in the academic literature, and that the need for access to systematic information about the functioning of parliamentary administrations is of course a global one. That is when the idea of a broader publication was born, and the enthusiastic response from Andrew Taylor at Routledge to our enquiries, and subsequently the favourable comments from the peer reviewers to our proposal, convinced us that there is indeed a place and a market for a handbook on the topic.

Selecting suitable contributions for such a major publication was no easy task. A balance needed to be struck between the aspiration towards truly global coverage and the practical impossibility of including all representative democracies in the world. The result is a collection

---

[1] Thomas Christiansen, Elena Griglio & Nicola Lupo (eds) *Administering Representative Democracy: The European Experience of Parliamentary Administrations in Comparative Perspective*, Special issue of the *Journal of Legislative Studies*, Vol.27, No.4 (2021), pp. 477–594.

that still has a strong focus on the editors' home region of Europe, but that also comprises chapters on parliaments from key democratic systems in every other global region. In addition to the 50 countries that we were able to include, a number of "horizontal" chapters discuss cross-cutting issues, while our introduction also looks across the many individual contributions to identify common trends as well as distinguishing features in the various national and supranational experiences.

As we commissioned chapters on such a large number of countries and issues, we were fortunate to be able to count on a group of exceptional authors willing to contribute. This includes both academic scholars and practitioners, and in many cases collaboration between these in the writing individual chapters. Just as with this team of editors, the combination of scholarly approaches and insights from the world of policymaking has facilitated the creation of this unique collection of up-to-date, insightful and well-informed accounts of parliamentary administrations around the world. We are very grateful to all our contributors for their diligence and reliability in writing their chapters, for their cooperation in dealing with requests for revisions, and for their patience in waiting for the publication process to come to a conclusion.

Thus, our initial idea of a small workshop bringing together a handful of colleagues eventually had expanded to become a major publication with almost 60 chapters and some 80 contributors. At this point, with the project reaching an almost industrial scale, it became a major challenge to maintain the overview, to manage the workflow and to ensure coherence. Fortunately, we could rely on the outstanding, reliable and ever-present assistance of Isabel Hernandez Pepe from Scuola Normale Superiore in Florence (formally of Luiss University) to meet this challenge. She managed the correspondence with authors, kept track of the state of the various chapters and finally prepared the manuscript for submission to the publisher. Isabel also provided valuable help with research on the topic and the aggregation of the data contained in the country chapters, an effort that also Alessandra Carraro contributed to. Our thanks go to both of them for their excellent assistance. The support, encouragement and valuable advice of Andrew Taylor, the commissioning editor at Routledge, was already mentioned. We are of course grateful to him, and also to Sophie Iddamalgoda at Routledge who was very helpful in the various stages of the production process of this volume.

We hope that readers and researchers will share our view that this handbook provides a valuable resource, whether to understand the arrangements in specific cases, to study the comparative dimension across a larger number of parliamentary administrations or to analyse a number of pertinent issues that affect all systems to varying degrees.

Rome, July 2022
The Editors

ABBREVIATIONS

AAD	Administrative Affairs Division
AFET	European Parliament's Committee on Foreign Affairs in Montenegro
AIPA	ASEAN Inter-Parliamentary Assembly
ANCI	National Association of Italian Municipalities
APH	Australian Parliament House
API	Denmark
APL	Asociación de Personal Legislativo
ASEP	Council for Civil Personnel Selection
ASGP	Association of the Secretaries General of Parliaments
ATE	Asociación de Trabajadores del Estado
BDBOS	Federal Agency for Digital Radio of Public Authorities and Organisations with Security Tasks
BiH	Bosnia and Herzegovina
BOLD	big open legal data
B-VG	*Bundes-Verfassungsgesetz* (1920 Federal Constitution)
CAO	collective labour agreement
CATV	Community Access Television
CBO	Congressional Budget Office
CC	Control Committees
CCC	Conference of Committee Chairs
CDPLW	Conference for the Direction and Programming of Legislative Work
CDT	Centre for Democratic Transition
CEDI	Center for Documentation and Information
CEFB	Committee on Economy, Finance and Budget
CEFOR	Center for Education, Training and Development
CEI	Central European Initiative
CFSP	common foreign and security policy
CGPO	Centre for Human Resources and Organisation Management
CHF	Swiss Franc
CIO	Chief Information Office
CIP	Centre for Innovation in Parliaments

Abbreviations

CNR	National Research Centre
CoF	Committee of Finance
CONLE	Legislative Consultancy
CONOF	Budget and Financial Inspection Consultancy
CoP	Conference of Presidents
COSAC	Conference of Parliamentary Committees for Union Affairs
CPA	Commonwealth Parliamentary Association
CRM	Customer Relationship Management
CRS	Congressional Research Service
CRTA	Centre for Research, Transparency and Accountability
CS	chamber secretariats
CSDP	Common Security and Defence Policy
CSOs	civil society organization
DAO	Department for Analysis and Research
DC	District of Columbia
DCAF	Geneva Centre for Security Sector Governance
DEM	*Democratas*
DG COMM	Communications Directorate-General
DG ITEC	Directorate-General for Innovation and Technological Support
DGs	Directorates-General
DHR	Department of the House of Representatives
DIP	Documentation and Information System for Parliamentary Processes
DOF	Department of Finance
DOS	Department of the Senate
DP	Democratic Party
DPL	Department of the Parliamentary Library
DPRS	Department of the Parliamentary Reporting Staff
DPS	Department of Parliamentary Services
EALA	East African Legislative Assembly
ECPRD	European Centre for Parliamentary Research and Documentation
EDC	European Documentation Centre
EEC	European Economic Community
EFSF	European Financial Stability Facility
EIF	European Interoperability Framework
EKDDA	National Center for Public Administration and Local Government
ELDIS	Electronic Document Information System
EMU	Economic and Monetary Union
ENA	*École nationale d'administration*
ENPLAC	Exchange Network of Parliaments of Latin America and the Caribbean
EP	European Parliament
EPIS	European Programs Implementation Service
EPRS	European Parliamentary Research Service
EPSO	European Personnel Selection Office
EPTA	European Parliamentary Technology Assessment
ERS	Evaluation and Research Secretariat
ESM	European Stability Mechanism
EU	European Union
EUDISYS	EU-Dokumenten- und Informations-System

Abbreviations

EUZBBG	Act on the Cooperation of the Federal Government and the Bundestag in European Union Affairs (Gesetz über die Zusammenarbeit von Bundesregierung und Bundestag in Angelegenheiten der Europäischen Union)
EUZBLG	Bill on the Cooperation of the Federation and the Länder in European Union Affairs (Gesetz über die Zusammenarbeit von Bund und Ländern in Angelegenheiten der Europäischen Union)
EWS	Early Warning System
EXPO	Directorate-General for External Policies of the Union
FinDel	Finance Delegation
FK	Finance Committee
FMC	(Montenegro)
GAO	Government Accountability Office
GIZ	The Deutsche Gesellschaft für Internationale Zusammenarbeit
GNAT	Grand National Assembly of Turkey
GO	Government Offices
GOG-NR	*Geschäftsordnung des Nationalrates* (Rules of Procedure of the National Council)
GPK	Control Committee
HATVP	High authority of transparency of the public life
HIS	Health Insurance System
HoP	House of Peoples
HoR	House of Representatives
HoUs	Heads of Unit
HR	Human Resources
HW&SW	Computer Management Branch
ICA	International Council for Archives
ICPPD	International Conference of Parliamentarians on Population and Development
ICPS	Institute of Constitutional and Parliamentary Studies
ICT	Information and Communication Technologies
ID	International Department
IDSCS	Institute for Democracy 'Societas Civilis' Skopje
IFLA	International Federation of Library Associations
IG	Instrument Government
IGs	interest groups
INAP	National Institute of Public Administration
INEGI	National Statistics Institute of Mexico
IPCs	interparliamentary conferences
IPEX	InterParliamentary EU information eXchange
IPIs	International Parliamentary Institutions
IPOL	Directorate-General for Internal Policies
IPSA	Independent Parliamentary Standards Authority
IPU	Inter-Parliamentary Union
IRI	International Republican Institute
ISTAT	Italian National Institute for Statistics
IT	Information Technology
JDP/AKP	Justice and Development Party

Abbreviations

JHD	Joint House Department
JPC	Joint Parliamentary Committee
JPSG	Joint Parliamentary Scrutiny Group
JRC	Joint Recruitment Cell
KATEF	Knesset Parliamentary Oversight Coordination Unit
KDCA	Korea Disease Control and Prevention Agency
KNA	Korean National Assembly
LAFEAS	Legislative, Financial, Executive and Administrative Service
LARRDIS	Library, Reference, Research, Documentation and Information
LCO	Legislative Counsel Office
LCSSE	Law on Civil Servants and State Employees
LDP	Liberal Democratic Party
LLR	Legal, Legislative and Research Services
LRD	Legal and Research Department
LSC	Legislative Service Commission
LSS	Legislative Sector Support
MDB	*Movimento Democrático Brasileiro*
MEPs	Members of the European Parliament
MESC	Mandate, Ethics and Submissions Commission
MISA	Ministry of Information Society and Administration
MoF	Ministry of Finance
MOPS Act	*Members of Parliament (Staff) Act*
MPLADS	Members of Parliament Local Area Development Division
MPs	members of parliament
NABO	National Assembly Budget Office
NAL	National Assembly Library
NARS	National Assembly Research Service
NATO	North Atlantic Treaty Organization
NCOP	National Council of Provinces
NDI	National Democratic Institute
NGO	non-governmental organization
NOK	Norwegian Krone
O&M	Organisation and Methods
OBCs	Other Backward Classes
OBU	Oireachtas Broadcast Unit
OCD	Office of the Chamber of Deputies
ODS	Civic Democratic Party
OECD	Organisation for Economic Co-operation and Development
OGP	Office of Government Procurement
OISD	Office on Institutions Supporting Democracy
OPECST	The Parliamentary Office for Scientific and Technological Assessment
OPPD	Office for the Promotion of Parliamentary Development
OSCE	Organization for Security and Co-operation in Europe
OWL	Oireachtas Work Learning
PA	parliamentary assembly
PABiH	Parliamentary Assembly of Bosnia and Herzegovina
PACE	Parliamentary Assembly of the Council of Europe
PAMO	Parliamentary Assembly of the Mediterranean

Abbreviations

PAS	Public Appointments Service
PBO	Parliamentary Budget Officer
PCA	Parliamentary Control of the Administration
PDT	*Partido Democrático Trabalhista*
PGPA Act	Public Governance, Performance and Accountability Act
PH	Physically Handicapped
PI	Department of Parliamentary Institute
PID	Parliamentary Information Direction
PMA	Parliament Museum and Archives
PMBs	Private Members' Bills
PNO	Parliamentary Notice Office
PP	*Partido Progressistas*
PPG	parliamentary party groups
PPR	Press and Public Relations Wing
PQs	parliamentary questions
PRIDE	Parliamentary Research and Training Institute for Democracies
PSA	Parliamentary Service Act
PSB	*Partido Socialista Brasileiro*
PSD	Property Services Division
PSDB	*Partido da Social Democracia Brasileira*
PSP	Parliament Support Programme
PT	*Partido dos Trabalhadores*
PWSS	Parliamentary Workplace Support Service
QMV	qualified majority voting
QuANGO	quasi non-governmental organizations
R&I	Research and Innovation
RoP	Rules of Procedure
RPP/*CHP*	Republican People's Party
RS	Republika Srpska
RSA	Republic of South Africa
RTI	Right to Information Act
SADC-PF	Southern African Development Community Parliamentary Forum
SAPC	the Stabilisation and Association Parliamentary Committee
SC	Senate Chancellery
SCT	Scheduled Tribes
SCTC	Scheduled Castes and Scheduled Tribes
SDC	Swiss Agency for Development and Cooperation
SEK	Swedish Crown
SFPALC	Senate Finance and Public Administration Legislation Committee
SO	Standing Orders
STV	Single Transferable Vote
TD	Teachta Dála (Member of the Lower House)
TGNA	Turkish Grand National Assembly
TLAC	Top-Level Appointments Committee
UK	United Kingdom
UN	United Nations
UNDP	United Nations Development Programme
UNESCO	United Nations Educational, Scientific and Cultural Organization

Abbreviations

UNFPA	United Nations Population Fund
UNICEF	United Nations Children's Fund
UPB	Parliamentary Budget Office
UPI	Union of the Provinces
US	United States
UVI	Impact Assessment Office
WFD	Westminster Foundation for Democracy
ZBB	Zero-based Budgeting

1
INTRODUCTION
A Global Perspective on the Role of Parliamentary Administrations

Thomas Christiansen, Elena Griglio and Nicola Lupo

1.1 Introduction

The idea of "parliamentary administration" might appear, at first sight, like an oxymoron: parliaments are the domain of politicians, the elected representatives of the people, whereas administrations are commonly understood as the executive bureaucracies carrying out the tasks of governments. Yet, perhaps paradoxically, also the work of parliaments, approving legislation and holding governments to account, requires administrative support, especially and increasingly in the modern age when the functions of public powers, and hence the demands on parliaments, have expanded significantly. Indeed, parliamentary administrations are essential for the proper functioning of representative democracy, albeit by a degree of separation: just as parliaments are central in the operation of a representative democracy, capable administrative support of elected representatives is critical for a meaningful execution of parliaments' functions. Or, to put it in reverse, in the context of the modern state, a parliament *without* adequate support from a dedicated staff – facilitating meetings, providing logistical assistance, undertaking research, keeping public records, offering legal advice, managing public relations and international liaisons – would be in no position either to legislate or to hold the executive effectively to account.

Yet, while this argument about the significance of parliamentary administrations can be easily made, the academic literature has paid surprisingly little attention to them. Perhaps in part due to the disciplinary separation between *parliamentary studies* and *public administration*, scholars have tended to focus either on the political and constitutional dimension of parliaments, or on the (dominant) executive dimension of public administration. Thus, on the side of parliaments, neither the *Oxford Handbook of Legislative Studies* (Shane, Saalfeld, and Strøm, 2014), nor the *Oxford Handbook of the American Congress* (Edwards, Lee, and Schickler, 2011), nor the *Handbook of Parliamentary studies* (Benoît and Rozenberg, 2020) devote any specific attention to their administrative dimension. In the same vein, on the public administration side, both the *Routledge Handbook of Public Administration* (Hildreth, Miller and Lindquist, 2021) and the SAGE Handbook of Public Administration (Peters and Pierre, 2012) do not contain chapters on the administrations of parliaments.

There have been selected publications on specific aspects of the topic,[1] to which also the editors of this volume have contributed (Christiansen, Griglio and Lupo, 2021; Högenauer, Neuhold and Christiansen, 2016), individual chapters in edited books (Egeberg, Gornitzka,

Trondal and Johannessen, 2015; Wise, 2003; Yong and Petit, 2018) and official/non-academic publications (ECPRD and Italian Chamber of Deputies, 2003; Grudzinski and Staskiewicz, 1992; IPU, 2020; Verrier, 2007; Vilella, 2019). However, no comprehensive or systematic account of the nature, the role, and the functions of parliamentary administrations has been published. It is in this regard that the present Handbook fills a gap in the literature and seeks to provide a definite account of the organization and work of parliamentary administrations around the world. Based on what was stated above, this volume contributes to our understanding of what makes representative democracy work, as well as highlighting the many challenges that need to be confronted.

While the systematic study of parliamentary administrations concerns to a large extent procedural, organizational, and technical aspects, it is also a highly political matter. A very basic question in this regard concerns the position of parliaments within a state's constitutional setting. Parliaments are ubiquitous around the global, yet liberal democracy is not. Indeed, according to latest data published in 2022, democracy has been in retreat, with growing numbers of "fully democratic" states being downgraded to "flawed democracies" or worse (Economist Intelligence Unit, 2021). Although also non-democratic regimes often maintain parliaments for a variety of reasons, our scholarly interest – and hence the coverage of this Handbook – is mainly focused on democratic polities, in which the function of parliaments is genuinely about representation of the people, and in which parliaments exercise essential functions such as providing a forum for public debate and holding executive institutions to account.

Within the wider understanding of liberal democracy, a further distinction between presidential and parliamentary systems can be made. As the name suggests, parliaments are – at least in principle – the centre-piece in parliamentary democracy, with governments depending on a majority of the elected members for their legitimacy and decision-making. The result is often a "fused system" where the government is closely allied with the majority in parliament. Presidential systems, by contrast, have alternative and independent channels of legitimation for the executive and the legislature. A system of checks and balances, and potentially competition between the two branches, results from such an arrangement.

1.2 The Content of the Handbook

Either way, parliaments are central in both of these systems of representative democracy, and hence also the presence and the good functioning of administrations to support their work matters. Consequently, the present Handbook, while focusing on the discussion of arrangements in democratic polities, includes contributions on both presidential and parliamentary systems. In providing the most comprehensive coverage of the topic, the volume includes individual studies from 50 countries around the globe, alongside a number of horizontal chapters that provide cross-cutting analysis of some of the key challenges that are common to contemporary parliamentary administrations.

The study of such a large number of country-specific experiences is valuable for a number of reasons. First, it provides a useful reference to the detailed arrangements that are being made in individual countries. While there has been access to information for some of the larger states and better-known parliaments, say the US Congress, the German Bundestag or the European Parliament (EP), for many others this kind of knowledge has been limited or non-existent, at least in the English language.[2]

Introduction

Second, beyond the value of understanding individual cases better, the Handbook also provides a unique comparative perspective. The authors of country-specific chapters have followed a common approach in selecting the relevant data and structuring their discussion, making it possible to identify both common themes and crucial differences across these many systems. In this regard, each chapter addresses (within the context of what is meaningful in each particular case) the following aspects:

- the historical evolution of the parliamentary administration
- key organizational aspects, including questions of hierarchy and resources
- the role of the administration in the context of parliamentary work, for example assistance in the context of legislative procedures
- the involvement in managing inter-institutional and external relations
- current challenges facing the parliamentary administration, including in particular the response to the Covid pandemic and its impact on parliamentary work

This collection of comparable data on a large number of national and, in the case of the EP, supranational systems facilitates comparative analysis, categorizing different models and drawing more general conclusions about strengths, weaknesses, and risks involved in the administration of parliaments.

Third, there is also a diachronic dimension to this analysis, as the various chapters present the historical trajectory of parliamentary administrations and chart the changes that have occurred over time. In the process, it becomes apparent how parliamentary administrations have needed to adapt to changing circumstances, ranging from constitutional reforms, societal change, technological progress to globalization, and new systemic and physical threats. It shows that parliamentary administrations, just like the representative democracies they serve, are living entities whose capacity to reform also determines their ability to perform.

For reasons of space, this Handbook could not include chapters on every parliamentary system in the world – a selection has had to be made, which reflects both editorial judgements (and perhaps bias) and the availability of relevant expertise. While the vast majority of the contributions deal with Western states, every effort has been made to also include chapters on key countries of the non-Western world and the Global South. The Handbook provides insights into experiences from every continent, with complete coverage of North America and the European Union and selected countries from the rest of Europe, Africa, Asia, and Oceania.

Europe receives extensive attention in this volume, partly not only because of the large concentration of parliamentary systems that can be found here but also because in the process of European integration a particular arrangement of multilevel governance has developed here. This has involved the creation of a transnational assembly that eventually evolved into the first ever directly elected supranational parliament with proper law-making and budgetary powers (Jacobs and De Feo, 2022). Beyond the emergence of this European Parliament as a novel kind of institution, the integration process also had repercussions on national parliaments in the EU's member states, involving both the threat of disenfranchisement and the creation of new opportunities for parliamentary cooperation. To varying degrees, national parliaments – and their administrations – have undergone a process of "Europeanization" as a consequence of these challenges (Christiansen, Griglio and Lupo, 2021; Högenauer, 2021). It is also due to this particular experience in Europe and the demands that it puts on parliamentary administrations that the Handbook includes contributions on all EU member states, as well as most of those countries that have candidate status or special arrangements with the European Union.

In terms of the cross-cutting analysis, authors have contributed to "horizontal" chapters on some of the key challenges that have been identified in the country-specific chapters and indeed have based their analysis on some extent on the information provided in the country chapters – this kind of cross-fertilization between individual country studies and cross-cutting analysis being the added value from a comparative perspective referred to above. The key challenges identified and addressed in this first part of the Handbook are:

- the impact of the distinction between presidential and parliamentary systems on parliamentary administrations
- the relationship between the speaker (or president) of parliament and the administration
- the peculiarities of the administration of parliaments in bicameral systems
- the challenge of digitalization
- the provision of scientific expertise in the context of parliamentary work
- parliamentary diplomacy and the facilitation of transnational parliamentary work (in the global and the European contexts)

Following this first part with "horizontal" analyses, subsequent parts of the Handbook discuss the individual experiences of parliamentary administrations around the world, distinguishing between EU member states, other states in Europe and, finally, around the world.

While this volume, designed as a Handbook and as such as a reference work, does not contain a concluding chapter, the following sections of this introductory chapter provide a discussion of the key findings that can be gathered from both country-specific and "horizontal" analysis. The following section engages more deeply with debates about the significance of parliamentary administrations and the relevance of systematic analysis. The next section then brings together the empirical insights from across the various country chapters, highlighting the value of a comparative perspective. A subsequent section addresses the current and future challenges for parliamentary administrations that have been identified across the Handbook's contributions, before a concluding section summarizes these findings and provides a future outlook.

1.3 The Significance of Parliamentary Administrations

The historical development of parliamentary administrations has taken different forms in different countries, making it difficult to generalize. Nonetheless, broadly speaking, we can observe that over time there has been a steady increase of the size and functions of parliamentary administrations. Initially, in 19th and in the early 20th century, the parliaments of nascent liberal democracies in Europe were supported by administrative staff in a variety of ways: assisting elected members during their meetings, providing procedural and logistical assistance, and collecting the required documentation, both *ex ante* through the management of parliamentary libraries and *ex post* by recording proceedings (minutes, reports of the debates, and voting results). As a matter of fact, members of parliamentary administrations developed high levels of excellence regarding the skills required for carrying out these initial tasks: many of the best librarians, stenographers, procedural experts – and even the founders of "parliamentary law" (Lupo and Thiers, 2020) – are among these first parliamentary administrators.

Beyond this administrative support, parliaments might rely on the personal skills and networks of relationships of elected MPs, who were usually chosen from among the most notable persons on each constituency – something which usually implied that they had the personal resources to hire one or more secretaries or support staff to manage their activity in their constituency. Fast forward to the present day, it clearly emerges – also from the contributions to this Handbook – that parliamentary administrations have grown significantly in size and are much more articulated and differentiated, both in terms of their functions and of their organizational structures.[3]

However, it is important to emphasize that the evolution of parliamentary administrations has not always been straightforward, registering both ups and downs, with their size depending on multiple factors (Otjes, 2022). What is also worth remarking is that this process has fallen significantly short of the growth of functions and dimension of the large bureaucracies that make up the executive branch of states. The expansion of state functions has led to an exponential increase in the quantity and nature of public structures as well as the number of officials working for them (Becker and Bauer, 2021), ironically while these are often barely politically accountable to legislatures (Benoît, 2020).

The development of the functions of parliamentary administrations is ongoing. Just a look at the effects of the Covid pandemic since 2020 illustrates the challenge on parliamentary administrations to adapt to changing circumstances, accelerating the digitalization of procedures and organization and requiring new human and material resources to manage all these largely unforeseen innovations.

Moreover, also as a consequence of digitalization, parliamentary administrations have been called upon to play new roles. The meaning of the "public" has expanded dramatically, not anymore limited to the press – or, better, to specialized journalists, asked to regularly report on parliamentary activity – but now including also the internet, social media, and potentially every individual citizen. The "public" of parliaments has been empowered by access to the internet, allowing citizens to follow parliamentary activity and thus of the positions expressed by individual MPs without much effort. In other words, "forced increased transparency" of parliamentary activity, depending on the opportunity to use old and new media as channels of institutional communication with citizens (Lupo and Fasone, 2015), has transformed the traditional features of legislative work, especially within standing committees, requiring new balances between efficiency and transparency (Voermans, ten Napel and Passchier, 2015).

Even some traditional functions of parliamentary administrations have been recently re-interpreted in profound ways due to contemporary challenges. One case in point concerns of the functions aimed to ensure the security of parliamentary activity. The risks deriving first by the renewed terrorist threats and violent manifestations – with the attack on the US Capitol on 6 January 2021 and the attack on Brazil Congress on 8 January 2023 as prime examples – have been reminders that the integrity of the symbolic and actual seats of representative democracy cannot be taken for granted and needs to be adequately protected. At the same time, this has to be balanced with the defence of parliaments' traditional autonomy and therefore without leaving this task entirely to the security forces directly controlled by the executive.

Another trend charted by the chapters in this Handbook is the increase of the functions of parliamentary administrations aimed at supporting the external role of parliaments. As parliaments, especially in the last three decades, have been developing interparliamentary cooperation (IPC) and the so-called parliamentary diplomacy, this has obliged their administrations to strengthen their specialization on international relations. Although the plenary chamber maintains its symbolic centrality, the attention of the parliamentary staff is more and more focused on other kinds of meetings, involving of course MPs but also foreign representatives and/or taking place outside the national borders (Stavridis, 2021).

The most delicate issue regarding parliamentary administrations concerns the nature of the activity they perform. The degree of impartiality and the mechanisms aimed at granting this impartiality within an institution that is inevitably highly politicized, fully pluralistic, and often strongly characterized by partisanship probably represent the most crucial and intriguing academic puzzle regarding parliamentary administration.

This is arguably the perspective from which most of the features of each parliamentary administration need to be analysed, be it comparatively or conceptually. Starting from the status of the parliamentary officials composing it, with their status similar to that of all other public officials – often with stronger mechanisms aimed at ensuring their independence and impartiality – or the staff directly supporting individual MPs or the various parliamentary groups, making their work by definition more politicized. Moving to the core role of parliamentary administration, this is very rarely entitled to a proper political function, but normally called upon to be in support of the many, often intertwined functions assigned to parliamentary institutions. Eventually, also its internal organization and hierarchy can be seen as a way to address the issue of impartiality, each time in consistency with the characteristics of the respective political system, its customs, conventions, and traditions.

1.4 A Comparative Perspective on Parliamentary Administrations

The comparative analysis of the data contained in the various country-specific chapters demonstrates several commonalities and differences in relation to certain fundamental organizational and functional options of parliamentary administrations. This initial overview of the contributions to the Handbook constitutes an opportunity to engage in a systematic comparative analysis, and this section provides some insights on this regard.

The very first observation in this context concerns the size of parliamentary administrations. Recent studies in this field (Otjes, 2022) debated the influence played by three factors (population, assembly size and parliamentary strength) on the size of parliamentary staff, demonstrating that population is a stronger predictor compared to the number of MPs, while the level of parliamentary powers does not act as a key explanation. In fact, as argued in the country-specific chapters, the ratio between the number of parliamentary staff and the number of MPs still remains a telling quantitative factor able to capture the scope and potential strength of the administration. Focusing on the staff/MPs ratio,[4] four groups of parliaments can be distinguished. A minority of parliaments (Malta, Spain and Switzerland) follows a ratio of approximately 1 staff/1 MP. In the large majority of parliaments, the ratio swings around 2 (with an interval of ± 0.5). In another minority of parliaments (Germany, Greece, Hungary, India, Israel, Latvia, Mexico), the ratio stretches the threshold of 5. Finally, two parliaments outstand the average trend: this is the case of the European Parliament that has reached a ratio of 7.7 staff/MPs, and Australia, that shows a 9.1 ratio. These can be considered the two most (relatively) numerous and staffed parliamentary administrations if we limit our analysis to permanent bureaucracies.

As a matter of fact, beyond these cases, it is worth mentioning the experience of those parliaments where either permanent staff is extremely marginal and political patronage is the rule (this is the case of the US) or the distinction between permanent and temporary staff is blurred due to the strong osmosis between the two categories. All these cases clearly stand outside the above-mentioned four groupings, showing high ratios of 11.6 staff/MPs in Turkey, 27 in Brazil, 37 in the United States, and 38 in Argentina. It is interesting to note that all these four cases correspond to presidential forms of government.

A second dimension of framing the distinctive features of parliamentary administrations is the degree of budgetary autonomy. Most of the national chapters refer to the size of budget as a relevant factor in support to a proper administrative autonomy of parliament. However, in a diachronic perspective, parliamentary administrations seem to be at the crossroads of their historical development. As a matter of fact, some parliaments have reported in the last few years an increase in the level of funding aiming at addressing the upcoming challenges in the field of recruitment, digitalization, or research. This common trend links parliaments (Australia, Greece, Latvia, Luxembourg, Mexico, Netherlands, Spain, UK) with a rather different history and constitutional role. In sharp contrast stand those parliaments that have lately recorded a rationalization of budget and hence a downscaling of parliamentary staff. Whereas in South Africa this trend is part of a broader State process leading to the containment of public expenditure, in the case of Japan, budgetary curtails and staff cutting were considered consistent with the reduction of the number of MPs in 2013 and 2017; they have been interpreted as a factor contributing to the relative empowerment of the executive vis-à-vis the legislative branch.

The previous remark confirms that budgetary autonomy as a prerequisite for administrative autonomy is one of the pivotal factors supporting parliaments' independence vis-à-vis the executive. Historically, this has accompanied the parliamentarization of many countries in the European Union and is now significantly characterizing the transition of a candidate country such as North Macedonia, which in 2020 has started promoting the budgetary and financial independence of the National Assembly in order to ensure its independence from the executive branch.

The third perspective regarding the comparison of parliamentary administrations relates to the internal set of administrative arrangements, which depend on staff recruitment, organization, roles, and functions; the governance of administration, including its political control and oversight. The combination of these two arrangements provides an idea of the relationship that links each parliamentary administration to politics, spanning from a situation of complete administrative neutrality to strong partisanship and politicization.

For what concerns staff recruitment, organization, roles, and functions, comparative analysis shows that – apart from the atypical model followed by the US Congress relying almost entirely on political patronage for staff recruitment – in most parliaments two categories of "human resources" can be distinguished: on the one hand, permanent administrative staff who are civil servants, and, on the other hand, support staff hired under private law/political patronage supporting either individual MPs or political groups. These two categories are usually clearly separated in terms of status and career perspectives, but some exceptions are worth mentioning. For example, in Albania and Luxembourg, support staff benefits from the same conditions as the permanent staff. The relative size of both these categories may vary between the two houses in bicameral parliaments (see the case of the Netherlands) and it may vary over time, as the experience of Brazil – where the decentralized and partisan staff has significantly grown in the last decade to the detriment of a centralized, non-partisan bureaucracy – confirms.

The recruitment and status of the first category of permanent officials in its turn fall under two main models. In the majority of parliaments, administrative staff follows the selection procedures and the status of civil servants: in these experiences, parliamentary officials do not substantially differ from the other public employees serving the executive branch. Only in some cases (Croatia and Spain, among others), specific adaptations to the parliamentary context are provided for the officials serving the legislative branch. The alternative model, adopted by Belgium, Canada, France, Hungary, India, Israel, Italy, Poland, Portugal,

Romania, Turkey, UK, foresees the establishment of a special administrative regime for parliamentary staff, completely separated from the general civil service.

Whereas the existence of a separate administrative regime is considered indicative of the degree of administrative autonomy and independence enjoyed by parliament vis-à-vis the executive (IPU, 2020), other organizational and functional features may contribute to support or endanger this prerogative in the regard of politics in general. These may include the career paths of parliamentary officials, their administrative functions, and the daily connection with MPs and political groups. As a matter of fact, most parliamentary administrations interpret the role of their permanent staff as deeply non-politicized and non-partisan. This is particularly true in those systems following a special administrative regime that regulate every single aspect of the career and activity of their officials following a merit-based system. In other cases, where the parliamentary administration lacks a formal statutory guarantee of independence, it is only through concrete working practices, from communication to transparency, that it can prove its political neutrality (Austria). Whereas the majority of parliamentary administrations find their dominant logic in the non-partisanship, the Turkish experience confirms the existence of parliamentary administrations which rather depend explicitly on partisanship for their activity and career due to political contingent factors, including the concentration of power in the hands of the Speaker and the lack of political alternation in the last 19 years. The Argentinean Congress is another example of highly politicized organization, guided by a partisan principle, led by the Speakers of the Chambers, and greatly influenced by the Parliamentary Labour Union.

In those systems more directly adopting the non-partisan logic (including Korea, Italy, Iceland, Ireland, Montenegro and Portugal), specific rules are introduced in order to prevent parliamentary employees to publicly support or oppose a political party or candidate. A significant exception is made in Germany, where parliamentary officials are asked to be politically neutral in the performance of their work, although they are allowed to be members of political parties and even run in local elections.

The impartiality requirement does not exclude that, while performing their duties, parliamentary officials tend to establish cooperative relationships with political actors (Norway), acting in close contact with the representatives of both ruling and opposition parties (Japan). Whereas some administrative units mainly deal with what can be categorized as fully administrative matters (i.e. security, IT systems and housekeeping activities), other units are tackling more sensitive tasks, directly supporting the political functions of parliament, such as legislation, budgeting, control of the executive, and public relations. This explains why some administrative positions (particularly within the secretariats at committee level) may be potentially influential actors in their respective policy domains (Finland).

In order to reconcile the prerequisite of administrative impartiality in a working context deeply embedded in politics and often polarized, Iceland has significantly adopted a code of ethics for the Althingi staff, which emphasizes avoidance of conflicts of interest, promoting impartiality and objectivity. Similarly, with the aim of decreasing the possibility of malpractice and wrong application of procedures, a set of mechanisms such as Integrity and Risk Managers was established in Montenegro (although they still need to reach their full potential).

The independence of parliamentary administrations from the political sphere is also grounded on the internal governance structure and hierarchy. The apex of parliamentary administration may be either the Speaker or a collective body (named Bureau, Presidium, Commission) consisting of parliamentarians from all key parties or groups. These bodies usually address political (administrative) guidelines to the Secretary General, who usually enjoys large margins of discretion in the daily administrative management but, at the same time, is responsible functionally and hierarchically of the whole bureaucratic sector, being answerable for the administrative performance before the political sphere.

The rules governing the appointment and removal of the Secretary general and of the other top officials are of great importance for the independence and autonomy of the administrative structure (Gianniti and Di Cesare, 2023). In most cases, the position of the Secretary General is rather stable, compared to similar positions at the executive level, being removable only through articulated procedures, involving broad political consensus. However, often beyond the narrative of independence and neutrality, forms of politicization can occur at the highest administrative levels. For instance, in the European Parliament, the staff policy of the Secretary General is closely monitored by the political authority (the Bureau of the European Parliament) which has come to exercise a strong political influence on certain nominations. Even the Canadian Parliament, which has a solid tradition of administrative neutrality, has lately experienced developments and controversies in the appointment of Clerks for both chambers, hinting at a possible new politicization of roles previously seen as highly impartial. Politicization of senior management may be spurred by competing behaviours of its members seeking for party group consensus aimed at renewing their position, as the experience of Austria, Bosnia, Brazil, and Czechia confirm. This reaches its maximum in the case of Turkey, where the many central units may be entrusted on external administrators, thus increasing the possibility of politicization and arbitrariness of administrative careers.

The general rule is that every parliament or house in bicameral parliaments has its own Secretary General, with the exception of France, Uruguay, and Mexico (in the Senate) where two SGs are present in each House (Gianniti and Di Cesare, 2023) and the opposite choice of Austria and Switzerland, which, consistently with the option for a joint parliamentary administration serving both houses, foresee the presence of just one single Secretary General heading up the entire administration of the bicameral parliament (Griglio and Lupo, 2023).

1.5 Contemporary Challenges for Parliamentary Administrations

Reference has already been made to the changes that parliaments, and hence their administrations, have undergone over the past century. Looking more closely at recent developments, a number of contemporary challenges can be identified that parliamentary administrations have had to confront in the 21st century. In the following, five such challenges will be introduced that are discussed in more detail in various chapters of this Handbook.

First, there has been an intensifying pressure on representative institutions to be more transparent in how they work, and what they debate. As already discussed above, there has been a long trajectory that has sought to communicate parliamentary proceedings to the wider public, starting with the publication of official records, the provision of citizens' access to the chamber, and eventually the broadcasting of debates on radio, television, and the internet. The aspiration towards accessibility has also been expressed in the architectural choices of modern parliamentary buildings making use of walls of glass, symbolizing the transparency of the institution. However, in line with the recognition that also in parliaments significant aspects of the decision-making process occur behind the scenes, the agenda of achieving greater transparency has involved the accreditation of independent media representatives, the creation of registers for organized interests, and the publication of minutes and voting records of committees, opening up parliamentary business to the public beyond the plenary chamber.

Transparency, rather than being an end in itself, is a tool towards a wider aim, namely enabling citizens to follow closely the activities of their elected representatives. Arguably, this capacity of the electorate to understand and evaluate the behaviour of MPs is elementary in ensuring that the choices being made at the ballot box are well informed. However, beyond this rather passive relationship between transparency of parliaments and the voting choices of citizens, there is also a more proactive dimension of this link, namely the direct engagement with citizens.

The aim of citizen engagement has led many parliaments to open up their proceedings and indeed their buildings to the public. Visitor galleries, guided tours, and organized visits for school classes are now common place for most parliaments. On a more substantive level, letters to elected members, petitions, and similar instruments allow citizens to comment on legislative affairs. What this means for parliamentary staff is the need for additional skills and resources in order to deal with the increased workload. Effective management of citizen engagement and a capacity to respond to petitions and individual requests can be seen as important at a time when political mobilization increasingly takes place through extra-parliamentary channels.

Another area of growing importance that places greater demands on parliamentary administrations is that of parliamentary diplomacy and IPC. Diplomacy is, of course, the traditional domain of the executive, conducted by heads of state, foreign ministers, and diplomats. Indeed, given its declaratory and secretive nature, foreign and security policy is traditionally an area in which parliaments have limited influence, though considerable constitutional variation exists in this field. However, parliaments themselves have developed a practice of engaging with matters of foreign policy. This includes activities such as passing resolutions that refer to current or past developments in other countries (e.g. condemnations of *coup d'etats* or the recognition of historical crimes as genocide), addressing speaking invitations to foreign leaders or international figures, sending delegations of parliamentary representatives abroad. Such activities, when carried out by parliaments without involvement of the government, do not formally commit the country, and as such are largely symbolic. However, such acts of parliamentary diplomacy can have a profound impact, especially in the context of highly sensitive or contentious matters.

IPC is more routine in that over the past century the regular interaction between parliaments have become institutionalized. Various international and regional fora have been set up that facilitate the regular exchange between representatives of parliaments. IPC offers the opportunity to parliamentarians – and their staff – to learn from their respective experiences, to establish best practices, and to identify opportunities for joint action. This can be useful both in terms of procedural and constitutional matters (e.g. defending parliamentary prerogatives vis-à-vis the executive) or on substantive matters (such as the promotion of the rule of law). To a certain degree, IPC has become institutionalized by the work of international organizations such as the Inter-Parliamentary Union or regional initiatives such as IPEX, the EU's "platform for inter-parliamentary exchange". At the same time, at a time when liberal democracy is in retreat in some countries, IPC may also constitute a support structure for beleaguered legislatures.

What matters in the current context is that parliamentary diplomacy and IPC activities also depend on skilled administrators to make these work. These international exchanges require knowledge about other countries' political and constitutional systems, a high degree of political sensitivity in engaging in the world of diplomacy, the presence of the requisite language skills, and the capacity to rely on or establish personal networks across national borders. With elected members being generally focused on their domestic electorates, it often falls on administrators not only to support MPs in their international activities but in fact also to take the initiative to create such contacts and initiatives in the first place.

A further issue that has come to prominence in the management of parliamentary affairs in the course of the 21st century has been the security of parliaments. What happened in Washington DC on 6 January 2021 when a violent mob attacked the US Capitol to interrupt the declaration of the results of the presidential election – in what was an apparent insurgency against the democratic process of the United States – demonstrated vividly the vulnerability of legislative institutions, and the need for physical protection of their structures. A strikingly similar assault on the premises of the parliament (and the buildings of other state institutions) occurred in Brazil on 8 January 2023. While such events have been exceptional in the context of modern democratic systems, there have been other breaches of the security of parliamentary buildings, including both politically motivated (such as the far-right protesters storming the steps of the Reichstag, the home of the German Bundestag in August 2020) and simply criminal instances (such as a bank robbery inside the European Parliament in 2009).

What these examples show is the need for parliaments to provide for security, not only for its members and staff but also to protect the democratic process and constitutional integrity of the institution of parliament. Given that public security is normally the domain of the executive, many parliaments have established their own police force or security agency in order to maintain their independence and ensure the separation of powers. In the context of greater polarization and increasing propensity for political violence, ensuring the physical security of parliamentary spaces has become a major challenge for parliamentary staff, coming together also with the heightened concern and additional responsibilities related to the personal safety of members and staff during the Covid pandemic.

Beyond these issues surrounding physical threats to parliaments, another growing concern for administrations has been the need to ensure a secure environment for data storage and transmission. As many institutions in both the private and the public sector, parliaments have been subjects of cyber-attacks which – again – are potentially particularly harmful given their centrality to the democratic process. Such attacks can be about accessing confidential or privileged information or seeking to influence the decision-making process. In a fast-evolving threat environment, the provision of cyber-security for parliaments is a demanding task that administrations need to adapt to on a constant basis.

Beyond cyber-security, digital transformation more generally poses new challenges for parliamentary administrations. Digitalization is a process touching on all the aspects of administrative work but at the same time has important consequences also for the political role of parliament. This is why ongoing political and administrative drives to promote a digital organization can be considered a necessary premise for implementing the perspective of a "paperless parliament".

Promoting a digital organization presupposes a radical change in the internal administrative machinery of parliament, and this change is not new to many parliamentary administrations (Israel, Ireland, Korea, Switzerland, among others), which have started this process quite a long time ago. Other bureaucracies can be considered latecomers in the digital challenge, but for all of them the pandemic has represented an accelerator of digitalization both in the field of the administrative procedures and daily practices and in the field of the political activity and connection with the society.

The transition to a digital parliamentary organization requires a series of adaptations both in terms of technology and human resources. On the one hand, it relies on the introduction of new technology infrastructures and equipment. For instance, in the case of Portugal, this has eventually led to the creation, in 2018, of a new Technology Infrastructure and Information

Systems Divisions, under the Information Technology Directorate. On the other hand, digitalization necessarily advocates the engagement of staff units with advanced digital skills (Greece) whose main task is granting parliament its own autonomy and technical capacity in the generation of IT resources and contents and in the IT management. In the pursuit of improving the IT support of parliament, Malta has promoted the collaboration with universities. By contrast, the experience of the Austrian Parliamentary Service that acts as service provider for the federal ministries (the entire public consultation procedure regarding draft bills is published on the parliament's website) witnesses how improvements in the digital administrative capacity of parliament may benefit the overall public sphere. Finally, the "human" challenge also includes the consolidation of a digital administrative culture both within employees (Ireland) and within MPs (Croatia), and in many cases, these may be long-term processes.

In a substantive perspective, similar priority goals are addressed by parliamentary bureaucracies in their approach to modern technologies and digital processes: openness and transparency of parliamentary activity (see for instance the applications to stenographic recording and minutes in Estonia and Japan); efficiency of parliamentary work; connection with the public and participation of civil society (see for instance the launch of e-petitions in Belgium, Estonia, Luxembourg, EP); modernization of parliamentary institutional communication (see for instance the opening of all parliaments to social media and the improvements in the use of podcasts and parliamentary TV programmes); digitalization of the legislative process (Bosnia, Brazil, Czechia, Denmark, Estonia); accessibility of parliamentary documents through the creation of open data platforms (France, India, Korea); and simplified datasets (France).

The pandemic has undoubtedly accelerated most of the digital processes that were already underway, and this resulted in formal changes in the political organization of parliament also. As a matter of fact, at the end of 2020, the Dutch Tweede Kamer established a parliamentary committee on Digital Affairs with its own parliamentary staff, including a clerk, information specialist, knowledge coordinator, as well as EU-advisor. In the same period, the Swedish Riksdag created a Sub-Committee on the Information Society and Digitalization within the Committee on Education, Science, Technological Development, and the Information Society. The possibility to have remote committee and plenary meetings, which was already among the administrative digital goals in some parliaments, has undoubtedly acknowledged a rapid acceleration under the pandemic. The backside of all these digital trends is - as mentioned before - in the increased exposition of parliament to cyberattacks, that's why - following some recent incidents - IT security has been incorporated by some parliamentary administrations (Norway, Italy) as one of the digital priorities.

1.6 Conclusion

As stated at the outset of this chapter, there is no representative democracy without a parliament and - at least in contemporary democracies - there is no parliament able to work without its own administration.

The instrumental contribution to the smooth functioning of representative democracy is what distinguishes the presence and role of parliamentary administrations worldwide. However, the way in which this objective is achieved varies substantially between national jurisdictions. Indeed, the comparative perspective and comprehensive analysis provided by the contributions to this Handbook confirm that the organizational and functional solutions implemented in response to this common need are extremely varied, to the point that it is difficult to identify general reference models. As a matter of fact, many factors contribute to determining the nature and structure of parliamentary administrations: first, the process of parliamentary institutionalization (Judge and Earnshaw, 2003) that led to the definition of the characteristic features of parliament; second, the form of government and its interaction with the executive power (Fasone, 2023); third, the reference legal system (belonging either to the common law or to the civil law families) and administrative tradition (Sager, Rosser, Hurni and Mavrot, 2012); and, fourth, the electoral system, party system, and presence of a majoritarian or consensual model of democracy.

None of these factors by itself would determine the shape of the administrative architecture of parliament. However, a combination of these factors allows us to distinguish between two main institutional solutions to the common need of "administering" representative democracy: the "bureaucratic model" and the "staffing model".

The bureaucratic model involves the presence of a centralized administrative apparatus within parliament, selected through different recruitment procedures – either autonomous or derived from the state's wider civil service – providing parliamentary officials with a permanent position, independent from politics. Institutionalization, centralization, political neutrality, autonomy from the political sphere, and hierarchical organization are the main characteristics of the bureaucratic model, which is the leading solution worldwide: it is the rule not just in most European parliaments (including Cyprus, which follows a presidential system) but also in extra-European parliaments, such as the Korean National Assembly, the Parliament of South Africa and, significantly, also the Mexican Congress, which has recently promoted the establishment of an autonomous parliamentary civil service.

The alternative of a staffing model is instead adopted by "legislatures" that follow the presidential model of the US Congress, including for example Argentina and Brazil. This model is based on a decentralized approach with staffers answering personally to individual MPs or political groups (Peters, 2023) and a limited number of non-partisan officials hired through public competition for permanent positions. Compared to the bureaucratic model, the staffing model shows on average a bigger size of personnel – and hence of budget – and, at least in the US experience, serves a "strong" parliamentary institution, solidly grounded in the constitutional architecture.

The two models differ in the emphasis that parliaments place on the activities, and hence on the administrative needs, of individual MPs (which are predominant in the staffing model) and of their collective structures and bodies (which prevail in the bureaucratic model). These alternative approaches raise some questions about the alignment of the administrative solution with the parliamentary archetype at stake given that the "legislatures" following the American presidential model are precisely the assemblies most inclined to operate – beyond the traditional internal political cleavages – on the basis of institutional (and therefore unitary) cleavages (Laver, 2008).

Notwithstanding these underlying differences, several instances of "contamination" across the two models can be identified. On the one hand, administrations following the staffing model are able to fulfil selected "shared" administrative needs associated with the collective dimension of parliamentary activities (mainly research and budget services) by establishing independent agencies (such as the US Congressional Budget Office). On the other hand, the bureaucratic model integrates the role of permanent officials selected through public competition with the presence of staff under the political patronage of party groups or individual MPs, whose size shows higher rates of increase compared to permanent officials (Fasone, 2023).

It is significant to observe how a sort of hybridization between the two administrative models has found success in the experience of the European Parliament. In the course of its institutionalization process (Corbett, Jacobs and Shackleton, 2016; De Feo, 2016), the European Parliament has tried to combine the aspiration to rely on a solid and well-funded staffing system with the experience derived from the parliaments of EU Member States based on the recruitment of parliamentary officials through the *concours*. Even today, the continuous oscillation between these two opposing requirements supports the existence, in the internal administrative practices of the European Parliament, of an intense mobility between the staff of party groups and the permanent officials serving parliament as a whole (Jacobs and De Feo, 2023).

The comparative picture therefore confirms that matter how parliaments satisfy their internal administrative needs insofar they are able to do this autonomously. The autonomy of the internal administrative structure from external influences is indeed an indispensable requirement for the autonomy of parliament, which in its turn is the premise for setting an autonomous administrative organization. This was true historically, in the process of parliamentary institutionalization (Sisson, 1974), but it is still topical today, when legislatures see their institutional role deeply challenged within democracies under threat (Ginsburg and Huq, 2018). As a matter of fact, parliaments' administrative autonomy nowadays implies the capacity to address in an independent manner both old and new requirements, stemming from the drafting of stenographic records to digitalization, from the management of plenary and committee sittings to research and documentation. The ability to adapt to these administrative changes is essential to the protection of parliamentary identity facing some of the epochal challenges of representative democracy (Costa, Kerrouche and Magnette, 2004): preserving the role of parliament vis-à-vis increasing executive dominance at both supranational and national level (Curtin, 2014; Dan Wood, 2011); meeting the expectations for increased transparency and citizens' participation in order to combat electoral abstention and populism; responding to the nature of political decision-making in an ever more interdependent world which demands a more globalized parliamentarism.

Notes

1 See the special issues published in *Legislative Studies Quarterly*, Vol. 6, No. 4 (1981), dealing with the growth of legislative bureaucracies in the United States and in Europe since the Second World War, and in *Revue française d'administration publique*, Vol. 68, (1993), focusing on the role of parliamentary administrations in France, with limited comparative case studies from Germany, Senegal, and United Kingdom. See also the "virtual issue" published by the European Consortium of Political Research – ECPRD (2013) – bringing together papers presented at the 2013 ECPR General Conference.
2 On the Spanish Parliament, see for instance Díez Picazo (1985). On the French Parliament, Coniez and Michon (2020). On the Italian Parliament, Zuddas (2004) and Pacelli and Giovannetti (2020).
3 On the US case, see Fox and Hammond (1979), Malbin (1980), Weiss (1989) and Lyons (2013). For the UK, see Ryle (1981) and Petit and Yong (2018).
4 In calculating the staff/MPs ratios, we refer only to the number of permanent staff for all parliamentary administrations. The categorization of staff is not always precise, which is why exceptions to this criterion have been made for some of the cases covered here, namely the US (whose staff is mainly under political patronage), Argentina, Brazil, and Turkey (where the relationship between temporary and permanent staff is rather blurred and does not enable to clearly distinguish the numerical consistency of the two categories).

References

Stefan Becker, and Michael W. Bauer, 2021. 'Two of a Kind? On the Influence of Parliamentary and Governmental Administrations', in *The Journal of Legislative Studies*, Vol. 27, No. 4, pp. 494–512.

Cyril Benoît, and Olivier Rozenberg (eds), 2020. *Handbook of Parliamentary Studies. Interdisciplinary Approaches to Legislatures*, Northampton, Edward Elgar.

Cyril Benoît, 2020. 'Legislatures and the Administrative State: Political Control, Bureaucratic Politics and Public Accountability', in C Benoît and O Rozenberg (eds), *Handbook of Parliamentary Studies. Interdisciplinary Approaches to Legislatures*, Cheltenham, Edward Elgar, 255–274.

José Antonio Cheibub, and Bjørn Erik Rasch, 2022. 'Constitutional Parliamentarism in Europe, 1800 2019', in *West European Politics*, Vol. 45, No. 3, pp. 470–501.

Thomas Christiansen, Elena Griglio, and Nicola Lupo, 2021. 'Making Representative Democracy Work: The Role of Parliamentary Administrations in the European Union', in *The Journal of Legislative Studies*, Vol. 27, No. 4, pp. 477–493.

Jacobs Corbett, Francis Jacobs, and Michael Shackleton (eds), 2016. *The European Parliament*, 9th edn, London, John Harper.

Hugo Coniez, and Pierre Michon, 2020. *Servir les assemblées. Histoire et dictionnaire de l'administration parlementaire française, de 1789 à la fin du XXe siècle*, 2 vol., Paris, Mare et Martin.

Olivier Costa, Eric Kerrouche, and Paul Magnette, 2004. 'Introduction. Le temps du parlementarisme désenchanté? Les parlements face aux nouveaux modes de gouvernance' in O Costa, E Kerrouche and P Magnette (eds), *Vers un renouveau du parlementarisme en Europe?*, Brussels, Ed de l'Université de Bruxelles, 9–32.

Deirdre Curtin, 2014. 'Challenging Executive Dominance in European Democracy', in *The Modern Law Review*, Vol. 77, No. 1, pp. 1–32.

B. Dan Wood, 2011. 'Congress and the Executive Branch: Delegation and Presidential Dominance', in George C. Edwards, Frances E. Lee, and Eric Schickler (eds), The Oxford Handbook of the American Congress, Online edn, Oxford Academic, pp. 789–811.

George C. Edwards, Frances E. Lee, and Eric Schickler (eds), 2011. *The Oxford Handbook of the American Congress*, Online edn, Oxford Academic.

Alfredo De Feo, 2016. *A History of Budgetary Powers and Politics in the EU: The Role of the European Parliament. Part II: the Non-elected Parliament 1957–1978*, Luxembourg, Publications Office of the European Union.

Luis Maria Díez Picazo, 1985. *La autonomía administrativa de las cámaras parlamentarias*, Zaragoza, Studia Albornotiana.

ECPRD, 2013. "Parliamentary Administration in EU Affairs: Assistants or Advisors", ECPR Virtual Special Issue, available at https://ecpr.eu/Events/Event/PanelDetails/980.

ECPRD and Italian Chamber of Deputies, 2003. *Seminar on Parliamentary Administrations and Legislative Cooperation: Reports*, Palazzo Montecitorio – 30–31 October 2003, Roma, Camera dei Deputati.

Morten Egeberg, Åse Gornitzka, Jarle Trondal, and Mathias Johannessen, 2015. The European Parliament Administration: Organizational Structure and Behavioral Implications, in Michael W. Bauer and Jarle Trondal (eds), *The Palgrave Handbook of the European Administrative System. European Administrative Governance*, New York, Palgrave Macmillan.

Cristina Fasone, 2023. 'A Distinct Role for Parliamentary Administrations in Presidential and Parliamentary Systems?', in T Christiansen, E Griglio and N Lupo (eds), *Handbook on Parliamentary Administrations*, London, Routledge.

Harrison W. Fox, and Susan W. Hammond, 1979. *Congressional Staffs: The Invisible Force in American Lawmaking*, New York, Free Press.

Luigi Gianniti, and Rosella Cesare, 2023. 'The Internal Administrative Structure and the Relationship with the Speaker', in T Christiansen, E Griglio and N Lupo (eds), *Handbook of Parliamentary Administrations*, London, Routledge.

Elena Griglio, and Nicola Lupo, 2023. 'The Administration of Bicameral Parliaments', in T Christiansen, E Griglio and N Lupo (eds), *Handbook on Parliamentary Administrations*, London, Routledge.

Przemysław Grudzinski, and Wiesław Staskiewicz, 1992. *A Parliamentary Research Organization: The Proceedings of the International Conference on Parliamentary Services in Central and Eastern Europe: June 21–23, 1992*, Warsaw-Pultusk, Warsaw, Sejm Publishing Office.

W. Bartley Hildreth, Gerald Miller, and Evert L. Lindquist (eds), 2021. *Handbook of Public Administration*, New York, Routledge.

Anna-Lena Högenauer, Christine Neuhold, and Thomas Christiansen, 2016. *Parliamentary Administrations in the European Union*, New York, Palgrave.

Anna-Lena Högenauer. 2021. 'The Mainstreaming of EU Affairs: A Challenge for Parliamentary Administrations', in *The Journal of Legislative Studies*, Vol. 27, No. 4, pp. 535–553.

Aziz Huq, and Tom Ginsburg (eds), 2018. 'How to Lose a Constitutional Democracy', in *65 UCLA Law Review*, Vol. 78, pp. 78–169.

IPU, 2020. *Comparative Research Paper on Parliamentary Administration*, available at: https://www.ipu.org/resources/publications/reference/2020-09/comparative-research-paper-parliamentary-administration.

Francis Jacobs, and Alfredo De Feo, 2023. in T Christiansen, E Griglio and N Lupo (eds), *Handbook of Parliamentary Administrations*, London, Routledge.

David Judge, and David Earnshaw, 2003. *The European Parliament*, New York, Palgrave Macmillan.

Michael Laver, 2008. 'Overview: Legislatures and Parliaments in Comparative Context', in B Weingast and D Wittman (eds), *Oxford Handbook of Political Economy*, Oxford, Oxford University Press, 195–211.

Nicola Lupo, and Cristina Fasone, 2015. 'Transparency vs. Informality in Legislative Committees. Comparing the US House of Representatives, the Italian Chamber of Deputies and the European Parliament', in *The Journal of Legislative Studies*, Vol. 21, No. 3, pp. 342–359.

Nicola Lupo, and Eric Thiers, 2020. 'Sources and Origins of Parliamentary Law', in C Benoît and O Rozenberg (eds), *Handbook of Parliamentary Studies. Interdisciplinary Approaches to Legislatures*, Cheltenham, Edward Elgar, 160–180.

Christina L. Lyons, 2013. 'Congressional Staff', in *How Congress Works*, 5th edition, Los Angeles, CQ Press, 185–222.

Michael J. Malbin, 1980. *Unelected Representatives. Congressional Staff and the Future of Representative Government*, New York, Basic Books.

Simon Otjes, 2022. 'What Explains the Size of Parliamentary Staff?', in *West European Politics*, Vol. 46, No. 2, pp. 374–400.

Mario Pacelli, and Giorgio Giovannetti, 2020. *Interno Montecitorio. I luoghi, l'istituzione, le persone*, Torino, Giappichelli.

B. Guy Peters, and Jon Pierre (eds), 2012, *The SAGE Handbook of Public Administration*, London, SAGE, 2nd ed.

B. Guy Peters, 2023. 'United States', in T. Christiansen, E. Griglio and N. Lupo (eds), *Handbook of Parliamentary Administrations*, New York, Routledge.

Sarah Petit, and Ben Yong, 2018. 'The Administrative Organization and Governance of Parliaments', in C Leston-Bandeira and L Thompson (eds), *Exploring Parliaments*, Oxford, Oxford University Press, 24–31.

Michael T. Ryle, 1981. 'The Legislative Staff of the British House of Commons', in *Legislative Studies Quarterly*, Vol. 6, No. 4 (Nov., 1981), pp. 497–519.

Fritz Sager, Christian Rosser, Pascal Y. Hurni, and Céline Mavrot, 2012. 'How Traditional Are the American, the French, and the German Traditions of Public Administration? A Research Agenda', in *Public Administration*, Vol. 90, No. 1, pp. 129–143.

Martin Shane, Thomas Saalfeld, and Kaare W. Strøm (eds), 2014. *The Oxford Handbook of Legislative Studies*, Online edn, Oxford Academic.

Richard Sisson, 1974. 'Comparative Legislative Institutionalization: A Theoretical Exploration', in Allan Kornberg (ed.), Legislatures in Comparative Perspective, New York, David McKay Company, Inc, 17–38.

Stelios Stavridis, 2021. 'Parliamentary Diplomacy: A Review Article', in *International Journal of Parliamentary Studies*, Vol. 1, No. 2, pp. 227–269.

June Verrier, 2007. Benchmarking Parliamentary Administration: The United Kingdom, Canada, New Zealand and Australia, in *Australian Parliamentary Review*, Vol. 22, No. 1, pp. 45–79.

Giancarlo Vilella, 2019. *The Working Methods of the European Parliament Administration in Multi-Actors Words. A Case Study*, Florence, European Press Academic Publishing.

Wim Voermans, Hans-Martien ten Napel, and Reijer Passchier, 2015. 'Combining Efficiency and Transparency in Legislative Processes', in *The Theory and Practice of Legislation*, Vol. 3, No. 3, pp. 279–294.

Carol H. Weiss, 1989. 'Congressional Committees as Users of Analysis', in *Journal of Policy Analysis and Management*, Summer, 1989, Vol. 8, No. 3 (Summer, 1989), pp. 411–431.

Lois Recascino Wise, 2003. Representative Bureaucracy, in B. Guy Peters and Jon Pierre (eds), *Handbook of Public Administration*, London, SAGE.

Benjamin Yong, and Sarah Petit, 2018. The Administrative Organization and Governance of Parliament, in Louise Thompson and Cristina Leston-Bandeira (eds), *Exploring Parliament*, Oxford, Oxford University Press.

Paolo Zuddas, 2004. *Amministrazioni parlamentari e procedimento legislativo: il contributo degli apparati serventi delle Camere al miglioramento della qualità della legislazione*, Milano, Giuffrè.

PART I

Cross-cutting Analyses of Parliamentary Administrations

2
A DISTINCT ROLE FOR PARLIAMENTARY ADMINISTRATIONS IN PRESIDENTIAL AND PARLIAMENTARY SYSTEMS?

Cristina Fasone

2.1 Introduction

What relationship, if any, is in place between a certain form of government[1] and the architecture and functioning of a parliamentary administration, which, in turn, affects the way parliamentary institutions work? Indeed, there is a consolidated body of scholarship highlighting the differences shown by democratic systems operating under various forms of government, with the main dichotomy being parliamentarism vs. presidentialism (Elia, 1970; Horowitz, 1990; Lijphart, 1992); however, almost non-existent, beyond this handbook, is the academic reflection on what this dichotomy may imply on the administrative structure of legislatures.

Gradually emerged in England in the aftermath of the struggle between the House of Commons and the Crown, parliamentarism has widely circulated abroad (see Verney [1959] 1992, pp. 31–30, on the defining features of this form of government), has been praised by many for its alleged capacity to resist authoritarianism (at least, until a few year ago: see Linz, 1990a; Ackerman, 2000, p. 664–670with regard to "constrained parliamentarism"), and is mainly concentrated in Europe as well as in former UK colonies (e.g. Australia, Canada, India, and New Zealand). The interdependence between the legislative and the executive branch – the "fusion of powers" according to the political science literature – is what shapes parliamentarism, through the confidence relationship (Lijphart, 1992, pp. 5–6). Such a relationship can take many different configurations: it can refer to both or either Houses in case of a bicameral legislature, it can be presumed or expressly voted at the beginning of the term, it can be in placed on the Head of Government/Cabinet solely or on the Government as a whole, it may be subject to various degrees of "rationalization" (Mirkine-Guetzévitch, 1954, 97 ff.), it can be terminated under stricter or looser conditions, and it can be more or less easy for the Executive to call for early elections. To speak about parliamentarism (singular) is in fact an oversimplification of the reality as behind the confidence relationship – the common feature therein – there exists many variations on the model.

DOI: 10.4324/9781003181521-3

Likewise, presidentialism, originated for the first time from the US Constitution of 1787, is not a monolithic category. If the US probably represents a benchmark, few systems have come close to it in terms of checks and balances. With a few exceptions (e.g. see the case of South Korea), in the various areas of the world where it has been "imported", notably, in South America, in Africa, and in Asia, presidentialism has typically paved the way to a iper-presidentialization and a too strong executive (Linz, 1990b, pp. 54–55; Scoseria Katz, 2016, p. 214 ff.). The concentration of powers in the hands of a directly elected official in charge as Head of State and Head of Government (Sartori, 1994, pp. 173–181; Dixon, Landau and Roznai, 2019, p. 54), though in presence of a legislature that cannot be dissolved beforehand, has often triggered a marginalization of the Congress (Valenzuela and Wilde, 1979, pp. 189–215; Crisp and Schibber, 2014, pp. 637–643).[2]

During the twentieth century, the "family" of forms of government has witnessed further additions. The Constitution of the French Fifth Republic, indeed, adapted the Weimarian (failed) semi-presidential experience to the post-Second World War democratic context in France, in order to create a system preventing political fragmentation and ensuring stability (De Gaulle, [1946] 1992). Especially after the referendum of 1962, the French model of dual executive has inspired other countries, for example Poland in Europe, Tunisia in Africa, Mongolia in Asia, and Haiti in America to name a few, although the *fait majoritaire* has hardly been replicable elsewhere (Duverger, 1980, pp. 165–187; see Shugart and Carey, 1992, pp. 55–75 and Elgie, 2011, p. 20 ff. on the sub-types of semi-presidential systems).

Although other forms of government have been identified during the last century, from the Swiss (originally in 1798 and, now, according to the 1999 Constitution) and the Uruguayan (1919–1933) directorial regimes, inspired by the Pennsylvania Constitution of 1776 and by the French *Directoire* of 1795, to the prime ministerial form of government, in operation at national level only in Israel and for a limited period of time (1992–2001), the main fundamental difference amongst those regimes lies in the presence or in the lack of the confidence relationship (Lijphart, 1992, p. 6, describing all the other systems as "mixed"). If the focus is the executive-legislative relationship through the confidence, it can be even questioned the categorization of semi-presidentialism as an autonomous form of government, besides its diarchical element: the alleged alternation between presidential and parliamentary phases has hardly materialized, even in France with three experiences of cohabitation only. That's why in this contribution, semi-presidentialism is mainly associated with parliamentary systems in the democratic countries examined.

What does the choice of a certain form of government imply for the legislature and for the parliamentary administration? In principle, it seems that the more autonomous a legislature is from the executive (e.g. in the US presidentialism), in terms of power to shape the political directions of a given system (and, potentially, to prevent the executive from implementing its agenda), the more its law-making and oversight capacity increases. By contrast, this could lead to think that the expectation for political systems based on the confidence relationship, notably parliamentary systems and even more so semi-presidential systems modelled on the French example (Kerrouche, 2007, pp. 336–340), is to have legislatures strongly dependent on the executive.[3] Should these hypotheses be confirmed, then we can expect particularly well-equipped congressional administrations (as for the size, the budget, and the status of autonomy), supporting the law-making and scrutiny activity of legislatures in presidential regimes, and a modest parliamentary staff in systems articulated around the confidence relationship, maybe even with a certain degree of reliance on the executive's administration.

However, not only scholars in the field of legislative studies have shown that a specific form of government is not necessarily the determinant of a legislature's strength (Polsby, 1975;

Mezey, 1979; Norton, 1990) but also similar conclusions are not that straightforward when applied to parliamentary administrations either, according to a comparative analysis carried out on the country chapters collected in this volume. On the one hand, the form of government is just one of the variables affecting the actual powers and influence of a legislature. The electoral system, the party system, the majoritarian or consensual model of democracy followed, the political composition of the Cabinet/Government (one-party majority government, coalition government, or minority government), the way the confidence is given and withdrawn, and the actual degree of separation of powers can trigger very different dynamics compared to what is expected. For example, in the presence of two parliamentary systems, normally the capacity of a Parliament to influence the legislative process is higher where coalition governments are paired with a consensual style of democracy, like in Germany (Saalfeld, 1996, p. 68 ff.; Fish and Krönig, 2009, p. 261–265), than in jurisdictions were coalition and minority governments (so far) have been the exception and there is a clear majoritarian imprinting in the political dynamics, like in the UK (according to a traditional understanding, see Griffith, 1974, which has been recently challenged by Russell and Gover, 2017, p. 47 ff.). By the same token, despite a system is formally presidential, the *modus operandi* can be far away from the US separation of power model and rely on (informal) coalition agreements with a heavily fragmented political landscape, like in Brazil (Mainwaring, 1997, p. 55; Santos and Saboia Vieira, 2022).

This contribution argues, in turn, that no conclusive evidence can be found about the relationship between a certain form of government and the size and organization of the administration of a legislature although a few trends can be detected. For instance, the size of the parliamentary administrations and the budgetary autonomy tend to be more prominent in presidential systems than in parliamentary systems, as well as the supporting apparatus/agencies carrying out research activities and the budget assessment. Likewise, the system of recruitment and the status of the parliamentary staff seem to be much more independent from party politics in parliamentary and semi-presidential systems compared to presidential regimes.

Much more blurred is the evaluation of other features like the administrative support Parliaments get at the committee level, which seems largely dependent on the actual powers and autonomy standing committees enjoy along the law-making process, or the ratio between MPs' staff and non-partisan parliamentary officials.

These conclusions are drawn from a comparative analysis of the legislatures in some presidential regimes (Argentina, Brazil, Cyprus, Korea, Mexico, South Africa, US, plus the European Union [EU], and the European Parliament),[4] showing different levels of autonomy from the executive and following various political dynamics; from a selection of parliamentary regimes (Germany, Israel, Italy, Spain, and the UK) and of semi-presidential systems (Austria, France, Poland, Portugal, and Finland, which is semi-presidential in name only and is, de facto, a parliamentarism).

2.2 Analytical Framework

The study first considers the level of budgetary autonomy of a legislature, the size of the parliamentary staff, and its status, notably its degree of independence from politics and the ratio between "partisan" and "non-partisan" staff. Relatedly, it delves into the methods of recruitment, including the autonomy of the parliamentary system of selection vis-à-vis the convergence with the career in the (general) civil service.

Indeed, one can hypothesize that the autonomy enjoyed by a Congress under the US archetype of presidentialism can lead legislatures in this regime to resort to more human and financial resources than in systems based on the confidence relationship, where they can rely on the active collaboration with the executive – and are to the same extent depend on the government – to fulfil the same functions. It can also be expected that in parliamentary and semi-presidential systems the parliamentary staff is predominantly independent from the civil service and less partisan compared to presidential regimes, where on average there is more emphasis on the individual work of congressmen and on their influence as legislators (according to the strand of scholarship applying behavioural studies and rational choice theory to the study of the Congress: see, critically, Shepsle and Weingast, 1984, pp. 150–152) rather than on parliamentary structures and bodies and in general on the collective dimension of parliamentary activities.

Second, the study is intended to shed light on the differences – if any – between presidential systems and regimes based on the confidence relationship for what concerns the research support offered to MPs by the parliamentary administration, in terms of resources devoted to research and the organization, for example whether research services are articulated by standing committees and whether they work on demand of individual MPs or just assist the activities of parliamentary bodies at large. For the reasons pointed out above, it could be anticipated that in presidential systems MPs are more likely to have direct access to individual research support compared to "fused power systems" and, possibly, given the alleged independence from the executive, also in terms of information supply, in presidential regimes, the "investment" on research resources a Congress has to bear is higher.

Third, the contribution focuses on the way the policy-making process on the budget is supported by the parliamentary administration, in particular if independent agencies – independent fiscal institutions – supporting the legislatures are set up to this end. Indeed, it is expected that, due to the strong ties between the Parliament and the Government, in parliamentary and semi-presidential systems, the legislature would be more inclined to rely on the budgetary inputs and information provided by the Treasury and, consequently, would be less likely to set up their "own" fiscal council (on these agencies, see Beetsma and Debrun, 2016; Closa Montero, González de León and Losada Fraga, 2020), besides the internal administrative support offered by budgetary services. Thus, one can envisage the creation of parliamentary budget offices predominantly in presidential systems, as Congresses there otherwise lack the knowledge to deliberate on fiscal issues.

2.3 Comparative Assessment

The three main areas of investigation, namely the physiognomy of the parliamentary administration (budgetary autonomy, size and composition of the staff, the method of recruitment, and its status), the administrative structures devoted to research in relation to the committee system, and the parliamentary agencies/bureaucracies dealing with the budget, form the object of a comparative assessment of various legal systems. This allows not only to draw evidence on similarities and differences amongst presidential, semi-presidential, and parliamentary regimes but also to consider variations within the same type of form of government aiming to detect further factors potentially affecting a certain configuration and functioning of the parliamentary administration.

To this end, the analysis includes parliamentary systems with a high level of political fragmentation and instability, like Italy and Israel, systems that have traditionally been defined as majoritarian, like the UK, or highly stable, like Spain, though they have recently experienced new dynamics, and systems featured by a consensual model of democracy (Germany and Finland). Likewise, the research on presidential regimes encompasses legal systems characterized by different degrees of separation between the legislature and the executive and of operation of checks and balances mechanisms ranging from the stable democratic systems in the US, Korea, and Cyprus to systems with tendencies to overstretch the executive and presidential powers, like Argentina, Mexico, and South Africa, to a country, Brazil, where this trend is combined with a highly fragmented political systems and coalition governments. Finally, in semi-presidential regimes, there are systems where the legislature is highly influential and resilient to change, like in Austria (Fasone, 2014, p. 22) and in Portugal (Jancic, 2016, pp. 242–243), and countries where the Parliament is marginalized and confined in its power *de iure*, like in France (Rozenberg, 2019, pp. 45–65), or *de facto* like in Poland since 2015 (Maatsch, 2021, p. 786 ff.). The comparison will also include the case of the European Parliament (EP) and the European Union, which is not easy to fit into one specific form of government. As well known, some highlight the EU's aspiration to resemble the US system (Fabbrini, 2010, pp. 53–79) and, consequently, the EP's attempt to look at the US Congress as a model (Kreppel, 2006, p. 137 ff.). Others, instead, have insisted on the necessary political "consonance" between the Commission's President (and the College of Commissioners) and the majority in the EP, also based on Arts. 14, para 1, and 17 post-Lisbon (Lupo and Manzella, 2019, pp. 63–67). Further to this, other scholars have hinted to the similarities with systems based on a dual executive, like semi-presidentialism – both collective in the case of the EU, looking at the European Council and at the Commission (Bonvicini, Matarazzo and Tosato, 2009, p. 179 ff.).

2.3.1 The Physiognomy of Parliamentary Administrations: Budget, Staff, and Method of Recruitment

A first element to look at is the degree of budgetary autonomy a legislature enjoys,[5] as in turn this determines the level of instrumental and human resources the institution is capable to mobilize. Most legislatures examined benefit from complete spending autonomy, even though the budget of the legislature is part of the general budget of state (see Konrath, Pollak and Slominski, 2022, on Austria; Karayianni, 2022, on Cyprus; Raunio, 2022 on Finland; Tacea, 2022 on France; Arndt, Högenauer and Koggel, 2022, on Germany; Kölling and Molina, 2022 on Spain), and/or the budget is requested to comply with the general spending rules for the public administration or with the ceilings set by the Government (see Santos and Saboia Vieira, 2022 on Brazil; Nieto-Morales, 2022 on Mexico; Meakin, Yong and Leston-Bandeira, 2022 on the UK). Even where complete budgetary autonomy is ensured (see Hattis Rolef, 2022 on Israel; Lupo and Gianniti, 2022 on Italy; Guahk, 2022 on Korea; Serowaniec, 2022 on Poland; Vargas, Dias Pinheiro and Fonseca, 2022 on Portugal; and McKay and Johnson, 2010, p. 94, on the US),[6] typically the resources at Parliament's disposal were committed from the general national budget (see for more details, Table 2.1). In a couple of parliamentary systems, notably Finland and Spain, the draft budget for the legislature is submitted by the executive, although the former can certainly amend it (European Parliament, Directorate-General for Research, 1997, p. 1). Interestingly, in a presidential system like South Africa, in addition to the tabling of the (congressional) budget by the Treasury, the budget of the two Houses of Parliament is set through the ordinary budget process and no "special" autonomous procedure is regulated (Layman, 2022).

No clear pattern can be detected between the level of budgetary autonomy of a Parliament and the form of government in which it is embedded. Rather, it seems that the way the budget of the legislature is devised depends on the status of the parliamentary administration – for example, whether it is part of the general civil service. Relatedly,

Table 2.1 Forms of government vis-à-vis budgetary autonomy, parliamentary staff's size, status, and system of recruitment

Country	Form of government	No of MPs/senators	Budget	Staff (2019–2021)	Method of recruitment
Argentina	Presidential	257 Reps in the Chamber and 72 senators	N/A	More than 12,500 people (5,000 in the Chamber, 5,000 in the Senate, and 2,500 in the supporting agencies, like the Library)	Mainly political patronage (most staff members are those of party groups and individual members), except for the Administrative Technical Staff. High level of unionism
Austria	Semi-pres.	18 members of the National Council; 61 members of the Federal Council (joint administration)	No complete budgetary autonomy included within the federal budget	432 permanent staff members plus contractors	Public competition as per the civil service rules for the permanent administrative staff. Staff recruited by parliamentary groups and MPs very influential to provide policy expertise
Brazil	Presidential	513 deputies (Chamber of deputies only)	Complete budgetary autonomy, but subject to the federal public administration spending rules	13,900 people: permanent employees (2,742), commissioned employees (1,787) and freely appointed employees (9,376)	Only permanent employees appointed following public competition and examination; commissioned employees recruited by political groups; the others appointed to support individual MPs
Cyprus	Presidential	56 MPs	The House of Representatives' Budget is part of the State budget, but spending autonomy	137 permanent staff members	Public competition
EU – EP	Mixed (strong presidential features in parliamentary setting)	705 MEPs	Complete budgetary autonomy	5,400 permanent staff members and 1,113 contract agents + staff of political groups (1,135) and of individual MEPs (1,941)	75% of the staff (permanent) recruited through the EPSO competition. Staff of political groups may manage to enter the Administration

(Continued)

A Distinct Role for Parliamentary Administrations

Table 2.1 Forms of government vis-à-vis budgetary autonomy, parliamentary staff's size, status, and system of recruitment *(Continued)*

Country	Form of government	No of MPs/senators	Budget	Staff (2019–2021)	Method of recruitment
Finland	Semi-pres., but with parliamentary dynamics	200 MPs	Budgetary autonomy in spending, but the Eduskunta's budget is part of the state budget (draft budget proposed by the Government)	520 staff members + party groups' staff and, to a lesser extent, individual MPs' staff	Staff within parliamentary administration recruited to public competitions/tenders or ad hoc contracts (for advisors)
France	Semi-pres.	577 MPs (National Assembly only)	Budgetary autonomy in the framework of the State budget	Around 1,300 parliamentary officials (1,110 public *fonctionnaires* and 184 contract agents). About 2,100 MPs' staff	Public competition for parliamentary officials
Germany	Parliamentary	709 MPs in the Bundestag (minimum 598) and 69 seats in the Bundesrat	Budgetary autonomy in spending, but the Bundestag's budget is part of the federal budget (Ministry of Finance involved)	Approximately 3,000 employees for the Bundestag plus political groups' staff and MPs' individual assistant (4,000): 7,000 on the whole	Public competition for the employees (or internal calls for the vacancies). Limited level of interchangeability between parliamentary staff and the staff of other public administrations
Israel	Parliamentary (formally Prime-ministerial from 1992 to 2001)	120 MPs	Complete budgetary autonomy	Over 700 Knesset's employees, plus 240 Knesset's Guards. Mostly with full-time permanent contracts	External tenders and internal call for applications for vacancies, with merit-based selection. Ad hoc selections procedure for the legal advisor
Italy	Parliamentary	630 deputies and 315 senators	Complete budgetary autonomy (resources committed from the State budget)	1,042 employees in the Chamber; 585 employees in the Senate + staff of the groups (increased substantially), and individual MPs and senators' staff	Public competition for the employees

(Continued)

Table 2.1 Forms of government vis-à-vis budgetary autonomy, parliamentary staff's size, status, and system of recruitment (Continued)

Country	Form of government	No of MPs/senators	Budget	Staff (2019–2021)	Method of recruitment
Korea	Presidential	300 MPs	Complete budgetary autonomy	Around 2,000 employees (civil servants)	Public recruitment process (national competition when there is a vacancy). Limited level of interchangeability between parliamentary staff and the staff of other public administrations
Mexico	Presidential	500 MPs in the Chamber of Deputies and 128 members in the Senate	Budgetary autonomy within the federal budgetary framework	Around 2,400 employees (civil servants) in the Chamber; around 600 civil servants and 130 non-tenured contract agents in the Senate	Recent establishment of parliamentary civil service. Officials recruited through a competitive selection procedure
Poland	Semi-pres.	460 members in the Sejm and 100 in the Senate	Complete budgetary autonomy	1,295 employees in the Sejm; 331 in the Senate	Parliamentary civil servants recruited through ad hoc public competition
Portugal	Semi-pres., but with parliamentary dynamics	230 MPs	Complete budgetary autonomy	418 employees (parliamentary civil service)	Employees recruited through a public competition
South Africa	Presidential	400 members in the National Assembly; 90 in the National Council	Budget of the two Houses of Parliament set through the ordinary budget process (for the federal budget) by the National Treasury	1,309 officials work for the Parliament of South Africa as a whole	Parliamentary staff part of the (general) public administration and subject to recruitment through a competitive procedure

(Continued)

Table 2.1 Forms of government vis-à-vis budgetary autonomy, parliamentary staff's size, status, and system of recruitment (Continued)

Country	Form of government	No of MPs/senators	Budget	Staff (2019–2021)	Method of recruitment
Spain	Parliamentary	350 deputies and 265 senators	Budgetary autonomy in the framework of the State budget (draft budget of the two Houses incorporated into the general budget and proposed by the Government)	383 parliamentary employees, 65 contracted staff members, and 280 temporary staff members in the Congress; 250 parliamentary employees and 72 contracted staff members in the Senate	Public competition for the selection of the parliamentary employees
UK	Parliamentary	650 MPs in the House of Commons; approximately 820 peers in the House of Lords	Budgetary autonomy within general ceilings set by the Government	Almost 4,000 permanent staff: around 3,000 in the Commons and 570 in the Lords. Additionally, around 3,200 staff for individual MPs in the Commons	Permanent staff qualified as "crown servants" (rather than civil servants). Competitive selections procedure for the recruitment
US	Presidential	435 Reps and 100 senators	Complete budgetary autonomy	Roughly 20,000 people, excluding the Library	Political patronage. Parliamentarians, the Legislative Counsel (bill drafters), Law Revision counsel (codifiers of enacted law), and Inspector General appointed solely on the basis of the ability to fulfil the office's duties (and impartiality)

Source: Country reports collected in the Handbook and websites of the selected legislatures.

it is affected by the length of the process of gradual autonomization of the recruitment and of the rules on the parliamentary staff from the staff of the public administration, which in some countries, like Austria, has taken decades (Konrath, Pollak and Slominski, 2022) and in South Africa is still underway (Layman, 2022). In general, a trend towards increasing budgetary autonomy of Parliaments does exist, in parallel with the consolidation of constitutional democracies, while the budgetary cuts and the spending review that have affected the public administration as a whole over the last decade also had an influence on legislatures, though to a lesser extent.

When it comes to the size of the budget, instead, hints of a connection with the form of government becomes more apparent. The capacity of the budget is indeed directly linked to the cost of the personnel working for the Parliament at large (including its independent agencies), and we do see that in presidential systems the size of the congressional staff is on average bigger that in parliamentary regimes, which is subsequently reflected on the financial resources needed. The cases of the US, Argentina, Brazil, and, to a lesser extent, Mexico, Korea, and the EP[7] are a testament to that, with a size of the staff in a few cases above 10,000 employees, and compared to the number of MPs served (see Table 2.1). Semi-presidential systems follow immediately after when looking at the budget and at the staff available compared to the seats in Parliament (see the cases of Austria, France, Poland, and Portugal). In comparison, in some parliamentary regimes, legislatures seem understaffed and with a much smaller budget, as the cases of Italy (Lupo and Gianniti, 2022) and Spain (Kölling and Molina, 2022) show. There are a few outliers in this respect, like South Africa in presidential regimes, with a limited-size parliamentary staff, or Germany amongst parliamentary systems, with over 3,000 permanent employees in the Bundestag only.

However, more interesting is to give a closer examination on the composition of the parliamentary staff. The cases of the US Congress and of the legislatures in presidential systems following this model show that only a slight minority of the employees there are hired as permanent officials, with a non-partisan "mandate". In the US Congress, only the parliamentarians (fewer than ten), the Legislative Counsel (bill drafter), the Law Revision counsel (codifying enacted laws), the Inspector General, the General Counsel, and the Historian are expected to act impartially like civil servants, although they are not recruited through a public competition (McKay and Johnson, 2010, p. 95; Peters, 2022). Likewise, in Argentina, the greatest part of the congressional staff is selected through political patronage by party groups or individual MPs (Bertino, 2022), and in Brazil, of the almost 14,000 staff members of the Chamber of deputies, "only" 2,742 are permanent employees recruited through public competition (Santos and Saboia Vieira, 2022). By the same token, in Mexico, the establishment of a fully fledged parliamentary civil service is very recent and the staff used to be recruited through a mechanism of "spoil system" (Nieto-Morales, 2022). What characterizes presidential regimes in the Americas, however, does not appear to apply to some presidential systems in other continents. For instance, the parliamentary staff of the Korean National Assembly – around 2,000 employees – enjoy the status of civil servants, selected through a public recruitment process based on a nation-wide competition whenever there is a vacancy (Guahk, 2022). Moreover, the practice shows a limited level of exchange between the parliamentary staff and the staff of the other administrations. The situation is very similar at the Cypriot House of Representatives (Karayianni, 2022) and, to some extent, at the EP, should one regard the EU dynamics as presidential. Indeed, while especially in the past it was not infrequent for the personnel of political groups to manage to enter the EP's administration, today more than 75% of the permanent staff working for this institution is recruited through the European Personnel Selection Office (EPSO) competition (Jacobs and De Feo, 2022). By the same token, the officials at the Parliament of South Africa are recruited through a competitive procedure but form part of the general public administration and a process of reform is currently underway to create an ad hoc unitary status and system of recruitment for the officials working at the legislatures placed at the various levels of government in the country (the proposed establishment of a Parliament and Provincial Legislatures' Service, on which see Layman, 2022).

By contrast, it is much more common in parliamentary and semi-presidential systems the attempt to keep the process of selection of the parliamentary administrators and their status separate from those of the other institutions and from the civil service in general (with a very limited, almost non-existent, level of inter-changeability between parliamentary employees and other civil servants). For instance, in the UK, the permanent staff at Westminster are qualified as "crown servants", different from the civil servants (Meakin, Yong and Leston-Bandeira, 2022). In connection to this, *ad hoc* public competitions are organized to select parliamentary officials, which by definition are expected to act in a politically neutral and impartial way (in Finland, see Raunio, 2022; in France, see Avril, Gicquel and Gicquel, 2021, pp. 131–138; in Germany, see Arndt, Högenauer and Koggel, 2022; in Italy, see Lupo and Gianniti, 2022; in Poland, see Serowaniec, 2022; in Portugal, see Vargas, Dias Pinheiro and Fonseca, 2022; in Spain, see Kölling and Molina, 2022; in the UK, see Meakin, Yong and Leston-Bandeira, 2022). In some legislatures, for example in the Israeli Knesset, the recruitment process may differ depending on the office, with the legal advisors selected through a very cumbersome and multi-step process (Hattis Rolef, 2022).

Overall, in the parliamentary and semi-presidential systems under review, there seem to be, on the one hand, an influence of the European continental-French model of recruitment of public administrators, preferably through *concours* (Campbell and Laporte, 1981, p. 522); on the other, the choice to separate the career of the parliamentary administrators from that in the civil service may depend from an attempt to strengthen parliamentary autonomy, in front of the government that in such systems tends to act as the "executive committee" of the legislature (Elia, 1951, pp. 59–66 drawing on Laski, 1944, pp. 347–359). In other words, the parliamentary administration appears instrumental to provide support to all MPs on an equal footing and in an impartial way regardless of their positioning within the majority or in the opposition.

While the patent partisan dynamics within the parliamentary administration are a feature of the US Congress and of the above-mentioned presidential systems that try to emulate it – administrators are chosen because of their political affiliation and no restrictions are set for the staff to run in electoral campaigns or to take political offices – it should be noted that the number of employees working as individual MPs' staff and for political groups, rather than as parliamentary officials (subject to different recruitment procedures and status), has increased in most of the legislatures analysed over the past few decades. The trend is possibly the outcome of two different factors. One influential factor is certainly the electoral system: majoritarian systems and, in particular the first-past-the post, may favour political dynamics that emphasize the individual activities of MPs, aiming to seek re-election, and their individual weight in parliamentary proceedings. As a consequence, MPs tend to give pre-eminence to gain the support from a numerous and well-experienced personal staff, which may be trusted more than the parliamentary officials. Another important factor paving the way to the increase in the personnel directly working for the groups and for individual MPs is the block in the turnover of the parliamentary officials and the lack of public competitions held to recruit new administrators as a consequence of budget cuts. In these circumstances, as demonstrated by the cases of Italy (Lupo and Gianniti, 2022) and Portugal (Vargas, Dias

Pinheiro and Fonseca, 2022), the resort to the "political staff" – however different is their contractual status – aims to compensate a too small body of parliamentary civil servants to cope with the many functions legislatures and legislators have to fulfil.

2.3.2 Support for Committees and Parliamentary Administrative Structures Devoted to Research

Committees, in particular the permanent ones, have famously been labelled as the "backbones" of legislatures (Westlake, 1994, p. 191, with regard to the EP). In law-making, the strength of committees is what defines the strength of a parliamentary institution, in terms of capacity to shape the content of legislation and to oversee the executive (Barthélemy, 1934, pp. 58–59; Shaw, 1998, p. 229; Strøm, 1998, pp. 21–59). It follows that the administrative support standing committees are given is of the utmost importance for a legislature to control the law-making procedures. An important part of this support consists in carrying out bill-related research activities that can inform a well-thought deliberation by MPs and especially committee members.

The extent to which a certain form of government influences the architecture and the functioning of the parliamentary standing committee system has been subject to investigation over the last decade (see, e.g. Fasone, 2012, pp. 197 ff.). In that case, it has been concluded that looking at some prototypical case studies of presidential (US), semi-presidential (France), and parliamentary (Italy and the UK) regimes, there is an expectation that for presidential systems to have powerful committees is instrumental to preserve the functioning of the checks and balances mechanism, while this presents some problems when a divided government is in operation (Wilson, [1885], 2009, p. 110). In parliamentary systems, one can expect for the physiological development of the executive-legislative relationship that the government can count on a solid parliamentary majority in committees seconding, wherever possible, the political direction of the executive (Capitant, 1934, p. 10). From this perspective, at least until the 1990s, the functioning of the Italian committee system and its overarching influence on law-making has resembled more that in the US Congress than in other parliamentary regimes (D'Onofrio, 1979; Della Sala, 1993). Finally, the example of the French Fifth Republic showed a deliberate attempt to confining the influence of the Parliament by limiting the power and the configuration of its few and big standing committees (Shaw, 1998, pp. 231–232).

Including more countries into the analysis reveals that there is indeed a connection between the presidential nature of the form of government, the centrality of committees and the level of support they get in terms of research. In the presidential regimes studied, standing committees are the linchpins of law-making, they are numerous, of small size, and well-staffed (perhaps with the exception of Cyprus, see Karayianni, 2022), and they can count on the supply of studies and information by a Research Service that also works upon request by individual MPs, whether they step up as committee members or not. While the Research Services always provide impartial and non-partisan support to committees' and MPs' activities, in some presidential systems, notably in the US and Argentina, the committee staff is eminently partisan. In the US House of Representatives, except for three committees, professional staff members are appointed for two-thirds by majority members and for one-third by minority members, whereas in the Senate staff appointment in committees reflects the overall ratio of senators from each party (McKay and Johnson, 2010, p. 377).

Such a level of partisanship is unknown to parliamentary and semi-presidential systems: committee members may well be assisted by their own staff or by the staff of their groups, but this comes in addition to parliamentary clerks and officials assigned to a specific committee as part of the legislature's administration. Beyond such a feature, it is almost impossible to trace a link between the organization of the research support towards committees and the parliamentary/semi-presidential nature of the form of government. The arrangements could not be more varied. In some legislatures, like the German Bundestag, the two Houses of the Italian Parliament, the Israeli Knesset, and the European Parliament (though, as anticipated, the placement of the latter in one specific form of government is troubled), there is a Research Service, inspired by the US Congressional Research Service (Peters, 2022), further articulated according to the committees' remits, and that supports parliamentary activities besides the parliamentary officials working in the secretaries of the various committees. In other parliamentary/semi-presidential regimes, like in the French, the Spanish, and the UK Parliaments, there is no "autonomous" Research Service or Division linked to the committees' competence by subject matters and the standing committees themselves are quite marginalized in law-making.[8] In Spain, their role in the legislative process is often bypassed and they have scarce resources (Kölling and Molina, 2022). In the UK, where there are no standing committees regularly involved in the legislative procedures, there is no even an ad hoc committee service (chamber and committees' staff are part of the same service), but there are teams of clerks (from 6 to 8) working for the select committees, in charge with the scrutiny and the oversight of the executive only (Meakin, Yong, Leston-Bandeira, 2022). Likewise, in the French National Assembly, besides lacking a Research Department, there is no dedicated committee service and the committees' secretariats are scattered around different thematic poles, each of which includes several divisions (Tacea, 2022). Some legislatures make extensive use of external advisors (e.g. in the UK and Finland), while the European Parliament regularly involves external experts by outsourcing studies and reports.

As such, unlike for presidential regimes, the presence of the confidence relationship only does not seem to be a determinant of the configuration of the administrative support run for committees nor of the setting up of a Research Department supplementing information to committees, more rarely to individual MPs (in the EP for instance). Looking at the cases considered, as a preliminary conclusion to be subject to further investigation in the future, it appears that important variables in this context are the influence exerted by and "imported" from the model of the US Congress, the powers granted to committees by the law, the consensual nature of the political dynamics, and the inclination to see in the committees the places where the compromise is reached along the law-making process (Strøm, 1998, pp. 27–28).

2.3.3 *Parliamentary Bureaucracy and Agencies Dealing with the Budget*

The power of the purse, grounded on the principle "no taxation without representation", is probably one of the most distinctive features of parliamentary institutions and, around that, the struggle for their autonomy and strengthening has been advanced over the last centuries. This does not mean, however, that the budgetary powers of legislatures are alike and manifest differences have emerged. Here the divide between presidential and parliamentary/semi-presidential systems appears to have an explanatory value.

Indeed, in regimes where the bond between the executive and the legislature revolves around the confidence relationship, the budgetary procedures and the content of the budget itself have become visibly shaped by the Government even though the Parliament can pass amendments and is ultimately called to approve the budget in order to have it in force (Bateman, 2020, pp. 5–13). The marginalization of Parliaments in the budget process has been a problem increasingly felt in Europe in the aftermath of the debt crisis and especially in those countries, like Greece, Ireland, Portugal, and Spain receiving financial assistance (Moschella, 2017, p. 243 ff.).

By contrast, in presidential regimes, the capacity of the Parliament to influence the budget seems higher, also due to the lack of confidence votes to be used by the executive (increasingly in parliamentary systems) as a leverage to pressure the legislature on budgetary procedures. Congresses tend to remain the *domini* of the budget process once it has started and from time to time they have not hesitated to delay and veto budgetary decisions (McKay and Johnson, 2010, pp. 226–305). The (in)famous cases of the budget shutdown in the US or the veto of the Cypriot House of Representatives to the first rescue package in 2013 confirm the reach and scope of the congressional power of the purse. Instead, the veto on a budgetary document and act by a legislature in a parliamentary regime, as occurred in Italy in 2011 and in Spain in 2019, are seen as a symptom of the mal-functioning of the system and of a de facto *remise en cause* of the confidence relationship, although formally speaking this could remain untouched.

All the legislatures included in the comparative analysis can rely on ad hoc budget services,[9] but their position in relation to the parliamentary administration and reach of functions vary a lot. In general, such administrative support on budgetary policy has been established from the 1970s onwards and the Congressional Budget Office (CBO), set up in 1974, has been a benchmark worldwide. The support offered is linked to the expertise in economic and fiscal matters, is non-partisan and objective, and the selection of the relevant employees is merit-based (Joyce, 2011; Peters, 2022).

Various organizational arrangements have been devised in parliamentary and semi-presidential systems. For example, in Italy, the Budget Services of the Chamber of Deputies and the Senate were created in 1988–1989, in the aftermath of an important reform of the State Budget (Law no. 362/1988) and supply information on the reliability of the budget accounts, on the effects of bills on the revenues and expenditures and they mainly support the Budget Committees, though not exclusively. In the French National Assembly, instead, the budget falls within the remit of one of the 12 legislative services, notably on public finances. What these budget services have normally in common in regimes based on the confidence relationship is that they are internal to the parliamentary administrative structure and they serve the activity of parliamentary bodies, in particular Budget Committees and the Assembly, but they do not act on demand of individual MPs.

In several presidential systems, namely in Argentina, Korea, Kenya, Mexico, South Africa, and US, the need to rely on autonomous sources of information and evaluation on the budget seems to have paved the way to the setting up of independent fiscal agencies, formally placed outside the Congressional administration, but in fact serving the Congress only.[10] Modelled on the CBO, these agencies tend to act as fiscal think tanks enhancing the transparency and the publicity of budgetary information and supplying figures and data also upon request of individual Congressmen.

While the World Bank and the OECD have been advocating for the setting up of these institutions since decades, only some of them, and preferably in presidential systems and outside Europe (Closa Montero, González de León and Losada Fraga, 2020), have been established having strong bond to the legislature: they are not part of the parliamentary administration, and that's why they are recognized as independent fiscal institutions, but their staff do work for the Parliament in an impartial and non-partisan manner. In a few parliamentary systems (Australia, Canada and Italy[11]), trying to emulate the US CBO, parliamentary budget offices have been established lately. Not by chance this move was done in systems whose legislatures have been trying to keep their influence on the budget process or to re-balance their marginalization against the backdrop of the mounting executive dominance (Wehner, 2010, p. 53; Bateman, 2020, p. 199 ff.). They are a minority, nevertheless, and most parliamentary/semi-presidential systems have created independent fiscal institutions as stand-alone bodies, within other independent authorities (the central banks or the courts of auditors) or within the executive, though remaining functionally autonomous (Merlo and Fasone, 2021, Appendix), and while keeping budget services inside the parliamentary administration.

2.4 Conclusion

There is no clear-cut influence of the form of government and, in particular of the presidential vs. parliamentary divide, on the structure and the functioning of parliamentary administrations. To be more precise, the comparative analysis reveals some common trends featuring prominently within the "family" of the presidential systems, like the high level of budgetary autonomy, the considerable size of the internal budget and of the staff as well as its partisanship, the operation of congressional budget offices, the key role of the administrative support vis-à-vis standing committees in addition to the relative autonomy and impartiality of Research Services, which also serve individual MPs. However, these considerations apply mostly to the presidential systems that have tried to follow, more or less successfully, the US Congress as a benchmark and one can hardly find all these characteristics together in every presidential democracy examined.

By the same token, also in parliamentary (and semi-presidential) systems, there is a high degree of variation besides some common traits. Amongst the latter one can include the presence of a predominantly impartial and non-partisan parliamentary bureaucracy, with a status different and autonomous from the general civil service, and recruited through public competitions; possibly in an attempt to build a certain level of autonomy from the executive and its administration. Another recurrent feature, with few exceptions, is the "incorporation" of budget services within the parliamentary administration compared to the model of the independent agencies like the parliamentary budget offices. When it comes to the administrative structures to support the standing committees and the research activities, the comparative assessment shows very different institutional arrangements, depending on the functions and the strengths of those committees.

On certain issues, there are more visible similarities across presidential and parliamentary/semi-presidential systems than within the same type of form of government. For example, on the recruitment and the impartiality of the parliamentary staff, the Congresses of countries like Cyprus and Korea come closer to most parliamentary systems in Europe than to other presidential systems. Likewise, in some parliamentary democracies, like Finland, Germany, and Italy (and in the EP), the centrality of the administrative support to committees and the design of the Research Service (deliberately) resemble more the US Congress than other fellow Parliaments across the EU.

Furthermore, a few general trends can be detected from the comparative analysis, again, regardless of the form of government. Amongst them, there is the global tendency of Parliaments to let the proportion of political groups and individual MPs' staff on which they rely increase compared to parliamentary officials and civil servants: a feature that may depend, on the one hand, on the difficulty to recruit new officials and related to budget cuts or to the lack of resilience of the parliamentary administration; on the other, this can derive from the dynamics of the electoral systems and of the party competition, especially in majoritarian regimes, that emphasize the individual dimension of the parliamentary activities rather than the MPs' membership of the various parliamentary bodies and the collective dimension of decision-making within legislatures.

Other factors triggering a convergence between forms of government and seemingly affecting the organization and functioning of parliamentary and congressional administrations are the widespread executive dominance on law-making (Curtin, 2014) and the shift of focus by Parliaments from legislation only (or predominantly) to scrutiny and oversight (Griglio, 2020). To react to what are in fact common challenges for legislatures, the US Congress is typically used as a source of inspiration in reforming the administrative structures, given its strength within the constitutional system (see the cases of the EP, of the Korean Assembly, and of the Israeli and the Italian Parliaments). This common benchmark, together with the development of an intense interparliamentary cooperation and exchange of best practices amongst legislatures (and parliamentary officials: Fitsilis, 2018; Christiansen, Griglio and Lupo, 2021, pp. 486–489), has probably led to intensify this convergence process. These and other elements require further investigation and a more fine-grained inquiry in order to better understand not only *what* is happening at the level of the parliamentary administrations operating under different forms of government but also *why* we observe such trends.

Notes

1 The notion of form of government used here refers to the distribution of the powers to give political directions (*indirizzo politico*) amongst the constitutional bodies and, in particular, between the executive and the legislative branch (Mortati, 1973, p. 74).
2 In this chapter, legislatures will be labelled as Congresses in presidential systems and as Parliaments in parliamentary-semi-presidential systems. On this point, see Kreppel (2014, pp. 84–85). The term "legislature", however, is much broader, according to a certain understanding, as "the body entitled to make laws" and may not necessarily overlap with representative institutions like Congresses and Parliaments (Fasone, 2019, p. 2): see the view of the US Supreme Court in *Arizona State Legislature* vs. *Arizona Independent Redistricting Commission et al.* (576 U.S. 787, 2015) arguing, 5 to 4, that the electorate can be qualified as a "legislature" when voting on a ballot initiative to withdraw from the State Congress the power to draw electoral districts and to grant such a power to an Independent Redistricting Commission.
3 According to Schlesinger ([1985] 1992), "(…) while the parliamentary system formally assumes legislative supremacy, in fact it assures the almost unassailable dominance of the executive over the legislature" (p. 91). By contrast, "The Congress is far independent from the executive, far more responsive to a diversity of ideas, far better staffed, far more able to check, balance, challenge, and investigate the executive government" (p. 92).
4 On the inclusion of the EU and of the European Parliament here, see the justifications provided in para. 2 below.
5 By budgetary autonomy, here we mean the extent to which the legislature is able to set its own budget regardless of external influence.
6 According to Rules 102–104 of the EP?s rules of procedure, this legislature enjoys complete budgetary autonomy but the salary of the EP's officials is subject to the same terms and conditions as the other EU civil servants (Corbett, Jacobs and Neville, 2016, pp. 258–259).
7 In the case of the EP, the figure of around 6,500 personnel, between permanent staff and contract agents, is also influenced by the multinational and multilinguistic nature of the institutions (see Jacobs and De Feo, 2022).
8 Although there is no "autonomous" Research Service in the Finnish Parliament either (there is an Information Service whose consultation by MPs has declined steadily), there is an ad hoc Committee Department to govern the staff assigned to the numerous and powerful standing committees. The French, the Spanish, and the UK Parliament can rely, nonetheless, on the libraries for carrying out in-depth studies or on administrative structures specialized on certain issues, like the UK Parliamentary Office of Science and Technology.
9 Although in some legislatures, like in the Israeli Knesset, the Budget Control Department is established within the Research and Information Centre (Hattis Rolef, 2022).

10 In the case of the Mexican Centre for Public Finance Studies, the independence of the body from the legislature has been put into question (OECD, 2015, p. 166).
11 In these countries, the setting up of the parliamentary budget offices has not led to dismantle or abolish the existing administrative budget services.

References

Ackerman, B., 2000. *The New Separation of Powers*, in *Harvard Law Review*, 113(3), pp. 642–729.
Arndt, F., Högenauer, A.-L. and Koggel, C., 2023. Germany's Parliamentary Administration Germany, in T Christiansen, E Griglio and N Lupo (eds), *Handbook on Parliamentary Administrations*, London, Routledge.
Avril, P. Gicquel, J. and Gicquel, J.É., 2021. *Droit parlementaire*, Paris, L.G.D.J., 6th ed.
Barthélemy, J., 1934. *Essai sur le travail parlementaire et le système des commissions*, Paris, Delagrave.
Bateman, W., 2020. *Public Finance and Parliamentary Constitutionalism*, Cambridge, Cambridge University Press
Beetsma, R.M.W.J. and Debrun, X., 2016. *Fiscal Councils: Rationale and Effectiveness*, in *IMF Working Paper*, WP/16/86, https://www.imf.org/external/pubs/ft/wp/2016/wp1686.pdf
Bertino, P., 2023. Argentina's Parliamentary Administration Argentina, in T Christiansen, E Griglio and N Lupo (eds), *Handbook on Parliamentary Administrations*, London, Routledge.
Bonvicini G., Matarazzo R. and Tosato G.L., 2009. *I partiti politici europei e la candidatura del presidente della Commissione*, in *Il diritto dell'Unione europea*, 1, pp. 179 ff.
Campbell, S. and Laporte, J., 1981. *The Staff of the Parliamentary Assemblies in France*, in *Legislative Studies Quarterly*, 6(4), pp. 521–531.
Capitant, R., 1934. *La réforme du parlementarisme*, Paris, Sirey.
Christiansen, T., Griglio, E. and Lupo, N., 2021. *Making Representative Democracy Work: the Role of Parliamentary Administrations in the European Union*, in *The Journal of Legislative Studies*, 27(4), pp. 477–493.
Closa Montero, C., González de León, F. and Losada Fraga, F., 2020. *Democracy vs Technocracy: National Parliaments and Fiscal Agencies in EMU Governance*, in RECONNECT Working Paper series, D.10.2., https://reconnect-europe.eu/wp-content/uploads/2020/11/D10.2.pdf.
Corbett, R., Jacobs, F. and Neville, D., 2016. *The European Parliament*, London, John Harper Publishing, 9th ed.
Crisp, B.F. and Schibber, C.F., 2014. *The Study of Legislatures in Latin America*, in Martin, S., Saalfeld, T. and Strøm, K.W. (eds.), *The Oxford Handbook of Legislative Studies*, Oxford, Oxford University Press, pp. 629–644.
Curtin, D., 2014. *Challenging Executive Dominance in European Democracy*, in *Modern Law Review*, 77(1), pp. 1–32.
De Gaulle, C., [1946] 1992. *The Bayeux Manifesto*, in Lijphart, A. (ed.), *Parliamentary versus Presidential Government*, Oxford, Oxford University Press, pp. 139–141.
Della Sala, V., 1993. *The Permanent Committees of the Italian Chamber of Deputies: Parliament at Work?*, in *Legislative Studies Quarterly*, 18(2), pp. 157–183.
Dixon, R., Landau, D. and Roznai, Y., 2019. *Term Limits and the Unconstitutional Constitutional Amendment Doctrine: Lessons from Latin America*, in Baturo, A. and Elgie, R. (eds.) *The Politics of Presidential Term Limits*, Oxford, Oxford University Press, pp. 53–70.
D'Onofrio, F., 1979. *Committees in the Italian Parliament*, in Shaw M. and Lees, J. (eds.), *Committees in Legislatures*, Durham, NC, Duke University Press, pp. 61–101.
Duverger, M., 1980. *A New Political System Model: Semi-presidential Government*, in *European Journal of Political Research*, 8(2), pp. 165–87.
Elgie, R., 2011. *Semi-Presidentialism: Sub-Types and Democratic Performance*, Oxford, Oxford University Press.
Elia, L., 1951. *Il Governo come Comitato direttivo del Parlamento*, in *Civitas*, II(4), pp. 59–66.
Elia, L., 1970. *Governo (forme di)*, in *Enciclopedia del diritto*, vol. XIX, Milano, Giuffrè, pp. 634–675.
European Parliament, Directorate-General for Research, 1997. *Budget of Parliament. What Are the Procedures Involved? How Are They Controlled?* National Parliaments series, PE 124.794mv. 1, Luxembourg.
Fabbrini, S., 2010. *Compound Democracies: Why the United States and Europe Are Becoming Similar*, Oxford, Oxford University Press, 2nd ed.
Fasone, C., 2012. *Sistemi di commissioni parlamentari e forme di governo*, Padua, Cedam.

Fasone, C., 2014. *Eurozone, Non-Eurozone and "Troubled Asymmetries" among National Parliaments in the EU. Why and to What Extent This Is of Concern*, in *Perspectives on Federalism*, 6(3), pp. 1–41

Fasone, C., 2019. *What Is a Legislature in the Twenty-First Century? Classification and Evolution of a Contested Notion*, in *Federalismi.it*, 15, pp. 1–20.

Fish, M.S. and Krönig, M., 2009. *The Handbook of National Legislatures. A Global Survey*, Cambridge, Cambridge University Press.

Fitsilis, F., 2018. *Inter-parliamentary Cooperation and Its Administrators*, in *Perspectives on Federalism*, 10(3), pp. 28–55.

Griffith, J.A.G., 1974. *Parliamentary Scrutiny of Government Bills*, London, Allen and Unwin for PEP and the Study of Parliament Group.

Griglio, E., 2020. *Parliamentary Oversight of the Executives. Tools and Procedures in Europe*, Oxford, Hart Publishing.

Guahk, Y., 2023. Korea's Parliamentary Administration Korea, in T Christiansen, E Griglio and N Lupo (eds), *Handbook on Parliamentary Administrations*, London, Routledge.

Guy Peters, B., 2022. *The Proposed Establishment of a Parliament and Provincial Legislatures' Service*, United States.

Hattis Rolef, S., 2023. Israel's Parliamentary Administration Israel, in T Christiansen, E Griglio and N Lupo (eds), *Handbook on Parliamentary Administrations*, London, Routledge.

Horowitz, D.L., 1990. *Comparing Democratic Systems*, in *Journal of Democracy*, 1, pp. 73–79.

Jacobs, F. and De Feo, A., 2023. European Parliament's Administration, in T Christiansen, E Griglio and N Lupo (eds), *Handbook on Parliamentary Administrations*, London, Routledge.

Jancic, D., 2016. *National Parliaments and EU Fiscal Integration*, in *European Law Journal*, 22(2), pp. 225–249.

Joyce, P.G., 2011. *The Congressional Budget Office: Honest Numbers, Power, and Policymaking*, Washington, DC, Georgetown University Press.

Karayianni, N., 2023. Cyprus' Parliamentary Administration Cyprus, in T Christiansen, E Griglio and N Lupo (eds), *Handbook on Parliamentary Administrations*, London, Routledge.

Kerrouche, E., 2007. *The French Assemblée nationale: The case of a weak legislature?*, in *The Journal of Legislative Studies*, 12(3–4), pp. 336–365.

Kölling, M. and Molina, I., 2023. Spain's Parliamentary Administration, in T Christiansen, E Griglio and N Lupo (eds), *Handbook on Parliamentary Administrations*, London, Routledge.

Konrath, C., Pollak, J. and Slominski, P., 2023. Austria's Parliamentary Administration, in T Christiansen, E Griglio and N Lupo (eds), *Handbook on Parliamentary Administrations*, London, Routledge.

Kreppel, A., 2006. *The Environmental Determinants of Legislative Structure: A Comparison of the U.S. House of Representatives and the European Parliament*, in Power, T.J. and Rae, N.C. (eds.), *Exporting Congress? The Influence of the U.S. Congress on World Legislatures*, Pittsburgh, The University of Pittsburgh Press, pp. 137–156.

Kreppel, A., 2014. *Typologies and Classifications*, in Martin, S., Saalfeld, T. and Strøm, K.W. (eds.), *The Oxford Handbook of Legislative Studies*, Oxford, Oxford University Press, pp. 83–97.

Laski, H.J., 1944. *The Parliamentary and Presidential Systems*, in *Public Administration Review*, 4, pp. 347–359.

Layman, T.P., 2023. South Africa's Parliamentary Administration, in T Christiansen, E Griglio and N Lupo (eds), *Handbook on Parliamentary Administrations*, London, Routledge.

Lijphart, A. 1992. Introduction, in, *Parliamentary versus Presidential Government*, Oxford, Oxford University Press, pp. 1–27.

Linz, J.J., 1990a. *The Virtues of Parliamentarism*, in *Journal of Democracy*, 1, 1990, pp. 84–91.

Linz, J.J., 1990b. *The Perils of Presidentialism*, in *Journal of Democracy*, 1, 1990, pp. 51–69.

Lupo, N. and Manzella, A., 2019. *Il parlamento europeo. Una introduzione*, Rome, LUISS University Press.

Lupo, N. and Gianniti, L., 2023. Italy's Parliamentary Administration, in T Christiansen, E Griglio and N Lupo (eds), *Handbook on Parliamentary Administrations*, London, Routledge.

Maatsch, A., 2021. *Disempowerment through the Backdoor: The Impact of Populist Parties on the National Parliament in Poland*, in *Parliamentary Affairs*, 74(4), pp. 786–801

Mainwaring, S., 1997. *Multipartism, Robust Federalism, and Presidentialism in Brazil*, in Mainwaring, S. and Shugart, M. S. (eds.), *Presidentialism and Democracy in Latin America*, Cambridge, Cambridge University Press, pp. 55–109.

McKay, W. and Johnson, C.W., 2010. *Parliament and Congress: Representation and Scrutiny in the Twenty-First Century*, Oxford, Oxford University Press.

Meakin, A., Yong, B. and Leston-Bandeira, C., 2023. United Kingdom's Parliamentary Administration, in T Christiansen, E Griglio and N Lupo (eds), *Handbook on Parliamentary Administrations*, London, Routledge.

Merlo, S. and Fasone, C., 2021. *Differentiated Fiscal Surveillance and the Democratic Promise of Independent Fiscal Institutions in the Economic and Monetary Union*, in *Swiss Political Science Review*, 27(3), pp. 582–600.

Mezey, M.L., 1979, *Comparative Legislatures*, Durham, NC, Duke University Press.

Mirkine-Guetzévitch, B., 1954. *L'échec du parlementarisme «rationalisé»*, in *Revue internationale d'histoire politique et constitutionnelle*, 1954, pp. 97 ff.

Mortati C., 1973. *Lezioni sulle forme di governo*, Padova, Cedam.

Moschella, M., 2017. *When Some Are More Equal than Others: National Parliaments and Intergovernmental Bailout Negotiations in the Eurozone*, in *Government and Opposition*, 52(2), pp. 239–265.

Nieto-Morales, F., 2023. *Mexico's Parliamentary Administration*, in T Christiansen, E Griglio and N Lupo (eds), *Handbook on Parliamentary Administrations*, London, Routledge.

Norton, P., 1990. *Parliaments: A Framework for Analysis*, in *West European Politics*, 13(3), pp. 1–9.

OECD, 2015. *Mexico - Centre for Public Finance Studies*, in *OECD Journal of Budgeting*, 2, pp. 165–173.

Polsby, N.W., 1975. *Legislatures*, in *Handbook of Political Science*, Reading, MA, Addison-Wesley, Vol. 5.

Raunio, T., 2023. *Finland's Parliamentary Administration*, in T Christiansen, E Griglio and N Lupo (eds), *Handbook on Parliamentary Administrations*, London, Routledge.

Rozenberg, O., 2019. *De la difficulté d'être un Parlement normal*, in Duhamel O. et al. (eds), *La Ve République démystifiée*, Paris, Presse de Sciences Po, pp. 45–65.

Russell, M. and Gover, D., 2017. *Legislation at Westminster: Parliamentary Actors and Influence in the Making of British Law*, Oxford, Oxford University Press.

Saalfeld, T., 1996. *The West German Bundestag after 40 Years: The Role of Parliament in a 'Party Democracy'*, in Norton, P. (ed), *Parliaments in Western Europe*, London, Frank Cass, pp. 68–89

Santos, F. and Saboia Vieira, F., 2023. *Brazil's Parliamentary Administration*, in T Christiansen, E Griglio and N Lupo (eds), *Handbook on Parliamentary Administrations*, London, Routledge.

Sartori, G., 1994. *Comparative Constitutional Engineering: An Inquiry into Structures, Incentives and Outcomes*, New York, Springer.

Schlesinger, A.M. Jr., [1985] 1992. *Leave the Constitution Alone*, in Lijphart, A. (ed.), *Parliamentary versus Presidential Government*, Oxford, Oxford University Press, pp. 90–94.

Scoseria Katz, A., 2016. *The President in His Labyrinth: Checks and Balances in the New Pan-American Presidentialism*, PhD Thesis, Yale Law School (unpublished), https://papers.ssrn.com/sol3/papers.cfm?abstract_id=3258783

Serowaniec, M., 2023. *Poland's Parliamentary Administration*, in T Christiansen, E Griglio and N Lupo (eds), *Handbook on Parliamentary Administrations*, London, Routledge.

Shaw, M., 1998., *Parliamentary Committees: A Global Perspective*, in *The Journal of Legislative Studies*, 4(1), pp. 225–251.

Shepsle, K.A. and Weingast, B.R., 1984. *Positive Theories of Congressional Institutions*, in *Legislative Studies Quarterly*, XIX(2), pp. 149–179.

Shugart, M.S. and Carey, J.M., 1992. *Presidents and Assemblies. Constitutional Design and Electoral Dynamics*, Cambridge, Cambridge University Press.

Strøm, K., 1998. *Parliamentary Committees in European Democracies*, in *The Journal of Legislative Studies*, 4(1), pp. 21–59.

Tacea, A., 2022. *The French Parliamentary Administration: A Bureaucracy inside the Parliament?* France.

Valenzuela, A. and Wilde, A., 1979. *Presidential Politics and the Decline of the Chilean Congress*, in Smith, J. and Musolf, L. (eds.) *Legislatures in Development: Dynamics of Change in New and Old States*, Durham, NC, Duke University Press, pp. 189–215.

Vargas, A., Dias Pinheiro, B. and Fonseca, T., 2023. *Portugal's Parliamentary Administration*, in T Christiansen, E Griglio and N Lupo (eds), *Handbook on Parliamentary Administrations*, London, Routledge.

Verney, D.V., [1959] 1992. *Parliamentary Government and Presidential Government*, in Lijphart, A. (ed.), *Parliamentary versus Presidential Government*, Oxford, Oxford University Press, pp. 31–47.

Wehner, J., 2010, *Legislatures and the Budget Process: The Myth of Fiscal Control*, New York, Palgrave.

Westlake, M., 1994. *A Modern Guide to the European Parliament*, London and New York, Pinter Publishers.

Wilson, W., [1885] 2009. *Congressional Government. A Study in American Politics*, New Brunswick, NJ, Transaction Publishers.

3
THE INTERNAL ADMINISTRATIVE STRUCTURE AND THE RELATIONSHIP WITH THE SPEAKER

Luigi Gianniti and Rosella Di Cesare

3.1 Introduction

Each Parliament has its own administrative structure, defined by different regulatory sources. The highest political authority, the Speaker, is also the person to whom the administrative structure generally refers. The strength of his or her powers in relation to the administration depends on the nature of the bodies which are called upon to support him/her: that is, whether they are purely political or mixed political-administrative bodies. The chief administrative officer, the Secretary General (SG), generally carries out a multitude of tasks, inevitably relating to the Speaker. Across the different systems, it is clear that the relationship between the Speaker and the SG is not dependent upon the fundamental choice in favour of bicameralism or monocameralism, but upon the organizational autonomy of each Chamber. Bicameral Parliaments – usually organized with two SGs – may feature two Chambers which are similarly organized or which feature significant differences in the role of the SG, regardless of the powers exercised by each Chamber in the constitutional system. Therefore, the arrangement of Parliamentary Administrations is also independent of the symmetrical or asymmetrical nature of bicameralism (Griglio & Lupo, 2021).

This chapter will analyse the relationship between Parliamentary Administrations and the Speaker, describing the characteristics of the former (autonomy, independence, and necessity) by reference to the system of appointment and the functions and tasks of the relevant SG, who in most cases is chosen from within the Administration. We will also examine the additional administrative figures who interface with the Speaker, and whose powers don't depend upon the SG from a hierarchical perspective.

3.2 Autonomy of Parliament and Autonomy of Parliamentary Administrations

The principle of the autonomy of Parliaments is expressed at both the political and administrative levels. As a political organization, Parliament has regulatory autonomy with respect to establishing its internal rules of operation and managing its own expenditure. Administrative autonomy permits a body to define its own structures without any interference and has a special role vis-à-vis political autonomy. The administrative dimension of parliamentary autonomy is instrumental (Tudela Aranda, 2010), since the functioning of legislative Assemblies requires the existence of a specific administrative bureaucracy, whose organizational models are influenced by the evolution of Parliaments (its functions, growth, and complexity) and by the predominant type of functions exercised by the relevant form of government (Zampetti, 2013). In this context, the case of the European Parliament shows that the progressive achievement of autonomy ran parallel with an increase in parliamentary bureaucracy (Costa, 2003; Egeberg, Gornitzka, Trondal, & Johannessen 2013). It is argued that in EP the extension of powers not only has implications for the directly elected Members of Parliament (MEPs) but also for officials employed (Högenauer, Neuhold, Christiansen, & Dobbels, 2016).

These administrations legitimize themselves by serving the purpose of implementing the original position of the Chambers within the constitutional organization, consolidating their autonomy by reference to their effectiveness. Legislative Assemblies can be effectively autonomous if they actually benefit from independent institutional support, regardless of the government's majorities and other constraints resulting from the constitutional system of allocation of powers. Parliamentary Administrations cannot legitimately be influenced in the carrying out of this task by external factors, for example by constraints imposed by the Executive or other constitutional bodies or powers of the State. This is considered to be the "guarantee statute" which covers the procedures for the performance of the functions properly exercised by the Chambers (Dickmann, 2014).

By contrast, efficient Parliamentary Administrations may affect the Chambers' ability to exercise their autonomy (Costa, 2003). This is the unique nature of Parliamentary Administrations: they serve a single institution, for theirs functions, for its pluralism, and for the eminently public and deliberative nature of almost all its activities (Tudela Aranda, 2010). Democratic Parliaments therefore need parliamentary bureaucracy: politicians have to delegate some tasks and decisions due to a lack of time and expertise (Högenauer & Neuhold, 2015) but they still want to monitor the behaviour of administration (Arnold, 1987).

3.3 Governing Principles of Parliamentary Administrations

The principle of the autonomy of legislative Assemblies means that the legislative provisions regarding the legal and economic status of civil servants apply to the employees of Parliament only when expressly stated in special provisions of the same laws or in special legislative measures, or when independently provided for by the Assembly itself (Finzi, 1934): this helps to make such bureaucracies "special". In the past, for example, in the experience of the Reichstag and the German States of the 1930s, there were some cases of total equality between Parliamentary employees and other civil servants. Presently, by comparison, Parliamentary employees' peculiar legal and economic position can be different from the position of civil servants, as a direct consequence of the autonomy constitutionally guaranteed to legislative Assemblies.

Autonomy presupposes specificity, and its exercise also requires continuity of operations, which is guaranteed by the administrative apparatus, capable of ensuring the "role of institutional memory" that elected representatives cannot by definition guarantee. The autonomy of Parliamentary Administrations also ensures their independence from the executive administrations (Inter-Parliamentary Union, 2020) and the ability to have permanent employees.

In many cases, administrations are exclusively subject to the rules of the civil service or belong to civil service (in Cyprus, including the SG) (ECPRD, 2003). In the United Kingdom, for example, the autonomy and independence (resulting in continuity and stability) of the administration are ensured first and foremost through a recruitment system which is common to the whole Civil Service,[1] but which includes specific additional tests to be completed by those applying for parliamentary service jobs (Cozzoli, 1997). A similar situation exists in Germany, where the Bundestag administration is part of the federal bureaucracy and it is possible for officials to move between the legislative and the executive branches (Blischke, 1981), and in Albania, where the rules of the "Law for the Civil Servant" are also applied in the event of parliamentary staff recruitment.

In France, on the other hand, the parliamentary staff do not come from the *Institut national du service public* (INSP) – and do not therefore already comply with the Government's demands for autonomy as from the selection stage (Campbell & Laporte, 1981) – but are always recruited from the public, on the basis of their possession of certain qualifications, by each Chamber separately (Mattarella, 1997); the rules of public competition are established by the two Bureau of the Chambers (Tacea, 2022). Similarly in Belgium (Dirck G. Caboor & Popelie, 2022) and in Italy (Lupo & Giannetti, 2022), the staff of the Chambers has its own statute and is distinct from the rest of the public administration. In Portugal, parliamentary staff form a special and permanent body governed by a special statute – the Statute governing Parliamentary Staff – and this career path is usually only accessed via their base category of staff and requires certain educational qualifications (Vargas, Dias Pinheiro, & Fonseca, 2022).

Sometimes the assimilation of the staff of the Legislative Assemblies with the civil servants is also intended to mark their difference from the other categories of staff within the Chambers, such as parties' staff and MPs' personal staff (Piccirilli & Zuddas, 2012).

It follows that Parliaments may have different legal bases for their respective administrations, characterized by their relationship with their employees arising from the relevant recruitment process governed by several sources: the Constitution, the laws (e.g. the Parliamentary Service Act for Commonwealth Parliaments,[2] with the exception of India[3]), parliamentary rules and regulations, and joint deliberations of the Bureaus (Inter-Parliamentary Union, 2020).[4]

There are, however, common principles regarding parliamentary staff in the broad sense (Association of Secretaries General of Parliaments, 2013): recruitment must be on the basis of fair and open competition; appointments must not be based on "personal or partisan political considerations"; Parliaments retain autonomous control of the recruitment process; recruits must possess the ability to be impartial and to preserve integrity; qualified recruitment must be based on the different professional profiles required; and the internal and external mobility of staff must be ensured. In the case of bicameral Parliaments, recruitment procedures may differ for each Chamber, or they may be common to both branches of Parliament. For example, in Spain, the Staff Regulations of the General Courts regulate the employment relationship with staff and permit the mobility of officials between the Congress of Deputies and the Senate de Santos Canalejo, 2018. In Switzerland, by comparison, the administrations of the two Chambers are fully integrated, meaning that all staff members work for both Chambers, as staff of the Federal Assembly (Griglio & Lupo, 2021).

Parliamentary Administrations can alternatively be based on a "career model" or on an "employment/function model". In the first, the administration recruits young, qualified, and generalist officials. In the pattern of jobs or functions, professional figures are recruited for a specific function and for a certain period. In 90 per cent of countries, parliamentary staff are recruited under the control of Parliament, with some exceptions – namely the European Parliament, which has a central office for all institutions (Jacobs & De Feo, 2022), and Ireland, in which there is an independent statutory body for staff recruitment (English & Murphy, 2022). These principles apply to Parliamentary Administrations strictly speaking, which is more pronounced in some national legislatures, but besides them there are other categories of staff (Piccirilli & Zuddas, 2012), namely employees of political groups (party group staff), individual assistants of Parliamentarians (MPs' assistants), and staff of committees (Committee staffing, divided into majority and minority staffs in the USA). While the Speaker obviously has relations with the Parliamentary Administration, there are no hierarchical relationships with respect to the other three categories of staff. In some legal systems (such as the USA), the personal staff of deputies and senators comprise the majority of the total staff.

Further distinctions within Parliamentary Administrations relate to the degree of independence from political forces: for example, in the American system there are so-called partisan officers, who are elected by the Houses,[5] and "bipartisan" or "non-partisan" officers (Battini, 1997). In other cases, such as in the European Parliament, mobility between the staff of political groups and that of the Parliament as a whole is also possible: usually the SG is selected from the staff of political groups or from the staff of the Presidents of the European Parliament,[6] with a different approach taken to the staff hired via regular competition by comparison with an internally selected SG. Similarly, in Austria, there have been cases of political staffers who have ultimately become heads of service, or heads of departments within the Parliamentary Administration (Konrath, Pollak, & Slominski, 2022). In Spain, there is also a temporary staff hired by the Parliamentary Administration but dedicated to the needs of the members of the Bureau and other parliamentarians institutions (Kölling & Molina, 2022). In France, on the other hand, transfers between these types of staff and the administration of the *Assemblée Nationale* are prohibited, as neutrality is one of the requirements of recruitment.

3.4 The Head of the Parliamentary Administration: The Secretary General (SG)

Autonomy is essential to guaranteeing the independence of the Administration, which is confronted with the pluralism of the political forces present in Parliament. At regular meetings, National Assemblies of the European Centre for Parliamentary Research and Documentation (ECPRD) have exchanged their views as to the role and position of their respective Parliamentary Administrations, and in particular, regarding the tasks of their chief officers. Information will be obtained from the results of survey questionnaires, because it is also necessary to understand the functioning of some processes that are not governed by written rules (Dale' Ha|l Wan Zahlr Sheikh Abdul Rahman, 1993). Thanks also to the results of questionnaires and comparative surveys undertaken by Parliaments themselves, it is possible to summarize the typical characteristics of parliamentary bureaucracies, in general, and of the SG, in particular: namely neutrality, independence, speciality from civil service, stability, and professionalism of staff. The neutrality and autonomy of the Administration are linked to a notion of continuity and a recruitment policy that does not take account of the election results.

The chairperson and head of each Chamber is the President, who liaises with the head of the administrative apparatus, the SG, as the true point of contact between the political body and the Administration, according to the traditional "hourglass" model (Bontadini, 1983). The SG supports the Speaker in the political elaboration phase and provides the guidelines for the administrative implementation phase.

It is no coincidence, therefore, that the term "General Secretariat" sometimes refers to the entire Parliamentary Administration, such as in the European Parliament (Alexander, 2020) or in Spain. On the other hand, the Clerk's Department represents one of the internal

Table 3.1 Organization of parliaments and presence of the SG

One SG for chamber		One SG for two chambers	Two SGs in each chamber
Bicameral parliament	Unicameral parliament		
Argentina, Australia, Belgium, Bosnia,[7] Brazil, Canada, Czech Republic, Italy, Poland, Romania, Slovenia, Spain[8], United Kingdom	Albania, Bulgaria, Cyprus, Denmark, Estonia, Finland, Greece, Hungary, Israel, Norway, Serbia, Slovakia, Sweden	Austria, Switzerland	France, Uruguay, Mexico (one SG in the lower Chamber, two SGs in the Senate)

articulations of Parliamentary bureaucracy (such as in Italy and in the United Kingdom). Different titles are used in different countries (including SG, Head of the Secretariat, Clerk, Officer of Parliament, and General Director), but in almost all cases, he/she is the highest official responsible for the direction of the different Parliamentary Services.

Usually, even in bicameral Parliaments, each Chamber has its own SG (Zampetti, 2000), but there are cases in which the two Chambers are headed by a single SG (such as Austria or Switzerland, where the SG is "of the Federal Assembly"), or in which each of the two Chambers has two SGs (such as France, Uruguay, and Mexico) (Table 3.1). These different organizational choices may highlight a "unitary" or "plural" model of parliamentary administration, which will be described in Section 3.6.

The Speaker, as representatives of the parliamentary institution, should also be the guardians of its autonomy (Zuddas, 2011). Relationships with the Administration can also vary according to the historical-political phases that characterize the life of Parliaments: Presidents can therefore be the greatest defenders of the autonomy of the Parliamentary bureaucracy (Posteraro, 2012–2013) or may view it as a counter-power to balance. The SG acts under the direction of the Speaker but is not subordinate to party leaders, according to his/her impartiality; in other words, his/her possible political affinity must never influence his or her advice. It is argued that the SG is "apolitical" because he or she never takes side, but he or she is "intensely political" because they have to understand the politics and motivations underlying different groups (Crewe, 2017).

Moreover, the first moment of contact between the Speaker and the SG is in the appointment procedure (see infra at 5) that may transform into a cause for political division. Furthermore, the procedures for selecting the SG may affect his legitimacy and accountability in relation to the bodies which appointed him.

All Parliament's Offices depend on the SG and this dependence is both hierarchical and functional (Toniato, 2007). The centrality of the SG is based on the pursuit of the independence and impartiality of the Administration, but, at the same time, it is aimed at implementing the guidelines established by the political governing bodies. Sometimes there may be a preponderance of "administrative power" – which indicates a strong Parliamentary Administration while on other occasions excessive politicization is evident – which indicates, by contrast, the weakness of the Administration. This scenario has always characterized the tension between politics and administration: value of bureaucratic expertise, on the one hand, and the desire for political control, on the other (Huber & McCarty, 2004). In the relationship between the Speaker and the SG, the main distinctive feature of successful Secretaries General and their staff is confidentiality, in addition to trust, integrity, and understanding.

3.5 The SG Appointment Procedure

The requirements for the appointment or election of the SG may be more or less stringent (Dale' Ha|l Wan Zahlr Sheikh Abdul Rahman, 1993). In some cases, it is possible to identify the SG outside the Administration, giving priority to mobility and flexibility of professional pathways, as the system allows movement between other branches of public administration. Other legal systems frame the position of the SG as the pinnacle of a career within the Administration, favouring continuity and experience, thus leading to a more specialized parliamentary career. The background and experience of the SG contributes to his/her authority in performing the role.

In some cases, for example the European Parliament, political affiliations, or an existing career within political groups does not preclude a person from becoming the SG. The highest officials within the Secretariat are considered "supranationalists" with a significant institutional memory, which is all the more important within an Assembly with a strong turnover (Judge & Earnshaw, 2003), thus mitigating the logic based on nationality. Similarly, in other legal systems, no restrictions on the basis of party affiliation apply the upper management of the administration (Finland, Netherlands, and USA).

On the other hand, there are countries where the SG is prohibited from having a political background (see, e.g., the United Kingdom, Canada, Denmark, Japan, Australia, and Poland). For example, in Spanish law, the *Letrado Mayor* of the Senate and the *Secretary General* of the Congress are expressly appointed from among the officials of the General Courts with at least five years of service, which exclude the possibility of the appointment of external staff. It is not uncommon, however, for the SG to receive a political appointment at the end of his/her term of office.[9]

The appointment process for the SG is another indicator of autonomy of the Parliamentary Administration (Inter-Parliamentary Union, 2020). In some cases, the appointment process is governed by legislative sources.[10] With the exception of very few cases where the SG is recruited through a public selection or competitive process (Austria, Cyprus, and Estonia), the following types of appointment and removal of the SG can be identified (Table 3.2):

a   *monocratic appointment by the Speaker of the Assembly, with or without the consent (or input) of other collegial bodies* – (Albania, Argentina, Austria, Brazil, Bulgaria, the Czech Republic, Denmark, the German Bundestag, Greece, Hungary, Israel, Poland, Portugal, and Slovakia). In Albania, the SG of the unicameral Parliament is chosen by the Speaker, following a competitive procedure, according to the "Law for the Civil Servant". In Argentina, all of SGs (four for the Chamber and three for the Senate) are selected by the President of each Chamber and three out of four are endorsed by the legislative body. In Australia, the appointment of the SG is monocratic after consultation with members of the House. In Austria, the appointment of the SG is entrusted to the Speaker after a public selection, with the advice of a small group of experts. In Denmark, the appointment is made by the President, following the approval of the Committee on the Rules of Procedure. In the German Bundestag, the SG is appointed by the President of the Bundestag with the consent of the Presidium (similarly in Bundesrat). In Israel, the SG is appointed by the Speaker and his Deputies. In Poland, the Speaker appoints the Chief of the Chancellery, in both Houses, after consulting the Rules and Deputies' Affairs Committee. In Portugal, the SG is appointed by the President after obtaining a favourable opinion from the Board of Administration[11] and remains in office until the appointment of a new SG. He or she may also be dismissed at any time by the President,

Table 3.2 Types of SG appointment procedures

Appointment by the Speaker	Appointment by restricted collegial bodies	Appointment by the whole House	Appointment by external bodies	
With/without the opinion of other collegial bodies	Bureau, Presidium, Committee, group of experts, members of the House	Through a direct election or through the approval of a resolution after proposal of other bodies	Formally nominated by Government	Nominated by the King on Government proposal
Albania, Argentina, Austria, Brazil, Bulgaria, Czech Republic, Denmark, Germany, Greece Israel, Hungary, Poland, Portugal	Australia, European Parliament, French Assemblée nationale, Ireland, Italy, Spain	Belgium, Bosnia, Finland, Japan, Mexico, Montenegro, Norway, Romania, Serbia, Slovenia, Sweden, USA	Canada, New Zealand	United Kingdom

also after obtaining a consenting opinion from the Board of Administration. In Slovakia, the SG is appointed and recalled by the Speaker;

b *appointment by restricted collegiate, political, or administrative bodies* – usually in these cases, the appointment is made by the Bureau of the Assembly, which includes the Speaker, Vice-Presidents, Negotiators, and other Parliamentarians in order to represent all the parliamentary groups (Australia, the European Parliament, France, Ireland, Italy, and Spain), typically on the proposal of a President. In Australia, Clerks of the House of Representatives and Senate are appointed by their respective presiding officers for a non-renewable period of ten years (Parliamentary Service Act 1999). In the European Parliament, the SG is appointed by the Bureau and also in the French *Assemblée nationale* the two SGs are designated by the Bureau. In Ireland, the SG is nominated by the House of Oireachtas Commission on the Speaker's recommendation, from among the persons identified through an "open competition". In Italy, the Bureau of each Chamber appoints, on the proposal of the President, the SG; the same thing happens in Spain;

c *election by the entire Chamber, through a direct election or through the adoption of a resolution, or appointment by the Chamber after an advisory phase* – (Belgium, Bosnia, Finland, Japan, Mexico, Montenegro, Norway, Romania, Serbia, Slovenia, Sweden, and the USA). In Belgium, in both Houses, the SG is elected by an absolute majority of votes and by secret ballot. In Bosnia, the SGs of the two Chambers are appointed by their respective Houses on the suggestion of the Collegium of the House. The Finnish Parliament elects the SG on the basis of a proposal from the Chancellery Commission, which is the uppermost political body.[12] In Japan, the Diet Law states that each Chamber elects the SG from among those who are not members of the Chambers, but the Rules of Procedure (Rule 17) of the House of Councillors (Upper House) provide for the Chamber to delegate the selection of the SG to the President. In Mexico, the SG of the Chamber of Deputies is elected by a two-thirds majority of the Chamber, while the two SGs of the Senate are elected by a simple majority. In Montenegro, the SG is appointed and dismissed by Parliament, following a proposal of the Speaker. In Romania, the SG is appointed in a plenary session, on the proposal of the Standing Bureau of the Chamber, after the political consultation of the Committee of the Leaders of the parliamentary group and after having informally been preapproved by the President of the Chamber's political group. In Serbia, the SG and deputy SGs are appointed and dismissed by the Assembly. In Sweden, the SG is elected by the Assembly, while in the Slovenian lower House the SG is appointed by the National Assembly on the proposal of the Council of the President. In the American House of Representatives, the Clerk is elected every two years by the full House adopting a resolution;

d *appointment by external bodies*. There are cases of formal government appointment (Canada), or of appointment by the King, on a proposal of the Government (the United Kingdom, New Zealand). In Canada, the Clerk of the House of Commons is formally appointed by the Government, but essentially by the House: the appointment comes after the Clerk has referred the nomination proposal to the Standing Committee on Procedures and House Affairs and following the ratification of the nomination by the House.[13] In the United Kingdom, the Clerk of the House of Commons is appointed by the Queen, along with his assistants, and can only be dismissed by unanimous decision of the House. The Clerk of the Parliaments (House of Lords)[14] shall be appointed by her Majesty and may only be removed by her Majesty, upon a request of the House of Lords to the Queen for that purpose. In the House of Representatives of New Zealand, the Clerk is appointed by the Governor General as the representative of the Crown, on the advice of the Speaker.

The role of the SG is conditioned not only by the appointment process but also by the length of his or her mandate, which is generally characterized by a certain stability. The SG's position is not usually affected by election results and as a result avoids the introduction of a spoils system mechanism. There have been very long-serving SGs: in the Czech Republic, the SG of the Chamber of Deputies remained in office for 27 years until 2017; in France (*Assemblée Nationale*), one SG spent 25 years in office from 1946 to 1971; in Finland, a SG was in office from 1992 to 2015 (23 years); in the Senate of the Italian Republic, another SG remained in office from 1975 to 1992 (17 years); and in the European Parliament, the current SG has been in office since 2009. However, the SG's term of office may have a predetermined duration (e.g.: seven years in New Zealand and in the Italian Chamber of deputies; a renewable five-year term in Austria; a four-year term in Sweden and in Montenegro) or may be linked to the re-election of the Chamber (Bosnia) or Government, on the basis of a specific resolution of each Chamber (Australia). Any attempt to remove the SG follows the same procedures as the appointment, with some peculiarities: for example, according to the Rules of the US House of Representatives, the Clerk – elected by the House – can be removed by the House itself or by the Speaker.

3.6 The Relationship between the Speaker and the Secretary General: Unitary vs Plural Model

The duties of the SG concern procedural, administrative, and international matters. In almost all cases, the SG is the highest official responsible for the direction of the different parliamentary services. The principal functions of the SG act in relation to the Speaker, to the Bureau, and to Members of Parliament, on one hand, and at an administrative level, on the other, are:

- to give assistance to the Speaker of the Parliament in all circumstances both during and outside sittings;
- to give advice on law, practice, and parliamentary procedure;

- to take the minutes of meetings and draft decisions;
- to prepare meetings of the Bureau and of the Assembly;
- to direct the administration of Parliament, to decide on the appointment and deployment of staff under the SG's direction;
- to draw up and submit to the Bureau a draft internal budget;
- to authorise certain expenditure within the limits of his powers.

The SG is responsible for the offices and is directly related to the political bodies, having the confidence of the President. In most legal systems, the SG carries out both administrative and management functions as well as functions related to the application of the rules and the correctness of the legislative procedure, according to a "unitary" model; in other legal systems, these functions are distinct, on the basis of a "plural" model.

In the unitary model, the SG usually plays a dual role of adviser in parliamentary law and of operational manager (Lomp, 2009): he or she has a double responsibility towards the President. The advantage of this system is to have a single administrative reference that interfaces with the supreme political authority. On the strictly legislative side, the SG sits next to the Speaker during plenary sessions to ensure the correctness of the legislative procedure and assists him in the planning of work in the Bureau. On the administrative side, the SG represents the administration and organizes it, ensures the security and safety of people and offices, is responsible for financial management and takes care of external relations. In some legal systems, such as the Hungarian one, there has been a (gradual) shift from a plural model, with different bodies independent of each other and in contact with the Speaker, to a unitary model, in which there is a single leader of the administration, who combines legislative and managerial tasks.

Within the plural model, there are different situations. For example, there are two senior officials at the top of parliamentary bureaucracy in France: in each Chamber, there are two SGs, one responsible for legislative services, the other for the administrative services, independent from one other hierarchically, both assisted by a Director-General and both accountable to the political authority (Mattarella, 1997). In the Mexican Senate, there are both a Secretary General of Parliamentary Services and a Secretary General of Administrative Services, while in the Mexican Chamber of Deputies these functions are performed by only one SG. In Denmark, there are a SG and two deputy secretaries general, of which one serves as Parliamentary Secretary (Clerk) for the Speaker. Thus, the functions of support and procedural assistance to the President are distinct from the administrative tasks: the Clerk, as a Parliamentary Secretary, answers to the Speaker but, as a deputy SG, depends on the SG. Additional administrative figures who are not dependent on the SG, or who are on an equal footing with the SG, are the heads of legislative offices, in those systems where this function is not exercised by the SG. In the US House of Representatives, there is a distinction between the Clerk and the Parliamentarian: the Office of the Parliamentarian provides the House with non-partisan guidance on parliamentary rules and procedures. A Parliamentarian is appointed by the Speaker, without regard to his or her political affiliation. In Japan, the Japanese Diet Act provides that each of the two Chambers of Diet has its own Legislative Office. In the Japanese House of Councillors (Upper House), this is an organ which is independent of the Secretariat of the House of Councillors and is under the supervision of the President of the House of Councillors: the Commissioner General of the Legislative Bureau, appointed by the President of the House of Councillors with the approval of the House. In Japan, the Legislative Bureau of the House of Representatives has a Commissioner General (Ashida & Takahashi, 2021).

Even in the legal systems that are aligned with to the "unitary" model, however, there are numerous functions relating to the Administration that the SG does not carry out completely autonomously but rather acts in concert with deputy SGs, other collegiate bodies, or a management board (in Italy, there are the Presidency Council and the College of Quaestors). In this context, the role of the SG clearly becomes essential both from a "descending" perspective (i.e., the SG conveys his/her administrative vision first to the President and then down to all other subjects) and from a "horizontal" one (i.e., in relation to the coordination of the activities of these same bodies) (Malaschini, 2013). The same administrative functions can therefore be exercised on the basis of a monocratic direction by the SG or shared with collegiate bodies.

Few examples: in the United Kingdom, the House of Commons features a federal administrative system, in which responsibility for the functions performed is spread across several administrative areas. The Clerk of the House chairs the Board of Management, which is the administrative management body (Ryle, 1981). In the House of Lords, on the other side, the administrative model still bestows the relevant responsibility on the Clerk of the Parliaments, which heads the Parliament Office, while the Black Rod's Department falls under the responsibility of the Gentleman Usher of the Black Rod, which is independent of the Clerk and relates to security and ceremonial functions (Cozzoli, 1997). Canada too has a collegiate body within the House of Commons, the Board of Internal Economy, chaired by the Speaker of the House, where majority and opposition members are equally represented. The Clerk of the House serves as a secretary to the Board. The Canadian Senate has a different structure, because the Clerk of the Senate does not act as secretary of the top collegiate administrative body (the Standing Committee on Internal Economy, Budgets and Administration), but serves as Chief Legislative Services Officer and is distinct from the Law Clerk, who has an independent relationship with the Standing Committees. These bodies are governed by the law (the Parliament of Canada Act). In Ireland, the SG is a member of the House Governing Board, the House of Oireachtas Commission, and is subject to its management.

There are also different forms of organization supporting the SG: in some cases, the SG is flanked by a management board made up of the directors of the main administrative structures. Others contemplate the presence of up to three deputy secretaries general. These deputies can be appointed in order to substitute the SG in certain areas of competence (sometimes distinguishing the "parliamentary/legislative" arena from the administrative; while in other cases – as in Israel – non-parliamentary functions are entrusted to a Director-General) and create a small management team. Otherwise, Heads of Departments or Services may report directly to the SG, with the Heads of the Secretariats of the Commissions or Offices answering to them, according to a vertical hierarchy. There are also offices directly employed by the SG which are linked "horizontally" to the General Secretariat.

3.7 The Speaker and the Other Administrative Bodies

Depending on the prevalence of a unitary or plural model, there may be administrative bodies that deal directly with the Speaker without the involvement of the SG and other administrative figures whose positions are not dependent on Parliament at all. In the USA and the Canadian systems, the Parliamentary Librarians are another example of bodies that relate directly to the Speaker, as the Library is a "third administration" by comparison with the two Chambers. In the USA, the Librarian of the US Congress is appointed by the President. In Greece, the Scientific Service – which is a unit of the Parliamentary

Administration – is directly linked to the Speaker and is governed by the President of the Scientific Council. The establishment of a Scientific Service is in fact provided for in the Greek Constitution and the discipline of its functioning is contained in the Standing Orders of the Hellenic Parliament (Fitsilis & Bayiokos, 2017). The President of the Scientific Council himself – who is part of the Scientific Service – oversees the Parliament's Library.

Finally, an additional body must also be mentioned in the context of the relationship between the Administration and the political bodies: the President's Cabinet, chosen at the discretion of the President even from beyond the members of the Parliamentary Administration. Each President forms his own Cabinet, which may consist of a Head of Cabinet (in some cases a Director-General), a Press Office Head, a Diplomatic Adviser, a Head of the Special Secretariat, and other advisers in the cultural or legal fields. They are responsible for the Speaker but not for the Chamber or for the Administration. These figures enjoy a personal and privileged relationship with the President, who sometimes uses them to convey his administrative address to the SG (Malaschini, 2013). There are, however, Assemblies, as in Romania, where the President's Secretariat/Cabinet consists of senior administration officials, hierarchically subordinate both to the SG and to the Speaker: this could create a dual channel to which officials may belong.

3.8 Final Considerations

Digital transition is, today more than ever, a crucial challenge not only for all production processes but also for public authorities and their organizations. For Parliaments, the transformations of the public space also result in a crisis of representative democracy and its traditional tools.

However, the autonomy of Parliaments and of Parliamentary Administrations can prove to be precious assets for addressing these challenges in an original and innovative way. In this perspective, the role of the Speakers can be increasingly crucial for developing administrative guidelines and organizational models of Parliamentary Administrations capable of meeting the challenges of the times.

Notes

1 According to House of Commons Staff Handbook, "staff of the House of Commons Service are not civil servants, however the House of Commons Administration Act 1978 says that terms and conditions of service of staff must be kept 'broadly in line' with the Home Civil Service".
2 For example, the Public Service Act 1902 regarding the Federal Parliament's administrative structure of Australia's Federal Parliament.
3 The Indian Constitution, in Article 98, states that each Chamber has "a separate secretarial staff". The legal framework of Indian Parliamentary Administration therefore derives from the Constitution but is refined in each House.
4 Article 72.1 of the Spanish Constitution provides that the two Chambers shall, by common accord, govern the Staff Regulations of the General Courts. The Staff Regulations of the Chambers were therefore approved and amended frequently by a joint decision of the Bureau (Mesas) of the Congress of Deputies and the Senate.
5 With the exception of the Parliamentarian, who can remain in office even in the event of a change of majority.
6 The current European Parliament SG Klaus Welle, appointed in 2009, was Head of the Cabinet of the President of the European Parliament and Secretary General of the EPP-ED Group in the European Parliament.

7 In Bosnia, there is a SG for each Chamber, as well as a third Secretary general for common services (Secretary of the Joint Service).
8 Only the SG of the Congress (and not the SG of the Senate) is the Chief Clerk of the *Cortes Generales* and the Head of all parliamentary staff.
9 In the United Kindom, the former Clerk of the House of Commons, Robert Rogers, was elevated to the House of Lords in 2015. Similarly, in Italy, the SG of the Senate of the Republic, Antonio Malaschini, was appointed State Secretary in 2011 and the SG of the Chamber of Deputies, Donato Marra, was appointed State Secretary in 1995, both at the end of their term of office. Instead the SG of the Senate, Gaetano Gifuni, was appointed Minister in 1987 and then returned to take over the position of SG.
10 Ireland: House of Oireachtas Act 1999, section 5; Japan: The Diet Law; United Kindom: Clerk of the Parliament Act of 1824; Israel: the Knesset Secretary General Law (5728–1968).
11 The Board of Administration is a consultation and management body comprising a maximum of seven Members of the *Assembleia da República*, representing each of the seven largest parliamentary groups, together with the SG and an elected representative of the parliamentary staff.
12 In Finland, the Chancellery Commission was not in unanimous agreement with respect to the selection of the current SG and instead needed to vote on its proposal: in the plenary vote, Maija-Leena Paavola (the current SG) was elected with 107 votes, with three other candidates receiving support from among the MPs.
13 In 2017, there was a division of the Canadian House of Commons regarding the appointment of the Clerk of the House, because no agreement had been reached.
14 The title is indicative of the clerk's mandate through successive Parliaments (Barrett, 2019).

References

Alexander, D. A. (2020), *The Committee Secretariat of the European Parliament: administrative mobility, expertise and keeping the legislative wheels turning*, in *The Journal of Legislative Studies*, https://doi.org/10.1080/13572334.2020.1832389.

Arnold, R. D. (1987), *Political control of administrative officials*, in *Journal of Law Economics and Organization*, Vol. 3, No. 2, pp. 279–286.

Association of Secretaries General of Parliaments. (2013), *Principles for the Recruitment and Career Management of Parliamentary Staff*. https://www.asgp.co/sites/default/files/documents//YLKBFHZZYVBGVWWYLRMYXYHOLTRBEG.pdf.

Barrett, V. (2019), *Parliamentary Administration: What does It Mean to Manage a Parliament Effectively?* The Australian National University ProQuest Dissertatios Publishing.

Battini, S. (1997), *Gli apparati degli organi costituzionali negli Stati Uniti d'America*, in C. D'Orta and F. Garella (eds.), *Le amministrazioni degli organi costituzionali: ordinamento italiano e profili comparati*, Laterza, p. 500.

Blischke, W. (1981), *Parliamentary staffs in the German Bundestag*, in *Legislative Studies Quarterly*, Vol. 6, No. 4, pp. 533–558.

Bontadini, P. (1983), *Strutture organizzative complesse e dinamiche*, in VV.AA. (ed.), *Burocrazia parlamentare. Funzioni, garanzie e limiti*, Ufficio stampa e pubblicazioni della Camera dei deputati.

Campbell, S. and Laporte, J. (1981), *The staff of the parliamentary assemblies in France*, in *Legislative Studies Quarterly*, Vol. 6, No. 4, pp. 521–531.

Costa, O. (2003), *Administrer le parlement européen: les paradoxes d'un secrétariat général incontournable, mais faible*, in *Politique Européenne*, No. 11, pp. 143–161, https://www.cairn.info/revue-politique-europeenne-2003-3-page-143.htm.

Cozzoli, V. (1997), *Gli apparati degli organi costituzionali nel Regno Unito*, in C. D'Orta and F. Garella (eds.), *Le amministrazioni degli organi costituzionali: ordinamento italiano e profili comparati*, Laterza, pp. 442 e 446.

Crewe, E. (2017), *Magi or Mandarins? Contemporary Clerkly Culture*, P. Evans (ed.), *Essays on the History of Parliamentary Procedure*, In Honour of Thomas Erskine May (Hart Studies in Constitutional Law), Oxford: Hart Publishing, p. 50.

Dale' Ha|l Wan Zahlr Sheikh Abdul Rahman (1993), *The Independence and Neutrality of the Parliamentary Service*, in *Constitutional and Parliamentary information*, pp. 42–50. https://www.asgp.co/sites/default/files/documents//YGWYQQJMMBXTKYKMWEMUIUAKXNXCXK.pdf.

de Santos Canalejo, E. (2018), *Evolución y retos de la administración parlamentaria en las Cortes Generales*, in *Revista de las Cortes Generales*, No. 105, pp. 17–50.

Dickmann, R. (2014), *Autonomia costituzionale e principio di legalità a garanzia dell'indipendenza delle amministrazioni degli organi costituzionali*, in *Forum di Quaderni costituzionali*, No 6, pp. 1–3.

Dirck G. Caboor, P. and Popelie, P. (2023), Belgium's Parliamentary Administration in T. Christiansen, E. Griglio and N. Lupo (eds.), *Handbook of Parliamentary Administrations*, Routledge.

ECPRD (2003), *Seminar on Parliamentary Administrations and Legislative Cooperation*, 30–31 October, Reports.

Egeberg, M., Gornitzka, Å, Trondal, J., and Johannessen, M. (2013), *Parliament staff: unpacking the behaviour of officials in the European Parliament*, in *Journal of European Public Policy*, Vol. 20, No. 4, pp. 495–514.

English, M. and Murphy, T. (2022), *Parliamentary Administration in Ireland*, in T. Christiansen, E. Griglio and N. Lupo (eds.), *Handbook of Parliamentary Administrations*, Routledge.

Finzi, C. (1934), *L'autonomia amministrativa ed economica delle Assemblee legislative*, Tipografia della Camera dei deputati, p. 176.

Fitsilis, F. and Bayiokos, V. (2017), *Implementing structured public access to the legal reports on bills and law proposals of the Scientific Service of the Hellenic Parliament, Greece*, in *Knowledge Management for Development Journal*, Vol. 13, No. 2, pp. 63–80.

Griglio, E. and Lupo, N. (2021), *Parliamentary administrations in the bicameral systems of Europe: joint or divided?*, in *The Journal of Legislative studies*, DOI: 10.1080/13572334.2021.1953268.

Högenauer, A. and Neuhold, C. (2015), *National Parliaments after Lisbon: administrations on the Rise?*, in *West European Politics*, Vol. 38, No. 2, pp. 335–354, DOI:10.1080/01402382.2014.990698.

Högenauer, A. L., Neuhold, C., Christiansen, T., and Dobbels, M. (2016). *Administrative Players in the European Parliament*, in *Parliamentary Administrations in the European Union*, European Administrative Governance Series. Palgrave Macmillan, 33, https://doi.org/10.1057/9781137596260_3.

Huber, J. D. and McCarty, N. (2004), *Bureaucratic capacity, delegation, and reform*, in *American Political Science Review*, Vol. 98, No. 3, pp. 481–494.

Inter-Parliamentary Union (IPU) (2020), *Comparative Research Paper on Parliamentary Administration*, https://www.ipu.org/fr/ressources/publications/reference/2020-09/etude-comparative-sur-ladministration-parlementaire.

Jacobs, F. and De Feo, A. (2023), European Parliament's Administration, in T. Christiansen, E. Griglio and N. Lupo (eds.), *Handbook of Parliamentary Administrations*, Routledge.

Judge, D. and Earnshaw, D. (2003), *The European Parliament*, Palgrave Macmillan, p. 176.

Kölling, M. and Molina, I. (2023), Spain's Parliamentary Administration, in T. Christiansen, E. Griglio and N. Lupo (eds.), *Handbook of Parliamentary Administrations*, Routledge.

Konrath, C., Pollak, J., and Slominski, P. (2023), Austria's Parliamentary Administration, in T. Christiansen, E. Griglio and N. Lupo (eds.), *Handbook of Parliamentary Administrations*, Routledge.

Lomp, A. (2009), *The Office of Secretary General*, in Association of Secretary General of Parliaments, Geneva, October.

Lupo, N. and Gianniti, L. (2023), Italy's Parliamentary Administration, in T. Christiansen, E. Griglio and N. Lupo (eds.), *Handbook of Parliamentary Administrations*, Routledge.

Malaschini, A. (2013), *Presidenti di assemblea e amministrazione del Senato*, in *Il Filangieri. Quaderno 2012-2013*, No. Jovene (publisher) 2012–2013, pp. 275–279.

Mattarella, B. G. (1997), *Gli apparati degli organi costituzionali in Francia*, in C. D'Orta and F. Garella (eds.), *Le amministrazioni degli organi costituzionali: ordinamento italiano e profili comparati*, Laterza, pp. 413.

Navilli, M. (2007), *Il personale degli apparati serventi delle assemblee parlamentari, Il pubblico impiego non privatizzato*, IV, in L. Viola (ed.), *Autorità indipendenti e organi costituzionali, a cura di Franco Carinci e Vito Tenore*, Giuffrè, pp. 177–231.

Piccirilli, G. and Zuddas, P. (2012), *Assisting Italian MPs in pre-legislative scrutiny: the role played by Chambers' counsellors and legislative advisors in enhancing the knowledge and skills development of Italian MPs: the assistance offered to an autonomous collection of information*, in *Parliamentary Affairs*, Vol. 65, pp. 672–687.

Posteraro, F. (2012–2013), *Presidenti di Assemblea e Amministrazione della Camera*, in *Il Filangieri, Quaderno 2012-2013*, pp. 267–274.

Romzek, B. S. and Utter, J. A. (1997), *Congressional legislative staff: political professionals or clerks?*, in *American Journal of Political Science*, Vol. 41, No. 4, pp. 1251–1279.

Ryle, M. T. (1981), *The Legislative Staff of the British House of Commons*, in *Legislative Studies Quarterly*, Vol. 6, No. 4, pp. 497–519.

Tacea, A. (2023), France's Parliamentary Administration, in T. Christiansen, E. Griglio and N. Lupo (eds.), *Handbook of Parliamentary Administrations*, Routledge.

Toniato, F. S. (2007), *Servizi e uffici delle amministrazioni parlamentari. Il Senato della Repubblica*, in *Rassegna parlamentare: Rivista mensile di studi costituzionali e di documentazione legislativa*, Vol. 49, No. 1, pp. 236–244.

Tudela Aranda, J. (2010), *La Administracion parlamentaria en la encrucijada de la renovacion*, in *Corts: Anuario de derecho parlamentario*, No. 23, pp. 157–191.

Vargas, A., Dias Pinheiro, B., and Fonseca, T. (2022), *Parliamentary Organisation, from Stability to Change*, in T. Christiansen, E. Griglio and N. Lupo (eds.), *Handbook of Parliamentary Administrations*, Routledge.

Zampetti, U. (2000), *The role of the Secretary General in the Administration of Parliament*, in *Constitutional and Parliamentary information*, Vol. 50, No. 180, pp. 107–260.

Zampetti, U. (2013), *L'evoluzione dell'amministrazione della Camera dei deputati nel quadro delle principali riforme istituzionali, regolamentari, legislative dell'Italia repubblicana*, in F. Lanchester (ed.), *Regolamenti parlamentari e forma di governo: gli ultimi quarant'anni*, Giuffrè, pp. 153–177.

Zuddas, P. (2011), *Prime osservazioni critiche su una proposta di revisione della disciplina della nomina del Segretario generale della Camera dei deputati: il segretario "di legislatura" e i rischi per la neutralità dell'apparato servente*, in *Osservatorio sulle fonti*, No. 1, pp. 1–13.

4
THE ADMINISTRATION OF BICAMERAL PARLIAMENTS

Elena Griglio and Nicola Lupo

4.1 Introduction. Bicameral Parliaments as Complex Institutions: The Puzzle of Administrative Organization

Parliaments are complex and pluralistic organizations (Amellier, 1966; Norton, 1990; Manzella, 2003; Benoit and Rozenberg, 2020). They are called upon to represent political and territorial diversities and to cover at least potentially any subject matter. This implies a rather structured architecture, able to support the high degree of autonomy demanded by each (individual or collegial) political actor and at the same time to promote the development of institutional common outcomes. Procedures are the essential mechanisms for reconciling these potentially diverging requirements: they ensure the involvement of different actors, assigning a prominent role to minor collegial bodies (groups, committees, delegations, bureaux, among others) in order to reduce the pluralism and the diversity at a level that is compatible with the need to achieve a decision (Lupo, 2019; Fasone, 2020).

In the case of bicameral parliaments, the level of complexity is at least doubled, as the internal structure is duplicated in two parallel Houses: these may either be of similar or of dissimilar composition (Mill, 1861), they usually hold different functions and act independently from one other (Rasch and Tsebelis, 1995). Whereas there is no one model of bicameralism and no unique arrangement (Llanos and Nolte, 2003), institutional complexity is a common outcome of all bicameral systems (Massicotte, 2001; Uhr, 2008), because the presence of two, parallel and autonomous, pluralistic structures fosters multiple patterns of interaction, either cooperative or competitive (Diermeir and Myerson, 1999; Bradbury and Crain, 2004). In these polyarchic and networking institutions, maintaining a minimum of structural consistency and institutional continuity is certainly not an easy task, which is up to parliamentary administrations performing.

Parliamentary officials are an essential point of reference both for individual MPs and for collegial bodies regarding any issue concerning the interpretation and application of procedures, the protection of the democratic values and organizational or functional guarantees that are the cornerstone of parliamentary activity (Barrett, 2019; Inter-Parliamentary Union, 2020; Christiansen, Griglio and Lupo, 2021). Since the hardware of parliaments is in their administrative structure, it is extremely important for their effective functioning to clearly identify the linkages between the political and administrative spheres.

"Legislatures" that follow the model of the US Congress[1] tend to adopt a decentralized approach with staffers answering personally to individual MPs (Peters, 2021; Fasone, 2022).[2] By contrast, in European "parliaments", the link between the political and the administrative sphere tends to be more centralized and ordered according to a hierarchical structure, which finds in the Secretary General, directly linked to the Speaker/President of the House, its pivotal actor (Association of the Secretary Generals of Parliaments [ASGP], 2000).[3]

The organizational model adopted in determining the link between politics and administration is the outcome of a series of delicate trade-offs and balances, for example between parliament and government; between unity and diversity; or between party politics and administrative traditions.

All these patterns of interaction are far more relevant when bicameralism is at stake. It can be argued that in bicameral parliaments the nature of the link between the political and the administrative sphere becomes even more of a puzzle: as each House has its Speaker/President and enjoys a certain degree of institutional autonomy, the shape given to the administrative structure creates the potential for a wide range of different arrangements.

The solution adopted in each case can be seen as the result of the stratification of long-standing features, deeply rooted in the history and political culture of each institution and each country (Coniez and Michon, 2020). At the same time, changes in the shape given to parliamentary administrations can be interpreted as an attempt to support and foster some of the major trends affecting the nature and internal structure of bicameral parliaments (Lupo, 2012).

This chapter aims to provide a comparative analysis of the various solutions that parliaments have arrived at in addressing this universal challenge. Based on previous research focused on bicameral parliaments in Europe (Griglio and Lupo, 2021) and on the findings provided by the contributions on individual countries in this Handbook, its purpose is to identify the main administrative formats adopted by bicameral parliaments. In doing so, it highlights the reasons behind the institutional choices and critically debates the advantages and disadvantages involved in these. Towards this aim, the next section presents an overview of the three main formats resulting from the comparative analysis of bicameral parliamentary administrations. Subsequent sections analyse the features of each of these formats, examining the motivations behind choices in favour of a more divided or a more integrated administrative arrangement in bicameral parliaments. This analysis provides the foundation for a summary and a discussion of the implications of the alternative arrangements in the final section.

4.2 Towards a Typology of Bicameral Parliamentary Administrations

The administrative organization of bicameral parliaments as complex institutions follows rather different formats. There is no one-size-fits-all format able to explain how the administrative sphere adapts to the requirements of a bicephalic parliament.

On the one hand, bicameral parliaments are composed of two Houses, each characterized by a well-defined internal political structure and a clear set of functional prerogatives, usually determined by the Constitution (Patterson and Mughan, 1999: 3 ff). The institutional autonomy of each House normally comprises also the administrative autonomy, i.e. the right to self-organize, which encompasses the creation of two autonomous administrative services, one for each House (Díez Picazo, 1985; Pacelli and Giovannetti, 2020). This arrangement aligns with the prevalence of asymmetrical over symmetrical bicameral systems: since asymmetries in the composition and role of the two Houses are the rule in the large majority of bicameral systems (Mughan and Patterson, 1999: 338; Borthwich,

2001), the provision of tailored administrative services in support to each House represents the most obvious answer.

On the other hand, bicameral parliaments often act as a single institution (Trivelli, 1975): this happens not just in the hypothesis of joint sessions but also in the recurring cases of bicameral committees entrusted with the most different tasks. Many spheres of parliamentary activity, including law-making, call for a strong coordination between the two Houses in order to ensure that their work may lead to a common output. In other spheres, including the management of foreign or supranational affairs, bicameral consistency is rather advocated in order to give unity and strength to parliament as a single institution in its interaction with third actors (Griglio, 2020: 133 ff). In response to these requirements, joint administrative support might turn out to be the best answer. As a matter of fact, the presence of single or closely integrated administrative structures serving both Houses may be the easiest way to compose the lines of activity and interests of two autonomous pluralistic institutions which are often asked to act with one single voice. In addition to these arguments, a practical remark would confirm that in symmetrical bicameral systems the two Houses have corresponding legislative and non-legislative prerogatives. Consequently, not just the *technical* functions (consisting in the management of organizational and purely administrative tasks) but also the *procedural* and *substantive* functions (that, respectively, deal with orienting decision-makers in the choices between existing alternatives and supporting MPs with information, knowledge, and expertise) could be easily served by unified administrative structures.

The search for a balance between the precondition of each chamber's autonomy and the call for bicameral synergies has spurred different administrative answers from bicameral parliaments. In a broad perspective, three main formats can be identified: divided, polylith, and joint administrations.

Divided administrations, composed of two autonomous administrative structures, one for each House, identify the basic format. This administrative solution perfectly mirrors the institutional autonomy attributed to each of the two Houses, but can coexist with forms of bicameral coordination among the two administrative services without giving origins to the creation of joint structures.

In some parliaments, the presence of two unicameral administrative services is integrated with the creation of a joint administrative service supporting different areas of shared needs and interests. *Polylith* administrations that follow this model can be considered an evolution from the basic format insofar the creation of the "third" administrative branch often turns out to be a more recent development, adopted in response to new challenges. A further variation lies in the multiplication of the joint administrative services, which may be created to satisfy different shared tasks of the two Houses beyond the ones served by the unicameral services. This format may be used to include the experience of Congress-type assemblies also, which are served by several groups of staff, however not structured as a real bureaucratic "service" (Peters, 2022).

Polylith administrations find their antithesis and at the same time their apogee in the format of *joint* administrations, characterized by the presence of a single administrative service supporting both Houses. This format maximizes shared structures incorporating them in a single bureaucracy.

These models revolve around two opposed dominant logics. *Administrative separateness*, which is at its maximum in divided administrations, offers the advantage of simplicity in the organization of the administrative services, tailored according to the asymmetric prerogatives of the two Houses, thus providing full coherence between the political and administrative autonomy and governance. However, it has a contraindication in the duplication of administrative structures and lines of activity between the two Houses which risk stimulating competing attitudes between the two Houses. By contrast, *administrative integration* is the dominant logic behind joint administrations and it finds in the burden/cost sharing and in the protection of parliament's unity and cohesion its inner ratio. Whereas this logic emphasizes the coordination interests and potential synergies between the two Houses, it has its side-backs in the complexity of the internal organization and governance and in the difficulties in managing the conflicting interests of the two Houses.

Previous research, focused on the comparison of parliamentary administrations in bicameral systems of Europe, demonstrates that the choice between these two logics, and hence between the two opposite formats of divided or joint administrations, is independent from the nature and type of the bicameral system (Griglio and Lupo, 2021). However, the presence of institutional asymmetries or symmetries might influence what can be defined the internal micro-organization of parliamentary administrations.[4]

Based on these preliminary observations, the following sections examine the main types of bicameral parliamentary administrations. Going beyond the European experience, this provides a global perspective, based also on the insights gained from the relevant cases discussed in this Handbook (see Table 4.1). The enlarged set of benchmarks, including also presidential systems and different parliamentary traditions, offers the opportunity to add further insights to our understanding of the administrative arrangements of parliaments and their relationship with the institutional features of bicameral systems.

4.3 Divided Parliamentary Administrations

4.3.1 Duplication or Adaptation to the House specificities?

Divided administration is the preferred format in bicameral parliaments. This is the easiest and the most obvious solution, given the constitutional and political autonomy that each parliamentary assembly – lower and upper Houses in bicameral systems – enjoys (Le Divellec, 2020). Simplicity in the organization of the administrative services and full coherence between the political and administrative governance are two clear advantages of this format. Since the interests of the two Houses may differ or even come into conflict, two entirely separate administrations would seem to offer the ideal answer to the requirement of providing full and equal protection to such interests.

The other side of the coin of such an arrangement, however, is the duplication of administrative structures and lines of activity in both Houses, which may bring about some disadvantages. In parliaments falling under this category, the two administrative services created to support the Houses of Parliament act as two separate and fully independent organizations, relying on an autonomous governance and on distinct internal rules, often based in the Rules of procedure (Inter-Parliamentary Union, 2020). In most cases (Brazil, Czech Republic, France, Italy, Poland, Romania), the administrative autonomy and independence results in the creation of two parallel structures which are rather similar in the internal organization and services provided.

From an organizational point of view, the administrative hierarchy is perfectly duplicated in both Houses, each run by a distinct Secretary General, usually linked to the respective Speaker/President.[5] Both administrations follow a rather similar division in macro-level (e.g. areas, departments, directions) and micro-level units (e.g. divisions, offices, units). Existing differences in the denominations used to identify corresponding units in the two administrative branches may often be considered cosmetic rather than substantial (Kaniok, 2023).

Table 4.1 Overview of administrative arrangements in bicameral parliaments

Bicameral parliament	Joint administrations (one administrative service for both Houses)	Divided administrations (two administrative services, one for each House)	Polylith administrations (three administrative services: one for each House + a joint service)	Polylith administrations (multiple administrative services/staffing)
Argentina				Five parliamentary services: one for the lower House, one for the upper House and three (Library, Print and Health Insurance System) shared by the two Houses.
Australia			The Federal Parliament's administrative structure comprises three Departments: the Department of the House of Representatives (DHR), the Department of the Senate (DOS) and the Department of Parliamentary Services (DPS), created in 2004 and serving both Houses, which derives from the merging in a single Department of the Department of the Parliamentary Reporting Staff (DPRS), the Department of the Parliamentary Library (DPL) and the Joint House Committee.	
Austria	Since 1945, both parliamentary chambers are served by a joint, deeply integrated parliamentary administration in which the President of the National Council has a dominating role.			
Belgium		The lower and the upper Houses have two distinct parliamentary administrations. However, they share the department of the Library of Parliament. Moreover, they are exploring forms of bicameral cooperation in certain fields (joint security, joint catering).		

(Continued)

Table 4.1 Overview of administrative arrangements in bicameral parliaments (Continued)

Bicameral parliament	Joint administrations (one administrative service for both Houses)	Divided administrations (two administrative services, one for each House)	Polylith administrations (three administrative services: one for each House + a joint service)	Polylith administrations (multiple administrative services/staffing)
Bosnia Herzegovina			Three administrative pillars: one for the lower House, one for the upper House and the Joint Service supporting both Houses for general technical tasks.	
Brazil		The administrative services of the two Houses are separate and function independently but are quite similar in their organization and the services they provide. Although independent from each other, the Chamber and Senate administrations have in common some of the services rendered to the members of parliament, especially regarding matters that are considered in mixed committees or deliberated in joint sessions of the National Congress, such as budget laws and presidential vetoes. Also some of the electronic systems for legislative monitoring have been integrated.		
Canada			The two Houses operate as highly separate organizations with their own administrative services. Only the third organization, the Library of Parliament, acts a joint structure.	

(Continued)

Table 4.1 Overview of administrative arrangements in bicameral parliaments (Continued)

Bicameral parliament	Joint administrations (one administrative service for both Houses)	Divided administrations (two administrative services, one for each House)	Polylith administrations (three administrative services: one for each House + a joint service)	Polylith administrations (multiple administrative services/staffing)
Czech Republic		The two chambers work independently, they have their own administration and internal rules governing it. Both administrations operate on the basis of very similar structures. They are both using almost identical departments.		
France		Two services – the Parliamentary Institute, tasked with a scientific, informative and educational mission, and the Library – are formally part of the lower chamber administration but serve the Senate as well.		
Germany		Each House has its own administration, with a bicephalic structure, divided into an administrative service and a legislative one. Both the *Bundestag* (lower House) and the *Bundesrat* (upper House) have their own administration. By comparison, the administration of the *Bundesrat* is much smaller. The administrations of the two Houses do not form a network as such. However, they cooperate closely on specific issues.		
Ireland	The Houses of the Oireachtas Service (the Service) is the joint administration that provides advice and support services to the Houses of the Oireachtas Commission, to the Houses of the Oireachtas and their Committees and to the Members of the Houses.			

(Continued)

Table 4.1 Overview of administrative arrangements in bicameral parliaments *(Continued)*

Bicameral parliament	Joint administrations (one administrative service for both Houses)	Divided administrations (two administrative services, one for each House)	Polylith administrations (three administrative services: one for each House + a joint service)	Polylith administrations (multiple administrative services/staffing)
Italy		Each House has its own administration. The same services and units are duplicated in each bureaucratic structure. In 2017, the two parliamentary administrations were formally merged, but this process has not led to structural consequences so far and bicameral coordination between the two bureaucracies continues in an informal manner.		
Mexico		Parliamentary administration in Mexico consists in each House of a secretariat and of the specialized units of the parliamentary civil service. Secretariats constitute the main part of the parliamentary administration in both the Chamber of Deputies and the Senate. The parliamentary civil service increasingly plays a significant role in the administration of both chambers.		
Netherlands		Both chambers have laid down the organizational structure of their administration in their respective rules of procedure. Both administrations are headed by a Secretary General. The organizational structure of the administration in the House of Representatives is considerably more complex than in the Senate.		

(Continued)

Table 4.1 Overview of administrative arrangements in bicameral parliaments (Continued)

Bicameral parliament	Joint administrations (one administrative service for both Houses)	Divided administrations (two administrative services, one for each House)	Polylith administrations (three administrative services: one for each House + a joint service)	Polylith administrations (multiple administrative services/staffing)
Poland		Each Chamber has separate administrative bodies in the form of the Chancellery of the Sejm and the Chancellery of the Senate. Chancelleries have a similar organizational structure, including the names of the units, the legal basis of their operations and the functions they perform.		
Romania		According to the article 64 of the Romanian Constitution, the organization of the two chambers is regulated by their own Standing Orders. Each House has its own parliamentary administration, run by a Secretary General, who is the representative of the chamber, managing the functional activity of the Assembly.		
Spain	The Spanish bicameral parliament has a formally joint administration which nonetheless finds a differentiated governance and special arrangements in the two Houses. Unicameral specificities sometimes seem to overcome the joint nature of the parliamentary bureaucracy.			

(Continued)

Table 4.1 Overview of administrative arrangements in bicameral parliaments (Continued)

Bicameral parliament	Joint administrations (one administrative service for both Houses)	Divided administrations (two administrative services, one for each House)	Polylith administrations (three administrative services: one for each House + a joint service)	Polylith administrations (multiple administrative services/staffing)
South Africa	The Parliament and Provincial Legislatures' Service provide the administrative services both to the national Parliament of South Africa and to the nine Provincial Legislatures (South African Legislative Sector – SALS), with an autonomous administrative staff apart from the public service.			
Switzerland	Switzerland has the most tightly integrated administrative organization: both Houses of Parliament occupy the same building and have a single administration. With the exception of a few functions directly related to the plenary sessions, all staff members work for the two chambers.			
UK				Each House has its own staff and a relatively similar set of administrative arrangements (the *governance of administration* – the political control and oversight of administration – and then *staff organization, roles and functions*). Following the passing of the Parliament (Joint Departments) Act 2007 and the move towards unifying some cross-Parliament services, five Joint Departments are now serving both Houses: Parliamentary Digital Service, Parliamentary Security Department, In-House Services and Estates, Parliamentary Archives, Parliamentary Procurement and Commercial Services.

(*Continued*) |

Table 4.1 Overview of administrative arrangements in bicameral parliaments (Continued)

Bicameral parliament	Joint administrations (one administrative service for both Houses)	Divided administrations (two administrative services, one for each House)	Polylith administrations (three administrative services: one for each House + a joint service)	Polylith administrations (multiple administrative services/staffing)
US				There are five major groups of staff serving Congress. The largest group are personal staffs of each Congressman and Senator. Then there are staffs for the committees in each house, as well as for several joint committees. The third group are the staffs for the leadership of the two houses, for example the majority and minority leaders and whips. The fourth group are the various officers of each house, for example parliamentarians, doorkeepers, clerks. Some of these posts are more ceremonial than functional, but they are still part of the Congressional staff. The final group of staff are the employees of the three major support agencies that provide research and analysis to Congress.
	5	10	3	3

From the point of view of the services provided, each House tends to create similar expert structures supporting either the functions of committee and plenary meetings or the highly specialized lines of activity, including IT, EU affairs or budget. The working style in the two Houses may also be rather similar, following shared principles, usually derived by a common (national) administrative tradition and by the existence of similar appointing procedures, status and institutional duties for the staff serving the two administrations.

However, the duplication of administrative services may coexist with relevant differences in their internal arrangement. The first and most obvious of these lies in the divergent size of staff serving lower and upper Houses, which in the large majority of cases follows the asymmetries in the number of MPs allocated to the two branches of Parliament. One extreme case here is Germany: the sizeable administration of the German lower House, the Bundestag, comprising approximately 3,000 members of staff, mirrors the size of this assembly, one of the largest in the EU, currently comprising 736 MPs following the 2021 elections. Conversely, the administration of the upper House, the *Bundesrat*, is composed of little more than 200 employees, serving an assembly of 69 representatives. This confirms the lack of any automatism in the ratio between the number of MPs and the size of the administration, with the lower House having a composition ten times bigger than that of the upper House (Högenauer, Arndt and Koggel, 2023). In a minority of cases, however, the staff numbers appear to be independent from the number of MPs allocated to each House – the experience of Argentina's Parliament is a case in point.[6]

It might be asked whether existing asymmetries in the dimension of the two administrations depend not just on the number of MPs allocated to the lower and upper House but also on existing asymmetries in their functions. Broadly speaking, there is no clear evidence in support to this perspective of inquiry. However, a counter-argument can be found in the rather unique case of the symmetric bicameral system of Italy which involves two parliamentary administrations that perfectly mirror each other in the internal organization (Griglio and Lupo, 2021; Lupo and Gianniti, 2023).

Some observations about the administrative impact exercised by functional or structural asymmetries arise from the comparison of the organizational charts of administrative services in lower and upper Houses (appearing in the chapters of this Handbook). In terms of macro-structures and micro-units activated, these charts show different levels of organizational complexity between the two Houses: upper Houses' administrations are not only composed of fewer units of staff but they also display a more basic structure, corresponding to fewer macro-structures and micro-units (e.g. France, see Tacea, 2023).

It is difficult to assess whether the asymmetries in the organizational charts do correspond to the functional and structural asymmetries between the two Houses. For instance, upper Houses' administrative units involved in the legislative services are usually more limited in size, scope and work pressure compared to lower Houses (Groen, 2023). This mirrors the fact that upper Houses usually have more narrow prerogatives and limited involvement in the decision-making. But there are also relevant examples of plenary or committee secretariats endowed with key tasks in facilitating and orienting the participation of upper Houses in law-making. An example can be drawn from the German *Bundesrat*, where committee secretariats play a pivotal role in drafting and channelling amendments, discussing them with state ministries and developing close contacts with relevant federal ministries and committees of the *Bundestag*. This proactive role can be considered a sort of administrative adaptation to the requirements of an atypical parliamentary assembly, composed not of elected members but of representatives of state governments, who – due to their executive responsibilities – tend to rely intensely on the *Bundesrat* administration as a sort of connecting belt and agreement facilitator (Högenauer, Arndt and Koggel, 2023).

Another relevant observation here concerns research services. With the important exception of the German *Bundesrat* – which is lacking a research service because it actually does not need one (since its members can rely on their state administrations for background research, advice and analytical support normally covered by research services – Högenauer, Arndt and Koggel, 2023) – these are usually set in upper Houses also. The latter may sometimes be encouraged to reinforce research units focused on core institutional activities and supported by an external visibility as a means of compensating for the weaknesses of their constitutional prerogatives. A significant example is provided by the creation in the Belgian Senate, in 2019, of the Center of Expertise for Institutional Affairs, tasked with collecting, developing and disseminating knowledge in institutional matters (art. 87.1 and 87.2 of the Senate Rules of Procedure). The creation of this new body follows the 2014 constitutional reform of the Belgian bicameralism (Sixth State Reform), which significantly revised the role of the upper House (Dandoy et al., 2015).

4.3.2 *The Search for Administrative Synergies*

Whereas existing asymmetries between the two Houses may give rise to divergencies in their administrative arrangement, administrative synergies might nonetheless facilitate cooperation on joint tasks or common needs of the two branches of Parliament. The search for such administrative synergies involves the provision of forms of cooperation and the pooling of resources and expertise between the two Houses without bringing about the establishment of a joint bureaucratic structure. Three areas of activity – respectively, related to the procedural, technical and substantive functions – can lead to the activation of such administrative synergies.

First, *procedurally*, all the structures or procedures underpinning both Houses, including meetings of the parliament in joint session and bicameral committees, are managed by means of a functional cooperation between the two bureaucracies (Högenauer, Arndt and Koggel, 2023; Lupo and Gianniti, 2023; Santos and Saboia, 2023). This is usually developed through the juxtaposition or rotation of each chamber's administrative inputs. Moreover, each chamber's administrative services normally cooperate in support of the legislative activities carried out independently by each of the two Houses. They do so by providing the timely exchange of documents and parliamentary acts. This comprises for example mutual access to documentation and information systems (Högenauer, Arndt and Koggel, 2023).

Second, administrative synergies between the two Houses may be activated for those *technical* functions that, due to economies of scale, are better served by pooling resources and that correspond to symmetrical needs of the two branches of parliament. One most relevant example is that of Belgium, where the administrative services of the two Houses are fully autonomous, but interestingly share the same building. In the last few years, relevant efforts have been made by the two administrations in order to pool forces and explore enhanced cooperation in selected *technical* fields, including joint security detail and joint catering operation (Popelier and Caboor, 2023). This trend can be interpreted as an administrative response to the sequence of constitutional reforms which have strengthened the asymmetric nature of the Belgian bicameral system, significantly limiting the prerogatives of the upper House, the Senate.

Not too dissimilar efforts have been shaping latest trends in the Italian parliamentary administrations. In 2017, the two parliamentary administrations were formally merged in response to a tempted, but failed, constitutional reform of the symmetric bicameral system. Rules on the creation of joint administrative services (from medical assistance to joint procurement) were introduced and these are still in force, although they remain formally unexecuted (Lupo and Gianniti, 2023). Digital arrangements, eventually leading to the integration of electronic systems for legislative monitoring electronic voting (e.g. Brazil: Santos and Saboia, 2023), is another field open to instances of bicameral administrative cooperation.

Third, the carrying out of *substantive* functions may occasionally see the establishment of forms of administrative cooperation between the two services. This is true particularly for Parliamentary Libraries, which even in divided administrations may lead to the creation of a joint department (e.g. Belgium: Popelier and Caboor, 2023), to the sharing of a department that, formally placed in the lower House's administration, serves the upper House as well (e.g. Czechia: Kaniok, 2023) or to the unification of the Libraries serving the two Houses (e.g. Italy: Lupo and Gianniti, 2023).

Not too dissimilar solutions have been activated for research services: this happens in the Czech Parliament, where the Parliamentary Institute formally belonging to the lower House also supports the Senate, and in Italy, where the administrative cooperation between the research services of the two Houses has now led to the release of joint dossiers of legislative bills that are always scrutinized independently by each House (Griglio and Lupo, 2021; Lupo and Gianniti, 2023).

On the whole, this overview demonstrates that, over time, divided administrations have come to adapt to the constitutional features of their respective bicameral system. While we can observe that in many cases bicameral symmetries and asymmetries do influence the internal organization and functioning of administrative services, no automatism can be drawn from these experiences. Administrative answers to the institutional inputs of a bicameral system are uneven and often unpredictable, especially when seen from outside. Ultimately, the shape of an administrative design is the outcome of a complex combination of structural and functional features, which are related both to the overall role of parliament in the constitutional design and to the established practice of internal organizational and procedural arrangements that support its activity (Lupo, 2019).

4.4 Joint Services in Polylith Administrations

In some bicameral parliaments, we see the presence of three or more administrative services: beyond the two general services supporting the lower and the upper House, other focused or sectorial services have been created to jointly manage common requirements or fields of shared activity.

Among those discussed here, five parliaments follow this format. Beyond the two services set for the lower House and the upper House, the Parliaments of Australia, Bosnia and Canada possess an additional joint administrative service. In the case of Argentina, the two Houses share three and in the UK even five different services.

Such joint services may fulfil different shared needs and manage multiple areas of activity. The comparative analysis shows two main sets of goals. The first set of goals deals with a *substantive* function, namely a common need faced by both Houses to rely on documentation, research evidence and reporting in order to increase the robustness of their decision-making (Rose et al., 2020). Following this logic, the Library of Parliament is in three cases – Canada, Argentina and Australia – devised as a joint service. In Australia, the joint department established in 2004, named the Department of the Parliamentary Reporting Staff (DPRS), does not only serve the joint Parliamentary Library but also covers the DPRS and the Joint

House Committee. This demonstrates the merging in a joint structure of different administrative units which are meant to cover all the reporting and documentation needs of parliamentarians and at the same time to support the activity of the Joint House Committee. Equally, the creation of the Parliamentary Archives in UK as a joint service derived from the House of Lords Records Office may be linked to the perceived need of a shared records management of the UK Parliament in order to collect, preserve and make archives accessible in an easy and simplified way.

The second set of goals attaches to the presence of joint services the management of *technical* functions (i.e. dealing with security, procurement or IT) which, for economies of scale, are better fulfilled by pooling resources of the two Houses. Bosnia has a Joint Service which supports both Houses in the conduct of general technical tasks. Argentina has two joint parliamentary services, respectively, for Print and Health Insurance System. UK has four Joint Departments, established in 2007,[7] all performing technical tasks: Parliamentary Digital Service, Parliamentary Security Department, In-House Services and Estates, Parliamentary Procurement and Commercial Services. Many of such services have been created in the last few decades in response to a common challenge to realign the administrative organization to the call for bicameral synergies in some core functions.

However, it is remarkable that joint services have *not* been set in those parliamentary administrations following the polylith model to support *procedural* functions. Such functions would clearly appear to call for a strong coordination between the two Houses in areas such as budgetary matters, foreign affairs or European integration. An explanation for this can be found in the strong political salience of these spheres of activity: in the exercise of these functions, the political will drives each House to keep full control over the substance, dominating the administrative handling of such matters and therefore avoiding the creation of a joint structure that might challenge the level of internal autonomy.

In conclusion, it can be argued that the creation of joint services, in addition to separate administrations of each House, is more likely in areas with a strong administrative and technical component. By contrast, it remains low when the procedural or substantive implications of such functions risk to interfere with the political sphere.

4.5 Joint Parliamentary Administrations

4.5.1 What Moves the Option for a Joint Bicameral Administration?

Joint administrations can be considered a minority format in the context of bicameral parliaments: only five cases covered in this Handbook fall under this type. Four of these are in Europe (Austria, Ireland, Spain and Switzerland) and one in Africa (South Africa). When investigating the reasons why two Houses might decide to pool their administrative resources and establish a joint administrative service, three elements need to be taken into consideration.

First, there is the historical process of the creation of joint parliamentary administrations as a means to reinforce parliamentary independence vis-à-vis the executive. Considering the search for balance between parliament and government, it is evident that setting up a single administration – or two administrations that are tightly coordinated – can be expected to strengthen the role both Houses can play; conversely, two independent administrative services would mutually check each other and weaken the overall position of the parliament in the institutional system. This is evident regarding the origins of certain joint parliamentary administrations. In Switzerland, for instance, the creation of the *Services du Parlement* is the result of a historic evolution that led the parliamentary administration to gain autonomy and independence from the Federal Chancellery. Initially, it had been the Federal executive that, in the 19th century and for large part of the 20th century (until 1972), had provided the Secretariat of the National Council and of the Council of States. The autonomy and unity of the *Services du Parlement* was only fully recognized by the new Constitution adopted in 1999 (art. 155).

Austria is an example of one of the most integrated parliamentary administrations and its rules have been outlined by Article 30.3 of the Constitution adopted in 1921, when parliament as an institution was defined in its fundamental organization and tasks. The administration is strongly grounded in the bicameral architecture of Parliament, as a single institution. It is remarkable to note that the Austrian Constitution formally recognizes as State organs the National and the Federal Councils, but not the bicameral legislature, and refers to the notion of the federal 'Parliament' only to identify the scope and the functions of the parliamentary administration.

In Spain, the unitary nature of the parliamentary bureaucracy – based on the statute of personnel, which is regulated 'by common agreement' between the two Houses (Díez Picazo, 1985; García-Escudero Márquez, 1998) – was recognized by art. 72 of the 1978 Constitution, which identified in the Parliament one of the fundamental democratic safeguards after years of dictatorship.

In South Africa, the creation of a joint bureaucracy is strongly rooted in the strengthening of the legislative institution as a means to reinforce constitutional democracy. The staff of Parliament was initially set up in 1974, outside of the Civil Service, as a single special bureaucracy serving both Houses.[8] This was part of the process of parliamentary institutionalization which further continued in 1996, when the staff of Parliament, named 'Parliamentary Services Administration', was referred to the South African Legislative Sector, the Parliament consisting of the two Houses (the National Assembly and the National Council of Provinces), as well as the nine Provincial Legislatures established by the Republic of South Africa (RSA) Constitution Act, No 108 of 1996 (Layman, 2023).

Finally, historical causes seem to have inspired also the establishment in Ireland, in 1959, of the joint staff of the Houses of the Oireachtas. The purpose of this reform was to make civil servants of the two Houses independent from the government.[9] This historical change can be connected to the autonomization of the Irish executive branch set by the Republic of Ireland Act 1948, which came into operation on 18 April 1949. As a matter of fact, the Act, severing the last ties with the British Monarchy, can be considered the birthday of a fully independent Irish executive power, which clearly activated some counter-measures on the side of Parliament.

Apart from such historical circumstances, a second element which can explain the option to create a joint parliamentary administration in bicameral systems lies in the search for unity and coherence of parliamentary action in the context of highly pluralistic and composite environments. A single administration following all the decision-making processes in the two Houses is likely to provide more unitarian results compared to the more fragmented and sectorial outcomes which could be expected when two distinct parliamentary administrations assist the two Houses.

This is evident from the fact that in three out of five cases (Austria, Switzerland and South Africa[10]) the upper House represents the sub-national entities of a Federal State. In South Africa, as discussed above, the Parliamentary Services Administration is exceptionally advising not just the national Houses but also the provincial legislatures, thus confirming the strong emphasis towards the unitary nature of the main representative assemblies. The willingness to develop such a system of 'cooperative governance' (Layman, 2023) takes into account the autonomy of legislatures in determining their own internal arrangements but at the same time strengthens the intrinsic nature of South Africa as 'a unitary state with federal features' (ibidem). This was later confirmed by the Memorandum of Understanding signed by all Speakers of Parliament and Provincial Legislatures in March 2010, which outlined the commitment of the institutions to collaborate and cooperate on matters of common interest based on their similar constitutional mandates. Probably, a best practice on how to accommodate and adapt political representation in multi-level settings.

Finally, a third possible explanation for the creation of joint services is the search for greater autonomy: having regard to the point of balance between politics and administration, the choice in favour of a single administration in a bicameral system – which is by definition composed of two Houses presided over by two distinct Speakers/Presidents – potentially gives the administration a higher degree of autonomy from the directions determined by politics and by MPs leadership bodies. Although, as discussed below, in joint services the administrative governance is not always equally distributed among the Speakers/Bureaux of both Houses, it can nonetheless be argued that parliamentary staff serving two Houses have a broader mission and a greater degree of administrative autonomy with regard to the political preferences of the elected members.

4.5.2 A Single Format, with Rather Different Levels of Administrative Integration

The format of joint parliamentary administrations offers a wide range of internal options ranging from the more cohesive arrangements, with only limited lines of separation between the two Houses, to a more divided approach, where a single bureaucracy splits into two administrative structures which are rather autonomous from one another. The determinants of these internal arrangements may be found both in the macro-level and the micro-level of the organization. On the one hand, they deal with the appointment and role of the Secretary General and the status of personnel. On the other hand, they relate to the scope and nature of unicameral administrative arrangements.

Having regard to both of these levels of analysis, the Swiss and Austrian administrations are examples of a deeply unified bureaucracy, with a high level of internal integration. In both countries, a single Secretary General serves the two Houses (even three in Switzerland, including also the Federal Assembly composed of the two Houses in joint session) and the staff of the joint administration has a common status modelled on the conditions set for federal employees. What differs in the two administrations is the governance of these aspects, and in particular the appointment of the Secretary General and the recruitment of staff: in Switzerland, they are based on bicameral procedures,[11] while in Austria they rest with the President of the National Council, the lower House.[12]

In the internal arrangement, the Austrian parliamentary administration provides joint structures for the large majority of internal tasks. Probably due to the strongly asymmetrical nature of the Austrian bicameral system, some unicameral administrative units, working at the level of each House, have been created in the legislative field to support the core advice and support services of the *Nationalrat* and the *Bundesrat*. However, the tasks and activities which are instrumental, but not inherent, to law-making (the legal, legislative and research services, the EU affairs services, the information and public relations services, the stenographic records, the archives and statistics) are supported by joint services. The degree of internal integration is even more extensive in the Swiss parliamentary administration, where, with the exception of a few functions directly related to the plenary sessions, all the other tasks are served by joint structures and all staff members work jointly and equally for the organs of both chambers.

Compared to the Swiss and Austrian cases, South Africa and Ireland can be considered examples of joint administrations with an intermediate degree of integration. The Parliamentary Services Administration of South Africa combines a strong coordination with some internal divisions between the two Houses. Alongside the Secretary to Parliament, the leading position introduced by the Parliamentary Service Act 1974 (§18) that must enjoy the confidence of the Speakers of both Houses, two distinct Secretaries, one for the National Assembly and the other for the National Council of Provinces, have been re-established. These cover the basic procedural and logistic advice and guidance to plenary and Committee sessions and liaison offices with national and sub-national governments. All the other functions (legal, research and advisory, external relations, corporate services) are jointly administered in support of both Houses. Interestingly, a separate joint program within the administration of Parliament – the Legislative Sector Support – was created in 2006 as part of the Legislature Support Programme funded by the European Union. Its task is to enhance the coordination of the whole legislative sector, supporting the aggregate bodies of the Speakers' Forum of South Africa and the Secretaries' Association of the Legislatures of South Africa.

Elements of integration and autonomy are also present in the internal arrangement of the Irish 'Houses of the Oireachtas Service' (Coughlan and Gunn, 2011; McKenna, 2011). Both Houses have their own clerk, but the clerk of the lower House, the Dáil, acts as the Secretary General of the administration, with a power of direction and control over all the officers and joint staff, subject to the orders received from the Speaker of the Dáil (art. 149 of the Standing Orders of the Dáil – art. 15 and 16 of the Houses of the Oireachtas Commission Act). The Secretary General is appointed by a bicameral body, the Houses of the Oireachtas Commission,[13] on a recommendation made by the Speaker of the Dáil (Houses of the Oireachtas [appointments to certain offices] Act 2015). However, the upper House, the Seanad, which in the last century has faced several attempts at reform even including a failed referendum on its abolition in October 2013, has a dedicated Seanad Office, dependent upon the Secretary General, providing advice and support services to its sittings and business.

Finally, Spain offers an example of the least integrated among joint parliamentary administrations. In its internal governance, notwithstanding its formal unity, it is intrinsically divided. Each House has its own head official, the *Secretario General* for the Congress and the *Letrado Mayor* for the Senate, appointed by the House Bureau, following the Speaker's proposal. The civil servants of the *Cortes Generales* have a composite status – partially based in joint *Estatuto del Personal de las Cortes Generales,* approved by the Bureau of the Congress and of the Senate on 23 June 1983, as integrated by each House (Gómez, 2002; Lozano Miralles, 2005) – that nevertheless does not hinder mobility between the two branches. In the internal organization, the Spanish Parliament features extensive unicameral administrative arrangements, covering most of the legislative and non-legislative offices, exception made for few joint administrative structures (responsible for the activity of the *Cortes Generales* and for the Technical Secretary of the Central Electoral Committee).

On the whole, multiple factors influence the internal degree of integration and cohesion of a joint parliamentary administration. Some major determinants can be identified in the symmetries and asymmetries of the bicameral system and in the *influence effectiveness*[14] of the lower and of the upper House. For instance, when the two Houses exercise similar constitutional functions, as in Switzerland, staff resources and expertise can be pooled easily and in an effective manner. Similarly, when the two Houses have a comparable institutional strength, as in Switzerland and South Africa, this favours the joint governance of the administration.

By contrast, in asymmetrical bicameral systems (such as Austria, Ireland and Spain), certain administrative units – related, for instance, to the exercise of core legislative tasks, to the knowledge and interpretation of the Rules of procedure, to the management of relationships with MPs – are working at the level of each House. When in asymmetrical bicameralism upper Houses are extremely weak in terms of status and prerogatives, it is the lower House that prevails in the provision of administrative governance. This happens in Austria and Ireland- but not in Spain- due to the intrinsically divided structure of the parliamentary administration.

4.6 Conclusions

The comparative analysis demonstrates the difficulty to find any underlying and universal rule behind the administrative arrangement of bicameral parliaments. The institutional complexity arising from the presence of two Houses is mirrored and indeed multiplied at the administrative level. A wide range of solutions, either shaped in terms of separateness and differentiation or supporting the call for administrative synergies and forms of integration, can be identified.

Even if there is no one-size-fits-all explanation for the mix between these two opposite requirements, we have observed that the way in which each parliament shapes its administrative organization is based on clear institutional preferences, with regard both to the basic choice between a divided or a joint administrative format and to the subsequent adjustments in the internal micro-organization. In most cases, the administrative format is defined alongside the historical process of parliamentary institutionalization (Polsby, 1968). The need to promote and strengthen parliamentary pluralism and enhance the autonomy entrusted on each House or, to the contrary, to sustain the unity of the parliamentary institution vis-à-vis the executive might be dominant reasons behind the choice for either a divided or a joint format.

Within each format, the decision on which structures and spheres of administrative activity are better served at the level of each House and which others instead require bicameral solutions depend on clear determinants: surprisingly, these determinants tend to be rather similar for the divided and the joint formats. On the one hand, divided administrations may prefer to address the needs for administrative synergy in different ways, ranging from informal coordination to the creation of joint services and the shift towards a polylith format. Calls for synergy mostly feature in those technical and specialized areas where economies of scale are particularly relevant or regard those *substantive* functions with a strong administrative component where interference from the political sphere tends to be low. On the other hand, joint administrations may decide to create divided units to support the specific requirements and needs of lower and upper Houses, up to the re-creation of strong lines of administrative division between the two branches of parliament. These arrangements can specifically cover the *procedural* or *substantive* functions that correspond to strong asymmetries in the institutional architecture of the bicameral system. These are fields of activity with a strong political dimension and sensitivity where the role of the administration is usually limited to the provision of support services (that are nonetheless crucial to the continuity of the institution's work).

This overview confirms that divided administrations, which find in *administrative separateness* their dominant logic, tend to compensate this structural choice with the development of forms of bicameral informal coordination up to the creation of joint services in support for shared functions, common needs or highly technical and knowledge-based requirements associated to economies of scale. By contrast, joint administrations, based on *administrative integration*, complement this dominant logic with the establishment of divided units to support the specific administrative necessities of lower and upper Houses, up to the re-creation of strong lines of bureaucratic division between the two branches of parliament in those fields of activity that meet broader institutional asymmetries. These opposed trends witness that the hybridization of the original organizational choice is a rule both in divided and in joint administrations and that, regardless of the referent model, bicameral parliaments rely on a composition of administrative services shared between the two Houses and of other services supporting each House separately. The mix between these two solutions is the outcome of national parliamentary designs evolving over the decades in support to changing institutional needs and choices.

Notes

1 On the difference between 'legislature' and 'parliament', Laver (2008) and Kreppel (2006). In fact, due to the variety of institutional denominations adopted, a certain degree of confusion surrounds the terms 'parliaments', 'legislatures' and 'legislative bodies'; see Fasone (2019).
2 Due to its specificities, the staffing model of the US Congress, which is not structured as a real 'bureaucracy', will not be examined in details in the article, but in Figure 1 it will be mentioned within the format of polylith administrations.
3 It is well known that the Speaker/President represents the only and final point of (political) unity of such a pluralistic and articulated organization, depending on the features of each Parliament and institutional system (Lippolis and Lupo, 2013).
4 On the difference between the macro- and micro-organization of parliamentary administrations, see Griglio and Lupo (2021, note no.1).
5 On the presence of two Secretary Generals for each House in some bicameral experiences, including France, see however Gianniti and Di Cesare (2023).
6 The administrative services supporting the Argentinean lower House (the Chamber of Deputies, composed of 257 representatives) and upper House (the Senate, composed of 72 senators) have the same number of people working as Parliamentary Staff, around 5,000 each.
7 The creation of Joint Departments in the British Houses of Parliament was preceded by the adoption of the Parliament (Join Departments) Act 2007, regulating the sharing of the functions, the staff mobility and all the organizational requirements.
8 The Parliamentary Service Act 1974 gave effect to a resolution of the Senate and of the House of Assembly to merge the administration of their personnel and resources with those of the Joint Parliamentary Establishment, a pre-existing joint administrative service.
9 Pursuant to art. 20 of the staff of the Houses of the Oireachtas Act, 1959, civil servants who are a member of the joint staff of the Houses of the Oireachtas cannot be removed from office by the government except after consultation with the Chairmen of the two Houses.
10 In Spain, the upper House is only formally composed by representatives of the sub-national entities and defined as 'Chamber of territorial representation' by art. 69 Cost., although in the constitutional practice it is acting more as a (weak) political assembly than as a place for the participation of the strong Spanish regions (Santolaya Machetti, 1983; Jimenéz Blanco, 1985; Solozábal Echavarría, 1995).
11 In Switzerland, the Secretary general is appointed by a parliamentary body, called the 'Coordination conference', and is therefore confirmed by the Offices of the two Houses. The recruitment of staff is deliberated through an ordinance of the Federal Assembly (art. 66 *Loi sur le Parlement*).
12 According to art. 30.3–6 of the Constitution and art. 14 of the Federal Law on the Rules of Procedure of the Austrian National Council, the President of the National Council ratifies the appointment of the Secretary General and acts as the supreme administrative organ in the internal organization and in the execution of administrative matters.
13 The Commission, which also acts as the governing body of the Service, is a composed of the Speakers of the two Houses, the Secretary General, a member appointed by the Minister and not more than 7 ordinary members.
14 This notion can be interpreted as an indicator of the amount of influence effectively achieved by parliamentary assemblies in the decision-making process, see Arter, 2006.

References

Amellier, M. 1966. *Parliaments: A Comparative Study on the Structure and the Functioning of Representative Institutions in Fifty-Five Countries*, 2nd ed., London, Cassell.

Arter, D. 2006. 'Introduction: comparing the legislative performance of legislatures', in *The Journal of Legislative Studies*, 12, 3–4, 245–257.

Association of the Secretary Generals of Parliaments (ASGP). 2000. Report of the Meeting 'The role of the Secretary-General in the administration of Parliament', Amman, 1–4 May 2000.

Barrett, V. 2019. *Parliamentary Administration: What Does it Mean to Manage a Parliament Effectively?*, The Australian National University ProQuest Dissertations Publishing.

Benoit, C. and Rozenberg, O. (eds). 2020. *Handbook of Parliamentary Studies*, Cheltenham, Edward Elgard.

Bontadini, P.L. 1983. 'Strutture e dinamiche organizzative degli apparati', in VV.AA. (ed), *La burocrazia parlamentare: funzioni, garanzie e limiti*, Roma, Camera dei deputati, 31–39.

Borthwich, R.L. 2001. 'Methods of Composition of Second Chambers', in N. Baldwin and D. Shell (eds), *Second Chambers*, London or Portland, Frank Cass, 19–26.

Bradbury, J.C. and Crain, W.M. 2004. 'Bicameralism', in C. Kershaw Rowleyand F. Schneider(eds), *Encyclopedia of Public Choice*, Vol. 2, New York, Kluwer, 39–41.

Christiansen, T., Griglio, E. and Lupo, N. 2021. 'Making representative democracy work: the role of parliamentary administrations in the European Union', in *The Journal of Legislative Studies*, 27, 4, 477–493.

Coniez, H. and Michon, P (eds). 2020. *Servir les assemblées. Histoire et dictionnaire de l'administration parlementaire française de 1789 à la fin du XXe siècle*, Paris, Mare & Martin.

Coughlan, K. and Cunn, E. 2011. 'Advising and Serving the Houses: From Clerk to Chief Executive', in M. MacCarthaigh and M. Manning (eds), *The Houses of the Oireachtas: Parliament in Ireland*, Dublin, Institute of Public Administration, 184–204.

Dandoy, R., Dodeigne, J., Reuchamps, M. and Vandeleene A. 2015. 'The new Belgian Senate. A (dis) continued evolution of federalism in Belgium?', in *Representation*, 51, 3, 327–339.

Diermeir, D. and Myerson, R.B. 1999. 'Bicameralism and its consequences for the internal organization of legislatures', in *American Economic Review*, 89, 1182–1196.

Díez Picazo, L.M. 1985. *La autonomía administrativa de las cámaras parlamentarias*, Zaragoza, Studia Albornotiana.

Fasone, C. 2019. 'What is a legislature in the twenty-first century? Classification and evolution of a contested notion', in Federalismi.it, 15.

Fasone, C. 2020. 'Parliaments in Comparative Legal and Political Analyses', in C. Benoit and O. Rozenberg (eds), *Handbook of Parliamentary Studies*, Cheltenham, Edward Elgard, 121–140.

Fasone, C. 2023. 'A Distinct Role of Parliamentary Administrations in Presidential and Parliamentary Systems?', in T. Christiansen, E. Griglio and N. Lupo (eds), *Handbook of Parliamentary Administrations*, Routledge.

García-Escudero Márquez, P. 1998. 'Articulo 72', in O. Alzaga (ed), *Comentario sistemático a la Constitución española de 1978*, VI, Madrid, Ed. Cortes Generales y Edersa, 392–430.

Gianniti, L. and Di Cesare, R. 2023. 'The Internal Administrative Structure and the Relationship with the Speaker', in T. Christiansen, E. Griglio and N. Lupo (eds), *Handbook of Parliamentary Administrations*, Routledge.

Griglio, E. 2020. *Parliamentary Oversight of the Executives. Tools and Procedures in Europe*, Oxford, Hart Publishing.

Griglio, E. and Lupo, N. 2021. 'Parliamentary administrations in the bicameral systems of Europe: joint or divided?', in *The Journal of Legislative Studies*, 27, 4, 513–534.

Gómez, M. C. 2002, October 8–11. Los retos de la gestión del personal en una administración parlamentaria neutral y moderna. Presentation at the VII Congreso Internacional del CLAD sobre la Reforma del Estado y de la Administración Pública, Lisboa, Portugal http://unpan1.un.org/intradoc/groups/public/documents/CLAD/clad0044006.pdf.

Groen, A. 2023. The Netherland's Parliamentary Administration, in T. Christiansen, E. Griglio and N. Lupo (eds), *Handbook of Parliamentary Administrations*, Routledge.

Högenauer, A., Arndt, F. and Koggel, C. 2023. Germany's Parliamentary Administration, in T. Christiansen, E. Griglio and N. Lupo (eds), *Handbook of Parliamentary Administrations*, Routledge.

Inter-Parliamentary Union. 2020. *Comparative Research Paper on Parliamentary Administration*. Geneva, IPU.

Jimenéz Blanco, A. 1985. *Las relaciones de funcionamiento entre el poder central y los entes territoriales. Supervision, solidaridad, coordinacion*, Madrid, Instituto de estudios de administracion local.

Kaniok, P. 2023. Czechia's Parliamentary Administration, in T. Christiansen, E. Griglio and N. Lupo (eds), *Handbook of Parliamentary Administrations*, Routledge.

Kreppel, A. 2006. 'Understanding the European Parliament from a Federalist Perspective: The Legislatures of the United States and the European Union Compared' in A. Menon and M.A. Schain (eds), *Comparative Federalism. The European Union and the United States in Comparative Perspective*, Oxford, Oxford University Press.

Layman, T. 2023. South Africa's Parliamentary Administration, in T. Christiansen, E. Griglio and N. Lupo (eds), *Handbook of Parliamentary Administrations*, Routledge.

Laver, M. 2008. 'Overview: Legislatures and Parliaments in Comparative Context' in B. Weingast and D. Wittman (eds), *Oxford Handbook of Political Economy*, Oxford, Oxford University Press.

Le Divellec, A. 2020. 'Parliament in Constitutional Law', in C. Benoit and O. Rozenberg (eds), *Handbook of Parliamentary Studies*, Cheltenham, Edward Elgar, 102–121.

Lippolis, V. and Lupo, N. (eds) 2013. 'Le trasformazioni del ruolo dei Presidenti delle Camere', in *Il Filangieri. Quaderno 2012–2013*, Napoli, Jovene, 1–308.

Llanos M. and Nolte, D. 2003. 'Bicameralism in the Americas: around the extremes of symmetry and incongruence', in *The Journal of Legislative Studies*, 9, 3, 54–86.

Lozano Miralles, J. 2005. La administración parlamentaria: Una visión comparada de los parlamentos autonómicos. Presentation at the VII Congreso Español de Ciencia Politica y de la Administración: democracia y Buen Gobierno, 21–23 September 2005. www.aecpa.es.

Lupo, N. 2012. Il ruolo delle burocrazie parlamentari alla luce dei mutamenti dell'assetto istituzionale nazionale e sovranazionale, in *Rassegna parlamentare*, 54, 1, 51–89.

Lupo, N. 2019. 'Parliaments,' in R. Masterman and R. Schütze (eds), *Cambridge Companion to Comparative Constitutional Law*, Cambridge, Cambridge University Press, 335–360.

Lupo, N. and Gianniti, L. 2023. Italy's Parliamentary Administration, in T. Christiansen, E. Griglio and N. Lupo (eds), *Handbook of Parliamentary Administrations*, Routledge.

Manzella, A. 2003. *Il parlamento*, III ed., Bologna, Il mulino.

Massicotte, L. 2001. 'Legislative unicameralism: a global survey and a few case studies', in *The Journal of Legislative Studies*, 7, 151–170.

McKenna, C. 2011. Staff of the Houses of the Oireachtas. In M. MacCarthaigh and M. Manning (eds), *The Houses of the Oireachtas: Parliament in Ireland*, Dublin, Institute of Public Administration, 222–233.

Mill, J.S. 1861. 'On Second Chambers', in J.S. Mill (ed), *Considerations on* (1861), reprinted Cambridge, Cambridge University Press, 2010, 238–248.

Mughan, A. and Patterson, A.C. 1999. 'Senates: A Comparative Perspective', in S.C. Patterson and A. Mughan(eds), *Senates: Bicameralism in the Contemporary World*, Columbus, Ohio State University Press, 333–349.

Norton, P. (ed). 1990. *Parliaments in Western Europe*, London, Frank Cass.

Pacelli, M. and Giovannetti, G. 2020. *Interno Montecitorio. I luoghi, l'istituzione, le persone*, III ed., Torino, Giappichelli.

Patterson, S.C. and Mughan, A. 1999. 'Senates and the Theory of Bicameralism', in S.C. Patterson and A. Mughan (eds), *Senates: Bicameralism in the Contemporary World*, Columbus, Ohio State University Press, 1–31.

Peters, G. 2021. 'Bureaucracy for democracy: administration in support of legislatures', in *The Journal of Legislative Studies*, 27, 4, 577–594.

Peters, G. 2023. United States' Parliamentary Administration, in T. Christiansen, E. Griglio and N. Lupo (eds), *Handbook of Parliamentary Administrations*, Routledge.

Polsby, N.W. 1968. 'The Institutionalization of the U.S. House of Representatives, in *The American Political Science Review*, 62, 1, 144–168.

Popelier, P. and Caboor, P. 2023. Belgium's Parliamentary Administration, in T. Christiansen, E. Griglio and N. Lupo (eds), *Handbook of Parliamentary Administrations*, Routledge.

Rasch, B.E. and Tsebelis G. 1995. 'Patterns of Bicameralism', in H. Döring (ed), *Parliaments in Western Europe: Majority Rule and Minority Rights*, New York, St. Martin Press.

Rose, D., Kenny, C., Hobbs, A. and Tyler, C. 2020. 'Improving the use of evidence in legislatures: the case of the UK Parliament' in *Evidence & Policy*, 16, 4, 619–638.

Santolaya Machetti, P. 1983. 'En torno al principio de cooperacion' in *Revista de Derecho politico*, 21, 83–109.
Santos, F. and Saboia, F. 2023. Brazil's Parliamentary Administration, in T. Christiansen, E. Griglio and N. Lupo (eds), *Handbook of Parliamentary Administrations*, Routledge.
Solozábal Echavarría, J.J. 1995, 'Estado autonómico', in *Enciclopedia jurídica básica*, Madrid, Editorial Civitas.
Tacea, A. 2023. France's Parliamentary Administration, in T. Christiansen, E. Griglio and N. Lupo (eds), *Handbook of Parliamentary Administrations*, Routledge.
Trivelli, L. 1975. *Le Bicamérisme. Institutions Comaparées. Étude historique, statistique et critique des rapports entre le conseil national et le conseil des états*, Lausanne, Diffusion Payot.
Uhr, J. 2008. 'Bicameralism', in R.A.W. Rhodes, S.A. Binder and B.A. Rothman (eds.), *The Oxford Handbook of Political Institutions*, Oxford, Oxford University Press. 474–494.

5
THE EUROPEANIZATION OF PARLIAMENTARY ADMINISTRATIONS

Anna-Lena Högenauer

5.1 Introduction

The role of parliamentary administrations in EU affairs has only recently caught the attention of academics. As a result, the body of literature is still small, and there is a dearth of broader comparative studies covering several national parliaments. This is not surprising, as the study of European parliamentary administrations in general is at best rudimentary compared to the breadth and depth of the literature on the staff of the US Congress.

The starting point for the comparative study of national and regional parliamentary administrations in EU affairs was the OPAL project (Observatory of National Parliaments after the Lisbon Treaty, 2011–2014). The project collected a range of basic data covering most national parliaments, complemented with a smaller number of qualitative case studies into select regional and national parliaments (Christiansen et al. 2014; Högenauer and Christiansen 2015; Gattermann et al. 2016; Högenauer and Neuhold 2015; Högenauer et al. 2016; Neuhold and Högenauer 2016). It inspired other authors to enquire into the political control of national parliamentary staff (e.g. Winzen 2014; Strelkov 2015) and the administrative capacity of regional parliaments in EU affairs (e.g. Buzogany and Häsing 2017).

This early literature revealed that parliamentary administrations – and especially committee staff – play a considerable role in EU affairs scrutiny. In most national parliaments, EU experts provide substantive advice on EU questions and are often involved in the drafting of committee decisions on EU affairs. They also play a key role in facilitating interparliamentary networking and information exchange. This has led authors to conclude that there was a considerable "bureaucratization" of EU affairs scrutiny (Högenauer and Neuhold 2015; Högenauer et al. 2016; Neuhold and Högenauer 2016). At the same time, they found that the nature of parliamentary work and the practices in place meant that bureaucratic input was subject to adequate political checks (Christiansen et al. 2014; Winzen 2014).

The aim of this chapter is to provide an overview of the state of the art as well as an empirical update. In February 2021, the members of the European Centre for Parliamentary Research and Documentation were asked to reply to a questionnaire on the administrative capacity of parliaments in EU affairs, the distribution of roles between the EAC and sectoral committees in EU affairs, the role of committee staff and research staff and interparliamentary cooperation. It was qualitative rather than quantitative in nature and required a description of structures, roles and processes. All 11 Upper Houses and 23 out of 27 Lower Houses replied to the questionnaire. The French, Italian, Dutch and Romanian Lower Houses are missing. For some parts of the analysis, the gaps can be filled with older data from the abovementioned studies on parliamentary administrations and from the Palgrave Handbook of National Parliaments (Hefftler et al. 2015).

The chapter will first explain the current context of national parliamentary scrutiny of EU affairs. It will then consider four aspects of the Europeanization of parliamentary administrations: the presence of EU experts, the role of committee staff in EU affairs, the role of staff in interparliamentary relations and the organization of research units.

5.2 The Role of National Parliaments in EU Affairs Post-Lisbon

National parliaments were long considered late-comers in EU policy-making: at the outset, they were represented in EU affairs through their delegations to the consultative European Assembly (later European Parliament [EP]). However, there was no systematic scrutiny of European initiatives within the national parliaments themselves. This only changed with the accession of new member states, whose parliaments were quicker to define scrutiny rights for themselves and establish European Affairs Committees (Norton 1996; O'Brennan and Raunio 2007). However, in 2001, Maurer and Wessels (2001) still classified most national parliaments as weak due to limited scrutiny powers and low motivation.

In the mid-2000s, national parliaments started to push for more formal recognition in the context of the negotiations of the Draft Constitutional Treaty. The Treaty ultimately failed at the negotiations stage, but the new rights that national parliaments had secured were incorporated in the Treaty of Lisbon that entered into force in late 2009. Indeed, the European Commission started to improve its cooperation with national parliaments even before 2009 in anticipation of the new treaty, and many national parliaments also started their preparations for Lisbon in the mid-2000s with revisions to their rules of procedures. As a result, the literature finds that national parliaments were reversing the trend of deparliamentarization in the 2000s (e.g. Raunio and Wiberg 2009; Winzen, 2012).

But what are these new opportunities? Some of the Treaty changes are primarily symbolic and have no practical relevance, such as the recognition of the contribution of national parliaments to the good functioning of the EU in art. 12 TEU. Other provisions do have practical relevance, such as the right of national parliaments to veto a decision to move from unanimity to qualified majority voting in the Council of Ministers. However, while this gives national parliaments control over changes to the decision-making procedures, this type of situation will be very rare. Ultimately, three developments were particularly important – improved information rights (1), the creation of an Early Warning System (EWS) (2) and the start of the Political Dialogue in 2006 (3).

Firstly, Protocol 1 of the Treaty of Lisbon guarantees national parliaments extensive information rights such as the right to a wide range of (pre)legislative documents such as draft legislation, White and Green Papers, impact assessments. Most importantly, they now receive this information directly from the European Institutions and therefore no longer depend on the support of their national government.

Secondly, Protocol 2 of the Lisbon Treaty defines the role of national parliaments in guarding the principle of subsidiarity. It creates the new so-called EWS (also called Early Warning Mechanism). Under the EWS, the European Commission has to send the national parliaments all draft legislative proposals in their own language. They then have eight weeks from the day they receive the proposal to review it for a potential breach of the principle of subsidiarity, that is to determine whether the goals of the legislation could also be achieved by action on the national or regional level or whether there really is an added value to European-level action. During this period, each chamber of each national parliament can adopt a reasoned opinion, if it finds that there is a breach of subsidiarity. Every national parliament has two votes, which are split even across both chambers in the case of bicameral parliaments. If the reasoned opinions on a draft legislative act represent at least one third of all the votes allocated to national parliaments (18/54), it is considered a "yellow card" and the European Commission has to review the draft. However, it can then decide to maintain, amend or withdraw the draft. If at least a simple majority object on grounds of subsidiarity, it results in an "orange card". But the European Commission can still maintain the proposal, which only fails if a majority of 55 per cent of the members of the Council or a simple majority of the votes cast in the EP bring the proposal down. The yellow and orange cards thus do not confer veto powers to the national parliaments but rather allow them to put the Commission under pressure to justify its proposals better (cf. Malang et al. 2017; Buskjaer Rasmussen and Kluger Dionigi 2018 for a discussion of the EWS and the Political Dialogue).

Finally, the European Commission established the Political Dialogue in 2006. Under the Political Dialogue, national parliaments can communicate substantive comments on EU legislative proposals to the European Commission. The European Commission is not obliged to take these comments on board, but it provides a channel of communication between national parliaments and the European Commission that did not previously exist.

In addition to these treaty changes, Gattermann et al. (2016) identify two external pressures for the growing Europeanization of national parliaments. Firstly, the steady expansion of EU competences makes effective EU affairs scrutiny increasingly important for national parliaments. The growing range of EU legislation squeezes the domestic political space slowly but steadily, so that the relevance of national parliaments risks declining unless they can carve out a role in EU affairs. This trend first led to the creation of European Affairs Committees (EACs) but now arguably increasingly requires a more active involvement of sectoral committees as the EU affairs-related workload expands.

Secondly, while European affairs were considered to be of low salience in the past (i.e. to attract little public interest beyond broadly pro- or anti-European attitudes), the Eurozone crisis, the migration crisis and the Covid-19 crisis have upped the stakes. Polarized debates about (re)distributive policies on the European level, EU-imposed austerity and "bailout" packages for struggling countries, a fairer distribution of migrants and the extent to which the EU should accept migrants blur the distinction between domestic and European politics and have electoral relevance in a number of member states.

Overall, the post-Lisbon years provided both institutional and political incentives to national parliaments to engage with EU policy-making. These changes also affect the presence and role of EU experts within parliamentary administrations.

5.3 The Administrative Capacity of National Parliaments for EU Affairs Scrutiny

The 2021 survey largely confirms the findings of Högenauer et al. (2016). While all chambers for which data was available employ staff specialized in EU affairs, the administrative capacity of national parliaments varies considerably (cf. Figure 5.1). On the one hand, three chambers have fewer than five EU experts (the Slovenian, Belgian and Dutch Upper Houses), on the other hand, the German Bundestag employs over 70 EU experts. It is difficult to explain

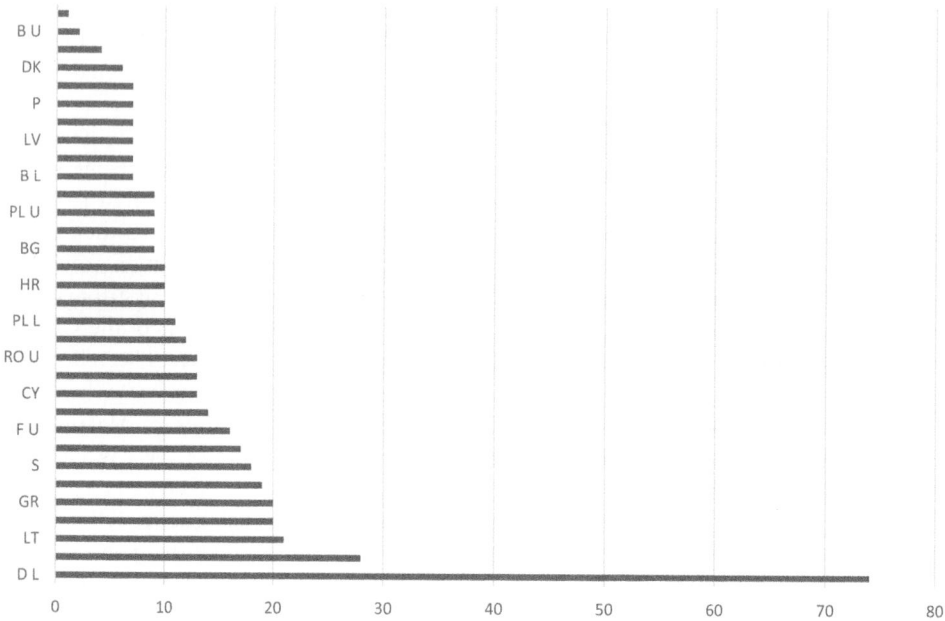

Figure 5.1 The number of EU experts in national parliaments (2021)

this variation. It does not correspond to the size of the state, as most of the better staffed parliaments are not in particularly large countries. Högenauer et al. (2016) showed that the number of EU experts in 2011–2013 also did not reflect the size of the parliament in terms of the number of MPs or to the size of the parliamentary administration in general. One can also easily see that the wealth of the country has no clear impact.

However, it does appear that Upper Houses have generally fewer EU experts than the corresponding Lower House. In 2011–2013, the two exceptions were the Czech parliament and the UK parliament, but Britain has since left the EU and the Czech Lower House has expanded its staff. On the whole, this reflects both the generally more prominent position of Lower Houses in the domestic political systems and the growing salience and importance of EU affairs. For example, the introduction of regular EU checks on the national budget mean that finance committees have been forced to engage with the EU far more than before the Eurozone crisis. Overall, most parliaments have between 7 and 15 EU experts, which suggests that this is perceived as the number required to provide sufficient procedural expertise and advice on the most important EU issues.

The findings also confirm a trend towards increasing Europeanization, despite the protracted Eurozone crisis and – most recently – the rather costly Covid-19 crisis. Högenauer et al. (2016) had already found that there number of EU experts working for national parliaments increased between 2006 and 2011–2013, albeit only in a good third of the chambers for which comparative data was available. The 2021 data reveals an important growth in the number of EU experts: In the 32 parliaments/chambers for which data was available, the combined number of EU experts rose from 292 in 2011–2013 to 430 in 2021. Of the 32 chambers/parliaments, 5 recorded a slight decrease in the number of EU experts, but 20 reported an increase. The German Bundestag reported the biggest growth with almost 30 additional EU experts, but the Hungarian, Finish, Swedish, Greek and Lithuanian parliaments and the

Czech Lower House also hired ten or more new staff. On the whole, the increase is mostly due to Lower Houses or unicameral parliaments, which further suggests that a shift in their political focus is underway.

5.4 The Organization of EU Affairs Scrutiny and the Role of Committee Staff

The responsibility for EU affairs scrutiny is organized differently across the national parliaments. Firstly, in some cases, committees can mandate the government, that is define the position that the government should defend in the Council of Ministers. Secondly, in some countries, committees can directly adopt opinions for the Political Dialogue or reasoned opinions for the EWS. In others, it is the plenary that decides. Thirdly, in some cases, EU affairs are primarily or exclusively the responsibility of the EAC. In others, the sectoral committees are responsible for (part of) the scrutiny ("mainstreaming").

Not all of these differences are important for the organization of staff support. For example, whether the plenary or the committee adopt a reasoned opinion, ultimately the drafting of the opinion usually happens in the lead committee. Thus, if staff is involved in providing substantive advice or assists with the drafting, it will usually be committee staff. However, which committee is in charge matters: If EU affairs fall predominantly under the responsibility of the EAC, arguably only the EAC needs EU experts. On the other hand, if sectoral committees are in charge of scrutinizing EU legislation that falls into their area of expertise, that is if scrutiny is mainstreamed, they might need EU expertise.

Previously, the most comprehensive study on mainstreaming (Karlas 2012) only covered the Lower Houses. Högenauer (2021) uses the data from the 2021 ECPRD survey, which covered all 11 Upper Houses and 23/27 Lower Houses, to provide a more up-to-date picture of the extent of mainstreaming (Table 5.1). The four missing Lower Houses (Netherlands, France, Italy and Romania) are added based on the data from the Palgrave Handbook of National Parliaments (Hefftler et al. 2015). It should be noted that the classification is based on the reported practice of scrutiny rather than formal rules.

Table 5.1 shows that sectoral committees have become Europeanized in most EU member states. In 15 chambers, sectoral committees are routinely involved in EU affairs scrutiny, either because their involvement is mandatory, or because it has become an established

Table 5.1 Committees responsible for EU affairs scrutiny

EAC only	EAC + occasional consultation of sectoral committees	EAC + regular consultation of sectoral committees	Sectoral committees are responsible for their areas
Slovenia Upper	Austria*; Croatia; Czech Lower; France Upper; Hungary; Latvia; Malta; Poland Lower; Romania Lower**; Romania Upper; Slovenia Lower; Spain*	Bulgaria; Cyprus; Czech Upper; Denmark; Estonia; Finland; France Lower**; German Upper; Greece; Italy Lower**; Italy Upper; Lithuania; Poland Upper; Portugal; Slovakia	Belgium Lower; Belgium Upper; German Lower; Ireland*; Luxembourg; Dutch Lower**; Dutch Upper; Sweden

Source: Högenauer (2021).
Notes:
* Both chambers conduct the scrutiny jointly.
** Based on Thomas and Tacea (2015), Tacea (2015), Högenauer (2015), Cavatorto (2015).

Table 5.2 Staff support for sectoral committees

	Only EAC	Mainly EAC	Regularly sectoral	Fully mainstreamed
NO ACCESS TO EU EXPERTS		Austria* (occasionally support from EAC); Latvia; Malta	Poland Upper	Dutch Upper
EAC STAFF AND/OR RESEARCH/ LEGAL SUPPORT SECTORAL	Slovenia Upper	Poland Lower; Slovenia Lower	Bulgaria (some); Estonia; France Upper; German Upper; Italy Upper; Portugal; Slovakia	Belgium Senate; Ireland (normal sectoral staff receive training); Luxembourg
A JOINT CENTRAL EU UNIT		Croatia; Czech Lower; Hungary; Romanian Senate; Spain	Cyprus; Czech Upper; Denmark; Greece;	Belgium Lower; German Lower;
SECTORAL HAVE OWN EU EXPERTS			Bulgaria (some); Finland; Lithuania	Dutch Lower**; Sweden

Source: Högenauer (2021).

Notes:
* Both Houses scrutinize jointly.
** Information based on Högenauer et al. (2016).

practice. Eight chambers are already fully mainstreamed. Overall, we would expect the sectoral committees of the 23 parliaments in the last two categories to need expert staff support in EU affairs. This support could either come from EU experts that work specifically for the sectoral committees, or from a central unit that advises all committees. Table 5.2 provides an overview over the different forms of support in practice.

It is important to note that Table 5.2 provides a simplified representation of staff support. In practice, parliaments can have multiple sources of staff support. Thus, sectoral committees could have both own EU experts and benefit from the presence of a joint EU unit, a unit in charge of interparliamentary relations and/or a research or legal service. The research and legal staff are put in a low category of support (one step up from "no support"), because the type of assistance they provide is more limited. A legal unit would typically provide answers to precise points of law, rather than on the more political concept of subsidiarity or on the substantive evaluation of a policy. The main task of the research service is to provide information to individual members of parliament (MPs) upon request and to draw up reports on wider issues on the request of a committee. However, they focus on background information and would not normally deal with an ongoing legislative process, the position of the government and the evaluation of proposals coming from Europe. They would definitely not be involved in the drafting of the position of a committee. In addition, the capacity of those units to provide EU expertise varies strongly across parliaments, as their total staff can be very small (four researchers, the Lativan parliament) or quite extensive (96 researchers, the Polish Lower House). Therefore, if a committee has no own EU experts or a central unit advising all committees on EU affairs, its "normal" staff would de facto have to take on EU responsibilities as well.

Secondly, while the table ranks EU affairs support for sectoral committees broadly from lowest to highest, there are exceptions where this ranking does not work: For example, the central EU unit of the German Bundestag with its 74 EU experts can arguably provide sectoral committees with more extensive support than a parliamentary administration where each committee has one dedicated expert (e.g. Finland).

On the whole, Table 5.2 illustrates that sectoral committees usually do not have their own EU experts but rather receive support from a central unit. In addition, a majority of sectoral committees have to rely primarily on their normal staff with assistance from EAC staff and/or from a legal or research unit, and in six cases, they have to rely (almost) exclusively on their "normal" staff. Contrary to what one might expect, there is no clear link between the role of the sectoral committee and the type of support. There are two reasons for this: administrative capacity and the strength of the parliament. The Dutch Senate has only 61 civil servants in total and is a part-time chamber. As committee staff usually look after several committees simultaneously, there is obviously insufficient capacity to provide committees with dedicated EU staff. The Luxembourgish parliament is in a similar position with regard to its size and the size of its administration (Högenauer et al. 2016), and the Belgian Senate and Irish parliament have comparatively weak scrutiny powers (Auel et al. 2015).

Mainstreaming appears to happen in two different types of parliament that follow different logics: they are either strong and want to become stronger (e.g. Sweden, Finland, Denmark, the German Lower House, the Dutch Lower House) and they invest in EU staff with expertise in at least some key policy areas (whether in a central unit or as dedicated committee staff). Or the parliaments are small and/or weak, in which case mainstreaming appears to be a strategy to overcome low *political* capacity, that is the problem of a small EAC with few MPs is resolved by involving other committees. However, they then still have a problem of low administrative capacity.

However, in some cases where the number of dedicated EU experts is low, parliaments reported that they offer EU training to normal staff (Ireland) and make EU affairs part of their normal duties (Dutch Senate, Poland). In those cases, the result is the Europeanization of the tasks of sectoral committee staff regardless of the presence of EU experts.

Overall, the secretariats of the sectoral committees of 20 of the 33 chambers/parliaments play some sort of a role in EU affairs (cf. Table 5.3). Of course, this question is not relevant in cases where the sectoral committees do not participate in EU affairs scrutiny. Data is missing for the Polish Senate and Bulgaria.

Table 5.3 confirms the findings of Högenauer et al. (2016) that EAC staff or the main EU unit perform a wide range of support task. Their role goes far beyond mere procedural support or organizational support with the setting up of meetings. Instead, in many cases, the EU staff perform the roles of agenda-shaper by providing assistance with the preselection of relevant dossiers. This typically involves staff participating in the scrutiny of the Annual Work Programme of the European Commission with the aim of highlighting relevant or potentially problematic proposals that will come out later in the year. In addition, staff are often in charge of filtering incoming EU documents, which can amount to several thousand documents per year, giving MPs more time to focus on the detailed scrutiny of important issues.

In addition, they play an important advisory role, in that they are often involved in the drafting of committee decisions and provide substantive advice. These two roles are particularly important in the context of the EWS, for example, where reasoned opinions have to meet certain formal requirements and contain an assessment of the principal of subsidiarity. Thus, if a parliament wants to use the EWS to protest against an EU legislative proposal that

Table 5.3 The role of staff in EU affairs scrutiny

		(Pre)selection	Subsid. adv.	Procedural adv.	Drafts
A	EU	x	x	x	(x) assists political groups
B Lo	EU	x	x		(x) on request
	SC	x		x	
B Up	EU	x		x	
	SC	(x) mostly MPs		x	
BG	EU	x	x	x	x
HR	EU	x	x	x	x
	SC	x	x	x	
CY	EU	x	x	x	x
CZ Lo	EU	x	x	x	x
	SC	x			x
CZ Up	EU		x	x	x
DK	EU	x	x	x	x
	SC	x	x		x
EST	EU	x	x	x	x
	SC			x	x
FIN	EU		x	x	x
	SC.		x	x	x
F UP	EU	x	x	x	x
	SC			x	
D Lo	EU	x	x	x	
	SC	x with group staff		x	x with group staff
D Up	EU	x		x	
	SC			x	
GR	EU	x	x	x	x
H	EU	x	x	x	x
	SC		x		x
IRL	EU	x	x	x	x
	SC		x		x
I Up	EU	x	x	x	x
	SC	x		x	(x) only Pol. Dialogue
LV	EU		x	x	x
LT	EU	x	x	x	x
	SC	x	x	x	x
L	EU	x	x		x
	SC	x	x		x
M	EU		x	x	x
NL Lo	EU	x	x	x	x
	SC	x	x	x	x
NL Up	EU			x	x
	SC			x	x
PL Lo	EU	x	x	x	x
PL Up	EU		x	x	x
P	EU			x	(x) on request
	SC	x	x	x	
RO Up	EU	x	x	x	x
	SC	x	x	x	x

(Continued)

Table 5.3 The role of staff in EU affairs scrutiny *(Continued)*

		(Pre)selection	*Subsid. adv.*	*Procedural adv.*	*Drafts*
SK	EU	x	x	x	x
SL Lo	EU	x	x	x	x
SL Up	EU	x	x	x	x
E	EU	x	x	x	x
S	EU			x	x (not EWS)
	SC		x		x

Source: Högenauer (2021).

Notes:
EU refers to the EAC staff or the main EU staff unit; SC to the staff of sectoral committees.

it dislikes because of its substance, it needs to find a way to present the proposal as being in breach of the principle of subsidiarity.

By and large, in those cases where the roles of EU staff are limited, this is either due to the EAC itself having a limited role, or to the parliament having limited resources. Thus, the EAC of the Swedish parliament usually does not deal with the EWS (which is left to sectoral committees). Therefore, logically, its staff does not need to draft reasoned opinions or provide subsidiarity advice. By contrast, in the case of the Belgian and the Dutch Senate, the low administrative capacity means that MPs cannot delegate as many tasks.

Table 5.3 also shows that the work of sectoral committee staff has become Europeanized in a majority of EU national parliaments. There is more variation in the type of tasks performed, as both the administrative capacity and the role of sectoral committees in EU affairs vary considerably across the cases. In Sweden, the sectoral committees are responsible for the EWS. Therefore, sectoral committee staff is in charge of subsidiarity advice and the drafting of opinions. By contrast, in Italy, the Senate EAC is in charge of the EWS. Consequently the sectoral committee staff do not deal with those issues.

Lastly, one relatively under-researched source of variation is the presence and role of personal assistants and "political" staff. The absence of research on this issue is problematic, as this will obviously have a wider impact on the organization of the central administration of parliaments and the delegation of tasks. For example, in the Danish parliaments, several MPs share a secretary. In the German Bundestag, one MP can have several assistants. Presumably, this means that German MPs can use their assistants as a source of research and advice. In addition, the political groups in the German Bundestag benefit from considerable staff and often employ multiple EU experts. Therefore, group staff can and does assist with "political" tasks like the drafting of decisions. However, there is no systematic data on the staffing levels of party groups and on the assistants of MPs that would allow us to map the situation in a comparative way across member states. As a result, we are missing an important piece of the puzzle of administrative capacity and the organization of advice.

5.5 The Role of Staff in Interparliamentary Cooperation

One area where staff plays a particularly important role is interparliamentary cooperation. There are different levels of interparliamentary cooperation that also affect staff. Firstly, there are institutionalized forms of cooperation. One of the most important of those in EU affairs is the Conference of Parliamentary Committees for Union Affairs of Parliaments of the

European Union (COSAC). This is a forum where delegations of the EACs and the EP meet twice a year to discuss current issues. In addition, several new interparliamentary conferences (IPCs) have been created, for example the IPC on economic policy and the IPC on the EU's Common Foreign and Security Policy and Common Security and Defence Policy. In addition, the first interparliamentary committee meeting to evaluate Eurojust was organized in 2020. These conferences require preparation and staff support also at the national level.

Secondly, the EWS requires for national parliament to stay in regular contact. If they wish to obtain enough votes for a yellow or orange card, they need to mobilize other parliaments to join them in issuing reasoned opinions. In the past, mobilization has been a problem. Only three yellow cards have been issued, and not all national parliaments participate actively. This need for regular exchanges in combination with a desire to have better access to information in Brussels has led to the emergence of a network of the permanent representatives of national parliaments in the EP, also known as liaison officers (Mastenbroek et al. 2014). Having started in the early 1990s, the network grew exponentially in the 2000s to include (almost) all national parliaments in 2015 (Neuhold and Högenauer 2016). The liaison officers are parliamentary officials who stay in close touch with their home parliament, either through regular visits or via video-conferences.

The liaison officers provide one of the most if not the most effective means of interparliamentary exchange. They meet on a weekly basis in so-called Monday Morning Meetings (MMMs). These meetings can be used not only to invite Commissioners (or other key figures) to brief the parliaments on key issues of common interest, but they are also used to alerted other parliaments to the fact that one is planning to conduct a subsidiarity-check on a proposal. As most liaison officers (with the exception of the German delegation) have an office in the EP, they can also meet easily throughout the week.

The key role of this network has been discussed in depth by Neuhold and Högenauer (2016), where they show, for example, how the yellow card on the Monti II regulation was the product of intense interparliamentary networking. In the end, 12 national parliaments representing 19 votes raised subsidiarity concerns, which lead to the first "yellow card" procedure, but two of the reasoned opinions were only adopted on the last possible day. The Danish parliament proactively used its liaison officer to mobilize other parliaments. It used the network to circulate its own reasoned opinion as "blue-print" to the other parliaments to help them raise subsidiarity concerns.

However, the EAC staff in the national parliaments are also heavily involved in interparliamentary coordination. In the 2021 study, most parliaments reported that their EAC staff had bilateral contacts with other parliaments on a weekly or at least monthly basis. Exceptions to this are mainly parliaments from Eastern Europe, namely the Slovenian chambers, the Croatian parliament, the Bulgarian parliament, the Polish Senate and the Romanian Senate. In Western Europe, only the French Senate staff reported having only sporadic contact with other parliaments.

Sectoral committee staff, by contrast, report only 1–4 contacts per year. Even in fully mainstreamed parliaments, where sectoral committees play an important role in EU affairs scrutiny, cooperation appears to run mainly via the EAC or a central unit dedicated to interparliamentary relations.

5.6 The Europeanization of Research Services

One aspect of the administration that is under-researched is the existence of parliamentary research services and their role in European affairs. While such a unit would not be directly involved in the legislative or control work of parliaments, it can provide important support in the background: One of the fundamental challenges of parliamentary democracy is that the executive has far more resources at its disposal (e.g. well-staffed ministries) and that the executive is closer to the source of information. This leads to the problematic situation where parliaments have to vote laws and hold ministers accountable largely on the basis of information provided by the executive. A parliamentary research service can act as an independent source of information (von Winter 2006; Rohleder und Schöler 2013).

The survey from 2021 could only scratch the surface of this issue. However, it seems that not all parliaments have a research service. At least five lower houses or unicameral parliaments (like the Belgium Lower House, the Croatian parliament or the Maltese parliament), only have a library, a documentation service and/or a legal service. In those cases, the capacity for independent research is limited, as those services mainly focus on legal support and the archiving of information. Thus, research would have to be undertaken by the main committee advisors, who have also other tasks.

However, the majority of parliaments did report having a research service. The overwhelming majority of those are Europeanized and frequently answer questions related to Europe or provide background research, reports and comparative studies to MPs. In six cases, the level of Europeanization is relatively low, in that the service only occasionally assists in EU affairs, and the bulk of the work falls on the shoulders of the main EU affairs unit or committee staff. In addition, the size of the research services also varies from a handful of staff to 92 in the case of the Polish Sejm, which of course affects the range of issues that the service can help with.

The precise function of research services would merit further research. In particular, it would be interesting to have studies on the impact of research services on government-parliament and on government-opposition relations. In other words, to what extent do (large) research services lead to a more independent parliament? Do they have an impact on the nature and content of debates? It should be noted that – at the time of writing – some parliaments like the Luxembourgish parliament are building up research services in the hope of gaining greater independence and improving the quality of parliamentary scrutiny.

5.7 Conclusion

The 2021 survey of national parliaments in EU affairs confirms the findings of the OPAL project that the EAC staff of a large majority of parliaments plays an extensive role in EU affairs scrutiny. They staff if often involved in the preselection of relevant issues from the Annual Work Programme of the European Commission and in the filtering of relevant documents on a regular basis. In addition, it is common for EAC staff to assist with the drafting of committee decisions and to provide substantive advice.

In addition, the 2021 study revealed that the staff of sectoral committees has also become Europeanized to a considerable extent. In 20 out of 33 chambers, sectoral committee staff provided procedural or substantive advice, assisted with the selection of relevant issues and/or the drafting of decisions. This is the result of a development whereby an increasing number of parliaments delegate EU-related tasks to their sectoral committees in order to benefit from their expertise. At the same time, while this trend increased the political capacity of parliaments to scrutinize EU affairs, it creates a challenge for the administrative capacity of parliaments, as the additional political actors also need support. This results in considerable disparity where some sectoral committees have extensive resources at their disposal, and others have to rely mainly on a small number of non-specialized staff.

Secondly, parliamentary staff plays a key role in interparliamentary coordination, especially in the context of the EWS. The liaison officers, in particular, are the main source of regular contact with other parliaments. However, the growing need for coordination has also impacted EAC staff, which in many cases is also in contact with other parliaments on a weekly basis. Even sectoral committee staff is sporadically involved in interparliamentary coordination, although this appears to coincide to some extent with the number of IPCs or joint committee meetings per year.

Thirdly, the new opportunities for parliamentary scrutiny created by the Treaty of Lisbon, the political crises of the European Union of the past decade have also left their traces in the staff support of parliaments. While the number of EU experts in national parliaments grew modestly between 2006 and 2011–2013, it experienced a sharp rise by 2021. In addition, while a few chambers are responsible for a substantial part of the increase, in total 20 chambers (out of 32) now have at least 1 EU expert more than in the past.

Overall, the Europeanization of parliamentary staff confirms the picture of uneven staffing levels and responsibilities that has emerged from previous studies. While the overwhelming majority of national parliaments appear to experience a trend towards an increasing Europeanization of their staff, the discrepancies between parliaments are huge – both in terms of staffing levels and in terms of the organization of support. Some parliaments focus on committee staff, others on central units. Some have research and legal departments or have access to external expertise, others have none of that (or only rudimentary structures with very few staff). In addition, there are still gaps in the availability of core data: we know almost nothing about the "political" staff available to party groups, or the assistants available to MPs. This makes it even more difficult to fully comprehend the resources available to every individual parliament. After all, tasks do not necessarily have to be delegated to one specific staff category: who drafts, who researches, who advises – that all depends on what kind of staff exists and which unit is best staffed.

Acknowledgements

The author thanks the members of the ECPRD network, who have supported this study by providing data on their parliaments.

References

Auel K., Rozenberg O. and Tacea A. (2015) Fighting Back? And, If So, How? Measuring Parliamentary Strength and Activity in EU Affairs. in C. Hefftler, C. Neuhold, O. Rozenberg and J. Smith (eds.) The Palgrave Handbook of National Parliaments and the European Union, London: Palgrave Macmillan, 60–93.

Buskjaer Rasmussen M. and Kluger Dionigi M. (2018) 'National Parliaments' Use of the Political Dialogue: Institutional Lobbyists, Traditionalists or Communicators?', Journal of Common Market Studies 56(5), 1108–1126.

Buzogany A. and Häsing J. (2017) 'Spokes in the Wheel. European Affairs and the Parliamentary Administration of German Landtage', Journal of Legislative Studies, 23(2), 200–220.

Cavatorto S. (2015) Italy: Still Looking for a New Era in the Making of EU Policy. in C. Hefftler, C. Neuhold, O. Rozenberg and J. Smith (eds.) The Palgrave Handbook of National Parliaments and the European Union, London: Palgrave Macmillan, 209–231.

Christiansen T., Högenauer A.L. and Neuhold C. (2014) 'National Parliaments in the post-Lisbon European Union: Bureaucratization rather than Democratization?' Comparative European Politics 12, 121–140.

Gattermann K., Högenauer A.L. and Huff A. (2016) 'Research Note: Studying a New Phase of Europeanisation of National Parliaments', European Political Science 15, 89–107.

Hefftler C., Neuhold C., Rozenberg O. and Smith J. (2015) The Palgrave Handbook of National Parliaments in the European Union, Basingstoke: Palgrave Macmillan.

Högenauer A.L. (2021) 'The Mainstreaming of EU Affairs: A Challenge for Parliamentary Administrations', The Journal of Legislative Studies 27(4), 535–553.

Högenauer A.L. and Neuhold C. (2015) 'National Parliaments After Lisbon: Administrations on the Rise?', West European Politics 38(2), 335–354.

Högenauer A.L., Neuhold C. and Christiansen T. (2016) Parliamentary Administrations in the European Union, Basingstoke: Palgrave Macmillan.

Högenauer, A.L. (2015) The Dutch Parliament and EU Affairs: Decentralizing Scrutiny. in C. Hefftler, C. Neuhold, O. Rozenberg and J. Smith (eds.) The Palgrave Handbook of National Parliaments and the European Union, London: Palgrave Macmillan, pp. 252–271.

Högenauer, A.L. and Christiansen, T. (2015) Parliamentary Administrations in the Scrutiny of EU Decision-Making. in C. Hefftler, C. Neuhold, O. Rozenberg and J. Smith (eds.) The Palgrave Handbook of National Parliaments and the European Union, London: Palgrave Macmillan, pp. 116–132.

Karlas J. (2012) 'National Parliamentary Control of EU Affairs: Institutional Design after Enlargement', West European Politics 35(5), 1095–1113.

Malang T., Brandenberger L. and Leifeld P. (2017) 'Networks and Social Influence in European Legislative Politics', British Journal of Political Science 49(4), 1475–1498.

Mastenbroek, E., Zwaan, P., Groen, A., Meurs, W., Reiding, H., Dörrenbächer, N. and Neuhold, C. (2014) Engaging with Europe. Evaluating national parliamentary control of EU decision making after the Lisbon Treaty, Report prepared for the Dutch Tweede Kamer.

Maurer, A. and Wessels, W. (eds.) (2001) National Parliaments on their Ways to Europe: Losers or Latecomers?, Baden-Baden: Nomos.

Neuhold, C. and Högenauer, A.L. (2016) 'An Information Network of Officials? Dissecting the Role and Nature of the Network of Parliamentary Representatives in the EP', Journal of Legislative Studies 22(2), 237–256.

Norton, P. (ed.) (1996) National Parliaments and the European Union, London: Frank Cass.

O'Brennan, J. and Raunio, T. (eds.) (2007) National Parliaments within the Enlarged European Union, London: Routledge.

Raunio, T. and Wiberg, M. (2009) 'How to Measure the Europeanisation of a National Legislature?' Scandinavian Political Studies 33(1): 74–92.

Rohleder K. and Schöler U. (2013) Die Europäisierung und andere aktuelle Herausforderungen für die Wissenschaftlichen Dienste des Deutschen Bundestages. in Eberbach-Born, B., Kropp, S., Stuchlik, A. and Zeh, W. (eds.). Parlamentarische Kontrolle und Europäische Union. Baden-Baden: Nomos, 151–180.

Strelkov A. (2015) 'Who Controls National EU Scrutiny? Parliamentary Party Groups, Committees and Administrations', West European Politics 38(2), 355–374.

Tacea A. (2015) The Slow Adaptation of a New Member State: The Romanian Parliament and European Integration. in C. Hefftler, C. Neuhold, O. Rozenberg and J. Smith (eds.) The Palgrave Handbook of National Parliaments and the European Union, London: Palgrave Macmillan, 613–631.

Thomas A. and Tacea A. (2015) The French Parliament and the European Union: 'Shadow Control' through the Government Majority. in C. Hefftler, C. Neuhold, O. Rozenberg and J. Smith (eds.) The Palgrave Handbook of National Parliaments and the European Union, London: Palgrave Macmillan, 170–190.

von Winter, T. (2006) Die Wissenschaftlichen Dienste des Deutschen Bundestages. in Falk, S., Rehfeld, D., Römmele, A. and Thunert, M. (eds.). Hanbuch Politikberatung. Wiesbaden: VS Verlag, 198–214.

Winzen T. (2014) 'Bureaucracy and Democracy: Intra-Parliamentary Delegation in European Union Affairs', Journal of European Integration 36(7), 677–695.

Winzen, T. (2012) 'National Parliamentary Control of European Union Affairs: A Cross-National and Longitudinal Comparison', West European Politics 35(3), 657–672.

6
PARLIAMENTARY DIPLOMACY

Jonathan Murphy

6.1 Introduction

This chapter explores the role of parliamentary administrations in parliamentary diplomacy. As is the case throughout this Handbook on the multiple roles of parliamentary administration, it is often difficult to clearly distinguish between the roles of elected parliamentarians and the parliamentary administrations. Further, parliamentary administrators have strong incentives to stay out of the limelight and to allow their political bosses to claim credit (and sometimes, accept responsibility) for the outcomes of their work. As elected officials, parliamentarians have both a public mandate and a constitutional responsibility to carry out Parliaments' roles of legislation, oversight of the executive, and voting the budget. Parliamentary administrators' role is to enable these institutional tasks to be carried out as smoothly as possible, a little like the behind-the-scenes work of theatre technicians. Only in the most egregious examples of set, malfunction is the audience aware of the silent labour going on behind the curtains. However, as the other chapters in this Handbook demonstrate, Parliament cannot function without the work of its administration, much as a theatre show could not go on, or a government department deliver public services without its professional experts and management.

This chapter will attempt to shine some light on how parliamentary administrations enable parliamentary diplomacy. It argues that parliamentary diplomacy is an important feature of parliamentary work, and that its role is essential in anchoring Parliament as the cornerstone institution of representative democracy. In turn, the parliamentary administration is a key actor in parliamentary diplomacy, both in supporting the parliamentary diplomacy led by MPs including through developing and maintaining the organizational infrastructure for such diplomacy, and also directly through networks of parliamentary officials. The administration, therefore, should not be viewed as merely assisting elected officials but also enabling the *institutionalization* of parliamentary norms internationally.

The chapter begins by exploring the definitional challenge posed by parliamentary diplomacy, suggesting that while there may be no immediately obvious alternative to the term, a too ready association of parliamentary diplomacy with state diplomacy can both mislead and circumscribe understanding of Parliaments' unique, institutional, contribution to democracy internationally. The chapter goes on to explore the extant literature on parliamentary administrative diplomacy, and then discusses several themes in international parliamentary diplomacy. The special case of the parliamentary diplomacy in the construction of the European Union is explored, including the relationships between national Parliaments and the European Parliament (EP). The emergence of a European polity has correctly led to considerable scholarly enquiry but may have eclipsed other manifestations of parliamentary diplomacy, some that predated the European project but that remain relevant. One development in international parliamentary life is the increasing technical sophistication of Parliaments, underpinned by a professional administration. As Parliaments seek to ensure that they can provide an effective balance of powers with the executive, they have gradually enhanced their administrative capacities. These new functions, discussed in this chapter in relation to Parliamentary Budget Offices (PBOs), have in turn generated international networking, as well as inter-institutional support for Parliaments seeking to establish and enhance their own PBOs. The greater the technical expertise required of Parliaments, the more crucial the role of its administration, and the more important the role of international benchmarking. The chapter explores the development of international parliamentary collaboration.

The Inter-Parliamentary Union (IPU) and its administrative affiliate, the Association of Secretaries General of Parliament (ASGP) play an important role in parliamentary diplomacy, and specifically in administrative diplomacy. Increasingly, IPU supports technical enhancement of Parliaments, again largely through administrative networking, and the chapter looks particularly at IPU's leadership in strengthening Parliaments' digital capacities, which extend well beyond technical norms and into the principles of Parliaments as institutions for open governance and citizen voice. The IPU and other international parliamentary associations have in recent years promoted explicit benchmarks of parliamentary performance, underpinned by administrations' documentation of parliamentary work, which establish standards for democratic Parliaments that can support international institutionalization of democratic governance practices.

The field of international parliamentary strengthening has expanded considerably in recent years in parallel with international efforts to embed and enhance democracy beginning in the 'Third Wave' of democratizations that commenced in the 1970s and extended through to the 1990s, and more recently, the Arab Spring of the 2010s. While in its earlier manifestations in the 1980s and 1990s, parliamentary development was often led by specialist democracy-promotion organizations, Parliaments – and particularly parliamentary administrations – have played a growing role in the development and delivery of capacity-building support to Parliaments in emerging democracies.

Finally, the chapter presents a short case study on the EP's diplomacy in Ukraine, one of the most ambitious bilateral parliamentary initiatives. The case study demonstrates how high-profile parliamentary political diplomacy was strategically underpinned by the EP administration, leading to a long-term partnership for institutional reform of the Ukrainian Parliament; an initiative that in retrospect assumes greater significance in light of the Russian Federation's 2022 full-scale invasion of Ukraine and attempts to suppress Ukrainian democracy.

There are inevitably limitations to the chapter. Its short length evidently precludes a comprehensive examination of administrative parliamentary diplomacy globally, and the author has chosen instead to survey specific aspects of administrative parliamentary diplomacy, particularly those that appear under-researched.

6.2 Defining Parliamentary Diplomacy

Parliamentary diplomacy is an unusually slippery concept to write about. While definitional debates take up a good chunk of many scholarly discussions in any domain, there is very little common ground among the various authors who have tackled the subject of parliamentary diplomacy. Understandings of parliamentary diplomacy range from international diplomacy adopting aspects of parliamentary traditions (such as, the General Assembly of the United Nations) to the efforts of parliamentarians on the international stage, to co-operation between Parliaments as institutions. Given such wide discrepancy of understandings, the literature about parliamentary diplomacy is quite diffuse in theme and focus. Some aspects of parliamentary diplomacy that are given a central role in certain accounts – for example, the development and role of the IPU and other inter-parliamentary bodies – are virtually non-existent in other studies that might focus instead on the role of individual parliamentarians in the context of, and sometimes in opposition to, inter-state diplomacy.

Another issue is that, while some Parliaments use the term parliamentary diplomacy, others prefer different descriptors, such as inter-parliamentary co-operation. Thus, a search for the term 'parliamentary diplomacy' will turn up many hits in the archives of one Parliament (e.g. that of Italy), and few or none in that of another Parliament (such as Ireland). This is not just a question of document classification, as the different nomenclatures tend to represent distinct visions of the phenomenon of 'parliamentary diplomacy'.

However, this chapter is not about parliamentary diplomacy more broadly but is rather a constituent chapter of a Handbook of Parliamentary Administration. The Handbook is an important endeavour in bringing together both geographic and thematic scholarship on parliamentary administrations, and also in beginning to redress an imbalance of representation in which Parliaments as institutions are often viewed as merely an empty stage in which the political drama is acted out, much as if we viewed the *Teatro alla Scala* in Milan as just a place that can be hired to put on a show.

The chapter will concentrate on aspects of parliamentary diplomacy where the administration plays a role clearly distinguishable (if not necessarily independent) from that of parliamentarians. This is not to suggest that the role of parliamentarians is somehow less important than that of administrators. Dialogue and interaction between parliamentarians are evidently an important aspect of parliamentary diplomacy (Beetham, 2006: 172). As we would expect, parliamentary administrators support and enable such conversations in various ways depending on these interactions' myriad manifestations, from organizational and logistical support to conceptual and strategic advice. It is quite difficult to generalize about this administrative support, and parliamentarian-parliamentarian diplomacy already has a considerable literature in which the role of administrators is recorded, though largely in passing (see particularly Stavridis and Jancic, 2017; Senate of the Netherlands, 2010; Weisglas and de Boer, 2007). The chapter will explore one case study involving the EP and the Verkhovna Rada, the Ukrainian Parliament, in which parliamentary diplomacy included important 'political' and 'administrative' aspects that help to illustrate ways in which these can intersect to follow political declarations with persistent follow-through in institutional reforms.

In this context, therefore, the author is on the one hand constrained by the necessity of grounding the research and discussion from the viewpoint of the *administration* of Parliament and on the other hand somewhat relieved of the need to adjudicate between the largely incompatible definitions outlined at the outset of the chapter.

The boundaries of a parliamentary administration are not necessarily hermetically sealed – for example – are the assistants of members of Parliament recruited by those MPs but paid by Parliament 'members of the administration'? Or the staff of parliamentary party caucuses, again selected by the individual parliamentary group, but paid from the central budget of the Parliament? Nevertheless, notwithstanding these examples of hybrid or anomalous status within an administration, the *essence* of a parliamentary administration is that it derives its existence from the presence of an *institution*, of Parliament as something that exists beyond the individual actions of its elected members. Just as we would never think of public administration as reducible to the thoughts and deeds of Ministers, neither can Parliaments be reduced to the actions of MPs; including in the sphere of parliamentary diplomacy.

6.3 Parliaments as Institutions

Once we start thinking about Parliaments as having a distinct institutional identity, we then need to think about their interactions not merely as constituent components of national states, but as bodies that play a particular role in governance, and particularly in *democratic* governance, with a supra-national salience. While it is uncommon for parliamentary diplomacy to seek to overtly contradict the objectives of the national executive – these rare examples often derive from a situation of contested power such as in Venezuela following the opposition's victory in 2015 parliamentary elections (Briceño-Ruiz, 2019) – parliamentary diplomacy can, and perhaps increasingly does, privilege the broader goals of deeper democratization and specifically of stronger Parliaments within representative democracy, goals that can be pursued largely or entirely independent of national government diplomatic priorities.

Parliamentary diplomacy from an institutional perspective can thus be seen as having at least two distinct though connected objectives; the first to pursue the political and strategic interests of Parliament and its members as representatives of a national polity, and a second in supporting the strengthening of Parliaments as institutions internationally, and of parliamentarism as an anchor of democratic governance, and specifically of representative democracy. Thus, where traditional diplomacy is fundamentally associated with the national state, an important aspect of parliamentary diplomacy is the propagation of the principle of representative democracy and the centrality of Parliaments within representative democracy (Senate of the Netherlands, 2010).

This chapter explores these dual objectives of parliamentary diplomacy, with a particular focus on the second, broader objective of promoting (democratic) parliamentarism, that has largely gone unnoticed in the existing literature. In this context, we will explore evidence for an expanding role of Parliament in theory and practice of democracy-promotion, which has typically been viewed within the context of state policy (Barany and Moser, 2009). A particular attention is paid to transnational parliamentary performance benchmarking exercises, largely carried out by parliamentary administrators, which implicitly or explicitly establish standards for democratic Parliaments.

The nature of Parliaments as forums for the exercise of representative democracy implies, or even requires, that parliamentary administrations operate largely 'behind the scenes'. This is also true for public officials more generally. Drawing from the Weberian conception of the impartial bureaucracy, state bureaucrats in western democracies were expected to provide advice behind closed doors, and to execute political decisions assuming the legitimacy of the elected leaders who made those decisions (Aberbach et al., 1981). However, particularly since the 1980s, public officials in many countries have assumed a higher profile. This has included being held publicly accountable when administrative mistakes are made where, previously, ministerial responsibility had been viewed as a governance principle; and, in being identified personally, in the propagation of government policies. With few exceptions, this added publicity and potential partisanship has not occurred within parliamentary administrations. Several reasons can be ascribed. First and most important, the fundamental purpose of Parliaments is to provide a forum for debate and decision-making by the people's *elected* representatives. Second, Parliaments are not executive bodies and thus normally do not develop or implement programmes whose public explanation may require technical expertise. Third, even where detailed technical support is provided to parliamentarians to enable them to carry out their functions of legislation and executive oversight, it is for the parliamentarians to decide if and how they make use of that expert counsel.

However, while parliamentary administrators generally remain behind the scenes, there are exceptions, and these may be expanding in an era where transparency in governance is widely, though not uncontroversially, viewed as an unalloyed virtue. The content and source of advice received by Parliament is increasingly viewed as pertinent in explaining and justifying decision-making (Yong et al., 2019). Within parliamentary diplomacy, a dual role of administrators can also be distinguished. On the one hand, administrators are responsible for supporting parliamentarians in their parliamentary diplomacy. This is seen, for example, in much of the work of national Parliament representatives to the EP, supporting their parliamentarians in making bilateral visits to the EP. Similarly, national parliamentary administrators regularly provide briefing as well as logistical support for parliamentarians attending international parliamentary institutions, or visiting other Parliaments. However, as Parliaments become technically more sophisticated, and the sphere of inter-parliamentary co-operation increases, including through expansion of international norms for parliamentary functioning, the opportunity and need for parliamentary officials to share their expertise and knowledge has increased. As we will discuss below, many Parliaments now have specialized expertise, for example in budgetary oversight, or in legislative drafting, that would previously have been concentrated exclusively in government.

There is only a very small extant literature on parliamentary administrations and parliamentary diplomacy. When Pegan and Högenauer (2016) published a chapter on the topic in a collection of inter-parliamentary co-operations, they stated that theirs was the first scholarly publication addressing the topic apart from two articles touching on the theme that Högenauer herself had recently co-authored. Fitsilis (2018) later published a paper on 'administrative parliamentary networks'. Hamilton (2016), then Secretary-General of the Netherlands Senate, and subsequently acting President of the Association of Secretaries-General of Parliaments (ASGP) outlined a useful overview on parliamentary diplomacy that, while covering the theme as a whole, places particular emphasis on its institutional objectives. Similarly, the Senate of Italy (2018) produced an invaluable compendium of parliamentary diplomacy that focuses particularly on institutions of parliamentary diplomacy.

The chapter focuses primarily on administrative contributions to parliamentary diplomacy that can be clearly distinguished from the support role provided by many parliamentary administrations to parliamentarians' diplomatic efforts. This is not to underestimate or devalue this important support work. In the case of larger Parliaments, where parliamentarians' diplomacy is often very extensive, and the administration's work involved in making it possible can be enormous. To cite one example, in its biannual reporting for 2017–2019 the German Bundestag (2019: 45–46) reports that 1133 parliamentary missions were carried out, including 99 committee delegations, 29 parliamentary group delegations, 34 missions of members of the Bundestag's praesidium, and 169 missions to conferences and meetings of international parliamentary assemblies, as well as election observation missions. Each of these missions involved various preparations, including research briefings, advance contacts, frequently the travel of staff advisors to support the mission, along with the logistical and administrative arrangements; this level of international engagement would not have been possible without such administration support.

6.4 Administrative Parliamentary Diplomacy in Europe

The European Union is a unique and emergent transnational governance institution. As Griglio and Lupo (2018) note, its 'composite poly-centric' nature, comprised national and pan-European democratic polities, inevitably creates specific forms of inter-parliamentary co-operation. As a governance system still in the process of construction, the exact relationship between national Parliaments and the EP, and indeed national Parliaments and the European Union as a whole, remains fluid and subject to continuing contestation. As European integration has developed, particularly following the adoption of the Treaty of Lisbon that aimed to formalize the jurisdictional relationships between national and European spheres, the scope of administration-level inter-parliamentary information-sharing and co-ordination has increased.

Pegan and Högenauer's (2016) chapter is part of an edited collection on inter-parliamentary co-operation in the emerging European constitution, focused particularly on the deepened role of both the European and national Parliaments as a result of the Treaty of Lisbon. They focus on three key institutions of European-level administrative co-operation: (1) Liaison officers of national Parliaments in Brussels, (2) Administrative staff of Conference of European Affairs Committees of the national Parliaments of the EU (COSAC), and (3) the European Parliament's Directorate for Relations with National Parliaments, along with the resources allocated by the EP to support the various aspects of these relations, including the information and documentation networks, European Centre for Parliamentary Research and Documentation (ECPRD), sponsored by the EU national Parliaments, the EP, and parliamentary institutions of the Council of Europe, and IPEX, the platform for EU Inter-parliamentary Exchange.

The network of liaison officers of European Union national Parliaments in Brussels has developed into a durable organization of administrative-level parliamentary diplomacy, focused particularly on liaison between the EP and national Parliaments. Almost all EU national Parliaments appoint at least one representative to a liaison office to the EP; most of whom are hosted within the EP. The tasks of the national liaison officers vary according to the mandate provided by their National Parliament but typically include gathering information on EP and European Union policy developments in areas of particular interest to their host Parliament. Most national Parliament liaison officers regularly facilitate bilateral meetings when their national parliamentarians visit the EP. The network of liaison officers meets weekly including also EP officials and staff from COSAC. This provides an opportunity both for information-sharing of EP developments and also informal networking between the different national Parliament liaison officers.

As well as examining the networks outlined by Pegan and Högenauer, Fitsilis (2018) underlines the parliamentary diplomacy involved in the engagement of parliamentary administrations in twinning programmes, as well as the networking of PBOs. The role of administrations in twinning programmes will be discussed below. PBOs are an important and growing phenomenon representing a further embedding of within the parliamentary administration of content expertise independent from the executive. While the emergence of PBOs has been addressed in scholarly literature (Chohan and Jacobs, 2017), the implications of PBOs and other specialized parliamentary offices on the nature of the parliamentary administration – including the parliamentary diplomacy of PBO networking – warrant a separate article or chapter.

Both Fitsilis and Koutsogiannis (2017) and Pegan and Högenauer (2016) explore the development of administrative parliamentary diplomacy through networks in the field of research and digital communication, through the ECPRD and IPEX networks. National Parliaments appoint correspondents to ECPRD, which operates as a clearing house for sharing information on different aspects of parliamentary functioning, both through responding to requests submitted by member Parliaments (in 2018, 333 requests generated 7174 responses[1]), which are maintained as an informational database, and through organization of regular conferences. ECPRD requests and responses, and the overall database, are restricted to ECPRD members – Parliaments in countries of the EU and of the Council of Europe, and a small number of non-EPs with affiliate status. ECPRD is funded jointly by the EP and the Parliamentary Assembly of the Council of Europe and also organizes regular conferences of correspondents.

IPEX, an exclusively European Union organization (with a small number of associate Parliament members from Europe but outside the EU), functions under the authority of the Speakers' Conference of EU national Parliaments and is directed by the Secretaries General of the EU's national Parliaments and co-funded by the EP and national Parliaments. The Treaty of Lisbon provides for national Parliaments to carry out subsidiarity oversight of European legislation, introducing an 'Early Warning System' (EWS) allowing national Parliaments to flag proposed European regulations that national Parliaments violate the subsidiarity principle (Malang et al., 2019). If one third of EU national Parliaments raise a concern, a 'yellow flag' is triggered, and the European Commission is required to review the proposed legislation. All European Commission draft legislative proposals are uploaded to IPEX, and in turn IPEX national Parliament correspondents may upload documentation on their review process for each legislative proposal. This process of institutionalized inter-parliamentary diplomacy has variable take-up, with some national Parliaments much more active than others. While overall the EWS had only generated three 'yellow flags' by 2020, van Gruisen and Huysmans (2020) demonstrate that even where the yellow flag trigger is not reached, the Commission is likely to make changes in response to reasoned concerns of national Parliaments. It is important to note that while IPEX is operated by parliamentary administrators and represents an institutionalized inter-parliamentary governance framework, the actual decision-making on triggering subsidiarity concerns is reserved to elected parliamentarians in each country.

Many Parliaments operate research and library services, and the International Federation of Library Associations and Institutions (IFLA) includes a Section on Library and Research Services for Parliaments,[2] bringing together parliamentary librarians and researchers in establishing and sharing good practices. Fitsilis argues that, beyond the specific information-sharing platforms and processes of ICPRD and IPEX, parliamentary administrations' research activities represent a promising area for parliamentary diplomacy. He outlines some practical institutional barriers to effective development of parliamentary researchers' communities of practice; including the absence of a publishing stream as exists for academic scholars; indeed, parliamentary researchers work may even have restricted access outside Parliament. It should be noted, however, that expert academics are frequently engaged by Parliaments to conduct specific research projects and that these interactions provide opportunities for enhancement of knowledge and capacity on both sides, and the development of communities of practice. Various formal and informal associations exist that include both parliamentary administrators and scholars; some involving several hundred members from across the world[3]; these play an important role in parliamentary diplomacy and the diffusion of innovations across Parliaments.

The emergence of a European-level parliamentary ecosystem, which has gradually become somewhat formalized, especially following the Treaty of Lisbon, has provided a considerable boost to inter-parliamentary co-operation and parliamentary diplomacy. However, it is important in the context of an overall account of parliamentary diplomacy to underline that this is by definition geographically circumscribed and represent largely an *addition* to the overall global picture of parliamentary diplomacy. This intra-EU parliamentary diplomacy, including at the administration level, has mainly if not exclusively focused on the relationships between national and EPs. Although opportunities have been created for international interactions – for example through the network of national Parliament representatives at the EP, these interactions still concentrate on the parliamentary dimensions of European Union governance.

6.5 The Inter-Parliamentary Union

Inter-parliamentary diplomacy exists beyond Europe, and globally. The Geneva-headquartered IPU, founded in 1889 and the oldest global multilateral institution, represents 179 of the world's national Parliaments (although with the notable exception of the United States) (Jönsson & Johnsson, 2018). The IPU was inspired from its outset by the underlying principle of Parliaments as a peaceful, dialogic approach to decision-making: 'from the First World War onwards, the Union associated democracy with parliamentarianism, and began to understand itself as a defender of both. It is difficult to determine exactly when democracy and parliamentarianism began to be seen as nearly coterminous' (Albers, 2012: 206–207). IPU has evolved substantially in its organization and thematic agendas since its foundation, from a focus on international arbitration in the early years, to an emphasis on international peacebuilding in the inter-war years, and in more recent times a multi-faceted interest in different thematic aspects of human development, as well as growing attention to the strengthening of Parliaments. While the formal leadership of the IPU is comprised Parliamentary Speakers and other elected parliamentarians, in practice, and to an increasing extent, parliamentary administrators play an important role in IPU initiatives to strengthen Parliaments.

Parliamentary administrations are formally engaged with IPU through the ASGPs, established in 1939, and 'constituted as a consultative body of the Inter-Parliamentary Union'.[4] The ASGP is an under-researched institution, in common with parliamentary administrations as a whole. Nevertheless, its importance as a clearing house for knowledge about Parliaments in general and parliamentary administration in particular can be gauged by the extensive use of the AGSP network as a source of information by parliamentary researchers. ASGP membership is restricted to Secretaries General and their deputies. Whereas IPU sessions tend to be dominated by formal political declarations, ASGP meetings focus mainly on issues of parliamentary management and practice. The Exceptional ASGP meeting of May 26 and 27, 2021, for example, focussed primarily on the ways in which Parliaments had adapted to the challenges of functioning during the Covid-19 pandemic,[5] with 31 presentations from SGs and deputy SGs from 29 different Parliaments. Beyond the formal meeting agendas, the ASGP meetings, held in conjunction with the IPU congresses, provide substantial opportunities for senior officials' inter-parliamentary diplomacy and networking. ASGP is thus a key vector for cross-institutional transfer of knowledge and innovation on parliamentary organization and functioning.

IPU has gradually expanded its engagement in normative principles of democratic governance.[6] It has established forums to promote broad participation and engagement with Women and Youth, as well as four standing committees on Peace and International Security; Sustainable Development, Finance and Trade; Democracy and Human Rights; and United Nations Affairs.

The IPU, and specifically its small secretariat, are increasingly engaged in parliamentary development activities corresponding to the organization's commitments to enhanced parliamentary action to support democracy, peace, human rights, and sustainable development. While these activities are politically led by parliamentarians, in practice IPU staff engage with parliamentary staff and experts in the development and use of resources to support these activities, ranging from collection and dissemination of data on parliamentary representation of women[7] and youth,[8] to development of toolkits to advance parliamentary work in specific priority areas such as the United Nations sustainable development goals,[9] to organization and delivery of parliamentary strengthening programming at the request of specific Parliaments (e.g. in Afghanistan, Côte d'Ivoire, and Djibouti[10]).

IPU maintains sophisticated databases of Parliamentary composition and functioning, such as Parline,[11] helping Parliaments to benchmark their functioning; these necessarily depend on parliamentary administrations to maintain and share the core data underpinning these databases. Increasingly, IPU supports informal norm-setting of parliamentary powers and performance; in 2019, it launched an ambitious project to develop a broad range of indicators of *de jure* and *de facto* parliamentary powers and performance. Once again, the exercise depends on the engagement of parliamentary administrations that maintain such data and have a day-to-day familiarity with data availability and collection methodologies. Some Parliamentary administrations, including from developing countries, have sophisticated data collection and monitoring and evaluation capacities (Watera, 2018).

The IPU indicator development follows on similar initiatives by parliamentary bodies, including the Commonwealth Parliamentary Association (CPA, 2018), the Association Parlementaire de la Francophonie, and SADC-PF (O'Brien et al., 2016). The first of these initiatives was that of the CPA, whose 2006 benchmarks were developed collaboratively with several other democracy-promotion organizations, building on work originally done by the US-headquartered National Democratic Institute. The benchmarks were updated and expanded in 2018. The CPA's benchmarking initiatives have typically involved a combination of elected officials, parliamentary staff, and parliamentary development experts, as was the case in 2018 where the new benchmarks were drafted at an intensive workshop in the United Kingdom.[12] Norm-setting, both statutory and voluntary, is a key aspect of contemporary governance (Brunsson & Jacobsson, 2010) and the centrality of parliamentary administrations to the expanding number of such initiatives is an important but little-researched development in legislative functioning, reflecting a growing institutionalization of transnational legislative norms and practices.

Fostering parliamentary digitalization is a particular focus area for IPU leadership in inter-parliamentary administrative co-operation and institutional strengthening. Activities are organized around the concept of the 'e-Parliament', defined as 'A legislature' that is empowered to be more open, transparent and accountable through ICT (IPU, 2018: 18). A dedicated unit of the IPU, the Centre for Innovation in Parliaments (CIP), acts to co-ordinate the exchange of knowledge, innovations, and best practices in (primarily digital) innovation. Each two years, the IPU produces a World e-Parliament Report. IPU also organizes the biannual World e-Parliament Conference, dedicated to sharing 'thought leadership discussions on digital Parliaments, good practices on parliamentary innovation, and collaborative creation of practical "how to" guides', geared for an audience of 'parliamentary staff working on digital technology, social media, parliamentary web sites, communications, library and research services, public engagement and other related fields'.[13] The CIP sponsors regional and thematic innovation hubs that are hosted by different Parliaments; there are five regional hubs around the world, as well as three thematic hubs on ICT Governance,

Open Data, and Transparency. The IPU's activities in parliamentary technological innovation have a very high level of engagement; 114 Parliaments around the world provided data for the 2018 e-Parliament Report with good responses from all regions, and the IPU's coordination in this field acts as a strong motivator for institutional development.

Beyond the IPU, there is a plethora of international parliamentary institutions (IPIs) ranging from regional parliamentary assemblies covering every part of the world (e.g., see De Vrieze, 2016) to global and often regional thematic bodies and assemblies from the Parliamentary Network to Fight AIDS, Tuberculosis, and Malaria to The International Conference of Parliamentarians on Population and Development (ICPPD). Rocabert et al. (2019) report a rise in the number of international parliamentary institutions from less than 5 in the 1940s to 40 in the 2010s. The Senate of Italy, using a broader definition (2018) enumerated 73 different international parliamentary bodies, in which the Italian Parliament participates in 12. Many of these bodies are affiliated with and receive support from particular international institutions, such as the relationship between ICPPD and the United Nations Population Fund (UNFPA).[14] Again, however, parliamentary administrators in national Parliaments provide support to organization of both national chapters and international events; often, staff from national Parliaments are seconded to international parliamentary bodies.[15]

6.6 Parliamentary Administrations and International Parliamentary Development

A final area of significant growth in administrative parliamentary diplomacy in recent years, which again has received little scholarly attention, is through Parliaments' engagement in explicit support to parliamentary development. The field of parliamentary development has been a constant, and generally growing, aspect of democratic development for the past quarter century, particularly associated with western democracies' desire to support the consolidation of third wave democracies that emerged from the 1970s through to the 1990s (De Vrieze & Meyer-Resende, 2015). Parliamentary development support has been primarily financed by national governments' foreign aid budgets[16] and delivered by a range of different organizations including United Nations agencies, as well as specialized democracy-promoting organizations such as those affiliated with the National Endowment for Democracy in the United States, the party foundations (Stiftungs) affiliated with political parties in Germany and some other European countries, and the Westminster Foundation for Democracy based in Britain. Increasingly, as the private sector has become widely involved in development assistance delivery, American and other private companies have also delivered parliamentary support programmes under contract to various government aid agencies. International institutions such as the World Bank, the International Monetary Fund, and OECD have also engaged in parliamentary development, though typically focused on specific aspects of Parliaments' functioning – in the case of the Bank and IMF, financial oversight – and usually without a particular mandate or interest in Parliaments' overall role as an anchor of representative democracy.[17]

The impetus for development of a parliamentary development community of practice (CoP) came originally from USAID and UNDP that independently established nuclei of parliamentary expertise in their headquarters during the 1990s. In addition, the National Endowment for Democracy, established by the US Congress in 1983, in turn created and funded two daughter organizations, the National Democratic Institute (NDI) and the International Republican Institute (IRI), that aimed to harness the democratic enthusiasm and technical capacities of their respective political parties in the service of international democratic development. While these two organizations' mandates extend to numerous aspects of democracy including political party and civil society strengthening, their arrival on the scene provided another impetus to the new field of parliamentary development. Also with its origins in Third Wave democratisation, the US House Democracy Partnership is another US-led initiative engaging both members of the House of Representatives and House and Congressional staff in peer-to-peer parliamentary development support activities with Parliaments in emerging democracies.[18] From the 1990s through the 2000s, UNDP, USAID, and NDI produced a number of resources including guides, handbooks, and practice notes on parliamentary development. By 2007, UNDP alone was supporting parliamentary development in 65 countries (UNDP, 2009). During the 2000s, the European Union greatly expanded its own democracy assistance, including in parliamentary development, establishing centralized expertise to support EU Delegations as they developed on-the-ground projects, and spending over €150 million on 73 different national and regional parliamentary strengthening projects during the first decade of the 21st century (Murphy, 2010).

Somewhat paradoxically, this blossoming of support to parliamentary development was mainly organized and delivered by non-parliamentary actors. While some of the staff and consultants engaged in parliamentary development projects had parliamentary experience as staff or former MPs, many did not, and with the exception of projects financed through the European Union's twinning programme for EU accession and European Neighbourhood states,[19] Parliaments and parliamentary administrations were not directly involved in most international parliamentary development projects. In 2008, the EP established the Office for the Promotion of Parliamentary Development (OPPD),[20] which organized numerous exchanges between emerging democracy Parliaments and the EP, conducted research programmes on parliamentary development, and provided some more technical support to emerging democracy Parliaments. In 2015, OPPD's operations were folded into the EP's Directorate for Democracy Support, which has continued to provide technical support to a small number of emerging democracies identified as priorities by the EP; in 2017, eight countries EP, 2019. At the time of writing, EP capacity-building support was focused mainly on European Neighbourhood and potential accession countries, including Albania, Bosnia and Herzegovina, Georgia, Macedonia, Montenegro, and Ukraine.

Several individual Parliaments and specifically, parliamentary administrations, have engaged in parliamentary development through their own initiative and in collaboration with parliamentary development organizations. Many larger Parliaments have international co-operation departments that organize exchanges and on-demand training for parliamentary staff as well as Members of Parliament. The German Bundestag is one of the most active in this domain. Between 2017 and 2019, advice was provided to parliamentary administrations from 25 countries from Africa, Asia, Europe, and South America, with a particular focus on Parliaments in countries in democratic transition (German Bundestag, 2019: 44). The Bundestag also organizes several exchange programmes, including the International Parliamentary Scholarship programme (German Ministry of Foreign Affairs, 2016). Operating since 1986, and with an annual intake of 120 young academics from up to 42 countries, the IPS is carried out in co-operation with three Berlin universities as well as the German political foundations. In the course of a five month internship, participants attend workshops and seminars on the German system of parliamentary democracy, spend a three-month internship in the office of a member of the Bundestag, and attend complementary seminars and lectures at the cooperating Berlin universities (German Bundestag, 2019: 44).

Other Parliaments have similar flagship parliamentary development programmes. The French Parliament has a long-running relationship with the United Nations Development Programme in which UNDP parliamentary development staff are provided intensive training in parliamentary operations. For a number of years, the Parliament of Finland's international department and the World Bank Institute organized an annual seminar for developing country Parliaments on Public Financial Management.[21] The Spanish Parliament, the Cortes Generales, regularly offers training in parliamentary processes in both Madrid and in Latin America and the Caribbean. Australian and New Zealand Parliaments work closely with developing democracies in the Pacific region, including through twinning of each of the federal and state legislatures of Australia with Pacific Island Parliaments.

The structured international parliamentary development engagements of European Union national Parliaments has grown in recent years, with the majority of the Parliaments of the 27 member states involved in regular administrative capacity-development work with developing democracy Parliaments, whether through the EU Twinning modality, in bilateral programmes with national parliamentary development institutions (such as the German Bundestag with the country's political party Stiftungs), and/or in collaborations with international organizations such as UNDP. The European Union recently financed the Inter Pares programme which aims to institutionalize peer-to-peer parliamentary strengthening activities between Members and staff of European Union national Parliaments and Parliaments in emerging democracies.[22] The programme, delivered by the intergovernmental organization International IDEA, offers a framework in which the development needs and objectives of partner Parliaments can be identified in a structured way, and support partnerships organized with EU national Parliaments to share matching skills and capacities. The programme reduces supporting Parliaments' organizational and financial overheads and enables integration of support from several European national Parliaments to meet diverse needs of particular partner Parliaments. Together, parliamentary twinning programmes, partnerships with parliamentary development organizations, and programmes such as Inter Pares in Europe and the House Democracy Partnership in the United States are facilitating the institutionalization of development-oriented administrative parliamentary diplomacy. Given growing authoritarian threats to democracy including in established democracies, these focused engagements of Parliaments in international capacity-building, combined with the definition of performance norms for democratic Parliaments, strengthen Parliaments' status as the key institution of representative democracy.

6.7 Case Study – Parliamentary Diplomacy in Ukraine

Finally, we will look at one example of parliamentary diplomacy illustrating the potential for interplay and integration between 'political' and 'administrative' parliamentary diplomacy; the EP's support to democratic transformation in Ukraine since 2012.[23] The importance of the EP's long-term engagement with the Verkhovna Rada, Ukraine's Parliament, is made manifest in the context of the Russian Federation's illegal full-scale invasion of Ukraine that began on February 24, 2022.

Ukraine, whose territory has hosted much of Europe's bloodiest conflicts of the past century, now lies again on an emergent fault line, between the European Union and a resurgent Russia, the latter seeking to re-establish itself after the collapse of the Soviet Union. Ukraine's independence has never been accepted by ideologues of Russian power, and from the 1990s Ukraine's elite has been divided between western (European) and eastern (Russian) orientations. The election of the pro-Russian leader Viktor Yanukovych to the Ukrainian presidency led to a spiralling crisis alimented by endemic corruption and the imprisonment of some of Yanukovych's political enemies, including notably former Prime Minister Yuliya Tymoshenko and former Internal Affairs Minister Yuriy Lutsenko. As the conflicts in Ukraine took on an increasingly geopolitical character, in 2012 the EP's President Martin Schulz appointed former EP President Pat Cox and former Polish President Alexander Kwasniewski to attempt to negotiate the release of Tymoshenko and other opponents of Yanukovych. Despite 27 Cox-Kwasniewski missions to Ukraine, although Lutsenko and other lower profile figures were pardoned, Tymoshenko was not released until the Maidan Revolution of 2014 overthrew Yanukovych, who fled to Russia.

Pro-western forces won post-Maidan elections in Ukraine in 2014, and Volodymyr Groysman, the new Speaker of the Verkhovna Rada, the Ukrainian Parliament, requested support from the EP in reforming the Parliament, long seen as a corrupt and inefficient institution. By agreement, Pat Cox, who had attained a high profile in Ukraine and respect from reform forces, was appointed to head a joint initiative of the European and Ukrainian Parliaments to analyse the functioning of the Rada and recommend a roadmap for reform (European Parliament, 2016). The Cox mission received substantial administrative support from within the EP, including from the Directorate for Democracy Support and the EP President's Office, as well as from Groysman's office, and international expertise. The findings and comprehensive recommendations of the 'Cox Report', which included both administrative and political reform recommendations, were adopted unanimously by the Ukrainian Parliament. The Report was launched at 'Ukrainian Days' organized in 2016 in the EP in Brussels, during which a convention for continuing administrative support to Rada reform was signed by the Secretaries General of the European and Ukrainian Parliaments. In addition, the European Union financed a multi-year 'Rada for Europe' programme for technical support to be delivered by UNDP to enable implementation of the Cox Report reforms, delivered in close collaboration with the EP's Directorate for Democracy Support. A second follow-up prong of the EP's support to parliamentary strengthening in Ukraine was the launch of the 'Jean Monnet Dialogue', again led by Cox. The Dialogue was designed by the Directorate for Democracy Support's Mediation and Dialogue Support Unit, which is in turn under the political direction of the Democracy Support and Election Coordination Group of MEPs. The Dialogue, involving extensive informal consultations between Cox and different political groups, followed by approximately biannual weekend workshops inside and outside Ukraine, fostered confidence-building and constructive interaction between the Verkhovna Rada's fissiparous factions. The Dialogues continued until elections of 2019 brought new political actors to power. A comparable process was also supported by the EP's Mediation and Dialogue Support Unit in North Macedonia between 2015 and 2017, supporting a peaceful resolution to longstanding debates about the country's geopolitical orientations (Fonck, 2018).

Ukraine has been one of a small number of priority countries for support through the European Parliament's Comprehensive Democracy Support Approach, involving multi-faceted supports including a Standing Rapporteur on Ukraine (Michael Gahler, MEP, Germany), collaboration in capacity development with on-the-ground parliamentary strengthening programmes delivered by agencies such as the United Nations Development Programme and the National Democratic Institute, and scheduled participation of Ukrainian parliamentary officials in the EP's Democracy Fellowship Programme.[24]

The continuing close ties between the EP and the Verkhovna Rada of Ukraine co-ordinated through the EP administration's Directorate for Democracy Support enabled the EP to respond quickly and effectively to the Russian invasion. On March 4, 2022, only a few days after the invasion began, and while Kyiv was under siege from Russian troops, EP President Roberta Metsola hosted an online meeting bringing together Verkhovna Rada Speaker Ruslan Stefanchuk and parliamentary Speakers from European Union national Parliaments, thus simultaneously leveraging both the parliamentary diplomacy network of European Union Parliaments along with the close diplomatic ties between the EP and the Verkhovna Rada.[25] On April 1, 2022, President Metsola travelled to Kyiv and spoke in person to the Verkhovna Rada expressing the solidarity of the EP and of the people of the European Union with Ukraine, 'you are fighting for what we all believe in: freedom, democracy, and the rule of law'.[26]

6.8 Conclusion

The chapter has illustrated the diversity of parliamentary administrations' roles in parliamentary diplomacy. It has been argued that parliamentary administrations are not merely adjuncts or supports to parliamentary diplomacy conducted by elected parliamentarians, but that, rather, administrations bring specific and essential elements to effective parliamentary diplomacy. Parliaments are key institutions of representative democracy; just as democracy cannot exist without elections, so representative democracy cannot function without Parliaments. Parliaments establish the formal mechanism for the reflection of the population's diversity in a formal process of debate and decision-making. This process, this set of norms and rules, is not invented at the beginning of each debate but rather reflects the institutionalization of practices that extend beyond national borders and represent humanity's learning and common understanding of how differences in interest and opinions can be peacefully mediated and legitimate decisions reached. Parliamentary administrations are responsible for administering, adjudicating, and documenting these practices. However, these are living principles that are not written down in tablets, but rather developed and refined as they encounter new challenges in the never-ending drama of human civilization. Inter-parliamentary diplomacy, involving both parliamentary administrations and elected parliamentarians, is a crucial vector for sharing of experiences, of mistakes made and lessons learned, leading to the strengthening and embedding of Parliaments at the heart of every democracy.

Notes

1 ECPRD Activity Report 2016–2018, Draft accessed at http://www.assembly.coe.int/LifeRay/APCE/pdf/ConfPres/2019Strasbourg/20191024-ActivityReport16-18ECPRD-EN.pdf.
2 https://www.ifla.org/publications/node/9759.
3 See for example the International Parliament Engagement Network, http://parliament-engagement.com/.
4 https://www.asgp.co/about.
5 https://www.asgp.co/sites/default/files/Orders%20of%20the%20day%20Ordre%20du%20jour_210525.pdf.
6 See IPU Strategy 2017-2021, accessed at https://www.ipu.org/resources/publications/about-ipu/2017-01/strategy-2017-2021.
7 https://www.ipu.org/news/press-releases/2017-03/new-ipu-and-un-women-map-shows-womens-representation-in-politics-stagnates.
8 https://www.ipu.org/our-impact/youth-empowerment.
9 https://www.ipu.org/our-impact/sustainable-development/sustainable-development-goals.
10 https://www.ipu.org/es/node/9556.
11 https://data.ipu.org/.

12 https://www.cpahq.org/what-we-do/institutional-parliamentary-strengthening/.
13 https://www.ipu.org/event/virtual-world-e-parliament-conference.
14 https://www.unfpa.org/parliamentarians.
15 See for example the secondment policy of the South African Development Community Parliamentary Forum (SADC-PF), https://www.sadcpf.org/index.php/en/documents/publications/sadc-finance-bulletin/secondment-policy, and the description of the practice at the Assemblée Parlementaire de la Francophonie, https://www.parl.ca/iiapublications/SmartBook/Documents/2d0e6fc7-cc88-431e-b44b-4f331f8a982d/2d0e6fc7-cc88-431e-b44b-4f331f8a982d.pdf.
16 And, increasingly, by the European Union.
17 Brian Levy (2010), a senior World Bank official, went so far as to explicitly declare the Bank to be 'agnostic' about democracy.
18 https://hdp.house.gov/about.
19 https://ec.europa.eu/neighbourhood-enlargement/tenders/twinning_en.
20 https://www.europarl.europa.eu/sides/getDoc.do?language=EN&type=IM-PRESS&reference=20100709STO78532.
21 https://www.worldbank.org/en/news/feature/2013/05/20/seminar-on-the-role-of-parliament-and-public-financial-management-pfm-in-fragile-states.
22 https://www.inter-pares.eu/.
23 Several published articles have discussed different aspects of EP diplomacy in Ukraine, including Nitoiu and Sus (2017); Fonck (2019); Redei (2019); Redei and Romanyshyn (2019); Kuzio (2017); and, Immenkamp and Bentzen (2019). The author provided technical support to the development of the 'Cox Report' (European Parliament, 2016).
24 European Parliament Democracy Support and Election Coordination Group Annual Work Programme for 2021, accessed at https://www.europarl.europa.eu/cmsdata/230327/DEG_Annual%20Work%20programme%202021.pdf.
25 European Parliament news release, March 4, 2022, "Kyiv is under siege and so is democracy – President Metsola to Ukraine Speaker", accessed at https://www.europarl.europa.eu/news/en/press-room/20220304IPR24713/kyiv-is-under-siege-and-so-is-democracy-president-metsola-to-ukraine-speaker.
26 European Parliament news release, April 1, 2022, "Metsola: Courage and hope to the people of Ukraine", https://www.europarl.europa.eu/news/en/press-room/20220401IPR26507/metsola-courage-and-hope-to-the-people-of-ukraine.

References

Aberbach, J.D., Putnam R.D., & Rockman, B.A. (1981). *Bureaucrats and Politicians in Western Democracies*. Cambridge, MA: Harvard University Press.

Albers, M. (2012). Between the Crisis of Democracy and World Parliament: The Development of the Inter-Parliamentary Union in the 1920s. *Journal of Global History*, 7(2), 189–209.

Barany, Z., & Moser, R.G. (Eds.). (2009). *Is Democracy Exportable?* Cambridge: Cambridge University Press.

Beetham, D. (2006). *Parliament and Democracy in the Twenty-First Century: A Guide to Good Practice*. Geneva: Inter-Parliamentary Union.

Briceño-Ruiz, J. (2019). The Crisis in Venezuela: A New Chapter, or the Final Chapter?. *Latin American Policy*, 10(1), 180–189.

Chohan, U. W., & Jacobs, K. (2017). The Presidentialisation Thesis and Parliamentary Budget Offices. *Parliamentary Affairs*, 70(2), 361–376.

Commonwealth Parliamentary Association (CPA), Recommended Benchmarks for Democratic Legislatures (2018), London, CPA, accessed at https://www.cpahq.org/media/l0jjk2nh/recommended-benchmarks-for-democratic-legislatures-updated-2018-final-online-version-single.pdf.

De Vrieze, F. (2016). The South-East European Cooperation Process and Its New Parliamentary Assembly: Regional Dialogue in Action. *The Hague Journal of Diplomacy*, 11(2–3), 215–234.

De Vrieze, F., & Meyer-Resende, M. (2015). Global Mapping and Analysis of Parliamentary Strengthening Programs: Report: A Study for the Swiss Agency for Development and Cooperation SDC, accessed at https://doc.rero.ch/record/279036/files/02-Global_mapping_and_analysis_of_parliamentary_strengthening.pdf.

European Parliament (2016). Report and Roadmap on Internal Reform and Capacity-Building for the Verkhovna Rada of Ukraine, Brussels, European Parliament, accessed at https://www.europarl.europa.eu/resources/library/media/20160229RES16408/20160229RES16408.pdf.

European Parliament (2019). EP Democracy Support Activities and Their Follow-Up, and Prospects for the Future, Brussels, European Parliament Policy Department for External Relations, accessed at https://www.europarl.europa.eu/thinktank/en/document.html?reference=EXPO_STU(2019)603474.

Fitsilis, F., & Koutsogiannis, A. (2017). Strengthening the Capacity of Parliaments through Development of Parliamentary Research Services. Working paper, 13th Workshop of Parliamentary Scholars and Parliamentarians, 29–30 July 2017, Oxfordshire, UK, accessed at.

Fitsilis, F. (2018). Inter-Parliamentary Cooperation and Its Administrators. *Perspectives on Federalism*, *10*(3), accessed at http://www.on-federalism.eu/attachments/307_download.pdf on 25 May 2021.

Fonck, D. (2018). Parliamentary Diplomacy and Legislative-Executive Relations in EU Foreign Policy: Studying the European Parliament's Mediation of the Macedonian Political Crisis (2015–17). *JCMS: Journal of Common Market Studies*, *56*(6), 1305–1322.

German Bundestag (2019). Report on the International Activities and Obligations of the German Bundestag, October 24, 2017 to September 30, 2019.

German Ministry of Foreign Affairs (2016). Bundestag and Foreign Policy, *AAIntern*, 7/2016.

Griglio, E., & Lupo, N. (2018). Inter-parliamentary Cooperation in the EU and outside the Union: Distinctive Features and Limits of the European Experience. *Perspectives on Federalism*, *10*(3), 56–82.

Hamilton, G. (2016). *Parliamentary Diplomacy: Diplomacy with a Democratic Mandate*. Geneva, Associations of Secretaries General of Parliaments, Inter-Parliamentary Union.

Immenkamp B., & Bentzen N. (2019) Parliamentary Diplomacy: Democracy Support at the European Parliament. In: Costa O. (ed) *The European Parliament in Times of EU Crisis*. European Administrative Governance. Cham, Switzerland: Palgrave Macmillan, 413–437.

Inter-Parliamentary Union (IPU) (2018). World e-Parliament Report 2018, IPU, Geneva, accessed at https://www.ipu.org/resources/publications/reports/2018-11/world-e-parliament-report-2018.

Jönsson, C., & Johnsson, A. (2018). Parliaments in Global Governance. *Global Governance: A Review of Multilateralism and International Organizations*, *24*(3), 309–320.

Kuzio, T. (2017). Ukraine Between a Constrained EU and Assertive Russia. *JCMS: Journal of Common Market Studies*, *55*(1), 103–120.

Levy, B. (2010). Democracy Support and Development Aid: The Case for Principled Agnosticism. *Journal of Democracy*, *21*(4), 27–34.

Malang, T., Brandenberger, L., & Leifeld, P. (2019). Networks and Social Influence in European Legislative Politics. *British Journal of Political Science*, *49*(4), 1475–1498.

Murphy, J. (2010). Engaging and Supporting Parliaments Worldwide: Strategies and Methodologies for EC Action in Support to Parliaments, Brussels, European Commission. Accessed at https://op.europa.eu/en/publication-detail/-/publication/b5494163-8654-48a1-8d5c-4e5f265ca6e2.

Nitoiu, C., & Sus, M. (2017). The European Parliament's Diplomacy—A Tool for Projecting EU Power in Times of Crisis? The Case of the Cox–Kwasniewski Mission. *JCMS: Journal of Common Market Studies*, *55*(1), 71–86.

O'Brien, M., Stapenhurst, R., & Von Trapp, L. (Eds.). (2016). *Benchmarking and Self-Assessment for Parliaments*. Washington, DC: The World Bank.

Pegan, A., & Högenauer, A-L. (2016). The Role of Parliamentary Administrations in Interparliamentary Cooperation. In *Interparliamentary Cooperation in the Composite European Constitution*. New York, Bloomsbury, 147–164.

Redei, L. (2019). MEPs as Mediators: An Emerging Trend of Parliamentary Diplomacy?. In *Parliamentary Cooperation and Diplomacy in EU External Relations*. Cheltenham, Edward Elgar Publishing.

Redei, L., & Romanyshyn, I. (2019). Non-Parliamentary Diplomacy: The European Parliament's Diplomatic Mission to Ukraine. *European Foreign Affairs Review*, *24*(1), 61–79.

Rocabert, J., Schimmelfennig, F., Crasnic, L., & Winzen, T. (2019). The Rise of International Parliamentary Institutions: Purpose and Legitimation. *The Review of International Organizations*, *14*(4), 607–631.

Senate of Italy (2018). Repertorio della diplomazia parlamentare mondiale, Rome, Senate of the Republic, accessed at https://www.senato.it/application/xmanager/projects/leg18/file/Repertorio_diplomazia_parlamentare.pdf on January 21 2021.

Senate of the Netherlands (2010). "Parliamentary Diplomacy", Memorandum Adopted by the Committee of Senior Members of the Senate of the States General on 16 November 2010, accessed at https://www.staten-generaal.nl/eu/id/vikslch65iv8/document_extern/parliamentary_diplomacy/f=/viksld10w1vg.pdf on 27 May 2021.

Stavridis, S., & Jancic, D. (Eds.). (2017). *Parliamentary Diplomacy in European and Global Governance.* Leiden, Brill.

United Nations Development Programme (UNDP) (2009). Parliamentary Development UNDP Strategy Note, UNDP, New York, accessed at https://www.undp.org/content/dam/aplaws/publication/en/publications/democratic-governance/dg-publications-for-website/parliamentary-development-strategy-note-/PD_Strategy_Note.pdf.

van Gruisen, P., & Huysmans, M. (2020). The Early Warning System and policymaking in the European Union. *European Union Politics*, *21*(3), 451–473.

Watera, J. (2018). Readiness Assessment of Parliaments to Engage with the Sustainable Development Goals: Application of the Self-Assessment Toolkit. *International Journal of Technology and Management*, *3*(2), 6.

Weisglas, F., & de Boer, G. (2007). Parliamentary Diplomacy. *The Hague Journal of Diplomacy*, *2*(1), 93–99.

Yong, B., Davies, G., & Leston-Bandeira, C. (2019). Tacticians, Stewards, and Professionals: The Politics of Publishing Select Committee Legal Advice. *Journal of Law and Society*, *46*(3), 367–395.

7
PARLIAMENTARY ADMINISTRATION FACING THE DIGITAL CHALLENGE

Fotios Fitsilis and Olivier Costa

7.1 Introduction

New technologies put organisations in front of some difficult choices. This is not least true for parliaments that need to change to adapt to the ongoing digitalisation of societal processes, while continuing being meaningful poles in institutional systems of governance (Orlikowski and Barley, 2001; Giddings, 2005; Fallon et al., 2011). One just needs to keep in mind that GovTech (Government Technology) is an already established term, while an analogon for parliaments, that is ParlTech (Parliamentary Technology), is still being forged (Bar-Siman-Tov et al., 2021; Koryzis et al., 2021). Administrative science has long dealt with the incorporation of technology in various public administration processes (see e.g. Thompson and Bates, 1957), yet recent advances in digital systems and tools that are based on the social (web 2.0) and the semantic web (part of web 3.0) pose serious challenges to parliamentary administrations (see e.g. Sartor et al., 2011). What is more, the evolution of intra-parliamentary processes does not seem to go hand in hand with the development cycle and the introduction of ever-complex electronic parliament (e-Parliament) systems.

Starting with a broad review of the technological state of play, this chapter addresses a series of digital challenges today's parliamentary administrations face. Herefor, the latest World e-Parliament reports by the Inter-Parliamentary Union (IPU) can be used as a point of reference (IPU, 2018; IPU, 2021b). Specific challenges that stem from the digital transformation of dedicated parliamentary functions, that is legislative drafting, oversight and parliamentary diplomacy, are discussed. In this regard, novel ParlTech approaches, such as legal informatics and systemic interoperability, and their overall positive effects in the parliamentary workspace are presented. In the light of the increasingly influential digital media, parliamentary communication, though not a distinct parliamentary function by itself, is tackled as it correlates with established parliamentary procedures and inclusive governance principles. One also needs to take into account that the parliament of the future is likely to involve systems and applications built around disruptive technologies, of the likes of artificial intelligence, augmented reality and recommender systems (de Campos et al., 2018; Fitsilis, 2019). The potential and the disruptive nature of such technologies for parliamentary administrations are analysed, jointly with a series of challenges that are necessary to be addressed to counterbalance lack of capacity and institutional inertia.

Having presented the above, the role of technology to the overall parliamentary response to the pandemic is briefly highlighted. Moreover, patterns are sought to support legislatures in developing realistic digital strategies and the role of inter-institutional cooperation is investigated. Ultimately, a set of broad research directions for the digital parliament is proposed in an effort to systematise international and interdisciplinary efforts to strengthen the role of parliaments using advanced digital tools and services.

7.2 State of Play

7.2.1 Parliaments and Technology: An Old Story

Since the Second World War (WWII), Members of Parliament (MPs) in Western democracies have faced an inflation of their work and duties, due to numerous factors: the growing number, length and complexity of laws; the increasing technicity of the work of control and scrutiny of the executive power; the rising pressure coming from constituents, civil society organisations and lobbies; the need to be more active on the ground and in the media; the crisis of democratic representation that increases the risk of electoral sanction; the professionalisation of political life, which requests more involvement in electoral campaigns, just to name a few. To face those pressures, the means of work of MPs have been constantly reinforced. Before WWII, most parliaments were only offering to Members access to meeting rooms, limited administrative staff and, in the case of more advanced institutions, a parliamentary library (Anghelescu, 2010). Progressively, they have acquired a very protective status (e.g. remuneration, privileges), a budget to hire personal assistants, more support from civil servants attached to the institution or to the party groups, as well as various means of work, such as personal office, budget to cover their expenses and telecommunication tools. In this context, parliaments and their administrations have been very keen to adapt to major innovations in the history of information and communications technologies (ICT). This has been the case with the telegraph, telephone, radio, television, internet and social networks, as well as with printing, typing machines, micro-films, computers, photocopiers, databases, office software or, more recently, artificial intelligence.[1]

The impact of new technologies and ICT on administration is not specific to parliaments – if one just thinks about how digital tools have transformed office work, writing, research, communication etc. However, parliaments have paid a specific interest in technological and IT innovation, for several reasons. First of all, MPs, as elected officials seeking for re-election, have always valued any means allowing them to be more efficient in their work, whether it is in their constituency or within the assembly. Second, chambers are also much concerned about their competitiveness, since they need to find a balance of power with the executive, which has far more resources. The internal competition within the house, between the various party-groups, is also a general incentive for MPs and groups' agents to take advantage of any new available technology – be it in the field of communication, office work, data collection or research. Furthermore, the various parliaments have always been quite active in exchanging information among them on how to increase the efficiency and impact of their work, especially through new technologies. Finally, another reason for introducing ICT in parliaments relates to transparency as a distinctive feature of their representation function. Modern technology may allow for increased transparency of several facets of parliamentary work, while favouring the establishment of new interaction channels with citizens, for instance through digital platforms.

7.2.2 The Impact of ICTs on Parliamentary Activities

There is a considerable literature on the impact of ICT on parliamentary work (Coleman et al., 1999; Hoff et al., 2004; Kies et al., 2004; Ward and Lusoli, 2005; Leston-Bandeira, 2007). However, those studies are mostly focused on the representation function of parliaments and the behaviour of individual MPs. Little is known about the way ICT has transformed the work of the institution, and more specifically of its administration, as a whole.

In the late 1970s, computers were already in use in Western democracies' parliaments to manage data and allow for simple tasks, such as the online retrieval and display of text records that could be used to track the elaboration of bills. Computers also permitted to inform administrators and members in real time about the latest developments of parliamentary activities, to manage correspondence with external stakeholders and keep track of it. Emailing functions already existed within the most advanced chambers, but they were only internal to a given institution. The main limitation of the first IT systems was indeed interoperability: each organisation had a proprietary network that could not communicate with others. Also, those systems were overall not very efficient: the number of computers was limited – as they were very expensive – and communications between them were slow and subject to failures.

The development of the personal computer (PC) in the 1980s has favoured a more massive use of ICT in all sorts of organisations. Within parliaments, actors – staff members, MPs, and parliamentary assistants – have started to perform many of their task using digital tools, but the real revolution came in the 1990s, with the internet and the advancement of high speed communication. Systems interoperability deeply transformed the overall organisation of work within legislatures and between institutions. The PC allowed world-wide access to data located on parliaments' servers and, later, their world-wide exposure. It also eased the communication of MPs with their collaborators at local level (Ward and Lusoli, 2005) and permitted distant working, especially from their constituency.

No parliamentary function was left unaffected by the ICT revolution. Electoral functions were the less concerned, if the activities of the administration are considered. ICT has massively modified the way MPs organise their constituency work, their relation with their voters and their campaigns for re-election (Allan, 2006), but all this does not involve directly the parliamentary administration. The activities of the parliament consisting in appointing ministers, agency heads or judges have neither been significantly influenced, even if it is easier today for MPs to gather information about those persons and their records. The impact of ICT has been evident on the legislative function. It has been transformed at several levels: research and data collection; organisation of impact assessments and evaluations; drafting of texts and amendments; communication on legislative activities. The oversight of governmental activities has also evolved thanks to new technologies. Parliamentary oversight requires processing of enormous amounts of information, now systematically gathered and organised by dedicated staff, and easily accessible to MPs in databanks or on the web. Finally, the role of parliaments in communication and in exchanges with the civil society and citizens has been greatly transformed by new technologies. They allow parliaments to swiftly communicate on their activities, for example via the diffusion of information, data, video and sound, and to dialogue with citizens and stakeholders via web platforms and social networks.

7.2.3 The Impact of ICT on the Main Parliamentary Activities

Since the end of the 1990, ICT has become key in the organisation of some of the main parliamentary activities. First, technology has completely changed the way data is managed and how research is conducted. Parliaments often enjoy important resources in that regard, for example to allow legislators to make their own mind on legislation and policies, in order to be independent from the executive power. This is not unrelated to the fact that the US Congress has the largest library in the world. PC and the web have totally modified the access to information, but it has to be organised and analysed by librarians, data scientists and researchers to be usable and helpful to MPs. This is why legislatures devote growing means to the constitution of databases for knowledge management and documentation.

ICT has massively changed the way parliamentary documents are prepared and diffused. Managing those documents – such as drafts of proposed legislation, committee reports, amendments, questions and records of debates – lies at the heart of the activities of parliaments' administrations. The whole process is subject to critical constraints of time and accuracy, as MPs need to quickly and easily access reliable documents. ICT has fundamentally modified those tasks and has also allowed MPs and their assistants to use a large set of tools to prepare their proposals (motions, amendments, questions etc.) and reports. Assigning of 'tags' (keywords) to any given text has permitted swift document retrieval and easy access to stored information not only for white-collar workers within the administration but also for actors belonging to other institutions, and, more recently, for every internet user.

Another central task of the administration is to support the work of parliamentary organs: plenary, committees, groups, delegations etc. This mainly implies the management of documents that need to be drafted, distributed and archived, and the preparation of meeting minutes. Even before the COVID-19 crisis, video-conferencing was occasionally an important issue, as parliamentary organs frequently organised hearings or exchanges of views with people not able to attend in person.

Such support activities are particularly important for the plenary meetings, for example transcription of the floor actions are needed nearly in real time, tasks that ICT tools – speech to text transformation – are able to deliver in sufficient quality. Technology also provides electronic voting. It makes the voting process more easy and efficient and permits to register votes in a reliable manner. A growing number of parliamentary activities are recorded, in audio or video, for matters of archiving or to permit the access to deliberations in real time. This may include the use of TV channels or live-streaming on various websites or social networks. In addition, internal as well as external stakeholders, such as journalists, civil society representatives, citizens and officials of the executive, need permanent access to parliamentary documents and information.

As mentioned, ICT has transformed the daily life of MPs (Hoff, 2004). While part of their activities are up their own staff, for instance, their personal website and presence on social networks, newsletter preparation, communication with the constituents, MPs also enjoy the support of the parliamentary administration, particularly when working remotely, making sure that they enjoy access to all the necessary parliamentary tools and resources.

ICT has also challenged the way legislatures communicate towards the outside world. This includes the production of public domain information or the dissemination of videos about the main parliamentary activities. Parliamentary portals are of key importance in this respect: all parliaments maintain websites not only integrating the information generated by their various bodies but also providing extensive material on the history of the institution, its organisation, composition and competences and the activities of its organs. Most parliaments propose sophisticated tools allowing citizens, civil society representatives, journalists, lobbyists and other stakeholders to track legislation and parliamentary work, also providing detailed information of each Member's activities. Today, in the logic of 'open data', parliaments are expected to widely share different kinds of, mostly unprocessed, information to let various actors make their own analysis of it. Some parliaments also encourage external stakeholders to express their views on various policy issues or pending proposals. Designing a website suitable for all the users – with contrasted levels of knowledge and different expectations – becomes a vital challenge.

Thanks to video-conferencing and virtual networks, new technologies enable robust and secure inter-parliamentary and inter-institutional communication. Parliaments can take advantage of ICT to share data, information and resources, to organise systematic benchmarks of solutions to common problems and exchange good practice. Not all legislatures, though, have the necessary budget, in-house skills and human resources to take full advantage of the opportunities offered by new technologies. Therefore, the international collaboration of parliaments on those matters has been proven to be fundamental. Once a digital solution has been developed and tested, it can be also be replicated in another similar context. In this sense, the IPU can play a pivotal role in sharing the knowledge and experiences of its members.

7.3 Digital Challenges

Innovations like radio, television or the internet have deeply metamorphosed politics – and thus parliaments and their administrations. In the recent period of time, the organisation of work within legislatures has been influenced by the many reflexions on the possible use of ICT as a tool to revitalise governance and renew democratic culture (Lawson, 1998). This is impacting the way parliaments work, especially in advanced democracies, with innovations like office automation, online campaigning, networking and mass communication (Davies, 1999). However, parliaments are also criticised for their inertia and their conservatism, regarding for instance the open data movement. Some chambers are attached to traditional political structures and are not very capable to reflect the evolutions that transform societies (Ferguson, 2006). Additionally, it took time for some representatives and civil servants to use digital technology – especially for interacting with citizens – and to accept the idea of e-Democracy and its disruptiveness (Campbell et al., 1999). Nevertheless, modern technology continues to represent an opportunity for parliaments to improve the efficiency of their main functions and to communicate with citizens, the civil society, executive organs and other chambers at the international level.

There are two main challenges, regarding internal production and management of documents, and the communication with citizens. The first is an organisational one: the tools and software in use in most parliaments to produce legal documents, such as reports, amendments and questions, are more complex to use than the average office ones, thus requiring constant training on the part of staff, Members and their assistants. This is also the case with open standards such as XML.[2] There needs to be an *ex ante* agreement on necessary technicalities that include document format, elements and structure. This additional level of technical complexity requires relentless effort in coaching and supporting the actors.

Second, external communication in massively impacted by digital technology. Parliaments' administration should devote massive efforts to reinforce the links between representatives and represented, and to contribute to the development of an open and equitable information society. The main challenge here is to develop new tools without deepening the digital divide by favouring users who have the capacities to take advantage of them, especially in order to influence legislators, to the detriment of less skilled citizens and actors (Wresch, 1996; Norris, 2001). It is crucial for representative institutions to allow citizens to express their views and, ideally, to participate in policymaking. This involvement can take, for instance, the form of participation to online forums and polls. Submission and support of electronic petitions is already a feature in several legislatures. Agents in charge of those new channels of participation need to take care of potentially dangerous issues for a democratic dialogue, such as the representativeness of contributors, the observed tendency to polarisation on online platforms and the possibility of instrumentalisation by 'trolls'. Transparency, open-data and participation cease to be valuable objectives if only lobbyists and extremists take advantage of them.

Parliaments need to take seriously the risks linked to technology. In large scale, such risks are visible in the constant attempts of foreign countries to interfere in the democratic life of others (Bressanelli, 2021). In sum, ICT must be a means to help parliaments becoming part of society based on equitable, transparent and inclusive information, capable to strengthen the democratic process, and to promote an e-Democracy (Lawson, 1998; Vedel, 2006). Constant efforts are thus needed to think about the way to favour citizens' access to information as well as their participation (Ferguson, 2006).

7.4 The Future of Parliamentary Administrations

What drives parliamentary change? This is a seemingly simple research question, but to identify and understand the parameters of change and their impact would require a broad historical and contemporary study of parliaments. Nonetheless, as societal components and human identities are transforming into the digital realm (see e.g. Montag and Diefenbach, 2018), it is safe to assume that parliamentary organisations – as representative institutions – are going to follow the same transformation path, perhaps with a time lag. Digital technology leaves no part of the parliamentary administration unaffected, which is why this chapter was conceptually designed as a horizontal one. On the other hand, the plethora of different technologies, the volume of necessary investments, the lack of standards and the usually introvert response of parliaments against innovation[3] are among the facts that make predictions on the future of parliamentary administration difficult.

To offer a full assessment of possible changes on parliamentary administrations would be out of the scope of this chapter. Instead, the authors opt to analyse closer the parliamentary potential of four specific technology sectors in a descriptive, non-exhaustive manner. A balanced approach between contemporary and future applications is attempted. The first two of them, parliamentary communication and legal informatics, are state-of-the-art technologies that are currently being used to advance parliamentary functions across the globe. The next two, disrupting technologies and rule-as-code, concern future parliamentary technology, or ParlTech.[4]

7.4.1 Digital Parliamentary Communication

Modern technology, particularly the rise of digital platforms, has initiated a profound shift in personal and political communication through the immense popularity and outreach of social media channels. As a result, political discourse is increasingly taking place via digital platforms within an algorithmic and weakly regulated environment (on the necessity to regulate algorithms, the institutional position of parliaments and the role of parliamentary research services in providing substantial scientific support, see Fitsilis, 2019). This trend can be related to the so-called 'representation gap' that in this context can be defined as a technology-induced disruption of the seamless link of trust between parliaments and citizens.

Parliaments were not left unaffected by change and tried to make good use of the digital medium (Williamson and Fallon, 2011; Griffith and Leston-Bandeira, 2012), which in some occasions altered established citizen engagement practices (Poblet et al., 2019). Leston-Bandeira (2019) reported on the effect of technology on citizen petitions, better known as e-petitions. On the use of digital platforms, particularly Twitter, by MPs and their effects on campaigning and policymaking, one may consult an increasingly rich body of literature (see e.g. Scherpereel et al., 2017; Agarwal et al., 2019).

Yet, as late adopters, legislatures still struggle to come up with individualised, let alone uniform, rules of conduct with the new media (IPU, 2018). Therefore, the IPU has recently issued its updated social media guidelines for legislatures and MPs (IPU, 2021a).[5] While digital communication may institutionally influence parliamentary communication, for instance by enhancing the parliamentary diplomacy function (Fitsilis and Stavridis, 2021), this has to be facilitated at the administrative level as well. Knowledge of digital marketing and social media analytics is essential for advancing parliamentary communication and to strengthen the link to broad parts of society that operate online. Organisational adaptation, for example in the form of a media unit, might prove useful to bundle the necessary efforts and to increase their overall efficiency.

Absorbing and leveraging the effects of the omnipresent and omnidirectional social media for own advantage is not the only way forward for parliaments. Advancements in the field of legal informatics have cultivated great expectations in GovTech and are expected to further boost parliamentary operation in the years to come.

7.4.2 Interoperability and Legal Informatics

It is not exaggerated to say that the new era for the digital parliament has been enabled through the definition of new semantic and legal document standards (see W3C, 2019; OASIS, 2020, respectively). These again have formed the base for the development of new tools and services in the legal domain, hence the term 'legal informatics'. Characteristic representation of such applications can be found in *LEOS*, an authoring tool for legislative drafting, the *AT4AM* (for all) system for drafting amendments and *ManyLaws* that, among others, offers timeline and comparative analysis among European, Austrian and Greek laws, while visualising potential correlations, dependencies and conflicts (further analysis of these applications is given by Malanga, 2015; Stavropoulou et al, 2020; Leventis et al. 2021, respectively).

These examples are purely indicative, yet characteristic of the benefits these web- and XML-based workflow technologies can offer. The incorporation of 'smart'[6] authoring tools into the parliamentary working processes will cater for instant transparency and accountability boost, as changes to bills and law proposals would be visible to all stakeholders in real time.[7]

This technology is not only limited to the drafting of laws but can also extend to efficient post-legislative scrutiny (de Vrieze and Norton, 2020), e-deliberation (Schlosberg et al., 2008) and possibly lead to new concepts of participatory legislation (Coutinho et al., 2017), thus covering the entire spectrum of parliamentary functions. While the advent of XML technology in a major legislature can be eventually traced back to the late 1990s and the US

House of Representatives (2018), it was the emergence of the *Akoma Ntoso* standard in 2018 that sparked hype across parliamentary and governance institutions.

The creation of machine-readable,[8] semantic web compatible laws is not an automatic process. The necessary systemic and procedural transformation is directly reflected on the administration of the parliament and the capacity of its staff to efficiently operate these novel tools. In this regard, timing for conducting training needs assessment and definition of the necessary digital skills constitute critical parameters. Introducing new legal informatics applications without properly preparing the organisational change will only lead to counter-productive internal tensions and operational delays.

To fully harvest the power of legal informatics, parliaments will additionally have to rely on interoperable systems that are built within a well-defined framework. The European Interoperability Framework (EIF) is a construct of this sort (Kouroubali and Katehakis, 2019). Currently offering a series of principles and recommendations, EIF seeks to make a leap forward by adopting standards-based approach.

7.4.3 Emerging and Disruptive Technologies

Emerging technologies are going to have an impact on every aspect of societal activity. So much is certain. The ones that are going to fundamentally change the way organisations function are called 'disruptive'.[9] With innumerable technologies emerging (see e.g. Gartner, 2020; Strawn, 2021),[10] how should they be prioritised for entering the parliamentary workspace and under which conditions? Several of these technologies deploy advanced algorithms at their core and generate great volumes of data which in the legal domain can be referred to as 'big open legal data' (BOLD). Their use, both within and outside parliament, needs to be carefully regulated to avoid unwanted side effects, for instance algorithmic bias, misinformation and black-box decision-making (Wachter et al., 2018).

Given the complexity of parliamentary organisations and in order to avoid such shortcomings, it is imperative to define a framework for the digital transformation of legislatures. At the same time, it is necessary to carefully screen existing technology options so as to come up with a limited set of emerging technologies, based on which 'proof of concepts' can be designed for parliamentary application. This is because ParlTech, that is emerging technologies for parliaments, is likely to remain a niche sector, possibly unable to carry on its own the significant investments necessary for the development and specialisation of a multitude of technologies. One of the first structured efforts to closer specify a subset of emerging technologies within a maturity vs. usefulness matrix has been attempted by Koryzis et al. (2021). Analysis therein isolated linked open data and advanced legal services, virtual parliament and social media analytics as technologies within the limits of the 'peak of inflated expectations', that is with the biggest hype. There are technologies worth studying when developing the digital parliament.

Parliaments also need to be aware of the risk that introduction of ParlTech can lead to counterproductive results if not accompanied by an adequate institutional strategy and the acquisition of new digital skills by employees – but also, to some extent, Members and their personal staff. As digital transformation goes hand-in-hand with organisational change, representative institutions need to re-define internal procedures and re-structure administrative units to facilitate incorporation of new tools and services, a process known as business process re-engineering (a reflection in the public sector is offered by McAdam and Donaghy, 1999). Thorough planning is presumed essential to avoid internal stress[11] and possible disruptions in organisational culture and institutional memory.

7.4.4 Rule as Code

The Rule as Code is a concept to automatically and transparently transfer law into code using structured language (Kelly, 2020, p. 3). Though the concept is not new (see e.g. Chasalow, 1961), it made a strong comeback in recent years through the emergence of a series of such structured languages, for instance *LogLaw*, *Blawx* and *Catala*, as well as proof-of-concepts that principally demonstrated usefulness in real-world applications. There exists a clear separation between the already known principles of Better Regulation and Rule as Code. In particular, Better Regulation is a policy development method (see e.g. Bürgin, 2019), while Rule as Code is the process of transferring rules – to which law may belong – into to machine-readable language, that is code (Barraclough et al., 2021, p. 2).[12]

The potential of the concept appears significant as machine-consumable rules may limit the gap between intended policies and their implementation, while in parallel increasing both speed and consistency of service delivery (Mohun and Roberts, 2020, p. 2). In addition, unlike XML-based representation formats, Rule as Code enables *ex-ante* testing and validation of the legal outputs based on any use case scenarios imaginable. As a result, it can be verified before enactment whether a rule causes the desired effects. Nonetheless, there are several concerns related either to the digitisation or to the interpretation of law (see, indicatively, Deakin and Markou, 2020).

An unambiguous legal meaning might not only be advantageous in strict regulatory environments as in banking, fiscal or employee benefit frameworks but can also result in loss of flexibility when implementing or interpreting legal provisions for unforeseen circumstances. The latter is often the case at the administrative and the judicial level.[13] It is possible to develop capacity in parliaments to oppose these concerns, by providing parliament with the ownership of the transformation of law into code. Hence, while laws will still be drafted according to established processes,[14] the parliament could take over the responsibility to prepare a codification layer, a move that seems to be compatible with institutional sovereignty (see Barraclough et al., 2021, p. 3) and the parliamentary oversight.[15] The term 'legal engineer' may apply for the parliamentary administrators who facilitate this undertaking. All in all, in an ideal scenario, natural language law, XML-based representation and Rule as Code would form an inseparable triplet that characterises different facets of a law (rule).

7.5 Effects of COVID-19 Pandemic on the Digitalisation of Parliamentary Administration

Beginning in early 2020, the COVID-19 pandemic started to impact parliamentary operation worldwide. With the shifting of the institutional equilibrium towards the side of the Executive, a much anticipated response was triggered on the parliamentary side and captured by a series of reports, surveys and trackers initiated by major national, regional and international organisations, such as the Westminster Foundation for Democracy (WFD, 2021), ParlAmericas (2020) and the IPU (IPU, 2021b). These studies confirmed original assumptions that response has not been uniform among parliaments and indicated a varying impact of technology in combating the crisis. The latter is also supported by broad academic research on the relation between technology and parliamentary activity during the pandemic (Bar-Siman-Tov et al., 2021), while Griglio (2020) offered evidence of digital solutions bridging the discontinuation of the parliamentary oversight function.

Without doubt, the challenges that parliaments faced were unprecedented and included different options to re-start parliamentary work. Initial distrust was short-lived as technology managed to deliver on its promises. According to the IPU, towards the end of 2020, one third of surveyed parliaments (n=116) have held virtual or hybrid plenary sittings due to the pandemic, whereas this figure rises to two thirds when it comes to committee sessions. Hence, the most widely used application of technology has been videoconferencing. Inevitably, the pandemic seems to have impacted voting as well, with 28% of parliaments (n=70) resorting to new voting methods when in plenary offered by videoconferencing tools or novel voting applications (IPU, 2021b).

One needs to take into account that other systemic aspects were influenced as well. For instance, as a significant part of parliamentary operation went digital, cyber security needed to be enhanced to ensure secure inter-parliamentary communications and voting.[16]

On the administrative side, horizontal ICT units took the first blow along with the responsibility of developing and putting into production digital systems and services to enable business continuation. Equally pressurised were units entrusted with the support of core parliamentary work, which had to switch on-the-fly from 'business as usual' to emergency operating procedures within a remote or hybrid environment.

While parliamentary employees are certainly no strangers to emergency or crisis situations, the pandemic presented a challenge of a whole new dimension. New digital skills needed to be acquired on-the-job, basically during project design and implementation, with a significant part of the work force serving from a home office environment, a situation that – if preserved – may lead to work-life imbalance and stress (Bellmann and Hübler, 2020). In this context, with every single study on employment trends showing that the future of work is home-based, parliament should at least be preparing to restructure their operational procedures and adjust their working premises. This seemingly contradicts the original notion of parliament as centralised institution (with a central administration), where representatives of the people convene at the same place and time. In reality, a profound transformation is taking place with parliamentary work being gradually elevated from the physical into the digital realm, where it is still conducted on e-Parliament platforms in a centralised manner.

This situation had a very strong yet unseen impact on the activities of MPs. Within a very short amount of time, chambers' administrations had to develop and integrate into procedure reliable and secure video-conferencing systems enough to allow for deliberations of the plenary rooms, the committees and the groups. Before the crisis, telework already existed in some parliaments for staff members, and MPs were already able to electronically access all kinds of resources. However, large scale remote participation of Members to the various parliamentary activities was not foreseen. With COVID-19, some assemblies had also to develop electronic voting systems to avoid the interruption of legislative activities. Even if technology allows for such adaptations, the use of online tools had a deep impact on the quality of deliberation, resulting, in several cases, a serious drop in the number of amendments and questions tabled by Members, and far less interaction between them. Obviously, informal exchanges, including those with staff members with technical or legal knowledge, are also missed.

As the pandemic evolves dynamically, parliaments continue adapting to changing conditions. Hence, any current plans so as to maintain COVID-19 induced working practices, including technological means, post-pandemic might be too ambitious. Extreme caution is also necessary not to over-interpret the results of the aforementioned surveys as the pandemic – as of early 2022 – is still ongoing and its extinction, even with ambitious vaccination programs, is far from being over (Fitsilis and Pliakogianni, 2021, p. 26).

7.6 Conclusions and Research Directions

The popular cliché 'the future is now' may indeed be proven true in the case of the migration of parliaments into the digital sphere. Significant alterations in the structure and working processes of parliament administration shall be needed to facilitate this change. Will parliaments manage? The still ongoing COVID-19 crisis and the rapid digital transition, though inconsistent across different legislatures, offer strong indications that – when prompted – parliaments have the inherent capacity to perform the necessary changes.

There are national parliaments that are actively pursuing or have assimilated several technological advancements, particular in the domain on digital engagement, such as the Chilean (Feddersen and Santana, 2021), the Brazilian (de Barros et al., 2016), the Austrian and the Hellenic ones (Fitsilis et al., 2017), just to name a few.[17] Institutional adaptation will not be easy for every single organisation, but help is just around the corner, for example in the form of technical assistance from stronger parliaments, donor organisations or the IPU. The role of the latter as innovation hub is considered decisive on the international scale to support and strengthen assemblies with limited inherent capacity.[18]

In the long term, emerging and disrupting technologies may contribute to make up lost ground. In the meantime, and provisionally neglecting the greater hype around ParlTech, the technology vector is rather pointing towards exploitation of digital media and the implementation of semantic web compatible solutions. The building of such parliamentary tools and services goes through carefully selected proof-of-concept applications that are based on agreed-upon principles and approaches, such as standard-based, user-friendly and mobile-first design, that are complemented by inclusiveness, data openness and personal data protection features. The authors point at the necessity to develop these applications jointly with parliamentary administrations, so as to avoid the fate of several information systems projects that ended up underperforming (Hughes et al., 2016).

On several occasions, one needs to differentiate between the effects of technology on the institution, on the one hand, and the administration, on the other. When studying parliamentary administrations, the focus of the discussion tends to be strongly user-centric. In the case of a paradigm shift in technology, any effects would have direct consequences on the operational procedures conducted by intra-parliamentary stakeholders. For the majority of stakeholders,[19] parliamentary administration constitutes a black box and interaction is limited to a few dedicated interfaces, for example the library or research service and secretariat support for plenary and committee sessions. With the help of technology and changes in the nature of employment, this interaction is possible to be further automated.

Emphasis must be placed on the necessary capacity of personnel to perform the relevant operations. This is because the efficiency of state-of-the-art and/or emerging digital technology might be limited without the support of a dedicated parliamentary administration. A whole new set of digital skills and competencies will be needed to build up the necessary capacity. For parliaments that do not have established internal training units, strategic cooperation with national schools of governance or international facilities (see e.g. the Interoperable Europe Academy in the European context; European Commission, n.d.) might prove useful. In this regard, the pandemic seems to have created a positive precedent as the majority of training courses have migrated online, thus being easily accessible at a low cost.

As a direct consequence of using integrated and interoperable digital systems, inter-institutional cooperation between parliament and the executive can be strengthened, while maintaining constitutional statutes of the separation of powers. Yet the ultimate question, whether digital transformation will ultimately advance the institutional position and status of legislatures, still remains to be answered. As remarked, technology offers notable opportunities to transform parliamentary functions through the use of legal informatics and the semantic web: the existence of legal digital twins can promote understanding and accessibility to legal information, with the potential to pave the way to an ecosystem of interconnected legal documents. In parliamentary oversight, advanced data collection and semantic analysis can lead to efficient application of post legislative scrutiny methods. Parliamentary diplomacy, tough multi-faceted and touching upon several layers of inter-institutional cooperation, could be pioneered through sophisticated use of new digital media and platforms.

To conclude the above discussion, it is possible to isolate some broad directions for future research on parliaments. For instance, further study could be directed on the development of a rigid framework for the digital parliament (Koryzis et al., 2021). Additional research is necessary to specify an extensible set of digital skills for personnel to support the digital transformation of legislatures (Tsekeris, 2019). A third independent research direction could not only be related to the wider transformation of complex organisations and the incorporation of smart organisational and management tools for efficient administration (Chew et al., 2020) but also the design of flexible labour schemes for administrators to facilitate parliamentary operation while in home office or part-time presence in parliamentary premises (Spurk and Straub, 2020).

Notes

1 In April 2021 the Committee for the Future in the Parliament of Finland organised a first of its kind hearing of two artificial intelligence personae.
2 XML stands for Extensible Markup Language and is a set of rules encoding documents in machine-readable formats.
3 The pandemic forms an obvious exception to be discussed in the next section.
4 In its present meaning, the term 'ParlTech' appears in Koryzis et al. (2021); the term is also used in a forthcoming article by Bar-Siman-Tov et al. (2021), but in a more restrictive manner to describe the 'use of digital devices to maintain legislative functions' during the COVID-19 pandemic.
5 At this point, it is necessary to point out that political and institutional communication is not one and the same thing. Individual MPs or parliamentary groups might follow distinct communication campaigns designed to maximise impact or readership for a given period of time and adjust marketing- and media-mix accordingly. Parliament as such may pursue broader objectives, such as institutional development and strengthening, by targeting a nation-wide or even – in the case of parliamentary diplomacy – international audience.
6 Here, 'smart' has to be decoupled from its usual link to artificial intelligence and characterises systems of enriched functionality.
7 This is made possible through the very nature of structured legal documents, whose elements (e.g. distinctive parts, articles or passages) or metadata (e.g. what has been changed, when it has been changed and who changed it) can be captured using appropriate 'tags'.
8 Machine-readability due to structural characterisation is to be separated from the Rule-as-Code approach, on which is going to be elaborated below.
9 Nonetheless, the discussion on which technologies can have 'disruptive' effects within parliaments has a lot of subjective elements.
10 Gartner presents an overview of user perception regarding emerging technologies in its annual hype cycles.
11 Typical for disruptive changes in organisation, stress situations among employees as well as between employees and leadership may arise; such a disruption has been caused by the COVID-19 pandemic and despite the overall positive response, as presented it in the next section, it has negatively impacted institutional functions and the status of the Legislative *vis-à-vis* the Executive.
12 The referenced publication originally uses the term 'better rules'. Instead, the authors here use 'Better Regulation', a term broadly acknowledged in the European context.

13 Under certain conditions though, semantic 'interpretative' issues can also be replicated in Rule as Code.
14 The use of legal document standards and authoring tools do not alter the very nature of the legislative process.
15 Advanced oversight schemata could provide for the missing flexibility by amending the code.
16 Apart from installing and configuring trustworthy Virtual Private Networks (VPNs) and software, this includes the implementation of an organisation-wide cyber security policy.
17 The European parliament, though a supra-national one, deserves a special mention for maintaining a unit dedicated to innovation (as part of DG ITEC).
18 The IPU has established several thematic and regional technology hubs as parts of its Centre for Innovation in Parliament. The latter could also contribute towards a reliable framework and agreed upon metrics for measuring the impact of digital transformation in parliament.
19 Reference is made here on intra-parliamentary stakeholders, such as MPs and their aides, parliamentary groups and some affiliated bodies, such as independent authorities, though the following argument may also be valid for external ones.

References

Agarwal, P., Sastry, N. and Wood, E. (2019) Tweeting MPs: Digital engagement between citizens and members of parliament in the UK. In *Proceedings of the International AAAI Conference on Web and Social Media* 13, pp. 26–37.

Allan, R. (2006) Parliament, Elected Representatives and Technology 1997–2005—Good in Parts? *Parliamentary Affairs* 95(2), pp. 360–365.

Anghelescu, H. G. (2010). Historical Overview: The Parliamentary Library from Past to Present. *Library Trends* 58(4), pp. 418–433.

Barraclough, T., Fraser, H. and Barnes, C. (2021) *Legislation as Code for New Zealand: Opportunities Risks and Recommendations*. Auckland, NZ: Brainbox Institute. Available at: https://www.brainbox.institute/law-as-code (accessed 27 March 2021).

Bar-Siman-Tov, I., Rozenberg, O., Benoît, C., Waismel-Manor, I. and Levanon, A. (2021) Measuring Legislative Activity during the COVID-19 Pandemic: Introducing the ParlAct and ParlTech Indexes. *International Journal of Parliamentary Studies* 1(1), pp. 109–126.

Bellmann, L. and Hübler, O. (2020) Working from Home, Job Satisfaction and Work–Life Balance–Robust or Heterogeneous Links? *International Journal of Manpower*. Available at: https://doi.org/10.1108/IJM-10-2019-0458 (accessed 25 March 2021).

Bressanelli, E. (2021) Investing in Destabilisation: How Foreign Money is Used to Undermine Democracy in the EU. Study Requested by the INGE Committee, European Parliament, PE 653.631.

Bürgin, A. (2019) The Implications of the Better Regulation Agenda for the European Parliament's Inter-and Intra-Institutional Power Relations. *Journal of European Integration* 41(2), pp.187–202.

Campbell, A., Harrop, A. and Thomson, B. (1999). Towards the Virtual Parliament – What Computers Can Do For MPs. *Parliamentary Affairs* 52(3), pp. 388–403.

Chasalow, I. (1961) The First National Law and Electronics Conference. *American Behavioral Scientist* 4(7), pp. 31–34.

Chew, M.Y.L., Teo, E.A.L., Shah, K.W., Kumar, V. and Hussein, G.F. (2020) Evaluating the Roadmap of 5G Technology Implementation for Smart Building and Facilities Management in Singapore. *Sustainability* 12(24), p. 10259.

Coleman, S., Taylor, J. and van de Donk, W. (1999) *Parliament in the Age of the Internet*. Oxford: Oxford University Press.

Coutinho, D.R., Kira, B., Lessa, M.R. and de Castro, H.A. (2017) Participatory Democracy and Law-Making in Contemporary Brazil. *The Theory and Practice of Legislation* 5(3), pp. 225–243.

Davies, R. (1999) *The Web of Politics: The Internet's Impact on the American Political System*. Oxford: Oxford University Press.

de Barros, A.T., Bernardes, C.B. and Rehbein, M. (2016) Brazilian Parliament and Digital Engagement. *The Journal of Legislative Studies* 22(4), pp. 540–558.

de Campos, L.M., Fernández-Luna, J.M., Huete, J.F. and Redondo-Expósito, L. (2018) Positive Unlabeled Learning for Building Recommender Systems in a Parliamentary Setting. *Information Sciences* 433, pp. 221–232.

de Vrieze, F. and Norton, P. (2020) *Parliaments and Post-Legislative Scrutiny*. London: Routledge.

Deakin, S. and Markou, C. (2020) *Is Law Computable? Critical Perspectives on Law and Artificial Intelligence*. Oxford: Hart Publishing.

European Commission (n.d.) Interoperable Europe Academy. Available at: https://joinup.ec.europa.eu/collection/digital-skills-public-sector/solution/interoperable-europe-academy.

Fallon, F., Allen, B. and Williamson, A. (2011) Parliament 2020: Visioning the Future Parliament - International Comparison: Australia, Canada, Chile and the United Kingdom. Hansard Society, London. Available at: https://www.readkong.com/page/parliament-2020-visioning-the-future-parliament-9309417 (accessed 8 November 2022).

Feddersen, M. and Santana, L. E. (2021) Unpacking the Democratic Affordances of CrowdLaw Concept and Practice: 'It feels like being part of the game', *Politics*. Available at: https://doi.org/10.1177/0263395720973850 (accessed 27 March 2021).

Ferguson, R. (2006). *Digital Dialogues*. London: Hansard Society.

Fitsilis, F. (2019) *Imposing Regulation on Advanced Algorithms*. Cham: Springer.

Fitsilis, F. and Pliakogianni, A. (2021) The Hellenic Parliament's Response to the COVID-19 Pandemic – A Balancing Act between Necessity and Realism. *IALS Student Law Review* 8(1), pp. 19–27.

Fitsilis, F. and Stavridis, S. (2021) The Hellenic Parliament's Use of Digital Media in its response to the 2019 Turkey-Libya Memorandum of Understanding on Maritime Boundaries in the Mediterranean Sea: A Preliminary Assessment. GreeSE Papers 163. London: Hellenic Observatory, London School of Economics and Political Science. Available at: http://eprints.lse.ac.uk/id/eprint/111929 (accessed 8 November 2022).

Fitsilis, F., Koryzis, D., Svolopoulos, V. and Spiliotopoulos, D. (2017) Implementing Digital Parliament Innovative Concepts for Citizens and Policy Makers. In Nah FH., Tan CH. (eds) *HCI in Business, Government and Organizations. Interacting with Information Systems*. HCIBGO 2017. Lecture Notes in Computer Science, vol. 10293. Cham: Springer.

Gartner (2020) 5 Trends Drive the Gartner Hype Cycle for Emerging Technologies, 2020. Available at: https://www.gartner.com/smarterwithgartner/5-trends-drive-the-gartner-hype-cycle-for-emerging-technologies-2020/ (accessed 30 March 2021).

Giddings, P. (2005). *The Future of Parliament: Issues for a New Century*. NYC: Palgrave Macmillan.

Griffith, J. and Leston-Bandeira, C. (2012). How Are Parliaments Using New Media to Engage with Citizens? *The Journal of Legislative Studies* 18(3–4), pp. 496–513.

Griglio, E. (2020) Parliamentary Oversight Under the Covid-19 Emergency: Striving Against Executive Dominance. *The Theory and Practice of Legislation* 8(1–2), pp. 49–70.

Hoff, J. (2004), Members of Parliaments' Use of ICT in a Comparative European Perspective. *Information Polity* 9(1, 2), pp. 5–16.

Hoff, J., Coleman, S., Filzmaier, P. and Cardoso, G. (2004) Use of ICT by Members of Parliament. *Information Polity* 9(1, 2), pp. 1–4.

Hughes, D.L., Dwivedi, Y.K., Simintiras, A.C. and Rana, N.P. (2016) *Success and Failure of IS/IT Projects. A State of the Art Analysis and Future Directions*. Berlin, Heidelberg: Springer-Verlag.

IPU (2018) World e-Parliament Report 2018. Geneva: IPU. Available at: https://www.ipu.org/resources/publications/reports/2018-11/world-e-parliament-report-2018 (accessed 16 March 2021).

IPU (2021a) *Social Media Guide for Parliaments and Parliamentarians*. Geneva: IPU. Available at: https://www.ipu.org/resources/publications/reference/2021-02/social-media-guidelines (accessed 16 March 2021).

IPU (2021b) Lessons from the Pandemic. In *World e-Parliament Report 2020*, Geneva: IPU.

Kelly, A.J. (2020) A Computer Language Model for Digitising New Zealand Statute Law. *Loophole* 1, pp. 2–25. Available at: https://www.calc.ngo/sites/default/files/loophole/Loophole%20-%202020-01%20%282020-02-09%29.pdf (accessed 16 March 2021).

Kies, R., Mendez, F., Schmitter, P. and Trechsel, A. (2004) Evaluation of the Use of New Technologies In Order To Facilitate Democracy in Europe. Public Report for the Scientific and Technological Option Assessment (STOA), European Parliament Directorate-General for Research, European Parliament, STOA 116 EN 10-2003.

Koryzis, D., Dalas, A., Spiliotopoulos, D. and Fitsilis, F. (2021) ParlTech: Transformation Framework for the Digital Parliament. *Big Data and Cognitive Computing* 5(1), pp. 15–31.

Kouroubali, A. and Katehakis, D.G. (2019) The New European Interoperability Framework as a Facilitator of Digital Transformation for Citizen Empowerment. *Journal of Biomedical Informatics* 94, p. 103166.

Lawson, G. (1998) *NetState: Creating Electronic Government*. London: Demos.

Leston-Bandeira, C. (2007) The Impact of the Internet on Parliaments: A Legislative Studies Framework. *Parliamentary Affairs* 60(4), pp. 655–674.

Leston-Bandeira, C. (2019) Parliamentary Petitions and Public Engagement: An Empirical Analysis of the Role of E-Petitions. *Policy & Politics* 47(3), pp. 415–436.

Leventis, S., Fitsilis, F. and Anastasiou, V. (2021) Diversification of Legislation Editing Open Software (LEOS) Using Software Agents—Transforming Parliamentary Control of the Hellenic Parliament into Big Open Legal Data. *Big Data and Cognitive Computing* 5(3), p. 45.

Malanga, K.N. (2015) Evaluation of open source software with QualiPSO OMM: a case for Bungeni and AT4AM for all. In *Paper Presented at the Free and Open Source Software Conférence (FOSSC-15) in Muscat*, February 18–19, 2015. Available at: http://41.89.227.156:8080/xmlui/handle/123456789/256 (accessed 27 March 2021).

McAdam, R. and Donaghy, J. (1999) Business Process Re-Engineering in the Public Sector: A Study of Staff Perceptions and Critical Success Factors. *Business Process Management Journal* 5(1), pp. 33–52.

Mohun, J. and Roberts, A. (2020) Cracking the Code: Rulemaking for Humans and Machines. OECD Working Papers on Public Governance, No. 42, OECD Publishing, Paris. Available at: https://doi.org/10.1787/3afe6ba5-en (accessed 21 March 2021).

Montag, C. and Diefenbach, S. (2018) Towards Homo Digitalis: Important Research Issues for Psychology and the Neurosciences at the Dawn of the Internet of Things and the Digital Society. *Sustainability* 10(2), p. 415.

Norris, P. (2001) *Digital Divide: Civic Engagement, Information Poverty, and the Internet Worldwide*. Cambridge: Cambridge University Press.

OASIS (2020) OASIS LegalDocumentML (LegalDocML) TC. Available at: https://www.oasis-open.org/committees/tc_home.php?wg_abbrev=legaldocml (accessed 21 March 2021).

Orlikowski, W. J. and Barley, S. R. (2001). Technology and Institutions: What can Research on Information Technology and Research on Organizations Learn from Each Other? *Management Information Systems Quarterly* 25(2), pp. 145–165.

ParlAmericas (2020) COVID-19 and Parliaments Role During a Pandemic. Available at: http://parlamericas.org/uploads/documents/COVID19_and_Role_of_Parliaments_ENG.pdf (accessed 30 March 2021).

Poblet, M., Casanovas, P. and Rodríguez-Doncel, V. (2019) Multilayered Linked Democracy. In *Linked Democracy* (pp. 51–74). Cham: Springer.

Sartor, G., Palmirani, M., Francesconi, E. and Biasiotti, M.A. (2011) *Legislative XML for the Semantic Web: Principles, Models, Standards for Document Management* (Vol. 4). Dordrecht: Springer Netherlands.

Scherpereel, J.A., Wohlgemuth, J. and Schmelzinger, M. (2017) The Adoption and Use of Twitter as a Representational Tool Among Members of the European Parliament. *European Politics and Society* 18(2), pp. 111–127.

Schlosberg, D., Zavestoski, S. and Shulman, S.W. (2008) Democracy and E-Rulemaking: Web-Based Technologies, Participation, and the Potential for Deliberation. *Journal of Information Technology and Politics* 4(1), pp. 37–55.

Spurk, D. and Straub, C. (2020) Flexible Employment Relationships and Careers in Times of the COVID-19 Pandemic. *Journal of Vocational Behavior* 119, p. 103435.

Stavropoulou, S., Romas, I., Tsekeridou, S., Loutsaris, M.A., Lampoltshammer, T., Thurnay, L., Virkar, S., Schefbeck, G., Kyriakou, N., Lachana, Z. and Alexopoulos, C. (2020) Architecting an innovative big open legal data analytics, search and retrieval platform. In *Proceedings of the 13th International Conference on Theory and Practice of Electronic Governance* (pp. 723–730). NY: ACM.

Strawn, G. (2021) Open Science and the Hype Cycle. *Data Intelligence* 3(1), pp. 88–94.

Thompson, J.D. and Bates, F.L. (1957) Technology, Organization, and Administration. *Administrative Science Quarterly* 2(3), pp. 325–343.

Tsekeris, C. (2019) Surviving and Thriving in the Fourth Industrial Revolution: Digital Skills for Education and Society. *Homo Virtualis* 2(1), pp. 34–42.

US House of Representatives (2018) Technology Timeline. Available at: https://xml.house.gov/resources/TechTimeline.htm (accessed 26 March 2021).

Vedel, T. (2006) The Idea of Electronic Democracy: Origins, Visions and Questions. *Parliamentary Affairs* 59(2), pp. 226–235.

W3C (2019) Main Page. The Standards. Available at: https://www.w3.org/2001/sw/wiki/Main_Page (accessed 25 March 2021).

Wachter, S., Mittelstadt, B. and Russell, C. (2018) Counterfactual Explanations without Opening the Black Box: Automated Decisions and the GDPR. *Harvard Journal of Law and Technology* 31(2), p. 841–887.

Ward, S. and Lusoli, W. (2005) 'From Weird to Wired': MPs, the Internet and Representative Politics in the UK'. *The Journal of Legislative Studies* 11(1), pp. 57–81.

WFD (2021) Pandemic Democracy Tracker. Available at: https://tracker.wfd.org/ (accessed 24 March 2021).

Williamson, A. and Fallon, F. (2011) Transforming the Future Parliament through the Effective use of Digital Media. *Parliamentary Affairs* 64(4), pp. 781–792.

Wresch, W. (1996) *Disconnected: Haves and Have-Nots in the Information Age*. New Brunswick: Rutgers University Press.

8
PARLIAMENTARY ADMINISTRATIONS AND THE PROVISION OF SCIENTIFIC EXPERTISE

Giovanni Rizzoni

8.1 Introduction

None of the main parliamentary functions could properly take place without being supported by adequate knowledge and information resources. This is a prerequisite for all modern parliaments but is particularly relevant today. In a "knowledge society", representative assemblies operate within a kind of "infosphere", which itself has reached an unprecedented degree of complexity (Floridi, 2014). Legislatures have to manage ever increasing information flows deriving from the broadening scope of government and a greater degree of societal interconnectedness (Bradley, 1980, Miller, Pelizzo and Stapenhurst, 2004).

One of the growing functions of parliamentary administrations involves the transformation of information into knowledge, which may then in turn be used for the purposes of political decision-making by the representative assemblies that they serve.

> Borrowing a famous metaphor from Claude Lévi-Strauss, it may be useful to think about information as something "raw", while knowledge has been "cooked". Of course, information is only relatively raw, since the "data" are not "objectively" given at all, but perceived by human minds that are full of assumptions and prejudices. However, knowledge is "cooked" in the sense of being processed. The processes (…) include verification, criticism, measurement, comparison and systematization.
>
> (Burke, 2012, 5)

In the modern information society we live in today, the legitimization of parliamentary decision-making can no longer rely solely upon the validation derived from the popular vote but must also be supported by knowledge. In some jurisdictions, this trend is confirmed by the jurisprudence of the constitutional courts that submit legislative acts to a reasonableness test in order to verify whether or not they are sufficiently based on objective fact and to avoid arbitrariness in their application to citizens (Morrone, 2009, Payandeh, 2011).

A significant flow of information reaches parliaments from other institutions in a way that varies according to the form of government in each country. In parliamentary systems, pursuant to the primacy of the fusion of powers, the primary supplier of information to legislative assemblies is ordinarily the government. The executive informs the Parliament through a number of channels, including via answers to parliamentary questions, reports accompanying draft laws, and different types of documents that the government may be required to forward to the Parliament (e.g. on the implementation of laws). However, to varying degrees, the information thus conveyed to Parliaments constitutes "politically qualified" information in that it is produced in accordance with the first principle governing the parliamentary form of government: the responsibility of the executive towards the Parliament. One of the main ways in which this principle is applied relates to the duty to properly inform the parliament (Teuber, 2006). In presidential systems, the dynamics of information flows to parliaments are different. In these contexts, dominated by the division of powers, parliamentary assemblies tend to acquire the knowledge they need through channels that are independent of the executive. Of these channels, prominence is often given to "independent knowledge agencies" specifically created to serve the legislature, such as, in the US system, the Government Accountability Office (GAO) or the Congressional Budget Office (CBO)

However, in both parliamentary and presidential systems, especially since the second half of the twentieth century, parliaments have developed their own administrative units specialising in producing and digesting knowledge for the benefit of parliamentary bodies (committees, commissions, and political groups) or individual parliamentarians. In a political environment increasingly dominated in the twentieth century by the equation of knowledge with power, the creation of these Parliamentary Research Services (PRSs) was inspired by the need to balance a double information asymmetry.

This double asymmetry comprises, on the one hand, the information differential affecting legislatures and their members vis-à-vis the executives and, on the other hand, the information disadvantage of the parliamentary opposition in relation to the majority. The first type of asymmetry was more pronounced in presidential systems, with the second being more prominent in the parliamentary forms of government. Both, however, converged to consolidate the critical political pressure required for the introduction of PRSs in the parliamentary administrations of several democracies across the world. Regardless of the form of government, the rationale underpinning the creation of such structures seems to be connected to the will to enhance scrutiny of the executive and improve its legitimacy in respect of citizens, and thus, to strengthen Parliament's autonomy and independence.

In this chapter, we will discuss the structure and functions of PRSs. The chapter starts with a brief analysis of the historical evolution of these services. It will then outline the main organizational solutions adopted by parliamentary administrations to carry out these activities. The services delivered by these structures and the different categories of recipients of their work will subsequently be analysed. I shall also consider the transformative factors currently at work, affecting PRSs (digitalization, changes in parliamentary representation, and changes in relations with citizens). Finally, we will draw some conclusions regarding current trends and the foreseeable future for PRSs.

8.2 The Historical Development of PRSs

Looking back on the history of PRSs, it is useful to understand some of the characteristics that still mark the organization and work of these structures. The first administrative units dedicated to meeting the information needs of modern legislative assemblies were parliamentary libraries. Since the nineteenth century, several modern parliaments have built up their own libraries dedicated to parliamentary users. In some cases, libraries were at the core of the administrative apparatus supporting parliaments, together with the reporting service (Venturini, 2019). This almost inextricable relationship between libraries and parliaments reflects some strong features of parliamentarism in the nineteenth century. The liberal culture of the time considered it essential to support parliamentary debate on a solid cultural basis: access to an adequate book collection was then the most secure way of ensuring this outcome. It is also interesting to note that most of the nineteenth-century parliamentary libraries were set up as generalist libraries, ready to receive works on all subjects of human knowledge. This choice reflected the humanist cultural background of much of the nineteenth-century parliamentary class and was consistent with the "encyclopaedic" orientation of modern parliamentarism (Benoit and Rozenberg, 2020, Rizzoni, 2021b). The ultimate outcome of this approach is represented by the Library of Congress, today the most remarkable, universal collection of human cultural products of all kinds. But the examples offered by the libraries of the British House of Commons or of the Italian Chamber of Deputies are no less noteworthy.

Parliamentary libraries soon began to provide MPs with additional services beyond those typical of this kind of institution by, for example, preparing bibliographies on certain topics. Such activities quickly broadened with the growing information needs of parliamentarians, especially since the second half of the twentieth century. This increased demand for information led, in many countries, to the creation of Information and Research Services distinct from parliamentary Libraries. These developments are consistent with the change which occurred with respect to the parliamentary class in the meantime: the type of "amateur politician" of the nineteenth century, who typically maintained a main profession, was replaced by the professional politician, whose working environment in the parliamentary committees was specialized by sector. The introduction of the system of standing committees for the preparation of parliamentary work and the increasing specialization of individual elected representatives reflected two aspects of the same trend. This explains why the first legislative assembly to introduce, as early as the nineteenth century, a system of standing committees specialized by subject, namely the US Congress, was also the first to have a Research Service created separately from the structure of the Congress Library (Cole, 2004). The correlation between research services and standing committees is, moreover, confirmed by the case of the UK House of Commons, which still lacks a system of permanent committees with legislative competence, and in which research and documentation functions are carried out by the Research directorate of the Commons Library.

Administrative structures dedicated to research were introduced in some European parliaments, especially from the second half of the twentieth century onwards, such as in the German Bundestag (1964) and the Italian Chamber of Deputies (1976). The case of the Greek Parliament, whose Research Service is expressly mentioned in the text of the 1975 Constitution, is particularly interesting. The emergence of the parliaments of new democratic countries in Eastern Europe, following the end of the Cold War, has also generally given rise to the establishment of PRSs. In most cases, the model followed was that of the Parliamentary Institute, which we will consider later. Among the newly established PRSs, a special mention should certainly be made of the European Parliamentary Research Service (EPRS): created in 2013 by the European parliament, the EPRS quickly became one of the most important and structured services in this field. Another interesting case is that of the French National Assembly which abolished its research service in 2007, in order to assign research and documentation functions directly to the secretariats of the standing committees.

Some parliaments have created specialized research units to respond to particular aspects of legislative work. For example, some units have been created to analyse the financial costs of the bills under consideration by the Parliament. Normally, these units are part of the parliamentary administration and must be distinguished from another category of agency, the Parliamentary Budget Offices (PBOs) or Fiscal councils that, where instituted, often enjoy a wide margin of autonomy even from parliamentary governing bodies in preparing their independent evaluations (Beetsma et al., 2018). A case partially similar to the PBOs is represented in some jurisdictions by special agencies specialising in the assessment of technological choices faced by parliaments. These structures have varying relationships with parliamentary administrations: sometimes they are mixed, technical-political bodies (e.g. in France), and sometimes they are autonomous agencies composed entirely of experts from outside the Parliament (e.g. in Germany) (Nentwich, 2016). Precisely because of their hybrid nature, these bodies will not be the subject of our analysis focussed on the work of parliamentary administrations.

Another emerging trend is the creation of ad hoc units specialising in the *ex ante* or *ex post* impact assessment of public policies. Sometimes these services are autonomous from PRSs, whereas in some jurisdictions, they are housed within these structures (as is the case with the EPRS).

Today, PRSs represent a very rich and diverse reality, which is constantly evolving. Mutual contacts and exchanges of experience between the structures of different Parliaments are facilitated by the existence of very active and structured international networks, such as the European Centre for Parliamentary Research and Documentation (ECPRD). The ECPRD was first established at the request of the Speakers of European Parliamentary Assemblies in June 1977. Its membership is reserved for Parliaments in which the President is a member of the European Conference of Presidents of Parliament. As stated in its Statute (ECPRD, 2019), the ECPRD promotes cooperation between member chambers through the exchange of information, compilation of documentation and studies, organization of seminars, and sharing of knowledge regarding parliamentary ICT application. Today, the ECPRD constitutes a true "community of knowledge" that connects PRS members of the network on a daily basis. Other regionally based networks exist in Latin America (the Exchange Network of Parliaments of Latin America and the Caribbean – ENPLAC), Nordic countries, Africa, Australasia, the Asia-Pacific, and Arab countries.

International comparisons and cooperation between PRSs are also supported at global level through the work of the Inter-Parliamentary Union (IPU) and the International Federation of Library Associations and Institutions (IFLA). In 2015, IPU and IFLA issued *Guidelines for parliamentary research services* (IPU and IFLA, 2015), a useful overview of the best practices around the world for establishing and developing PRSs.

We now turn to the analysis of some structural characteristics of PRSs.

8.3 The Structure of PRSs

The analysis of the status of PRSs within parliamentary administrations demonstrates a variety of different organizational solutions. As mentioned above, some parliaments inspired by the Westminster tradition follow the example of the UK Parliament, like the libraries of the Canadian and Australian parliaments. In these parliaments, PRS functions are carried out by dedicated internal units set up within the Parliamentary Library. In other parliaments, like the European Parliament and the German Bundestag, PRSs are autonomous structures, although sometimes part of larger administrative units, which also include libraries. In some parliaments,

PRSs enjoy a special autonomous status from the rest of the parliamentary administration, which is also confirmed by the composition of their governing bodies. This is the solution adopted in some Eastern European parliaments, through the Parliamentary Institute model (e.g. Czech Republic and Slovak Republic). This type of organizational choice is usually intended to provide an enhanced guarantee of the PRS's scientific independence (Papazoski, 2013). In some parliaments, there is no dedicated PRS structure. As already mentioned, this is the case of the French National Assembly in which the structures relating to legislative matters, on the one hand, and those dealing with research and studies, on the other hand, have been merged, since 2006, into six large operational areas (legal affairs, cultural and social questions, economic and scientific assessment, public finances, European affairs, international affairs, and defence). These structures, in addition to their principal activities, are responsible for research and expertise functions (EPRS, 2016).

In some bicameral parliaments, a unified structure serves both chambers, as in Canada and Australia with their parliamentary libraries. In other countries, the two chambers have distinct PRSs, even if, in some cases, there is a consolidated tradition of cooperation between the two services, as is the case with the PRS of the Italian Chamber of Deputies and Senate (Giannetti and Lupo, 2021).

The size of PRSs can also vary greatly. The broadest structure is certainly that of the Congressional Research Service (CRS), which currently employs around 400 specialists in a wide range of public policy areas. In other Parliaments, PRSs comprise only a few staff, while in Parliaments such as the Bundestag, the Italian Chamber of Deputies, or the Polish Sejm, the staff complement ranges from 50 to 100. Of course, the different dimensions of these services reflect differences in their functions and purposes: a structure like the CRS to some extent seeks to offer first-hand parliamentary expertise in every field of public policy. Its structure therefore reflects that of the government through a very complex articulation. PRSs like most European ones, which operate within parliamentary forms of government, assume that much of the politically relevant information reaches Parliament through the Government. They then operate in order to provide a "second opinion" on information provided by the government, with the aim of offering briefings on the bills proposed by the government and *ex ante* or *ex post* impact assessments on the policies initiated by the executive branch. These varying functions also influence the composition of staff. In PRSs in presidential systems, specialists are active in the various fields of intervention, while in the PRSs of parliamentary systems, staff with generalist skills, especially in law, social sciences, and economics, are predominant. The EPRS sits in the middle of these extremes: the size of its staff – around 300 people, of whom about half are policy analysts – makes it more aligned with the American CRS.

Of course, each PRS has its own way of finding the right blend between specialist knowledge and generalist expertise in order to best meet parliamentarians' demands.

8.4 The Functions of PRSs

Turning to a more detailed analysis of the functions of PRSs, it should be noted from the outset that their activity is inspired by a set of principles, which are largely common to this type of service. We can identify the following guiding objectives: capacity to provide independent, timely, and authoritative analysis, lack of advocacy, pursuit of "usable knowledge", transparency, and confidentiality. As a rule, the services provided by PRSs are offered to both governing and opposition parties, with the aim "to inform the parliamentary and public debate on issues facing the parliament, not to lead the debate" (IPU and IFLA, 2015). This work is carried out in a neutral, objective, and trustworthy manner and its format is defined in order to provide the MPs and the parliamentary bodies with the information required at each stage of the parliamentary decision-making process. In other words, one of the key missions of PRSs is to counteract the information overflow that affects parliament by selecting the knowledge that can actually be used by parliamentarians.

While these are the common values, the emphasis placed on each component of this constellation differs. For example, for the CRS, confidentiality has traditionally been the guiding principle for briefing its parliamentary clientele, with the publication of non-confidential CRS products only occurring since September 2018 following a long history of challenges to this principle by members of Congress. In other contexts, the opposite rule applies, that is to say, all information and briefing products are systematically published, subject to specific exceptions (e.g. in Italy and United Kingdom). Of course, these different options have a significant impact on the functioning of these structures, as will be seen in more detail below.

The services provided by PRSs also differ with respect to the degree in their complexity. According to the list in the IPU-IFLA Report, these activities include the synthesis and analytical presentation of legislative topics; general and customized products; analysis of a broad range of proposed legislation and policies considered by parliament; expertise in a wider range of public policy fields; support for legislative drafting; and *ex ante* and *ex post* impact assessment.

Beyond these typical functions, in some jurisdictions, PRSs also conduct educational and training activities for the benefit of MPs and staff. This is the case with respect to the Parliamentary Institutes of the Czech Chamber of Deputies and of the National Council of the Slovak Republic (Papazoski, 2013). The CRS is also very active in this field: through the Federal Law Update Series, for example, the Service offers continuing legal education credits to Members and congressional staff. The programme consists of 12 sessions offered over two weeks. Attorneys provide updates on issues of law and policy directly related to the legislative agenda (CRS, 2020).

These activities are indicative of one of the implied functions of PRSs: the preservation of the institutional memory of the parliamentary institution and of the knowledge accumulated by it. This mission is invaluable in an age dominated by the decline of parliamentary seniority and by an accelerated turnover in the composition of parliamentary assemblies.

The users targeted by PRSs may be individual MPs, parliamentary committees, or parliamentary groups. If these are the traditional recipients of PRS products, it should be noted that here too different priorities emerge depending on the context. In some cases, parliamentary committees are the predominant beneficiaries of PRS activity. In other parliaments, individual parliamentarians are the main clients of PRSs. The diverse composition of the clientele targeted by PRSs also influences the modes of the analysis work carried out by these structures. When the main users are individual members, PRS services tend to be offered on a customized supply and demand basis, whereas more general products are normally delivered to parliamentary bodies, like the standing committees, with a proactive role played by the PRS. Of course, in the latter case, it becomes crucial for the PRS to set clear criteria for selecting the topics to be covered by their analysis. In some cases, like in Italy, the coverage is systematic, in the sense that all the bills under consideration by the standing committees are submitted to specific analysis by the Research service.

In addition to the institutional recipients of PRS products, however, other subjects are to be included among the beneficiaries of their work, such as media actors, representatives of established interests, and parliamentary monitoring organizations. Beyond these stakeholders, the public at large too, via parliamentary sites and search engines, increasingly benefits from PRS products. These developments, as we shall see, are of the utmost importance to understanding current trends in the work of PRSs.

The extent to which PRSs are involved with parliamentary decision-making also affects the content of their products. In some cases, PRSs are in direct contact with parliamentary bodies, such as committees, and also support their work through the provision of informal advice, for example, when it comes to drafting legislative proposals and amendments (this is the case for the Italian Parliament). Several PRSs ensure that their officials attend the relevant committee meetings in order to provide "on the spot" expertise to MPs.

In other cases, PRSs produce information and documentation on the subjects dealt with by the Parliament, but with a more "scientific" approach and a less direct link with the parliamentary decision-making process. Of course, the differing attitudes of Parliaments with respect to their roles as "arena parliaments" or as "transformative parliaments" have a significant impact on these different working styles. In the case of the latter, the need for internal expertise to define the content and technicalities of parliamentary decisions is, of course, stronger (Robinson and Miko, 1994).

The role played by other actors in meeting parliamentary demands for information also contributes to defining the fields covered by the PRSs. For example, the presence of parliamentary political groups with their own knowledge processing structures can make a significant contribution to defining the content of parliamentary decisions. The role of lobbies can be equally important.

PRSs must therefore find their niche within a complex cognitive ecosystem in which MPs are exposed to multiple sources of information. One of the main conflicts within this environment comes from the material difference in information MPs receive on the one hand from their own political group or representatives of vested interests, which provide MPs with politically biased knowledge, and on the other, sources like PRSs, which are obliged to adopt a non-partisan and neutral approach. It's up to parliamentarians themselves to identify the most convenient blend between these different sources. Some country reports included in this volume (e.g. Brazil and the United States) indicate that the former group of sources are gaining ground – in terms of audience and capacity to influence parliamentary decision-making – vis-à-vis the services provided by PRSs.

A final consideration regarding PRS functions concerns their "encyclopaedic" mission within the complex cognitive system activated by parliamentary procedures. We already noted how PRSs are given the function of digesting the rich information flow conveyed to parliaments: they operate with the aim of transforming this flow into "usable knowledge" for the benefit of the MPs. In order to discharge this function, most PRSs use complex cognitive grids devoted to the classification and retrieval of the information made available to the Parliament. In doing so, PRSs respond to the need to connect each individual action taken by the parliament to broader areas of intervention evident in one of the major contemporary public policies (such as the fight against climate change, women's empowerment, and digitalization). In some cases, PRSs are responsible for preparing and continuously updating a list of the major legislative topics. The architecture of these platforms can vary, but they share the same objective of offering a cognitive map for the navigation of the immense ocean of information faced by parliamentary business. Figures 8.1 and 8.2 are some of the examples taken from parliamentary websites.

These interesting examples demonstrate how PRSs can contribute to the development of a modern "parliamentary encyclopaedia" as a reference tool aimed at unifying – for

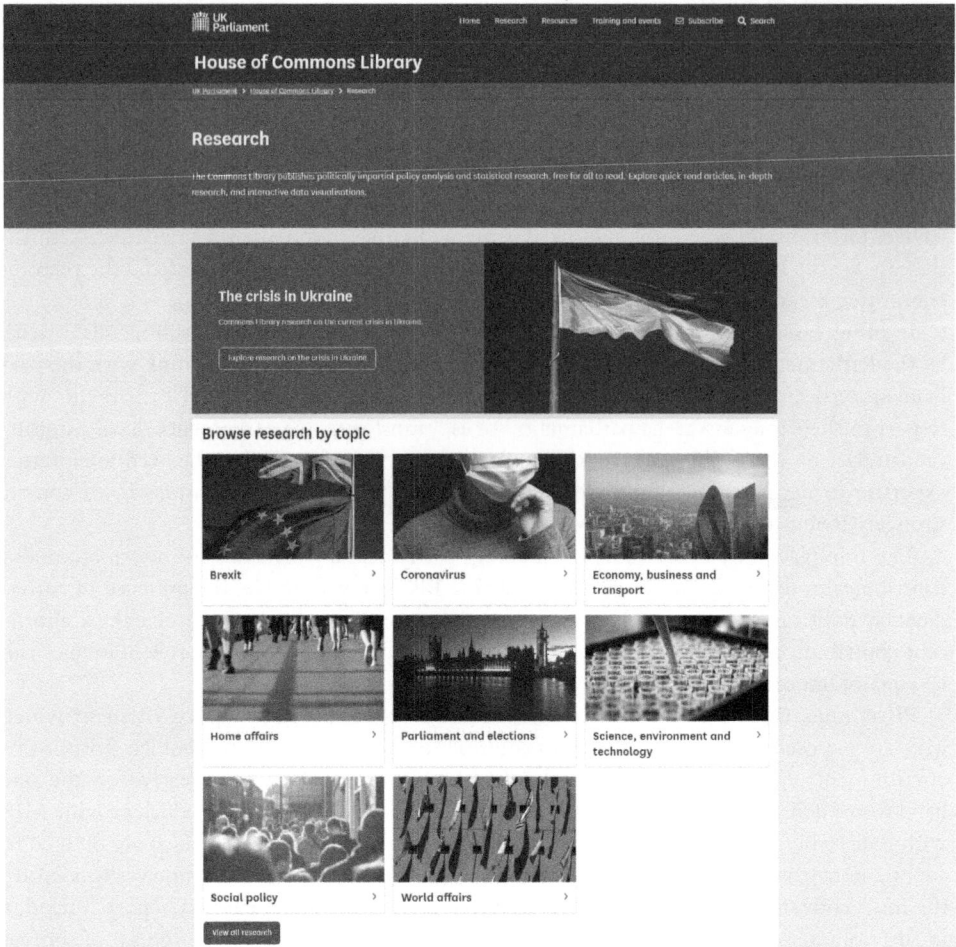

Figure 8.1 Web portal of the House of Commons Library

the benefit of both parliamentarians and citizens – the otherwise highly fragmented and dispersed sphere of contemporary policymaking. This endeavour seems in line with the "encyclopaedic" approach adopted by some great international organizations dealing with public policies. This is the case of the United Nations, whose General Assembly, in 2015, approved, together with the 2030 Agenda for Sustainable Development (Figure 8.3), its broad programme of public policy action, according to which all acceding States commit to 17 objectives, which are in turn divided into 169 sub-targets.

Similar programmes of action have been developed by the European institutions with the launch in 2020 of the Next Generation EU Strategy, which provides the financial framework for the policies to be adopted by Member States in order to overcome the economic crisis caused by the Covid-19 pandemic. The EU Plan sets out a few broad objectives (green transition, digital transition, equity and social and territorial cohesion, and macroeconomic stability) that will be implemented through the Member States' national plans.

It is now worth analysing the most important transformations affecting the operation of PRS and how these services are responding to such pressures.

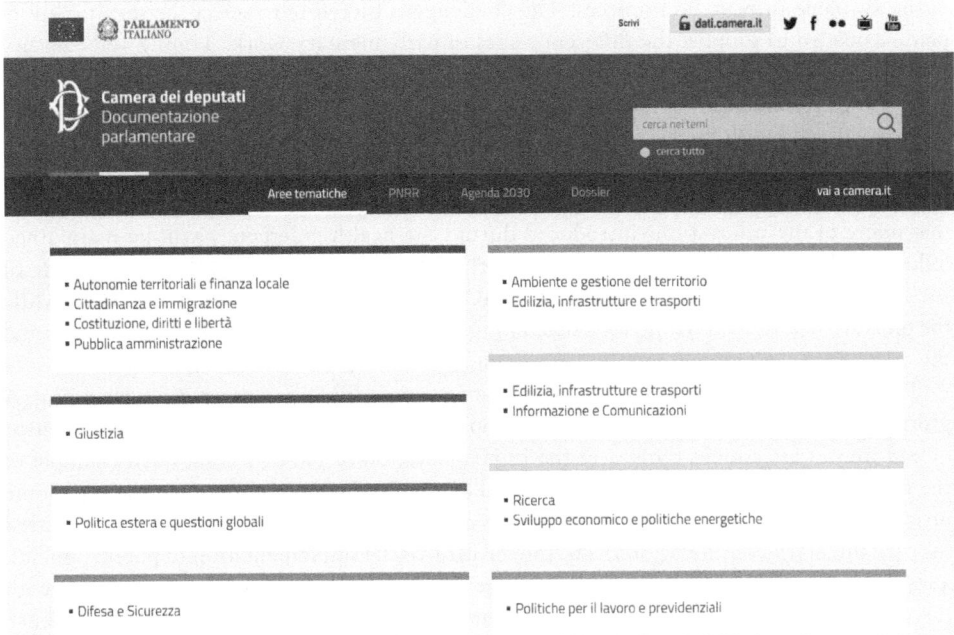

Figure 8.2 Web portal of the Italian Chamber of Deputies research service

8.5 Transformation Factors Affecting PRS Work

Digitization processes are among the most significant factors that are currently transforming the work of PRSs. First of all, of course, the profound changes in the relationship between parliaments and the public sphere brought about by the advent of the internet had considerable consequences on the work of PRSs. Nowadays, they are operating within a vastly more complex and interconnected informative environment than in the past.

Today, parliamentarians can directly encounter a potentially infinite volume of information, thus undermining the traditional intermediary work of PRSs. As a result, the role of these structures is increasingly evolving towards the synthesis, comparison, and verification

Figure 8.3 2030 agenda Sustainable Development Goals
Source: European Commission Website.

of the available information sources. The challenge is therefore to select the specific information needed to support the different stages of parliamentary work. Timing and capacity to synthesise become crucial for this purpose.

The recent pandemic has led to a great acceleration in the digitization of the products and services offered by PRSs. In several parliaments, PRSs have had to learn – practically overnight – to operate in a completely new setting, in which parliamentarians and parliamentary staff were forced to work remotely. From the first surveys conducted on this subject, it appears that many of the innovations introduced during the health emergency will be maintained following the end of the crisis, becoming part of the "new normal" of the everyday life of PRSs. It is, for example, likely that part of PRS staff will continue to work remotely, while the pressure will remain strong for a stricter digital integration between the PRS services and the other documentation activities carried out by parliamentary administrations.

The demands expressed by parliamentarians towards PRSs are also rapidly changing. A growing interest is emerging in securing support for oversight functions and for *ex ante* or *ex post* impact assessment tools over the implementation of public policies. An example of the response to these new demands is offered by gender impact assessment, which in some jurisdictions is produced by PRSs or similar structures with respect to the bills submitted for parliamentary consideration. As to the scrutiny of the implementation of public policies, a significant number of European PRSs are now engaged in assisting their parliaments with the complex translation into concrete measures of the National Recovery and Resilience Plans.

Carrying out such difficult tasks would hardly be possible without developing effective partnerships. Today, cooperation is as crucial as ever for PRSs, primarily with other administrative units of the parliamentary administration (e.g. the Library and other structures specialising in the analysis of specific profiles, like the Budget Services). We have already mentioned the growing role of the networks, like the ECPRD, that connect the PRSs of different parliaments. But partnerships are also crucial with other institutions, such as the national statistical agencies, offices of auditors general, think tanks specialising in public policies, and academia.

As regards the dissemination of their products, most PRSs have followed the recent change of strategy adopted by Parliaments: the "passive" approach consisting of making PRS products publicly available is now accompanied by proactive and interactive communication strategies, with the aim of reaching out to potential users interested in PRS work. This option includes the creation of social media accounts or applications that make it possible for PRSs to provide information to parliamentarians and to other potentially interested subjects according to the interest profiles of individual users. Moreover, in accordance with the practice of other institutions (think tanks, etc.), PRS are increasingly using visual information methods, such as graphics and animations. There is also widespread use of the podcast format, with automatic reading of texts. It has become increasingly crucial for PRS products to be presented in a user-friendly and intuitive manner in order to meet the expectations of parliamentarians and other stakeholders.

These developments have other significant consequences. The range of users of PRSs is expanding considerably, including not only parliamentarians and practitioners (staff of parliamentary groups, journalists, and stakeholders) but also citizens at large. Most members of the public ordinarily access PRS products not via parliamentary sites, but through search engine queries. This phenomenon alters the composition of PRS users and gives rise to strong pressure to ensure that their products are useful not only to specialists but also to a wider audience.

On the other hand, PRSs face some undeniable challenges in their current activity. The most serious concerns seem to be the following:

Polarization of the political debate. Even in consolidated democracies, public debate tends to be characterized by a strong polarization between ideologically conflicting positions, with little or no room left for recourse to "neutral" voices such as those expressed by PRSs. In these contexts, politically biased *doxa* tend to prevail over the *episteme* (Thompson, 2016), with the obvious consequential risk of diminishing the incentives for parliamentarians to rely on the support of "epistemic agencies" like PRSs.

Growing rejection of expertise. The decline in the confidence placed in specialist knowledge is a widespread phenomenon that occurs in most western democracies (Nichols, 2017). The rejection of "expertocracy" can also infiltrate the parliamentary ecosystem, with the consequence of marginalising the role of PRSs.

Time constraints. The dramatic succession of "black swans" (Taleb, 2007) that seem to keep pervading our political communities (economic crisis, environmental disasters, and, last but not least, the catastrophic Covid-19 pandemic) exercises enormous pressure on democracies to deliver rapid and effective action to tackle such disruptive emergencies. One consequence of this trend is an evident shift of power from the Parliaments to the Executives. Another is the dramatic acceleration of the decision-making processes which must very often be concluded without the support of an adequate and complete informative basis. The contribution of "reflexive" structures like PRSs may therefore be sacrificed in the name of urgency.

Highly technical content of political decision-making. Most contemporary public policies (on climate, public health, energy, and digital transition) are centred on choices that can only reasonably be made with the benefit of a highly technical understanding of the components of any alternative option (Holst and Molander, 2017). Very few RDSs, as generalist services, are able to provide the kind of specialist expertise required to evaluate such matters.

These defying (and somewhat contradictory) challenges can be successfully overcome by PRSs only through innovation regarding the methods and contents of their action. In this endeavour, PRSs can help make a crucial contribution to rethinking the traditional parliamentary institutions, supporting their transition from modernity to contemporaneity (Rizzoni, 2021a). Through experimentation with new products and a proper reinterpretation of their role in the new communicative context, PRSs therefore have the potential to become "drivers of innovation in many traditional parliamentary domains, such as openness, transparency and citizen's empowerment" (Fitsilis and Bayiokos, 2017).

8.6 Conclusion

The question regarding the relationship between knowledge and political decision is one of the central problems of modern life. This is particularly the case when scientific knowledge is at stake, as this cognitive sphere is controlled by strict and highly specialized verification rules. More than a century ago, Max Weber (Weber, 2004 [1919]) identified the scientist and the politician as two opposing figures, led by two missions inspired by radically different values and targeting inevitably divergent purposes. Later, Hannah Arendt (Arendt, 2006 [1968]) reiterated the idea of an irremediable opposition between science and politics, giving the former the task of acting as a "constitutional limit" vis-à-vis the destabilising freedom of the latter. She was of the view that such freedom could even come into conflict with the factual data established in the scientific arena.

In contradiction with these theories, modernity has reaffirmed the need for a continuous relationship between science and political decision-making. While in the nineteenth century, humanistic culture served as a common baseline for a political class predominantly composed of "amateur" politicians, this model became obsolete during the following century. Policymaking had to deal directly with increasingly complex problems with highly technical content. In order to tackle these issues, governments have built up huge administrative structures, largely composed of highly specialized experts. The expertise of scientists and academics from outside the administration was equally extensive. The influence of experts on political decision-making has been growing, often blurring the boundaries between the two spheres and pushing both democracies and authoritarian regimes towards becoming more "technocratic" (Esmark, 2017).

The recent pandemic has made the relationship between politics and science even more problematic when decisions, unprecedented in democracy as to citizens' fundamental freedoms, were made on the basis of the scientific evidence available regarding the spread of the epidemic. However, the crisis has also confirmed the difficult nature of this necessary relationship between politics and science (Antonelli, 2020). The emergence of Covid has once again demonstrated that scientific research, by virtue of its very status, is incapable of establishing absolute truths. Rather, the guidance it is able to offer relies upon provisional and continuously reviewed evidence. These limitations are all the more obvious when scientists are asked to make predictions about complex situations subject to a multitude of determinants, such as pandemics (Böcher, 2019). The crisis has revealed that experts are often in conflict with one another and clearly struggle when asked to express an opinion on issues that extend beyond the narrow scope of their specialization (Watt, 2016). On the other hand, the pandemic has also highlighted the absolute need for politicians to refer to scientific evidence in order to secure legitimation for extremely difficult decisions, especially when the public is exposed to the influence of misinformation and "fake news".

Compared to the other powers (executive and judicial), parliaments have to deal with the difficult relationship between politics and knowledge in a very specific way. On the one hand, they are the institutions responsible for representing the conflict and they cannot therefore avoid reflecting, at least to some extent, the disputes which are also affecting the scientific world. On the other hand, one of the historical missions of modern parliamentary assemblies, as places of popular representation, is precisely to democratically control and balance the growing strength of the government's administrative and technical apparatus. In order to carry out this constitutional task, parliaments must also have access to highly qualified expertise capable of providing adequate assessment bases for public policy decisions. It is, however, up to the parliamentary bodies themselves to carry out this assessment, which is an eminently political act as it necessarily involves a balance between conflicting interests and values.

The main function of PRSs is to support this assessment. They are, therefore, not so much called upon to provide scientific expertise themselves, but to act as a *knowledge brokers* for the formulation of political judgement by parliamentary bodies. From this point of view, PRSs perform a "bridging function", as they strive to reduce the gap between the world of specialist academic research and the world of politics (Schick and Hahn, 1994). They are asked to facilitate the critical process of collecting the adequate amount of knowledge to support political decisions. In doing so, they assist the "institutional thinking" (Douglas, 1986) of parliaments, provided that the cognitive basis for parliamentary decision-making is not only fed by knowledge coming from outside the institution, but – in a very special way – *releasing the implied knowledge already present within the institution*. This process is the outcome of a complex relationship between the logic of democratic legitimization and that of the verification of scientific evidence. This interaction normally implies phenomena of the democratization of science and the "scientification" of politics (Krueper, 2016).

Judgements made by parliaments, as political acts, always take place in a confrontational context and necessarily have future action as their horizon. Their content is therefore the result of cognitive, but also imaginative, action. Political representation, as a reflective form, does not pertain to an existential or factual presence to be replicated or mimicked, but a presentation through ideas and communication that the political actors (representatives and represented) create (Urbinati, 2006). PRSs act as facilitators of this crucial process. For this reason, they cannot be viewed as an intellectual luxury, but rather as an institutional necessity belonging to the very core of any effective parliamentary administration, at least those serving a certain type of parliament, that is, parliaments which are reflexive institutions making fundamental choices addressing the future of the democratic communities they represent.

References

Antonelli, F. (2020), *Emerging Aspects in Technocratic Politics at the Time of the SARS COVID19 Crisis*, Rivista trimestrale di Scienza dell'Amministrazione, 2, http://rtsa.eu/RTSA_2_2020_Antonelli.pdf

Arendt, H. (2006) [1968], *Truth and Politics in Between Past and Future*, London, Penguin.

Beetsma, R., Debrun, R., Fang, X. et al. (2018), *Independent Fiscal Councils: Recent Trends and Performance*, Washington, IMF Working Papers. Available at https://www.elibrary.imf.org/view/journals/001/2018/068/001.2018.issue-068-en.xml?Tabs=contentSummary-102775

Benoit, C. and Rozenberg, O. (2020), *Introduction*, in C. Benoitand O. Rozenberg (eds.), *Handbook of Parliamentary Studies. Interdisciplinary Approaches to Legislatures*, Cheltenham, Northampton, Elgar Publishing.

Böcher, M. (2019), *Politikberatung – notwendig, aber auch erfolgreich? Modelle und Kontroversen wissenschaftlicher Politikberatung*. Available at https://www.researchgate.net/publication/333652432_Politikberatung_-_notwendig_aber_auch_erfolgreich_Modelle_und_Kontroversen_wissenschaftlicher_Politikberatung (accessed on 15 April 2021).

Bradley, R.B. (1980), *Motivations In Legislative Information Use*, Legislative Studies Quarterly, V, (3) (August), 393–406.

Burke, P. (2012), *A Social History of Knowledge. From the Encyclopédie to Wikipedia*, Cambridge, Polity Press.

Cole, J.Y. (2004), *The Congressional Research Service*, in J.Y Cole and J. Aikin (eds.), *Encyclopaedia of the Library of the Congress: For Congress, the Nation and the World*, Washington, DC, The Library of the Congress.

CRS – Congressional Research Service (2020), *Annual Report 2019*. https://www.loc.gov/crsinfo/about/crs19_annrpt.pdf

Douglas, M. (1986), *How Institutions Think*, Syracuse, Syracuse university Press.

ECPRD – European Centre for Parliamentary Research and Documentation (2019), *Statutes of the EPRS*. Available at https://ecprd.secure.europarl.europa.eu/ecprd/public/page/about

EPRS – European Parliament Research Service (2016), *Parliamentary Democracy in Action. Knowledge Support Functions: European Parliament, US Congress, German Bundestag, UK House of Commons, Italian Camera dei deputati, French Assemblée Nationale*.

Esmark, A. (2017). *The Technocratic Take-Over of Democracy: Connectivity, Reflexivity and Accountability*. Paper prepared for *ICPP 2017*, Singapore. Retrieved from: https://www.ippapublicpolicy.org/file/paper/594bba371f736.pdf (accessed on 30 May 2020).

Fitsilis, F. and V. Bayiokos (2017), *Implementing Structured Public Access to the Legal Reports on Bills and Law Proposals of the Scientific Service of the Hellenic Parliament*, Knowledge Management for Development Journal, 13 (2), 63–80.

Floridi, L. (2014), *The Fourth Revolution: How the Infosphere is Reshaping Human Reality*, Oxford, Oxford University Press.

Gianniti, L. and Lupo, N. (2023), Italy's Parliamentary Administration, pp. 306–319, in T Christiansen, E Griglio and N Lupo (eds), *Handbook on Parliamentary Administrations*, London, Routledge.

Holst, C. and Molander, A. (2017), *Public Deliberation and the Fact of Expertise: Making Experts Accountable*, Social Epistemology, 31 (3), 235–250.

IPU and IFLA (2015). *Guidelines for Parliamentary Research Services*. [online] Inter-Parliamentary Union (IPU) and the International Federation of Library Associations and Institutions (IFLA). Available at http://www.ipu.org/pdf/publications/research-en.pdf (accessed on 10 July 2017).

Krueper, J. (2016), *Das Wissen des Parlament*, in M. Morlok, U. Schliesky and D. Wiefelspuetz (eds.), *Parlamentsrecht. Praxishandbuch*, Baden, Nomos, pp. 1141 ss.

Miller, R., Pelizzo, R. and Stapenhurst, R. (2004). *Parliamentary Libraries, Institutes and Offices: The Sources of Parliamentary Information*, Washington, DC: World Bank Institute. Available at http://siteresources.worldbank.org/PSGLP/Resources/ParliamentaryLibrariesInstitutesandOffices.pdf (accessed on 11 July 2020).

Morrone, A. (2009), *Constitutional Adjudication and the Principle of Reasonablness*, in G. Bongiovanni, G. Sartor and C. Valentini (eds.), *Reasonableness and Law*, Berlin, Springer, pp. 215–242.

Nentwich, M. (2016), *Parliamentary Technology Assessment Institutions and Practices. A Systematic Comparison of 15 Members of the EPTA Network*, Vienna, Institute of Technology Assessment.

Nichols, T. (2017), *The Death of Expertise. The Campaign Against Established Knowledge and Why It Matters*, Oxford, Oxford University Press.

Papazoski, Z. (2013). *Development of Parliamentary Research Services in Central Europe and the Western Balkans*. [online] Washington, DC: National Democratic Institute for International Affairs. Available at https://www.ndi.org/sites/default/files/developmentof-parliamentary-research-services-CEE.pdf (accessed on 11 July 2017).

Payandeh, M. (2011), *Das Gebot der Folgerichtigkeit – Rationalitaetgewinn oder Irrweg der Grundrechtsdogmatik*, Archiv des oeffentlichen Rechts, 136, 578–625.

Rizzoni, G. (2021a), *Il Parlamento dal moderno al contemporaneo. A proposito dell'Elogio dell'assemblea, tuttavia di Andrea Manzella*, Diritto pubblico, 243–260.

Rizzoni, G. (2021b), *Parliamentarism and Encyclopaedism. How Parliaments Produce and Elaborate Knowledge*, Luiss School of Government Working Papers, 65.

Robinson W.H. and Miko, F. (1994) *Political Development Assistance in Central Europe and the Former Soviet Union: Some Lessons From Experience*, in L.D. Longley (ed.), *Working Papers on Comparative Legislative Studies*, Appleton, Research Committee of Legislative Specialists of IPSA, pp. 409–430.

Schick, R. and Hahn, G. (1994), *The Reference and Research Services of the German Bundestag*, Government Information Quarterly, 12 (2), 141–161.

Taleb N.N. (2007). *The Black Swan: The Impact of the Highly Improbable*, New York, NY, Penguin Random House.

Teuber, C. (2006), *Parlamentarische Informationsrechte. Eine Untersuchung and den Beispielen des Bundestages und des Landtages Nordrhein-Westfalen*, Berlin, Duncker & Humblot.

Thompson, M. (2016), *Enough Said. What is Wrong with the Language of Politics*, London, Badley Head.

Urbinati, N. (2006), *Representative Democracy. Principles and Genealogy*, Chicago and London, The University of Chicago Press.

Venturini, F. (2019), *Libri, lettori e biblioteche a Montecitorio. Storia della Biblioteca della Camera dei deputati*, Milano, Wolters Kluwer, Cedam.

Watt, I., 2016, *Agnotology and Knowledge Management in Parliamentary Research Services and Libraries*, Paper for the ECPRD Seminar 'Innovative Services for Parliamentary Libraries, Research Services and Archives', 9 September 2016, Oslo, Norway. Available at https://www.researchgate.net/profile/Iain_Watt3/publication/308900243_Agnotology_and_knowledge_management_in_parliamentary_research_library_services/links/57f6228a08ae91deaa5e743e/Agnotology-and-knowledge-management-in-parliamentary-research-library-services.pdf?origin=publication_detail

Weber, M. (2004) [1919], *The Vocation Lectures: Science As a Vocation, Politics As a Vocation*, Indianapolis, IN, Hackett Publishing.

PART II

Administrations of National Parliaments

PART II.I

In the EU

9
AUSTRIA'S PARLIAMENTARY ADMINISTRATION

Christoph Konrath, Johannes Pollak and Peter Slominski

9.1 Introduction

Research on the Austrian parliamentary administration is scant and mainly conducted by historians and legal scholars (e.g. Schefbeck 2013a, Posnik 2016). The existing knowledge is largely scattered and descriptive. For the first time, this chapter offers an empirically informed overview of the main features of Austria's parliamentary administration focusing in particular on its legal and political context. After presenting the constitutional and legal framework, it then gives an overview of the size of Austria's parliamentary administration and its evolution over the last decade in terms of budget, staff, the growing focus on expert support and public relations. The chapter draws on a wide range of legal and political documents as well as quantitative data to shed light on the recent developments and main challenges the parliamentary administration faces today. It also draws on five expert interviews with individuals from the parliamentary administration.

9.2 The Federal Legislature: Austria's Bicameral Parliament

The legislative power consists of two parliamentary chambers, the National Council (*Nationalrat*) and the Federal Council (*Bundesrat*). The National Council has 183 members who are directly elected every five years by the Austrian citizens, the electoral threshold being four per cent of the votes. Since the late 1980s, it is common that up to six political parties are represented in the National Council (Konrath 2017). The Federal Council has currently 61 members who are delegated by the respective provincial parliaments. As a result, the Federal Council's political composition changes with every provincial election. Internally, the Federal Council is also organised along party lines and its composition usually mirrors that of the National Council (Steininger 2001).

As an asymmetrical bicameral parliament, federal statutes are mainly adopted by the National Council. The role of the Federal Council is to represent the interests of the provinces (*Länder*) in the legislative process at the federal level. In doing so, the Federal Council has the power to raise a reasoned objection against an enactment by the National Council. However, the National Council can override this suspensive veto by reiterating its previous position. This decision (*Beharrungsbeschluss*) only requires a higher number of representatives present but no greater majority than it has already received in the first enactment (Hausmaninger 2000: 49–53; Grabenwarter 2015: 7).

Since 1945, both parliamentary chambers are served by a joint, deeply integrated parliamentary administration in which the President of the National Council has a dominating role. Historically, the administrations of the two chambers of the Imperial Council, the legislature of Cisleithania or the Western half of the Habsburg Empire, shared only some services. After World War I, in the years 1918–1920, the newly founded Republic of Austria had a unicameral parliament. After the adoption of the 1920 Federal Constitution (*Bundes-Verfassungsgesetz*, B-VG) and the establishment of a bicameral parliament, the National Council was supported by its own administration whereas the Federal Council was administered by the Federal Chancellery until 1934 (Schefbeck 2013a).

The Parliamentary Administration was a rather small organization until the early 1970s. A considerable part of its staff were civil servants who were formally employed by various federal ministries but seconded to work for the parliamentary administration. This development along with the dominant role of the party groups left a lasting imprint on the self-conception of staff members who have considered themselves primarily as neutral facilitators of parliamentary procedures. Therefore, many developments that have been observed in parliamentary administrations in other European countries such as providing expert knowledge for the legislative process have started only in the 1990s or later (Schefbeck 2013a).

It is noteworthy that the joint administration mirrors the organization of the parliamentary party groups. The respective party groups of each chamber form a joint party group for the purpose of public funding and expert support (Pogatschnigg 2006; Group of States against Corruption [GRECO] 2011, 2017). Here again, the support for party group members of the National Council seems to take precedence in practice. There is, however, a significant difference between the support for members of the National Council and those of the Federal Council: Every member of the former can claim expenses for employing parliamentary assistants. In the latter, this right is restricted to the party group chairpersons.

9.3 The Institutional Setting and the Role of the Parliamentary Administration

The Austrian Federal Constitution stipulates a distinction between legislative and executive powers. This distinction has procedural, material, and organizational implications and is of crucial importance for the status and the activities of the parliamentary administration. As a rule, every activity of the parliamentary administration must be assigned either to legislative or executive powers. While "legislative" activities take place in an autonomous sphere (and cannot be legally challenged), "executive" activities are conducted within the framework of general administrative law (Siess-Scherz 2019). Thus, a political and constitutional concept of "parliamentary autonomy" that extends to the parliamentary administration exists in the sphere of "legislative powers" only.

The main institutional features of the parliamentary administration are enshrined in Article 30 of the B-VG. It is complemented by Art. 30b B-VG that establishes an independent disciplinary authority for the civil servants of the parliamentary administration. Additional rules can also be found in the Rules of Procedure of the National Council and the Federal Council. The President of the National Council is the supreme authority of the parliament's administrative affairs. She or he appoints parliamentary employees and has all competences in personnel matters. The President of the National Council is a so-called monocratic organ that has sole decision-making power in all matters of the parliamentary administration's organization. Therefore, the President of the National Council also shapes the administrative support of the Federal Council, including infrastructure, research, and communications. However, the President of the Federal Council has to be involved in matters pertaining to the second chamber's secretariat and office. This underlines that the parliamentary administration is deeply integrated and that all services are available for both chambers thus requiring a high-level of co-operation. The status of the President of the National Council is unique also with regard to the fact that neither the Federal Constitution nor the Rules of Procedure of the National Council (*Geschäftsordnung des Nationalrates*, GOG-NR) foresee a duty of the president to act impartially. It is a common feature of Austrian parliamentarism that the president will act in close collaboration with the government and the majority groups in the National Council. Although there are no formal rules, the president is always nominated by the largest party group.

It is upon the President of the National Council to decide which services of the parliamentary administration shall be directly available to parliamentary bodies, individual members of the parliament (MPs) or parliamentary groups and which can only be requested through him or her. The staff of the parliamentary administration is responsible for the assistance of parliamentary tasks and the conduct of administrative matters of the Austrian Parliament as well as of similar tasks concerning the Austrian Members of the European Parliament (MEPs).

The situation is different, though, when it comes to decision-making in procedural matters and services for core parliamentary work and infrastructure (offices, information and communications technology, security etc.). While the Rules of Procedure of both chambers assign this power to the President of the National Council, she or he usually seeks consensus with all parliamentary groups. This is primarily done in the President's Conference (*Präsidialkonferenz*), a consultative body formed by the President, her or his deputies and the chairpersons of the parliamentary groups. It is complemented by a range of other advisory bodies, for example for information technology, building and security. This approach allows the parliamentary groups to exert considerable power in the day-to-day management of parliamentary affairs (Konrath 2020: 206). The influential role of parliamentary groups is further strengthened by the Rules of Procedure and agenda-setting powers (Konrath 2017) as well as the considerable amount of public subsidies they receive (see Figure 9.1 [Budget]). Thus, the Austrian Parliament belongs to the type of parliament in which parliamentary groups are relatively strong administrative actors (Pegan 2015). This also becomes evident with regard to specialised units of the parliamentary administration and support for committees and the plenary.

9.4 Budgetary and Personnel Resources

The Austrian Parliament has no budget autonomy and the parliamentary budget is part of the federal budget. The President of the National Council can only propose the parliamentary budget plan to the Minister of Finance. However, it is the National Council, which adopts the federal budget, and it has the power to amend certain elements of the draft budget but only on a highly aggregated level. The President of the National Council – in practice in consensus with the parliamentary groups – can then exert considerable powers of budget allocation on the administrative level.

The overall budget of the Austrian Parliament has grown significantly between 2010 and 2020 (see Figure 9.1). Growth is especially strong with regard to communication activities, information and communications technology. Budget debates show that members often

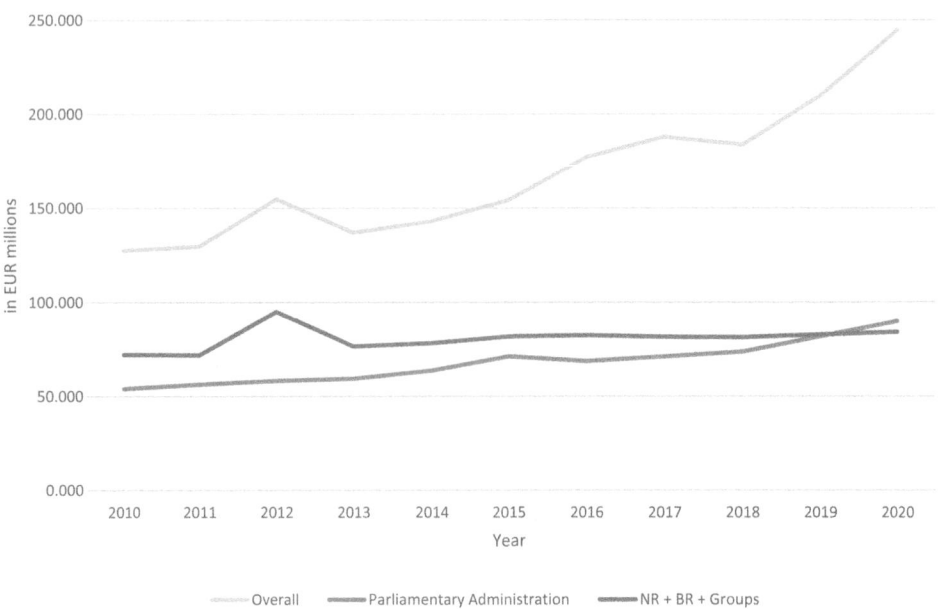

Figure 9.1 Budget development 2010–2020

emphasize services, which they regard as important for the electorate or which coincide with the political objectives of their parliamentary group. By contrast, while MPs also emphasise the will to strengthen specialized organizational units as being an indispensable element of a mature and autonomous parliament (cf. Parlament 2020b), these units show only slow growth and have until recently remained rather small compared to other national parliaments of comparable size such as Ireland, Slovenia, Sweden, or Slovakia (Interview 1).

Between 1970 and the 1990s, the number of personnel remained rather stable (ca. 200 staff) (Schefbeck 2013a). Ever since, it has grown constantly and the period between 2010 and 2020 has witnessed an especially strong rise in staff numbers (see Figure 9.2).[1] In 2020, the

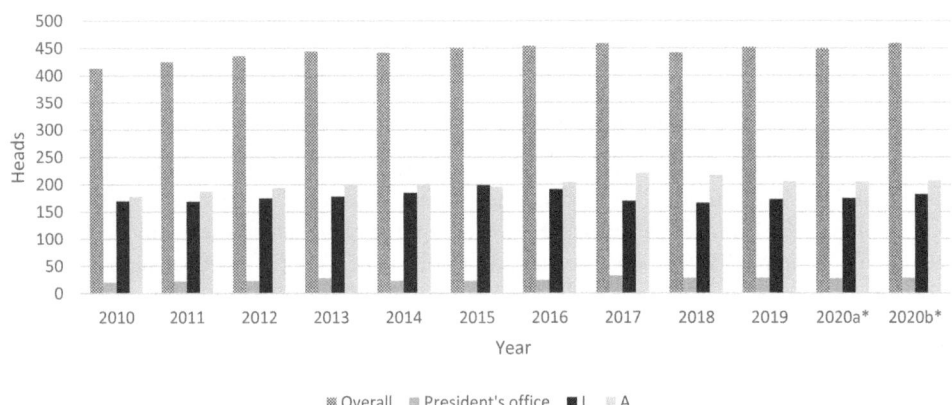

Figure 9.2 Staff 2010–2020

parliamentary administration had a staff of 432 people not counting contractors assisting security and facility services. Unfortunately, it is not possible to compare these numbers with those of the parliamentary groups.[2]

9.5 Selection and Status of Staff

With regard to the appointment of staff, the parliamentary administration follows the established rules and practices for civil servants at the federal level. However, until recently, work in the parliamentary administration was considered highly specialized and focused on parliamentary core activities. Thus, there was almost no cross-mobility between the parliamentary administration and other branches of government or the private sector. Civil servants who were seconded from other government departments remained in parliament. This practice has changed with the growth of the administration and the commitment to further professionalization. In the time between 2010 and 2013, almost a third of middle- and senior-management positions was filled with persons who had not worked in the parliamentary administration (or a president's office) before. This re-orientation becomes visible in staff training programmes, too. New staff has to complete a course programme at the Austrian Federal Academy of Public Administration, internal trainings, and at least two months of internships in other departments or external agencies. Further, the parliamentary administration offers internship programmes for graduates and co-operates with universities and government agencies to ensure educational and professional exchange (Interview 2).

Only senior management positions (Secretary General and deputies, heads of services) are appointed for a renewable five-year term. In light of available data on the federal (ministerial) administration, we assume that this can imply politicization of the senior management as its members have a strong interest in a renewal of their position (cf. Kneucker 2020: 273 ff.). The politicization also correlates with the paradigm of party group consensus and aligns the work of the parliamentary administration with common interests of the President and the party groups. This assessment is supported by the fact that the Parliamentary Budget Office is the only unit within the administration that has been authorized to publish its own views and analysis independently and that a political agreement among all party groups was considered necessary for this step. Yet, we have to take into account that senior management is expected to have good working-relations with all party groups. Given that the number of parliamentary groups has increased since the late 1980s, we reason that this development has had a mediating effect on the politicization of the parliamentary administration. Similarly, the party affiliation of the Presidents of the National Council has varied more often than that of comparable line ministers in the period from 2000 to 2020. As a result, the level of politicization of the parliamentary administration through appointments of (former) political staffers seems to be lower than in the ministries. Between 2010 and 2020, we can identify three (high level) political staffers that became heads of service. However, only one of these assignments was renewed. In addition, six political staffers became heads of departments. One of them had worked in a political group; the others were staffers in the offices of the President of the National Council (Interview 3).

9.6 Internal Organisation and Hierarchies

The internal organization of the parliamentary administration is particularly complex due to its size and the practice of multiple staff assignments. Since 2005, the parliamentary administration has undergone major organizational reforms. Only the chamber services and the

Legal, Legislative and Research Services (LLR) remained largely unaffected as they have to support parliamentary core activities in a stable manner. All other services were re-organized several times and underwent substantial reforms in 2020 with the aim to make it more efficient and service-orientated (Parlament 2020a). However, many institutional issues seem to be unclear. For example, there is an imbalance between management positions and the total size of the administration. It implies that a substantial number of junior and middle management are pre-dominantly involved in day-to-day work (Interview 3).

Since 2020, the Secretary General and two Deputy Secretary Generals act as management board of the parliamentary administration. Each board member supervises two or three of the eight internal services of the parliamentary administration. The first group of services comprises the National Council Service, the Federal Council Service, and the LLR, which are considered to support parliamentary core activities. The second group comprises communications, education programmes and citizen services as well as the library, and support for EU and international affairs. The common focus of this group may not be evident and there seem to be obvious overlaps and intersections with other services. The third group comprises resource management and general services (e.g. human resources, finance and security) and information and communications technology, and infrastructure operations. Each service comprises 4–5 departments, which amounts to a total of 34 departments.

Since 2005, we have also witnessed a significant increase of staff in the President's office. This development corresponds with the growth of ministerial secretariats in the line-ministries and the creation of parallel "political" and a "professional" administration. Given the strong position of the President of the NR vis-à-vis the parliamentary administration, this means that there is a growing demand to co-ordinate administrative decisions with the office of the President (cf. Kneucker 2020: 258 ff.).

Those developments correlate with a growing emphasis on compliance rules, mission statements and internal review of the parliamentary administration (Parlament 2021). However, the parliamentary administration lacks a formal statute or legal basis that would guarantee its independence. It is only through its concrete practices, communication activities and transparency measures that the parliamentary administration can prove its impartiality and equidistance to all parliamentary groups.

9.7 Parliamentary Administration's Support of the Legislative Process

The staff of the parliamentary administration supports the federal legislature primarily in organisational and procedural matters. There are no dedicated committee secretariats. However, committee and plenary work is organized on basis of multiple staff assignments. For long, this meant that more than a third of the administration's staff supported committee and plenary proceedings either as a clerk or by performing ad-hoc functions such as vote counting in addition to their regular duties. This work has decreased over the years due to the expansion and professionalization of activities in other areas of parliamentary activities. However, in 2020, about a quarter of staff is still assigned to committee and plenary tasks. There are two main reasons for multiple staff assignments: The majority of committees of both chambers meet only four times per year and there are rarely more than three (National Council) or two (Federal Council) plenary sitting days per month and two months of parliamentary recess. With the exception of the budget office and the EU Affairs department, the parliamentary administration does not systematically offer policy expertise to the MPs or committees, which is mainly provided by the parliamentary groups. This system of support for committees and plenary traditionally relies upon political group staff who are familiar with parliamentary procedures. While the cooperation between them and the administration works well, this may be difficult to be maintained in case of further party fragmentation or an increase of turnover rates among group staff (Interview 1).

The administration's focus on procedural support has led to a high identification with and knowledge of parliamentary procedures among staff (interview 1). However, it remains open whether this system can be maintained in light of the parliamentary administration's growing workload and demands for professionalization. Nowadays, it is mostly staff of the National Council Service, the Federal Council Service (both are responsible for the administration of parliamentary core activities), and the LLR that support the committee and plenary work, and there is a de-facto committee secretariat for investigation committees of the National Council.

In light of the changes in staff-assignments and procedural assistance, the parliamentary administration aims to digitalize parliamentary processes as far as possible. For example, it has established a reliable electronic workflow for legislation in co-operation with the Federal Chancellery and other ministries (Schefbeck 2013b), a real-time information system documenting all parliamentary procedures, and a document managing systems for parliamentary control activities and EU-documents. The implementation of these measures was also necessary as the parliamentary administration staff does not have centralized office space available and staff offices are dispersed in Vienna's city centre. In turn, the parliamentary administration has been able to uphold full services throughout major building renovation works or the Covid-19 pandemic as staff has accommodated to remote work. However, further ideas such as the digital introduction of written questions and members' bills require amending of the Rules of Procedure and thus the consensus of all parliamentary groups.

9.8 Specialized Units and Expert Support

Specialized units of the parliamentary administration have evolved slowly since the mid-1970s (Schefbeck 2013a). The gradual growth and creation of new units reflects the changes in the size and internal organization of the parliamentary groups and the attempts to increase parliament's institutional autonomy. Only the parliamentary library dates back to 1869 and holds one of Austria's foremost collections of legal and political literature as well as political pamphlets. It offers only library service and does not provide any other form of research or assistance. In 1974, the library was supplemented by a media documentation unit that provides comprehensive media monitoring services (including social media, think tanks. and academic blogs) of all relevant policy fields for MPs and their staff.

The LLR was founded in 1993 and remained a very small unit until 2010. Since then, it has grown slowly but continuously. In 2013, a Parliamentary Budget Office (PBO) was installed as part of the LLR but with a special mandate based on a consensus of the political groups. It includes analysis of all fiscal affairs debated in parliament, review of ex-ante impact assessments of government draft bills and fiscal advice for the National Council. The PBO is the only unit of the parliamentary administration that can be directly approached by a committee or members of the budget committee with research requests. While the PBO is part of the administration and has no formal independence, it has published all briefings and analysis, and has thus secured a reputation in the expert community and the wider public (Interview 1).

Requests for services of the other LLR units can only be made upon approval by the President of the National Council. In most cases, though, it is the President who requests legal opinion which he/she can share with the parliamentary groups or the general public. The same applies to legal drafting. This service is usually provided for all matters pertaining to parliamentary procedures and parliamentary affairs (including constitutional amendments). The LLR cannot represent parliament at court but it will prepare legal briefs and opinions. The same applies to all legal affairs of the administration, including public services law and procurement. Given the changes in the composition and size of the political groups and the growing public interest in parliamentary affairs, the parliamentary administration is confronted with a growing demand for impartial expertise and support. Therefore, the LLR has – like the PBO – defined a number of research products that are prepared in a pro-active manner and are publicly available since 2021 (Interview 1).

The evolution of the LLR mirrors the transformation of political group staff (with growing tendencies towards political co-ordination and communication) and their expectation of services that should be carried out by the parliamentary administration. The same applies to support in EU affairs. This unit was created upon Austria's accession to the EU in 1995 with the view to assist the EU committees of both chambers to identify political and legislative priorities based on the Annual Work Programme of the European Commission and the Council Presidency (Miklin 2015). This mirrors the traditional understanding of EU-affairs as separate from other parliamentary business. However, the PBO's role in EU-related matters is growing in the context of the European Semester and its influence on the day-to-day business of the Budget Committee (Högenauer 2021). The EU-Affairs Unit pre-checks all new draft EU legislative acts and advices the EU committees on possible breaches of the principle of subsidiarity. Upon request, it will also advise political group staff on drafting (reasoned) opinions or other decisions of the EU committees. Moreover, the EU Affairs Unit is managing relations with the European Parliament and other national parliaments in EU-affairs. Together with a department managing inter-parliamentary and bilateral exchange programmes, it organises study visits and staff exchanges to foster inter-parliamentary co-operation. In this context, it offers training programmes in EU affairs for staff and the possibility to take part in inter-parliamentary conferences in Brussels (Interview 4).

9.9 Communicating Parliamentary Activities

A substantial part of staff is engaged in communication and information services. These services have grown significantly since 2010, and they have been twice substantially reorganized in this period. Their growth correlates with general trends in public communications and with a growing public interest in parliament. This period has seen a growing political pluralisation of the National Council, the strengthening of parliamentary minority rights (Konrath 2017), and the re-taking of the parliamentary arena, for example in the wake of the financial crisis and debates on transatlantic free trade agreements (cf. Auel, Eisele and Kinski 2016). Traditionally, the parliamentary administration saw its role in documenting parliamentary procedures in detailed stenographic records of plenary sittings (including interjections and the description of placards and objects brought to the chamber) and in-depth reports of the committee proceedings (which are predominately in-camera). Both practices are kept because of demand from members and the public. They complement the detailed documentation of parliamentary materials on the website (which is maintained by the National Council Service and the Federal Council Service) that makes the Austrian

Parliament the most transparent of all public institutions in Austria. It is noteworthy that the full and structured publication of parliamentary proceedings has been and remains mainly an initiative of administrative staff (cf. Schefbeck 2007). Gradually, the documentary approach has been complemented by proactive communication and public relation activities comprising social media activities, podcasts, and parliamentary TV programmes aligned with otherwise in-camera committee debates and the publications of the LLR. These activities have evolved fairly recently and are still evolving. They are based on a strictly neutral and descriptive and documentary approach refraining from any engagement with party politics. At the same time, the parliamentary administration is gradually changing its communication approach, that is by providing explanations of current parliamentary affairs. In the past, this was the domain of political groups' speakers or public academics (Interview 5).

Considering communication and information services, the parliamentary administration focuses on citizens' services, educational activities and events. The citizens' service handles ca. 8,000 requests per year, including individual complaints or questions about legislative proceedings. It co-operates closely with other units of the administration and reports to the President of the National Council on a monthly basis in order to provide citizen-feedback on parliamentary affairs. On average, 70% of requests dealing with factual information on the political system and legislative activities. More than 25% of them concern expressions of opinions about specific issues, politicians or public institutions (Blümel 2022).

Since political or civic education is not part of the school curricula, the Austrian Parliament has become one of the most prolific providers of political education. Since 2007, the administration organizes the so-called democracy workshop (*Demokratiewerkstatt*) for pupils aged 8–15 years. On average, 9,000 pupils attend the workshops per year and many more use the extensive web resources (Pollak and Slominski 2014).

On average, 90 public events (e.g. book presentations, debates, exhibitions, concerts) are held in parliament per year. Most of them are by invitation of the Presidents but they are organized and curated by the parliamentary administration. Of particular importance is the Austrian parliament's role in the public commemoration of the Holocaust. Since 1998, the administration prepares up to three major commemorative events per year that often are accompanied by exhibitions and publications.

The Austrian political system foresees only a limited number of participatory instruments. In this context, it is the task of the parliamentary administration act as a liaison to citizens, while political parties often refrain from direct involvement with petitioners (Blümel 2021). Uniquely, the parliamentary administration acts as service provider for the federal ministries as the entire public consultation procedure regarding draft bills are published on the parliament's website (Uhlmann and Konrath 2017). Since 2021, statements can also be submitted during the parliamentary proceedings (Rattinger and Wagner 2021: 247 ff). The increased utilisation of this tool has kept significant numbers of staff of the National Council Service and the Citizens Service occupied with processing these interventions (Interview 3). From 2015 to 2020, the Austrian Parliament offered the possibility of crowdsourcing for legislation (Parlament 2018). However, this tool was never used for legislative activities.

9.10 External Relations

The relations between the executive and the parliamentary administration are clearly dominated by the former. The latter is mainly expected to manage the (electronic) workflow of the legislative procedures. Moreover, a lot of working relations are maintained with regard to ICT-matters, professional trainings, security affairs, and administrative innovation programmes. The relationship is different, though, when it comes to expertise in constitutional, fiscal and European affairs, and the development of specialized units of the parliamentary administration. As there is no legal basis to obtain information and knowledge from the government, the parliamentary administration relies completely on the willingness of the executive to share relevant information (cf. Downes et al. 2018: 65). Attempts to strengthen the position of the parliamentary administration, that is by creating a legal basis for the services of the parliamentary administration, have not succeeded so far (Interview 1).

Being a federal state, each Austrian province has its own (unicameral) parliament, the *Landtag*. Relations between the federal parliament and the Landtage are managed by the Federal Council Service. Also, the LLR has close working relations with the administrations of the Landtage and the latter make use of the LLR's research products.

Since 2010, the Presidents of the National Council have intensified their international activities, especially with regard to parliamentary diplomacy and inter-parliamentary cooperation (Heinisch and Konrath 2022). The International Affairs Service of the parliamentary administration supports the President and parliamentary delegations in the preparation of international meetings and participation in international assemblies and organizations. Those activities culminated in the organization of the 5th World Conference of Speakers of Parliaments in 2021. It was the first of its kind to be held in a national parliament. If necessary, staff will also accompany the President or MPs to relevant international events. Since 2020, the International Affairs Service takes a more active role, monitors pertinent international developments and prepares briefings and situation reports for the President and for MPs. In addition, the administration's staff has also increasingly been involved in international activities. The parliamentary administration organizes staff exchange programmes and operates a grant programme for staff of parliamentary administrations of the Western Balkan states. Particular emphasis is put on the engagement of the specialised units of the LLR in international networks like the European Centre for Parliamentary Research and Documentation or the OECD Network of Parliamentary Budget Offices and Independent Fiscal Institutions. In this regard, the LLR runs a newsletter on parliamentary practice and procedure in Europe, organizes expert exchanges on parliaments and data protection regulations in the EU or lends its services to the establishment and peer reviews of PBOs (Interview 1 and 4).

9.11 Conclusions

Both chambers of the Austrian Parliament are served and supported by a joint and deeply integrated administration in which the President of the National Council and the parliamentary groups have long played a dominant role. As a result, the parliamentary administration conceives itself as a neutral facilitator of parliamentary procedures and communicator of parliamentary activities without getting involved in party politics. Since 2010, the budget of the Austrian Parliament has grown significantly which also improved the financial and personnel resources of the administration. Enhanced resources and an increased level of professionalization ensure that the parliamentary administration is able to meet its manifold tasks.

Austria's Parliamentary Administration

Organizational chart of the Austrian Parliamentary Administration

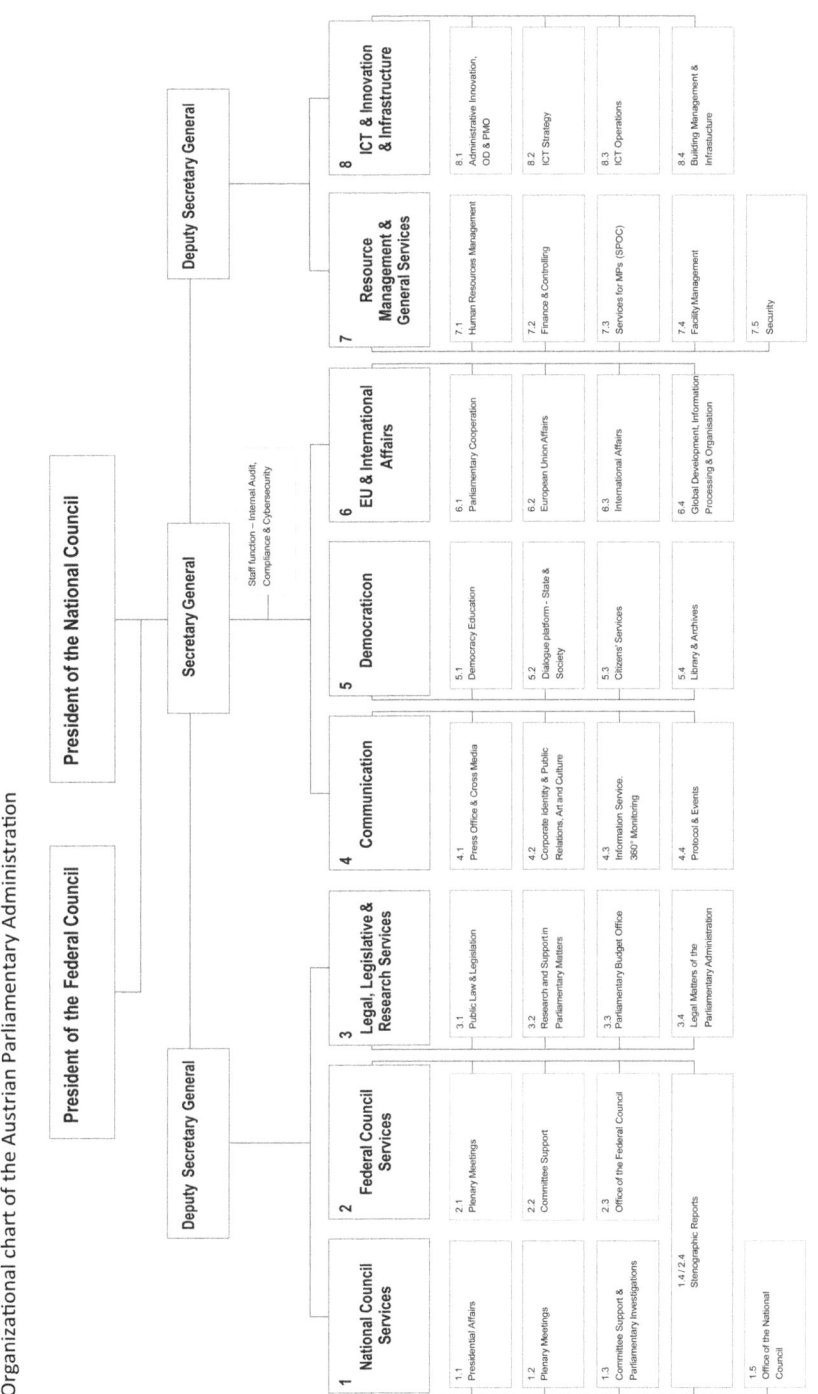

Notes

1 The rise was especially significant in ICT and communications where former free-lancers and contractors transferred to the administration.
2 Only the group of the liberal party Neos discloses data on group staff and finances (https://parlament.neos.eu).

References

Auel, Katrin, Eisele, Olga and Kinski, Lucy (2016): From Constraining to Catalysing Dissensus? The Impact of Political Contestation on Parliamentary Communication in EU Affairs. *Comparative European Politics*, 14 (2), pp. 154–176.
Blümel, Barbara (2021): Anliegen der BürgerInnen. Petitionen und Bürgerinitiativen im Parlament, in Sieglinde Rosenberger and Benedikt Seisl (eds.), *Petitionen in Österreich. AkteurInnen – Prozesse – Funktion,* Wien: Parlamentsdirektion, pp. 74–81.
Blümel, Barbara (2022): Report on Enquiry Service of the Austrian Parliamentary Administration, *International Journal of Parliamentary Studies*, 2 (2), (online first), https://doi.org/10.1163/26668912-bja10042.
Downes, Ronnie, von Trapp, Lisa and Jansen, Juliane (2018): Budgeting in Austria. *OECD Journal on Budgeting* 18 (1), pp. 1–84.
Grabenwarter, Christoph (2015): Constitutional Law, in Christoph Grabenwarter and Martin Schauer (eds.), *Introduction to the Law of Austria*, Alphen aan de Rijn: Wolters Kluwer.
Hausmaninger, Herbert (2000): *The Austrian Legal System*, Wien: Manz.
Heinisch, Reinhard and Christoph Konrath (2023): Bundespräsident, Bundesregierung und Parlament, in Markus Senn, Franz Eder and Markus Kornprobst (eds.), *Handbuch Außenpolitik Österreichs*, Wiesbaden: Springer VS, pp. 51–75.
Högenauer, Anna-Lena (2021): The Mainstreaming of EU Affairs: A Challenge for Parliamentary Administrations. *Journal of Legislative Studies*, (online first), https://doi.org/10.1080/13572334.2021.1965364.
Kneucker, Raoul (2020): *Bürokratische Demokratie, demokratische Bürokratie*, Wien: Böhlau.
Konrath, Christoph (2017): Parlamentarische Opposition in Österreich: Recht und Praxis in Zeiten eines fragmentierten Parteiensystems. *Zeitschrift für Parlamentsfragen*, 48 (3), pp. 557–574.
Konrath, Christoph (2020): Regierung und Parlament: Organisation und Praxis, in: Reinhard Heinisch (ed.), *Kritisches Handbuch der österreichischen Demokratie*, Wien: Böhlau, pp. 203–256.
Miklin, Eric (2015): The Austrian Parliament and EU Affairs: Gradually Living Up to Its Legal Potential, in: Claudia Hefftler et al. (eds.), *The Palgrave Handbook of National Parliaments and the European Union*, Houndsmills: Palgrave Macmillan, pp. 389–405.
Pegan, Andreja (2015): An Analysis of Legislative Assistance in the European Parliament, Doctoral Thesis University of Luxembourg.
Pogatschnigg, Ilse (2006): *Die Klubbildung im österreichischen Parlament*, Frankfurt: Peter Lang.
Pollak, Johannes and Slominski, Peter (2014): The Silence of the Shepherds: How the Austrian Parliament Informs its Citizens on European Issues. *Journal of Legislative Studies*, 20 (1) 2014, pp. 109–124.
Posnik, Rosi (2016): Tätigkeit der Parlamentsverwaltung für BürgerInnen – ein Überblick, *Journal für Rechtspolitik*, 24, pp. 27–31.
Rattinger, Christof and Wagner, Gerlinde (2021): Aktuelle Rechtsfragen zum Gesetzgebungsverfahren und zum Ibiza-Untersuchungsausschuss, in Gerhard Baumgartner (ed.), *Öffentliches Recht Jahrbuch*, Wien: Neuer Wissenschaftlicher Verlag, pp. 246–278.
Schefbeck, Günther (2007): Auf dem Weg zur E-Konsultation? Zur Praxis „deliberativer Politik" in Österreich, in: Alexander Prosser and Peter Parycek (eds.), *Elektronische Demokratie in Österreich*, Wien: Österreichische Computer Gesellschaft.
Schefbeck, Günther (2013a): Parlamentsverwaltung auf dem Weg zur Autonomie, *Mitteilungen des Österreichischen Staatsarchivs* – Sonderband 12.
Schefbeck, Günther (2013b): Law-Making Support through ICT: The Austrian "E-Law" System. *eGov Präsenz* 12 (2), pp. 82–84.
Siess-Scherz, Ingrid (2019): Artikel 30 Bundes-Verfassungsgesetz, in: Georg Lienbacher and Benjamin Kneihs (eds.), *Rill-Schäffer-Kommentar Bundesverfassungsrecht*, Wien: Verlag Österreich.

Steininger, Barbara (2001): Der Bundesrat, in: Wolfgang C. Müller, et al. (eds.), *Die österreichischen Abgeordneten. Individuelle Präferenzen und politisches Verhalten*, Wien: WUV, pp. 421–454.

Uhlmann, Felix and Konrath, Christoph (2017): Participation, in: Ulrich Karpen, and Helen Xanthaki (eds.), *Legislation in Europe. A Comprehensive Guide For Scholars and Practitioners*, Oxford: Hart, pp. 73–95.

Media

Parlament (2018): Präsidiale des Nationalrats gibt grünes Licht für Crowdsourcing-Pilotprojekt. *Parlamentskorrespondenz* 646 – 2018-06-07.

Parlament (2020a): Parlamentsdirektion: Fünf neue Dienstleiterinnen und Dienstleiter eingesetzt. *Parlamentskorrespondenz* 160 – 2020-02-17.

Parlament (2020b): Budgetausschuss startet Detailberatungen über Budget 2021 mit Parlamentsbudget. *Parlamentskorrespondenz* 1153 – 2020-11-09.

Parlament (2021): GRECO-Empfehlung zur Korruptionsprävention: Verhaltensregeln für ParlamentarierInnen veröffentlicht. *Parlamentskorrespondenz* 834 – 2020-07-24.

Reports

Group of States against Corruption (GRECO) (2011): Evaluation Report on Austria – Transparency of Party Funding (Theme II).

Group of States against Corruption (GRECO) (2017): Corruption Prevention in Respect of Members of Parliament, Judges and Prosecutors.

10
BELGIUM'S PARLIAMENTARY ADMINISTRATION

Pieter Dirck G. Caboor and Patricia Popelier

10.1 Introduction

Any discussion of parliamentary administrations in Belgium is inevitably interwoven with the complex state structure in which these administrations are functioning. Linked with the absence of solid scholarship on Belgian parliamentary administrations – as is the case for parliamentary administrations in general – this forces us to make choices.

First, we need to decide which parliament will be the unit of analysis. Article 1 of the Belgian Constitution states that Belgium is a federal State composed of Communities and Regions, which hides a complex and multi-level government architecture that revolves around the antagonism between the major Dutch and French language communities. This is, moreover, in constant motion: next to chocolate, waffles, and beer, Belgium is also known for forever fiddling with its institutional architecture. This way, Belgium transformed from a unitary state into a federation with confederal traits in less than five decades, and a seventh state reform is in the offing. As a result, Belgium has many parliaments. As of 1995, the six Communities and Regions all have their own single-chamber parliaments, and in addition, the assemblies of two smaller Brussels entities have also gained legislative powers. This chapter, however, focuses on the federal parliament. One reason is that it is the oldest parliament, having come into being with the creation of Belgium in 1831. Another reason is that its bicameral composition and the division in language groups reflect the multinational and federal nature of the Belgian state structure.

The bicameral structure brings us to our second choice. The six state reforms so far also included a remodelling of the federal bicameral parliamentary system. Up until 1995, the system was symmetrical, with the House of Representatives[1] and the Senate[2] having the same responsibilities. Ever since, the balance has shifted in favour of the House. It has budgetary power, oversight power, full legislative power, inquiry power, and so on. By contrast, the Belgian Senate is no longer elected directly but composed of members of the Community and Regional parliaments (and a few co-opted members), does not vote on the federal budget, has no oversight responsibilities, and has only a limited legislative power shared with the House. The chapter therefore concentrates on the lower chamber, the House of Representatives, and its administration[3]. Though the administration only serves the House of Representatives, it shows traces of the bicameral nature of the federal parliament. For example, the Library of

Parliament is a common department to the House of Representatives and the Senate. Also, a Parliamentary Committee for Post-Legislative Scrutiny has been established with members of both assemblies and is supported by both the House and Senate administrations.

This leaves us with the last and most difficult choice. The fact that there is hardly any academic research on Belgian parliamentary administrations is both a challenge and a gift. It allows us to set the beacons but at the same time forces us to make choices as to the topics to be discussed. In this chapter, we focus on political-administrative relations. This way, we avoid the pitfall that by describing the supportive role of parliamentary administrations towards the parliament, it is ultimately the parliament instead of its administration that is being discussed.

10.2 Key Aspects of the Organization of the Parliamentary Administration

The House and its administration are Siamese twins: they are separate organizations, but inextricably linked. This results in a multi-layered structure with a political and an administrative component. The political component (the MPs) focuses on policy, that is finding the right solution for social needs. The administrative component focuses on procedure, that is applying the right constitutional process for the selected solutions. Both complement each other, which means that the House administration is not involved at all in policy design. Moreover, the multinational structure of the Belgian society leaves its marks in the organization of both components. This is most visible in the language groups in the House. In the administrative component, it led to the creation of specific departments for simultaneous interpretation of oral discussions and for the translation of reports, questions, and other documents. Interestingly, unlike other federal administrations, there are no hard language quota among staff. Nevertheless, the House administration recruitments focus heavily on bilingualism and guard a balance between Dutch and French native speakers. During their career, staff are offered language courses and are encouraged to perfect their language skills. And the House administration offers translation and interpretation capabilities to facilitate a bilingual operation of the House parliamentary business.

The political component consists of 150 MPs. They are elected in 11 constituencies and adhere to either the French or the Dutch language group. The political groups – up to 10 at the moment of writing – are each headed by a chair. The administrative component has evolved organically from a three-person administration in 1831 to an administration that today counts 580 civil servants divided over a multitude of directorates-general and departments (Röttger *et al.*, 2003).

Under Article 60 of the Constitution, the House of Representatives determines the way in which it exercises its duties. The House administration is therefore independent from the executive administrations and ruled by a specific set of human resources rules adopted by the House. The challenge for the House administration is to deploy the available people and resources flexibly and rationally in order to facilitate (not: direct) the parliamentary process. This is all but stating the obvious: after all, the activities of the House and its administration are subject to "the hurry and strife of politics" (Wilson, 1887, p. 209), the political ups and downs. A week full of committee meetings and plenary sittings can be transformed in the blink of an eye in a week of political crisis and no parliamentary meetings at all. Conversely, a political incident can lead to urgent committee meetings or plenary sittings during the weekend, late at night or on holidays. Urgent procedural briefs might be requested at the eleventh hour, catering might be needed though none was anticipated initially, and so forth.

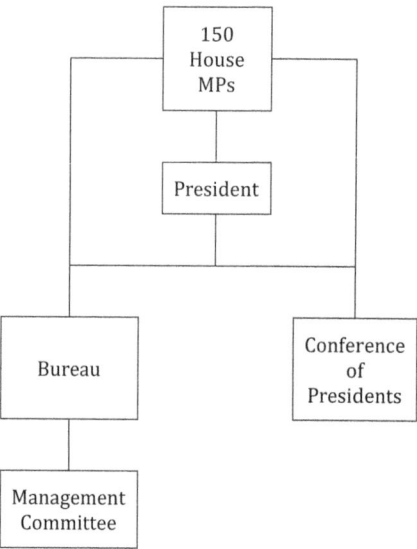

Figure 10.1 Political component of the House of Representatives

The administration facilitates all of these ups and downs. It is therefore crucial that the administration is managed flexibly.

The political component is steered by three formal bodies, all chaired by the President of the House: the Bureau, the Management Committee, and the Conference of Presidents (Figure 10.1).

- The Bureau of the House is a political and more-or-less proportional body comprising the President, the Vice-Presidents, the Bureau members, and the chairmen of the political groups (House Rule 3). It has a general authority regarding the management of the House (House Rule 9). Specifically, it lays down the statutes of the MPs, the staff, and the organs of the House; it appoints and dismisses the members of staff. No expense may be incurred if not authorized by the Bureau. The latter can delegate this competence to the Management Committee or the officials-general.
- Six members of the Bureau, under the direction of the House President, form the Management Committee. That Committee is an integral part of the Bureau; the officials-general of the House assist the Management Committee in fulfilling its tasks. The Management Committee is entrusted with preparing the Bureau's decisions, more particularly with regard to the House's staff, buildings, implements, and expenditure, and with following up the implementation of these decisions. It draws up the draft budget and draft accounts of the House and submits them to the House Accounts Committee.
- The Conference of Presidents is quite akin to the Bureau, but with a different role (House Rules 14–18). Where the Bureau and the Management Committee are tasked with the management of the organization, the Conference of Presidents has a political directing role. It regulates and organizes the political agenda of the House, discusses and proactively settles procedural disagreements, thereby ensuring that the public plenary and committee meetings of the House are devoted as much as possible to substantive debate rather than formal procedural incidents.

Whereas the Bureau and the Management Committee shall decide on staff recruitments, promotions, human resources rules, department mergers, new assignments for departments, and so forth, and the Conference of Presidents' decisions will affect the way that the administration needs to organize or reorganize the parliamentary activities in the short term, the House administration has no voice in these entities other than the presence or the assistance of the officials-general. This clearly demonstrates that the administration is inextricably linked and submissive to the political component.

The administrative component is under the direction of the Secretary General, the lead official of the House administration or staff (House Rules 168 and 169). In that capacity, and "in the name of the Bureau", he has authority over all the administrative departments of the House and their staff. The House administration is governed by the political component but enjoys some degree of operational autonomy under the direction of the Secretary General to execute its mission.

In 2021, the House administration counts 580 officials in 20 departments, ranking under the Secretary General and 3 directorates general (Figure 10.2): the directorate general of the Legislative Departments, responsible for the management of the parliamentary work of the House; the directorate general of Public and International Relations; and the directorate general of the Administrative Departments, which is a collection of departments that support the broader organization of the parliament in terms of human resources, ICT, infrastructure, security, maintenance, and so on. The Secretary General has a proper department – Secretariat General – that supports the day-to-day operations of the Secretary General. The Accounting Department also reports directly to the Secretary General. Next to the Secretary General (or Clerk), two Directors General act as Deputy Secretary General and assists the Secretary General. They are foremost the lead officials for the directorates general of Public and International Relations and of the Legislative Departments. A third Director General is responsible of the Administrative Departments.

The House administration is appointed, promoted, and dismissed by the House Bureau and the Management Committee. Nevertheless, the administration is in no way to be considered a politicized administration. New appointments to the House staff are subject to objective and comparative recruitment exams, promotions have to be thoroughly motivated and might be subject to promotion exams, and dismissals must rely on substantive grounds and be thoroughly motivated. In most cases, the Secretary General's preliminary advice will be followed. Moreover, upon appointment, the administration officials enjoy a permanent position, safeguarding them against the ruptures and fracture lines that elections trigger between the outgoing and the incoming parliament. A new parliament with a new majority will for sure change the House's operational dynamic but will not imperil a House administration official's job. Moreover, under pressure from the Belgian Constitutional Court (No 31/96, 15 May 1996), the House staff nowadays enjoys legal protection against alleged wrongful human resources decisions by the Bureau or the Management Committee. Officials can lodge a request for stay or annulment with the Council of State, Belgium's highest administrative court, as is the case for executive administration officials.

10.3 The Role of the Administration in the Context of Parliamentary Work

It is the administration's task to support the MPs without getting involved in policy-making itself. This strict division between policy-making and administration is reflected in the organization of the administration. For example, the House of Representatives has no

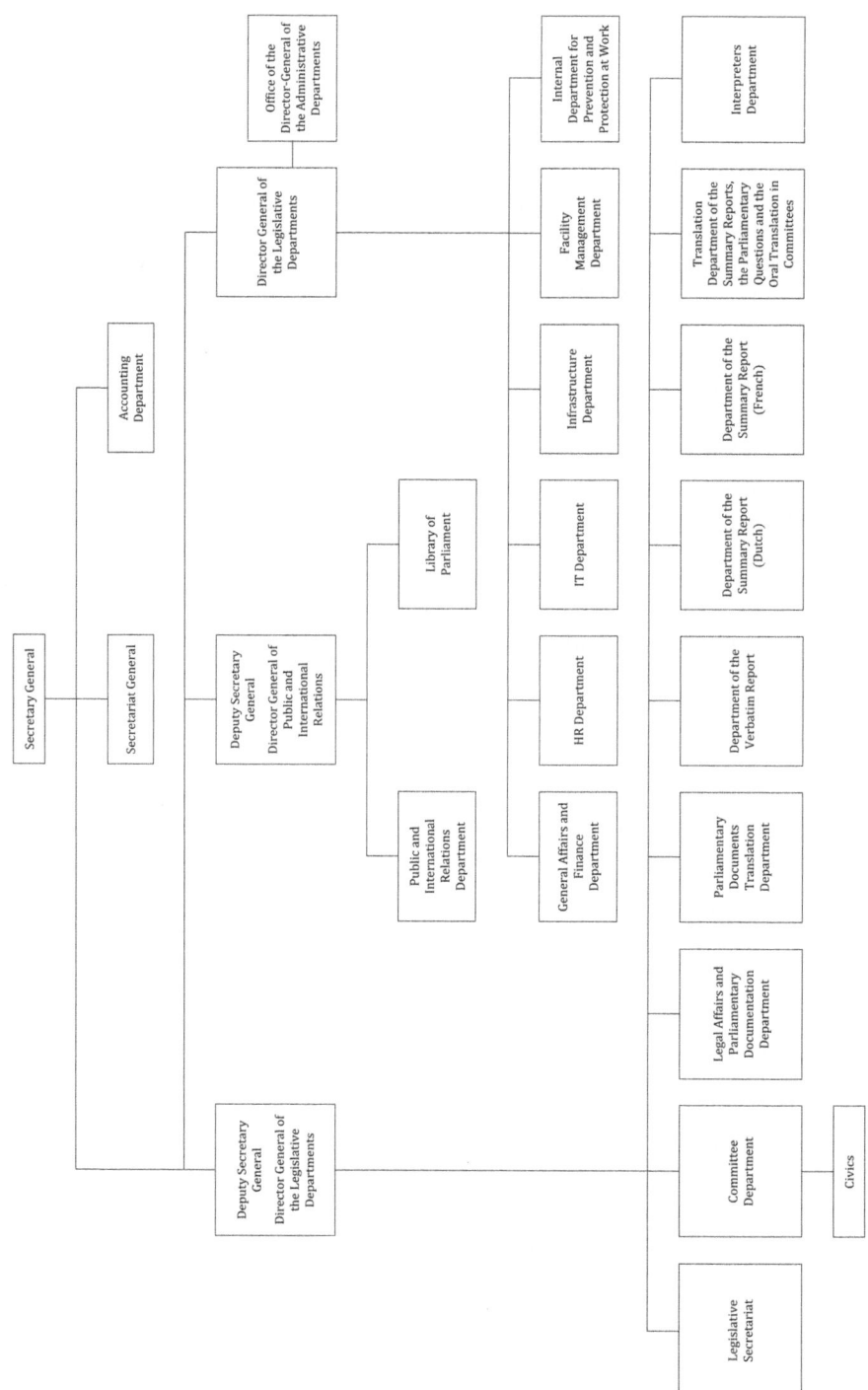

Figure 10.2 Administrative component of the House of Representatives

so-called Research Department that prepares policy briefs or drafts legislative initiatives or legislative amendments. Some of the general research capacity is part of the duties of departments such as the Legal Affairs and Parliamentary Documentation Department or the Library. But in general, policy research is the task of the political assistants. Each House MP can employ a political assistant. They work for and within the political component of the House and focus on policy and, therefore, separately from the House administration staff who focus on procedure.

For this reason, the House administration is not involved in drafting legislative initiatives or amendments on government or private member's bills. Nevertheless, private member's bills are briefly scrutinized before printing, and an advice is issued by the Legislative Secretariat in order to solve procedural issues early on. Moreover, the Committee Department will offer technical-legislative advice on bills that are discussed by the committees. Finally, in a second reading procedure, the Legal Affairs Division will often issue a technical-legislative advice on the text as adopted by the committee in first reading. All of those administrative interventions concern legislative technique and not legislative substance.

The House of Representatives and the Senate have a bicameral Parliamentary Committee for Post-Legislative Scrutiny, composed of 11 House MPs and 11 Senators. This is a parliamentary, political committee. The House and Senate administrations offer support to the Committee and make the first assessments of the cases before it, but the ultimate decision always falls within the jurisdiction of the elected MPs who are member of the Committee. For the sake of completeness, it must be noted that the Committee's bicameral composition is under review since the Sixth State Reform of 2014, that reduced the implication of the Senate in the legislative process. But even before, it never operated smoothly, as can be deduced from the activity reports (https://www.comitewetsevaluatie.be/indexN.html#).

The administration is actively involved as an advisor when it comes to parliamentary practice and procedure. This relies mainly on House Rule 169, where it provides that the Secretary General assists the President in all circumstances, maintains the archives, and keeps up to date the registers and files of matters before the House, as well as the precedents. Many departments execute part of those tasks. The Committee Department supports the committees and their presidents, the Legal Affairs and Parliamentary Documentation Department registers parliamentary precedents and regularly offers advice on issues of parliamentary procedure, the Legislative Secretariat guarantees a smooth process of the plenary sittings, and so on. It must be stressed that the administration has an advisory and reactive responsibility in this field. This task is part of its facilitating mission to ensure that the parliamentary activities proceed without a hitch. Though the officials can rely on their experience to anticipate certain legal questions or operational requests, in most cases, their intervention is expressly requested by the political component via the Secretary General.

All this, however, cannot prevent that at times there is a thin line between politics and administration. This is particularly evident when the administration is called upon for advice to help the Parliament to decide on a politically salient matter. For example, when, in December 2018, the largest Flemish political party withdrew from the government coalition, turning the latter into a minority government, a burning political issue that divided constitutional scholars revolved around the question whether this should be considered a new government that had to ask the House for a new vote of confidence. This was answered positively in a note from the Legal Affairs and Parliamentary Documentation Department. That legal opinion was used, quoted, rejected by some, and praised by others during the ensuing plenary debate (House plenary sitting, 12 December 2018, CRIV 54 PLEN 0260). A week later, the government resigned.

10.4 Managing Inter-Institutional and External Relations

The supportive role of the administration is also reflected in the House's external relations. Staff officials are involved in the organization, preparation, and secretariat of numerous parliamentary diplomatic events in parliament's premises in Brussels and abroad.

The House administration is also involved in the administration of the Benelux Parliament. Moreover, members of the House administration interact in their own capacity with their homologues from others parliaments. They act as secretary or support staff of the Belgian Inter-Parliamentary Union (IPU) Group, as IPU Parline Correspondent or IPU Parline Focal Point for Europe, as Correspondent and Deputy Correspondent of the European Center for Parliamentary Research and Documentation, and as secretaries of House delegations to numerous international organizations.

Belgium being a Member State of the European Union, there are specific venues and instruments within the House to deal with EU affairs. There is a (Federal) Advisory Committee for European Questions, supported by House staff. The House is also involved in the Early Warning Mechanism. According to House Rule 35*bis*, paragraph 2, draft legislative acts of the European Union sent to the House of Representatives are forwarded to the standing committee concerned in order to be examined in the light of the principles of subsidiarity and proportionality. Under House Rule 37*bis*, opinions, dealing inter alia with compliance with the principles of subsidiarity and proportionality, can be issued by the relevant standing committees on the European Commission's legislative proposals and other texts of the European institutions. Unless a third of the Members of the committee asks that the opinion be put on the agenda of the plenary sitting, this opinion is sent forthwith to the relevant European institutions. The preparation of these opinions can be carried out in two ways. The relevant standing committee can instruct the committee's Europromotor (an MP appointed as such by and among committee members) to formulate a draft opinion. More often, the House's administration, and more particularly, the EU-Desk within the Committee Department, examines European Commission's legislative proposals and other texts of the European institutions. This gives the administration a gatekeeping role, which it takes up under pressure of the large quantity of EU documents. Less than 15 per cent of the documents received from the EU institutions are transmitted by the secretariat to the MPs (Delreux and Randour, 2015, p. 159). The EU-Desk drafts, on its own initiative, at the request of the chairman or of a third of the Members of a standing committee or at the request of the President of the House, a note dealing inter alia with compliance with the principles of subsidiarity and proportionality. These notes are sent to the Members of the relevant standing committee and to the Members of the Advisory Committee for European Questions. All this ensures that the House has by far the highest activity rate with regards to subsidiarity-scrutiny compared to other legislative assemblies in Belgium, which are less well organized to deal with EU affairs. Also, the prominence of legal reasoning in the House's opinions reveals the input of the administration in the drafting stage (Vandenbruwaene and Popelier, 2017, p. 195).

Even though Belgium has numerous parliaments, they all operate independently and autonomously. So do their administrations. Of course, there is some degree of interaction and cooperation. Formally, the assemblies' presidents and secretaries general regularly meet to discuss issues of common interest. Informally, administration officials often know and consult their counterparts in other parliaments.

Obviously, the House of Representatives has a privileged relationship with the Senate. Together they form the federal parliament, and therefore, some constitutional and legislative procedures are interconnected. They also share a building but have distinct administrations. This is not surprising, because the interests of both assemblies can conflict. Nevertheless, over the last few years, efforts are being made to join forces as much as possible. Harmonized human resources rules have been issued and will be gradually implemented; there is a joint security detail, a joint catering operation, etc. The presidents of both assemblies have expressed their intention to explore further collaboration on whatever field that is suitable to it.

10.5 Managing Current Challenges

As in most other democracies (Holmberg *et al.*, 2017), the Belgian Parliament is trusted by less than half of the population. According to the Eurobarometer's last survey before the corona crisis (November 2019), 41% of the Belgian citizens trust the national parliament. This must be put in perspective: a low level of trust can be a sign of critical citizenship (Norris, 1999), the percentage is higher than the EU27 average, and citizens put even less trust in the national government (35%) and the political parties (21%). It is nevertheless a disturbing finding that forces Parliament to be responsive.

Communication with the public is therefore among the most urgent challenges for the House of Representatives. However, it has been observed that "increased levels of parliament accessibility, transparency, visibility and communication have not coincided with increasing levels of trust" (Leston-Bandeira, 2012, p. 521). This is also evident from the Belgian experience, given the frequent efforts to communicate with the public. The administration hosts numerous visits from citizens, schools, associations, and journalists. Professional guides show visitors around in the parliament's premises and make the political activities alive for young and old. Journalists are recurring visitors and bring the parliamentary activities to the citizens through broadcasting, paper press, and more and more through digital media. House officials are available to make all visitors and journalists feel at home, while at the same time safeguarding a smooth parliamentary debate and process. The House and its administration are increasingly active on social media and are transitioning towards a modern digital organization. A new website is being developed as we write this chapter in the summer of 2021. Moreover, new participatory instruments are being explored and developed. Recently, a new website to address petitions to the House was launched, pursuant to the Federal Legislative Act of 2 May 2019, that allows citizens under certain conditions to be officially invited by the House for a hearing on the topic of their petition. In the end, trust in Parliament depends on several factors on which the Parliament alone cannot easily impact, such as personality traits of the trustor, and contextual factors such as the level of corruption and government performance (for an overview: Popelier, 2020). It is nevertheless held that Parliament should still invest in engaging with the public, to maintain the trust of those who already trust the Parliament (Leston-Bandeira, 2012, p. 524; Dunn, 2015).

Like other parliaments world-wide, the House of Representatives faced another challenge when the Covid-19 virus hit Belgium in March 2020. The social distance measures that were adopted to contain the virus spread are difficult to reconcile with the very nature of legislative assemblies, which is to assemble together to discuss political issues, and with the mandatory quorum rules that often apply (Bar-Siman-Tov, 2020, pp. 14–15). A study covering 159 countries showed that parliamentary activity during the crisis was not so much linked with mortality rates and thus the gravity of the situation, but with the state of democracy (Waismel-Manor et al., 2020, p. 11). In Belgium, the House of Representatives continued to function as usual (Elst and Caboor, 2020), after some amendments to the Rules of Procedure and with the help of technological solutions such as an eVoting application (Caboor et al., 2020, p. 125), and even managed to adopt urgent legislation despite the Covid-19 restrictions (Mussely and Caboor, 2021, pp. 31–36). Both the House Rules amendments and the technological solutions were actively and urgently prepared, developed, and implemented by the House administration, even though staff, like everyone else, suddenly had to work from home. This, however, was not sufficient to retain the citizens' trust. According to the Eurobarometer of July 2020, citizens' trust in the national parliament dropped to 33%, close to trust in the national government (33%) and lower than the EU27 average (36%). Criticism of the Parliament's failure to provide a solid and well-considered legal basis for government action had not yet fully erupted at that time, which shows once more that it is not entirely in the hands of the parliament itself to win the public's trust. In particular, trust in Parliament remains closely linked to trust in the government. The forming of a new government in October 2020 did, according to the last Eurobarometer (Winter-Spring 2020–2021) not only result in a rise of citizen's trust in government (41%) but also in parliament (44%).

In order to transform the House of Representatives from an old stately lady to a trendy one that keeps the pulse of society, both the political and the administrative component of the House will need to contribute to the effort. The House administration has therefore initiated a major modernization effort to align it to the standards of the 21st century and to be ready to cooperate with the MPs to bring the House closer to the citizens. To achieve that goal, the administration has started from within its own structure and has clearly defined its mission, its values, and its ambitious vision. The mission has been defined throughout the preceding text: the House administration provides quality expertise and support to the House and the MPs. The core value that translates best the political-administrative relations discussed in this chapter is flexibility: to be ready and available whenever parliamentary democracy requires it. The vision for the next five to ten years is centred around six pillars. The House administration aims to (1) professionalize its processes and procedures, (2) be flexible while offering a modern work-life balance, (3) implement a solid internal communication overhaul and (4) invest in modern and interactive communication with the citizens, (5) orient its investments towards durability, and (6) develop that vision in close partnership with the political component. This will result in strategic and operational goals, such as a project-based decision-making process, internal and external communication plans, innovative evaluation and reward programs, and so forth. The main achievement is that the administration finally has taken the time to reflect about its proper functioning in a structured way, to identify the internal and external challenges ahead (e.g. technology, work from home facilities, balancing work-life, better education) and to define its future goals as an organization, while at the same time assuring the current supportive services towards the MPs. This forward-looking effort has been initiated in collaboration and with the participation of the administration staff and departments. At the moment of writing, strategic and operational goals are being defined so that a next chapter on the

Belgian House of Representatives, five to ten years from now, can present a state of the art 21st century parliamentary administration.

10.6 Conclusion

This chapter highlighted the administration's supportive role in political-administrative relations. For the Belgian House of Representatives, this results in a multi-layered organization, with an administration that serves parliamentary democracy, is subject to the opinion of 150 masters and is governed by the political component of the House. In and of itself, this is a challenge for the House administration. But thanks to the current modernization effort, the administration will be refurbished and prepared for the next few decades. Doing so, it will be ready to deploy the available people and resources flexibly and rationally in order to facilitate the parliamentary process and steadfastly face Wilson's "hurry and strife of politics".

Notes

1 The House of Representatives, often abbreviated as "House", is the lower chamber of the Belgian federal Parliament. Original nomenclature: Chambre des représentants (in French), Kamer van volksvertegenwoordigers (in Dutch), Abgeordnetenkammer (in German).
2 The Senate is the upper chamber of the Belgian federal Parliament. Original nomenclature: Sénat (in French), Senaat (in Dutch), Senat (in German).
3 The House administration is commonly referred to as "les services de la Chambre" (in French), "de diensten van de Kamer" (in Dutch).

References

Bar-Siman-Tov, I. (2020) 'Covid-19 meets politics: the novel coronavirus as a novel challenge for legislatures', *The Theory and Practice of Legislation*, 8(1–2), p11–48.
Caboor, P., Van Koekenbeek, S. and Mussely, H. (2020) 'De wetgevingsprocedure in tijden van social distancing: een overzicht van enkele parlementaire reglementswijzigingen' *Tijdschrift voor Wetgeving*, 23(2), p124–127.
Delreux, T. and Randour, F. (2015) 'Belgium: Institutional and Administrative Adaptation but Limited Political Interest' in Hefftler, C., *et al.* (eds.) *The Palgrave Handbook of National Parliaments and the European Union*. London: Palgrave MacMillan, p153–169.
Dunn, K. (2015) 'Voice, representation and trust in parliament', *Acta Politica*, 50(2), p171–219.
Elst, M. and Caboor, P. (2020) 'Wetgevingsprocedure aangetast door corona of immuniteit opgebouwd?' *Tijdschrift voor Wetgeving*, 23(4), p320–330.
Holmberg, S., Lindberg, S. and Svensson, R. (2017) 'Trust in parliament', *Journal of Public Affairs*, 17, p1–9.
Leston-Bandeira, C. (2012) 'Conclusion: 'Parliaments' endless pursuit of trust; refocusing on symbolic representation' *The Journal of Legislative Studies*, 18(3–4), p514–526.
Mussely, H. and Caboor, P. (2021) 'Spoedwetgeving tijdens de COVID-19-pandemie' *Tijdschrift voor Wetgeving* 24(1), p31–36.
Norris, P. (ed.) (1999) *Critical citizens: Global Support for Democratic Government*. Oxford: Oxford University Press.
Popelier, P. (2020) 'The Duty of Parliament to Adopt Reliable Legislation: Linking Trust in Parliament with Legitimate Expectations' in De Benedetto *et al.* (eds) *The Crisis of Confidence in Legislation*, Oxford: Hart, p243–257.

Röttger, R., Van der Hulst, M. and Van der Jeught, S. (2003) 'L'organisation interne de la Chambre des représentants', in Gerard, E. *et al.* (eds) *Histoire de la Chambre des Représentants de Belgique 1830-2002*, Brussels: Belgian House of Representatives, 2003, p179–216.

Vandenbruwaene, W. and Popelier, P. (2017) 'Belgian Parliaments and the Early Warning System', in Jonsson Cornell, A. and Goldoni, M. (eds.) *National and Regional Parliaments in the EU Legislative Procedure Post-Lisbon: The Impact of the Early Warning Mechanism*, Oxford: Hart 2017, p181–198.

Waismel-Manor, I. *et al.* (2020) 'Covid-19 and Legislative Activity: A Cross-National Study' [online]. Available at file:///C:/Users/ppopelier/Downloads/Covid-19Legislatures-26-6-20-FW1.pdf (Accessed: 8 August 2021).

Wilson, W. (1887) 'The study of administration' *Political Science Quarterly*, 2(2), p197–222.

11
BULGARIA'S PARLIAMENTARY ADMINISTRATION

Martin Belov

11.1 Key Aspects of the Organization of the Parliamentary Administration

There are four layers of stakeholders in the Bulgarian Parliament (the National Assembly). These are the politicians (the MPs), the governing administrative personnel (e.g. the secretary general), the experts and the administrative staff. Only the first layer has explicit constitutional standing being provided by the Bulgarian Constitution of 1991. The other three layers are regulated by the legislation and especially by the Regulation for the Organization and the Activity of the National Assembly. The first layer is *per se* political one. The second level is *de facto* based on party politics. Political influence is rather visible also in the third layer. Thus, only the administrative staff is to an extent shielded from direct party political influence.

The structure of the Parliament is provided by the 1991 Constitution and the Regulation for the Organization and the Activity of the National Assembly. The Constitution contains detailed provisions for the competences of the Chairman/Chairwoman of the National Assembly and for the standing and competences of the MPs. The parliamentary groups and the parliamentary committees are briefly and incompletely institutionally shaped by the Constitution. However, they are extensively regulated in the Regulation for the Organization and the Activity of the National Assembly. Horizontally, the National Assembly is structured in plenary, parliamentary committees, parliamentary groups and parliamentary delegations. Vertically, the Parliament is structured in Chairman/Chairwoman of the National Assembly, Chairman's Council and plenary.

The organization, structure and functioning of public administration in Bulgaria is regulated by the Administration Act. Its provisions apply also for the parliamentary administration. The Parliament has the discretion to further develop its administrative structure in its Regulations for the Organization and the Activity of the National Assembly. The question whether the provisions of this Regulation can deviate from the Administration Act has neither been theoretically clarified, nor has been raised in the practice. Nevertheless, there is a potential for possible collisions because according to Decision № 7 of 2010 of the Constitutional Court, the Regulations for the Organization and the Activity of the National Assembly has the hierarchical standing of an act of Parliament, so it is formally coequal to the Administration Act. However, such collision may be relatively easily solved since both the Administration Act and the Regulations for the Organization and the Activity of the National Assembly are adopted by the Parliament.

DOI: 10.4324/9781003181521-14

According to article 4 of the Administration Act, the administration is organized in directorates. Departments may be attached to the directorates, while sectors may be attached to the departments.

Following the above-mentioned legislative provisions administration of the Parliament is structured in general administration, specialized administration, administrative bodies responsible directly to the Chairman or the Chairwoman of the National Assembly and other administrative units which are secondary spenders of budgetary subsidies. The general and specialized administration forms the main part of the parliamentary administration. It consists of directorates, departments and sectors.

The National Assembly elects on proposal of the parliamentary groups some of the MPs as secretaries of the Parliament. These secretaries are not part of the parliamentary administration *per se* because they remain MPs but they accomplish some administrative functions. They support the Chairman or Chairwoman of the National Assembly for the counting of the quorum, the accomplishment of voting via the electronic voting system, the prevention of voting with electronic cards of other MPs, the counting of votes and the announcement of the result of open voting. Moreover, they aid the accomplishment of the secret voting, read the names of the MPs in case of voting name by name, sign and certify stenographic protocols and accomplish other tasks that have been assigned to them by the Chairman or Chairwoman of the National Assembly.

The general administration includes seven directorates, one separate department and one separate sector both of which are not directly attached to a directorate. The department that is not attached to a directorate is the 'Parliamentary Library' department. The sector which is not attached to a directorate is the sector 'Quaestors'.

The directorates are 'Parliamentary Chancellery', 'Parliamentary Budget and Finance', 'Legal Activities and Public Procurement', 'Human Resources', 'Information and Communication Systems', 'Property Management' and 'Car Park Service and Garage'. Three of the directorates contain departments. 'Parliamentary Chancellery' Directorate includes 'Administrative Service' Department and 'Registry and Reception' Department. 'Parliamentary Budget and Finance' Directorate includes 'Budget', 'Salaries', 'Payments' and 'Material Equipment' Departments. 'Legal Activities and Public Procurement' Directorate is divided into two departments – 'Legal Activities' Department and 'Public Procurement' Department.

The directorates are administrative units which functions are not directly related to the core activity of the Parliament. For example, the 'Legal Activities and Public Procurement' directorate does not tackle the acts of Parliament. It is not involved in the drafting or preparation of any legislative or other legal acts of the National Assembly. The same is true for the 'Parliamentary Budget and Finance' directorate which is not involved in the parliamentary budgetary process but just administers the implementation of the budget of the National Assembly. Furthermore, 'Human Resources' have no influence on the standing of the MPs (apart from maintaining their labour files) and 'Information and Communication Systems' assures the proper technical functioning of these systems while not otherwise impacting of the information, communication and deliberation processes in the Parliament. It is also visible that the structure of the general administration includes directorates with more substantial role (e.g. 'Parliamentary Chancellery', 'Parliamentary Budget and Finance', 'Legal Activities and Public Procurement' and 'Human Resources') and directorates with purely technical tasks (e.g. 'Information and Communication Systems', 'Property Management' and 'Car Park Service and Garage').

The quaestors are administrative officials of the Parliament. They are appointed and removed by the Chairman or the Chairwoman of the National Assembly. The quaestors are instrument for maintenance of the order in the buildings of the Parliament at full disposal of the Chairman or the Chairwoman of the National Assembly. They must respect and apply his/hers orders related to the maintenance of the order in the plenary hall of the National Assembly and at its balconies. The quaestors aid the secretaries of the Parliament when counting the votes in open voting as well as for the preparation and accomplishment of secret voting or voting via the electronic voting system. The quaestors help the secretaries of the National Assembly for prevention of voting with the electronic card of other MPs. They safeguard that only the MPs, the ministers or other officially allowed persons (e.g. accredited journalists, participants in parliamentary internships) are present in the premises of the National Assembly. The quaestors are allowed to remove from the parliamentary session persons (including MPs) who are disturbing the parliamentary order. This can be done only after an order of the Chairman or the Chairwoman of the National Assembly.

The library of the National Parliament is in possession of approximately 350000 books and periodic journals. It has also collection of copies of all legislative acts adopted after 1990. There is a student's internship program which is administratively attached to the library of the National Parliament because its main aim is to deliver comparative legal surveys that are ordered by the MPs as an aid of their legislative activity. The library of the National Parliament not only serves mainly the MPs and the parliamentary administration but is also open to other state institutions and to the citizens.

The specialized administration of the National Assembly is divided into five directorates. These are: 'Plenary Sessions, Parliamentary Control and Final Text Versions' Directorate, 'Legislative Activity and EU Law' Directorate, 'Coordination, Interaction, Analysis and Information' Directorate, 'International Relations and Protocol' Directorate and 'Public Relations' Directorate. The first of these directorates – the 'Plenary Sessions, Parliamentary Control and Final Text Versions' Directorate – has more complex structure than the other. It includes four departments – 'Plenary Sessions', 'Parliamentary Control', 'Final Text Versions' and 'Stenographic Services and Word Processing'.

There are several administrative services which are at the direct disposal of the Chairman or the Chairwoman of the National Assembly. These are the 'Security of Information' Department, the 'Internal Audit' Department and the 'Financial Control' Sector. The stenographers of the Parliament have similar status. The quaestors of the Parliament are also under the direct control and orders of the Chairman or the Chairwoman of the National Assembly but they form part of the general parliamentary administration and are also under the guidance of the secretary general of the National Assembly.

Finally, there are several separate units which are secondary disposers with budgetary credits and are part of the specialized parliamentary administration. These are the Economic and Social Council, the State Gazette (the official journal of Bulgaria) Editorial Board, the National Centre for Parliamentary Studies, the Regional Secretariat for Parliamentary Cooperation in South-Eastern Europe, the Health Recreational Complex 'Velingrad', the Publishing Activity Unit and the Alimentary Complex.

11.2 The Status of the Members of the Parliamentary Administration, Their Independence and Training

Most of the members of the administration of the National Assembly have the status of public servants. They are recruited, perform their functions and have the rights and duties prescribed in the Public Servants Act. The recruitment of the public servants is accomplished via competitive public procedure. There are also some members of the administrative staff who are hired on the basis of labour contract or civil contract. Another important exceptions are the non-permanent assistants which work on the basis of civil contract and do not conclude either labour contract or public servant contract. There are three types of non-permanent assistants. These are the non-permanent assistants of the MPs, the non-permanent assistants of the parliamentary groups and the non-permanent assistants of the parliamentary committees.

The appointment of all types of non-permanent assistants usually follows party lines. This is not especially visible in the case of non-permanent assistants of MPs and parliamentary groups (and is naturally understandable here) but is also visible with regard to the non-permanent assistants of the parliamentary committees. The recruitment of the members of the administrative staff who are public servants is formally impartial and is supposed to be based on meritocracy, competence and experience. Nevertheless, the party political influence can be experienced also here.

The Parliament has also access to external consultancy. The parliamentary groups and to lesser extent the parliamentary committees and the units belonging to the general or the specialized administration may hire external consultants usually on a case by case basis.

The Parliament does not have special rules or programs for the organization of staff training and development. Courses for improvement of the qualification are organized in an irregular basis which has no special legal background. There are also no institutionalized mechanisms in place promoting and enabling the professionalization and the development of functional expertise of the administrative staff. Thus, the qualification and the improvement of skills and competences are accomplished in a spontaneous way by the public servants and the other members of the parliamentary administration on their own initiative or on the initiative of the administrative directors.

There is no sharp distinction between central services and committee secretariats. The general and specialized administration of the National Assembly serves both the Parliament in general and its particular composite bodies, including the parliamentary committees.

The Bulgarian constitutional law does not contain explicit provisions concerning the interaction of the parliamentary administration with the stakeholders of the political process. The political parties' influence on the parliamentary process is institutionalized mainly through the parliamentary groups that are formed by the parties represented in the Parliament. Channels for party political influence are also the MPs that represent the party in the plenary of the National Assembly, it is parliamentary committees and delegations and in the leading bodies.

In 2009, the Prevention and Disclosure of Conflict of Interests Act has been adopted. Its article 12 requires that all office holders of public positions have to disclose possible conflict of interests by submitting an annual declaration for conflict of interests. The person who has been elected or appointed as office holder has to submit such declaration not later than 30 days after his/hers election or appointment.

11.3 The Role of the Chairman/Chairwoman of the National Assembly and the Chairman's Council in the Context of Parliamentary Work

The Bulgarian Parliament has clear institutional hierarchy. On the top of it stands the Chairman or Chairwoman of the National Assembly. He or she has range of important competences provided by the Constitution and the Regulation for the Organization and Activity of the National Assembly, most of which are concentrated within the parliamentary corporation, while some of them allow him or her to participate in the general political life of the Republic of Bulgaria.

The Chairman or Chairwoman of the National Assembly has strong standing within the parliamentary corporation and enjoys central place also in the inter-institutional relations between the central constitutional players. He or she not only plays representative and symbolic role but has also important substantial competences related to directing the parliamentary process in general and the legislative and especially the controlling process in particular. For example, the Chairman or Chairwoman of the National Assembly distributes the submitted draft acts of Parliament to the standing committees and assigns the role of leading committee. He or she, together with the Chairman's Council, determines the weekly work schedule of the Parliament. The Chairman or Chairwoman of the National Assembly directs the parliamentary process, including the procedures for parliamentary control. He or she has also disciplinary power within the parliamentary corporation, which assures the maintenance of the order in the parliamentary buildings and the financial and material conditions for the proper functioning of the National Assembly. He or she is important safeguard for the parliamentary autonomy and its organizational, financial, material and institutional aspects.

The Chairman's Council is consultative body supporting the activity of the Chairman or Chairwoman of the National Assembly. It consists of the vice-chairmen of the National Assembly and the chairmen of the parliamentary groups. The Chairman's Council has several important competences. It accomplishes consultations for the legislative program and the weekly work schedule of the Parliament. It facilitates the achievement of consensus and the conflict resolution between the parliamentary groups on issues related to the parliamentary procedure. The Chairman's Council must be periodically, at least monthly, informed by the Chairman or Chairwoman of the National Assembly for the implementation of the parliamentary legislative program and for the work of the parliamentary committees on the draft acts of Parliament and other acts that have been assigned to them.

The Chairman or Chairwoman of the National Assembly has also several competences beyond the parliamentary process and as part of the overall constitutional order and political system. The Chairman or Chairwoman of the National Assembly represents the Parliament in the inter-institutional relations with the other state organs. He or she represents the Parliament in front of the civil society especially in official celebrations and occasions. Moreover, the Chairman or Chairwoman of the National Assembly has external representative functions. He or she represents the Parliament in different international forums and generally in the external relations (within and outside the EU). Last but not least, the Chairman or Chairwoman of the National Assembly has also reserve function. He or she temporarily fulfils the functions of the President of the Republic in case of pre-term termination of the functions of the President when there is also vacancy of the position of the Vice President of the Republic who is the typical substitute of the President in such extraordinary situation. In contrast to the Vice President of the Republic, who becomes President until the end of the term of office, the Chairman or Chairwoman of the National Assembly just accomplishes the functions of President until the election of a new President in the pre-term presidential elections.

11.4 The Role of the Parliamentary Administration in the Context of Parliamentary Work

According to article 8 of the Administration Act, the administrative direction of the administration of a state institution should be accomplished by a secretary general. The secretary general directs the administration by coordinating and controlling the administrative units with regard to the correct application of the legal acts. He or she is responsible for the planning and the accountability for the accomplishment of the yearly targets of the administration. The secretary general is appointed by the institution which administration he or she directs.

The secretary general of the National Assembly is appointed by the Chairman or Chairwoman of the National Assembly who also appoints the public servants at its cabinet, at the cabinets of the vice chairmen or chairwomen of the Parliament and at the parliamentary groups' offices, the latter on the proposal of these groups. The secretary general of the National Assembly accomplishes the overall administrative guidance over the parliamentary administration and controls its activity in accordance with the Administration Act, the Regulations for the Organization and the Activity of the National Assembly and the orders of the Chairman or Chairwoman of the National Assembly. He accomplishes urgent administrative functions falling into the scope of competences of the Chairman or Chairwoman of the National Assembly when his or hers term of office has expired (e.g. during parliamentary elections after the lapse of the term of the old Parliament while the new Parliament is still not summoned) or in case of pre-term removal of the Chairman or Chairwoman of the National Assembly from office until new one is elected.

The main aspects of the role of parliamentary administration can be systematized according to two main criteria: the subject to which the supportive activities are directed and the type of activity.

The administration of the National Assembly has supportive functions for the plenary of the Parliament, its internal structures and the MPs. Most parts of the parliamentary administration support all institutions that form the parliamentary corporation, while some of them have supportive functions only for a specific institution. The first group encompasses most of the administrative entities enlisted and analysed above. The second group includes the non-permanent assistants which are attached to the MPs, the parliamentary groups and the parliamentary committees; the chief of the cabinet of the Chairman or the Chairwoman of the National Assembly; and the members of the administrative staff attached to the parliamentary groups and the parliamentary committees.

According to the functions they perform, one can differentiate among administrative-managerial institutions, advisory institutions, financial-budgetary institutions and administrative-material support institutions. Some of the institutions that belong to the parliamentary administration perform more than one of these functions. Thus, they should be included in more than one group.

The main institution belonging to the parliamentary administration that possesses administrative-managerial functions is the chef secretary of the National Assembly. The chief of the cabinet of the Chairman or the Chairwoman of the National Assembly also performs such functions.

The administrative units with advisory functions include the non-permanent assistants of the MPs, the parliamentary groups and the parliamentary committees, the chief of the cabinet of the Chairman or the Chairwoman of the National Assembly, the 'Plenary Sessions, Parliamentary Control and Final Text Versions' Directorate, the 'Legislative Activity and EU Law' Directorate, the 'Coordination, Interaction, Analysis and Information' Directorate, the 'International Relations and Protocol' Directorate and the 'Public Relations' Directorate. These directorates have also functions related to the administrative and material support.

The main administrative unit with financial-budgetary institutions is the 'Parliamentary Budget and Finance'.

The institutions that offer material support can be divided into two main groups. The first of them supports the fulfilment of the typical functions of the Parliament. The administrative units belonging to this group are: the quaestors, the parliamentary secretaries, the parliamentary library, the State Gazette (the official journal of Bulgaria) Editorial Board, the 'Parliamentary Chancellery', 'Legal Activities and Public Procurement', 'Human Resources' and 'Information and Communication Systems'.

The second group aids the MPs in their overall pronounced social standing serving as material safeguards for their status. Here one can include 'Property Management' and 'Car Park Service and Garage' Directorates, the Health Recreational Complex 'Velingrad', the Publishing Activity Unit and the Alimentary Complex.

11.5 The Role of Parliamentary Administration in the Legislative Process

There are two institutions which are empowered to introduce legislation. Hence, the right to legislative initiative belongs to the Council of Ministers and the single MPs. All draft acts of Parliament can be introduced in the National Assembly only if they are supplied with impact assessment report drafted by the initiating subject. The MPs structure the impact assessment report in accordance with special methodology which is attached in the form of Appendix to the Rules for Organization and the Activity of the National Assembly. Draft acts of Parliament which are not supplemented with impact assessment report are not taken into consideration and are not distributed to the parliamentary committees by the Chairman or the Chairwoman of the National Assembly until such report is presented by the initiating subject.

The permanent committees of the National Assembly may assign the accomplishment of posterior impact assessment. Its purpose is to establish the efficiency of the implemented acts of Parliament and the achievement of their goals.

According to the 1991 Bulgarian Constitution, the legislative process is structured in two reading. The draft acts of Parliament are introduced first in the parliamentary committees and then in the plenary of the Parliament for adoption on first and then on second reading. During the first reading, the MPs vote on the principles of the draft act of Parliament, its overall outlook and general design, whereas on the second reading the voting is on the details.

After its adoption by the Parliament, the draft act of Parliament is certified by the Chairman or the Chairwoman of the National Assembly and is sent to the President of the Republic for promulgation and publication in State Gazette (the official journal of the state). The President may impose a suspensive veto on the draft act of the Parliament in which case it is returned to the National Assembly for reconsideration. The Parliament may reject the veto with absolute majority of the MPs.

The interaction between the National Assembly and the President of the Republic in the course of the legislative process involves also intensive work of the administrations of both institutions. It includes the work of the legal advisors and other experts as well as the staff of the State Gazette which is part of the administration of the National Assembly as has been explained above.

The parliamentary administration supports both the committee phase and the plenary phase. The workload is balanced between the parliamentary committees and the plenary. It is the emphasis of the work in the committee and the plenary phase which differs thus engaging different players. For example, while in the committee phase the workload is on the advisors and the committee administration, the plenary phase involves also the quaestors, the parliamentary secretaries, the stenographers and the units responsible for finalization of the text.

11.6 The Parliamentary Administration, the Civil Society and the Public Sphere

There are several instruments of the participatory democracy through which the National Assembly can be addressed with issues by the citizens. The most important of them is the national legislative citizens' initiative and the petition. Moreover, under certain conditions, citizens may be allowed to participate as audience to the meetings of the parliamentary plenum and the parliamentary groups. From socio-legal perspective, the instruments for civic communication and engagement with the Parliament are rather meagre and weak.

The Parliament maintains relations with traditional and new media mainly via its 'Public relations' Directorate and the parliamentary press centre. There is a special page on the website of the National Assembly allowing for media monitoring and online visits of the Parliament. Some of the parliamentary sittings have been broadcasted online via the Internet site of the National Assembly. The Parliament has created an official Facebook page in 2011 but until March 2021 it is still not really active since no news have been published on it. In 2021, due to high turbulences in the Bulgarian political life, the parliamentary debates have been extensively directly translated via range of media, including TV and the web pages of newspapers.

11.7 Managing Inter-Institutional and External Relations. The Parliamentary Administration's Role in EU Matters

The administration of the National Assembly is fully autonomous from the administrations of the other state institutions. More precisely, it is independent from the administration of the government and the President of the Republic. It has to be noted that this independence is organizational and institutional and not functional. In other words, while there is clear organizational and institutional separation of administrative powers between the administrations of the main constitutional institutions, there is also functional interdependence between them.

This is especially visible in the sphere of legislation and in the budgetary process. The Council of Ministers is the main initiator of draft acts of Parliament. Thus, most of the draft acts of Parliament are elaborated by the governmental administration and especially by the experts of the ministries. This is due to the fact that Bulgaria is hybrid parliamentary republic and the main driving force of the legislative process is the single power unit composed by the government and its parliamentary majority (Kirov 2004). Moreover, it is the ministries that have both the political incentives and the administrative capacity for drafting acts of Parliament.

Nevertheless, the National Assembly is free to approve, reject or amend the draft acts of Parliament proposed by the government. It has also the administrative capacity to draft its own proposals for both amendment of the acts introduced by the government and for legislative reforms proposed by the MPs and the parliamentary groups. There are different reasons for the initiation of draft acts of Parliament by the single MPs. Many of them come from the parliamentary opposition or independent MPs. However, there are also draft acts of Parliament which are initiated also by MPs from the parliamentary majority due to political considerations such as blame-shifting, tactical manoeuvring.

It has to be taken into account that the Bulgarian National Assembly belongs to the prototype of the 'speaking parliament' (Beyme 1999; Laprat 1995; Lijphart 1999).[1] It is much more a forum for public deliberation of draft acts of Parliament in the course of the legislative process than power centre for legislative drafting and source of ideas for legislative reforms different from or alternative to the ones proposed by the government. This is due to many reasons: the parliamentary form of government, the domination of the governmental over parliamentary administration in terms of quantity of its members, administrative capacity and expertise specialization, the political culture, the leadership type of parties, the strong prevalence of the figure of the Prime Minister dominating the government and overshadowing the institutional independence of the Parliament, the rather week parliamentary opposition during the last decade etc.

The parliamentary administration is weakly involved in the Parliament's external relations. This counts for in its inter-institutional relations, for the parliamentary diplomacy and inter-parliamentary cooperation and for the EU affairs.

The EU integration clause of the Bulgarian Constitution is rather laconic. According to article 4, paragraph 3 of the Constitution the Republic of Bulgaria shall participate in the construction and development of the European Union. The inter-institutional relations related to the membership of the Republic of Bulgaria in the EU are not concentrated in a special chapter or part of the Constitution. They are spread in different constitutional chapters. Pertaining to article 105, paragraphs 3 and 4 of the Constitution the Council of Ministers shall inform the National Assembly on matters concerning the obligations arising for the Republic of Bulgaria from its membership of the European Union. When participating in the drafting and adoption of acts of the European Union, the Council of Ministers shall inform in advance the National Assembly and shall render account for the actions thereof. Hence, the Bulgarian Constitution briefly reproduces the minimal framework of the inter-institutional relations between the Parliament and the government required by the EU law.

The National Assembly adopts annual working program for the participation in EU matters. They are coordinated with the Annual Program for the Participation of the Republic of Bulgaria in the Decision-Making of the EU that is adopted by virtue of a decision of the Council of Ministers.

The National Assembly has adjusted its structure to the minimal requirements of the EU membership. It has specialized parliamentary committee on EU matters. There is also European Documentary Centre at the National Assembly. However, the Bulgarian Parliament is not eager to massively engage in EU policy-making. It restrains its activity to the minimal degree of parliamentary involvement required by the EU law and does not show appetite for expansion of its role. This is especially visible in the sphere of parliamentary control over the governmental activity in the EU decision-making processes which is rather underdeveloped and pale. The Bulgarian Parliament typically refrains from involvement in EU affairs and particularly in the Early Warning System. Thus, the activity of the National Assembly related to EU matters is concentrated mainly in the sphere of legislation and more precisely in the implementation of EU directives in Bulgarian acts of Parliament.

11.8 Managing Current Challenges Facing the Parliamentary Administration

The main challenge to the functioning of the National Assembly and its administration has obviously been the Covid-19 pandemic which has deeply impacted the rhythm of parliamentary work. Naturally, this is not unique challenge to Bulgaria since pandemic has challenged the parliamentary process and the parliamentary routine all over the world.

The Covid-19 pandemic has impacted the two most important functions of the National Assembly – its legislative and controlling function (Belov and Tsekov 2021). The Parliament has adopted several important decisions related to the Covid-19 pandemic and which regulated or impacted on its functioning in times of pandemic. These are Decision for Declaration of State of Emergency (State Gazette № 22 of 13.03.2020), Decision for Prolongation of the State of Emergency (State Gazette № 33 of 7.4.2020), Decision on the work of the National Assembly during the State of Emergency (State Gazette № 22 of 13.03.2020) and the three Decisions for Amendment of the Decisions on the Work of the National Assembly during the State of emergency that have been adopted on 26 March 2020, 3 April 2020 and 15 May 2020. Finally, on 6 November 2020, the National Assembly has adopted Decision for Adoption of Rules for Participation in the Plenary Sittings of MPs which are under Quarantine due to Covid-19.

The immediate conclusion stemming from the number and the frequency of the decisions of the Parliament is that the National Assembly did not have very clear idea how to cope with the institutional challenges of the pandemic. This led to dysfunctionality of the parliamentary activity, to a shift of power from the National Assembly to the government and even to non-elective and not constitutionally provided bodies such as the National Operative Headquarters (consisting of medical specialists). Altogether this has produced visible deparliamentarization of the Bulgarian parliamentary republic.

The impact of all these decisions of the National Assembly on parliamentary procedure during the time of emergency (13 March 2020–13 May 2020) can be summarized as follows (Belov and Tsekov 2021). Important group of changes concerns the parliamentary timing. The Parliament has reorganized the timing of its functioning. The periods of parliamentary holidays have been changed and the parliamentary process has been speeded up to the detriment of the quality of the debates, the quality of the legislation and the efficiency of the parliamentary control. The terms for introduction of suggestions for improvement of the draft acts of Parliament adopted on first reading by the MPs have been reduced to 24 hours before the parliamentary debate. Draft Acts of Parliament have been submitted only to one standing committee and have been adopted only in one reading in the parliamentary committee phase. Oral deliberations have been restricted. Parliamentary control has been limited only to written questions and answers. During the times of emergency, only draft acts of Parliament related to it have been taken for consideration.

The number of MPs that were allowed to be present at the plenary debates was limited to ¼. The access of external persons to the parliamentary premises has been restricted. The Parliament has made partial recourse to new digital means for minimizing the personal presence of the MPs in the building of the Parliament.

The pandemic emergency has been replaced with an extraordinary epidemic situation that has been introduced by virtue of amendments in the Health Act. Although the Constitutional Court has confirmed its constitutionality by virtue of its Decision № 10 of 2020, it is actually unconstitutional. This is due to the fact that the Bulgarian Constitution provides only for three forms of emergency – war, state of siege and state of emergency, and the legislative invention of a fourth form of emergency – the extraordinary epidemic situation – although confirmed by the Constitutional Court is clearly unconstitutional (Belov 2021).

On 6 November, the National Assembly has adopted Decision for Adoption of Rules for Participation in the Plenary Sittings of MPs which are under Quarantine due to Covid-19. This decision allowed these MPs to participate in the plenary sessions of the National Assembly remotely via the electronic system for videoconferences of the Parliament. This participation should be direct and personal. In order to be allowed to participate in the parliamentary session, the MPs should inform personally and in advance the Chairman or Chairwomen of the National Assembly if they are independent MPs. Such information has to be transmitted via the chairman of the parliamentary group if the MPs belong to such group. The MPs that will participate remotely in the sitting of the Parliament have to be included in publicly announced list. They can vote orally via the electronic system for videoconferences of the Parliament.

A group of MPs have approached the Constitutional Court with a demand to declare this decision of the National Assembly unconstitutional. The Constitutional Court has rejected their motion for unconstitutionality by virtue of its Decision № 2 of 2021. This decision of the Constitutional Court is in compliance with its previous case-law. In its Decision № 8 of 2003, the Constitutional Court has decided that 'the requirement of article 81, paragraph 3 of the Constitution that "voting is personal" is a fundamental constitutional principle related to the work of the National Assembly'. Regardless of the type and specifically chosen manner of voting, the right of each MP to participate in it is a personal constitutional right which is inadmissible to be exercised by person different from the entitled MP. The content of this right is that the voting upon the adoption of the acts of the National Assembly is an act of personal discretion, in which the MP expresses immediately, freely and independently his or her personal will in accordance with his or her conscience and convictions (Belov and Tsekov 2021). Hence, Decision № 2 of 2021 seems to be correct and in compliance with the Bulgarian Constitution.

11.9 Conclusion

The organization and functioning of the administration of the Bulgarian National Assembly has borrowed from both the Bulgarian national traditions and the achievements of the parliamentary administrations of the EU Member States. It is adequate to the size, competences and the workload of the Bulgarian Parliament. In the last, more than three decades tendencies of professionalization and meritocracy have been intermingled with cases of political appointment of the members of the parliamentary administration. These trends not only have advantages (e.g. the assurance of the connection between the political and administrative domains of power within the parliamentary corporation) but also raise issues of concern such as the challenges to professionalism and competence produced by politically motivated appointments of the members of the administration.

The administration of the Bulgarian Parliament has gradually increased its expertise in participation in external and international relations. Since 2007 – the year in which the Republic of Bulgaria has joined the EU – the Parliament in general and its administration in particular had to get used to participate more extensively in pan-European parliamentary networks.

Visible efforts have been put also in increasing the publicity of the activity of the National Assembly. An important role has been played by the integration of the digital infrastructure of the Parliament in the overall process of digitalization of the public administration in Bulgaria. Nevertheless, quite naturally, the digitalization and publicity has impacted mostly the accomplishment of the constitutional functions of the Parliament and especially its legislative, budgetary and especially controlling procedures. Thus, they have concerned rather the activity of the MPs and the political part of the parliamentary corporation and not that much the functioning of its administration. This is understandable since policy-making requires publicity while parliamentary administration has much more supportive, expert and technocratic functions. Generally, there has been clear trend toward offering Internet-based visibility of the parliamentary activity. This has been especially true for the 45 and the 46 National Assemblies.

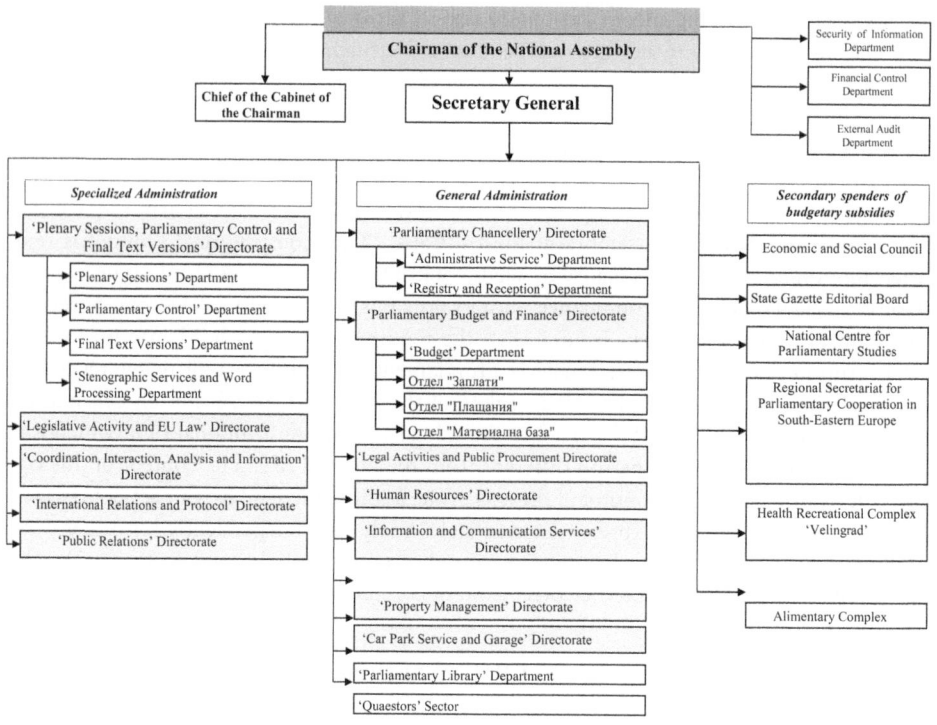

Organizational chart of the National Assembly in Bulgaria

Source: https://www.parliament.bg/en

Note

1 For the difference between 'speaking' and 'working' parliament see von Beyme, K 1999, *Die parlamentarische Demokratie. Entstehung und Funktionsweise 1789–1999*. Opladen/Wiesbaden: Westdeutscher Verlag, p. 188, Lijphart, A 1999, *Patterns of Democracy. Government Forms and Performance in Thirty-Six Countries*, Yale University Press, London, p. 72, Laprat, G 1995, *Parliamentary scrutiny of Community legislation: an evolving idea* – in Laursen, F, S Pappas (eds.) *The Changing Role of Parliaments in the European Union*, EIPA, Maastricht, Marschall, St 2005, *Parlamentarismus*, Nomos, Baden-Baden, p. 115 and the following.

References

Belov, M 2021, Mastering Emergency Situations: The Activist Role of the Bulgarian Constitutional Court in Redefining the Constitutional Design of War, State of Siege and State of Emergency in: Courts and Judicial Activism under Crisis Conditions: Policy Making in a Time of Illiberalism and Emergency Constitutionalism, Routledge, Abingdon.

Belov, M, A Tsekov 2021, Covid-19 Pandemic and Its Impact on Parliamentarism in Bulgaria. A self-restricting of the control power in The Parliament in the time of coronavirus, Robert Schuman Foundation Study papers, available at https://www.robert-schuman.eu/en/doc/ouvrages/FRS_Parliament_Bulgaria.pdf, pp. 1–9.

Beyme, K 1999, Die parlamentarische Demokratie. Entstehung und Funktionsweise 1789 – 1999. Opladen/Wiesbaden: Westdeutscher Verlag, p. 188.

Kirov, V 2004, *Public Power*, Ciela, Sofia, p. 208 (in Bulgarian).

Laprat, G 1995, Parliamentary scrutiny of Community legislation: an evolving idea, in Laursen, F, S Pappas (eds.), The Changing Role of Parliaments in the European Union, EIPA, Maastricht, Marschall, St 2005, Parlamentarismus, Nomos, Baden-Baden, p. 115.

Lijphart, A 1999, Patterns of Democracy. Government Forms and Performance in Thirty-Six Countries, Yale University Press, London, p. 72.

12
CROATIA'S PARLIAMENTARY ADMINISTRATION

Jelena Špiljak

12.1 Introduction

Croatian Parliament (*Hrvatski sabor* or Sabor for short) is a unicameral national legislature, defined by the Croatian Constitution as a representative body of the people, vested with legislative power. The word *sabor* is an old Croatian expression that means "assembly". The first such recorded assembly took place in Zagreb already in 1273, but the first democratically elected parliament convened in 1990, originally as a bicameral parliament, with the Representatives' House and the House of Counties. The Representatives' House was directly elected and vested with legislative powers, while the House of Counties was a deliberative, advisory and, to some extent, supervisory house (Deren-Antoljak 1993), assembled on territorial principle – gathering representatives of the Croatian Counties. Representatives' House held comparatively greater importance, as it was the first institution elected in democratic, multiparty elections, enacting initial decisions concerning Croatian independence. House of Counties seized to exist in 2001, after the constitutional reform saw Croatia shift from semi-presidential to parliamentary system of governance.

In 2021, Sabor was in its 10th parliamentary term, gathering 151 directly elected MPs, assisted in their work by the Staff Service, a structure ensuring continuity and maintenance of the institutional memory. This chapter aims to provide overview of the structure and main functions of Sabor's Staff Service in the observed period of March to October 2021, with analysis of main challenges and development tendencies. Recent challenges will also be addressed, particularly issues arising from organization of parliamentary work during the COVID-19 pandemic and ensuing swift digitalization that was essential in order to maintain the dynamic of Sabor's daily operations.

12.2 Parliamentary Administration in the Context of Civil Service

The Republic of Croatia established a central Civil Service, to perform core business tasks in all state bodies. Supplementary and technical tasks are performed by a special category of employees, the governmental employees. In the broader context of the Croatian labour legislation, the key difference between civil servants and governmental employees is in the type of contracts they hold. Civil servants are subject to admission to Civil Service and assignment to specific posts within the Civil Service, while governmental employees conclude labour contracts with state bodies that employ them. This makes civil servants privileged in relation to governmental employees, as they get to negotiate the terms of their employment through *lex specialis*, rather than through a much more general Labour Act.

General provisions governing the work of Civil Service are found in the Civil Servants Act, and the specific job titles with corresponding remuneration coefficients are prescribed by the Regulation on Titles of Posts and Complexity Coefficients of Civil Service Tasks, enacted by the Government.

Staff Service of Sabor is part of the Croatian Civil Service; therefore, their employment, labour relations, remuneration, professional training, advancement, as well as all matters concerning regulation of their rights, duties and accountability, are determined by the Government and through the abovementioned acts. As the Civil Service is protected against political staffing, this protection extends to Sabor's Staff Service; however, Staff Service is precluded from negotiating even more favourable employment conditions for themselves. Even though Civil Service is essentially professional, civil servants are not prohibited from being members of political parties but are not allowed to express their political alignment when acting in their official capacities.

Recruitment of the Staff Service is conducted via public vacancies procedure, or through permanent or temporary transfers from other state bodies. The latter has predominantly been the case since 2010, as new employments into Civil Service have been either prohibited or discouraged, due to budgetary issues.

12.3 Legal Framework and Structure of Staff Service

The Staff Service of the Sabor is established by the Standing Orders of the Croatian Parliament. Any member of the Staff Service is obliged to provide the MPs with assistance in the performance of their parliamentary duties and the MPs may seek information and expert explanations from the Staff Service.

Structure and functions of the Staff Service are set out in the Decision on the Staff Service of Parliament and further elaborated in the Ordinance on the Internal Structure of the Staff Service, an internal document that lists all positions in the Sabor and their respective job descriptions. Through these documents, Staff Service is entrusted with professional, analytical, administrative, security implementation, technical and other tasks, performed in order to assist Sabor in its work, particularly when it comes to operations surrounding Sabor's plenary sessions, the work of its committees and political groups (Deputy Clubs).

Tasks and duties of the Staff Service are conducted by civil servants and several appointed officials, hired in the following organizational units: (i) Secretariat; (ii) Office of the Speaker of Parliament; (iii) Offices of Deputy Speakers; (iv) Protocol Office; and (v) Office for International and European Affairs.

Staff is further deployed to offices and services: (i) Office of the Secretary General; (ii) Committees Service; (iii) Deputy Clubs (Political Groups) Service; (iv) Session Preparation and Processing Service; (v) Service for Preparation of Acts of Parliament for Publication; (vi) Human Resources and Legal Service; (vii) Press Office; (viii) Citizens Service; (ix) Information and Documentation Department; (x) Library; (xi) General Administration Service; and (xii) Guard.

This administrative division does not precisely reflect the reality of Sabor's Staff Service position within the overall parliamentary organization, where the main division can be drawn between offices and services headed by civil servants and those headed by elected and appointed officials, as interpreted by the author in Figure 12.1.

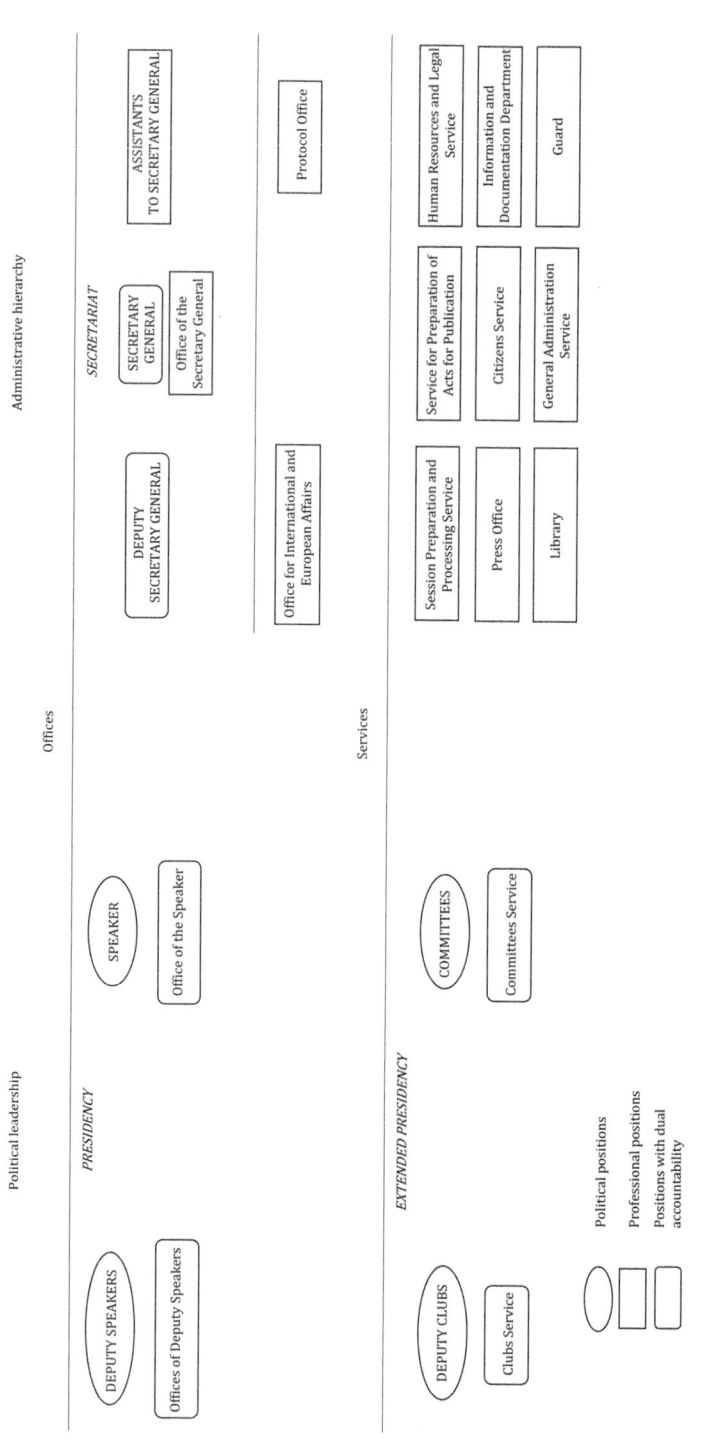

Figure 12.1 Organizational chart of the Croatian Parliament

At the top of the administrative hierarchy is the Secretariat, headed by the Secretary General – an official elected by Sabor, at the proposal of the Speaker. Secretary General is assisted in their work by the Assistants to the Secretary General, selected among the high-ranking civil servants, and is accountable to the Speaker. Their position is often a political appointment; however, the Secretary General in the observed period came from within the ranks of Sabor's Staff Service, possibly indicating the Speaker's tendency to professionalize the function. The Deputy Secretary General is *ex officio* Plenary Sessions Secretary and is also elected by Sabor, at the proposal of the Speaker.

Offices of the Speaker and Deputy Speakers are *de facto* headed by elected officials – holders of titular offices, but they may appoint heads of their offices. Head of the Speaker's Office is an official appointed by Sabor, while heads of Offices of Deputy Speakers are civil servants, assigned to those posts at the request of the respective Deputy Speaker, and for the duration of their term of office. At the end of their terms, those civil servants will be reassigned to different posts within Sabor, or elsewhere in the Civil Service.

Protocol Office and Office for International and European Affairs are headed by civil servants, as are all the services, with the exception of the Committees Service and the Deputy Clubs Service that are both in practice decentralized.

Sabor's Political leadership should be distinguished from the administrative hierarchy, even if political leadership has a say in the development of the Staff Service. Speaker and Deputy Speakers form the Presidency of Sabor. Secretary General, chairpersons of political groups and chairpersons of committees may be invited to participate in the meetings of the Presidency. This informal "extended Presidency" meets ahead of every plenary session to set up the first draft agenda and agree on procedural details, or to discuss specific issues. Presidency and extended Presidency may instruct the Secretary General on issues pertaining to the Staff Service, but those instructions will be further streamlined through the hierarchy exclusively by the Secretary General.

12.4 Distribution of the Staff Service

As a bicameral parliament Sabor had a joint Staff Service of both houses with 226 employed civil servants in 2001, as reported by the Human Resources and Legal Service in March 2021. At the beginning of March 2021, Staff Service consisted of 284 civil servants, or 188 civil servants per MP (of whom there were 151). The numbers show Sabor has been continuously operating with a relatively small Staff Service, even though it had grown by 26 per cent in 20 years. The ratio of Civil Servants to MPs indicates another specific feature of Sabor – MPs do not have their own assistants, nor do they have an option to employ them. Only civil servants employed in the Staff Service are authorized to perform tasks and duties in the scope of work of Sabor, so even if an MP wanted to privately employ an assistant, he could not do so. In practice this means that MPs who do not hold offices within Sabor have to rely on themselves in many of their day-to-day operations, such as analysing draft legislation and writing speeches for the plenary session.

12.5 Political Groups

MPs are primarily gravitating towards their political groups, or Deputy Clubs, as they are called in Sabor, for political instructions and expertise on issues appearing in the plenary. Political groups are specific in terms of staffing, as their staff can exceptionally be employed without going through the process of admission into the Civil Service. They must, however, meet all the requirements for the post they are assigned to, and they are considered civil servants with temporary assignment, limited to the duration of the parliamentary term, or until dissolution of the political group that employs them.

In March 2021, there were 13 Deputy Clubs in Sabor, employing 30 staff,[1] with tendency to grow – by October 2021, there were 15 Deputy Clubs, employing 32 staff. Each Deputy Club is entitled to hire its secretary, by a decision of its chairperson, and one additional official, to perform professional and administrative tasks for the Club. Clubs with more than 15 members can employ additional officials: one if they have between 16 and 30 members, two if they have 31–45 members and so on. In October 2021, only the two largest political groups had more than the minimally guaranteed two employees.

Even though the Deputy Clubs Service was listed as a special service, suggesting existence of a coordinative body or official, in practice this is not the case. Each political group functions independently and its employees are responsible directly to their chairperson. While political groups may choose to assign civil servants already working in Sabor, or elsewhere in Civil Service, to the posts within their groups, if they employ officials from outside of the Civil Service, these officials cannot be reassigned to any other post within Sabor or any other state body. In this way, professional civil servants in the Staff Service are protected from losing their posts to political appointments, while political groups are given opportunity to hire staff of their own choosing.

12.6 Committees

There are 29 standing committees (NDI 1996) in Sabor, as established by the Standing Orders. Majority of committees can be characterized as sectoral and legislative committees, mirroring governmental portfolios and are tasked with scrutinising draft legislation before it reaches the plenary. There are several specialized committees assigned with specific tasks, such as the Petitions and Appeals Committee, dealing with petitions submitted by citizens, the Credentials and Privileges Commission, dealing exclusively with MPs mandates and immunities, or the Elections, Appointments and Administration Committee, which is in charge of all political appointments in Sabor. Chairmanship of committees reflects election results, in terms that majority of the committees are chaired by the MPs from within the ranks of the ruling party or coalition, while the rest are chaired by the MPs from within the ranks of parliamentary opposition. Details of chairpersons' seats distribution are agreed among political groups, but regardless of whether the chairperson comes from majority or opposition, ruling party or coalition will always hold majority of membership in every committee.

As is the case with political groups, while the Committees Service is established as a special service, in practice, committees' secretariats function in a highly decentralized manner.

The 29 committees employed 84 officials in March 2021, making them the largest group in parliamentary staff, accounting for 30 per cent of total Staff Service. In contrast with the number of Deputy Clubs and their staff, in the committees, the situation remained stable in the observed period. Most committees employ the head of the committee secretariat, one advisor, and an administrative secretary. Even though the workload varies greatly among the committees, due to prominence of topics they cover in daily parliamentary procedures, this staffing pattern is consistent across all committees. There are some committees with no advisors assigned, as well as committees (European Affairs Committee and Foreign Affairs Committee) that are entitled to more than one advisor but did not employ them in the observed period.

All committee officials are civil servants with permanent posts. Since the post of the Head of the Committee Service has never been filled, committee officials respond directly to the Secretary General. However, since the job descriptions require committee staff to perform tasks directly for the chairperson of the committee they are assigned to, they are also accountable to the chairperson. This dual accountability is not clearly demarked in documents governing the work of Civil Service or Sabor's Staff Service, but in practice chairpersons are those who propose annual evaluations of "their" officials and even give their approval for the use of vacation days. However, all final decisions concerning Staff Service are in the scope of the Secretary General, and in case of any conflict of jurisdiction, ultimately, committee staff is accountable to the Secretary General.

Even though the separation between committee officials and the political level would be difficult to achieve due to the very nature of committee work, committee staff is protected against unjust and unreasonable reassignment. Heads of secretariats of individual committees are all long-term officials in Sabor and so are most of committee advisors and administrative staff, all with considerable parliamentary experience. Their main challenge is adjustment to what is usually a new chairperson every four years or less. Generally considered permanent fixtures in their committees, with no "forced mobility" (Alexander 2020), committee staff guarantees continuity through parliamentary terms.

12.7 Offices and Services Headed by Civil Servants

Along with the Protocol Office and the Office for International and European Affairs, there are nine other services headed by civil servants that are established to provide assistance in the preparation of draft legislation and other acts adopted by Sabor, draft reports and minutes of plenary sessions, provide the analysis of materials and draft legislation and facilitate publication of enacted legislation. Additionally, Office for International and European Affairs assists parliamentary delegations to international bodies and organizations, and Protocol Office facilitates official engagements of the Speaker, Deputy Speakers and committee chairpersons.

Job descriptions of the offices and services are mostly self-explanatory, but small staff numbers mean that most of them deal with at least some jobs that are not necessarily in their logical scope of work. Heads of these offices and services, together with their other staff – advisors and administrative secretaries, enjoy high degree of independence in their work, as they are accountable directly to the Secretary General. As is the case with committee staff, large majority of civil servants in offices and services are long-time employees of Sabor, with significant experience and expertise.

Services usually do not work directly with MPs but are tasked with specific expert assignments for Sabor as a whole. The Office for International and European Affairs and the Protocol Office are in a specific position, as they do communicate daily with MPs and provide assistance directly to them, but at the same time their accountability is solely to the Secretary General. As opposed to Deputy Clubs' and committees' staff, MPs do not have a role in evaluation of the work of the staff of offices and services, except in case of three of Sabor's parliamentary delegations[2] that are granted by the Standing Orders the status of a committee. The staff of these delegations is a part of the Office for International and European Affairs, but they also operate directly under the supervision of their head of delegation.

Services providing direct support to the work of the plenary session are coordinated by the Plenary Sessions Secretary (Deputy Secretary General), while the rest of the services are given more general goals to achieve, with certain freedom in ways in which to achieve those goals, and even in selection and implementation of their own projects. Some of these projects have proven to be very successful, such as publication and maintenance of an extensive web-based legislative database by the Information and Documentation Department, or participation of the Library in the ECPRD Network.

12.8 Supplementary Jobs

Sabor shares its technical services with the Government (the two institutions are situated in close proximity of each other). The General Administration Office of the Croatian Parliament and the Government has been set up to provide supplementary services to both institutions, such as building maintenance and catering. These posts are assigned to governmental employees and they are not considered part of Sabor's Staff Service. Additionally, Sabor has its own General Administration Service, employing civil servants and dealing with Sabor-specific general tasks, such as IT, audio and video technology used for plenary sessions and committee meetings.

The largest supplementary service in Sabor is the Guard, employing 39 civil servants as of March 2021. Members of Sabor's Guard make up the parliamentary security service, in charge of control of persons, objects and vehicles entering Sabor premises and ensuring overall safety of people and property in Sabor's buildings. The Guard is also in charge of maintaining the order in the plenary session as a last resort – if an MP fails to follow instructions of the Speaker or presiding Deputy Speaker behaves disruptively or dangerously, the Guard will remove them from Plenary Hall.

Expert analysis and similar supplementary jobs can only exceptionally be outsourced to experts outside of the Civil Service, and only to perform tasks that are not considered core business of the state body. In case of Sabor, free-lance interpreters are often hired for specific events. During the Croatian EU Council Presidency in the first half of 2020, two external experts were hired on the basis of temporary contractual employment, outside the scope of the Civil Service.

12.9 International and European Affairs

Arguably the greatest paradigm shift the Staff Service encountered since the abolishment of the House of Counties in 2001 was the Croatian entry into the membership of the European Union in 2013. The beginning of the pre-accession process coincided with the constitutional reform in 2000/2001, when the newly unicameral Sabor took over tasks of political and legal control of the Croatian bid for EU membership and the ensuing processes. Sabor participated in the pre-accession process primarily through its committees: the European Integration Committee, the National Committee for Monitoring of Accession Negotiations and the Croatia-EU Joint Parliamentary Committee.

In July 2012, the Office for International and European Affairs was established as one of the five main organizational units in Sabor. It has since consistently been the largest of all expert offices and services, employing 20 civil servants as of October 2021. The number of civil servants in the Office was at times higher, reaching up to 25, but staff turnover has remained relatively high, in contrast with most of the other offices and services.

The Office consists of two departments, for international and European affairs, respectively. International Affairs Department, employing 12 civil servants, acts as the secretariat to Sabor's permanent delegations to interparliamentary organizations and monitors interparliamentary cooperation in general. All MPs and committees are to some extent involved in various international activities, and in doing so they can count on the expertise from the International

Affairs Department. European Affairs Department, with eight employed civil servants, provides assistance in European affairs to MPs who are not normally directly dealing with the EU. All committees are in charge of monitoring EU policies pertaining to their scope of work, so most MPs can expect to encounter EU affairs in some form or another.

The European Affairs Department also coordinates participation of the Staff Service and MPs in various twinning and other technical assistance projects. Since the establishment of the Office for International and European Affairs was itself the result of a twinning project implemented in Sabor prior to Croatian membership in the European Union, being able to carry out new twinning projects for candidate and potential candidate countries is an indicator of the Office's success.

On the political level, international and European affairs are, in the conditions of EU membership, dealt with in the European Affairs Committee, the Foreign Affairs Committee and the Interparliamentary Cooperation Committee. European affairs are normally handled by the European Affairs Committee on behalf of Sabor as a whole, but in close cooperation with other committees. Sabor conducts European affairs indirectly, by monitoring the activities of the Government in EU institutions, which Sabor prioritises, and directly, by exercising the powers from the Lisbon Treaty (Briški and Špiljak 2014). Foreign Affairs Committee is in charge of the EU's Common Foreign and Security Policy and any ensuing documents, along with more "national" tasks, such as participation in diplomatic appointments procedure. Interparliamentary Cooperation Committee performs political scrutiny of Sabor's delegations to parliamentary organizations and coordinates the work of interparliamentary friendship groups. Each of the three aforementioned committees operated with three civil servants in the observed period – head of committee secretariat, administrative secretary and one advisor.

Creation of the system governing the conduct of European affairs in Sabor was another major challenge for the Staff Service. The comparative advantage was that Croatia was the first country to become an EU Member State after entry into force of the Lisbon Treaty (Briški and Špiljak 2014). Sabor was therefore able to avoid creation of parallel documentation flows that occurred in some of the national parliaments when the Lisbon Treaty introduced direct delivery of all EU documents to national parliaments, thus also avoiding duplication of tasks in the Staff Service. Nevertheless, in relation to the total number of civil servants in the Staff Service, number of officials directly dealing with EU affairs remains relatively high, with 11 employees of the European Affairs Committee and the European Affairs Department combined, confirming the findings of Högenauer et al. (2016), indicating that parliaments with small administration tend to have relatively high proportion of EU experts. Of these 11 officials, 10 were experts with tertiary education degrees, which is proportionately more than in most of Sabor's services. Similarly, of 12 civil servants working in the International Affairs Department, 10 are experts with tertiary education degrees.

As is the case in the Office for International and European Affairs, and unlike in most other committees, staff turnover in the European Affairs Committee is high. Sabor's EU affairs experts tend to relatively quickly advance to higher positions in Sabor or elsewhere, not only confirming their qualifications and expertise but also bringing challenges in terms of maintaining the level of quality and consistence in conduct of European affairs.

12.10 Addressing Current Challenges

The COVID-19 pandemic caught Sabor in the midst of implementation of the parliamentary dimension of Croatian Presidency of the Council of the European Union and coincided with Sabor's buildings suffering serious damages in an earthquake that struck Zagreb in March 2020.

Consequently, two of the planned five interparliamentary conferences had to be cancelled, including the COSAC plenary meeting. Experts in the Office for International and European Affairs, as well as political leadership and staff of the European Affairs Committee showed flexibility and initiative, managing to organize an alternative video conferential meeting of the Chairpersons of COSAC, working mostly in home office. As luck (or misfortune) would have it, many of the solutions implemented in organization of this meeting remained in place by October 2021, as ensuing Council presidencies held all of their interparliamentary events online.

Even though most of the Staff Service worked from home and parliamentary facilities could not be used for several months, Sabor was continuously in session throughout 2020 and 2021. Staff Service showed dedication and adaptability in organising alternative premises for plenary sessions and facilitating the work of committees through electronic means. Digitalization remained a challenge though, as by October 2021, many of the MPs and officials still required significant degree of support in the use of digital tools. Arguably, Civil Service cannot offer competitive remuneration to IT experts, resulting in their high turnover and limiting the extent of support that can be offered.

Since 2001, Sabor has been under constant pressure from the civil society to increase its openness. Staff Service has been mostly successful in responding to these requests, notably with the efforts of two specialized services – the Citizens Service and the Press Office. Sabor's website is constantly increasing public availability of information on parliamentary work. The Citizens Service regularly organized Simulated Parliament for students, "open days" and a volunteering programme. Sabor also offers institutionalized representation of civil society, in the form of external members of committees. These members are elected by Sabor on proposal of NGOs, academia and professional associations, having same rights and duties as the committee members, except for the right to vote.

Taking into consideration that MPs come from both the position and the opposition, Sabor can seldom express a unified position. Due to this particularity, Sabor does not use social media, to preclude questions of accountability for the shared content. That being said, newly emerging patterns of political communication utilized by some of the MPs remained somewhat of a conundrum to main political groups and the Staff Service alike, presenting another challenge to be addressed in the near future.

12.11 Conclusion

Throughout its contemporary history, Sabor has been operating with a small and professional Staff Service, enjoying a relatively high political independence. However, Sabor's Staff Service, as a part of the Croatian Civil Service, is legally and administratively tied to the executive. This tension reflects Sabor's own position in Croatian political life, where the concept of political power remains imbalanced in favour of the executive (Deren-Antoljak 1993), and Sabor is perceived as largely subordinate to the Government, even though constitutionally it is the highest institution of public power.

Unlike in the executive, where the instructions from the superiors are disseminated down a clear vertical line, administrative hierarchy in Sabor is more fluid, almost with a dual line of command – political and professional. This duality is ultimately personified in the Secretary General, who, as a politically appointed official, is expected to uphold the Staff Service to the highest professional standards. Secretary General's success in balancing between political demands and best interests of civil servants determines the success of the Staff Service in their work.

Relatively low staff turnover is contrasted by the high turnover of MPs from term to term (see Ilišin 2007 and *Parlametar* 2021). In such circumstances, Sabor's Staff Service is the guardian of institutional memory. Officials must be careful to maintain their political neutrality in order to be able to perform adequately regardless of who is currently in power, while always treating members of position and opposition as equals.

Some political developments suggest that the (im)balance of power may shift towards the parliamentary branch in the future, as MPs show more political initiative and political groups become more influential within their own parties (see Heidar and Koole 2000). In this newly emerging environment, Sabor's Staff Service will need to either adapt rapidly to carrying out a much higher variety of tasks in their individual positions, or it will have to significantly grow in numbers. Maintaining a small Staff Service works only for as long as legislative behaviour is predictive, which is increasingly more often not the case. If the real meaning of "policy" does really come only through bureaucratic action (Kettl 2006), then Sabor's future as a policy-maker depends on its Staff Service.

Notes

1. This and all following numbers of civil servants in offices, services and departments were derived from author's analysis or obtained directly from parliamentary officials in March 2021, with updates in October 2021, where available.
2. Delegation to the Parliamentary Assembly of the Council of Europe, Delegation to the NATO Parliamentary Assembly and Delegation to the Parliamentary Assembly of the Organization for Security and Co-operation in Europe.

References

Alexander, David A. (2020): The Committee Secretariat of the European Parliament: administrative mobility, expertise and keeping the legislative wheels turning. The Journal of Legislative Studies. DOI: 10.1080/13572334.2020.1832389.

Briški, Tatjana & Jelena Špiljak (2014): Posredno uključivanje nacionalnih parlamenata u europski zakonodavni process: prioritet Hrvatskoga sabora u europskim poslovima. Suvremene teme god 7., br. 1. 7–28.

Deren-Antoljak, Štefica (1993): Odnos Zastupničkog i Županijskog doma Sabora Republike Hrvatske. Politička misao Vol. XXX, No. 4. 74–86.

Heidar, Knut & Ruud Koole eds. (2000): *Parliamentary Party Groups in European Democracies – Political Parties Behind Closed Doors*. London: Routledge.

Högenauer, Anna-Lena, Christine Neuhold & Thomas Christiansen (2016): *Parliamentary Administrations in the European Union*. Hampshire: Palgrave Macmillan.

Ilišin, Vlasta (2007): Hrvatski sabor 2003.: obrasci političke regrutacije parlamentarne elite. Politička misao Vol. 44, No. 4. 55–92.

Kettl, Donald F. (2006): 'Public Bureaucracies' in Rhodes R. A. W., Sarah A. Binder & Brent A. Rockman eds. *The Oxford Handbook of Political Institutions*. Oxford: Oxford University Press. 366–84.

National Democratic Institute for International Affairs NDI (1996): Committees in Legislatures: A Division of Labor. Legislative Research Series: Paper #2.

Internet sources

The Constitution of the Republic of Croatia (Consolidated Text), https://www.sabor.hr/en/constitution-republic-croatia-consolidated-text, Article 71; accessed on 9 March 2021

Zakon o državnim službenicima (Official Gazette Narodne novine nos. 92/05, 140/05, 142/06, 77/07, 107/07, 27/08, 34/11, 49/11, 150/11, 34/12, 49/12, 37/13, 38/13, 01/15, 138/15, 61/17, 70/19, and 98/19), https://www.zakon.hr/z/108/Zakon-o-dr%C5%BEavnim-slu%C5%BEbenicima; accessed on 9 March 2020 (Croatian Text Only)

Standing Orders of the Croatian Parliament (Consolidated Text) (Official Gazette Narodne novine nos. 81/13, 113/16, 69/17, 29/18, 53/20, 119/20 – Decision of the Constitutional Court of the Republic of Croatia, and 123/20), https://www.sabor.hr/en/information-access/important-legislation/standing-orders-croatian-parliament-consolidated-text; accessed on 9 March 2021

Odluka o stručnoj službi Hrvatskoga sabora (Official Gazette Narodne novine no. 64/12), https://narodne-novine.nn.hr/clanci/sluzbeni/2012_06_64_1518.html; accessed on 9 March 2021 (Croatian Text Only)

Parlametar, https://parlametar.hr/; accessed on 9 March 2021 and 11 October 2021

13
CYPRUS' PARLIAMENTARY ADMINISTRATION

Natia Karayianni

13.1 Introduction

The Republic of Cyprus came into existence in 1960 as a presidential democracy. The Constitution of the Republic of Cyprus sets out the role of each branch of government and is permeated throughout by the principle of separation of powers. The House of Representatives (*Voulì ton Antiprosòpon*) is vested with legislative power (Constitution of the Republic of Cyprus, 1960, Article 61).

The House is unicameral and, as per Article 62 of the Constitution, comprises 50 Members of Parliament, of which two-thirds were to be Greek Cypriot and one-third Turkish Cypriot. In 1985, the House of Representatives, by decision, raised the number of Members from 50 to 80, retaining Greek Cypriot and Turkish Cypriot representation proportion so that there is provision for 56 Greek Cypriot and 24 Turkish Cypriot Members of Parliament.

It should be noted that, after the intercommunal strife of December 1963, the Turkish Cypriot representatives withdrew from the House of Representatives and the Turkish Cypriot seats have since remained vacant. As a result, the House currently comprises 56 Greek Cypriot Members of Parliament, representing 7 parties. For the purposes of this chapter, no analysis will be made of the particular circumstances and events which led to the current situation in Cyprus. Rather, the focus will remain on the administration of the House of Representatives as it stands today.

The House of Representatives convenes in one ordinary session each year, usually commencing in September and ending in July, with regular committee meetings taking place throughout the working week and a plenary meeting once a week.

Despite the importance of the administration in the functioning of the House, as will be seen in this chapter, little or no attention has been focused on its contribution to the works of the House.[1]

13.2 The organization of the Administration of the House

In following with the principle of separation of powers, the running of the House of Representatives is under the sole authority of the House itself as provided for in Article 73.1 of the Constitution, which holds that "Subject to the ensuing provisions of this Article, the

House of Representatives by its Standing Orders regulates any matter of parliamentary procedure and of functions of its offices".

In 1961, shortly after the Republic came into being, the House voted into law the Services and Personnel of the House of Representatives Law 1961, which provides for the setting up of its services.

13.2.1 Status of Parliamentary Personnel

The Services and Personnel of the House of Representatives Law 1961 provides that all members of the House Administration, including the Secretary General, are part of the Civil Service (*section 7, Law 24/1961*). The appointment of the personnel of the House is made against permanent posts, approved by the House as part of its budget, which in turn is part of the state's budget. In 2019, the House of Representatives amended the Constitution to reinforce its independence, as enshrined in the oft quoted principle of separation of powers, so that the House's budget is subject to the approval of the House alone and is included in the state's budget as a separate budget, without the prior approval of the Ministry of Finance.

As members of the Civil Service, the personnel of the House enjoy job security and thus are not subject to political pressure in terms of their employment. Posts in the Civil Service may be transferable and non-transferable. The House's organogram includes clerical, administrative, and auxiliary personnel as transferable posts, all in supporting roles to the House administration. The rest of the positions in the House's administration are non-transferable, which means that most House personnel spend their entire career in positions within the House.

As with all positions in the Civil Service, the specific terms of employment for each position, such as the duties, responsibilities and required qualifications, are set out in schemes of service. For the House the Speaker has the right to amend the schemes of service for the administration.

The Civil Service in Cyprus is a career-based service and discretion and political neutrality is expected of all civil servants. Under the Civil Service Law (1990) and the Political Rights of Civil Servants, Education Officials, Municipal Employees, Community Employees and Public Law Organization Employees Law (2015), all civil servants may freely express their views (*section 62 Law 1/1990*), including their political views and beliefs outside their working hours (*section 3 Law 102(I)/2015*). Furthermore, they have the right to join a union (*section 63 Law 1/1990*) or a political party and may even hold office in a political party, so long as they first secure permission to do so from the appropriate authority (*section 4 Law 102(I)/2015*).

These rights are accompanied by corresponding obligations. Civil servants must be impartial, serve the interests of the public, avoid conflicts of interest, abide by the Constitution and the laws, serve citizens objectively, fairly, impersonally and impartially and act with dignity (*section 60 Law 1/1990*). Furthermore, they may not use their position or exercise their influence to act in such a way as to persuade any person to join a political party or organization or to influence any person in favour of a political party or a politician (*section 5 Law 102(I)/2015*).

It should be noted that the House's administration is strictly separate from the political advisors to Members of Parliament. All Members and parliamentary parties receive funds from the House's budget to hire personal personnel which serve under a private employment contract. The prerequisites, remuneration and rights of the political personnel are set out in the Parliamentary Advisors and Other Relevant Issues Law (2019). While there is great interaction and cooperation between the House's administration and the political personnel, their duties and status are clearly demarcated.

The separation between the political personnel and the administration does not transfer to the relationship between the administration and the Speaker or the Members of Parliament. Although the head of the administration is the Secretary General, the personnel of the House may, and does, receive instructions directly from the Speaker and the Members, particularly in the case of committee secretariats from the chairperson of the committee. The accountability of the House personnel to their political superior is not explicitly set out in their scheme of service; it is an integral part of their functions within the parliament.

Nowhere is political impartiality more important than in the House of Representatives. The culture of the House's administration is such that even personnel members who are politically active, function neutrally within the walls of the House. The permanence of the personnel of the House makes it that much more important for the personnel to maintain political neutrality, treating all Members in the same way, regardless of political affiliation. In the face of the ever-changing political membership of the House, not just in terms of individual Members but also with a balance of power that is subject to change with every election, the administration guarantees continuity of knowledge and experience.

13.2.2 Services of the House

The Services and Personnel of the House of Representatives Law 1961 provided for the creation of a Publications Service, a Committees Service, a Protocol Service, each comprising two officials, as well as four stenographers, five messengers and three telephone operators (*section 4 Law 24/1961*). Further personnel were to be transferred from other parts of the Civil Service (*section 5 Law 24/1961*).

Over the ensuing decades, the needs of the House have grown as the Republic matured and the obligations of the House grew both in relation to internal affairs and as regards external relations. The competences of the services of the House have developed to follow the changing of the House's needs and the expectations from Members of the personnel of the House. The services of the House and their respective competences, as they stand currently, are shown in Table 13.1.

In terms of numbers, the Services of the House have grown in tandem with their competences. A comparative view of the personnel of the House, not including supporting services, in 2013 and 2021, as shown in the state budget is set out in Table 13.2.

As can be seen from Table 13.2, the personnel of the House has substantially increased in the past few years. Overall, there was a 77.9% increase, since 2013, of which 40% in Directors, with the expansion of the Communications Service and the planned creation of the new Budget Administration Service and a 333%, 93% and 51% increase in middle management, lower management and personnel, respectively, resulting from the expansion of all services in the administration.

Per service, there is a 79% increase in the personnel of the Parliamentary Committees Service, 53% in the personnel of the International Relations Service, 50% in the European Relations Service, 300% in the Financial Management Service and 150% in the Communication Service.

Table 13.1 Services of the House of Representatives

Services of the House of Representatives	
Parliamentary Committees Service (including the Legal Affairs Sector)	Responsible for the technical aspects of the legislative process and the operation and work of the parliamentary committees.
International Relations Service	Responsible for the planning, organization and development of the political, cultural, economic and other relations of the Republic of Cyprus with other countries at the bilateral and multilateral parliamentary level.
Research, Studies and Publications Service	Responsible for the language editing, indexing and publication of the minutes of the plenary session of the House, the linguistic editing of all texts issued by the House, the curating of all publications of the House, scientific research and methodical collection of data related to the history and action of the House and organizes cultural and other events.
European Relations Service	Responsible for the provision of legal or other scientific support in relation to any matter falling within the scope of the European acquis or European affairs in general, including the drafting of reports and legal studies on harmonizing bills/regulations and chapters of the acquis communautaire.
Financial Administration Service	Responsible for the coordination and management of the expenditures of the House, including the preparation of the annual Budget, the auditing of expenditures and revenues and the maintenance of the building and the equipment of the House.
Communications Service	Responsible for the dissemination of information to the media and citizens about the House's activities, facilitating journalists in their work, the maintenance of the House's website and providing technical support to the personnel and Members.
Library (The Library is part of the Research, Studies and Publications Service)	Serves the Members, the political personnel, the House's administration and any interested external users for research purposes in the legal science, history and politics of Cyprus.

Source: Website of the House of Representatives

13.3 The Role of the Administration in the Context of Parliamentary Work

As with all legislatures, the personnel of the House provide various supporting services to the Members. The work of the House services is generally considered to be of good standard, although no formal evaluation has been performed, other than the annual evaluation of individual members of personnel by the Head of their service and the Secretary General.

Table 13.2 Comparative view of the personnel of the House

Service	Positions	2013	2021
Parliamentary Committees Service	• Director of Parliamentary Committees Service	1	1
	• First Secretary to Parliamentary Committees	1	5
	• Senior Secretaries to Parliamentary Committees	4	8
	• Secretaries to Parliamentary Committees A′	6	12
	• Secretaries to Parliamentary Committees	12	17
		Total: 24	**Total: 43**
International Relations Service	• Director of International Relations Service	1	1
	• First International Relations Officer	1	3
	• Senior International Relations Officer	3	6
	• International Relations Officer A′	5	8
	• International Relations Officer	7	10
		Total: 17	**Total: 28**
Research, Studies and Publications Service	• Director of Research, Studies and Publications Service	1	1
	• First Research, Studies and Publications Officer	1	3
	• Senior Research, Studies and Publications Officer	2	4
	• Research, Studies and Publications Officer A′	4	9
	• Research, Studies and Publications Officer	12	14
		Total: 20	**Total: 31**
European Relations Service	• Director of European Relations Service	1	1
	• First European Relations Officer	–	1
	• Senior European Relations Officer	–	2
	• European Relations Officer A'	3	5
	• European Relations Officer	6	6
		Total: 10	**Total: 15**
Financial Administration Service[2]	• Director of the Financial Management Service	1	1
	• First Officer of the Financial Management Service	–	1
	• Senior Officer of the Financial Management Service	1	1
	• Financial Management Service Officer	–	2
	• Assistant Processing Officer	–	3
		Total: 2	**Total: 8**

(Continued)

Table 13.2 Comparative view of the personnel of the House *(Continued)*

Service	Positions	2013	2021
Communications Service	• Director of Communications Service	–	1
	• First Communications Officer	–	–
	• Senior Communications Officer	1	1
	• Communications Officer A'	1	2
	• Communications Officer	2	6
		Total: 4	**Total: 10**
Budget Administration Service[3]	• Director of Budget Administration Service	–	1
	• Budget Administration Officer	–	1
		Total: –	**Total: 1**
All Services	• Directors	5	7
	• Middle management (First Officers)	3	13
	• Lower management (Senior Officers and Officers A')	30	58
	• Personnel	39	59
		Total: 77	**Total: 137**

Source: State budget 2013 and 2021.

13.3.1 Legislative and Parliamentary Scrutiny

The work of the House, as analysed in the annual reports of the House for the 2013–2014 (House of Representatives, *Èkthesi Pepragmènon 2013–2014*,) and 2018–2019 parliamentary sessions (House of Representatives, *Èkthesi Pepragmènon 2018–2019*), show no significant changes in the deposition of government bills and regulations. However, there is a marked upward trend in the submission of private members' bills, (66 in 2009, 125 in 2013 and 149 in 2019).

There are currently 16 standing committees in the House, 4 ad hoc committees and 2 subcommittees. The bulk of the work of the legislative and parliamentary scrutiny of the House is performed at a committee level. Parliamentary committees scrutinize bills and regulations in depth and submit them, often with substantial amendments proposed by the committee, to the plenary of the House for final decision on the issue at hand. The same is true of parliamentary scrutiny of the executive. The committee examines an issue, as registered by any Member and, upon conclusion of the scrutiny, drafts a report which is submitted to the plenary. Such issues range from local interest matters to the scrutiny of the way in which specific laws are applied.

Unlike most other legislatures, private members' bills play an important role in the works of the House, as the only limitation placed on them, other than constitutionality which is true of all bills, is that they cannot increase the expenditure of the state. The importance of private members' bills is evident in the increase of their number, as mentioned hereinabove. The personnel of the House are responsible for drafting all private members' bills. The role of the personnel in drafting private members' bills is not to interfere with the political will of the rapporteur but rather to advise Members on any legal or technical issues arising from their proposal and to transfer their political will to the proposed legislation.

The standing committees of the House are on verge of being underpersonneled. Each committee is typically supported by one secretary, assisted in issues of harmonising legislation by an officer of the European Affairs Service. Of the 16 standing committees, only 8 are supported by more than one secretary and only the Committee on Financial and Budgetary Affairs has a fully dedicated secretariat. The rest of the committees share their secretaries with other committees. Until recently, the situation was even more dire, with all secretaries responsible for two committees each. With the recent increase in the personnel of the Parliamentary Committees Service, it is expected that each committee will soon have a dedicated secretariat.

As mentioned above, one of the basic principles of the Constitution of the Republic is the strict separation of powers amongst the executive, the legislative and the judicial branches. As a consequence, the administration of the House has to work independently of the rest of the Civil Service. This is of particular importance in relation to the legislative procedure as neither the plenary nor the parliamentary committees can direct the Attorney-General to advise them on issues of a legal nature, although there has been a good level of cooperation between the two institutions and the Attorney-General may decide to offer advice on any issue pending before the House.

The schemes of service of the House personnel involved in the functioning of the parliamentary committees task the said personnel with providing all the support required by the committee in the discharge of its functions, from procedural support to the provision of expert knowledge. In practice this includes all the procedural issues involved in the preparation of the agenda and the meetings of each committee, the preparation of detailed briefing material for the chairperson and the members of the committees, the legislative vetting of all bills and regulations deposited by the government, the drafting of private members' bills, the evaluation and analysis of relevant data, the conduct of research on the legislation and best practices of other states and the evaluation of the level of harmonization with the European Union acquis.

During the financial debt crisis, the House of Representatives has been called upon to act swiftly and scrutinize legislative measures in record time so as to deal with the fallout. Following the agreement on the Economic Adjustment Programme, a number of complex issues were set before the House, whether in the form of government bills and, on occasion, private members' bills, or for the purposes of parliamentary scrutiny of government decisions.

The year 2020 was also a significant year for the Republic of Cyprus, as it has completed 60 years of life. During the past 60 years, society has progressed and the Republic's institutions have grown and with them the need to institute new legislation and revise the existing one in a number of areas. In the past five years alone, the House has scrutinized and passed legislation on a number of important and complicated issues, including eight amendments of the Constitution and legislation to revise and update the legal framework on road safety, to regulate the lifting of the right to privacy of personal communication, for the establishment of a national health service and for the establishment of a criminal justice system for juveniles.

All the above, and many more issues and bills, were analysed in depth and vetted in legal and legislative terms by the administration personnel. The personnel of the House drafted private members' bills, vetted and redrafted government bills following instructions from committees, brought legal and technical issues to the attention of the committees and advised them on the best way to resolve such issues, as well as on the best way to incorporate the House's political will into the proposed law.

Further to the work performed on the level of parliamentary committees, parliamentary scrutiny is also performed via questions submitted by Members to Ministers of the government, who have an obligation to reply in good time. The said questions and the answers submitted by the Ministers are curated by the Research, Studies and Publications Service. In the 2018–2019 parliamentary session, 763 questions were submitted via the Service (House of Representatives, *Èkthesi Pepragmènon 2018–2019*).

13.3.2 International Relations

Parliamentary diplomacy is particularly important in the case of Cyprus, in view of the "Cyprus question", stemming from the invasion of the Republic on 20 July 1974, by Turkish armed forces, as a result of which over 36% of the territory of the Republic of Cyprus is illegally occupied by Turkey (Ministry of Foreign Affairs, *The Cyprus Question*). As mentioned in the introduction of this chapter, no further analysis of the Cyprus question will take place, other than to note that it forms a significant part of parliamentary diplomacy for the Republic of Cyprus.

In general terms, the House has no direct responsibility for foreign policy, as in a presidential system especially, this responsibility falls to the executive branch. However, the work done by Members is important in terms of the promotion of Cyprus abroad and the dissemination of information on various issues the Republic has to deal with, both in a multilateral level through membership of international organizations and in a bilateral level through strengthening relationships with individual states.

The personnel of the International Relations Service are responsible for providing technical support and expertise to the Members who take part in international activities on behalf of the House, as well as for the organization and technical support of international parliamentary activities taking place in Cyprus, including the conduct of research, the evaluation of the relevant data and the drafting relevant texts such as reports, memoranda and press releases.

13.3.3 External Relations with Society

The House has a long tradition of providing technical support for the operation of a Parliament of Elders, a Youth Parliament and a Children's Parliament, which convene annually under the auspices of the Speaker of the House.

The House has also digitized all the content of the House's library, including the minutes of the House from 1960 onwards, and upgraded the website so that it best facilitates access by the citizens and affords them opportunity to express their views on a number of issues.

Furthermore, the Research, Studies and Publications Service and its officers are tasked with the organization of cultural and educational events, open to the public, as well as with the organization of educational visits to the House from all levels of education, from primary schools to universities.

In the 2018–2019 parliamentary session alone, the Service organized two conventions, five cultural events and one theatre performance as well as issued two publications (House of Representatives, *Èkthesi Pepragmènon 2018–2019*).

In 2019, the House also established the House of the Citizen, which is housed in a restored historic building near the parliament, which was retrofitted with technology to provide the citizens with the ability to be properly informed on the work of the parliament and promote interactive communication between the legislature and the citizens. The project was to be supported by the administration personnel, but due to Covid-19 restrictions, the scheduled events did not take place. Once the pandemic crisis is over, it is expected that the House of the Citizen will resume its work.

In an attempt to bring the House closer to the citizens, in 2019, the previous Speaker established the Parallel Parliament, whose main purpose is to bring society into dialogue with the House and involve them in the decision-making process by making use of the knowledge and expertise of the citizens of Cyprus (House of Representatives, *Èkthesi Pepragmènon 2018–2019*). The administration of the House was actively involved in setting up the Parallel Parliament and provides technical support for its continuing function, adding to the responsibilities and obligations of the personnel.

13.3.4 Covid-19 and the House

Covid-19 hit the House of Representatives as unexpectedly as it did all legislatures. The second half of the 2019–2020 parliamentary session was conducted in the midst of the first measures taken in Cyprus, including a lockdown, which precluded the usual way of conducting parliamentary committee meetings and plenary sessions.

The administration was called upon to find ways to allow the House to function to the best of its ability. Constitutional restrictions precluded the utilization of teleconference tools for the plenary, although parliamentary committees conducted consultations, rather than official meetings, via such tools. At first, the plenary only convened in relation to measures concerning the pandemic, under a political agreement between the parliamentary parties that the minimum number of Members would be present to ensure a quorum was reached. In particular, between March and July 2019, parliamentary committees conducted 60 teleconferences, with the support of the Communications Service on technical issues.

As the public health crisis grew, the House decided via resolution to move the work of the parliamentary session to a conference centre, which afforded enough space for the House's work to be conducted safely. In order to facilitate this move, the House relied heavily on the utilization of technology both by the administration and the Members. Tools developed prior to the pandemic took on increased importance since a major part of the work of the House was, and continues to be, conducted in some distance from the physical offices of the personnel and the Members. The personnel of the House were also urged to work from home, with a small contingent of emergency personnel physically present at the House. Great use was made of the "e-cooperation" system, which allows access to the necessary documents for both the plenary and the committees, from any computer outside the House, as well as the live-streaming of plenary sessions, allowing personnel to follow the meetings without being physically present in the room at the time.

Outside parliamentary committee work, the House continued to function in the face of Covid-19 restrictions, with Members submitting no less than 607 questions to Ministers (House of Representatives, *Èkthesi Pepragmènon 2019–2020*).

In terms of parliamentary diplomacy, as with all aspects of parliamentary operations, alternative methods were employed for the House to continue to fulfil its role. Members continued to take active part in the international and European levels via teleconference, with 48 such teleconferences taking place by the end of August 2020 (House of Representatives, *Èkthesi Pepragmènon 2019–2020*).

The House also continued to engage with the public through the organization of six cultural events and one conference, which took place either prior to Covid-19 measures being taken or with strict application of these measures. Further, four publications were issued and the material given in the context of educational visits from students of all levels of education was revised.

During the Covid-19 crisis, parliamentary personnel rose to the occasion and continued to provide all the necessary support to the Members in adapting to the new environment and the new demands made for the use of technology, ensuring that the House continued to function with its usual efficiency. This is evident in the annual report of the House for the 2019–2020 parliamentary session (House of Representatives, *Èkthesi Pepragmènon 2019–2020*), which notes no significant changes in parliamentary functions.

13.4 Challenges

The changing face of society inevitably affects the administration of the House. The House of Representatives has moved towards a more open relationship with society, promoting transparency and citizen engagement. This has taken the form of the establishment of new institutions such as the Youth Parliament, the Parallel Parliament and the House of the Citizen, as well as the digitalization of the minutes of the House from 1960 onwards, upgrading the website and live-streaming the plenary sessions.

The revision of the Republic's legislation on a number of areas has also stretched the administration's human resources as, despite the recent increase in personnel, no time was afforded to properly train new recruits, laying the onus of the work to the more experienced personnel, which is low in numbers.

Because of the financial debt crisis beginning in 2013, the construction of a new House building was postponed, which was again postponed due to the financial consequences of the Covid-19 crisis. As a result, the personnel of the House perform their duties in cramped circumstances, an issue that has only heightened by hiring new personnel. The House personnel are currently split between two locations, as the current building cannot accommodate them all, with all the ensuing challenges and difficulties this brings.

The drive towards a deepening independence of the House, as evident in the constitutional amendment which ensures the financial autonomy of the House, rendering it solely responsible for the drafting of its own budget, has led to the first independent budget for 2020 and the creation of the new Budget Administration Service. The House is currently in the process of drafting legislation regulating the execution of its budget, providing for effective auditing mechanisms and for any other relevant issue relating to the ensuring of full financial autonomy.

13.5 Conclusion

The administration of the House of Representatives is small in numbers, although it has recently expanded as a response to the added expectations and duties assigned to its personnel. As part of the Civil Service, its personnel are not subject to political pressure in terms of their employment, which allows them to maintain their political neutrality. The terms of service of the administration personnel and the fact that they spend their entire career within the House ensure continuity and accumulated experience in parliamentary functions.

In the drive for ensuring the independence of the House from the executive, this continuity and experience must be safeguarded.

The changing needs of society, heightened by the consequences of the Covid-19 pandemic, have put added pressure on the administration to swiftly adapt in order to allow the House to continue to function at peak efficiency, which it appears to have done admirably. In the past few years, the personnel of the House has had to manage additional responsibilities and increased complexity in its work, while facing human and material resources shortages and is currently undergoing an evolution, with new responsibilities assigned to it and the addition of new personnel, which must be integrated into new and existing structures. The results of this evolution cannot yet be evaluated as it takes time for the ongoing changes to show any effects in the work done by the administration.

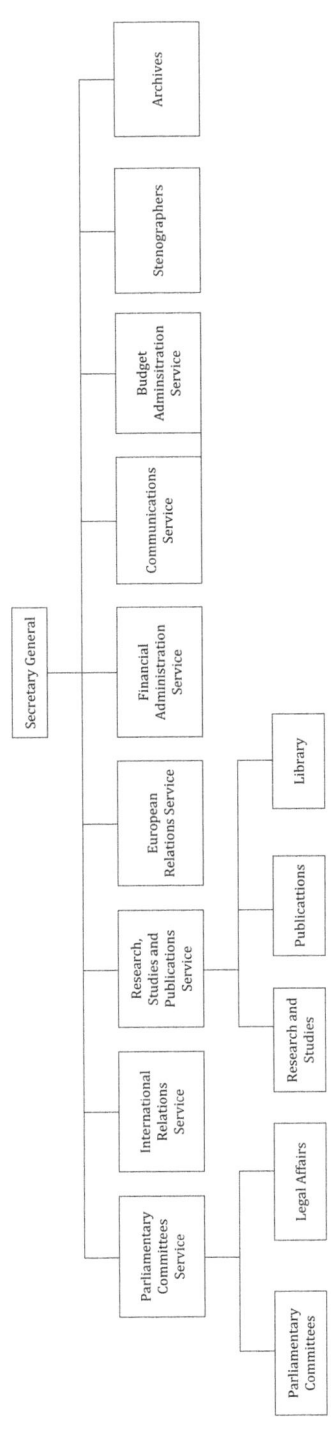

Notes

1 The only remotely relevant academic work found was this author's LLM thesis [Karayianni, Natia (2013) *The Contribution of the Drafter in Parliament to the Quality of Legislation in Cyprus*. Master's thesis, Institute of Advanced Legal Studies].
2 The Financial Management Service is also staffed by transferable staff which is not included in the budget of the House.
3 The Budget Administration Service is a new service to be established in 2021.

References

Civil Service Law 1990, Law 1/1990.
Constitution of the Republic of Cyprus, 1960.
House of Representatives, http://www.parliament.cy/en/general-information [Accessed 25 July 2021].
House of Representatives, 2019, *Èkthesi Pepragmènon 2018–2019,* [Activities Report 2018–2019], Available at: http://www.parliament.cy/el/%CE%B1%CF%81%CF%87%CE%B5%CE%AF%CE%BF/%CE%B5%CE%BA%CE%B8%CE%AD%CF%83%CE%B5%CE%B9%CF%82-%CF%80%CE%B5%CF%80%CF%81%CE%B1%CE%B3%CE%BC%CE%AD%CE%BD%CF%89%CE%BD/-%CE%B5%CE%BA%CE%B8%CE%B5%CF%83%CE%B7-%CF%80%CE%B5%CF%80%CF%81%CE%B1%CE%B3%CE%BC%CE%AD%CE%BD%CF%89%CE%BD-2019 [Accessed 25 April 2021].
House of Representatives, 2014, *Èkthesi Pepragmènon 2013–2014,* [Activities Report 2013–2014], Available at: http://www.parliament.cy/images/media/assetfile/APOLOGISMOS%202013-2014.pdf [Accessed 25 April 2021].
House of Representatives, 2020 *Èkthesi Pepragmènon 2019–2020,* [Activities Report 2019–2020], Available at: http://www.parliament.cy/el/%CE%B1%CF%81%CF%87%CE%B5%CE%AF%CE%BF/%CE%B5%CE%BA%CE%B8%CE%AD%CF%83%CE%B5%CE%B9%CF%82-%CF%80%CE%B5%CF%80%CF%81%CE%B1%CE%B3%CE%BC%CE%AD%CE%BD%CF%89%CE%BD/-%CE%B5%CE%BA%CE%B8%CE%B5%CF%83%CE%B7-%CF%80%CE%B5%CF%80%CF%81%CE%B1%CE%B3%CE%BC%CE%AD%CE%BD%CF%89%CE%BD-2020 [Accessed 28 April 2021].
House of Representatives 2020, *Proedrikì Demokratìa versus Proedrevòmenis Koinovouleftikìs Demokratìas* [Presidential System versus Presidential Parliamentary System], Government Printing Office, Nicosia.
Ministry of Foreign Affairs, 2021 *The Cyprus Question*, Available at: https://mfa.gov.cy/historical-background.html [Accessed 28 April 2021].
Parliamentary Advisors and Other Relevant Issues Law 2019, Law 41(I)/2019.
Political Rights of Civil Servants, Education Officials, Municipal Employees, Community Employees and Public Law Organization Employees Law 2015, Law 102(I)/2015.
Services and Personnel of the House of Representatives Law 1961, Law 24/1961.

14
CZECHIA'S PARLIAMENTARY ADMINISTRATION

Petr Kaniok

14.1 Introduction

The Czech parliament consists of two chambers with a different history.[1] Whereas the Chamber of Deputies (*Poslanecká sněmovna, Sněmovna*),[2] serving as the lower chamber and consisting of 200 MPs, has been existing since 1 January, 1993, when the Czech Republic as one of the two states succeeding former Czechoslovakia, started its existence, the Senate (*Senát*),[3] the upper house of the Parliament consisting of 83 senators, has been counting its existence since Autumn 1996. Both chambers work independently, they also have their own administration and internal rules governing it. From the broadest perspective, the working of both administrations is defined by the law, more specifically by three acts. Firstly, both administrations were created by Act 59/1996 Col. on the Seat of the Parliament of the Czech Republic and subsequently – as the second important act involved – defined as "organizational parts of the state" by Act 219/2000 Col. On the property of Czech Republic and its actions in legal affairs. More specifically, in case of *Poslanecká sněmovna*, whose administration is organized as *Kancelář Poslanecké sněmovny* (the Office of the Chamber of Deputies, OCD), the third key legal document is Act 90/1995 Col. on the rules of procedure of the Chamber of Deputies. In the case of *Senát* and its *Kancelář Senátu* (Senate Chancellery, SC), a similar function plays Act 107/1999 Col. On the rules of procedure of the Senate. Both administrations have their own organizational rules which in detail specify the internal functioning and working of both bodies.

14.2 Key Aspects of the Organization of the Parliamentary Administrations

Internal organization and structure of both bodies are very similar and follow the principles which arise from the functions both administrations have. That means that they provide professional, organizational, and technical support for the activities carried out by the Czech Parliament, its bodies and offices, deputies and senators, political groups, and members of the European Parliament elected within the territory of the Czech Republic. Both bodies are managed by Secretary Generals and are divided into numerous departments. Their overview can be found in Annex (Organizational Chart of the Chamber of Deputies in Czech Republic; Organizational Chart of the Senate in Czech Republic).

Both charts suggest that both administrations operate on the basis of very similar structures. They are both using almost identical departments – additionally, they are in both cases divided into divisions fulfilling particular tasks (Articles 4–21, OCD Organization Rules, Annex II SC Organization Rules). The differences are rather cosmetic and concern titles and names of units or departments. In general, both administrations contain structures supporting elected representatives of each chamber – secretariats of Presidents and Vice-presidents – specialized and expert parts such as EU affairs units or IT departments and structures created for committees and commissions.

A specific position within the internal structure is granted to two institutions which are serving – although not formally – both Houses. The first one is the Parliamentary Institute, an analytical department working within OCD. Even that being part of the lower chamber administration, it serves in *Senát* as well (Article 18, OCD Organizational Rules). The purpose of the Institute is to resolve the tasks of scientific, informative, and educational nature for *Poslanecká sněmovna*: Deputies, Committees and other authorities, Office of the Chamber, *Senát* and its offices, senators, and Senate authorities. To provide the best possible services, the Institute has been divided into three departments, each dealing with a particular agenda. The Department of General Analysis deals predominantly with Deputy and Senator requests and provides general analyses and analyses in the field of foreign relations. The Department of EU Affairs serves mostly as an expert base for the Committee for European Affairs of *Poslanecká sněmovna*. For example, the department elaborates and holds the database of incoming EU documents and those that have some relation to EU. The Department of Communication and Education provides services for the public and operates Information Center of *Poslanecká sněmovna*.

Similar specific position is granted to the Parliamentary Library. Likewise, the Parliamentary Institute, it is a part of OCD administration, but it serves for *Senát* and its members as well. The library also provides a public library and information services. Since its inception, the Library has collected nearly 220,000 volumes of legal publications, legislation, political science, modern history, philosophy, sociology, economics, culture, encyclopaedias, and reference books. The core of the book collection consists of Czech parliamentary documents and laws from 18 other foreign parliaments.

In terms of hierarchy, OCD and SC are organized in slightly different ways. The Head of OCD is the leading position within the administrative structure. The second level consists of directors/heads – this concerns, secretariats/offices of elected representatives, departments, independent units, and secretaries of committees and commissions. Third level is then created by particular employees.

SC is formally organized in two tiers. They are so-called managerial employees who are appointed – chancellor, director of the office of the President of the Senate, heads of departments, and committees' secretaries – and other employees. In fact, the structure is more nuanced as the managerial employees do not operate on the same level – the chancellor is the key figure in the hierarchy. Additionally, there are heads of units within departments or deputies of departments' heads present in the structure.

In the case of both administrations, a clear distinction can be made between central services and committees'/commissions' secretariats. Although the latter is in both bodies part of the same central structure – and is interlinked with the central administration through the Secretary General – their real functioning is more in the hands of the committees'/commissions' chairs. From the point of view of the administration role, the key position here is the committee's/commission's secretary. In both chambers, it is an appointed position crucial for the smooth functioning of either a committee or a commission. Even that committee/commission secretaries are formally organizational and supportive positions, officials interviewed argue that due to their knowledge of committees' agenda and continuity – many of them used to serve for decades – they can have strong informal power over a particular structure, also due to close personal links with committee chairs or people responsible for a particular agenda – mostly deputy ministers – in executive.

Although the organization structure of both administrations is often perceived as very stable, internal dynamics and changes can be identified. Both administrations were affected by the Czech Republic access to the EU – as a consequence, EU units within both were created. Officials interviewed confirm that the EU membership affected both administrations in even more aspects – for example, it attracted younger and differently motivated employees or increased pressure on staffs' language skills. In the case of OCD, changes often happen in departments and units related to the elected representatives of the Chamber of Deputies. Parts of the administration that are subordinated directly to the president and vice-presidents are usually adjusted after each parliamentary election, reflecting, for example, the number of Vice-presidents. In the case of other departments, changes happen gradually time to time echoing external events or demands. Typically, security departments or PR/media departments were enlarged or restructured on the basis of such influence. This applies for both administrations.

SC internal structure was changed twice in its history. The first reorganization occurred in 2006 when the SC transformed its managerial structure and cut the number of managerial positions by ten. It also decreased the number of total staffs employed from 214 to 200. This reform was explained by a need to make the SC more efficient (Senát 2006). The second reconfiguration occurred in 2021 caused by challenges related to, for example, digitalization. Within the second reform, in particular PR and media department and IT department were internally reorganized (SeznamZprávy 2021).

In terms of size of staff, both administrations can be described as pretty stable. OCD staffing is approximately twice as it is in the case of SC. This reflects the fact that the size of both chambers – in terms of elected members – has similar proportions. If staffs' numbers are compared during the last 15 years, periods of small ups and downs can be identified. However, in general, no turbulent events causing substantial increase or decrease occurred. Particularly in the most recent years, shifts happen in terms of units and are rather cosmetic. Table 14.1 offers a summarization of staffs' development, evolution, and trends.

The process of staff recruitment combines political appointments as well as regular job calls. The former is typical – but not necessary – for leading positions and functions within the respective administration. In particular, the General Secretary is appointed/removed by the respective President after approval of such nomination by the organizational committee of the particular chamber (Article OCD Organizational Rules, Article 6 SC Organizational Rules). However, OCD was in this regard remarkably stable. In the last three decades, there were just two OCD General Secretaries – the first one, Petr Kynštetr serving for almost 27 years quitting in 2017. In the case of SC, changes in the chancellor position emerged more frequently. For example, since 2005, there were different four chancellors in the helm.

As the General Secretary appoints/removes all departments' heads as well as committees/commissions' secretaries, there is a limited space for political appointments. However, according to officials interviewed, those are very rare, and if those occur, occur only in departments which are directly related to the elected representatives such as the Office of

Table 14.1 Number of staffs in Senát and in Poslanecká sněmovna

Year	Office of the Chamber of Deputies	Senate Chancellery
2020	348	190
2019	354	193
2018	356	188
2017	353	191
2016	355	193
2015	360	192
2014	362	187
2013	362	193
2012	343	192
2011	343	194
2010	342	196
2009	348	196
2008	343	195
2007	365	200
2006	353	200
2005	348	211

Source: Author on the basis of SC Annual Reports 2005–2020.

the President. Nevertheless, such appointments are not perceived as a kind of protégé as it is widely believed that President or Vice-presidents have the right to choose their closest colleagues who directly shape elected MPs' activities. All other employees are recruited on the basis of standard job calls where pressure for political appointments is minimal and nonexistent.

The fact that both administrations appear to be de-politicized does not exclude controversies around top officials that may occasionally raise. SC was in this regard more in the spotlight. In 2020, the current chancellor, Mrs Vohralíková was anonymously accused of economic misconducts and clientelism (DeníkN 2020). One of her predecessors, Jiří Uklein, serving as a chancellor in the period 2012–2018, was indirectly forced to resign due to conflicts with one of the senators, Jan Horník, and an accusation of bad relations with SC employees (Aktuálně 2018). On the contrary, OCD almost three decades acting General Secretary Petr Kynštetr was highly respected by politicians across the party scene, called "Czech Sir Humprey" (Idnes 2016) and after his resignation in 2017 was appointed as a Czech ambassador in the Republic of Ireland. On the other hand, his high profile among politicians was caused to a certain degree by the fact that he was fully loyal to them, blocking, for example, any attempt for greater transparency in the Chamber of Deputies (Respekt 2006).

Regarding promotion, there are no formal procedures. As officials interviewed point out, the very flat internal structure of the administration does not provide much space for any promotion or staff mobility. As already mentioned, both administrations have in practice a three-/four-layer structure consisting of the General Secretary, the heads of departments (in some cases heads of units), and employees. The possibility of promotion is thus limited and practically can happen only within departments. Additionally, there is no system of internal rotation within departments which also makes the internal set-up pretty rigid and resistant to changes.

Staff training and development opportunities are neither regulated nor formally outlined in detail. From the formal point of view, all such activities are in the hands of the respective HR department. Employees can go through various seminars and educational programmes – for example, language training – but their participation is often based on their own activities or agreements with direct superiors. On the other hand, SC situation is in this sense more robust as SC Organizational Rules (Annex II, Article 13) outlines the responsibilities of HR in a very detailed way, including, for example, "the preparation of a personal strategy of SC" or "language training". OCD Organizational Rules are in the same agenda vaguer and do not go into such depth and details (Article 21).

Staff training in both administrations can be divided into three groups. The first one consists of language courses, dominantly in the English language. The second group contains courses that employees have to go through as they are prescribed by the employment law, for example, by Labor Code, such as first aid training or work safety training. The last group of courses offered then consists of specialized expert courses as, for example, on IT, ethics, or public procurement. Table 14.2 offers an annual overview of staff training of these three categories in SC, providing the number of staffs involved in each category.

As access to external consultancy is concerned, both central administrations have to rely on their staff and their expertise. External services are purchased only in case of bigger and complex logistic or IT activities such as important social events or total web page redesign. Regarding expertise, employees of both administrations are not expected to seek any kind of external consultancy. Moreover, apart from this "internal institutional culture", external consultancy is not included in both administrations' budgets. On the contrary, paid external consultancy is allowed and rather common for MPs, and from time to time, it is requested by committees and commissions.[4] However, this again usually demands a committee or commission chair – elected politicians. However, the total number of such orders is low and the Czech parliament in this regard does not differ from any medium size parliamentary system.

Table 14.2 Staff training in SC

Year	Language courses	Employment law courses	Other courses
2020	34	0	28
2019	58	0	148
2018	60	0	95
2017	28	135	54
2016	33	0	132
2015	34	100	0
2014	30	0	100
2013	33	0	111
2012	69	0	39
2011	40	0	50
2010	43	26	14
2009	52	48	120
2008	61	0	150
2007	NA	NA	NA
2006	153	0	75
2005	64	NA	NA

Source: Author on the basis of SC Annual Reports 2005–2020.

In neither administration, there are no formal rules defining relations between employees and staff related to MPs such as assistants or secretaries or parliamentary clubs. According to officials interviewed, mutual contacts are minimal, most likely to happen in the case of Parliamentary Institute, which may be asked by parliamentary club staff to prepare a particular analysis. However, as officials interviewed emphasized, such analyses are always prepared on a neutral and unbiased basis, not promoting a particular political perspective.

14.3 The Role of the Administration in the Context of Parliamentary Work

Administrators in both chambers conduct multiple activities which mirror the colourful internal structure of both bodies. It can explain, hardly be said, that one type of work that prevails over the other departments has various sizes in terms of staffing and duties assigned. As an example, Table 14.3 offers an overview of the main types of SC[5] activities between 2016 and 2020 period.

As the main activity of both chambers is legislative work, the substance of both SC and OCD activities are related to this as well. Administrations' assistance does not limit to legal advice. It also contains preparatory documents serving as underlying materials for political debates and decisions. The administration is also responsible for the recording of all plenary meetings. The work of legislative departments is however crucial as their staff incorporate political demands and changes raised by MPs. Usually, such employees are policy sector specialists focusing only on one or a limited number of areas. Furthermore, a high degree of interdepartmental cooperation is required. This is caused by the high degree of complexity and internal interdependency of the Czech legislation as a proposed change in one piece of legislation – for example, in the Civic Conduct – may affect other laws.

Another important area is the agenda of EU affairs. Particularly *Senát* profiled itself, especially during the centre-right ODS, a strong influence there, as a chamber focusing on EU affairs (Hrabálek – Strelkov 2015). Annually, both administrations obtain around 40,000 documents from the EU level through the electronic system EU Extranet, the main task of the respective EU units is to choose those which are suitable for further scrutiny and discussion by MPs. For example, in 2012, EU unit chose 727 documents from which Committee for the EU affairs discussed 106. From those, 69 were furthermore discussed by the plenary (SC Annual Report 2012).

Both administrations are very active in public and media relations. Regarding the former, OCD as well as SC has to deal with a considerable number of requests coming from citizens. They may have the form of telephonic questions, written, and questions or requests on the

Table 14.3 Overview of SC main activities

	2016	2017	2018	2019	2020
Preparatory of senate materials	642	610	535	426	535
Legal advice for legislative work	155	131	98	92	157
Requests/submissions from citizens	1997	2812	3341	2520	7102
Press releases	104	91	171	217	200
Foreign visits accepted*	62	64	52	59	16

Source: Author on the basis of SC Annual Reports 2016–2020.

* These numbers do not include visits by ambassadors in *Senát*.

Table 14.4 Overview of citizens' requests for information between 2005 and 2020

Year	OCD	SC
2020	1323	7102
2019	967	2520
2018	860	3341
2017	810	2812
2016	1413	1997
2015	977	2196
2014	906	1585
2013	1271	1497
2012	1792	1539
2011	1866	1700
2010	8422	1617
2009	1382	1573
2008	1415	1634
2007	1746	1052
2006	1744	1146
2005	2142	3372

Source: OCD Annual report on information providing 2005–2020 and SC Annual Reports 2005–2020.

basis of the 106/1999 Col. Law on free access to information. Since 2000, each administration has had to provide an annual report on providing information to citizens. Details provided in Table 14.4 suggest that this activity creates a substantive burden for both administrations as numbers are remarkably high across years.

Apart from assistance to MPs in substantive matters and relations with citizens, both administrations also conduct various logistics tasks and activities such as catering service, technical service, or IT.

14.4 Managing Inter-Institutional and External Relations

The inter-institutional relations do not exist in vacuum but are in the Czech case predefined by the 300/2017 Col. Law on the principles of negotiation and contact between the Chamber of Deputies and the Senate. Even that this act does not mention parliamentary administrations explicitly, as it sets ground for the political cooperation of both chambers, it also creates legal context for the clerks' contact.

The cooperation between two Czech administrations is according to officials interviewed most important in the area of legislative work. Mutual links are in this case predefined by the nature of legislative work in the Czech political system (Zbíral 2020). Two issues are important in this regard. Firstly, the legislative process – in terms of parliamentary and executive involvement follows a standardized pattern. Typically, each policy area is in each particular administration covered by a clerk specialist. The same applies for the executive level where the number of staffs involved may be higher. These employees are usually in close contact when in their area a new legislative proposal or an amendment to an existing law is prepared. More specifically, each piece of legislation has one responsible officer from the government (in case the proposals come from the executive), one responsible officer from OCD, and once it has been approved and handed over to *Senát*, one officer from SC. These three officers plus two rapporteurs (one from each chamber) share most of the work on a particular proposal. Secondly, inter-chamber cooperation and communication is organized by the organizational departments of both chambers. As the officials interviewed confirmed, they closely watch the specific deadlines and duties of each chamber and inform each other.

Although in the legislative area – which represents the key mission of the Czech parliament – this process reproduces in almost every case, these contacts are however rather informal and they are not regulated by any framework or document. Relying on personal ties and contacts is characteristic for the majority of other departments and their units – for example, departments responsible for EU affairs cooperate on such a basis. However, also in the case of other departments, employees know who are their partners in the same or similar department in the second chamber's administration. Although the degree or intensity of inter-administrational cooperation cannot be measured, all interviewed officials perceived existing ties as well working, correct, and unproblematic. Moreover, correct routine was described with cooperation at the executive level of state administration.

Both chambers' administrations are active in external relations, in the EU affairs in particular. Interestingly, SC Organizational Rules in this area explicitly expect close cooperation with a similar department in the OCD – this applies both for foreign relations as well as for the EU affairs. In case of the lower chamber, its permanent representative to the EP has been existing since 2008, in the case of *Senát* since 2004. In the period 2004–2008, the Czech parliament was represented only by Senate's representative. Both administrations tasked their representatives with similar functions – weekly monitoring of EU agenda, updating the respective chamber on important events, monitoring of early stages of decision-making process, cooperation with other national parliaments' representatives, or assistance during MPs visits in Brussels. Each administration has its own IPEX correspondent.

14.5 Managing Current Challenges Facing the Parliamentary Administration

The current challenges such as digitalization, increased demands on parliamentary security, or calls for greater transparency and dialogues with the public are in both administrations perceived as uncontroversial. Starting with the latter, particularly SC is used to organize events for the general public and is also very transparent regarding its own work. For example, the SC publishes very detailed and structured annual reports summarizing all activities that occur within SC responsibilities. Its website is instructive and provides detailed information on competences and roles of SC departments. The OCD is not that much open – its annual reports are treated as interim document of the OCD and thus not publicly accessible. Information about OCD provided on website are relatively limited only to the basic facts. Anyway, both administrations have established departments and units for the public as information centres.

Increasing push for transparency is in both chambers secured by the fact that all plenary meetings are transmitted and recorded. Furthermore, full transcripts of all plenaries are available – all such activities fall into the responsibilities of administrations. Both administrations have to report on an annual basis how they complied with duties associated with information provided – in particular, if a request is submitted according to the 106/1999 Col. Law on free access to information, the content of the request, and the way it was dealt with must be specified. However, each administration obtains around 20 such requests annually.

As the Czech Republic has not been affected by any terrorist attacks so far, security issues or related restrictions do not represent a major topic for parliamentary administrations. There cannot be identified any event which would lead to the increase or decrease of security measures within, for example, parliamentary buildings. More attention is on the contrary devoted to the IT dimension of the security agenda. Officials interviewed confirmed that constant improvement of IT processes is often linked to cybersecurity measures.

The IT security area to some extent relates to digitalization. In this regard, both chambers as well as their administrations have been active since the 1990s. All materials and documents are available on-line; there have been also created legislative databases.

COVID-19 pandemic affected the administrators in the same way as the rest of the Czech society. Employees were offered home-office working mode – if possible – but they could access parliamentary buildings on the same conditions as other employees in the public sector. This means, for example, obligatory testing on a weekly basis and wearing protective masks.

14.6 Conclusion

The Czech parliamentarism represents a case where each of the chambers fulfil different roles. Both chambers have different roles, different processes of composition, different sizes, and different traditions (Linek – Mansfeldová 2007). Contrary to all these differences, the working of both chambers' administrations, as this chapter demonstrates, is surprisingly similar and follows almost identical principles. This can be explained by various factors.

The first one is a common and shared historical origin. Although the OCD and *Poslanecká sněmovna* have been existing for four years longer than SC and *Senát*, both chambers and their administrations were formed during the 1990s. The same societal and political contexts were reflected in the same administrative culture as well as approach towards the style of both OCD and SC internal organization. In addition, the legislative set-up of administration is defined by a similar type of rules and laws. Both administrations are also highly de-politicized, which contributes to their stability and similar profile. They also influence each other as inter-chamber administrations' cooperation is in particular influenced by informal relations, often in the form of close personal links. Finally, both administrations have developed organically avoiding turbulent and politically motivated reforms. If a change occurred, it usually reflects broad social events or needs. Due to the rooted stability, both SC and OCD manage to cope with current challenges such as digitalization, security threats, or public involvement.

As the foreseeable future is concerned, there are no signs of any substantive reform or changes which could change the course of Czech parliamentary administrations. Although Czech politics, especially its party scene, has been coping with change and reconfiguration since 2010, its parliamentary institutional part appears to be solid and resistant to such processes.

Organizational Chart of the Senate in Czech Republic

- Office of the President of the Senate
  - Head of Secretariat of the President of the Senate
  - Protocol Department
  - The Secretariats of the vice-presidents of the Senate

- Head of the Senate Chancellery
  - Internal auditor
  - Internal auditor
  - Press secretary
  - Security director
  - Internal auditor

- The Secretariats of the Senate's committees
- The Secretariats of the Senate's standing commissions

Departments:
- Organizational department
- Legislative Department
- HR Department
- Internal Office department
- Foreign Relations Department
- Senate Services and Public Relations Department
- Financial Department
- Technical services Department
- IT Department
- Catering Services Department

Organizational Chart of the Chamber of Deputies in Czech Republic

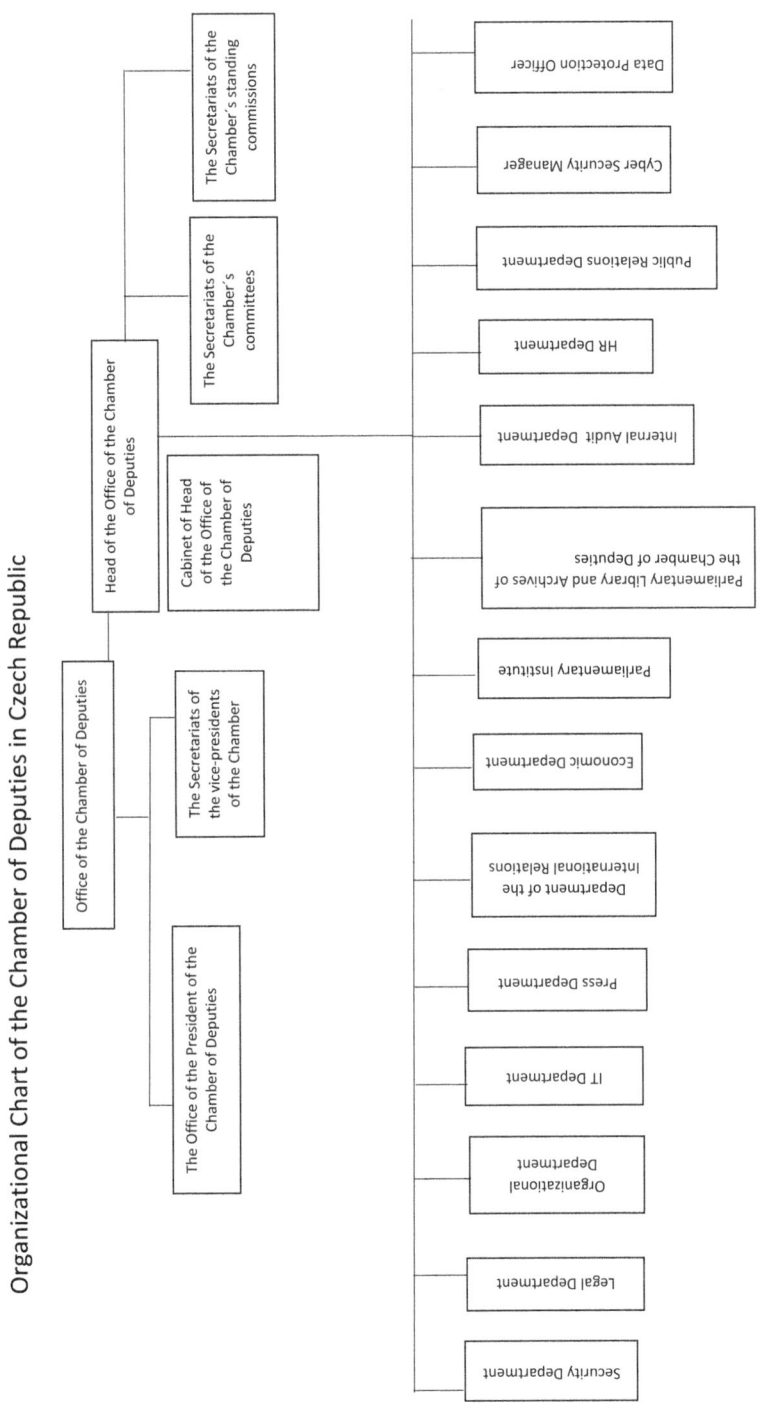

Notes

1 For details on the history and political development of the Czech parliament, see for example Zbíral (2020) or Mansfeldová (2014).
2 The Chamber of Deputies.
3 The Senate.
4 The commission is a working body established by the *Senát* decision. It usually has a specific purpose; its mandate may be either permanent or temporary.
5 OCD annual reports are treated as internal documents which are not publicly available.

References

Act 219/2000 Col. On the property of Czech Republic and its actions in legal affairs.
Act 90/1995 Col. On the rules of procedure of the Chamber of Deputies.
Act 107/1999 Col. On the rules of procedure of the Senate.
Act 300/2017 Col. On the principles of negotiation and contact between the Chamber of Deputies and externally.
Aktuálně (2018). Senátní kancléř Uklein končí na vlastní žádost ve funkci. Available at (https://zpravy.aktualne.cz/domaci/senatni-kancler-uklein-konci-na-vlastni-zadost-ve-funkci/r~44d855ac89e011e8a4080cc47ab5f122/).
DeníkN (2020). Kancléřka Senátu čelí nařčení z nekalostí. Pochybení odmítá, čeká ji ale vysvětlování. Available at (https://denikn.cz/493829/kanclerka-senatu-celi-narceni-z-nekalosti-pochybeni-odmita-ceka-ji-ale-vysvetlovani/#).
Hrabálek, Martin – Strelkov, Alexander (2015) The Czech Parliament and European Integration. In: Hefftler C., Neuhold C., Rozenberg O., Smith J. (eds) The Palgrave Handbook of National Parliaments and the European Union. Palgrave Macmillan, London.
Idnes (2016). Skončí ve službách státu český „sir Humphrey"? Přežil vlády od roku 1990. Available at (https://www.idnes.cz/zpravy/domaci/skonci-petr-kynstetr-sir-humphrey-snemovna.A161214_092310_domaci_hro).
Interview with OCD employee, 12.3.2021.
Interview with OCD employee, 16.3.2021.
Interview with SC employee, 12.3.2021.
Linek, Lukáš – Mansfeldová, Zdena (2007). The Parliament of the Czech Republic, 1993–2004, The Journal of Legislative Studies, 13:1, 12–37, DOI: 10.1080/13572330601165238.
Mansfeldová, Zdena (2014). The Czech Parliament on the Road to Professionalization and Stabilization. In: Semenova E., Edinger M., Best H. (eds) Parliamentary Elites in Central and Eastern Europe: Recruitment and Representation. pp. 33–53. Routledge: Oxon/New York.
OCD Annual report on information provided 2005–2020, available at (https://www.psp.cz/sqw/hp.sqw?k=33#zpravy).
Organizational rules of the Office of the Chamber of Deputies.
Organizational rules of the Office of the Senate Chancellery.
Respekt (2006). Utajený vládce českého sněmu. Available at (https://www.respekt.cz/tydenik/2006/28/utajeny-vladce-ceskeho-snemu).
SC Annual Report 2005–2020, available at (https://senat.cz/kancelar/index-eng.php?ke_dni=18.3.2021&O=13).
Senát (2006). Kancelář Senátu mění organizační strukturu. Available at (https://www.senat.cz/zpravodajstvi/zprava.php?ke_dni=28.5.2019&id=290).
SeznamZprávy (2021). Kancelář Senátu po patnácti letech změnila své uspořádání. Available at (https://www.seznamzpravy.cz/clanek/kancelar-senatu-po-patnacti-letech-zmenila-sve-usporadani-144942).
Zbíral, Robert (2020). Legislation in the Czech Republic. In: Karpen U., Xanthaki H. (eds) Legislation in Europe: A Country by Country Guide. pp. 119–137. Hart: Oxford/New York/Dublin.

15
DENMARK'S PARLIAMENTARY ADMINISTRATION

Helene Helboe Pedersen[1]

The Danish parliament, the Folketing, is a one-chamber legislature with 179 members representing about 11 political parties.[2] Members are elected at least every fourth year, but the Prime Minister can dissolve parliament and call for election at any time. The electoral system is proportional, and members are elected in ten multimember districts in Denmark while two are elected in Greenland and two in the Faroe Islands. Parties can use different types of ballots, but open lists are most common, making candidates compete for personal district votes to win their seats. Governments are typically minority (coalition) governments. There is no investiture vote, but parliament can force the government or any individual minister to withdraw by a simple majority vote of no confidence. Compared to other Western European parliaments, the Folketing has strong institutions for controlling government and influencing legislation (Sieberer 2011).

Still, concern has been uttered regarding Folketing's strength relative to the government, who has privileged access to the expertise and administrative support in the ministries and ministerial agencies. Critics are concerned that members of parliament do not receive sufficient support to scrutinize the increasing amount of complex regulation initiated by government or the EU, which weakens the democratic control of important societal decisions. Members of parliament receive direct support from two main sources.[3] First, the state provides financial support directly to individual members (9,375 Euro per month in 2021) and to the parliamentary party groups (59,817 Euro per month in 2021) (Folketinget 2021a). The support is adjusted every year and has increased over time, resulting in an increased number of staffers in the parliamentary party groups who support the political work of MPs (Pedersen 2020). Second, the Folketing has its own administration tasked with HR issues, maintenance, parliamentary documentation, and political support of MPs' work. However, systematic analyses and knowledge of Folketing's administration are lacking. There is very limited knowledge of how political support is provided through the parliamentary administration, who makes use of this support, and for what purposes. This chapter, therefore, focuses on Folketing's administration (Folketing's administration) and its political tasks in particular.

The chapter is based on information available in parliamentary documents and interviews with key staffers in the administration,[4] who have been crucial for describing the procedures for how the administration supports parliamentary activity. The chapter first analyses the organization and resources of the administration. Second, it analyses the way the administration supports the political work of MPs in standing committees, and third, it analyses how administration supports the parliament's international relations and the activities regarding the EU in particular. Finally, it concludes by discussing the challenges and opportunities facing Folketing's administration both in the short term – such as the Covid-19 pandemic – and in the long term.

15.1 Organization and Resources

The parliamentary administration answers to the parliamentary presidium, which consists of the speaker of the house and four vice-speakers, who are elected by and among MPs. The administration is organized with a management consisting of three persons headed by the secretary general and supplemented with two deputy secretary generals, of which one serves as the parliamentary secretary (clerk) for the speaker. The secretary general answers to the parliamentary presidency and is thus under the control of the parliament alone and answers to no other governmental or private agent. The clerk answers to the speaker of parliament in his role as parliamentary secretary and to the general secretary in his role as deputy secretary general. As illustrated in the organizational chart in Figure 15.1, each management office is responsible for multiple functions and units. The focus of this chapter is on how the parliamentary administration supports the political work in parliament. These functions are primarily handled by the parliamentary secretariat, which is organized into five subunits.

The legal service secretariat (*Lovsekretariatet*) plans plenary meetings and provides relevant documents for the parliamentary chair to lead the meetings according to Rules of Procedure. An important task is to coordinate the order and timing of bill readings with the ministries and the parliamentary committees. The committee secretariat (*Udvalgssekretariatet*) assists committee members and chairs in running committee meetings. This includes coordinating visits from stakeholders (deputations), producing relevant analyses for committee meetings, organizing hearings or excursions, and assisting committee members in formulating motions or parliamentary questions. Each standing committee is assisted by a committee secretary and a committee assistant. The international secretariat (*Det Internationale Sekretariat*) focuses on all parliamentary activities related to foreign policy and the EU in particular. This includes assisting the work of the European Affairs Committee and the Foreign Policy Committee, which are two crucial parliamentary committees scrutinizing the government's foreign and EU policy (Sousa 2008). Further, the international secretariat assists members of parliament when they participate in international parliamentary conferences, and it runs the EU information service. The library (*Biblioteket*) makes relevant literature and documents available for members of parliament and serves as a contact and information point for citizens interested in political procedures, documents, or institutions. Finally, the parliamentary records (*Folketingstidende*) document activities in parliament by transcribing debates in the chamber and in open committee hearings and making them publicly available.

As evident from the chart and indicated by the number of staff employed in each subunit, the parliamentary administration is a significant institution in the Danish parliament. It clearly outnumbers the MPs and attends to multiple functions important for running a parliament efficiently. A third of all employees in the administration are tasked with supporting the political activities in parliament. Over time, the resources of the parliament administration have increased. Figure 15.2 illustrates developments in budgets and number of man-year staff from 2007 to 2019. The economic resources increase from 45.8 million

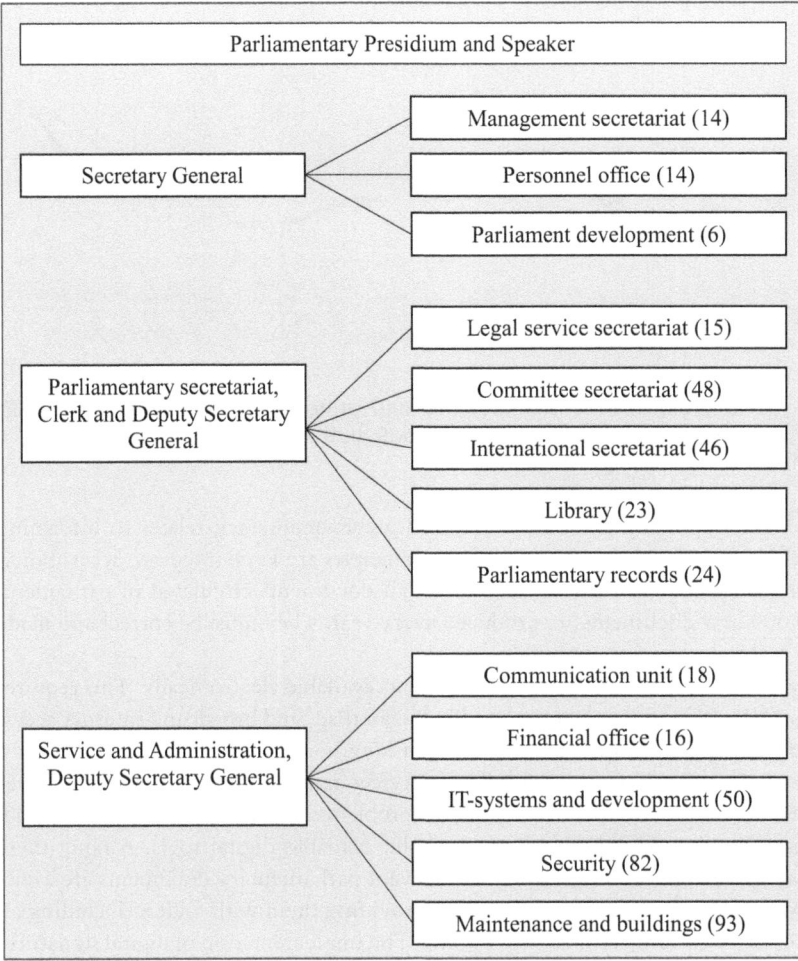

Note: The chart is developed based on the illustration on the parliamentary website: https://www.ft.dk/da/organisation/folketingets-adminstration/administrationens-arbejde. Numbers in parentheses refer to the number of staff in each unit and are provided by the parliamentary secretariat.

Figure 15.1 Organizational chart of the parliament administration

euros in 2007 to 58.0 million euros in 2019, which constitutes an increase of 27 percent in 12 years. This budgetary increase is reflected in the number of staff, which increases from 390 to 419 (7 percent).

Figure 15.3 shows that staff with an academic degree constitutes about 25 percent from 2012 onward. When engaging new staff, the administration follows a procedure very common to procedures in other public institutions in Denmark. Job openings are advertised in open calls, and candidates are interviewed by a hiring committee in which the leadership, co-workers, and union representatives participate. For very specific jobs, the administration can recruit directly from the ministries, ministerial agencies, or the like.

Beyond staffing, digitalization is an increasingly important resource. The IT management is divided into two sections: development and management, and together, they work toward creating the best possibilities for E-governance and E-democracy. E-governance relates to the

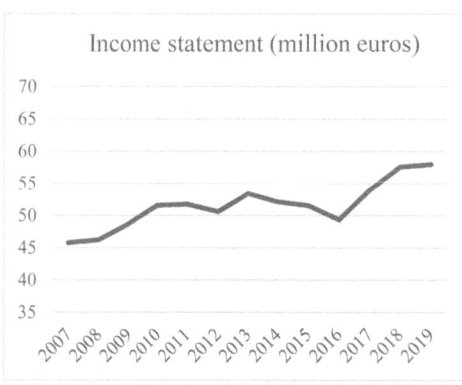
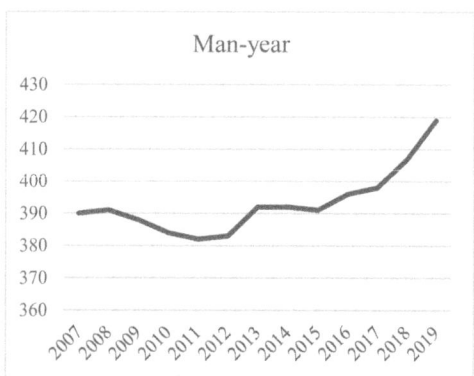

Figure 15.2 The resources of Folketing's administration 2007–2019. Note: Numbers are drawn from the yearly accounts of Folketing: https://www.ft.dk/da/organisation/folketingets-adminstration/folketingets-regnskaber

internal procedures supporting parliamentary activities. E-democracy relates to informing and involving the public. For E-governance, three principles are keys: integrity, accessibility, and security. Integrity relates to the correctness of all documents circulated in parliament. More than 100,000 new documents are produced every year. They must be correct and made available in the right place as fast as possible.

Accessibility refers to making all relevant documents available electronically. This requires hardware. Each MP is offered two laptops, an iPhone, an iPad, and broadband internet access at their home address. The IT service centre is open long hours a day, including weekends, and constitutes the access point for all kinds of services ranging from dry-cleaning, over building maintenance issues to soft- or hardware problems. New MPs are offered an IT mentor assisting them in using the hardware and the available digital tools. Among these digital tools is an app (*Tinget*) through which all relevant parliamentary documents are available. Further, MPs can sign up for specific services providing them with folders, including all relevant documents for committee meetings or bills. The implementation of digital signatures in the early 2000s has made it possible to run a paperless parliament, although some MPs still prefer to have their documents in paper, which are then delivered by the library and committee secretariat.

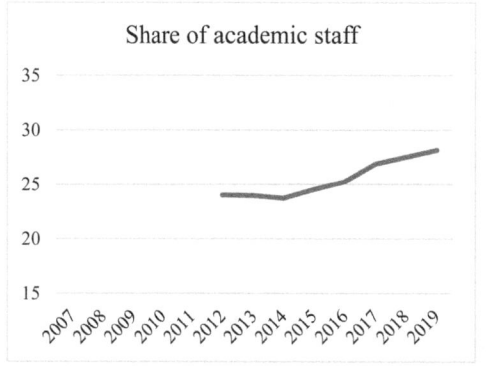

Recruitment procedures

- Job calls are announced internally and externally on the same day
- Job calls are published on the parliamentary website, LinkedIn and the national portal Jobnet
- Hiring committees consist of the head of the relevant unit, an employee from the unit, a HR person, and a union representative

Figure 15.3 Academic staff and procedures for recruitment

With accessibility comes security issues. This is particularly relevant as confidential documents are also electronically accessible for MPs. Security is supported by multi-factor authorization processes and careful instructions regarding IT-responsible behaviour. The IT-offices make efforts to build a responsible and open culture signalling their role as supporters rather than controllers to make MPs trust that they can receive help if they end up with security issues.

With regard to E-democracy, Folketing's administration has hosted a public website since 1997 and has continuously worked to increase transparency and accessibility for the public. This includes digitalizing, archiving, and indexing all parliamentary documents – also going back in time. For more advanced users, such as journalists or researchers, the IT development section initiated an open API (*oda.ft.dk*), making data easily accessible. For ordinary citizens, IT development works to provide more information via parliamentary TV and launch a new initiative to visualize plenary procedures. Based on a political initiative, IT is now being developed to increase access for disabled citizens by, for instance, providing read-out-load services for written documents and subtitling plenary debates and public committee meetings.

Often E-democracy and E-governance supplement and reinforce each other, but, in some situations, they may conflict. For instance, services that trace activities of individual MPs or procedures for involving citizens directly in parliamentary proceedings may be relevant for E-democracy but less so for E-governance. In such instances, the parliamentary administration constitutes a service for parliament and answers to the decisions reached in the parliamentary presidency.

15.2 Administration in Parliamentary Work: Tasks and Relations

The tasks and position of the parliamentary administration relate to many relevant actors. Internally, administrative subunits interact when solving their overall task of running parliament as a building and as a legislative assembly. As part of parliament, administrative staff stands in direct relation to MPs and, through them, also the party political staff. Externally, the parliamentary administration coordinates with the government and, to some extent, interacts with citizens and stakeholders. The parliamentary administration describes no relations to the press but emphasizes its task of providing neutral and objective information to parliament and the public.

The relationship between the administrative subunits is characterized by strong interdependence and respect for specific expertise. For instance, consideration for maintenance and guards is emphasized when the importance of planning plenary and committee meetings is explained, and cooperation with the library providing relevant information and the legal service secretariat for legal support is highlighted when it is explained how committee staff supports MPs' legislative activities. Interviews reveal that "no mistakes culture" is a key value for the administrative proceedings across all subunits. They set great pride in securing that information shared with MPs or citizens is absolutely correct. The administration serves as a correctness guard – MPs can trust that the plenary agenda is specified correctly so that they vote on the right amendment, majorities are correctly interpreted in committee reports, and all information received from the administration is correct. Moreover, the committee secretariat assists MPs in being correct by reviewing their bill proposals (if they draft them themselves) and confirming the sources they refer to in, for instance, their parliamentary questions.

The MPs are the centre of attention of the parliamentary administration, but the direct contact with MPs differs across subunits. The IT unit provides a great deal of crucial and practical service and therefore stands in direct contact with MPs. The committee secretaries are the most important political and parliamentary advisors for MPs in the parliamentary administration. Their services include formulation of parliamentary questions, motions, private bills, information and analysis of committee-relevant matters, and organization of hearings and excursions besides managing the committee meetings. Committee secretaries not only deliver on request but also make MPs aware of issues within the jurisdiction of the committee or highlight specific elements in a bill that may be of importance. When it comes to the committee meeting, committee secretaries primarily interact with the committee chair or deputy chair to plan the agenda. However, individual members may also ask for assistance. Opposition MPs are more likely to ask for the assistance of the parliamentary administration than MPs representing parties in government, who have better access to information and assistance from government bureaucrats. In particular, MPs from parties that never entered government refer to the parliamentary administration to receive assistance.

The cooperation between committee secretaries and MPs sometimes evolves into a close, informal, and trusting relationship so that MPs may seek support from "their" committee secretary even if they move on to another committee. The committee secretary offers a different kind of support than the parliamentary party group. New MPs are welcomed by a committee secretary mentor, who guides them with regard to formal and informal procedures in parliament. For instance, they might make new MPs from a governing party aware that it is uncommon to call their own ministers for questioning in the committee, and new MPs may also seek advice from the committee secretary rather than party staff or fellow party MPs to avoid revealing uncertainties that may undermine their status within the party group. Such relationships between MPs and committee secretaries are supported by the norm that all contact between individual MPs and the committee staff is confidential (Folketinget 2019). The staff in the committee secretariat – committee secretaries, committee assistants, and two consultants – perceive MPs as their main "customers" and prefer to interact with them directly rather than through their party staff. Hereby, they try to separate the parliamentary and party political support of MPs and ascertain MP knowledge of all actions taken by the administration on their behalf. This priority limits the contact with party staff, and the two lines of financial support outlined in the introduction therefore seem to also work in practice.

The government is central for activities in parliament and, therefore, of great relevance to the parliamentary administration. Government and parliament are responsible for legislation, and therefore, the legal service secretariat continually coordinates with the ministries to plan the legislative agenda. Parts of this coordination are institutionalized with the government's October announcement of the planned bills and the following reports on progression and adjustments in December, March, and April. These documents help the legal service secretariat plan and organize bill readings in the plenary. Other parts of the coordination are less institutionalized and take place informally on a day-to-day basis. Typically, coordination issues can be handled with a phone call, but, if necessary, the legal service secretariat can refer to parliament's Rules of Procedure, which for instance specify that at least 30 days have to pass between the bill being introduced and the final vote (Folketinget 2018). If ministries struggle to get first in line, this is left for the government to handle, while the Speaker – according to Rules of Procedure – always has the final say on this matter.

The committee secretaries are also in contact with ministries to ask for information, inform about questions, and coordinate and plan questioning sessions. Political negotiations often take place in the ministries rather than in the committees. Information shared in these meetings is not automatically sent to the committee. Committee members may issue a question to the minister to obtain the relevant information, but there is no procedure for such information exchanges. Similarly, there are no formal procedures for sharing information regarding secondary legislation. In some committees – such as the committee on environment – a practice has been established for sending delegated acts to the committee, but in most committees, this is not the case, and it seldom happens (Christensen et al. 2020). The committee secretary does not participate in meetings in the ministry unless the whole committee is formally invited as parliamentary committee.

Finally, the parliamentary administration also interacts with citizens and stakeholders. For subunits focusing on supporting the political work of MPs, which is the focus of this chapter, direct interactions with citizens are rare. However, with the introduction of citizen proposals in 2018, the legal service secretariat got in more direct contact with citizens, and the committee secretaries coordinate with citizens and stakeholders planning deputations in the committee. This involves informing citizens about the procedures for deputations and also perhaps reminding committee members that the committee guidelines specify that committees should make efforts to represent parliament when welcoming citizens and stakeholders (Folketinget 2019).

Overall, the parliamentary administration attends to a multitude of tasks related to running parliamentary activities. Interviews and documentary material describe rather cooperative relationships between administrative subunits as well as relevant actors in parliament, government, and the public. The administration defines MPs – individual, committee chairs, or speaker – as their key focus and makes efforts to offer a flexible, qualified, and correct service to them. However, they draw clear boundaries to government and political parties. Service is provided to MPs personally, not to party staff, inter-ministerial coordination issues are left for the government to handle, and committee secretaries assist the parliamentary committee as a unit when interacting with ministries.

15.3 Administrative Support for Parliamentary Activities Related to the EU and Beyond

The parliament has two main tasks when it comes to international relations. First, it scrutinizes and mandates the government's foreign and EU policy, which primarily takes place within the framework of the Foreign Policy Committee and the European Affairs Committee. Second, it promotes policies and political ideas in interaction with other parliaments through various international, European, and regional networks. The international secretariat provides the administrative support for these activities.

Scrutinizing and mandating EU policy is a major task. The task is complicated by the massive amount of issues to consider, the uncoordinated timing of national and EU decision-making processes, and the low saliency of EU issues in national politics (Senninger 2017). The international secretariat therefore faces a special task of making MPs attend to issues most important to Denmark and to increase knowledge and understanding of the EU decision-making process. The secretariat attends to all issues brought forward by MPs interested in EU politics, but they are also proactive in calling attention to issues that might be of special interest to Denmark, such as EU regulation of minimum wages. The international secretariat therefore serves as a crucial filter that assists parliament in prioritizing EU issues. An important part of this prioritizing task is to prepare a list of the most salient issues that the members of parliament should pay special attention to during a term. This crucial task is conducted in cooperation with the Ministry of Foreign Affairs, the European Affairs Committee, and the standing committees. When the Commission publishes its program, the international secretariat's consultants with EU expertise scrutinize the program and discuss the relevance of the many issues with the standing committees. The committees may express interest in specific elements of the program, and these initial discussions result in a gross list of relevant issues. The gross list is then discussed in the European Affairs Committee, which will narrow the list down to five to ten issues. Issues are prioritized based not only on the principle of subsidiarity but also on political "weight" of the issue (Folketinget 2021b), which may relate to national interest and political saliency. The prioritized issues are subjected to more detailed scrutiny and political activity. The task of prioritizing issues is thus of great political and parliamentary importance.

The international secretariat further supports the parliamentary control of EU politics by being the secretary of the European Affairs Committee. This includes preparing annotated agendas, which are needed and important for members of the committee in order to make informed decisions on the many and complicated issues debated in this committee.

The international secretariat is key for building and sharing information and expertise on EU matters. It manages the EU Information Centre, which gathers and systemizes information on EU and produces material for educating the public on EU matters. It also conducts analyses, gathers information, and advises members of parliament on EU issues in general, and a consultant from the secretariat is permanently positioned in Brussels to stay close to the action. The secretariat assists all MPs, but also, on this matter, mainly MPs from the opposition without privileged access to the ministries make use of the available expertise. Consultants in the secretariat are more likely to work with party staff to provide the relevant information to MPs and are also in close contact with committee secretaries to coordinate and arrange discussions of EU-related issues in the standing committees.

The Folketing not only scrutinizes EU and foreign politics but it also works actively to assist MPs in promoting parliament's interests and values in international settings. As such the Danish parliament also has a lobbying task trying to promote Danish interests, values, or policies internationally. The administration assists by building and maintaining networks and by following the decision-making processes in EU. This is necessary information for the parliaments to act timely and efficiently in the EU political context. This task is highly relevant not only within the EU but also in other international settings. The Danish parliament is engaged in multiple inter-parliamentary networks (See Table 15.1).

The work in international parliamentary networks is organized through delegations of MPs. Delegations are appointed by parliament and typically represent political parties proportionally. The international secretariat assists these delegations by preparing conferences, providing relevant information and documents, and taking care of all practical issues. The importance and aim of these inter-parliamentary networks vary, depending on the political agenda. For instance, the Conference of Artic Parliamentarians has become more important over the last

Table 15.1 List of parliamentary networks

- The UN General Assembly
- The Inter-Parliamentary Union
- The OSCE Parliamentary Assembly
- The Parliamentary Assembly of the Council of Europe
- The NATO Parliamentary Assembly
- The Nordic Council
- The Conference of Artic Parliamentarians
- The Baltic Sea Parliamentary Conference
- The Parliamentary Assembly of the Union for the Mediterranean (passive member)

years, making activities related to this network increasingly important. The aim may be more or less focused on Danish interests. For instance, as many other parliaments, the Folketing is involved in supporting institutional developments in parliaments around the world.

The complexity and proactive nature of the administrative tasks related to assisting the international work of parliament requires substantial resources and expertise. The quality of parliamentary control and parliamentary influence on EU politics depends on the resources invested. In particular, because of low national political saliency, resources may be more efficiently invested in the parliamentary administration than in individual MPs or parliamentary party groups on this matter. However, beyond resources, the administration also cooperates with parliament to develop better structures and procedures for involving parliament in EU politics. The aim is to involve standing committees with relevant expertise more and earlier in the decision-making process in order to strengthen the parliamentary control.

15.4 Conclusion: Challenges and Opportunities

The administration of the Danish parliament, the Folketing, is substantial and growing. It is dedicated to supporting the parliamentary work of the members of parliament. Formally as well as reflected in the perceptions of the role of the parliamentary administration, the administration answers to parliament and takes care to guard borders to government on the one hand and political parties on the other. Interviews reveal that the administration emphasizes easy access for MPs by creating single access points for multiple services ranging from practical issues to advice on legal or political matters. Further, the administration is proactive when it comes to developing digital solutions and informing MPs on politically relevant issues, particularly with regard to EU politics, where the administration plays a crucial role in filtering and prioritizing among the massive amount of complex issues to attend to. Still, all interviewees emphasize that requests made and initiatives taken by MPs are given first priority.

The Covid-19 pandemic has put the parliamentary administration under pressure. Practical issues of allocating rooms spacious enough to hold the relevant number of people, organizing new voting procedures, and establishing digital infrastructures to work from a distance have made great demands on the administrative resources. Such pressure has revealed important strengths of the parliamentary administration, particularly with regard to IT solutions. Only a day after the first closure of society was announced, the IT management offered an online conference solution that was highly secure and easy to use. Yet, issues remained for confidential meetings, for instance in the Foreign Policy Committee, which had to meet on site in order to respect principles of confidentiality. Political issues of handling fast-track legislation of high complexity to meet the need for decisive and swift political action to contain infection were also demanding on the administration. Bills were processed through the same procedures but in a few hours rather than days or weeks (Pedersen & Borghetto 2020), which made it difficult for the administration as well as MPs to collect and evaluate information relevant to the decisions. These experiences have resulted in initiatives regarding how to handle fast-track legislation in the future – such as introducing fast-track public hearings – and how to strengthen control of delegated legislation – such as introducing specific oversight subcommittees. These are political decisions, but they will influence the work and tasks of the administration.

The potential tasks of a parliamentary administration are almost unlimited, and, consequently, it is almost impossible to evaluate when resources allocated to the administration are sufficient. There are two main debates on this issue. First (permanent), opposition parties tend to push more strongly for increasing the resources of the parliamentary administration as a way to increase the parliamentary capacity to control the government and proactively promote a parliamentary political agenda. Governing parties tend to be less eager as their dependence on the parliamentary administration is reduced by access to the ministerial departments. Second, the distribution of resources through parliamentary party group support or parliamentary administration is debatable. The parliamentary administration is neutral and offers no political assistance in writing political speeches or planning political campaigns, which are crucial elements of the MPs' representative tasks. The party staffers are solely dedicated to promoting the interests of the individual party and may care less about substantially important but politically insignificant issues. Party group support as well as budgets for parliamentary administration have increased over the years. However, the balance has changed. While the budget for the parliamentary administration was three times as large as state subsidies for parliamentary party groups in 2007, it was only twice as large in 2017. State subsidy for parliamentary party groups has increased by 69 percent in ten years, while the budget for the parliamentary administration has increased by 18 percent. This at least reflects a political priority of strengthening the capacity of political parties to support the activities of their MPs more than strengthening the support provided by the parliamentary administration. Whether this development will continue is hard to predict, as it depends on political agenda setting and political priorities. As such, the two main debates regarding the resources of the parliamentary administration interact. The parliamentary administration is a product of political decisions, which require majorities. Opposition parties may find it more difficult to muster the needed majorities. However, the experiences from the Covid-19 pandemic may create a window of opportunity as it has revealed the importance and fragility of parliamentary control. This analysis highlights how effective and professional parliamentary administrations are crucial parts of making that control work in practice.

Notes

1 The chapter is written with the support of Torben Jensen, who is parliamentary secretary (clerk) and deputy secretary general of the parliament administration. Torben Jensen has provided relevant information and verified its correctness, while the author is responsible for all conclusions made based on these information.
2 At the time of writing, 14 parties were represented. This includes four single-member party groups elected in Greenland and the Faroe Islands.
3 Indirectly, MPs may also receive support from their party. Political parties also receive public funding.
4 I have conducted interviews with Liselotte Astrup (Head of IT development), Johanne Albjerg (Head of IT), Birgit Thostrup Christensen (Head of legal services department), Lis Grønnegård Rasmussen (Head of Committees), and Pernille Deleuran (Head of International Department). The one-hour interviews were conducted and recorded over teams in March 2021. The participants are interviewed as informants (Allen 2017) to provide insider information about processes, procedures, and mission statements of the administration. I am interested in this information to provide a precise and comprehensive analysis of the way the parliamentary administration works rather than understand staff perceptions and opinions. As such I include this information as part of describing the functions of the parliamentary administration rather than using explicit citations.

References

Allen, Mike (2017) Informant Interview. In Allen, Mike (ed.) *The SAGE Encyclopedia of Communication Research Methods*, New York: SAGE Publications, pp. 700–703.
Christensen, Jørgen Grønnegård, Jensen, Jørgen Albæk, Mortensen, Peter Bjerre, & Pedersen, Helene Helboe (2020). *Når Embedsmænd Lovgiver*. Copenhagen: Djøf Forlag.

Folketinget (2018). Folketingets forretningsorden, https://www.ft.dk/da/dokumenter/bestil-publikationer/publikationer/forretningsorden/forretningsorden-for-folketinget (accessed March 12 2021).

Folketinget (2019). Udvalgsvejledningen. Præsidiets guide til arbejdet i Folketingets stående udvalg, https://www.ft.dk/-/media/sites/ft/pdf/publikationer/udvalgsvejledningen2019.ashx (accessed March 12 2021).

Folketinget (2021a). Gruppestøtte og regnskaber, https://www.ft.dk/da/partier/om-politiske-partier/gruppestoette-og-regnskaber (accessed January 29 2021).

Folketinget (2021b). EU-note, https://www.ft.dk/samling/20201/almdel/EUU/eu-note/27/2355849.pdf (accessed March 25 2021).

Pedersen, Helene Helboe & Borghetto, Enrico (2020). *Fighting COVID-19 on Democratic Terms. Parliamentary Functioning in Italy and Denmark during the Pandemic*, paper presented at the ECPR general conference 2020, P491: Lessons Learned, Lessons Missed.

Pedersen, Helene Helboe (2020). The Parliament (Folketinget): Powerful, Professional, and Trusted? In Christiansen, Peter Munk, Elklit, Jørgen, & Nedergaard, Peter (eds.) *The Oxford Handbook of Danish Politics*, Oxford: Oxford University Press, pp. 88–106.

Senninger, Roman (2017). Issue expansion and selective scrutiny–how opposition parties used parliamentary questions about the European Union in the national arena from 1973 to 2013. *European Union Politics*, *18*(2), 283–306.

Sieberer, Ulrich (2011). The institutional power of Western European parliaments: A multidimensional analysis. *West European Politics*, *34*(4), 731–754.

Sousa, Maja Møller (2008). Learning in Denmark? The case of Danish parliamentary control over European Union policy. *Scandinavian Political Studies*, *31*(4), 428–447.

16
ESTONIA'S PARLIAMENTARY ADMINISTRATION

Leif Kalev, Ott Lumi and Tõnis Saarts

16.1 Introduction

The following article discusses the administration of the Estonian Parliament. Called Riigikogu (State Assembly), it has functioned in its current form since 1992 and has roughly a century of parliamentary tradition. The people attained the right to elect first a provincial assembly in 1917 and then directly the national parliament in 1919. This was interrupted by the Soviet and Nazi occupations of 1940–1991.

The restored republic has been parliamentary. This was predominant also between the World Wars, although semi-presidentialism was used from 1933 to 1940. Riigikogu is and has mostly been unicameral, with a brief interlude in 1937–1940. Now and during all the period of restored independence, Riigikogu has 101 members (historically, it has been 100 ± 20 members).

The key body of the parliamentary administration is the Riigikogu Kantselei – the Chancellery of Riigikogu. The structure of the Chancellery can be generally characterized as four blocks: (1) central departments, (2) secretariats for parliamentary commissions and offices of board members of Riigikogu, (3) secretariats of factions, and (4) autonomous units. The Chancellery with its approximately 230 employees is roughly the size of a typical ministry (core unit), but as this includes the technical functions that are separated from the ministries, the numbers are modest.

In the following chapter, we will first generally characterize its functions, structure, budget, staff, and position in the constitutional system. Then we will focus on the work practices, autonomy, and the political dimension and consider the knowledge and support services, main activities, and mechanisms for ensuring professionalism. We will then discuss the key findings.

Our study is based on several documents and materials that are available from Riigikogu website. Additional numerical data has been provided by the Chancellery. We also conducted eight interviews, mostly with senior parliamentary administrators and one with an experienced politician, a former Speaker of Riigikogu (Kalev, Lumi and Saarts, 2021). The selection of interviewees aimed to cover the main functions of the Chancellery. We have analysed the content, harmonized our interpretations through internal discussions, and received additional comments to the draft from our interviewees. For brevity, the references are limited but further material is available from the authors.

16.2 Functions and Position

According to its statutes, the Chancellery of the Riigikogu is an official public agency that supports the national parliament in performing its constitutional functions. As its main functions, the Chancellery:

1. advises Riigikogu, its bodies and members on legislative matters and parliamentary control, and in the performance of other functions; analyses parliamentary law and practice, and makes proposals for improving the work of Riigikogu;
2. services Riigikogu, manages its records and creates the conditions necessary for Riigikogu to perform its functions; manages the issues relating to the benefits related to membership in Riigikogu;
3. assists Riigikogu in communicating with other government bodies and the public, and manages its foreign relations;
4. prepares the draft budget of Riigikogu and implements the approved budget; organizes the administration of state assets in accordance with the State Assets Act; with the authorization of the Board of Riigikogu, represents Riigikogu in court and in other government institutions;
5. services the National Electoral Committee and the Political Parties Financing Surveillance Committee.

The strategy of the Chancellery gives priority to professional advising that considers the needs of the members of the Riigikogu and gives priority to clear, fast, and inclusive communication that helps both the general public and the media better understand the proceedings of the Riigikogu.

The authority and activities of the Chancellery arise from those of the Riigikogu. While the Riigikogu is the formal centrepiece of the representative democratic constitutional order, the reality is influenced by the executive drift broadly similar to the other Western democracies. The Chancellery is relatively autonomous from the vastly bigger government administration; thereby also remaining aside of its developments while not necessarily having the funding and authorization to innovate on its own.

The budget of Riigikogu for 2021 is slightly below 25 million euros, including slightly below 10 million for the Chancellery. The share of Riigikogu in the national budget has steadily decreased. While it was 0.4% in 2005, it was 0.3% in 2015, and is below 0.2% in 2021 (Riigikogu Kantselei, 2021). This reflects the weak position of Riigikogu in budgetary planning and negotiations, diverging from the usual doctrine of the power over the purse.

The draft national budget is composed by the Ministry of Finance and in this process Riigikogu applies for funds similarly to the departments of the executive. The Ministry of Finance consolidates the proposal, and the government negotiates the budget bill as for any other state institution. Riigikogu is not directly represented in the government meetings and has a relatively limited role in discussions over its budget. While in principle the budget bill can be changed during its readings in Riigikogu, this is rather limited in practice. This can be explained both by the small expert staff of Riigikogu and the party government. The coalition parties' MPs are influenced by their leaders who are usually in the government and support a smooth passage of the government budget bill in the parliament.

16.3 Structure, Personnel, and Hierarchy

The political structure of the parliament is headed by the annually politically elected parliament's board. The board is elected in late March and consists of three members: the Chairman and two Vice Chairmen. Political tradition dictates that the second Vice Chairman of Riigikogu belongs to the biggest opposition party, while the first Vice Chairman and the Chairman belong to the ruling coalition parties.

The support structure of board members of the parliament is quite modest for its size. Currently, each of the board members of the parliament has one political advisor and each of them has two political assistants and one aide. The MPs have no advisors or assistants, it is considered sufficient to support them via the central departments and secretariats.

There has been a long discussion on introducing the personal aides for MPs to reduce the technical workload. So far, the MPs have to personally manage their calendars, submit the receipts for their expenses to the bookkeeping, etc. Also a political personal adviser for MPs has been proposed. While these discussions have lasted well over a decade, there have been no decisions. Riigikogu already decided to adopt these in 2007, but with the clause that it will be enacted by the next composition in 2011. It never happened, though, due to the fact that it is considered politically unpopular.

The structure of the Chancellery is presented in Figure 16.1.

The Chancellery is headed by the Secretary General of the Riigikogu who is appointed for a term of five years by the Board of the Riigikogu following a public recruitment procedure. The Secretary General is assisted by the Deputy Secretary General (substantive support functions) and the Administrative Director (technical support functions). The Chancellery is accountable to the Board of the Riigikogu.

The central departments provide services to Riigikogu and are specialized as the Sittings Department, the Foreign Relations Department, the Personnel Department, the Public Relations Department, the Finance Department, and the Verbatim Records and Translation Department that report to the Secretary General of the Riigikogu. The Legal and Research Department (LRD) reports to the Deputy Secretary General of the Riigikogu. The Facilities Department reports to the Administrative Director who heads the Information Technology Department. There can be some members of staff who are not members of the departments and other units of the Chancellery.

The politically more relevant services will be discussed below but there are also tens of people who are responsible for the general maintenance that is often laborious in the historical building. There are also traditions such as the daily raising and lowering the national flag that require personnel.

The autonomous units the Riigikogu are the Foresight Centre, the Political Parties Financing Surveillance Committee, and the National Electoral Office, which serves National Electoral Committee. The Foresight Centre is a think-tank analysing long-term developments in the economy and society that was attached to Riigikogu after the dissolution of Estonian Development Fund – where it was a structural unit. This institution is not functionally related to Riigikogu but acts rather as an outer body. However, its reports are used in parliamentary discussions and events.

The parliament library, reading hall, and some information and publishing services are provided by Estonian National Library that is a fully autonomous public legal entity that operates under its own law, leadership, and budget. There is some practical and human interaction with the Chancellery but otherwise the activities are separate.

Estonia's Parliamentary Administration

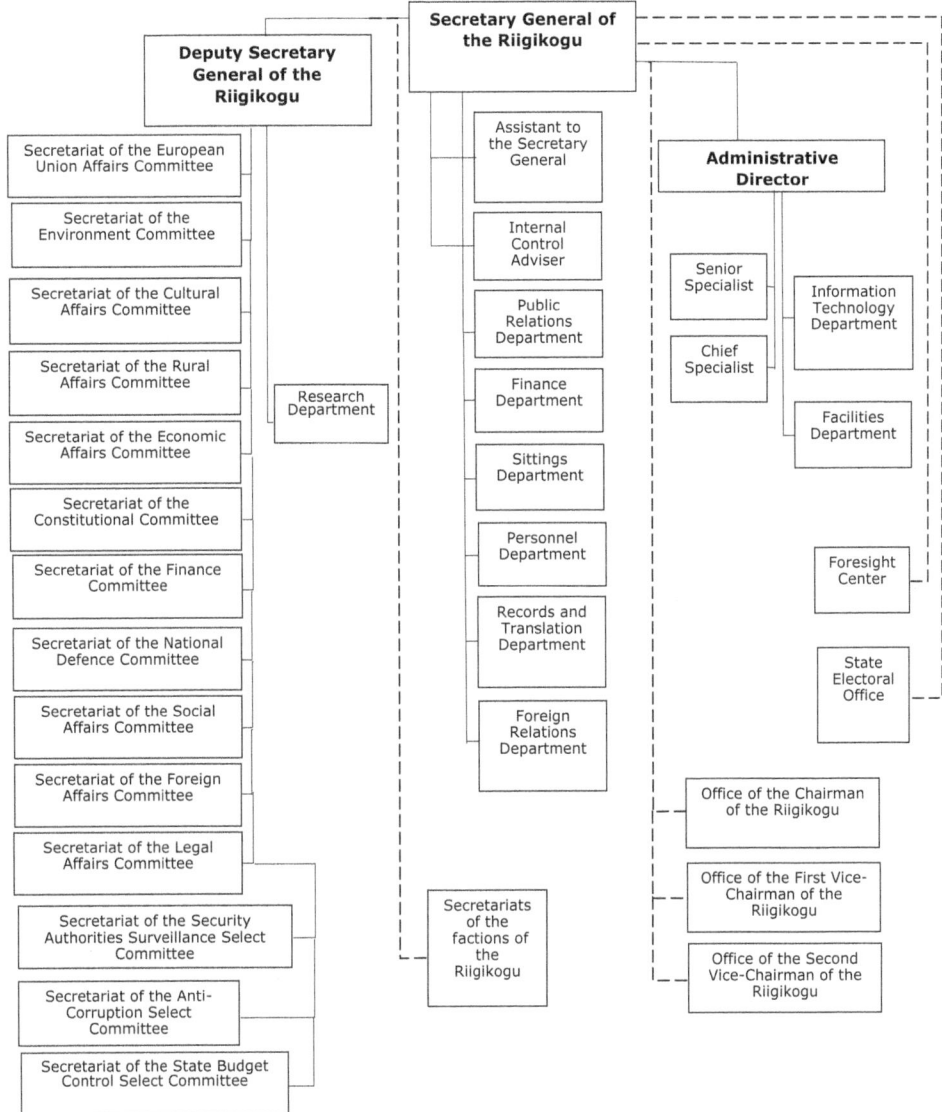

Figure 16.1 Structure of the Chancellery of Riigikogu
Source: Riigikogu website, modified.

The structure and personnel numbers of the Chancellery have been remarkably stable over the decades. We can see a slight overall decline as compared to the year 1996 when the Chancellery was already fully functional (Table 16.1). The positive side is manageability and flexibility, the downside is gradual decline in terms of relevance and expertise.

The staff of the Chancellery is non-political except for the factions – which are regarded as the political domain and also as an exception. In the main structure, party political experience is seen as a factor that reduces an applicant's chances to be hired. This is to avoid any

Table 16.1 General trends in personnel

	1992	1996	2000	2005	2010	2015	2017	2019	2020	2021
Management	16	20	19	19	14	19	19	17	16	16
Legal and analytical support	14	16	18	18	14	14	14	14	14	14
Documentation and interpretation	33	34	38	38	37	33	34	33	33	31
Public relations	5	5	8	11	12	13	14	12	12	12
Foreign relations	6	17	12	11	9	9	9	9	9	9
Personnel	3	4	5	6	6	6	5	5	5	5
Maintenance, finance, and ICT	46	67.5	93.5	67	62	54	51	51	51	51
Committee secretariats	37	49	50	51	49	51	53	55	55	55
Faction secretariats	28	45	45	40	40	40	40	40	40	40
Total	188	261.5	292.5	265	247	244	239	236	235	233
Foresight centre							6	8	8	8
National electoral office (up to 2015 elections office inside the main structure of the Chancellery)		4	4	4	4	5	8.5	14.5	13.5	13.5

Source: Riigikogu Kantselei (2021)

suspicions of bias. Over the decades, there have been also cases of employing a formerly politically attached person, usually after a period in some other job.

In terms of staff, the backbone of the Chancellery are the advisers – some having already worked since its establishment. There is a high turnover in junior positions. Faction support structures experience more changes after the elections. As the number of specialized positions in the Chancellery is limited, the career possibilities in the executive for consultants are considered rather competitive. Thus, the Chancellery is currently often an early career stage for public servants as the salary level in the Chancellery is lower compared to similar positions in the executive.

The Chancellery does not have any special training programme for raising the level of expertise among their staff. Of course, there are the 'freshman courses' for the new workers and the brand-new MPs, but they focus on technical and practical knowledge. It should be noted that if a staff member finds a suitable training course for advancing expertise (e.g. on a specific policy area), the Chancellery would compensate it for an attendee.

Politically, the two most important administrative structures of the Estonian parliament are the **faction and committee secretariats**. From 1990s, the committee and faction support structures have not gone through transformative changes but rather incremental shifts, reflecting the conservative nature of the institution.

There are 11 standing committees in the Riigikogu. In committee level, the most significant change has been creation of European Union Affairs Committee after Estonia's accession. In addition, Riigikogu has three other types of committees: select committees, investigation, and study committees. Select committees are the most permanent ones, currently these are the Security Authorities Surveillance Select Committee (has acted from the regaining of independence), the Anti-Corruption Select Committee, and the State Budget Control Select Committee.

The secretariat of a committee is headed by a head adviser of the secretariat or an adviser who is appointed by the director of the Riigikogu, based on the proposal of the deputy director. Other officials of the secretariat of a committee of the Riigikogu shall be appointed by a director based on the proposal of the head adviser of the committee or the adviser in accordance with the deputy director. The head of the secretariat reports to the deputy director. In matters directly related to advising and servicing the commission, the head of the secretariat reports directly to the chairman of the commission. Other officials of the commission report to the head of secretariat.

The staff of the secretariat consists usually of two to five civil servants (depending on the scope of the topics). One of them deals with transcription of the meetings. The others are usually assigned functions based on the committee policy spheres that mirror the main areas of the respective ministries (e.g. in the case of Social Affairs Committee – the areas of health, labour, and social policy). The committee's communication needs are covered by the public relations department. The communication specialists from PR unit cover the needs of several committees simultaneously (usually two to three). Most of the heads of secretariats have a degree in law. Legally, these are permanent positions and there is also relatively little volatility in practice, so it typically is a long-term job.

As it was revealed in the interviews, there is a tendency that the staff of a committee becomes increasingly its chairman's support structure due to their more hierarchical relationship. This is different for the other members who attend the committee hearings a similar number of times.

The structure of the Chancellery includes also secretariats serving the factions of the Riigikogu which main task of which is to advise the faction and its members and to organize their administration. These are rather autonomous from the everyday functioning of the Chancellery and are considered a mostly political domain. The number of positions in the secretariat that a faction has is determined by the chairman of the faction of the Riigikogu; however, it is in accordance with seats acquired by party forming the faction. Currently, the number of staff varies from 4 to 10 per faction.

The heads of the faction secretariats are party political appointees. They are usually either long-time party-related staffers or rising stars of the party, potentially leaders of the youth organizations. For the political parties in Estonia, the faction secretariats can be also considered extensions of the party office, as traditionally it is hard to draw a line between party political work and party faction work. Yet, it must be added that usually each of the factions also obtains some highly professional (in strategic or juridical competences) party-related experienced employees. The functions traditionally covered by faction staff are media coordination for MPs, planning the work in electoral districts, and coordinating between faction and party headquarters.

16.4 Knowledge Services and Legislative Drafting

The main function of the Chancellery is to provide support for the politicians. These include the **knowledge and support services**, in the form of legal or policy expertise, at two different levels: (1) LRD, (2) the expert staff assigned to the parliamentary committees and factions. In terms of the roles (Högenauer, Neuhold and Christiansen, 2016), the parliamentary administrators cover well, those of administrative assistants, agenda-shapers, and coordinators are better. Analyst and advisor roles are less well-covered.

The LRD advises the members of the Riigikogu, the Board, the committees, the factions, and their employees in order that the discussion in the parliament would be knowledge-based. The department also has the right to order research from outside. The budget is not always sufficient and the experts in the department cover only basic expertise; however, this functionality at least somewhat supports knowledge-based policy analysis and decision-making.

In practice, the constant challenge is to make the parliamentarians use this opportunity. The LRD's services are primarily used by the opposition politicians, while the government parties usually rely on the expertise from the executive. However, even the opposition has not been overly eager to use the services, and they rarely seek comprehensive, balanced, and elaborate analyses on policy matters – pieces of specific advice that support a partisan policy agenda are sought after instead. The LRD often lacks the appropriate funds and expertise to conduct the more ambitious research projects on its own. For a more profound analysis, the LRD turns to the universities, law companies, or think-tanks. The LRD does not make ex-post assessment of the impact of a particular policy; they rather offer expertise in policy formulation.

The parliamentary committees provide the main avenue for how the MPs can get support from the experts. The committee staff can offer some expertise or legal advice. In addition, committees often invite experts, public officials, representatives of advocacy groups, or civil society organizations to the committee meetings. This is not fully institutionalized and happens in an *ad hoc* manner: it depends on the particular policy or bill and the committee members' attitudes on the involvement of external expertise. Inclusion traditions in different committees vary significantly (Allik, 2009).

Consequently, there are three major reasons why the Chancellery is not fully prepared to provide extensive expertise or knowledge support to the MPs: (1) the executive dominance, which makes the budget for the research activities limited. The MPs from the government parties usually do not need the support from the LRD while relying on the resources of the executive; (2) the attitudes of the politicians – usually they do not seek for the balanced and elaborated analyses, but there is an interest in getting specific pieces of information to support a narrow political agenda; and (3) the major locus for providing the expertise is not the LRD but the staff and experts assigned to the specific committees. These limitations do not mean that the Chancellery does not offer its expertise if needed, in case such advisory capacity exists.

Legislative drafting is regulated by the Riigikogu Rules of Procedure and Internal Rules Act. According to the regulations, a bill can be initiated by an individual MP, faction, parliamentary committee, or the government. Like in many countries, the executive dominance is strongly pronounced. Over time, the proportion of Riigikogu-initiated bills has fallen – this is especially true as a proportion of adopted bills.

Factions and individual members of the parliament were rather active in preparing and presenting the bills in the 1990s when 40–50% of the bills initiated by Riigikogu were finally adopted, but currently predominately the opposition parties' MPs are active here (Solvak, 2012). While in IX Riigikogu (1999–2003) the share of Riigikogu-initiated bills was 42% of all and 30% of the adopted bills then in the XIII Riigikogu (2015–2019) it was 35% and 15%, respectively (Riigikogu, 2007, 2019). Also, the bills of Riigikogu are usually shorter or initiated by the governing coalition through parties.

The government has to give its opinion to the bills initiated by the members, factions, or committees of the Riigikogu. In the case of single members, as well as in the case of factions, the drafting advisory is usually given by faction staff. In case the bill is initiated by committee, the legislative drafting is done by committee staff. The same logic applies also in the case of potential amendments to laws. It may happen that there are some informal exceptions to this rule.

There is some support for the members of Riigikogu available to make sense of the **budget**. They receive initial training on how to read the budget proposal of the government and its explanatory note. The Finance Committee is supported by three advisers and two consultants. The more numerous experts from the Ministry of Finance provide additional explanations to the bill.

16.5 Openness, Digitalization, and External Relations

A large amount of information can be found on the Riigikogu website. Riigikogu is also represented on social media having its own Facebook groups (14000+ followers). Since 1998, there have been different projects in cooperation with the civil society organizations for high-school and college students, where they can simulate either the work of the Riigikogu or European Parliament. Because of the covid restrictions, no such project was held in 2020.

It has been possible for the citizens to follow the live plenary sessions via the web, and one can read all the transcripts of the sessions on the website (the recordings are available at the digital archive since 1990, video recordings on YouTube since 2014). Since 2020, the plenary sessions have been automatically transcribed by a robot and later only edited by humans. The committees publish their protocols, but not full recordings of their sessions, on the webpage.

Since the 2000s, there has been a digital platform for sharing legislative bills and the accompanying documents. The Chancellery has provided regular training sessions for the MPs for using this platform.

The Covid-19 crisis has forced many MPs to advance their digital skills. However, the major challenge brought by the Covid-19 has been that the plenary sessions and committee meetings had to be moved to the web-based platforms. So far, it has worked relatively well. In fact, the broadcasts of plenaries have been used for years. The Covid-19-related challenge was to move to an interactive platform so the parliamentarians could work from home.

In Estonia, there are several online portals that aim to promote e-democracy and citizen's participation: the Petition Web (two versions: https://rahvaalgatus.ee, https://petitsioon.ee/) and the Participation Web (https://www.osale.ee/) – the latter one is used for collecting policy proposals from citizens. According to the law, Riigikogu has to discuss these if a petition has more than 1000 verified signatures. Currently, the petitions are usually submitted through rahvaalgatus.ee and discussed in the parliamentary committees.

There is a special Department of Information Technology responsible for maintaining and developing the digital platforms and infrastructure of Riigikogu. They provide IT services, assistance, and training for the whole staff of Riigikogu. The department is also responsible for cybersecurity. Estonia has been one of the forerunners of digitalization and e-governance in Europe (Velmet, 2020) and Riigikogu started developing the website and digital platforms already by the end of the 1990s. A major update to the website was made in 2015.

The Public Relations Department of Riigikogu is responsible for the external and internal communication of the institution. It coordinates communication with the media, provides access for journalists, organizes the press-briefings/conferences, assists the administration, committees, and delegations in their public relations, and deals with the image of Riigikogu. Factions have their own consultants for public relations and they issue press-releases and help MPs with communication related to the factions.

The support for **external and EU relations** is threefold. Political steering of foreign affairs takes place in the committee of foreign relations. Its obligation is to guarantee the coordination of foreign relations activities of the parliament committees and the parliament board. The committee is also responsible for maintaining good contacts with other parliaments as well as coordinate the state's activities in the Nordic countries and Baltic states' parliamentary cooperation bodies. The committee has three advisors on staff.

The coordination of EU-related issues is the responsibility on the European Affairs Committee that has a total staff of six people (head, four advisors, representative of Estonia's Permanent Representation to the EU). The cooperation of government and parliament civil servants in EU affairs is well organized (Riigikogu, 2007, Aarma, 2005). Especially important is the European Affairs Committee's members as well as staffers right to access to government's European legislation database. The staffers have the right to participate in the meetings of European Union Coordination Committee meetings.

The foreign relations department in the Chancellery has eight employees, which is a significant number in the overall scale of the departments. It consists of head of department, head of protocol, four advisors (each responsible for a block of different international organizations) and two staffers for administrative tasks. The focus is in the Riigikogu and its Chancellery foreign relations, developing relations with other foreign parliaments, international organizations, and foreign embassies located in Estonia and Inter-Parliamentary Union (IPU). It also organizes visits, meetings, etc. for parliamentary groups, members of the board, and top managers of the chancellery. They also plan the foreign visits of the speaker and supply him or her with necessary background materials.

16.6 Discussion and Conclusions

There has been a remarkable stability of the Riigikogu and its Chancellery in restored Estonia, especially if seen on the background of the dynamics of the executive and more generally of society, politics, and economy in the last three decades.

The stability has its pluses and minuses. For the Chancellery, this has meant the evolution of a persistent core of competent employees. It also has supported the formation of the traditions in the parliament that enable to mediate periodic changes, turbulence, and possible conflicts after elections. The administrative autonomy of the Chancellery is broader as compared to a regular department in the executive and it doesn't have to follow all of the administrative frameworks established by the Ministry of Finance.

It is also possible that the decidedly non-partisan composition of the Chancellery is fostered by this stability. However, while the predominantly formal and legalist organizational culture may protect officials from politicians, it also does not encourage taking a more proactive role.

The downside is that in a dynamic setting the stable institution risks being less able to act in a proactive and innovative role. In recent decades, there have been several reforms to support more elaborate planning, policy preparation, coordination, information processing, and other capacities in the executive, while the Chancellery has remained broadly stable. Here the changes have mostly resulted from outside influence such as the accession to European Union, dissolution of the Development Fund, or the Covid-19 outbreak. The Chancellery is influenced by the decline of the relative position of Riigikogu among the branches of power as characterized by the decline in legislative initiative and the share in national budget.

This is well-reflected also in case of the Chancellery – which can be characterized by the stability of its functions and a decline in personnel and share in the budget. It is not always necessary to have a larger budget share but the little-attended functions such as policy (design) advice and planning, as well as being outcompeted by the executive in salaries for similar administrative positions, demonstrates that the aspiration for efficiency takes its toll. With its current resources and competences, the Chancellery can offer only limited support for a substantive legislative role of the parliament.

Even if the Chancellery excels in bookkeeping (e.g. of the checks every MP has to submit for expenses), data protection of MPs, or raising the national flag every morning, this doesn't help to overcome the public frustration about the ability of the parliament to operate as relevant in politics and policy formulation. While a MP focuses on voter contacts and publicity may pay off in terms of election results, the focus on legislative and policy initiative would be an arduous path also in terms of support. This parallels the downward spiral of the political role of the parliament.

There may be some historical explanations. The reliance on the premises of the 1920s parliamentarism and the wish to avoid 1930s-style authoritarianism resulted in a strong formal role of the parliament in the restored republic. However, the constitutionally underregulated government started to evolve based on practical needs and dynamics while Riigikogu remained rather stable. At the turn of the millennium, when the resulting weakening of the parliament was already well visible, the politicians lacked motivation for readjustment. It was a period of stable governments dominated by Reform Party that enjoyed their broad autonomy. Also, the emerging new generation of public servants and politicians was more executive oriented.

There have been surprisingly little efforts to strengthen Riigikogu and even less the Chancellery. One of the developments has been the introduction of the issues of national importance in the parliament that has allowed to enhance parliamentary outreach and visibility. A persistent issue is the question of personal aides or advisors of the Riigikogu that is debated every couple of years but so far dismissed. There were some reform ideas during the 2011–2012 societal discontent, but these produced little in practice. Enhancing the capacities of the Chancellery is little considered.

The slightly outdated expectations upon which the restored parliamentarism was established (such as the cabinet of ministers operating as an executive committee of the parliament) were further eroded by the rise of the party government and the evolution of autonomy and expertise in the executive, especially related to Europeanization and policy learning. The risk of parliamentary prerogative and autonomy due to specialization and additional requirements is not considered a major problem by the interviewees; however, it is difficult to see how a little-resourced parliament can meet these challenges. However, should more ambitious parliamentary politicians and leaders emerge, there is a firm ground for development.

References

Aarma, O. (2005). 2004. aastal ühinenud riikide parlamentide kaasatus Euroopa Liidu otsustusprotsessi. *Riigikogu Toimetised*, 12, pp. 151–156.
Allik, M. (2009). Kaasamine Riigikogus: komisjonide tavad ja liitude arvamused. *Riigikogu Toimetised*, 20, pp. 130–139.
Högenauer, A.-L., Neuhold, C. and Christiansen, T. (2016). *Parliamentary Administration in the European Union*. Basingstoke, New York: Palgrave Macmillan.
Kalev, L., Lumi, O. and Saarts, T. (2021). *Interviews with 7 parliamentary administrators and 1 politician*.
Riigikogu (2007), *Riigikogu X koosseis: Statistika ja ülevaated*. Tallinn: Riigikogu, Kantselei, Rahvusraamatukogu.

Riigikogu (2019), *Riigikogu XIII koosseis: Statistika ja ülevaated*. Tallinn: Riigikogu, Kantselei, Rahvusraamatukogu.
Riigikogu, (2021). *Riigikogu website*. [online] Available at: https://www.riigikogu.ee/ [Accessed 6 July 2021].
Riigikogu Kantselei (2021). *Finance and Personnel Data by Riigikogu Chancellery Based on Authors Query*. Tallinn.
Solvak, M. (2012). Kakskümmend aastat Riigikogu: kas tööparlamendist kõneparlamendiks? *Riigikogu Toimetised*, 26, pp. 83–94.
Velmet, A. (2020). The Blank Slate E-State: Estonian information society and the politics of Novelty in the 1990s. *Engaging Science Technology and Society*, 6, pp. 162–184.

17

FINLAND'S PARLIAMENTARY ADMINISTRATION

Tapio Raunio[1]

17.1 Introduction

The Finnish political system is normally categorized as semi-presidential, with the executive functions divided between an elected president and a cabinet that is accountable to the Eduskunta, the unicameral national legislature. However, the new constitution,[2] which entered into force in 2000, completed a period of far-reaching constitutional change that curtailed presidential powers and brought the Finnish political system closer to a normal parliamentary democracy. Cabinet formation is now based on partisan negotiations and the president is almost completely excluded from the policy process in domestic matters. European Union (EU) matters belong to the competence of the government, while foreign policy is co-led between the president and the government. These constitutional changes mean that the Eduskunta is much more at the centre of things than before (Karvonen et al. 2016).

In terms of internal organization, the Eduskunta is, without any doubt, an institutionalized legislature. Its internal structures have evolved gradually over the decades, and parliamentary decision-making is based on interaction between party groups and committees (Raunio 2022). The 200 members of parliament (MP) are elected every four years under an open-list system where voters choose between individual candidates. Yet, party discipline is strong and MPs are expected not to deviate from the positions of their parties. The Finnish party system is characterized by high degree of fragmentation, and parties are used to regular cooperation across the political spectrum. Typically, the governments are broad oversized coalition cabinets that rule with the support of their Eduskunta party groups.

This chapter analyses parliamentary administration in Finland. Reflecting the overall institutionalization of the Eduskunta, the structure and functions of administration display stability. The lines between MPs and civil servants are for the most part clear, and it is expected that the latter focus on keeping the machinery working and do not intervene in political conflicts. However, particularly committee secretaries are potentially influential actors in their respective policy domains. At the same time, the resources of party groups and individual MPs have increased quite considerably.

17.2 Structure and Functions of the Parliamentary Administration

The Eduskunta employs around 500 persons, roughly two-thirds of whom are women. This figure includes staff working for the parliament, such as lawyers, secretaries, record clerks, custodians, librarians, security personnel, but neither the party group staff nor all of the personal assistants of MPs – as explained later in the chapter, currently most of the assistants are employed by the party groups. The total number of staff has decreased gradually since the turn of the millennium: 676 persons worked for the Eduskunta in 2008, and in 2020 the figure was down to 520. In 2019, the average age of a parliamentary civil servant was 50, while that of an MP's assistant was 36.[3]

Party membership has facilitated access to key positions, but, reflecting the overall trend in public administration, such party links are noticeably less important than before. Open positions are advertised publicly and are filled with standard, national practices used in the public sector. It is commonplace for staff members to move 'up the ladder' inside the Eduskunta. There are specific resources for staff training, and as public sector employees, the staff enjoy essentially the same benefits as their colleagues in other public sector institutions and agencies.

The Eduskunta administration is not regulated by the constitution. Instead, the relevant provisions are in the parliamentary rules of procedure.[4] At the apex of the administrative, hierarchy is the Chancellery Commission (*kansliatoimikunta* in Finnish; the Eduskunta's rules of procedure refer to it as the Office Commission), which consists exclusively of MPs: the Speaker, the two Deputy Speakers, and four MPs. It decides Eduskunta's annual budget proposal, appoints civil servants to key parliamentary offices (apart from the Secretary-General), agrees on the conditions of employment for parliamentary civil servants, and takes decisions concerning how Eduskunta's facilities are allocated as well as procurements. Matters are presented to the Chancellery Commission by the Secretary-General or other officials in the Parliamentary Office.

The task of the Parliamentary Office (*Eduskunnan kanslia*) is to establish the necessary conditions for Eduskunta to carry out its duties. It functions under the supervision of the Chancellery Commission. The Parliamentary Office is divided into six units that operate under the Secretary-General: the Central Office (65 persons in 2019), the Committee Secretariat (69), the Administrative and Service Department (156), the International Department (20), the Information and Communication Department (69), and the Security Department (44). The Parliamentary Office is also in charge of the system of providing personal assistants to MPs.

The Secretary-General (*pääsihteeri*) is the head of the Parliamentary Office. Seppo Tiitinen has held the position longest, from 1992 to 2015, and he was known both as a strong defender of the Eduskunta and as a strong-willed person wielding considerable influence behind the scenes. The current Secretary-General, Maija-Leena Paavola (2016–), is the first female to serve in that position and has kept a much lower public profile than her predecessor. The Eduskunta elects the Secretary-General on the basis of a proposal from the Chancellery Commission. In the case of Paavola, the Chancellery Commission was not unanimous and needed to vote on its proposal. In the plenary vote, Paavola was elected with 107 votes, with also three other candidates receiving support among MPs (Länkinen 2015). Plenary minutes are signed by the Secretary-General, and together with the Speaker, the Secretary-General also signs all parliamentary replies and communications.

The Central Office (*keskuskanslia*) helps prepare and implement plenary sessions and provides related services. More precisely, it prepares plenary session plans to the Speaker's Council (which brings together the Speaker, the Deputy Speakers, and the committee chairs), and handles administrative cooperation related to the plenaries with the government and the parliamentary committees. It also drafts the minutes and publishes parliamentary documents and registers, translates key parliamentary documents into Swedish, and distributes and stores the documents.

17.2.1 *The Potential Weight of Committee Secretaries*

The Committee Secretariat (*valiokuntasihteeristö*) provides secretarial services for the committees as well as handles the preparation of matters to be brought before the committees and the arranging of related support functions. The number of committees has increased gradually, and the 2019–2023 Eduskunta has 17 committees. Each committee has a secretariat led by the committee secretary. Several committees have four clerks, whilst others, particularly those with broader jurisdictions, have more staff (six to ten). The secretariats draft the committee agendas, reports, and statements, compile the initial list of expert witnesses to be heard, and handle general matters related to committee organization and meetings. Regarding hearings, the committees have their 'usual suspects' and the committee secretary draws up a list of who should be heard on any particular issue. Committee members can suggest additional names, and typically such additions are accepted (Seo 2017: 124–139). Media and civil society activists have argued for the introduction of a transparent lobbyist registration system, but the Eduskunta has been reluctant to adopt such a lobby registry (Sutinen 2017).

Committee secretaries also coordinate matters with other sectoral Eduskunta committees, the Parliamentary Office, and the executive branch. Often same committee secretaries serve multiple electoral terms in the same committee, building thereby considerable expertise and potentially also influence. The relationship between the committee secretary and the committee chair is fundamentally important, and their exact respective roles can vary. MPs appreciate the know-how and expertise of committee secretaries, both regarding the preparation and conduct of meetings and the substance of the issues. However, committee secretaries are not expected to become involved in party politics, and in any case governing parties control also majorities in the committees.

The Administrative and Service Department (*hallinto- ja palveluosasto*) handles affairs such as finances, real estate management, information and communications technology, as well as personnel administration. It prepares matters for the Chancellery Commission and handles the implementation of the Commission's decisions. The Security Department (*turvallisuusosasto*) is responsible for the parliamentary security system, in addition to which it handles rescue and civil defence activities.

The International Department (*kansainvälinen osasto*) assists the Speakers, MPs, and various parliamentary organs in the handling of international affairs. It assists in international parliamentary speakers' conferences, foreign visits by MPs and parliamentary civil servants, and participation in international inter-parliamentary institutions. The Eduskunta's expert in Brussels is part of Eduskunta's EU Secretariat, which also consists of the committee secretariats of the Grand Committee (the EU committee of the Eduskunta) and the Foreign Affairs Committee (responsible for EU's foreign and security policy issues). The Brussels-based expert monitors EU legislative initiatives beginning at the earliest possible stages with the aim of facilitating parliamentary involvement in Helsinki. The expert follows closely the European Parliament and its Finnish members, sends information and documents to Eduskunta, including various reports and summaries that often provide relevant background details behind specific issues, participates in the meetings of national parliaments' representatives in the EU, and assists MPs visiting Brussels.

17.2.2 Information to MPs and the Public

The Information and Communication Department (*tieto- ja viestintäosasto*) is responsible for parliamentary communication, including via digital and social media channels. The Eduskunta's information office disseminates information on plenary sessions, committee work, international affairs, and other parliamentary matters. The Visitor's Centre, opened in 2004, stages around 250 public seminars or conferences per year in which MPs meet citizens. It also provides information on the Eduskunta, operates guided tours, holds an annual open day, and has hosted the Youth Parliament since 1998. The Eduskunta boasts on its website being one of the most open parliaments in the world. While there are good grounds for refuting such claims, certainly in terms of media access the rules are open, as reporters and photographers registered to work at the Eduskunta can easily interview MPs and ministers in the halls, lobbies, and cafés of the parliament buildings. The Eduskunta library and the Information Service operate under the Information and Communication Department. The library has been open to the public since 1913 and parliamentary documents have been available online since 1995. The services and materials found in the library are selected with the primary aim of supporting the work of the Eduskunta. The Information Service directed at the public assists people, normally free of charge, in finding information on various aspects of societal issues and broadly law and social sciences, not just information related to parliamentary work.

However, there is another information service, the Research Service, which formally is under the Parliamentary Office. It acquires data and background material as well as carries out various studies for MPs, party groups, and the parliamentary administration. The Research Service handles roughly 1300 information requests per year. The availability of online information has resulted in a significant drop in such requests, as previously the Service handled as many as 5500 tasks annually. As MPs and party groups can easily find factual information and documents online, nowadays a larger share of the tasks are broader, more in-depth analyses and reports that can take several weeks to produce. If needed, the Service can also draw on external experts. The share of international requests, often carried out jointly with other legislatures, has increased over the years. In 2011, the Service established a special unit for economic forecasts, which employs four economists. Interviews indicate that the Research Service has been particularly important in assessing the economic consequences of planned reforms, and opposition parties have benefitted from the Service when preparing their annual alternative, so-called shadow budgets (Aula & Konttinen 2020). If an MP publicly refers to the information provided by the Research Service, the information itself becomes also publicly available. However, while the Eduskunta has its own publication series, the Research Service is nonetheless relatively small and in general there is the expectation that, if needed, the government or external experts produce more in-depth reports and additional memos on issued handled by the Eduskunta, including various follow-up documents such as impact assessments. The Service is also careful not to become embroiled in political conflicts. As commented by the Antti

Rautava, the head of the Research Service: 'We do not want to cross over to the side of politics. You can only lose trust once' (Uusikumpu 2018).

17.2.3 Clear Division of Labour

A recent study examining the internal organization of the Eduskunta found that MPs had no clear view of what the Parliamentary Office does or how it exactly functions. At the same time, MPs expressed satisfaction with the support and skills of the bureaucracy (Aula & Konttinen 2020). The parliamentary bureaucracy handles procedural, technical, and legal matters, and while certain individuals, notably committee secretaries, are potentially very influential, the division of labour is clear: the Eduskunta civil servants are not expected to intervene in the substance of issues or to take sides in party-political bargaining.

The extent of interaction with the executive branch, notably with civil servants in the ministries, is regular and occurs via multiple avenues and is not regulated by any statutes. Particularly the committee secretaries are routinely in touch with their respective line ministries. When the government has failed to keep the parliament properly informed, also the Secretary-General or the committee secretaries can publicly defend the rights of the Eduskunta. Contacts with other stakeholders, such as trade unions, businesses, and civil society actors are also primary handled by committee secretariats. However, apart from processing Citizen's Initiatives (introduced in 2012), the Eduskunta does not offer any participatory instruments beyond the standard hearings of stakeholders in the committees (Seo & Raunio 2017). Overall, the parliamentary administration stays relatively hidden from the public view. It is not considered appropriate for the administrative staff to comment publicly on the substance of issues, and by and large this norm has been followed.

17.3 Party Group Staff and MPs' Assistants

In order to understand the functions of the party group staff and MPs' assistants, it is necessary to provide contextual information about party-political dynamics and the electoral system. Starting with party groups, the Finnish party system is noted for its high degree of fragmentation. Since the declaration of independence in 1917, no party has even come close to winning a majority of parliamentary seats (the post-Second World War high is 28.3% won by the Social Democrats in the 1995 elections), and this fragmentation contributes to cooperation between the main parties. Despite the entry into the Eduskunta of new party families such as green, Christian, and populist parties, the party system has remained rather stable, with the three core parties – the Social Democrats, the Center Party, and the National Coalition – largely holding on to their vote shares in recent decades. The rise of the populist Finns Party has produced a situation where the party system has four quite equally sized large parties. Forming majority cabinets is, therefore, not possible unless the government has at least three parties. This means that Finnish parties are used to active cooperation, not least in the Eduskunta and its committees.

Party discipline is strong. This applies particularly to governing parties. It is commonly accepted among the coalition partners that the government programme forms the backbone of the cabinet and that it is binding on all the parties and their MPs. The government parties also monitor that their party groups support the programme. The cooperation rules between the governing parties' parliamentary groups that have been in use since the early 1980s effectively prevent any disagreements or public conflicts between the government and the party groups. Dissenting MPs can expect tough sanctions, including expulsion from their parliamentary group. The only exceptions are matters that are clearly 'local' by nature and certain questions of conscience. The Eduskunta is thus a party-dominated legislature – and has become more so since the 1990s as a result of constitutional reforms.

MPs are elected from one single-member and 12 multi-member electoral districts, with the Åland Islands entitled to one seat. Voters choose between individual candidates who appear on party lists in alphabetical order. The 'party brand' is an electoral asset, but at the same time, there is arguably more competition within than between parties. The combination of an 'open list' and decentralized candidate selection means that the whole system is very local or district-based – and this creates strong incentives for cultivating ties with constituents (Arter 2011; Raunio & Ruotsalainen 2018). Therefore, MPs must in their work strike a balance between the party-dominated environment of the Eduskunta and maintaining contacts with their constituents. As seen in this section, the personal assistants of MPs are important in both aspects.

17.3.1 Stronger Party Groups

Public funding of political parties and their party groups has since 1967 been decided by the Eduskunta, with parties' electoral success determining their level of public subsidies. Since their inception, these subsidies have accounted for the vast majority of parties' total incomes – on average nearly 80% in the case of party central office and almost 100% in the case of Eduskunta party groups. Over the decades, the financial resources of party groups have strengthened significantly, while the respective subsidies of the extra-parliamentary party organization have by and large stagnated. In fact, since the early 1980s the staff levels of central party offices have declined, while the opposite applies to parliamentary groups. In the early 1960s, the party groups had no paid workforce at all, but between the late 1960s and the late 1980s their staff increased threefold. Despite the great recession, party group resources continued to grow also in the 1990s, albeit at a slower rate. In addition, since 1997 all MPs have received an allowance to hire a personal assistant. Overall, the resources of the party groups have increased considerably during recent decades, although the number of full-time party group staff (excluding MPs' assistants) has hardly increased since the 1990s (Koskimaa 2016, 2020).

The majority of the Eduskunta party groups operate a so-called group secretariat model (*ryhmäkanslia*), where the MPs' assistants are employed by the party group, not by the individual MPs (although formally those assistants working directly for the MP are employed by the Eduskunta). Particularly the Social Democrats have long-standing experience of this model, while the Centre Party adopted it in the beginning of the 2019–2023 electoral term. In March 2021, the largest party group, the Social Democrats (40 MPs), had in their group secretariat ten persons working for the whole group: the general secretary, an assistant, a lawyer, a service and administration manager, a person handling media relations, and policy specialists in the fields of EU and international affairs, economy, social policy, administration, and environment and economic policy. A total of 29 persons assisted MPs, with 11 of them assisting two social democratic MPs. Most of the 29 also had specific duties for the whole group.

The National Coalition (conservatives), the Finns Party (populists), and the Swedish People's Party do not operate the group secretariat model. For example, in March 2021, the National Coalition had 11 persons working for the party group, with conservative MPs in addition having their own personal assistants. MPs have often resisted the group secretariat model, as they fear the consequences of losing their own assistants. When the assistant is accountable only to the MP, the latter obviously has more freedom in determining what the assistant does. Yet at the same time, the group secretariat model has its advantages, especially in terms of intra-group coordination and policy expertise. For example, the general secretary of the Centre Party's parliamentary group, Seija Turtiainen, defended the move to the group secretariat model by referring to the cost-effective use of resources, avoiding the duplication of work carried out by MPs' assistants, and the need to develop policy expertise (Lampi 2019). Interviewed MPs have also agreed that the group secretariat model results in more cost-effective use of resources (Aula & Konttinen 2020).

17.3.2 Similar Practices, Important Assistants

There are practically no written rules about how party groups organize their internal work. Hence there is a myriad of unwritten norms and codes, but nonetheless the groups have adopted largely similar organizational arrangements. Regardless of whether the party groups operate the actual group secretariat model, the group secretariats coordinate the work of the party groups, provide support for the group leadership, prepare issues and documents for group decision-making, and in general keep the wheels turning. In their preparatory work, the group secretariats often benefit from cooperation with the Eduskunta's internal information unit (see above). Links to the information unit and potentially also use of external experts are more important for the opposition party groups, as they do not enjoy similar direct access to the ministries and the government as the party groups of the cabinet parties. The substantive weight of group secretariats has clearly increased. Party group decisions and policies are prepared under the guidance of the secretariats.

Assistants are very important for the MPs. The assistants must be at least 18 years old, but otherwise there are no real criteria. Some of the assistants are seasoned veterans of party politics, while others are still undergraduate students, or relatives of MPs. Finnish MPs do not operate local, constituency offices. Hence, the assistants primarily work in Helsinki in the Eduskunta, although some of the assistants are based in the constituency. The job description of assistants varies to some extent, depending largely on what the MP chooses to do herself. Essentially all assistants are the personal secretaries of the MPs: they manage the MP's calendar, arrange meetings, and handle email and perhaps social media accounts. In terms of policy-making, assistants can prepare documents or speeches, acquire background information and material, and interact with other assistants or group secretariats. In the group secretariat model, the assistants do not only assist one or two MPs but they also work for the entire group, not least through helping with data collection and preparation of documents. Again, there is considerable variation: some assistants, particularly those who assist two MPs, may have little time for group duties, while others focus primarily on group-level tasks.

Every week the general secretaries of the party groups hold a joint meeting with the leading civil servants from the Parliamentary Office to plan the parliamentary week ahead. However, the party group secretariats nonetheless operate in the world of party politics, while the actual parliamentary administration sticks to keeping the Eduskunta running. It is this division of labour that we shall discuss in the concluding section.

17.4 Conclusions

The Eduskunta is an institutionalized legislature. Reflecting similar features in the executive branch, the parliamentary rules of procedure as well as more informal behavioural codes display continuity and stability. Both MPs and civil servants know the rules of the house, and there is no larger pressure – either from the inside or the outside – for changing how the Eduskunta functions.

In line with the rules of procedure, the Parliamentary Office 'shall create and maintain the conditions in which the Parliament can perform its tasks as an organ of the State'. As a result, the administration focuses on procedures and legal issues – that meeting schedules are adhered to, that documents are delivered on time, and that MPs and party groups receive the needed technical and substantive support in policy-making. There is no denying the practical importance of the parliamentary administration, but it is almost invisible to the broader public. In fact, several key administrative personnel have in interviews emphasized that they prefer to and also should stay in the background. Occasionally the Secretary-General or committee secretaries appear in the media, but normally only to explain some parliamentary procedures or to defend the information rights of the Eduskunta.

The Parliamentary Office and the party group staff live in parallel, vastly different worlds. The former keeps the wheels of the institution turning but does not intervene in party-political bargaining. The latter in turn operate in the sphere of party politics, with the aim of contributing to the electoral and policy success of their parties. Interestingly, also the party group staff are invisible beyond the walls of the legislature. Even the general secretaries of the party groups – the leading figures in group secretariats – remain hidden from the public view. The resources of the party groups have increased substantially in recent decades. Particularly important was the introduction of personal assistants to MPs in the late 1990s. As most party groups have a model wherein the assistants work simultaneously for the entire group, the assistant system further empowers the party groups also inside their respective party organizations.

The existence of two different spheres – administrative and party-political – does not rule out senior civil servants wielding even significant influence inside the Eduskunta. This applies particularly to committee secretaries that can develop considerable expertise and authority within their policy domains. Yet such influence is difficult to measure or capture, as there is no concrete evidence of it and as MPs are always in the end politically responsible for the decisions. And maybe that is a good solution for both sides: bureaucrats facilitate and influence parliamentary and party group decision-making behind the closed doors of the Eduskunta, while MPs and political parties get the credit for the policies.

In terms of the future development of the parliamentary administration, the COVID-19 crisis has intensified discussions concerning both digitalization and better communication inside the Eduskunta and with the broader society. These challenges are highlighted in the action and financial plan of the Parliamentary Office for 2021–2024, but it is not evident that the pandemic will usher in any major reforms. To be sure, the Eduskunta administration adapted rather quickly to the 'crisis mode', switching to online meetings and remote working, but how much of these practices will continue after the crisis is unclear. The existing organizational arrangements and behavioural norms are widely accepted in the Eduskunta, both among MPs and the civil servants, and hence there is no real pressure to change the established practices.

```
                    CHANCELLERY COMMISSION
                       Consists of MPs
```

| Security Department | PARLIAMENTARY OFFICE
Secretary-General | Administrative and Service Department |

| Committee Secretariat | Central Office | International Department | Information and Communication Department |

Notes

1 I am grateful to Kristiina Hakala, chief information specialist at the Library of the Finnish Parliament, and Tuomas Kuoppala, a political science doctoral student at Tampere University, for their valuable inside information on how the Eduskunta administration works.
2 The Constitution of Finland, 11 June, 1999 (731/1999, amendments up to 817/2018 included). An English translation is available at http://www.finlex.fi/en/laki/kaannokset/1999/en19990731.pdf.
3 The staff figures reported in this section are primarily from the latest annual report of the Parliamentary Office (*Eduskunnan kanslian toimintakertomus 2019*) and the action and financial plan of the Parliamentary Office for 2021–2024 (*Eduskunnan kanslian toiminta- ja taloussuunnitelma 2021–2024*). Both are available, together with older reports, at https://www.eduskunta.fi/FI/naineduskuntatoimii/julkaisut/Sivut/default.aspx, accessed 19 March 2021.
4 *Eduskunnan työjärjestys* 17.12.1999/40 v. 2000. An unofficial translation is available at https://www.eduskunta.fi/EN/naineduskuntatoimii/Documents/parliaments_rules_of_procedure.pdf, accessed 19 March 2021.

References

Arter, David (2011): The Michael Marsh question: How do Finns do constituency service? *Parliamentary Affairs* 64:1, 129–152.
Aula, Ville & Lea Konttinen (2020): Miten kansaa edustetaan? selvitys kansanedustajien työstä eduskuntatyön uudistamiseksi. Sitran selvityksiä 165.
Karvonen, Lauri, Heikki Paloheimo & Tapio Raunio eds. (2016): *The Changing Balance of Political Power in Finland*. Stockholm: Santérus Academic Press.
Koskimaa, Vesa (2016): *Towards Leadership Democracy: The Changing Balance of Power in Three Finnish Political Parties 1983–2012*. Tampere: Tampere University Press, Acta Universitatis Tamperensis 2224.

Koskimaa, Vesa (2020): The 'genetic' effect: Can parties' past organizational choices condition the development of their internal distribution of power in the cartel party era? Evidence from Finland, 1983–2017. *Politics* 40:3, 313–331.

Lampi, Santeri (2019): 'Keskusta siirtyy ryhmäkansliamalliin – kansanedustajien avustajajärjestelmä menee remonttiin', *Suomenmaa*, 4 January 2019, https://www.suomenmaa.fi/keskusta/keskusta-siirtyy-ryhmakansliamalliin-kansanedustajien-avustajajarjestelma-menee-remonttiin/, accessed 21 March 2021.

Länkinen, Tiina (2015): 'Eduskunta äänesti Maija-Leena Paavolan pääsihteerikseen', *Yle*, 11 December 2015, https://yle.fi/uutiset/3-8521620, accessed 19 March 2021.

Raunio, Tapio & Taru Ruotsalainen (2018): Exploring the most likely case for constituency service: Finnish MPs and the change towards personalised representation. *Representation* 54:1, 37–53.

Raunio, Tapio (2022): Committees in the Finnish Eduskunta: Cross-party cooperation and legislative scrutiny behind closed doors. In Sven T. Siefken & Hilmar Rommetvedt (eds) *Parliamentary Committees in the Policy Process*. London: Routledge, 79–97.

Seo, Hyeon Su & Tapio Raunio (2017): Reaching out to the people? Assessing the relationship between parliament and citizens in Finland. *The Journal of Legislative Studies* 23:4, 614–634.

Seo, Hyeon Su (2017): *Reaching Out to the People? Parliament and Citizen Participation in Finland*. Tampere: Tampere University Press, Acta Universitatis Tamperensis 2264.

Sutinen, Teija (2017): 'Eduskunta tuhoaa päivittäin tiedot talossa käyneistä vierailijoista – hävittäminen alkoi, kun oikeus määräsi tiedot julkisiksi', *Helsingin Sanomat*, 12 September 2017, https://www.hs.fi/politiikka/art-2000005363066.html, accessed 23 March 2021.

Uusikumpu, Maarit (2018): 'Ilman näitä miehiä kansanedustajat olisivat hukassa – Eduskunnan tietopalvelun Antti Rautava ja Martti Tanskanen välittävät päättäjille faktaa, jotta valheet eivät myrkyttäisi politiikkaa', *Motiivi*, 11 December 2018, https://motiivilehti.fi/lehti/artikkeli/ilman-naita-miehia-kansanedustajat-olisivat-hukassa-eduskunnan-tietopalvelun-antti-rautava-ja-martti-tanskanen-valittavat-paattajille-faktaa-jotta-valheet-eivat-myrkyttaisi-politiikkaa/, accessed 22 March 2021.

18
FRANCE'S PARLIAMENTARY ADMINISTRATION

Angela Tacea[1]

France has a hybrid political system, categorized as *semi-presidential* (Duverger, 1962), *presidentialist* (Gicquel and Gicquel, 2014) or *parliamentary with presidential capture* (Le Divellec, 2011). The executive is divided between the President, endowed with important prerogatives, directly elected by the people and not accountable to the Parliament, and the Cabinet, accountable only to the Assemblée nationale. Cabinet formation is based on the results of the legislative elections. Yet, contrary to other parliamentary systems, the President has a discretionary power to designate the Prime Minister, who is rarely the leader of the majority party. The Constitution does not foresee a confidence vote.

The French Parliament is rather weak compared to other European (EU) legislatures. According to the index of parliamentary powers developed by Fish and Kroenig (2009), the French Parliament ranks 24 out of 26 EU member states. Indeed, the legislature is often reduced to a mere rubber-stamping of the decisions that have been taken by the executive. The Cabinet dominates the Parliament though different instruments. First, legislation is the application of policies that are decided by the Cabinet (article 20 of the French Constitution). Second, the presence of ministers during the votes reinforces party disciple (Avril, 2013). Third, despite the different constitutional reforms, the Cabinet still controls large parts of the parliamentary agenda.

In contrast to the political (inter)dependence between the executive and the legislative, the parliamentary administration is defined by its autonomy and political independence. In this sense, it exercises its role in an impartial manner with no political or individual interference (Rosanvallon, 2008). The present chapter will highlight how the autonomy and independence of the French parliamentary administration reinforces its democratic legitimacy.

The Assemblée nationale and the Sénat have their own administration. However, the responsibilities and the legal status of parliamentary clerks are similar. In this sense, the term parliamentary administration can be used with regard to both chambers of the French Parliament. However, this chapter will mainly focus on the administration of the lower house, the Assemblée nationale, although occasional comparative references will be made to the Sénat.

18.1 The Organization of the Parliamentary Administration

To organize 1,139 hours and 30 minutes of plenary debates, to adopt 560 legislative texts, to table 70,956 amendments and 1,143 oral questions and 9,299 written ones[2] and to support the activities of 577 members of the parliament (MPs), the Assemblée nationale has a high-functioning infrastructure. The total number of permanent staff (hereinafter parliamentary officials) is fixed at 1,349 by the Assemblée Nationale's *Internal rules of procedure on the organization of services related to the staff regulations*. In March 2018, the Assemblée nationale employed a total number of 1,278 parliamentary officials (all categories included) as follows: 1,094 public servants *(fonctionnaires)* and 184 agents employed under a public or a private contractual contract, a ratio of 2.2 employees per MP. This ratio is lower compared to the House of Commons or to the Bundestag (Secrétariat général de l'Assemblée nationale et de la Présidence and Secrétariat Général de la Questure, 2018, p.20). On 31 December 2016, the average age of parliamentary officials was 50.1 years. Around 56% of them were more than 50 years old and 30% of them were between 30 and 40 years old. Only 14% were less than 40 years old (Assemblée nationale b). The Sénat employed in 2021 approx. 1,100 parliamentary officials (all categories included), though the total number is not clearly indicated by the institution. This makes a higher ratio compared to the lower chamber, of 3.1 employees per senator.

The parliamentary administration of the French lower chamber is made up of four different general administrative bodies[3]: clerks (180), deputy-clerks (115), secretaries of administrative services (172) and agents (409) and 20 specialized bodies (security, IT, drivers, drafting of parliamentary minutes, real estate, catering, nurses etc.) (Saint-Dizier, 2014; Assemblée nationale a). These bodies have a four-level hierarchical organization: level 1: clerks, parliamentary minutes editor, chief-engineer, chief architect and IT engineers; level 2: deputy-clerks, technical director of restaurants and restaurants' employees of the 4th category; level 3: secretaries of administrative services, restaurants' employees and professional workers of the 3rd category and level 4: agents, security personnel, restaurants' employees, and professional workers of the 2nd category. Each category is divided in grades, and each grade in classes. Class and grade advancement follows a merit base, while a salary increase is automatically undertaken every two years. The same structure applies in the upper house.

One of the key features of the French parliamentary administration is its bicephalic structure (art 2 of the Internal Rules and Procedures). Two senior officials, designated by the Bureau of the Assemblée nationale, are leading two different poles: an administrative service and a legislative one. In theory, the two officials are chosen among the clerks of all categories. In practice though, they are chosen among the general directors or directors based on their competence and experience. Each secretary general is assisted by a director general of legislative services and, respectively, of administrative services (Assemblée nationale b). The Sénat is organized following the same bicephalic structure between a Directorate General for Institutional Missions and a Directorate General for Resources and Means.

The General Secretariat of the Assemblée nationale and of the Presidency assists the President of the chamber during plenary meetings and supports him with everything that touches upon the institutional organization of the Assemblée nationale, particularly the relationship with public authorities and the government. Some secretary generals have been quasi-irremovable, such as Émile Blamont who spent 25 years in office (1946–1971). Nonetheless, this is rather an exception, secretary generals spend between 6 and 10 years in office. Figure 18.1 gives an overview of the different legislative services that are subordinated to the General Secretariat of the Assemblée nationale and of the Presidency.

FRANCE

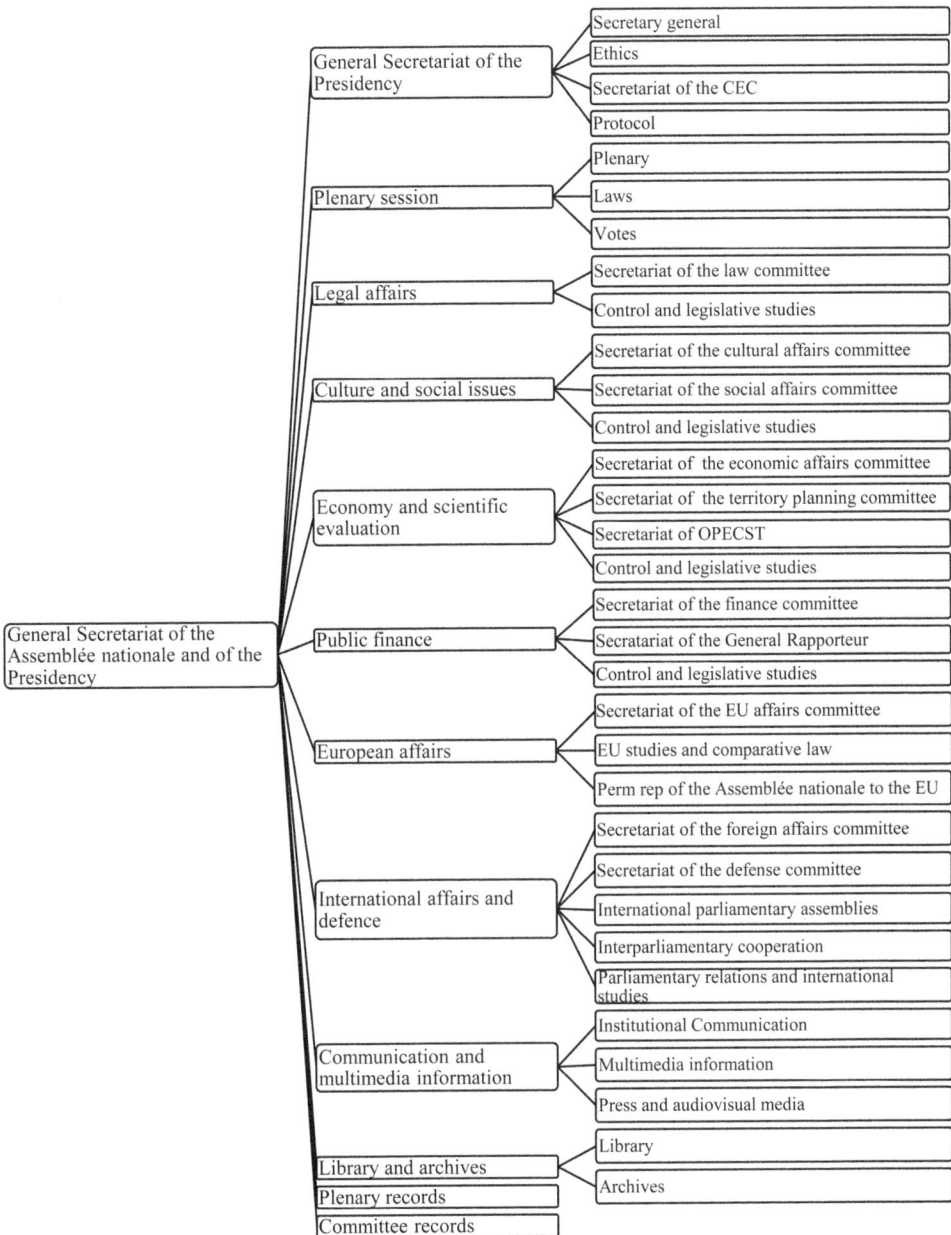

Source: Author's compilation from the website of the Assemblée nationale

Figure 18.1   The organization of the General Secretariat of the Assemblée nationale and of the Presidency

The secretary general of the Assemblée and of the Presidency is responsible before the President of the Assemblée nationale for the good functioning of 12 legislative services: the General Secretariat of the Presidency, the plenary session, legal affairs, culture and social issues, economy and scientific evaluation, public finance, European affairs, international affairs and defence, communication and multimedia information, library and archives, plenary records and committee records. Figure 18.1 shows the organization of each legislative services into several divisions. Committee secretariats are divided into thematic poles and each pole includes a control and legislative studies division. This complex organization is sometimes confusing for MPs who have difficulties in identifying the appropriate interlocutor. For this reason, a recent report submitted to the President of the Assemblée nationale suggested a reorganization of legislative services, into two new directorates: one in change of the legislation and another one in charge of the control and evaluation.

Since the IIIrd Republic, French parliamentarians considered that their work should not be disrupted by administrative issues. To this end, they have designated among themselves three specialized members in charge of the administrative and financial management of the assembly. On 20 December 1803, a *sénatus-consulte* officially created the term and function of questor. Since 1973, two questors belong to the parliamentary majority and one to the opposition (article 10 of the Rules and Procedures). Questors oversee the elaboration, the execution and the control of the budget of the Assemblée nationale, as well as every administrative issue related to the institution: staff management, social protection and pensions, the preservation of the cultural heritage of the Assemblée nationale, the car fleet, the restaurants and every material aspect related to the work of their fellow MPs. The three questors are assisted by a General Secretariat of the Questure. Figure 18.2 details its organization.

The General Secretariat of the Questure is accountable before the questors regarding the performance and smooth running of five administrative services: general administration and

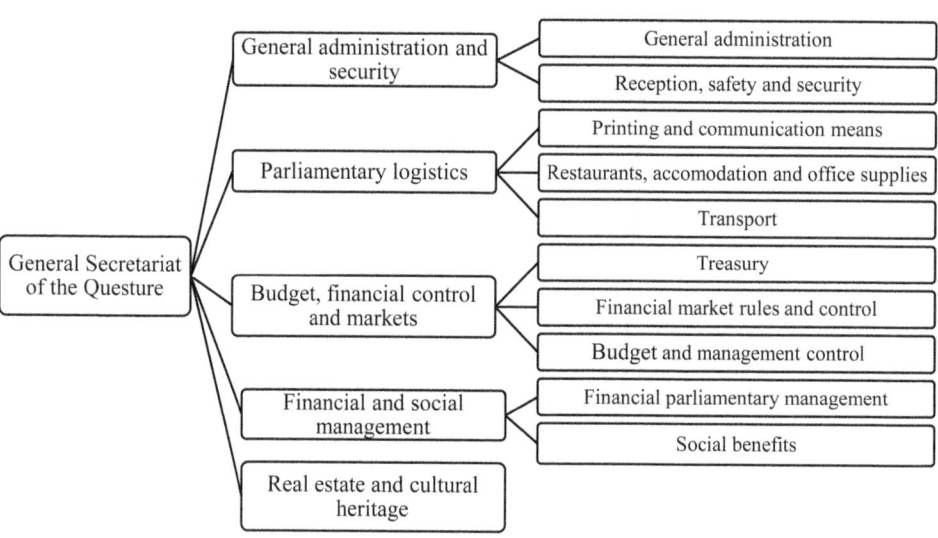

Source: Author's compilation from the website of the Assemblée nationale

Figure 18.2 The General Secretariat of the Questure

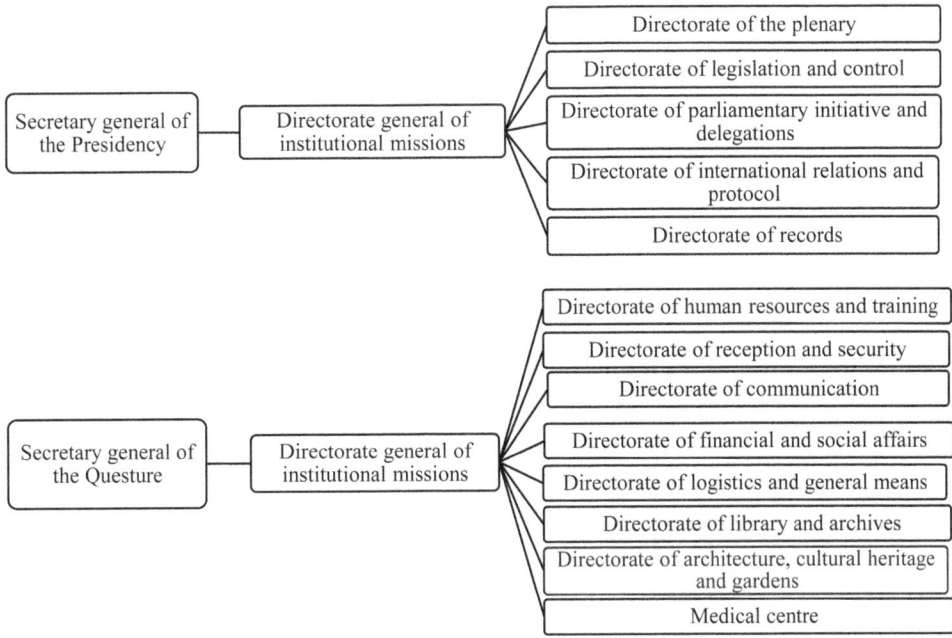

Source: Author's compilation from the website of the Sénat

Figure 18.3 The organization of the administrative structures of the Sénat

security, parliamentary logistics, budget, financial control and markets, financial and social management and real estate and cultural heritage.

As shown in Figure 18.3, the structure of the parliamentary administration in the Sénat is similar to that of the Assemblée nationale.

This dual structure is unique in Europe. Though other European parliaments have questors (e.g., the European Parliament, the Italian Parliament), they all have only one secretary general. In principle, the secretary general of the Assemblée and of the Presidency and the legislative services of the Assemblée nationale cannot buy a pencil without the approval of the General Secretariat of the Questure. In the same way, the secretary general of the Questure cannot speak to the President without the authorization the secretary general of the Assemblée. Even though the practice is more flexible, the duality between the administrative and the legislative secretariats is often a source of conflicts and administrative burdens. Consequently, their fusion has been proposed on several occasions in 1985, 2009 and 2019, with no success, however.

In addition to the legislative and administrative services, the Assemblée nationale has also two common services (Figure 18.4): the IT and the human resources service.

The financial and administrative autonomy of the parliamentary assemblies, which stems from the principle of the separation of powers (decree no. 58-1100 of 17 November 1958), confers a specific legal status to the parliamentary administration. Though parliamentary officials are public servants, they are independent from the executive and their status is regulated by the Assemblée Nationale's *Internal rules of procedure on the organization of services*

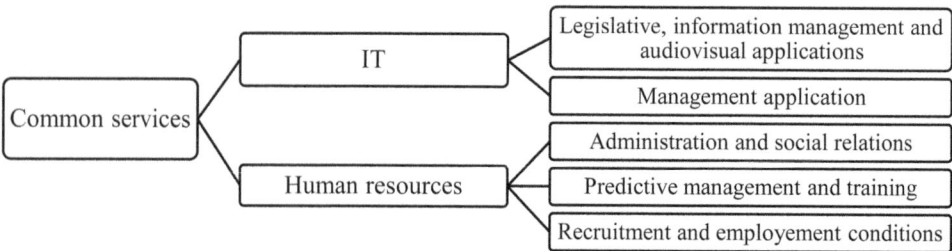

Figure 18.4 Organization of the common services

related to the staff regulations. Yet, to avoid any denial of justice and any arbitrary decision of the assembly regarding its agents, the same decree stipulates that the administrative jurisdiction may solve any individual legal dispute regarding parliamentary agents following the general principals of law and the fundamental guarantees of civil and military public servants.

Members of the parliamentary administration are recruited by competition *(concours)*, the rules of which are established by the Bureau of the Assemblée nationale and of the Sénat. The competition for parliamentary clerk is one of the most difficult public competitions in France together with that for the *École nationale d'administration* (ENA). Its attractiveness is given both by a very attractive salary and the opportunities for career development. The admitted candidates complete a one-year internship before being officially appointed to their respective grade. During their career, parliamentary officials belonging to the general administrative bodies can be assigned to different services of the Assemblée nationale. Starting with 2007, the maximum time spent in the same service has been established at eight years (Assemblée nationale, 2012). Originally, the autonomy of the parliamentary administration prevented any secondment of its officials to another public administration or service. At present, parliamentary officials can benefit both from an internal and an external mobility either through a supply service of personnel or a secondment (Avril, Gicquel and Gicquel, 2021, p.136). Supply service of personnel can be used for service abroad in the EU institutions, international organizations, foreign parliaments or for independent administrative authorities (Commission nationale de l'informatique et des libertés, Conseil supérieur de l'audiovisuel, Commission de Régulation de l'Energie) or judicial authorities (Conseil constitutionnel). In such a case, the parliamentary official continues to receive his/her salary from the Assemblée nationale. In the case of secondment, for example in the local administration, the salary is provided by the host institution. Several parliamentary officials joined ministerial cabinets: Bernard Rullier became deputy-director and then chief of cabinet of the Minister in charge with the relation with the Parliament (1997–2002), before becoming the parliamentary advisor of François Hollande (2012–2017). Eric Thiers has been the chief of cabinet of the Minister in charge with the relation with the Parliament (2007–2009) and special advisor in charge of constitutional matters for the Minister of Justice (2017–2019) (idem) and since 2022 advisor in change of institutions and public action for the Cabinet of the French President. If parliamentary officials can work in another administration, the opposite is not possible because of the separation of power between the executive and the legislative. Indeed, a parliamentary official working in a local administration can hardly be accused of trying to influence the administration in favour of the Parliament. However, the opposite is less straightforward. As Guy Carcassonne noted, 'we have seen too many public servants, in a secondment to the Parliament, lobbying in favour of their administration of origin, tearing down the scrutiny of the legislative texts, particularly in regard to the budget, becoming the advocates of those who they were supposed to control' (Carcassonne, 1985, p.35).

Besides internal and external mobility, parliamentary officials can benefit from continuous training. The aim of this training is to adapt the profile of parliamentary officials to the permanent evolution of the activities and interests of the Assemblée nationale, such as the development of European and international relations, the raise of new technologies, the enforcement of security etc.

18.2 Administration in Parliamentary Work

Parliamentary administration's tasks are extremely diverse and range from helping MPs with their daily life at the Palais Bourbon to providing valuable expertise and inform the legislative and control activities exercised by the members of the parliament.

From a practical point of view, several services 'discharge the MP of time-consuming contingences' (Carcassonne, 1985, p.31). Fifteen agents make photocopies, print documents, reports and all the necessary documentation for the parliamentary activity. The printed bills and their reports can be picked up by MPs or their assistants at the Library. Forty-five chauffeurs drive MPs to party meetings, talk shows, meetings with members of the executive etc. Out of these 45 chauffeurs, 15 are dedicated to all MPs and protocol missions, 6 to the Presidency and 18 to different personalities (Secrétariat général de l'Assemblée nationale et de la Présidence and Secrétariat Général de la Questure, 2018). In addition, nine agents take care of flight and train tickets. A Post Office offers mailing services. Twenty-one agents offer catering services in one of the two restaurants, two self-service restaurants and the refreshment bar *(buvette des parlementaires)* and a hotel room can be booked by MPs in one of the 51 hotel rooms situated inside the 101 rue de l'Université building of the Assemblée nationale. Two doctors, three nurses and two sport coaches help MPs, their assistants and any parliamentary employee to stay healthy and fit. And even a hairdresser offers her services inside the Palais Bourbon. This comprehensive and meticulous organization of every detail of the day-to-day life is meant to help MPs dedicate all their time to the parliamentary work. In practice, though, it often disconnects them from the outside word. Some MPs, namely those coming from the regions, never go outside the buildings of the Assemblée nationale during the time they spend in Paris.

At a more intellectual level, the legislative services presented in the previous section provide studies and documentation and accompany MPs and their assistants in accomplishing the legislative, control or evaluation missions. Parliamentary officials, in particular clerks and deputy-clerks have mainly an advisory role, supporting MPs from a technical and legal point of view in the law-making process and the scrutiny of the government. In this sense, they are fulfilling research, drafting and implementation tasks related to the legislative procedures. Indeed, independently of the expertise or the interest of an MP for a particular topic – not to mention that in most of the cases such an expertise is missing – the MP will never have, nor the comprehensive knowledge required by her/his mandate, neither the time to fully master a particular topic. In addition, when an MP is designated rapporteur for a legislative text or an informative/inquiry mission, s/he needs to organize hearings and/or field work, discuss with the members of the government, explain the topic to her/his colleagues, table and examine amendments, draft her/his report, present it in the committee meetings and defend it in the plenary. There is no doubt that this work cannot not be done by the MPs alone.

The relationship between MPs and parliamentary clerks depends very much on the personality, the experience and the interest of MPs. For those who have a long-established parliamentary career and an appropriate knowledge of the topic, parliamentary clerks act more as a technical and logistic support. They help with the organization of hearings, draft reports and amendments. To organize hearings, every committee secretariat has a list of academics, NGOs, experts etc. on the topic of their specialization. The list can be updated, and the MPs can suggest other names, but most of the times MPs leave this work to the parliamentary clerks. No wonder that the same personalities are often heard by the respective committee. For those MPs who act as a rapporteur with the aim of increasing their legislative activity, parliamentary clerks might be a real substitute for the legislator (Carcassonne, 1985, p. 35). Yet, in most of the cases, the reality is somewhere in between. Parliamentary clerks place their legal and technical expertise at the service of the MP's political will. In addition to these hard skills, the work of parliamentary clerks requires negotiation and conflict management competences. For example, it has become a tradition that two rapporteurs, one belonging to the majority and another one to the opposition, are designated for parliamentary information missions. The different political opinions of the rapporteurs might result in real clashes instead of a smooth cooperation. Though divergent opinions can be included, the final information report should reflect a certain form of consensus. In such cases, parliamentary clerks must deal with the unwillingness of rapporteurs to cooperate, the absence of response to their e-mails or MPs' opinions that change last minute. If the senior management might intervene to unblock this type of political deadlocks, most of the times through their long experience, their professional deontology and their resilience, parliamentary clerks manage to unblock even the most complicated situations. They organize 'conciliation' meetings, and they write and re(write) the draft report until it perfectly reflects the views of the two rapporteurs.

The recruitment and the career trajectory of parliamentary officials discourage specialization. Indeed, the competition includes five eligibility written examinations: (1) on political, international and economic issues; (2) on political science and constitutional law; (3) a summary note on legal issues; (4) on economy and public finance and (5) on EU law/administrative law/civil or criminal law/social law and three oral examinations on (1) parliamentary law; (2) a foreign language and (3) an interview (Arrêté du Président et des Questeurs no 03-102 du 17 septembre 2003). After recruitment, parliamentary clerks are encouraged to move from one service to another and their term in one service is limited to a maximum of eight years. This type of generalist profile corresponds to the advisory role that parliamentary clerks play. Yet, the increased specialization of the legislative texts raises the question of employing experts on certain matters. Though the Assemblée nationale can use the expertise of external institutions, such as the Court of Auditors, this expertise seems insufficient for the needs of the institution. The recent report submitted to the President of the Assemblée nationale (Secrétariat général de l'Assemblée nationale et de la Présidence and Secrétariat Général de la Questure, 2018, p.8) suggested the creation of a parliamentary evaluation agency that could provide the Assemblée nationale with an independent expertise.

18.3 Managing Current Challenges Facing the Parliamentary Administration: Digitalization, Transparency and Citizens' Engagement

In September 2017, the former president of the Assemblée nationale, François de Rugy launched an extensive reflection process with the aim of reforming the institution. Seven working groups composed of ten MPs from all parliamentary groups have worked on several institutional and legislative aspects.[4] Some of these aspects, such as the control and evaluation means, the legislative procedure and the rights of the opposition, were an anticipation of the future Constitutional bill that was initiated by the government on 9 May 2018. Others, such as the digital and participatory democracy and the opening-up of the parliamentary institution to civil society, were meant to adapt the Assemblée nationale to the current societal and technological challenges. Though the government suspended the examination of the Constitutional bill in July 2018 and François de Rugy quitted the presidency of the Assemblée nationale in September 2018 to become Minster for ecological transition, some of the measures proposed by the working groups were nonetheless implemented. They mainly relate to the transparency and openness of the institution and to citizens engagement.

To increase the transparency and openness of the institution, the Assemblée nationale launched, in 2015, an open data platform to make available in reusable formats under a free license all parliamentary documents, except for parliamentary reports. The open data platform is managed by the IT service of the Assemblée nationale and fed by the legislative services. There is no IT team dedicated to the open data platform. Instead, the entire IT staff (30 parliamentary officials) work daily to manage the platform. The open data has been made part of the IT architecture of the Assemblée nationale. For example, every day parliamentary clerks send to the Official journal the list of MPs who are present to the committee meetings. The attendance record is nonetheless kept only for permanent committee meetings. Documents such as the list of current and former MPs, the legislative files, the plenary debates, the amendments, the votes, the parliamentary questions are made available in three formats: XML, JSON and CSV. However, the hearings undertaken by the working group on transparency highlighted three main issues: some data is still not available in open source, the accessibility of data is still problematic, and the platform lacks visibility. The initial list of new data to be uploaded on the open data platform included the list of the persons heard by the rapporteur, the list of members of interest groups who enter the Assemblée nationale, the list of parliamentary assistants, the international activities of MPs (missions abroad) and the votes by delegation. This information is publicly available, but most of the times it is published in PDF format, with no systematization, which makes it difficult to use. Only the list of parliamentary assistants has been recently added on the platform. With the aim of increasing the transparency of the institution, the conclusions adopted by the Bureau of the Assemblée nationale, the Conference of Presidents and the meetings of the Questure have also been made public. The publication of members of interest groups has been a very sensitive and controversial topic. The Presidency of the Assemblée nationale decided not to publish them on the grounds that the High authority for the transparency of the public life (*La Haute Autorité pour la transparence de la vie publique* - HATVP) is publishing the lists of the representative of interest groups in open data format. The actualization of the data has also been improved as it is now possible to download data related to the legislative texts, the legislative reports, the records of the committee meetings and the amendments. Some of the data, such as the plenary sittings, is published in real time, while other type of data is updated three times per day. In addition, the open data platform has been made more visible on the website of the Assemblée nationale.

In practice, though, making available a large amount of data does not necessary increase the transparency of the institution, nor does it make it more open to citizens. Indeed, one of the criticisms addressed to the open data platform is that the data set is too difficult to use because the formats, the size and the information provided are too complex for users who do not have access to the digital infrastructure, nor to the hardware and/or software, and do not possess the necessary skills to make effective use of data. Indeed, until very recently, the IT services published very large. XML,. JSON files, which were unexploitable by ordinary citizens or journalists. For the reason, the competent services of the Assemblée nationale decided to publish also simplified data sets, such as the list of MPs or of amendments. In an informal discussion with the IT services of the Assemblée nationale, parliamentary clerks reported that this has significantly increased the use of parliamentary data by journalists. The most common users of the open data platform are journalists, such as Contexte – a web media specialized in institutions, public polices and legislation – associations, such Regards Citoyens a parliamentary monitoring organization and different state institutions, such as the General Secretariat of the Government and the Gandermarie nationale. The Gandermarie nationale makes an impressive number of queries to the point that the IT services of the Assemblée nationale asked them to limit the number of their requests. The organization of a hackathon to facilitate citizens' comprehension of the legislative process and to specify users' needs regarding the formats, the exploitation and the actualization of the data set has been proposed. Though two hackathons have been organized by the Assemblée nationale, one on 23 March 2019 and the second one on 24 and 25 January 2020, none of them used the Assemblée nationale's data set.

A second important aspect relates to the engagement of citizens during the legislative procedure. The Assemblée nationale has been often criticized for being an ivory tour, where the voice of the citizens is rarely heard. Articles 147 to 151 of the Rules and Procedures organize a petition right for citizens. However, in practice the secretariat of the Law committee, in charge with the examinations of petitions, proceeds only occasionally to an examination of the petitions submitted to the Assemblée nationale. To compensate for this obsolete procedure, the current legislature started to make an increased use of public consultations.[5] This practice was inspired by the success of the public consultation organized by the working groups in charge of reflecting upon the reform of the Assemblée nationale which gathered 17,321 votes and was made public in open data format.[6] Contrary to the analysis of petitions, which was the sole responsibility of the secretariat of the Law committee, the public consultations are directly integrated to the legislative procedure, when bills are examined, or to the control process, during the information missions. Thus, citizen's direct participation is treated as part of the evidence that parliamentary clerks are collecting. The use of public consultations is limited to two per committee per parliamentary session. In practice, the rapporteur at its own initiative or that of the parliamentary clerk who assists him/her makes an official request to the presidency of his/her committee. An administrator from the IT department is assigned and s/he takes care of the technical parts of the consultation (online publication, type of questions – opened/closed and management of answers).

The last measure that has been implemented following the recommendations of the working group on the openness of the Assemblée nationale has been the redesign of the website of the Assemblée nationale. In software design, the main component is the *persona*, which is a fictitious, specific and concrete representation of target users. During an informal discussion, the members of the IT services reported that the former website of the Assemblée nationale was designed for expert users. During the redesign process, the *Personas* have become the citizens. To this end, several working groups with 30 randomly selected and representative citizens have been organized. The aim of the workshops was to simplify the access to citizens to the institution. Citizens were first given a list of tasks, such as finding an MP or a certain legislative text; second, they were left navigate alone on the website of the institution, while they were observed by parliamentary clerks. For example, it has been observed that most of the citizens do not know the name of their MP; but they know their postal code. Consequently, the search tool of the Assemblée national includes now the possibility to search for an MP by the postal code.

18.4 Conclusions

The principle of separation of power and its internal organization makes the parliamentary administration the most independent public French administration. This independence is clearly reflected by its financial autonomy and its specific statutory powers. The bicephalic organization of the administration of the Assemblée nationale reinforces its independence. Indeed, though the President of the Assemblée nationale can be considered the 'chief of the administration' (Duverger, 1973, p. 272), in practice, the Bureau of the Assemblée holds 'the power to regulate the deliberations of the Assembly and to organize and manage all its services' (article 14 of the Rules and Procedures), while the Questure holds the financial power (article 15 of the Rules and Procedures).

Parliamentary clerks follow a strict deontology based on neutrality that helps them support MPs independently of their political affiliation. From their recruitment by *concours*, to the development of their career, every organizational detail is meant to protect parliamentary officials from external directives and to favour a search for generality. The impartial conduct of parliamentary clerks is guided by the concern to consider all the possible dimensions of a problem and analyse it in its complexity. In this sense, it comes to no surprise that the expertise is one of the defining characteristics of parliamentary clerks' profiles, with more than 50% of parliamentary officials being more than 50 years old. In addition, though parliamentary clerks can benefit from external mobility in other public administrations, the autonomy of the Assembly has constantly been presented as an impediment for other public servants to temporary integrate the parliamentary administration. This independence, which can be assimilated to that of quasi non-governmental organizations (QuANGO), pushed some scholars to praise for the democratic legitimacy of the parliamentary administration (Balnath, 2016).

The new practices related to the open data movement and the increased used during the current legislature of public consultations as a means of evidence-based policies provides the French parliamentary administration with a 'proximity legitimacy' (Rosanvallon, 2008, p.267). Lately, citizens have become more and more demanding when it comes to their association to the political and administrative decisions. They ask for their voice to be heard by decision-makers, for their individual situations to be taken into consideration and for political decisions be transparent. Or, by organizing online public consultations, hackathons and opening all the aspects of the legislative procedure to citizens, the administration of the Assemblée nationale aims to respond to these new social demands.

Notes

1 Between 2017 and 2018, the author has been a parliamentary assistant in the Assemblée nationale.
2 Numbers for the Parliamentary Session 2019–2020 (1 October 2019–30 September 2020).
3 Numbers on the 1 March 2017.
4 https://www2.assemblee-nationale.fr/qui/pour-une-nouvelle-assemblee-nationale-les-rendez-vous-des-reformes-2017-2022
5 https://data.assemblee-nationale.fr/autres/consultations-citoyennes
6 https://data.assemblee-nationale.fr/autres/pour-une-nouvelle-assemblee-nationale

References

Arrêté du Président et des Questeurs n° 03-102 of 17 September 2003 relatif à la nature des épreuves et à la composition du jury
Assemblée nationale (2012). *Les concours de l'Assemblée nationale*, Paris: Assemblée nationale.

Assemblée nationale a, *Fiche de synthèse n°69: Les secrétaires généraux*, retrieved at: https://www2.assemblee-nationale.fr/decouvrir-l-assemblee/role-et-pouvoirs-de-l-assemblee-nationale/l-administration-de-l-assemblee-nationale/les-secretaires-generaux

Assemblée nationale b, Fiche de synthèse n°67: Statut et carrière des fonctionnaires de l'Assemblée nationale, retrieved at https://www2.assemblee-nationale.fr/decouvrir-l-assemblee/role-et-pouvoirs-de-l-assemblee-nationale/l-administration-de-l-assemblee-nationale/statut-et-carriere-des-fonctionnaires-de-l-assemblee-nationale

Avril, P. (2013). Renforcer le Parlement: qu'est-ce à dire?. *Pouvoirs*, 146, (3), 9–19.

Avril, P., Gicquel, J.-E. and Gicquel, J. (2021). *Droit parlementaire*, Paris: L.G.D.J.

Balnath, M. (2016). Un mandat représentatif peut en cacher un autre: lumière sur l'administration parlementaire sous la Cinquième République. *Cahiers Jean Moulin*, 2. https://doi.org/10.4000/cjm.273

Carcassonne, G. (1985). L'appareil de l'Assemblée, *Pouvoirs*, 34 – L'Assemblée – September, 31–36

Duverger, M. (1962), *Le Système politique français*, Paris: PUF.

Duverger, M. (1973). *Sociologie de la politique*, Paris: PUF.

Fish, M. S., and Kroenig, M. (2009). *The Handbook of National Legislatures: A Global Survey*. New York: Cambridge University Press.

Gicquel, J. and Gicquel, J.-E. (2014). *Droit constitutionnel et institutions politiques*, 28e édition, Paris: LGDJ.

Le Divellec, A. (2011). Vers la fin du "parlementarisme négatif"? Une problématique introductive à l'étude des réformes constitutionnelles de 2008, *Jus Politicum*, 9 (October), 1–3.

Rosanvallon, P. (2008), *La légitimité démocratique. Impartialité, reflexivité, proximité*, Paris: Éditions du Seuil.

Saint-Dizier, A.-L. (2014). Parlementaire (administration) in Kada N. eds, *Dictionnaire d'administration publique*. Grenoble: Presses universitaires de Grenoble, 363–364.

Secrétariat général de l'Assemblée nationale et de la Présidence and Secrétariat Général de la Questure (2018). Rapport au Président de l'Assemblée nationale. Quelle administration parlementaire en 2022? Les misions, l'organisation et le statut de l'administration de l'Assemblée nationale, retrieved at: https://fr.irefeurope.org/SITES/fr.irefeurope.org/IMG/pdf/rapport-au-president-de-l-assemblee-nationale-quelle-adminsitration-parlementaire-en-2022.pdf

19
GERMANY'S PARLIAMENTARY ADMINISTRATION

Felix Arndt, Anna-Lena Högenauer and Claus Koggel

19.1 Introduction

The German legislature consists of the Bundestag and the Bundesrat. Although the Bundesrat is not a classic second chamber of a unified legislative body with regard to its composition and functions, it participates in the legislative process on equal footing with the Bundestag. Consequently, Germany is considered a bicameral system.

The members of the Bundestag are directly elected every four years. The size of the Bundestag varies from election to election: the minimum number of members of parliament (MPs) are 598. The complex electoral system which combines party lists and constituency votes while trying to maintain a proportional distribution of seats results in so-called overhang seats and equalization seats and can lead to more than 100 additional members. Thus, the Bundestag is fairly large compared to other European parliaments. The head of government (the chancellor) is elected by the Bundestag following elections. German governments are typically coalition governments with a parliamentary majority in the Bundestag. The main functions of the Bundestag are its participation in the legislative process, the election of the chancellor and the oversight over the executive and its control over the federal budget.

The second legislative organ, the Bundesrat, consists of the representatives of the 16 federal state (Länder) governments. There are no elections to the Bundesrat and thus no legislative terms. The composition of the Bundesrat changes gradually over time after elections in the Länder, which are held at different times. In constitutional parlance, the Bundesrat is an "eternal organ". Although all Bundesrat members belong to a political party, there are no political groups. The decisive factor is the affiliation of the members to one of the 16 Länder. Pursuant to art. 50 of the German Basic Law, the Länder – via the Bundesrat – participate in the legislation and the administration of the Federation and in matters concerning the European Union. Every land has – depending on the number of its population – between three and six votes in the Bundesrat. This amounts to 69 votes (and 69 seats) in total. Decisions have to be taken with an absolute majority of at least 35 votes.

On the whole, the German parliament is considered to be a comparatively strong parliament. For example, Fish and Kroenig (2009) give it a score of 0.84 in the Parliamentary Powers Index, one of the highest scores in the world. With regard to EU affairs scrutiny, Auel et al. consider the Bundestag to be the second strongest chamber in the EU (0.78) and the Bundesrat the eighth strongest chamber (0.62) (Auel et al. 2015). Nevertheless, while the political strength of the German parliament is subject to numerous studies, we know less about its administrative capacity. These support structures are important, though, as they provide MPs with the information and support that they need to be able to effectively use their formal powers. For this reason, the chapter will examine the general structure of the administrations of the Bundestag and the Bundesrat as well as their roles in the legislative process, the scrutiny of EU affairs and interparliamentary cooperation.

19.2 The Organization of the Administration

The German Bundestag is not just one of the largest national parliaments in the EU in terms of the number of MPs, but it can also rely on a sizeable administration. Thus, the Bundestag comprises approximately 3000 employees. However, as German MPs also benefit from generous allowances for personal assistants and political groups also receive financial support, the total number of people working in the Bundestag (as opposed to just the central administration) is around 7000 (https://www.bundestag.de/parlament/verwaltung). While the chapter will mainly focus on those parts of the central administration that support the political process, we will briefly provide an overview over the main elements of the administration here (cf. Figure 19.1).

The President of the Bundestag nominates the Secretary-General, who is responsible for the day-to-day management of the administration. The administration itself is subdivided into five departments (parliament and members, research and external relations, information and communication, technical services, central services), the Permanent Representative of the Parliamentary Oversight Panel over the intelligence services and the administration of the Parliamentary Commissioner for the Armed Forces.

The Department "Parliament and Members" supports the political work of the Bundestag. It is in charge of EU affairs and of services to the plenary, the committees and members. The parliamentary service prints and distributes all documents related to the legislative process or to motions and creates the minutes of meetings. It also supports the question hour and the chair of the plenary. The directorate "committees" comprises the secretariats of the permanent committees and the special committees. EU affairs are not only in the hands of a separate directorate "Europe", which comprises the secretariat of the European Affairs Committee, but also EU affairs in general. It deals with questions related to Economic and Monetary Union (EMU), analyses EU issues, assists committees in the selection of EU-related priorities, advises them and manages EU-related documents. It also produces legal advice on EU law and politics. The Liaison Office of the Bundestag in Brussels is also part of this subdivision with the responsibility to provide early information on EU legislative processes (cf. Neuhold and Högenauer 2016). In addition, the directorate for members takes care of the legal issues surrounding the past and current MPs and MEPs, the hiring of their personal assistants and the management of state funding for political parties.

The Department "Research and External Relations" comprises three Directorates. The Directorate Research Services is in charge of managing information, writing reports and providing information-related services to MPs. The aim is to provide MPs with information independently from the government, so as to enable them to fully exercise their legislative and scrutiny functions. The Directorate for external relations is in charge of relations with parliaments world-wide and of relations with interparliamentary assemblies. Furthermore, the Bundestag's Language Service is part of this directorate. The Directorate for petitions manages the petitions submitted by citizens (Art. 17 Basic Law).

Germany's Parliamentary Administration

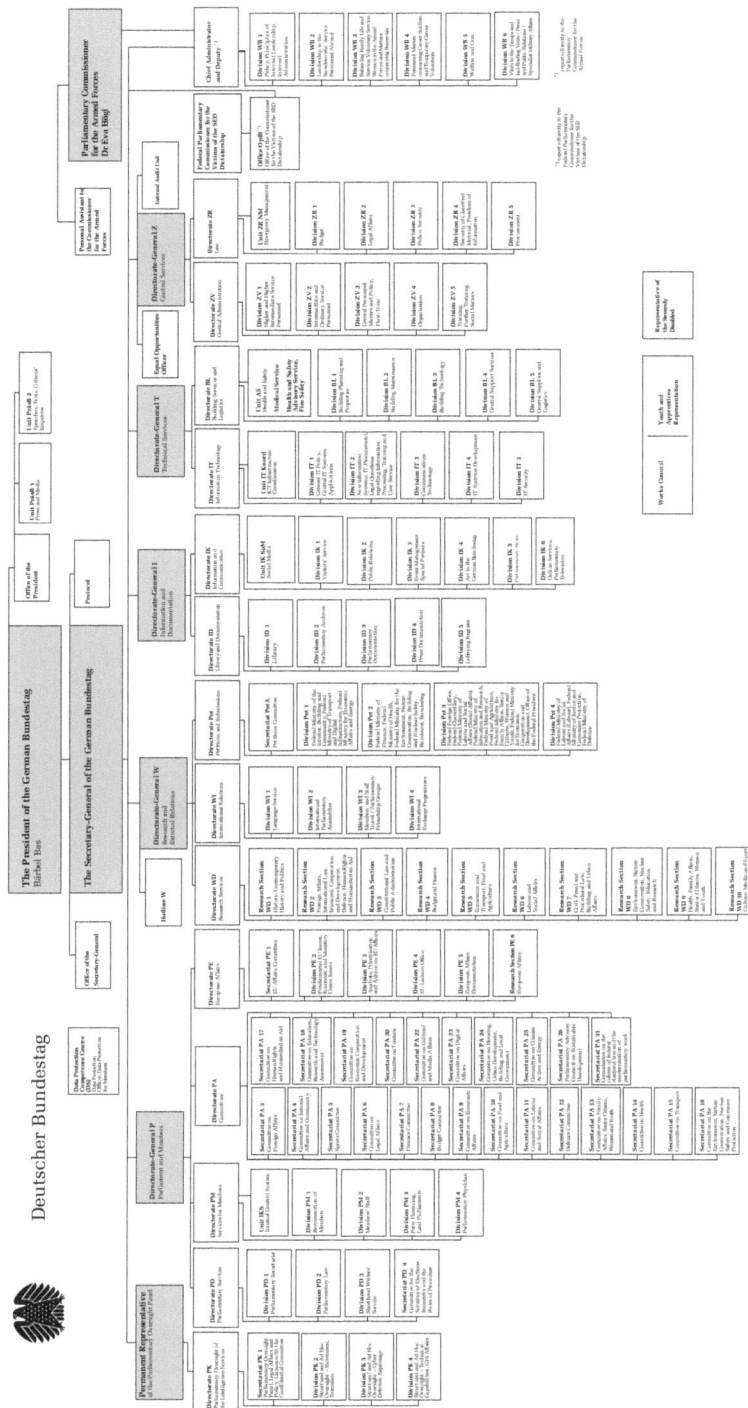

Figure 19.1 The administration of the Bundestag, for a current version see https://www.bundestag.de/en/parliament/administration

The Department "Information and Documentation" provides information on the functioning of the Bundestag to citizens and MPs. This includes the visitor service, the provision of free print publications and videos and an "Infomobil" that allows the Bundestag travel around Germany. It publishes a weekly magazine "Das Parlament", informs several times per day about committee meetings and plenary work in its newsletter "heute im bundestag" and runs the TV coverage of all plenary sessions and public committee sessions. It is also in charge of managing exhibitions, events, art in the Bundestag etc. Finally, the library service runs one of the largest parliamentary libraries in the world with around 1.5 million books and 8600 journals. The archive houses around 7000 meters of shelves worth of printed documentation (https://www.bundestag.de/en/parliament). It is publicly accessible. The Documentation and Information System for Parliamentary Processes (DIP) documents the legislative and scrutiny work of parliament. The press documentation service provides a daily media summary to MPs and staff.

The Department for technical services comprises the IT service and is in charge of construction issues and logistics. Finally, the Central Department is in charge of managing the administration in terms of its staff and finances. Finally, the Bundestag has its own police in charge of security.

Civil servants in the Bundestag's administration are recruited following a public advertisement and on the basis of applicants' skills and qualifications. For positions in the non-technical departments that require a University degree ("higher service") predominantly fully qualified lawyers are employed, even if a number of positions are also open for persons with other academic backgrounds. Other common qualifications, inter alia for positions in committee secretariats, include degrees in political or social sciences, history and philosophy. One reason for the more diverse professional background of committee staff is that a number of important committees play a limited role in the legislative process. These committees mainly exercise political scrutiny (e.g. the Foreign Affairs Committee, the Defence Committee or the Human Rights Committee). For the filling of leadership positions, the assent of the Presidium of the German Bundestag is required (Rule 7(4) RoP).

By comparison, the administration of the Bundesrat is much smaller (cf. Figure 19.2). Its secretariat comprised 208 employees in 2021.

The administration of the Bundesrat is headed by a Secretary General and a Deputy Secretary General who are elected by the Bundesrat's plenary.

In terms of structure, the administration is mainly divided into three Directorates-General: Committees (Directorate General A), Parliament (Directorate General P) and Central Administration (Directorate General Z). The Directorate-General A comprises 16 standing committees which are grouped in seven committee secretariats. The committee secretariats usually consist of around five people each – a head, a desk officer, a clerk and two secretaries.

The Directorate-General P consists of the division Parliamentary Service/Parliamentary Law (P 1), which is among others responsible for the organization of the plenary meetings, the division Parliamentary Relations/Language Service (P 2), the division President's Office/Protocol (P 3), the division Press and Communications (P 4) and the division Visitor Service/Events/Public Relations (P 5).

The Directorate-General Z has a division for Human Resources (Z 1), a division for Central Administration (Z 2 – legal affairs, internal services, property administration, maintenance measures, internal and technical services), an IT-division (Z 3), the documentation division (Z 4), which also includes a small library, the division Organization/Stenographic Service (Z 5) and the division New Build Projects, Occupational Safety and Health, Fire Protection (Z 6). The Director General Z additionally exercises the function of Budget Officer. Unlike the Bundestag, the Bundesrat does not have a research service. As its members

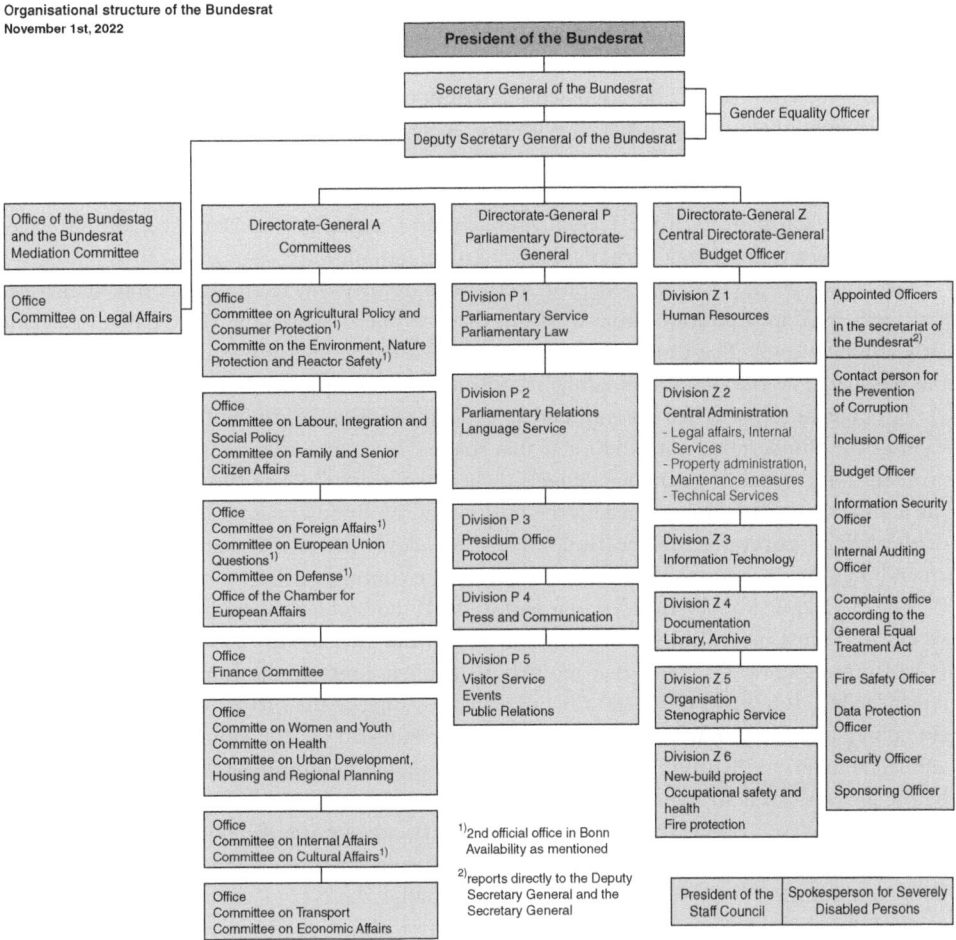

Figure 19.2 Organizational structure of the Bundesrat

are members of the 16 Länder governments, they can thus rely on their ministries for background research, expertise and scientific advice. Moreover, Bundesrat members do not have any staff or personal assistants in the Bundesrat administration but rely mainly on their staff in the 16 Länder.

Job vacancies are advertised externally. In case of higher ranking positions (e.g. management functions), these are first advertised internally. The selection of candidates for job vacancies involves two stages, a written exam and a structured interview. The hiring of a candidate requires the agreement of representatives of interest groups (e.g. the staff council, the representative for disabled persons and the Equality Officer). In the Bundesrat, the committee staff are often expected to be fully qualified lawyers or have an equivalent degree.

Employees are required to stay politically neutral in the exercise of their functions. They are bound by the current law and have to swear an oath to respect the Basic Law (i.e. the German constitution). However, while employees have to be politically neutral in the performance of their work, they are allowed to be members of political parties and even run in local elections, for example.

19.3 The Administration in the Legislative Process

The Bundestag and Bundesrat are the two legislative organs of the Federal Republic of Germany. All laws have to be discussed in both houses. Both the Bundestag and Bundesrat share the right of legislative initiative with the federal government. As in most Western democracies, most legislative proposals are initiated by the government (around 80 per cent), but each of the two houses accounts for around 10 per cent of legislative proposals (for detailed statistics, see Chapter 10 of the Datenhandbuch zur Geschichte des Deutschen Bundestages and https://www.bundestag.de/parlamentsdokumentation).

Legislative proposals of the federal government are first sent to the Bundesrat, which has six weeks to adopt a position (nine weeks in the case of changes to the Basic Law or particularly complex laws). The proposals are first discussed in the relevant committees and then in the plenary. The Bundesrat can adopt recommendations for amendments. Its vote can also be "no objections" or it can recommend a "general rejection" of the bill. However, the position of the Bundesrat is not binding at that stage. The vote is then sent to the federal government for a so-called counter statement ("Gegenäußerung"). The Bundestag then receives the legislative proposal together with the position of the Bundesrat and the counter statement of the federal government. The Bundestag then adopts the law or amends it. In practice, amendments are almost exclusively made during the committee stage after the first reading.

The bill adopted by the Bundestag is sent to the Bundesrat for a second passage. It has three weeks to discuss the bill in the committees and in the plenary. In the case of a consent bill ("Zustimmungsgesetz"), a bill that requires its explicit consent, the Bundesrat can adopt or reject the bill. If it wants to amend the bill, it has to convene the mediation committee of the Bundestag and the Bundesrat. This committee is composed of 16 members of the Bundesrat and 16 members of the Bundestag: Its task is to elaborate a compromise that requires approval by the plenaries of both houses.

If the Bundesrat rejects the bill adopted by the Bundestag, the federal government or the Bundestag can also convene the mediation committee in order to save their bill and negotiate for a compromise. Consent bills are all bills that change the Basic Law, transfer competences to the EU or affect the finances of the Länder or their administrative sovereignty.

If the bill adopted by the Bundestag is a bill of objection ("Einspruchsgesetz"), the Bundesrat can raise an objection within two weeks after a failure to reach a compromise in the mediation committee. However, the Bundestag can overrule the objection with an absolute majority of its members.

Bills originating in the Bundestag are sent to the Bundesrat only after they have been adopted; there is only the second passage as described above: Draft bills initiated by the Bundesrat are sent to the Bundestag. There are no fixed deadlines within which the Bundestag must discuss the draft bill. The Bundestag shall consider and vote on bills within a reasonable time. In case the Bundestag adopts the bill, it is sent back to the Bundesrat for the second passage.

The administrations of the Bundestag and the Bundesrat cooperate closely in the legislative process. For example, the parliamentary service of the Bundesrat and the parliamentary secretariat of the Bundestag coordinate the exchange of documents. The two services discuss the timing of the transmission of documents and when legislative proposals should be processed faster than the normal period. The Bundestag has access to the document webserver of the Bundesrat, where recommendations, decisions etc. are stored. Similarly, the Bundesrat has access to the DIP documentation and information system of the Bundestag and can upload documents there.

The administration of the Bundestag and its committee secretariats do not play a role in drafting bills initiated by the Bundestag. This task rests solely with the political groups that introduce a bill. In case of the political groups supporting the government, the competent ministries will usually provide assistance in this respect.

Committee secretariats primarily exercise an organizational role and advise the chairperson on questions of procedure. Aside from organizing deliberative sittings and hearings, they coordinate and prepare the committee recommendations and the report by the rapporteurs on the basis of the committee deliberations. Proposals for amendments to a bill are written by the political groups.

The committee secretariats of the Bundesrat support the 16 Länder in the formulation of draft bills initiated by the Bundesrat, of amendments to draft bills initiated by the federal government or of motions convening the mediation committee. In particular, they have to ensure that the appropriate legal language is used and that the Bundesrat's rules of procedure are observed. Once a week, the Secretary General, the Deputy Secretary General, the Directors General, the heads of the committee secretariats and the heads of all other Bundesrat divisions meet for an exchange on current Bundesrat business. At the centre of the meeting is the agenda of the next plenary session. The heads of the committee secretariats inform about the latest state of legislative proposals. In addition, the committee secretariats have established an informal exchange with the relevant federal ministries and committees of the Bundestag. These channels allow for a continuous discussion of core questions of the legislative procedure.

The secretariat of the mediation committee of the Bundestag and Bundesrat has always been located in the administration of the Bundesrat. The Deputy Secretary General of the Bundesrat acts as the committee's Executive Director; the tasks of the secretariat are performed by the staff of the secretariat of the Bundesrat's Legal Affairs Committee.

In the case of the Bundesrat, the administration usually does not draw up impact assessments. Hearings are also extremely rare. In the few cases where they occur, the role of the administration is mainly to support them with the logistics and the drafting of the minutes.

19.4 The Administration in EU Affairs

The participation rights of the Bundestag and the Bundesrat in EU affairs are guaranteed through art. 23 of the German Basic Law since the early 1990s. This article both requires the involvement of the Bundestag and the Bundesrat in EU affairs and specifies that the federal government has to inform them comprehensively and at the earliest possible time. The rights of the Bundestag are further elaborated in the Act on the Cooperation of the Federal Government and the Bundestag in European Union Affairs (Gesetz über die Zusammenarbeit von Bundesregierung und Bundestag in Angelegenheiten der Europäischen Union – EUZBBG). The Bundestag has to be informed of all Council negotiations, reports must be made in writing and oral reports in committees can only be seen as complementary to written reports and the government also has to report on the informal Eurozone summits. EU affairs (and thus parliamentary participation rights) are deemed to cover activities outside the legal framework of the EU (e.g. the EFSF, the ESM) if they are sufficiently close to EU law. All unofficial documents must be forwarded to the Bundestag upon request. In addition, should the government deviate from a resolution of the Bundestag in negotiations, one quarter of the members can request that the government publicly justifies this decision.

Within the Bundestag, according to its Rules of Procedure, all committees deal with EU-Affairs within their respective areas of responsibility. However, the Committee on EU-Affairs is as a cross-cutting committee involved whenever EU-legislation is concerned and in most strategic documents as well as EU-Budget-related documents. Two sectoral committees (Budget Committee and Committee on legal affairs) have set up internal subcommittees on EU-Affairs. Meetings of the Council of ministers can be discussed in the EU-Affairs committee as well as in the sectoral committees when members see the need to address the issue. However, the EU-Affairs Committee puts all ministerial meetings on the agenda and closely monitors them (cf. Deutscher Bundestag, 2020).

The European Affairs Directorate in the Administration of the German Bundestag assesses important EU initiatives, researches the timetables for the EU institutions' deliberations and analyses the state of discussion on legislative proposals in order to enable a timely exercise of the Bundestag's participatory rights in EU affairs. All documents transmitted to the Bundestag are included in EuDoX, the Bundestag's internal information system on EU affairs. This database is managed by the Division PE 5 in the European Affairs Directorate, which is also tasked with monitoring if the Federal Government is complying with its notification obligations. The Brussels-based Liaison Office of the Bundestag provides information about forthcoming EU decisions at an early stage and assists MPs and committees when they engage in dialogues with EU institutions.

The participation of the Bundesrat or the Länder in EU affairs is extensive and apart from art. 23 guaranteed additionally through art. 50 of the Basic Law. The participation rights are set out in more detail in the Bill on the Cooperation of the Federation and the Länder in European Union Affairs (Gesetz über die Zusammenarbeit von Bund und Ländern in Angelegenheiten der Europäischen Union – EUZBLG). In principle, the Länder have the opportunity to bring their experience from the execution of laws to bear on the Federal Government via the Bundesrat, so that the Federal Government can take the Bundesrat's position into account in its negotiations in the Council (§ 3 EUZBLG). Depending on the precise content of the EU proposal, the federal government has to take the position of the Bundesrat into account or even decisively into account in the formulation of its position. The latter is the case where the EU legislative proposal primarily affects the legislative competences of the Länder or their administrative procedures. In those cases, the Bundesrat really has the final say in determining the German position in the Council of Ministers.

In addition, where core interests or participation rights of the Länder are affected the Bundesrat is authorized to send a representative as part of the German delegation to the EU negotiations. In specific cases of exclusive Länder competences – like education in schools, culture or radio and television broadcasting – the negotiations are led by a representative of the Länder. These rights cover all levels of the Council and all stages of the negotiations.

In the Bundesrat, the discussion of EU affairs takes place in the Committee on Questions of the European Union and the sectoral committees that are affected by the contents of the respective legislative proposals. The recommendations of the committees are sent to the plenary, which adopts the final position of the Bundesrat.

The Bundesrat has also established a Chamber of European Affairs, whose decisions have the same effect as the decisions of the Bundesrat's Plenary. The Chamber deals with urgent and confidential matters pertaining to the European Union, particularly draft legislation. Its purpose is to avoid having to arrange special plenary sessions of the Bundesrat. Each land appoints one member but has the same number of votes as in the plenary.

The participation rights of the Bundesrat are thus quite extensive and allow for a certain level of control over the negotiation strategy of the federal government. The representatives of the Bundesrat, who participate in the negotiations, report in writing on the course of the discussions and indicate whether and to what extent positions of the Bundesrat are taken up and presented by the Federal Government. In those cases when negotiations move in new directions and require an adaptation of positions, the representatives can alert the Bundesrat to the need to discuss its position again with the government in a monitoring-process with the aim of providing a so-called follow-up decision.

Administratively, the Bundestag has a large body of staff at its disposal to support its political work. The Directorate PE (EU affairs) employs 74 staff members in total, 38 of those in the "höhere Dienst" (i.e. in jobs that require university degrees). The EAC secretariat is part of this structure and has six staff members. This large central unit supports EU affairs scrutiny across the Bundestag, as the sectoral committees can and do follow EU affairs in their areas of expertise (see above). This large central unit is the result of a reorganization of resources in 2013, as it was felt to be more efficient to incorporate all EU experts in one structure. The Directorate includes six permanent divisions, namely PE1 – EU Affairs Committee Secretariat, PE2 – Fundamental EU Issues, EMU Issues, PE3 – Analysis, Prioritization and Advice on EU Affairs, PE4 – EU Liaison Office, PE5 – European Affairs Documentation and PE6 – European Affairs Research Section. Until 30 June 2021, a temporary additional unit, PE RP – Organizational Task EU Council Presidency, supported the implementation of the Parliamentary Dimension of the German EU Council Presidency.

The role of the Directorate is to support the committees through the identification of priorities when it transmits EU documents. It also monitors the decision-making on the EU level – including the Council of Ministers. It advises committee secretariats on the drafting of the agenda with regard to EU documents and provides expertise on highly topical dossiers or notes on the subsidiarity check. The EU staff also assists with the drafting of EU-related decisions (e.g. reasoned opinions) and provides procedural advice (cf. Högenauer et al. 2016). More specifically PE 2 assists with questions related to the EMU. The fact that there is a separate staff unit dedicated to this issue underlines its increasing political salience as a consequence of the financial and eurozone crises. It also follows the European Semester and supports the relevant sectoral committees. PE 2 and 3 offer EU-related analyses, substantive advice and help identify EU priorities among the dossiers. PE 5 supervises the transmission of documents by the government and manages the Bundestag's EU information system EuDoX. PE 6 provides legal assessments upon request and PE 4 is in charge of gathering information in a timely manner about current political processes in the EU via the liaison office of the Bundestag in Brussels. For each sitting week of the Bundestag, PE 4 publishes the briefing "Report from Brussels" on current EU developments. The unit also coordinates and facilitates contacts between Bundestag committees and high-ranking EU officials.

In the Bundesrat, EU affairs scrutiny involves primarily the secretariat of the Committee on Questions of the European Union on the administrative level, which also has the function of secretariat of the Chamber for European Affairs. It consists of 14 colleagues (1 head, 1 senior officer, the national representative to the EU, 1 committee clerk, 4 secretaries and 6 clerks responsible for the management of EU documents). The committee staff prepares the committee meetings, draws up the minutes and drafts the committee recommendations for the final vote in the plenary incorporating also the recommendations of the sectoral committees. The committee secretariat also advises the chair and the members on procedural issues. In the case of scrutiny of EU proposals, especially under the Early Warning System, the role of the committee staff is to preselect documents for further discussions. This preselection is not based on the Annual Work Programme but takes place on a rolling basis and takes into account the issues of interest of the Länder. This requires a certain experience and understanding of the mindset of the members of the Bundesrat and their priorities.

The committee secretariat is also in charge of incorporating all EU-related documents into the central EU-database EUDISYS (EU-Dokumenten- und Informations-System). This has to happen in a timely manner, so that the Länder have access to the relevant current documents. EUDISYS also contains an "early warning list" with the relevant EU documents, the deadlines of the dossiers and the possible plenary meetings for each dossier.

In addition, the Bundestag and Bundesrat participate in the network of the representatives of the national parliaments on the EU level, where an intensive informal exchange on subsidiarity concerns takes place. In case of the Bundesrat, there is close trilateral cooperation with the second chambers of Poland and France, where information and opinions on the principle of proportionality and other concerns about EU proposals are shared. The national parliamentary representative of the Bundesrat in Brussels summarizes and discusses the subsidiarity concerns of all other parliaments in a report. The committee staff add the information to EUDISYS. The Bundestag and the Bundesrat also participate in the interparliamentary platform IPEX, where official positions to EU proposals and especially the Early Warning System are shared. Furthermore, the positions of the Bundestag and the Bundesrat in the framework of the Political Dialogue with the European Commission, the Commission's replies and, in case of the Bundesrat, an English-language summary produced by the committee secretariat are published.

The national parliamentary representative of the Bundesrat is also in charge of coordinating with the German MEPs and informing them of the positions of the Bundesrat in writing. She also maintains relations with the staff of the European Parliament. The EP also receives English-language summaries of the positions that the Bundesrat addresses to the European Commission.

The two committees of the Bundestag and the Bundesrat have a good working relationship in EU affairs. Especially in the framework of the COSAC meetings, the two units assist the close coordination of the joint German delegation. There are also occasionally joint political initiatives of the two committees in EU affairs, such as joint committee meetings or joint hearings, which are prepared and occasionally initiated by the staff. Close coordination also takes place between the employees responsible for IPEX and the national representatives to the EU.

In individual cases, the EU committee secretariats exchange detailed information on specific processes. This concerns both the positions of the houses, for example on ratification issues for the implementation of individual EU legal acts, and on fundamental EU matters (such as conferences or EU primary law).

19.5 The Administration in Interparliamentary Cooperation

With EU integration and the greater emphasis on national parliamentary control since the mid-2000s, the intensity of interparliamentary cooperation has also increased. In addition to the cooperation of the committees for EU affairs in COSAC, there is a variety of interparliamentary conferences (IPCs) and parliamentary assemblies (PA) (Arndt 2013).

The Bundestag and Bundesrat pursue interparliamentary relations on different levels: on the level of the presidents, the members and the staff. Both the presidents of the Bundestag and Bundesrat maintain bilateral contacts to other presidents of parliaments world-wide during travels abroad or their visits in Berlin, with a particular focus on presidents of Upper Houses for the Bundesrat. There are also a number of conferences of Presidents of Parliaments in different formats where both houses are actively involved (Conference of Presidents of Parliaments of the EU member states and the European Parliament, of the member states of the Council of Europe or the G20 and the World Conference of Presidents of Parliaments in the context of the Inter-Parliamentary Union [IPU]). Moreover, the Bundestag is represented in the Conference of Presidents of Parliaments of the G7 member states, whereas the Bundesrat President regularly participates in the meetings of the Association of European Senates.

The members of the Bundestag and Bundesrat have joint delegations in a number of IPCs and PAs, like the NATO PA, the PA of the Union for the Mediterranean, COSAC, the IPC for CFSP and CSDP, the IPC for Stability, Economic Coordination and Governance in the EU, the Joint Parliamentary Scrutiny Group (JPSG) for Europol, the interparliamentary committee for Eurojust, the various conferences of the acting EU Council presidency or committee meetings of the European Parliament. In addition, the Bundestag sends delegations to the PA of the Council of Europe, the PA of the Organization for Security and Cooperation in Europe (OSCE), the PA of the Black Sea Economic Cooperation, the Conference of Parliamentarians of the Baltic Sea States and the IPU.

Moreover, the Bundestag and the Bundesrat have established numerous parliamentary friendship groups, the Bundesrat with a focus on selected second chambers of bicameral parliaments.

Contacts have also become very dense on the level of Secretaries General. Both the Secretaries General of the Bundestag and Bundesrat are very active in the world-wide Association of the Secretaries General of Parliaments (ASGP) and in the meetings of Secretaries General of the EU Parliaments. In addition, there are numerous bilateral contacts. On staff level, both the Bundestag and the Bundesrat are very committed in the network of parliamentary representatives in the EU, IPEX, the European Centre for Parliamentary Research and Documentation (ECPRD), staff exchange programmes (e.g. with the US-Congress, Italy, France and Poland), study programmes (for the staff of Upper Houses in the case of the Bundesrat) and the secondment of short-term experts in the context of capacity building measures for parliaments abroad, especially in young or developing democracies.

The delegations of the Bundestag to the interparliamentary assemblies are supported by the Division WI 2, which bundles the delegation secretariats. It consists of 18 civil servants, including its head and 4 senior officers. The division is responsible for the organizational preparation of the meetings and accompanying the delegation. In order to provide substantive preparation, the division gathers information, in particular from the competent ministries of the federal government or parliamentary committees. After the meetings, the division prepares the reports by the respective delegations to the plenary, see cf. https://dserver.bundestag.de/btd/19/290/1929025.pdf.

In the Bundesrat, interparliamentary relations are the responsibility of the division on Parliamentary Relations P 2. It consists of its head, three senior officers, two clerks and three office clerks. However, the responsibility for trips abroad of the President – except interparliamentary meetings – and visits of foreign Presidents of Parliament to the Bundesrat lie within the competence of the division President's Office, Protocol. It consists of a head, one senior officer, two clerks and two office clerks. The two units are in charge of both the organizational/logistic preparation of the travel/meetings and of their substantive contents. This involves, for example, requesting information on the political stance of the German federal government or the diplomatic representations of Germany. Both units also have to work closely with the relevant foreign parliamentary administrations for the preparation of the meetings/visits. Usually the staff of both divisions accompanies the president on his/her visits so that they can assist him/her and offer advice constantly.

COSAC and IPEX, by contrast, are handled by the secretariat of the Committee for Questions of the European Union. This includes the preparation and follow-up of the meetings, accompanying the members of the Bundesrat participating in these conferences as well as the opportunity to network and exchange views. The committee for Questions of the European Union and the division for Parliamentary Relations have a very good and close working relationship supporting each other with information on EU or interparliamentary matters.

19.6 Outlook: The Administrations and the Challenge of COVID-19

Because of the distinct nature of the Bundestag and the Bundesrat, their administrations also vary greatly in size and in their specific role in the policy-process. The COVID-19 pandemic has also affected them differently, in that the need for social distancing could be more easily met by the Bundesrat due to the smaller number of members and staff involved.

In the Bundestag, the large number of MPs made it necessary to amend the rules of procedure temporarily to provide for hybrid or remote meetings of committees (rule 126a). Discussions whether this should be a permanent possibility are still ongoing. In the Bundesrat, the existing rules of procedure did not allow virtual or hybrid meetings of the plenary. However, there was no need to change these rules to keep the Bundesrat operational. In the plenary, the votes of the 16 Länder have to be cast en bloc, that is to say one member for each land acts as so-called vote caster. Therefore, during the pandemic, the Bundesrat had a quorum with only one-member present per land and thus could continue to meet in person. The Bundesrat's committees extensively used the – already existing – possibility to decide in so-called written procedures. Nevertheless, the Bundesrat administration quickly decided to set up video conference rooms which have since been used by committees for preparatory exchanges of ideas among members and the federal government before taking votes in written procedures or by members or Bundesrat staff participating remotely in IPCs. Since 2022 committee meetings may be held by videoconference for a certain period of time if the President of the Bundesrat approves (rule 37a of the Bundesrat's rules of procedure). Due to security reasons, the Bundesrat opted for a video conference tool specially developed by the Federal Agency for Digital Radio of Public Authorities and Organizations with Security Tasks (BDBOS) which enables secure conferencing even on confidential or classified contents. In cases when the Bundesrat is obliged to use video conference tools by commercial providers, the respective rooms are equipped with computers not linked to the internal IT network.

However, the pandemic led to a shift towards remote work for staff: Since July 2021, employees of the Bundestag's administration can work remotely for up to two days per week, depending on the concrete circumstances and tasks of the employee. This arrangement will be evaluated after two years, that is it could become a permanent fixture. As regards the working methods of the Bundesrat, staff could already work remotely to a limited extent before the pandemic. However, starting in March 2020, more laptops were purchased across the board at short notice, enabling most employees to work remotely at home. The presence of staff in the Bundesrat building was reduced to an absolute minimum and the possibility was given to work in so-called alternating team models. Since October 2022 it is possible that Bundesrat staff work up to half of the monthly working time remotely depending on the tasks and functions of the employee. However Bundesrat staff is obliged to two days of presence in the office per week. This regulation will be evaluated after 12 months.

References

Arndt, F. (2013). Parliamentary Assemblies, International in: Max Planck Encyclopedia of Public Law.
Auel K., Rozenberg, O., Tacea, A. 2015. 'Fighting Back? And, If so, How? Measuring Parliamentary Strength and Activity in EU Affairs', in C. Hefftler, C. Neuhold, O. Rozenberg and J. Smith, eds., The Palgrave Handbook of National Parliaments and the European Union, Basingstoke: Palgrave MacMillan.

Datenhandbuch zur Geschichte des Deutschen Bundestages [Online], https://www.bundestag.de/datenhandbuch. (consulted in 2021).
Deutscher Bundestag. (2020). Wegweiser in EU Angelegenheiten. Referat Öffentlichkeitsarbeit.
Fish, M. S., Kroenig, M. 2009. The Handbook of National Legislatures, Cambridge: Cambridge University Press.
Högenauer A. L., Neuhold, C., Christiansen, T. (2016). Parliamentary Administrations in the European Union, London: Palgrave.
https://www.bundesrat.de/DE/bundesrat/sekretariat/sekretariat-node.html, consulted on 12/11/2021.
https://www.bundestag.de/en/parliament/administration, consulted on 12/11/2021.
https://www.bundestag.de/parlament/verwaltung, consulted on 12/11/2021.
https://www.bundestag.de/parlamentsdokumentation, consulted on 10/01/2022.
Neuhold C., Högenauer, A. L. (2016), "An Information Network of Officials? Dissecting the Role and Nature of the Network of Parliamentary Representatives in the EP", Journal of Legislative Studies 22(2), 237–56.
Written response by the Bundesrat to a request for information, April 2021.
Written response by the Bundestag to a request for information, April 2021.

20
GREECE'S PARLIAMENTARY ADMINISTRATION

Fotios Fitsilis

20.1 Introduction

The year 2021 marked the 200th anniversary of the modern Greek State. Its top representative institution, the Hellenic Parliament,[1] is now operating not far away from where the Pnyx stands, the birthplace of Athenian Democracy during the golden age of Perikles two and a half millennia ago (Saripolos, 1874; Sakellariou, 2012). To celebrate this occasion, it is worth mentioning the timeline and the historical milestones of the past two centuries following liberation from Ottoman rule that led to the materialization of the Hellenic Parliament.

Following operation of pre-revolutionary regional assemblies and the beginning of the war of independence in 1821, national assemblies were founded that inaugurated the three constitutions of the revolutionary period (1821–1830), which, despite their provisional character, were both innovative and progressive. The assemblies ceased to exist during absolute monarchy by King Otto (1832–1843). A period of constitutional monarchy (1843–1862) followed, during which the legislative power was to be exercised by the King along with the parliament and the senate. In October 1862, King Otto was dethroned and, after two years of a 'governing parliament' system,[2] a period of crowned democracy came forth (1864–1909) (Kyrkos, 2006; Babounis, 2013).[3] A second period of crowd democracy was interrupted by the Declaration of the Republic, in 1924. During the third period of crowned democracy (1952–1967), the explicit institutionalization of parliamentarism was established. Cheibub and Rasch (2022) discuss the constitutional developments in Europe from 1800 onward and the post-WWII stabilization of parliamentarism visible also in the Greek case.

In the meanwhile, in 1935, the parliament was transferred to the former palace of King Otto in its today's location, in *Syntagma* (Greek word for constitution) square. Finally, following the 1974 referendum, the establishment of a presidential parliamentary republic with a unicameral parliament took place in 1975 (on the 1974 referendum abolishing monarchy, see Tridimas, 2010). The constitutional structure in Greece combines the separation of powers with a system of checks and balances to ensure accountability (Gerapetritis, 2020; for a more comprehensive study of constitutional aspects, see Mavrias, 2016).[4] As per electoral law, there are 300 Members of Parliament (MPs),[5] who are engaged in parliamentary work through multiple committees, permanent or ad hoc, dedicated to different facets of parliamentary work.[6]

In recent years, the Hellenic Parliament faced significant challenges, for instance in implementing Lisbon Treaty provisions to scrutinize European Union (EU) legislation and facilitate its participation in the Early Warning System (see Auel and Christiansen, 2015, and in particular, Sotiropoulos, 2015) or in relation to the sovereign debt crisis (see e.g. Sigalas and Blavoukos, 2014; Repousis, 2017). The impact of the latter on the institutional operation will be discussed closer in the next section. However, little to no scholarly attention has been vested in the study of the parliamentary administration, which forms a core organizational component that breathes life into parliamentary functions as per constitutional provisions under the Constitution of 1975. An exception is to be found in Foundethakis (2003), who studied enhancements in research and administrative support toward parliamentarians and committees following the 2001 constitutional revision.

This chapter is dedicated to the form, functions and challenges of the Hellenic Parliament. While it explains the general structure, the contribution also sheds light on particular and maybe unusual aspects of the parliamentary administration of the Hellenic Parliament that present notable differentiation compared to what is considered 'typical' in legislatures.

The next section discusses the development of both personnel strength and budget over the past two decades and presents key organizational aspects (Section 20.2). It is followed by a description of the main activities of the parliamentary administration (Section 20.3). Inter-institutional and inter-parliamentary cooperation are highlighted in Section 20.4, before going over to the analysis of contemporary parliamentary challenges, such as digital transformation and the response to the Covid-19 pandemic (Section 20.5), and the general conclusions (Section 20.6).

20.2 Organization of the Parliamentary Administration

The parliamentary administration of the Hellenic Parliament has considerably evolved over the past two decades, in terms of staff, tools and resources (see Figure 20.1). The 2000s found the state budget growing at a fast pace, a trend that the parliamentary budget also followed, eventually reaching an all time maximum in 2009 (224M Euro). This was the time when the Hellenic Republic entered a severe debt crisis, which saw major components of the state budget experiencing an abrupt decline. The parliamentary budget decreased almost as quickly as it had risen, reaching local minimum in 2015 (132M Euro), a decrease of 41% within six years (2009–2015). The budget has yet to recover from this local minimum, which appears to be the new 'state of normalization'. A minor increasing trend can be measured though, that is a rise of approx. 9% in six years (2015–2021).

When studying the evolution in the number of employees, a significant correlation with budget development can be determined between 2004 and 2015. Again, the number of employees follows an increasing trend reaching a peak of 1435 in 2010,[7] before dropping back to a local minimum of 1256 permanent employees in 2015 (−12.5%). But unlike the budget, the number of employees rebounded quickly, almost to match the overall 2010 maximum value. Currently, the employee to MP ratio is 4.78. This is attributed to two major effects. First, one needs to have in mind that the aforementioned major budgetary decrease had a profound effect on several budget lines, not least to the wages and benefits of parliamentary administrators. This led several senior staffers to prematurely leave the administration. Second, in the absence of structured knowledge buffers and methods to efficiently capture and manage institutional memory, the parliamentary leadership needed to swiftly cater for replacement to maintain existing levels of functionality.[8]

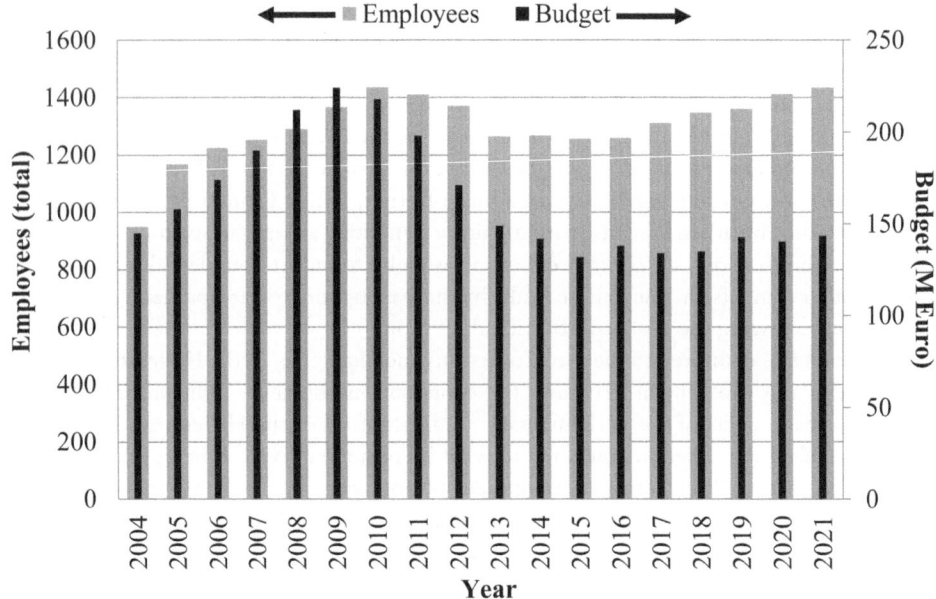

Figure 20.1 Evolution of budget size and number of personnel, from 2004 to 2021, in Greece

Other non-elected, non-permanent staff working in the parliament premises are political consultants and aides, collectively called 'advisors'. Each MP is entitled to appoint up to five advisors, one or two of which can originate from the private sector with the rest being public administrators.[9] Apart from individual MPs, parliamentary parties and the leadership can also contract non-permanent staff, with one significant difference: contrary to MP advisors, the latter are considered parliamentary employees.[10] Their numbers are rising during the past 20 years but still remain a fraction of the parliamentary workforce, that is less than 10% by the end of 2020. Cooperation with the parliamentary administration is generally seamless and happens through certain main interface points, such as the Personnel Department, the Special Service to the Committee for MP and Party Audits, and the Department for MPs and Parties. The Hellenic Police guards the premises of the parliament with sufficient security force headed by a senior police officer.

The organizational structure of the administration is subject to constant change to efficiently adapt to new challenges and to support the evolutionary nature of the functions of parliament.

Parliamentary administration in the Hellenic Parliament is currently organized in five main units, four Directorates-General (DGs) and the Scientific Service (see Chart 20.1). To the Secretary General, through delegation of the necessary authority by the Speaker, is attributed the role of chief administrative officer of the four DGs, that is DG for Parliamentary Work, DG for International and Public Relations, DG for Finance and Administrative Support and DG for e-Administration, Library and Publications. On the other hand, the Scientific Service, which enjoys a firm foundation in art. 65 para 5 (C)onstitution, is governed by the President of the Scientific Council and is directly linked to the Speaker[11] to ensure organizational and functional independence.

Apart from the above, there are also several stand-alone, specialized administrative elements that take the form of an office, a service or a unit.[12] To these belong the Health Service unit, the Civil Emergency Planning and Civil Protection Unit and the Strategic Planning and Management Functions Re-engineering Unit. Parliamentary communication and diplomacy is performed through the Press and Parliamentary Information Office, the Television Station and the Bureau of the Diplomatic Advisor to the President, respectively. Other significant functions are implemented by the Parliamentary Budget Office (PBO),[13] the European Programs Implementation Service (EPIS) and the Special Service to the Committee for MP and Party Audits. The main competences and outputs of the administration will be discussed in the section that follows.

A series of reforms have been conducted aiming to strengthen the professionalization and the development of functional expertise within the parliamentary administration. Starting from 2009, recruitment of permanent staff needs to follow the provisions and procedures of the Supreme Council for Civil Personnel Selection (ASEP), a constitutionally consolidated independent state body competent for the entire civil service (art. 103 para 7 C). The administration has three basic hierarchy levels common for the entire civil service (from lower to higher level): Head of Department, Head of Directorate and Head of General Directorate. Promotion is following criteria and procedures set out in the Civil Service Code, which are further specified in the Standing Orders (SO) for use in the parliamentary environment.[14] Evaluation includes a desk review of an applicant's qualifications and a structured interview, among others, by representatives from the political leadership, superior administrative officials and the service council.

In the absence of internal training and knowledge dissipation mechanisms, the Hellenic Parliament signed in 2013 a memorandum of understanding with the National Center for Public Administration and Local Government (EKDDA). The agreement enabled access to EKDDA's training methods and trainer pool through the parliamentary Directorate for Human Resources and Training. From an institutional point of view, training needs assessment allows for the tackling of specific needs and building up digital capacities within the administration, while this is also a significant vehicle for advancement of individual expertise. Further measures for employee development include conditional paid leaves for taking exams or conducting postgraduate studies.

The Hellenic Parliament has gradually built up solid internal expertise, particularly in the legal/constitutional domain, through establishment of the Scientific Service in 1987, since it was considered beneficial to have an in-house consultancy to rely on for politically sensitive or even confidential issues compared to external advisory services. The intense links of members of the Scientific Service to academia, that is adjunct or tenured positions in domestic or foreign universities, have also contributed to the incorporation of advanced research methods and scientific excellence in parliamentary practice. Though positional dualism – administrative and academic – can create friction with other units, the Scientific Service is well respected because of its swift, unbiased and non-politicized scientific advice and reporting.

In other cases, access to external consultancies, information or specialized services has been made possible through signing of program and/or cooperation agreements. Characteristic examples can be found in the 2008 agreement with the National Technical University of Athens for the purpose of restoration of the parliamentary premises and the shaping of the Old Tobacco Factory in Athens to host part of the Library of the Hellenic Parliament and a cultural centre and the 2018, more specialized, cooperation with the National Theater of Greece for content sharing and transmission through the parliamentary television channel.

20.3 Administration and Parliamentary Work

The described organizational scheme facilitates parliamentary operation (see above at 2). This section describes the primary competencies of the administrative units and the main outputs of their work.[15] The DG for Parliamentary Work runs the legislative and parliamentary control functions of the parliament (an overview of parliamentary control in the Hellenic Parliament is offered by Fitsilis and Koryzis, 2016). Moreover, administrative support to parliamentary committees is provided. The necessary tasks for institutional representation in Greece and abroad are performed by the DG for International and Public Relations. This involves planning and organizing of official missions in parliamentary assemblies and national and international forums as well as communication activities. As such, the DG constitutes a vital gear in inter-parliamentary cooperation, which is discussed in the next section. The DG for Finance and Administrative Support is the glue that keeps the administration together. It performs the horizontal tasks that are necessary for the operation of the parliamentary organization, such as financial back office and procurement, personnel and equipment management, infrastructure maintenance and support – technical and administrative – to MPs and political parties. Under its auspices also operate a crèche and a nursery school.

The DG for e-Administration, Library and Publications is responsible for the Information and Communication Technologies (ICT) infrastructure, including issuing and management of digital certificates, and the publishing of parliamentary material. For the latter, the relevant Directorate of Publications and Printouts operates a state-of-the-art vertical printing facility. The Library of the Hellenic Parliament, a nationally leading library bearing international imprint,[16] forms its own Department under the Directorate-General.[17] The Library displays extensive cultural/educational activities with frequent, quality exhibitions (see e.g. Angelis, 2017; Kamilaki, 2019). The major outputs of the Scientific Service are the publicly available legal reports on bills. Their structure and the process of legal reporting are described in detail by Fitsilis and Bayiokos (2017). Other forms of assistance include scientific support to parliamentary committees (Vassilouni, 2001, p. 6),[18] the aforementioned in-house advisory services and the archiving and documentation of parliamentary material (Fitsilis and Koutsogiannis, 2017, p.5).

The Hellenic Parliament is a complex organization that evolves over time. The Strategic Planning and Management Functions Re-engineering Unit was forged in 2017 exactly to study the inherent evolutionary dynamics and had significant merit in creating the first parliamentary strategic plan for the years 2018–2021 (Hellenic Parliament, 2018). On-going work by this unit reveals more than 300 actual competencies (as per Standing Orders, objective analysis) that correspond to approximately 1400 tasks (subjective estimation).

The Civil Emergency Planning and Civil Protection Unit plays an increasingly important role within the administration, since the Hellenic Parliament belongs to national critical infrastructure, also called vital governmental infrastructure. It is part of a large network of similar units that exist at all levels of public administration, whose action plans are coordinated by the Ministry of Defense. The unit contributed to combating the Covid-19 pandemic by organizing disinfection measures and the procurement of sanitary supplies,[19] while supporting the operation of an intra-parliament *ad hoc* Health Crisis Management Center for tracking and recording Covid-19 cases among parliamentary personnel. In this on-going effort, the Health Service, an in-house, fully equipped and staffed medical unit, has the primary role.

While there is not any type of structured ex-post impact assessment of laws in the sense of post-legislative scrutiny (de Vrieze and Norton, 2020), support to legislative drafting is *ex ante* provided by the Scientific Service through the legal reports on bills, which evaluate legality, constitutionality and conformity with EU law for incoming draft legislation. In addition, the Hellenic Parliament has gradually built a strong framework for scrutinizing public finances, including those of MPs and political parties. The Special Service to the Committee for MP and Party Audits conducts annual controls (audits) financial statements, asset declarations and electoral campaign expenses.[20] In its work, it is assisted by certified accountants. The Directorate for Financial Services is responsible for the related tasks around compilation, implementation and monitoring of the parliamentary budget. However, when it comes to the state budget, a PBO has been established in 2010 to support the financial oversight function of the institution.

As representative institution, the parliament and the political personnel need to be both accountable and transparent when conducting their respective duties. One way to achieve this is by efficiently utilizing all available means of communication and to maintain open and honest relations with traditional and new media. The institutional contact point for parliamentary communication is the Press and Parliamentary Information Office (in short: Press Office), which is directly linked to the Speaker. Apart from institutional events, its staff, mostly journalists and photographers, covers the official meetings of the Speaker and Deputy Speakers as well as the ones of committee Chairs. Starting in 2020, the Press Office publishes its own parliamentary e-magazine called *Epí tou... Peristylíou* (Greek for On the... Peristyle, see Hellenic Parliament, 2021).

For accredited journalists from traditional and digital media, a parliamentary press gallery with approximately 80 fully equipped offices operates within the premises of the Hellenic Parliament. Parliamentary journalists are independent and have no financial relationship with the institution. From their gallery, they have access to the CATV (Community Access Television) system to follow the raw live feed from all meetings taking place at any given time.[21] Furthermore, they are given full access to parliamentary minutes.

The Hellenic Parliament operates a television station that broadcasts the main volume of parliamentary works. For this, plenary and committee rooms are equipped with robotic cameras operated by skilled operators from the control room. Selected feeds from CATV, with priority in plenary sessions, are broadcast nationwide. The TV signal and feed from committee meetings, live or recorded, is transmitted online via three web channels. The TV station forms a separate autonomous unit within the parliament. It is led by a coordinator by Speaker's appointment. Its technicians, journalists and administrative personnel are all parliamentary employees. As such, the channel offers a full television program with parliamentary sessions, political debates on draft laws, documentaries on political and parliamentary history, cultural events and a morning show.

As regards to the nature of institutional hierarchy, the Speaker is elected by the absolute majority of the total number of MPs (art. 7 para 3 SO). The Speaker then appoints the political posts within the administration, that is the Secretary General, the Special Secretary, the Special Topic Secretary, the commanding officer of the parliamentary guard, as well as the members of the Speaker's office. The Speaker presides over the highest governing body in the parliament, the Conference of the Presidents. The Conference organizes parliamentary work and includes, among others, Deputy and former Speakers (provided they are elected MPs), the Chairs of Standing Committees and the presidents of parliamentary groups (art. 13 para 1 SO).

In general, the conduct and interaction among parliamentary stakeholders are regulated by a comprehensive set of Standing Orders. Nonetheless, for managerial positions in parliamentary administration, the degrees of (administrative) freedom are not always clear and usually leave room for manoeuvring. Hence, soft law always plays a significant role at all levels of management, especially when leading in urgent or critical occasions (for the use of soft law for crisis response at the EU level, see e.g. Stefan, 2020).

20.4 Managing Inter-Institutional and External Relations

In line with European tradition in parliamentary law, the legislative in Greece is historically and conceptually independent *vis à vis* other powers. The resulting autonomy and the uncontrollability of the *interna corporis* are embedded in the Constitution and the Standing Orders of the Parliament (Gerapetritis, 2012). There are, however, well-defined administrative and procedural interfaces, through which the Hellenic Parliament interacts with the Executive and Judiciary. For instance, permanent offices for the legal advisor of the State and the Commissioner of the Court of Auditors are foreseen. The parliament further supports inter-institutional cooperation by providing dedicated space within its premises for the Secretariat General for Legal and Parliamentary Affairs, a governmental service that is responsible, among others, for the effective implementation of the principles and tools of 'better regulation' and the coordination of the legislative process.

The five constitutionally consolidated independent state bodies enjoy special protection and support by parliament. Not only are their members appointed with a special majority by the Conference of the Presidents (three fifths, art. 101A para 2 C) but they may also refer to parliament for promoting any issue related to the accomplishment of their mission (art. 138A para 7 SO). Hence, in this case, parliament can operate as a formal 'broker' between these independent authorities and the Executive. The latter provision has been also used to administratively support independent state bodies through EPIS for taking part in funded projects, national or EU.

Institutionally, the Hellenic Parliament is deploying a series of instruments for participating in foreign policy; an activity that is sometimes called 'parliamentary diplomacy' (Karabarbounis et al., 2004; Stavridis, 2018; Fitsilis and Stavridis, 2021). International activity is coordinated by the Bureau of the Diplomatic Advisor to the President, which is headed by a senior diplomat originating from the Ministry of Foreign Affairs. The institution's multi-faceted external relations, a considerable part of which is inter-parliamentary cooperation, are mainly administered through the DG for International and Public Relations. European affairs form a significant sector of the parliament's external relation with homologue institutions. This is covered by the Directorate for European and Bilateral Affairs, which additionally handles relationship building for the parliamentary friendship groups.[22] Cooperation with International Parliamentary Institutions, so-called IPIs, and non-EU parliaments is regulated by the Directorate for International Affairs. This unit is also administratively responsible for the relations with the diaspora. The contribution of the DG's third main unit, the Directorate for Public Relations and Protocol, is not to be neglected, as it indirectly supports external relations, for example by organizing relevant events and conferences.

With the roles of the administrators and their general links with inter-parliamentary cooperation have already been highlighted elsewhere (see e.g. Högenauer et al., 2016; Fitsilis, 2018), it is imperative to note the engagement of a growing pool of employees in the use of digital technologies to promote the goals and objectives of parliamentary diplomacy. Their tasks include content generation and web management for the parliamentary portal and magazine, as well as for the Global Hellenism News website/newsletter, digital TV broadcasting and the management of the official Twitter account (@PressParliament). However, there is still unused potential that can be tapped by acquiring additional digital skills, for instance in digital marketing and analytics.

Hellenic Parliament employees actively participate in a multitude of administrative parliamentary networks, such as the National Parliament Representatives in Brussels, the InterParliamentary EU information eXchange (IPEX), the European Centre for Parliamentary Research and Documentation (ECPRD) and the PBO networks. In addition, the promotion of inter-parliamentary cooperation through institutional Twinnings with representative institutions in candidate or European neighbourhood countries has been pursued. To date, the Hellenic Parliament has been awarded four EU-funded Twinning projects with the National Assembly of the Republic of Serbia, the Parliament of Albania, the Grand National Assembly of Turkey and the National Assembly of the Republic of Armenia.[23]

20.5 Current and Future Challenges

In a rapidly changing environment, the Hellenic Parliament administration will continue facing numerous challenges. The degree of responsiveness and adaptation will shape the future of the institution as well as its status among governance bodies. Digital transformation of parliament has never been a walk in the park (Philippidou et al., 2008), yet this has not prevented uptake of an aggressive approach on digitalization. Recently, an electronic system for the collection of (digital) responses by ministries to written parliamentary questions has been introduced. Other innovations include a speech-to-text system for semi-automatic minute extraction and advancements in the cyber security and collaboration infrastructure.

The parliament has a long tradition participating in innovative research projects (Fitsilis et al., 2017). Still, exploitation is poor, as state-of-the-art results have not flown into production within the parliamentary workspace. This, however, did not prevent parliament from taking part in lighthouse projects, such as the ManyLaws (Virkar et al., 2020).[24] This goes hand-in-hand with other relevant governmental activities, such as the initiation of the development of a national codification portal, effectively an end-to-end lawmaking system with the aim to promote inter-institutional cooperation (Stasis et al., 2020).

Transparency in parliamentary operation is firmly embedded in the Standing Orders and the strategic plan. Administratively, this is manifested through the establishment of the Press Office, the parliamentary TV channel and the press gallery that facilitates accredited media representatives. At the same time, transparency constitutes a complex challenge in the era of digital communication. Parliamentary information is mainly propagated through the web portal and official social media accounts (Twitter and Instagram). The administrative acts and decisions of the Speaker and Secretary General are posted on 'Parliamentary Transparency', a dedicated section under the web portal (art. 164ST SO part B).

Citizen engagement is constantly promoted through various activities such as public events, exhibitions and publications.[25] For a range of outreach activities, the Hellenic Parliament relies on the services of the closely related Foundation for Parliamentary and Democracy (in short: Foundation), a subsidiary organization founded in 2004, whose study however goes beyond the scope of this chapter. One of the most significant citizen-centric activities has been the school visit program organized since 1994. The program annually hosts approximately 60,000 students from more than 1,600 schools across the country. Moreover, since 1996, the *Voulí ton Efívon* program (Greek for Youth Parliament) takes place.[26] There is also a structured petition process, according to which citizens may bring any issue to the attention of the parliament (art. 125 SO).[27]

The Covid-19 pandemic has changed the work patterns, both at the political and the operational levels. Parliamentary response has not been uniform but rather dynamic during the pandemic. This has allowed for the necessary administrative adjustments according to the development of the crisis situation. Under those circumstances, a combination of digital technology and social distancing measures has been utilized to enable remote/hybrid parliamentary sessions and meetings, which the majority of administrators needed to switch to remote working. In order for these measures to work, the use of digital signatures has been rapidly widened and teleconferencing facilities have been installed. Professional training, through the mentioned agreement with EKDDA, migrated online and enabled the strengthening of digital skills for many administrators. Hence, it is safe to conclude that the pandemic has had a positive fingerprint on the institution's path to digitalization. Fitsilis and Pliakogianni (2021) discuss in detail the effects of pandemic on parliamentary work during the first pandemic wave.

Overall, it is difficult to quantitatively assess the impact of the pandemic on parliamentary operation while it is surging. Nevertheless, there are indications that yield in two of the most significant parliamentary functions, the production of laws and the discussion of parliamentary questions, has not been affected; Hellenic Parliament, 2021). This would imply that despite the unprecedented crisis parliamentary administrators kept up and – in some cases – levelled up their productivity to meet the revised needs. More dedicated studies following extinction of the pandemic are necessary to further support this claim.

20.6 Conclusions

The Hellenic Parliament is a modern unicameral representative institution undergoing a transition phase, accelerated both through the sovereign debt crisis of the past decade and the Covid-19 pandemic. Despite the extraordinary circumstances, leadership and the administration maintained control of the situations and managed to perform their respective duties efficiently. In recent years, personnel has been renewed to a significant extent and seamlessly integrated into the existing organogram. Advances in legal informatics did not go unnoticed by the parliamentary organization and the involvement of several internal experts in national and co-funded ICT research and development projects will potentially support the parliament's future path (see also the relevant book chapter by Fitsilis and Costa, 2022). At the same time, building up internal digital know-how might have played a role in the parliament's overall positive pandemic response. As the current strategic plan expires by the end of 2021, the parliament could benefit from a complementary horizontal digital strategy to facilitate implementation of the updated institutional objectives.

Participation of Greek parliamentary professionals in institutional Twinning projects contributes to the advancement of inter-parliamentary cooperation and the strengthening of the Rule of Law in the European Enlargement and Neighbourhood areas. Such projects support the development of soft skills among participating experts, such as management by objectives, negotiation tactics, crisis response and risk mitigation. Yet, the future appears to be digital and special skills will be necessary to design and operate the tools and services of a 'smart parliament'. In this regard, a strengthened cooperation with public administration training centres, such as EKDDA, and European facilities of the likes of the Interoperability Academy are deemed necessary to prepare the parliamentary administration for imminent challenges. As resources are scarce and the necessary investments significant, strengthened cooperation with other peers under the umbrella of the Open Government Partnership and Inter-Parliamentary Union's Center for Innovation in Parliament appear to be the *non plus ultra* for achieving and maintaining a high degree of excellence in digital parliamentary governance.

Hellenic Parliament organigram (2021) - Concise version with administrative view down to Directorate level, with special units

[Organigram showing the structure of the Hellenic Parliament:

Leadership Level: Speaker, Special Topic Secretary, Secretary General, Special Secretary, Scientific Council

Special Units (under Speaker): EPIS, PBO, Commissioner of the Court of Auditors, Press Office, Legal Advisor of the State, Security Service, Special Agency to the C. for MP and Party Audits, Diplomatic Advisor, TV & Radio Station

Under Secretary General: Strategic Planning & Management Functions Re-engineering Unit

Under Special Secretary: Civil Emergency Planning & Civil Protection Unit, Health Service Unit

Directorate General Level (DG):
- Scientific Service
- DG for Parliamentary Work
- DG for International & Public Relations
- DG for Finance & Admin. Support
- DG for e-Admin., Library & Publications

Directorate Level (D):

Under Scientific Service:
- 1st D of Scientific Studies
- 2nd D of Scientific Studies
- D for Scientific Supervision

Under DG for Parliamentary Work:
- D for Legislative Work
- D for Parliamentary Control
- D for Stenografic Services & Minutes
- D for Standing Committees
- D for Special Perm. Committees

Under DG for International & Public Relations:
- D for International Affairs
- D for European & Bilateral Affairs
- D for Public Relations & Protocol

Under DG for Finance & Admin. Support:
- D for Financial Services
- D for Procurement & Equipment mgmt
- D for HR & Training
- D for Technical Services
- D for MPs and Parties

Under DG for e-Admin., Library & Publications:
- D for ICT
- D of Parliamentary Library
- D of Publications & Printouts

Legend: Leadership Level, Directorate General Level (DG), Directorate Level (D), Special Units, Offices & Services]

Notes

1 In Greek, the original name of the national parliament is Βουλή των Ελλήνων (transliterated as *Voulí ton Ellínon*). However, the article uses the official naming in English, that is 'Hellenic Parliament', throughout. In the following, the transliterated form of Greek words shall be used.
2 Definition of 'governing parliament': Executive and Legislative unified and exercised through parliament.
3 The crowned democracy established the principle of people's sovereignty, instead of the monarch's as in the previous constitution. Here, the legislative power was exercised by the King, who also had the right to ratify laws, along with the Parliament and the Senate.
4 During the past 200 years of complex parliamentary history, the presence of a bicameral system has been recorded at least twice, for example 1844–1864 and 1927–1935.
5 However, constitutional provision allows for a range between 200 and 300 MPs; see art. 51 para 1 (C)onstitution.
6 An updated list of the categorized parliamentary committees can be found on the Hellenic Parliament website: https://www.hellenicparliament.gr/en/Koinovouleftikes-Epitropes/Katigories
7 The maximum number of employees was recorded on 31/12/2009; see also *supra* note 5.
8 The latter has proven to be a vital decision as the country (and its institutions) suffered the effects of the Covid-19 pandemic.
9 The Hellenic Parliament provides Greek Members of the European Parliament (MEPs) with the same right.
10 This is primarily a legal distinction as advisors are hired by MPs through private contracts, while administrative decisions are necessary for the ones who support institutional bodies and figures.
11 The official title of the Speaker in the Greek institutional order is 'President of the Hellenic Parliament'.
12 Similar to the case of the Scientific Service, several such units, e.g. the EPIS and the Special Service to the Committee for MP and Party Audits, are equipped with special rules of procedure that regulate internal conduct.

13 The Greek PBO, www.pbo.gr/, has been established in 2010, but activated in 2013, and operates according to its own internal special regulation. The Office monitors State Budget implementation and supports the work of the relevant working body (Special Standing Committee on the Financial Statement and the General Balance Sheet and on the implementation of the State Budget).
14 The organization of parliamentary administration and the status of its employees are regulated in the second part of the Standing Orders of the Hellenic Parliament.
15 Here, the author makes reference to high-level competencies, as mentioned in the Standing Orders, rather than distinct tasks. Competencies are objective and their manifestation is expressed by the administrative division in units. By convention, from general to specific, the chapter separates among functions, competencies and tasks.
16 Among others, the Library is a member of the International Federation of Library Associations (IFLA), the International Council for Archives (ICA) and the European Documentation Centre (EDC).
17 It is to be noted that the President of the Scientific Council exercises scientific (but not administrative) supervision over the work of the ICT department and the Library.
18 This comes in addition to the administrative support provided by the committee secretariat.
19 This material primarily originated from the relevant military factory and medical supplies depot.
20 The service is both responsible for auditing MPs and MEPs, candidate or elected. Once again, the competency of the Hellenic Parliament in matters of Greek MEPs comes forth.
21 Non-accredited journalists may too attend plenary sessions from two dedicated plenary galleries, for domestic and foreign press representatives, respectively.
22 As of the beginning of the 18th Legislature (17/7/2020–to date), there were 78 such groups.
23 Since 2016, the project in Turkey has been stalled, awaiting state approval.
24 ManyLaws, https://www.manylaws.eu/, provides users with structured access to legal information across different legal orders.
25 The Directorate for Public Relations and Protocol under the D.G. for International and Public Relations, and the Library are among the units that have a leading role in outreach activities.
26 Both programs are supported by the Ministry of Education and Religious Affairs and carried out by the Foundation.
27 The process heavily relies on manual submission and processing of documents and its transformation into an e-petitioning system could be considered.

References

Angelis, V. (2017) A Milestone Exhibition by the Hellenic Parliament; "Loannis Kapodistrias: His Path in Time". The Clarity of Historical Vision. *Days of Art in Greece*, 6, pp. 88–101.

Auel, K. and Christiansen, T. (2015) After Lisbon: National Parliaments in the European Union. *West European Politics*, 38 (2), pp. 261–281.

Babounis, C. (2013) *I kyvernósa voulí katá tin ellinikí mesovasileía* [The governing parliament during the Greek interregnum]. Athens: Stochastis.

Cheibub, J.A. and Rasch, B.E. (2022) Constitutional Parliamentarism in Europe, 1800–2019. *West European Politics*, 45 (3), pp. 470–501.

de Vrieze, F. and Norton, P. (2020) *Parliaments and Post-Legislative Scrutiny*. London: Rutledge.

Fitsilis, F. (2018) Inter-Parliamentary Cooperation and Its Administrators. *Perspectives on Federalism*, 10(3), pp. 28–55.

Fitsilis, F. and Bayiokos, V. (2017) Implementing Structured Public Access to the Legal Reports on Bills and Law Proposals of the Scientific Service of the Hellenic Parliament, Greece. *Knowledge Management for Development Journal*, 13 (2), pp. 63–80.

Fitsilis, F. and Costa, O. (2022) Parliamentary Administration Facing the Digital Challenge. In *Handbook of Parliamentary Administrations*. London: Routledge.

Fitsilis, F. and Koryzis, D. (2016) Parliamentary control of Governmental actions on the interaction with European organs in the Hellenic Parliament and the National Assembly of Serbia. *Online Papers on Parliamentary Democracy*, V. Available at: <https://www.pademia.eu/wp-content/uploads/2014/02/Fitsilis_Koryzis_PademiaOnlineSeries.pdf> [Accessed: 1 March 2021].

Fitsilis, F. and Koutsogiannis, A. (2017) Strengthening the Capacity of parliaments through development of parliamentary research services. *Paper presented at the 13th Workshop of Parliamentary Scholars and Parliamentarians*, Wroxton, UK. 29–30 July 2017. Available at: <https://wroxtonworkshop.org/wp-content/uploads/2017/07/2017-Session-5A-Fitsilis-and-Koutsogiannis.pdf> [Accessed: 19 November 2022].

Fitsilis, F. and Pliakogianni, A. (2021) The Hellenic Parliament's Response to the COVID-19 Pandemic – A Balancing Act between Necessity and Realism. *IALS Student Law Review*, 8 (1), pp. 19–27.

Fitsilis, F. and Stavridis, S. (2021) The Hellenic Parliament's use of digital media in its 2019 Turkey-Libya Memorandum of Understanding on maritime boundaries in the Mediterranean Sea: a preliminary assessment. LSE Hellenic Observatory, GreeSE Paper No. 163.

Fitsilis, F., Koryzis, D., Svolopoulos, V. and Spiliotopoulos, D. (2017). Implementing digital parliament innovative concepts for citizens and policy makers. In International Conference on HCI in Business, Government, and Organizations (pp. 154–170). Cham: Springer.

Foundethakis, P. (2003) The Hellenic Parliament: The New Rules of the Game. *The Journal of Legislative Studies*, 9 (2), pp. 85–106.

Gerapetritis, G. (2012) *Sýntagma kai Voulí. Aftonomía kai anélenkto ton esoterikón tou sómatos* [Constitution and Parliament. Autonomy and uncontrollability of the body's interna corporis]. Athens: Nomiki Bibliothiki.

Gerapetritis, G. (2020) The Parliament. In: Featherstone, K. and Sotiropoulos, D.A. (eds), *The Oxford Handbook of Modern Greek Politics*. Oxford: Oxford University Press, pp.154–169.

Hellenic Parliament (2018) *Stratigikó Schédio 2018-2021* [Strategic Plan 2018–2021]. Available at: <https://www.hellenicparliament.gr/UserFiles/8158407a-fc31-4ff2-a8d3-433701dbe6d4/Strategic_Final.pdf> [Accessed: 4 March 2021].

Hellenic Parliament (2021) Periodikó tis Voulís ton Ellínon. Available at: <https://www.hellenicparliament.gr/Enimerosi/periodiko/> [Accessed: 24 June 2021].

Högenauer, A.-L., Neuhold, C. and Christiansen, T. (2016) *Parliamentary Administrations in the European Union*. London: Palgrave Macmillan.

Kamilaki, M. (2019) Exhibitions at the service of Parliaments: The case of "Glossopolis". In Presentation at the 35th Annual Pre-Conference of Parliamentary Research and Library Services, 22–23 August 2019, Athens. Available at: <https://www.ifla.org/files/assets/services-for-parliaments/conference/2019/kamilaki_exhibitions_at_the_service_of_parliaments.pdf> [Accessed: 9 March 2021].

Karabarbounis, H., Mastakas, P. and Dalis, S. (2004). *Koinovouleftikí Diplomatía kai i Voulí ton Ellínon* [Parliamentary diplomacy and the Hellenic Parliament]. Athens: Sakkoulas A. N.

Kyrkos, H. (2006) *I B' en Athínais Ethnikí ton Ellínon Synélefsis* [The 2nd National Assembly of the Greeks in Athens]. Athens, Thessaloniki: University Studio Press.

Mavrias, K. (2016) *Syntagmatikó Díkaio* [Constitutional Law]. 6th edn. Athens, Thessaloniki: P.N. Sakkoulas.

Philippidou, S., Karageorgiou, M., Tarantilis, C., Soderquist, E. and Prastacos, G. (2008) Meeting the Challenge of Technology-Driven Change within an Institutional Context: the Greek Case. *Public Administration*, 86 (2), pp. 429–442.

Repousis, S. (2017) Is the Third Greek Memoranda of Understanding and Loan Agreement of August 2015 odious? Truth Committee on Public Debt in Greek or Hellenic Parliament and Criticism on Results. *Journal of Money Laundering Control*, 20(3), 220–230.

Sakellariou, M.B. (2012) *I Athinaïkí Dimokratía*. Athens: Panepistimiakés Ekdóseis Krítis.

Saripolos, N. I. (1874) *Pragmateía tou syntagmatikoú dikaíou*. 2nd edn. Athens: M.N. Aggelidou.

Sigalas, E. and Blavoukos, S. (2014) The response of the Greek parliament following the financial crisis: In search for evidence. Paper presented at the ECPR 42nd Joint Sessions of Workshops, University of Salamanca, Salamanca, Spain, 10–15 April. Available at: <https://www.academia.edu/6827979/Parliamentarism_in_Crisis_The_Response_of_the_Greek_Parliament_Following_the_Financial_Crisis_Early_Evidence> [Accessed: 1 March 2021].

Sotiropoulos, D.A. (2015) The Greek Parliament and the European Union After the Lisbon Treaty: A Missed Opportunity to Empower Parliament. In Hefftler, C., Neuhold, C., Rozenberg, O., and Smith, J. (eds), *The Palgrave Handbook of National Parliaments and the European Union*. London: Palgrave Macmillan, pp. 335–352.

Stasis, A., Dalakou, V., Karakatsanis, I., Demiri, L., Valatsou, G. and Sarantis, D. (2020). Better access to law by codification and consolidation of legal acts: the case of the Hellenic Law Codification Portal. In Proceedings of the 13th International Conference on Theory and Practice of Electronic Governance (pp. 696–704). New York: Association for Computing Machinery.

Stavridis, S. (2018) Greek parliamentarians and Greek foreign policy (2004–2014). LSE Hellenic Observatory, GreeSE Paper No. 121. Available at: <https://www.lse.ac.uk/Hellenic-Observatory/Assets/Documents/Publications/GreeSE-Papers/GreeSE-121.pdf> [Accessed: 4 March 2021].

Stefan, O. (2020). COVID-19 Soft Law: Voluminous, Effective, Legitimate? A Research Agenda. *European Papers*, 5 (1), pp. 663–670.

Tridimas, G. (2010) Referendum and the Choice Between Monarchy and Republic in Greece. *Constitutional Political Economy Volume*, 21, pp. 119–144.

Vassilouni, S. (2001) The role of the directorate of studies in the legislative work of the Hellenic Parliament. In Presented at the 67th IFLA Council and General Conference in Boston. August 16-25, 2001. Available at: <https://files.eric.ed.gov/fulltext/ED459776.pdf> [Accessed: 1 March 2021].

Virkar, S., Alexopoulos, C., Stavropoulou, S., Tsekeridou, S. and Novak, A.S., 2020, September. User-centric decision support system design in legal informatics: a typology of users. In Proceedings of the 13th International Conference on Theory and Practice of Electronic Governance (pp. 711–722). New York: Association for Computing Machinery.

21
HUNGARY'S PARLIAMENTARY ADMINISTRATION

Zsolt Szabo

21.1 Introduction

The Office of the Hungarian National Assembly (*Országgyűlés Hivatala*, hereinafter: Office) is a single, independent administrative body, supervised by the President of the National Assembly (*Országgyűlés Elnöke* or *házelnök*, hereinafter: Speaker). It provides administrative, legal, communication, security and technical support for the unicameral Assembly. On the other hand, it is also responsible for the maintenance and public accessibility of its seat, the Parliament Building (*Országház*), which is, together with its recently opened historical museum, a major cultural and touristic attraction of the country.

21.2 The Evolution of the Office of the National Assembly of Hungary (1990–2020)

The first major step in the evolution of three decades ago was characterized by the gradual transition of the political system from socialist dictatorship to democracy. Before the regime change, there was no need for a professional parliamentary organization with well trained staff to assist the legislation, as the National Assembly had no weight in policy-making, and its sessions were few and far between. Careful political reforms in the 1980s, like the introduction of the obligation to have at least two candidates in each constituency in 1983, providing for opposition MPs in the 1985–1990 term, resulted in a more active and partisan parliamentary life, requiring professional organization and assistance.

In May 1989, already one year before the convocation of the first free elected, multiparty parliament, a new organization of parliamentary administration was introduced. It consisted of three internal organs on equal footage replacing the formerly rather small and centralized structure:

- the General Secretariat assisted in law-making, preparing plenary and committee session (with the General Secretary participating on the plenary, assisting the Speaker or his deputies in conducting the sessions and interpreting the rules of procedure),
- the Office of the National Assembly was responsible for the financial, maintenance and administrative tasks,

- the Secretariat of the Speaker assisted the elected office holders (deputy speakers, notaries) and managed the international and press relations.

The three managers of these branches were fully independent from each other, standing on an equal footage. All three of them were assigned by the Speaker directly (Soltész, 2017). In May 1990, after the first free parliamentary elections, as new institutions, the offices of the political groups – at the beginning, with very few and mostly administrative-technical staff – were also established.

During the 1990s and 2000s, both the number of experienced professionals and the yearly budget gradually grew to reach the current number. Since 2012, Chapter XII of the Act on the National Assembly[1] sets forth the essential duties of the parliamentary administration, while the provisions of the Rules of Procedure[2] lay down those duties in detail. The Act declares that the Office is "a central budgetary organ in charge of performing organisational, operational, administrative and decision-preparing functions for the National Assembly".

Since 2012, also the Parliamentary Guard (*Országgyűlési Őrség*) belongs to the organization of the Office, commanded by its own chief commander, supervised by the Speaker. Previously, the guard was part of the internal armed forces under the auspices of the Ministry of Interior. With the 2012 reform, the original situation of 1912 returned, when the parliamentary guard was originally established.

In the current organizational structure, introduced in 2013, a single person, the General Director is the leader of the parliamentary administration, supervising legislative tasks as well as financial management and operations. The formally centralized structure in practice preserved the far-reaching autonomy of the directors (*igazgató*) of the – already six – directorates (*igazgatóság*). The branches correspond to the parliaments tasks:

- Office of the Speaker,
- Directorate for Legislation (the former General Secretariat),
- Directorate for Financial Management and Operations,
- Directorate for Foreign Affairs,
- Media Office,
- Directorate for Public Collections and Public Education, (established in 2013, consisting of the Library, the Parliamentary Museum, the Public Relations Office and the Information Service for MPs).

In 2014, the number of MPs was reduced from 386 to 199, but this did not result in a reduction of positions in the administration. The contrary happened: the same legislative tasks with less MPs need more administrative assistance. Also the volume of activities (plenaries, committee meetings) remained the same (Erdős, 2016).

The Office adopted a four-year medium-term institutional development strategy in 2017. The overarching goal was the efficient performance of the basic tasks (law-making, strengthening the IT-assistance of the administrative activities), sustainment of professionalism, institutional and HR-development, acclimatizing the strategic approach, and efficient communication. However, these visions are not clearly translated into activities in everyday practice.

The parliamentary administration enjoys plenty of resources. Both the budget and the number of employees raised almost constantly in the past decade, with a big jump in terms of budget in 2018, caused by the status reform of the parliamentary staff (Table 21.1).

Table 21.1 Budget and number of employees (2010–2021)

Year	2010	2011	2012	2013	2014	2015	2016	2017	2018	2019	2020	2021
Budget*	16,900	17,139	18,903	21,000	21,345	21,420	22,560	21,872	20,343	28,066	37,478	41,304
Staff	855	847	847	892	912	943	947	947	950	1005	1005	994

Source: parlament.hu

* In million HUF.

21.3 The Legal Status of the Office and Its Relation to the Speaker

The Office enjoys full institutional independence within the Hungarian public administration. The Speaker supervises its activities, external bodies, like the Government, have no influence on its operation. The Speaker also performs employers' rights above the leading positions and appoints the General Director, therefore he has a relatively major influence on the personnel of the Office.

The Speaker may not only issue formal rulings (*házelnöki rendelkezés*), which are sources of internal parliamentary law, but some of them also effect external persons. One of them regulates the organization and functions of the Office,[3] another important one governs the access to the Parliament building for the press and the general public.[4] Being internal rules by legal nature, they might affect external persons nevertheless, yet no judicial remedy is available against them: neither the general courts, nor the Constitutional Court has the jurisdiction to control these norms.

It needs to be added that the Speaker in Hungary is traditionally not a neutral moderator, but an active political actor of his party – Speakers sometimes tend to make political statements even during chairing the plenary sessions. Within the Office, the Speaker has a Secretariat at his disposal, which is not only responsible for coordinating the duties and programmes but also for answering petitions, queries from the general public, related to the Assembly or to the Speaker.

The budget of the Office is prepared independently and separate from other bodies' budget, after discussions with the Ministry of Finance, by the Director General under the direction of the Speaker. The proposal is then sent to the Government, with the consent of the House Committee (consisting of the Speaker, his deputies and the leaders of the political groups), after obtaining the opinion of the budgetary committee. The Government is then required to submit it in unchanged form to the National Assembly, as a part of the legislative proposal on the central budget.[5]

21.4 The Current Organizational Structure and Functions

The primary functions of the Office are centralized in the largest unit, the Directorate for Legislation and its five departments (see organization chart at the end of the article). The largest of them, the Department of Committees, provides all committees' secretariats, which are responsible for scheduling, formally preparing the meetings (e.g. preparing scripts for committee chairs) and the committees' decisions, meeting protocols and statistics. One administrative and one or two professional staff are deployed at the secretariat of each committee. This is only sufficient for running the committees' workflow but does not allow for supporting in-depth committee activities, since there is no political need from the committees for such performing hearings, commissioning reports. The main, almost exclusive item on committees' agenda, is the second reading of bills, therefore the foremost committee activity at the meetings is the selection of amendments submitted to bills, frequently without substantial debate, by quick votes. Therefore, the main task of the Department is to support the smooth committee proceedings by organizational means.

The Codification Department (composed of lawyers) provides occasionally on-demand assistance for MPs and committees on legislative drafting, but in the past few years, as secretariats of the political groups develop their professional legislative staff, this is rather exceptional. The main activity of the Department therefore is to analyse and give opinion on all bills and amendments on the Assembly's agenda, in terms of legislative drafting rules. General legal or constitutional problems may also be addressed, but this rarely happens in practice. The proponents themselves also rely on the Department not as normative, but legislative drafting control body. As a rule, this task is performed not by compiling official opinions, but rather by reporting back to the drafter, in most cases, the line ministry, on an informal basis. The overwhelmingly technical correction suggestions appear than at a later stage of the legislative process as amendments, submitted by one of the parliamentary committees. Rarely, the Department also submits reports about constitutional-legal problems, the correction also here is responsibility of the submitter, which rarely results in changes after the political decision (the formal submission) on the bill.

It needs to be added that within the Office, none of the units perform any ex ante or ex post assessments of bills, and the focus in this phase is on formal and drafting requirements towards bills. In case of governmental bills, ex ante assessments are part of the preparatory phase done by the responsible line ministries (Szabó, 2020). On rare occasions, committees organize hearings on implementation of certain laws, but this activity decreased in the last decade. Therefore, the main activity of the parliamentary administration in terms of legislation is checking bills against legislative drafting rules.

The Codification Department further prepares the consolidated versions of a bill during the legislative procedure, after the approval of the amendments by the committees. It also runs the secretariat of the two parliamentary committees closely related to legal matters, the Committee on Legislation and the Committee on Privileges. Preparing in-depth legal and constitutional analysis of each bills is not a requirement. Furthermore, the Department gives legal opinions on parliamentary law and rules of procedure on request of other departments or committees.

The Department of Organization is responsible for the preparation of the plenary sessions (coordination of the agenda, scheduling presiding officers), and for running the secretariat of the House Committee (the coordinative body of the political groups and the Speaker). The other tasks cover the coordination of secret ballot votes of the MPs and the supervision of the Room Service of the plenary hall, which is also responsible for maintaining the order on the public gallery.

Within the Directorate for Legislation, there are further two smaller units. Units of more than 15 people are called department (*főosztály*), smaller ones are simply offices (*iroda*). The Office of information and documentation keeps and provides information, statistics on legislation and MPs and makes them available for the general public. It also supervises the register of parliamentary documents (bills, amendments, questions). The Office of the Notaries coordinates the work notaries of the National Assembly, who are elected from among the MPs, two of them have to be present during the plenary sessions. This unit prepares the detailed script to be read out by the chair of the plenary, it also edits the minutes of the plenary prepared by the stenographs and provides Hungarian linguistic assistance for parliamentary documents. Coordinating questions and interpellations to be discusses on the plenary is also within its domain.

The Directorate for Maintenance and Finances provides back-office services for the Office: among others, it is responsible for the budgetary tasks, the preparation of internal financial and public procurement regulations, the maintenance of estates (Parliament building and three office buildings around it), the room management, the IT-networks, the access control system, the internal and external televising network, the electronic voting system in the plenary hall, the HR-tasks (performance assessment, internal training), and the public procurement tasks (planning, implementing). The activities of the branches of the Directorate for Public Collections and Public Education are to be discussed further below in Chapter 6 (museum, library, participatory instruments).

21.5 Human Resources

The Office puts a continuous effort on skilled, flexible and permanent (loyal) staff. The workload is generally not overwhelming, but sometimes overtime work is required, especially if the House sits in late hours or works with busy agenda. To serve within the parliamentary administration is traditionally a long-term occupation, with good financial conditions. Many staff members serve decades long, the majority of the current top leaders, the directors have been serving for more than 20 years.

In order to provide competitive wages on the long run, a significant personnel reform took place in 2018, consisting of a 45% wage rise in average, and a change in status of the parliamentary officials. Parliamentary officials are now among the best paid civil officials in the Hungarian public administration, enjoying a special status "parliamentary public official" (*országgyűlési köztisztviselő*), regulated by the Act on the National Assembly, Chapter XII/A, instead of the general act on public service officials. Parliamentary public officials now have their own selection procedure, classification, advancement, renumeration, performance assessment, annual leave and promotion systems.

Classification categories with higher education degree range between "parliamentary counsellor" and "special senior lead parliamentary counsellor", and without secondary education from "parliamentary assistant" to "special senior lead parliamentary administrative officer". The amount of the remuneration basis is equal to the amount of the average monthly gross earnings in the national economy relating to the previous year, officially published by the Hungarian Central Statistical Office. This results in a stable, rather yearly increasing wage level. The starting salary for secondary degree holders at entering the career is 1.5 times of the basis at secondary level educations employees, raising up to a multiplier of 2.6 after 36 years. The starting multiplier is 0.9 at officers with high school graduation and may reach 1.7 after 36 years. Lead positions are eligible for a multiplier of 3–3.7. Just to compare: MPs' renumeration is set at three times of the average gross earnings, which can be increased by committee membership supplement.

The employer may increase the above salary level in case of good performance by not more than 50% or reduce by not more than 20% the basic remuneration. If a parliamentary public official (except from the lead positions) serves in a position where the use of a foreign language is necessary, a language supplement is eligible. The employer may also award a parliamentary public official fulfilling the conditions the title of "parliamentary expert advisor" or "senior parliamentary expert advisor". The total number of the holders of these titles shall not exceed 20% of the staff.

In 2018, about half of the employees on the Office's payroll had secondary degree, 30% of them are lawyers, almost 20% are economists. The other half of personnel are employed by work contracts, they are mostly dealing with secondary functions of the Office. Other common professions are administrative managers, foreign relation experts, public relations, event management and media professionals, financial and IT specialists. The Office staff also includes architects to plan and coordinate the jobs relating to maintaining and renovating the particularly valuable Parliament Building, including skilled joiners, upholsterers and tinsmiths who have acquired the fine skills of old-time craftsmen. The Office also employs parliamentary stenographers, who regularly win world championships in shorthand speech capturing.[6] The protocols are stenographed (short hand writing on the meeting, typing in text afterwards) at all plenary and committee meetings.

21.6 Special Functions

21.6.1 Staff of Political Groups

The size of the offices of the political groups corresponds to the size of the political group in the Assembly. Governing parties traditionally have larger staff, since they play a more active role in legislation. Opposition factions submit many bills, yet those are hardly ever discussed on the plenary. The number of public officials and employees with secondary or higher education assigned to parliamentary groups is set by law: it shall be 5 for groups with fewer than 10 members, 7 for groups with 11–20 members, 10 for groups with 21–34 members, 12 for groups with 35–50 members and 15 for groups with over 50 members.[7] Moreover, parliamentary groups may be assisted by a staff of public officials and employees, whose number corresponds with that of the parliamentary group members.

The personnel decisions on staff rely primarily on the leader of the political group. Since he/she is not a civil officer, formally the General Director appoints and dismisses faction staff, upon recommendation of the leader of the political group, and also the exercise of employer rights requires his/her consent. Faction employees are contracted with work contracts, not as parliamentary public officers. This allows flexibility in staff management, to be able adjust to the changes in the size of the political group after elections.

The Office provides parliamentary groups with the following supply free of charge: suitable office space in the Parliament building or in a block nearby; basic supplies (office furniture, equipment etc.) as required for the operation of the parliamentary groups and the work of the Members; and web access that allows Members to perform their work (up to the limit of the related budget appropriation). Persons employed by parliamentary groups are entitled to be paid up to the limit of the funds allocated for employee wages. Parliamentary groups are entitled to an amount corresponding to 10% of the funds allocated for wages to cover other benefits at the discretion of the party authorized to act as employer and to cover bonuses.

21.6.2 External Relations

External relations play an important role both on the Assembly's agenda and within the Office. Most tasks result from EU-, foreign and national affairs. The National Assembly has three standing committees dealing – at least partly – with foreign affairs: the Committees on European Affairs, the Committee on Foreign Affairs and the Committee on National

Cohesion. The Assembly also hosts the Forum of Hungarian Representatives from the Carpathian Basin, a consultative forum of deputies of Hungarian nationality in parliaments of the neighbouring countries (Romania, Slovakia, Ukraine, Serbia, and Croatia).

Within the Office, the Directorate for Foreign Affairs coordinates the international relations and international programme planning of the Assembly and its members by organization and preparing incoming and outgoing parliamentary delegations' programmes, background papers. It also coordinates relations with international organizations, the European Parliament and its members. It further coordinates technical assistance (twinning) projects implemented by the Office with non-EU-member countries. Furthermore, the Directorate supports the national policy activities of the National Assembly and its members (relations with Hungarian organizations, MPs in countries with Hungarian minority or diaspora).

There are three departments within the Directorate: Department on EU-affairs (directing also the Brussels offices of the Assembly, one within the European Parliament and one protecting Hungarian national minorities' rights), Department on National Integration and Protocol Department, to assist foreign delegations and international events. There also three Secretariats within the Directorate: one for the Hungarian National Group of the Interparliamentary Union, one for the parliamentary relations and one for Security Policy and Defence.

21.6.3 Research Department

As a branch of the Directorate for Public Collections and Public Education, the Information Service (Infoservice) provides the MPs and their staff, the committees, and other departments of the Office with information and research services on an impartial and confidential basis. In addition to answering individual requests, it supports MPs' legislative activities also with proactive background materials, related to legislative agenda items, like briefings on policy issues, which include references of the legal background, international treaties, EU legislation, national professional, political and civil opinions as well as statistical data. Analyses are longer papers, prepared on demand of the MPs, focussing on the international comparative analysis of the related issue.

21.6.4 Library

The Library of the National Assembly (*Országgyűlési Könyvtár*) fulfils three different functions: is a legislative library, a public library and a special collection library as well. Law and public administration, political science, 20th century and contemporary history are its main interests. The library acts as a non-lending library, open for the general public, and an information centre of national scope for law and political sciences, modern age Hungarian and universal history and the documents of the National Assembly. As a national scientific special library, one of its primary functions is to collect and process the full scale of domestic professional publications and the selection of foreign publications in this realm, as well as to collect and process the publications of the United Nations and its specialized organizations, and the publications of the European Union's organizations. The library is to be entitled to have one copy of the nationally provided legal deposits in its scope of collection.

The size of the library's holdings is close to 700,000 volumes, the number of subscriptions to periodicals in law, history, political science and social sciences is close to 1000, the annual acquisitions are close to 6000 pieces. In the reading room, approximately 45,000 documents are available in 12 different subject areas. The staff of the Library are also on the Office payroll, which provides for high salaries compared to other libraries.

21.6.5 ICT Development

The beginnings of e-legislation at the late 2000s were marked by the internal amendment management system of the regular laws on the annual national budget. In order to secure accurate legislative drafting and smart correction of drafting errors, the Office later developed its own web-based document editing and workflow management application, the ParLex. Decided in 2013 and launched in practice 2017, ParLex meets the highest requirements of data security. Covering the entire legislative procedure, it is possible to draft, submit, share and track parliamentary documents (laws, amendments) within the transparent and paperless system.[8] ParLex enables not only MPs and their staff to create, edit, propose bills, amendments and other legislative documents in XML but supports also the work of the parliamentary officers in charge. The legislative tasks within the Office – for example framing legal opinions, creating background materials for committee sittings – are covered by the system from the formulation of a legislative proposal to the automatic publication on the website.

From the onset of the running parliamentary cycle (May 2018), more than 2480 legislative proposals (bills, resolutions etc.) and over 3370 subsidiary motions were introduced via the system. In 2019, ParLex was awarded with Best Practice Certificate of the European Institute of Public Administration. Since 2020, ParLex is part of the Integrated Legislation System, operated by the Ministry of Justice.

21.6.6 Participative Instruments

The Office puts increasing efforts on public relations, an evident signal of this is the establishment of the Directorate on Public Collections and Public Education in 2013. As part of the Directorate, the Public Relations Office deals with parliamentary model programmes designed for the youth since the early 2000s. The two programmes offered target different age groups: the "Game of Democracy" is tailored for high school students with a bill and several amendments prepared by the staff, which they have to discuss and select during committee and plenary phases, and finally, adopt as a whole at the end. The "Model Parliament" attracts students above 18, who have to prepare and submit the bill on the agenda of their own. Mostly student groups of various universities register to the programme, which results in a kind of competition between faculties and other secondary education institutions.

These programmes, based on active participation and the method of learning-by-doing, present a model of parliamentary practice by role playing. During these programmes, students follow the process of law-making in rooms of the real parliament in a shortened, one-day form, while they get acquainted with key players, key skills such as rhetoric and argumentation and discuss their peers' opinions. As part of these programmes, participants take part in plenary sessions, meetings of committees and political groups. Besides, they make a decision and cast a vote about previously discussed proposals and amendments. The day closes with a press conference based on the work achieved (Kerekes and Andrási, 2020).

In 2015, another initiative of the Directorate, the Parliamentary Museum opened. It is a national museum in charge of collecting, safeguarding, processing and presenting the cultural values connected to the history of the National Assembly. A permanent, interactive exhibition on the 1000-years history of Hungarian parliamentarism attracts visitors mostly, but lectures, pre-booked school programmes and other events are also available.

The Directorate is also responsible for running the new, modern visitor centre, opened in 2014. Since the Parliament building is a top touristic magnet, the country's number one sight, the indoor tours, available in several languages, are highly overbooked. The Directorate employs many tour guides, contracted as freelancers on seasonal demand (they are not included in the Office's payroll). The income of touristic activities is nonetheless almost negligible in the annual budget (ca. 2.5%).

21.6.7 *Press Relations*

The Press Office, previously part of the Secretariat of the Speaker, became a separate unit in 2012. Its primary task is to inform the press on the activities of the plenary, committees, elected officers of the National Assembly. It also coordinates the access of journalists to the building by temporary (sessional or daily) licences. The answer to public information requests belongs also to its domain.

Organigram of the National Assembly in Hungary

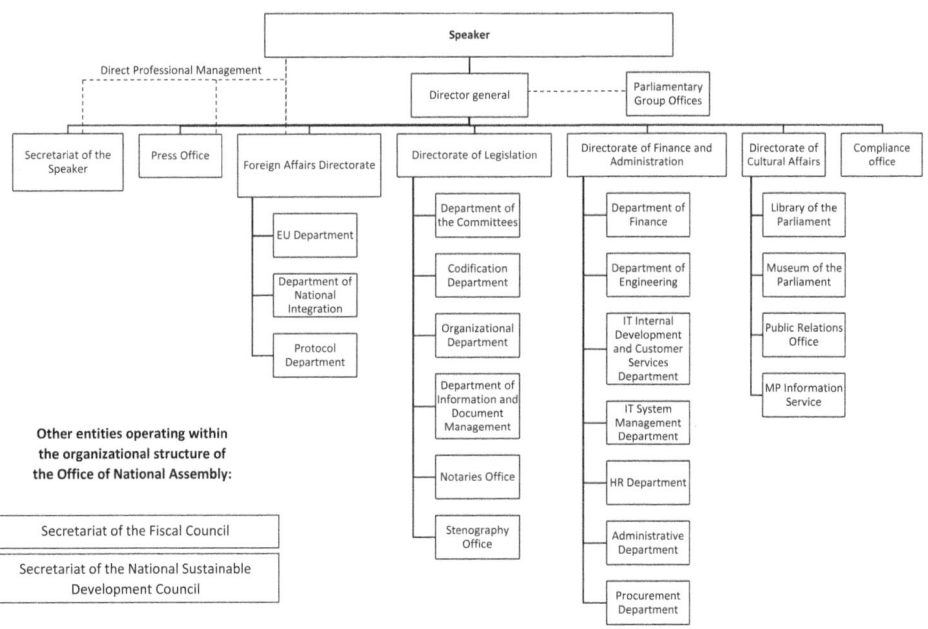

Notes

1 Act XXXVI. of 2012 on the National Assembly, Articles 123–124/A.
2 Resolution 10/2014 (II. 24.) of the National Assembly on certain standing orders.
3 Available in Hungarian: https://www.parlament.hu/hivatal/szmsz.
4 Speaker's ruling 9/2013.
5 Article 124 (1) Law on the National Assembly.
6 Look for the category 'speech capturing' here: https://www.intersteno.org/competitions-classification-lists/.
7 Article 115 Law on the National Assembly.
8 ParLex users manual, available: https://www.parlament.hu/documents/10181/773675/Parlex+k%C3%A9zik%C3%B6nyv+I.+r%C3%A9sz/f72a4bae-ce41-4dda-9d84-f228d277181e (downloaded: 13.01.2021).

References

Erdős, Csaba: How much does the operation of a parliament cost? In: Péter Smuk (ed.): Costs of Democracy, Gondolat, Budapest, 2016, 87–104.p. https://dfk-online.sze.hu/images/egyedi/Smuk_Costs_of_Democracy%20.pdf.

Kerekes, Margit – Andrási, Réka: Az Országgyűlés Hivatala törvényhozást modellező ifjúsági programjai, In: Parlamenti Szemle, 2020, volume 5, issue 2, pp. 155–170.

Soltész, István: Az Országgyűlés Hivatalának története: az irodától a professzionális hivatalig, In: Parlamenti Szemle, 2017, volume 2, issue 2, pp. 145–158.

Szabó, Zsolt: Hungary, In: Zbiral, Robert (szerk.) The Cradle of Laws: Drafting and Negotiating Bills within the Executives in Central Europe, Baden-Baden, Nomos, 2020, pp. 85–105, 21 p.

22
IRELAND'S PARLIAMENTARY ADMINISTRATION

Mellissa English and Tara Murphy

22.1 Introduction

The Irish Parliament is known as the Houses of the Oireachtas (the Oireachtas). It is a bicameral legislature, consisting of Dáil Éireann[1] and Seanad Éireann.[2] The current (33rd) Dáil has 160 members, each known as a Teachta Dála or TD. The current (26th) Seanad has 60 members, each known as a Senator.

Ireland's parliamentary administration is known as the Houses of the Oireachtas Service (the Service). The Service provides advice and support services to the Houses of the Oireachtas Commission (the Commission), to both Houses of the Oireachtas and their committees, and to the members (TDs and Senators) of the Houses.

The Commission is the governing board of the Service. It was established on a statutory basis as a body corporate[3] in 2004, pursuant to the Houses of the Oireachtas Commission Acts 2003–2021 (the Commission Acts) and is independent in the performance of its functions.

The Commission has no role in relation to parliamentary business or procedure; these are matters for the Oireachtas itself through the relevant committees, such as the Dáil Business Committee, the Committee on Standing Orders and Dáil Reform, and the Seanad Committee on Parliamentary Privileges and Oversight (see below at Section 22.3.1).

The Commission accounts to the Oireachtas through annual reporting and annual estimates of expenditure, and is required to ensure value for money in the use of resources. The Commission has a three-year budget set out in statute which is financed from the Central Fund (the main accounting fund used by the Government of Ireland). As a result, the Commission has control over current expenditure and, to a considerable degree, over staffing numbers. Appropriate corporate governance procedures and structures are in place to enable the Commission to effectively discharge its functions as a governing board, including a Finance Committee and an Audit Committee.

The Commission consists of the Ceann Comhairle (Speaker/Chairperson) of Dáil Éireann who acts as Chairperson of the Commission, the Cathaoirleach (Speaker/Chairperson) of Seanad Éireann, the Secretary General of the Service (who is the Clerk of Dáil Éireann and the Chief Executive of the Commission), a member of the Oireachtas appointed by the Minister for Public Expenditure and Reform, four members appointed by Dáil Éireann, and three members appointed by Seanad Éireann. Commission members serve in a corporate capacity and do not represent their parties, groups or their own interests.

The Secretary General/Clerk of the Dáil is appointed by the Commission on the recommendation of the Ceann Comhairle from among the one or more persons selected for that purpose by the Top-Level Appointments Committee (TLAC) following an open competition. The appointment process is laid down in section 5 of the Staff of the Houses of the Oireachtas Act 1959, as amended. The Secretary General is both a member of the Commission and is accountable to it for the implementation of its policies, and subject to its direction (other than in relation to the management of staff and in his/her role as Clerk of Dáil Éireann, as provided by section 16(5) of the Commission Acts).

Various divisions and units within the Service provide the parliamentary corporate services that keep the Oireachtas running smoothly (see below at Section 22.3). A statutory basis for the functions of the Service is provided by the Commission Acts.

The Service is staffed by civil servants of the State (general service, professional and technical) who are employed by the Commission. It is headed by the Secretary General who is responsible for the day-to-day management of the Service and implementation of the Commission's policies.

The Secretary General assigns responsibility at Assistant Secretary level for leading the delivery of functions and services in the Service. The degree of discretion at various organizational levels is informed by the Oireachtas' Corporate Governance Framework, which defines the relationships and the distribution of rights and responsibilities among those who work with and in the Oireachtas, determines the roles and procedures through which the Oireachtas objectives are set, provides the means of attaining those objectives and monitoring performance, and defines where accountability lies throughout the organization. Also, all staff are required to adhere to Service policies, procedures, circulars, and Office Notices in the performance of their duties.

The Secretary General is assisted by the Management Board. The Management Board is chaired by the Secretary General and comprises four Assistant Secretaries in the Service, the Clerk of the Seanad, an external non-executive member, and the chair of the Service's Principal Officers Network.

The Board has overall responsibility for the implementation of the strategic plan for the Service. It oversees and accounts for the performance of the Service through collective leadership. It also decides on issues of strategic, operational, and financial importance which may then be referred to the Commission for decision as appropriate.

The Management Board has established five strategic committees, each chaired by a board member, to provide a co-ordinated approach to the management of strategic and operational matters in the Service that have a cross-divisional dimension: Governance, Performance and Accountability Committee; Openness, Public Engagement and Campus Development Committee; People and organization Committee; Technology and Digital Transformation Committee; and Rannóg 2024 Committee.[4]

22.2 Key Aspects of the Organization

The Service comprises approximately 545 civil servants and has a three-year budget of €442 million for the period ending 2021. The Service has grown over the past decade due to the establishment of the Parliamentary Budget Office, the expansion of certain units (such the Office of Parliamentary Legal Advisers and the Information and Communications Technology Unit), and the need to support an increased number of Oireachtas committees. This growth is demonstrated in Table 22.1.

Table 22.1 Staffing levels in the Service

Staffing levels in the Service	
Year	Number of staff
2020	545
2019	520
2018	510
2017	530
2016	450
2015	545
2014	410

Note: For the years prior to 2014, the number of staff was in or around 370–375.

Members of the Oireachtas employ their own staff, who are hired directly by the members and their political parties, in accordance with terms and conditions set by the Department of Public Expenditure and Reform, with the Service operating payroll on their behalf. These staff are on fixed-term contracts and are only employed for as long as their employing parliamentarian holds a seat in the Oireachtas.

The Commission determines the number of Service staff (up to and including Principal Officer level) within the overall financial allocation approved by the Dáil. The sanction of the Minister for Public Expenditure and Reform is however required for senior posts at or above Principal Officer Higher level.

The recruitment practice of the civil service is independent of Parliament and Government. The Public Appointments Service (PAS), an independent statutory body, recruits civil servants for general service grades, while the Houses of the Oireachtas Service recruits specialist and State industrial staff directly. All recruitment to the civil and public service is underpinned by legislation and regulated by the Commission for Public Service Appointments. Staff seeking promotion may apply to open competitions run by PAS or internal competitions run by the Service. (Secretary General recruitment process: see above at Section 22.1.)

The Civil Service Code of Standards and Behaviour and Circular 09/2009: Civil Servants and Political Activity require civil servants, including staff of the Service, to conscientiously serve the Government of the day and advise on and implement policy impartially. With the exception of some subordinate grades, no civil servant may be a member of a political party, contribute to political debate or publicly support or oppose a political party or candidate for election.

In addition, there are various rules and arrangements in place for managing relationships with stakeholders, including, for example, the Regulation of Lobbying Act 2015, the Ethics Acts (comprising the Ethics in Public Office Act 1995 and the Standards in Public Office Act 2001), and the Civil Service Code of Standards and Behaviours.

22.3 The Role of the Service in the Context of Parliamentary Work

22.3.1 *The Main Activities of the Service*

The Service comprises a Parliamentary Services Division (staff who interpret and apply the rules and Standing Orders, and can advise the chairs and members of the Houses and their committees); a Parliamentary Information and Research Services Division (Library and

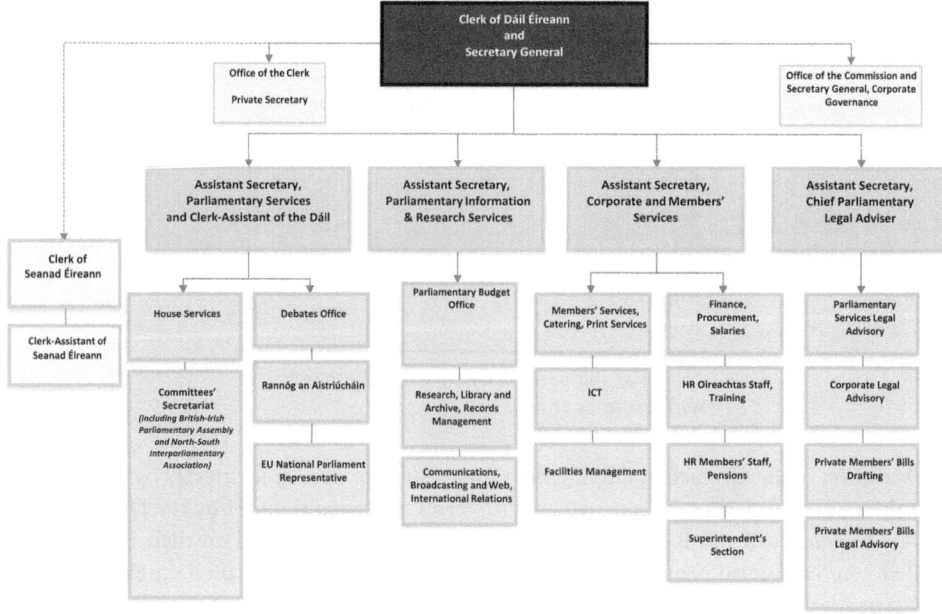

Figure 22.1 The Oireachtas' organizational chart

Research Services, Parliamentary Budget Office and Communications); a Corporate and Members' Services Division (including security, catering, finance, HR, IT etc.); and an Office of Parliamentary Legal Advisers (see Figure 22.1).

The General Election in 2016 returned a minority Government and this brought about a number of challenges for Parliament. A Sub-Committee on Dáil Reform was established and published three reports to the Dáil which included a series of recommendations for the reform of procedures and practices. As can be seen above at 2, the Service's staff increased by approximately 80 in response to these reforms.

Changes brought about as a result of Dáil reform included:

- the establishment of a Business Committee which gave more power to the Dáil to plan and make arrangements for its own business;
- the establishment of the Parliamentary Budget Office, an independent specialist unit which enables members and the Committee on Budgetary Oversight to conduct ex-ante scrutiny of all budgetary matters;
- the expansion of the Office of Parliamentary Legal Advisers to provide specialist drafting and advisory services in respect of members' private member bill (PMB) proposals;
- the establishment of eight Special Committees to report on particular policy areas; and
- many other practical initiatives in relation to the running of sittings and questions.

Many of the changes, introduced during a minority Government, continue and prove the need for certain specialist advices for members, irrespective of the political make-up of either House.

The Service is currently engaged in a major strategic programme of Digital Transformation (see below at Section 22.5.1) which includes a focus on technology in the Chambers.

No aspect of the Parliamentary Administration can function without the whole of it. Details of the main functions of each aspect of the Service are set out below.

22.3.1.1 Office of the Commission and Secretary General, Corporate Governance

The Office of the Commission and Secretary General supports the work of the Commission, Finance Committee, Audit Committee and Management Board. It also supports the Secretary General in the implementation of the governance framework for the Service, including coordination of the Service's three-year strategic plans and performance review and reporting. The Office has responsibility for the Service's customer service function. The Head of the Office is the Service's Chief Risk Officer and Head of Internal Audit.

22.3.1.2 Clerk of Dáil Éireann

The Clerk of Dáil Éireann provides advice on parliamentary procedure and practice to the Ceann Comhairle and to all members of Dáil Éireann. The Clerk is supported in this role by the Clerk-Assistant and Office of the Clerk. The Office of the Commission and Secretary General supports the Clerk in his/her capacity as Secretary General.

As Secretary General, the Clerk manages the Service, implements and monitors Commission policies regarding the Service, and delivers outputs as determined by the Commission.

22.3.1.3 Clerk of Seanad Éireann

The Clerk of Seanad Éireann provides advice on parliamentary procedure and practice to the Cathaoirleach and to all members of Seanad Éireann. The Clerk is supported in this role by the Clerk-Assistant and the Seanad Office.

22.3.1.4 Seanad Office

The Seanad Office supports the sittings and business of the Seanad, and its committees, by producing procedural documents, including the Seanad Order Paper; providing procedural advice; maintaining and drafting the Standing Orders for the Seanad; and providing the secretariat to the Seanad Committee on Parliamentary Privileges and Oversight, the Seanad Committee of Selection and the Seanad Public Consultation Committee. The current Principal Officer of the Seanad Office holds the office of Clerk-Assistant of Seanad Éireann.

22.3.1.5 Parliamentary Services

22.3.1.5.1 House Services

House Services comprises the following sections:

- Journal Office and Business Committee
- Bills Office
- Questions Office

The **Journal Office** has responsibility for the production of the Dáil Order Paper, the Journal (minutes) of Proceedings, and the Standing Orders of the Dáil. The Journal Office is the repository of precedents regarding parliamentary procedures in the Dáil and also provides the secretariat for the Committee on Parliamentary Privileges and Oversight (which, amongst other things, considers matters relating to the remit of Dáil committees).

The secretariat for the Business Committee and for the Committee on Standing Orders and Dáil Reform is also contained within the Journal Office.

The Business Committee makes recommendations to the Dáil in relation to the arrangements for sittings of the Dáil and the taking of Business, which are then decided in the Dáil on the Order of Business. The Business Committee also acts as the Committee of Selection, to nominate members to serve on Dáil committees.

The Committee on Standing Orders and Dáil Reform considers matters relating to Dáil parliamentary procedure.

The **Bills Office**:

- prints and circulates both government bills and PMBs, including versions of bills that have been amended by the Houses, as well as printing vellums (i.e., the copy of a bill which is signed by the President for the purposes of the promulgation of the Act as law), and Acts of the Oireachtas;
- seeks to ensure that the Constitution, Standing Orders and Rulings of the Chair are complied with during the passage of legislation;
- examines bills and amendments for compliance with the Constitution and the Standing Orders;
- provides procedural support to both Houses of the Oireachtas, their committees and members in their consideration of legislation; and
- provides procedural advice to Chairs of both Houses and committees, and to government departments, members and their staff.

The **Questions Office** receives and processes parliamentary questions for Dáil Éireann, as well as examining them for compliance with Standing Orders. It also publishes the Questions Paper and issues the replies to parliamentary questions received from government departments to members of the Dáil.

22.3.1.5.2 Committees' Secretariat

Each committee is generally assigned a team of between three and four staff headed up by a Committee Clerk (which is the Secretariat for that Committee). The Committee Secretariat:

- coordinates all the administrative arrangements for the committee, including all necessary arrangements for meetings and whatever steps are necessary to implement the decisions of the committee and sub-committees;
- advises on matters of procedure based on the committee's Orders of Reference, Standing Orders of the Dáil and Seanad, Rulings of the Chair, and precedent;
- liaises with government departments and other outside bodies, including those that are State funded and voluntary and private organizations that have relevance to the remit of the committee; and
- organizes policy advice and papers, and coordinates the drafting and publication of committee reports.

22.3.1.5.3 EU National Parliament Representative – Based in Brussels

The Representative:

- liaises with the EU institutions, in particular the European Parliament, the European Council, the Council of the European Union, and the European Commission;
- liaises with the Irish Permanent Representation to the European Union;
- liaises and builds strategic alliance, through the National Parliament Representatives, with parliaments of the other Member States;
- provides the Oireachtas with relevant and timely information on proposals selected for Scrutiny;
- provides support for inter-parliamentary events (Conference of Speakers, COSAC, JPSGs, Secretary General Meetings, Committee Delegations) and general liaison events; and
- promotes general interest in the Oireachtas' involvement in the running and activities of the EU institutions, by building relevant networks and circulating regular information bulletins.

22.3.1.5.4 Debates Office

The Debates Office produces and publishes the Official Report of the Debates for both Houses of the Oireachtas, their committees, and for committee inquiries held under statute; and publishes replies to parliamentary questions tabled by members to ministers. The Official Report is produced and published in the language spoken on the floor of the Houses and in committees (i.e., Irish or English).

22.3.1.5.5 Irish Translation Section/Rannóg an Aistriúcháin

Rannóg an Aistriúcháin:

- provides official translations of Acts of the Oireachtas and, on the request of a Minister, the translation of Statutory Instruments;
- translates material for the Order Papers of both Houses of the Oireachtas and for other units of the Oireachtas;
- provides simultaneous interpretation for both Houses and their committees;
- provides the Irish text of the Standing Orders of both Houses;
- manages the Irish Language Strategy and the statutory Irish Language Scheme in the Service, and
- provides a correspondence translation service for members.

22.3.1.6 Parliamentary Information and Research Services

22.3.1.6.1 Communications, Broadcasting and Web, International Relations

The **Press Office** works with a wide variety of print, broadcast, and online media outlets. The Press and Public Relations Officer has overall responsibility for the management of press and media queries for the Oireachtas. The Committee Press Officers have the responsibility of all press and media queries for committees.

The **Social Media Team** manages the Oireachtas' four official social media accounts on Twitter, Facebook, Instagram, and LinkedIn.

The **Broadcasting Unit** has responsibility for producing, recording, archiving, and broadcasting the proceedings of Dáil Éireann, Seanad Éireann and Oireachtas committees. Live coverage of all proceedings is made available via streaming to oireachtas.ie. The Unit is also responsible for the production and broadcast of Oireachtas TV, the Oireachtas' dedicated 24/7 television channel.

The **Web Team** manages the design and content on the oireachtas.ie website, including the daily publication of documents and business papers, and updating members' profile pages. The Web Team is also responsible for the provision of live streaming and downloadable video files of proceedings from both Chambers and all committee rooms on sitting days.

The **Events Team** is responsible for the management of official Oireachtas events and programmes.

The **Inter-Parliamentary Relations and Travel Unit** coordinates outgoing and incoming visits; provides secretarial support to Oireachtas delegations attending various inter-parliamentary assemblies, including the Inter-Parliamentary Union Assembly, the Parliamentary Assembly of the Council of Europe and the Parliamentary Assembly of the Organization for Security Co-operation in Europe, and inter-parliamentary conferences; and administers the Irish Parliamentary Association and provides secretariat support to Parliamentary Friendship Groups.

The Communications Unit is also responsible for graphic design and branding, merchandising and internal communications.

22.3.1.6.2 Parliamentary Budget Office

The Parliamentary Budget Office is an independent specialist unit within the Service. It provides the Houses of the Oireachtas and their committees with fiscal and economic information, analysis and advice that is independent and impartial relating to the particular macroeconomic conditions in the State; developments affecting public finances; the management of public finances; and the financial implications of proposals affecting the public finances.

22.3.1.6.3 Research, Library and Archive, Records Management

The **Library and Research Service** comprises the Oireachtas Library and the Parliamentary Research Service and provides research and information services to both Houses and their committees and individual members in respect of their parliamentary duties.

The **Oireachtas Library** delivers information services, including information skills training for political and parliamentary staff, and manages the contemporary and historical collections.

The **Parliamentary Research Service** publishes research on proposed legislation and other topical issues and delivers a commissioned research service to support the work of individual members and committees.

The **Records Management Unit** is responsible for records management policy and procedures in the Service as well the establishment of a Parliamentary Archive. It also has responsibility for the coordination of Freedom of Information requests and the data protection function within the Service.

22.3.1.7 Corporate and Members' Services

22.3.1.7.1 Facilities Management Unit

The Facilities Management Unit has responsibility for:

- Covid-19 compliance;
- maintenance of the parliamentary estate;
- safety and health matters;
- business continuity planning;
- sustainability;
- the creche;
- the fitness Room; and
- stationery stores.

22.3.1.7.2 Finance, Procurement, Salaries

The **Finance Unit** is responsible for the proper planning, processing, and management of the Commission's finances. Its key tasks include:

- processing payments for the Commission;
- the administration of the financial management software;
- providing advice and support to the Commission on financial management matters and ensuring the Commission's compliance with legislative and governance obligations;
- preparing the annual estimates and annual accounts of the Commission;
- reporting on expenditure to line sections and senior management on a regular basis; and
- accommodating and coordinating the audits of the Comptroller and the Auditor General.

The **Procurement Unit's** responsibilities include:

- governance and planning, including developing the Service's procurement plan and advising senior management on procurement performance and compliance;
- providing best practice advice for the staff of the Service in relation to Public Procurement;
- ensuring that tendering by contract managers is carried out in compliance with national and EU legislation and in line with the Office of Government Procurement (OGP) circulars and directions; and
- acting as the main liaison between the Service and the OGP.

The **Salaries Section** administers over 2,000 payroll payments spread across weekly, fortnightly, and monthly deadlines.

22.3.1.7.3 HR Services

The **HR Unit for Staff** provides HR services and support to Oireachtas staff.
   The **HR Recruitment Unit** manages the resources and recruitment in the Service.
   The **Training and Development Unit** organizes courses and programmes for Oireachtas staff, members, and political staff, and manages the organization development programme.

The **HR Systems and Change Unit** is responsible for HR systems improvement and integration **and** progresses organizational development strategies, policies and reform, including Civil Service Renewal and Public Service reform. It is also responsible for employee engagement, HR strategy and health and safety strategies for Covid-19.

The **Equality Diversity and Inclusion Unit** has been established focusing on our Equality, Diversity and Inclusion Strategy and programmes in the Oireachtas.

The **HR Unit for Members** provides HR services and supports to members as employers for political staff.

The **Pensions Unit** administers superannuation schemes for civil service staff, political staff, and members.

22.3.1.7.4 Information and Communications Technology

The Information and Communications Technology Unit provides information and communications technology facilities to members, staff, and qualifying parties.

22.3.1.7.5 Members' Services, Catering, Print Services

Catering Facilities has responsibility for hospitality services encompassing a table-service restaurant, self-service restaurant, bar, and coffee dock. The hospitality services also cater for functions and meetings.

The **One Stop Shop** is an information service for all members relating to salary and allowances. The office processes and administers members' salaries and allowances. It also assists members in accessing any other Oireachtas office service.

The **Print Facility** undertakes printing work for members of both Houses and qualifying parties. Members are entitled to use the facility *solely* in connection with their parliamentary duties. In addition, the Service may submit work to the Print Facility when the Print Facility has a reduced workload.

22.3.1.7.6 Superintendent's Section

The Superintendent's Section:

- manages protocol and security, including Garda vetting;
- manages the electronic pass card system;
- manages visitor access to the Houses;
- works with the Facilities Management Unit to protect the safety and health of all those who work in and visit Leinster House;
- provides operational support and security for sittings of the Houses and their committees and high-level parliamentary meetings; and
- offers public tours of the complex.

22.3.1.8 *Office of Parliamentary Legal Advisers*

The Office of Parliamentary Legal Advisers is the Oireachtas' in-house legal team, which offers a range of independent legal services.

The **Parliamentary Legal Advisory Unit** provides legal advice and services to members, officeholders, committees, and the Commission. In addition, it can assist members and committees to test government policy. It is also responsible for managing litigation.

The **Corporate Legal Advisory Unit** provides legal advice to the Service in relation to corporate matters.

The **Private Members' Bills Legal Advisory Unit** provides legal advice in relation to PMBs. Separately, if requested, legal advice may be provided to committees conducting pre-Committee Stage scrutiny of PMBs.

The **Private Members' Bills Drafting Service** drafts PMBs, can assist in the preparation of explanatory memoranda for PMBs and prepares Committee and Report Stage amendments for PMBs drafted by the Drafting Service.

22.3.2 Main Emphasis of Administrative Input among Tasks Such As

22.3.2.1 Support for Committees and/or Plenary Debates

The primary units providing support to committees include the Committee Secretariat, Bills Office, Debates Office, Broadcasting Unit, Press Office, Library and Research Service, and the Office of Parliamentary Legal Advisers. The primary units providing support to plenary debates include the Office of the Clerk of Dáil Éireann, the Seanad Office, Houses Services (comprising the Journal Office, Bills Office, and the Questions Office), Debates Office, Rannóg an Aistriúcháin, Facilities Management Unit, and Superintendent's Section.

22.3.2.2 Budgetary Issues

Regarding the national budget, the Parliamentary Budget Office provides evidence-based research and analysis to support the consideration by the Houses of the Government's annual Budget, including publishing analysis on the main Budget-related documents throughout the year. In addition, it supports the Committee on Budgetary Oversight in its scrutiny of budgetary-related matters and many individual Dáil committees in their scrutiny of the annual Estimates (i.e., government spending proposals).

Regarding the Oireachtas budget, the Finance Unit prepares the annual estimates and annual accounts of the Commission. The Office of the Commission and Secretary General provides secretariat administration services to the Commission and its Finance Committee, including in relation to the preparation of the Commission's budget.

22.3.2.3 Legislative Drafting

The Office of Parliamentary Legal Advisers provides advisory and legislative drafting services to members seeking to introduce PMBs to the Houses. In addition, the Office of Parliamentary Legal Advisers may commission policy research from the Library and Research Service on behalf of members in relation to PMBs.[5]

Before a bill can be initiated, the Bills Office will examine it to assess whether it complies with the Constitution and the Standing Orders of the House and will advise the Chair accordingly. The bill cannot proceed if it is ruled out of order.

Most government bills undergo scrutiny prior to publication (known as "pre-legislative scrutiny"). PMBs undergo scrutiny after second reading and prior to being considered in committee, unless a waiver is granted in respect of scrutiny for the particular bill; this scrutiny on PMBs is known as pre-Committee Stage scrutiny. Various units, including the Committee Secretariat, Office of Parliamentary Legal Advisers and Library and Research Service, support the committees in conducting this scrutiny process.

Various units support the committees when they conduct an ex-post impact assessment of a bill that has been enacted. This occurs where a committee decides to examine a post-enactment report that has been submitted pursuant to Standing Order 197 of the Dáil Standing Orders (which requires such a report to be laid 12 months following enactment).

22.3.2.4 Participative Instruments

Various units support the committee on Public Petitions, which receives and processes public petitions on matters of general public concern or interest. Other committees regularly invite public submissions as part of their examination of a particular issue.

22.4 Managing Inter-Institutional and External Relations

22.4.1 Relations with (and Degree of Autonomy from) the Executive

The Commission is independent in the performance of its functions. It receives its three-yearly budget on a legislative basis, directly from the Central Fund, and is not subject to Executive approval in the way in which government departments are.

22.4.2 Involvement of Parliamentary Staff in the Institution's External Relations

22.4.2.1 Inter-Institutional Relations

The Service is involved with a range of other institutions in relation to policy, procedural, advisory, and research matters. These include, for example, the British-Irish Parliamentary Reporting Association, the Hansard Association of Canada, the Commonwealth Hansard Editors Association, the Intersteno Parliamentary Reporters Section, clerking networks, the Conference of Inter-Parliamentary Lawyers of the UK and Ireland, and the Science Foundation of Ireland.

22.4.2.2 Parliamentary Diplomacy and Inter-Parliamentary Cooperation

The Service facilitates the parliament in its work with other parliamentary assemblies within Europe and beyond.

For example, there is significant engagement between Oireachtas committees and committees of other national parliaments. The Committee Secretariat provides administrative support for these inter-parliamentary activities and to Oireachtas delegations to the North/South Inter-Parliamentary Association, which is co-chaired by An Ceann Comhairle and the Speaker of the Northern Ireland Assembly, and the British-Irish Parliamentary Assembly.

(Inter-Parliamentary Relations and Travel Unit: see above at Section 22.3.1.)

22.4.2.2.1 European Union Affairs

In addition to bilateral engagement, Oireachtas committees participate fully in all inter-parliamentary conferences in which the European Parliament and national parliaments of the Member States of the European Union also participate. The Secretariat to each committee provides the necessary supports for this activity.

Regarding the EU Scrutiny process, Oireachtas committees are charged, in the first instance, with the scrutiny of all draft legislative acts and engagement with Ministers in relation to meetings of the relevant Council of Ministers of the European Union. An EU Co-ordination Unit within the Committee Secretariat together with the Oireachtas National Parliament Office in Brussels supports committees in this work.

The Service also participates in the activities of the European Centre for Parliamentary Research and Documentation (ECPRD).

(Oireachtas National Parliament Office: see above at Section 22.3.1.)

22.5 Managing Current Challenges

22.5.1 Digitalization

In 2016, the Service commenced a major strategic programme of Digital Transformation. The aim of the Strategy is to create an open and accessible parliament for all, transformed by intuitive, collaborative, and integrated digital solutions. The Digital Transformation comprises 7 programmes with over 100 projects up to 2027 which will enable the adoption of a digital culture across all areas of the Oireachtas, fundamentally changing how the Oireachtas operates and delivers value to members, staff, and citizens.

The Digital Transformation introduces modern technology to support members and staff with enhanced collaboration tools to improve communications and ways of working.

The Digital Parliament Programme under the Strategy will deliver an integrated Dáil Business System which will be completed by 2023. A Members Portal application also provides a range of online resources for members.

Further enhancements with regard to digitalization successfully supported the move to remote working during the Covid-19 pandemic and, thereafter, enabled a smooth transition to a blended working environment.

22.5.2 Transparency and Citizen Engagement

Having an "Open Parliament" that strengthens its engagement with the people is a key priority of the Commission. For example, the Oireachtas promotes citizen engagement through a variety of means.

22.5.2.1 Social Media and Broadcasting

The Oireachtas continues to achieve greater engagement year-on-year through the use of social media, with official accounts on Facebook, Twitter, Instagram, and LinkedIn.

The Oireachtas Broadcast Unit (OBU) produces the television channel "Oireachtas TV" which is available across all major platform providers. Oireachtas TV provides a curated feed of the live proceedings of the day across the Dáil, Seanad, and committees. It also produces a range of ancillary programming, across a variety of subjects and themes.

The OBU also participates in the Broadcasting Authority of Ireland Sound and Vision Scheme which allows it to work with the independent sector to produce documentaries around the themes of the parliamentary system and democratic participation.

22.5.2.2 Press Office

(Press Office: see above at Section 22.3.1.)

22.5.2.3 Oireachtas.ie Website

In recent years, the Oireachtas website has been extensively redesigned to facilitate greater engagement, access to parliamentary information, transparency, and openness in relation to the business of the Houses. It received over 2.3 million visits in 2019.

Research briefings by the Library and Research Service and Parliamentary Budget Office are published on the website.

22.5.2.4 Tours and Events

Visitors to the Oireachtas can avail of a guided tour of Leinster House. In 2019, the Ushers conducted 2,789 tours for 41,610 visitors.

The Oireachtas also holds multiple official events including visits by delegations from other parliaments and political leaders from around the world.

22.5.2.5 Education Programmes

In 2018, the Oireachtas became the first parliament to establish a programme for people with intellectual disabilities – the Oireachtas Work Learning (OWL) programme.

The Oireachtas makes educational materials available on its website. The Oireachtas also provides students and teachers of the Leaving Certificate subject, Politics and Society, with teaching material and lesson plans facilitated by the Parliamentary Education Officer in the Communications Unit.

The Service facilitates the Oireachtas Student Placement Programme for third-level students. This provides students with an opportunity to learn and apply that learning while working directly with members on projects/work relevant to their studies. The student receives accreditation for the completion of the placement towards their final assessment in their course of study.

22.5.2.6 Annual Report

Pursuant to section 6 of the Commission Acts, the Commission is required to publish an annual report, which is laid before both Houses and is also published on the Oireachtas website. The annual report sets out information on the work carried out by the Commission and the Service in supporting the Houses and members, as well as accounting for the expenditure of public funds in the running of the Houses for that particular year.

22.5.2.7 Accounts

The Commission's annual accounts are audited by the Comptroller and Auditor General and published in the Commission's annual report. The Commission is accountable to the Committee of Public Accounts of Dáil Éireann for the findings of the public audit.

22.5.2.8 Collaboration with Library and Research Service

The Library and Research Service invites academic researchers to collaborate with the parliamentary research service.

22.5.3 Changing Work Patterns due to the Covid-19 Pandemic

At various points, during the Covid-19 pandemic, both Houses sat with reduced attendance and in an external venue to facilitate social distancing. Most staff, apart from those required onsite to facilitate parliamentary sittings, worked remotely. A Covid-19 Compliance Team ensured compliance with public health guidance.

In 2021, the Government published a National Remote Work Strategy which seeks to have 20 per cent of public sector employees working from home or remotely. The Service published its own Blended Working Policy in 2022, enabling blended onsite and remote working.

Notes

1. "Lower house" is Dáil Éireann.
2. "Upper house" is Seanad Éireann.
3. "Body corporate" is an entity that is legally authorized to act as a single individual and has legal rights and duties (Oxford English Dictionary 2021).
4. This Strategic Committee is responsible for a five-year plan to address arrears in the publication of official translations of Acts into the Irish language through measures to improve capacity in the Translation Unit.
5. Government bills are drafted by the Office of the Attorney General.

23
ITALY'S PARLIAMENTARY ADMINISTRATION

Luigi Gianniti and Nicola Lupo

23.1 Introduction

The Italian Parliament is characterized by a perfectly symmetrical structure, with the two Houses – the Chamber of Deputies and the Senate of the Republic (from now on referred to as the Chamber and the Senate, respectively) – both directly elected by the citizens[1] and exercising exactly the same powers, in terms of lawmaking as well as of their relationship with the Executive. As Italy is a parliamentary form of government, this means that the Executive needs the confidence of both Houses (Article 94 of the 1947 Constitution).

A strong sphere of autonomy is granted to each of the Houses. This is provided directly by Article 64 of the 1947 Constitution, which requires the adoption, by an absolute majority of the members, of the parliamentary rules of procedure. However, the autonomy ensured by this constitutional provision has been interpreted more widely, even extending to the internal organization of each House, in its administrative, financial and even judicial dimensions (the latter with the so-called *autodichia*, or self-justice). This broad interpretation was first adopted by each of the two Houses, in continuation of the pre-republican experience, and has subsequently been confirmed by the Constitutional Court (starting from the judgement no. 129/1981, up to the judgement no. 262/2017).[2]

Consistently with these principles, two autonomous bureaucratic bodies, completely independent not only from the executive's bureaucracy but also from one another (with the exception of some limited, although recently increased, forms of cooperation), currently serve the two Houses (D'Orta and Garella, 1997; Griglio and Lupo, 2021). This is also why, in analysing the features of the Italian parliamentary administration, this chapter considers the administrations of the Senate and of the Chamber distinctively, although several common trends and initiatives are pointed out, wherever they exist, and a recently attempted unification process was launched in 2017, without being implemented so far.

23.2 The Dimensions of the Two Distinct Parliamentary Administrations

Each House is assisted by its own administration. In the pre-republican period, the reciprocal independence of each House was based on the clear asymmetry of the bicameral system, with differences arising with respect both to the legitimation (only the Chamber was elected) and to the powers (the Senate's vote could not determine a crisis of the Government) of the two Houses (Soddu, 1992). Since the election of the first Italian Republican Parliament, in 1948, and the introduction of a symmetrical bicameralism, a new political and institutional arrangement has shaped the role of the two Houses. During this period, the strengthening of the two independent parliamentary administrations has contributed to defining the respective positions and autonomy of the two Houses, based on the impartiality of the role of the two Speakers, from the Executive as well as from each other.

In response also to pressures from the political system, the size of the two parliamentary administrations increased steadily in the 1970s and in the 1980s, when the Chamber – whose Speakers, between 1976 and 1994, have been members of the main opposition party – could count, at the end of the XX century, on slightly less than 2,000 staff members (and a little more than 1,000 in the Senate). In the last two decades, both Houses have experienced a remarkable reduction of their staff, which has substantially been halved, due to a suspension of employee turnover and a stalemate in the recruitment procedures.

Senate staff now amount to 585 employees, just over half the number of employees who were in service as of 1 January 2006 (1,074): 88 senior officials, 29 stenographers, 104 documentalists, 204 secretaries and 160 assistants. In parallel, in the Chamber, between 2005 and 2019, there has been a reduction of 44%, from 1,856 to 1,042 employees: 125 advisers (among whom 10 are former stenographers), 159 documentalists, 266 secretaries and 445 assistants.

These numbers include all the permanent and independent staff normally recruited by public competition and hired directly and permanently by the administration. They do not include either the staff enlisted by parliamentary groups (which, in the meantime, have increased in number, so as to compensate for the weakening of proper party structures, following the almost complete cessation of public funding for the functioning of political parties), or the staff hired by single MPs (who are still regulated rather informally, through funds directly assigned to each MP, although some rules have been set, starting from 2022) (Caroli Casavola, 2014).

The halving of this dimension of both parliamentary administrations may be contextualized by reference to the more general process of reduction of public expenditure and progressive limitation of State administrative costs, but it is also the result of two other additional factors. First, it represents a reaction to the increased criticisms aimed at politics and politicians, which has been accused, especially since the 2008 economic crisis, of being a closed and privileged "cast" ("*la casta*"), to which the parliamentary administration has often (although inappropriately) been assimilated. Second, it accompanied the process of empowerment of the executive that, after 1993, followed the Italian political system's turn towards majoritarianism, under the (flawed) assumption that a majoritarian system requires a weaker and less autonomous Parliament.

23.3 The Internal Organization of the Two Parliamentary Administrations

The internal administrative organization of the Senate and of the Chamber is regulated by the "major" rules of procedure of each House, approved through a plenary vote by an absolute majority of its members, pursuant to Article 64 of the Constitution. These rules of procedures are complemented by other, hierarchically subordinate, internal rules adopted by the Bureau: this is a body chaired by the Speaker, composed of four deputy speakers, three quaestors, and at least eight secretaries, usually representing all the parliamentary groups.

In each House, the Bureau, the College of Quaestors and the Speaker are tasked with a number of regulatory, policy-setting and oversight functions concerning the structure and the management of the administration, including the appointment of directive positions.

The two parliamentary administrations advise and provide support services to parliamentary activities, ensuring technical, legal, procedural, documentary and administrative assistance with regard to the institutional functions of each House. Support services to legislative and oversight functions are still the core activity of both parliamentary administrations.

Parliamentary administrations perform their own tasks according to the principles of autonomy and fairness. They are not politicized by nature. Both of them are organized into Departments and Offices and headed by a Secretary General: a figure first appointed in the Chamber of the Kingdom of Italy in 1907 (Camillo Montalcini, under the Speaker Giuseppe Marcora) and then replicated, after the fall of fascism, in both Houses. In this way, the role of the parliamentary administration was able to emerge more clearly, during a phase in which the dimension of the State bureaucracy developed rather steadily under the direction of Giovanni Giolitti, and in which Italy's transformation from a liberal State into a welfare State took place. At the same time, the new figure of the Secretary General symbolized the unity and the impartiality of the parliamentary administration (Pacelli and Giovannetti, 2020, 113 ff.), two features which are still relevant today: the Secretary General directs its administration and is accountable for it before the Speaker (Articles 67 and 166 of the rules of procedure of the Chamber and of the Senate, respectively). The Secretary General is appointed by the relevant Bureau, on the proposal of the Speaker and among senior officials of each House.

Several Deputy Secretaries General, whose tasks are delegated by the Secretary General, coordinate vast operational areas, encompassing a number of Offices/Departments. For example, all Departments directly related to the parliamentary activity – which includes functions exercised by the Assembly and the standing Committees – make up an integrated operational area headed by a Deputy Secretary General. Moreover, some Offices/Departments – which are slightly different in each House – report directly to the Secretary General: this is the case for the General Affairs Office, the Legal Affairs/Counsel Office, the Press Office, the Information Technology Office, and the Office for the assessment of administrative action.

Bicameral Committees, including many Inquiry Committees,[3] are not assisted by a joint department either. The two Houses have separate departments for these joint bodies, and the choice of the department advising each bicameral committee follows the appointment of the Chair, who is either a Member of the Senate or a Member of the Chamber. The Chair also determines the rules of procedure applicable to the committee's work, either those of the Chamber, when the chair is a deputy, or those of the Senate, when the chair is a senator (critically, Gianniti, 2007, p. 77 f.).

From a broader perspective, this overview confirms that one of the most symmetrical bicameral systems has given rise to two distinct parliamentary administrations driven by independent and often competitive behaviours (Regonini, 2012, pp. 45 f.). These factors are partly the cause and partly the effect of the dominant interpretation of the Constitution, according to which each House was created as a distinct and autonomous constitutional body (Mazziotti di Celso, 1981, p. 762 f.). The opposite "unitarian" reading, which views the Italian Parliament as a single constitutional body, although with a complex structure (Manzella, 1977, p. 65; Id. 2003, p. 111), has not prevailed, at least with respect to the institutional side of the parliamentary dynamics (Lupo, 2021, p. 20 f.).

Over the last two decades, also in reaction to the financial crisis and to the uprising of anti-political movements, the two parliamentary administrations have gradually overcome their strict unicameral perspectives, engaging in several forms of bicameral administrative cooperation (Zampetti in VV.AA., 2013, pp. 24 ff.) and even pre-designing a process of unification between the staff of the two Houses. This evolution, which was foreseen by a transitional provision embedded in the constitutional reform of bicameralism attempted by the Renzi government but rejected by a referendum on 4 December 2016 (Lupo, 2015 and 2019), has not (yet) been fully accomplished and the unification process for the staff of the two Houses has, for the moment, been suspended (Griglio and Lupo, 2021).

23.4 Budgetary Autonomy and Recruitment Procedures

Like the other constitutional bodies – that is, the President of the Republic and the Constitutional Court – the Chamber and the Senate enjoy financial and accounting autonomy: each year they draw up and approve their own budget plan and balance sheet, establishing how the financial resources reserved in the State budget by means of a yearly budgetary commitment for each of the two Houses are going to be used.

As established by the rules of procedure of both Houses, these documents need to be debated and voted in the plenary after being drafted by the Quaestors and approved by the Bureau. The budgetary documents and the verbatim reports of the related plenary sittings are published in full in the parliamentary records and they often represent a useful moment of self-analysis regarding the main transformations taking place as to the role of each House and its administration.

In each House, the provisions governing the budget and the checks on the expenditure are outlined in special internal rules approved by the Bureau. Specifically, issues concerning financial, accounting and asset management as well as contractual matters are governed by the "Administration and accounting regulation", which includes rules regulating the appropriate planning, execution and supervision of works contracted by both the Houses.

As anticipated, recruitment of parliamentary staff takes place exclusively on the basis of public competition, organized independently by each House, although following a common and rather traditional structure. The types of examinations and the qualifications required for admission vary according to the careers of the staff. Even "vertical" progression from one career to another can only take place through public selection open to all.

The economic and legal status of the staff of the two parliamentary administrations is thus completely distinct from that of the Executive's administration. In order to protect the Houses' autonomy, controversies regarding staff's recruitment, careers and salaries are excluded from the review of the judiciary and are instead determined autonomously by each House, which has given rise to the creation of some *ad hoc* quasi-judicial bodies (so-called bodies of *autodichia*), of first and second instance, mainly composed of MPs, but anyway rather independent, pursuant to the requirements of the Constitutional Court (judgement no. 154/1985), and of the European Court of Human Rights (Savino case, 2009).[4]

23.5 The Assembly's and the Standing Committees' Support Structures

In both the Senate and the Chamber, the Assembly Department, performing functions related to the Plenary, is clearly distinguished from the Standing Committees Department.

The former, divided into several offices, provides assistance during the sittings of the plenary, registers the bills submitted and, on behalf of the Speaker, assigns them to the competent Committee, publishes non-legislative acts such as questions, interpellations and motions, and collects and maintains the precedents on the rules of procedure (in the Chamber, this last function is actually performed by the Office for the rules of procedure, directly headed by the Secretary General: see above, par. 2). The Assembly Department also supports the formation of the parliamentary agenda, decided either by the Conference of the Presidents of parliamentary groups or, in the event of lack of consensus within this Conference, by the Speaker (alone in the Chamber, upon possible amendments voted by the plenary, in the Senate).

The Standing Committee Department includes, in each House, the secretariats of all the Standing Committees (14 at the Chamber, 10 at the Senate): one secretariat for each Standing Committee, whose jurisdiction covers one or more subject matters (with some differences between the two Houses). Each standing committee, pursuant Article 72 of the Constitution, is allowed to approve legislative bills, substituting the plenary, although in practice this role has declined in the last three decades (Fasone, 2012). In each Committee, the secretariat is in charge of organizing, convening, supporting and reporting on the proceedings related to the law-making process as well as to the oversight function.

During plenary and committee sittings, the Secretary General and the relevant committee secretariat provide assistance to the Speaker and to the Committee Chair, respectively. The Assembly Department and Committees Secretariats, in their areas of competence: (a) take care of preparatory work for sittings, including keeping in touch with competent Government departments; (b) examine and report on the admissibility of the amendments, resolutions and other proposals, publish and hand them out; (c) guarantee the regularity of the procedure and of the voting results; (d) draw up the minutes of public sittings; (e) take note of Members due to speak and of leaves of absence and (f) draft verbatim and summary reports (for plenary sittings, this function is performed by the Department for parliamentary reports).

23.6 Parliamentary Documentation and the Role of Research Departments

In addition to the Departments supporting the functioning of the Assembly and of the Standing Committees, both Houses are endowed with several specialized units, whose main aim is to provide MPs with the documentation required to do their job.

The oldest units are the two Parliamentary Libraries: originally aimed at providing documentation to MPs,[5] they are currently open also to the general public. They also organize conferences, exhibitions and book discussions and publish proceedings of conferences and seminars promoted by the Senate and by the Chamber. The two libraries, although still managed by two distinct directors, have experienced the most intense form of joint bicameral administration in Italy: together, the Chamber's and the Senate's Libraries form the Joint Parliamentary Library. The Library of the Chamber is also involved in issuing documentation about comparative law, which has traditionally been in high demand from the lawmakers, who are always eager to know how the same problem has been addressed elsewhere (Lupo and Rizzoni, 2014, p. 131 ff.).

Connected to the Libraries, although enjoying an even larger autonomy from politics, are the two historical archives that collect and retain historical documents owned by the two Houses. They are also involved in publishing volumes containing historical sources and collections of parliamentary speeches.

The bulk of parliamentary documentation – now publicly available online – is currently prepared by the Research Departments of the Chamber and of the Senate. This represents another example of bicameral cooperation between corresponding administrative units, which has led the two Research Departments to jointly issue all the ordinary documentation: the report ("dossier") that accompanies and explains the contents of every legislative bill examined in Parliament is jointly drafted by the Departments of the two Houses. Further forms of collaboration on other topics or documents are becoming more frequent, as well as research cooperation with a few, highly qualified, national research structures, such as the Research Department of the Constitutional Court, the Italian National Institute for Statistics (ISTAT) and the National Research Centre (CNR).

Some attention should also be devoted to the historical evolution of the Research Departments, which have the delicate task of publishing high level studies about each ongoing proposal without expressing opinions that could interfere with political decisions. Important steps in the development of the Research Departments were made in the 1970s in the Chamber, and around two decades later in the Senate. In the Chamber, this step coincided, not by chance, with the new practice of electing members of the main opposition party as Speaker.[6] The aim was to set up a rather small, but qualified and comprehensive, unit – mirroring the system of standing committees, both of which offer an encyclopaedic approach to parliamentary business (Rizzoni, 2021) – capable of offering all MPs, and in particular members of the opposition, autonomous information, independent from the information channel under the Executive domain (Cheli, 1987; Simoncini, 1987; De Caro, 1991; Chimenti, 1994). In the Senate, two decades later, after the approval of a mainly majoritarian electoral law, a less ambitious aim was pursued: namely, to seek to counterbalance the increase in staff directly hired by MPs, strengthening standing committees' ability to verify the reliability of the information submitted by the Executive, consistently with the 1988 reform of parliamentary rules of procedure and the 1996 presidential directives requiring some kind of pre-legislative scrutiny and evidence-seeking within standing committees (Zuddas, 2004; Piccirilli and Zuddas, 2012).

The reference model for these administrative reforms derived, to a large extent, from experiences of presidential forms of government. In fact, especially during the 1980s, the US Congress was intensively studied by Italian scholars and parliamentary staff, focusing, among other issues, on the role of standing committees, on budgetary procedures and on parliamentary oversight of security services (Lupo and Rizzoni, 2014; Griglio, 2020). The US Congress was also viewed as a model at the level of parliamentary administration: the Congressional Research Service, the Congressional Budget Office and also the Office of Technology Assessment (later removed in 1994) were studied and often proposed as reference models, despite these experiences being hardly applicable to the Italian context and indeed being rather distant from the features of a parliamentary form of government.

This apparent contradiction can instead be explained perfectly well in light of the peculiarities of the Italian political system. In the 1960s and 1970s, Parliament was the engine of most of the legislation, while the Government, generally acting through short mandates and being internally extremely fragmented, played a rather subordinate role in the legislative process. For a Parliament that carries out its often autonomous role in the legislative process and which manages to emphasize to the maximum degree its own institutional alterity with respect to the Government, the need is broadly felt for strong autonomous documentation facilities (as are undoubtedly those of the US Congress), by contrast with the Government's offerings, which are capable of guaranteeing adequate fact-finding support to all MPs. These resources are obviously particularly useful for those parties which, finding themselves in the opposition or providing external support to the Government (Cotta and Verzichelli, 2007,

42 ff.), cannot take advantage of ministerial bureaucracies, but need sources of alternative and reliable knowledge.

Within the Research Department of the Chamber, an office called Observatory on legislation monitors the implementation of the legislative acts and publishes annual reports on the legislation, as well as produces documentation for the Committee on legislation ("Comitato per la legislazione"), a body equally composed of deputies from the majority and from the opposition, which is called upon to express its views on the quality of legislative text. A similar organ has been established in the Senate in 2022, when the rules of procedure have been amended.

In the Senate, there is an office called the "Observatory on the implementation of legislation", which periodically publishes reports on the status of implementation of legislative acts through secondary legislation.[7]

More specialized documentation is issued by the two Departments for State Budget, which are responsible for the technical assessment of the budgetary impact of bills, amendments and other legislative texts. These were established in 1988, soon after a reform of State budget legislation through which Parliament was called upon to play an active role in the process of keeping the expenditures under control and reducing public debt (Palanza, 1998). In 2012, the constitutional law no. 1/2012 amended the Constitution to introduce the principle of budget balance and, in compliance with what was required by EU law, established the Italian Fiscal Council. Also in this case, the fascination with the US model prevailed, and this Council, called the "Parliamentary Budget Office" ("Ufficio Parlamentare di bilancio-UPB"), was situated within the Parliament, although provided with a high degree of independence and assisted by its own specialized administrative structure, completely independent from the two parliamentary administrations. The Parliamentary Budget Office was designed according to a rather peculiar model: its links with the Houses derive uniquely from the procedure for appointment of their members, in which the two Speakers play a crucial role. For the rest, it acts independently, verifying the economic forecasts issued by the Government (Fasone and Griglio, 2013; Gianniti and Goretti, 2013; Vernata, 2020).

Within the two parliamentary administrations, two operational Departments are concerned with legislative drafting. In the Senate, this structure is more properly named the "Department for the quality of regulatory documents" ("Servizio per la qualità degli atti normativi"). They are tasked with receiving and publishing bills after proof-reading draft laws approved by either the Assembly or the Committees, in compliance with the specific guidelines on legislative drafting (Petta, 1994). In the Senate, this Department also collects and monitors impact assessment reports issued by the Government and by independent authorities.

23.7 The Relational Dimension: Inter-Institutional Relations and Inter-Parliamentary Cooperation

Besides their relations with the national Government on legislative, oversight and budgetary issues illustrated above, both Houses maintain relationships with Regional and Local entities. At the core of these relations is the Parliamentary Regional Affairs Committee, a bicameral committee, set up by the Constitution (Article 126), comprising 20 senators and 20 deputies. According to the constitutional law no. 3/2001 (Article 11), the Regional Affairs Committee should include, in addition, representatives of Regions and Local Authorities on the basis of the Rules of Procedure of both Houses. However, the implementation of this constitutional provision, which would have implied some kind of integrated activity between the national and regional parliamentary administrations, has not yet taken place, after 20 years (Bifulco, 2017). In the meantime, pending such integration, a form of cooperation with the Conference of Presidents of the regional legislative assemblies of the Regions and Autonomous Provinces, the Conference of Regions of the National Association of Italian Municipalities (ANCI) and the Union of the Provinces (UPI), has been established, pursuant to the internal rules of procedure of the Regional Affairs Committees, implementing a legislative provision.[8]

Over the last three decades, especially since the end of the Cold War, so-called Parliamentary diplomacy has considerably intensified (De Caro and Lupo, 2009). All the political bodies of both Houses take part in international and supranational activities: including the two Speakers and their respective Bureau, Parliamentary Committees and their Chairpersons, Delegations to International Assemblies and Parliamentary Cooperation Committees with foreign Parliaments set up under the terms of protocols of cooperation.

Administrative cooperation with the Parliaments of new and emerging democracies pursues the dual purpose of fostering exchanges with such assemblies and of helping them to strengthen their representative bodies. Sometimes, this cooperation takes place exclusively at an administrative level, and sometimes mainly at the political level, in any case generally by reference to a specific geographical area or within forms of multilateral organizations (Inter-parliamentary Union, NATO, OECD).

As far as multilateral cooperation is concerned, both Houses play an active role in raising a "parliamentary" awareness regarding any intergovernmental relation involving Italy. The main area of multilateral cooperation is the Euro-Mediterranean one, the core of which is the Euro-Mediterranean Parliamentary Assembly and the Parliamentary Assembly of the Mediterranean (PAMO), a parliamentary body within the Interparliamentary Union. Both Houses also cooperate with the countries of the Eastern Partnership, as well as with various African, Asian and Latin American countries.

The Italian Parliament has the following five delegations: to the Parliamentary Assembly of the Council of Europe, comprising 18 members and 18 substitutes; the NATO Parliamentary Assembly, comprising 18 members; the Parliamentary Assembly of the Organization for Security and Cooperation in Europe (OSCE), comprising 13 members; the Parliamentary Assembly of the Central European Initiative (CEI), comprising 7 members; and the Euro-Mediterranean Parliamentary Assembly, comprising 3 members. All these parliamentary delegations are necessarily composed of both senators and deputies and assisted by the staff of the two Houses, embedded in their International Relations Departments. They provide assistance to the delegations of their own House, to international Assemblies and to delegations on missions abroad. They also prepare documentation on the organization and activities of international institutions. Also in this case, the criterion used by the Chamber's and Senate's administration to support delegations is based on the Presidency of the delegation.

The action of the Italian Parliament in relation to the activities of the European Union has developed in different ways, both at the political and the administrative level, in each of the two Houses.

Even the procedures for taking part to the Early Warning System are different: more blurred with respect to the scrutiny of the substance of EU acts in the Senate, and more autonomous and exclusively in the hands of the standing committee for EU Affairs in the Chamber (Lupo, 2017), although the difference has diminished since the 2017 reform of the Senate's rules of procedure. In the exercise of this role, both Houses can consult the Regional Assemblies. Some joint activities take place, such as hearings of the Minister for EU Affairs or other Ministers. The communications that the President of the Council of Ministers regularly carries out before European Council meetings are normally organized separately in the Chamber's and Senate's Plenaries, one after the other.

In each House, the EU Affairs Committees are assisted by an Office for EU Affairs, and their documentation tends to be produced jointly by the two Offices.

Both Houses have always played an active part in interparliamentary cooperation with the EU, mainly in the form of participation in meetings of representatives of all EU parliaments (national parliaments and the European Parliament) on themes of mutual interest. The strategic choices in this activity are sometimes mutually agreed, thanks also to the support and documentation that the above-mentioned administrative structures develop in relation to the interparliamentary conferences organized within the EU: the Conference of Parliamentary Committees for Union Affairs of Parliaments of the European Union (COSAC), the Inter-Parliamentary Conference for the Common Foreign and Security Policy and the Common Security and Defence Policy, the Inter-Parliamentary Conference on Stability, Economic Coordination and Governance in the European Union, the Joint Parliamentary Scrutiny Group on Europol, the Inter-Parliamentary Committee Meeting for the Joint Evaluation of the Activities of Eurojust and other interparliamentary meetings organized by the Parliament of the Member State holding the rotating Presidency of the Council of the EU and the European Parliament.

23.8 The Challenges Ahead: The Reduction of Deputies and Senators After Constitutional Law No. 1/2020 and the Increased Digitalization

After the rejection, by the 2016 referendum, of the constitutional amendment aimed at reforming symmetrical bicameralism, a new constitutional amendment has been approved by Parliament and then confirmed by a referendum held in September 2020: with the beginning of the 19th legislative term (October 2022), the Senate is composed of 200 elected senators (instead of 315), plus life senators, and the Chamber of 400 deputies (instead of 630). As far as the Chamber's rules of procedure are concerned, this has taken the form of a mere voting thresholds update, while at the Senate the rules of procedure have been changed in a more comprehensive manner. The new MPs are called upon to represent wider territories and possibly to be members of more than one standing committee and will probably require a stronger parliamentary administration.

The effects of the Covid-19 pandemic similarly called for a renewal of the parliamentary organization and of its administration, dramatically accelerating its digitalization. Both Houses, without modifying their rules of procedure, allowed participation from remote uniquely for the committees' sittings without votes and denied any form of remote or proxy voting. In any case, a "window of opportunity" for the innovation of the primary features of the Italian Parliament seems to be opening, to find a better means of functioning as a symmetrical bicameralism. The outcome of this challenge will probably prove decisive, also in the perspective of promoting or preventing further attempts of constitutional reform of the Italian Parliament.

Italy's Parliamentary Administration

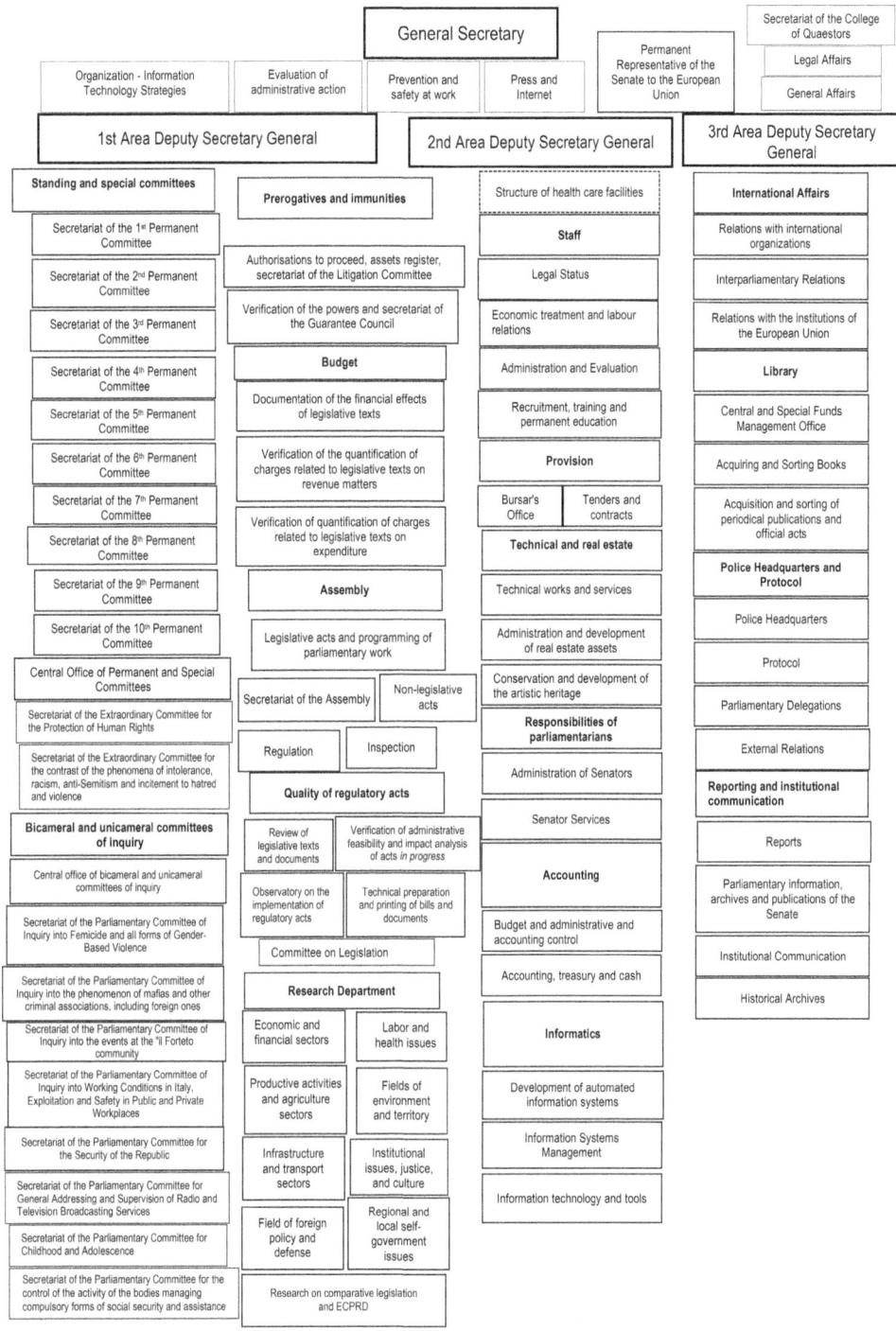

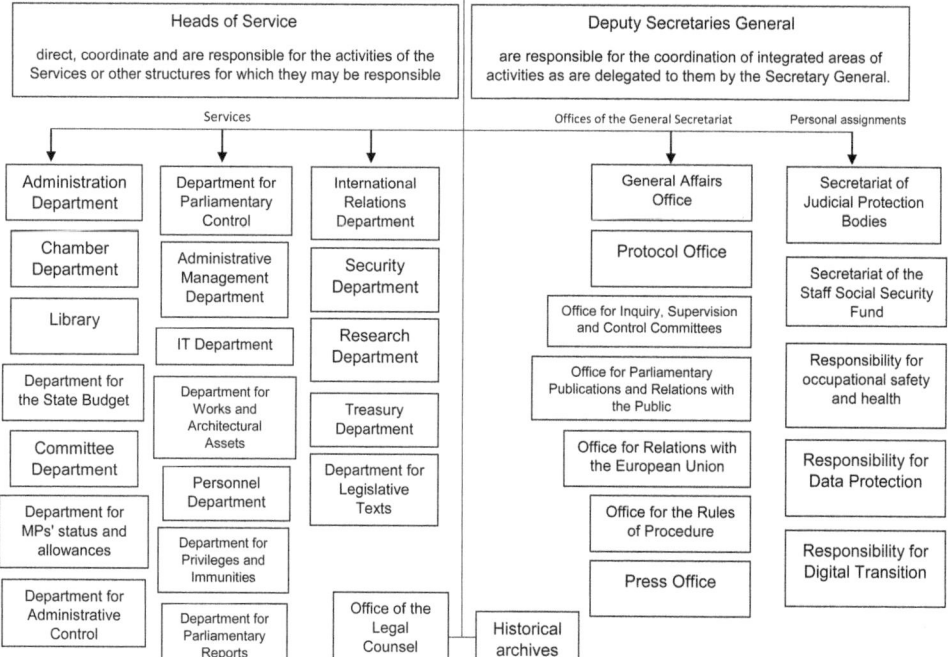

Organigram of the Italian Chamber of Deputies

Notes

1. With the only exception of a limited number of life senators, namely: all the former Presidents of the Republic and up to five senators appointed by the President of the Republic.
2. As the judgement no. 262/2017 concisely states, the "Rule-making autonomy logically carries over to organizational aspects, including matters related to the functioning of the administrative bureaucracies, which allow the constitutional bodies to carry out their constitutional functions freely and in an efficient way". Moreover, "This same foundation supports the authority of constitutional bodies to adopt labor rules for their employment relationship with their staff members. Indeed, good exercise of the high constitutional functions granted to the constitutional bodies in question depends to a crucial degree on how their personnel is selected, regulated, organized, and managed".
3. For instance, in April 2021, there were 14, excluding those not exclusively comprising MPs, which were normally hosted by the Executive (which is responsible for their secretariat).
4. On the Savino judgement (28 April 2009), in which the European Court of Human Rights condemned Italy only for the lack of independence and impartiality of the Judicial Section of the Bureau of the Chamber, while for the rest recognized the lawfulness of the rules of procedure on the *autodichia* system, and on the consequent amendments to the parliamentary rules of procedure, see, among others, Lo Calzo, 2018 and Castelli, 2020.
5. For the history of the Library of the Chamber, see Venturini (2019).
6. These were all members of the Italian Communist Party. The first was Pietro Ingrao, elected in 1976. Then came Nilde Iotti, elected for the first time in 1979, and then re-elected in 1983 and in 1988. In 1992, Giorgio Napolitano, member of Democratic Party of the Left, was elected, and was succeeded by Oscar Luigi Scalfaro when he was elected as President of the Republic. Since 1994, following the entry into force of a mainly majoritarian electoral system, the two Speakers have again been elected from amongst the members of the majority. See Lupo (2010).
7. In the Senate, there is another office, called the Impact Assessment Office ("Ufficio Valutazione Impatto-UVI"), presided over directly by the Speaker, which is responsible for verifying the administrative feasibility and analyzing the impact of legislative acts under consideration and already in force. The latter, established in 2017, issued some interesting reports (either on methodology or on single policies), before being "suspended" in 2018, at the beginning of the new legislative term (Griglio and Lupo, 2020).
8. Article 5-bis decree law no. 91/2017, as converted by law no. 123/2017. See also the Senate's rules of procedure approved in 2022 (Article 138-bis).

References

Bifulco, R. 2017. 'La lunga attesa dell'integrazione della commissione parlamentare per le questioni regionali', in F. Bassanini, A. Manzella (eds), *Due Camere, un Parlamento. Per far funzionare il bicameralismo*, Firenze: Passigli, pp. 137–149.

Caroli Casavola, H. (ed) 2014. *I collaboratori dei parlamentari. Il personale addetto alla politica*, Napoli: Editoriale Scientifica.

Cheli, E. 1987. 'Ruolo del Parlamento e nuovi caratteri della burocrazia parlamentare', in VV.AA. (ed), *Studi in memoria di Vittorio Bachelet*, Milano: Giuffrè, pp. 187–204.

Chimenti, C., 1994. 'Ruolo delle Camere e amministrazioni parlamentari', in *Lo stato delle istituzioni italiane: problemi e prospettive*, Milano: Giuffrè, pp. 236 *et seq*.

Cotta, M. and Verzichelli, L. 2007, *Political institutions in Italy*, Oxford: Oxford University Press.

De Caro, M. 1991. 'L'evoluzione degli apparati nel sistema della documentazione nel Parlamento italiano: l'esperienza del Servizio Studi', in *Associazione per gli studi e le ricerche parlamentari, Quaderno No. 1. Seminari 1989-1900*, Milano: Giuffrè, pp. 173 *et seq*.

De Caro, M. and Lupo, N. (eds), 2009. *Il dialogo tra i Parlamenti. Obiettivi e risultati*, Roma: Luiss University Press.

D'Orta, C. and Garella, F. (eds). 1997. *Le amministrazioni degli organi costituzionali: ordinamento italiano e profili comparati*, Roma-Bari: Laterza.

Fasone, C. 2009. 'L'autodichia delle Camere dopo il caso Savino. Una condanna (lieve) da parte della Corte di Strasburgo', in *Diritto pubblico comparato ed europeo*, Vol. 11, No. 3, pp. 1074–1089.

Fasone, C. 2012. *Sistemi di commissioni parlamentari e forme di governo*, Padova: Cedam.
Fasone, C. and Griglio, E. 2013. 'Can Fiscal Councils enhance the role of National Parliaments in the European Union? A comparative analysis', in B. De Witte, A. Héritier, A.H. Trechsel (eds), *The Euro Crisis and the state of European Democracy*, Fiesole: European University Institute e-book.
Gianniti, L. 2007. 'Per un ragionevole bicameralismo paritario', in A. Manzella, F. Bassanini (eds), *Per far funzionare il Parlamento. Quarantaquattro modeste proposte*, Bologna: Il Mulino.
Gianniti, L. and Goretti, C. 2013. 'Prime note sull'Ufficio parlamentare di bilancio', in *Rivista giuridica del Mezzogiorno*, Vol. 1–2, pp. 81–90.
Griglio, E. 2020. *Parliamentary oversight of the executives. Tools and procedures in Europe*, Oxford: Hart.
Griglio, E. and Lupo, N., 2020. 'Parliaments in Europe Engaging in Post-legislative Scrutiny: Comparing the French, Italian and Swiss Experiences', in *Journal of Southeast Asian Human Rights*, Vol. 4, No. 1, pp. 100–127.
Griglio, E. and Lupo, N., 2021. 'Parliamentary Administrations in the Bicameral Systems of Europe: Joint or Divided?', in *The Journal of Legislative Studies*, Vol. 27, No. 4, pp. 513–534.
Lupo, N. 2010. 'Presidente di Assemblea', in *Digesto delle Discipline Pubblicistiche. Aggiornamento*. Vol. IV, Torino: Utet Giuridica, pp. 444–480.
Lupo, N. 2012. 'Il ruolo delle burocrazie parlamentari alla luce dei mutamenti dell'assetto istituzionale nazionale e sovranazionale', *Rassegna parlamentare*, Vol. 54, No. 1, pp. 51–89.
Lupo, N. and Rizzoni, G., 2014. 'Foreign influences on (the procedure and on the content of) the Italian legislative process', in N. Lupo, L. Scaffardi (eds), *Comparative law in legislative drafting. the increasing importance of dialogue amongst parliaments*, The Hague: Eleven International Publishing, pp. 121–138.
Lupo, N. 2015. 'Prospettive di unificazione degli apparati di Camera e Senato: una mossa "difensiva", ma "opportuna"', in M. Bertolissi (ed), *Riforme. Opinioni a confronto*, Padova: Cedam, pp. 103–118.
Lupo, N. 2017. 'The Scrutiny of the principle of subsidiarity in the procedures and reasoned opinions of the Italian chamber and senate', in A. Jonsson Cornell, M. Goldoni (eds), *National and Regional Parliaments in the EU-Legislative Procedure Post-Lisbon. The Impact of the Early Warning Mechanism*, Oxford: Hart, pp. 225–252.
Lupo, N. 2019. 'The failed constitutional reform of the Italian Senate'. In *DPCE Online*, n. 2, pp. 1595–1608. Available at: <http://www.dpceonline.it/index.php/dpceonline/article/view/747>.
Lupo, N. 2021. 'L'evoluzione dei regolamenti delle Camere in relazione alle trasformazioni del sistema politico ed elettorale', in V. Lippolis (ed.), *Il Filangieri. Quaderno 2021. A cinquant'anni dai regolamenti parlamentari del 1971: trasformazioni e prospettive*, Napoli: Jovene, pp. 11–42.
Manzella, A. 1977. *Il parlamento*, I ed., Bologna: Il mulino.
Manzella, A. 2003. *Il parlamento*, III ed., Bologna: Il mulino.
Mazziotti di Celso, M. 1981. 'Parlamento', in *Enciclopedia del diritto*, XXXI, Milano: Giuffrè.
Pacelli, M. and Giovannetti, G. 2020. *Interno Montecitorio. I luoghi, l'istituzione, le persone*, Torino: Giappichelli.
Palanza, A., 1998. 'L'informazione tecnica nelle procedure parlamentari: l'esperienza dei Servizi del bilancio della Camera e del Senato', *Rivista trimestrale di diritto pubblico*, Vol. 48, pp. 753 *et seq*.
Pegan, A. and Högenauer, A.L. 2016. 'The role of parliamentary administrations in interparliamentary cooperation', in N. Lupo, C. Fasone (eds), *Interparliamentary cooperation in the composite European Constitution*, Oxford: Hart, pp. 147–166.
Petta, P. 1994. 'Le prime esperienze del servizio "drafting" del Senato', in *Rassegna Parlamentare*, Vol. 36, pp. 79 *et seq*.
Piccirilli, G. and Zuddas, P. 2012. 'Assisting Italian MPs in Pre-legislative Scrutiny: The Role Played by Chambers' Counsellors and Legislative Advisors in Enhancing the Knowledge and Skills Development of Italian MPs: The Assistance Offered to an Autonomous Collection of Information', in *Parliamentary Affairs*, Vol. 65, pp. 1–16.
Regonini, G. 2012. 'Parlamenti analitici', *Rivista Italiana di Politiche Pubbliche*, Vol. 1, 33–87.
Rizzoni, G. 2021. 'Parliamentarism and encyclopaedism: how Parliaments produce and elaborate knowledge, *Luiss School of Government Working Paper Series*, no. 65.
Simoncini, A. 1987. 'L'apparato conoscitivo del Parlamento italiano', *Rassegna parlamentare*, Vol. 29, pp. 166 *et seq*.
Soddu, F. 1992. *L'amministrazione interna del Senato regio. I. Dallo Statuto albertino alla crisi di fine secolo*, Sassari: Dessì.

VV.AA. 2013. *Il ruolo degli apparati serventi delle assemblee legislative tra tradizione e linee di sviluppo: atti del convegno, Palermo 20 gennaio 2012*, Napoli: Jovene.

Venturini, F. 2019. *Libri, lettori e bibliotecari a Montecitorio. Storia della Biblioteca della Camera dei deputati*, Padova: Cedam.

Vernata, A. 2020. *L'Ufficio parlamentare di bilancio. Il nuovo organo ausiliare alla prova del primo mandato e della forma di governo*, Napoli: Jovene.

Zuddas, P., 2004. *Amministrazioni parlamentari e procedimento legislativo. Il contributo degli apparati serventi delle Camere al miglioramento della qualità della legislazione*, Milano: Giuffrè.

24
LATVIA'S PARLIAMENTARY ADMINISTRATION

Daunis Auers and Visvaldis Valtenbergs

24.1 Introduction

Latvia's 100-member parliament – the *Saeima* (which means gathering or assembly in Latvian) – celebrated its centenary in 2022. It is Latvia's third legislative institution, following an unelected People's Council that was established in November 1918 and wrote the law on elections to the Constitutional Assembly, Latvia's first elected legislative body which functioned from 1920 to 1922 and drafted Latvia's Constitution (*Satversme*). There were four *Saeima* elections in the inter-war period before Latvia belatedly followed its neighbours and slipped into authoritarianism following a self-coup by Prime Minister Kārlis Ulmanis in 1934. The *Saeima* was suspended. Latvia experienced three occupations during the Second World War and was eventually absorbed into the Soviet Union for a near half-century. Latvia regained sovereign independence in 1991 and held elections to a reestablished *Saeima* in 1993. As a result, the *Saeima* has actually only functioned for 41 of these last 100 years.

The October 2022 *Saeima* elections were the tenth national legislative elections since 1993. The last three decades have seen a steady growth in the *Saeima's* budget as well as its administrative and analytical capacity. The Speaker of the parliament is the head of the *Saeima* Presidium which determines the internal rules and work procedures of the *Saeima*. The key administrative body of the legislature is the *Saeima* Administration (known as the *Saeima* Chancellery until 2015) which is headed by a Secretary-General.

This chapter studies the work of the *Saeima* Administration. The first section considers the functions, structure, personnel, and external relations the *Saeima* Administration in the parliament. The second part analyses the knowledge and legislative drafting services. The third and final part considers recent developments in openness and digitalization. The conclusion reflects on the development of the *Saeima* over the last three decades, identifying both strengths and weaknesses.

24.2 Functions, Structure, and Foreign Relations

The role and key functions of the *Saeima* Administration are laid out in the Rules of Procedure of the *Saeima* and more specifically in the by-law on the *Saeima* Administration.[1] The *Saeima* Administration's main task is to support the work of the legislature so that it can exercise the powers specified in the Constitution, the *Saeima* Rules of Procedure and other relevant legislation. The Latvian legislature has five main functions: (1) the adoption of laws and legislative amendments; (2) parliamentary scrutiny; (3) adopting the state budget; (4) appointing and approving public officials; and (5) developing foreign policy.

The 2015 amendments to the Rules of Procedure state that the *Saeima* Administration is managed by a Secretary-General appointed by, and subordinate to, the *Saeima* Presidium. The Secretary-General manages parliament personnel, supervises parliamentary financial and other resources, monitors strategic planning, represents parliament in international meetings, and manages relations with other national parliaments. The Secretary-General is responsible for administrative management of the parliament and has no term limit. Since the Secretary-General is not recruited from the political sphere, the position is considered generally independent from political interests (although the first Secretary-General was a former politician).

The political leadership of the *Saeima*, which is made up of both government and opposition party members, is located in the Presidium, which is composed of five members of parliament (MPs) holding the offices of Speaker, (two) Deputy Speakers, the Secretary, and the Deputy Secretary. The Presidium is elected in the first session of the parliament following an election and usually sits for a full four-year term. The Presidium appoints and dismisses heads of the organizational units of the *Saeima* Administration. Parliament officials are not considered to be a part of the civil service and the parliament administration is autonomous in the criteria and procedures for selecting its staff, typically using open competition recruitment procedures.

The *Saeima* Administration has five main structural units (see Figure 24.1): (1) Information and Communication Technology; (2) Executive (with responsibility for finances and infrastructure); (3) Legal; (4) Protocol; and (5) Security. Figure 24.2 tracks employment trends in the *Saeima* from 2006 to 2020. In 2020, the *Saeima* employed 544 individuals (including 100 parliamentary assistants but not including parliamentary deputies). Despite a steep climb in comparison to the previous year, this still remained less than the number of staff prior to 2009. The big fall in *Saeima* employees at that time is explained by the economic crisis of 2008–2010, which saw a severe contraction of Latvia's economy and accompanying austerity measures that cut the number of public jobs by one-third and average public sector salaries were cut by a quarter. In 2020, 86% of *Saeima* employees had a higher education, 8% a high-school education, and 6% a vocational education (Saeima, 2021). Since 2015, *Saeima* employees go through an annual performance review process that also identifies personal and professional development needs. A total of 255 employees raised their qualifications through professional courses in the year 2020.

A similar trend can be seen in the *Saeima's* budget for the 2006–2020 period (see Figure 24.3). A rapid increase between 2006 and 2008 is followed by a rapid fall in the size of the budget (indeed, the 2009 budget was cut by 3 million EUR from the originally agreed figure of 22.1 million EUR). However, since 2015, every year but one has seen the *Saeima* have a budget larger than the previous peak year of 2008.

Support for MPs, parliamentary groups, and committees is not within the direct remit of the *Saeima* Administration (see Figure 24.1). Members of the *Saeima* each have one paid assistant, although this salary (which is around 1,000 EUR, gross, a month) can be split between up to two assistants (as a result, parliamentary assistants tend to be party members, rather young, and often early career professionals, or students. In 2020, just three quarters of assistants (76%) had a higher education).[2] Each parliamentary group (known in Latvia as a "fraction") also has a technical assistant, a senior consultant, and a small number of

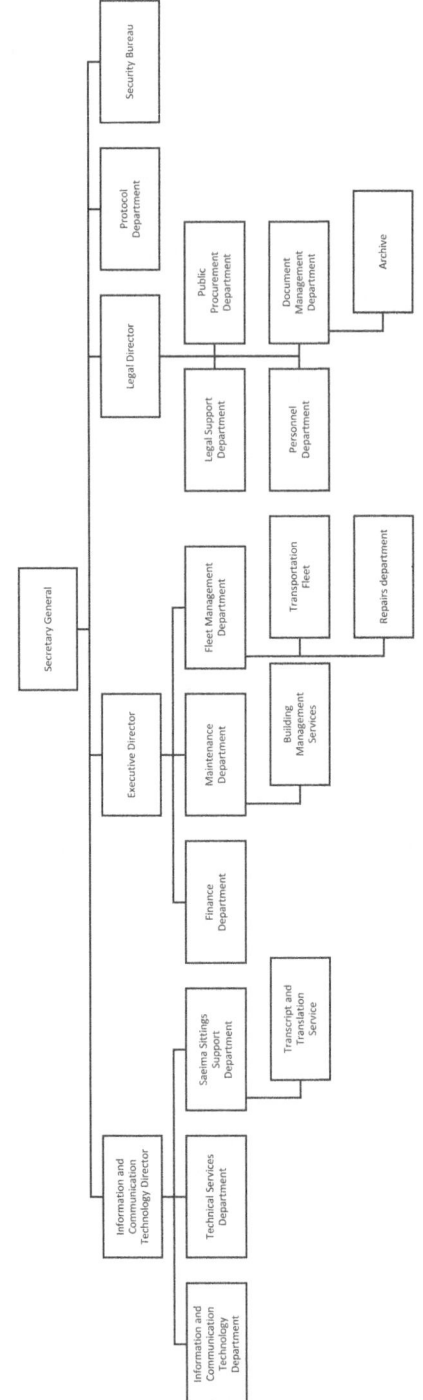

Source: Saeima 2022. https://www.saeima.lv/img/Saeimas_struktura_organizatoriska_struktura_2013_ENG.pdf

Figure 24.1 Structure of the *Saeima* Administration

Latvia's Parliamentary Administration

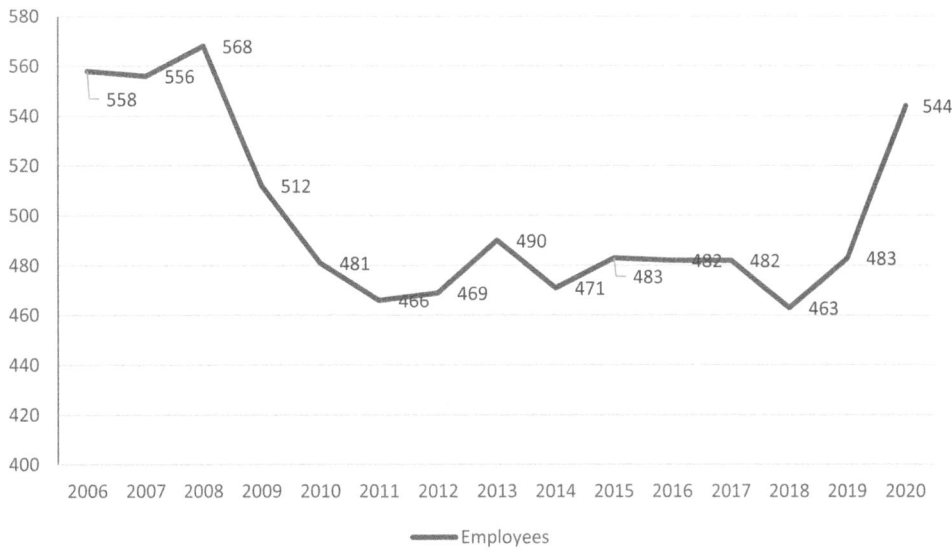

Figure 24.2 Saeima Administration employees 2006–2020

other consultants dependent on the number of seats the fraction won in the previous *Saeima* election. Each of the 15 standing committees in parliament has a limited number of consultants who are responsible for both organizing and scheduling the work of the committees as well as providing some expert advice. The chairs of the committees also have small annual budgets of just a few thousand euros that can be spent on external advice or research. Summing all this up, MPs have little autonomous expert capacity and are rather

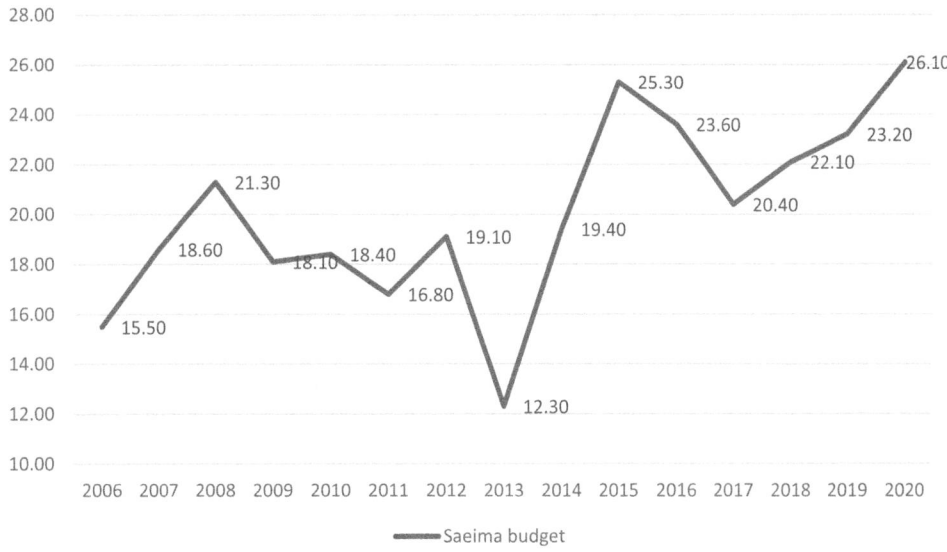

Figure 24.3 Annual *Saeima* budget 2006–2020 (millions, EUR)

dependent on services provided by the *Saeima* Administration (the analytical and legal services are discussed in greater detail in part two below). The *Saeima* has no register of outside member interests, although MPs do have to submit a detailed annual financial declaration of income and liabilities.

24.3 Analytical and Legal Support

Until 2017, the Latvian parliament was one of the few parliaments in Europe which lacked a research unit to provide MPs with research and evaluation support. The gap was partially filled by outsourced service providers, MP assistants, or advisers commissioned by parliamentary commissions or groups. *Ad hoc* evaluations (or rather investigations) were carried out by special commissions established for investigation of specific cases or accidents (Veitners, 2020). After lengthy discussions in 2017, the Analytical Service was finally established. Its objectives are to provide descriptive and analytical research to improve the quality of draft laws to be reviewed by the *Saeima*, to assess the effectiveness of the laws adopted by the *Saeima*, and to provide support to the legislator in the decision-making process. As of January 2021, the Analytical Service consisted of four full time researchers, a director, and library staff that provided library and reference services. Two researchers held doctoral degrees in political science, one in environmental science, one is a candidate for a doctoral degree in business management.

In terms of administrative hierarchy, the Analytical Service is controlled by the Presidium. Analytical Service reports are conditional to the prior approval of the Presidium and are sent to the primary commissioner of the study only after the Presidium has approved it. This built-in dependency on the Presidium, rather than parliament administration, can potentially limit the Analytical Service's autonomy from potential political influence (Veitners, 2020). Being potentially aware of this risk, the Service places political neutrality, evidence, and a fact-based approach as their principal work values (Saeima, 2018).

The Analytical Service delivers original studies (comparative research, *ex-ante*, and *ex-post* evaluations) as well as compact synthesis reports for MPs on specific issues of legislation or policy, annotations of draft laws. The reports are published digitally on the subsection of the parliamentary website[3] and are disseminated in printed form to individual MPs or parliamentary committees. The number of undertaken studies is linked to current capacity of the Analytical Service and rose to eight studies in 2020. In 2021, the Analytical Service delivered five studies (see Table 24.1).

The work of the Analytical Service is organized on an on-demand basis. At the beginning of each year, the Service usually circulates an invitation to submit research topics. Research topics can be submitted by Presidium and the Council of Parliamentary Factions, committees,

Table 24.1 Number of studies carried out by the Analytical Service 2017–2022

	2017	2018	2019	2020	2021	2022
Total number of studies	1	3	6	8	5	10
Original studies	1	3	4	2	2	6
Compact reports	0	0	3	7	3	4

Source: Saeima. Latvijas Republikas Saeimas Analītiskā dienesta pētījumi un apskati. Available: https://www.saeima.lv/lv/par-saeimu/publikacijas-un-statistika

chairs of at least two factions or their deputies that are signed by at least 20 MPs. The themes then undergo capacity assessment by the Service during which they are ranked according to its research capacity. The Analytical Service may consult with theme applicants to clarify certain aspects and limitations of research. The Presidium approves the final research plan. After the research has been completed, it is returned to the Presidium. Once it grants the permission to release the research, it is presented in the committees and published online.

Parliamentary research is usually composed of compact reviews of existing research and secondary data directly related to research questions, reviews of the known impacts of different policy instruments in selected countries are usually provided. One to two page short summaries of key findings and one to two infographics are provided in reports to draw the attention of MPs to the main conclusions of the reports. Unlike the Legal Bureau of the *Saeima*, which provides legal advice to the parliamentary committees and MPs, the Analytical Service does not develop proposals or draft laws nor does it provide legal advice. It is also not involved in writing speeches, letters, presentations, translations of texts or defending political positions. However, it has become customary to develop policy scenarios instead of recommendations. For example, the Report about Inclusive Education for the Children with Special needs, published in 2020, highlights the advantages and shortcomings of fully inclusive, segregated, and combined policy scenarios.[4] A report on the use of research based evidence in policy making in the Latvian parliament found that the interactions between MPs and researchers tend to be situational depending on political needs, the availability of relevant research findings, and *ad hoc* activity of particular individuals (Kalniņš, 2019). A PowerPoint presentation is the main vehicle for conveying research findings. On some occasions, parliamentary researchers have also spoken to the media but are limited to only commenting on their research findings.

Research and regulatory impact assessment (RIA) are increasingly used as sources of reference explaining the reasoning, meaning, and justification of legal acts and policies.[5] The Analytical Service faces increasing demand from parliamentarians and growing interest from various stakeholder groups. At the same time, the limited current capacity of the Service leaves the *Saeima* in an inferior position to the executive in terms of institutional analytical capacity. Although the Analytical Service has not yet fully engaged in systematic RIA of concrete policy initiatives from the government, its analytical reports are sometimes debated at parliamentary committees and working groups. One such example, where the report of the Analytical Service aided the discussion on a policy topic in a Committee's working group, was the development of draft legislation on lobbying during 2019–2021.[6] In addition, the Legal Bureau and Legal Committee do carry out RIAs of laws initiated by the government, but there is still a long way to go to match the executive in terms of legal and policy expertise.

24.4 Openness and Digitalization

The main source for obtaining information on parliamentary work is the website of the *Saeima* which mainly informs society on parliamentary activities, without offering direct citizens' involvement in legislation, such as commenting on draft laws or sending messages direct to politicians. Civil society organizations have argued that the website of the Parliament is rather complicated to navigate for the average person (Valtenbergs, Čaplinska, 2021). *Saeima* social media profiles are hosted on *Facebook, Flickr, YouTube, Twitter,* and *Instagram* and mostly consist of one-way communication content with the aim of raising awareness of parliament and its legislative work, making announcements and promoting the activities of the parliament.

The Parliament does not take any special approach to target specific segments of population other than the press. The *Saeima* website hosts a few easy-to-read infographics about the inner workings of the parliament and changes in important legislative acts which are quite popular. For example, the infographics about changes to the administrative penalty law and *Covid-19* restrictions were among the most downloaded in 2020 (Saeima, 2021).

The website allows the public to access agendas and other documents for committee meetings, plenary sessions, and Presidium decisions. However, civil society representatives argue that this information is not always easily accessible to those with limited knowledge of parliamentary decision-making processes. The transparency of the parliamentary law-making process still has to be improved (Valtenbergs, Čaplinska, 2021). In terms of the provision of electronic information, civil society experts complained about a lack of uniform approach among parliamentary committees in providing their meeting agendas and information materials (Valtenbergs, Čaplinska, 2021). Although parliamentary committees regularly consult with civil society organizations and interest groups, there is no e-consultation system in the Latvian parliament. Face to face consultations are mainly carried out in parliamentary committees who decide who will be invited and what methods for submitting comments and questions will be allowed. Under the Covid-19 social distancing restrictions, virtual meeting platforms, such as *Zoom* and *Webex* became part of the ordinary parliamentary working routine.

In response to unpredictable law-making processes, there have been some extra parliamentary efforts to facilitate access to the information and promote the targeted involvement of civil society organizations and interest groups in the parliamentary work. As part of their advocacy and interest representation efforts, the Civic Alliance – Latvia NGO compiles and sends information that was gathered manually by reviewing all official websites of the state and municipal institutions – the State Chancellery, the Cabinet of Ministers, Secretaries of State, the *Saeima,* Municipality of Riga, and the State Revenue Service – to its member organizations and social media followers. The information on upcoming events is disseminated on a weekly basis through a closed Facebook group, Twitter, and is published on the website of Civic Alliance – Latvia (Valtenbergs, Čaplinska, 2021). In late 2021, the Latvian Government launched a Joint Law portal facilitating citizen's access to documentation of the Cabinet of Ministers and Secretaries of State.[7] The portal allows public input to draft laws. It remains to be seen how e-consultations actually take off and what would be the future role of the portal in parliamentary work.

Internally, the Parliament uses the Electronic Document Information System (ELDIS), which ensures the reception, verification, processing, and sending of electronically signed documents. ELDIS also serves as an online channel between the *Saeima* and The Cabinet of Ministers. *HCL Notes* tool is used to provide e-mail and document management services. A single e-mail address is used to receive e-mail in the Parliament. In addition, correspondence can be sent via Latvia's main e-government hub Latvija.lv. According to the Annual Report of the Parliament, 16,800 documents addressed to the *Saeima,* its units and MPs were received at the official e-mail address of the *Saeima* and from *Latvija.lv* in 2020. Roughly, half were received electronically. About half of those in turn were signed with a secure electronic signature (4,033 documents) and the number of electronically signed documents is growing every year (Saeima, 2021).

Latvia is among the countries where at least 10,000 citizens can present collective legislative initiatives directly to parliament. The process is regulated by the Rules of the Procedure of *Saeima* (Saeima, 1994a). The Rules do not specify the form (digital or paper) or e-platform from which initiatives can be submitted, potentially opening multiple opportunities for different platforms (Saeima, 1994a). The niche is currently filled by one e-participation platform – *MyVoice* (*Manabalss.lv*) which was established by the Civic Participation Foundation NGO founded in 2011, the same year when the right to directly petition the parliament was introduced. The platform operates independently from the parliament and is neither financed nor administered by the parliament or the government. Since 2011, the citizen initiatives coming through the platform have changed several laws and even led to one constitutional amendment. By the end of 2021, 50 citizen initiatives have been submitted to the Parliament and 27 of them have been adopted by the *Saeima*.[8] The constitutional amendment concerned using open voting for the election of the state president in parliament. Other notable policy successes have been the introduction of a bottle deposit system, the right to use public transportation lanes for motorcycles, the provision of state support for the treatment of lung cancer, hepatitis C and melanoma, automatic reimbursement of over-paid income tax, reduced VAT rate for certain fruits and vegetables, and many others. Although the policy record of *MyVoice* seems impressive, the MPs are under no legal obligation to change the legislation in response of citizen legislative initiatives. In fact, several popular citizen initiatives challenging the course of action of the governing coalition have not led to any changes or parliamentary action.[9]

Initiatives have occasionally been stuck in the *Saeima*. At the end of 2020, there were 29 initiatives (dating back from 2015) awaiting action by the *Saeima*. According to interviews with MPs, key factors in determining the policy outcome of citizen initiatives are fiscal considerations, the political position of the ruling coalition as well as party orientation, and coalition agreements (Kozins, 2021). After an initiative has gathered at least 10,000 signatures, it is submitted to the Mandate, Ethics and Submissions Commission (MESC) of the Parliament, which is obliged to review it within one month. MESC then invites the authors to a public hearing. Though *MyVoice* staff is also present at the hearing, they abstain from taking any position regarding the initiative. In this phase, the authors of the initiative can bring their own selected experts to the MESC meeting. As a general rule, MESC transfers the initiative to the relevant Commission of the Parliament or to the relevant Ministry with a request to provide an opinion. The initiative is never rejected by MESC. MESC maintains a public website on the portal of the Parliament with a list of citizen initiatives. The website lists the name of the initiative, the date in which the initiative was received by the Parliament, a short summary of the initiative, and key milestones in the advancement of the initiatives.

The popularity of collective initiatives in Latvia may be partly attributed to the relatively low threshold of 10,000 signatures which is much lower than the required number of signatures for citizen-initiated draft laws (which is one tenth of the electorate or about 150,000 citizens in 2021). The threshold for citizen-initiated laws has been criticized as too high and a popular initiative to lower the bar to 50,000 citizen signatures was launched in January of 2022 by the campaign site *referendums.info*[10] (Central Electoral Commission (CEC), 24.01.2022).

The Latvian parliament was one of the first parliaments in the world to be ready to work remotely during the Covid-19 crisis. Thanks to the new *e-Saeima* tool, parliamentary sittings could be held remotely. The first sitting of the remote parliament, using the *e-Saeima* tool, took place on 26 May 2020 at which MPs debated a substantial draft law on administrative-territorial reform. The e-Saeima tool was developed in an emergency mode in just a few weeks, in response to the restrictions on assembly caused by *Covid-19* (Saeima, 2020).

The *e-Saeima* tool provides the most important functions of the parliamentary sitting – an opportunity for deputies to both debate and vote on the issues on the agenda of the *Saeima* sitting. MPs can connect to the *e-Saeima* environment on a special website using a secure authentication by electronic signatures. In the *e-Saeima* environment, participants can follow the agenda of the sitting, as well as the list of debaters on the current issue. Members of the sitting may apply to debate both the subject under consideration and subsequent items on the agenda. Voting in the electronic environment is provided by three "buttons" – "for", "against", and "abstain". Allowed voting time is 30 seconds, during which MPs can also change their choice. After the vote, the results appear on the screen according to the physical placement of the deputies in the *Saeima* Plenary Chamber. The course of the parliamentary sitting on the *e-Saeima* platform can also be followed by anyone online on the Saeima website.

Finally, the external relations of the *Saeima* are supported at a number of different levels. In 2019, the last full year before the Covid-19 pandemic, the Speaker of the *Saeima* went on nine official foreign visits and the parliament had delegations to nine different international organizations (including the Baltic Assembly, the NATO Parliamentary Assembly, and the European Council's Parliamentary Assembly). As of 2022, there were 51 bilateral cooperation deputy groups with other national legislatures (ranging from the US Congress to the Lebanese Parliament). In addition to its legislative and oversight duties, the *Saeima* Foreign Affairs Committee (FAC) is also responsible for maintaining relations with other FACs, particularly at the level of the Baltic States (B3), the Baltic States and Nordic countries (NB8), and the European Union. The European Affairs Committee (EAC) has been parliament's official representative on all EU issues, thus giving the Committee a broad mandate, since 2001. The EAC's key power is *ex-ante* oversight and approval of national negotiating positions before they are presented at the Council of the EU and the European Council. EAC decisions are binding on the cabinet. However, EAC Committee Chairs have complained about a lack of substantive expert analytical support to help committee members in the many different policy issues – from agriculture to research and innovation – that come up in the committee (Auers, 2020).

24.5 Conclusions

The Latvian *Saeima* has steadily modernized and enhanced its administrative capacity over the last three decades. The administration was initially headed by the *Saeima* Chancellery, but a major restructuring in 2015 saw the creation of a Secretary-General post (which was initially filled by Karīna Pētersone, a political heavyweight who had spent four years as a Minister of Culture) and the Chancellery reduced to a financial administration role. The Secretary-General has broader powers and control over five structural units (1) Information and Communication Technology; (2) Executive (with responsibility for finances and infrastructure); (3) Legal; (4) Protocol; and (5) Security. At the same time, however, the Presidium of the *Saeima* has maintained hiring and firing powers and, crucially, controls the agenda and output of the Analytical Service.

Indeed, analytical support remains the Achilles heel of the *Saeima*. MPs have only one assistant and the low salary dictates that the assistant will likely have little policy expertise. The Analytical Service was only created in 2017 and is critically understaffed when compared to the parliamentary services in Estonia and Lithuania (see relevant chapters in this volume). The already limited research output of the service is further limited by the significant role that the Presidium (a political rather than administrative institution) plays in planning the Analytical Services agenda.

The *Saeima* also has a mixed record when it comes to its digital services. There remain constraints to the extent to which the public can engage with MPs and parliament as a whole, with the *Saeima* web-page and social media being informative rather than functioning as a resource providing two-way communication. At the same time, however, the *MyVoice* collective initiative platform and the *e-Saeima* tool adopted during the Covid-19 pandemic have shown the *Saeima's* ability to absorb new technology and rapidly adapt to changes in the environment. This bodes well for what is likely to be an increasingly digital future for Europe's parliaments.

Notes

1. Rules of Procedure of the Saeima. https://likumi.lv/ta/en/en/id/57517 and the 2017 by-law on the *Saeima* Administration ("Par Saeimas Administrācijas nolikuma apstiprināšanu") which, rather curiously, is available to read in the parliament but is not publicly available on the Saeima's website.
2. *Saeima* Annual Review 2020, p. 43. Available at: https://www.saeima.lv/files/PP/Saeimasgadaparskats2020.pdf Accessed: 30.12.2021.
3. The reports of the Analytical Service are available at: https://www.saeima.lv/lv/par-saeimu/publikacijas-un-statistika
4. Beizītere, I., Grumolte-Lerhe, I., Ziemane, I., Valtenbergs, V. (2020). Iekļaujoša izglītība bērniem ar īpašām vajadzībām. Aprīlis. LR Saeimas Analītiskais dienests [In Latvian]. Available: https://www.saeima.lv/petijumi/Ieklaujosa_izglitiba_berniem_spec_vajadzibam_Latvija.pdf. Accessed: 30.12.2021.
5. At the executive level, regulatory impact assessment (RIA) in Latvia is regulated by the Instruction of the Cabinet of Ministers (Cabinet of Ministers, 2021). At the legislative level, RIA is regulated by Rules of the Procedure of Parliament (Saeima, 1994a,b).
6. Valtenbergs, V., Kalniņš, V., Grumolte-Lerhe, I., Beizītere, I. (2019). Lobēšanas normatīvais regulējums un tā problemātika Latvijā un Eiropā. Novembris [In Latvian]. Available: https://www.saeima.lv/petijumi/Lobesana_Latvija_un_Eiropa_2019.pdf. Accessed: 30.12.2021.
7. The Portal of Draft Legislation. https://tapportals.mk.gov.lv/legal_acts. Accessed: 04.02.2022.
8. Data based on annual reports of *MyVoice*. https://manabalss.lv/pages/paveiktais. Accessed: 03.02.2022.
9. As of February of 2022, there were several citizen initiatives backed over 20,000 signatures that had not lead to changes proposed by the public. These initiatives were "For the abolishment of the income tax for the sole property" (58,715), "The vaccination has still to remain voluntary" (55,836), "For legal recognition of all families" (23,278), "Allow children to breathe freely at school (against wearing masks in schools)" (29,607), "Abolish the existent model of road tax and implement it according to Estonian example" (25,128). Source: www.manabalss.lv. Accessed 03.02.2022.
10. https://www.referendums.info/. Accessed: 03.02.2022.

References

Auers, D. (2020). Europeanization of Latvia's political system. In D. Auers (ed.), *Europeanization. Latvia Human Development Report 2019/2020*. Riga: University of Latvia Press, pp. 17–25.

Beizītere, I., Grumolte-Lerhe, I., Ziemane, I., Valtenbergs, V. (2020). Iekļaujoša izglītība bērniem ar īpašām vajadzībām. Aprīlis. LR Saeimas Analītiskais dienests [In Latvian]. Available: https://www.saeima.lv/petijumi/Ieklaujosa_izglitiba_berniem_spec_vajadzibam_Latvija.pdf. Accessed: 30.12.2021.

Cabinet of Ministers. (2021). Cabinet of Ministers Instruction No 617 "Procedure for assessing the initial impact of a draft law", 7 September. Available: https://likumi.lv/ta/id/325945-tiesibu-akta-projekta-sakotnejas-ietekmes-izvertesanas-kartiba. Accessed: 20.01.2022.

Central Electoral Commission (CEC). (24.01.2022.). CVK reģistrē parakstu vākšanai grozījumus Satversmē, kas rosina samazināt nepieciešamo parakstu skaitu likumu un tautas nobalsošanas ierosināšanai. Available: https://www.cvk.lv/lv/jaunumi/cvk-registre-parakstu-vaksanai-grozijumus-satversme-kas-rosina-samazinat-nepieciesamo-parakstu-skaitu-likumu-un-tautas-nobalsosanas-ierosinasanai-921. Accessed 03.02.2022.

Kalniņš, V. (2019). *The Use of Research-Based Evidence in the Latvian Parliament. The Case of Demography and Migration policies*, Rīga: University of Latvia. https://www.izm.gov.lv/images/zinatne/SMP_study.PDF

Kozins, I. (2021). Sabiedrisko iniciatīvu portāla "Manabalss.lv" ietekme uz likumdošanas procesu Latvijā: likumdevēja perspektīva lēmumu pieņemšanā. Master's Thesis University of Latvia [In Latvian].

Saeima. (1994a). Saeimas kārtības rullis, pieņemts 28.07.1994. *Latvijas Vēstnesis*, Nr. 96 (227). Available: https://likumi.lv/ta/id/57517-saeimas-kartibas-rullis. Accessed: 03.02.2022.

Saeima. (1994b). Likums "Par tautas nobalsošanu un likumu ierosināšanu un Eiropas pilsoņu iniciatīvu", pieņemts 31.03.1994. *Latvijas Vēstnesis*, Nr. 47 (178), 20. apr.; 2012. gada 20. septembra redakcija. Available: https://likumi.lv/ta/id/58065-par-tautas-nobalsosanu-likumu-ierosinasanu-un-eiropas-pilsonu-iniciativu. Accessed: 03.02.2022.

Saeima. (2018). Saeimas Prezidija 2018. gada 15. oktobra lēmuma "Par analītiskā dienesta nolikuma apstiprināšanu" pielikums. 15. oktobris. Dok. Nr. 611-237-12/18 [In Latvian]. Available: https://titania.saeima.lv/ELDIS/webpublic.nsf/0/2E366FC67A2BD39AC22583240044464F. Accessed: 21.01.2022.

Saeima. (2020). Parlaments gatavs darbam e-Saeimas režīmā. 25 May. Available: https://www.saeima.lv/lv/aktualitates/saeimas-zinas/28981-parlaments-gatavs-darbam-e-saeimas-rezima. Accessed: 04.02.2022.

Saeima. (2021). 2020. gada publiskais pārskats. LR Saeima. Available: https://www.saeima.lv/files/PP/Saeimasgadaparskats2020.pdf. Accessed: 04.02.2022.

Saeima. (2022). Sabiedrības līdzdalība. Available: https://www.saeima.lv/lv/sabiedribas-lidzdaliba. Accessed: 04.02.2022.

Valtenbergs, V., Čaplinska, L. (2021). *Introducing Digital Advocacy Tool for Civil Society Organisations in Latvia: Pilot Study*. MyVoice Group. Available: https://manabalss.lv/system/cso-advocacy-tool-eng.pdf. Accessed: 04.02.2022.

Valtenbergs, V., Kalniņš, V., Grumolte-Lerhe, I., Beizītere, I. (2019). Lobēšanas normatīvais regulējums un tā problemātika Latvijā un Eiropā. Novembris [In Latvian]. Available: https://www.saeima.lv/petijumi/Lobesana_Latvija_un_Eiropa_2019.pdf. Accessed: 30.12.2021.

Veitners, K. (2020). Latvia. In R. Stockmann, W. Meyer, L. Taube (eds.), *The Institutionalisation of Evaluation in Europe*, Cham, Switzerland: Palgrave Macmillan, pp. 377–403.

25
LITHUANIA'S PARLIAMENTARY ADMINISTRATION

Modestas Gelbūda[1]

25.1 Introduction

The parliamentary tradition has a long history in Lithuania marked by notable achievements and interruptions associated with the loss of independence (Gumuliauskas et al., 2020; Jurgaitis, 2016). After the World War One, Lithuania restored Independence and, despite manifestation of authoritarian tendencies on the part of President, this enabled the country maintain parliamentary tradition until 1940 (Blažytė-Baužienė et al., 2009; Svarauskas, 2020). Since 1991, the Seimas has taken a path of becoming a truly European parliamentary institution. However, the imprinting effects of the Soviet past and half a century separation from the democratic developed world have left their marks.

Currently, the Seimas operates as a single-chamber legislature body with 141 members elected in a mixed electoral system; 70 members are elected in individual constituencies and the remaining 71 by way of the proportional electoral system. Since 1992, most of the governments were formed by coalitions of three to four political parties and, except the 1992 and 1996 elections, they enjoyed a slight majority over opposition parties.

Much like in some other European parliaments, the Seimas is in a somewhat weaker position relative to the government for several reasons. Firstly, in addition to retaining seats in the Parliament, political party leaders often take up government positions, which provide access to larger resources in terms of budget allocations and in-house technical expertise. Secondly, the government tends to expect from Parliament support to proposed draft bills rather than interference into the difficult job of executing the programme. Thirdly, MPs are overly sensitive to public pressure, especially media attention, when making decision and approving the budget for the parliamentary administration. In other words, the parliamentary administration has been slightly under-financed compared to the ministries.

25.2 The Seimas Administration (Which Is Called Chancellery (*kanceliarija*, in Lithuanian)

The scientific research on parliamentary administration in Lithuania is close to non-existent, although there are several books, edited volumes and scholarly journal *The Parliamentary Studies*. Thus, this chapter draws on various internal documents, interviews with current and former leaders of the organization and also on a direct experience and daily observations as a secretary general. Some of the interviewed employees have a long institutional memory as their experience covers all the period from the early 1990s, when Lithuania restored the Independence, until today. Thus, in many ways this chapter is, to some extent, prepared following the guidelines of single case methodology (Yin, 2018). The chapter has the following structure. First, it reviews the organization and resources of the administration. Second, it describes the way the administration supports the political work of MPs in standing committees, and third, it analyses how administration supports the parliament's international relations and the activities regarding the EU in particular. Finally, it concludes by discussing the challenges and opportunities facing the Seimas administration both short and long terms.

25.3 Human and Financial Resources of the Parliamentary Administration

Overall, the Seimas as a legal entity employs 1,086 people. These include 532 civil servants under political patronage, 413 employees of the parliamentary administration and 141 MP. Thus, the secretary general, or chancellor, has less than 50% of employees listed in the public register under his/her direct managerial control. Table 25.1 provides an overview of the employment structure.

Political groups and individual MPs are entitled to employ staff members of political (personal) confidence at their own discretion, that is, without following any formal competitive recruitment and selection procedures. Party groups receive one full time position for ten MPs.

Individual MPs usually have three full time positions at their disposal to employ advisors and assistants of political and personal confidence. Technically, altogether, 141 MP can employ 423 full time advisors and assistants of political confidence at any single point in time. However, as shown in Table 25.2, this number often exceeds 500 and fluctuates between 213 and 571. This is due to a fact that MPs often employ their politically selected advisors and assistants in part-time positions and on short-term basis. Such employment pattern leads to higher number of servants employed than there is a number of full time positions. Furthermore, some MPs practice mixed employment solutions, whereby the same person acts as an advisor and assistant of political confidence. Naturally, high turnover and a short-term employment have a negative impact on the quality of the service.

Table 25.1 Structure of employees

Date	Civil servants	Staff under employment contracts	Civil servants of political (personal) confidence	Members of the Seimas
31 December 2021	253	160	532	141

Source: The Seimas Chancellery HRM Office

Table 25.2 Employment dynamics at the parliamentary administration

Date	Civil servants and Staff under employment contracts	Civil servants of political (personal) confidence
31 December 2002	454	230
31 December 2003	468	222
31 December 2004	479	213
31 December 2005	487	236
31 December 2006	473	514
31 December 2007	477	542
31 December 2008	483	395
31 December 2009	472	514
31 December 2010	480	526
31 December 2011	479	527
31 December 2012	475	418
31 December 2013	491	563
31 December 2014	478	563
31 December 2015	466	571
31 December 2016	442	466
31 December 2017	424	521
31 December 2018	412	535
31 December 2019	414	527
31 December 2020	405	411
31 December 2021	413	532

Source: The Seimas Chancellery HRM Office

The financial resources available to the Seimas administration for performing its functions are slightly more modest than those available to the government and the ministries and are significantly less than those allocated for the example the parliamentary administrations of the Nordic countries. Nonetheless, since 2001 to 2021, the annual budget more than doubled. It is quite consistent trend that the payroll of all people employed in the administration, including MPs, consumes around 80% of the annual budget, leaving circa 20% for the investment and operational activities. Table 25.3 provides an overview of how the annual budgets have increased over time.

25.4 The Governance and Organization of the Parliamentary Administration

According to the Statute of the Seimas (2021), the administration is accountable to the Seimas board, which consists the speaker and seven deputy speakers, usually representing most, if not all, political parties. The board approves the organizational structure, sets the

Table 25.3 The annual budgets from 2001 to 2021

	2001	2005	2010	2015	2016	2017	2018	2019	2020	2021
Budget in EUR, millions	16.0	20.6	24.1	28.6	30.7	29.8	30.1	31.8	36.0	35.2

Source: Finance department

largest possible number of positions of civil servants and staff under employment contracts and approves the regulations and rules of the Seimas administration. The board submits the budget request of the parliamentary administration to the Ministry of Finance and provides informal support in negotiation process. However, the decision power with regard to allocating budgets to the parliamentary administration rests with the government.

The secretary general, who officially carries the title of chancellor, leads the administration. Seimas, in the plenary sittings, appoints the secretary general under nomination of the speaker. The chancellor is accountable to the Seimas and its board. However, in reality, the secretary general primarily works with the board and very seldom, if ever, the Seimas requests the secretary general to make reports or to answer questions during plenary sittings. The Seimas exercises its authority over the head of administration during weekly board meetings, where, in addition to regular business, the board members usually ask the secretary general questions. Moreover, the Seimas may exercise its authority over the head of administration in the form of meetings with political party groups, where issues related to different activities of the administration are debated. Currently, the secretary general does not have deputies. Historically, however, such a position existed and, given the complexity of the organization, it will be re-introduced in the near future.

The development of the parliamentary administration, including its organizational structure, has been influenced by four major factors. First, historically the administration has been strongly influenced by political leaders, who primarily influenced recruitment, performance evaluation and promotion decisions. From 1991 to 2000, the chancellor's role was mainly performed by MPs, who had a dual responsibility of being a member of the Seimas and a board member with special responsibilities of overseeing the parliamentary administration. Second, over the last 20 years, the majority of the chancellors have been appointed from within the public sector. Hence, with some notable exceptions, there was a tendency to reproduce the same patterns of thinking and acting prevailing in the public sector setting. Third, the chancellors' professional field of expertise had a clear influence on the organizational structure. As none of the chancellors had a strong exposure to the western management and education, they enacted their professional and cultural background into organization. Finally, chancellors enjoyed and practiced relatively tight control and centralized decision-making, while employee initiatives and suggestions were, at times, treated as exceeding their mandate especially, if they were coming from outsiders to the "inner circle" of the chancellor.

The administration employs over 400 people and yet does not have any vice-chancellor positions. One of the reasons behind this centralization was the intention to make the organizational structure flatter; the negative side is that chancellor becomes deeply engaged in hundreds of operational matters. Figure 25.1 provides an organizational structure.

The Seimas administration is highly hierarchical organization with the power mostly consolidated within the position of the secretary general. However, the hierarchical thinking and tight control logic is visible in a number of functional departments and independent units. Recently, with arrival of new secretary general, there have been several significant initiatives to delegate decision-making power and authority to sign certain documents to the lower levels of organizational hierarchy. Although managers at different levels are now more empowered, the culture of seeking informal approval of their own decision by the chancellor still exits for various reasons. In some cases, this is a clear manifestation of the old routine, while in other cases this has to do more with a lack of shared understanding between a new leader coming from the outside and the incumbent managers. The third reason for seeking informal approval is associated with "higher risk" decisions, especially, if they have a potential to draw media attention and eventually reflect on the reputation of the whole parliament, not just parliamentary administration, which does not have an independent identity within the society.

Lithuania's Parliamentary Administration

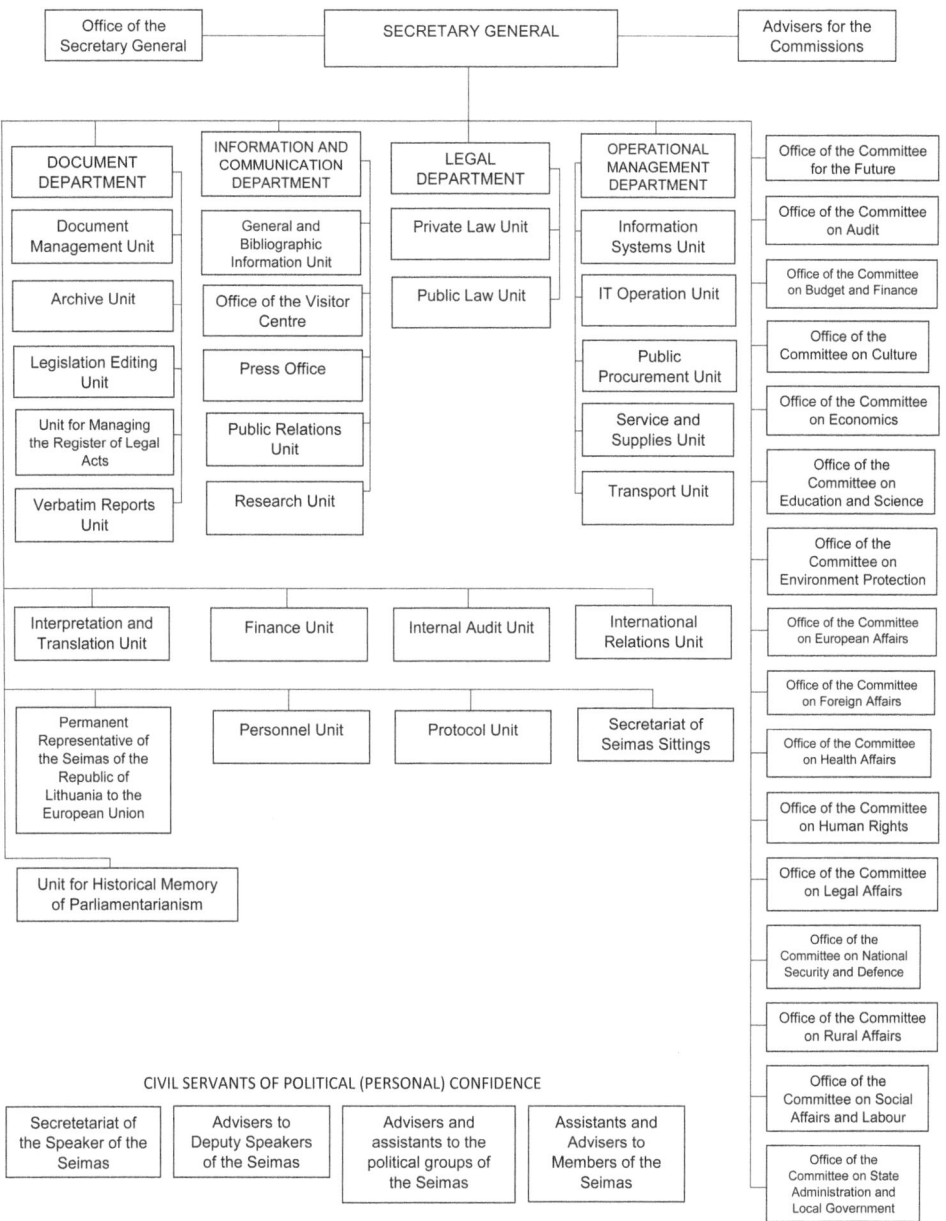

Figure 25.1 Organizational structure chart of the Seimas administration (Lithuania)

Historically, the degree of politicization of administrative careers has been high. The Seimas administration did not have any career plans neither hierarchical nor horizontal. The annual performance review was performed in a ceremonial manner rather than sought objective performance appraisal with clear career implications. Thus, communicating their expectations to the secretary general through MPs was a viable option.

25.4.1 The Distinction between Central Services and Committee Secretariats

The distinction between central services and committee secretariats is quite clear within the current structure. However, it is worth noting that each MP is a member of two standing committees and one commission. Like in many other European countries, the Seimas administration supports standing committees via committee secretariats, which employ 6–11 professionals. The list of committees is provided in Appendix 25.1.

In addition to the 16 committees, there are 16 commissions, but only 10 have regular activities and significant workload. Appendix 25.2 provides a list of all parliamentary commissions. A usual rule is that a single advisor provides both expert and technical support to a commission. Such a single advisor–based support to the commission structure has both advantages and disadvantages. The advantage is the focus, which means that an advisor is deeply engaged in the commission activities and works very closely with its chairperson. On the other hand, disadvantages include substitution problems and asymmetric workload, which very seldom is close to a full time position.

25.4.2 Specialized Units

The Seimas administration has all typical specialized units, such as library, research, legal service, IT, international relations, protocol, internal audit, finance and others. Some of these units are part of Departments, while others are independent units. Notably, per regulation, the National library also performs the function of Parliamentary library.

The administration does not provide security service, which is a responsibility of Dignitary Protection Service, operating within the Ministry of Interior system.

The Research unit supports standing committees, commissions, political party groups and individual MPs with research on various issues related to the current or future legislative initiatives. Typically, requests submitted to the service concern reviews of current regulatory practices, serving as a point of reference for formulating parliamentary decisions or orienting legislative and oversight initiatives. The production of a research report takes from one to three months, and the unit is usually overbooked with requests for research. Currently, the research unit is recruiting new staff members for more long-term policy-oriented research. The growth of the research unit is closely related to the decision of the current coalition to establish a separate multi-domain standing committee dedicated to the Future, which is a key driver of the National Development Strategy "Lithuania 2050".

The Legal Department provides legal services not only to various political bodies, including committees, commissions and the plenary proceedings, but also to the parliamentary administration. The Legal unit acts as a critical quality controller and gatekeeper in the law-making process. The usual procedure is that the central government and the relevant ministries submit their draft bills to the Seimas, where the bill is assessed and submitted to the appropriate standing committee. The relationship between MPs and the Legal department is subtle, primarily because the Seimas administration is independent from political influence and furthermore because the Legal department is independent in that it prepares and adopts conclusions on draft bills without any formal or informal approval by the chancellor. It happens that the Legal department receives unjustified informal critique by individual political groups or MPs, who do not agree with the content of its legal conclusion.

The second function of the Legal unit is gate-keeping. The more critical comments the Legal department provides in its conclusion, the more leverage is given to the opposition and the more heated discussions are promoted at committee level. All this makes the law-making procedure longer. Speed is another crucial dimension of gate-keeping, and, very often, the Legal department is asked to provide conclusions within one to three working days instead of formally allocated seven days in response to specific political requests. Table 25.4 reveals that the number of different legislative activities and decisions made by the Seimas is very high, which certainly puts pressure on the administration.

25.4.3 Professionalization and the Development of Functional Expertise

The Seimas administration recruits and promotes employees following different procedures. One of the latest developments has been the centralization of the recruitment process of the civil servants within the Civil Service Department under the Ministry of the Interior, whose purpose is to cope with the lack of transparency, equal opportunity and fair competition among the different public sector organizations, including the Seimas administration. Therefore, the Seimas administration does not currently have a chance to recruit civil servants by drawing on internal processes and rules. When the Seimas administration advertises a new open position, the candidates have to submit their application the Civil Service Department, but they can only apply if they have passed a special examination, which tests their basic knowledge and competence. The selection committee is formed in such a way that the Civil Service Department delegates 2/3 of its members, while the Seimas administration or any other institution delegates 1/3. The two best candidates selected in the first round undergo a second selection round, which was carried out by the Seimas administration alone. If the pre-selected candidates meet minimal critical requirements, the administration is, to some extent, "forced" to recruit him/her.

Such mechanism, while securing a more independent and transparent process, limits the impact of personal preferences by the organization leaders, has been criticized for being a too lengthy process and for not being able to account for the specific needs of the public sector organization. In response to these critiques, the Seimas administration began hiring staff under employment contracts for the available positions, which, under normal circumstances, are performed by the public servants. This is compatible with the Seimas administration's legal prerogatives. One critical step in recruiting "staff under contracts" is that, at first, the Seimas administration must advertise such a position internally. Only if there are no qualified internal candidates, the administration can seek external candidates.

Opportunities for staff training and development have been quite limited for a long time, except for the period when Lithuania held the Presidency of the EU. The Seimas administration does not use competency models or thorough skill assessment to identify training needs; however, opportunities for introducing such tools are being investigated now.

The Seimas administration has access to external consultancy. However, it primarily employs consultancy services in IT, engineering, maintenance and construction projects. There have been no significant external consultancy projects with regard to upgrading functional expertise, or improving management and innovation activities within functional departments. Primarily, the expertise of functional departments grows through learning by doing.

Table 25.4 Comparison of the legislative activities in different parliamentary terms of the Seimas

Parliamentary term	Number of registered draft legislation	Number of adopted legal acts	Number of adopted laws	Number of laws considered under special urgency procedure	Number of sittings	Percentage of laws considered under special urgency procedure, %	Number of legislation adopted per sitting	Number of adopted draft legislation	Percentage of adopted draft legislation, %
1992–1996	2,773	1,690	1,039	160	634	15.4	2.7	1,905	68.7
1996–2000	3,003	2,141	1,613	382	528	23.7	4.1	2,224	74.1
2000–2004	3,947	2,631	1,896	510	571	26.9	4.6	2,752	69.7
2004–2008	3,499	1,901	1,177	287	471	24.4	4.0	2,099	60.0
2008–2012	5,052	2,487	1,790	940	489	52.5	5.1	2,558	50.6
2012–2016	4,878	2,804	2,105	769	394	36.5	7.1	2,632	54.0
2016–2020	5,413	3,440	2,572	233	455	9.1	7.6	3,387	62.6

25.5 The Role of the Administration in the Context of Parliamentary Work

25.5.1 Support for Committees and/or Plenary Debates

The Seimas administration plays a critical role in supporting parliamentary work. The most important contributions come from the Seimas sittings secretariat, committee secretariats, commission advisors, legal department and research unit.

The sittings secretariat assists the chairperson in running the proceedings prepares all the related documents and distributes them to the MPs. It also develops the comprehensive and detailed programmes for Fall and Spring sessions and specific sittings' agendas. The second critical function performed by the sitting secretariat is consultancy, particularly during the first two years of the political cycle, since after each election there are significant changes in the Seimas political leadership team. In addition, the secretariat provides consultancy on draft laws and suggested amendments, preparation of written inquiries, development of plenary session programs, sittings agenda, electronic voting system and others. The consultancy also covers initiation of temporary parliamentary groups and inter-parliamentary groups.

The committee secretariats play a vital supportive role in securing smooth and effective execution of legislative, parliamentary control and other functions. Table 25.5 provides an overview of the different activities performed by committee secretariats. The table reveals wide asymmetries in the activities performed by secretariats. This poses a serious challenge to the procedures of fair performance appraisal and equitable reward of staff members. Moreover, the activity report demonstrates the relatively high productivity of standing committees. Such a high productivity has been considered a manifestation of the "legislative inflation", which

Table 25.5 The standing committee secretariats activity report for 2021

	Committee sittings organized	Committee hearings organized	Number of draft bills prepared	Number of conclusions on draft bills	Number of parliamentary scrutiny items examined	Number of proposals for EU legislation and other documents considered	Number of stakeholders' proposals for draft legislation received
AAK	53	6	46	112	28	33	262
ATK	35	0	0	7	36	5	0
ADK	36	6	15	70	65	1	156
BFK	65	1	87	222	51	17	420
EKK	60	7	92	157	53	21	257
ERK	155	0	1	10	343	252	101
KK	54	2	52	61	44	2	163
KRK	48	9	9	62	83	15	259
NSGK	79	6	27	68	58	19	153
SRDK	53	1	65	124	23	15	138
SRK	51	8	37	69	47	15	255
ŠMK	48	5	44	65	65	2	224
TTK	39	48	148	273	51	12	388
URK	128	3	22	42	278	12	127
VVSK	42	0	35	91	12	4	165
ŽTK	16	1	14	52	21	9	382
Viso:	962	103	694	1,485	1,258	434	3,450

means that the government drafts and the parliament adopts a high number of bills, but the quality, clarity and consistency of the legislation has not increased, and the legal environment for citizen and organizations has not been improved.

Legislative process, including drafting, suffers from a number of serious problems. In the Seimas administration report, Lukošaitis and Juknevičiūtė (2021) identified ten major problems. Here, it is only worth mentioning that ex-ante and ex-post impact assessment is performed for a relatively small number of draft bills.

25.6 Managing Current Challenges Facing the Parliamentary Administration

25.6.1 Digitalization

The digitalization is one of the areas where the Seimas administration has made significant progresses.

Several years ago, the administration implemented documents management system (DMS), which effectively means that all chancellor's decisions, all key activities and part of the communication within parliament and with citizens are carried out electronically. Notably, the implementation of DMS started five to seven years later than at the government level. DMS covers the activities of the standing committees, of parliamentary commissions and the plenary sittings. Communication with the ministries is carried out with a support of DMS. Most of new processes, which the Seimas administration initiates, are immediately moved to DVS, and the only major barrier in this regard is the limitation of IT resources.

The second major trend in digitalization is virtual meetings. Prior to COVID-19, virtual meetings and remote work were nearly non-existent. Over the last two years, most formal meetings of the political bodies such as standing committees, regular and temporary commissions, the Seimas Board and conference chairs are virtual or mixed. Except the initial pandemic period, the plenary sittings have been conducted in a face-to-face mode. The Seimas made attempts to run plenary sittings in a mixed mode, however, experience was not very positive in that technological solutions were not able to provide the same experience and equal rights of participation and voting to all MPs irrespective of their physical location.

On the people management side, the Seimas administration has a rather radical internal regulation, which allows most employees to work remotely all the time. The exceptions are the employee groups, which need to work in presence. Most of the administrative meetings were therefore carried out virtually.

The third element of digitalization is a digital environment for standing committees. The standing committees and their committee secretariats have as a secure shared digital environment to store, organize and access relevant information from any device. Naturally, committee secretariats act more as information providers, while committee members are information users. Although the absolute majority of PMs has sufficient IT skills, a minority of MPs tend to rely either on their own staff or on the secretariat staff to access documents.

The first digitalization efforts started in 2008 when the Seimas adopted a bill on the Information system of legal acts. The overarching purpose of such system is to improve openness, transparency, effectiveness and quality of the legislative process by transferring it to the electronic space. More specific objectives are meant to create a centralized, all-encompassing, reliable and secure system covering the all the different stages of the legislative process, from the submission of a legislative initiative to the submission of amendments up to the final approval. It is worth mentioning that the Lithuanian Parliament assigned its administration the duty of managing the Register of legal acts, established in 2014. Thus, the Seimas administration manages both information systems and secures access to the legislation in progress and already adopted legal acts to all interested parties.

One rather traditional area of digital development is called "E-services". This area primarily belongs to the interaction with citizens and society at large. Currently, there are five digital ways for the citizens to interact with the parliament and its administration. First of all, they can write an electronic letter, and usually the client service unit responds to all electronic emails or transfer them to other relevant institutions. Secondly, the website of the parliament registers the legislative proposals submitted by individual citizens or their groups. Thirdly, the Seimas website has a special functionality and interface called "E-petition", where it is possible to submit petition in electronic format. Fourth, it is possible to submit a document to the Parliament through an e-document interface. Finally, the digital solution is used to order documents from the archives. Citizen participation in the political processes, including legislation, is one of the lowest in the European Union. Through its commitment to digitalization, therefore, the Seimas administration is aiming at improving the user-Parliament interface and lifting other barriers that may discourage public engagement.

25.6.2 Democratization, Engagement and Global Learning

With the arrival of new secretary general, the Seimas administration has taken a path of becoming fully democratic organization, where employee voice is encouraged, supported and rewarded, where evidence-based debates and challenges are valued, and where psychological safety of employees is a critical component of emerging organizational culture (Edmondson, 1999). The new management philosophy invites all employees to propose new ideas, join problem-solving teams, which change the way administration works and serves the MPs and other stakeholders. The path taken during the last year is a shift from "the fixed mindset" exemplified by narrow task focus to "the growth mindset" embodied in a collaboration and contribution across all organization (Dweck, 2006). Based on the growth mindset logic, each manager within the administration has been assigned improvement goals, consistent with recent trends in public service operations management (Radnor and Bateman, 2016).

To support new management philosophy, the decision has been made to establish the Strategy and Innovation unit, which would act as an internal consultancy. Recent study on the effectiveness of the parliamentary administrations reveals parliament's claims to be "unique" and an ensuing emphasis on differences over similarities with other public organizations have reduced the potential for learning from outside (Barrett, 2019). The management philosophy at the Seimas administration seeks to overcome such a learning trap by explicitly focusing on and incentivizing global learning from other parliamentary administrations, other public sector institutions, businesses and NGOs.

25.7 Conclusion

Since restoring Independence in 1991, the parliamentary administration has undergone a remarkable evolution. In the early 1990s, the administrative and political processes were tightly intertwined. During the first decade, MPs and, especially, political leaders had a lot of formal and informal influence. The formal influence manifested itself through formal appointments of MPs and board members (deputy speakers) acting as secretaries general. The informal influence was enacted through the perceived power of the political leaders relative to the administration leaders and employees, and in particular, it was reinforced by the absence of formal regulations on how to recruit, reward and promote. Currently, the interaction between the political leadership and the management of administration is based on mutual trust, collaboration, respect of formal mandates and share vision to make Seimas administration one of the most forward-looking organizations of its kind.

The set of activities have expanded dramatically within traditional functions and, particularly, in attempt to become more open, transparent and engaged with society. The Seimas administration has a separate unit called the Visitors Center, which is deeply engaged in education activities. The number of school visits, art exhibition and other cultural and memorial activities is extremely high. The Seimas hosts many national and international conferences, under the sponsorship of the Seimas board or committees. Given the Lithuanian history, it is natural to have a special unit for historical heritage and parliamentarism, which works very close with various communities, schools and freedom fighter organizations to nurture a sense of history, statehood and democracy.

Digitalization has been at the centre of attention in recent years, and its activities in this area will continue to grow. The key focus areas are the civic-tech, user experience, cyber security, consolidation and moving IT resources to the centralized clouds, and upgrading major operation systems related to critical parliamentary activities.

On the organizational development side, the key strategic directions are competence development, continuous improvement, service excellence, employee engagement and well-being.

Note

1 Modestas Gelbūda is a secretary general at the Seimas administration and professor at ISM University of Management and Economics in Lithuania. The chapter is written with a support of the Research Council of Lithuania under contract Nr. S-MOD-17-15.

References

Barrett V. (2019). Parliamentary administration: what does it mean to manage a parliament effectively? Doctoral dissertation. The Australian National University.
Blažytė-Baužienė, D., Tamošaitis, M. and Truska, L. (2009). Lietuvos Seimo istorija. XX-XXI a. pradžia. Vilnius: Baltos lankos.
Edmondson, A. C. (1999). Psychological safety and learning behavior in work teams. Administrative Science Quarterly. 44 (2): 350–383.
Dweck, C. S. (2006). Mindset: The new psychology of success. Random House.
Gumuliauskas, A., Anušauskas, A., Juršėnas, Č. and Sinkevičius, V. (ed.) (2020). Parlamentarizmas Lietuvoje. Vilnius, Lithuania: Lietuvos Respublikos Seimo kanceliarija.
Högenauer, A.-L., Neuhold, C. and Christiansen, T. (2016). Parliamentary Administration in the European Union. Basingstoke, New York: Palgrave Macmillan.
Jurgaitis, R. (2016). Nuo bajoriškosios savivaldos iki parlamentarizmo: Vilniaus seimelio veikla, 1717-1795 m. Parlamentarizmo istorijos tyrimų centras.
Lukošaitis, A. and Juknevičiūtė, D. (2021). Teisėkūra Lietuvos ir kitų Europos valstybių parlamentuose: racionalumo ir sprendimų kokybės užtikrinimo problemos (analitinė apžvalga, AN 21/46). Vilnius: Lietuvos Respublikos Seimo kanceliarijos Informacijos ir komunikacijos departamento Tyrimų skyrius.
Radnor, Z. and Bateman, N. (2016). Debate: the development of a new discipline—public service operations management. Public Money & Management. 36 (4): 246–248. doi: 10.1080/09540962.2016.1162586
Seimas of the Republic of Lithuania Statute (2021) Vilnius, Lithuania.
Svarauskas, A. (2020). Steigiamasis Seimas ir Lietuvos Respublikos kūrimas 1920–1922 metais. Vilnius, Lithuania: Lietuvos istorijos institutas.
Yin, R. K. (2018). Case Study Research and Applications: Design and Methods. Sixth edition. Los Angeles: SAGE.

Appendix 25.1 Standing Committee Secretariats

List of the committees of the Seimas:

1 Committee on Environment Protection;
2 Committee for the Future;
3 Committee on Audit;
4 Committee on Budget and Finance;
5 Committee on Economics;
6 Committee on European Affairs;
7 Committee on Rural Affairs;
8 Committee on Culture;
9 Committee on National Security and Defence;
10 Committee on Social Affairs and Labour;
11 Committee on Health Affairs;
12 Committee on Education and Science;
13 Committee on Legal Affairs;
14 Committee on Foreign Affairs;
15 Committee on State Administration and Local Authorities;
16 Committee on Human Rights.

Appendix 25.2 The List of Parliamentary Commissions

List of the standing commissions:

1 Anticorruption Commission;
2 Commission for Ethics and Procedures;
3 Commission for Addiction Prevention;
4 Commission for Energy and Sustainable Development;
5 Commission for Youth and Sport Affairs;
6 Commission for Parliamentary Scrutiny of Criminal Intelligence;
7 Commission for Suicide and Violence Prevention;
8 Commission for the Cause of Freedom and the National Historical Memory;
9 Commission for the Rights of People with Disabilities.
10 Petitions Commission

List of the other commissions:

1 Commission of the Seimas of the Republic of Lithuania and the Lithuanian World Community;
2 Commission for the Traditions and Heritage of Lithuanian Studies;
3 Freedom Prize Commission.

26
LUXEMBOURG'S PARLIAMENTARY ADMINISTRATION

Astrid Spreitzer[1]

26.1 Introduction

The key element of the administration of the Luxembourgish parliament – as of the country – certainly remains its size. With its 60 members[2] and as a unicameral parliament, the Chambre des Députés (Chamber of Deputies) is among the smallest national parliaments in the European Union (EU). Not surprisingly, Parliamentary administration too is rather small. Although its workforce increased during the last 20 years, the Chamber still counts on very limited human resources (HR). From 2001 to 2021, the staff of the Chamber more than doubled from 47 to 120. A sharp increase in headcount shows in 2021, when external staff integrated the Chamber administration.

Although this number still seems to be very small, staff growth largely exceeds population growth in the same period. Luxembourg's population increased from 433,600 in 2000 to 634,700 in 2021,[3] and thus 1.5 times of its size. Parliament administration increased 2.6 times of its size between 2001 and 2021 (cf. Figure 26.1). Government administration on the other hand increased by a factor of 0.7 from about 19,100 in 2001 to 32,851 in 2021.[4]

The total expenditures of the Chamber increase from 21 million in 2001 to 44 million in 2019. And this will come as no surprise, staff spending grows as well from 3.4 million to 11.8 million in the same period. In relative terms, staff spending augments from 17 per cent of total costs in 2001 to 27 per cent in 2019 (cf. Figure 26.2.).

26.2 The Organisational Structure of Parliamentary Administration

The functional bureaucratic principle defines the organisation of the Chamber. The 13 divisions split the workforce, mostly depending on its specialisation. Besides, three micro-units of one collaborator each with the aspiration to be independent add to the organisation chart (the financial control, a data protection officer and an independent auditor). We may further add that the Chamber holds a staff committee, which includes at least one representative of each career in the Chamber. In December 2021, it is composed of six members. Its mission consists in a representation of the collective interests of the Chamber staff as a whole or of specific groups. It is consulted when modifications are foreseen in the organisation or

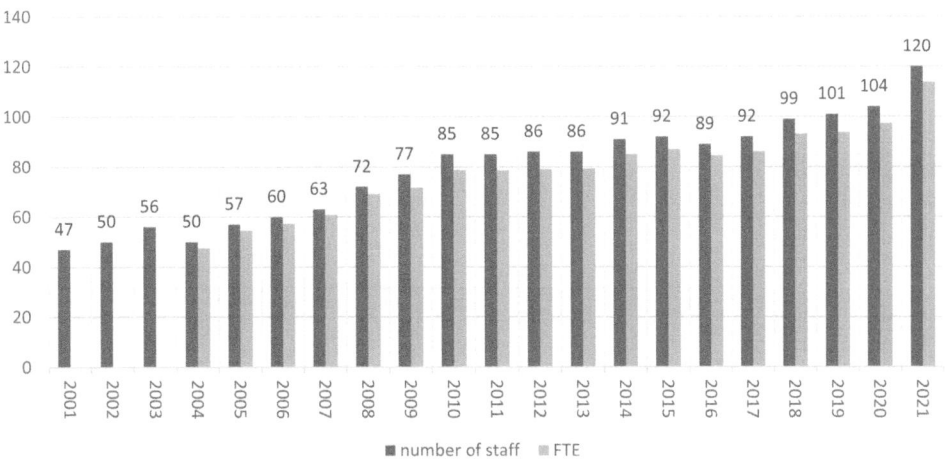

Figure 26.1 Size of parliamentary administration in the Luxembourg chamber of deputies, 2001–2021 (n, FTE)

functioning of the Parliamentary administration. More specifically, it promotes training and professional development and proposes improvements of the work organisation and working conditions, as well as security measures.

The services directly supporting the political work of the members of parliament (MPs) are the Plenary service (including the general secretariat), the Service of international relations, the Public relations service, the Minutes service and the Committee service. The latter is the largest service and comprises 20 per cent of the staff of the Chamber. It carries a heavy responsibility for the functioning of the Chamber, and its recent and foreseen growth in staff requires reflection for its future organisation (cf. Figure 26.3).

A duo of an administrator ("secrétaire administrateur") holding a university degree, and an administrative collaborator without university degree, constitute the committee secretariats. They provide above all a thorough application of law-making principles. In 2021, the Chamber

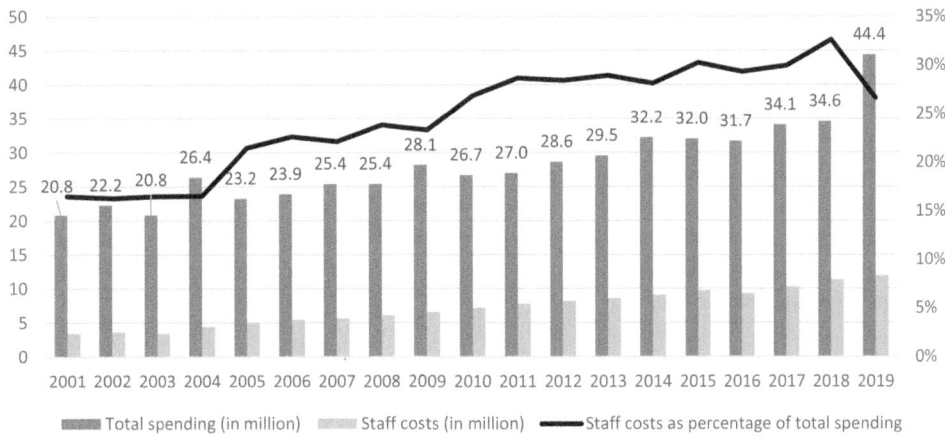

Figure 26.2 Total expenditures and staff costs, 2001–2019 (in million)

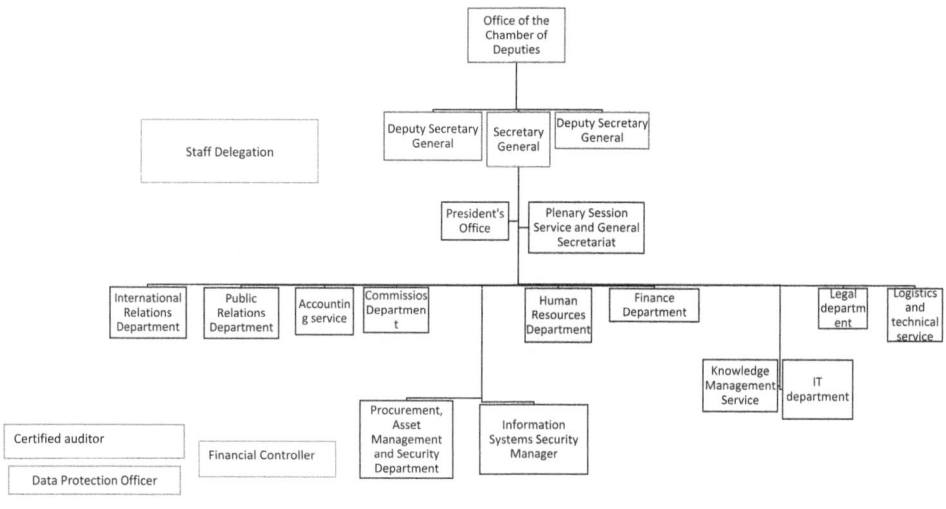

Figure 26.3 Organisational chart of the parliamentary administration in the Luxembourg chamber of deputies (2021)

has 20 permanent and 4 regulatory committees, which tend to meet more and more often: the number of committee meetings come up to more than 780 in 2021, from about 550 meetings in 2001. Due to the perimeter of a respective committee, its activity level and the frequency of its meetings, a secretary administrator may be responsible for one or several committees. Staff of other services supports the Committee service. This is the case for the European affairs committee (EAC),[5] for instance, where staff out of the International relations service ensures the committee secretariat.

Specialised support services include the HR service, the Finance service, the Legal service, the Logistics and technical service, the IT service, the Knowledge management service, the Purchases, asset management and security service and the Information system security service. Attached to the Plenary service, a Scientific service, based on the model of the Wissenschaftliche Dienste in the German Bundestag, assures advice in science and constitutional matters since 2017. Formally, the Conference of presidents[6] of the Chamber commissions a scientific study, which is supposed to cover all aspects of a subject matter in a neutral and independent manner. So far, the Scientific service is composed of four collaborators. While they may provide general knowledge on multiple areas, their main purpose consists in identifying relevant external actors, who could provide expertise in specific fields. Thus, their networks in the scientific community are systematically mobilised by the Chamber, which equals to an outsourcing of most scientific advice. At the same time, the Scientific service also promotes the work of the Chamber, not least, as the collaborators continue publishing their research.

26.3 The Role of the Administration in the Context of Parliamentary Work

In terms of staff attribution, Parliamentary administration puts most of its efforts into the support of the political work of MPs. At least 57 per cent of the Chamber's personnel work for political support services, which represent the largest divisions (Figure 26.4).

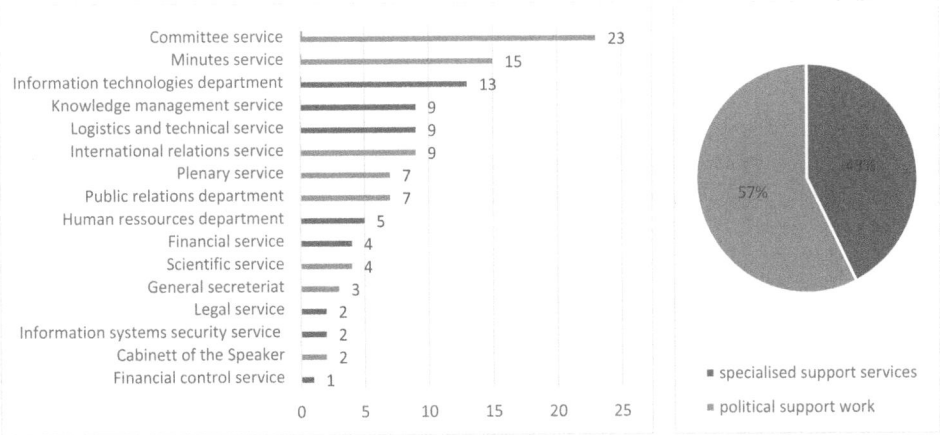

Figure 26.4 Number of staff per service and percentage of staff attributed to political support work and specialized support services, 2021

Thus, the main function of the Chamber is to facilitate the political work of MPs. While the political support work is important, it cannot function without the specialised support services. Internally, no service is considered more important than another is, and cooperation and horizontal and transversal work is promoted. This is true not only for the internal services, but also for the Chamber as a whole. While research often discusses the independence of legislatures from government (Maurer and Wessels, 2001), the Chamber engages in active cooperation and collaboration with other institutions, such as the Council of State and the government in order to reinforce its role and efficiency. Traditionally, one example of such cooperation concerns the work of the committee secretariats, which are in permanent formal and informal exchange with the secretariats in the Council of State and the government. Another recent example regards the cooperation with the Government IT Centre[7] concerning the digitalisation of different aspects of Chamber work (see below in Section 26.6).

26.3.1 *The Nature of Institutional Hierarchy*

The institutional hierarchy of the Chamber consists of a political layer in form of the Bureau and the Speaker and an administrative layer topped by the Directorate and covering the 14 divisions.

The **Directorate** tops the administrative layer consisting of the General Secretary and his two deputies. The Chamber elects the **Secretary General** with an absolute majority in a plenary session for the legislative period (normally five years). The nomination is renewable, and a vote takes only place if five MPs demand for it. The last election took place in February 2020 as the former General Secretariat retired. The vote confirmed a candidate from within the Chamber: neither a deputy Secretary General nor a head of division took over the office but a simple team member of the Service of international relations with no apparent links to a political party. Former Secretary Generals had clear linkages to majority parties.

The Directorate directly reports to the **Executive Office (Bureau)**, composed of the Speaker, three vice-speakers, a maximum of nine members and the General Secretary. The Bureau represents the Chamber at national and international levels. It is concerned with all financial and organisational questions except the agenda of the plenary sessions.[8] Most interestingly in this context, the Bureau is responsible for all decisions concerning the Chamber administration, i.e. staff conduct and discipline.

The duties of the **Speaker** are to represent the Chamber, maintain the order in the assembly, to enforce the Standing Orders, to judge the formal admissibility of texts, motions and other proposals, to grant the floor, to ask questions and put them to the vote, announcing the results of votes and ballots, to pronounce the decisions of the House. The **Speaker's office (Cabinet)** supports the Speaker in his functions. It is composed of the Secretary General who heads the Cabinet and two members of staff.

The political and administrative layers intersect at the level of the Chamber leadership and management. The General Secretary is the head of administration. However, the fact that the Bureau takes all formal decisions cushions his formal responsibility. The close working relationship with the Speaker adds to this picture. Many tasks are executed by the two of them, for instance, the establishment of the agenda of the Bureau, the proposal for the selection of new collaborators or the confirmation of the results of votes or minutes of plenary sessions. What is more, the Bureau includes the Secretary General, although without voting rights. As mentioned, staff questions are a matter of the Bureau.

The administrative procedures and principles are accepted and they prevent from political interference in administrative matters. They establish autonomy and independence and allow for discretion at all administrative levels. In recruitment for instance, those administrative procedures mostly consist in entry exams. The Speaker and the Secretary General propose the two best candidates from the exam's ranking to the Bureau, which accepts those proposals without discussion.

If candidates hold a political background when applying for a position in the Chamber, for instance when they work for a political faction, and if they pass the entry exam as one of the two best in the ranking, they are invited to the interview and surely may be recruited: In this case, they enter Parliamentary administration not because of their political background but because of their fit to a post. In the daily work, politicisation is neither appreciated nor helpful and every MP is regarded in the same way.

MPs may however propose trainees, which systematically integrate to reinforce the Chamber administration. Having the support of a MP is however no pre-condition of becoming a Chamber trainee. Discussions on staff matters arise in the Bureau, when administration affects the political logics. Summing up, the degree of politicisation of the Chamber staff is low.

The administrative logic of impartiality even spills over into the political sphere, for instance in the office of the Speaker. His role requires impartiality and formality in decision-making. The support of the Secretary General, who is also Head of the Cabinet, contributes to meet those needs.

26.3.2 Human Resources Management in the Chamber and Its Challenges

Despite discussions, whether its unique function in the democratic system necessitates a distinct management of its HR, in 2021 the Luxembourgish parliament integrated into the serviced system of the government. The State Centre for Human resources and Organisation management (CGPO)[9], manages all of the around 33.000 public servants of the Luxembourgish state administration (in 2022). The CGPO acts similarly to a trustee for the Chamber: without giving up any decisional power concerning its HR management, this allows Parliament to benefit from the economies of scale of a larger organisation. This regards the entire lifecycle of personnel management *...from initial recruitment, through the calculation and management of remuneration and careers of active state officials, to the management of retired state officials' files and others beneficiaries of a pension* (CGPO, 2021).

Notwithstanding recent trends, the Luxembourgish Civil service – and the Chamber administration as part of it – classifies as a traditional career system (Demmke and Moilanen, 2010). Commonly, public officials enter directly after finishing their studies or in their early work life and stay in the public service until their retirement. Their career advances with their seniority. Mobility within the civil service is low and quasi non-existent towards the private sector.

This is even more the case in the Chamber administration, as the staff of the Chamber in many regards enjoys favourable conditions compared to civil servants working for government concerning remuneration or retirement for instance. The Rules of Procedures of the Chamber (RoP) govern those conditions in Annex 4 on the legal statute of Chamber officials.

The amount of expertise available is a major concern and linked to the size of a legislature, be it in political or administrative terms. The more MPs and the larger the administrative personnel, the more specialisation is possible. The smaller the area to cover by one person, the easier expertise may potentially be developed. This leads us to conclude that the administrative staff of the Chamber as well as Luxembourgish MPs are generalists rather than specialists. Nevertheless, some possibilities exist to facilitate specialisation, in small-scale settings too. The number of committee meetings may increase the intensity of dealing with a subject matter, for instance (Spreitzer, 2014). What is more, a small parliament may decide on a few priorities to cover in depth and ignore less important topics. The prioritisation of the parliament's agenda and a strong focus on essential topics help further expertise.

Recruitment in the Chamber decidedly helps to acquire competencies and specialisation. The centralised HR decision-making of the CGPO organises the entry of an official-to-be through a general exam, with the objective to guarantee a baseline for a reserve list of candidates eligible to apply for posts. In a second step, in order to select the appropriate candidates, administrations may organise specific tests.

When the Chamber entry exam for functionaries provided ever less candidates for specific posts, it asked for access to the state entry exam and its reserve lists of candidates. Recently, with the integration of the Chamber into the centralised state HR-services, this became possible. Thus, Parliament may recruit functionaries by organising its own entry exam, or using the centralised government services, depending on its needs.

The Chamber entry exam is still based on the idea that every functionary masters editorial competences and text analysis in the three official languages. State entry exam was reformed in 2017 and uses tests based on logical and analytical aptitudes (abstract, verbal and numeric reasoning, as well as a mailbox-exercise testing problem-solving and decision-making capacities). The expectation is that this new possibility delivers a larger choice for the recruitment of Chamber functionaries. In the meantime, the recruitment of employees provides an alternative.

The Luxembourgish Civil service certainly is an outstanding case as it still privileges the employment of staff on a public law status. Still, the staff of the Chamber consists of two populations: recognised Chamber functionaries and employees under private law.

As a functionary, the RoP applies and changes towards government administration are possible without any problems and with a recognition of career paths and seniority. The inverse is also possible: a transfer of a government agent into the Chamber administration. As the Chamber statute is advantageous compared to the statute of government officials, the more favourable conditions are applied in either case, that is: at the integration of a collaborator; obviously, the further career advancement depends on the place of affectation.

Chamber employees underlie private law but benefit from the same conditions as their functionary colleagues, when it comes to their career path, for instance. Formerly an exception, difficulties in finding the required profiles have made that out of the staff, more than one fourth (27 per cent) are employees.

The difference between the two populations lies in the recruitment procedures and requirements. Employees do not undergo the state exam and may be exempted from mastering the three official languages, that is, Luxembourgish, French and German.

While each new official undergoes a trial period of a maximum of two years, the internal formation foreseen for onboarding is the one of government officials and thus not specific to the Chamber. Expertise is bought in with specialised profiles. Once in place, a job in the Luxembourgish Chamber brings about a great variety of tasks. The number of different dossiers and subject matters to cover by one collaborator is certainly high due to the small size of the administration. The staff does not rotate internally. At the time of recruitment, the idea is to keep a staff member for her whole career in the service she starts. Specialisation thus comes in through recruitment and with the time, on the job.

As mentioned, promotion mechanisms come with seniority. After 12 years of service, a civil servant moves from the general level to the upper level. The only requirement is to have attended 12 training days before the end of the general level. The Chamber employs staff of five careers defined by the diploma attained: higher university degree (A1), lower university degree (A2), secondary degree (B1), artisans (D1) and bailiffs (D2). After 15 years of service, it is possible to change from a lower to a higher career, by taking a promotion exam, which mainly consists of writing a paper, and presenting the work done.

Training and external consultancy are further possibilities for professionalisation. The staff of the Chamber has access to the offer of the National Institute of Public Administration (INAP),[10] concerning both basic and continuous training. Attending the initial training of state civil servants is obligatory for new Chamber recruits. They are exempted from the exam at the end of the training. Instead, the Chamber requires its future officials to write a paper and to solve a practical case study at the end of their trial period.

Access to external consultancy was one of the main reasons to introduce a scientific service in 2017. The small but highly qualified staff of the service (four civil servants in the end of 2021), with specialisation in science and legal matters, acts as door opener and provides a network of scientific expertise and methodological knowledge. It helps identify pertinent external actors who may provide consultancy on specific matters.

26.4 Managing Inter-Institutional and External Relations

It is a unicameral parliament, as political elites considered that the country was too small for a bicameral system.[11] Moreover, while the State Council may have ambitions to upgrade to an upper parliamentary chamber,[12] it is a non-elected body, and its tasks are other than that of a Senate.[13] Its main mission is to check the constitutionality of draft laws and their accordance to superior law, that is, international agreements and general legal principles.[14]

The administrative relations between the State Council and the Chamber are thus intense. All law initiative and every amendment has to be checked by the State Council. In its organisation, the State Council somewhat mirrors the committee system of the Chamber, and committee secretariats are in frequent contact. During the state of emergency and the necessity to manage the Covid pandemic, this relationship became even more intensive. Legislative work had to speed up, which required more coordination between the Chamber and the State Council in order to quickly adopt urgent legal proposals. Informal cooperation between the upper management of the two institutions also intensified in this period, including the Ministry of State, and it resulted in a perfect mesh of administrative acts. At the committee level, we may observe similar developments.

Besides inter-institutional relations at national level, the Chamber is busily engaged in **international relations**. The Chamber is member in 12 inter-parliamentary bodies at international, European and regional level.[15]

Parliamentary administration occupies nine staff members at the **Service of international relations**. This department differs from other services, as it is concerned with a special mission on the one hand and the backup of a committee on the other hand. It supports parliamentary external affairs and relations with international bodies, delegations, ingoing and outgoing visits, and it assures the protocol service. What is more, it ministers EU affairs.

The Chamber takes EU affaires seriously, as staff attribution shows: In 2004, the then "International relations and Protocol department" consisted of 4.5 posts. At that time, one position was vacant. In 2009, three posts were vacant, at a staff of seven, and in 2010, those vacancies were mostly filled with 2.75 employments (Spreitzer, 2015). Thus, since 2004, the Service for International relations has more than doubled. This is due to the installation of the Europe unit ("*Cellule Européenne*") intended by its Europe strategy of 2005.[16]

Also attached to the International relations department is the **permanent representative of the Chamber in Brussels**. She represents the Chamber at the European institutions in Brussels and thus covers all events taking place in Brussels and regarding EU matters (i.e. COSAC events of the EU presidency country). The post was created in 2006, right after the Luxembourgish Council and COSAC presidency. The permanent representative does not have any support in Brussels but relies on the resources of the International relations department of the Chamber (Spreitzer, 2015).

EU affairs at the Chamber include the distribution of information on European dossiers and, what is more, the support of the **EU Committee of the Chamber (EAC)**[17]. Contrary to other committees, which count on the "*Committees Service*" department of the Chamber, the EAC is larger in scope and may draw on extended staff. Formally, two administrators plus one assistant are attributed to the EAC. Other committees rely one administrator plus one assistant at the most and half of the committee administrators are assisted by one person and responsible for two committees.

In 2010, the Luxembourgish parliament extended its provisions on EU scrutiny to enable the application of rules on the EWM (Spreitzer, 2015). The Europe unit manages the inflow of all documents sent by the European institutions and evaluates them according to the Chamber's priorities concerning subsidiarity and proportionality. It classifies EU documents into A and B and creates lists for the use in the sectoral committees.

The Europe strategy foresaw in a second phase to attribute a larger role to the civil service in this process. Clerks should conduct profound research and draft the political opinion or motivated opinion, respectively.[18] The administrative burden prevented this extension of the staff's role in EU affairs. Still, the Europe unit pays a crucial role in the selection of documents committees shall examine.

Not only from the **administrative point of view** does the procedure work in a satisfying manner. Judged by its output, the Europe strategy of the Chamber and its system of EU document screening has been very effective.[19] It represents, however, a large burden to a parliament, which used to adopt around 90 laws per parliamentary session. The number of incoming EU documents is many times higher than the number of law initiatives (ibid, 2015).

26.5 Recent Changes in Work Patterns: A Pandemic and a New Leadership

Hand in hand with its increase in staff, Parliament's organisation and work patterns underwent a fundamental transition during the last couple of years. It is difficult to disentangle the reasons for the transformation: contributing to this was a change in the Chambers leadership with a new Secretary General taking office after a 17 years reign of his predecessor,[20] and the Covid-19 pandemic, both starting of early 2020. The most accurate is perhaps to say that a clever instrumentalisation of the necessities the pandemic pushed forward helped implement the agenda of the new Secretary General.

We have already mentioned the intensified coordination between the Chamber, the State Council and the government ministries, necessary in order to increase the speed of lawmaking during the Covid-19 state of emergency.

The Covid-19 pandemic forced the introduction of telework for its entire staff. So far, only the Minutes service could work from home, which made the Chamber a pioneer of telework. The Chamber's leadership is much in favour of this generalisation, and remote work will remain possible for the Parliamentary administration after the pandemic. A separate article will be introduced in the Chambers RoP. Telework brought geographical distance, and in order to prevent from isolation and conflict, the Chamber introduced team building in order to get co-workers together again.

Not only remote work changed the work patterns of Parliamentary administration and MPs. The pandemic brought along challenges, which revealed and re-enforced existing structural weaknesses at first. It allowed to question otherwise rigid structures and give more flexibility to the organisation.

The main accomplishment of the former Secretary General was to delegate tasks formerly attributed to his position. Consequently, the number of divisions increased during his office. The present leadership makes efforts to bring those divisions together and engage in a more transversal way of working. The pandemic made it possible to work on procedures and the organisation chart.

The two deputy Secretary Generals, one formerly responsible for the functioning of the services directly supporting the political work of the MPs and the other heading the supporting services, switched to lead the important projects of the Chamber transversally. In order to do so, middle management had to take over more responsibilities than it did beforehand. Previously a pure matter of seniority and bringing about few obligations, being head of service now actually means to manage the division and to report to the Secretary General.

26.6 Digitalization Strategy

A new digitalization strategy is guiding these changing work patterns in the Chamber. And it remains a priority of the Luxembourgish parliament in its service to the citizen and MPs. Citizens will soon benefit from a modernisation of the Chamber's website and an increase in its internet presence. Newly in place is a specific website for petitions (petitiounen.lu), which facilitates the access of citizens to this tool of direct democracy. The Chamber was one of the first EU parliaments to introduce an electronic vote for plenary ballots. This system has come to age and needs updating.

The Chamber makes large efforts to digitalise its internal working procedures, with its integration in a centralised management of HR. All personnel files had to be scanned, in a remake of publications of legislative acts (together with the State ministry) and in a project to automatize the production of minutes of meetings using artificial intelligence (together with the Government IT Centre[21]). Recently introduced are the massive use of telework and videoconferences, which were quickly made possible and will now remain in place. For this purpose, the IT service reorganized into four sub-divisions and integrated external expertise.

Notes

1 I wish to thank Laurent Scheeck, General Secretary of the Chamber and Manon Hoffmann, Head of Human resources of the Chamber who have agreed to an interview and give me insight on their daily work and professional experiences. Special thanks go to Anne Tescher, Deputy Director of the State Centre for Human resources and Organisation management for her valuable input and comments on this chapter.
2 Before 1988, the number of MPs varied as it was dependent on the size of population.
3 STATEC: Affichage de tableau – Évolution de la population totale, luxembourgeoise et étrangère au 1er janvier 1961–2021 (public.lu), viewed 9 January 2022.
4 Apart from the general administration, these numbers include staff of the sectors education, judiciary and the armed forces.
5 « Commission des Affaires étrangères et européennes, de la Coopération, de l'Immigration et de l'Asile »
6 The Conference of Presidents is the parliamentary steering organ, including the Speaker, the Secretary General and the leaders of all parliamentary factions. It is responsible for the organisation of works in the Chamber.
7 Centre des technologies de l'information de l'Etat (CTIE), https://ctie.gouvernement.lu/en.html, viewed 20 April 2022.
8 The Conference of presidents decides over the agenda of plenary sessions.
9 Centre de gestion du personnel et de l'organisation de l'État, State Centre for Human Resources and Organisation Management (CGPO) // The Administration (cgpo.gouvernement.lu/en.html), viewed 23 January 2023.
10 Institute national d'administration publique, National Institute for Public Administration // The Luxembourg Government (gouvernement.lu), viewed 10 November 2021.
11 Dumont, P. / Spreitzer, A. (2012) The Europeanization of Domestic Legislation in Luxembourg, Springer, p. 217. Schmit (2009), p. 60.
12 The State Council holds an observer status in the Association of European Senates, http://www.senateurope.org/eng/members.html, viewed 30 January 2022.
13 Schroen, M. (2008) Parlament, Regierung und Gesetzgebung, chapter in Das Politische System Luxemburgs, VS Verlag für Sozialwissenschaften, p. 115.
14 "S'il estime un projet ou une proposition de loi contraire à la Constitution, aux conventions et traités internationaux, ainsi qu'aux principes généraux du droit, le Conseil d'Etat en fait mention dans son avis. Il en fait de même, s'il estime un projet de règlement contraire à une norme de droit supérieure." art. 2(2), Loi du 12 juillet 1996 portant réforme du Conseil d'Etat.
15 For details check out the Chamber website: https://chd.lu/wps/portal/public/Accueil/Organisation EtFonctionnement/RoleInstitutionnel/ActivitesInternationalesEuropeennes, viewed 29 January 2022.
16 The Chamber's *"Europe strategy"* was initiated by the Bureau in March 2004 and decided by the end of 2005. It was set out twofold: first, the Chamber made efforts to better communicate Europe to its citizens via its TV channel and website, among others. Second, it included a reform of the EU scrutiny procedure and an active engagement in the screening of EU documents.
17 Commission des Affaires étrangères et européennes, de la Coopération, de l'Immigration et de l'Asile (Committee of Foreign and European affairs, for Cooperation, Immigration and Asylum)
18 La stratégie européenne de la Chambre des Députés (2005), point IV.
19 Clerk of the Chamber of Deputies, face-to-face interview, 18 June 2013.

20 Laurent Scheeck took on his responsibilities as the new Secretary General in early 2020, following the 17 years in office of Claude Frieseisen.
21 Centre des technologies de l'information de l'Etat (CTIE), https://ctie.gouvernement.lu/en.html, viewed 20 April 2022.

References

Demmke, C. / Moilanen, T. (2010) Civil Services in the EU of 27. Reform Outcomes and the Future of the Civil Service, Peter Lang, p.188.

Maurer, A. / Wessels, B. (2001) National Parliaments on Their Ways to Europe: Losers or Latecomers? Nomos.

Spreitzer, A. (2014) Effects of European integration on parliamentary control of government: the case of Luxembourg, *1999–2011*, PhD thesis, University of Luxembourg, Luxembourg, https://orbilu.uni.lu/bitstream/10993/16868/1/PhThesis%20AS_20140521.pdf, viewed 23 April 2022.

Spreitzer, A. (2015) Luxembourg's Chamber of Deputies and EU Affairs, Chapter in The Palgrave Handbook of National Parliaments and the European Union, Palgrave Macmillan, p.232–251.

27
MALTA'S PARLIAMENTARY ADMINISTRATION

Mark Harwood

27.1 Introduction: Westminster in the Mediterranean

Malta, the EU's smallest member state, is situated midway between Europe and Africa with a history of occupation. In 1802, the Maltese inhabitants petitioned the British king for his protection, and from 1813 until 1964, Malta was a British crown colony; during this period, Malta's political system took shape, from the increased inclusion of Maltese representatives in the political system (culminating in the 1921 constitution which created a Government of Malta), the evolution of Maltese political parties (from 1880 onwards) and the establishment of its electoral system with STV (Single Transferable Vote) being first used in 1921 and for all subsequent elections. On independence in 1964, the new constitution, formulated in conjunction with the British, entrenched a political system considered a variation of the Westminster/Whitehall model with the British monarch as Queen of Malta and Head of State. Subsequently, Malta became a two-party political system from 1966 onwards and a republic in 1974. As a small, part-time parliament where one party has always dominated parliamentary business, this chapter will analyse the implications this has had on parliament's administration (is-Servizz Parlamentari, the Parliamentary Service) as well as how the latter have been impacted by digital technology and the COVID-19 pandemic.

Chapter VI of the Maltese constitution states that there shall be a Parliament of Malta consisting of the Head of State (President) and the House of Representatives. The unicameral House of Representatives was designed to comprise 50 members (on independence) but the number has grown steadily and changes to the Constitution and the electoral laws now mean that the number is not fixed (in addition to the 65 elected members representing 13 districts, there is a system of compensation which ensures that the final configuration of the House reflects the first count votes cast in the general election and, since 2022, an additional mechanism to ensure greater female representation, hence, currently there are 79 MPs). Elections must take place every five years, and once a new parliament is sworn in, the first order of business must be the election of the Speaker, while the leader of the party commanding a parliamentary majority becomes prime minister with ministers appointed from among the elected members of the House. As outlined by parliament itself "throughout the years, the Maltese Parliament has functioned through simplicity and pragmatism" (Parliament of Malta 2021a), and while it operates under rules of procedure modelled on those of the UK's House of Commons, these have been adapted to suit a much smaller parliament (Parliament of Malta 2021a). As with other parliaments, the principal innovation in the working of the legislature post-independence was the decision, in 1995, to establish Standing Committees to facilitate the work of the plenary, while other important developments include the country's 2004 membership of the EU, the move to a new parliament building in 2015 as well as the entry into force of the Parliamentary Service Act in 2017.

In addition to the fact that the Maltese parliament is quite small, several other factors impact how it operates and its administrative needs. As stated, parliament is a part-time house meeting from 4 to 7:30 pm on Monday to Wednesday (Parliament of Malta 2021b). As one of the few parliaments not meeting fulltime, this has several ramifications, including creating time pressures on parliamentary business as well as meaning that MPs are not fulltime parliamentarians, placing additional pressure on their ability to prepare for parliamentary work and their availability during normal office hours (when committees can meet). Additionally, Malta has been a two-party system since 1966. This means that every ruling party has enjoyed an absolute control of the House and its operating procedures (except the Public Accounts Committee which is chaired by the Opposition (with the right to request investigations) though the majority of members remain from the ruling party). When there have been moments when the ruling party has lost control of the House, this has normally led to a general election (as in 1998 and 2013). In 2017, the opposition Christian Democrats entered an electoral coalition with the Democratic Party which saw the latter secure two seats but this did not impact the ruling party's (Social Democrats) absolute control of the House and the Maltese parliament can be considered to remain a two-party parliament. In this way, Malta conforms to the Westminster Constitutionalised model (Hazell 2008) and "can be described as a two-party majoritarian democracy existing under weak, but nevertheless extant, constitutional constraints" (Bulmer 2014, 249), and while this creates an executive "who have virtually unlimited domestic discretion in making legislation and policy; these majoritarian party-political powers are constrained … by peripheral institutions of legal constitutionalism such as the Constitutional Court, the Presidency, and the Ombudsman. Such constraints … ensure the peaceful transfer of power through free, fair and regular elections" (Bulmer 2014, 249).

27.2 The Parliament's Administrative System

27.2.1 The Speaker and the Clerk of the House

Article 59 of the Maltese constitution outlines the conditions for the election and potential vacation of the office of Speaker, while Article 64 refers to the office of Clerk of the House and states that "the office of the Clerk to the House of Representatives and the offices of the members of his staff shall be public offices" (Maltese Constitution Art. 64.2.). As outlined by parliament itself, the House executes its business based on the constitution, Standing Orders of the House, the House of Representative's (Privileges and Powers) Ordinances, Rulings from the Chair (based on written and unwritten practices) and also usage practices of the UK parliament. As outlined by parliament, the Speaker's main role is to "ensure that order is maintained during sittings of the House and that the parliamentary rules are respected" (Parliament of Malta 2021e), while Art. 4 of the Parliamentary Services Act states that "the legal and judicial representation of the (Parliamentary) Service shall lie in the Speaker" and also states that the officers of the House comprise the Clerk, other officers required to sit at the table of the House and "such officers as the Speaker may establish".

According to parliament's mission statement, the Office of the Clerk, under the direction of the Speaker, "is duty bound to deliver effective, apolitical, professional and innovative services to support the efficient conduct of the House of Representatives, its committees as well as a range of services and facilities for Members of Parliament" (Parliament of Malta 2021c). The 1962 Standing Orders of the House state that the Clerk's principal responsibilities include:

- "The delivery of services requested by Members of Parliament, Ministries, Government departments, the press and the public within existing financial and human resources;
- The ongoing task of ensuring that the Parliamentary Chamber, its precincts and Office of the Clerk remain a functional working location that is accessible to the public within security constraints
- The provision of a wide range of services and facilities to ensure that Parliament functions effectively. While these services primarily consist of the keeping and publishing of Parliamentary Minutes and Transcripts they also include research support, audio/visual broadcasting of debates and the provision of IT services to Members of Parliament" (Parliament of Malta 2021d).

27.2.2 Administrative Divisions

Figure 27.1 provides an overview of the staffing divisions to be found in the Maltese parliament in 2021. As can be seen, parliament's administration is divided into four principal divisions with tasks focused on the work of the House and the committees, information services, international affairs and support services. In addition to the units listed in the organigram, there are five additional units which sit 'outside' the hierarchy: the Speaker's secretariat,

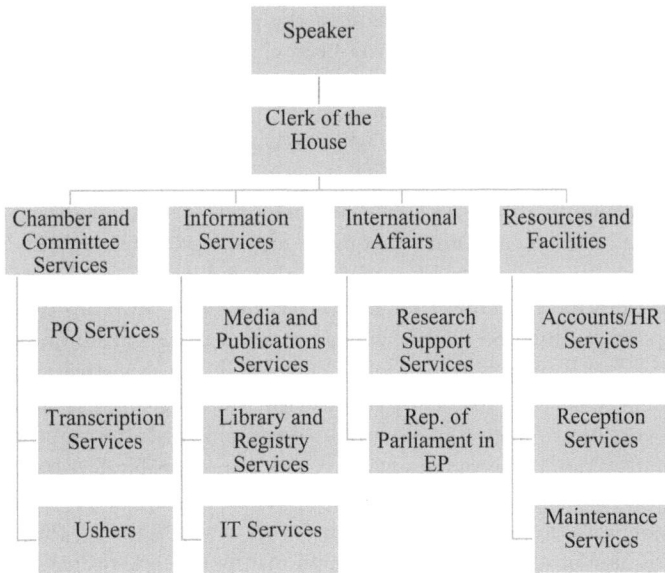

Figure 27.1 The Maltese parliament's governance structure

the legal services (legal services have been outsourced for the past 15 years), security, the Administrative Board and the Parliament of Malta Foundation.

The work of parliament has been impacted by three important developments over the last two decades which have impacted its staff numbers and budget. The first relates to Malta's membership of the EU in 2004; from membership onwards, parliament was given the additional role of scrutinising the government's EU negotiating positions as well as participating in the EU's early warning system for subsidiarity. These developments placed increased pressure on the Foreign and European Affairs Committee of the House and a number of Research Analysts were recruited to assist the committee and to draft parliament's decisions as part of the early warning mechanism, representing a new type of official within the parliamentary administration. Subsequently, the role of these Research Analysts has been widened to also assist the delegations assigned to the various inter-parliamentary forums within which the Maltese parliament participates, see Section 27.4. Extending beyond the remit of EU affairs, these Research Analysts have also been assigned to various parliamentary committees to help in the preparation of meetings and to assist in the drafting of reports which are then presented to the House. In this way, Research Analysts have become a new and important addition to the work of the House over the last two decades and the evolution in their role reflects the pragmatic approach of small states in dealing with expanding responsibilities. In 2020, the number of Research Analysts was five, which means that there is a ratio of 1:13 in terms of Research Analysts to MPs.

The second important development was the move to new premises in 2015. Based historically in the Grandmaster's Palace in the centre of Valletta (itself an office complex for the President and a museum), a new parliament designed by Renzo Piano was built at the entrance to Valletta, the capital. An imposing array of local stone and glass, the building was immediately short on space with the result that most of the staff working in transcription and editing moved to telework, an arrangement that served well once the COVID-19 pandemic began. The move also necessitated other changes for the parliament's administration; with a state-of-the-art building all to itself, maintenance agreements had to be negotiated with the intention, in the near future, to outsource the management of these contracts, while parliament's security, which had previously been the responsibility of the Armed Forces, shifted to the police.

Third, the most significant recent innovation in the work of parliament's administration was the 2017 Parliamentary Service Act. The Act meant that, for the first time in the history of the Maltese parliament, the House had its own, autonomous administrative service responsible for providing all the necessary support services for the running of the House. The Act means that parliament is now responsible for establishing its own budget, managing its resources and making its own recruitment. To that end, parliament has been taking steps to detach itself from the centralized public service, including in terms of grade structures and accounting systems (while still observing good governance and administration of public funds). In this way, parliament is in the process of negotiating a collective agreement with the staff's two main unions, while the new grade structure should enable parliament to issue calls for new employees better catered to the needs of parliament. In terms of these new grade scales, job specifications and promotions, the Clerk is responsible for drafting and issuing calls as well as establishing the criteria to use in selection boards, a role which is undertaken after consultation with the Speaker. Further, in terms of staff training, the Clerk is responsible for the provision of ad-hoc training and sponsorships of work-related academic courses.

As can be seen, the administrative service of the Maltese parliament has seen several key innovations over the last two decades with a sharp increase in the demands placed on it.

Reflective of this, we see that its staff contingent has more than doubled over the last 20 years from a staff complement of 30 in 2002 to 73 at present. Those currently engaged with parliament include public servants detailed to parliament when the service was established in 2017 as well as new recruits who have been employed directly with the new service (the 73 employees do not include the 20 police officers guarding the building, maintenance personnel nor cleaning staff though the funds for the wages of these employees are provided for by parliament). In terms of budget, in 2002, this stood at €2,336,363 (recurrent) with no capital budget, while the budget in 2020 now stands at €10,472,000, with a capital budget of €2,176,000 (Parliament of Malta 2019).

27.3 Administrators in the Context of Parliament's Work and Its Political Parties

In its broadest terms and as highlighted in Figure 27.1, the administration of the House involves: work related to the running of the House and its various committees; research support provided to committees and delegations travelling abroad; the transcription and editing of parliamentary debates and committee meetings for publication; as well as the parliament's general service, such as Human Resources or IT support. The third and fourth functions are squarely administrative roles which are not particularly conditioned by the nature of the organisation within which they are situated, whereas the first and second functions, in supporting the House and its committees, relate directly to the work of a legislative body and can be considered the most sensitive functions of the parliamentary administration. In relation to these functions, the parliamentary staff are involved in preparing and disseminating the agendas and minutes of the plenary and the various committees and maintaining their respective pages on parliament's website (committees and parliamentary debates can be viewed online). Parliamentary staff also process and vet all parliamentary questions (PQs) (there were 4,118 PQs in 2019 [Parliament of Malta 2020]), produce edited proceedings of debates and also provide procedural advice to the Speaker or Deputy Speaker as well as the chairs and members of various committees.

In supporting the work of the House and the various committees, the work of the research department, library and ICT resources are central. As outlined previously, Research Analysts are increasingly being assigned tasks outside their original remit (of supporting the Foreign and European Affairs Committee), and to this end, they are not being assigned to a single committee, allowing their services to be used by parliament as needs arise. Their work is facilitated by the parliament's library and archive which were overhauled and moved to a purpose-built safe area under parliament's main building in 2022. Reflective of the needs of the new state-of-the-art building and the heavy investment in streaming of parliamentary business online, there has been an expansion in the ICT section over the last few years with four people currently working in this department as IT officers.

It should be stressed that, in supporting the work of the House and committees, the parliamentary administration is careful not to get involved in the partisan, political business of the parliament, even in the case of Research Analysts whose work is primarily advisory. To this end, the administration does not assist in the work of drafting legislation, which is normally undertaken by the principal ministry responsible for piloting a bill through parliament (with the assistance of the Legislation Unit of the State Advocate); the degree to which Committee Clerks assigned to the Committee for the Consideration of Bills are involved relates to checking that the published version of the Acts are as they were amended and approved by the Committee and then the House. They also make orthographical or necessary renumbering of articles while also ensuring that the Maltese and English text fully reflect each other (Malta has two official languages). In this way, the support given is purely administrative. This approach is reflected in the fact that there are no procedures for the parliamentary service to conduct any *ex ante* or *ex post* assessment of the legislation passed by parliament.

This purely administrative role is seen in the work extended to participative instruments, including the right of permanent committees to invite representatives of civil society to address committees, while experts can also be summoned as witnesses to advise the committees and to answer questions. In addition to these provisions, the general public can also petition parliament directly. To facilitate this work, an online portal allows submissions, which must follow specific guidelines to be considered admissible to the Petitions Committee. In all cases, it is the work of the administrative staff to administer and make arrangements for witnesses or guests to address committees or for petitions to be processed. The purely administrative role is also seen in budgetary affairs. With the entry into force of the Parliamentary Service Act, financial estimates are submitted by the Clerk of the House to the Speaker who then passes these estimates to the House Business Committee for eventual approval by way of a resolution in the House. A degree of consultation exists in that the Ministry for Finance is an ex officio member of the House Business Committee but the parliamentary service's role is primarily focused on providing the estimates.

Further, and in maintaining the purely apolitical line of the administration, the parliamentary service does not have a communications unit or press officer. All press statements which are issued by the Speaker are prepared by senior parliamentary staff and sent directly to the media houses or issued by the Department of Information which comes under the Government and is part of the general service. Parliament does not have its own social media platforms though several initiatives have been undertaken in the last decade to increase transparency, including the launch of the publication 'Mill-Parlament' ('From Parliament' and published by the Office of the Speaker, comprising articles on the work of parliament and its MPs) in 2013 as well as the establishment of Parliament TV in 2015. It should also be stated that parliament's website allows for an easy search of parliamentary debates and PQs, including transcripts of all plenary debates stretching back to 1992.

In this way, we see that there is a strong logic of appropriateness underscoring the behaviour of both the political and administrative classes within Parliament, which ensures that the parliamentary service is principally an administrative structure with limited principal-agent delegation, thus limiting any concerns of bureaucratic drift, underscored by an understanding to protect the apolitical nature of the service which reinforces trust on both sides. Ultimately, the parliamentary service is too small to go beyond a largely administrative role which, in turn, protects it from accusations of political bias. That said, the dynamic between the Clerk and the Speaker is the principal point at which the apolitical nature of the Service can be questioned but two key points would indicate that both political (Speaker) and administrative (Clerk) offices strive to uphold the politically neutral ethos of the Office of Clerk. The first relates to the history of appointments to the office of Clerk where we see that since 1947 there have been 24 Speakers of the House but only 8 Clerks. The second relates to the tendency for politicians to depend on their party or their personal secretariat to provide political input and to keep public officials at arm's length. As with all senior office holders, the Speaker of the House has his own secretariat, who are all employed on a 'person of trust' basis, thus freeing the Speaker from needing to seek political advice from outside his secretariat. In this way, the parliamentary service can be largely apolitical because it does not have the push or pull factors to make it otherwise and the concerns seen in other parliaments with the principal-agent balance and efforts to avoid bureaucratic drift (Högenauer et al. 2016, 18/19) are much less of a concern in Malta.

Additionally, the ability to not be drawn into partisan politics is helped by the fact that the parties do not have political staff that can infiltrate the parliamentary service. In terms of the political parties and their staff within parliament, there are two main groupings recognised and they are each entitled to a part-time secretary, who is funded by the parliamentary service. These individuals are recruited and managed by the parties. In all cases, there are no formal links between these individuals and the parliamentary service other than payment for their contracts. Additionally, each political grouping is entitled to €100,000 annually but these funds are not used for the employment of support staff within parliament so there is no hierarchical relationship in this instance. The parliamentary service also does not fund or control any staff attached to individual MPs.

27.4 Inter-Institutional and External Relations

As outlined in Section 27.2.2, a principal innovation post-EU membership was the recruitment of Research Analysts to help in parliament's work in the area of EU affairs. Subsequently, their remit was widened to assist with the work of various committees and external relations by assigning Research Analysts to delegations. As listed above, a Research Analyst is now assigned to each formal inter-parliamentary forum in which the Maltese parliament participates regularly. Apart from assisting the delegates and the drafting of speeches and post-meeting reports, the advantage of this new system is that this ensures continuity in the participation of the Maltese parliament in these fora irrespective of any changes in the delegation. This work can be quite onerous, with delegations having travelled abroad 10 times in 2019 in relation to the EU institutions, 13 times for the Parliamentary Assembly of the Council of Europe, 3 times for the Parliamentary Assembly of the Mediterranean, 3 times for the Commonwealth Parliamentary Assembly and that of the OSCE, 2 times for the International Parliamentary Union and once for the Parliamentary Assembly of the Union for the Mediterranean (Parliament of Malta 2020).

In terms of EU membership, the Foreign and European Affairs Committee scrutinises the government's position for negotiations within the Council of the EU and participates in the early warning system for subsidiarity, a task which necessitated an increase in its Research Analysts from two to five. In terms of the early warning system, this can be considered the closest the parliamentary service comes to acting in a political fashion; while the Maltese parliament has issued red cards as part of the early warning mechanism on numerous occasions, there appears to be a tendency for parliament to issue opinions as a way to consolidate the government's stated opposition to EU proposals, as with the proposals for a consolidated community tax base (Harwood 2014; Viola 2019). This is not surprising; the opinions drafted by the Research Analysts are based on the government's memorandum as part of its scrutiny of pipeline acquis (Harwood 2014). In this way, in drawing up their recommendations for use in the early warning mechanism, the Research Analysts are often guided by the government's own stated opinion and are primarily driven by the government's established position on an EU proposal, thus involving a limited degree of principal-agent delegation.

27.5 Current Challenges

Digitalisation has been on parliament's agenda since the early 1990s when computers were introduced into parliament for the transcription of debates. With respect to audio-visual facilities, parliament shifted from analogue to digital technology in 2003 when all plenary and committee meetings began to be streamed online, both live and on-demand, via parliament's website. With the move to its new premises in 2015, this audio service was complemented with video streaming and continued to be offered live and on-demand not only through the website but also, from 2015 onwards, through the establishment of the TV channel, Parliament TV. Technology has also been extended to facilitate the internal work of parliament and the material provided to MPs, with the use of emails and SMS to keep MPs, ministerial staff and the press informed of agendas, upcoming meetings and PQs as well as sharing audio and text extracts where needed.

In the pursuit of further improving the ICT support of parliament, the House has invested heavily in scanning technology, first introduced in 2010. The principal focus now, in consultation with the National Archive Office, is the procurement of equipment and document management applications for the full scanning and retrieval facilities of parliament's archive. An example of the progress made in this regard can be seen with the publishing of PQs over the years; at present, the House is developing new software in conjunction with the Department of Artificial Intelligence at the University of Malta which shall permit MPs to submit and view the PQ database through their mobile phones. Through the collaboration with the University, two apps have already been launched to increase accessibility for the general public to the work of parliament; in 2017, the parl.eu2017.mt app was launched which provided access to the parliamentary meetings linked to Malta's presidency of the Council of the EU, while the PQViz app provides a visualisation tool for the work associated with parliamentary questions (Office of the Speaker 2017, 17). Ultimately, the provision of these services, including the streaming of debates and online portals for the searching of parliamentary information, all contribute to the transparency of parliament.

In terms of the COVID-19 pandemic, parliament introduced a number of measures to complement the global and national measures taken. Fears that Malta would be heavily impacted by COVID stemmed from its status as the most densely populated country in Europe as well as the EU country with the fastest growing population due to inward migration. However, even considering these risks, Malta never introduced a strict lockdown with people, including the public service, being encouraged to work from home and to minimise social interaction. In light of the pandemic, the parliamentary administration focused its resources on teleworking where possible, making the actual building safe, suspending all travel for parliamentary staff while also introducing flexible work arrangements for all staff considered critical and therefore needing to work from within the building. The administrative staff supported the continuation of the work of the various committees by establishing a system for committee witnesses to deliver their interventions online and for the House to continue to work and meet within the Parliament building; throughout the pandemic and reflective of parliament's small size, the House functioned as normal with members wearing masks and maintaining social distancing. The only principal change was that the Visitor's Gallery was closed (Office of the Speaker 2020, 3).

27.6 Conclusion

The Maltese parliament is a product of Malta's colonial past, its smallness as a political system and the polarised nature of its politics since independence. With a House controlled absolutely by every successive government and with power centred in the executive branch of politics, parliament can often seem like a rubber stamp, but as outlined above, the regular, open and clean transfer of power after elections is one of the cornerstones of Malta's democracy. Ruling parties will inevitably be reconstituted as the 'loyal opposition' at some point and both parties have a vested interest to maintain the effective operation of parliament within the Maltese political system.

As outlined above, while parliament is dominated by a single party with the Speaker from the ruling party, and while the Speaker has extensive power over the running of the House and its administrative staff, it is clear that the parliamentary service is considered to be apolitical and to deliver its work in a non-political manner. With limited principal-agent delegation of responsibilities above largely administrative functions and with a small service with limited potential to go beyond administrative roles, the Maltese parliamentary service appears to operate in much the same way the House operates, pragmatically. There appears to be mutual trust in that the political class expects administrative input from the service, while the administrative staff appear to have little inclination to undermine their apolitical status for some temporary gain, there being a distinct logic of appropriateness in their actions. This is surprising considering the heavy pressures under which parliamentarians work but it seems that MPs expect any policy-input to come from more trusted sources such as the party itself or their own 'people of trust' and not the parliamentary service. Where the service goes beyond purely administrative functions, as with the work of Research Analysts, their work is largely grounded in the processing of opinions drawn from outside parliament, in particular the information gathered by government in the drafting of their position on EU proposals.

In conclusion, it can be said that the administrative system of one of the smallest parliaments in Europe tends towards pragmatism with a clear delineation between the political class and the parliamentary service where roles are largely administrative in terms of the latter. That said, with the enactment of the Parliamentary Service Act in 2017, the distinction between the parliamentary service and the rest of the Public Service will grow and efforts are being made to make parliament a fulltime House which will impact the demands placed on the administrative staff. In this way, as parliament enters its second century of operation (2021 having been the 100th anniversary since its first sitting), the potential for change may increase.

Acknowledgement

The author would like to express his thanks to the Clerk of the House, Mr Raymond Scicluna, and his staff for their help and assistance throughout the writing of this chapter.

References

Bulmer, W. (2014) 'Constrained Majoritarianism: Westminster Constitutionalism in Malta', *Commonwealth and Comparative Politics*, Vol. 52(2) 232–253, Routledge, UK.
Harwood, M. (2014) *Malta in the European Union*, Routledge, UK.
Hazell, R. (ed.) (2008) *Constitutional Futures Revised: Britain's constitution to 2020*, Macmillan, UK.
Högenauer, A., Neuhold, C., Christiansen, T. (2016) *Parliamentary Administration in the European Union*, Palgrave Macmillan, UK.
Office of the Speaker (2017) *mill-Parlament*, no. 16. Available online at: https://parlament.mt/media/89384/mill-parlament-nru-16.pdf.
Office of the Speaker (2020) *mill-Parlament*, no. 24. Available online at: https://parlament.mt/media/107592/periodical-no-24.pdf.
Parliament of Malta (2019) *Interim Expenditure Report 2019*. Available online at: https://www.parlament.mt/media/102833/03745.pdf.
Parliament of Malta (2020) *Annual Report 2019*. Available online at: https://parlament.mt/media/110105/annual-report-2019.pdf.
Parliament of Malta (2021a) 'Historical Background'. Available at: Parliament of Malta – Historical Background (parlament.mt).

Parliament of Malta (2021b) 'Parliament Practice'. Available at: Parliament of Malta – Parliament Practice (parlament.mt).
Parliament of Malta (2021c) 'Mission Statement'. Available at: Parliament of Malta – Mission Statement (parlament.mt).
Parliament of Malta (2021d) 'Objectives and Responsibilities'. Available at: Parliament of Malta – Objectives & Responsibilities (parlament.mt).
Parliament of Malta (2021e) 'Speaker of the House of Representatives'. Available at: https://parlament.mt/en/13th-leg/political-groups/speaker-farrugia-anglu/
Viola, D. (2019) 'Scrutinising European Union Legislation in Light of Subsidiarity: the Maltese Parliament', *Commonwealth and Comparative Politics*, Vol. 52 (2) 208–222.

28
THE NETHERLANDS' PARLIAMENTARY ADMINISTRATION

Afke Groen[1]

28.1 Introduction

The administration of the Dutch parliament can be considered effective and of high quality. Nevertheless, it faces a number of challenges, which have surfaced in internal and external reports particularly since the late 2000s. A recurring theme has been the relatively small size of the administrative support to Members of Parliament (MPs) in comparison to parliamentary administrations in other countries (Van der Woude, 2014, p. 331–332). Amongst other issues, this had led to limited capacity and high work pressure in view of the increasing number of topics and depth and scope of information on the agenda; growing media and social media attention (Tweede Kamer, 2012, p. 10); the relatively small number of MPs per capita (Staatscommissie parlementair stelsel, 2018, p. 279); and the increasingly high turnover of MPs with national elections (Tweede Kamer, 2008, p. 14).

The question of expanding the parliamentary administration has been sensitive to political parties, as increasing the expenditure on one's own resources is perceived to be an unpopular measure (Van der Wilde, 2019). Since the late 2010s, the size of the parliamentary administration has become part of a broader, public debate on the functioning of the Dutch parliamentary system and the state of representative democracy. After an influential report recommended more administrative support to parliamentary committees (Staatscommissie parlementair stelsel, 2018) and a – small-scale – public petition called for increased support to individual MPs (Waling, 2019), the parliament's lower house adopted a motion to structurally expand its administrative resources (Tweede Kamer, 2019a).

Against this backdrop, this chapter provides an analysis of the organizational structure of the Dutch parliamentary administration, its role in the context of both day-to-day and more exceptional parliamentary work, its relations with other actors, and the external challenges facing the administration. By and large, the chapter focuses on the parliamentary administration of the House of Representatives, known as the *Tweede Kamer* (second chamber). The House is the most important and influential of the two chambers of the Dutch parliament. As a "part-time chamber" (Högenauer, this publication), the Senate, known as the *Eerste Kamer* (first chamber), has its own, small administration. It additionally makes use of various elements of the services of the administration of the House of Representatives (De Leeuw, 2014, p. 5). Where relevant, the chapter highlights differences between the two branches of the administration.

28.2 Key Aspects of the Organization of the Dutch Parliamentary Administration

28.2.1 The Development of Parliamentary Resources

In 2014, an external evaluation characterized the Dutch parliamentary administration as "relatively cheap and efficient" in international comparison (De Leeuw, 2014, p. 2). Indeed, the budgets of the administrations of both the House and the Senate are small. Figure 28.1 displays the evolution of the overall budget of the Dutch parliament over the past two decades, while Figure 28.2 displays the division of expenditures between the different parts of the budget in the House. Three observations stand out.

First, the Senate has very few resources in comparison to the House. This can be best understood not just by differences in size – the Senate has 75 members who work on a part-time basis; the House has 150 full-time MPs – but particularly by the less extensive powers and involvement in day-to-day politics and policymaking of the Senate. Indeed, in comparison to the House, the Senate has a "much smaller administrative organization, different work processes, different work pressure due to a concentration of meetings, limited or no party group support to the Members, and extensive support to Members by the Directorate Content" (Tweede Kamer, 2011, p. 8).

Second, the budget shows smaller increases and decreases over the years, as well as a gradual overall increase over the past two decades. Smaller budgetary changes can, for instance, be the result of temporary projects (e.g. Tweede Kamer, 2020a, p. 8), political decisions to cut down on public expenditure in times of austerity (e.g. Tweede Kamer, 2010), or national elections. Regarding the latter, party groups in the House are, in case of electoral loss, entitled to funding for their own administrative support based

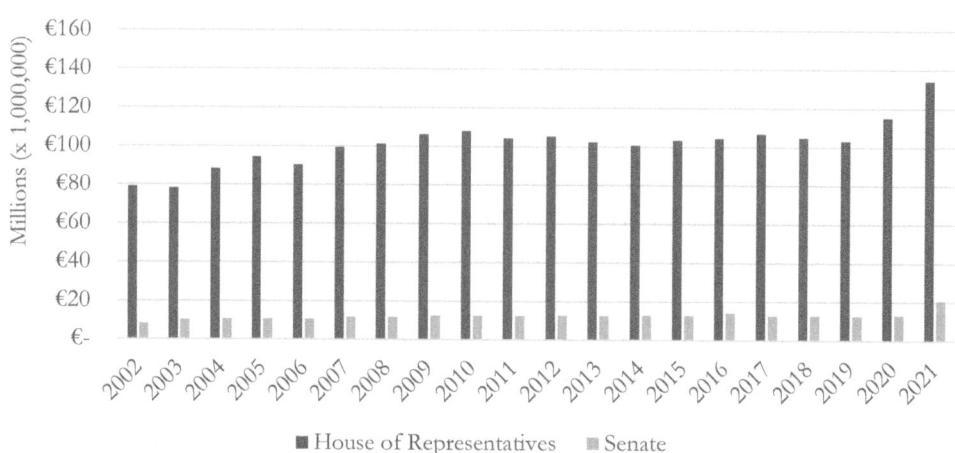

Figure 28.1 Evolution of the budget for scrutiny and legislation of the Dutch House of Representatives and the Senate (2002–2021)

Source: Own compilation based on data drawn from the yearly budget bills for both houses. Note that the numbers are hence estimated expenditures. The budget of the House excludes the expenditure on pay and expenses for MPs, the budget for the Senate includes these. The years 2002–2019 have been indexed for inflation (base year 2020). Before 2002, the annual government budget did not break down the estimated expenditure for the five High Councils of State in the Netherlands.

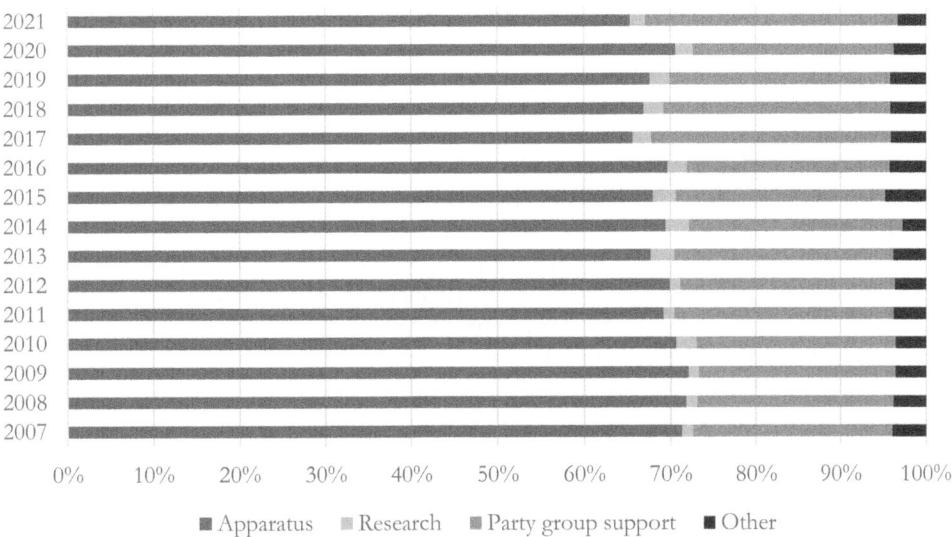

Figure 28.2 Percentage of total budget earmarked for apparatus, research, and party groups in the Dutch House of Representatives (2007–2021)

Source: Own compilation based on data drawn from the explanatory memorandums to the yearly budget bills. Note that the percentages thus reflect estimated expenditures.

on their number of seats during the previous parliamentary term (Regeling financiële ondersteuning, 2020). As far as the overall increase in financial resources is concerned, this can best be understood by the increasing workload that the Dutch parliament faces (see e.g. Tweede Kamer, 2012, p. 10). Other explanations for the gradually expanding size of the budget are growing structural expenses on the security of parliamentary buildings and the digitalization and automation of work processes. As such, the growth of the parliamentary administration fits in a historical pattern that can be observed internationally (Christiansen et al., 2021, p. 481).

Third, the structures of administrative support in the House are quite strongly tilted to the partisan dimension, rather than to the impartial, politically independent dimension (Christiansen et al., 2021, p. 482). That is, the House provides considerable funding to administrative support at party group level, namely about 25% of its total budget. This is an important difference from the Senate, which does not provide funding to party group support. Party groups can spend the resources on support staff and material costs at their own discretion, through foundations they dedicate specifically to this purpose. About 70% of the budget is allocated to the operation and management of the House, including both material costs and staff.

The rather stable division of resources between the various parts of the organization is worth highlighting, as the years 2007–2021 saw both an internal evaluation of the parliamentary administration (Tweede Kamer, 2008), a revised regulation on financial support to party groups (Tweede Kamer, 2014a), and the reorganization of the administration in view of the 2014 evaluation (De Leeuw, 2014). The budgetary amendments resulting from the 2019 motion to structurally expand the resources of the administration, however, allocate more than 80% of new funds to party group support, less than 15% to the parliamentary administration, and 2.5% to the administration of the Senate (Tweede Kamer, 2019b). This once more reflects the relative importance that MPs in the House attribute to their "own" support staff at the level of the party group.

28.2.2 The Organizational Structure of the Parliamentary Administration

Given the analysis of the parliamentary budget, it is of no surprise that the organizational structure of the administration in the House is considerably more complex than in the Senate. Both chambers have laid down the organizational structure of their administration in their respective rules of procedure. Also, both administrations are headed by a Secretary General, who is in charge of the day-to-day administrative management of the parliament.

The Senate has two further administrative directorates, organized alongside a division between central services and work in parliamentary committees. The Directorate Organization is concerned with the operation, communication, and protocol of the Senate. It is oriented mostly towards the work of the Secretary General and the secretariat of the speaker of the Senate. Amongst other responsibilities, it takes care of all affairs established by protocol – including foreign affairs – security and the parliamentary buildings, financial management, and postal and archival services. The Directorate Content, for its part, is focused on the work of the Senate in the parliamentary committees, as well as on other work of the speaker and the individual members (see Ambtelijke organisatie, no date). In 2021, a total of 7 clerks supported the work of 13 parliamentary committees and 1 temporary research committee. In total, the administration of the Senate counts 61 staff members (Högenauer, this publication).

The parliamentary administration of the House relies on a more extensive organizational structure that contains various specialized sub-units. In total, the parliamentary administration of the House counts 17 permanent services and over 200 different job descriptions (Tweede Kamer, no date). The organization has three main branches (see Figure 28.3). The first branch includes the various departments concerned with the facilities and premises of the House. The second branch is headed directly by the Secretary General. She or he is supported by the Departments for Communication, Financial and Economic Affairs, and Human Resources. The branch further focuses on assistance to the parliamentary activities of the MPs. The Chief Information Office (CIO) oversees the third branch of the organization, which is responsible for activities such as parliamentary reporting, automation, and information security.

The responsibilities of the administration are rather diffused. In 2016, the House established a Management Team of the administration with a three-tier structure, including the Secretary General, the Facilities Director and CIO. The aim of this was to address a perceived accumulation of responsibilities with the Secretary General (Tweede Kamer, 2017a, p. 12–16).

The administration is furthermore relatively focused on the work of the parliamentary committees (Christiansen et al., 2021, p. 482; see Figure 28.4). In 2021, support staff focused on the plenary counted 31 employees, whilst the various parts of the administration focused on the work of committees and activities such as parliamentary inquiries counted 120 employees. In 2022, this has been further institutionalized: between 2021 and 2022, 19 employees were added to the staff focused on parliamentary activities, whilst no additions were made to plenary staff (Tweede Kamer, 2022a). In the past, there has also been a reallocation of resources from the Departments of Communication, Human Resources, and Information to those of Research, Legislation, and the clerks. This was the result of the process of reorganization that started in 2014 kicked off by the general feeling that the division of resources and personnel between the departments was found not to be ideal and difficult to change (De Leeuw, 2014, p. 4).

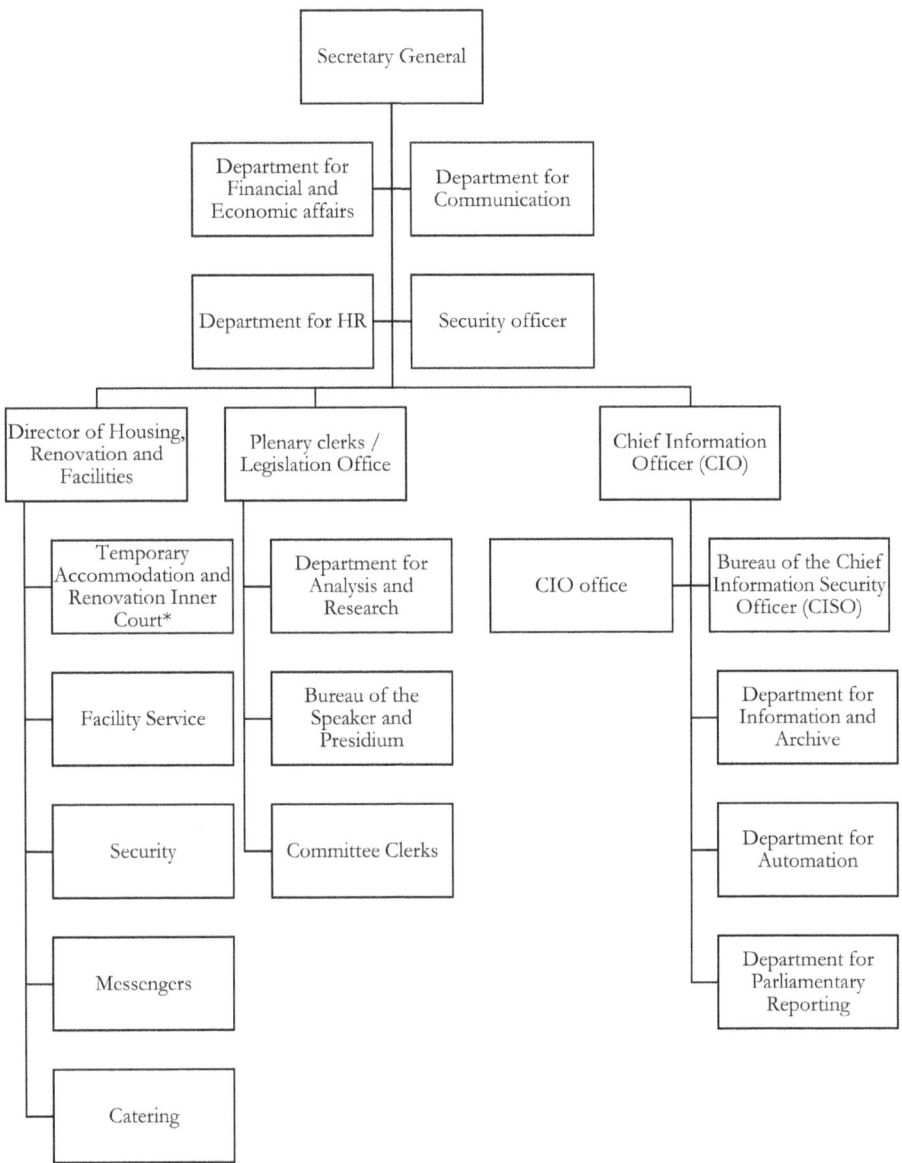

Figure 28.3 Organogram of the Dutch House of Representatives (2021)

Source: Organogram (no date).

*A large, multi-annual renovation project of the parliamentary premises, whereby all parliamentary work moved to temporary premises, started in 2021.

28.2.3 *Relation between the Administration and the Presidium*

In the institutional hierarchy of the parliamentary administration of the House, the Presidium – consisting of the Speaker and seven other MPs – and the Secretary General are highest up. The House appoints and dismisses the Secretary General, while the Presidium

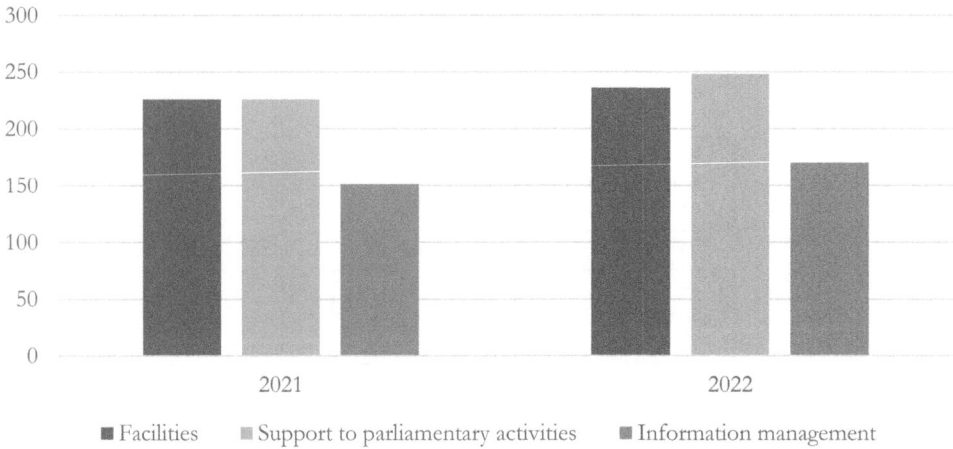

Figure 28.4 Division of staff members across three main administrative branches of the administration of the Dutch House of Representation (2021–2022)

Source: Tweede Kamer (2022a).

carries out all other legal authorities vis-à-vis the Secretary General. The Presidium, for its part, appoints and dismisses the two other members of the Management Team, while the Secretary General carries out the legal authorities vis-à-vis these two Directors. She or he also appoints and dismisses all other administrators. The hierarchy in the Senate bears great similarity to this arrangement, although it additionally has a College of Seniors with an advisory role vis-à-vis the Speaker. The Senate's counterpart of the Presidium, called the Household Committee, formally seems to have a stronger role in appointing and dismissing all other administrators.

One could thus say that the Presidium in the House functions "as if it were a Supervisory Board", while the Management Team of the parliamentary administration functions "as if it were an Executive Board" (Besluit tot instelling, 2008, p. 146). The 2014 evaluation on the functioning of the administration, however, found that these terms did not always capture actual practice well. That is, the members of the Presidium also have other roles and responsibilities that might become difficult to distinguish in practice (De Leeuw, 2014, p. 6). The report furthermore concluded that actual relationships were imbalanced, not least because the Presidium at times intervened in the work of the administration and too often concerned itself with matters that should be picked up by the administration – resulting in little mutual trust (2014, p. 6).

28.2.4 Staff Development and Professionalization

When it comes to procedures for recruitment, the parliamentary administration follows general practices in the government sector. The House and the Senate publicly advertise vacancies on their respective websites and applications proceed through an online recruitment system. The terms of employment at the parliamentary administration are those of the collective labour agreement (CAO) of the government sector. These also include general provisions for staff training and development.

Further to the 2014 evaluation and the taking office of a new Secretary General in 2016, the parliamentary administration of the House embarked on an agenda of professionalization.

One of the key aims of this agenda was to enhance the mobility and employability of staff members within the own organization. This included introducing a regular survey of in-house availability of and demand for staff competences and expertise, as well as a yearly cycle of appraisal interviews in which mobility, flexibility, and professional development would more formally come up for discussion (Tweede Kamer, 2015a, p. 9). The administration also established a trajectory for management development (Tweede Kamer, 2017b, p. 16).

If necessary, the parliamentary administration can additionally draw on (temporary) external services. In the House, this practice has particularly existed within the Department of Automation, which has been tasked with a number of major IT-projects (Tweede Kamer, 2020b, p. 9–10). The parliament, however, is committed to the so-called *Roemernorm* within publicly funded organizations, which limits expenditure on external personnel to 10% of all expenditure on both internal and external personnel.

Finally, given the confidential and sensitive nature of the work of the parliament, the administration has put in place various procedures to ensure the good conduct of its staff members. As part of the recruitment procedure, applicants are required to submit a certificate of good conduct. Permanent staff members take an oath or make a solemn affirmation, including keeping professional secrecy. Other staff members, such as interns, temporary, and external staff sign a nondisclosure agreement (Regeling vertrouwelijke stukken, 2018).

28.3 Role of the Administration in the Context of Parliamentary Work

When it comes to the function that the parliamentary administration fulfils, it follows from the discussion above that the various tasks and responsibilities are divided over various units in the House. In the Senate, however, the two key functions of providing support to MPs and registering parliamentary activities are combined into the Directorate Content. The role of this Directorate is to provide substantive preparation of both the plenary and committee meetings. It also supports members in preparing the consideration of legislative proposals and in corresponding with the government. Moreover, it is tasked with reporting and executing decisions taken by the members (Ambtelijke Organisatie, no date).

To better understand the role of the parliamentary administration in the House, it is helpful to further elaborate on five core tasks. The formal responsibilities of the administration, and in particular those of the clerks, are laid down in the House's rules of procedure (Tweede Kamer, 2020c).

28.3.1 *Supporting the Debates and Legislative Work of the Plenary*

Together, the plenary clerks and the Legislation Office carry out a central role in supporting, preparing, and advising the House when it meets in plenary session. This firstly concerns ensuring a smooth running of procedures as established by protocol and regulation. During the plenary session, the Secretary General, for instance, is seated next to the Speaker of the House. The Legislation Office furthermore advises parliamentarians on the overall constitutional process. Secondly, the clerks manage the large amount of information that the parliament deals with. They receive all documents that are sent to the House, register these documents in the parliamentary information system *Parlis*, and share documents with MPs, party groups, and parliamentary committees. This, for instance, also means that the clerks play an important role in managing confidential information (Regeling vertrouwelijke stukken, 2018).

Thirdly, the administrators can advise MPs in the law-making process. The legal experts in the Legislation Office are available to advise and support parliamentarians if they make use of their right to initiative to propose legislation, their right to amendment of legislative proposals, or if they want to submit an initiative note containing proposals on a particular policy issue. For example, they can provide research for and co-write on a legislative proposal initiated by an MP, as well as on its explanatory memorandum (Handreiking ambtelijke bijstand, 2018, p. 3).

28.3.2 Supporting the Debates and Legislative Work of the Parliamentary Committees

Like the plenary clerks, the committee clerks prepare and ensure the smooth running of the committee meetings and other activities. However, they have an even more important role in advising the respective MPs on the committee and the committee chair. This includes procedural advice, advice regarding parliamentary instruments, and advice regarding legislative proposals. When it comes to the latter, the clerk advises the parliamentary committee about whether or not it is desirable to publish a legislative report on a new proposal. She or he is subsequently responsible for drafting this report, which includes an assessment of matters such as the advice of the Council of State, matters concerning the entering into force of the legislation, and relevant EU-legislation.

All in all, the clerks play a key role in guarding the quality of the legislative process and the quality of legislation as such. Their work is mostly oriented towards parliamentary processes (see also Becker & Bauer, 2021). Nevertheless, clerks are experts in the field of the parliamentary committee that they support, given their important advisory role on the handling of legislation. Work pressure among clerks is, however, high. Because the parliamentary committees also work according to varying procedures, the committee secretariats that support them are different from each other, which may result in little flexibility and a tendency to "reinvent the wheel" (De Leeuw, 2014, p. 5). Although the number of clerks has been expanded several times since the late 2010s, enlarging administrative support to the parliamentary committees is still one of the key priorities for strengthening the overall functioning of the House (see also Staatscommissie parlementair stelsel, 2018).

28.3.3 Supporting Parliamentary Research Activities

Over the years, it has been the explicit ambition of the House to strengthen its independent knowledge and information position vis-à-vis the government to bolster its legislative function and enhance scrutiny and control (Loeffen, 2013). In 2017, the Presidium of the House took the initiative to install a "Sounding Board" to advise on strengthening the knowledge and research functions of the parliamentary administration (Tweede Kamer, 2017a). After a reorganization, the Department for Analysis and Research (DAO) was established to, on the one hand, better attune to information requirements and reduce information overload, on the other hand, harness external expertise and knowledge (see Christiansen et al., 2021, p. 482). The Department is heavily focused on the work of the parliamentary committees, as it has a dedicated information specialist and knowledge coordinator in every committee. The latter act as "knowledge brokers between the committee and scientific and advisory bodies" (Tweede Kamer, 2017a, p. 3). Moreover, DAO supports parliamentary inquiries, the most powerful instrument of the House to scrutinize the government.

Since the late 2010s, there has been political and public momentum for the House to further act on its ambition to strengthen its knowledge and information position vis-à-vis the government. Important junctures have been an advice of a weighty state commission in 2018, as well as two political scandals in early 2021 that were indicative of a lack of what became publicly known as the "countervailing power" of the parliament. Subsequently, the House by motion further expanded the resources of DAO with ten full-time equivalents in the 2022 parliamentary budget. As such, the House can be seen to adjust its administrative support in response to an increasing – public and political – demand for stronger scrutiny and control, specifically in the domains of constitutional law, budgetary rights, and policy implementation (Tweede Kamer, 2022b, p. 2).

28.3.4 *Managing and Controlling the Budget*

The Presidium – the political leadership of the House – is responsible for developing the yearly estimate of the expenditure, including the expenditures on the administration. Importantly, this estimate also sets the political priorities for budgetary expenditure. The Management Team supports the yearly budgetary cycle and involves the party groups in this process, for instance through its regular, institutionalized meetings with the secretaries of the party groups. These meetings aim to facilitate a regular exchange of information and collaboration on organizational matters and facility management (Besluit tot instelling, 2008, p. 147).

On behalf of the Speaker, the Secretary General is responsible for day-to-day management of the entire budget of the House, but it is the Department of Financial and Economic Affairs that is mandated with the necessary competences. Perhaps the most important task of the Department is to ensure that the parliament's resources are allocated most efficiently over the various activities, services, and aims of the House. When it comes to the financial resources allocated to the party groups, foundations of the party groups are responsible for financial management and control (Regeling financiële ondersteuning, 2020).

28.3.5 *Providing Access to Parliamentary Activities and Media Communication*

The Editorial and Reporting office is tasked with creating the verbatim reports of both plenary and committee meetings, in the House as well as in the Senate. Beyond its responsibility for written records, the office plays an important role in providing digital access and visibility to parliamentary activities, as it manages the video-streams of the House that broadcast parliamentary meetings both live and previously recorded.

The Communications Office of the House, for its part, is responsible for external (social) media relations and internal communication. The external communication covers both the daily affairs of the House and the parliamentary working procedures. In essence, the Office is oriented towards three actors or platforms. First, it provides communication advice for the MPs and staff members and may act as the spokesperson when it concerns the Speaker, Presidium, parliamentary committees, or Management Team. Second, it organizes the facilities for external media and press, including accreditation, as well as advice on visual material, sound, and new media. And third, the Office develops the House's own media communication, including press releases, short explanatory videos, and social media, on Twitter, Facebook, and Instagram.

28.4 EU Affairs and Inter-Parliamentary Relations

The parliamentary administration plays a crucial role in supporting the work of the House and the Senate in EU affairs and inter-parliamentary relations. The administration has a clerk's office specifically dedicated to inter-parliamentary relations. Up to 2008, this office had a rather isolated position, as it was part of a joint committee of the Senate and House (Eerste Kamer, 2008). Since, it has been part of the authority of the Secretary General of the House. Its tasks are to maintain administrative relations with inter-parliamentary organizations and platforms; advise MPs, the Speakers, and the political leadership of both chambers on inter-parliamentary affairs; as well as support the participation of MPs in inter-parliamentary meetings (Reglement griffie, 2020).

Both chambers have fully mainstreamed administrative support to EU affairs. That is, as the sectoral committees are responsible for the scrutiny of EU affairs, the administrative support for EU affairs is also focused on the sectoral committees (Högenauer, this publication; see also Gattermann, Högenauer & Huff, 2016; Högenauer, Neuhold & Christiansen, 2016). Given the vast differences in the size of the administration of the House and the Senate, it should not come as a surprise that the House has substantially more in-house resources and expertise dedicated to EU affairs than the Senate. Crucially, while EU affairs are part of the normal duties of committee staff in the Senate (Högenauer, this publication), the House employs dedicated EU-advisors to the parliamentary committees.

The EU-advisors perform a number of key tasks. First, they support the committees in employing the various parliamentary instruments and possibilities for scrutiny and control in EU affairs, such as regular debates and questions, as well as the scrutiny reserve and the subsidiarity check.[2] This includes strategic advice on how and when to employ such instruments. Second, they follow up on all Commission proposals in their respective domain. They also prepare the parliamentary scrutiny in terms of substance, for instance by writing memos. Third, they are responsible for managing relations with other national parliaments, the European Parliament, and the Commission, as well as for managing intra-parliamentary relations with the EU-advisors and staff of other committees (Högenauer & Neuhold, 2015, p. 346; Mastenbroek et al., 2014).

The position of the EU-advisors results from a process of increasing attention to, as well as constant evaluation of, the scrutiny of EU affairs in the Dutch House. In 2002, the House for the first time recommended the institution of an EU staff unit (Tweede Kamer, 2002), which resulted in the delegation of a liaison officer for both chambers (see also Neuhold & Högenauer, 2016). More administrative support for EU affairs followed only in 2006, with the hiring of four experienced EU-advisors additional to the four members of staff to the European affairs committee. By mid-2007, the EU-advisors started to focus their work on the sectoral committees. This has subsequently been institutionalized (Bovenop Europa, 2011, p. 23; see also Mastenbroek et al., 2014), although it has taken time for the EU-advisors to become the single point of contact for MPs in the stream of information on EU affairs (Tweede Kamer, 2014b, p. 16).

28.5 Conclusion and Future Challenges

The administration of the Dutch parliament performs crucial functions, not just in terms of managing parliamentary procedures and information processes but also in terms of preparing the substantive work of the MPs. In response to changes in political priorities and the substantive focus of the parliament, the structure of the administration has changed. One example is the reform of administrative support to EU affairs in the House in the mid-2000s, following new European realities and political priorities. Another example is the reorganization and growth of administrative units dedicated to parliamentary research activities, in response to a growing emphasis on an independent information position of the House.

The parliamentary administration similarly seems to adjust to new challenges, including changing work patterns due to the Covid-19 pandemic and the demands of digitalization. During the pandemic, most of the procedural parliamentary meetings went online and administrative staff worked from home. For the longer term, the House has made adjusting to the demands of the "modern workplace" one of its priorities for 2022 and 2023. It will introduce a new environment for digital meetings in the first quarter of 2022 and, over the next years, will work on improving cloud solutions (Tweede Kamer, 2022b, p. 5). More generally, the scrutiny of digital affairs was already one of the key challenges facing the parliament as well as its administration prior to the pandemic. In 2020, this led to the decision to establish a parliamentary committee on Digital Affairs with its own parliamentary staff, including a clerk, information specialist, knowledge coordinator, as well as EU-advisor (Tweede Kamer, 2020d).

The relatively small size of the administration has, however, posed difficulties before embarking upon the challenges of Covid-19 and digitalization already. High work pressure hampers the ability of the administration to effectively respond to political demands. In the House, for instance, MPs will carry out no less than three parliamentary inquiries in the parliamentary term 2021–2025, putting a heavy strain on administrative capacities. This is even more problematic as the work pressure amongst MPs is also found to be very high.

Moreover, public and political debates are ongoing about, first, the independent position of the parliament vis-à-vis the government and, second, the parliament's capacity to make good legislation. To accomplish the ambitions to strengthen the position of the parliament on both fronts, it is imperative to expand administrative support – most importantly to the parliamentary committees, where the centre of gravity is (Staatscommissie parlementair stelsel, 2018). Indeed, as Christiansen et al. (2021, p. 480) observe, "legislative work requires the availability of reliable documentation at its basis and above all the skills of ensuring the quality of legislative drafting with respect to bills and amendments being passed in parliament". The turn of events since 2021 might be a juncture to finally act on the many reports that have recommended expanding the capacities of the Dutch parliamentary administration. Both chambers have taken some steps in this direction (Tweede Kamer, 2021, p. 49–52; Eerste Kamer, 2022; Tweede Kamer, 2022b).

Notes

1 The author would like to thank two anonymous interviewees.
2 With the scrutiny reserve, the House makes special agreements on information provision with the government on Commission proposals it deems of high political interest. With the subsidiarity check, the House has implemented the Early Warning System for the principle of subsidiarity.

References

Ambtelijke organisatie (no date). Available at: https://www.eerstekamer.nl/begrip/ambtelijke_organisatie (Accessed: 20 January 2021).
Becker, S. & Bauer, M. (2021). 'Two of a kind? On the influence of parliamentary and governmental administrations', *The Journal of Legislative Studies*, 27(4), p. 494–512.

Besluit tot instelling van een regulier overleg tussen het managementteam van de Tweede Kamer en de fractieorganisaties (2008). In Tweede Kamer, *Reglement van Orde*. Den Haag: Tweede Kamer der Staten-Generaal, p. 146–149.

Bovenop Europa: Evaluatie van de versterkte EU-ondersteuning van de Tweede Kamer, 2007-2011 (2011). Den Haag: Tweede Kamer der Staten-Generaal.

Christiansen, T., Griglio, E. & Lupo, N. (2021). 'Making representative democracy work: the role of parliamentary administrations in the European Union', *The Journal of Legislative Studies* 27(4), p. 477–493.

De Leeuw, J. (2014). *Meer verzakelijking en verdere professionalisering: Externe validatie van het functioneren van de ambtelijke ondersteuning van de Tweede Kamer*. Den Haag: ABTOPConsult.

Eerste Kamer (2008). *Wijziging van het Reglement van Orde van de Eerste Kamer en van het Reglement voor de Griffie voor de interparlementaire betrekkingen in verband met het toevertrouwen van de zorg voor de Griffie voor de interparlementaire betrekkingen aan de Tweede Kamer der Staten-Generaal*. Den Haag: Eerste Kamer der Staten-Generaal.

Eerste Kamer (2022). *Raming der voor de Eerste Kamer in 2023 benodigde uitgaven, evenals aanwijzing en raming van de ontvangsten*. Den Haag: Eerste Kamer der Staten-Generaal.

Enthoven, G. (2011). *Hoe vertellen we het de Kamer? Een Empirisch Onderzoek naar de Informatierelatie tussen Regering en Parlement*. Delft: Eburon.

Gattermann, K., Högenauer, A-L. & Huff, A. (2016). 'Research note: studying a new phase of europeanisation of national parliaments', *European Political Science* 15, p. 89–107.

Griglio, E. & Lupo, N. (2021). 'Parliamentary administrations in the bicameral systems of Europe: joint or divided?', *The Journal of Legislative Studies*, 27(4), p. 513–534.

Handreiking ambtelijke bijstand bij initiatiefwetgeving (2018). Available at: https://www.rijksoverheid.nl/documenten/rapporten/2018/08/28/tk-bijlage-handreiking-ambtelijke-bijstand-bij-initiatiefwetgeving (Accessed: 29 March 2021).

Högenauer, A-L. & Neuhold, C. (2015). 'National Parliaments after Lisbon: administrations on the rise?, *West European Politics*, 38(2), p. 335–354.

Högenauer, A-L., Neuhold, C. & Christiansen, T. (2016). *Parliamentary administrations in the European Union*. Basingstoke: Palgrave Macmillan.

Loeffen, S. (2013). 'Naar een sterker parlement: meer (ruimte voor) onderzoek', *Montesquieu Instituut Policy Papers*, 1.

Mastenbroek, E., Zwaan, P., Groen, A., van Meurs, W., Reiding, H., Dörrenbächer, N. & Neuhold, C. (2014). *Engaging with Europe: Evaluating national parliamentary control of EU decision making after the Lisbon Treaty*. Radboud University Nijmegen.

Neuhold, C. & Högenauer, A-L. (2016). 'An information network of officials? Dissecting the role and nature of the network of parliamentary representatives in the European Parliament', *The Journal of Legislative Studies*, 22(2), p. 237–256.

Organogram (no date). Available at: https://www.tweedekamer.nl/over_de_tweede_kamer/organogram (Accessed: 20 January 2021).

Regeling financiële ondersteuning fracties Tweede Kamer 2014 (2020). BWBR0035068. Available at: https://wetten.overheid.nl/BWBR0035068/2020-01-28 (Accessed: 30 March 2021).

Regeling vertrouwelijke stukken (2018). Available at: https://wetten.overheid.nl/BWBR0031383/2018-04-17 (Accessed: 30 March 2021).

Reglement griffie interparlementaire betrekkingen Staten-Generaal (2020). Available at: https://wetten.overheid.nl/BWBR0024419/2020-01-28 (Accessed: 15 April 2022).

Staatscommissie parlementair stelsel (2018). *Lage drempels, hoge dijken: Democratie en rechtsstaat in balans*. Amsterdam: Boom.

Tweede Kamer (no date). *Functielijst ambtelijke organisatie*. Available at: https://www.tweedekamer.nl/kamerstukken/detail?id=2020D16659&did=2020D16659 (Accessed: 21 January 2021).

Tweede Kamer (2002). *Liaisonfunctie Brussel-Den Haag en ondersteuning inzake Europees Beleid: Brief van de algemene commissie voor Europese Zaken*. Den Haag: Tweede Kamer der Staten-Generaal.

Tweede Kamer (2008). *Parlementaire zelfreflectie 2007-2009*. Den Haag: Tweede Kamer der Staten-Generaal.

Tweede Kamer (2010). *Vaststelling van de begrotingsstaat van de Staten-Generaal (IIA) voor het jaar 2011: Brief van de minister van Binnenlandse Zaken en Koninkrijksrelaties*. Den Haag: Tweede Kamer der Staten-Generaal.

Tweede Kamer (2011). *Vaststelling van de begrotingsstaat van de Staten-Generaal (IIA) voor het jaar 2012: Memorie van toelichting.* Den Haag: Tweede Kamer der Staten-Generaal.

Tweede Kamer (2012). *Vaststelling van de begrotingsstaat van de Staten-Generaal (IIA) voor het jaar 2011: Memorie van toelichting.* Den Haag: Tweede Kamer der Staten-Generaal.

Tweede Kamer (2014a). *Regeling financiële ondersteuning fracties Tweede Kamer: Brief van het presidium.* Den Haag: Tweede Kamer der Staten-Generaal.

Tweede Kamer (2014b). *Democratische legitimiteit: Verslag van de rapporteur.* Den Haag: Tweede Kamer der Staten-Generaal.

Tweede Kamer (2015a). *Raming der voor de Tweede Kamer in 2016 benodigde uitgaven, alsmede aanwijzing en raming van de ontvangsten: Begrotingstoelichting (uitgaven en ontvangsten).* Den Haag: Tweede Kamer der Staten-Generaal.

Tweede Kamer (2015b). *Vaststelling van de begrotingsstaat van de Staten-Generaal (ILA) voor het jaar 2016: Memorie van toelichting.* Den Haag: Tweede Kamer der Staten Generaal.

Tweede Kamer (2017a). *Raming der voor de Tweede Kamer in 2018 benodigde uitgaven, alsmede aanwijzing en raming van de ontvangsten: Nota naar aanleiding van het verslag.* Den Haag: Tweede Kamer der Staten-Generaal.

Tweede Kamer (2017b). *Jaarverslag en slotwet Staten-Generaal 2016.* Den Haag: Tweede Kamer der Staten-Generaal.

Tweede Kamer (2019a). *Nota over de toestand van 's Rijks Financiën: Motie van het lid Jetten c.s.* Den Haag: Tweede Kamer der Staten-Generaal.

Tweede Kamer (2019b). *Vaststelling van de begrotingsstaat van de Staten-Generaal (IIA) voor het jaar 2011: Amendement van het lid Sneller c.s.* Den Haag: Tweede Kamer der Staten-Generaal.

Tweede Kamer (2020a). *Vaststelling van de begrotingsstaat van de Staten-Generaal (IIA) voor het jaar 2021: Memorie van toelichting.* Den Haag: Tweede Kamer der Staten-Generaal.

Tweede Kamer (2020b). *Raming der voor de Tweede Kamer in 2021 benodigde uitgaven, alsmede aanwijzing en raming van de ontvangsten: Nota naar aanleiding van het verslag.* Den Haag: Tweede Kamer der Staten-Generaal.

Tweede Kamer (2020c). *Reglement van orde.* Den Haag: Tweede Kamer der Staten-Generaal.

Tweede Kamer (2020d). *Update vereist: Naar meer parlementaire grip op digitalisering.* Den Haag: Tweede Kamer der Staten-Generaal.

Tweede Kamer (2021). *Versterking functies Tweede Kamer: Meer dan de som der delen.* Den Haag: Tweede Kamer der Staten-Generaal.

Tweede Kamer (2022a). *Aantallen medewerkers.* Den Haag: Tweede Kamer der Staten-Generaal.

Tweede Kamer (2022b). *Raming der voor de Tweede Kamer in 2023 benodigde uitgaven, alsmede aanwijzing en raming van de ontvangsten: Geleidende brief.* Den Haag: Tweede Kamer der Staten-Generaal.

Van der Wilde, D. (2019). 'Het Haagse Taboe: De capaciteitsproblemen van de Kamer zijn 'een bloody shame'', *NPO Radio 1*. Available at: https://www.nporadio1.nl/politiek/17236-het-haagse-taboe-de-capaciteitsproblemen-van-de-kamer-zijn-een-bloody-shame (Accessed: 19 January 2021).

Van der Woude, W. (2014). 'Staten-Generaal en wetgeving', *RegelMaat*, 29(6), p. 322–333.

Waling, G. (2019). 'Steun de Kamer, versterk onze democratie'. Available at: https://steundekamer.nl (Accessed: 19 January 2021).

29
POLAND'S PARLIAMENTARY ADMINISTRATION

Maciej Serowaniec

29.1 Introduction

In the light of Article 95 of the Constitution, the Polish Parliament has a bicameral structure, consisting of the Sejm (the lower Chamber of the Parliament) and the Senate (the upper Chamber of the Parliament).[1] Each Chamber is vested with a separate administrative body in the form of the Chancellery of the Sejm (Polish: Kancelaria Sejmu) and the Chancellery of the Senate (Polish: Kancelaria Senatu). These are the legal, organizational, advisory, financial and technical bodies serving the Chambers and their organs, guided in performing their tasks by the principle of impartiality. The internal organization of both Chancelleries is determined by parliamentary regulations and their statutes.

29.2 Organizational Structure of the Parliamentary Administration in Poland

The Chancelleries are complex institutions. They perform organizational, technical and advisory tasks connected with the activities of Parliament and its bodies. Moreover, they are responsible for creating favourable working conditions for parliamentarians and for the exercise of their parliamentary mandate (Witkowski, 2021, p. 272).

The basic organizational unit functioning within the structures of both Chancelleries is the Bureau (Polish: Biuro), although this word may not be found in the name of a given organizational unit (e.g. the Sejm Library, the Parliament Guard or Sejm Sittings Secretariat). The Bureau performs the tasks set out in the organizational rules as well as the tasks assigned by the Chief or Deputy Chief of the Chancellery, to whom it reports as an organizational unit. Currently, the structure of the Chancellery of the Sejm comprises 21 bureaus (Figure 29.1), while the structure of the Chancellery of the Senate 18 bureaus (Figure 29.2).

The adopted functional division of the Chancellery's organizational units allows each unit to be staffed by personnel with qualifications in a particular, relatively narrow area (i.e. service of the plenary sessions; committee meetings; legislative drafting; budgetary issues or European Union affairs and inter-parliamentary cooperation). The adopted system favours more effective supervision exercised by persons performing managerial functions, who need to be familiar with the narrow range of qualifications. However, this division has certain disadvantages as well. The first is the relatively large number of executives. The second is the slower and more bureaucratic decision-making process.

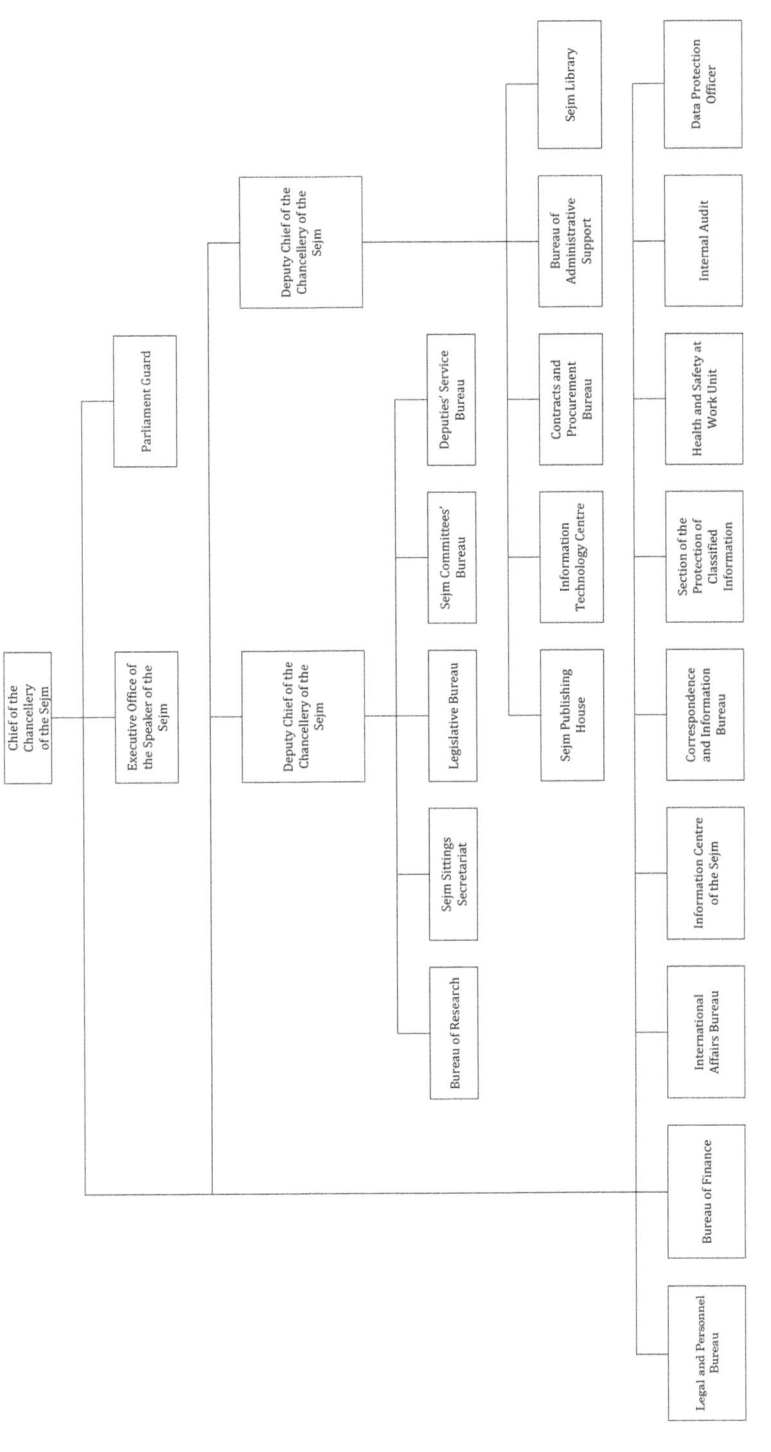

Figure 29.1 Organizational chart of the Chancellery of the Sejm

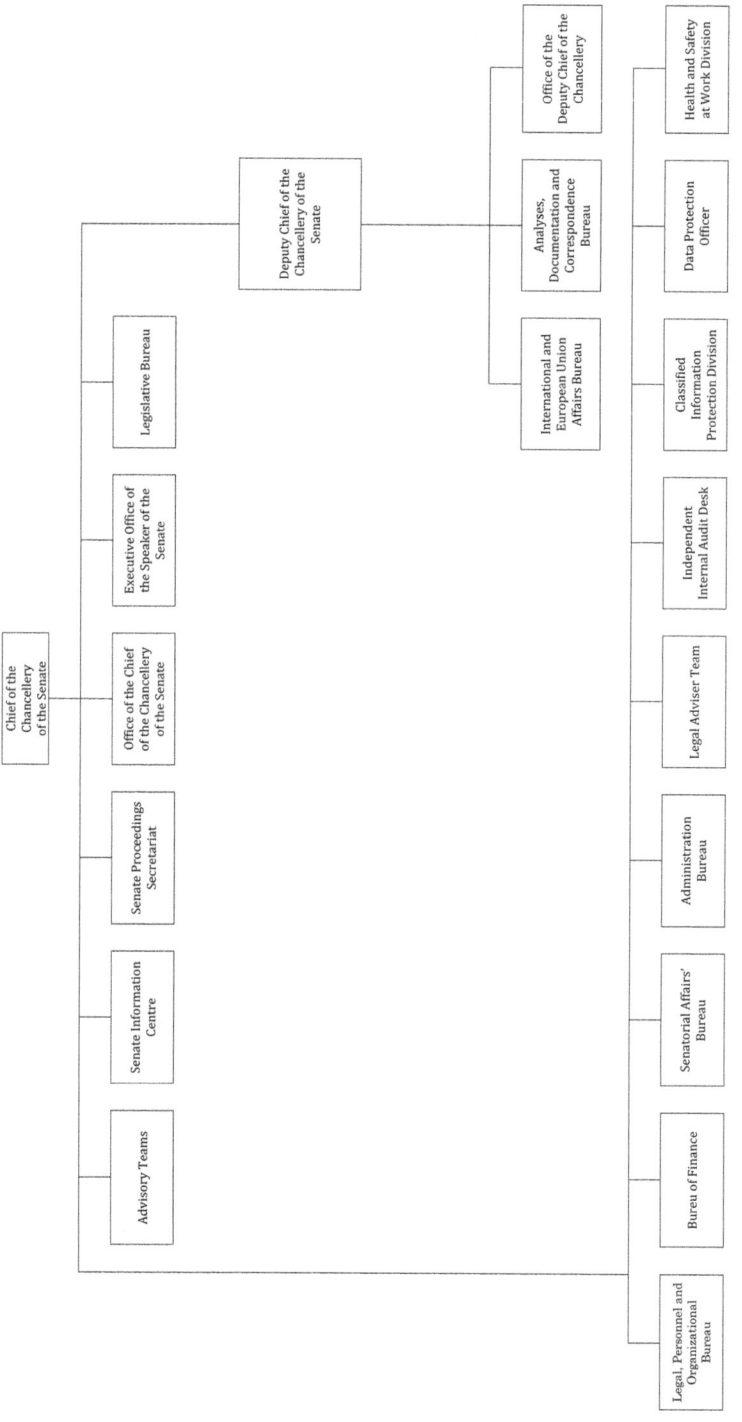

Figure 29.2 Organizational chart of the Chancellery of the Senate

29.2.1 Presence of Specialized Units in the Polish Parliamentary Administration

The functioning of the Chancellery of the Sejm and the Senate is based on a specialized bureaus that perform three basic functions:

1. provide procedural, organizational and clerical support for the work of the Parliament;
2. provide scientific and expert support for the legislature;
3. provide financial and organizational services and look after the assets and properties of Parliament (Woś, 2010, pp. 102–103).

The organizational unit with the longest tradition is the Sejm Library. From the beginning, the library's purpose has been to support the legislative process by providing library and information services to the Sejm and its bodies. The second task of the Library is to document the legislative process by collecting and storing all types of documents produced in the course of the Sejm's activities, as well as those related to its activities and to the history of the Polish parliamentary system (Art. 26(1)(1) of the Organizational Rules). The structure of the Library of the Sejm includes the Archives of the Sejm, which collects archival records produced in the course of the Sejm's activities. The collections of the Sejm Library are available to senators and the employees of the Senate Chancellery.

The Parliament Guard, a uniformed parliamentary protection force subordinate to the Speaker of the Sejm, can also take pride in its long tradition. The tasks of the Parliament Guard include the protection of parliamentary buildings and facilities, as well as the execution of the orders of the Speaker of the Sejm issued on the basis of the Regulations of the Sejm. Additionally, the Guard performs representative tasks, as well as those relating to security, order and fire protection for the Senate.

The legal service of the Chancellery of the Sejm consists of staff from the Legislative Bureau and the Bureau of Research. The Legislative Bureau plays the leading role in handling work on bills and resolutions. The tasks of the Legislative Bureau include "issuing initial opinions on bills, resolutions, declarations, appeals and statements of the Sejm submitted to the Sejm, before submitting them for the first reading" (Art. 24(1)(1) of the Organizational Rules). In turn, the task of the Bureau of Research is to "perform and organize scientific consultancy for the Sejm, its organs, its Deputies and the Chancellery of the Sejm" (Art. 17(1)(1) of the Organizational Rules). Moreover, the Bureau provides expert assistance in the exercise of parliamentary mandate, conducts research work related to legislative proceedings, analysing the legal, economic and social effects of the enacted laws. In addition, it provides advice and opinions on matters relating to Poland's membership in the EU (Radziewicz, 2013, pp. 36–37).

The Information Technology Centre (IT Centre) is responsible for the proper functioning of the Sejm's on-line information system, systems supporting the legislative process and the voting system. In addition, it maintains the Internet System of Legal Acts, a database containing descriptions and texts of legal acts published in the Journal of Laws and the *Monitor Polski* from 1918 to the present, as well as Constitutional Tribunal decisions.

29.3 The Role of the Administration in the Context of Parliamentary Work in Polish Sejm and Senate

The Chancelleries ensure the proper organization of the sittings of the Chambers, the work of their internal bodies and the office and expert services for Deputies and Senators. Among the tasks of the Chancelleries is the preparation and presentation to the Speakers and Presidiums of both Chambers of Parliament of motions, opinions and comments on matters that are the subject of the work of Parliament. In practice, they also oversee the keeping of timetables and agendas of sessions of the Sejm and Senate, and of parliamentary committees, and are responsible for collecting and disseminating materials to MPs and senators (Zubik, 2003, p. 407).

29.3.1 *Support for Committees and Plenary Debates*

From the early 1990s, the tasks performed by the Chancellery of the Sejm to service the plenary sessions were clearly separated from those related to the activities of the Sejm's committees, which brought transparency to the service of the various spheres of the Sejm's activities.

One of the primary tasks of the Chancellery of the Sejm is to provide substantive, organizational and technical services to standing committees, extraordinary committees and committees of enquiry. The implementation of this task is the responsibility of the Sejm Committees' Bureau. Its structures include the permanent secretariats of the parliamentary committees, which support committees in their work. The exceptions to this rule are the EU Affairs Committee, which is supported by the International Affairs Bureau, and the Legislative Affairs Committee, which is supported by the Bureau of Research.

The secretariats organize committee meetings as agreed by their chairmen and bureaus. They notify Deputies and certain State bodies of the dates and subjects of committee meetings and provide committee members with the required materials for those meetings. They are responsible for gathering and inputting information on committee proceedings into databases and for verifying the attendance of Deputies at committee meetings. The committee secretariats also draft minutes of their meetings and compile and collect all documentation of committee proceedings for information and archiving purposes. They are responsible for the form and timeliness of transmitting to the bodies of the Sejm the committee's recommendations, opinions, bills and resolutions, as well as reports on the bills, resolutions and positions of the Senate that have been considered. In the area of handling legislative and resolution work in committees, the staff of the secretariats cooperate with the Legislative Bureau and the Bureau of Research.

The tasks relating to the handling of plenary sittings of the Sejm fall within the remit of the Sejm's Sittings Secretariat. It prepares draft agendas for Sejm sessions, as well as the final versions of the agendas following the amendments introduced by the decision of the Sejm or the Speaker. At the stage of preparatory work, the tasks of the Secretariat also include registering and collecting motions submitted by the parliamentary clubs and groups[2] relating to the subject matter of the Sejm's sittings. On their basis, a draft schedule of sessions of the Sejm and a draft thematic plan of the work of the Sejm are drawn up. During the sitting, the staff of the Sejm's Sittings Secretariat are responsible for providing services to those presiding over the session and for the ongoing analysis of the proceedings of the Sejm. They also operate the voting machine and the light panels in the plenary Chamber, register Deputies for the floor and collect motions and amendments tabled at the second reading of bills and draft resolutions. Moreover, officials of the Sejm's Sittings Secretariat prepare supporting materials for the consideration of items on the agenda (the so-called sitting script). The Secretariat is further responsible for the stenographic reports and minutes of the Sejm's sittings, which are the only official statements of the proceedings of the Sejm.

In the case of the Chancellery of the Senate, there is no clear separation between the tasks performed for the service of plenary sessions and those related to the service of committee activities. Implementation of both these tasks is the responsibility of the Senate Proceedings Secretariat.

29.3.2 Legislative Drafting

The Rules of Procedure of the Sejm require the Chancellery of the Sejm to ensure the participation of a representative of the legal service in proceedings concerning bills and resolutions. The legal service is constituted by the employees of the Legislative Bureau, as well as the Bureau of Research, to the extent of its participation in the legislative process. Legislative lawyers participate in all stages of intra-Sejm proceedings with bills and resolutions.

Legislative Bureau staff prepare a preliminary legislative opinion on submitted bills, resolutions, declarations, appeals and statements of the Sejm. This includes an assessment of meeting the formal statutory requirements for a given bill. In the course of legislative proceedings, employees of the Legislative Bureau monitor the plenary session of the Sejm or participate in the committee meeting when the first reading of a bill is held. The legislator entrusted with the handling of a particular bill or resolution is required to actively participate in all meetings of the committee or subcommittee. The legislator is responsible for observing the principles of legislative technique and is obliged to formulate comments and objections to the bill itself and the amendments tabled to it. When drafting committee reports on a given bill for a sitting of the Sejm in cooperation with the secretariats of the parliamentary committees, the legislator is responsible for preparing and checking the text of the bill and the attached minority and legislative committee motions. The expert opinions and opinions provided by the Legal Service are not binding on either MPs or the parliamentary committees (Iłowiecki, 2010, pp. 28–30).

Once the Sejm passes laws and resolutions, legislators draft the texts of these acts and present them to the Speaker of the Sejm for signature. The role of the Legal Service does not cease with the passing of the passed law for signature by the President of the Republic of Poland or even with the publication of the Act in the Journal of Laws. In connection with the control of the constitutionality of the enacted law, carried out by the Constitutional Tribunal, the employees of the Bureau of Research also work out drafts of the Sejm's positions on the appealed bills, as well as prepare other materials for the MP – the Sejm's representative participating in the proceedings before the Constitutional Tribunal. The Bureau of Research prepares for the needs of the Sejm's bodies' numerous notes and analyses any information concerning the Sejm's activities in the scope connected with the jurisprudence of the Constitutional Tribunal (Radziewicz, 2013, p. 36).

The tasks assigned to the Chancellery of the Sejm in the area of legislative activity extend to the preparation of consolidated texts of laws.[3] On the basis of an analysis made by the Legislative Bureau, with a view to fulfilling the conditions set forth in this Act, a consolidated text is drafted. The final, agreed consolidated text is presented to the Speaker of the Sejm for signature, and then forwarded to the Prime Minister together with an application for publication in the Journal of Laws (Art. 16(1) of the Act of 20 July 2000 on Publishing Normative Acts and Certain Other Legal Acts).

On similar principles, legal and legislative assistance to the Senate, its bodies and senators is provided by the Legislative Bureau of the Senate Chancellery.

29.3.3 European Union Affairs, Parliamentary Diplomacy and Inter-Parliamentary Cooperation

The International Affairs Bureau plays a key role in initiating and coordinating cooperation with the European Parliament and the national parliaments of EU Member States. It draws up programmes of international parliamentary cooperation of the Sejm, handles visits of Sejm delegations to foreign parliaments, international assemblies and parliamentary organizations, as well as visits of delegations of these parliaments, assemblies and organizations to the Sejm (Art. 19(1)(1) and (2) of the Organizational Rules). It is also responsible for servicing the Sejm's EU Affairs Committee (Art. 19(1)(8) of the Organizational Rules). The Bureau for International Affairs prepares and organizes interpretation and translation services for the Sejm and its bodies as well as the Chancellery of the Sejm, edits the information bulletin and prepares information materials for foreign visitors to the Sejm (Art. 19(1)(3) of the Organizational Rules).

The Bureau of Research is responsible for preparing opinions on the compliance of draft laws with EU law and on legal issues related to the process of implementing EU law. It provides opinions on draft EU legal acts, including a review of their legal bases, assesses the legal, economic and social effects of the proposed solutions and assesses their compliance with the principles of subsidiarity and proportionality. In this respect, it cooperates with academic groups and with EU legal and parliamentary research services of other countries, including Interparliamentary EU Information Exchange (IPEX), European Centre for Parliamentary Research and Documentation (ECPRD), International Federation of Library Associations and Institutions (IFLA) and European Parliamentary Technology Assessment (EPTA).

29.3.4 Budgetary Issues

The budgetary procedure provides for a mode for establishing the budget of the Chancellery of the Sejm. The adoption of specific solutions in this respect is an expression of the Sejm's autonomy. The draft budget of the Chancellery is prepared by the Bureau of Finance and, as regards the part relating to MP's allowances, by the Deputies' Service Bureau. The revenue and expenditure draft signed by the Chief of the Chancellery of the Sejm is finally approved by the Speaker of the Sejm after consultation with the Rules and Parliamentary Affairs Committee. The draft budget thus established is incorporated by the Minister of Finance into the draft budget act (Art. 139(2) of the Public Finance Act). The Minister of Finance and the Council of Ministers do not enjoy the right to modify these draft budgets. They may be amended only by the Sejm and the Senate in the course of parliamentary work. The budget of the Chancellery of the Sejm, as adopted, is a summary of projected revenues and expenditures earmarked for the performance of the tasks performed by the Sejm and the Chancellery of the Sejm. Under similar principles, with the involvement of the Senate Bureau of Finance, the budget of the Chancellery of the Senate is drafted (Zientarski, 2011, pp. 187–189; see also Table 29.1).

Table 29.1 The expenditures of the Chancellery of the Sejm and Chancellery of the Senate (2000–2020, in thousand PLN)

	2000	*2005*	*2010*	*2015*	*2020*
Chancellery of the Sejm	289,308	353,887	395,323	419,911	557,535
Chancellery of the Senate	112,324	123,009	79,700	85,261	110,225

Source: Analysis of the execution of the state budget and assumptions of the monetary policy by the Supreme Audit Office in the years 2000–2020, on-line access: www.nik.gov.pl

29.4. Rules/Arrangements for Interaction with Stakeholders (e.g. Political Parties, Organized Interests and Civil Society)

29.4.1 Technical, Organizational and Financial Support for Parliamentary Clubs and Groups

The Chancelleries provide the technical, organizational (in terms of premises) and financial conditions for the activities of the parliamentary clubs and groups' offices. The Chancellery's Bureaus of Finance are responsible for providing the individual clubs and groups with lump sums to cover the costs of their activities and the activities of their offices. These funds are used to finance, among others, salaries of club and group offices' employees, purchases of press and publications, as well as costs connected with the organization of seminars, conferences and other meetings by a club or group in the parliamentary premises. It should be noted that the staff employed in the offices of the clubs and groups do not have the status of parliamentary staff. With the support of the IT Centre, club and group offices are also equipped with the necessary IT and office equipment. In addition, the Chancelleries organize training for staff working in the clubs and groups' offices, for example in the field of service to Parliament, its bodies, clubs and groups, and the operation of parliamentary and senatorial offices.

29.4.2 Service to Non-Attached Parliamentarians

The Chancelleries provide also organizational and office support for non-attached parliamentarians. They also ensure them work premises with IT and office equipment. In turn, the Chancellery's Bureaus of Finance provide the non-attached parliamentarians with lump-sum funds for their services. These funds are used, inter alia, to finance expert reports and opinions commissioned by MPs without the assistance of the Chancellery, to finance purchases of newspapers and magazines, as well as the costs associated with organizing seminars, conferences and other meetings on parliamentary premises.

29.4.3 "Dialogue with Citizens" within the Direct Democracy Institutions

The Chancellery of the Sejm assists the Speaker with regard to the activities relating to the adoption of a citizens' motion for a nationwide referendum. The determination of whether the motion has been supported by the required number of at least 500,000 citizens is the responsibility of the Correspondence and Information Bureau. A negative assessment of the Bureau in this respect constitutes grounds for the Speaker of the Sejm to request the National Electoral Commission to determine whether the required number of signatures has been submitted and, consequently, to decide on refusal to accept the request. The tasks of the Correspondence and Information Bureau further include the analysis of petitions submitted to the Sejm and the preparation of draft letters of the Speaker addressed to the petitioners.

Similar tasks are undertaken by the Chancellery of the Sejm in the exercise of legislative initiative by citizens. A group of citizens, numbering at least 100,000 persons having the right to be elected to the Sejm, may put forward a legislative initiative by placing their signatures under a bill. Upon collecting 1,000 signatures, the committee's plenipotentiary notifies the Speaker of the Sejm of the committee's establishment. All the organizational and formal tasks preceding the issuance of the provisions above by the Speaker of the Sejm are performed by the Chancellery of the Sejm, and in particular by the Legal and Personnel Bureau, in cooperation with the Legislative Bureau and the Bureau for Research.

The tasks of the Sejm Committees' Bureau and its permanent committee secretariats, in turn, include the organization of public hearings by the Sejm committees and the performance of tasks relating to lobbying activities conducted on the grounds of the Sejm. In the latter case, the Chancellery of the Sejm is responsible for issuing a periodic access card to a person engaged in professional lobbying activity and for making available in the Information System of the Sejm the proposed legal solutions, expert opinions and legal opinions submitted by said persons.

29.4.4 Relations with Traditional and New Media

The Information Centre of the Sejm is responsible for maintaining contact with and handling the media. The Centre's tasks include: maintaining permanent contact with representatives of domestic and foreign mass media; providing information on the work of the Sejm, its bodies and the Chancellery of the Sejm; providing information on events taking place at the Sejm, including press conferences, briefings and thematic conferences and seminars. The Information Centre of the Sejm contacts journalists by phone, e-mail (newsletter), via the website www.sejm.gov.pl, Twitter accounts (@PLParliament) and via an SMS gateway. However, to cover the work of the Sejm and its bodies, media representatives are required to hold a one-off, periodic or permanent press accreditation.

The Information Centre of the Sejm is moreover responsible for disseminating knowledge about the Sejm. To this end, it prepares materials documenting the work of the Sejm and its organs as well as educational materials, organizes meetings, seminars and competitions, and organizes tours of Sejm buildings. The Senate Information Centre performs its tasks under similar principles in the Senate of the Republic of Poland.

29.5 The Nature of Institutional Hierarchy

29.5.1 Management of the Chancellery of the Sejm and Senate

The Chancelleries of the Sejm and Senate are built on the principle of hierarchical subordination, which is typical of most state offices. The Chancellery is headed by the Chief of the Chancellery, who is responsible to the Speaker of the House for the actions of employees subordinate to him/her, and in particular for the execution of the Chancellery's budget and the State Treasury's assets under its management. The legal position of the Chief of the Chancellery is primarily determined by the provisions of parliamentary regulations.

By definition, the Chief of the Chancellery of the Sejm holds an apolitical official position, which should be filled according to the criterion of expertise and professional experience. He/she is appointed and dismissed by the Speaker of the Sejm "upon consultation with the Rules of Procedure and Parliamentary Affairs Committee" (Art. 200(2) of the Rules of Procedure of the Sejm). The Speaker is also vested with the power to appoint and dismiss not more than two Deputies, after consultation with the Chief of the Chancellery of the Sejm (Art. 200(3) of the Rules of Procedure of the Sejm); there are no more than two of them (Art. 200(1) of the Rules of Procedure of the Sejm). The characteristic feature of such an employment relationship is the lack of protection of permanence, expressed in the fact that the appointing authority may dismiss the Chief of the Chancellery of the Sejm or his/her Deputies from their positions. The purpose of this regulation is to give the Speaker of the Sejm, as the appointing authority, the freedom to select persons to be entrusted with managerial positions in the Sejm administration. The employment relationship by appointment of the Chief of the Chancellery and the Deputies is established for an indefinite period of time. The positions of the Chief of the Chancellery of the Sejm and the Deputies thereof belong to the group of positions subject to special anti-corruption rigour. Pursuant to Article 4 of the Act of 21 August 1997 on Restriction on Conduct of Business Activities by Persons Performing Public Functions, such persons may not conduct business activities on their own account or jointly with other persons, nor manage such activities, nor be members of bodies of business entities. As regards the powers of the Chief of the Chancellery of the Sejm, first of all, it is necessary to mention the authority provided for in Article 201(1) of the Rules of Procedure of the Sejm over all the employees of the Chancellery of the Sejm. The Chief of the Chancellery participates, in an advisory capacity, in the work of the Presidium of the Sejm and the Convention of Seniors. As the head of the State budget unit, the Chief of the Chancellery is responsible for the execution of the State budget in the "02 Chancellery of the Sejm" section, as well as for all State assets under the Chancellery's management. The Chief of the Chancellery of the Sejm is also in charge of the protection of classified information produced, processed, transmitted or stored at the Chancellery of the Sejm.

During the Chief of the Chancellery's absence, the deputy authorized by this officer manages the Chancellery of the Sejm. On a day-to-day basis, the Deputies of the Chief of the Chancellery coordinate the activities of the organizational units subordinate to them, and in particular: accept plans, reports, documents and studies pertaining to the activity of the subordinate offices and keep the Chief of the Chancellery informed about their work. The formal subordination of individual offices directly to the Chief of the Chancellery and his/her Deputies is established by way of a separate order issued by the Chief of the Chancellery.

Bureaus are headed by directors who manage their work and are responsible for all the activities of the organizational unit. Directors carry out the tasks entrusted to them by the Chief of the Chancellery or his/her deputy, to whom the organizational unit reports. They are responsible for the proper performance of their tasks, for observing working time and order and for complying with the law, including the rules on health and safety at work and on the protection of classified information.

29.5.2 *Parliamentary Service of the Sejm and Senate of the Republic of Poland*

Despite the changing political situation in the country, the standard of work performed by the parliamentary service has been crucial, consisting in the professional and politically neutral performance of tasks serving the efficient functioning of Parliament. Employees of both Chancelleries form a professional group in which employment relations are governed by the provisions of the Act of 16 September 1982 on Employees of State Offices. The employees of the Chancelleries are employed on the basis of an employment contract. A person who is a Polish citizen is over the age of 18 and has full capacity to enter into legal transactions and enjoys full public rights, as well as being of irreproachable character, has the appropriate education and has completed an administrative internship, while the state of their health allows them to be employed on a given position and may become an officer of the Chancellery. The Constitution introduces in Article 103(1) the prohibition on combining employment at the Chancellery with a parliamentary mandate. The *incompabilitas* principle, in this case, is intended to prevent the mixing of the decision-making functions of Parliament and its organs with the subservient and auxiliary functions of the Chancellery of the Sejm, as well as to limit the ability of MPs to pursue gainful employment in a state institution.

Employees newly hired at the Chancellery who have no work experience in public administration are required to complete an administrative traineeship. In the Chancellery of the Sejm, the administrative traineeship is called the Sejm traineeship. Appointed civil servants and graduates of the National School of Public Administration are exempt from the Sejm traineeship. The traineeship lasts 12 months and ends with an appraisal issued by the Appraisal Committee following an examination.

An official employed by the Chancellery is obliged to protect the interests of the state and safeguard the rights and legitimate interests of citizens. He/she is also obliged to observe the binding legal order, rationally manage public funds, perform the entrusted tasks reliably, impartially, efficiently and in a timely manner, observe state and official secrecy, develop his/her professional knowledge and behave decently at work and outside of work. An official submits a statement of his or her financial standing upon the commencement of the employment relationship and at the request of the Chief of the Chancellery of the Sejm. Individuals taking up the official position may not undertake additional employment without the prior consent of the Chief of the Chancellery of the Sejm.

Under the law, employees of the Chancellery of the Sejm are entitled to special privileges, as compared to the general provisions of the labour law. These include an allowance for long-standing work in state offices, jubilee awards, awards from the internal bonus fund, as well as retirement or disability severance pay. The Chief of the Chancellery of the Sejm has at his/her disposal an additional award fund for the Chancellery's officers, and he/she may increase it within the limits of the funds available for remuneration (Art. 48(1c) of the Officials Act).

Employment at the Chancellery of the Sejm is stable, with the majority of employees being employed for an indefinite period of time. As shown by the practice to date, as a rule, the Speaker of the Sejm does not influence the staffing of lower official positions, leaving the freedom of personnel decisions to the Chief of the Chancellery.

The Chancellery of the Sejm currently employs 1271 staff, while the Senate Chancellery employs 331 employees (Table 29.2).

29.5.3 Operation in the Era of the COVID-19 Pandemic

As early as 6 March 2020, Order No. 3 was issued by the Speaker of the Sejm, acting in consultation with the Speaker of the Senate, on special organizational arrangements related to the threat of SARS-CoV-2 virus infection. It specified the rules for remote working by employees of the Chancellery of the Sejm and the Senate, as well as imposed limitations on the access to parliamentary buildings. Apart from MPs and senators, only those employees of the Chancellery may enter parliamentary buildings whose presence in the Sejm and Senate is justified by ensuring the continuity of parliamentary work and efficient functioning of the Chancellery.

Table 29.2 Number of employees in the Chancellery of the Sejm and Chancellery of the Senate (2000–2020)

	2000	2005	2010	2015	2020
Chancellery of the Sejm	1,154	1,160	1,196	1,199	1,295
Chancellery of the Senate	321	274	284	287	331

Source: Analysis of the execution of the state budget and assumptions of the monetary policy by the Supreme Audit Office in the years 2000–2020, on-line access: www.nik.gov.pl

29.6 Conclusion

Over the years, with the development of Polish parliamentarism, the Chancelleries of the Sejm and Senate have improved their functioning and adjusted their potential to systemic challenges. The efficiency and functionality of operations, and above all the professional, stabilized parliamentary service, are the hallmarks of the administrative services of the Sejm and Senate worth highlighting in the context of their performance to date.

Notes

1. The Constitution of the Republic of Poland of 2 April 1997 vests legislative power in the Sejm and the Senate (Art. 95). The legislative competence of both Chambers is not symmetrical. The Constitution provides the Sejm with a dominant role in the legislative process. The inequality of the two Chambers of the Polish Parliament is also expressed in the fact that only the Sejm is vested with the right to control the Council of Ministers.
2. In Polish Parliament, Deputies and Senators are often grouped into a clubs (Polish: kluby) or groups (Polish: koła). For example, the Sejm club consists of at least 15 Deputies; group consists of at least 3 Deputies. The Senate club consists of at least seven Senators; group consists of at least three Senators.
3. In Poland, the official consolidated text is published in the form of a notice in the official journal in which the normative act was announced. The consolidated text constitutes an annex to the announcement. Since 1 January 2016 onward, the Speaker of the Sejm announces the consolidated text of the Act at least once every 12 months, if it has been amended.

References

Legal Acts

Konstytucja Rzeczypospolitej Polskiej z dnia 2 kwietnia 1997 r. [The Constitution of the Republic of Poland of 2 April 1997], J. of L. 1997, No. 78, item 483 as amended.

Ustawa z dnia 16 września 1982 r. o pracownikach urzędów państwowych [Act of 16 September 1982 on Employees of State Offices], consolidated text: J. of. L of 2001, No. 86, item 953, as amended.

Ustawa z dnia 21 sierpnia 1997 r. o ograniczeniu prowadzenia działalności gospodarczej przez osoby pełniące funkcje publiczne [Act of 21 August 1997 on Restriction on Conduct of Business Activities by Persons Performing Public Functions], J. of L. of 1997, No. 106, item 679, as amended.

Ustawa z dnia 20 lipca 2000 r. o ogłaszaniu aktów normatywnych i niektórych innych aktów prawnych [Act of 20 July 2000 on the Publishing Normative Acts and Certain Other Legal Acts], J. of L. of 2000, No. 62, item 718.

Ustawa z dnia 27 sierpnia 2009 r. o finansach publicznych [Act of 27 August 2009 on Public Finance], J. of. L. of 2009, No. 157, item 1240, as amended.

Uchwała Sejmu Rzeczypospolitej Polskiej z dnia 30 lipca 1992 r. Regulamin Sejmu Rzeczypospolitej Polskiej [Resolution of the Sejm of the Republic of Poland of 30 July 1992. Rules of Procedure of the Sejm of the Republic of Poland], consolidated text: M.P. 2020, item 476, as amended.

Uchwała Senatu Rzeczypospolitej Polskiej z dnia 23 listopada 1990 r. Regulamin Senatu [Resolution of the Senate of the Republic of Poland of 23 November 1990. Rules of Procedure of the Senate of the Republic of Poland], consolidated text: M.P. 2018, item 846, as amended.

Załącznik do zarządzenia nr 6 Marszałka Sejmu z dnia 21 marca 2002 r. Statut Kancelarii Sejmu [Annex to Order No. 6 of the Speaker of the Sejm of 21 March 2002: The Statute of the Chancellery of the Sejm], online access: https://www.sejm.gov.pl/sejm9.nsf/page.xsp/KS_statut

Załącznik do zarządzenia nr 6 Marszałka Senatu z dnia 20 października 2006 r. Statut Kancelarii Senatu [Annex to Order No. 6 of the Speaker of the Senate of 20 October 2006. The Statute of the Chancellery of the Senate], online access: https://www.senat.gov.pl/kancelaria/statut-kancelarii-senatu/

Literature

Iłowiecki, R. (2010) Status legislatora w organach władzy publicznej. Zawód legislator [Status of Legislative Drafting. The profession of Drafter], *Przegląd Sejmowy*, no. 6, pp. 28–30.

Radziewicz, P. (2013) Doradztwo naukowe w pracach Sejmu [Scientific Consultancy Services in the work of the Sejm]. *Przegląd Sejmowy*, no. 5, pp. 36–37.

Witkowski, Z. (2021) 'Sejm [The Sejm]' in Witkowski, Z., Lis-Staranowicz, D. Serowaniec, M. (eds.), *Polskie prawo konstytucyjne w obliczu wyzwań współczesności [Polish constitutional law in the context of contemporary challenges]*. Toruń: TNOiK Publishing House, pp. 272–273.

Woś, K. (2010) *Kancelaria Sejmu – zadania, struktura, funkcjonowanie [The Chancellery of the Sejm – tasks, structure, functioning]*. Warsaw: The Sejm Publishing House.

Zientarski, P.B. (2011) *Organizacja wewnętrzna Senatu. Studium prawnoustrojowe [The internal organization of the Senate: A legal and organizational study]*. Warsaw: The Chancellery of the Senate.

Zubik, M. (2003) *Organizacja wewnętrzna Sejmu RP [Internal organization of the Sejm of the Republic of Poland]*. Warsaw: The Sejm Publishing House.

Netography

Analysis of the execution of the state budget and assumptions of the monetary policy by the Supreme Audit Office in 2000–2020, online access: www.nik.gov.pl [accessed: 27.03.2021]

Maciej Serowaniec – Associate Professor, Department of Constitutional Law, Faculty of Law and Administration, Nicolaus Copernicus University in Toruń (Poland), ORCID: 0000-0003-4693-7977, e-mail: mserowaniec@umk.pl

30
PORTUGAL'S PARLIAMENTARY ADMINISTRATION

Ana Vargas, Bruno Dias Pinheiro and Teresa Fonseca

30.1 Parliamentary Organization, from Stability to Change[1]

After the Revolution of 25 April 1974, which overthrew the dictatorial regime, the first free elections were held for the Constituent Assembly, one year later. The Constitution was approved in 1976, creating a Parliament with one single chamber (*Assembleia da República*), with political and legislative powers and competences to scrutinise the Government.

Furthermore, the Constitution establishes that "the Assembly and its committees shall be assisted in their work by a permanent body of technical and administrative staff, and by specialists who are on assignment or are temporarily contracted. The number of such staff and specialists shall be the number which the President deems necessary", as a form of ensuring the autonomy and the independence in relation with the Government, because till there, the parliamentary staff was assigned by the Government.

Since then, the staff of the *Assembleia da República*, together with the parliamentary members and bodies, have been able to accommodate and even initiate organizational reform processes in order to respond to the challenges that the institution is increasingly facing.

In a constantly rotating organization, such as a Parliament, the staff is the guardian of parliamentary memory and *praxis*. They ensure its day-to-day operation and are also the key element for its continuity, change and evolution. However, parliamentary staff is the least visible side of Parliaments. These are people who usually go anonymous, but are often seen in the background of the events taking place in the Parliament.

30.2 Key Aspects of the Organization of the Parliamentary Administration

The dimension of the parliamentary staff should be weighted according to the number of the members of Parliament. The *Assembleia da República* is composed of 230 Members since 1991. The *ratio* of parliamentary staff to MPs never reached 2.[2] Although it was around 1.5 in the first decade of this century, it dropped between 2010 and 2015, as can be seen from Table 30.1 and Figure 30.1.

Table 30.1 Dimension of the parliamentary staff

Year	2000	2005	2010	2015	2020
No. of Staff	365	379	383	340	418

It should be recalled that, between 2011 and 2014, Portugal was under a Financial Assistance Programme, agreed between the Portuguese authorities and the Troika (European Commission, the European Central Bank and the International Monetary Fund). During this period, there was no staff recruitment. As a result, the evolution of staff in the *Assembleia da República* shows a **U** curve over the last decade, and, from 2015 on, there has been a reversal of the downward trend that had led to a staff loss of more than 10%.

Several competitive procedures to recruit parliamentary staff have been launched in recent years to compensate for exits, provide qualified staff to deal with new challenges and reverse the ageing index. However, we remain far from a *ratio* of two parliamentary staff members *per* MP.

30.2.1 Recruitment and Career

Parliamentary staff form a special and permanent body governed by a special statute – the statute governing parliamentary staff – and access to this career is usually made through the starting grade of the category and requires certain educational qualifications.

The three parliamentary careers – advisor, support officer and operations assistant – differ in terms of the educational qualifications required at the time of entry[3] and their functional content.

Under the Statute, recruitment is carried out using a competitive appointment procedure which must respect several principles, such as freedom to apply, equal conditions and opportunities for all candidates, the neutrality of the composition of the appointment panel, implementation of objective evaluation methods[4] and also the right of challenge and appeal.

Depending on the performance evaluation,[5] parliamentary staff advance in their career through different remuneration scale points, but access to a higher category (senior advisor, support coordinator and senior assistant) is subject to a competitive appointment procedure,

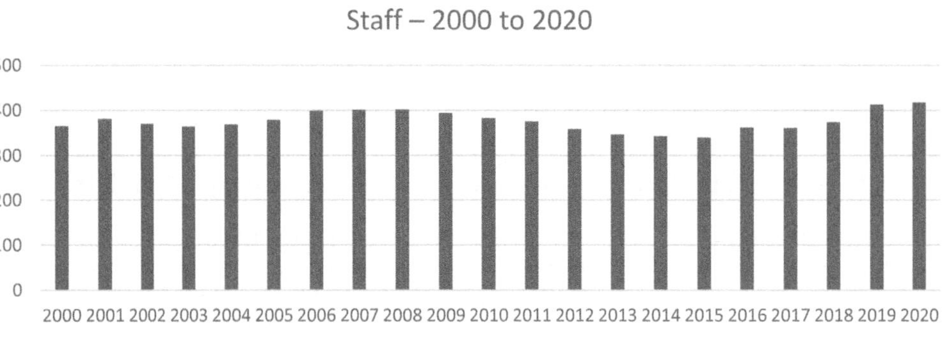

Figure 30.1 Graph of development of staff size of the Assembleia da República

in which case the selection methods are a public discussion of a paper on a topic relevant to exercising the functions, of an eliminatory nature, a *curriculum vitae* evaluation and a competence evaluation interview.

Parliamentary staff take up their duties as interns for a probationary period of 18 months, with two phases: an initial phase, mostly consisting on training, and a second phase, of a practical nature, involving the performance of duties in different parliamentary services.

Among the rights and duties of parliamentary staff is the duty of developing, strengthening and enhancing their professional skills through an appropriate training system, which is ensured through access to internal and external training activities.

Each parliamentary group has the right to have technical and administrative staff of its trust, which are not part of the staff of the *Assembleia da República* nor subject to their Statute[6] and who are freely employed and dismissed by the parliamentary groups.

Concerning parliamentary committees, provision is made for the possibility of committee chairs proposing to the Speaker (President of the *Assembleia da República*) that technical experts be assigned to them from the public or private sector to provide technical advisory services. This solution has not been frequently used, apart from assigning a military staff member to advise the National Defence Committee, for several legislatures now.

Staff on assignment exercise their functions under the committee chair's direct guidance, without prejudice to the general and special duties to which parliamentary staff are subject.

30.2.2 The Legal Status of Personnel

Employment in the *Assembleia da República* is carried out on an exclusive basis and is incompatible with holding any public or private office, role or activity which could affect the independence of parliamentary employees and their full compliance with the duties established in the Statute.

Exceptionally, employment in the *Assembleia da República* may be combined with other public employment if there is an obvious public interest in such accumulation and the latter is unpaid. If it is paid, it may be authorized in certain cases which are exhaustively listed.

Whether paid or not, private functions or activities that compete with, or are similar to the parliamentary functions carried out, and are in conflict with them, undermining the duties laid down in the Statute, are excluded.

The Secretary-General and heads of services may not accumulate other public functions or offices, except those which result from inherent unremunerated situations, missions and studies of a transitory nature, or participation in committees and working groups that result directly from the exercise of their functions. There are exceptions for certain activities, such as teaching activities, that can be authorized by the Speaker. The exercise of private functions by heads of services also requires authorization which may only be granted if it is not liable to compromise or interfere with the exemption required to exercise those functions.

Parliamentary staff are subject to duties of impartiality and of political neutrality, which consist of not revealing, in the performance of their work, any party-political inclination or preference for any legislative policy solution, and not to perform or omit to perform any act which may in any way favour or hinder a political position to the detriment or advantage of others.

They are also subject to professional secrecy concerning all facts and information of which they may be aware only in the course or as a result of the performance of their functions, and to professional confidentiality, which consists of a prohibition on supplying any non-public information or documents related to the work of the *Assembleia da República* without prior authorization by a superior.

30.2.3 The Structure of Administrative Departments

Concerning services organization although there have been changes brought forward with the creation of departments and the allocation of new functions, the basic structure of parliamentary services has remained the same and is based on the following areas:

- Parliamentary Support;
- Information and Culture;
- Administrative and financial;
- International relations and Protocol;
- Information Technology.

In 2004, a Citizen Information Centre and Public Relations and a Parliamentary and Interparliamentary Training Centre were established. The Technical Budget Support Unit was subsequently set up, operating under the guidance of the committee responsible for the budget area, supporting it by preparing studies on budgetary and financial management. In 2015, the Control and Audit Office was set up to monitor and control the budget implementation and the financial, asset and accounting situation of the parliamentary services and the independent administrative bodies with administrative autonomy operating within the *Assembleia da República*.

More recently, in 2018, the Communication Office and the Museum and Citizenship Division were set up, and the services created in 2004 were abolished. The creation and recreation of these services show the search for solutions to the new areas of parliamentary competences focusing on citizens and the importance of communication, in addition to the allocation of internal capacity in terms of (own and state) budgetary control.

In terms of specialized units, in addition to the departments supporting parliamentary activity and its bodies, the administrative support and international relations and protocol and public relations services, the *Assembleia da República* has a library (established in 1836), a legislative and parliamentary information division, a bookshop and historical archives.

The security service – which is the structure especially in charge of the prevention, control, surveillance, protection and defence of the premises and property of the *Assembleia da República*, its services and the people working within it or visiting it – and the legal auditor, who exercises functions in the field of legal advice and administrative litigation, depend directly on the President.

Also, in 2018, the technological dimension has been strengthened through the creation of the Technology Infrastructure and Information Systems Divisions, under the Information Technology Directorate, as can be seen from Figure 30.2.

The Rules of Procedure allow the Speaker to establish memoranda of understanding and assistance protocols with higher education institutions. However, the use of this possibility has not been common practice. Nonetheless, academics often participate in and contribute to parliamentary work.

In certain areas, as is the case of information and communication technologies, either because they correspond to new competences or functions that are not permanent or even due to recruitment difficulties, it has been common practice to hire companies to provide specific services.

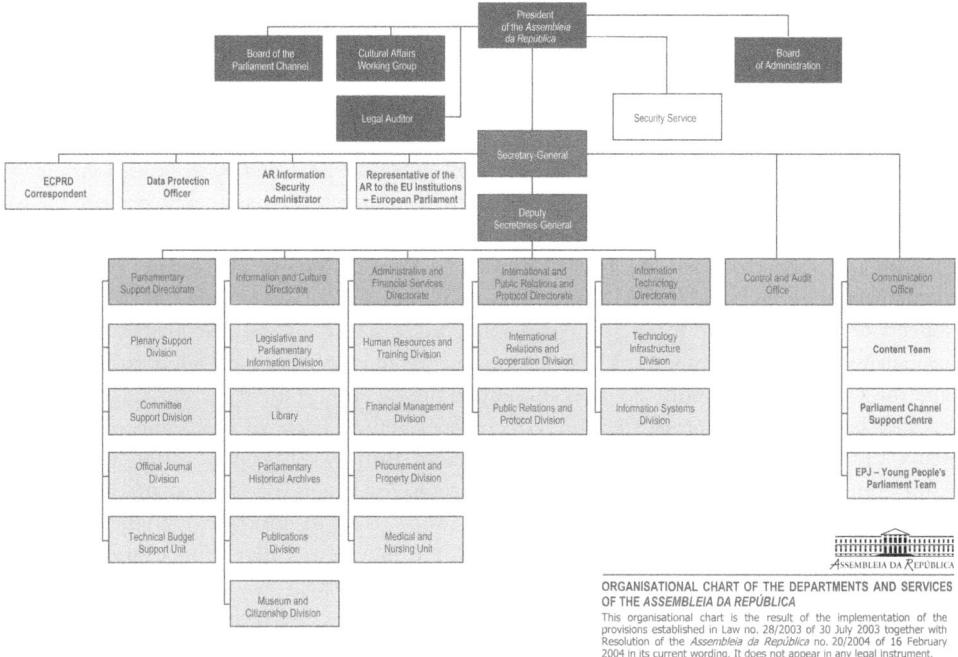

Figure 30.2 Organizational chart of the *Assembleia do República*

30.3 The Role of the Administration in the Context of Parliamentary Work

30.3.1 The Internal Governance

In what concerns internal governance, there is a hierarchical structure with the Speaker overseeing the administration of the Parliament and exercising authority over all staff and security forces.

The Secretary-General is appointed by the Speaker, under an assignment regime and for the term of the legislature, after obtaining a favourable opinion from the Board of Administration.[7] He remains in office until the appointment of a new Secretary-General and may be dismissed at any time by the Speaker, also after obtaining a favourable opinion from the Board of Administration. Till now (2021), all secretary-generals had no prior parliamentary experience as a staff member.

The Secretary-General, who has two deputies, oversees and coordinates all departments of the *Assembleia da República* and refers those matters which do not fall within his competence to the Speaker for the issuing of an order thereon. He is responsible, among others, for the day-to-day management of the human and financial resources and the assets of the *Assembleia da República*, for authorising the works projects and the lease or acquisition of goods and services that fall within the scope of his financial competences, for coordinating the preparation of draft activity plans, the draft budget and the draft management report and accounts, for proposing changes to the organizational structure of parliamentary services and to the staff and for regulations needed for the internal organization and operation of the departments and services.

Regarding parliamentary work, the Speaker is responsible for chairing the Bureau,[8] the Standing Committee,[9] the Conference of Leaders and the Conference of Parliamentary Committee Chairs.

The Conference of Leaders meets regularly and consists of the Speaker and the presidents of the parliamentary groups. It is responsible for scheduling plenary sittings and setting the order of business. Meetings of the Conference of Leaders are attended by those responsible for the Parliamentary Support Directorate and the Plenary Support Division, who prepare the list of the legislative initiatives and petitions that should be scheduled.

The Conference of Parliamentary Committee Chairs consists of the Speaker and the parliamentary standing or *ad hoc* committee chairs and meets regularly to monitor the functional aspects of their work and to assess the general conditions of the legislative procedure and the proper implementation of laws. Those responsible for the Parliamentary Support Directorate and the Committee Support Division also attend the meeting.

The list of parliamentary standing committees and each committee's specific competence are approved by the Plenary, on a proposal from the President, after hearing the Conference of Leaders. The Speaker is responsible for arranging their formation, supervising and facilitating their work and making every effort to ensure compliance with the time limits that the Parliament sets for them. He may also convene meetings with the chairs of the parliamentary committees and subcommittees to inform himself about their work.

30.3.2 Administrative Support to Legislative Work

Parliamentary work is primarily reflected in three dimensions: legislative, control and representation and, in any case, the support provided by the staff is indispensable. However, it is in support of legislative work that it is the most visible.

Every legislative initiative is analysed by the services before being admitted by the Speaker.[10] The memorandum on admissibility concludes if there are grounds for refusing to admit the initiative – either because it does not comply with the formal requirements, it is unconstitutional or does not comply with the budget cap rule.[11]

Before the relevant committee draws up an opinion, a technical note is prepared by the staff and included as an annex to the opinion. The technical note, which results from the collaboration of various services,[12] contains, where possible, an analysis of the compliance with formal, constitutional and regulatory requirements; the legal and theoretical background to the issue, including at the European and international level; a list of other pending Portuguese and EU initiatives on the same subjects; a brief analysis of the facts, situations and realities concerned and an historical overview of any problems raised. It also includes references to contributions from persons and bodies with interest in the matters concerned, particularly any opinions they may have issued on the topic.

This technical note includes an *ex-ante* evaluation in the form of an assessment of the consequences of its adoption and the foreseeable cost of its implementation.

As of recently, gender impact assessments are now also carried out.

In terms of an *ex-post* evaluation, at the end of each legislative session the staff prepares a progress report on the adoption and entry into force of the laws and their regulations, which, after being sent to the Government for its opinion, is examined by the Conference of Parliamentary Committee Chairs. This Conference may determine that the contents of some of the laws passed, the resources allocated to their implementation and their practical effects should be subjected to a qualitative analysis.

Parliamentary committees may also ask the MP who is acting as rapporteur, or any MP on the parliamentary committee, for a report on the qualitative monitoring of the regulation and implementation of given legislation.

In some cases, as is the case in the field of promoting gender equality, the Parliament has asked the Government to assess the impact of certain legislation. This is done through regular reporting to the *Assembleia da República*.

30.3.3 *Administrative Support to State Budget*

In what concerns the State Budget, there is a special procedure. The Technical Budget Support Unit prepares two reports, a preliminary report, which is submitted before the hearing of the Minister of Finance on the general principles, and a second report, which is final and submitted before the beginning of the debate on the general principles (Bernardo, Cipriano, 2019, p. 268).

Monitoring dossiers are prepared by the staff with the articles and the list of forthcoming votes to support the debate and vote on the details. Due to the time limits and the complexity of the procedure, it has been common practice to set up a task force involving staff from various services, who categorise and systematise the draft amendments submitted by MPs (it should be noted that over 1,000 draft amendments have been tabled in recent years).

After the State Budget Bill's final overall approval, the Plenary support services prepare the final wording, merging the agreed rules, systematising the text and its style, which is considered and decided on by the relevant parliamentary committee. It is an important moment in all legislative procedures, but it takes on greater importance in this case due to the complexity, the scale and the time limits involved in adopting the Budget.

30.3.4 *Administrative Support to Public Consultations*

In the Portuguese legal system, public consultation of initiatives is mandatory in the case of labour legislation and where it is deemed relevant to gather input from civil society. Increasing emphasis has been placed on the involvement of citizens and representative organizations within the scope of the legislative procedure, and in recent years there has been a variety of mechanisms available to citizens, ranging from the creation of discussion *fora* to the possibility of sending contributions to initiatives under discussion and participating in hearings or audiences.

Initiatives under public discussion are published in a separate issue of the Journal of the *Assembleia da República*[13] and the opening of the procedure is announced in two nationally distributed newspapers, indicating the subject matter, the period during which contributions can be received and the contact information to do so. Parliamentary committees also hold mandatory or optional hearings of bodies representing the addressees of the rules.

In addition to publicising the initiatives under discussion and involving the addressees of the rules, it is also important to ensure transparency regarding the bodies heard and the contributions received. Therefore, the audio or video recordings of the hearings and seminars held as well as any documentation received during the process are made available on the page of each initiative, notwithstanding being broadcast live or later by the Parliament Channel.

The Constitution, the Rules of Procedure and several separate laws provide for mandatory or optional consultations. Due to the multitude of consultation requirements, a handbook on public consultations in the parliamentary legislative procedure has been drawn up – by parliamentary staff – and recently updated.

Plenary meetings are fully recorded, transcribed and published – in the *Journal of the Assembleia da República* – and are also broadcast live by the Parliament Channel, the internet portal and social media by parliamentary staff.

Most committee meetings are recorded and broadcast live. The video recordings are available on the Parliament Channel website and can be freely accessed and downloaded at any time.

30.4 Managing Interinstitutional and External Relations

30.4.1 *Relations with the Government*

The *Assembleia da República* has a specific financial regime and approves its budget, which is designed as part of a procedure other than that used for the consideration and passage of the State Budget (Gonçalves, 2019, p. 92), accordingly. The funds included in the Budget of the *Assembleia da República*, once approved, are inserted in the State Budget, even if they are not dependent on the Government. The *Assembleia da República* is subject to the preparation and presentation of its accounts to the Court of Auditors.

Although, as a rule, the remuneration structure and raises are identical to those set by the Government for civil servants, in the case of parliamentary staff, the remuneration scheme is set by the President on a proposal from the Board of Administration, internally discussed with the Parliamentary Staff Union.

In terms of the organization of parliamentary work, the Government appears before the *Assembleia da República* every month and Ministers attend parliamentary meetings in their area of competence at least four times per legislative session, regardless of further appearances in the framework of parliamentary scrutiny functions.

The Government has the right to be represented at the Conference of Leaders and may intervene in matters that do not solely concern the *Assembleia da República* itself.

30.4.2 *External Relations*

In terms of external relations, the *Assembleia da República* has delegations to various international parliamentary organizations and parliamentary friendship groups, which are formed each legislature and are supported by parliamentary staff.

External relations are also increasingly handled by both the Speaker and the parliamentary committees and their chairs.

The increasing role of the Parliament in the international sphere has, in recent years, given rise to the concept of parliamentary diplomacy (Araújo, Ferreira, 2019, p. 368), which, in the Portuguese case, is particularly geared towards Europe and Portuguese-speaking countries.

In the case of the latter, in parallel with political cooperation, there has been administrative cooperation provided by parliamentary staff, embodied in bilateral cooperation plans and implemented by training and exchange of best practices between the parliaments concerned.

In recent years, the *Assembleia da República* has also been involved in twinning projects in the framework of the European Union through the participation of staff in beneficiary countries (Kosovo, Bosnia and Albania) in training or evaluation activities.

The enhanced role of national Parliaments in European Union Affairs is another trend worth mentioning, especially after the entry into force of the Treaty of Lisbon. This posed a set of new challenges which required institutional and administrative adaptation for all national Parliaments, not only internally but also in terms of interinstitutional relations at the EU level and the deepening of interparliamentary cooperation with other Parliaments.

For that reason, the *Assembleia da República* has decided to assign one staff member as its representative in Brussels: attached at first to the COSAC Secretariat during the 2007 Portuguese Presidency of the EU Council and, from 2008 onwards, as a fully fledged Permanent Representative of the Parliament to the EU institutions. Based at the European Parliament, this so-called *Antena* is responsible for managing relations with all EU Institutions, especially the EP, the European Commission and the Council. Furthermore, this staff member is also responsible for monitoring and reporting on all major EU issues that are deemed politically and institutionally relevant to the work of the Parliament in EU affairs. Finally, the *Antena* is also responsible for preparing and advising the delegations of MPs who attend the multiple interparliamentary cooperation *fora*.

Moreover, this Permanent Representative is embedded in the network of representatives from all the 39 Parliamentary Chambers present in Brussels, enabling daily coordination and real-time exchange on multiple topics, namely on the Early Warning Mechanism or on other issues of common concern. Examples of the latter include the flow of information related to measures taken in the context of the COVID-19 pandemic, Brexit or the national Recovery and Resilience Plans in the context of Next Generation EU.

Finally, it should be noted that this Permanent Representative is appointed by the Parliament's Secretary-General following an internal competitive procedure for the position, open to any career staff member of the Parliament experienced in EU affairs.

30.5 Managing Current Challenges Facing the Parliamentary Administration

30.5.1 Towards a Digital Parliament

The process of digitising parliamentary work has been gradual, keeping pace with developments in information and communication technologies, and is one of the Parliament's main challenges. The need to adapt to the reality brought by the COVID-19 pandemic accelerate some of these processes, namely the possibility of remote meetings, hybrid plenary sittings or the organization of the teleworking framework.

In 2016–2018, the Working Group for the Digital Parliament, composed of MPs and heads of services, was set up "with the aim of harnessing the potential of new technologies to strengthen and enhance the relationship between citizens and the *Assembleia da República*".

The *Assembleia da República* makes available on its internet portal all the public information relating to parliamentary work and Members. Information tends to be structured in a database and is largely available in open data for re-use by other bodies or citizens.

The portal is based on a content management system, which allows the information to be made available immediately through decentralized uploads by the various parliamentary services, according to the principle that data is published by those who first receive it. It is adapted to mobile devices and includes citizen engagement platforms.

It also ensures accessibility for citizens with special needs, by adapting it for screen readers, and includes an audio version and alternative image description.

A parliamentary Web TV platform, launched in 2015, allows spectators, among other features, to select the live broadcast they wish to watch when several meetings are taking place simultaneously.

The main ongoing projects in the area of digitalization are the dematerialization of the legislative procedure (in conjunction with other sovereign bodies) and the implementation of a document management system and a digital preservation plan.

Parliament presents itself as a plural, transparent institution scrutinized by society and close to voters, raising awareness to the sovereign body and its activities and promoting the participation of citizens through the internet portal, the Parliament Channel, social media (Facebook, Instagram, YouTube, LinkedIn and Twitter), a monthly newsletter, sending information by email, the publication of newspaper advertisements and, of course, face-to-face or telephone contacts.

30.5.2 Tools for Citizen Participation

In addition to those already mentioned regarding legislative procedure, the following are tools for citizen participation in the Parliament's activity managed by the staff:

- The right to petition, to exercise legislative initiative and to referendum, which have digital platforms for the submission, collection of signatures and follow-up of the subsequent proceedings[14];
- the "Citizens' Mailbox", which enables citizens to contact MPs and services by email; and
- the "Suggestions Box", which is intended to collect on the website, on an informal basis, suggestions for the political action of MPs.

The *Assembleia da República* is also open for guided tours of the building and attendance of parliamentary meetings. It has the following areas open to the public: Parliamentary Bookshop, Archives and Library. The Parliament is open for free visits and cultural activities (theatre, cinema, music concerts, book launches) on special occasions.[15]

The annual Youth Parliament programme, an initiative of the *Assembleia da República* targeting young people of basic and secondary education, aims to stimulate young people's participation in political and parliamentary activity.

30.5.3 Relations with Media

Deepening the media relationship has been a key aspect in the Parliament's communication strategy to reach out to the public. The Communication Office gathers all the functions and staff connected to communication.

The relationship with the media is based on the following goals: ensuring that the Parliament's activities are rigorously disseminated and ensuring that journalists and technicians have all the necessary support to accomplish their mission.

The accreditation of journalists and image reporters or photojournalists is obtained for each legislative session.

Four journalists and two image reporters or photojournalists named by the (national) media have access to permanent accreditation. However, many others are accredited daily to cover parliamentary activity.

Journalists and image and sound technicians from television and radio stations have access to and can move around and remain in the Parliament's areas where meetings, ceremonies, sittings or events open to the media are held. They may also visit reserved areas if they have due authorization to do so.

The Session Chamber includes seats for the media and dedicated spaces in the galleries for photographers and image reporters.

The media have a room with computers, internet, telephones and copiers, a press conference room and radio and television control rooms.

Parliamentary television provides the signal from live broadcasts of the Plenary, committees and other events to other TV stations. The internet portal has a dedicated area for the media.

The parliamentary services also provides all the replies to requests for clarification from journalists made in person, by telephone or email, and issues press releases regularly.

30.5.4 Working during the Pandemic

During the period of the epidemiological crisis, the *Assembleia da República* maintained its legislative activity, as well as the political supervision of the Government, in particular regarding measures to combat the health and economic crisis caused by the COVID-19 epidemic and authorizations for declarations of a state of emergency.

A contingency plan was adopted on 3 March 2020 and parliamentary proceedings, as well as the functioning of the services, were successively adapted in line with developments in the situation.

The main steps taken were as follows: reduction in parliamentary meetings and in the number of parliamentarians in meeting rooms in person; videoconference and mixed meetings (face-to-face and via videoconference); placing of parliamentary staff working from home on a rotation basis; cancellation of cultural events; restrictions on visitors' access to the building and closure of services open to the public (Archives, Library, Bookshop).

30.5.5 Security in the Parliament

In terms of security, in addition to the Security Service[16] mentioned above, there are various security procedures in place, such as the X-ray inspection of bags and other items carried by staff and visitors or of correspondence deemed suspicious, as well as the distribution of cards with different colours to those visiting the *Assembleia da República*, in accordance to the areas they can visit.

As mentioned above, the *Assembleia da República* has an area of information security administration, which has recently been created and whose Chief Information Security Officer is currently implementing the ISO 27001 standard.

30.6 Conclusion

After several years without recruiting staff, recruitment procedures resumed, ensuring the rejuvenation of parliamentary staff and a commitment to new areas.

Developments in parliamentary services reflect the parliamentary reforms that have been undertaken and have allowed adjustments to new challenges and demands from MPs, citizens and the media.

The successful adaptation to telework during the pandemic has highlighted the flexibility of parliamentary staff and services, which, at a distance and through electronic means, ensured the quality and quantity of work.

Notes

1. We thank Cristina Correia and João Amaral for the critical review of this article.
2. On the ECPRD website, in the summary of replies to a question from the Congress of Deputies, Spain, 2013, Request 2213 – Number of Civil Servants/Numbers and MPs and Ratio, we can see that, in terms of the *ratio* of staff to Members, Portugal was close to Spain and Denmark, but far away from other parliaments indicating a *ratio* above 2 (Italy, Finland, Poland) or even above 4 (Belgium and Greece).
3. Parliamentary advisors are required to hold an undergraduate degree prior to the Bologna Process or the 2nd Bologna cycle; parliamentary support officers are required to have completed the 12th year of schooling or an equivalent course, plus a specific training course, and parliamentary operations assistants are required to have completed compulsory schooling.
4. Competitive appointment procedures obligatorily include the following selection methods: Written knowledge test; Psychological evaluation; Written and oral test of English or another language deemed appropriate; IT literacy test; and Interview to evaluate the competences required to exercise the functions.
5. Classifications range from *Very Good*, to *Good* and *Fair*, corresponding to three, two and one points, respectively. A *Poor* classification equals minus one point.
6. The statute governing parliamentary staff governs the recruitment and advancement arrangements, as well as the set of rights and duties of parliamentary staff.
7. The Board of Administration is a consultation and management body made up of a maximum of seven Members of the *Assembleia da República*, representing each of the seven largest parliamentary groups, together with the Secretary-General and an elected representative of the parliamentary staff.
8. The Bureau of the *Assembleia da República* is composed of the President of the *Assembleia da República*, four Vice-Presidents, four Secretaries and four Vice-Secretaries.
9. The Standing Committee operates when the *Assembleia da República* has been dissolved or is not in full session.
10. Legislative initiatives may be prepared and submitted by Members of the *Assembleia da República*, the Government, the Legislative Assemblies of the Autonomous Regions and citizens.
11. This rule prevents the admission of initiatives by Members of the *Assembleia da República*, citizens or the Legislative Assemblies of the Autonomous Regions which increase expenditure or decrease the revenue provided for in the State Budget.
12. The technical note brings together contributions from committee and plenary support staff, legislative and parliamentary information staff and also Library staff.
13. The Official Journal of the *Assembleia da República* is published only in electronic format.
14. As forms of conventional participation, they are also forms of direct participation, since their authors do not need to exercise these rights, the intermediation or sponsorship of a Member of the *Assembleia da República* or any body (Fernandes, Tibúrcio, 2019, p. 313).
15. These activities were suspended during the epidemiological crisis caused by COVID-19.
16. Carried out by a deployment of the National Republican Guard and the Public Security Police.

References

Araújo, J. M. and Ferreira, R. P. (2019) 'Diplomacia parlamentar' in Vargas, A. and Fonseca, T. (eds.) *Como funciona o Parlamento*. Lisboa: Assembleia da República, p. 368.

Bernardo, A. P. and Cipriano, V. (2019) 'O Orçamento do Estado' in Vargas, A. and Fonseca, T. (eds.) *Como funciona o Parlamento*. Lisboa: Assembleia da República, p. 92.

Dias Pinheiro, B. and Ribeiro Lopes, C. (2019) 'A Assembleia da República e a União Europeia' in Vargas, A. and Fonseca, T. (eds.) *Como funciona o Parlamento*. Lisboa: Assembleia da República, p. 368.

Fernandes, T. and Tibúrcio, T. (2019) 'Raio-X da participação dos cidadãos no Parlamento' in Vargas, A. and Fonseca, T. (eds.) *Como funciona o Parlamento*. Lisboa: Assembleia da República, p. 313.

Gonçalves, F. P. (2019) 'Autonomia parlamentar' in Vargas, A. and Fonseca, T. (eds.) *Como funciona o Parlamento*. Lisboa: Assembleia da República, p. 268.

31
ROMANIA'S PARLIAMENTARY ADMINISTRATION

Alexandra Alina Iancu

The rebuilding of the Romanian parliamentarism brought about the restoration of democratic principles. During the constitutional moment of 1991, elements of the past have joined momentary political improvisations and institutional mimicry (Iancu, 2009, p. 183). Following similar patterns in the region, Western European transplants inspired the reforms (Semenova et al., 2014, p. 16). The members of the Constituent Assembly placed a central emphasis on the executive-legislative relations (Parau, 2015; Selejan-Gutan, 2016). Political leaders decided to follow the French imprint and to adopt a semi-presidential regime (Elgie, 2011, p. 29; Dima, 2009; Tănăsescu, 2015). The president is directly elected yet relatively weak, lacking for instance discretion over the procedure to dissolve the Assembly (Gherghina et al., 2016). Bicameralism has been reinstated (Iorgovan, 1998; Guțan, 2016), after the interwar model. Under the current arrangements, both the lower Chamber – *Camera Deputaților* (330 deputies) – and the upper Chamber – the Senate (136 senators) – are elected for four-year terms according to the same electoral formula (proportional representation on closed-party lists) and have almost identical powers, except over the legislative procedure, where the two houses have different decisional powers over separate subjects (Gherghina and Chiru, 2018).

The Romanian Constitution provides formally for a strong and stable Parliament (Tacea, 2015). The Assembly is defined as the sole legislative authority and the supreme body of representation (art. 61). The legislative branch in joint session gives a vote of confidence at the formation of a new government and can dismiss the cabinet through a vote of no-confidence (art. 103, lit c), approves the state budget, may declare a state of emergency, exercises oversight over the intelligence services (art. 65), and plays an important role in the appointment of 2/3 of the constitutional justices (each house appoints three justices, art. 142) or in the procedure of suspension from office (impeachment) of the Romanian president or indictment for high treason (arts. 95–96).

In the 1990s, Parliament did little to maximise its constitutional prerogatives, due to political fragmentation and inherent weakness. However, starting in the 2000s, the Assembly became institutionalized (Roper & Crowther, 1998; Chiva, 2007). The logic of the parliamentary debate at committee level (after the constitutional revision of 2003) and the increasing number of bills that the MPs initiated suggested a rapid empowerment. Furthermore, the adoption of several motions of censure led to cabinet dismissals; oversight committees exposed abuses of power; the Assembly triggered twice the procedure for the suspension from office of the president (Perju, 2015). The MPs also developed critical selectivity in endorsing various bills (except in cases of bills related to the European policies or the adoption/ratification of international treaties – Chiru and Gherghina, 2018). Even in the case of European affairs, Parliament has become – despite its lacking sufficient know-how increasingly active (Tacea, 2015, pp. 621, 624).

The main paradox in the evolution of the Romanian Parliament towards autonomy and empowerment is that this transformation was unrelated to a process of professionalization of the parliamentary administration. Against the backdrop of pre-accession conditionalities, the adoption in 2006 of a Parliamentary civil service act had a limited effect both in terms of personnel reshuffling and efficiency-wise (in restructuring the internal functioning of the Assembly). For example, a review of the laws adopted by Parliament reveals the overwhelming share of bills initiated by the executive. Between 1989 and 2011, out of 5,486 laws, 4,825 originated with the executive (87.95%) (Iancu, 2013). Even though this percentage slightly decreases in the subsequent legislatures to 74% (IPP, 2012, 2016), the governmental capture of the Parliament's political agenda remains the current practice. At first glance, the percentage is similar to other parliamentary democracies (Sajó and Uitz, 2017, p. 151). Nevertheless, IPP reports on the 2008–2016 parliamentary activity showed that the executive centralism results – at least in part – from a lack of administrative know-how. Parliamentary initiatives are not scarce (about 70% of all bills) but they are poorly drafted. For instance, in 2012–2016 legislature, about 97% of the MP's bills were rejected on formal grounds (e.g., poor legislative drafting techniques and juridical faults – see IPP, 2012, 2016). Conversely, the Romanian MPs continue to complain about the absence of a parliamentary administration able to match the executive in terms of expertise (see interviews in Iancu, 2013).

The present chapter focuses on the configuration and functioning of parliamentary administration (of the lower Chamber of the Parliament), in order to explore the potential causes for a lack of substantial changes in the parliamentary administration after the adoption of the Parliamentary civil service act (Law 7/2006). The first section presents the organization of Camera Deputaților. The second part focuses on the material and personnel resources available to the house. The conclusions touch on recent trends in the articulation of the parliamentary administration as a potential explanandum for the ongoing lack of expertise both in relation to the law-making process and to the recent demands of the Europeanization.

31.1 The Reform of Parliamentary Administration: Structure and Functioning

According to article 64 of the Romanian Constitution, the organization of the two Chambers is regulated by their own Standing Orders. The two Chambers elect their Speakers for the entire term and the members of the Standing Bureaus for each session. MPs are enrolled in parliamentary Committees and, based on their political affiliation, in political groups. Parliamentary staff is appointed within the specialized structures of the two Chambers and serves the Chamber to fulfil their functions, procedures, and constitutional duties. Individual MPs receive allowances that they can use in order to hire parliamentary staff (full- or part-time). Despite the adoption of a parliamentary service law in 2006, enabling the creation of an independent and professionalized parliamentary civil service, the employees of the Romanian Parliament remain highly vulnerable to political influences.

The parliamentary administrations of each of the two Chambers are run by a Secretary General. He or she is the representative of the Chamber, managing the functional activity of the Assembly (art. 4, Standing Orders of Camera Deputaților). Formally, the Secretary General is in charge of administering the entire staff, managing financial resources, performing functions in the legislative process, or overseeing that parliamentary services are providing the much-needed documentation and advice. The Secretary General is appointed and dismissed in plenary session, on the proposal of the Standing Bureau of the Chamber, after the political consultation of the Committee of the leaders of the Parliamentary Group (art. 223, Standing Orders of Camera Deputaţilor). According to parliamentary practice, the proposal is first informally preapproved by the President of the Chamber's political group (Gaspar, 2014, p.35). While at first glance the Secretary General is a high civil servant with extensive prerogatives in managing the parliamentary administration, his role was partially amputated through in-house regulations.

The adoption of a Statute of the parliamentary civil servants followed the general reluctance in creating an autonomous public administration (Ionascu, 2006) and has been delayed until the mid-2000s. Procedurally, the Secretary General was in charge of all the staff's appointments and dismissals (Decision 10/21.03.1995). Officially, only the leading positions of the administration – chiefs of departments and the General Director of the Parliament required the prior authorization of the Permanent Bureau (art. 3, D10/1995). Starting with 1997, political preauthorization has been extended to other categories of staff-members. The initiative to dismiss some of the employees has been transferred to the members of the Permanent Bureau (for their cabinet members), the Parliamentary Group, and the Bureau of the parliamentary Committees (Decision 18/2.06.1997). This procedure has been maintained ever since (e.g., the decisions 30/24.04.2001, 23/5.07.2006, 21/18.06.2013). According to the current Standing Orders of the lower house, the parliamentary staff working at the Speaker's cabinet, the employees attached to the cabinets of the members of the Permanent Bureau or to the Parliamentary Groups, and the cabinets of the presidents of the parliamentary Committees are directly subordinated to the respective structures (and thus to political leaders). The dismissal of the parliamentary employees is not *discretionary* in the sense in which the Standing Orders specify: "if an employee working for a Parliamentary Group should no *longer accepted* by the Members of the same Parliamentary Group or if the Group should cease to exist, the Secretary General of the Chamber of Deputies shall see to it that the employee(s) of that Parliamentary Group be transferred to equivalent offices" (art. 16, 2). However, the role of the Secretary General in regard to these members of the staff is reduced to overseeing their professional training and the application of the internal regulations (Standing Orders of Camera Deputaţilor 2018, art. 25).

The variability of the Secretary General's administrative capacity is not linked to the distinction between the so-called political/patronage appointees (contract-based staff) and the creation of a new set of employees, namely the parliamentary civil servants. Indeed, until the adoption of a Statute in 2006, the members of the staff were the subject of the general labour code, being hired and released from office discretionarily, on the basis of political decisions. The late adoption of Law 7/2006 created the opportunity of reforming the parliamentary staff. First, similarly to the French case (Campbell and Laporte, 1981), the parliamentary employees have been set apart from the other members of the public administration. Second, the law clearly differentiated amongst categories of staff, by introducing the career-system of civil service which offered the much-needed job stability. The new regulations are distinguished between political appointees (e.g., the Speaker's cabinet, the cabinet members of the Permanent Bureau, the cabinets of the Parliamentary Groups and of parliamentary commissions) and the professional civil servants (art. 4). However, such provisions proved difficult to implement for several reasons. First, the law secured the offices of the pre-existent parliamentary staff (most of them in effect political appointees) and provided at the same time the parliamentary employees with extensive reward structures. Second, the application of the law was initially suspended by emergency governmental ordinance (EGO 2/2006), on the grounds that it set unreasonable benefits and discriminated against other categories of civil servants. The EGO 2/2006 was rejected by the Parliament a few months later (Law 271/2006). The end-result was the creation of a window of opportunity for the new staff to join a position in the newly created and autonomous parliamentary civil service. Third, in 2010, a new revision to the law (Law 113/2009, art. 5) allowed the backdoor entry in the parliamentary administration. Article 10(3) of Law 7/2006, as amended, indicated that political appointees working in the above-mentioned parliamentary structures could be either considered contractual staff or civil servants (on a fixed-term contract or open-ended employment contracts). The political will of packing the civil service position with party loyalists is therefore entrenched in the legislative text. Furthermore, seniority requirements have been exempted in the case of the employees working in the Speaker's cabinet, Permanent Bureau, and Parliamentary Groups. Article 13 reinforces the patronage-oriented direction of the regulations as it states that the political leaders (the Speaker, the members of the Permanent Bureau, and the leaders of the Parliamentary Groups) are in charge of the appointment of civil servants working within the respective parliamentary structures (evidently after validating a public examination).

Under current regulations, parliamentary civil servants have to be Romanian citizens with an impeccable record (no past criminal convictions, no collaboration with the former (communist) secret police, and no dismissal from public office). Potential candidates have to comply with the education and seniority requirements (art. 12) and have to pass an exam. There are three different categories of staff: high civil servants, leading positions, and execution positions (Law 7/2006, art. 7). The right to an exam-based promotion for parliamentary employees is guaranteed. This entails, in the absence of vacancies, the automatic upgrade of their previous positions (since 2011, Law 284/2010). The staff should participate in annual trainings (courses, exchanges, etc.) and they receive at the end of their careers "special pensions". Similar to magistrates (judges and prosecutors), qualified recipients (30 years of seniority – among which at least 14 years in Parliament) have the right to the net equivalent of 80% of the average of the calculation base used for their gross salaries during their last year in office (art. 73). Other benefits include meal tickets, leave of absence, etc. The members of the parliamentary administration have to comply with stringent incompatibility requirements (art. 9) and cannot hold other public offices (except as university professors). However, differently from other civil servants and somewhat paradoxically, they can work in the private sector – under the condition that there is no direct connection between their parliamentary activity and their job in the private sector (Law 284/2010).

The newly created structure of incentives has only partially contributed to the creation of a parliamentary civil service. While the regulations clearly incorporated the need of a public exam in order to join the administration, the stability in office of these parliamentary employees remains highly questionable. According to Law 7/2006, the Secretary General may demote a parliamentary civil servant, provided that the person had received two "insufficient" assessments in two consecutive years (art. 26). If there are no vacancies on lower hierarchical positions or if the proposal is rejected, the civil servant is dismissed. Other provisions suggest that the entire idea of a lifelong career in the parliamentary administration has no grounding under the current provisions. Article 66 clearly specifies that the Secretary General can dismiss a member of the parliamentary administration in case of a reduction in the size of the staff or in order to integrate another civil servant wrongly dismissed from office. No additional clarifications are provided in the law as to the conditions, criteria of selection, etc.

The Secretary General benefits from high levels of administrative discretion in regard to the parliamentary staff. Nevertheless, his decisional leeway is contained by the organizational chart, previous practices of hiring public servants, and more importantly the creation of a smaller body of employees placed under the protection of the political leaders. Such functional differentiation in terms of the Secretary General's latitude goes beyond the recruitment procedures in order to bend other decisional competencies. In the current architecture of the lower Chamber, various bodies within the Assembly can be easily insulated. For example, the Speaker's cabinet is formally led by a high civil servant subordinated to the Secretary General (a directorate) and includes parliamentary advisors, the permanent representative of the Chamber with the EP – a contractual position created in 2006 (Standing Orders 2018, art. 36). The cabinet is primarily subordinated to the Speaker of the Chamber, despite the former's important coordination prerogatives such as setting and implementing the agenda of the President and ensuring the cooperation with the other public institutions such as the Presidential Administration, the Senate, the Government, mass-media, and economic agents(Standing Orders 2018, art. 37). Such a structure has been instrumentalized in the past, packed with contract-based patronage-oriented advisors and activated in cases of political conflicts (i.e., amongst the members of the governing coalition) or of lack of reliability between politicians and the members of the staff.

31.2 Human and Financial Resources in Building Up a Modern Parliamentary Administration

The financial autonomy of the two Chambers is constitutionally guaranteed. According to the art. 64 (1), "Financial resources of the Chambers shall be provided for in the budgets approved by them". Every year, each of the two Chambers votes the respective budget and advances the document to the government prior to the adoption of the state budget (Standing Orders, art. 224). Although less significant than in the case of other public institutions (Iancu, 2019), the budget of the Assembly has grown over time. Until 2005, most of the increases were impaired by inflation. After the mid-2000s, due to a relative financial stabilization of the currency, there is a clear spike in the financial means of the Assembly (see Figure 31.1 for Camera Deputaților). In 2020, the budget of the lower Chamber was the equivalent of 108.5 M. Euros. On occasion, budgetary allocations are rectified to cover ongoing deficits.

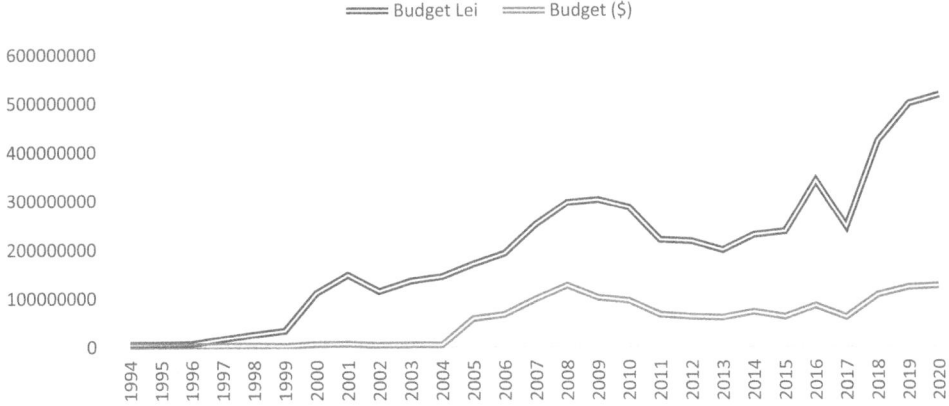

Figure 31.1 The budget of the Romanian Chamber of Deputies – Camera Deputaților

The Parliament's expenditure patterns have not gone unnoticed. In recent years, the Parliament has been amply criticized on many occasions for the so-called financial privileges. Paradoxically, the parliamentary parties were in charge of the populist exploitation of the idea that the Parliament is overcrowded, too expensive, and overpaid (Dragoman, 2019; Gherghina, 2019). It is no coincidence that the citizens – on the occasion of a consultative referendum launched by Romanian President Băsescu in November 2009 (for the adoption of a unicameral Parliament and the reduction of the number of MPs to a total of 300) – practically plebiscited the two presidential proposals. Despite the massive vote in favour, the referendum results have not been yet implemented. Nevertheless, the results are still instrumentalized and rhetorically rekindled in local political debates.

The personnel costs cover a large part of the projected budgets (about 70% of budget of the lower Chamber in 2020). The share of personnel costs has been related to the changes in the definition of the parliamentary structures and staff. While in terms of career projection parliamentary employees do not resemble other categories in the public sector, from a functional perspective, their attributions and role(s) are similar to those of the other parliamentary administrations in the EU (Gaspar, 2014). During the last three decades, the parliamentary organizational chart grew more complex to include new departments and directorates. The members of the administration are currently attached to six departments (Parliamentary Studies and EU policies, Legislative, Technical secretary, Transportation and Administrative, Economics, Technical) or to the Directorate of Human Resources (Decision 26.06.2018). The departments are in charge of the preparation and support of all parliamentary activities, such as organising the plenary sessions, recording the parliamentary activity, preparing technical and specific standpoints concerning legislative acts, organising the committees work, and developing in-house summaries or comparative research, policy briefs, and documentation (art. 7). The staff also manages the financial, material and human resources, ensures the coordination with other national and international authorities and the citizens, and conducts internal auditing (arts. 6–7).

The size of the parliamentary staff is assessed and then approved by the Permanent Bureau's decision (Decision 42/2018). There are no official data communicated to the public as to the size and type of budgetary spending by category of parliamentary employees. Furthermore, the various types of contracts and the numerous changes in their statutes often blurred the public reporting on the configuration of the parliamentary staff. Some public information suggests a gradual increase in the total number of persons working for the Parliament (Ziare.com, 2014; Badea, 2019). Nevertheless, the increase does not concern the parliamentary public servants as such (these represent on average only one-third of the staff). In December 2014, the total number of employees of the lower house was 1593 among which 695 parliamentary civil servants, 788 contract-based employees, and 110 positions for activities publicly financed (Ziare.com, 2014). Five years later, in 2019, the staff was increased to 1617 employees – both civil servants and contract-based employees (Badea, 2019). Based on the current declaration of assets available on the website of the Camera Deputaților, 662 civil servants are assigned to different departments. Most of them are allocated to the legislative (186) and in the technical departments (186), which are in charge of the law-making process administration, general documentation, and the organization of the parliamentary sessions. Other departments are visibly smaller: Department of Parliamentary Studies and EU policies counts 42 employees, while the staff of the Foreign Affairs and Protocol Department currently numbers 44 members.

The civil servants are a narrow stratum within the parliamentary staff. They are certainly well rewarded for their activities, when their incomes are compared to the general level of salaries in Romania (the average gross for 2021 is the equivalent in Romanian Lei of roughly 867 Euros). According to the salary rates posted on the Chamber's website, the Secretary General receives a gross of about 5000 Euros/month, while the pay for a parliamentary adviser is about 2500 Euros/month. However, salaries are not the only incentive for those joining the parliamentary administration. These positions are often instrumentalized as a rapid entry point in the higher regular civil service. Joining the parliamentary administration secures the promise of further promotions. A recent example is paradigmatic in this regard. The liberals (currently the governing party), in order to ease the way for the nomination of the future prefect of Bucharest, facilitated the fast-track hiring of Traian Berbeceanu as a civil servant working for the liberal group in Parliament. The strategy enabled Mr. Berbeceanu to secure a civil-servant tatute, one of the eligibility criteria to be appointed as prefects (G4Media, 2020).

Parliamentary civil service positions represent a small fraction within the parliamentary staff. Conversely, the number of the personal (cabinet) MP aides has grown steadily from the 1990s onwards. In 2010, Romanian MPs hired on average three parliamentary assistants, paid from the lump-sum allocated to each MP (Protv, 2010). In 2013, immediately after the parliamentary elections, the media revealed that the MPs appointed a record number of 2265 employees (1154 parliamentary assistants in the lower Chamber). The total salaries of the assistants exceeded 500,000 Euros/month (Dădăcuş, 2013). Moreover, other parliamentary assistants are working at the constituency level, within the MPs' territorial bureaus. In 2017, in one month alone, the members of the Chamber hired about 600 (592) assistants in constituency offices (Postelnicu, 2017). The salaries of parliamentary assistants working within the territorial bureaus are less impressive and range around 1.670 Euros/month (Profit, 2021). These political appointees are in contact with the electorate at the constituency level, but in practice they represent one of the most important recruitment pools for the civil service. Starting with 2006, the MPs openly lobbied for blurring the legal distinction between the two categories of parliamentary staff (civil servants and political appointees). A legislative proposal in 2016 wanted to certify the ongoing practice of "internal transfers" from contract-based employees to the parliamentary civil-servant Statute by legislating the right of the contract-based employees (that met the requirements set by Law 7/2006 and had a seniority of over 5 years) to be heaved automatically into the civil servants' body (Zf, 2016). The main paradox is that, while the bill has not been adopted, the practice of transferring contract-based personnel to public office institutions has been informally institutionalized. Contract-based personnel receive in practice almost the same tenure right, emoluments, and protections as the members of the parliamentary administration. In recent years, a new practice emerged concerning the transfer through secondment of MP aides to public institutions (e.g., autonomous agencies and directorates), circumventing the regular tests or public competitions, as required by the Statute of civil servants in Romania (Petcu, 2020).

31.3 Conclusion

Despite the parliamentary empowerment in Romania, the newly found political activism did not alter the negative public perception regarding the activity of the legislature. Trust in the Assembly is constantly low, below 10% of the total population (Ionescu,

2018). In public debates, the erosion of confidence in Parliament is primarily attributed to *political* practices, namely, the lack of full endorsement of integrity policies/practices (Iancu, 2018), financial privileges, and the lack of legislative effectiveness. This image also reflects negatively on parliamentary administration, which is perceived as an extension and as a mirror of the representatives. The system of special pensions, high salaries, and artful technicalities used to distinguish between the diverse categories of parliamentary employees strengthened even further the perceived parallelism between the administrative staff of the institution and the politician-representatives. The negative perception is partially justified. Despite a degree of professionalization of the parliamentary administration, the ineffectiveness of slow, overwrought parliamentary processes and work is perceptible. Normative acts based on legislative delegation sometimes outnumber or outweigh the ordinary legislative procedures (Selejan-Guțan, 2016). Increasing experience and specialization of personnel (quantity) did not bring with it a qualitative leap in the adoption rates of parliamentary bills.

The Romanian MPs were initially reluctant to implement regulations on the creation of the parliamentary public administration. Soon after the adoption of Law 7/2006, they changed their minds and rallied in favour of the civil servants, strongly lobbying to maximise the reward structure for this category of personnel. In practice, the regulations failed, at least in part, to create a genuine parliamentary administration. The civil servants remain a minority within a parliamentary staff dominated by political appointees. The status of the narrow stratum of civil servants also remains highly vulnerable stability-wise. The design of these new regulations facilitated an ongoing process of politicization, as such positions continue to be exploited as patronage-oriented barter tokens.

Organizational Chart of Romanian Chamber of Deputies

Source: http://www.cdep.ro/pls/dic/site.page?den=servicii2-schema

References

Badea, C. (2019) 'Câți salariați plătim la Camera Deputașilor și cât ne costă consilierii lui Dragnea', *Ziare.com*, 17 January 2019 [Online], Available at: https://ziare.com/politica/camera-deputatilor/cati-salariati-platim-la-camera-deputatilor-si-cat-ne-costa-consilierii-lui-dragnea-1545976 (Accessed: 7 March 2021).

Campbell, S., and Laporte, J. (1981) 'The Staff of the Parliamentary Assemblies in France', *Legislative Studies Quarterly*, VI(4), pp. 521–531.

Chiva, C. (2007) 'The Institutionalization of Post-Communist Parliaments: Hungary and Romania in a Comparative Perspective', *Parliamentary Affairs*, 60(2), pp. 187–211. doi: https://doi.org/10.1093/pa/gsm012

Dădăcuș, L. (2013) 'Exclusiv, Parlamentarii au 2265 de angajați pentru care decontează peste 3 milioane de lei lunar – lista completă a parlamentarilor și a numărului de angajați', *Mediafax*, 15 November 2013 [Online]. Available at: https://translate.google.com/translate?hl=en&sl=ro&u=https://www.mediafax.ro/politic/exclusiv-parlamentarii-au-2-265-de-angajati-pentru-care-deconteaza-peste-3-milioane-de-lei-lunar-lista-completa-a-parlamentarilor-si-a-numarului-de-angajati-11689769&prev=search&pto=aue (Accessed: 21 January 2021).

Dima, B. (2009) 'Semiprezidențialismul românesc postdecembrist', *Sfera Politicii* 17(139), pp. 14–29.

Dragoman, D. (2019) *Democratic Transition and Consolidation in Romania: Civic Engagement and Elite Behavior After 1989*. Berlin: Peter Lang.

Elgie, R. (2011) *Semi-presidentialism: Sub-types and Democratic Performace*. Oxford: Oxford University Press.

G4Media (2020) 'Traian Berbeceanu a fost angajat ca funcționar public la grupul deputaților PNL. Pentru a fi numit prefect, el trebuie să facă parte din corpul funcționarilor publici', *G4 Media*, 20 October 2020 [Online]. Available at: https://www.g4media.ro/traian-berbeceanu-a-fost-angajat-ca-functionar-public-la-grupul-deputatilor-pnl-pentru-a-fi-numit-prefect-el-trebuie-sa-faca-parte-din-corpul-functionarilor-publici.html (Accessed: 27 January 2021).

Gaspar, I. (2014) 'Evoluția instituției secretarului general în sistem parlamentar', *Drepturile omului*, 2, pp. 34–39.

Gherghina, S. (2019) 'Hijacked Direct Democracy: The Instrumental Use of Referendums in Romania', *East European Politics and Societies*, 33(3), pp. 778–797. doi: 10.1177/0888325418800553.

Gherghina, S. and Chiru, M. (2018) 'Romania: an ambivalent parliamentary opposition' in: De Giorgi, E. and Ilonszki, G. (eds.) *Opposition Parties in European Legislatures: Conflict or Consensus?* Series: Routledge studies on political parties and party systems. Abingdon: Routledge, pp. 191–209.

Gherghina, S. et al. (2016) 'Former Presidents and their parties: making post-mandate carriers. Insights from Bulgaria and Romania', *European Consortium of Political Research General Conference*, 7–10 September 2016, Prague [Online]. Available at: https://ecpr.eu/Events/PaperDetails.aspx?PaperID=30116&EventID=95 (Accessed: 28 January 2021).

Iancu, A. (2013) 'Searching for Representation. Romanian Parliamentary Elites and their Political Roles', *Studia Politica. Romanian Political Science Review*, 2, pp. 225–256.

Iancu, A. (2018) 'Questioning Anticorruption In Post-Communist Contexts: Romanian MPs from Commitment to Contestation', *Südosteuropa. Journal of Politics and Society*, 66(3), pp. 392–417. https://doi.org/10.1515/soeu-2018-0030

Iancu, A. (2019) *La démocratie roumaine à ses débuts: Élitisme, apolitisme et informalité gouvernementale*. Iasi: Institutul European.

Iancu, B. (2009) 'Constitutionalism in Perpetual Transition: The Case of Romania' in: Iancu, B. (ed.) *The Law/Politics Distinction in Contemporary Public Law Adjudication*. Utrecht: Eleven International Publishing.

Ionascu, A. (2006) 'The Evolution of Parties Supporting Government forms of Patronage in Post-Communist Romania', *Sfera Politicii*, 123–124, pp. 62–77.

Ionescu, V. (2018) 'Sondaj CURS: Încrederea în Parlament a scăzut cu 9%, până la 14%. Încrederea în Justiție a crescut la 34%', *Curs de guvernare.ro*, 10 July 2018 [Online]. Available at: https://cursdeguvernare.ro/sondaj-curs-incredere-parlament-scazut-cu-9-pana-la-14-increderea-justitie-crescut-la-34.html (Accessed: 9 February 2021).

Iorgovan, A. (1998) *Odiseea elaborării constituției. Fapte și documente, oameni și caractere, cronica și explicații, dezvăluiri și meditații*. Târgu Mureș: Uniunea Vatra Românească.

IPP (2012) 'Sinteza activității parlamentarilor în mandatul 2008 – 2012', Institute for public policies, *Seria de Rapoarte de monitorizare a activității parlamentare,* September 2012 [Online]. Available at: http://www.ipp.ro/protfiles.php?IDfile=162 (Accessed: 15 May 2015).

IPP (2016) 'Parlamentul Absent. Scurt bilanț al legislaturii 2012–2016', Institute for public policies, *Seria de Rapoarte de monitorizare a activității parlamentare,* 2016 [Online]. Available at: https://www.ipp.ro/wp-content/uploads/2016/12/Bilanț-al-principalelor-aspecte-care-au-marcat-activitatea-actualului-legislativ-în-perioada-2012-–-2016.pdf (Accessed: 15 January 2021).

Law 7/2006 (Legea 7 din 11 ianuarie 2006 privind statutul funcționarului public în parlamentar), *Monitorul Oficial,* 345, 25 mai 2009, Available at: http://legislatie.just.ro/Public/DetaliiDocument/106147 (Accessed: 15 December 2020).

Parau, C. (2015) 'Explaining Governance of the Judiciary in Central and Eastern Europe: External Incentives, Transnational Elites and Parliamentary Inaction', *Europe-Asia Studies* 67(3), pp. 409–442. DOI: 10.1080/09668136.2015.1016401.

Perju, V. (2015) 'The Romanian Double Executive and the 2012 Constitutional Crisis', *International Journal of Constitutional Law,* 13(1), pp. 246–278. https://doi.org/10.1093/icon/mov011

Petcu, T. (2020) 'Statul la stat. Cabinetele parlamentare, trambulină pentru ocuparea fără concurs a unui post bine plătit în instituții publice', Digi24, 8 October 2020, [online]. Available at: https://www.digi24.ro/special/statul-la-stat/statul-la-stat-cabinetele-parlamentare-trambulina-pentru-ocuparea-fara-concurs-a-unui-post-bine-platit-in-institutii-publice-1380656 (Accessed: 25 January 2021).

Postelnicu, V. (2017) 'Asta, da, viață de parlamentar! 800 de angajați în slujba aleșilor noștri', *Libertatea,* 7 April 2017, [online]. Available at: https://www.libertatea.ro/stiri/exclusiv-peste-800-de-persoane-si-au-angajat-parlamentarii-de-la-inceputul-legislaturii-campionul-angajarilor-un-deputat-pnl-care-10-colaboratori-vrancea-1798921 (Accessed: 5 January 2021).

Profit (2021) 'Parlamentarii au stabilit salariile pentru angajații de la propriile cabinete. Cât vor câștiga oamenii de încredere ai aleșilor', *Profit,* 24 February 2021 [Online]. Available at: https://www.profit.ro/stiri/politic/parlamentarii-au-stabilit-salariile-pentru-angajatii-de-la-propriile-cabinete-cat-vor-castiga-oamenii-de-incredere-ai-alesilor-20004318 (Accessed: 1 March 2021).

Protv (2010) 'Consilierii parlamentarilor: multi si foarte bine platiti din bani public', *Stirile Protv,* 23 June 2010 [online]. Available at: https://stirileprotv.ro/stiri/politic/consilierii-parlamentarilor-multi-si-foarte-bine-platiti-din-bani-publici.html (Accessed: 15 February 2021).

Roper, S. and Crowther, W. (1998) 'The Institutionalization of the Romanian Parliament: A Case Study of the State-building Process in Eastern Europe', *Southeastern Political Review,* 26(2), pp. 401–426. https://doi.org/10.1111/j.1747-1346.1998.tb00488.x

Sajó, A. and Uitz, R. (2017) *The Constitution of Freedom. An Introduction to Legal Constitutionalism.* Oxford: UP.

Selejan-Guțan, B. (2016) *The Constitution of Romania A Contextual Analysis.* Oxford: Hart.

Semenova, E., Edinger, M. and Best, H. (2014) 'Parliamentary elite formation after communism: an introduction' in: Semenova, E., Edinger, M. and Best, H. (eds.) *Parliamentary Elites in Central and Eastern Europe Recruitment and representation.* London: Routledge, pp. 1–31.

Tacea, A. (2015) 'The slow adaptation of the new member states: the Romanian parliament and the European integration', in: Hefftler, C. et al. (eds.) *The Palgrave Handbook of National Parliaments and the European Union.* Basingstoke, Hampshire: Palgrave Macmillan, pp. 613–631.

Tănăsescu, S. (2015) 'Conflicting revisions to the Romanian constitution give rise to questions about semi-presidentialism', in: Liao, D.C., Shen, Y.C. and Wu, Y-S. (eds.) *Semi-Presidentialism Across Continents: A Dialogue Between Asia and Europe.* Taipei: Wunan Books, pp. 57–87.

Zf (2016) 'Consilierii aleșilor ar putea deveni funcționari publici parlamentari', Ziarul Financiar, 7 May 2016, 7.05.2016, [Online]. Available at: https://www.zf.ro/print/15289891 Accessed: 18 January 2021).

Ziare.com (2014) 'Deputatii si-au aprobat bugetul pe 2015: Cati bani primesc in plus', *Ziare.com,* 9 December 2014 [Online]. Available at: https://ziare.com/politica/camera-deputatilor/deputatii-si-au-aprobat-bugetul-pe-2015-cati-bani-primesc-in-plus-1337766 (Accessed: 17 December 2020).

32
SLOVAKIA'S PARLIAMENTARY ADMINISTRATION

Natália Švecová

32.1 Introduction

The National Council of the Slovak Republic (hereinafter referred to as "National Council") is a unicameral Parliament consisting of 150 Members of Parliament (hereinafter referred to as "MPs") elected in one nationwide multimember constituency for the period of four years in accordance with the principle of proportional representation. Like in many other parliamentary democracies, the National Council performs legislative and oversight powers, together with legally defined roles in the European and foreign affairs, and in the appointment process of certain public officials.

To ensure smooth operation of the National Council and its working bodies, one institution called *Kancelária Národnej rady Slovenskej republiky*, in English the Chancellery of the National Council of the Slovak Republic (hereinafter referred to as "Chancellery"), performs all the parliamentary administration services. The Chancellery is a state budgetary organization with its status enshrined at the level of law, specifically in the Act on Rules of Procedure of the National Council of the Slovak Republic, No. 350/1996, as amended. It is autonomous from executive administration, in particular in terms of budget, hierarchy, organizational structure and decision-making. The Chancellery provides expert, organizational and technical services necessary for the operation of the National Council, its committees and special oversight committees, including parliamentary documentation, record-keeping and printing services (Act of the National Council of the Slovak Republic on the Rules of Procedure of the National Council of the Slovak Republic 1996 as amended, s. 143). It also carries out duties set out by other legal regulations, particularly in the area of civil service acting as the service office under the Civil Service Act, No. 55/2017, as amended, employment relations, and public property protection and management.

The Chancellery is administrator of individual budgetary chapter of the State Budget, with approved receipts for 2021 in the amount of 1,400,000 EUR and expenditures amounting to 35,702,322 EUR, which constitutes 0.15 per cent of the total State Budget expenditures for 2021 (Act on the State Budget for 2021, s. 1 and annexes) and equals to 0.04 per cent of the annual Gross Domestic Product in current prices in 2020 (Statistical Office of the Slovak Republic, 2021). It is to be noted that the Chancellery administers the Bratislava Castle, having also recreational-conference facility Častá-Papiernička located approx. 50 kilometres from the Parliament. Therefore, the parliamentary administration budget covers not only costs related to parliamentary activities and wages of MPs, their assistants and parliamentary staff members but also expenses linked with maintenance and restoration of this historical monument, and the facility operation.

32.2 Evolution of the Parliamentary Administration

After the Velvet Revolution in 1989 triggering transition to democracy, the position of the Chancellery was vested firstly in the then Act on Rules of Procedure of the Slovak National Council, No. 44/1989, as amended, which was later repealed by the current Rules of Procedure from 1996 (Act No. 350/1996). The first interim organization structure from 1990 counted with 250 employees – 140 staffers dealing with expert and administrative tasks and 110 blue-collars (Slovak National Council, 1990). Since then, the historical milestones linked with gaining the independence of the Slovak Republic in 1993 and its subsequent development have marked the evolution of the Chancellery. Evolution of parliamentarism went hand in hand with branching out the parliamentary administration tasks, for example in relation to international and European affairs (e.g. creation of a new Department for European Affairs in 2004).

The total number of civil servant positions in the Chancellery is determined by the Secretary General as administrator of the budgetary chapter, within staff limits approved for financial year concerned. The Chancellery is obliged to notify the Government Office twice a year about the number of civil servant posts, and arrangement thereof according to organizational structure (Act on Civil Service and on Amendment and Supplementation of Certain Acts 2017 as amended, s. 23 para. 1).

As can be seen from Figure 32.1, throughout the last 18 years, the total number of civil and public servants working for the Chancellery has a declining tendency dropping from 491 to 391 with an average number of 394 employees. During the V. electoral term (2010–2012),

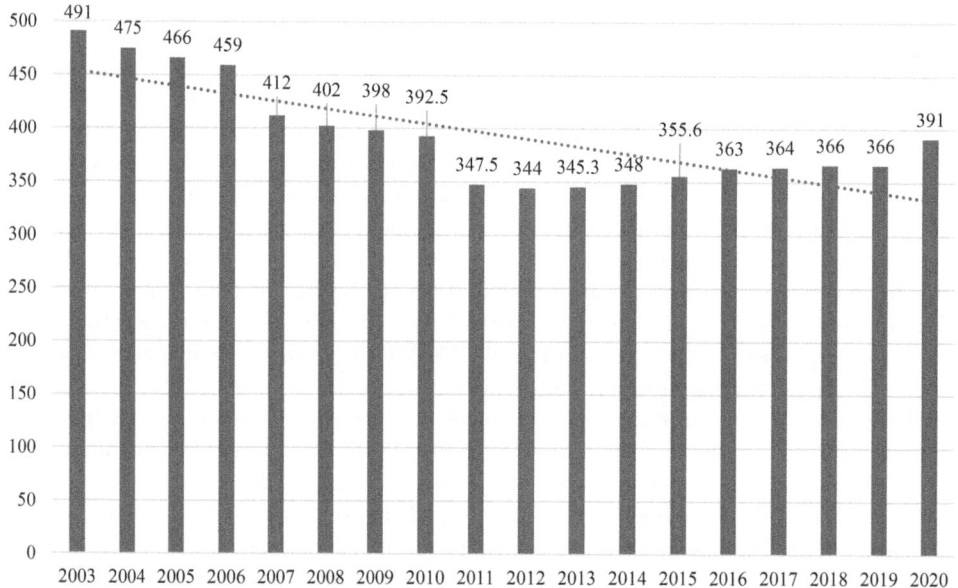

Figure 32.1 Average number of employees of the National Council of the Slovak Republic

the Chancellery implemented several organizational changes to fulfil its intention to reduce wage costs by 10 per cent (National Council of the Slovak Republic, 2021a). On the other hand, especially in 2015 and 2016, slightly more employees were hired than discharged (see Table 32.1 and Figure 32.2), as resources were needed to prepare and organize parliamentary dimension of the Slovak Presidency in the Council of the EU in the second half of 2016. Nevertheless, the figures and evidence from the parliamentary annual reports show that over time the parliamentary administration remains adequately stable without any regular disruptive political interferences ensuing from the changes in power after parliamentary elections, or politically motivated fluctuation of staff members. Just to bring one example, the secretaries of parliamentary committees have status of civil servants employed for indefinite period, not replaced after the change of respective committee chair.

32.3 Employment and Contractual Relationship

The tasks of the Chancellery are carried out by civil servants in state-employment relationship under the Civil Service Act, No. 55/2017, as amended, and employees performing the work in the public interest under the Act on Performing Work in the Public Interest,

Table 32.1 Selected aspects of employment statistics

Year	2010	2011	2012	2013	2014	2015	2016	2017	2018	2019	2020
Number of approved positions of civil servants	175	164	161	161	161	155	156	155	155	155	165
Number of approved positions of employees performing the work in the public interest	276	262	217	217	217	223	222	238	238	238	244
Average number of civil servants and employees performing the work in the public interest	392.5	347.5	344	345.3	348	355.6	363	364	366	366	391
Average monthly wage (in EUR)	1226	1272	1258	1271	1327	1365	1475	1575	1667	1919	1796
Newly hired or transferred civil servants to the Chancellery	22	56	69	42	47	40	29	21	18	19	33
Hired employees performing the work in the public interest	(combined above)						37	22	16	22	25
Discharged employees performing the work in the public interest	36	95	70	54	30	29	20	25	19	17	18
Discharged, or retired civil servants, or civil servants transferred to other service offices	(combined above)						32	18	18	24	33

Source: Author based on the Annual Reports of the National Council of the Slovak Republic (National Council of the Slovak Republic, 2021a).

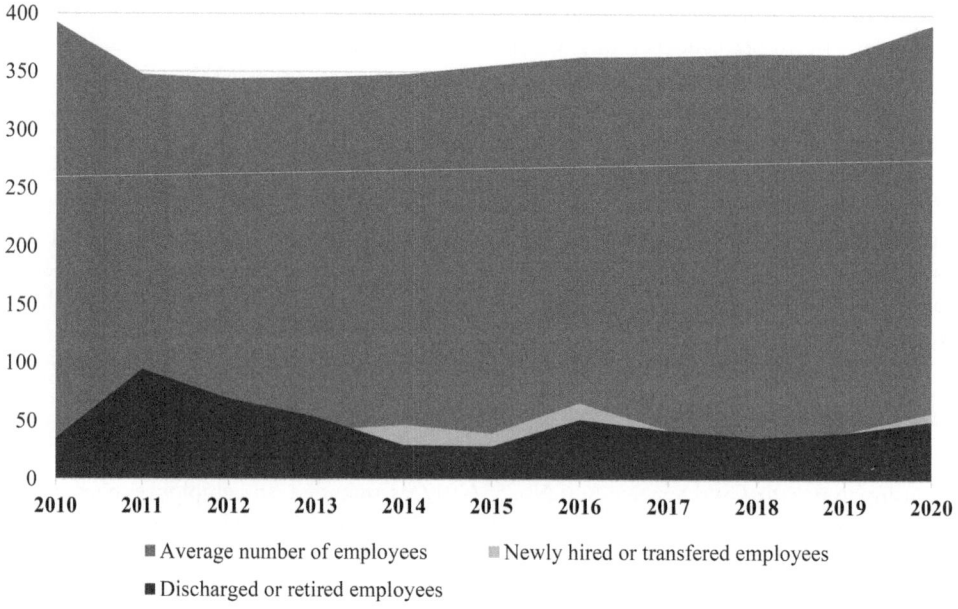

Figure 32.2 Evolution of the size of the parliamentary administration in Slovakia

No. 552/2003, as amended. *Lex generalis* for both categories of the parliamentary administration staff members is the Labour Code, No. 311/2001, as amended.

The Chancellery is the service office within which civil servants perform civil service in state-employee relation to the Slovak Republic, not directly to the Chancellery as an institution. Civil service is an activity, by which the civil servant, to the extent provided by the Civil Service Act or a special regulation, performs tasks of the respective state body in the execution of state administration, or performs tasks in conducting state affairs in the service office concerned, which includes management, decision-making, drafting law proposals, including professional activities related to deliberation of draft laws, approval and signing of laws, as well as expert activities related to the laws vetoed by the President, drafting conceptual and strategic documents, development of documents for the performance of state affairs, legal representation, control, surveillance or inspection, internal audit or government audit or decisions drafting (Act on Civil Service and on Amendment and Supplementation of Certain Acts 2017 as amended, s. 6 para. 1).

The Salary Order, annexed to the Act on Rules of Procedure of the National Council of the Slovak Republic, No. 350/1996, as amended, contains qualification requirements and catalogues of activities of civil servants, employees performing the work in the public interest with prevalence of mental work ("white-collar") and employees performing the work in the public interest with prevalence of manual work ("blue-collar"). Thus, to distinguish between the civil servants and employees performing the work in the public interest, it is inevitable to take into consideration two major aspects. Firstly, to analyse whether a particular position is bringing to constitutional-legal powers of the National Council, ergo is directly linked with the execution of state administration by the Parliament. Secondly, further guidance is provided by the catalogues of activities of civil servants and employees performing the work in the public interest attached to the parliamentary Rules of Procedure. For example, among the civil servants, one can find lawyers reviewing draft laws, who work for the Department of Legislation and Law Approximation, or researchers from the Department of Parliamentary Institute. Employees performing the work in the public interest with prevalence of mental work are, for example, librarians, who work for the Parliamentary Library, or payroll accountants working for the Economic Department. Employees performing the work in the public interest with prevalence of manual work are for instance technicians or drivers working for the Department of Operations and Services.

Staff members of parliamentary groups are employees performing the work in the public interest upon a public service contract with the Chancellery concluded for the duration of the electoral term. Each group might have one, working as treasurer of the respective faction, with work schedule conditioned by the group size. The Chancellery assigns dedicated subsidies for daily operation of parliamentary groups, the amount of which, together with management rules thereof, are determined by the Speaker of the National Council (National Council of the Slovak Republic, 2021c). The treasurer is responsible, *inter alia*, for administration of these contributions to cover day-to-day operating costs (e.g. cell phone plans and office supplies) of the faction. Thus, the Chancellery does not employ any political advisers of parliamentary groups, as might be the case in other countries. The political parties themselves may hire such political personnel independently, covering remuneration thereof from the party budget, i.e. from state subsidies that they receive for votes and mandates after the parliamentary elections, membership fees and donations.

Employees working for Chancellery of the Speaker and Secretariats of Vice-Speakers are temporary civil servants, who are in their civil service relationship subordinated to the Secretary General, although they perform tasks upon assignments of parliamentary dignitaries concerned.

The Chancellery also covers the salaries of MPs' assistants, who are neither civil nor public servants. Each MP is entitled to not more than three personal assistants, with each assistant working for one MP only (Act on Salaries of Certain Constitutional Officials of the Slovak Republic 1993 as amended, s. 4a para. 2). The assistants are freelancers. Upon MP's agreement, the Chancellery concludes with assistants' contracts under the Commercial Code for a definite period, i.e. maximum for the duration of term of office of the respective MP. The salary of assistant/s and operating expenses of MP's constituency office together shall not exceed 2.7 times the average nominal monthly wage of an employee in the Slovak economy for the previous year (Act on Salaries of Certain Constitutional Officials of the Slovak Republic 1993 as amended, s. 4a para. 3). Therefore, MP's assistant salary is not fixed; it depends on the operational costs of the MP's constituency office, number of assistants and the decision of the respective MP on how to divide the available sum among assistants.

Moreover, the Chancellery through its Department of Parliamentary Institute organizes every year internships for undergraduate university students, the purpose of which is to acquaint the students with roles and responsibilities of the National Council and its administration. More than 700 students completed this programme in its 22-year duration so far. In academic year 2020/2021, the department organized, by applying teleworking protocols, already XXIII season of this programme. Interns work for various organizational units of the Chancellery, especially committee secretariats and selected departments. The internship lasts from October to May (eight months), with work schedule of maximum 15 hours weekly providing study breaks for university exams. It is preceded by a selection procedure (oral interview with shortlisted candidates), which takes place in June. After completing the internship, the graduates receive certificate.

32.3.1 Civil Service at a Glance

Whereas the work of civil servants is directly linked with the execution of parliamentary powers, it is inevitable to shed a light on the civil service, enshrined in the Civil Service Act, No. 55/2017, as amended, and other related regulations. Performance of civil service is guided by the principles of political neutrality, legality, transparent employment, effective management, professionalism, transparent and equal pay, stability and equal treatment (Act on Civil Service and on Amendment and Supplementation of Certain Acts 2017 as amended, arts. 1–9). Thus, the civil servants are not political nominees and their admission to the service and career path are governed by the rules stipulated at the level of law and implementing by-laws. The Civil Service Act 2017, aiming to professionalize the civil service, established a new independent institution – Civil Service Council – to coordinate and oversee compliance and protection of the above-mentioned principles and observance of the civil servants' code of conduct, laid down by the Government Decree No. 400/2019. In relation to this ordinance, the Secretary General of the Chancellery issued on 7 January 2020 an internal directive on principles of ethical conduct of a civil servant in connection with the performance of the civil service in the parliamentary administration. Another novelty brought by the new Civil Service Act 2017 is the existence of so-called mentorship as a form of workplace induction available to new civil servants during the three-month probationary period.

The civil service may be performed as permanent of indefinite duration or temporary for a fixed period (e.g. for duration of maternity leave of civil servant who is being substituted). Admission to or promotion within the permanent civil service is based upon the selection process, which can be conducted as internal from among civil servants of the respective service office, internal open to applicants from all services offices, or external open to all citizens, who meet the qualification criteria under the Civil Service Act and annex to the parliamentary Rules of Procedure. Vacant positions are announced through the register of competitions on central web portal (the so-called central portal of public services to the people *slovensko.sk*). The selection process consists of written part and oral part, or just oral part. The selection committee evaluates the results and determines the order of successfulness of applicants upon total score achieved in individual parts of the process. The order of applicants is binding for filling the post (Act on Civil Service and on Amendment and Supplementation of Certain Acts 2017 as amended, ss. 40–41). Such rules and principles are bringing to independency of the parliamentary staff from politics and professionalization of the service.

32.4 Organization of Work in the Parliamentary Administration

The Secretary General is the statutory body of the Chancellery, managing and organizing its activities, being the highest senior official, superior to all employees and civil servants in the Chancellery. He/she is appointed and recalled by the Speaker of the National Council. The current Secretary General has been in office since April 2013, *ergo* throughout three electoral terms, working with different Speakers. Nevertheless, previously it was quite common for a new Speaker to appoint a new Secretary General.

As of April 2021, the parliamentary administration has six specialized units: (1) Chancellery of the Speaker, (2–5) four Secretariats of Vice-Speakers and (6) Employees of Parliamentary Groups. Moreover, there are in total 33 organizational units (see Chart 32.1); it is to be noted that 17 Committee Secretariats have status of departments). Some departments are further divided into divisions or units, depending on their scope of work. The tasks of individual parliamentary administration departments are clear-cut, stipulated in the Organizational Rules, issued by the Secretary General.

32.4.1 Selected Roles of the Parliamentary Administration in Context of Parliamentary Work

One of the cornerstones of parliamentary administration in the context of parliamentary work is the Organizational Department, which performs conceptual and coordination activities, and administrative tasks in preparation of plenary sessions, as well as activities related to ensuring the National Council functioning and implementation of state affairs within the constitutional powers of the National Council and its Speaker. In practical terms, the department prepares, just to make some examples, the draft annual parliamentary schedule for approval of the so-called parliamentary gremium (i.e. collective body summoned by the Speaker composed of representatives of all parliamentary groups), the draft plenary session agendas and procedural guidelines for the Speaker/Vice-Speakers, the draft resolutions of the Parliament, and develops expert opinions for decision-making of the parliamentary leadership. Moreover, it performs coordination, administrative and record-keeping tasks related to oversight function (Question Time and interpellations) and appointment activities (National Council of the Slovak Republic, 2021b, pp. 31–33).

Legislative services play one of the focal roles in operations of modern parliamentary democracies, enabling smooth performance of parliamentary committees as well as ensuring continuous support for the plenary sittings. Forasmuch as the draft law might be markedly amended throughout the legislative process, an eye should be kept on it. One of the most effective ways to provide such purpose is to establish and maintain proper legislative services. Thus, the role of the Department of Legislation and Approximation of Laws is to review the compliance of draft laws with Constitution, constitutional laws, laws, international treaties and EU law. In practice, two types of legal assessments are conducted. Firstly, it is the so-called 24-hour information, which serves as a basis for decision of the Speaker of the National Council regarding the admissibility of a draft law, i.e. assessment of whether the submitted draft law meets the requirements under the Rules of Procedure Act and Legislative Rules of Law-Making. Secondly, it is the legislative standpoint issued for draft laws that passed the first reading, providing constitutional and legal review of the draft law that is available to MPs, particularly to common rapporteur appointed by the lead committee. Moreover, lawyers from this department cooperate with committee secretaries in tracking amendments and drafting lead committee reports. Once the law is adopted, they prepare its fair copy and perform emendation of its wording before publication in the Official Gazette (National Council of the Slovak Republic, 2021b, pp. 36–37).

Nevertheless, it is to be noted that the parliamentary administration drafts neither law proposals, nor amendments. Such tasks are in hands of the authors (i.e. MPs or line ministries). The Department of Legislation and Law Approximation may provide consultations and practical advice thereof.

Moreover, legislative and legal services are distinguished within the parliamentary administration. While the Department of Legislation and Law Approximation performs legislative and legislative-technical tasks, the Department of Legal Services and Public Procurement drafts contracts, legal opinions, objections and submissions, represents the Chancellery in court proceedings and ensures public procurement.

Laws require the National Council to set up the Mandate and Immunity Committee, Committee on Incompatibility of Functions, Committee on European Affairs, Constitutional and Legal Affairs Committee, three special oversight committees and the Committee for Review of Decisions of the National Security Authority. Other sectoral committees are established during constituent session of the National Council on proposal of MPs or parliamentary groups. In the current VIII electoral term, altogether 19 parliamentary committees have been appointed.

Committee secretariats are directly subordinated to the Secretary General as equally as other parliamentary administration departments. On average two employees work for a committee (one secretary and one assistant); except for the special oversight committees with fewer employees or merged secretariats, and European Affairs Committee supported by a separate department (Department for European Affairs). The secretaries and assistants are permanent civil servants, employed in the Chancellery as non-partisan and independent professionals for indefinite period. Their focal role is to ensure smooth committee operations, including documents drafting (e.g. agenda setting upon agreement with the committee chair, preparation of invitations, drafting resolutions, minutes and committee reports, tracking the legislative process and amendments and providing office management for the committee and its chair) (National Council of the Slovak Republic, 2021b, pp. 33–34).

Qualified parliamentary research helps to improve the effectiveness of the legislature. Parliamentary research services may enhance the decision-making on particular policy issues. Reliable facts and analyses may eventuate in better understanding of the problem and comparative analysis of the matter may broaden horizons to find the most appropriate solution. Forasmuch as information technologies have been changing almost every aspect of our lives, high-quality information potentiates the legitimacy of the legislature. Yet important, regardless of the form of government, there is a growing desire for the legislature to be more active within the existing constitutional framework and therefore its outputs need to be based on relevant and sustainable facts.

The Department of Parliamentary Institute (hereinafter referred to as "PI") is the information-analytical hub providing parliamentary research, library and archival services in the Chancellery. The status of the PI is defined at the level of law, by Section 144 of the Act on Rules of Procedure of the National Council of the Slovak Republic, No. 350/1996, as amended, according to which the PI performs analytical, educational, documentation and information tasks related to activities of the National Council and its Members. The PI also includes the Parliamentary Library Division and Parliamentary Archives Division.

As part of its analytical and research activities, the PI regularly develops not only on-demand analyses upon requests of MPs or parliamentary committees but also proactive research papers, issued in three editions (Comparative analyses, Information papers and Factsheets), focused on topical issues discussed in the National Council and its committees, which are disclosed to all MPs and published online on the parliamentary website. Moreover, it cooperates with the European Centre for Parliamentary Research and Documentation and provides replies to queries from foreign Parliaments and international organizations.

In the field of education, the PI, *inter alia*, issues briefing books and organizes induction programme for newly elected MPs at the beginning of each electoral term and provides various *ad hoc* study visits or workshops for domestic audience or foreign participants as part of the parliamentary development assistance.

What is to be considered in connection with structure of parliamentary research services is the organizational relationship between the research department and the parliamentary library. In Slovakia, the Parliamentary Library is the division under the Department of Parliamentary Institute. It is not a public library. According to the Library Act, No. 126/2015, as amended, it has the status of a special library. The services are provided to MPs, staff of the Chancellery, special users and university students (only for on-site reading). The book collection consists of approximately 95,000 books and 850 titles of periodicals (Parliamentary Library of the National Council, 2021).

32.4.2 Management of European Affairs, Inter-Parliamentary and Inter-Institutional Cooperation

The National Council applies a mixed system of parliamentary scrutiny of EU matters. Hence, the Committee on European Affairs regularly checks the compliance of draft EU legislative acts with the principle of subsidiarity on one side, and on the other hand it approves the government positions before meetings of respective EU institutions (i.e. National Council has the right to give binding mandates to government members before meetings of the Council or the European Council). The Department for European Affairs provides coordination, expert and conceptual tasks thereof, ensuring also the function of committee secretariat. It continuously follows legislative process at the EU level and cooperates with EU institutions, national Parliaments of EU Member States, government bodies, permanent representation in Brussels, other parliamentary committees and administration departments (National Council of the Slovak Republic, 2021b, pp. 34–35).

The Chancellery has long-standing and wide-ranging experience in implementing capacity building activities and institutional reforms aimed at strengthening the representation, law-making and oversight functions of partner Parliaments. These activities date back to 2004, when the Slovak parliamentary experts provided guidance during parliamentary Rules of Procedure drafting in Montenegro. Since then, the Chancellery has co-organized many events for MPs and/or parliamentary staff members mainly from Western Balkan countries. Moreover, between September 2017 and December 2019, the Chancellery implemented in consortium with the Czech Parliament and Hungarian National Assembly the EU-funded Twinning Project Strengthening the capacities of the Parliament of Moldova for EU approximation process (MD 13 ENPI OT 02 17 (MD/28)), which conducted 70 institutional and capacity-building activities. To ensure smooth on-the-spot management of this Project, the Chancellery seconded one of its experts as the Resident Twinning Adviser.

In addition, parliamentary diplomacy is implemented in standard ways, as bilateral or multilateral, or through permanent delegations to international organizations such as Inter-Parliamentary Union, Parliamentary Assembly of Council of Europe and NATO Parliamentary Assembly. Department of Foreign Relations and Protocol provides expert, organizational and information activities thereof and cooperates with the Ministry of Foreign and European Affairs, Slovak Embassies abroad and other state authorities (National Council of the Slovak Republic, 2021b, pp. 41–42). Staff members of the department act as secretaries of permanent delegations and provide logistical, protocol and contextual support in relation to inward and outward visits.

In compliance with Section 143 paragraph 11 of the Act on Rules of Procedure of the National Council, No. 350/1996, as amended, the Chancellery may demand from state authorities and legal entities any information, which may be necessary for the operation of the National Council and its committees. These authorities are obliged to meet such requirements. Thus, for example, the Department of Parliamentary Institute often cooperates with ministries, governmental agencies and other public institutions (such as the Statistical Office), by exchanging information. Nevertheless, external experts are involved occasionally, although the Rules of Procedure enable it. By means of Section 54 of the Rules of Procedure, committees may invite to their meetings various specialists and request their opinions and expert analyses. Committees may also create commissions as their advisory bodies, composed of MPs and various experts from academia, business or civil society.

32.5 Managing Current Challenges

The first recorded case of COVID-19 in Slovakia was confirmed on 6 March 2020, shortly after the parliamentary elections of 29 February 2020, won by the opposition. Constituent session of the National Council took place on 20 March 2020, with the new government appointed one day after. Throughout 2020 (March to December), the new Parliament held 20 in-person plenary sessions lasting 67 sitting days, keeping the agreed schedule with few extraordinary sessions due to the pandemic. Depending on the local epidemic situation, access to the parliamentary building was restricted, and the Chancellery serially applied telework protocols for staff in March, April and October 2020, and in January to April 2021, with consent of director of each respective organizational unit, if the individual scope of work allowed. For instance, the Department of Parliamentary Institute initially organized the induction programme for newly elected MPs in the form of narrated presentations available on the internal network of the Chancellery together with three briefing books (*How the Parliament Works*, *Practical Guide to Member's Work* and *Short Parliamentary Dictionary*). With relaxation of the COVID-cautious measures, the PI subsequently continued with in-person seminars in summer 2020.

32.6 Conclusion

To ensure smooth operation of the Slovak Parliament and its working bodies, one institution called the Chancellery of the National Council of the Slovak Republic performs all the parliamentary administration services. The Chancellery is well-rooted and professional administration, having the status of state budgetary organization. Thus, it is autonomous from executive administration, in particular in terms of budget, hierarchy, organizational structure and decision-making. As of April 2021, the Chancellery is composed of 6 specialized units and 33 organizational units (including 17 committee secretariats). Scope of work of individual parliamentary administration departments is clear-cut without any significant overlaps. The statutory body is the Secretary General, who is appointed and recalled by the Speaker of the Parliament. The current Secretary General has been in office since April 2013, *ergo* throughout three electoral terms, working with different Speakers. Evidence from the parliamentary annual reports show that over time the parliamentary administration remains adequately stable without any regular disruptive political interferences ensuing from the changes in power after parliamentary elections, or politically motivated fluctuation of staff members. Just to bring one example, the secretaries of parliamentary committees have status of civil servants employed for indefinite period, not replaced after the change of respective committee chair.

Slovakia's Parliamentary Administration

Organizational Structure of the Chancellery of the National Council of the Slovak Repulic

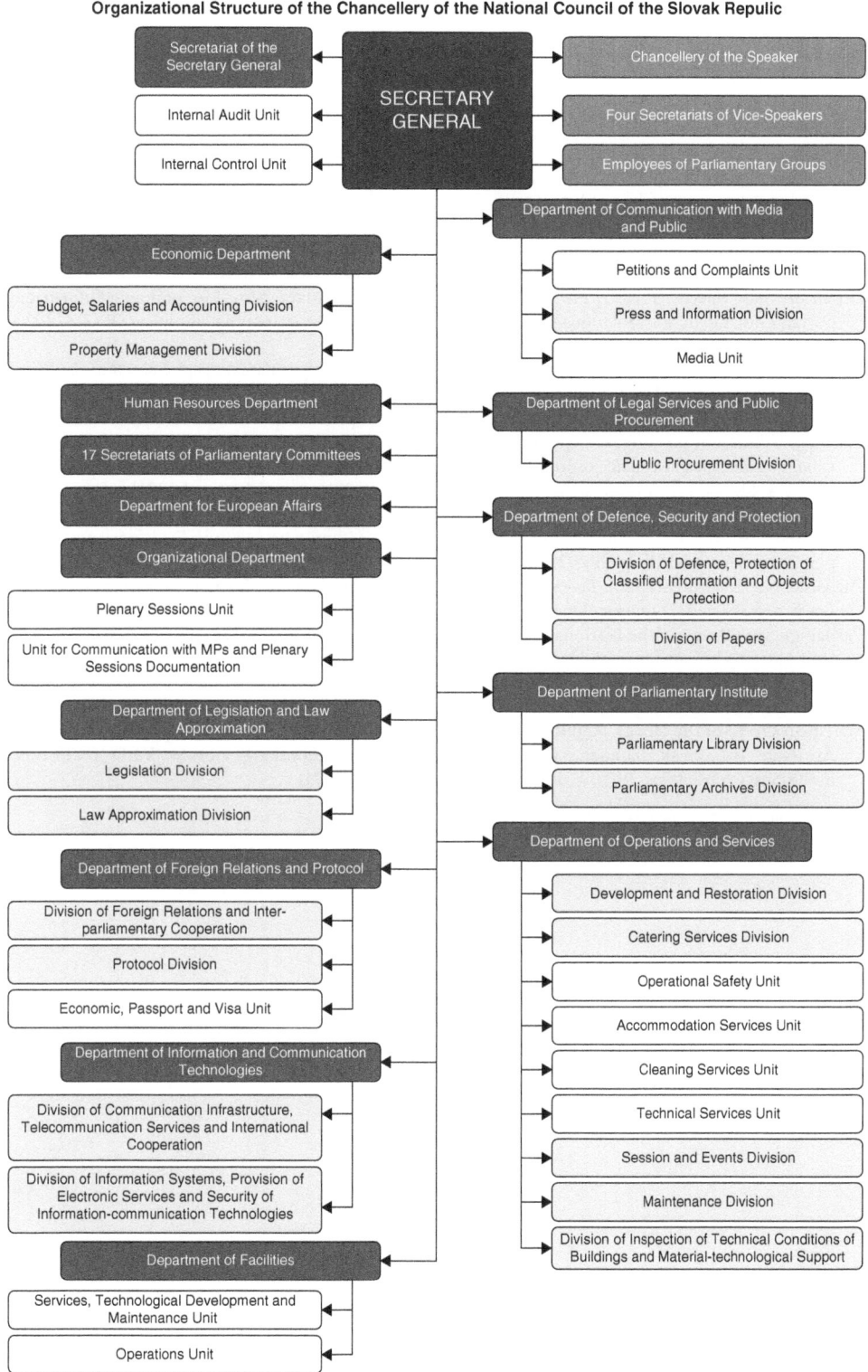

References

Act of the National Council of the Slovak Republic on the Rules of Procedure of the National Council of the Slovak Republic 1996 as amended, No. 350/1996, Bratislava: Slov-Lex právny a informačný portál, available in Slovak language from: https://www.slov-lex.sk/pravne-predpisy/SK/ZZ/1996/350/20210101.html [accessed 30 March 2021].

Act on Salaries of Certain Constitutional Officials of the Slovak Republic 1993 as amended, No. 120/1993, Bratislava: Slov-Lex právny a informačný portál, available in Slovak language from: https://www.slov-lex.sk/pravne-predpisy/SK/ZZ/1993/120/20210101 [accessed 12 April 2021].

Act on Civil Service and on Amendment and Supplementation of Certain Acts 2017 as amended, No. 55/2017, Bratislava: Slov-Lex právny a informačný portál, available in Slovak language from: https://www.slov-lex.sk/pravne-predpisy/SK/ZZ/2017/55/20210301 [accessed 30 March 2021].

Act on the State Budget for 2021, No. 425/2020, Bratislava: Bratislava: Slov-Lex právny a informačný portál, available in Slovak language from: https://www.slov-lex.sk/pravne-predpisy/SK/ZZ/2020/425/20210101.html [accessed 30 March 2021].

National Council of the Slovak Republic. (2021a). *Annual Reports of the National Council of the Slovak Republic for years 2003–2020* [online]. Available in Slovak language from: https://www.nrsr.sk/web/?sid=nrsr/kancelaria/pi/oa/vyrsprava [accessed 10 April 2021].

National Council of the Slovak Republic. (2021b). *Organizational Rules of the Chancellery of the National Council of the Slovak Republic* [online]. Available in Slovak language from: https://www.nrsr.sk/web/Static/sk-SK/NRSR/organizacny_poriadok_20190515.pdf [accessed 10 April 2021].

National Council of the Slovak Republic. (2021c). *Roles and Responsibilities of Parliamentary Groups* [online]. Available in Slovak language from: https://www.nrsr.sk/web/?sid=poslanci/kluby/postavenie [accessed 10 April 2021].

Parliamentary Institute. (2020). *Information Bulletin* [online]. Available in Slovak language from: https://www.nrsr.sk/web/Dynamic/DocumentPreview.aspx?DocID=489575 [accessed 10 April 2021].

Parliamentary Library of the National Council. (2021). *Welcome* [online]. Available in English language from: https://kniznica.nrsr.sk/index.php/en/welcome [accessed 15 April 2021].

Slovak National Council. (1990). *Draft of the Interim Organizational Structure of the Chancellery of the Slovak National Council No. 643/1990*. Bratislava: Parliamentary Archives.

Statistical Office of the Slovak Republic. (2021). *Quarterly GDP data by industry in current prices* [online]. Available in Slovak language from: http://datacube.statistics.sk/#!/view/sk/VBD_INTERN/nu0005qs/v_nu0005qs_00_00_00_sk [accessed 30 March 2021].

33
SLOVENIA'S PARLIAMENTARY ADMINISTRATION

Alenka Krašovec[1]

33.1 Introduction

Slovenia took its first steps in transitioning to a democracy at the end of the 1980s, with the final step in the institutional arrangement of the newly democratized and independent country coming when the new Constitution was adopted in December 1991. Under the Constitution, the Slovenian Parliament formally has two chambers and consists of the Državni zbor (lower house)[2] and the Državni svet (upper house),[3] with the latter having 22 indirectly elected representatives of local and 18 representatives of local and functional interests.[4] The Državni svet's relatively limited *de iure*, but also *de facto* power[5] (some legal experts even contend that Slovenia has one-and-a half houses), has seen the Državni zbor often being referred to as the parliament. The Državni zbor has 90 members, including 2 seats reserved for representatives of the country's Italian and Hungarian national minorities. Slovenia uses a proportional (PR) electoral system with a relatively low threshold for Državni zbor elections – since 2000 the threshold has been 4%, whereas before then it was three seats (i.e. 3.3%–3.4%) – and quite a fragmented (at least numerically) party system. Typically, governments in Slovenia are majority coalitions of several parties, but with a clear tendency to drop out during the legislative term (Krašovec & Krpič 2019).

Although most Slovenian constitutional scholars view the country's constitutional system of 1991 as a parliamentary one, several well-known comparative analyses mostly describe Slovenia as a semi-presidential system (e.g. Elgie & Moestrup 2008; Samuels & Shugart 2010), although this is chiefly because the President of the Republic is directly elected while does not possess legislative powers.

This chapter analyses Službe državnega zbora (the Services or administration of the Državni zbor), headed by generalni sekretar (Secretary General). New institutional arrangement was set up during the democratization process way back in 1992 at the time of the first elections to the Državni zbor.

33.2 Administration of the Državni zbor

33.2.1 Structure and Functions

Generally speaking, the parliamentary administration and its regulation concerns questions of a parliament's autonomy, more precisely its administrative autonomy. The Državni zbor in Slovenia enjoys a comparatively high level of such autonomy as it decides about both the internal organization and the organization of its services alone (Velišček 2011; Sancin et al. 2018). Moreover, Members of the Parliament (MPs) perceive this kind of autonomy as the highest of the various forms of autonomy held by the Državni zbor (Sancin et al. 2018, p. 199). The administration of the Državni zbor is not regulated by the Constitution but by several legal acts. The first elections to the Državni zbor were held at the end of 1992, the same year the Law on MPs was passed. It was the first such legal act to (indeed briefly) mention the Zbor's administration, stating (among the conditions of MPs' activities) that the Državni zbor determines the organization and functioning of its administration, while an MP has the right to require expert explanations and all other services from the administration needed to carry out their functions. Two other regulations adopted in 1993 (Rules of Procedure of the Državni zbor; Decree on the Organization and Functioning of the Državni zbor's Services) more extensively dealt with the Zbor's administration. Since 1992, all three legal acts have been amended several times and some new ones passed to regulate this area, including the Law on the Državni zbor of 2019 that also sought to assure greater consistency in the different forms of autonomy, including administrative and financial, held by the Državni zbor.

The way the Zbor's administration is organized has changed over the years by learning from new insights, needs and experiences, yet without amounting to a major reorganization, and thus may be characterized as upgrades of the existing structure (Velišček 2011, p. 86).

As Figure 33.1 reveals, one can talk about the considerable diversification of the Zbor's services whose structure is similar to certain other parliamentary administrations across Europe but is closest to the 'Scandinavian model' (Lončar 2008, p. 133, 151).

With respect to personnel, some changes in the number of Državni zbor administration employees can be seen since 1992 – very slow growth in the 1992–2011 period, followed by a drop (see Table 33.1) due to a comprehensive package of austerity measures adopted in 2012 to deal with the Great Recession, and small increase in 2018–period. As a result of most of the expert staff working for the old, socialist representative body having decided to join the administration of the Državni svet in 1992, the Državni zbor commenced work with only a limited number of employees, who generally provided administrative and technical support (Velišček 2011, p. 80). People employed in the Državni zbor administration hold the status of a civil servant, inter alia meaning they are selected according to a merit system and under a public sector employment procedure. The career and salary promotion of those working in the administration are regulated by general rules that apply to the public sector, with the biggest changes to these rules coming in 2008 for the whole public sector.

The Državni zbor has its own systematization of working positions. Yet, the Zbor administration has constantly employed fewer people than the systematization has called for. As evaluated by former President of the Državni zbor, mainly due to a wish, or a need to show the public that the Zbor is working hard to save taxpayers' money (Brglez 2021). Employees are entitled to participate in various types of staff training/development, including foreign languages, ICT, leadership and collaboration skills, different expert meetings, conferences

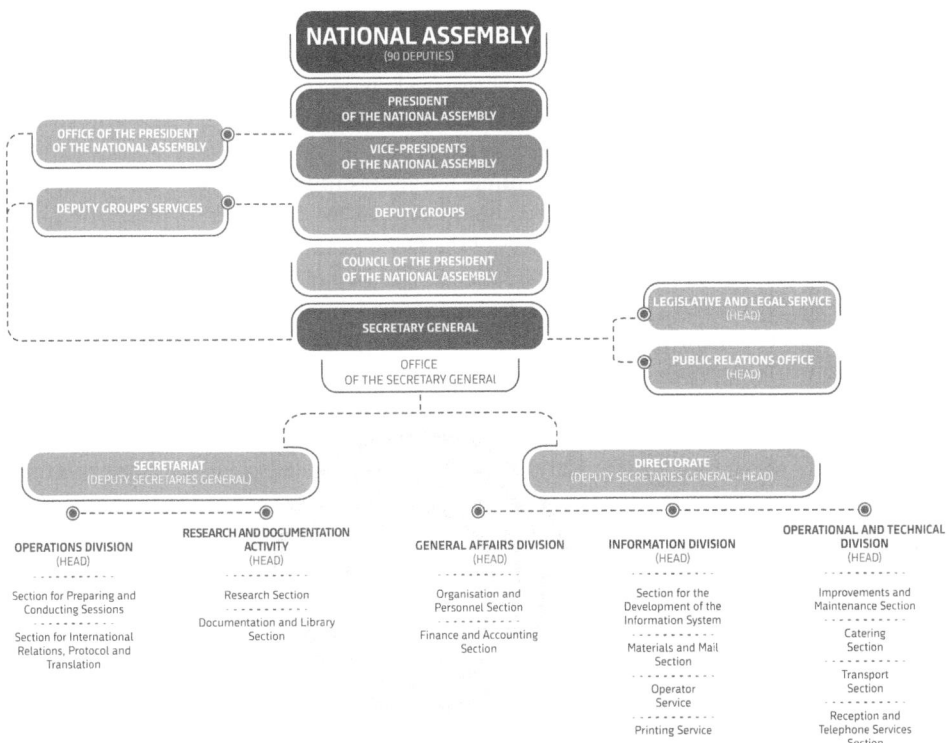

Figure 33.1 Organizational chart of the Državni zbor in 2021

Table 33.1 Number of employees in the Državni zbor administration (1992–2020)

Legislative term (data on the last day of the mandate)	Zbor's administration (without PPG)
1992–1996 (28.11.1996)	256
1996–2000 (27.10.2000)	259
2000–2004 (22.10.2004)	270
2004–2008 (15.10.2008)	281
2008–2011 (21.12.2011)	282
2011–2014 (1.8.2014)	257
2014–2018 (22.6.2018)	247
2018–2022 (data as at 31.12.2020)	259

Source: Državni zbor, 2021

and seminars that are organized internally or externally and held in Slovenia or abroad, including, for example, ECPRD seminars. It is important that the Zbor has its own counsellor for staff training or development and that such activities have been engaged in continually. During the Covid-19 pandemic, online education and trainings have also been on offer, including on how to handle remote work.

The Državni zbor's services are responsible for performing expert, administrative, technical and other tasks that ensure the conditions needed for the work of the Zbor and its MPs. As shown in Figure 33.1, the services of the Državni zbor are headed by the Secretary General. The Secretary General directs, organizes and coordinates the services, arranged into different divisions that work for and execute tasks for the Državni zbor, its working bodies, the parliamentary party groups (PPGs) and the MPs, provides for the coordinated functioning of the services, takes care of the development of the organization and work and performs other tasks according to the Državni zbor's Rules of Procedure and other regulations (Article 14 of the Decree on Internal Organization and the System of Positions in the Services of the Državni zbor 2019). The Secretary General holds the status of a functionary and is appointed by the Državni zbor (by a plurality vote) at the proposal of the Council of the President of the Državni zbor until the end of the term of the Državni zbor that appointed him/her. He/she is accountable to the Zbor, but his/her responsibility is not just to direct, organize and coordinate the Zbor's administration but is also responsible for its agenda-setting and the planning of its work (Zajc 2009). The Secretary General is namely a member of the Council of the President of the Državni zbor (together with the President and Vice-Presidents of the Zbor and the PPG leaders) who among others decides on: proposals to adopt a law through an urgent procedure, proposals to discuss a draft law in a shortened procedure, proposals to hold a preliminary discussion on a law, the duration of the Državni zbor's sessions and the time allocated for the discussion of individual agenda items, as well as on the allocation of speaking time to MPs and PPGs and other participants. Taking all these into account, it is possible to say, the Secretary General is on administrative-political intersection (Brglez 2021). Despite his/her appointment is the most obvious indicator of the spoil system, the Secretary General should be neutral in relation to all MPs and parties. As evaluated by former President of the Državni zbor, the Secretary General has indeed several, more indirect ways to be also important political actor but this has not been the case, at least not on the open stage (Brglez 2021).

In the 1993 Decree on the Organization and Functioning of the Državni zbor's Services, the Zbor's services were led by three functionaries: Secretary General, Secretary of the Državni zbor and Secretary of the Secretariat for Legislative and Legal Services. Each was appointed by the Državni zbor on the proposal of the Zbor's Committee for Elections, Appointments and Administrative Affairs (today called the Committee for Public Office and Elections). The Secretary General organized and coordinated the work of all services to ensure the implementation of tasks and affairs for the Zbor's needs and those of its working bodies and MPs, was responsible for the smooth functioning of all of the Zbor's services and took care of developing the organization and work, while performing other tasks in line with the Državni zbor's Rules of Procedure. The Secretary of the Državni zbor led the secretariat in the preparation and implementation of Državni zbor sessions, was responsible for assuring expert opinions within the Zbor's working areas, organized, led and coordinated expert work for the Zbor and its working bodies and prepared plenary sessions of the Državni zbor. The Secretary of the Secretariat for Legislative and Legal Services was responsible for delivering opinions on the conformity of draft laws, other acts and amendments with the Constitution and the legal system as well as on legislative and technical aspects of drafts. In 1994 (with changes to be enforced after the 1996 elections), the positions of Secretary General and Secretary of the Državni zbor were merged together – the Secretary General. Under new Rules of Procedure of the Državni zbor passed in 2002, the position of the Secretariat for Legislative and Legal Services was also changed to become the Legislative and Legal Service and in legal and organizational terms it lost the complete independence it once possessed (Stanič Igličar 2007, p. 45). These days, this service is directly accountable to the Council of the President of the Državni zbor as well as the Secretary General. Generally, the Decree on the Organization and Functioning of the Državni zbor's Services in 1997 is a turning point in how the parliamentary administration in Slovenia is organized not only by more precisely establishing the power held by the Secretary General but also with a more exact definition of the parliamentary administration in terms of its departments and sectors, or divisions (Zajc 2009, p. 100).

As seen in Figure 33.1, the Secretary General has two deputies. One of these deputies leads the Secretariat. One Section within the Secretariat is responsible for (a) carrying out expert and administrative tasks related to preparing and implementing the Zbor's sessions and the sessions of the working bodies and (b) international activities and protocol. There is also a Research-Documentation Division and within that the Research Section which only started to work in 1998. As argued by Zajc (2000), this Section is very valuable since it assures expert, objective and politically impartial/neutral support for MPs. The Section prepares tasks (analyses, comparative overviews, reports etc.) based on requests by the Državni zbor, its working bodies, PPGs, individual MPs and the Secretary General, or upon its own initiative. Within one month of their completition, all tasks are available at the Zbor's portal and intranet, while the commissioner of the task receives the results prior to that. In 2020, for example, most requests for research came from MPs in the opposition (12), followed by MPs in the government coalition (9), while working bodies and PPGs requested two of such tasks each, as did the Secretary General. In 2020, this Section also prepared 13 research tasks on its own initiative and 5 reports on the Državni zbor's work (Report on Work of the Research Section in 2020). The Section has developed to become an important service (Zajc 2009), despite employing quite a small number (eight) of people.

33.2.2 Working Bodies

Support for performing both expert and administrative tasks, but mostly with regard to preparing and implementing activities of the Državni zbor's working bodies (the purpose of these bodies – their members are MPs – is to monitor the state of affairs in individual policy areas, prepare policy decisions in such areas, formulate positions on particular issues and discuss draft laws and other acts of the Državni zbor at different stages of the legislative process), is also assured within them.

As Olson and Mezey (1991) noted, the working bodies of modern parliaments are typically where most of the parliamentary policy-making processes take place. Similarly, the Državni zbor's working bodies have held an important role in parliamentary policy-making since 1992. The 2002 Rules of Procedure added some formal competences to working bodies in the legislative process, while simultaneously shortening it. The majority of parliamentary experts believe these Rules have significantly empowered the Zbor's working bodies, largely because these bodies were given very important competences in the first and second readings of the legislative process (Fink-Hafner & Krašovec 2005, p. 409). Many working bodies had been formed in each legislative term, with the numbers varying a little, partially depending on the number of ministries in governments (some working bodies are permanent or standing commissions); in 1992, for example, 24 of such bodies were established (as well as 6 Committees of Inquiry), while 21 working bodies were formed in 2020 (as well as 6 Committees of Inquiry) (Report for the Period 23.12.1992 to 16.10.1996; Report on Work of the Državni zbor in the 2018–2022 Period: Third Year of the Term). Each working body is entitled to a secretary, one or more experts/counsellors and at least one administrative worker; the number of staff in the working bodies depends on the size of the body and the field it covers.

As described by Velišček (2011, p. 82), in the Državni zbor's first legislative term (1992–1996), support for the personnel mainly went precisely to the working bodies. Although those who work in these bodies have always been civil servants, early on some presidents of the working bodies repeatedly proposed that the president of a working body has the right to select the personnel (Stanič Igličar 2007, p. 34).

Zajc (2009, p. 101) observed that, more generally, expert support for policy- and decision-making processes in the Državni zbor is compared to other parliaments still weak in personnel terms, especially when we note that quite a small number of MPs must deal with a similar extent of work as other MPs in bigger parliaments must. Especially at the beginning, there was considerable fluctuation among employees in the Zbor's services due to distrust in their performance as well as poor appreciation of their work (Zajc 2009, p. 101).

Despite the relatively small number of employees in the Zbor's administration and notwithstanding the considerable workloads, a survey among MPs conducted in 2018 revealed that more than 70% of them evaluated the expert, administrative and technical support provided by the Zbor's services as good (30%) or very good (42%) (Sancin et al. 2018, p. 204).

33.2.3 Relations with the Public, Participation of the Public

As indicated by Figure 33.1, the other deputy Secretary General leads the Directorate with three Divisions responsible for (a) organization and personnel (HR department), finances and accounting; (b) information (ICT, post, printing …); and (c) operational/technical activity (investments, catering, receptionist activities …).

There is also a Public Relations Office, which takes care of relations with not only different external publics but also different publications of the Državni zbor. The Office is directly accountable to the Secretary General.

There are different ways the public/citizens can participate and/or collaborate with the Državni zbor, in addition to them having the right to initiate legislation and to demand that a referendum be held on the issue. Someone must prepare, organize and implement such participative instruments and the parliamentary administration has an important role to play here, especially the Public Relations Office, the working bodies' services but also the Information Division and the employees in the PPGs. The public/citizens can, for example, send their opinions and messages to MPs, working bodies …, including by e-mail, they can be invited to take part in working bodies' sessions (in 2020, 1,155 citizens did so, and in the 1992–1996 period, for example, 2,840) (Report on Work of the Državni zbor in the 2018–2022 Period: Third Year of the Term; Report for the 23.12.1992–16.10.1996 Period), they can follow sessions of the working bodies and plenary sessions of the Državni zbor when they are open to the public, prepare petitions (the working body responsible received 133 petitions in 2020) (Report on Work of the Državni zbor in the 2018–2022 Period: Third Year of the Term), participate in the public presentation of opinions within working bodies and send initiatives as an organized civil society (up to 461 initiatives were received in 2020) (Report on Work of the Državni zbor in the 2018–2022 Period: Third Year of the Term). Local communities are also invited to submit opinions when a draft law touches on their status or rights. Still, the parliamentary administration also engages in the preparation, organization and implementation of events like exhibitions, the Kids' Parliament, open-door days and organized tours of parliament (Žagar & Blažič 2008).

33.3 Parliamentary Party Groups and Their Staff

In Slovenia, MPs elected to the Državni zbor regularly establish PPGs – MPs elected on the same list of candidates establish a PPG for this party. Given the PR electoral system, the considerable importance of parties, and despite trends towards the presidentialization and/or personalization of parties and politics (Fink-Hafner & Krašovec 2019), not one MP has been elected outside of a party candidate list. Slovenia's party system has seen parties splitting and merging, while in the last decade also electorally very successful new parties have flourished yet frequently experienced major internal conflicts even before managing to properly institutionalize themselves (Krašovec 2017; Fink-Hafner 2020; Haughton & Deegan Krause 2020). The outcome is that several MPs have switched parties and PPGs during the legislative term, but it has also led to the establishment of a PPG of unaffiliated MPs, while some MPs decided to act as an independent MP. The general rule is that at least three MPs are needed to establish a PPG, the exception being the two representatives of the Hungarian and Italian national minorities who together hold the status of a PPG with all the procedural rights and different resources that are attributed to PPGs.

In addition to the parliamentary administration, PPGs also employ several people. However, like in many other countries, they do not form part of the parliamentary administration in the classic sense (Krašovec 2004, p. 59).

The issue of resources for the PPGs has frequently been on the Državni zbor's agenda. While in Slovenia the party regulation allows different kinds of resources for parties, in reality they have depended heavily on various forms of public subsidies, including staff, or funding for the staff in PPGs (Krašovec 2000, 2018; Krašovec & Haughton 2011). Such a public subsidy was first introduced by the Decree on the Organization and Functioning of the Državni zbor's Services in 1993, which provided that each PPG has a secretary, formally employed by the Državni zbor but at the proposal of the PPG leader. In 1997, this form of subsidy to the PPGs was increased as the new Decree stated that each PPG was entitled to a secretary, an expert and one administrative employee with one extra member of administrative staff allocated for every additional eight MPs. Moreover, the PPGs received certain amounts (on a monthly basis) of 'additional professional help' – each PPG was entitled to one-third of the monthly salary of one counsellor for each MP it had engaged. In addition, the PPGs were (and still are entitled) to a monthly subsidy to ensure the work of the MPs in their electoral constituencies. As stated by Velišček (2011, p. 82), at the start of the third term (in 2000), demands to strengthen the expert support provided to the PPGs grew, with some ideas for how to achieve this aim even anticipating the redistribution of civil servants from the Zbor's administration to the PPGs. At the end, these ideas were not realized, although support for the PPGs has grown over the years. The 2019 Decree on Internal Organization and the System of Positions in the Services of the Državni zbor provides for a secretary of a PPG, a counsellor for PR, two experts and one member of administrative staff for each PPG, and one extra administrator allocated for every additional eight MPs, and an expert for every additional six MPs, but only when the PPG has at least eight MPs. Even today, every PPG receives additional expert support, namely, for every MP it contains, it receives funds in the form of a monthly salary for one undersecretary.

Table 33.2 Number of people employed in PPGs (1992–2020)

Legislative term (data on the last day of the mandate)	Number of employees
1992–1996 (28.11.1996)	24
1996–2000 (27.10.2000)	35
2000–2004 (22.10.2004)	63
2004–2008 (15.10.2008)	83
2008–2011 (21.12.2011)	82
2011–2014 (1.8.2014)	64
2014–2018 (22.6.2018)	70
2018–2022 (data as at 31.12.2020)	109

Source: Državni zbor, 2021

Not surprisingly, a trend is evident in terms of an increase in the number of staff employed in the PPGs, with the exception of 2011–2014 period due to the Great Recession, followed by a big increase in 2018–period (Table 33.2). Still, their number also depends on the number of PPGs and MPs in each PPG. Generally speaking, and unsurprisingly given the rules, the PPG with the most MPs has the most employees.

Yet, from the outset the status held by the PPG's personnel has been distinguished from those who are employed by the Državni zbor's services. The former are employed only for a fixed period of time – the maximum with respect to the time of the PPG's existence, the staff are selected by the PPG leader, not necessarily following the Law on Civil Servants – for example a public sector process, although the employment contract must be signed by the Secretary General. Employees in the PPGs are also entitled to staff training and development and regularly participate in different forms and types of them.

The PPGs in Slovenia have their own internal rules, which they mostly design and adopt themselves, although the central office of a respective party frequently 'intervenes' while forming the rules and organization of PPGs, at least by giving its approval for the rules (Krašovec 2000; Zajc 2009).

33.4 Conclusion

The administration of the Državni zbor in Slovenia has experienced several changes in the last three decades, notably in terms of organization (greater complexity) and the support provided to PPGs (more resources intended for them), albeit to a smaller extent given the employee numbers in the Zbor's administration. The 2019 Law on the Državni zbor regulates the Zbor's autonomy, including administrative, regulative, financial and security autonomy, and can therefore also importantly influence the parliamentary administration in the future. Assuring these kinds of autonomy was for decades an important challenge for Zbor; therefore, it is not a surprise that the draft law was in a big part prepared by administration itself, while politics adopted it and added only several things (Brglez 2021).

While Lončar (2008, pp. 142–148) years ago identified several challenges the Državni zbor administration had faced in the past, it seems that it has managed to successfully deal with many of them. Yet, as Zajc (2009) already warned, the number of personnel is still quite low (and lower than envisaged in the systematization), especially if the Zbor's administration wishes to provide even higher quality services than now.

One challenge that many institutions in the Slovenian public sector have encountered is digitalization, with the Državni zbor not being an exception. Digitalization in this regard has not been important itself but mainly for assuring even higher transparency, and Državni zbor has already made important progress in this regard (Brglez 2021). However, the Covid-19 pandemic has further intensified discussions on digitalization, also forcing broader society to think about it more intensively. The Državni zbor administration has switched over to remote work where possible and of course introduced other protective measures for all jobs where such work is not possible (Državni zbor, 2021), also exhibiting the ability of the Državni zbor and its services to adapt to changes in their environments quickly notwithstanding its relatively high level of institutionalization.

Notes

1 I am grateful to the Research Section and some other services of the National Assembly of Slovenia for their valuable help and information regarding the Assembly's administrative services.
2 Državni zbor is the National Assembly.
3 Državni svet is the National Council.
4 There are representatives of trade unions, employers, farmers, universities etc. and therefore Slovenia is frequently described as a country with elements of corporatism (Lukšič 2003).
5 The Državni svet has the right to initiate legislation (it is not a frequently used power) and may convey to the Državni zbor its opinion on all matters within the competence of the latter. The Državni svet has some restricted influence on governance as it can issue a veto on passed laws (the veto can be overridden by a majority of all MPs, which is almost the norm). Until 2013, it could demand the holding of a nationwide referendum on the laws passed by the Državni svet (it demanded 2 such referendums out of the 20 held in the 1996–2013 period).

References

Elgie, R. and Moestrup, S. eds., (2008). *Semi-Presidentialism in Central and Eastern Europe*. Manchester, New York: Manchester University Press.
Fink-Hafner, D., (2020). Destabilizacija slovenskega strankarskega sistema po letu 2000. In: A. Krašovec and T. Deželan, eds. *Volilno leto*. Ljubljana: Fakulteta za družbene vede. pp. 5–35.
Fink-Hafner, D. and Krašovec, A., (2005). Is Consultation Everything? The Influence of Interest Groups on Parliamentary Woking Bodies in Slovenia. *Czech Sociological Review*. **41**(3), 401–421.
Fink-Hafner, D. and Krašovec, A., (2019). The Presidentialisation of Parties in Slovenia: Leaders and Parties. In: G. Passarelli, ed. *The Presidentialisation of Political Parties in the Western Balkans*. Cham: Palgrave, MacMillan. pp. 145–167.
Haughton, T. and Deegan Krause, K., (2020). *The New Party Challenge*. Oxford: Oxford University Press.
Krašovec, A., (2000) *Moč v političnih strankah*. Ljubljana: Fakulteta za družbene vede.
Krašovec, A., (2017). A Hint at Entrepreneurial Parties? The Case of Four New Successful Parties in Slovenia. *Politologicky Časopis*. **24**(2), 158–178.
Krašovec, A., (2018). Evolution of Party Regulation in Slovenia and the Party System: From Some to Marginal Impact? In: F. Casal Bertoa and I. van Biezen, eds. *The Regulation of Post-Communist Party Politics*. London and New York: Routledge. pp. 236–256.

Krašovec, A. and Haughton, T., (2011). Money, Organization and the State: The Partial Cartelization of Party Politics in Slovenia. *Communist and Post-Communist Studies.* **44**(3), 199–209.
Krašovec, A. and Krpič, T., (2019). Slovenia: Majority Coalitions and the Strategy of Dropping out of Cabinet. In: T. Bergman, G. Ilonszki and W. C. Müller, eds. *Coalition Governance in Central Eastern Europe*. Oxford: Oxford University Press. pp. 475–521.
Krašovec, T., (2004). Parlamentarne Administracije. In: T. Krašovec, ed. *Zbornik 2004*. Ljubljana: Državni zbor RS. pp. 46–75. Available from: https://fotogalerija.dz-rs.si/datoteke/Publikacije/Zborniki_RDS/Zbornik_RDS_-_2003.pdf [Accessed 22 April 2021].
Lončar, L., (2008). Organiziranost služb Državnega zbora Republike Slovenije – izkušnje in novim izzivom naproti. *Uprava*. **6**(3), 131–153.
Lukšič, I., (2003). Corporatism Packaged in Pluralist Ideology: The Case of Slovenia. *Communist and Post-Communist Studies*. **36**(4), 509–525.
Olson, M. D. and Mezey, L. M., (1991). Parliaments and Public Policy. In: D. M. Olson and M. L. Mezey, eds. *Legislatures in the Policy Process: The Dilemmas of Economic Policy*. Cambridge: Cambridge University Press. pp. 1–23.
Samuels, D. J. and Shugart, M. S., (2010). *Presidents, Parties, and Prime Ministers: How the Separation of Powers Affects Party Organization and Behaviour*. New York: Cambridge University Press.
Sancin, V. et al., (2018). *Avtonomija državnega zbora v vseh vidikih njene pojavnosti*. Ljubljana: Pravna fakultete Univerze v Ljubljani. [Viewed 15 April 2021]. Available from: https://fotogalerija.dz-rs.si/datoteke/Publikacije/Raziskovalni_projekti/Avtonomija_Drzavnega_zbora_v_vseh_vidikih_njene_pojavnosti.pdf
Stanič Igličar, H., (2007). *Parlamentarni uslužbenci v Sloveniji*. M.A. Dissertation, Faculty of Social Science, University of Ljubljana.
Veliščk, J., (2011). *Avtonomija parlamenta na primeru Državnega zbora Republike Slovenije*. M.A. Dissertation, Faculty of Social Science, University of Ljubljana.
Žagar, K. and Blažič, J., (2008). *Sodelovanje med državljani in Državnim zborom: Raziskovalna naloga št. 4/08*. Ljubljana: Državni zbor Republike Slovenije.
Zajc, D., (2000). *Parlamentarno odločanje*. Ljubljana: Fakulteta za družbene vede.
Zajc. D., (2009). *Sodobni parlamentarizem in proces zakonodajnega odločanja*. Ljubljana: Fakulteta za družbene vede.

Other Sources

Decree on the Organization and Functioning of the Državni Zbor's Services. Official Gazette 12/1993.
Decree on the Organization and Functioning of the Državni Zbor's Services. Official Gazette 19/1997.
Decree on the Organization and Functioning of the Državni Zbor's Services. Official Gazette 124/2000.
Decree on the Internal Organization and the System of Positions in the Services of the Državni Zbor's. Official Gazette 45/2021.
Interview with Milan Brglez, former President of the Državni Zbor's. Interview with an author, 20 June 2021.
Law on the Državni Zbor's. Official Gazette 66/2019.
Law on Members of the Parliament. Official Gazette 48/1992.
Report for period 23.12.1992–16.10.1996. Ljubljana: Državni zbor. [Viewed 17 April 2021]. Available from: https://fotogalerija.dz-rs.si/datoteke/Publikacije/PorocilaDZ/1992_%E2%80%93_1996/Mandatno_porocilo_1992-1996.pdf
Report on Work of the Državni Zbor's in the 2018–2022 period: Third Year of the Term (2021). Ljubljana: Državni zbor. [Viewed 17 April 2021] Available from: https://fotogalerija.dz-rs.si/datoteke/Publikacije/PorocilaDZ/Mandat_2018%E2%80%9 32022/Porocilo_o_delu_Drzavnega_zbora_v_letu_2020.pdf
Report on Work of the Research Section in 2020 (2021). Ljubljana: Državni zbor.
Rules of Procedure of the Državni Zbor's. Official Gazette 40/1993.
Rules of Procedure of the Državni Zbor's. Official Gazette 35/2002.

34
SPAIN'S PARLIAMENTARY ADMINISTRATION

Mario Kölling and Ignacio Molina

34.1 Introduction to the Parliamentary Administration in Spain[1]

The political form of government of Spain is constitutionally defined as a parliamentary monarchy, although the executive branch is clearly dominant in determining policymaking and steering popular leadership. The national sovereignty is primarily exercised through the *Cortes Generales*, which represents the Spanish people, exerts the formal legislative power and holds the prime minister and other members of the government accountable.

The *Cortes Generales* is a bicameral assembly: the lower Chamber is named the *Congreso de Diputados* (Congress of Deputies) and the upper Chamber as the *Senado* (Senate). Both have a term of four years. All members of the 350-seat lower Chamber are directly elected in closed party-lists by a proportional system which is, however, biased in favour of the larger parties, since many of the 52 constituencies are too small to achieve enough proportionality. Of the 265 senators, 208 are also directly elected by a malapportioned majority system, with sparsely populated provinces overrepresented, while the rest (currently 57 seats) are appointed by the Parliaments of the autonomous communities according to population.

The Spanish bicameralism is quite asymmetric being the lower Chamber much stronger in all functions, legislation, representation and control of the executive, and therefore in legitimacy. Indeed, the Spanish upper Chamber is too weak to constrain or check the government, almost incapable of vetoing or delaying legislation coming from the lower Chamber, and ineffective to articulate the country's complex centre-periphery relations, which, at least in theory, would be its main constitutional role as the Chamber of territorial representation.

Besides the high asymmetric bicameralism, the parliamentary administration is on the one hand formally a single bureaucracy, with several joint institutions. On the other hand, the administration is divided between both chambers into two branches with a high level of autonomy.

The Spanish transition to democracy was also a new start for the parliamentary institutions in Spain. The administrative structure of both chambers evolved since the ratification of the 1978 Spanish Constitution. According to Santos Canalejo, three phases can be distinguished. A first one, between the first democratic elections after the Franco Dictatorship in 1977 until 1982, was dominated by the uncertainty about the future nature of the parliamentary organization, especially in relation to the creation and role of a common "Secretariat of the Cortes", which historically existed, for example in the Cortes de Cadiz, and the efforts to create a collegiate administration between both chambers. A second stage between 1982 and 2007 was characterized by the consolidation of the General Secretariats in both chambers and the adoption of specific rules of procedure in both chambers. And a third stage was initiated by the "Europeanisation" of public procurement law through the approval of Law 30/2007 on Public Sector Contracts. Law 30/2007 included for the first time in its general provisions the upper and lower chambers, together with other State institutions and the autonomous communities, ending the specific role of the parliamentary administration in procurement law (Santos Canalejo, 2018).

34.2 The Organization of the Parliamentary Administration in Both Chambers

Article 72 of the Constitution (SC) establishes the general framework for the parliamentary administration underlining the regulatory autonomy, the financial autonomy and the functional autonomy of the upper and lower chambers. Thus, the Constitution ensures the organizationally independence and non-subordination of the parliamentary administration vis-à-vis any other constitutional powers. The parliamentary autonomy, however, cannot deviate from the material content (guaranteeing the independence of Parliament)[2] and does not mean impunity of both chambers from compliance with the law, or the decisions of the Judiciary.[3]

34.2.1 The Functional and Regulatory Autonomy of the Parliamentary Administration

Article 72.1 SC refers to the regulatory and functional autonomy, projected in the power of both chambers to establish "their own rules of procedure" and to elect "their respective Speaker and the other members of their Bureaus". In this regard, the Spanish parliamentary administration is intrinsically divided. The rules of procedure of the lower Chamber remain basically the same as the one approved in 1982.[4] The upper Chamber's rules of procedure, although reformed in 1994, continue to follow the basic parameters of the 1982 version.

According to article 72.1 SC "The Speakers of the chambers exercise on behalf of the latter all administrative powers and disciplinary functions within their respective chambers". The outstanding position of the Speakers of the chambers in the internal hierarchy can also be deduced from their tasks established by the rules of procedures. In the case of the lower Chamber, "the Speaker shall [...] declare the Congress constituted, and shall adjourn the sitting."; "2. The constitution of Congress shall be notified by the Speaker to the King, the Senate and the Government" (art. 4). "3. The Speaker directs and coordinates the action of the Bureau" (art. 30). In addition, the Speaker of the lower Chamber has some specific constitutional tasks laid down in articles 99.1, 99.5 and 64.1 SC.

Each Chamber has its own Secretariat General which works independent form each other. The Secretaría General is responsible for assisting, supporting and providing legal, technical and administrative advice to the different parliamentary bodies. The origin of this divided organizational structure was based on comparative experience from other parliamentary administrations.[5]

The Secretario General of the lower Chamber and the Letrado Mayor of the upper Chamber are the heads of the General Secretariats. The Statute of Personnel of the *Cortes*

Generales establishes their election procedure (6.1), according to which the Secretario General and Letrado Mayor are appointed by the Bureaus, at the proposal of the Speakers, from among the members of the corps of clerks.

The Secretario General and the Letrado Mayor report directly to the respective Speaker and the Bureau, draw up the minutes of Bureau meetings and ensure, under the supervision of the Speaker, the implementation of the decisions taken (art. 35 in RPC and RPS).[6] The Secretario General and the Letrado Mayor are responsible for directing all other clerks (*Letrados*) who, in turn, advise the rapporteurs and committees and carry out all legal and administrative functions of the parliamentary institutions (Tudela 2010). In this regard, the Secretario General and the Letrado Mayor play the twofold role of being the principal adviser on law, practice, parliamentary procedures and of a top manager with a directive function over the internal administrative activity (Griglio and Lupo, 2021). In this sense, there is a clear 'hierarchical' line which works in both chambers.

The Secretario General and the Letrado Mayor are outstanding high-ranking parliamentary civil servants, with great expertise, and are politically impartial. While there are many dismissals in the executive branch when a government changes, changes among these high positions in the parliamentary administration are less frequent. From 1990 to 2021, there were only two different Letrados Mayor in the upper Chamber, and from 2004 to 2021, only two different Secretarios Generales in the lower Chamber.[7]

Each Secretariat General is based on two administrative macro-areas – the Secretaria General for parliamentary affairs and the Secretaria General for administrative affairs who coordinate nine twin Directorates in each Chamber, each overseen by an Adjunct Secretary General. According to García-Escudero, the Secretaria General for parliamentary affairs acts "as the engine room" of the lower Chamber, preparing all background documents for the works of the Bureau, the Board of Spokespersons and the Plenary, as well as the agenda and proposals for decisions, and their implementation (García-Escudero 2021:11). In concrete, the Directorates of the Secretaria General for parliamentary Affairs in each Chamber are responsible for the following tasks:

- Directorate of Technical parliamentary Assistance: Preparation, advice, assistance, support and implementation for matters within the scope of Plenary Sitting, Permanent Deputation, Bureau and Board of Spokespersons.
- Directorate of Committees: Preparation, advice, assistance, support and implementation for matters within the scope of committees.
- Directorate of Studies, Analysis and Publications: Conducting analysis related to constitutional and parliamentary activity, as well as EU affairs[8]
- Directorate of Documentation: Compiling material for legislative procedures
- Directorate of International Relations: Preparation, organization and management of international affairs and inter-parliamentary cooperation.

The parliamentary staff is also involved in the institution's external relations, specifically inter-parliamentary relations and parliamentary diplomacy. However, the resources available have been reduced, which obliges the administrations to a "titanic" workload and makes it difficult for them to offer value-added services (Astarloa, 2017). Regarding the EU affairs, a Joint Committee on EU affairs, created at the time of accession in 1986, facilitates the coordination and avoids the duplication of political and administrative work in both chambers. The specialized scrutiny of EU legislation has also been reinforced thanks to the gradual Europeanization of all the other parliamentary standing committees. The EU

Joint Committee has at its disposal only two clerks, a librarian and three administrative personnel. The involvement of both chambers in EU affairs (including inter-parliamentary dialogue through the COSAC mechanism) or contact with the EU institutions is quite modest and the lower Chamber was actually the last national Parliament to open an office in Brussels.

34.2.2 Human and Financial Resources

Article 72.1 of the Constitution also refers to the independence of both chambers to provide themselves with the personal and material means that make possible the free and effective exercise of their constitutional functions. The rules of procedure of the lower Chamber state in article 60 that "the Congress shall have all necessary personal and material means and facilities available for the conduct of its business. In particular, technical, documentary and advisory services". Article 60 RPD makes further reference to the Budget Committee, which shall "be provided with the suitable allocation of personal and material means to enable technical advice on those aspects of legislative proceedings bearing upon revenue and public expenditure". Article 60 RPD also establishes that the list of staff and its functions falls under the responsibility of its Bureau. The rules of procedure of the upper Chamber refer to the parliamentary administration in its additional provision, according to which the regulation of the rights, duties, situations, functions and powers of civil servants should be established in the Statute of Personnel of the *Cortes Generales* (see below). In fact, the economic status, recruitment and basic conditions of service of personnel are set in this joint Statute of Personnel of the *Cortes Generales*, approved by the Bureau of the Congress and of the Senate on 23 June 1983 – BOE of 29 June 1983. However, such rules are integrated by each Chamber (Gómez, 2002; Lozano Miralles, 2005). The civil servants working in both chambers have the same statute, which means that they can work in both chambers. The staff of the *Cortes Generales* can be appointed either in the lower or upper Chamber and is functionally and organically autonomous from the executive bureaucracy. This formula has worked remarkably well in Spain without any dysfunction in this respect.[9]

Admission to the different bodies of civil servants is made on the occasion of a vacancy, by means of a public and free call for applications, in accordance with the principles of merit and ability. Training is regularly encouraged, not only in technological means but also in skills, including team management, effective presentations or conflict resolution. Compared to the rest of the public administration, the entry criteria and selection procedures are stricter, but the working conditions are comparably better, for example compatibility with secondary employments and salaries. In 2020, there were 383 civil servants of the *Cortes Generales* appointed to the lower Chamber, as well as 65 contracted staff and 280 temporary staff (see Table 34.1). As for the upper Chamber, there were 250 civil servants and 72 contracted staff appointed (2000: 190 civil servants and 83 contracted staff).

Clerks (*Letrados*) are high-ranking parliamentary civil servants, who act as legal advisers to the Parliament's different bodies. "The origin of the Letrados de las Cortes Generales goes as far back as the Rules of Procedure of the Cortes de Cádiz in 1810, which established a Technical Secretariat of the Cortes Generales, comprised of four officers" (García-Escudero 2021:6).

Clerks provide technical and expert assistance to the parliamentary bodies, for example Committees and members of the lower and upper Chamber. Their tasks also include the drafting of reports, opinions and resolutions on legislative initiatives. According to García-Escudero clerks follow "the bill from the moment it enters the House until the law is published

Table 34.1 Human resources of Congress and Senat (2020)

	Clerks	Consultants (not permanent)	Archivists-librarians	Editors, stenographers and stenotypists	Administrative technicians	Administrative staff	Ushers
Lower chamber	40	10	23	37	33	131	119
Upper chamber	20	6	13	24	25	96	72

in the Official Journal, and even afterwards, revising possible mistakes or differences between the published text and the one approved by the Parliament" (García-Escudero 2021:15). Their work as independent advisors is focused on the legal field without entering into political considerations.

Clerks are also involved in the management of the parliamentary administration. Those who work in the administrative area deal with budget management, human resources in the chambers and the supervision of expenses of parliamentarians. However, some MPs and some of the trade unions consider that these powers should not correspond to the clerks because their training only entitles them to provide legal advice and in no case to keep the accounts of the Parliament or to hire staff.[10] The oversight of parliamentarians' travel expenses is particularly important here. Clerks are the ones who ultimately approve travel (expenses) for MPs. Finally, clerks are also responsible for representing and defending the *Cortes Generales* before the ordinary Courts as well as before the Constitutional Court.

The relevance of the clerks during the Spanish transition (as experts in constitutional law, of which there was a shortage) can still be confirmed, although the parliamentary party groups hired their own staff. In times of an increasing fragmentation of the Parliament, in which new political parties have representation in both chambers, the role of clerks is essential to improve the quality of bills, whichever its origin, throughout the legislative procedure. New parties "have little to none previous experience in legislation and often lack qualified assistants. Hence the urgent need to reinforce Parliament's role in scrutinizing the quality of legislation" (García-Escudero 2021:3). Moreover, the long-standing support provided by a clerk to a specific committee makes him or her a real asset to that committee "[…] with his or her remarks and advice more likely to be accepted" (García-Escudero 2021:20). A former clerk once stated, "an independent legal advisor, will always be much more honest with a MP than someone whose salary depends on his or her affinity to a political party" (Santamaría Pastor, 2016).

The entry to the corps of clerks requires passing a competitive examination, for which a degree in law is required. The promotion of clerks up to the rank of Head of Directorate, as is the case for high-level civil servants in the administrations, is done by means of an open call for applications and according to certain merit point scales. The access to Directorates requires a prior call for applications from those civil servants. The decision is then taken by the bureau of each Chamber on the proposal of the Secretary General/ Letrado Mayor.

Although most staff of the parliamentary administration are civil servants, there is also a small number of temporary staff hired by the parliamentary administration through a procurement system with a public call for applications. These consultants provide direct assistance to the members of the Bureau and other parliamentarians institutions and offer specific expertise, for example in economy and budgetary affairs or journalism.

The parliamentary groups should receive strictly the "premises and material means" and the budgeted subsidies recognized by the rules of procedures of the chambers (art. 28 RPD; arts. 27.5 and 34 RPS). Nevertheless, the interpretation of "premises and material means" has become during the years very broad.[11] The parliamentary groups are assigned funds to hire personnel, with budget allocations dependent on the party's electoral results.

In 1997, the figure of the deputy's assistant was created and organized in the lower house through an office of the General Secretariat (called "the deputies' secretariat"), with the aim of guaranteeing one assistant per MP. Nevertheless, the parliamentary groups which have the power to propose appointments ended up absorbing the assistants, and the deputies' secretariat was closed very soon. Today individual members of Parliament lack even a single assistant, some may have a trainee. In general terms, the staff assigned to the parliamentary groups is shared among some members of the parliamentary groups. The Speakers have a small cabinet, each member of the Bureau has two assistants, the committee chairmen have one assistant and the former Speaker has one assistant.

According to Santos Canalejo, over the past decade, an increasing gradation of categories (from the initial basic one of an "assistant" to the three current ones, of "assistant", "assistant-technician" and "adviser") can be stated, which not only created an enormous bureaucratic apparatus (Santos Canalejo, 2018) but also led to precarious work situations, where assistants are sometimes paid only the minimum wage.[12] Moreover, due to the increasing number of parties represented in the Parliament, the total number of temporary staff for parliamentary Groups/MPs increased (see Table 34.2).

Regarding the budget autonomy, the Constitution (art. 72.1) points out that both chambers "autonomously approve their budgets". Both chambers have mostly made use of this autonomy within the framework of government directives. The lower Chamber's budgetary autonomy has only recently created conflict with the executive, and since 2015, several conflicts between minority governments or caretaker governments and the legislative power emerged.[13]

The budget of the lower Chamber for the year 2021 contemplates an expenditure forecast of 97,106,570 euros,[14] which represents an increase of 11.6% compared to the one approved for the year 2019. As for the upper Chamber, the budget for the year 2021 contemplates an expenditure forecast of 58,251,540 euros, which constitutes a rise of 7.7% compared to the budget approved in 2019 (see Figure 34.1).

An important guarantee for the parliamentary budgetary autonomy is the Remainder Fund (Fondo de Remanentes). In both chambers, the bureaus agree on the transfer of annual budgetary surpluses and income from interests to the Remainder Funds. The Funds, in

Table 34.2 Evolution of staff assigned to political groups and individual members 2000 and 2020

	Temporary staff for MPs	*Temporary staff parliamentary groups*
2020	244	199
2000	50	166

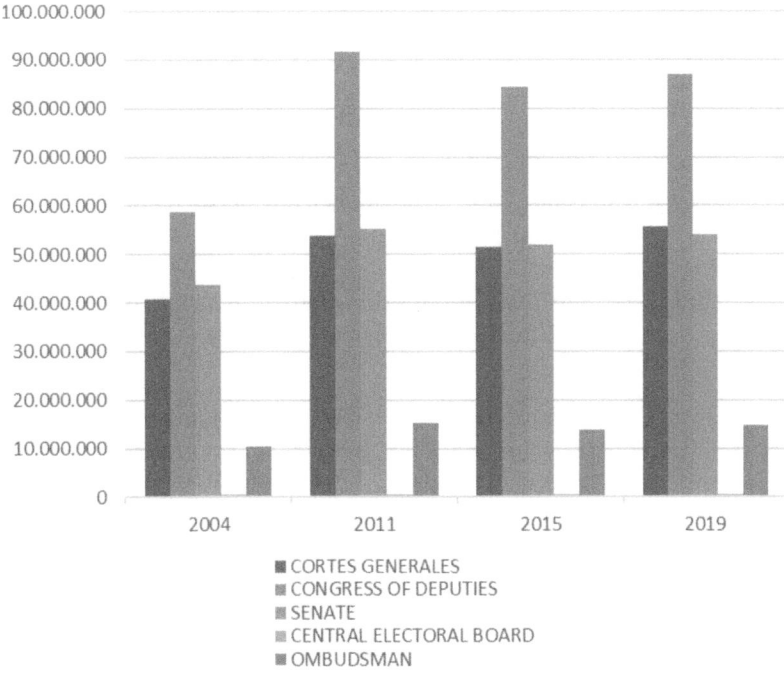

Figure 34.1 Evolution of the budget of the Cortes Generales (2004–2019) in euros

addition to guaranteeing the budgetary autonomy, offer liquidity to the treasury of both chambers in specific situations since the Parliaments lack the possibility of extraordinary credits. At the end of 2019, the amount of the Remainder Fund of the lower Chamber was 104,700,000 euros (more than an annual budget).

Although the separation of the parliamentary administrations of both chambers is very visible, article 72 of the SC also found the unitary nature of the parliamentary administration. Due to constitutional requirements, and for practical reasons, a constant coordination and cooperation is needed to harmonize services and procedures. In this sense, although the two chambers have separate organizational charts, there are close links between the administrations. Both administrations belong to the *Cortes Generales* and coordinate the budgetary decisions, the legislature procure and the international representation in shared commissions. Although both chambers lay down their own rules of procedures, the common Personnel Statute of the Cortes Generales regulates the personal issues.

Moreover, there are some joint committees in areas such as EU policy or national security as well as for monitoring the work of the ombudsman and the audit's office, which are two autonomous constitutional bodies linked to the *Cortes*. Both chambers jointly may appoint enquiry committees on any matter of public interest. Although, according to article 72.2 SC, joint sittings shall be governed by the Rules of Procedure of the *Cortes Generales*, this common provision is still pending 40 years after the entry into force of the Constitution.

However, there is also a clear 'hierarchical' line which works at the Parliament level. The Secretario General of the lower Chamber is the Letrado Mayor (Chief Clerk) of the *Cortes Generales* and, in this sense, the Head of all parliamentary staff, who is responsible for the Technical Secretary of the Central Electoral Committee – a joint institution of the Cortes. Despite this formal 'hierarchical' order, permanent contacts within the joint boards and long-standing informal contacts between the Secretary Generals of both chambers have led to a consensus-oriented relation which minimizes conflicts between both chambers.[15]

34.3 The Role of the Administration in the Context of Parliamentary Work

34.3.1 *The Parliamentary Administration as a Provider of Advice and Technical Expertise*

The availability of expertise and technical advice are essential in order to guarantee that MPs carry out their Constitutional role as lawmakers with a thorough understanding, analysis and prosecution of often complex realities. Despite the provision of article 60 of RPC, the administrative means to provide members of Parliament with multidisciplinary advice are limited. The lack of technical support for deputies and senators, who cannot effectively oversee all dimensions of public policy, has been frequently criticized. Besides the Directorate of Budgets and Staffing in both chambers, no real parliamentary research units exist, and economic resources for parliamentary committees are scarce. The Directorate for documentation in both chambers delivers important comparative analysis and documentation but does not carry out own research. Nevertheless, the salience of topics and the interests of the parliamentary groups play an important role in the parliamentary resources available for a legislative project.

The rules of procedure of the upper and lower Chambers state that parliamentary committees may request, through their respective Speakers, "the attendance of persons competent in the subject-matter for the purposes of reporting to and advising the committee" (art. 44 RPC); in this regard, the rights of parliamentary committees to send invitations to independent experts are not limited by any legal constraint. Requests to summon experts have increased in number in recent years, particularly at the beginning of the legislative process or in specialized subcommittees. Nevertheless, the limited nature of the Parliament's staffing and financial resources prevented so far the systematic involvement of university scholars, think tank analysts and other experts in the lawmaking process. There are formal or informal collaboration with other public administrations or the Bank of Spain, although this information cannot be considered autonomous and include political judgement of the executive.[16]

There is, strictly speaking, no ex-ante nor ex-post analysis of the impact of the regulation, beyond the reports that the draft laws themselves provide. Nor is there an institutionalized channelling of participatory mechanisms.[17] Both chambers have not adopted any legislative drafting guidelines to scrutinize the quality of bills (García-Escudero 2021: 5). However, specific preliminary RIAs[18] for legal norms are not only developed by the executive. On occasions, special parliamentary Committees or Subcommittees are established by both chambers to study a particular issue, and their final reports can be the basis for a legislative project tabled by a parliamentary political group. Moreover, the rules of procedure of the lower house specify that legislative projects should contain explanatory memorandums. Finally, clerks advising committees draw up reports which include, among other, the impact of the new legislative initiative on current legislation in the field, indicating the regulatory background, case law, regional legislation concerned, EU law and models of foreign law that may be helpful for the assessment of the bill. The lower Chamber is also beginning to feel responsible for the effects of the laws they adopt (García-Escudero 2021).

In March 2021, the Ministry of Science and Innovation signed a collaboration agreement with the lower Chamber to set up the Science and Technology Office in Parliament. The Office will prepare impartial and independent reports which will cover the scientific and technical state of the art on prospective topics of interest for MPs. The estimated annual budget of the Office will be 324,000 euros, of which the lower Chamber will contribute 200,000 euros and the Ministry 124,000 euros.

34.3.2 Current Challenges Facing the Parliamentary Administration

Digitalization and transparency as well as citizen engagement are important challenges for the Spanish parliamentary administrations which include also the administration of regional Parliaments. But also the Covid-19 pandemic had an important impact on the work of parliaments in Spain. During the coronavirus crisis, both chambers demonstrated a remarkable ability to continue their legislative business thanks to a largely digital working environment that was already in place. Both chambers were the only EU national Parliaments allowed to vote remotely in plenary sessions before the pandemic (art. 82 RPC and art. 92 PPS). The remote vote can only be applied if MPs cannot attend plenary sessions because of specific justified circumstances. However, the pandemic caused serious interference with the functioning of the *Cortes* as the parliamentary activity was reduced to a minimum, basically, to the voting of the extensions of the state of alarm and the validation of the Royal Decree Laws. This situation already reinforced the traditionally weak position of the Spanish Parliament vis-à-vis the executive (García-Escudero, 2020).

The upper house already started to adapt its administration towards a digital Parliament in 2010 and has since then implemented new administrative procedures and updated its regulations (Inter-Parliamentary Union, 2020). This digital transformation project was driven by a set of laws passed between 2007 and 2015, aiming to provide citizens with electronic access to public services and transparency, access to public information and good governance, as well as enhancing electronic communication within the public administration.

Regarding transparency and citizen engagement, there is no lobbying register. However, a Code of Conduct for MPs was adopted in October 2020. The relations of the chambers with the media, both classic and digital, have always been coordinated by the respective Directorates for Communications. Only rarely has the coordination of these Directorates led to political problems and the traditional commitment to neutrality has prevailed. The Speaker cabinets usually have a person in charge of communication, who is responsible for the Speakers but not for the chambers.

34.4 Conclusion

The Spanish parliamentary administration can be characterized by its institutional strength and has been an important factor of the stability of democracy. However, the subordination of the Parliament to the government and the parties has been growing during the past decades. The recent changes in the party system, which makes the executive weaker vis-à-vis the Parliament, may transform this situation. There are not only some potential elements to take advantage (the prestige and expertise of the senior civil servants – Clerks in this case – the synergies between both chambers and the financial and regulatory autonomy) but also shortcomings (the lack multidisciplinary expertise).

As Griglio and Lupo pointed out, the Spanish is an example of a bicameral parliamentary architecture which coexists with a joint administration (Griglio and Lupo, 2021: 3). In this regard, the Spanish parliamentary administration represents some unicameral arrangements but serves a highly asymmetrical bicameral system. Certain administrative units – related, for instance, to the exercise of legislative procedures or to the management of relationships with MPs – might be better served at the level of each chamber. Moreover, one Chamber can start new initiatives independently from the other, as we can see in the upper house adaption towards a digital Parliament in 2010. However, personal issues and procurement might be better served jointly in order to archive advantages because of economies of scale.

Organizational Diagram of the Spanish Secretariat General of the Senate

- CHIEF CLERK
- SENATE SECRETARIAT GENERAL

- CABINET
- ADVISORY UNIT; COORDINATION, CONTROL AND PROJECT EVALUATION UNIT

- ASSISTANT SECRETARIAT GENERAL FOR PARLIAMENTARY AFFAIRS
  - Directorate of Technical Parliamentary Assistance
  - Directorate of Committees
  - Directorate of Studies
  - Directorate of Documentation
  - Directorate of International Relations

- DEPUTY SECRETARIAT GENERAL FOR ADMINISTRATIVE AFFAIRS
  - Directorate of Human Resources and Internal Governance
  - Directorate of Budgets and Staffing
  - Directorate of Sustainability and Infrastructure
  - Directorate of Information and Communication Technologies

- Directorate of Institutional Relations
- Intervention of the Senate
- Legal Advisory
- Security Provisions

https://www.senado.es/web/composicionorganizacion/administracionparlamentaria/secretariageneralestado/organigrama/index.html

Organizational Diagram of the Spanish Secretariat General of the Congress

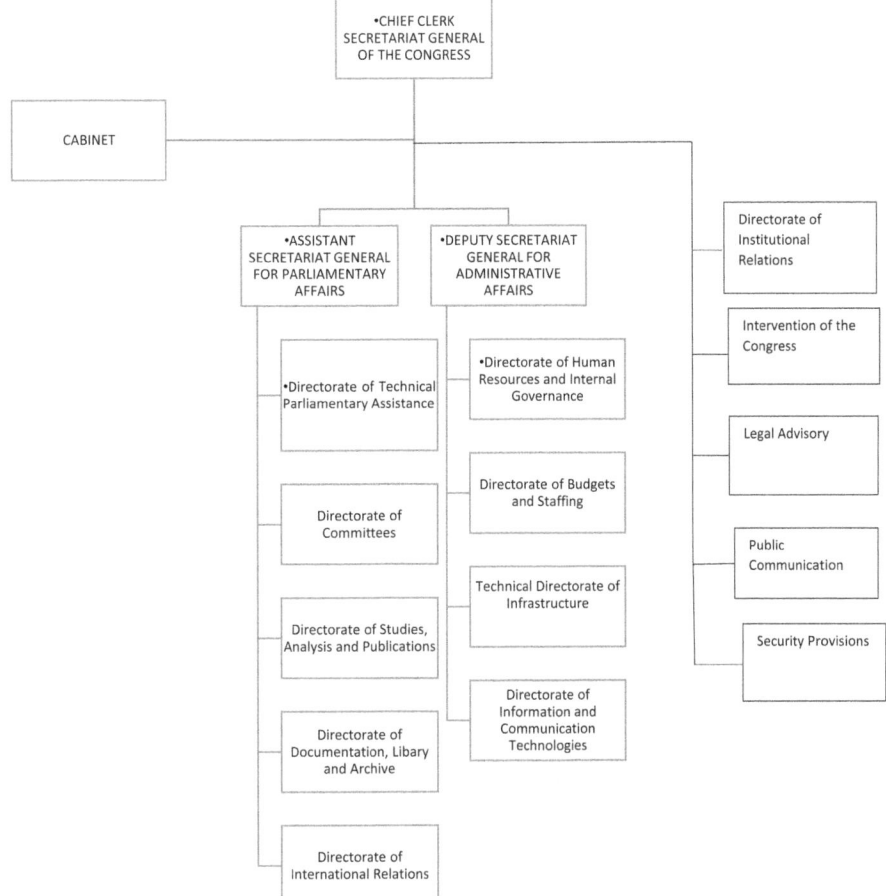

Source: https://www.congreso.es/docu/transp/Organigrama_Internet_tr.pdf

Notes

1 The authors are very grateful for inputs received from Piedad García-Escudero and Manuel Alba. Both have been Chief Clerks of the *Cortes* and Secretaries-General of the Congress for many years. Moreover, they also want to thank Jose Tudela Aranda for his comments. Jose Tudela Aranda was Chief Clerk of the regional parliament of Aragon. Research was supported by the Spanish research project: El Control y responsabilidad política en el estado constitucional con especial referencia al Parlamento en el contexto multinivel, PID2019-104414GB-C31.
2 According to the Supreme Court (SSTS of 10 November 2006 and 8 April 2008).
3 Article 118 of the Spanish Constitution and article 18 of the Judiciary Power Organic Law.
4 See official version in English of the Standing Orders of the Congress available at https://www.congreso.es/webpublica/ficherosportal/standing_orders_02.pdf
5 Interview with a former secretary general of the Congress.
6 In the case of the Senate, the Secretary General is formally known as *Letrado Mayor* (Chief Clerk).
7 Interview with a former Secretary General of the Congress.

8 They also organize seminars, conferences and training courses and bring support for researchers in the field of parliamentary studies.
9 Interview with a former Secretary General of the Congress.
10 http://www.ahorasemanal.es/los-gestores-del-congreso-y-el-senado
11 Interview with a former Secretary General of the Congress.
12 Interview with a former Secretary General of the Congress.
13 See Appeal No. 4931/2016 and Constitutional Court Judgment 4/2018, 22 January.
   Morales Arroyo, J. M. (2020). El conflicto presupuestario Gobierno/Cortes generales como 'perpetuum mobile'. FORO. Revista De Ciencias Jurídicas Y Sociales, Nueva Época, 22(2), 313–329. https://doi.org/10.5209/foro.69066; https://revistas.ucm.es/index.php/FORO/article/view/69066/4564456555803
14 https://www.congreso.es/web/guest/cem/infeco
15 Interview with a former Secretary General of the Congress.
16 Interview with a former Secretary General of the Congress.
17 Interview with a former Secretary General of the Congress.
18 Real Decreto 931/2017.

References

Astarloa, I. (2017) *El Parlamento moderno. Importancia, descrédito y cambio*. Madrid: Iustel.

García-Escudero, P. (2021) 'Parliamentary scrutiny of the quality of legislation in Spain. The role of parliamentary clerks', *The Theory and Practice of Legislation*, DOI: 10.1080/20508840.2021.1904565.

García-Escudero, P. (2020) 'Actividad y funcionamiento de las Cortes generales durante el estado de alarma por COVID-19', *Cuadernos Manuel Giménez Abad*, 19, pp. 18–27.

Griglio, E. and Lupo, N. (2021) 'Parliamentary administrations in the bicameral systems of Europe: joint or divided?', *The Journal of Legislative Studies*, DOI: 10.1080/13572334.2021.1953268.

Santamaría Pastor, J.A. (2016), Los gestores del Congreso y el Senado, in http://www.ahorasemanal.es/los-gestores-del-congreso-y-el-senado

Santos Canalejo, E. de. (2018) 'Evolución y retos de la Administración Parlamentaria en las Cortes Generales' *Revista de las Cortes Generales*, 105 pp. 17–50.

Tudela, J. (2010) 'La Administración parlamentaria en la encrucijada de la renovación', *Corts: Anuario de derecho parlamentario*, 23 pp. 157–191.

35
SWEDEN'S PARLIAMENTARY ADMINISTRATION

Ingvar Mattson and Thomas Larue

35.1 Key Aspects of the Organization of the Parliamentary Administration

The Riksdag fulfils traditional functions of parliaments in a democracy (Loewenberg and Patterson 1979) and according to the constitution it enacts laws, determines state taxes, decides how state funds shall be employed and examines the Government.

35.1.1 Basic Facts and Cornerstones of the Riksdag Administration

The role of the Riksdag Administration can be summarized in one sentence: to support the Riksdag and the processes and bodies within it as well as its members. These tasks are formally described in Chapter 14 of the Riksdag Act and mainly Articles 1–3 in the Act with Instructions for the Riksdag Administration. Thus, the primary assignment is to provide efficient support to the work of the Chamber, the Speaker, the Committees and other Riksdag bodies (and eight boards) as well as efficient support and services to members of the Riksdag and party group secretariats. In addition, the administration informs the public on the Riksdag's work and decisions and preserves the buildings owned by the Riksdag. Also, according to its instruction, the Riksdag Administration must consider the requirements of the total defence and is responsible for the Riksdag's security and emergency preparedness.

The administration is governed by the Riksdag Board which is chaired by the Speaker and consists of ten MPs. The administration is headed by a secretary-general (SG) elected by the Riksdag for a four-year tenure with unlimited re-election possibilities. She or he works closely with the Speaker in steering the administration's activities. The relationship between the Speaker and the SG, regarding the running of the administration, is similar, but not identical, to the relationship in companies between a board chairman and a CEO.

The Riksdag Administration strives to create the best possible conditions for the work of the Riksdag and the MPs in five distinct areas of responsibilities:

- providing efficient support to the work in the Chamber and the parliamentary committees
- ensuring efficient support and services to members of the Riksdag and party secretariats

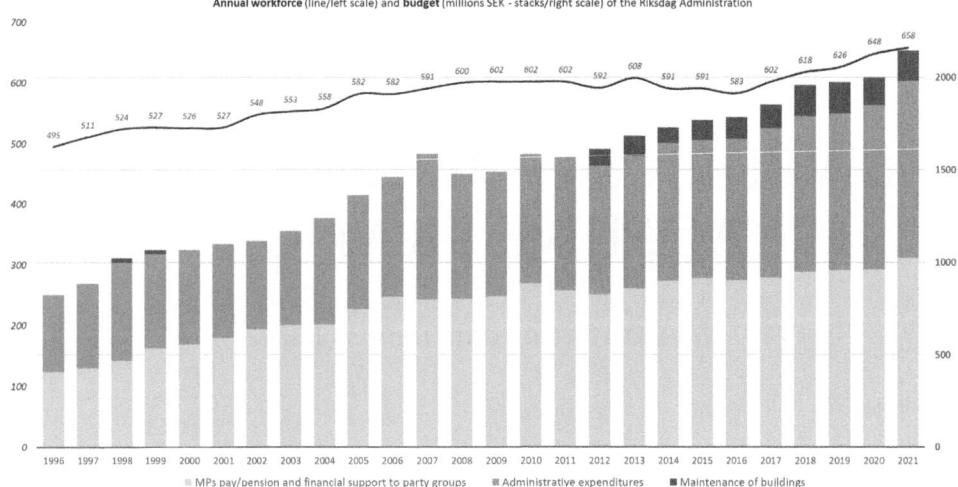

Figure 35.1 Annual workforce (line/left scale) and budget (millions SEK – stacks/right scale) of the Riksdag Administration

- promoting knowledge about the Riksdag and its work
- maintaining and preserving the buildings and collections of the Riksdag
- being an efficient and forward-looking authority and employer

The strategic plan decided by the Riksdag Board for each election period of four years pinpoints goals for each area which are then broken down to activities in an annual plan and an internal, managerial budget decided by the SG.

To accomplish its tasks, the administration employs numerous staffs, from carpenters and lawyers to wellness educator and security guards. Figure 35.1 shows both the size of the administration (in annual workforce) and the total appropriations (in Swedish crowns, SEK) for the last two decades.

As shown in Figure 35.2, the administration is sectioned into seven divisions: Chamber Division, Committee Division, Administrative Affairs Division, IT Division, Property and Service Division, Security Division and Communications Division. These divisions' staff size varies from circa 60 (AAD) to roughly 150 (PSD).

Lately, staff increases have foremost been in IT- and Security Divisions, predominantly because of security upgrades and conversion of IT-consultancy into permanent staff (cf. Sections 35.4.1 and 35.4.4 below).

35.1.2 Central Services – Chamber and Committees Secretariats – and Other Units

The Chamber and all the committees each have secretariats. The size of committee secretariats varies from 5 to 12 employees. The committees' ubiquitous role emanates from Chapter 4 Article 5 of the Instrument of Government (IG) which states that any matter raised by the Government or by an MP shall be prepared by a committee before it is settled. The committees devote comparatively much resources to the exceptional volume of private members motions (Mattson 1995). With increased opposition activity in the Riksdag

Figure 35.2   Riksdag Administration

(Bolin and Larue 2016), the committees' mandatory preparation of parliamentary business, including private members motions, has become more complex and thus demanding for their secretariats (cf. Section 35.4.5 below).

Even though committee secretariats have a crucial role for the parliamentary process, many other specialized units also provide vital support for the functioning of the Riksdag. The Secretariat of the Chamber's assures due-process executions of debates and votes. The Research Service and the Riksdag Library provide facts and analysis not only to mostly party group secretariats but also MPs and their drafting of private members motions. Different IT-units provide support in the increasingly digitalized work environment of MPs, parties and civil servants within the Riksdag Administration. Specialized units continuously make risk assessments increasingly not only on information security but also on physical security. Since 2017, a Democracy Centennial Secretariat organizes different events for the centenary of Swedish universal suffrage and the Riksdag's commemoration during 2018–2022.

35.1.3 Many Different – Sometimes Unique – Tasks

One unique aspect of the Riksdag Administration compared to other state agencies in Sweden is that it manages several old buildings in central Stockholm. These are primarily used as offices for all 349 MPs and around 425 employees at the eight party group secretariats. Some of these buildings have overnight flats, since MPs registered as resident further than 50 km from the Riksdag are entitled to overnight accommodation. Rules for these accommodations are set out in the Compensation Act (2016:1108). As shown in Figure 35.1, maintenance costs have increased over time, not least due to the start of a major renovation cycle – approximately 15–20 years – of the largest buildings. Renovations are also examined on the basis of energy consumption, indoor environment and materials.

The Riksdag Administration distributes around 310 million SEK each year to party groups and their secretariats in accordance to the Act (2016:1109) on Support for Party Groups for the MPs work in the Riksdag. An important task for all public authorities and for the Riksdag Administration is the free access to official documents to which everyone is entitled according to Freedom of the Press Act, one of Sweden's four constitutional laws. Demands for such access have legal priority.

The Riksdag Administration's mixed tasks and their emphasis on service are exemplified by the administration's duties enumerated in the Instruction Act (2011:745), for example the administration is responsible for offering MPs travelling services, parking spaces, technical and electronic equipment, children's activities, insurance and occupational health care, and for ensuring that MPs who leave the Riksdag are offered support for transition to a gainful employment.

35.2 The Role of the Administration in the Context of Parliamentary Work

Support for the 15 permanent committees, respectively, plenary debates is mainly given by the committees' secretariats, respectively, the Chamber secretariat (CS). For the latter, this principally not only includes taking verbatim minutes and documenting the parliamentary record including votes but also aiding in the Speaker's planning of the debates. Both the record and individual MPs votes are quickly published on the Riksdag's website. Plenary debates are chiefly held not only on committee reports (see below) but also on interpellations or the specific Government question time each Thursday. Besides the CS, various other functions support Chamber proceedings, such as media technicians and communication officers. The former ensure that all meetings are broadcasted live on the website and the latter compose summaries and press releases of decisions. Below the amount of debate hours in the Chamber and the numbers of interpellations since 2007 is shown in Figure 35.3.

Committee secretariats' main task is to draft committee reports which contain committees' proposals for Chamber decisions on all matters, mainly Government bills and private members' motions. Every bill and motion must be decided by the Chamber, thus so-called killing in committees is not possible in the Riksdag. The reports are structured according to

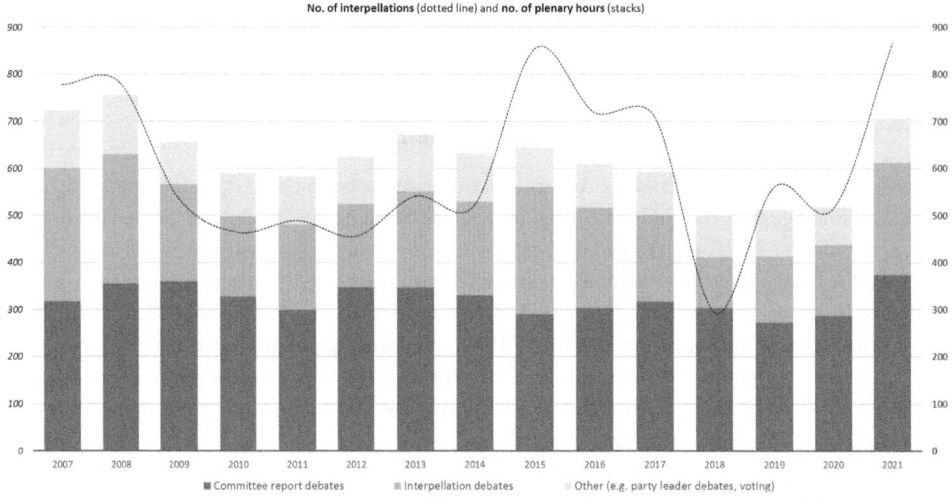

Figure 35.3 Number of interpellations (dotted line) and no. of plenary hours (stacks)

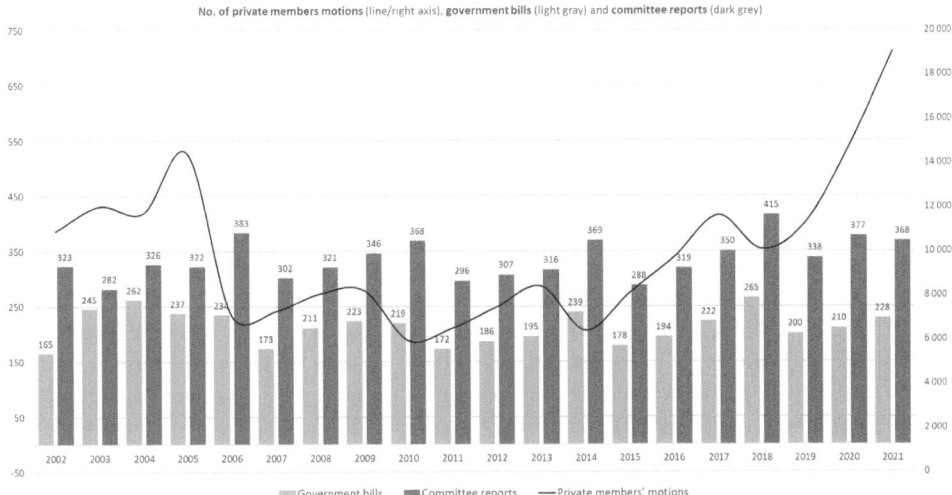

Figure 35.4 Number of private members motions (line/right axis), Government bills (light grey) and committee reports (dark grey)

the committee majority's instructions but they also contain the minorities' reservations and amendments. The numbers of private members motions, Government bills and committee reports are shown in Figure 35.4.

The secretariats also support the committees' monitoring of European Union (EU) affairs (see Section 35.3.2 below). In addition to the permanent committees, a specific committee on EU Affairs Committee (EAC) handles voting mandates prior to Council of Ministers meetings. While the EAC lacks legislative and budget powers, it requires a deft secretariat to handle vast amounts of complex – often last-minute – documents from Brussels.

An Evaluation and Research Secretariat (ERS) assists all committees – in cooperation with their secretariats – in their evaluations of previous Riksdag decisions and research overviews. Secretariats also aid committees with other tasks, for example public hearings with stakeholders and scientists or study visits domestic and overseas.

35.2.1 Budgetary Issues

In the mid-1990s, Sweden fundamentally reformed its budget process thus rearranging parliamentary decision-making, including voting processes and committees' roles. Since then amendments to Government's budget bills in committees used to be rare (Wehner 2007), even if it has risen in recent years and the opposition has even some years had the last say on major budget issues. The current budget process introduced 1996 thus mandates two decisions: the first – so-called framework decision – sets the total amount of all expenditures and incomes is prepared by the Committee of Finance (CoF). The second decision or more correctly 27 decisions details the final spending in each (of the 27) expenditure areas and is handled by the individual committees. Within the Riksdag Administration, the CoF's staff is of course heavily involved in this process. The CoF is entitled, for purposes of economic policy, to take so-called committee initiatives also on a matter falling within the remit of another committee. The CoF is also the committee which handles amendments to budget.

Though these are normally rare, in times of crises they may increase and during the covid pandemic the committee has handled a record of 18 extra amending budgets above the two regular spring- and fall amending budgets.

Another unit which has a heavy workload in the budget process is the Research Service and mainly its Economic Analysis section. They provide advanced fiscal policy calculations for the opposition parties' budget alternatives – including different taxation and income levels – introduced as party motions within the two weeks following the Government's submission of its Budget Bill. The Riksdag Administration also has a computerized system in order to administrate the different expenditure appropriations in the Government's budget bill as well as the opposition parties' alternative budgets.

Article 3 in Chapter 10 of the Budget Act (2011:203) requires the Government to present in its budget bill an account of the results achieved in activities relative to the targets expenditure areas adopted by the Riksdag for each expenditure area. This account is then reviewed by each committee, with the help of their secretariats and the ERS. Some committees have institutionalized a political dialogue between state secretaries and committees in order to improve this result account.

35.2.2 Legislative Drafting and Impact Assessments

Though the Swedish committees are formally powerful in international comparison (Mattson and Strøm 1995), boasting for example unlimited rights to freely initiate or amend legislation and budget, this rarely happens. In reality, the Riksdag's committees lack the resources required for drafting complicated legislative bills. Thus, legislation is mainly drafted by the Government and prepared by its numerous commissions of inquiry. The majority of ex-ante impact assessments of new legislation are executed in these commissions and the Government's ministries.

However, the Riksdag often gives the Government the task of preparing specific legislation, through resolutions (Bolin and Larue 2016). These resolutions have increased over time, especially demands taken by opposition parties against Government parties' will (particularly after 2005, see Oscarsson et al. 2021: 73). Resolutions are mainly found in demands made by parties and individual MPs in private members' motions and to a smaller – but increasing and accelerating tempo during the last three to four years – extent in committees initiatives. Motions are in many cases prepared with the help of expert civil servants in the Research Service. Below, in Figure 35.5, the number of inquiry assignments given to the Research Service since 2000.

A few ex-post impact assessments are made by individual committees with the assistance of the ERS and committee secretariats, though the vast majority of such assessments are executed by sectoral state agencies or general evaluating agencies such as the National Audit Office (a state agency under the Riksdag) or the Swedish Agency for Public Management. The Riksdag also often instructs the Government to make specific ex-post impact assessments.

35.2.3 Institutional Hierarchy – Political and Administrative Leaderships

The Riksdag elects the secretary general (SG) of the Riksdag at the start of the parliamentary session following an ordinary election to the Riksdag. The election is prepared by a group consisting of the Speaker and the parties' group leaders. At the request of the Riksdag Board,

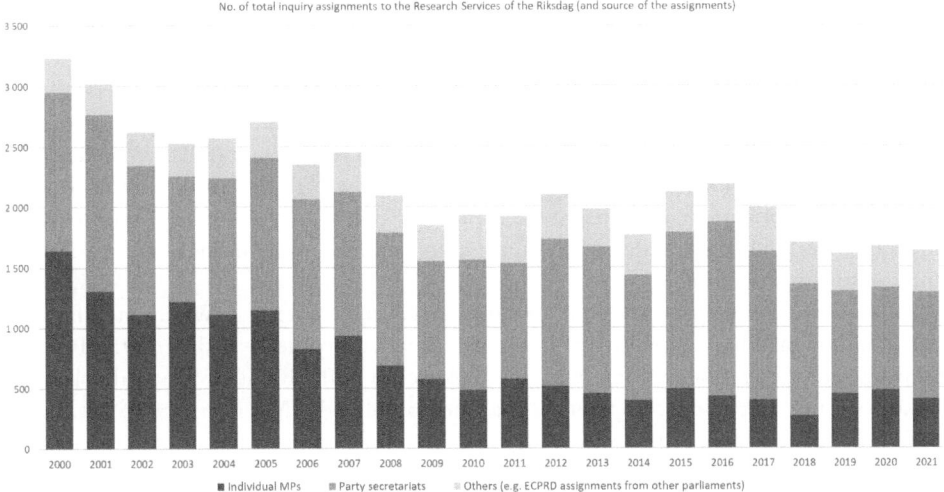

Figure 35.5 Number of total inquiry assignments to the Research Services of the Riksdag (and source of the assignments)

the Riksdag may dismiss an SG who has grossly neglected his or her commitments to the Riksdag. The next level of institutional hierarchy is constituted of the management team composed of the SG and all seven Division heads.

The direction and planning of the work of the Riksdag is led by the Speaker or in his or her place one of the Deputy Speakers. Each of the parties appoints a group leader (and a deputy group leader) to confer with the Speaker concerning the work of the Chamber. The meetings of group leaders are also important as an arena for informal and strategical aspects of both daily business in the Riksdag and more long-term choices. The formal decisions are then taken by the Riksdag Board which formally leads the Riksdag Administration. This Board thus deliberates and decides on the organization of the work of the Riksdag. The Board also delegates decisions and assignments to the SG. The Board meets behind closed doors. The Deputy Speakers, group leaders who are not members of the Board and the SG may participate in the deliberations of the Board.

The Chairmen's Conference consists of the Speaker, acting as chair, and the chairs of each committee. The conference meets approximatively four to five times per year to deliberate on matters of common concern for the activities of the Chamber and the committees. The latest topics discussed range from the monitoring of EU affairs to checklists for both evaluation and research projects within the committees.

Each committee's chair and vice-chairs constitute its presidium. These presidiums commonly have a more pronounced role in the weekly planning of the committees' activities – though all formal decisions are taken by the committee. Each presidium works closely with the head of their committee's secretariat in the planning of activities.

Since the administration's main goal is to support the Riksdag and the processes and bodies within it as well as its members, *all* civil servants in the Riksdag Administration operate with an intrinsic devotion to the hierarchical axiom of the aforementioned sources of political leadership. Of course, this devotion is exercised under the constitution, the laws and within the framework of the budgetary resources available to the Riksdag Administration. All parliamentary staff is party neutral, including the SG.

35.2.4 Degree of Discretion at Various Organizational Levels and Recruitment Procedures

According to Article 16 of the Act (2011:745) with Instructions for the Riksdag Administration, the SG of the Riksdag may delegate his decision-making power to other officials within the administration. According to the SG's Regulation (2011:15) on decisions in finance and personnel administration issues within the Riksdag Administration, other official executives may decide on procurements and other contracts within the following limits of allocated budget: heads of divisions up to 5 million SEK, heads of secretariats and units up to 1 million SEK.

In Sweden, no politicization of administrative careers exists. When making official appointments, both in courts of law and in state authorities – including the Riksdag Administration – the constitution (Chapter 12 Article 5 of the IG) states that only objective factors, such as merit and competence, shall be considered. "Merit" refers to familiarity with the requirements of the position acquired over time and is usually measured in years of service. "Competence" refers to general and special understanding of importance for the position. In the Riksdag Administration, all positions are appointed by the head responsible for recruiting with the exceptions of the following appointments: deputy SG of the Riksdag and heads of committee secretariats. These categories of appointments are decided by the Riksdag Board.

The Riksdag Administration aims at being an efficient and forward-looking authority and employer. Several opportunities for staff training and development exist, for example a competence exchange with the Government Offices (GO). The officials are recruited from the open labour market, in contrast to civil service systems in several other countries where recruitment is made from lists of applicants rated after their results in competitive examinations.

35.3 Managing Inter-Institutional and External Relations

International relations – or parliamentary diplomacy – has been a growing activity for parliaments worldwide. These interactions take place on many levels and in many forms. However, two strains are worth describing in some detail because they are the most formalized, namely cooperation among parliamentarians in international organizations and the parliamentary dimension of Sweden's EU membership.

Besides these formalized forms of international external relations, there are many informal but nevertheless well-established forms and fora for international exchanges, most notably, the interactions between Parliaments' speakers and presidents. One can mention the cooperation among the Nordic countries, the NB8 (including the Nordic and Baltic parliaments) and the EU member states. With regard to the inter-institutional relations with Governmental authorities, these relations are concentrated to the tasks which emanate from the activities and roles of the Riksdag and its organs, mainly the committees.

35.3.1 Parliamentary International Organizations and Assemblies

The oldest international organization for parliamentary cooperation is the Inter-Parliamentary Union (IPU) for the parliamentarians and more recently paralleled by the Association of Secretary Generals (ASGP). However, the most well-established international organization, from a Swedish perspective, is the Nordic Council. Permanent delegations from the Riksdag participate in totally eight international assemblies. These delegations are supported by staff from the International Department (ID). Apart from this support, the ID, which is comprised of 20 staff members, also support the Riksdag's other international interactions such as arranging international conferences.

35.3.2 European Union Affairs

The Riksdag deals with EU matters in many different ways. The MPs work with EU matters in the parliamentary committees, the EAC and in the Chamber. In bald terms, the Riksdag:

- monitors the Government's EU policies
- ensures that EU legislation, proposed by the Government, is implemented in Sweden
- monitors important documents from the EU Commission
- early warning system examination of proposal for new EU laws according to the subsidiarity principle
- cooperates with the European parliament and national parliaments in the other EU member states

In order to support these activities, many functions are engaged within the Riksdag Administration. Most notably, the secretariat for EU matters (which includes a staff representative to the European parliament based in Brussels). This is the key organizational resource for handling the ominous flow of documents from and to the EU. Expert support with EU competence is provided to every committee, including the EAC. The Riksdag's ambition is to engage all MPs and all committees in their respective EU affairs, rather than concentrating EU matters to the EAC. Thus, support from the administration is provided for in many facets.

35.3.3 Inter-Institutional Relations

The relations with the GO and other Government agencies are concentrated to the tasks which emanate from the activities and roles of the Riksdag and its organs, mainly the committees as well as the Chamber. Some informal early contacts between the GO and both the Chamber's and the committee's secretariats are essential in order to plan the orderly handling of Government bills. In times of crisis, the Government can propose a shortened private members' motions period on specific bills which requires a contact from the ministry to for example relevant secretariats. Other contacts between GO or Government agencies and committee secretariats include preparing for visits from ministers and/or agencies' Director Generals at the committees' requests.

The Riksdag Administration's degree of autonomy from the GO and agencies is total in both formal and other terms, though good but sparse contacts are maintained.

35.4 Managing Current Challenges Facing the Parliamentary Administration

35.4.1 Digitalization

Digitalization represents both ever growing challenges and fantastic opportunities for the Riksdag's Administration's efficiency and service to Sweden's elected representatives. The evolution is staggering, from 49 employees and an operating budget (salaries of employed excluded but external consulting fees included) of around 41.5 million SEK in 2007 in the IT Division, these numbers in 2021 have risen to 92 employees, respectively, around 98 million SEK. The administration has prioritized digitalization in its strategic plan. One of the most profound challenges to this strategy is caused by the EU Court of Justice's Schrems II verdict on GDPR. Briefly, the verdict makes it practically impossible to use public cloud services from US companies' servers.

Apart from this urgent challenge, the Riksdag's ambition is set on a completely digital parliamentary process, including documents such as digital originals, digital archives and digital signatures. While several steps have been taken this aim are still a few years away. Nowadays, Government bills and other parliamentary documents, such as committee reports, are signed and archived on paper and only completed with digital versions.

35.4.2 Citizen Engagement, Transparency and the New Media Landscape

The Swedish constitution does not provide the kind of instruments – which are common in other countries – to promote citizens engagement, for example no petitions or citizens' initiative to the national parliament exist. The constitutional discourse presumes that the citizens' political wills should mainly be canalized through political parties and their MPs. Referendums are possible but they are consultative with the exception of binding referendums on constitutional changes (on the local level so-called people's initiatives are possible).

The Riksdag Administration's role has a clear focus on transparency. Emphasis is put on communication and education. Plenty of methods and channels are applied for that purpose. Of course, the website is pivotal for the communication strategy. It is used to inform citizens about all parliamentary activities with focus on formal matters such as final Chamber decisions and debates, interpellations, committees' considerations. The website also contains information on individual MPs and their parliamentary activities. Informing the public about the constitutional roles of parliament is also an important part of the website.

Educational activities include a workshop for pupils in which they can roleplay as MPs for a day, guided tours for school children, citizens and tourists, and tutoring seminars for teachers and journalists. The Riksdag Administration also produces classroom material for teachers and students.

The Riksdag Administration promotes new ways to communicate through rich options offered by the Internet and social media (see below). Recently, short educational films have been prioritized in light of Internet consumption patterns. That is an important method to reach many groups, not least younger generations. The Riksdag Administration is responsible for Riksdag-accounts for the on Twitter, Instagram, YouTube and LinkedIn. These channels are mainly used for informational purposes. A lot of the material used by media is from the Riksdag's official website, where all parliamentary decisions are summarized in brief accessible texts.

35.4.3 Changing Work Patterns due to the Covid-19 Pandemic

The pandemic has had huge impact on work patterns in most parliaments around the world, and also in Sweden. That regards both the parliamentary processes and the MPs activities. Despite the pandemic being one of the most urgent challenges for parliament and its administration in recent times the Riksdag was able to fulfil all its constitutional obligations, for example voting a full state budget as well as numerous laws (both emergency laws and financial support schemes as well as regular laws).

Some general safety measures have been at hand during the whole pandemic, including recommendations regarding keeping social distance, staying at home on mild symptoms, frequent hand-washing, work from home if possible etc. Other measures have been adjusted depending on the evolution of the pandemic situation in society as a whole. Recommended use of masks in the Chamber was, however, introduced later than in many other countries.

Since the constitution do not allow for digital plenary meetings, the strategy has been to reduce the number of persons present in the Chamber. This has been accomplished by voluntary agreements among the party groups. In simple terms, there is only one MP from each party during debates, that is 8 persons, and the number of MPs in votes has been restricted to 55, chosen in order to preserve the parties' share of mandates in the full parliament (with 349 MPs).

In addition to this change in Chamber voting and debate, keeping distance has been recommended and facilitated for in the large plenary hall. In order to avoid crowds, the number of people present on the Riksdag's premises has been minimized. Seminars are cancelled as are all visiting companies from for example schools and tourists.

As for the committees, they now mainly meet digitally. This was made possible through a hurried change of the Riksdag Act in June 2020. Before that, no formal decision-making in committees was allowed through digital meetings. Nowadays, committees only meet physically on highly sensitive matters connected to for example defence and national security, and then only in extra-large meeting rooms and with masks recommended.

35.4.4 Ensuring Parliamentary Security

Security is one of the most profound areas of change for the Riksdag Administration. This also shows in numbers, 39 employees worked at the Security Department in 2007 and the budget for external security contractors was around 6.2 million SEK. In 2021, 80 employees work at the same department and the budget for external contractors is close to 33 million SEK. From 2022, the department has been upgraded to a Division. Two decades ago, the doors to the parliamentary buildings were open and visitors had almost free access into parliament, not only the plenary galleries but also members offices. This has changed dramatically mainly due to increased security threats marked by different tragic events, including the assassination of the Minister of Foreign Affairs Anna Lindh in 2003 and the "Stockholm terrorist attack" in 2017. Both occurred in the city centre of Stockholm, but away from the parliamentary premises. Also, the assassination of Prime Minister Olof Palme in 1986 had implication on security issues for parliament, but less so than one could presume because it was, at the time, regarded as an exception. Both the 9/11 attacks in 2001 and the 22 July attacks in Norway 2011 also contributed to heightened security demands. On top of these events, analysis of the security situation, both domestic and international, also motivated increased efforts, including more resources. Only in the last five years, the level of annual funds allocated to security purposes in the Riksdag Administration budget has risen with 60 million SEK. The security improvements' modus operandi has not however been driven by the incidents above, but rather by a systematic and strategic method of change, based on a model that focuses on three cornerstone elements:

1. what should be protected (e.g. MPs personal security, parliamentary processes, information, IT-systems and physical integrity of the Riksdag's premises)
2. what are the threats (e.g. personal attacks on MPs, political demonstrations, terrorist attacks and fire)
3. which measures should be taken (e.g. strengthened entrance controls, cf. airports)

This systematic approach has been applied in order to minimize risks of missing necessary preventing measures against future incidents because of narrow-mindedness triggered and driven by previous incidents.

The complexity of parliamentary security means that the Riksdag Administration cannot get the job done alone. The Swedish Security Service is responsible for providing personal security for the key leadership of the state, including ministers but more crucially the Speaker and every MP. The Swedish Police Authority is responsible for the general security. Thus, cooperation between these authorities is essential, in terms of both actual operations and training. The Riksdag Administration performs various activities, including access protection, information security, security clearance, fire protection, emergency preparedness etc.

At first glance, one could believe that there is a 1:1 trade-off between security and openness. However, proportional security measures can also, at best, facilitate openness. Parliament does not want to build fences and close out the public, the easiest measure. Instead, security measures are tailor-made to allow for some open meetings, hearings and seminars on the premises as well as groups of visitors, including school children.

The storming of United States Capitol in January 2021 has shown that physical security of the premises is of utmost importance to any parliament. It also shows that security threats can be complex and unexpected.

35.4.5 Final Words – Future Challenges

At the horizon, we are starting to make out the contours of the future return to a "new normal" after the global pandemic shockwave. What this exactly will imply for the ways in which MPs and parties wish to work in parliament is yet unknown. As are the consequences for the administration. Probably the metamorphosis of digitalization is far from over as this global calamity breaks down old habits and creates new ones.

Other future challenges are however already known to us since some time, for example the Swedish political party landscape has seen a steadily increasing fragmentation (see Sartori 1976, Lindvall et al. 2017). This creates both amplified dynamism and unexpectedness in parliamentary processes. In the public debate, calls for a more active role for the Riksdag are often heard (Lindvall et al. 2017, Bäck & Hellström 2018), even though opposite views exist (Petersson 2020). Processes concerning both Government formation (Teorell et al. 2020) and budget are getting more complex. The budget rules from mid-1990s – a cornerstone of a stable budget process – and especially some of these rules' more informal aspects and prerequisites are starting to crack at the seams. These budget rules are considered semi-constitutional and many attempts to patch them in order to guarantee stable budget processes have failed.

This puts the Riksdag at the very heart of Swedish politics. But it also creates a pressure on the Riksdag administration, especially committee secretariats, to deal with complicated and sudden political processes (such as military aid to Ukraine). A tangible illustration of this is the previously almost unseen increase in committee initiatives taken by opposition parties against Government parties' will (see Hajdarevic & Larue 2021).

References

Bäck, Hanna and Hellström, Johan, (2018). "Sverige behöver underlätta för minoritetsstyren", *Svenska Dagbladet*, 2018-12-01, available on <https://www.svd.se/sverige-behover-underlatta-for-minoritetsstyren>, quoted 2021-04-20.
Bolin, Niklas and Larue, Thomas, (2016). "The Reparliamentarization of Sweden? The Use and Relevance of Parliamentary Resolutions to the Government", *Statsvetenskaplig tidskrift* 118(3), pp. 307–337.

Hajdarevic, Asmir and Larue, Thomas, (2021). "Swedish Parliamentary Committees' Right to Initiative – The Opposition's New Hammer?", *Statsvetenskaplig tidskrift* 123(3), pp. 471–510.

Lindvall, Johannes, Bäck, Hanna, Dahlström, Carl, Naurin, Elin and Teorell, Jan, (2017). *SNS Demokratirapport 2017 – Samverkan och strid i den parlamentariska demokratin*. Stockholm: SNS Förlag.

Loewenberg, Gerhard and Patterson, Samuel C., (1979). *Comparing Legislatures*. Lanham: University Press of America.

Mattson, Ingvar, (1995). "Private Members' Initiatives and Amendments" in H. Döring (ed.), *Parliaments and Majority Rule in Western Europe*. Frankfurt: Campus Verlag and New York: St. Martin's Press, pp. 448–87.

Mattson, Ingvar and Strøm, Kaare, (1995). "Parliamentary Committees" in H. Döring (ed.), *Parliaments and Majority Rule in Western Europe*. Frankfurt: Campus Verlag and New York: St. Martin's Press, pp. 249–307.

Oscarsson, Henrik, Bergman, Torbjörn, Bergström, Annika and Hellström, Johan, (2021). *SNS Demokratirapport 2021: Polarisering i Sverige*. Stockholm: SNS förlag.

Petersson, Olof, (2020). "Kan vi få en riksrättsprocess som den i USA här i Sverige", *Dagens Nyheter*, 2020-01-28, available on <https://www.dn.se/debatt/kan-vi-fa-en-riksrattsprocess-som-den-i-usa-har-i-sverige/>, quoted 2021-03-14.

Sartori, Giovanni, (1976). *Parties and Party Systems: A Framework for Analysis*. Cambridge: Cambridge University Press.

Teorell, Jan, Bäck, Hanna, Hellström, Johan and Lindvall, Johannes, (2020). *134 dagar – Om regeringsbildningen efter valet 2018*. Göteborg: Makadam förlag.

Wehner, Joachim, (2007). "Budget Reform and Legislative Control in Sweden", *Journal of European Public Policy* 14(2), pp. 313–332.

PART II.II

In the Wider Europe

36
ALBANIA'S PARLIAMENTARY ADMINISTRATION

Afrim Krasniqi

36.1 Introduction

Albania is a young democracy. Its current parliamentary system has only 30 years of age. Its relatively diminutive parliamentary track record between the two world wars (1920–1924) left little or no trace in the memory of the current parliamentary administration. Since 1990, Albania is a parliamentary republic, with a unicameral parliament composed of 140 MPs. The only exceptions of note took place in the parliamentary sessions of 1991–1992 that took place with 250 MPs and those of 1997–2001 that saw a total composition of the parliament of 155 MPs. Article 64 of the Constitution of Albania stipulates that the Assembly consists of 140 MPs, elected according to a system of proportional representation with regional competition and a national threshold. The Assembly is recognized as Albania's main representative political institution, but the Constitution does not provide any definition of the role and function of the Assembly and of its position in relation to other constitutional bodies, describing it only as the highest body that exercises legislative power (Krasniqi, 2020). The Constitution stipulates the obligation of the Assembly to hold its proceedings in two annual sessions, with the first session starting in the third week of January and the second on the first Monday of September. The constitutional and political mandate of the Assembly defines the role and size of the parliament.

Kuvendi (The Assembly) has a separate structure between the political part and the administrative part, the last one headed by the Secretary General (Sekretari i Përgjithshëm).

36.2 Key Aspects of the Organization of the Parliamentary Administration

The "human capital" of the Assembly of Albania consists of distinct three categories: MPs, civil administrative staff and support staff. The relations of each category with the Assembly are regulated by different pieces of legislation. The last two categories – civil servants and support staff – are considered parliamentary administration. The official administrative structure can be found attached. Civil servants are selected through competition and enjoy a guaranteed career statute; the rest of the administration consists of the political support staff of the Assembly leaders and parliamentary groups, as well as of those staffers providing technical support services in the Assembly. The annual state budget does not distinguish between these three categories, considering them as public employees in the general staffing table.

36.2.1 Size of the Parliamentary Administration 2002–2021

The available publications of the annual state budget and the reports on the Albanian parliament provide exhaustive data on the human resources of the Assembly. Usually, this information combines the number of the MPs, their political staff, the support staff and the civil servants of the parliament. Compared to the institution of the President and to the Office of the Prime Minister, over the last two decades, the Assembly of Albania has had on average six to seven times more administrative staff than the President of the Republic, but two to three times less than the administrative staff of the Office of the Prime Minister. Table 36.1 displays the official data on the human resources of the Assembly over the last two decades (2001–2021). The first column gives the total number of human resources, the second the number of the political, administrative and support staff (all staffers without the MPs).

The data in the below table show that over the last two decades the share of the administrative and support staff of the Assembly accounted on average for about 66% of the overall human resources in the parliament. The most obvious deviations are related to changes in the overall number of MPs, the number of parliamentary groups and their political support staff, the competitions for new recruitments in the administration, political rotations etc. In almost no single year has the Assembly managed to fill its staff structure at 100%, due to lengthy selection processes, political changes in the Assembly and ongoing changes in the administration. The number of vacancies between 2014 and 2020 was 56 (2014), 40 (2015), 35 (2016), 60 (2017), 61 (2018), 19 (2019) and 25 (2020). As of the beginning of 2021, the total human resource structure of the Assembly consists of 409 persons, of which 269 are administrative staff and, of them, only 177 are staffers having the status of civil servant according the law 152/2013 "On civil servants". The rest consists of MPs (140), and their political staffers (92). In total, civil servants make up only 43% of the total number of administrative staffers engaged in the Assembly.

36.2.2 Administrative Structure and Services of the Assembly

The overall staffing table of the Assembly has been constantly changing. Overall, the staffing table of the Assembly changed 25 times over the last 27 years. Only in the five-year period 2007–2012, the Bureau of the Assembly took 21 decisions to change the staffing table of the Assembly (AP, 2014). These changes made it difficult to have a staffing structure in place that would compare to previous legislatures. They came about not only because of the evolving responsibilities of the Assembly, the growing focus on increasing transparency, but also because of the short-term needs for staff changes and political relations between parliamentary groups and parties.

The structure of the parliamentary administration has not changed over the recent years. The parliamentary administration provides five main services: legislative, information and documentation services, foreign relations, monitoring of independent institutions and administrative services. The constituent sections of each of the services are reflected in more detail in the staff of the Assembly, accompanied by the number of staff for each unit. As shown in Table 36.2, the administrative services have the highest percentage of administrative staff, with 34% of the total, followed by information and documentation services (28%) and legislative services (27%).

Table 36.1 The number of employees of the Assembly 2002–2021

	2002	2003	2004	2005	2006	2007	2008	2009	2010	2011	2012	2013	2014	2015	2016	2017	2018	2019	2020	2021
Total human resources	320	404	407	414	440	440	440	477	349	349	349	359	361	396	405	405	405	405	405	409
Administrative staff	190	274	277	284	284	310	310	347	219	219	219	229	231	231	275	275	275	275	275	269
Administrative staff in (%)	59	68	68	69	65	70	70	73	63	63	63	64	64	58	68	68	68	68	68	66

Source: Author on the basis of the information of Ministry of Finance

Table 36.2 Parliamentary services (in %)

Legislative service	27%
Information and documentation	28%
Foreign relations	7%
Monitoring service	4%
Administrative service	34%

Source: Author on the basis of the information of annual reports of the Assembly

Table 36.3 displays the administrative structure of the Assembly in the years 2018–2021. The structure accounts only for civil servants and staffers of support services, categorized into five main departments. The monitoring service is a new structure set up in the framework of the efforts geared towards improving transparency and strengthening the constitutional role of the Assembly. Of the main services, the most complete subcategories are the services of parliamentary publications (26), maintenance services (23) and the service of parliamentary committees (22).

According to the current parliamentary practice, the Assembly has eight standing parliamentary committees. Each committee has one secretary and one to two advisors. The rest of the support staff in the commissions consists of technical specialists and managers. In each session of the legislatures held from 2002 onwards, the Assembly established special parliamentary committees, committees of inquiry or subcommittees in specific areas, for which assistance, technical staff and additional budgets were required. All these needs were covered by the administrative staff of the standing committees, with the difference that in some cases the Assembly engaged additional external experts from the largest political groups. The need for additional expertise and technical support staff is felt by other structures of the Assembly, such as the Bureau of the Assembly, the Conference of Presidents, the Permanent Secretariats, the Parliamentary Councils etc. Even in these cases, the additional needs are covered by the internal administrative staff of the Assembly, not by additional staff beyond the annually approved structure of the administration.

In recent years, the Assembly of Albania has focused on strengthening its specialized units, such as the parliamentary publications unit, the EU integration unit, the institutions monitoring unit, the legal services unit, the security and IT unit etc. In 2001, the Assembly started publishing the debates for one of the parliamentary legislatures, but only in 2009 the regular publication of the parliamentary debates from 1991 onwards started and currently all the parliamentary debates over the years have been published. In addition, in 2010, the Assembly launched the online publication of the minutes of committee meetings and of the plenary sessions. In 2017, the Assembly started with the online publication of data on the budget, financial entitlements of MPs as well as a large number of documents related to the programme of transparency (ISP, 2017, 2019).

The Parliament is equipped with a library with historical documentation; however, in parliamentary practice, the library is used more by administrative staff and researchers than by MPs. The Assembly has a unit dedicated to parliamentary research. The Parliamentary Rules of Procedure recognize the obligation of each standing parliamentary committee to conduct studies and research on legislative and law enforcement activity, development risks and strategies etc. The Assembly itself has drafted for the first time a strategy for the development of the institution, specifically that for the years 2020–2023. The Assembly has not yet established a tradition in drafting analytical and research documents related to parliamentary

Table 36.3 The administrative structure of the assembly in the years 2018–2021

Secretary General (1)				
Office of the Secretary General (3)				Archives (4)
Projects Unit (2)				
MONITORING OF THE INSTITUTIONS SERVICE (7)	LEGISLATIVE SERVICE (54)	SERVICE OF INFORMATION AND DOCUMENTATION (56)	ADMINISTRATIVE SERVICE (67)	FOREIGN RELATIONS SERVICE (14)
	Legal Service (14)	Service of Parliamentary Research and Library (9)	Service of Budget and Finances (9)	Protocol Directorate (4)
	Service of Parliamentary Committees (22)	Service of Information Technology (11)	Service of Human Resources and Support for MPs (6)	Directorate for Multilateral and Bilateral Relations (6)
	Service of Plenary Sessions (8)	Service of Public Relations (9)	Procurement (6)	
	Service of Approximation of Legislation (6)	Service of Parliamentary Publications (26)	Transport (18)	Translation Unit (3)
	Secretariat of the National Council of EU Integration (4)		Maintenance (23)	
			Protocol Unit (3)	
			Reception (3)	

Source: The official page of the Assembly http://parlament.al/Administrata/Struktura

activity, legislation and issues of the constitutional position of the Assembly. Until 2021, the Assembly has no study on the development of staff and human resources, on parliamentary budgeting or on the parliamentary balance for the last 30 years. In 2020, Albania marked the 100th anniversary of the first parliament, and the scientific papers of the conference, with research authors and academics, constitute some of the few reference sources on Albanian parliamentarism (ISP, 2020).

36.2.3 Recruitment, Training and External Consultancies

The size of the political support staff in the parliament varies, depending on the outcome of the parliamentary elections, changes in the parliamentary groups and in the presidency of the Assembly. On the other hand, the public administration domain is based on an uninterrupted career system and should not be influenced by political changes in the Assembly. The recruitment of parliamentary staff is based on the legislation on the civil servants, the Labour Code and the bylaws issued by the Bureau of the Assembly. Specifically, the Rules of Procedure of the Assembly and the Labour Code apply to the political support staff, while the legislation on the civil servant applies to the part of the public administration. The Organic Law on Civil Servants was first adopted in 1999 and then amended in 2013. It is a right and responsibility of all independent institutions (including the Assembly) to administer their civil service staffers, but in any case acceptance in the civil service is done through open competition and selection between a minimum of three candidates for the same vacant position (Sigma, 2003).

The current recruitment practices consist of public competitions, written and oral exams, based on strict criteria defined in legislation and the respective bylaws. In practice, parliament has always been accused of formal recruitment practices, of predetermining the winners, especially in the case of senior executives (general directors, service directors, heads of departments etc.). The announcements for vacancies and the progress of the competition are published on the official website of the Assembly (ISP, 2020).

A recurring concern for the sustainability and efficiency of the parliamentary administration in Albania is the impact of political developments on the structure and its practices of recruitment. The last political rotation in Albania took place in June 2013. In the new Assembly convened in September, the administrative staff consisted of 225 employees, of which 17 political staff, 143 having the status of civil servant and 65 support staff. The new political leaders announced a restructuring reform, which fired 35 civil servants out of a total of 69 staffers dismissed, including 90% of directors and senior management officials, as well as the Secretary General (Annual Report, 2013). These mass dismissals sparked a political debate in the plenary session of the Assembly on December 2013. Most of the dismissed employees were granted by the court the right to return or should this be unfeasible, for a financial compensation for the lost salaries. Generally, Albanian state institutions, including the Assembly, prefer to resort to the financial compensation of the unjustly fired staffers through funding from the state budget, rather than to proceed with the reinstatement of the dismissed officials for political reasons.

On the other hand, the Assembly provides a symbolic budget for the training of parliamentary staff, yet most of the training and qualification is provided by the parliament through bilateral or multilateral support projects funded by other states and international organizations. The data from the Assembly show that all administrative staff has completed several levels of periodic or topical training, being numerically the most trained administration compared to the administrations of other central institutions.

36.2.4 Rules and Arrangements for Interaction with Stakeholders

Over the last couple of years, the access of the Albanian public, media and civil society to parliamentary information has increased thanks to advanced legislation adopted in 2014 to this end. The Assembly itself publishes statistics and reference data on its activity, including data on requests for information and parliamentary initiatives, on the work of parliamentary committees etc. With the adoption of the Code of Conduct (2018), the Assembly has established a more transparent system of data, activity and decision-making. Part of the changes was the creation for the first time of the Register of Lobbyists, which includes civil society organizations attached to each parliamentary committee, the Register of Conflict of Interest where cases of incompatibility between parliamentary decision-making and private engagements are declared, as well as the Register of declarations for gifts and participation in third party activities. From 2015 onwards, the Assembly drafts and publishes annually a report on public participation in the parliamentary decision-making process. From 2013 onwards, the Assembly regularly publishes an annual report on the detailed balance of parliamentary activity, budget, decision-making etc.

The Assembly regularly organizes public consultations in committees or special sessions. From 2020 on, the consultation process takes place directly online. In recent years, most of the minutes of the meetings, the reports of the committees, the votes of the deputies, the database of legal acts and other documents important for public information on the parliament have been published. Investment towards transparency and openness is part of the legal obligations and comes as a direct contribution of the engagement of the parliamentary administrative staff. The increase in workload in the context of such developments has not been accompanied by an increase in administrative staff, but by investment in new communication technologies.

36.3 The Role of the Administration in the Context of Parliamentary Work

Based on the Rules of Procedure of the Assembly and on the internal regulatory documents of the parliament, the administrative staff, especially the archival research staffs, the legal service staff and the experts, are tasked to provide complete and detailed briefing materials for the chairs of the parliamentary committees and the highest parliamentary structures. None of their reports is published online or given to the media, as this is considered internal technical assistance. This practice has been criticized, as the requests for information to be provided by the support staff might be made according to political interest of the chairs of committees and other structures, preventing the provision of quality information for the public, interest groups, media and MPs who are excluded by of privileged political access (ISP reports 2017–2020).

The process of drafting legislation entails preliminary evaluations not only provided by the ministries but also the assistance and evaluations made by numerous institutional actors, the provision of domestic and international expertise, opinions of stakeholders etc. Albania has been consistently praised for the quality of the laws passed but has been criticized for the low level of their implementation (BTI, 2021). In this regard, the parliament does not yet have a mechanism for verifying and monitoring the level of the implementation of laws, including the adoption of bylaws by the responsible institutions. The practice of interpellations, hearings etc. is more political than technically effective in enforcing laws. With the amendments to the Rules of Procedure of the Assembly (2019), Parliamentary committees should draft and publish annual information and self-assessment reports, but by March 2021, no committee has yet fulfilled this responsibility (ISP, 2021). The drafting of such reports requires in-depth expertise and quality support staff, two indicators that parliamentary committees as a whole do not possess the necessary competence, neither in their current composition, nor in the additional technical resources made available through the preferential decisions of committee chairpersons who select assistants for the committees.

Since several years, the parliamentary staffs record all sessions and meetings of the committees or other decision-making structures in the Assembly. It also publishes the minutes of their meetings. The lack of complete minutes or delays in their publication face criticism from civilian monitoring groups and the media but are justified by the Assembly with its heavy workload and lack of sufficient human resources. These arguments stand, as often the complete or timely non-publication is also a matter of political decision-making of the leaders of the Assembly or committees.

In contrast to this problematic aspect, over the last decade, the Assembly has made steps ahead with regard to modern technology and inclusion of new media in its public outreach. The Parliament's efforts towards the "open parliament" model have led to improved mechanisms aiming at the public involvement in parliamentary decision-making, as well as to increased public transparency. Legislation on the right to information and public consultation (2014) had a major impact on improving the Rules of Procedure of the Assembly and the implementation of the transparency programme. The Assembly's greatest success came during the COVID-19 pandemic, as it was among the first parliaments in Southeast Europe and beyond to hold online meetings of its committees and governing bodies (Krasniqi, 2021). The database of online meetings can be found on the official website of the parliament, on YouTube networks and on the Assembly's accounts on various social media. Plenary sessions continued to be attended in person. On the other hand, during the pandemic, the parliament made changes to the Constitution and some of the essential laws, such as the Criminal Code, the Electoral Code, media legislation etc., which received hefty criticism from civil society, the media and some international institutions (HC, 2020). Transparency in form did not go hand in hand with more transparency in content and this remains one of the main features of Albanian parliamentary life during the pandemic.

Since 2015, Albania's only public broadcaster, TVSH, runs a channel dedicated to parliament, covering plenary sessions and parliamentary activity. Investments towards transparency in the new media have been accompanied by investments in technology, in the information systems in the Assembly, in the project for establishing an information centre on the Assembly and in the establishment of an institution for professional studies on the Assembly. In parallel, the Assembly continues to publish since 2014 a periodical scientific journal "Kuvendi" (The parliament), with contributions from experts in parliamentary and political studies, as well as in special cases from experts in legislative technique.

The Albanian Parliament has a history of about two decades of running debates on its budget, and a solid mechanism related to its review and approval. The first initiative to establish an independent parliamentary budget dates back to 2003. Accordingly, the budget of the Assembly is part of the state budget and is approved every year by a special law. It accounts for 0.3% of the state budget (IPA, 2010). The Assembly has no additional revenues other than various international projects and donations. According to the Regulation, the Secretary General submits the draft budget proposal, which is then reviewed by the Permanent Secretariat for the Budget, which consists of five MPs from the main political parties. The Secretariat for the Budget of the Assembly, in cooperation with the Secretary

Table 36.4 Budget assembly (2010–2020)

The budget (in %)	2020	2019	2018	2017	2016	2015	2014	2013	2012	2011	2010
Legislative Programme (%)	42	61	64	69	63	61	61	56	56	60	64
Administrative Programme (%)	58	39	36	31	37	49	39	44	44	40	36

General, supervises all the procedures for drafting the annual and medium-term draft budget of the Assembly from its initial stage until its proposal to the Bureau of the Assembly.

The budget of the Assembly consists of two main items: the legislative programme and the administrative programme. Data for the years 2010–2020 divided along these two items are presented in the attached table (Table 36.4). In total, expenditures on salaries and health insurance account for about 59%–60% of the Assembly budget. The remaining about 40%–41% of the budget goes to the legal services of MPs and to parliamentary activity. The financial control of the budget and the Assembly is made externally (Supreme State Audit) whilst a unit of specialists in the parliamentary staff is tasked with the internal budgetary control. Reports with findings and annual budget reports are published on the official website of the parliament from 2014 onwards. A careful reading of the annual reports reveals that almost every year the Assembly has not been able to absorb the entire budget and, as a result, the leftover is paid back to the state budget to be reallocated to the Assembly for the following year.

36.3.1 Nature of Institutional Hierarchy

The functioning of the Assembly of Albania and of its parliamentary administration is regulated through several bylaws adopted by the Assembly itself. Specifically, the Assembly has drafted and approved its own Rules of Procedure, the Rules of Procedure for the organization and functioning of the parliamentary services, the decisions of the Parliamentary Bureau on "On the approval of the structure of the administration of the Assembly" and one technical document approved by the Secretary General "The Manual for the description of the roles in the administration of the Assembly". The first group of documents is public and available on the official website of the Assembly, while the second has never been made public.

The parliamentary administration is headed by the Secretary General, chosen by the Speaker of the Assembly out of three candidates through a competition procedure, held according to the law "On Civil Servants". In the parliamentary practice of the last 20 years, stretching over five parliamentary elections, the Assembly has changed five Secretaries General. In each and every case, the Speaker of the Assembly has proceeded with the temporary appointment of a handpicked individual for the position of the Secretary General and then, the latter, has organized the legal procedure of the formal competition, resulting in the Secretary being confirmed in office with the status of civil servant. According to the Regulation, the Secretary "ensures and takes care of the progress of affairs in the Assembly and is accountable to the Speaker of the Assembly and to the Bureau of the Assembly".

The Assembly has several other leadership structures such as the Parliamentary Bureau, the Conference of Presidents, the Secretariats of the Assembly, the Parliamentary Groups, the Parliamentary Councils, the Committees and the Subcommittees, but de facto the only officials influencing the parliamentary activity and controlling the administration are the Speaker and

Secretary General appointed by him. The Speaker directs all parliamentary decision-making and agenda, the Secretary General supports him through his control over the parliamentary services. The form of organization of the parliamentary administration is such that it is impossible for parliamentary officials to freely express opinions or make proposals that may not be in line with the opinion of the highest political and administrative leader of the Assembly.

Over the last four legislatures, the Speakers of the Assembly consisted habitually of one of the two main political figures of the party in government, so their activity fell largely in line with the political and parliamentary agenda of their party. The Cabinet of the Speaker has seven advisors. On the other hand, the main parliamentary service, the legal directorate, covering the whole of the legislative activity of the parliament, has just 11 advisors. In the parliamentary hierarchy, the role of the chairs of the parliamentary committees has increased, mainly regarding the internal organization of the committees, but their influence on the overall parliamentary activity is still minimal. Each small parliamentary group has two support staff, a secretarial assistant and an advisor. The two main parliamentary groups have a secretariat and four advisors each. The analysis of the parliamentary practice for the period 2010–2021 has shown that the advisors of the parliamentary groups are not experts, but rather political and electoral figures of their respective political parties.

Until 2013, MPs did not possess individual offices and had no support or office equipment in the parliament. Only the parliamentary groups had offices in use and the right to access dedicated office space for their weekly meetings. In 2014, all MPs received individual offices; however, none of the MPs can count on administrative support staff. In 2014, an OSCE project prompted the establishment of local parliamentary offices in the regional centres of 12 national constituencies, providing them with office equipment and a secretary.

36.3.2 Managing Inter-Institutional and External Relations

The current political relations between national parliaments and the international projects in place in the field of parliamentary exchange greatly influence the level of cooperation between the parliamentary administration of the Assembly of Albania and their colleagues in the parliaments of other countries. The Parliament of Albania does not have a budget dedicated to international exchange of parliamentary staff. The same applies to bilateral or multilateral parliamentary activities, parliamentary diplomacy and interparliamentary cooperation in the framework of the European Union integration process.

The parliamentary activity in this regard is not conditioned by the agenda of the government. It takes place in parallel and in conjunction to it (Shllaku, 2005). When it comes to the relations with the European Parliament, the parliament is more dominant than the government in shaping communications, while in regional cooperation the government is dominant over the parliament. The government assists the parliament in its international activity, but the system of coordination of agendas during international partnership talks and developments is still fragile. Concepts such as early prevention, risk analysis and early warning system are rarely articulated in the parliament. Overall, the international parliamentary activity is passive and focused mostly on lobbying on Albanian national interests (Pano, 2016). It is greatly shaped by the priorities set by the President of the Assembly during his/her term of office.

36.3.3 The New Challenges Facing the Parliamentary Administration

The effectiveness of the parliamentary administration of the Assembly of Albania is the biggest challenge and this has been specifically assessed in some of the European Union's annual progress reports on Albania. In 2008–2019, the EU suggested strengthening the capacity of the parliamentary administration to assist the legislative process, to control this process and to monitor the activity and obligations of the Assembly in the EU integration process. The National Plan for the implementation of the EU-Albania Association Agreement 2008–2013 considered a priority the increase of human capacities and parliamentary infrastructure, the increase of transparency, the publication of acts and documentation, the continuous training of staff and the strengthening of legislative capacities (IPA, 2010). According to the 2015–2016 report, the organizational structure and administrative capacity of the parliament need to be further improved, which requires the allocation of sufficient funds to recruit and train staff, especially in relation to research and analysis (EU, 2015).

Further challenges are related to the increase of independence from the political influences, as well as to the improvement of the conditions and the relationship between the deputies and the parliamentary administration. In a survey conducted with Albanian MPs at the end of 2018, over 91% of MPs asked to have administrative support staff available, 85% asked to have a personal budget for running parliamentary activities, only half of them positively assessed the local offices provided by the OSCE programme, 79% requested annual training from the parliament, 64% confirmed that they were regularly assisted by the Assembly staff, 8% stated that their request for assistance were rejected by the Assembly staff, only 51% assessed that the Assembly has staff able to provide expertise, over 70% stated that Committees should have more technical staff and annual budget, 81% noted that Committees should have more control powers, 85% suggested live broadcasts of committee meetings, 73% were in favour increasing the access of citizens in terms of participating in the sessions of the commissions, 55% demanded more competencies for the chairmen of the commissions and 47% considered that the payment for the work in the commissions is discriminatory (ISP, 2018).

36.4 Conclusions

This is the first research paper covering the parliamentary staff, its size, role, structure and relations with the overall parliamentary activity in Albania. The lack of other studies bears witness to the fragile situation of parliamentary research in Albania. In over 30 years of parliamentary experience, and since the first law on civil servants, the administrative staff has collected only 21 years of experience. Its functioning is based on the legislation on public servants. The constant changes of staff, the vertical nature of decision-making, political influences, as well as considerable deficits in parliamentary research and professional expertise are some of the causes behind the overall low level of effectiveness of the parliamentary administration in Albania.

The progress of the last years towards an open parliament, the introduction of new technologies, the completion of a modern legal framework, the increase of financial and organizational autonomy, as well as the increase of public transparency are encouraging developments and a good starting point for the future. The main challenges for the quality of the parliament in Albania are related to the quality of parliamentary representation, the need for increased legislative and democratic controls of the parliament.

The parliamentary administration has to meet the challenge of strengthening its independence and professional capacities, achieving structural stability and managing its transformation from an assistive administrative body to a professional service endowed with research, advisory and professional skills able to contribute to the integrity and image of the parliament in Albania.

Administrative Structure of the Albanian Assembly in the Years 2018–2022

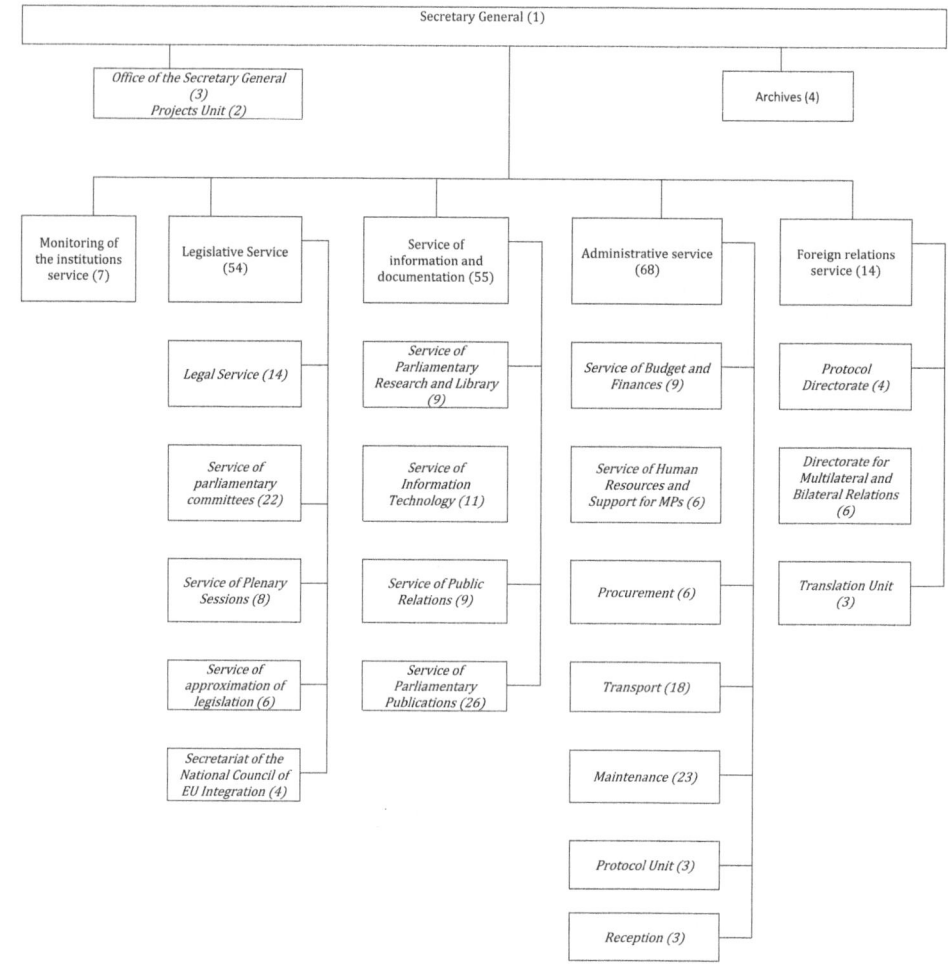

References

Act 166/2004 (amending). Rules of procedure of the Assembly of the Republic of Albania, https://www.legislationline.org/download/id/8100/file/Albania_Rules_of_procedure_assembly_as_of_2011_en.pdf

Assembly annual reports 2005–2020, available at http://staging.parlament.al/Files/Informacione/Buletini%20statistikor%202021-2025..pdf

Bufi, Y. (2010). The Temple of Democracy, Ombra GVG, Tirana. https://shtetiweb.org/leksione-shtetiweb/leksione-mbi-procedurat-parlamentare/

BTI (2021) Albania Country Report 2020 tps://www.bti-project.org/en/reports/country-report-ALB-2020.html

EU (2020) Progress Reports on Albania, available at https://ec.europa.eu/commission/presscorner/detail/en/COUNTRY_20_1794

European Commission. (2014). Enlargement Strategy and Main Challenges 2014–15' 1, the Commission put forward the following conclusions and recommendations on Albania: https://wbc-rti.info/object/document/14456/attach/20141008-albania-progress-report_en.pdf

Helsinki Committee (2020). Assessing Human Rights and the Rule of Law as Albania chairs the OSCE, https://ahc.org.al/wp-content/uploads/2021/01/Vleresimi-i-te-Drejtave-te-Njeriut-dhe-Shtetit-te-se-Drejtes-teksa-Shqiperia-kryeson-OSBE-ne.pdf

Interview with Budget Director, Ministry of Finance, 19.03.2021.

Interview with parliamentary employee, 18. 3. 2021.

IPA National Programme (2010) for Albania Project fiche no 4: "Strengthening the Assembly of Albania" https://ec.europa.eu/neighbourhood-enlargement/sites/near/files/pdf/albania/ipa/2010/pf4_parliament_en.pdf

ISP (2016–2020). Monitoring Reports on the Assembly, available at http://deputetim.al/index.php/publikime/

ISP (2019). The Parliament in the time of Covid-19, pg.25, http://isp.com.al/wp-content/uploads/2020/09/ISPPARLAMENTI-GJATE-PERIUDHES-SE-COVID-19.pdf

ISP (2018). Parliament and representation: survey, monitoring and issues, Tirana. http://isp.com.al/wp-content/uploads/2019/02/ISP-RAPORT-ANKETIMI-I-DEPUTETEVE-2018.pdf

ISP (2020) Survey/Citizen perception on MPs and the Assembly, http://isp.com.al/index.php/2020/08/28/isp-perceptimi-qytetar-mbi-deputetet-dhe-parlamentin-anketim-2020-2/

Krasniqi, A. (2020) The Albanian Parliament in transition. Kuvendi, No. 12, pp.25–45, https://www.parlament.al/Files/Informacione/Revista%20nr.%2012.pdf

Krasniqi, A. (2021). Impact on Democracy of Emergency Measures Against Covid-19: The Case of Albania, https://journals.sas.ac.uk/lawreview/article/view/5268/5104

Law no. 8550/1999. On the Status of MPs. http://parlament.al/Files/Informacione/ligji-per-statusin-e-deputetit.pdf

Law no 8549/1999. On the Status of Civil Servants. http://dap.gov.al/legjislacioni/per-sherbimin-civil

Laws and acts for public administration, http://dap.gov.al/legjislacioni/per-administraten-publike

Law no. 8417/1998, (amending). The Constitution of the Republic Of Albania, http://parlament.al/Files/sKuvendi/kushtetuta.pdf

Pano, M. (2016). The role of the Assembly in European integrations process. Kuvendi, no.6, pp.45–63. https://www.parlament.al/Files/Informacione/Revista%20nr%206.pdf

SIGMA (2003). Public management profiles of Western Balkan Countries: Albania http://www.sigmaweb.org/publications/35039571.pdf

Shllaku, A. (2005). The legistative process. Kuvendi, No.4, pp. 19–27, https://www.parlament.al/Files/Informacione/Revistanr.4.pdf

37
BOSNIA AND HERZEGOVINA'S PARLIAMENTARY ADMINISTRATION

Damir Kapidžić and Lejla Tafro-Sefić

37.1 Introduction: The Political System and Parliamentary Assembly of Bosnia and Herzegovina

Bosnia and Herzegovina (BiH) is a country with a very complex political system and the structure of the national Parliament as well as the parliamentary administration reflects this complexity. The country has a bicameral Parliament with one house elected by proportional representation and the other house appointed by subnational units. The composition of Parliament is designed to reflect both the territorial and ethnic diversity of the country, but it is one of the smallest national parliaments in the world. This creates noticeable challenges for Members of Parliament and many tasks are assigned to the parliamentary administration. While the competences of the national Parliament are limited in scope, they are complex in nature and it is the primary legislative body to engage with the international environment on numerous issues.

The current political system of BiH is a direct outcome of the 1995 General Framework Agreement for Peace in BiH, commonly known as the Dayton Peace Agreement. The Agreement put an end to the Bosnian War and through Annex 4 introduced a new Constitution for the country. The essence of the political system of BiH is a consociational democracy built on the idea of balancing national sovereignty and subnational autonomy with power-sharing between two territorial entities, and three constituent peoples (the main ethnic groups) but with strong emphasis on individual human rights. In a population of 3.5 million, Muslim Bosniaks comprise 50.1%, Christian Orthodox Serbs 30.8%, and Catholic Croats 15.4% (Agency for Statistics of BiH 2016, 54) and 3.7% of citizens who do not identify with a constituent ethnic group. The country consists of two *entities*, the Federation of BiH (FBiH) and the Republika Srpska (RS), as well as an independent unit, the District Brčko of BiH. There are multiple subnational levels of decision-making that have larger scopes of jurisdiction than the national Parliament (Kapidžić 2019). At lower levels, decisions are often made by the majority ethnic group, yet it is at the level of the national Parliament that all elements of power-sharing come together and interact. This complexity in identifying the basis of decision-making power (individual citizens, ethnic groups, and territorial units) is reflected in the rules governing composition, decision-making, and the administration of the Parliament.

The bicameral Parliamentary Assembly of Bosnia and Herzegovina (*Parlamentarna skupština Bosne i Hercegovine* or Парламентарна скупштина Босне и Херцеговине; PABiH) consists of the upper House of Peoples (*Dom naroda* or Дом народа; HoP) and the lower House of Representatives (*Predstavnički dom, Zastupnički dom* or Представнички дом; HoR). The HoP has 15 members, of which 5 Bosniak and 5 Croat Members are appointed by their respective ethnic delegates in the FBiH Parliament's House of Peoples, and 5 Serb Members by the RS National Assembly. The HoR has 42 members elected through open list proportional representation in general elections, 14 from RS and 28 from FBiH. The composition of both Houses strongly takes into account ethnic and subnational criteria (Central Election Commission 2021). With 57 members across both Houses, the PABiH is one of the smallest national parliaments in size worldwide, especially a bicameral parliament, and in relation to population size. The primary role and competences of the PABiH are to amend the Constitution, enact legislation and budget, ratify international treaties, and confirm the appointment of the executive branch (the Council of Ministers of BiH and the Chairman of the Council, effectively the prime minister). Policy areas in BiH are constitutionally delineated in a way that limits legislative competences at the national level (Constitution of BiH, art.III and art.IV.4.), and they have since only been expanded intermittently. The PABiH is marked by symmetric bicameralism. The HoR and the HoP have equal power and legislation must pass both Houses. In the HoP, a majority vote within any of the three ethnic groups of delegates can trigger an ethnic veto. The Houses are each headed by a Collegium of the House that includes the Speaker and two Deputy Speakers.

The parliamentary administration of BiH is referred to as *Sekretarijat Parlamentarne skupštine Bosne i Hercegovine, Tajništvno Parlamentarne skupštine Bosne i Hercegovine,* or Секретаријат Парламентарне скупштине Босне и Херцеговине in the three official languages of BiH, Bosnian, Croatian, and Serbian, respectively. In this chapter, we will use the English name: Secretariat of the Parliamentary Assembly of BiH, or short just the **Secretariat**. The Secretariat is a joint body that consists of three organizational pillars: two Administrative Services for the two Houses and a Joint Service, each with several task or policy-related subdivisions. The heads of each Service form a joint three-member professional body that coordinates and manages the work of the parliamentary administration.

There have been several publications that describe the history, role, composition and functioning of the PABiH (PABiH 2010; Pejanović 2017; Flessenkemper & Moll 2018; Kapidžić & Komar 2022, Banović, Gavrić & Barreiro Marino 2021). However, this chapter aims to give the first academic overview of the Secretariat. The following section will present organizational aspects of the Secretariat, including its development over time. The third will give an overview of the functioning and role of parliamentary administration. The fourth will examine inter-institutional and external relations, towards subnational and international institutions. The fifth will focus on current challenges. The final section concludes.

37.2 Organizational Aspects of the Secretariat of the Parliamentary Assembly of Bosnia and Herzegovina

The development of the Secretariat of the has been both gradual and constant. The first post-war Parliamentary Assembly of BiH convened after the 1996 elections. During the initial years, from 1996 to 1998, technical and administrative tasks for the Houses and Working

Committees were performed by the employees of the Assembly of the Republic of BiH and the National Assembly of RS, working from different locations. This was due to war-related mistrust and devastation of the BiH Parliament building which was located on the front lines of the conflict. After partial reconstruction in late 1998, the administration moved back into the Parliament premises. An Interim Secretariat was formed in March 1999 consisting of only six members who worked with the Administrative Offices of both Houses. It was transformed into a permanent Secretariat the following year (Službeni glasnik BiH 2000). In 2000, both Houses adopted their respective Rules of Procedure that define their work and decision-making procedures, which lay the groundwork for the role of the parliamentary administration. New Rules of Procedure were adopted in 2006 and 2014. With the adoption of the Decision on the Organisation of the Secretariat of the PABiH in 2005, the parliamentary administration was reorganized which facilitated professionalization and expansion of administrative capacities (Službeni glasnik BiH 2005; PABiH 2006; Službeni glasnik BiH 2008). This created the current organizational structure of the Secretariat with subsequent minor changes.

Civil servants, employees, and the three Secretaries of the administrative and Joint Services, as well as staff in the Offices of the speakers of the HoR and HoP employed on a fixed-term basis, make up the staff of the Secretariat. Expansion of the parliamentary administration happened at a gradual pace. In 2000, with limited budget and premises, only 20 civil servants were employed. During the following years, positions were staffed following priority areas at particular moments in time. Areas of legislative support, internal control, international cooperation and information and outreach activities saw a rise in staff. In early 2021, the Secretariat has 174 staff, of which 103 are civil servants and 71 employees. Table 37.1 gives an overview of the development in size of the Secretariat.

The Secretariat is a joint body and consists of the Administrative Service of the HoR, the Administrative Service of the HoP, and the Joint Service of the PABiH (Službeni glasnik BiH 2000, Službeni glasnik BiH 2005). Each of the three Services is headed by a Secretary (one from every constituent ethnic group). The Secretariat follows a hierarchical structure along the three distinct Services, but there is no hierarchy between different Services. Each Secretary is responsible for the work of the Service they oversee, including civil servants and employees. Together, the Secretaries form the **Collegium of the Secretariat**, a joint professional administrative body which coordinates and manages the work of the three Services.

Table 37.1 Number of staff in the Secretariat

Year	Civil servants	Employees
1999	/	6
2000	20	1
2005	31	18
2007	64	41
2010	93	61
2015	106	67
2016	102	64
2017	100	69
2018	100	66
2019	101	70
2020	103	71

The **Administrative Service of the HoR** includes the Offices of the Speaker and two Deputy Speakers of the HoR, the Office of the Secretary of the HoR, seven Offices of Committee Secretaries of the HoR, and the Section for Preparation of Sessions of the HoR. The **Administrative Service of the HoP** includes the Offices of the Speaker and two Deputy Speakers of the HoP, the Office of the Secretary of the HoP, three Offices of Committee Secretaries of the HoP, and the Section for Drafting and Publication of Legal Documents. The **Joint Service** consists of the Office of the Secretary of the Joint Service, six Offices of Secretaries of Joint Committees of both Houses, ten Administrative Departments (some with several sections), and the Internal Audits Unit. The detailed organizational map is provided in Figure 37.1.

The Administrative Services of the HoR and HoP are managed by the **Secretary of the HoR** and **Secretary of the HoP**, respectively. The Secretaries of the Houses are responsible for preparing, organizing, holding, and concluding parliamentary sessions, for implementation of any conclusions, decisions, and other acts of the Houses and the Collegiums of the Houses, and for coordinating the work of the Committee Secretaries of their respective House. The Joint Service is managed by the **Secretary of the Joint Service**. This Secretary is authorized to conclude all agreements on behalf of the contracting authority of the PABiH, to correspond directly with other BiH institutions, and to convene sessions of the Collegium of the Secretariat. Personnel and employment related issues within the parliamentary administration are also handled by this Secretary. The Office of the Secretary of the Joint Service is responsible for all administrative, organizational, and technical tasks in preparation for joint sessions of both Houses of the PABiH, sessions of the Joint Collegium of both Houses, and for sessions that include members of several Administrative Services.

Given the complex structure of the Secretariat, there is a functional need for clear and efficient internal communication. The main responsibility for ensuring smooth coordination between the semi-autonomous structures of the administration lies with the **Collegium of the Secretariat**, composed of the three Secretaries. The Collegium heads the parliamentary administration, coordinates between all organizational units, and manages the daily work of the administration in all its aspects. It is also responsible for financial transparency of the parliamentary administration, it decides on rights, obligations, and responsibilities of staff, as well as other tasks related to the functioning of the administration. There is no hierarchy in the Collegium, but its work is based on principles of equality and consensus. This body holds regular meetings and ensures a smooth functioning and exchange of information between different organizational units of the parliamentary administration.

In total, there are 16 **Offices of Committee Secretaries**, 7 affiliated with the HoR, 3 with the HoP, and 6 Joint Committees of both Houses. They each provide services and support to the Chairman of the respective Committee and his deputies on all issues related to commission work, especially organizational, administrative, and advisory issues. When the Committee is discussing legislation within its purview, the Secretary's Office prepares expert opinions and reports, sessions for public hearings, minutes from Committee sessions, and other related tasks. Each Committee Secretary works with the respective Chairman to inform the House(s) about the Committees' work. They also cooperate with relevant outside institutions on tasks arising from the Committee's work and monitor the implementation of decisions and recommendation by the Committees.

The ten **Administrative Departments** perform various specifically designated tasks for the needs of the PABiH. There are specialized departments that assist with legislative tasks, international relations and protocol, information and documentation, research, public relations, IT, and finance, among others. One of the primary tasks is to provide

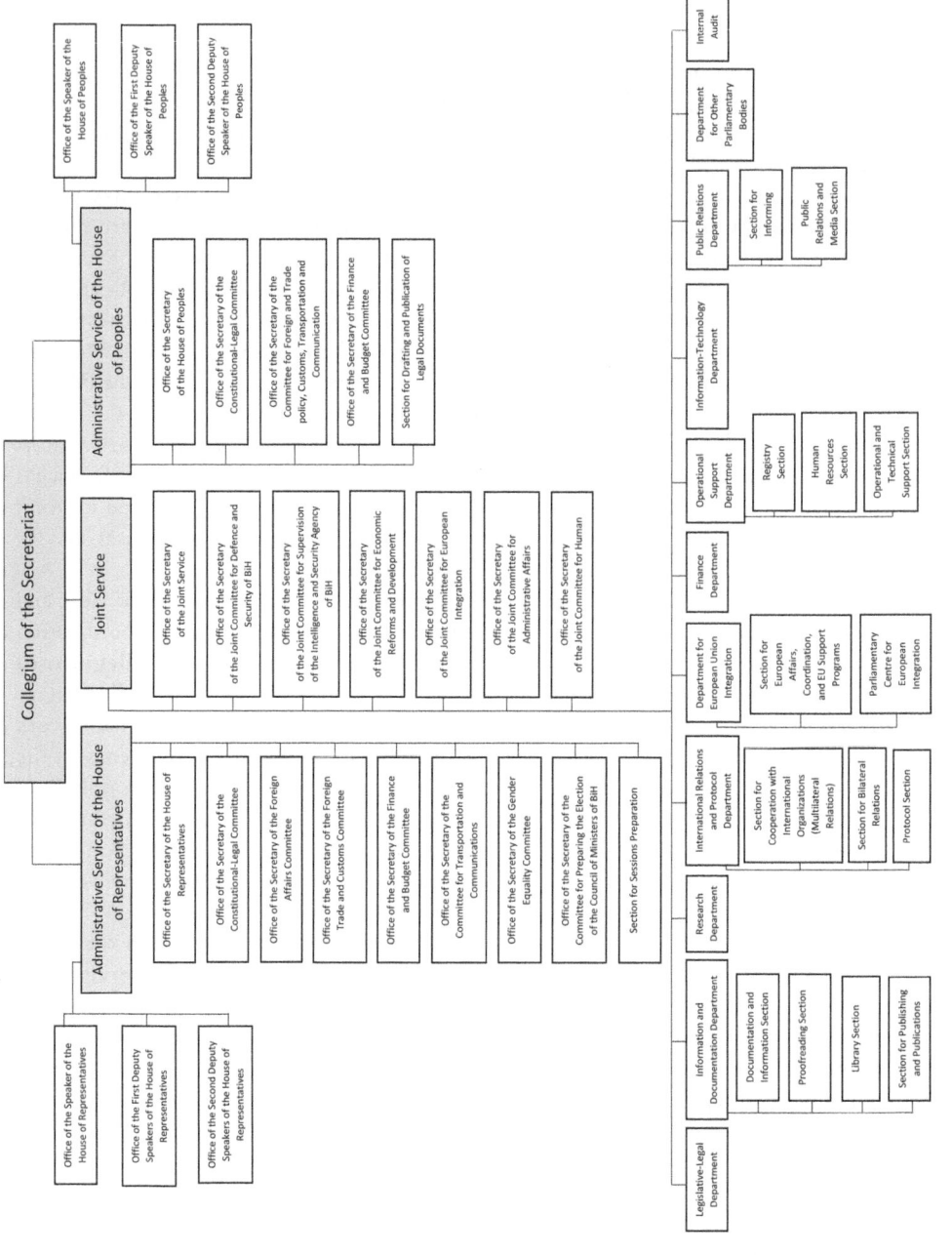

Figure 37.1 Organization chart of the Secretariat of the PABiH

legal and technical support to parliamentary working bodies during drafting of laws and other acts. This includes consulting services and expert opinions, as well as review, translation, and proofreading of legislation and preparation of adopted acts for publication in the "Official Gazette of BiH". Other tasks include technical and protocol duties for parliamentary delegations and reception of international delegations, public relations tasks, IT support, and financial administration of the entire Parliament. Dedicated departments deal with documenting and providing information and expertise to MPs, staff, and external users on issues related to the work of the PABiH, providing in-house research and analysis, and support for European integration affairs, including coordination of EU support programmes. The Parliament Library is also part of the Joint Service, re-established in 2002. Earlier library stock was destroyed during the Bosnian War and library premises were devastated. Through individual donations, international assistance, interlibrary exchange, help from the National and University Library of BiH and own purchase the Parliament Library now has over 4500 library units and 20 databases, as well as all official gazettes published in BiH. It is open to MPs and all staff of the Parliament and other BiH institutions, as well as regular citizens, with all library process digitalized. It is relevant to note that the number of staff in the Administrative Departments of the Joint Services of the PABiH is relatively small considering the breadth of assigned tasks.

There are three types of permanent staff with the Secretariat: the three Secretaries of the Houses and Joint Service, civil servants, and other employees. The Secretaries are appointed officials. The Secretary of the HoR and the Secretary of the HoP are appointed by the respective House on suggestion of the Collegium of the House. The Secretary of the Joint Service is jointly appointed by both Houses, at the proposal of both House Collegiums. The Rules of Procedure of the HoR and the HoP of the PABiH, respectively, prescribe the manner of their appointment (PABiH 2014a; PABiH 2014b). Each Secretary is responsible for his work to the respective House that appointed him. In this sense, there is a certain amount of political influence on the leadership of the Secretariat, with the role of the House Collegiums consisting of the two Speakers and four Deputy Speakers being especially prominent. As an informal rule, the three Secretaries come from three different ethnic groups. The mandate of any Secretary cannot be longer than the electoral mandate the PABiH, but the same person can be appointed again as Secretary. Any Secretary can be dismissed by the House who appointed him.

Civil servants employed in the PABiH can, in a hierarchical sense, be managerial civil servants such as Heads of Departments and Secretaries of Commissions, and other civil servants such as heads of sections, advisors, senior officers, and officers. Civil servants in the parliamentary administration have permanent contracts and are assigned a specific position by an administrative act, in accordance with provisions and the Law on Civil Service in the Institutions of Bosnia and Herzegovina (Civil Service Agency of BiH 2017a; Civil Service Agency of BiH 2017b). Employees work on the basis of a contract specific to their position, in accordance with the Law on Labour in the Institutions of BiH and parliamentary provisions (PABiH 2017a; PABiH 2020a). Approximately 60% of permanent staff of the Secretariat are civil servants. Additionally, advisors and technical staff (such as drivers) of Speakers and Deputy Speakers of the Houses are employed as needed on a temporary basis, corresponding to the term of the (deputy)speaker.

Recruitment and professional career development of civil servants is based on public competition and professional ability. The recruitment process is through public announcements and follows a set procedure (Civil Service Agency of BiH 2017a, art.21; Civil Service Agency of BiH 2017c, art.7). The BiH Civil Service Agency ensures and implements procedures for hiring civil servants by announcing vacancies, appointing independent selection commissions, and determining the character and content of public and professional exams. Civil servants are appointed by the Agency in accordance with the result of the selection process, while civil servants in managerial positions are appointed by the relevant institution from a list of successful candidates and based on the Agency's opinion. While the Law on Civil Service in the Institutions of BiH stipulates that the structure of civil servants in the civil service should reflect the national structure of the population according to the last census, criteria such as ethnic identity are not key and party membership is not relevant to employment and promotion. The Law highlights the right to fair and equitable treatment regardless of identity, gender, personal and political beliefs etc. Promotion of civil servants to higher positions is done through an internal or public competition, while promotion of a civil servant to a higher category, higher internal salary grade, is based on a positive evaluation of work and is decided by the institution in accordance with regulations on salaries and allowances. Civil servants in the PABiH have an obligation to pursue professional development and further education (Službeni glasnik BiH 2017).

Interaction within and with outside stakeholders is defined through the Rulebook on Communication (PABiH 2018). It regulates internal and external forms of communication and reporting between different levels in the Secretariat and outside them. Internal communication within the parliamentary administration is hierarchical with horizontal linkages. Vertical communication is mostly formalized, especially top-down communication, through meetings, written or email correspondence, decisions or internal regulations, the intranet and bulletin board, and reporting. Bottom-up communication also relies on these forms but includes informal communication through oral notifications and consultations. Horizontal communication is realized between all organizational units, regardless of which Service of the Secretariat they belonged, both formally and informally, through meetings and written and oral correspondence. In the communication of civil servants from different Services of the administration, the Secretaries of those Services can also be present if necessary. Special attention is paid to external communication and relations with the general public and civil society, using different means of communication.

37.3 The Work and Role of the Secretariat

The Secretariat with its two Administrative Services of the Houses, the Joint Service, and Collegium of the Secretariat works to secure the legal, professional, efficient, rational, and timely exercising of the power of the PABiH. The two Administrative Services of the Houses perform a number of activities for the needs of the two Houses. Especially relevant are activities in relation to preparing and conducting plenary sessions, assisting the Speakers and Deputy Speakers of the Houses, technical and administrative support for Committee sessions, and technical assistance in drafting and publication of legislation. Within the Joint Service, there are ten specialized departments: the Legislative–Legal Department, Information and Documentation Department, Research Department, International Relations and Protocol Department, Department for European Union Integration, Finance Department, Operational Support Department, Information–Technology Department, Public Relations Department, Department for Other Parliamentary Bodies, and the Internal Audit Unit (see Annex, Figure 37.1). Each of these performs a specific task related to the work of the Parliament and Secretariat, assisting the work of both Houses, while the examples below focus on interactions between the administrative and political dimensions of the PABiH.

One of the tasks of the **Legislative–Legal Department** is to perform legal and technical processing of documents to be considered by both Houses. After a draft law is submitted in regular procedure to the Speaker of either House, it is forwarded it to the Legislative–Legal Department to provide legal opinion on conformity with the Rules of Procedure of the Houses (PABiH 2014a, PABiH 2014b) and the Common Rules for Drafting Legal Regulations in the Institutions of BiH (PABiH 2017b). This Department also provides consulting and assistance to Members of Parliament and caucuses of the Houses during the drafting of proposed laws and amendments. Members of Parliament and parliamentary groups can request assistance through a request form, either in person, via email or intranet message, as defined by internal regulations (PABiH 2014c).

The **Information and Documentation Department** works through four sections that bring together a variety of documentation and publishing-related tasks to assists the work of Members of Parliament. One is to collect and process all parliamentary documentation, including records of proceedings of the PABiH, and to keep track of the legislative process, including statistical analysis of the work of Parliament. The Department makes this information available in both in printed and electronic form through the searchable database of all legislative activities *e-z@k PSBiH*. A second is to provide professional expertise to the Members of Parliament, staff, and others in identifying relevant information, research, and documentation. Requests for expertise assistance can be made in person or via email and intranet message. The Parliament uses three official languages of BiH in its work, Bosnian, Croatian, and Serbian, written in Latin and Cyrillic script. The Department is tasked to adapt and edit all relevant documents for the House sessions into three languages, including legal acts for publication in the Official Gazette of BiH, and official correspondence of Members of Parliament. The Parliament Library provides access to library holdings to users, both MPs, administration staff and external users, and support in researching thematic requests. Members of Parliament have direct access to electronic catalogues via intranet. This Department further controls adherence to corporate identity guidelines of Parliament, and it publishes publications and promotional material, among others the "Guide for Members of Parliament and Delegates" that synthesizes all information for newly elected parliamentarians, and a quarterly publication on all parliamentary activities.

Members of Parliament can send a request the **Research Department** in person, by email or intranet message to prepare information on topics or laws to be discussed during sessions (both brief reports and comparative studies), or an analysis of other relevant topics. The procedure and period for such requests is defined through internal regulations (PABiH 2011). The **International Relations and Protocol Department** functions through three sections that carry out work related to official visits, the participation of parliamentary delegations in international organizations at the multilateral level and the establishment and development of bilateral parliamentary cooperation. For Members of Parliament who participate in meetings abroad the Department facilitates issuing of diplomatic passports, makes hotel and flight reservations, and facilitates visa applications, when necessary, in addition to various protocol-related tasks. In its work, it cooperates with the BiH Ministry of Foreign Affairs. The **Public Relations Department**, through its two sections, publicly communicates the work of the PABiH towards domestic and international media, and citizens. On request of any, Member of Parliament is can call and prepare a press conference. Apart from that it regularly prepares announcements, media conferences, compiles daily clippings of relevant published news, and updates the PABiH website.

37.4 Inter-Institutional and External Relations

When it comes to external relations, there are several levels of interaction that are important. The most relevant for everyday work is with national government institutions and ministries, and when required with subnational (entity) parliamentary administrations. The Secretariats of the PABiH exchange relevant information on important issues within their scope of work with the Secretariats of the institutions of BiH and the Secretariats of the subnational Parliaments of FBiH and RS on a regular basis. Occasionally, seminars are jointly organised for experts and civil servants from the administration of these institutions. All cooperation necessarily takes into account the complex and sometimes limiting framework of the Constitution as well as separate laws, guidelines, and rules of procedure of the individual institutions.

The PABiH is involved in a range of bilateral and multilateral activities as laid out in the Houses' Rules of Procedure and the Rulebook on International Activities (PABiH 2009; PABiH 2014a; PABiH 2014b). The most noticeable are the standing parliamentary delegations of the PABiH, such as the Delegation to the Inter-Parliamentary Union (IPU), the Delegation to the Parliamentary Assembly of the Council of Europe (PACE), the Delegation to the Parliamentary Assembly of the Organization for Security and Co-operation in Europe (OSCE), the Delegation to the Parliamentary Assembly of the North Atlantic Treaty Organization (NATO), and others. Parliamentary staff is tasked with providing the necessary conditions for implementation of all planned international activities of the delegations. The Secretary for the delegations is a civil servant from the International Relations and Protocol Department, responsible for technical operation of all delegations and correspondence with the Secretariats of the international organizations. The PABiH has established Inter-Parliamentary Friendship Groups based on a regional approach, such as for neighbouring countries, Western European countries, Central and Eastern European countries, Asian countries, African and Near East countries, and for North and South America, Australia, Oceania, and Japan. The friendship groups have a Secretary, who is employed in the International Relations and Protocol Department, with similar tasks as the Secretary for the Delegations.

Administrative staff cooperates with the European Parliament through the Department for European Union Integration that regularly communicates with the Directorate for Democracy Support of the European Parliament on behalf of the PABiH. The Department for International Relations and Protocol also cooperates with the Secretariat of the European Parliament, primarily with units in charge of training parliamentarians and parliamentary staff. This cooperation includes drafting and implementing yearly programmes for cooperation activities that include both MPs and Staff of the PABiH. These programmes cover a broad spectrum of activities such as capacity building, political conferences, and study visits to European institutions. Under non-pandemic circumstances, yearly coordination meetings of staff from the European Parliament and the PABiH are organized with the purpose of identifying points of cooperation between the two parliaments, in a broader framework of cooperation with parliaments from the Western Balkans.

37.5 Current Challenges Facing the Secretariat

Among the main identified challenges, three stand out. These are the issues of European integration of BiH, e-legislation and digitalization, and COVID-19 responses. European integration is not only conditioned on political developments in BiH and the EU but is also a capacity-related issue for parliamentary administration. Fully engaging in the EU accession process with requirements to adopt large amounts of legislation from the Acquis will significantly increase the workload of administrative staff. This requires additional personnel, skills, and knowledge to the administration's current capacities.

E-legislation and digitalization go hand in hand. The implementation of a significant e-legislation project is currently underway, which aims to completely digitize the process of legislative acts. The digitalization process in the BiH Parliament began in 2010 and most is planned to be completed in 2022. Some organizational units have completely digitized their business processes. Staff can access cases, documents, and records of acts through the intranet portal and a mobile app, based on their access permissions. This has proven particularly useful while working from home during the COVID-19 pandemic. For everyday work, the collaboration platforms within the Microsoft Office 365 system are used on a regular basis. The Parliament is currently completing the process of establishing a dedicated Virtual Private Network, as well as more permanent network solutions for online sessions and meeting. Currently, three to four online meetings are held every day at the PABiH.

The COVID-19 pandemic had a noticeable impact on work of the Secretariat. Epidemiological restrictions on in-person meetings, travel, and changeable lockdown restrictions that impact everyday life have limited the ability of staff to fully carry out their work. Protective measures for BiH institution include increased disinfection of premises, social distancing, wearing face coverings, and at times working in shifts from the office and from home (Službeni glasnik BiH 2020; PABiH 2020b). A number of administrative staff were always present at Parliament, while those working from home were as required to be available via telephone and email. Several issues related to digitalization were made more urgent by the pandemic. The need to hold meetings of Members of Parliament and parliamentary staff online due to epidemiological restrictions was solved urgently by procuring the WebEx solution for collaboration. All these measures are valid only temporarily, but they have sped up processes of digitalization, and can possibly lead to more innovative forms of work in the future.

37.6 Conclusion

The Secretariat of the Parliamentary Assembly of BiH is small in size but complex in the institutional setup and nature of its work, which reflects the BiH Parliamentary Assembly it serves. The structure is made up of three Services, two of which serve the bicameral BiH legislature and a Joint Service that carries out administrative, advisory, and technical tasks. Coordination among the Services is key and handled by a joint body, the Collegium of the Secretariat. Although there is political influence in appointing the Secretaries of the three Services, professional criteria are relevant in the case of civil servants and employees. In its current form, the Secretariat has existed since 2005 without substantial changes since then. Under changing circumstances and current challenges, this has created pressure on parliamentary administration to adapt and develop innovative solutions.

References

Agency for Statistics of BiH 2016, *Census of Population, Households and Dwellings in Bosnia and Herzegovina, 2013 – Final Results*. Sarajevo, June 2016.

Banović, D, Gavrić, S & Barreiro Marino, M 2021, *The Political System of Bosnia and Herzegovina. Institutions – Actors – Processes*, Springer, Cham.

Central Election Commission 2021, *Izborni Zakon Bosne i Hercegovine (Tehnički prečišćeni tekst)*, viewed 22 March 2021, <https://www.izbori.ba/Documents/documents/ZAKONI/Tehnicki_precisceni_tekst/Tehnicki_precisceni_tekst_IZ_BiH-hrv.pdf>.

Civil Service Agency of BiH 2017a, *Zakon o državnoj službi u institucijama Bosne i Hercegovine – Integralni tekst*, viewed 22 March 2021, <https://www.ads.gov.ba/en/articles/82/zakon-o-drzavnoj-sluzbi-u-institucijama-bosne-i-hercegovine-integralni-tekst>.

Civil Service Agency of BiH 2017b, *Pravilnik o uslovima i načinu obavljanja internih konkursa, internih i eksternih premještaja državnih službenika u institucijama Bosne i Hercegovine – integralni tekst*, viewed 22 March 2021, <https://www.ads.gov.ba/bs-Latn-BA/articles/96/pravilnik-o-uslovima-i-nacinu-obavljanja-internih-konkursa-internih-i-eksternih-premjestaja-drzavnih-sluzbenika-u-institucijama-bosne-i-hercegovine-integralni-tekst>.

Civil Service Agency of BiH 2017c, Pravilnik o karakteru i sadržaju javnog konkursa, načinu provođenja intervjua i obrascima za provođenje intervjua – Integralni tekst, viewed 22 March 2021, <https://www.ads.gov.ba/bs-Latn-BA/articles/97/pravilnik-o-karakteru-i-sadrzaju-javnog-konkursa-nacinu-provo-enja-intervjua-i-obrascima-za-provo-enje-intervjua-integralni-tekst>.

Constitution of Bosnia and Herzegovina (as Amended in 2009).

Flessenkemper, T & Moll, N 2018, *Das politische System Bosnien und Herzegowinas. Herausforderungen zwischen Dayton-Friedensabkommen und EU-Annäherung*, Springer VS, Wiesbaden.

Kapidžić, D 2019, 'A Mirror of the Ethnic Divide: Interest Group Pillarization and Elite Dominance in Bosnia and Herzegovina'. *Journal of Public Affairs*, vol. 19, no. 2, pp. 1–12.

Kapidžić, D & Komar, O 2022, 'Segmental Volatility in Ethnically Divided Societies: (re)Assessing Party System Stability in Southeast Europe'. Nationalities Papers, vol. 50, no. 3, pp. 535–553.

PABiH 2006, *Pravilnik o unutrašnjoj organizaciji i sistematizaciji radnih mjesta u Sekretarijatu Parlamentarne skupštine BiH*, nr. 03-34-7-251/06, adopted 6 April 2006.

PABiH 2009, *Pravilnik o međunarodnim aktivnostima Parlamentarne skupštine BiH*, numbers: 01/7,02/3-50-1-17-4-20/06 adopted 26 July 2006. and 03/5-50-1-17-20,9/08 adopted 22 January 2009.

PABiH 2010, *Parlamentarna Skupština Bosne i Hercegovine*, PABiH, Sarajevo.

PABiH 2011, *Interna pravila o dostavljanju i obradi zahtjeva za istraživanje*, number 03-34-6-1448-2/10 adopted 3 February 2011.

PABiH 2014a, *Poslovnik Zastupničkog doma Parlamentarne skupštine BiH*, adopted 6 June 2014.

PABiH 2014b, *Poslovnik Doma naroda Parlamentarne skupštine BiH*, adopted 14 May 2014.

PABiH 2014c, *Interna pravila o dostavljanju i obradi zahtjeva za stručnu pomoć pri izradi prijedloga zakona i amandmana na prijedloge zakona*, number 03-02-4-1237/14 adopted 23 December 2014.

PABiH 2017a, *Zakon o Radu u Institucijama Bosne i Hercegovine (Neslužbeni pročišćeni tekst)*, viewed 22 March 2021, <https://www.parlament.ba/law/DownloadDocument?lawDocumentId=dbc1328e-41fd-4108-9620-8eb1fd9cb145&langTag=hr>.

PABiH 2017b, *Jedinstvena pravila za izradu pravnih propisa u institucijama BiH (Neslužbeni pročišćeni tekst)*, viewed 16 August 2021, <https://www.parlament.ba/law/DownloadDocument?lawDocumentId=8ff2657b-1df7-48c0-8e72-12a5d6737b9b&langTag=hr>.

PABIH 2018, *Pravilnik o komunikaciji*, number 03-02-4-568/17 adopted 30 May 2018.

PABiH 2020a, *Pravilnik o radu zaposlenih u Sekretarijatu Parlamentarne skupštine Bosne i Hercegovine*, numbers: 03-34-6-1415/10 adopted 29 December 2010, 03-02-4-1332/12 adopted 29 November 2012, 03-02-4-771/14 adopted 26 March 2015, 03-02-4-2433/17 adopted 05 June 2018, and 03-02-4-652/20 adopted 29 September 2020.

PABiH 2020b, *Instrukcija o organizaciji rada i pravima i obavezama zaposlenih u Sekretarijatu Parlamentarne skupštine BiH za vrijeme trajanja epidemije COVID-19*, number 03-02-4-1928/20 adopted 28 September 2020.

Pejanović, M 2017, *The State of Bosnia and Herzegovina and Democracy*, University Press-Magistrat Izdanja, Sarajevo.

Službeni glasnik BiH 2000, *Pravilnik o unutrašnjoj organizaciji Sekretarijata Parlamentarne skupštine Bosne i Hercegovine*, Službeni glasnik BiH, nr. 36/00.

Službeni glasnik BiH 2005, *Odluka o organizaciji Sekretarijata PSBiH*, Službeni glasnik BiH, nr. 92/05.

Službeni glasnik BiH 2008, *Odluka o organizaciji Sekretarijata PSBiH*, Službeni glasnik BiH, nr. 63/08.

Službeni glasnik BiH 2017, *Odluka o načinu provođenja obuke državnih službenika u institucijama Bosne i Hercegovine*, Službeni glasnik BiH, nr. 15/17.

Službeni glasnik BiH 2020, *Odluka o postupanju institucija BiH i pravima i obavezama zaposlenih u institucijama BiH tokom trajanja epidemije COVID-19*, Službeni glasnik BiH, nr. 58/20.

38
ICELAND'S PARLIAMENTARY ADMINISTRATION

Þorsteinn Magnússon

38.1 Introduction

Iceland is a parliamentary democracy. Its unicameral parliament, the Althingi, comprising 63 Members, is one of the smallest national parliaments in Europe. This is reflected in the size of its administration, the official name of which in Icelandic is "Skrifstofa Alþingis" (Althingi Secretariat). The total number of the administrative staff in March 2021 was 111. In addition, there are 30 people in the employ of the eight parliamentary party groups. The party groups' employees are though in actuality Althingi staff in the same manner as the administrative staff of the Secretariat (Skrifstofa Alþingis 2018). However, this chapter will focus primarily on the Althingi Secretariat and its permanent non-political staff.

The Althingi has been served by an administrative staff since the restoration of parliament in 1845 as an elected representative body. Until 1911, parliament normally assembled only every two years, with each session lasting up to two months. Administrative staff was hired temporarily for each session. The Secretary General was the first employee to be hired permanently, in 1915. Since 1909, the length of each annual session has gradually increased, and in recent decades sessions have normally lasted for up to nine or ten months each year (Skrifstofa Alþingis 1996, 2019). The Secretariat was for a long time quite weak in terms of the number and expertise of the staff that assisted Members, but since the mid-1980s the staff has gradually been strengthened.

As in the case of many other national parliaments, very little has been written about the administration of the Althingi. Scholars interested in the Althingi have focused their attention on the Members themselves and parliamentary business. This chapter is therefore to large extent based on the author's personal knowledge and experience as an employee of the Althingi Secretariat since 1988 and his writings on various aspects of the working of the Althingi (Magnússon, 1987, 2005, 2011a, 2011b).

38.2 The Legal Framework of the Althingi Secretariat

The Standing Orders of the Althingi constitute the legal basis for parliamentary administration in Iceland (Skrifstofa Alþingis 2021a). The Standing Orders are established by law, as provided in the Constitution (Stjórnarráð Íslands 2021a).

In June 2021, the Althingi passed a bill on the Standing Orders that included a separate chapter on the Secretariat. Previously, the Standing Orders had only included provisions on the Secretary General of the Althingi and his or her role and certain services to be provided by the Secretariat to the Althingi and its Members. These provisions were dispersed in different chapters of the Standing Orders. The bill consolidated these provisions in a separate chapter on the administration (Skrifstofa Alþingis 2021b). The bill also included several new provisions among other things on the role of the Secretariat. The objective of including a separate chapter on the Secretariat in the Standing Orders was to make the Secretariat more "visible" and to strengthen its status.

Although the foundation of the Althingi's administration was laid in 1845, the Secretary General of the Althingi is first mentioned in the Standing Orders in 1915, while the Secretariat is not referred to until 1991. However, the Secretariat has *de facto* been in existence since 1875, when it was set up under the management of a Secretary General, and his predecessor, the Secretary to the Speaker, was in office from 1845 to 1875 (Skrifstofa Alþingis 1875, 1915, 1996, 2021a).

In addition to the Standing Orders, various other laws have relevance for the parliamentary administration and apply to the Secretariat and its staff, the most important being the Government Employee Act, which, among other things, includes provisions on the rights and obligations of government employees, the Freedom of Information Act, which provides for public access to information on the administration of the Althingi, and the Government Employee Wage Agreements Act, which, amongst other things, provides that the right to strike does not apply to the staff of the Althingi Secretariat and entrusts the conclusion of wage agreements with Althingi employees to the Speaker of the Althingi. As regards political staff, the Members' Salaries and Expenses Act lays down provisions on the hiring of staff and defines their rights and obligations.

38.3 Management of the Secretariat and Its Organizational Structure

According to the Standing Orders of the Althingi, the Speaker has the supreme authority in the administration of the Althingi. However, the day-to-day running of the Secretariat is supervised by the Secretary General, as stated in the Standing Orders: "the Secretary General shall manage the Secretariat of the Althingi and is responsible for the operation, finances and property of the Althingi with the authority vested in the office by the Speaker". The Secretary General is ranked at the top of the list of civil servants in the Government Employee Act.

The Secretary General is appointed by the Speakers' Committee, which is composed of the Speaker and the six Deputy Speakers. The Secretary General is selected by open competition, and the Speakers' Committee is assisted in the selection process by an advisory committee that scrutinizes applications and conducts preliminary interviews.

The Secretary General is appointed for a term of six years, but there is technically no limit to the number of six-year terms that he or she may serve. Those who have held the office of Secretary General have historically remained in office for a long time. Since 1915, no Secretary General has resigned before reaching the maximum age permitted to serve in public office (now 70 years). Over a period of 105 years, from 1915 to 2019, five individuals have held the office of Secretary General, and their average length of service has been 21 years. In contrast, the Speaker of the Althingi normally only remains in office for single parliamentary term, which is four years. A long time in office can create a position of strength and influence. Over 30 years (1991–2021), 11 parliamentarians have served as Speakers, but over the same period only three individuals have served as Secretaries General.

The Secretary General is the chief adviser to the Speaker and the Speakers' Committee on everything relating to the work of the Althingi and its operation. He or she attends meetings of the Speakers' Committee (along with other members of the Management Board) and meetings held by the Speaker with the chairpersons of the parliamentary party groups. Although the Secretary General works closely with the Speaker and other political parliamentary bodies, his or her chief obligation is to the Althingi itself and its Members in general. The Secretary General therefore also serves in an advisory role vis-à-vis Members of the Althingi. This means that it is important for the Secretary General to have the trust of all Members of the Althingi, both the Government supporters and the Opposition (Bernódusson 2012).

The Althingi Secretariat is a unified and highly centralized parliamentary service, and the Secretary General is in charge of both the parliamentary and operational aspects of the administration. The Secretary General, the Deputy Secretary General, and the Director of Finance and Operations form a Management Board that leads the work of the Secretariat and coordinates its activities. Respectively, they supervise three of the Secretariat's units. A team of nine managers reports to the Management Board, each in charge of a specialized unit. The largest units are referred to as departments, while the smaller units are referred to as offices. A manager can divide a unit into sections with the approval of the Management Board. The main tasks of each unit are described in Table 38.1 (Skrifstofa Alþingis 2021c).

Table 38.1 The main functions of the Secretariat's organizational units

Unit	Main functions
Chamber Department	Prepares and services plenary meetings, administers the recording, broadcasting, and publication of debates, edits parliamentary documents for publication, and edits the statute book on the Althingi website.
Committee Department	Prepares and services meetings of committees and inter-parliamentary delegations. Provides legal advice and assists in drafting committee reports and amendments, as well as legislative bills and resolutions.
General Service Department	Responsible for security matters, catering services, maintenance and cleaning of buildings and general services for Members and staff.
Information Technology Department	Responsible for monitoring and maintaining computer systems and networks. Provides user support, technical supervision of the website and the Secretariat's records management system.
Speaker's Office	Services the Speaker, the Secretary General, and the Management Board. Manages the Speaker's international activities.
Office of Legal Affairs	Assists and advises the Speaker, the Speakers' Committee, and the Management Board on legal matters. Prepares legislation relating to the operation of the Althingi.
Research and Information Office	Responsible for research and data gathering, promotional material for the public, and editorial responsibility for the website and manages the reception of school children.
Finance Office	Responsible for preparing the Secretariat's budget and financial accounts, Members' remuneration, travel bookings and settlement of expenses, and various other financial matters.
Humans Resources Office	Responsible for staff matters, including human resource policy, salaries, staff recruitment, and career development. Responsible for gender equality policy and the operation of an equal pay system.

Table 38.2 The highest level of management by gender 2000–2020

Year	Management Board		Heads of Departments and Offices		Total in Figures		Total in Percentages	
	Women	Men	Women	Men	Women	Men	Women	Men
2000	0	3	3	4	3	7	30	70
2010	1	3	4	2	5	5	50	50
2020	2	1	5	4	7	5	58	42

The role of women in the Secretariat's management has changed significantly over the last 20 years, as shown in Table 38.2. In 2000, women were 30% of senior managers, but by 2020 this number had reached 58%, and currently there are two women on the three-member Management Board. In 2021, three of the four departments are led by women (Magnússon 2020).

38.4 The Staff of the Secretariat

38.4.1 Size and Composition

In the course of the last two decades of the 20th century, there was a growing recognition of the importance of improving services and staff assistance for Members (Magnússon 2005, 2011a). Accordingly, the Althingi Secretariat was systematically reinforced. The trend towards greater professionalism that started in the early 1980s led to a reorganization of the Secretariat in the summer of 1989, with the introduction of a formal organizational chart for the first time.[1] In addition, there was a greater emphasis on hiring well educated and trained staff. Figures from 2017 show that about 70% of the staff of the Secretariat possessed a university education. The rest of the staff had completed either secondary education, 20%, or primary education, 10% (Félagsvísindastofnun Háskóla Íslands 2017).

As Table 38.3 shows, there has been a gradual increase in the number of staff over the last two decades. Between 2000 and 2020, the increase was 31%, with the biggest leap in 2019 and 2020. This was due to a decision made by the Althingi in 2018 to increase the number of political staff. As a part of this decision, the Secretariat staff that had specifically served the party groups were transferred under the parties' authority. The table also shows that over the last 20 years the gender composition of the Secretariat staff has remained stable.

Table 38.3 The size and gender composition of the Althingi staff 2000–2020

Year	Men		Women		Total	
	No.	%	No.	%	No.	%
2000	39	41	57	59	96	100
2005	44	42	60	58	104	100
2010	52	45	64	55	116	100
2015	49	42	68	58	117	100
2020	61	44	78	56	139	100

It is also noteworthy that women outnumber men among the Althingi staff. However, this situation is characteristic of the public sector in general (Stjórnarráð Íslands 2021b).

The table refers to the number of employees in full-time equivalent positions. The numbers have been rounded.

38.4.2 Staff Recruitment and Turnover

As mentioned in Section 38.3, the Speakers' Committee appoints the Secretary General, who is then responsible for hiring other personnel of the Secretariat. The Secretary General also hires the staff of the party groups on the recommendation of the respective party groups. The salaries and other terms of employment of the party groups' personnel are governed by the wage agreement between the employees of the Althingi and the Speaker of the Althingi.

According to the Althingi's Standing Orders, the hiring of staff was jointly in the hands of the Speakers of the three chambers until 1991,[2] but in most cases the Secretary General was also involved in the process. With the new Standing Orders enacted in 1991, when the Althingi became a single chamber, it was provided that the Secretary General should submit proposals to the Speaker regarding the recruitment of other employees of the Althingi. The Speaker would traditionally approve the Secretary General's proposals, meaning that in practice recruitment was the domain of the Secretary General. In 2007, the Standing Orders were amended, and the Secretary General was explicitly entrusted with recruiting other employees for the Althingi Secretariat. This change was justified by the fact that the new provisions simply codified the practice that had been in place for many years. Although the Secretary General has been vested with full authority to hire staff, it is customary to keep the Speaker informed of intentions to fill senior management positions. In general, there has been no political interference in the recruitment of the Secretariat's staff since 1991, but the hiring of political staff is obviously based on other criteria.

Recruitment of the Secretariat's staff takes place through open competition, and all vacancies are advertised in accordance with legislation on the rights and obligations of government employees. The Secretariat has adopted special rules of procedure for the recruitment process, emphasizing that the process is conducted on a professional basis. Staff selection and careers are based on merit, with the emphasis on impartial and qualified staff; employment is generally for an indefinite term.

The turnover rate of the Althingi staff has been quite stable over the years, as evidenced by the figures in Table 38.4. In 2005, 2010, and 2020, the turnover rate was around 7.5%, but there was a slight upturn in 2015, when the figure was 12.55%. The average turnover rate for 2005–2020 was 10.1% (Fjársýsla ríkisins 2021).

The figures in the table show that the average length of service for the staff of the Secretariat is rather high. In March 2021, the average length of service was 11 years, and

Table 38.4 The Althingi's staff turnover rate in 2005–2020[3]

Year	Turnover rate in percentages
2005	7.64
2010	7.30
2015	12.55
2020	7.63
Average	10.12

44% of the staff had served for more than 10 years. The Management Board and the heads of units had noticeably the longest tenures. About 83% of the team had served for more than 10 years, which ensured both a degree of stability in the working of the Secretariat and a strong institutional memory (Skrifstofa Alþingis 2021d).

As one might expect, the turnover rate for political staff will tend to be higher than among the Secretariat's non-political staff, as the employment contracts of these employees expire at the end of each parliamentary term. Obviously, the outcomes of general elections have a decisive influence on whether employees of parliamentary party groups are re-hired. Also, there are always some political staff who have ambitions to leave their job to seek political office, for example by standing as candidates for parliamentary seats.

It is interesting, but not surprising, that the average age of the political staff is considerably lower than that of the Secretariat's permanent staff. In March 2021, the average age of the political staff was 36 years, whereas the figure for the Secretariat was 49 years. The average age for both groups of the Althingi staff was 46 years (Skrifstofa Alþingis 2021d).

38.4.3 Professional Development of the Secretariat's Staff

The Secretariat's emphasis on staff development has intensified over the last three decades. The Secretariat's policy in this regard falls into three categories. Firstly, opportunities are provided to engage in continuing education at recognized educational institutions. Staff can apply for paid leave for up to six months, but the studies must be work-related. Secondly, staff can apply for a grant to pay for courses that can be taken without need for a leave of absence. Thirdly, the Secretariat, or its individual units, regularly organize seminars and courses of study. It is also worth mentioning that staff exchanges organized between the Althingi Secretariat and the Government Offices have proven useful and informative for both parties (Skrifstofa Alþingis 2021e).

In addition to this, participation in meetings and conferences abroad has been a form of continuous education. This applies to meetings where issues concerning the functions of parliaments and the complementary role of parliamentary administrations are topics of discussion. In this context, Nordic co-operation has been particularly important to the Althingi. Many units of the administrations of the Nordic parliaments meet on a regular basis to exchange information on issues of mutual interest, for example on parliamentary business, general management, information technology, international co-operation, library services, and research services. These meetings have been beneficial for the Althingi Secretariat, which has placed importance on the information that participants gain from these meetings and conferences being shared with other staff of the Althingi. The experience obtained from these meetings has in some cases inspired changes in the working of the Althingi. In addition to these regular meetings, special fact-finding missions have also been arranged for individuals or groups of staff.

38.4.4 Relations with Parliamentarians and Political Staff

The Althingi is a polarized setting, where parliamentarians are divided into two distinct and opposed partisan groups: the Government and its supporters and the Opposition. This polarization is reflected in the long tradition of filibustering in the chamber (Magnússon 2011b).

This political environment places even more pressure on the Secretariat's staff to maintain impartiality and respect for all political views and to show professionalism in their work, as staff are required to serve Members of very different political persuasions. In 2021, eight political parties are represented in the Althingi. The code of ethics for the Althingi staff, established by the Speaker, therefore emphasizes avoidance of conflicts of interest and anything that could compromise, or be perceived to compromise, their impartiality and objectivity (Skrifstofa Alþingis 2021e). When recruiting, specific emphasis is for this reason placed on impartiality and professionalism. Applicants who are hired and have participated actively in political work are asked to refrain from further participation in such activities.

It follows that the staff of the Secretariat do not see it as their role to influence policy making; their job is to assist parliamentarians in their work. However, it is unavoidable that staff who have worked in the Althingi for a long time, amassed a wealth of knowledge on the workings of the Althingi and gained the trust of Members, will exert some indirect influence on various decisions made within the Althingi.

As mentioned in Section 38.4.1, a new "political staff system" was introduced in 2018. From the start, the relationship and co-operation between the Secretariat staff and the political staff has been successful. The political staff has been relatively small in the past, so it will be interesting to see how things develop in the future. The relaxed and friendly atmosphere that exists between these two groups is at least a good and promising sign. After all, it is the role of both groups to facilitate the work of the parliamentarians, so good co-operation is of cardinal importance.

38.5 The Role of the Althingi Secretariat

The role of the Secretariat falls into four main categories.

38.5.1 Assisting the Speaker

As mentioned in Section 38.3, the Speaker of the Althingi has "the supreme authority in its administration". It therefore follows as a matter of course that assistance to the Speaker is a significant part of the service provided by the Secretariat in support of the work of the Althingi.

An important element of this assistance involves preparations for the day's sitting, like drafting the agenda, preparing the schedule for the business of coming weeks, and preparing the necessary documents, such as speaking notes and voting papers. Also, the Secretariat provides the Speaker with advice on procedural matters.

Another element of the assistance to the Speaker relates to his or her administrative role. For example, this involves advising the Speaker on administrative matters, implementing decisions taken by the Speaker and the Speakers' Committee, and carrying out decisions taken at meetings of the Speaker and the chairpersons of the parliamentary party groups. Related to this is advising the Speaker on various constitutional and legal matters.

It is customary for the Speaker to take the initiative when it comes to formulating policy regarding matters pertaining to the Althingi. In this regard, the Secretariat has a pivotal role when it comes to drafting amendments to the Standing Orders and other laws that concern parliament.

The Speaker's participation in international work has taken up an increasing amount of the Speaker's time over the last three decades. Consequently, this has become a more important element of the service provided by the Secretariat to the Speaker.

38.5.2 Assisting Members in Their Parliamentary and International Work

The assistance provided by the Secretariat to Members of the Althingi in their normal parliamentary work chiefly concerns Members' work in the plenary chamber and in the eight standing committees, which have both legislative and supervisory functions. In the chamber, this assistance can concern procedural or practical matters relating to Members' participation in debates, as well as drafting Members' requests for reports from ministers or the National Audit Office. As regards the work of Members in the standing committees, the Secretariat assists in the review of legislative bills and draft resolutions, in preparing committee reports and amendments, in collecting data and information, and in organizing and preparing committee meetings.

In addition, the Secretariat, along with the staff of the parliamentary party groups, assists Members in the preparation and drafting of bills, resolutions, amendments, and written questions to ministers. There are no restrictions on the number of bills and resolutions that individual Members and committees can introduce. Members' bills, for example, are about equal in number to the bills introduced by the Government, and even though they are generally shorter than Government bills, and mainly aim at changing existing legislation, they still require extensive assistance from the Althingi staff.

In providing their assistance to Members, the staff of various units of the Secretariat are in regular contact with their counterparts in the Government Offices. This applies particularly to the staff who serve the committees, and, to a lesser extent, the chamber department, the legal office, and the research and information office. The reason for the close relations between the committee staff and their counterparts in the executive branch is that the great majority of the legislative bills passed in parliament are introduced by the Government, and when a committee reviews a bill, it normally requests officials from the relevant ministry or agency to attend the meetings to respond to questions that committee members may have. As committee staff are more of a generalist than a specialist bent, major substantive changes to government bills are primarily formulated in the ministries at the request of the relevant committees. The committee staff are also in frequent contact with interest groups, as it is a normal procedure for the committees to request written opinions from entities affected by proposed legislation. Representatives of these groups are also frequently asked to attend committee meetings to discuss matters. In fact, any citizen or group can submit opinions to a committee on any draft legislation. Such opinions are mainly submitted by e-mail.

The Secretariat provides Members (and the public at the same time) with essential information regarding day-to-day parliamentary work through the Althingi website. The website provides online access to the parliamentary database, which includes, among other things, parliamentary documents, records of debates, and minutes of plenary meetings and committee meetings.

In addition, the Secretariat has since 1991 hosted an induction programme for new Members of the Althingi. This is normally a one-day programme in the plenary chamber, with follow up programmes focusing on the role of the Althingi, and the services provided by the individual units of the Secretariat.

Finally, the Althingi is affiliated to eight international parliamentary associations, and Members participate in various other international activities. The Secretariat assists Members in this work. Staff provide the delegations with advice on international affairs, assist in preparations for attendance of international meetings, and collect data and information. Staff are also responsible for preparing international parliamentary meetings held in Iceland.

38.5.3 Dissemination of Information about the Althingi to the Public

The creation of the Althingi website in 1994 revolutionized the ability of the Secretariat to disseminate information about the work of parliament to the public. The Althingi website is now the most important and most widely used window for the outside world on the work of parliament and an essential element for the maintenance of an open and transparent relationship between the Althingi and the public.

An important part of the disseminating function of the Secretariat is aimed at young people. As part of its effort in this regard, the Secretariat publishes educational material about the role and working of the Althingi, using part of the official website of the Althingi for that purpose. Also, in furtherance of the aims of democracy, the Secretariat has since 2007 run a School Parliament for young people in their final year of primary school, where students participate in a role-playing event. Guided tours of the Althingi House offered to the public also include tours that are specifically tailored to young people.

The Secretariat regularly receives enquiries from the public on matters related to the Althingi. Responses to such enquiries are mainly by e-mail.

38.5.4 General Management of the Althingi

The Secretariat is entrusted with varied tasks concerning the general management of the Althingi. The largest part of these tasks concerns the provision of support services to both Members and staff. The support services primarily involve financial administration (including payment of the salaries of Members and staff), research services, computer services, information technology, security, property administration, building maintenance and renovation, catering, and cleaning.

In addition to the support services, the Secretariat is responsible for the administration of personnel matters, including staff recruitment and professional development. Also, as the Althingi Archives are independent of the National Archives of Iceland, the preservation of parliamentary documents is an important part of Secretariat's functions.

38.6 Managing Current Challenges

The Althingi Secretariat needs to deal with a variety of challenges in its work. These can be illustrated using three examples. Since the collapse of the banking sector in 2008, surveys have shown a low level of trust in the Althingi. In the last Gallup poll before the collapse, 42% of the population had trust in the Althingi; after the collapse, however, the level of trust lingered for a long time in the range of 11–12%. According to Gallup's measurement in 2020 and 2021, trust has increased somewhat, to 23% in 2020 and 34% in 2021 (Skrifstofa Alþingis 2021f). It is possible that this improvement may stem to some extent from the fact that the Althingi responded vigorously to the COVID-19 pandemic by passing various laws to mitigate its negative impact. Although it falls primarily to the Members of Parliament themselves to enhance trust in the Althingi through their work, it is also clear that the Secretariat needs to make greater efforts in this area, for instance with increased education about the work of the Althingi.

Another important challenge faced by the Secretariat is the discussion that has been ongoing for some time with the political leadership about reforming the working procedures of the Althingi to make it easier for both the parliamentary staff and Members themselves to reconcile their family and work responsibilities. Members are generally aware that the organization of parliamentary work and working procedures needs to be improved, but it has proven difficult to achieve a political consensus on the means of achieving this objective. One of the obstacles is that no agreement has been reached regarding changes in the arrangement of debate on parliamentary business. For example, during second readings of legislative bills, Members can speak as often as they wish, which opens the door to lengthy filibustering. Improvements in this regard are an important prerequisite for making the Althingi a more accommodating and attractive workplace for qualified and ambitious employees.

As in the case of other parliaments, the coronavirus pandemic has presented the Althingi and its Secretariat with complex challenges. The practical response to these challenges has been in the hands of the Secretariat. The main objective of the measures that were taken was to keep the Althingi operational, and especially to enable parliament to pass the legislation made necessary by the pandemic. The measures taken have proven successful and had the effect that the Althingi has remained capable of carrying out its principal functions.

It is now clear that the pandemic measures taken will have a lasting effect on the work patterns of the Althingi and its Secretariat. For instance, the Althingi has changed its rules on committee meetings and made it easier for committees under normal circumstances to conduct its business (including decision-making) using teleconference technology. Furthermore, the Management Board of the Secretariat has adopted rules for a trial period that permit staff who wish to continue to work remotely from home to do so partly each week.

38.7 Conclusions

During the last two decades of the 20th century, the Althingi Secretariat was strengthened and transformed into a modern and progressive workplace with emphasis on staff impartiality, professional competence, and gender equality. This process has continued, and the Secretariat has established itself as an important professional body in support of the work of the Althingi.

These changes have been so extensive that it is safe to say that Members who served in the Althingi up to the general election of 1987, or even 1991, would not recognize the Althingi as the same workplace in terms of services to Members. In this transformation, the Secretariat has played a significant role in bringing about a variety of reforms regarding the parliament's functions and procedures.

It applies to the Althingi as much as it applies to the labour market in general that new generations of Members are more self-sufficient and have greater knowledge of, and familiarity with, the use of the latest technology than their predecessors, including information technology. This has led to a shift of emphasis in the services provided to Members. The Secretariat now gives greater priority to analytical work and specialist assistance, while various earlier support services have been given less weight, such as the services of switchboard operators, typists, and receptionists.

Although the Secretariat is not, and will never be, on an equal footing with the administrative organs of the executive branch in terms of expertise in the various fields of public policy, it contributes importantly to the working of the Althingi. Its strengthening over the last three to four decades has been of cardinal importance for the working of the Althingi and has facilitated Members' ability to carry out their parliamentary duties.

Organisation of the Althingi Secretariat (Skrifstofa Alþingis 2021g)

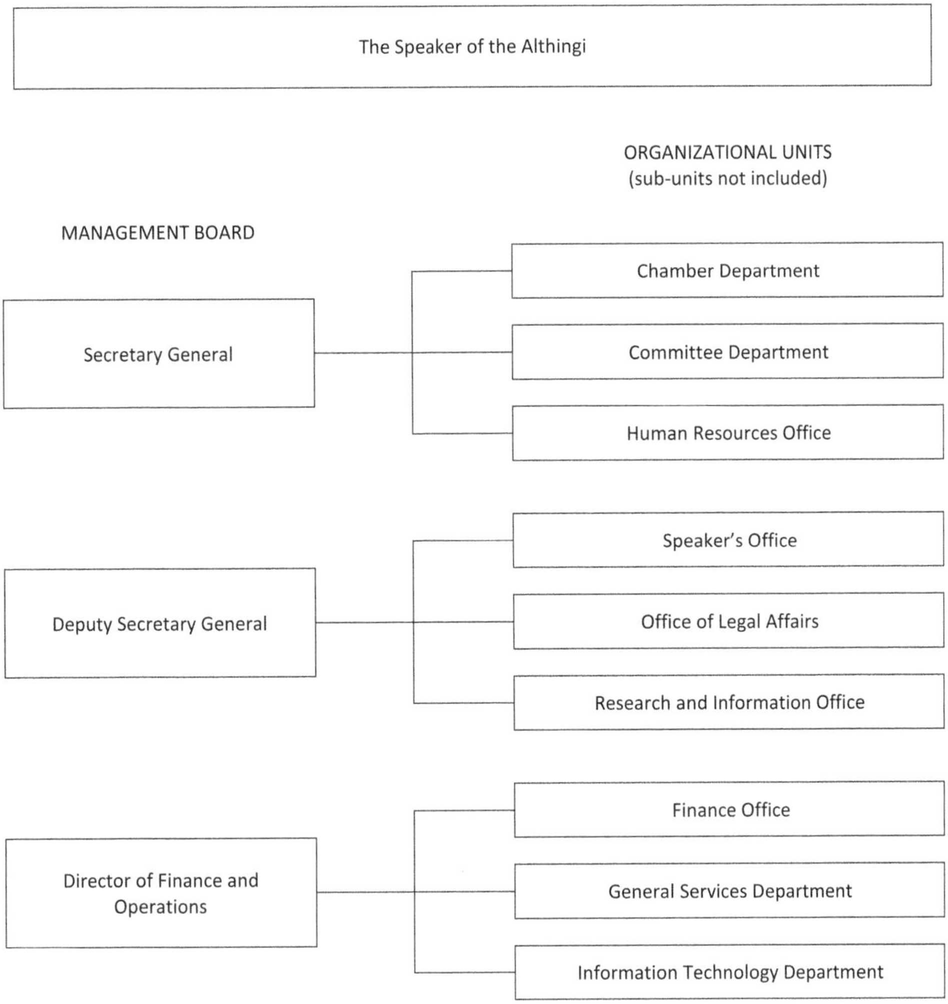

```
The Speaker of the Althingi
```

ORGANIZATIONAL UNITS
(sub-units not included)

MANAGEMENT BOARD

Secretary General
- Chamber Department
- Committee Department
- Human Resources Office

Deputy Secretary General
- Speaker's Office
- Office of Legal Affairs
- Research and Information Office

Director of Finance and Operations
- Finance Office
- General Services Department
- Information Technology Department

Notes

1. Since 1989, the organizational structure of the Secretariat has been changed three times; in 1996, 2006, and 2018. These changes reflected changing ideas about the way in which the Secretariat could better carry out its functions.
2. The Althingi operated in three chambers until 1991 when the Althingi became a unicameral body.
3. The turnover rate formula is as follows: the total number of employee departures is divided by the average number of employees for a given year, multiplied by 100. The average number is calculated by adding the number of employees on 1 January to the number of employees on 31 December, dividing the resulting figure by 2 and multiplying by 100. Only full-time employees are included in the figures.

References

Bernódusson, H. (2012). Parlamentsdirektørens lod og opgaver. In B. Brenno, ed. *I Stortingets tjeneste: artikler ved Hans Brattestås fratreden som Stortingets direktør [In the Service of Stortinget: articles on the occasion of the retirement of Secretary General Hans Brattestås]*. Oslo: Stortinget, pp. 13–22.

Félagsvísindastofnun Háskóla Íslands (2017). *Úttekt á launum starfsfólks á skrifstofu Alþingis [Analysis of the salaries of Althingi Secretariat personnel]*. Reykjavík: Félagsvísindastofnun Háskóla Íslands, p. 13.

Fjársýsla ríkisins (2021). *Starfsmannaupplýsingar – Alþingi [Althingi staff statistics]*. [e-mail].

Magnússon, Þ. (1987). *The Icelandic Althingi and Its Standing Committees*. PhD. Exeter University.

Magnússon, Þ. (2005). Alþingi í ljósi samþættingar löggjafarvalds og framkvæmdarvalds. *Stjórnmál og stjórnsýsla [The Icelandic Review of Politics and Administration]*, [online] Volume 1 (1), p. 38–42. Available at: http://www.irpa.is/article/view/a.2005.1.1.2/pdf_1 [Accessed 27 February 2021].

Magnússon, Þ. (2011a). Samþætting valdþáttanna og þróun Alþingis. In R. Helgadóttir, H.S. Kjartansson, and Þ. Magnússon, eds. *Þingræði á Íslandi [Parliamentary Democracy in Iceland]*. Reykjavík: Forlagið, pp. 424–430.

Magnússon, Þ. (2011b). Samþætting valdþáttanna og hlutverk Alþingis. In R. Helgadóttir, H.S. Kjartansson, and Þ. Magnússon, eds. *Þingræði á Íslandi [Parliamentary Democracy in Iceland]*. Reykjavík: Forlagið, pp. 403–422.

Magnússon, Þ. (2020). *Punktar um sögu Skrifstofu Alþingis [Notes on the history of the Althingi's Secretariat]*. Author's manuscript.

Skrifstofa Alþingis (1875). *Umræður [Debates]*. [online, p. 6] Available at https://www.althingi.is/altext/althingistidindi/L001/001_thing_1.pdf [Accessed 20 February 2021].

Skrifstofa Alþingis (1915). *Þingsköp Alþingis [Althingi's Standing Orders]*. Reykjavík: Skrifstofa Alþingis.

Skrifstofa Alþingis (1996). *Alþingismannatal* [Biographical Directory of Members of Althingi]. Reykjavík: Skrifstofa Alþingis, pp. 482–484.

Skrifstofa Alþingis (2018). *Frumvarp um breytingu á lögum um þingfararkaup alþingismanna og þingfararkostnað* [Bill amending the Members' Salaries and Expenses Act]. [online] Available at https://www.althingi.is/altext/149/s/0704.html [Accessed 13 February 2021].

Skrifstofa Alþingis (2019). *Handbók Alþingis 2017 [The Althingi Handbook]*. Reykjavík: Skrifstofa Alþingis, pp. 212–217.

Skrifstofa Alþingis (2021a). *Þingsköp Alþingis [Althingi's Standing Orders]*. [online] Available at https://www.althingi.is/lagas/151a/1991055.html [Accessed 13 February 2021].

Skrifstofa Alþingis (2021b). *Frumvarp um breytingu á þingsköp Alþingis [Bill amending the Althingi's Standing Orders]*. [online] Available at https://www.althingi.is/altext/151/s/0790.html [Accessed 20 February 2021].

Skrifstofa Alþingis (2021c). *Skipurit og hlutverk [Organisational chart and role]*. [online] Available at https://www.althingi.is/um-althingi/skrifstofa-althingis/skipurit-og-hlutverk/ [Accessed 6 March 2021].

Skrifstofa Alþingis (2021d). *Tölur varðandi skrifstofuna [Althingi staff statistics]*. [email].

Skrifstofa Alþingis (2021e). *Starfsmannahandbók [Staff Handbook]*. [online] Available at https://innri.althingi.is/starfsmannamal/starfsmannahandbok [Accessed 27 February 2021].

Skrifstofa Alþingis (2021f). *Traust til Alþingis vaxandi [Increased trust to the Althingi]*. [online] Available at https://www.althingi.is/tilkynningar/traust-til-althingis-vaxandi [Accessed 19 August 2021].

Skrifstofa Alþingis, (2021g). *Organisational chart*. [online] Available at https://www.althingi.is/english/information-and-enquiries/organisational-chart/ [Accessed 19 August 2021].

Stjórnarráð Íslands (2021a). *Constitution of Iceland*. Available at: https://www.government.is/Publications/Legislation/Lex/?newsid=89fc6038-fd28-11e7-9423-005056bc4d74 [Accessed 6 March 2021].

Stjórnarráð Íslands (2021b). *Tölfræði og útgefið efni [Statistics and publications]*. [online] Available at https://www.stjornarradid.is/verkefni/mannaudsmal-rikisins/tolfraedi-og-utgefid-efni/ [Accessed 19 March 2021].

39
MONTENEGRO'S PARLIAMENTARY ADMINISTRATION

Dražen Malović and Mirko Mijanović

39.1 Introduction

In Montenegro, the political authority is regulated by the Constitution following the principle of the division of powers into the legislative, executive, and judicial (Official Gazette of Montenegro, 2007). The legislative power is exercised by the Parliament of Montenegro, a unicameral legislature consisting of 81 members. The primary duty of MPs is to represent the citizens, their views, and interests. Therefore, one of the basic functions of the Parliament is to adopt laws in accordance with interests and needs of citizens, harmonized with the EU acquis.

One of the key functions of the Parliament is to oversee the work of the Government. The Parliament has at its disposal several tools for exercising parliamentary oversight, first and foremost the right of Parliament to adopt the budget and oversee the spending of budget funds. Parliamentary tools for examining and challenging the work of the government also include: a motion of no confidence, interpellation, parliamentary enquiry, hearings, and parliamentary questions.

As the highest representative body, it allows citizens to actively participate in parliamentary life. For this reason, parliamentary business is public and a special attention is paid to its openness and accessibility.

39.2 Key Aspects of the Organization of the Parliamentary Service

The Parliamentary Service performs expert and other tasks for the needs of the Parliament, its working bodies, MPs, and certain tasks for the MPs Groups.

Parliamentary staff participates in preparing and organizing sessions of the Parliament, meetings of the committees, and the Collegium of the President of the Parliament. They also draft texts of adopted laws and prepare them for submission to the President of Montenegro for promulgation and publication. Furthermore, they perform professional and other tasks regarding preparation of bills and other material upon the request of the chairperson, deputy chairperson of the committees, and MPs, as well as other affairs in relation to ensuring international parliamentary cooperation (Rules of Procedure of the Parliament of Montenegro, 2006).

In addition, parliamentary staff performs tasks in respect of exercising employment rights of the parliamentary officials and staff, as well as office operations, accounting, material and financial services, and numerous other affairs.

39.2.1 Evolution of the Parliamentary Service of Montenegro

From the midst of the last century up to the early 21st century, the Parliamentary Service had rather simple but valuable organizational scheme. A significant number of responsibilities set out in that period are also valid today and exercised by the following: Sector for Support to Legislative and Oversight Functions of the Parliament, the Cabinet of the President of the Parliament, the Secretary General's Office, and partly by the Sector for Legal, Human Resources, Financial and General Affairs (Rulebook on Organisation and Systematization of the Parliamentary Service of Montenegro, 2021).

Regarding the process of modernizing the Parliamentary Service, it is important to mention the year of 2006 and Montenegrin independence. The then Rulebook introduced for the first time the following jobs: *public relations and protocol, research and documentation, ICT,* while the *Library,* whose field of work had been recognized earlier, was further improved. In 2010, the Internal Audit Department as well as the Public Procurement Bureau were formed.

Wishing that the MPs' business is always available to public eyes, the Recording and Broadcasting of the Parliamentary Sittings Department was formed, tasked with recording and broadcasting the parliamentary sittings as well as other meetings and conferences. Broadcasting activities where even further developed, so since March 2021, Parliamentary TV Channel started operating, completely managed by the parliamentary administration.

As previously said, in the 2006, posts for research and analyses were created, which in 2010 became part of the Parliamentary Institute, which is, alongside with the Research Centre, Library, and Documentation Centre, part of the newly formed Education Centre.

Through Memorandum signed in 2016 between the Parliament of Montenegro and the Westminster Foundation for Democracy (WFD), aimed at strengthening financial oversight of the Parliament, the Parliamentary Budget Office (PBO) was formed.

The human resources component within the Parliamentary Service, starting from only one person in charge of labour issues, developed into individual units such as the Human Resource Management Bureau and the Legal Affairs Bureau.

The active Rulebook (2021) includes 281 posts, organization scheme can be found in the Annex of the book.

39.2.2 Structure of Employees

The term employee at the Parliamentary Service means employees occupying posts formulated through the Rulebook. Aside from civil servants and state employees, this includes Secretary General (SG), Deputy SG, Assistants SG, and Advisors to the President and vice-presidents of the Parliament, as well as trainees.

As the role of the Parliament changed and improved, accordingly the organizational change within the Service occurred, therefore the number of employees gradually increased. Consequently, using 2006 as a staring referential point, the number of employees has multiplied compared to the early 2021, from initial 55 employees to the current 198, namely 70% women and 30% men. The fluctuation of the total number of employees is presented in Figure 39.1.

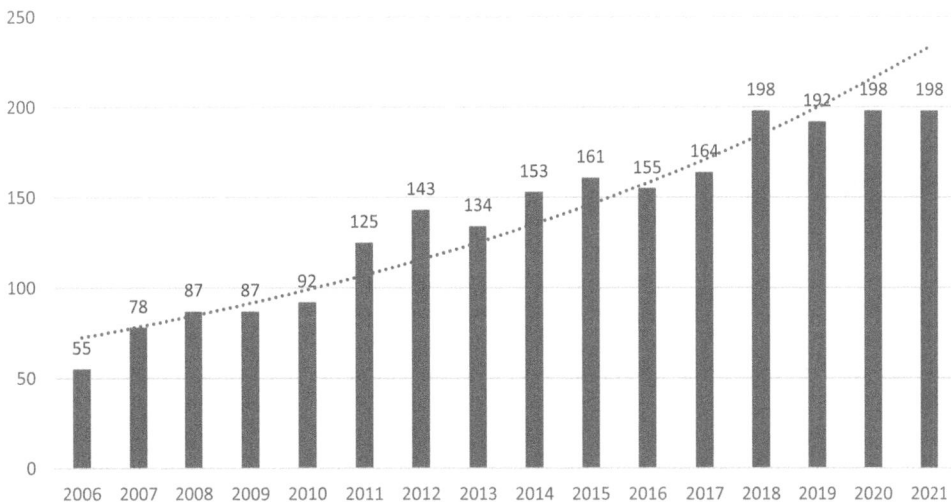

Figure 39.1 Number of employees 2006–2021 in the Parliamentary Service of Montenegro

Staff of MP groups are not employees of the Parliamentary Service, although groups receive certain funds from the Parliament for their engagement. Security officers in the Parliament are employees of the Police Authority, while a certain number of persons carrying out maintenance of facilities and premises used by the Parliament are employees of the Property Authority.

Also, for the needs of the Service, people are hired through contract or based on the decision on recruiting experts for the needs of working bodies; however, they do not have the status of employees at the Service.

39.2.3 Mechanism of Professionalization and the Development of Functional Expertise

Inter-Parliamentary Union's (IPU's) PARLINE survey, presented in the Comparative research paper on parliamentary administration 2020, defined multiple principles of governing parliamentary administration. Parliamentary Service Act (PSA) is the most common legal basis for regulating its autonomy. Having in mind that there is no PSA for the Parliamentary Service of Montenegro, its autonomy on number of procedures has been obtained through the exceptions in the Law on Civil Servants and State Employees – LCSSE (2013), which created a legal basis for adopting special acts, regulating the recruitment process, trainings and development of staff, as well as the staff's appraisal.

The same level of autonomy has been retained by the current LCSSE (2018a), which defines that vacancies are filled through deployment, public competition, and internal or public job vacancy announcements, while the Parliamentary Service adopts bylaws regulating the recruitment procedure (Official Gazette of Montenegro, 2018b). Like majority parliaments, Parliamentary Service of Montenegro is primary responsible authority for the recruitments of staff (The Inter-Parliamentary Union, 2020).

The positions of assistant SG are filled through a public competition, while any full time employed civil servant and/or state employee in Montenegro, who meets the requirements of the post, except those who are on probation, may apply for the internal announcement. The public announcement is being used for the initial positions of the categories, or if the vacancy is not filled during deployment and internal announcement process.

The filling of vacancies can also be done through deployment, temporary or permanent, horizontally – to a job for which the same requirements are prescribed as for the position presently covered by the employee, or vertically to a higher rank, if there is available vacancy, the employee meets requirements and was evaluated with the highest grade in the previous year, or to a lower rank due to the replacement of an absent employee or increased workload, while employee retains all the rights from the post from which he was deployed (Ibid).

With regard to professional development of the Parliamentary Service, during the staff's appraisal, the superior officers give proposals for the improvement of their abilities, which, together with the organization's aims, serve as a basis for preparing and adopting the Annual Plan for Trainings and Development (Official Gazette of Montenegro, 2018c).

One of the challenges arising during this process is potentially unclear goals of the institution or employees are not sufficiently aware of them, which creates dilemma what is important for further development. In these cases, it is questionable whether the trainings represent an added value for the staff and the institution, because when carried out in this manner, they represent only activities towards sharing the know-how and not the means to achieve organizational goals through learning and developing abilities (The European Commission, 2017).

The staff also attend trainings by the Human Resources Management Authority, as well as those organized by domestic and international organizations and institutions.

39.2.4 Access to External Consultancy

For its activities, the Parliamentary Service uses professional or expert assistance provided through projects, or by recruiting experts for the needs of working bodies.[1]

The Parliamentary Service participates in cooperation projects with numerous international organizations which, within the project activities, provide support for strengthening the legislative and supervisory role of the Parliament, thus improving transparency, openness and strengthening the capacity of working bodies and other units, and organizing bilateral and regional meetings. Most prominent project partners with whom activities were carried out in the previous period are:

- OSCE Mission to Montenegro
- WFD
- National Democratic Institute
- Die Deutsche Gesellschaft für Internationale Zusammenarbeit (GIZ)

Joint activities are also organized with the: UNDP Representation Office and UN Women, UNICEF Representation Office and Save the Children, Friedrich Ebert Foundation, DCAF, ERSTE Stiftung, British Council, and many others.

39.2.5 Rules for Interaction with Stakeholders

Transparency and openness of the legislature are important preconditions for greater citizen participation in the decision-making process and for monitoring political and social processes. The positive effects of civil society involvement are reflected in providing feedback on the results of implementation of policy and reforms, public oversight of parliamentary work, and providing insights from civil society perspective on monitoring sectoral policies, especially within the EU integration process.

In order of defining the aims related to the strengthening of institutional dialogue between the Parliament and NGOs, strengthening trust and creating sustainable partnership based on the principles of transparency, openness, and mutual respect, the Cooperation Agreement between the Parliament and NGOs in Montenegro (2016) was signed.

Representatives of scientific and professional institutions, other legal entities, and NGOs, as well as individual professional and scientific workers, can participate in meetings of working bodies, upon invitation, or at their request, with the consent of the chairperson of the committee, without the right to decide (Ibid).

Furthermore, representatives of the civil society are given the opportunity to submit an opinion to the working body regarding certain issues that are the subject of consideration by the working body, via prescribed Opinion Form of CSOs.

39.3 The Role of the Parliamentary Administration

Parliamentary Service ensures quality, professional and timely execution of tasks and business for the Parliament, its working bodies, and parliamentarians, in conducting their functions.

39.3.1 The Main Activities

The largest or core part of the structure are secretariats of the committees and the commission, which belongs to the Sector for Support to Legislative and Oversight Functions of the Parliament (Parliament of Montenegro, 2021). The Sector performs expert and other tasks for the needs of Chairpersons and Deputy Chairpersons of working bodies, MPs and the SG, formulates wording of adopted laws and other adopted acts (decisions, declarations, and resolutions). Staff is in charge of producing reports and minutes from the meetings of the working bodies, preparing proposals for acts and other materials as requested by the President, vice-president of the Parliament, a Chairperson of the working body or MPs, keeping track of EU acquis and the Regulatory Impact Assessment (RIA), as well as providing expert materials on the issues to be considered by the Parliament. Also, they prepare information papers, analysis, and research papers and assist working bodies in exercising their oversight, scrutiny, and communication roles and duties and provide expert assistance to MPs in wording the amendments (Ibid).

The Sector also drafts the text of the minutes from the parliamentary sittings, performing editing, preparing, and issuing of phonographic records.

Preparing research and analytical papers for the needs of parliamentarians and the parliamentary staff, drafting parliamentary publications and other education, and information materials is done by the *Sector for Research, Documentation and IT Network*. Work of the PBO is focused on assisting MPs in terms of analysing budget, controlling its implementation, analysing key budget documents and laws with fiscal impact, and responding to MPs' requests. The outcomes of this unit's work are research and briefing papers on the topics important for implementing economic and fiscal politics, especially in connection to economic and financial tendencies in Montenegro (Ibid).

The Parliamentary Service makes a continued progress in terms of transparency and publicity of its work, with significant role of the Department for Public Relations. This unit performs tasks related to the: informing the public on activities of the Parliament, the President, the vice-presidents and the SG, working bodies and MPs, preparing and issuing press releases, hosting press conferences, planning, preparing and organizing communication with the public, providing expert support for appearances in the media, issuing daily and annual press credentials to representatives of the media outlets, keeping records of accredited journalists, and organizing citizens' visits.

The Department communicates with the media and through journalistic requests prepares answers to questions from the interested public, communicates with the Public Broadcaster regarding live broadcasts of sessions and other important events organized by the Parliament.

Having in mind that the Parliamentary Service wants to keep up with the contemporary standards of modern European administrations, this unit also presents the parliament via social platforms such as Facebook, YouTube, Instagram, Flickr, and Twitter. Information on the platforms are posted intensively, in real time, with all follow-up material – texts, videos, and photos.

39.3.2 Institutional Hierarchy

As defined by the Rules of Procedure of the Parliament of Montenegro (2006), the SG manages the Parliamentary Service, whereby he or she is appointed and dismissed by the Parliament, upon the proposal by the President of the Parliament for the period of four years. This method of appointing the SG clearly indicates the autonomy of Parliamentary administration from the executive. This matches with the findings of the mentioned PARLINE survey, where majority of participant countries specify the appointment of the SG by the parliament, President, or some form of governing body, confirming the autonomy of their administrations.

Aside from administering the Parliament, the SG is in charge of:

- assisting the President and Vice-President of the Parliament in applying the Rules of Procedure;
- taking care of drafting the original laws and other acts of the Parliament;
- ensuring the implementation of the conclusions of the Parliament;
- preparing the proposal application for provision of budgetary funds for the operation of the Parliament and Parliamentary Service;
- the ordering issuer for financial and material business of the Parliament and Parliamentary Service and submitting the report on use of the funds to the Collegium of the President and the CEFB, if required by them.

The SG has two Deputies, also appointed for the four-year period.

The SG and Deputies report to the Parliament for their work (Ibid). These posts are political with no prescribed job requirements. Agreements on who will hold the post of the SG and Deputies are not public. Political and professional backgrounds of the SGs have been various. This is no different from the findings of PARLINE survey which showed that some of the SGs, covered by this survey, had other previous professions unrelated to the parliament and political parties, while number of them at some point showed recent political affiliations before being appointed.

President of the Parliament, Vice-Presidents of the Parliament, heads of MP groups, and the SG are members of the Collegium of the President, which, given its composition, constitutes a political body in charge of:

- the issues of organization and improvement of operations of the Parliament and its committees;
- planning the work of the parliamentary sessions and sittings;
- cooperation with bodies and organizations in Montenegro, parliamentary cooperation with parliaments of other countries, and parliamentary assemblies of international organizations;
- establishing and submitting an application for provision of funds for the work of the Parliament and Parliamentary Service upon the proposal of the SG of the Parliament.

Qualification and job requirements are prescribed for the assistant SG, position which is filled via open competition. The next levels in the hierarchy are civil servants and state employees who go through the process of internal or public vacancy announcement during the recruitment process.

The efforts have been continuously made towards making the recruitment and promotion of employees fair and transparent. In addition, staff of the MP groups is directly recruited by the political parties, which means they cannot become, by default, members of parliamentary staff.

The LCSSE (2018) states, the parliamentary staff must not discriminate citizens on the ground of their political views or affiliation to a political party. They are obliged to perform the tasks in politically neutral and impartial manner, in accordance with public interest, with an obligation to restrain from public demonstration of their political convictions. We believe that the existing legal framework does not regulate this issue sufficiently, and that it is rather necessary to consider it more thoroughly.

With the aim of decreasing the possibility of malpractice, and wrong application of procedures, the Service has established a set of mechanisms such as FMC Manager, Integrity Manager, and Risk Manager, which yet need to reach their full potential.

Speaking about impartiality, we could also reflect on possible influence of the MPs and politicization of the Service.

Although there was no official record of such a case, that certainly does not mean that there is absolutely no room for it, and that it probably exists in some lower extent. Current legal framework and procedures definitely prevent predominant influence of MPs on parliamentary staff, but nevertheless they do not exclude that possibility in total, since they do not regulate this issue sufficiently, and there is a room for their further improvement.

39.4 Inter-Institutional and External Relations

39.4.1 Relations with the Executive Administration

Regarding the relation between the Parliamentary Service and state administration, the rights and obligations of employees are essentially the same, regulated by the common legal framework. As said before, there are certain areas where the Parliament enjoys autonomy and independently adopts bylaws regulating the recruiting, evaluation of staff' performance, trainings and development of staff, as well as pay grades of certain categories among employees.

The employees of the Parliament take part in the work of a number of inter-institutional bodies, hence they are members of working groups for preparing and running the negotiations for the EU Accession. They have the possibility to get the insight into the EU acquis regarding individual chapters that the national legislation should be harmonized with, as well as to have a complete overview of the existing level of harmonization of Montenegro's legislation with the primary and secondary EU acquis.

In addition, the parliamentary staff is involved in various networks and associations both at international and domestic level, such as: Network of Parliamentary Committee on Economy, Finance, and European Integration of Western Balkans (NPC), ECPRD, Montenegro's Human Resources Network, etc.

39.4.2 Parliamentary Diplomacy and Inter-Parliamentary Cooperation

The Parliament cooperates intensively with parliaments of other states both bilaterally and multilaterally, through visits of delegations or individual MPs, and/or by hosting parliamentary delegations and foreign parliamentarians, participating in international gatherings, sharing information or via other cooperation forms.

Friendship groups are a special form of parliamentary cooperation among parliaments, allowing continuous inter-parliamentary cooperation and maintenance of political, economic, social, and cultural relations between countries. They are composed of no more than ten MPs, whereby each has its secretary from the Secretariat of the Committee in charge of carrying out the expert and administrative tasks for the needs of the Group.

An important segment of the international cooperation is related to the multilateral level within parliamentary bodies of international organizations as well as within several regional initiatives. The Parliament takes part in the work of these bodies, their plenary sessions, meeting of the committees, visits, missions, and other activities through their permanent delegations.

The expert and technical support to the work of permanent delegations is provided by secretaries who belong to the Parliamentary Service, therefore representatives of the parliamentary staff are members of delegations to the:

- IPU
- Parliamentary Assembly of the Council of Europe
- OSCE Parliamentary Assembly
- NATO Parliamentary Assembly
- South-East European Cooperation Process Parliamentary Assembly
- Central European Initiative – Parliamentary Dimension
- Parliamentary Assembly of Mediterranean
- Parliamentary Assembly – Union of the Mediterranean

Special attention is dedicated to the cooperation between the Parliament of Montenegro and the EP, which has been continuously improved and strengthened, achieved not only through numerous bilateral visits, including those at the highest level, the participation of EP representatives in events organized by the Parliament of Montenegro, but also the visits by representatives of the Montenegrin Parliament to the EP.

The important form of cooperation is conducted through the EU's Support Programme for the Parliaments of the Enlargement countries.

After the renewal of Montenegro's independence in 2006, the EP and the Parliament of Montenegro established regular dialogue where holding of inter-parliamentary meetings had been initiated between representatives of the EP Delegation for relations with South-Eastern countries and parliamentary Committee on International Relations and European Integration. Significant intensification of relations happened after 2010, when cooperation was raised to a higher level with the establishment of the first joint body of the EP and the Parliament of Montenegro – *the Stabilisation and Association Parliamentary Committee (SAPC)* – and furthermore after obtaining EU candidate status, when representatives of the Parliament were given the opportunity to attend as observers a number of meetings organized by the EP and the parliaments of the countries holding the EU Council Presidency.

A representative of the parliamentary staff is part of the SAPC standing delegation, in the capacity of the Delegation Secretary.

Intensive cooperation is also manifested through numerous meetings, including visits of the parliamentary speakers. Likewise, meetings were held with representatives of the AFET, especially with rapporteur for Montenegro, and EP's members to the SAPC. In connection to parliamentary committees, they held majority of meetings within conferences, inter-parliamentary meetings of committees, study visits, and other events, including ones organized within the Support Programme for the Parliaments of the Enlargement countries.

This Programme includes cooperation activities with the WB and Turkey parliaments, whose aim is to strengthen democracy, build institutions, and raise awareness of the EU processes and values.

It is carried out in line with annual plans formulated by DEG and includes conferences, roundtables, study visits, and Fellowship programme.[2]

Representatives of the parliamentary staff regularly take part in the IPEX, as well as in the previously mentioned ECPRD.

39.5 Managing Current Challenges Facing the Parliamentary Administration

39.5.1 Transparency and Digitalization

Aside from the previously mentioned cooperation with the civil sector, the significant part of the parliamentary transparency rests upon the regular provision of answers to all requests for free access to information and media questions. Data on the request for free access to information are published in the annual performance reports of the Parliament, prepared by the parliamentary staff.

The parliamentary transparency is also boosted by the Action Plans for the Strengthening of Legislative and Control Role of the Parliament, passed annually by the Collegium of the President.

The Centre for Democratic Transition (CDT) from Montenegro, in collaboration with their partners from the *ACTION SEE,* regional NGO network, prepares annual analysis of the level of transparency, openness, and responsibility of the WB legislative bodies. According to these researches, the Parliament of Montenegro has been recognized as the most open parliament in the region for a number of past years, with openness indicator 79% recorded in the last published report (Center for Democratic Transition, 2019).

Further transparency improvement contributes to the implementation of activities towards the digitalization of the legislative process. The first phase of the project was carried out in cooperation with the EU Delegation to Montenegro and included installing hardware infrastructure for the future digitalization of the parliamentary operations. The Parliament was provided with contemporary DATA centre, server equipment with the accompanying software, etc. In the next phases, the implementation of the e-parliament software solution is planned, to allow MPs, among other things, to have access to the system from anywhere and in any time, as well as the overall support to the legislative process.

39.5.2 Changing Work Patterns Due to the Covid-19 Pandemic

The functioning of the Parliamentary Service faced a major challenge due to Covid-19 pandemic. In response to the newly emerged situation, steps have been taken to reduce the opportunity for infection spreading and also towards the reduction of risk in terms of health safety of the staff.

The introduction of work from home for all employees was one of the first moves, which later has been adapted to the situation, so now, on a rotation basis a number of staff work from home and a number from office, while adhering to the preventive measures in the parliamentary premises.

When possible, meetings are organized online, as well as trainings and other activities requiring the participation of a larger number of persons.

In line with the Rules of Procedure, it was mandatory for MPs to be physically present for the purpose of taking part in the parliamentary sessions and meeting of the working bodies, therefore they were modified so that MPs have the possibility to participate online. In addition, for the purpose of enabling the necessary distance among MPs, during the plenary sittings, MPs are accommodated in parliamentary meeting rooms, participating online in the work.

39.6 Conclusion

The evolution of the Parliamentary Service of Montenegro has been gradual, based as well on the challenges, as on experiences or good practices from other parliamentary administration or its own.

Being most transparent parliament in the region for a number of years, with high openness indicator, we are also perceived by various international organizations as a very efficient representative body. Recognizing the importance of staff development and their welfare, building our capacities has been prioritized in recent years.

The future development and role of the Parliamentary Service will mostly be influenced by couple of factors.

First, the EU accession negotiations gives new momentum in the development process, which will certainly be based on further development of administration, more dynamic, assertive and flexible. Already complex accession process, in light of recent global events, will become even more challenging, and administration will have to put additional effort to keep up with new requests and standards. This implies further development of skills and knowledge of employees, introduction of new practices and simplification of procedures.

Second, in the light of the events of the last year, conclusions will be drawn and incorporated in future work of the Service, especially regarding the alternative ways of work, stressing the importance of already initiated process of the parliament digitalization. We are positive that after the entire situation gets back to normal, many of the innovations will be used in the future as well, giving thus additional incentive to further advancement of the digitalization procedure towards the full digitalization of the Parliament.

Montenegro's Parliamentary Administration

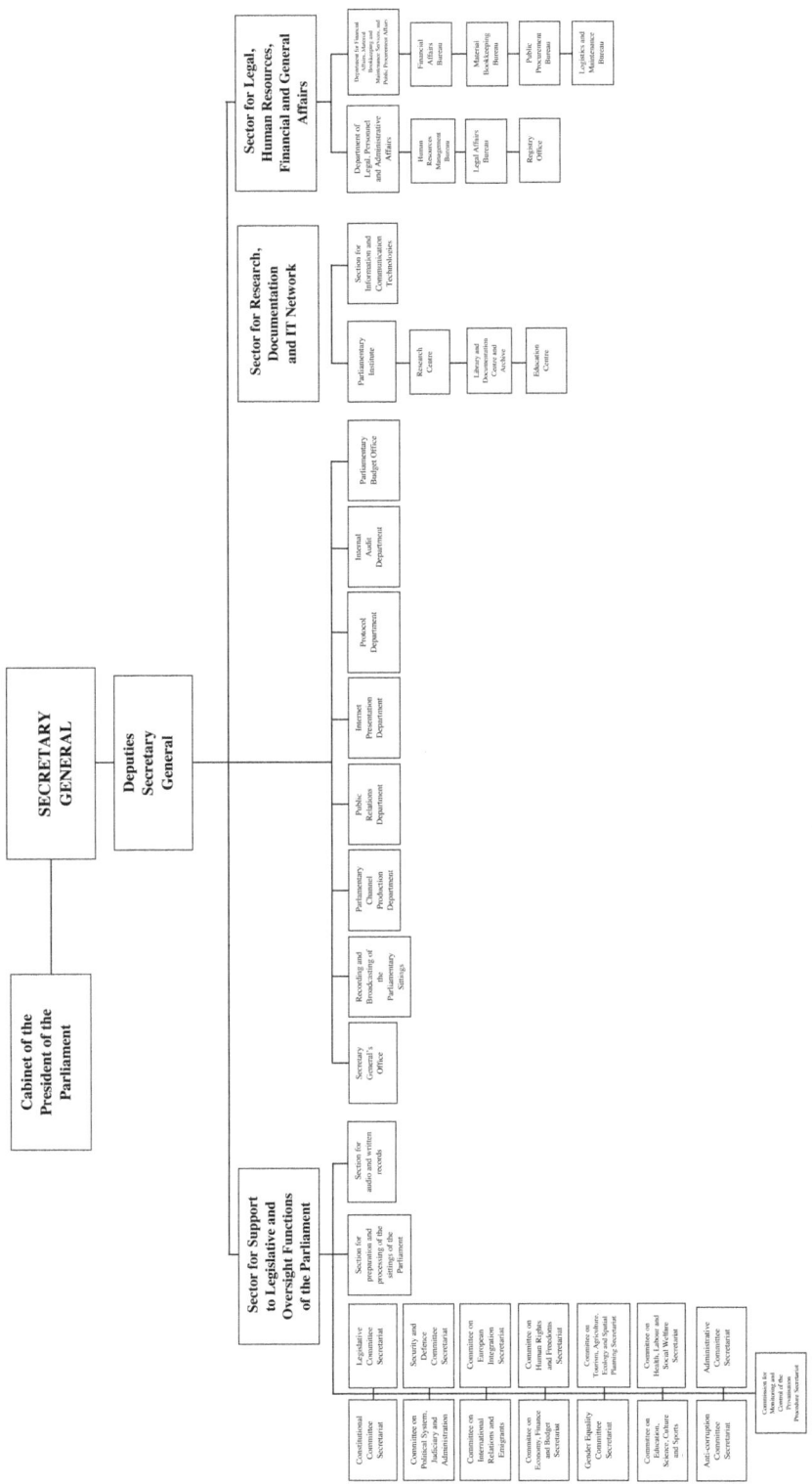

Notes

1 As stated in the Decision on determining remuneration for work of scientific and professional consultants, (2011), the working body of the Parliament may, for a certain period and for a maximum of 120 working days, recruit for its needs scientific and professional consultants from certain fields.
2 The Fellowship Programme for parliamentary staff members at the EP, which is also a key type of training intended for members of parliamentary administrations, is conducted within this programme.

References

Center for Democratic Transition (2019), *Parliament Openness in the Region and Montenegro*, Podgorica: Center for Democratic Transition.
Official Gazette of Montenegro (2007), Constitution of Montenegro, No 1/07, 38/13, Podgorica: Official Gazette of Montenegro.
Official Gazette of Montenegro (2013), Law on Civil Servants and State Employees, No, 39/11, Podgorica: Official Gazette of Montenegro.
Official Gazette of Montenegro (2018a), Law on Civil Servants and State Employees, No 2/18, Podgorica: Official Gazette of Montenegro.
Official Gazette of Montenegro (2018b). Rulebook on the Method of Assessment of Knowledge, Abilities, Competencies, Skills and Criteria and Method of Rating of Candidates During the Assessment of Knowledge, Abilities, Competencies and Skills in recruitment process in the Service of the Parliament of Montenegro, No 81/18, Podgorica, Official Gazette of Montenegro.
Official Gazette of Montenegro (2018c), Rulebook on the Content, Method or Preparation and Adoption of the Program of Professional Training and Development of the Parliamentary Service of Montenegro, No 81/18, Podgorica, Official Gazette of Montenegro.
Parliament of Montenegro (2021), Rulebook on Organisation and Systematization of the Parliamentary Service, No 00-57-2/21-44/7, Podgorica: Parliament of Montenegro.
Parliament of Montenegro (2006), Rules of Procedure of the Parliament of Montenegro, No 51/06, Podgorica: Official Gazette of Montenegro.
The European Commission (2017), *Quality of Public Administration – A Toolbox for Practitioners*, Brussels: The European Commission.
The Inter-Parliamentary Union (2020), *Comparative research paper on parliamentary administration*, Geneva: The Inter-Parliamentary Union.
The Parliament of Montenegro (2016), *Cooperation Agreement between the Parliament and NGOs in Montenegro*, Podgorica: The Parliament of Montenegro.

40
NORTH MACEDONIA'S PARLIAMENTARY ADMINISTRATION

Vlora Rechica

40.1 Introduction

The first Constitution of the independent Republic of North Macedonia was adopted in November 1991, declaring North Macedonia a parliamentary democracy. According to Article 61 of the Constitution, the Assembly (*Sobranie*) of the Republic of North Macedonia is the representative body of the citizens and holder of the legislative power. The Assembly is unicameral, in permanent session, and it is served by the Staff of the Assembly (*Sobraniska sluzhba*). The current Assembly is the successor of the Assembly of the Socialist Republic of Macedonia, which ceased to exist with the breakup of Yugoslavia. For a new democracy, such as North Macedonia, a functional and independent legislative body is crucial for the perseverance of the check and balances system and democracy itself. However, to build a strong legislative body, a broader view of what is necessary to ensure its functionality and independence is needed. While there is an abundance of research focusing on the political functions and role of the Assembly of North Macedonia, there is scarce information on the role of the assembly staff in establishing a strong and independent Assembly. The Members of Parliament (MPs) depend on a competent and impartial staff that supports them in carrying out their work; thus, an autonomous and resilient assembly is frequently accompanied by a strong and independent staff, particularly in the face of external uncertainties, as witnessed recently with the Covid-19 pandemic. This chapter outlines the efforts for the financial and administrative independence of the assembly staff in recent years while also giving an overview of the overall function and organization of the Staff of the Assembly of North Macedonia.

40.2 The Constitutional and Institutional Setting of the Assembly of North Macedonia and the Assembly Staff

North Macedonia gained its independence through a referendum on 8 September, 1991, after the breakup of Yugoslavia, becoming a sovereign parliamentary democracy in its own right ("The Consitution of North Macedonia", 2019). However, due to the name dispute with Greece, the UN General Assembly recognized the country only in 1993, under the provisional name *the Former Yugoslav Republic of Macedonia*. The 28-year name dispute with Greece was a defining factor in the country's democratic development, as its EU and NATO prospects were blocked for almost three decades (Nimetz, 2020). However, in 2019, after nearly three decades of independence, the country finally resolved the name dispute with Greece, changing its official name to the Republic of North Macedonia (Nimetz, 2020). In the meantime, despite outside contestations, democratization efforts were ongoing, including efforts to develop the Assembly's role as an independent body. The Assembly of the Republic of North Macedonia is the representative body of the citizens and holds the legislative power of the Republic. The MPs, elected by a proportional electoral system, have a four-year term, while the Assembly elects the prime minister, head of Government, and holds most executive power. The Assembly and the MPs gain legitimacy in elections by the will of the citizens. It is their duty to determine the political path of the state through the consideration, discussion, and adoption of laws to fulfil the legislative role of the Assembly, as well as to perform its oversight role over the work of the executive and its representative role, which is crucial in a parliamentary democracy.

The Assembly is unicameral, in permanent session, and consists of 120–140 MPs; although, in practice, the Assembly has not numbered more than 123 MPs in 30 years since the independence. The organization and functioning of the Assembly are regulated by the Constitution of the Republic of North Macedonia and the Rules of Procedure of the Assembly. Further, the work of the Assembly is also regulated by the Law on Assembly as well as internal acts and rulebooks. The work of the Assembly is organized into 21 permanent working bodies (committees) and three councils; the Council of the Assembly Channel, the Budget Council of the Assembly, and the National Council for European Integration. The Assembly also has the competency to establish other working bodies, such as the Standing Inquiry Committee for Protection of Civil Liberties and Rights, the Inter-Community Relations Committee, the Women Parliamentarians' Club, and the Interparty Parliamentary Group for the Rights of Persons with Special Abilities. Parliamentary diplomacy is organized into nine delegations to international parliamentary assemblies and other multilateral forums and 46 parliamentary groups for bilateral cooperation. The Assembly, according to the Rules of Procedure, also establishes party parliamentary groups. One parliamentary group comprises at least five MPs that belong to one or more political parties ("Rules of Procedure of the Assembly of the Republic of North Macedonia", 2013). The party parliamentary groups in the Assembly have one assistant per five MPs, and each MP has an office with an assistant in their constituency. The legislative process is supported by information programmes such as e-parliament, e-library, e-legislative archive, electronic communication, and information technology systems. Each MP has a personal office. The administrative work of the Assembly, led by the Secretary-General, is supported by the assembly staff composed of 255 administrative staff as of December 2020 ("Assembly Yearly Report (August–December 2020)", 2021).

The work of the assembly staff is regulated by the Rules of Procedure of the Assembly, the Law on Assembly, the Law on Administrative Servants, the Rulebook on systematization of jobs of the assembly staff, and the Rulebook for the Internal Organization of the Staff of the Assembly. According to the Rulebook for Internal Organization, which the Secretary-General adopts after previous approval from the President of the Assembly, the assembly staff is a set of administrative services that serves the MPs. The staff is organized into one cabinet and 15 sectors, 49 departments within the sectors and the cabinet, one separate organizational unit – Parliamentary Institute (PI), and two separate organizational units as departments. The staff offers expert, technical, and administrative support to the President of the Assembly, vice-presidents of the Assembly, the Assembly working bodies, MPs, and the Secretary-General of the Assembly. The assembly staff also serves all other working bodies formed by the Assembly, such as the Inter-Community Relations Committee.

The staff performs several tasks, according to the Rulebook for Internal Organization, including "professional-administrative tasks, normative-legal, research-analytical, statistical, administrative-supervisory, planning, IT, human resources, material, financial, accounting, informative, auxiliary-technical support and other matters of administrative nature under the competencies of the Assembly" ("Rulebook for the Internal Organization of the Service of the Assembly", 2021). These duties and competencies of the assembly staff generally remained unchanged over the past three decades; though, there have been several significant developments in terms of the technological modernization and independence of the staff throughout the years. These developments are generally supported by the international donor community and CSOs through funds and capacity-building activities. However, as of 2016, with the change of political leadership in the country after the wiretapping scandal (Jakov Marusic, 2017a) and a series of protests (Ozimec, 2016), these processes have significantly shifted towards in-house ownership by the Assembly, mainly influenced by then newly elected Assembly leadership and its reform agenda.

Meanwhile, these recent developments did not go uninterrupted. Both the MPs and assembly staff went through a harrowing day on April 27, 2017, when the Assembly building was stormed by a group of violent protesters, endangering both the lives of the MPs and the staff. The protesters' dissatisfaction, as reported, was caused by the decision of the winning coalition to elect Talat Xhaferi as the first Albanian President of the Assembly since the independence of the country (Jakov Marusic, 2017b). In July 2021, the Criminal Court in Skopje convicted four former senior officials, including the former President of the Assembly, Trajko Veljanovski, of the criminal act "terrorist endangerment of the constitutional order and security"(Dimitrievski, 2021). The Assembly was only able to constitute and continue its work in May of the same year.

The new leadership showed greater commitment to the reform process of the Assembly, both political and technical, which also included several processes and actions aimed at the Staff of the Assembly. In November 2017, the Assembly established a working group to develop the Open Parliament commitments as part of the fourth Open Government Plan, implemented by the Ministry of Information Society and Administration (MISA). Besides MPs, the working group included members of the assembly staff, civil society organizations, and international organizations. The Assembly adopted the first Open Parliament Action Plan in July 2018. This was a first step taken by the new leadership, showing commitment to the reform process of the Assembly.

The reform efforts of the Assembly were laid out in the 2019–2021 Strategic Plan and, more recently, the 2021–2023 Strategic Plan, as well as the 2018 Open Parliament Action Plan. The strategic plans also addressed the administrative and financial independence of the Assembly. The strategic goals, as defined in the 2021–2023 Strategic Plan, are a functional parliamentary democracy, open parliament, proactive parliamentary diplomacy, and *advanced and efficient services and assembly staff* ("Assembly Strategic Plan (2021–2023)", 2021). To achieve an advanced and efficient service and assembly staff, according to the 2021–2023 Strategic Plan, the Assembly must strive for a modern and functional infrastructure; strengthened financial independence and efficient financial management; independent, professional, and efficient parliamentary service, and valued staff; and a safe parliament. These goals require considerable efforts by both the President of the Assembly and the Secretary-General.

The President plays a crucial role in the Assembly, carrying great political importance, as he or she sets the strategic goals of the Assembly in coordination with the Secretary-General and the assembly staff. The President of the Assembly is elected from among the MPs by a majority vote, with a four-year mandate. The President represents the Assembly, convenes the sessions of the Assembly and chairs them, takes care of the implementation of the Rules of Procedure, signs the decrees for the promulgation of laws, and performs other activities determined by the Constitution and the Rules of Procedure. He or she takes care of the coordination of the activities of the Assembly with the President of the Republic and the Government, cooperates with the coordinators of the parliamentary groups, and realizes international cooperation on behalf of the Assembly. The President of the Assembly also monitors the work of the Staff of the Assembly, takes care of the improvement of its work and the creation of conditions for its modern and efficient operation, and entrusts the performance of specific tasks to the Secretary-General of the Assembly.

On the other, the Secretary-General plays a more technical role as head of the assembly staff. The Assembly appoints the Secretary-General of the Assembly upon the proposal of the Committee on Elections and Appointments within the Assembly. The Secretary-General assists the President in preparing and organizing the sessions of the Assembly and performs other activities determined by the Rules of Procedure and the Law on Assembly. The Secretary-General organizes and coordinates the work of the staff and establishes the Council of Assembly Staff as his/her advisory body. The Council prepares a functional analysis, proposes the act for internal organization and systematization of the jobs of the assembly staff, proposes filling vacancies through internal and public calls, etc. The Assembly also appoints one or more deputies of the Secretary-General who assist or replace them during their absence or disability ("Law on Assembly", 2020). According to the Law on Assembly, the Secretary-General of the Assembly, during the employment of the professional staff of the Assembly, observes the principles of adequate and equitable representation at all levels while respecting the criteria of professionalism and competence.

40.2.1 The Assembly Reform Process and Its Effect on the Assembly Staff

The Strategic Plan 2021–2023 defines several activities through which the Assembly intends to reach its strategic goals (see above, Section 40.2). To achieve a *modern and functional infrastructure*, which would ease the workload of the service, the Assembly must create functional and contemporary electronic systems that include a document management system, electronic processing of the documentation material, improved communication, intranet, and Internet, and general advancement of the ICT infrastructure. While some of these activities are purely technical, they are crucial for the smooth day-to-day operation of the assembly staff. Despite the strategic commitment, digitally, the Assembly still faces several challenges, mainly due to the outdated ICT infrastructure. However, the Parliament Support Programme (PSP), a ten-year programme funded by the Swiss Agency for Development and Cooperation (SDC), has announced that the cross-party PSP Steering Council, as PSP's management body, decided to increase the Assembly's transparency and accountability through legislative changes and improved digital access.

To achieve the Assembly's strategic goal for *financial independence and efficient financial management*, it is crucial to strengthen the financial independence of the Assembly through legislative change. To ensure the overall independence of the Assembly from the executive, the Assembly started the process of budgetary and financial independence in 2020. However, the initiative for financial independence required amendments to the Law on Assembly, which were only adopted in July 2021, though with an overwhelming majority. These amendments state that the Assembly decides independently on the use, distribution, and purpose of its funds, including funds concerning the assembly staff. In the meantime, in November 2020, as a sign of good faith, the Ministry of Finance (MF) decided not to amend and introduce changes to the Assembly budget submitted by the Assembly to ensure the Assembly's independence (Vasilevski, 2020). While a step in the right direction, the one-time practice did not substitute the necessity for legislative changes.

According to the amendments, the Assembly's independence is mainly to be secured through the Budget Council of the Assembly, the body currently in charge of the financial needs of the Assembly, while the assembly staff performs the professional-administrative affairs for the Budget Council. The Council also determines the strategic priorities of the Assembly for the next year and their inclusion in the country's budget. It is headed by one of the Assembly's vice-presidents, while the vice-president is the Chairman of the Committee on Finance and Budget and nine members from the ranks of the MPs. While in the past the Council proposed to the Government in cooperation with the MF the maximum amount of funds for the Assembly, with the changes adopted in July 2021, the President of the Budget Council submits the draft budget of the Assembly approved by the Budget Council to the President of the Assembly. The President of the Assembly then submits it to the Government and the MF. The MF incorporates the Draft Budget of the Assembly without changes in the Draft Budget of the Republic, and the Government adopts it without changes as an integral part of the Draft Budget of the Republic, which is then considered and adopted in the Assembly (Assembly of North Macedonia, 2021). Moreover, according to the changes, in the procedure of preparing the amendments of the country's budget, the funds in the submitted Budget of the Assembly cannot be reduced without the consent of the Budget Council of the Assembly (Assembly of North Macedonia, 2021). How these changes will contribute to the Assembly's independence is yet to be seen in the years to come; however, they are a step in the right direction.

According to the Assembly strategic plan, the leadership is also committed to ensuring a safe and secure parliament, which would require changes to the Law on the Assembly. The changes were partially inspired by the April 27th events and require legal reform of the security system in the Assembly, design of security protocols, and modernization of the external infrastructure and perimeter. However, there has been no progress on this matter in the past years.

Lastly, a crucial step towards Assembly independence is *ensuring an independent, professional and efficient parliamentary service and valued staff*. In 2020, the Assembly undertook crucial steps, which considerably contributed to securing Assembly independence. In January 2020, the President of the Assembly and the coordinators of all parliamentary groups in the Assembly proposed several amendments to the Law on Assembly. The specific aim of the proposed amendments was to achieve administrative independence of the assembly staff; however, more broadly, the objective is to contribute to the strengthening of the independence of the Assembly. These amendments to the Law on Assembly were adopted in January 2020, with an overwhelming majority. The following changes were introduced: the arrangement of the internal organization of the service will be created in accordance with a previously prepared functional analysis; the establishment of the Council of Assembly Staff as an advisory body to the Secretary-General, which will have the authority to propose the acts for internal organization and job systematization; the acts for internal organization and systematization on the proposal of the Council of Assembly Staff will be adopted by the Secretary-General upon the approval of the President of the Assembly; financial approval of the annual employment plan will be given by the Budget Council of the Assembly instead of the MF, which will ensure financial independence in terms of this procedure; individual consents for new employments on all grounds will be realized after obtaining financial consent from the President of the Assembly within the funds provided in the Budget for the Assembly instead of the previous individual consents given by the MF; the classification of the levels and titles of the parliamentary officials will be adequately determined, i.e., instead of the codes "UPR"[1] which indicate the bodies of state administration (*Uprava*), they will be renamed to the code "SOB"[2] which refer to the Assembly (*Sobranie*); lastly, the changes foresee cabinet officers and special advisers for the needs of the Secretary-General, in accordance with the Law on Public Employees and the Law on Administrative Servants.

While the changes towards administrative independence of the assembly staff started in 2019, formalized with the amendments on the Law on Assembly in 2020, they were finally enacted in January 2021, when the Assembly adopted the new Acts on internal organization and systematization. These Acts put in motion the long-awaited processes in ensuring that the staff's workflow will run smoothly, without pending approvals from central government institutions such as the MF. However, the processes of professional development and promotions of the assembly staff are still regulated by the general provisions of the Law on Administrative Servants, which regulates the status, classification, employment, promotion, professional development and training, measurement of the effect, and other issues related to the employment of administrative employees ("The Law on Administrative Servants", 2020).

40.3 Organization and Job Systematization of the Assembly Staff

The Rulebook on systematization of jobs of the assembly staff adopted in January 2021 foresees 357 job placements for the staff, distributed by organizational units defined in the Rulebook on Internal Organization. Considering that every employment is dependent on the MF's approval, greater efforts by the Assembly to get support for the proposed staff increase were required. However, with the new changes on the Law on the Assembly, the Secretary-General is only obliged to prepare a draft-annual plan for employment and draft-budget request to submit for approval to the Budget Council, instead of the MF. The effects of this change on the size and structure of the assembly staff are yet to be seen in the coming years. In general, the assembly staff's size has steadily grown since 2003, with a slight increase in 2010 and some minor fluctuations afterwards as seen in Figure 40.1. The

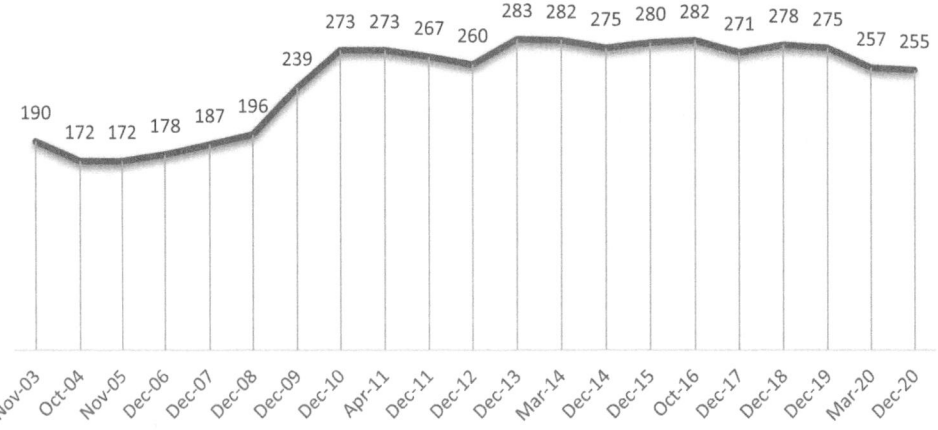

Figure 40.1 The progression of the assembly staff size over the years, North Macedonia

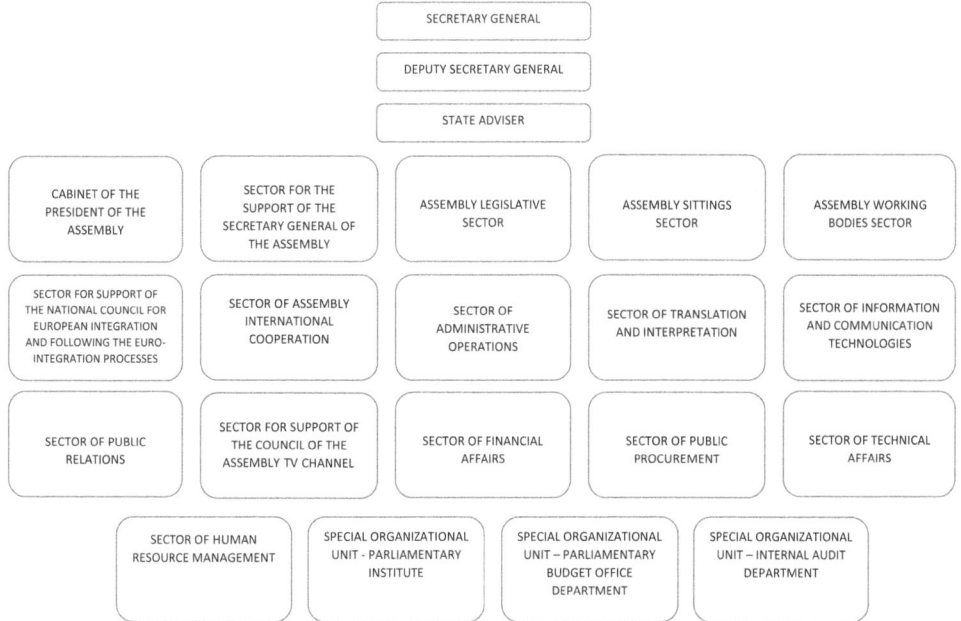

Figure 40.2 Sector for support of the Council of the Assembly TV Channel

sudden increase in staff in 2010 can be partially attributed to the PI establishment as a special organizational unit, which required new hirings.

According to the type, the volume, and the scale of complexity of the working tasks and other conditions required for their completion, the staff is organized in several organizational sectors, such as the Cabinet of President of the Assembly, sectors, departments, special organizational units, and special organizational units as departments. The new organizational structure of the Assembly, as defined in the 2021 Rulebook on systematization of jobs of the assembly staff can be seen in Figure 40.2.

According to Article 40-e of the Law on Assembly, the staff consists of parliamentary servants and auxiliary-technical employees. The parliamentary servants are persons with the status of administrative employees, regulated by the Law on Administrative Servants and the regulations on labour relations. The persons employed in the service who perform auxiliary-technical work do not have the status of administrative employees. Their status is regulated by the provisions of the Law on Public Employees and the labour relations. Moreover, each parliamentary group in the Assembly, depending on the number of MPs and a certain number of independent MPs, has the right to hire an assistant. The assistants are engaged for the duration of the mandate of the MPs based on a working contract concluded by the Secretary-General. The funds for hiring the external collaborators are provided from the funds of the Assembly and international donors.

The professional development and promotion of the service are regulated by the Law on Administrative Servants. Within the Assembly, the Human Resources Management Department performs the activities within the scope of human resource planning and staffing. The Unit for Employment, Promotion, and Development of Human Resources prepares annual employment plans, conducts procedures for public calls, promotion procedures through internal calls, coordination of the evaluation process of staff, evaluation and analysis of the training needs of the employees, and preparation of the annual training plan for the employees, and takes care of the motivation of the employees and conducting surveys for measuring the satisfaction of the staff regarding working condition. Besides the Assembly's annual plan for training, which offers possibilities for professional development, the service is also supported by the Swiss Fellowship Programme, implemented by the Parliamentary Support Programme (PSP). The Fellowship is designed to offer possibilities for obtaining financial support for Master's and Ph.D. studies and courses and training for the assembly staff. The goal of the Fellowship is to increase the quality of work in the Assembly through the increased academic knowledge of the employees.

The involvement of assembly staff in the institution's external relations is regulated by the Rulebook for Internal Organization. While the President holds the highest political function and represents the Assembly to third parties, his or her activities can only be implemented with staff support from the Department for International Cooperation. This department provides the Assembly with information and other materials in the field of international activities of the Assembly and of professional and informative material for the needs of the MPs for the bilateral meetings with the representatives of the parliaments of other countries to the preparation of reports, analyses, and other information materials for the needs of the parliamentary groups for cooperation with the parliaments of individual states and European Parliament. Moreover, the Department for Support of the National Council for European Integration and Monitoring of Euro-integration process, as a special department, provides the Assembly with research, analyses, reports, and information on realized activities of the Assembly in the process of European integration, as well as monitors the process of EU integration of the country.

40.3.1 Special Organizational Unit – The Parliamentary Institute (PI)

In 2010, to support the research capacities of the Assembly, the National Democratic Institute (NDI), with the financial support of SDC, supported the establishment of the PI. The PI was established to strengthen the legislative and supervisory analytical-research capacity of the Assembly. The PI, as a research center, has to provide the MPs with timely, objective, and independent professional research and analysis for the performance of the parliamentary function. The PI is regulated as a special organizational unit by the Law on Assembly and other internal acts. It is divided into two sectors, the Sector for Analysis and Research, which prepares research and analysis at the request of MPs and on its own initiative, and the Sector for Education, Communication and Library, which provides services related to education, specific communication with the public, transparency, and openness of the Assembly and library services. As part of the PI, the Library Unit procures library materials, provides access and use of the library fund, and provides access to electronic databases, among other services. Management and supervision over the work of the PI are performed by a Steering Council composed of the coordinators of the parliamentary groups, the Secretary-General, and other representatives appointed by the President in coordination with the vice-presidents of the Assembly and coordinators of the parliamentary groups. PI submits an annual report on its work to the Steering Council and the President of the Assembly. According to the Rules of Procedure and internal rulebooks of the Assembly, PI also prepares an Annual Plan for Education and Specific Public Communication to support the realization of the strategic priorities of the Assembly.

40.3.2 Special Organizational Department – The Parliamentary Budget Office (PBO)

The Parliamentary Budget Office (PBO) was established with the support of the Westminster Foundation for Democracy (WFD) and the British Embassy in North Macedonia in February 2018. According to WFD, the establishment of the PBO was also recommended by the "Report on the Assessment of Financial Supervision Practices in the Assembly of the Republic of North Macedonia" (WFD, 2020). Following these recommendations, a Memorandum of Understanding was signed in December 2018 among the Assembly, the British Embassy, and the WFD, establishing a Steering Committee for the needs of PBO. In September 2019, the PBO Steering Committee adopted the decision to establish the PBO within the service of the Assembly (WFD, 2020). The PBO is a special organizational unit – a department within the Service of the Assembly, the establishment of which is provided by Article 42-a of the Law on the Assembly, introduced with the legislative changes in January 2020. According to article 42-a, the PBO is a special organizational unit established to improve the parliamentary financial supervision and prepare expert financial and budget analyses for the needs of the MPs and the working bodies.

These financial analyses refer to information materials, briefings, short studies related to the budget, the budget rebalances, and the final account of the country's budget, the annual and other financial reports of the State Audit Office, and other independent bodies established by the Assembly. PBO can also perform different fiscal and monetary policy analyses and prepare financial calculations of policy proposals, and cost-benefit assessments of the draft laws submitted by MPs. PBO monitors the work of the Committee on Finance and Budget, the Budget Council, and other working bodies in the Assembly and prepares analyses and statistical macroeconomic reviews for their needs. PBO can also organize seminars and workshops in fiscal policy related to the financial and budgetary oversight of the Assembly of North Macedonia and exchange information with other parliaments, other state administration institutions, and international financial institutions. PBO's mission is to strengthen constitutionally established legislative and oversight roles of the Assembly by providing timely, impartial, and objective analyses available at the legislature.

40.4 Covid-19 and the Assembly

According to the annual survey of the Institute for democracy (IDSCS) on the perceptions of the citizens on the work of the Assembly, 35% of the surveyed citizens support the online work of the Assembly, while 37% support the online inclusion of MPs who are Covid-19 positive and in self-isolation (Rechica and Jovevska Gjorgjevikj, 2021). However, the opposition in the Assembly did not support the amendments to the Rules of Procedure submitted in December 2020 by the President of the Assembly, which refer to, as stated in the proposal, the realization of the sessions of the Assembly and the working bodies at a distance, that is, online work. With the rejection of this proposal, the Assembly continued its work in person. However, as the majority could not secure a quorum, the Assembly's work was blocked for months. In the meantime, in March 2020, an internal protocol for protection against Covid-19 was adopted, following the recommendations of the Ministry of Health of the Republic of North Macedonia and the World Health Organization. This protocol provided a procedure for entry and movement of employees and MPs in the Assembly, a schedule of disinfection of the premises, installation of automated hand sanitizers, and rotation of employees according to the work tasks and space conditions. In preparation for the constitutive session in August 2020, a working group was formed, which, together with the Institute of Public Health, developed and implemented a detailed protocol for the sessions and the functioning of the Assembly. As of January 2021, all staff has returned to the Assembly premises.

40.5 Gender Equality in the Assembly

The Assembly of North Macedonia is generally male-dominated, both in its leadership and the assembly staff's parity. There has not been a single woman President of the Assembly since the country's independence in 1991. On the other hand, there have been only two women in the position of Secretary-General of the Assembly, with the current Secretary-General serving her second term, becoming the longest serving woman in the position. The last parliamentary mandate, formed after the July 2020 early parliamentary elections, consists of 47 women MPs, out of 120 MPs or 39.1% of the Assembly composition, the highest number of women MPs since independence. While women are represented in higher numbers in the Assembly, only 5 working bodies are headed by women MPs out of 21 working bodies (Parliamentary Institute, 2021). Of the total number of staff, 68.5% are women, while 31.5% are men; on the other hand, 28.8% of the managerial positions are held by men, while women only hold 18.8% of these positions (Parliamentary Institute, 2020). Although women make up the majority of employees in the Assembly, they hold fewer decision-making positions in the staff organizational structure of the Assembly.

40.6 Conclusion

The Assembly of North Macedonia is one of the pillars of the country's developing democracy. However, with a turbulent political scene, the country has had difficulties building and strengthening its democratic institutions, including the Assembly. With the political change in 2016, the Assembly has positioned itself as the country's central legislative, oversight, and representative body. Moreover, with the new changes to the Law on Assembly, greater administrative and financial independence for the assembly staff was secured. These changes enable the assembly staff to perform its duties without constraints by the executive. Although these processes are relatively recent, they are a beacon of hope that the Assembly moves in the right direction. While there are still challenges ahead, such as improving the ICT infrastructure, developing openness and transparency, and the Assembly's complete financial and administrative independence in practice, the Assembly is slowly making progress towards fulfilling its strategic goals.

Notes

1 The code "UPR" stands for "Uprava", which translates to public administration.
2 The code "SOB" stands for "Sobranie", which translates to Assembly.

References

Assembly of North Macedonia, 2021. Draft law amending the Law on the Assembly of the Republic of Macedonia, shortened procedure [WWW Document]. URL https://www.sobranie.mk/materialdetails.nspx?materialId=a716e92d-7626-429a-a24e-422c119b4cda (accessed 7.31.21).
Assembly Strategic Plan (2021–2023) [WWW Document], 2021. URL https://www.sobranie.mk/strateshki-plan-na-sobranieto.nspx (accessed 4.1.21).

Assembly Yearly Report (August–December 2020) [WWW Document], 2021. URL https://www.sobranie.mk/godishen-izveshtaj.nspx (accessed 7.14.21).

Dimitrievski, A., 2021. 25 years in prison for "The April 27th Organizers" [WWW Document]. URL https://360stepeni.mk/25-godini-zatvor-za-organizatorite-na-27-april/ (accessed 7.30.21).

Jakov Marusic, S., 2017a. Macedonia's Wiretap Whistleblower Hails 'Fairytale' Ending. Balk. Insight. URL https://balkaninsight.com/2017/09/01/whistleblower-sheds-light-on-macedonia-wiretapping-scandal-09-01-2017/ (accessed 3.30.21).

Jakov Marusic, S., 2017b. Violence Erupts as Protesters Storm Macedonia Parliament. Balk. Insight. URL https://balkaninsight.com/2017/04/27/macedonia-elects-parliament-speaker-amid-ongoing-tension-04-27-2017-1/ (accessed 4.1.21).

Law on Assembly [WWW Document], 2020. URL https://www.sobranie.mk/zakon-za-sobranieto-na-rm.nspx (accessed 4.1.21).

Nimetz, M., 2020. The Macedonian "Name" Dispute: The Macedonian Question—Resolved? *Natl. Pap.* 48, 205–214. https://doi.org/10.1017/nps.2020.10

Ozimec, K., 2016. Macedonia: "Colorful Revolution" paints raucous rainbow | DW | 21.04.2016 [WWW Document]. DW.COM. URL https://www.dw.com/en/macedonia-colorful-revolution-paints-raucous-rainbow/a-19203365 (accessed 3.30.21).

Parliamentary Institute (2020) 5 November. Available at: shorturl.at/jqvQ2 (accessed:30.3.21).

Parliamentary Institute (2021) 8 March. Available at: shorturl.at/alvI7 (accessed 30.3.21).

Rechica, V., Jovevska Gjorgjevikj, A., 2021. Parliament Watch: Results from the field survey on citizens' perception about the work of the Assembly of Republic of North Macedonia (17 February–10 March 2021). IDSCS. URL https://idscs.org.mk/en/portfolio/parliament-watch-results-from-the-field-survey-on-citizens-perception-about-the-work-of-the-assembly-of-republic-of-north-macedonia-17-february-10-march-2021/ (accessed 7.30.21).

Rulebook for the Internal Organization of the Service of the Assembly [WWW Document], 2021. URL https://www.sobranie.mk/akti-generalen-sekretar.nspx (accessed 4.1.21).

Rules of Procedure of the Assembly of the Republic of North Macedonia [WWW Document], 2013. URL https://www.sobranie.mk/rules-procedures-of-the-assembly-ns_article-rules-of-procedure-of-the-assembly-of-the-republic-of-macedonia-precisten-tekst-2013.nspx (accessed 7.14.21).

The Consitution of North Macedonia [WWW Document], 2019. URL https://www.sobranie.mk/the-constitution-of-the-republic-of-macedonia-ns_article-constitution-of-the-republic-of-north-macedonia.nspx (accessed 4.1.21).

The Law on Administrative Servants [WWW Document], 2020. Minist. Inf. Soc. Adm. URL https://mioa.gov.mk/?q=en/documents/legislation (accessed 4.1.21).

Vasilevski, M., 2020. Minister Besimi officially handed over the Draft Budget for 2021 to the President of the Assembly [WWW Document]. URL https://finance.gov.mk/2020/11/12/%D0%BC%D0%B8%D0%BD%D0%B8%D1%81%D1%82%D0%B5%D1%80%D0%BE%D1%82-%D0%B1%D0%B5%D1%81%D0%B8%D0%BC%D0%B8-%D0%BE%D1%84%D0%B8%D1%86%D0%B8%D1%98%D0%B0%D0%BB%D0%BD%D0%BE-%D0%BC%D1%83-%D0%B3%D0%BE-%D0%B2%D1%80/ (accessed 4.1.21).

WFD, 2020. Parliamentary Budget Office in North Macedonia presents their work and their first analysis to new MPs. Westminst. Found. Democr. WFD. URL https://www.wfd.org/2020/09/21/parliamentary-budget-office-in-north-macedonia-presents-their-work-and-their-first-analysis-to-new-mps/ (accessed 7.30.21).

41
NORWAY'S PARLIAMENTARY ADMINISTRATION

Hilmar Rommetvedt

The aim of this chapter is to analyze the development and current state of the administrative functions of the Norwegian Parliament, the Storting. As we will see, there is a close relationship between the development of the Storting's administration and the parliamentary functions and political activities of the Storting. Consequently, we need to take into consideration both the central, shared administration of the Storting (*Stortingets administrasjon*) and the separate administrations or secretariats of the parliamentary party groups (*gruppesekretariatene*).

In the following, I will give a brief overview of the historical development of the Storting in Section 41.1 and the present organization of the Storting's administration and party group secretariats in Section 41.2. We will then have a closer look at the growing staff resources of the Storting and party groups and see how the growing administrative resources are paralleled by a rising level of activity in the Storting in Section 41.3. We will also see how the Storting has dealt with opportunities and risks associated with digitalization and the Covid-19 pandemic in Section 41.4, before I conclude the study in Section 41.5.

41.1 Historical Developments

The Norwegian Parliament, the Storting, was established by the adoption of the Constitution on 17 May 1814. The Constitution, which is supposed to be the second oldest still existing written constitution in the world, was founded on the principles of sovereignty of the people and separation of powers. Prior to the adoption of the Constitution, Norway had been under Danish rule for 400 years. Denmark had sided with Napoleon, and after his defeat, Denmark accepted to hand over Norway to Sweden. The Norwegians refused, but Norway was forced into a union with Sweden. An amendment to the Constitution was accepted, stating that Norway was 'united with Sweden under one King'. Nevertheless, legislative power should still be exercised by the people through an independent Norwegian Parliament.

Until 1871, the Storting assembled every third year, and for a few weeks only. The administrative tasks were indeed limited. In 1818, the Storting decided to employ an 'archivarius' to handle its documents. The new keeper of the archives became editor of the minutes of the Storting and combined these tasks with his job as a secretary of the Supreme Court.

The Storting's library was officially established in 1871, but the first librarian was not appointed until 1887. In 1857, the Storting decided that verbatim minutes of the deliberations should be issued, and shortly after 14 stenographers were employed by the Storting (Figved 2012:193–195).

The principle of parliamentarianism got its breakthrough in 1884, when the Storting decided that members of the King's Council (the Government) should meet in the Parliament.[1] There is no investiture required by the Constitution. A new government does not need a positive vote of confidence, but it needs to be accepted by the majority of the Storting. In case of a vote of no confidence, the Government (or a single minister) has to resign. General elections are now held every fourth year, and the Storting cannot be dissolved by the Government.

The first political parties, *Venstre* (Liberal Party) and *Høyre* (Conservative Party),[2] were established in 1884, followed by *Arbeiderpartiet* (Labor Party) in 1887. MPs who are appointed government ministers have to leave their seats in Parliament. They are replaced by a substitute representative from their own party and constituency.

On 7 June 1905, after decades of struggles over power between the King in Stockholm and the Storting in Oslo, the Storting declared that the union with Sweden was dissolved. Sweden accepted full independence for Norway. In two referendums, overwhelming majorities decided that Norway should still be a monarchy, and that a Danish prince (married to a British princess) should be installed as King Haakon VII of Norway. Today, the role of the King is purely symbolic.

From 1945 to 1957, the Labor Party won the majority of the seats in the Storting and consequently Norway was governed by single-party majority governments until 1961. In subsequent periods, most of the governments have been single-party minority governments or minority coalitions. Majority coalitions governed from 1965 to 1971 (*Senterpartiet* [Centre Party], Høyre, *Kristelig Folkeparti* [Christian People's Party/Christian Democrats] and Venstre), from 1983 to 1985 (Høyre, Kristelig Folkeparti and Senterpartiet), from 2005 to 2013 (Arbeiderpartiet, Senterpartiet and *Sosialistisk Venstreparti* [Socialist Left Party]), and from 2019 to 2020 (Høyre, Kristelig Folkeparti, Venstre and *Fremskrittspartiet* [Progress Party]).[3]

For a long time, the political and administrative capacity of the Storting was indeed limited. During Labor's single-party majority governments, executive-legislative relations were characterized by executive dominance. Most Norwegian scholars and commentators adhered to the 'decline of parliaments' thesis. In the 1960s, Rokkan (1966:107) claimed that 'The crucial decisions on economic policy are rarely taken in the parties or in parliament'. The 'central arena' was the bargaining table where government authorities met representatives from trade unions, the employers' and farmers' associations. Kvavik (1976:188ff) found that 'parliamentary institutions receive[d] an exceedingly weak evaluation' among interest group representatives. And in the beginning of the 1980s, Hernes (1983:300, 303) described 'the weakening of the parliament' and argued that power had changed 'away from the Storting towards the public administration and interest organizations'.

However, over the last few decades, the Storting has become much more active, less predictable and more influential. No doubt, the Norwegian Parliament has strengthened its position vis-à-vis the executive (Olsen 1983, Rommetvedt 2003, 2017, Grønlie 2014). There are various reasons for this development, such as the minority status of most governments, an increased number of parties represented in the Storting, increased volatility among voters and stronger competition among the parties. Nevertheless, it is difficult to see how the strengthening of the Storting would have been possible without a considerable growth in administrative resources (Section 41.3).

41.2 The Administrations of the Storting and Parliamentary Party Groups

The administration of the Norwegian Parliament comprises two organizational elements: the Storting's (central) administration and the parliamentary party group secretariats.

41.2.1 *The Storting's Administration*

The Storting is a unicameral parliament[4] with a common central administration headed by the Secretary General (*stortingsdirektøren*). She/he acts as secretary to the Presidium (the president and five vice presidents elected among the MPs). The Secretary General is supported by the *Executive Office* which is responsible for secretarial, clerical and administrative tasks, assistance to the members of the Presidium, reception services and press inquiries to the Presidium and Secretary General and the *Strategic Security Team* which provides strategic advice on security and preparedness. The security team was established in 2020 and reflects the increased challenges related to both physical and cyber security (Section 41.4).

The administration is organized in 7 departments with 29 sections, see Figure 41.1. The departments have the following responsibilities[5]:

The *Constitutional Department* deals with all functions associated with the constitutional activities of the Storting, including parliamentary procedures and working plans, the Rules of Procedure, the appropriations regulations and secretarial functions for the plenary. The department includes the secretariat of the standing committees and the respective committee secretaries and provides expert legal services on draft legislation.

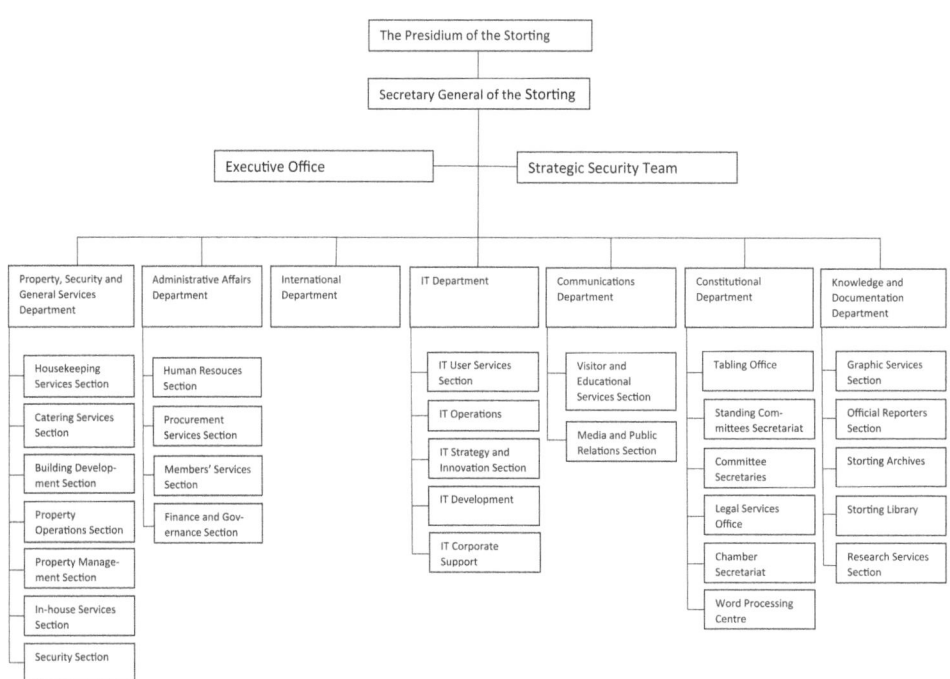

Figure 41.1 Organizational chart of the Norwegian Storting's administration (2019)

Traditionally, foreign affairs is a prerogative of the executive. However, in a globalizing world, foreign and domestic affairs are increasingly intertwined. Like other parliaments, both the Storting and the MPs have become more involved in foreign affairs (Rommetvedt, Zajc & Langhelle 2009). The *International Department* supports the Storting and MPs in all international activities, including practical assistance as well as expert advice on policy and political developments. The department provides services to committees on foreign and European affairs and delegations to inter-parliamentary assemblies and organizations.

The Storting has a modern computer system and the MPs have laptops, tablets and mobile phones at their disposal. The *IT Department* is responsible for IT training and user support and operates, maintains and updates the computer-based information systems and telematics solutions.

The *Communications Department* is responsible for external and in-house communication. The department includes the web editorial unit, and the management of intranet, media and public relations, guided tours, educational services and courses for teachers. The department administers accounts on various social media, and plenary meetings and open committee hearings are televised via the Storting's online TV channel.[6] In addition, the parliamentary party groups employ numerous communications advisors (Section 41.2.2).

The *Knowledge and Documentation Department* is responsible for obtaining and organizing information to assist the work of the Storting and keeping records about the activities. The department includes sections for graphic services and the production of official reports, the Storting's archives and library and a research services section. The latter was established in 1999 and provides expert assistance to individual MPs. It collects and processes factual background material and publishes memos on various topics. However, with 13 employees, the capacity of the research services section is limited, and most of the politically relevant information is collected by the political advisors in the party group secretariats (Section 41.2.2).

The *Property, Security and General Services Department* is responsible for the management and development of the Storting's property, security and service functions. It provides housekeeping and catering services, development and maintenance of buildings, in-house meeting room services and practical arrangements. The main building of the Storting in the center of Oslo was built in the 1860s and enlarged in the 1950s. For many years, several MPs had to share an office with one of their colleagues, but today all MPs have separate offices, and the Storting has a variety of offices and meeting rooms in surrounding buildings at its disposal.

The *Administrative Affairs Department* assists the administrative management in matters relating to employer obligations, human resources administration, finance and governance, general administration and various services to the MPs regarding salaries, allowances, trips, housing, pensions, insurance, working conditions and benefits.

Important elements of the ex post scrutiny and control function of the Storting are delegated to external bodies, including the Office of the Auditor General, the Parliamentary Ombudsman, the Parliamentary Ombudsman for the Armed Forces, the Parliamentary Intelligence Oversight Committee (EOS Committee) and the National Human Rights Institution.[7] These are independent of the Government and its administrative units and report directly to the Storting.

The label Storting's administration indicates that it deals with administrative matters, not politics. Recruitment of personnel to the central administration of the Storting is based on professional criteria. Members of the administrative staff are supposed to be politically neutral. In the 1950s, the secretary of the Standing Committee on Finance was criticized for serving the Labor Party rather than the Storting (Syse 2012), but today MPs and observers generally agree that the employees of the Storting's administration act in non-partisan ways, serving the Parliament as a whole. This is the case even though in her former career, the Secretary General from 2018 to 2022 had held positions as political advisor and state secretary in Labor governments.

However, the Storting is first and foremost a political institution and there is of course no sharp line of separation between administration and politics. Some of the departments and sections take care of what we quite easily may categorize as administrative matters, such as security, IT systems and housekeeping activities. Other departments of the Storting's administration are more closely involved in or related to the democratic and political roles and functions of the Parliament, such as legislation, budgeting, control of the executive and public relations. However, the political aspects of legislation and oversight are first and foremost the responsibility of the MPs and the parliamentary parties. Consequently, we need to take a look into the party group secretariats.

41.2.2 The Parliamentary Party Group Secretariats

Personal assistance to Norwegian MPs is provided by the parliamentary party groups. MPs do not have any individual assistants. The party group secretariats employ a number advisors (*rådgivere*, formerly called *gruppesekretærer* [group secretaries]) who assist MPs in their dealing with political issues. They collect information, prepare committee recommendations, debates and speeches, convey contacts with external institutions and interest groups, and coordinate activities with the extra-parliamentary party organization. The Parliament offers a basic amount of NOK 5.1 million (appr. €0.49 million as of July 2021) to each of the party group secretariats and an additional amount of NOK 834.000 per MP per year. Opposition parties with two or more MPs get an extra NOK 3.2 million per year (2020).[8]

The organizations of the secretariats varies among the parties. In general, the secretariats include political advisors, communications advisors and administrative personnel. The advisors specialize in the policy areas of the various standing committees and assist their party's members of one or more specific committee(s). To illustrate the variations, we may have a quick look at how the largest and one of the smallest parties have organized their secretariates.

The Labor Party, with a total of 48 MPs (2017–2021), is organized and staffed in the following way: the parliamentary leadership and its administration with seven persons, including political advisors to the parliamentary leader and deputy leader, the secretariat's leadership and administration comprising four persons, the communications team with seven communications advisors and the standing committees' factions supported by 27 political and administrative advisors.[9]

The parliamentary secretariat of the Green Party, with only one MP (2017–2021), employs eight persons, including the leader of the secretariat, four political advisors, a head of communications, a press contact and a secretary.[10]

It should be added that not all of the positions mentioned here are full-time employees, but the numbers are the result of a long-time increase in the parties' staff resources.

41.2.3 The Interplay between the Storting's Administration and the Party Group Secretariats

Parliamentary work is centred around specialized committees (Martin 2014, Siefken & Rommetvedt 2021). With a handful of exceptions, the 169 Norwegian MPs are assigned to 1 – and only 1 – of 12 standing committees. Almost all of the matters to be decided by the

Storing are firstly submitted to one of the committees for preparation. The committee will then prepare a report (*innstilling*) with recommendations to the plenary. The report includes (1) a 'technical' abstract (based on a bill or report submitted by the government or an MP), (2) comments supported by the whole committee, a majority of the members or various minorities (factions), (3) the committee's (majority's) concluding recommendation(s) to the plenary, and (4) alternative proposals from various minorities. Debates and voting in the plenary are based on the committee reports. Committee meetings are held in private, while committee hearings are open to the public (and televised).

The work of the standing committees and their members is supported by the Storting's administration and the party group secretariats. The Storting's Constitutional Department includes a joint committee secretariat together with one or two secretaries assigned to each of the committees. The committee secretaries plan and organize the work of the standing committees and provide practical and expert assistance. In addition, the joint committee secretariat arranges committee hearings, organizes committee trips, provides information to the press and general public and gives practical assistance in the day-to-day businesses of the committees.

Traditionally, parliamentary committees are considered to be the 'workhorses' of parliaments. However, recent studies clearly indicate that the real decisions are frequently negotiated and made outside the committees (Siefken & Rommetvedt 2021). In a survey among the Norwegian MPs in 2019, only 21 per cent answered that the real decisions are very or fairly often made in the formal committee meetings. Overall, 80 per cent said that the real decisions are often made in negotiations *outside* the formal committee meetings (Heidar & Rommetvedt 2020:146, Rommetvedt 2021). Compromises are negotiated among committee members from a range of parties that may control a majority of the Storting. The negotiating committee members are supported by political advisors from their party group secretariates. Committee secretaries do not participate, but they process the outcome of the negotiations.

Table 41.1 presents the standing committees and key figures regarding members, secretaries, meetings and recommendations. The numbers of meetings, hearings and recommendations are substantial, while the administrative staff of a total of 26 persons (10 in the joint committee secretariat and 16 in specific committees) is limited.

41.3 Growing Staff Resources and Rising Level of Activity

The number of seats in the Storting has been relatively stable. The number of MPs has increased from 150 prior to 1973 to 169 since 2005 onwards (see Table 41.2). However, over the years, there has been a much stronger growth in the staff resources of the Storting's administration and the party group secretariats. From 1971 to 2020, there was a 13 per cent increase in the number of MPs, while the number of people employed by the Storting's administration and the party groups' secretariats increased by 226 and 778 per cent, respectively! The average number of employees in the party secretariats increased from 4.6 persons per party in 1971 to 22.4 in 2020.

In the 1960s and 1970s, various scholars claimed that the power of the Norwegian Parliament was indeed limited (Section 41.1). However, Olsen (1983:72, 42) found that 'during the last part of the 1970s the Storting became a more rather than a less significant institution'. He suggested 'an ebb-and-flow perspective' on the importance of the Storting. More recent studies clearly demonstrate that Olsen's perspective is still relevant, but it could be added that 'ebb-and-flow' now varies around a much higher 'average sea level' than before. The

Table 41.1 The standing committees of the Norwegian Storting

Standing committee on	Committee members 2017–2021[i]	Committee secretaries 2020	Ordinary meetings per year 2013–2017	Committee hearings per year 2018–2020	Recommendations (reports) per year 2018–2020
Labour and Social Affairs	11–13	1	29	10	30
Energy and Environment	17	1	32	5.5	32.5
Family and Cultural Affairs	11–12	1	33	12.5	27
Finance and Economic Affairs	20	2	24	6	35
Health and Care Services	14–15	1	39	12	38
Justice	11–12	1	23	3	31
Local Government and Public Administration	14–15	1	34	12	39
Scrutiny and Constitutional Affairs	9–10	2	35	5.5	40.5
Business and Industry	15	1	32	14.5	41
Committee on Transport and Communications	15	1	32	4	30
Education and Research	14–15	1	30	7.5	17.5
Foreign Affairs and Defence	16	3[iii]	32	7.5	26.5
Total	172[ii]	16 + 10[iv]	375	100	388

i Changes in the numbers of committee members may occur during the election period.
ii Total number of MPs is 169, but a few MPs from small parties are members of two committees.
iii Two committee secretaries and a senior adviser.
iv A total of 16 assigned to specific committees and 10 in the joint committee secretariat.

Source: Author's compilation of data from www.stortinget.no

government parties suffer defeat in parliamentary voting more frequently, and they accept changes in their proposals after negotiating compromises with one or more opposition parties (Rommetvedt 2017:88, 99). The 'exceedingly weak evaluation' of the Storting reported by Kvavik (1976) has been replaced by much more positive assessments among interest groups, and they increasingly lobby the Storting (Rommetvedt et al. 2013).

The rising level of activity in, and strengthening of, the Storting should be related to the massive growth in staff resources and the subsequent increase in the working capacity of the Storting. The more or less parallel developments shown in the following graphs illustrate the point. Figure 41.2 shows the growth in staff resources, while Figures 41.3–41.5 show the rising levels of selected activities of the Storting.[11]

MPs' questioning of government ministers are mechanisms for agenda setting and control of the executive. The Storting has different types of questioning. For a long time, there was a steady increase in the number of questions, particularly during the ordinary question time where MPs deliver questions in writing and the ministers answer orally the following week. A peak was reached in 1988–1989 with a total of 883 questions, while a decline in

Table 41.2 Parties, MPs and administrative personnel in the Norwegian Storting (selected years)

Year	Parties	MPs	Storting's administration[i]	Party group secretariats	Storting employees per MP	Party employees per MP	Party employees per party	Total employees per MP
1971	5	150	151	23	1.0	0.2	4.6	1.2
1979	6	155	212	41	1.4	0.3	6.8	1.6
1983	7	155	223	50	1.4	0.3	7.1	1.8
1986	6	157	236	46	1.5	0.3	7.7	1.8
1990	7	165	276	59	1.7	0.4	8.4	2.0
1994	8	165	308	79	1.9	0.5	9.9	2.3
1999	8	165	349	109	2.1	0.7	13.6	2.8
2006	7	169	406	176	2.4	1.0	25.1	3.4
2009	7	169	442	184	2.6	1.1	26.3	3.7
2015	8	169	471	185	2.8	1.1	23.1	3.9
2018	9	169	484	186	2.9	1.1	20.7	4.0
2020	9	169	492	202	2.9	1.2	22.4	4.1

i The external bodies presented in Section 41.2.1 are not included in these figures.
Sources: Rommetvedt (2017) and author's compilation of data from www.stortinget.no

the 1990s was followed by a dramatic increase after the introduction of questions to be both asked and answered in writing. An all-time high with a total of 3158 questions was reached in 2019–2020. The party group secretariats assist the MPs in the formulation of questions, and questions and answers are then processed by the Storting's administration.

With help of the party groups' political advisors, MPs may formulate and table private members' bills and proposals. Figure 41.4 shows ups and downs in the numbers, but clearly the long-term trend is upwards. In the 2020–2021 session, the MPs submitted a total of 298 private members' bills and proposals.

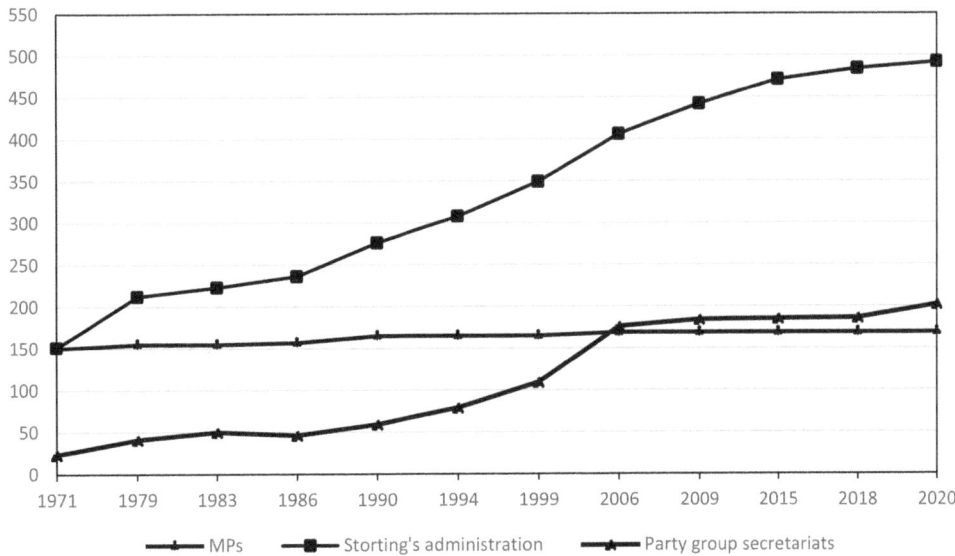

Figure 41.2 MPs and staff resources in the Storting (1971–2020)

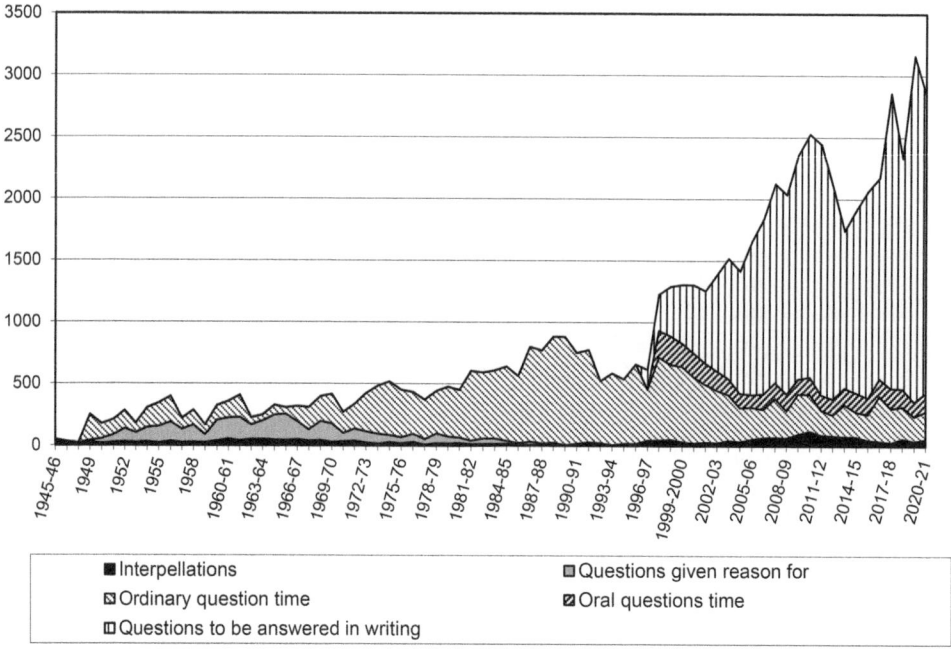

Figure 41.3 Parliamentary questioning by type of questions (1945–2021)

Deliberations and voting in the plenary are based on recommendations from the standing committees. The number of recommendations has been relatively stable over time, but as shown in Figure 41.5, the committees have become more dissensual. The share of recommendations with dissenting remarks and proposals from different committee factions representing one or more parties has increased dramatically.[12] Until the beginning of the

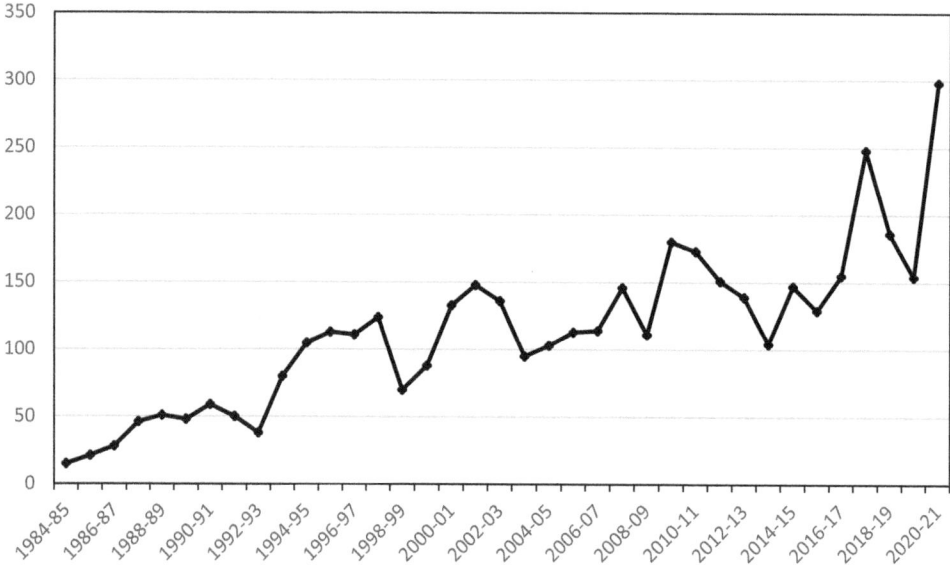

Figure 41.4 Number of private members' bills and proposal submitted (1984–2021)

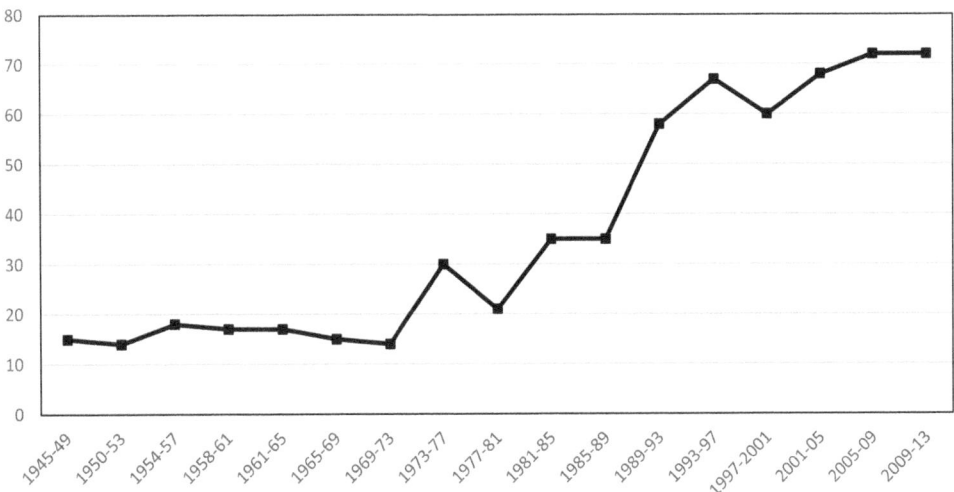

Figure 41.5 Per cent of committee recommendations with dissenting remarks (1945–2013)

1970s, approximately 85 per cent of the reports were unanimous. From 2005 to 2013, only 28 per cent of the recommendations were unanimous. The formulation of alternative proposals and arguments for the numerous dissents nowadays requires a large amount of work. It is difficult to see how this would have been possible without the growing staff resources of the party group secretariats.

41.4 'Viral' Opportunities and Risks

The growing staff resources are crucial factors in the explanation of the rising level of activity and strengthening of the Storting vis-à-vis the executive. However, we should also take into consideration physical and technical factors. Here, I will draw attention to two types of 'viral' opportunities and risks, one related to digitalization and communication 'going viral' through the use of inter- and intranet and social media, the other related to virus in its biological meaning.

For decades, Norwegian MPs had to share an office with a colleague. One can only imagine how the work was disturbed by the other MP's telephone calls or personal visits. According to a story from the 'old days', there were only a few typewriters at the disposal of the MPs, and they were chained to the wall to prevent MPs from running away with them. Today, MPs have separate offices, personal computers, laptops and mobile phones.

No doubt, the working capacity of the individual MPs has increased considerably. This is also the case at the institutional level. As an institution, the Storting has to deal with numerous inquiries from the media, interest groups and individuals and to process enormous amounts of documents such as Government proposals, questions to ministers, committee recommendations, minutes of debates, final resolutions and information to the public through the website, social media and printed matters. Behind the scene, administrative personnel have to operate the IT systems, formulate and format the content, provide training and user support etc. Furthermore, the Storting's communication with the public now relies heavily on digital media. In earlier days, one had to wait a couple of months for the printed minutes of the plenary debates, while now you can watch the debate live on internet and print out the written minutes a few hours later.

Digitalization represents not only an opportunity to increase the working capacity of the Storting and the MPs but also a risk related to electronic 'viruses' and hackers. In 2020 and 2021, the Storting experienced two serious cyberattacks, allegedly from Russia and China. Hackers succeeded to download data from the Parliament and the e-mail accounts of some of the MPs.

Both cyber security and the physical security of the MPs include new challenges to the Storting's administration. The relevance of the two-sided meaning of 'viral' has been demonstrated by the coronavirus and the Covid-19 pandemic. The pandemic represented a big challenge, both politically and administratively. In March 2020, various regulations were implemented by the Storting in order to prevent infections. At first, meetings, travels and visits were stopped, and for a few weeks, only highly necessary and urgent matters were dealt with. It was decided that only 87 of the 169 MPs should meet in the plenary (keeping the political balance). Online committee meetings and hearings were introduced, and to a much larger extent, both MPs and administrative personnel have worked online from their home offices.

Even though the Storting has dealt with a large amount of extraordinary matters related to infection control and economic compensations for the close-down of companies and losses of work, the Storting has managed to perform its parliamentary functions. According to the yearly report from the administration, due to the corona crises, the Storting has strengthened its digital competencies and ability to work online (Stortingets administrasjon 2021:14).

41.5 Conclusion

Up until the late 1970s and early 1980s, the power of the Norwegian Parliament was widely considered to be limited compared to that of the Government. However, from then on, the Storting became more active and influential. Potentially, the passage from one-party majority governments to coalition and minority governments in 1961 strengthened the power of the Parliament. At first, nothing much happened, but from the second half of the 1970s onwards, the level of activity increased. The development gathered momentum, and the influence of the Storting has increased significantly.

It seems quite obvious that the rising level of parliamentary activities and manifestation of power vis-à-vis the executive should be related to the growing staff and technical resources of the Storting. The rising activity and influence reflect an increase in the Storting's working capacity which would not have been possible without the massive increase in the staff resources of the central administration of the Storting and the secretariats of the parliamentary party groups. No doubt, the interplay between the party group secretariats and the central administration is crucial for the political functioning of the Norwegian Storting.

Notes

1 As Nordby (2000) has shown, Norwegian parliamentarism was not fully developed until the beginning of the 20th century.
2 Literally, Venstre and Høyre mean Left and Right.
3 Prime Minister's party listed first.
4 Until 2009, the Storting was a (semi) bicameral parliament with an *Odelsting* (lower house) and a *Lagting* (upper house).
5 https://www.stortinget.no/en/In-English/About-the-Storting/Administration/ Accessed 08.03.2021. See also Brenno et al. (2012) and Østbø (2010).

6 https://www.stortinget.no/no/Hva-skjer-pa-Stortinget/Stortinget-akkurat-na/nett-tv/#storting Accessed 10.03.2021.
7 https://www.stortinget.no/en/In-English/About-the-Storting/Control/ Accessed 08.03.2021.
8 https://www.stortinget.no/no/Stortinget-og-demokratiet/Organene/Partigruppene/Arsregnskap-for-stortingsgruppene/ Accessed 08.03.2021.
9 https://www.arbeiderpartiet.no/om/kontakt-oss/ Accessed 08.03.2021.
10 https://www.mdg.no/kontakt Accessed 08.03.2021.
11 Sources: Rommetvedt (2017) and the author's collection of data from www.stortinget.no.
12 Sources: Norwegian Centre for Research Data (NSD) and Grønlie (2014). Originally, the data were collected by the author of this chapter and later supplemented by NSD and Grønlie with the assistance of Torstein Monsen. See NSD: Fraksjonsmerknadsarkivet, http://www.nsd.uib.no/polsys/index.cfm?urlname=storting&lan=&institusjonsnr=1&arkivnr=7&MenuItem=N1_1&ChildItem=&State=collapse Accessed 27.01.2021.

References

Brenno, B., Grønn, H., Sandgrind, G. & Skjørestad, J. (eds.) (2012). *I Stortingets tjeneste*. Oslo: Stortinget.
Figved, I. L. (2012). Storting og samfunn – informasjons- og dokumentasjonsavdelingen. In Brenno, B., Grønn, H., Sandgrind, G. & Skjørestad, J. (eds.) *I Stortingets tjeneste*. Oslo: Stortinget, 192–200.
Grønlie, T. (2014). Til forsvar for folkestyret. In Narud, H. M., Heidar, K. & Grønlie, T. (eds.) *Stortingets historie 1964-2014*. Bergen: Fagbokforlaget, 21–196.
Heidar, K. & Rommetvedt, H. (2020). Er fagkomiteene eller partigruppene Stortingets «politiske verksteder»? In Bergh, J., Haugsgjerd, A. H. & Karlsen, R. (eds.) *Valg og politikk siden 1945*. Oslo: Cappelen Damm Akademisk, 140–153.
Hernes, G. (1983). *Det moderne Norge 5. Makt og demokrati*. Oslo: Gyldendal.
Kvavik, R. B. (1976). *Interest Groups in Norwegian Politics*. Oslo: Universitetsforlaget.
Martin, S. (2014). Committees. In Martin, S., Saalfeld, T. & Strøm, K. W. (eds.) *The Oxford Handbook of Legislative Studies*. Oxford: Oxford University Press, 352–368.
Nordby, T. (2000). *I politikkens sentrum. Variasjoner i Stortingets makt 1814-2000*. Oslo: Universitetsforlaget.
Olsen, J. P. (1983). *Organized Democracy. Political Institutions in a Welfare State – The Case of Norway*. Oslo: Universitetsforlaget.
Østbø, I. B. (2010). *Storting og regjering*. Oslo: Schibsted.
Rokkan, S. (1966). Norway: numerical democracy and corporate pluralism. In Dahl, R. A. (ed.) *Political Opposition in Western Democracies*. New Haven: Yale University Press, 89–105.
Rommetvedt, H. (2003). *The Rise of the Norwegian Parliament*. London: Frank Cass (now Routledge).
Rommetvedt, H. (2017). *Politikkens allmenngjøring. Stortinget, regjeringen og de organiserte interessene i et nypluralistisk demokrati*. 3rd edition. Bergen: Fagbokforlaget.
Rommetvedt, H. (2021). Norwegian parliamentary committees: split and sidelined in the policy process. In Siefken, S. T. & Rommetvedt, H. (eds.) *Parliamentary Committees in the Policy Process*. London: Routledge.
Rommetvedt, H., Thesen, G., Christiansen, P. M. & Nørgaard, A. S. (2013). Coping with Corporatism in Decline and the Revival of Parliament: Interest Group Lobbyism in Denmark and Norway, 1980-2005. *Comparative Political Studies*, 46 (4), 457–485.
Rommetvedt, H., Zajc, D. & Langhelle, O. (2009). The Internationalisation of National Parliaments: The Norwegian Storting and the Slovene Drzavni zbor. *Politics in Central Europe*, 5 (1), 55–85.
Siefken, S. T. & Rommetvedt, H. (eds.) (2021). *Parliamentary Committees in the Policy Process*. London: Routledge.
Stortingets administrasjon (2021). *Årsrapport 2020*. Oslo: Stortinget.
Syse, C. (2012). Trekk av utenrikskomiteens historie – dens ledere, medlemmer og sekretærer. In Brenno, B., Grønn, H., Sandgrind, G. & Skjørestad, J. (eds.) *I Stortingets tjeneste*. Oslo: Stortinget, 253–274.

42
SERBIA'S PARLIAMENTARY ADMINISTRATION

Davor Jančić

42.1 Introduction

Serbia's unicameral parliament bears the name of National Assembly *(Narodna skupština)* and is composed of 250 members. Its functions and operation are regulated by a multitude of legal acts of legislative and non-legislative nature. While the Constitution, which came into force on 8 November 2006, only regulates the Assembly's status and key functions, the contours of its internal organization are set out in the National Assembly Act of 2010 and thrashed out in the Rules of Procedure and numerous administrative acts.

The political layer of the Assembly is composed of the Speaker, Deputy Speaker(s), Members, Collegium of the National Assembly and working bodies. The working bodies consist of committees and sub-committees as permanent bodies, and committees of enquiry and commissions as temporary bodies.

The administrative layer consists of the Service of the Assembly *(Služba)* and staff working within parliamentary committees and parliamentary groups. The Decision on the Organisation and Operation of the Service of the National Assembly, which the Assembly adopted on 19 April 2018, lays down that the Service ought to perform its tasks in an impartial and politically neutral fashion, a requirement which is also foreseen in Article 5 of the Civil Servants Act of 2006. The Decision also states that the Service espouses the functional principle and operates as a monolithic unit. Although there is therefore no clear formal distinction between central and non-central levels of parliamentary administration, this is to some extent possible to discern on the basis of internal institutional arrangements presented below.

42.2 Key Aspects of the Organization of the Parliamentary Administration

The central administrative services are provided by the said Service, which, excluding external consultants, counts a total of 510 civil servants. It consists of two special bodies – the Cabinet of the Speaker and the Secretariat-General – and four sectors, as described in turn below.

The Cabinet of the Speaker, headed by the Chief of Cabinet, supports the Speaker and Deputy Speaker(s) by: analysing acts under discussion in the Assembly, organizing and coordinating the Speaker's cooperation with other state organs and international organizations, preparing information, expert analyses and opinions for the Speaker's and Deputy Speakers' attention, managing their agendas and organizing meetings and public appearances, preparing the annual workplan of the Assembly, helping with communication with citizens and organization of citizen visits to the Assembly.

The Secretariat-General is composed of a Secretary-General and one or more Deputy Secretary-Generals. These officials are appointed by the Assembly to assist the Speaker and Deputy Speakers in preparing Assembly sessions and to ensure the implementation of the decisions and conclusions of the Assembly. The Secretary-General and her/his deputies are accountable to and can be dismissed by the Assembly. The Secretary-General manages and, with the consent of the competent parliamentary committee, decides the internal organization of the Service, which is tasked with technical and other duties.[1] The security of the Assembly and the keeping of order is ensured by the Ministry of the Interior with the consent of the Secretary-General. As outlined below, within the Secretariat-General there are six departments and an Internal Auditor.

The Department for the Preparation and Processing of Assembly Sessions is charged with preparing and organizing parliamentary sessions, collecting the documents and data needed for these sessions, preparing the acts adopted for publication in the Official Gazette of the Republic of Serbia, preparing the original copies of the acts adopted by the Assembly, formulating MPs' questions, informing MPs of the sessions and other tasks. There is a Shorthand Notes Section within this department.

The Group for the Protection of Confidential Data engages not only in ensuring data protection and handling data access, but it also organizes occasional trainings for MPs and Assembly staff and ensures the implementation of laws relating to defence, the operation of the Assembly during war and emergencies and the fulfilment of tasks set by the state's Defence Plan.

The Library, holding some 60,000 books and periodicals in Serbian and foreign languages, is of a closed type, but access to it can be granted on approval by the Secretary-General. The Library fulfils not only the traditional tasks of creating and maintaining the database for use by MPs and other users, but it also conducts research and produces information and analyses on the Assembly's legislative activity. In this sense, it carries out expert studies and comparative analyses not only for MPs and working bodies of the Assembly, but also for international organizations, other national parliaments and institutions, notably within the European Centre for Parliamentary Research and Documentation, a network of which Serbia is a member. However, in practice, the Library's investigative and research capacity is extremely limited: it only employs six staff, of whom two librarians and four researchers (of whom one is the Library director).

The Public Relations Department is responsible for informing the public of the Assembly's activities, enhancing public relations, cooperating with national and international media, preparing digests of media reports about the work of the Assembly and managing the Assembly's webpage (including updates and translation). To enable traditional press and media coverage, Articles 257 and 258 of the Assembly's Rules of Procedure establish the right of media representatives to freely access plenary and committee sessions. Accredited journalists can also access stenographic notes, draft legislative proposals and other informative or documentary materials of the Assembly.

The Protocol Department is in charge of organizing protocollary affairs. These activities include the preparation of ceremonial events and the organization of international meetings of the Speaker, MPs and Assembly delegations. Another important role concerns communication with diplomatic representatives and officials of international organizations. Within this Department, there is a Section for International Parliamentary Activities. It prepares draft decisions on the sending of MPs and staff on official business trips for the attention of the Speaker and Secretary-General and draws up annual reports on these trips. It also provides logistical support in terms of travel and accommodation arrangements for MPs and staff.

The Group for Education and Presentation of the Assembly's Heritage prepares digital and print versions of educational materials about the Assembly's work and coordinates visitor programmes for citizens as well as for national and foreign delegations to the Assembly. It also organizes visits by Assembly representatives to citizens and devises other means of opening the Assembly up to the public. To increase the publicity of the Assembly's activities and bring them closer to the citizens, Serbian NGO CRTA (Centre for Research, Transparency and Accountability) has implemented the Open Parliament project, which has since 2012 reported on the activities of MPs and the Assembly on a dedicated online portal and Facebook page.

Other than these special bodies, the Service consists of four sectors, which are divided into departments (at least eight employees), sections (at least five employees) and groups (at least three employees).

The Legislation Sector plays a significant role in supporting the Assembly's legislative work. It focuses inter alia on: preparing and processing various kinds of acts and documents for the working bodies; preparing materials for the parliamentary groups; analysing draft legislative proposals, enacted legislation and other general acts; organizing committee meetings; producing reports and issuing expert opinions for the working bodies; drafting and reviewing amendments to bills and other proposals; monitoring the implementation of the working bodies' conclusions; organizing public hearings; providing analyses and information about the initiatives, petitions and proposals of the citizens, associations and organizations. The Sector's five departments perform these tasks by providing direct administrative and technical support to sectoral committees as presented in Table 42.1.

The International Relations Sector shoulders the international and European dimensions of the Assembly's work and is accordingly divided into two departments.

The Foreign Affairs Department supports activities related to international parliamentary cooperation and parliamentary diplomacy, which take the form of the Assembly's participation in the activities of international and regional organizations as well as that of study visits to and from foreign parliamentary institutions. The Department provides MPs with the background papers, information and documents needed. There is also a dedicated Translation and Interpretation Section. The Department directly supports the Foreign Affairs Committee and parliamentary friendship groups.

The European Integration Department supports the harmonization of Serbian law with EU law. It specifically concentrates on evaluating the compliance of draft national legislation with the EU acquis communautaire, preparing relevant concordance tables and comparative analyses of EU law and assessing the grounds for using the expedited legislative procedure. Additionally, the Department engages in communication with relevant EU institutions as well as national parliaments within the EU with a view to enhancing Serbia's EU integration process. The Department directly supports the Assembly's European Integration Committee.

The General Affairs Sector has three departments and two units: the Human Resources Department, the Department for Administrative Affairs, the Department for Budgetary, Financial and Accounting Affairs, the Public Procurement Section and the Legal Affairs Section.

Table 42.1 The Legislation Sector within the National Assembly of Serbia

Department	Committees supported
Department for the Constitutional and Legal System and the Organisation of Government (additionally assists the drafting of the Assembly's budget and deals with MPs' immunity)	The Committee on Constitutional and Legislative Issues; the Committee on the Judiciary, Public Administration and Local Self-Government; the Committee on Human and Minority Rights and Gender Equality; the Committee on Administrative, Budgetary, Mandate and Immunity Issues; and the Committee on the Rights of the Child
Department for Economic and Financial Affairs	The Committee on the Economy, Regional Development, Trade, Tourism and Energy; the Committee on Finance, State Budget and Control of Public Spending; the Committee on Agriculture, Forestry and Water Management; and the Committee on Spatial Planning, Transport, Infrastructure and Telecommunications
Department for Defence and National Affairs	The Committee on Defence and Internal Affairs; the Committee on Diaspora and Serbs in the Region; the Committee on Kosovo and Metohija; and the Committee on Security Services Control
Department for General Social Affairs	The Committee on Education, Science, Technological Development and the Information Society; the Committee on Culture and Information; the Committee on Labour, Social Issues, Social Inclusion and Poverty Reduction; the Committee on Health and Family; and the Committee on Environmental Protection
Department for the Affairs of Parliamentary Groups	9 currently existing parliamentary groups

Source: Own compilation based on the National Assembly website

The Operations and Technical Affairs and Information Technology Sector is composed of the following bodies: the Department for Electronics, Telecommunication and Information Technology, the Department for the Investment-Related Maintenance of Facilities and the Protection and Maintenance of Cultural Property, the Department for Technical and Current Maintenance, the Fire Protection Department and the Copy Office Section.

At non-central administrative level, Article 29(3) of the National Assembly Act requires all parliamentary committees to be assisted by a clerk. Parliamentary groups furthermore have advisers, who have the status of external consultants and are thus not part of the Assembly's Service as such. Article 13 of the Regulations on the Internal Organisation and the Systematisation of Positions within the Service of the National Assembly, adopted by the Secretary-General on 15 March 2019, envisages the appointment of 50 such consultants with differing levels of expertise. They provide crucial expert and administrative support to members of parliamentary groups through the analysis of legislation and bills, preparation of acts which the group wishes to submit to the Assembly, drafting of amendments, advice on the implementation of law, handling of petitions and other requests addressed to the group by citizens, associations and organizations, as well as through the organization of meetings. They are answerable for their work to the head of the parliamentary group and the Secretary-General. Their employment lasts during the existence of a parliamentary group or for the duration of the period for which the Assembly has been elected.

As regards the professionalization and development of functional expertise of civil servants, Articles 10–11 of the Civil Servants Act establish that civil servants have equal rights to progress in their role, which only depends on their performance and the needs of a given state organ. The Assembly has several mechanisms to ensure staff professional development and they are regulated by administrative acts. The Service's Human Resources Department is tasked with monitoring the professional abilities of the civil servants, preparing education and training programmes (e.g. courses, seminars, conferences, roundtables, workshops) and evaluating their outcomes. This department also implements the programme of socialization and mentorship, which is a form of induction process for new staff that usually lasts three to six months, but can, where needed, be extended to a year or longer. Additionally, the education of civil servants is both their right and duty, for which purpose the Secretary-General adopts annual and multiannual plans. In the realization of these plans, the Secretary-General is assisted by a three-member Staff Education Commission. To ensure the provision of professional education and training, the Service not only cooperates with other state institutions, universities, civil society organizations and individual experts but also with the missions of international organizations and EU institutions. The educational offering of the Service is therefore provided both in-house and elsewhere in Serbia and abroad through different study visits.

In addition to these arrangements, Article 27 of the National Assembly Act enables the working bodies to invite experts, scholars and professionals to participate in their work. If more comprehensive input is necessary, the Speaker may, on the request of a working body, commission scientific and expert institutions as well as individual experts to research matters falling within the remit of the Assembly's competence. Importantly, the Assembly can enter into agreements, often in the form of memorandums of understanding, with external organizations aimed at the implementation of joint projects. One such project was agreed in 2009 between the Assembly and the National Democratic Institute, with the support of the United States Agency for International Development. It consisted of the opening of parliamentary constituency offices whose objective was to enhance MPs' direct relations with citizens. There currently exist 34 such offices across Serbia, with some of them serving multiple MPs. Examples of other agreements enabling joint projects include those concluded: with the United Nations Children's Fund (UNICEF) in 2008 on the protection of the rights of the child and adolescents; with the United Nations Development Programme (UNDP) in 2009 on the strengthening of the Assembly's accountability; with the Organisation for Security and Cooperation in Europe (OSCE) in 2010 on the e-Parliament initiative on the electronic management of the legislative procedure; with the Westminster Foundation for Democracy (WFD) in 2011 on the strengthening of legislative and controlling capacities of the Assembly; and with the Swiss Embassy and UNDP in 2012 on the strengthening of the supervisory functions and publicity in the work of the Assembly.

Finally, when it comes to external influence over the Assembly, Serbia adopted the Lobbying Act in 2018 (effective since 13 August 2019). This Act establishes a register of lobbyists which is managed by the Anti-Corruption Agency and imposes financial penalties for violations of the lobbying rules. The penalties range from 50,000 to 2,000,000 dinars (equal to some €425–€17,000 at the time of writing). At the same time, the Corruption Prevention Act of 2019 establishes the principle of independence in the work of public servants and outlaws the different forms of conflict of interests, which are policed by the Anti-Corruption Agency.

42.3 The Role of the Administration in the Context of Parliamentary Work

As demonstrated above, the Service possesses an intricate system of internal administration which foresees extensive assistance to MPs in all aspects of their work, facilitating their performance of legislative, controlling and representative functions. To these ends and within its means, the Service produces documents ranging from research studies generated by the Library's researchers to legal advice, legislative analyses, minutes, reports, background papers, brochures and handbooks for MPs.

In the *legislative* sphere, the Service provides expert and administrative assistance for the conduct of plenary and committee sessions and MPs' meetings with domestic and foreign institutions and stakeholders. It helps to draft bills and maintains an electronic register of the MPs' presence in sessions and votes. The Legislative Sector, the Library and the International Relations Department are the bodies most closely involved with impact assessments in terms of ex ante and ex post analysis and review of legislation and legislative proposals. This is important because Article 151 of the Assembly's Rules of Procedure requires legislative proposals to be accompanied by an explanation. In legislative practice, this explanation takes the form of a questionnaire and furnishes an extensive analysis of the reasons for legislating (including consideration of the status quo) and of the legal and financial impacts of the proposed legislation, illustrated by quantitative and qualitative indicators and by an analysis of the legal solutions drawn from comparative law. Apart from general legislation, an important segment of the Secretariat-General's work concerns enabling access to information of public interest and monitoring the application of anti-corruption and gender equality laws.

With respect to the Assembly's role of *democratic control*, the Service provides MPs with any information that they may request to enable them to exercise this function effectively. The Shorthand Notes Section of the Secretariat-General plays a notable facilitating role in one further respect. Its staff help to formulate MPs' questions to the Government and ensure that any unanswered questions are sent to the relevant Ministry for reply within 8 days but no later than 30 days. They also process MPs' requests for information and explanation and submit them to relevant state institutions for reply within 15 days.

Regarding *budgeting*, the Secretary-General, as the manager of the Service, has budgetary functions to the extent that she/he prepares a draft of the Assembly's budget, which itself forms part of the overall state budget. As an illustration, Article 8 of the Budget of the Republic of Serbia for 2021 Act allocates, for the stated year, a total of 2,254,927,000 dinars to the Assembly (equal to some €19 million at the time of writing). Control over the Assembly's budget is performed by its Internal Auditor who is accountable to the Secretary-General. The Secretary-General is also responsible for the lawful management of the Assembly's property and is in charge of authorizing the Assembly's expenditures.

Regarding the Assembly's relations with the *media*, the National Assembly Act establishes the principle of publicity, whose practical implementation is the remit of the abovementioned Public Relations Department.

42.4 Managing Interinstitutional and External Relations

When it comes to interinstitutional relations, the Service directly cooperates with other state organs and organizations as necessary for its work, ensures the mutual exchange of information and data, and may to these ends set up joint expert bodies.

The Assembly's international cooperation is expressly foreseen in Articles 59–61 of the National Assembly Act. The objectives are set very widely and seek to preserve and promote peace, good neighbourly relations and cooperation based on the equality of all the nations and countries of the world. The various forms of parliamentary diplomacy envisaged by this statute explicitly encompass multilateral and bilateral cooperation. These particularly include: the creation and dispatch of standing delegations to parliamentary assemblies of international organizations and, where relevant, international organizations as such; MPs' participation in international meetings and conferences; interparliamentary dialogue and cooperation with the European Parliament (EP); engagement in joint projects with the representative institutions of third countries, parliamentary assemblies and international organizations; bilateral parliamentary relations through outgoing visits by the Speaker, delegations of individual MPs to national parliaments of third countries and the latter's incoming visits; mutual exchange of information, materials and publications with parliamentary counterparts; and the establishment of parliamentary friendship groups.

The Assembly has both standing and ad hoc delegations for international relations. While the composition of the standing delegations is decided by the Assembly, that of ad hoc delegations provides more flexibility. Under Articles 290–291 of the Assembly's Rules of Procedure, decisions on visit initiatives and on the composition of Assembly delegations for meetings with representatives of foreign legislative and executive institutions is made by the Foreign Affairs Committee, or by the Speaker if the Committee cannot reach a decision. It is furthermore explicitly foreseen that MPs, acting as Assembly delegation members, may participate in the regular and special sessions of the United Nations and its specialized bodies, agencies and international conferences, as well as other sessions of international organizations. Cooperation with the United Nations can yield tangible results. For instance, the aforesaid 2008 joint project with UNICEF led to the establishment of a Working Group on the Rights of the Child in the Assembly in 2009, which was then upgraded to the status of a parliamentary committee in 2010. This is a significant development because, as at December 2022, the Committee on the Rights of the Child is the largest parliamentary committee in the Assembly, counting 30 members, while all other committees count 17 members (15 committees), 16 members (three committees) or nine members (one committee).

When it comes to the establishment of Assembly delegations, Article 26 of the Rules of Procedure states that they are appointed on the proposal of the Speaker, acting in consultation with delegation heads and taking into account the proportional representation of political parties and genders. Importantly, delegations receive all-round support from an advisor in the Assembly's Foreign Affairs Department, who organizes their travel, prepares their documentation and attends all their meetings abroad if she/he accompanies the delegation. The advisor then drafts a report on the visit and, following potential revisions based on delegation members' comments, submits it to the Foreign Affairs Committee for adoption. To further inform the work of delegations, in 2012, the Assembly published a handbook for MPs which explains the functioning of various international parliamentary institutions (IPIs) and offers recommendations on the best practice that could be followed by delegation members. As at December 2022, the Assembly has 11 standing delegations as presented in Table 42.2, while the ad hoc ones are formed on request depending on the needs of the proposed incoming or outgoing parliamentary visit.

When it comes to friendship groups, the right to establish them is explicitly foreseen in Article 61 of the National Assembly Act. Their role is to facilitate bilateral international

Table.42.2 Serbian National Assembly delegations to international parliamentary institutions

Name of IPI	Year of establishment of IPI	Year of Assembly's affiliation	Type of affiliation	Number of delegation members
The Parliamentary Assembly of the Council of Europe (PACE)	1949	2003	Full member	14
Parliamentary Assembly of the Mediterranean	2006	2006	Full member	10
Parliamentary Dimension of the Central European Initiative	1993	2001	Full member	10
Inter-Parliamentary Union (IPU)	1889	1891	Full member	9
NATO Parliamentary Assembly	1955	2007	Associate member	10
OSCE Parliamentary Assembly	1990	2001[2]	Full member	8
South East European Cooperation Process Parliamentary Assembly	2014	2014	Full member	8
Parliamentary Assembly of the Black Sea Economic Cooperation (PABSEC)	1993	2004	Full member	6
Parliamentary Assembly of the Collective Security Treaty Organization	2006	2013	Observer	5
Assemblée parlementaire de la Francophonie	1967	2008	Observer	4
Interparliamentary Assembly on Orthodoxy	1993	1995	Full member	2

Source: Own compilation based on data drawn from the National Assembly website and the websites of the IPIs mentioned

relations of the Assembly with a given country. The Foreign Affairs Committee decides about the creation of friendship groups, appoints their heads and members and approves exchanges with friendship groups of third country parliaments. Membership of friendship groups is voluntary. As at December 2022, there are 161 friendship groups in the Assembly.

Among the Assembly's bilateral international relations, the EP is particularly important given Serbia's status as an EU candidate country with a Stabilization and Association Agreement, which entered into force in 2013. The importance of this status lies in increased contacts between the Assembly and the EP, which inter alia take the form of: (a) discussions between the EP and the Assembly within EU-Serbia Stabilization and Association Parliamentary Committee; (b) opportunities for members of the Assembly's Service, since 2013, to undertake traineeships in the EP; and (c) the Inter-Party Dialogue which has since October 2019 focused on fostering consensus across political parties in Serbia in order to improve the level playing field in parliamentary elections.

42.5 Managing Current Challenges Facing the Parliamentary Administration

Among the key contemporary challenges facing the Assembly and its Service have been digitalization and the handling of the Covid-19 pandemic.

In relation to *digitalization*, the Assembly maintains an effective institutional website and ensures the online availability of the recordings and live streams of plenary sessions and committee meetings. It also embraces digital platforms and maintains Facebook, YouTube and Twitter accounts. The Assembly's presence profited in 2016 from a UNDP-sponsored strategy for social media presence tailored specifically to the needs of greater parliamentary engagement with the public (UNDP Serbia 2016), as well as from a short seven-page guide on digital political communication, prepared by WFD in December 2020. The theme of digitalization is also reflected in the Assembly's organizational structure. On 9 December 2020, a Sub-Committee on the Information Society and Digitalisation was created within the Committee on Education, Science, Technological Development and the Information Society. A public hearing on digitalization organized by this Sub-Committee in February 2021 highlighted its importance, among other things, in the post-Covid period. Indeed, the use of digital technologies has been one of the reasons why Serbia has excelled at vaccination rollout (Minevich 2021; The Economist 2021). To further address pressing digital challenges, on 30 March 2021, the Assembly inaugurated within its midst an informal Parliamentary Network on Digital Security composed of 17 MPs. The Network, which has a dedicated Instagram account, aims to place significant focus on the online safety of children. The workplan of these Assembly bodies goes hand in hand with the UN General comment no. 25 (2021) on children's rights in relation to the digital environment, adopted on 2 March 2021. In more general terms, the Assembly, and especially its Service, actively cooperate with the Government's Office for IT and e-Government. Since February 2021, a telehousing agreement with the state's data centre has been in place to ensure safe storage and access to parliamentary data.

Regarding the *Covid-19 pandemic*, its key impact was the declaration of the state of emergency on 15 March 2020 by a joint decision of the President, Prime Minister and Speaker of the Assembly. As a consequence, the Assembly was suspended and no online sittings were organized. Only 44 days after this did parliamentary sittings resume and did so in person and involved temperature measurements on entry to the Assembly building and the use of masks, gloves and plexiglass screens. These measures were agreed virtually among the Speaker, Deputy Speakers, heads of parliamentary groups and the Assembly's Secretariat (Radojević and Stanković 2020: 4). The state of emergency was lifted on 6 May 2020, 54 days after its introduction. The suspension has been criticized for preventing the Assembly from scrutinizing the Government and for reducing the Assembly's role to rubberstamping Government regulations (Krstić and Davinić 2021). However, the Constitutional Court decided on 21 May 2020 that the declaration of the state of emergency did not violate the Constitution. At the same time, the EP held in a resolution that the suspension undermined the Assembly's position as the key institution of parliamentary democracy (EP 2021: point 38). This was followed by a letter which 21 MEPs sent to the Neighbourhood and Enlargement Commissioner, Olivér Várhelyi, underlining their concern about the "extremely serious" constitutional and human rights situation caused by the measures implemented during the state of emergency (European Western Balkans 2020). Yet, as things began to normalize, the Assembly responded to Covid-19 with internal reforms. On 2 February 2021, a temporary Sub-Committee on Covid-19[3] was established within the Committee on Health and

Family. In the three meetings that it held during its existence, this Sub-Committee followed information on the different variants of the virus, transmission and infection rates, vaccine efficiency and the progress of vaccination, while keeping abreast of some of the foreign parliamentary debates on the coronavirus.

Other than structure and working practices, Covid-19 also caused elections to national, provincial and local assemblies to be postponed from the initially planned date of 26 April 2020 to 21 June 2020. Furthermore, Covid-19 impacted the Assembly's relations with the citizens. To wit, citizen visits to the Assembly have fluctuated between 7000 and 11,000 in the period 2008–2020, but, unsurprisingly, dropped to a little over 1200 in 2020.

42.6 Conclusion

The foregoing review of the legal and practical arrangements for the administrative organization of Serbia's National Assembly paints a mixed picture, which is best encapsulated by the chasm between the institution's *de jure* and *de facto* operation (Tepavac 2019: 40).

As *positive aspects*, two important characteristics stand out. The first is the existence of a good legal framework for the organization of the administrative structures and activities of the Assembly. A series of legal acts provide often minute detail on the procedures applicable to the institutional mechanics and the expected operation of the Assembly's Service. The second is formal institutional agility and responsiveness. The swift creation of different institutional bodies and the implementation of various democracy-related projects are praiseworthy. An example of this legal and institutional entrepreneurship is that the digitalization and Covid-19 measures taken by the Assembly correspond to some of the policy recommendations on legislative leadership in the pandemic provided by the WFD (Gordon and Cheeseman 2021: 27–28).

The key *negative aspects* are rooted in the insufficient practical implementation of the otherwise solid legal framework as well as poor political culture, which comparative analyses demonstrate to be strongly mutually interlinked (Verrier 2007). Both the European Commission and the EP have voiced concerns about the functioning of Serbia's parliament and democracy in general. The shortcomings identified include the absence of a viable opposition, the quality of the legislative process (e.g. the frequent use of urgent procedures, filibustering, the use of inflammatory language against political opponents), transparency issues (Djurbabić 2013), the ineffectiveness of political oversight over the Government and the need for better cooperation with independent regulatory bodies (European Commission 2020: 4; EP 2021). Similarly, the EP highlighted that some MPs' use of abusive language, intimidation and slander in plenary debates amount to a "breach of democratic practice and fundamental democratic values" (EP 2021: point 39). It is not surprising that MPs speaking in the plenary have been compared to "gladiators in the arena" (Orlović 2012: 39), focused not on public policy but on battling their political opponents. The misuse of public sessions of the Assembly for politicians' personal and political purposes is part of a wider systemic problem, which has rightly been assessed as "irreversibly degrading" this institution's democratic credentials (Slavujević 2013: 68). These problems have been brought to the fore by the pandemic-propelled restrictions on personal and democratic freedoms in Serbia and the wider region of the Western Balkans, which have been questioned for their proportionality and vulnerability to executive power accumulation and state capture of the media (Bieber et al. 2020).

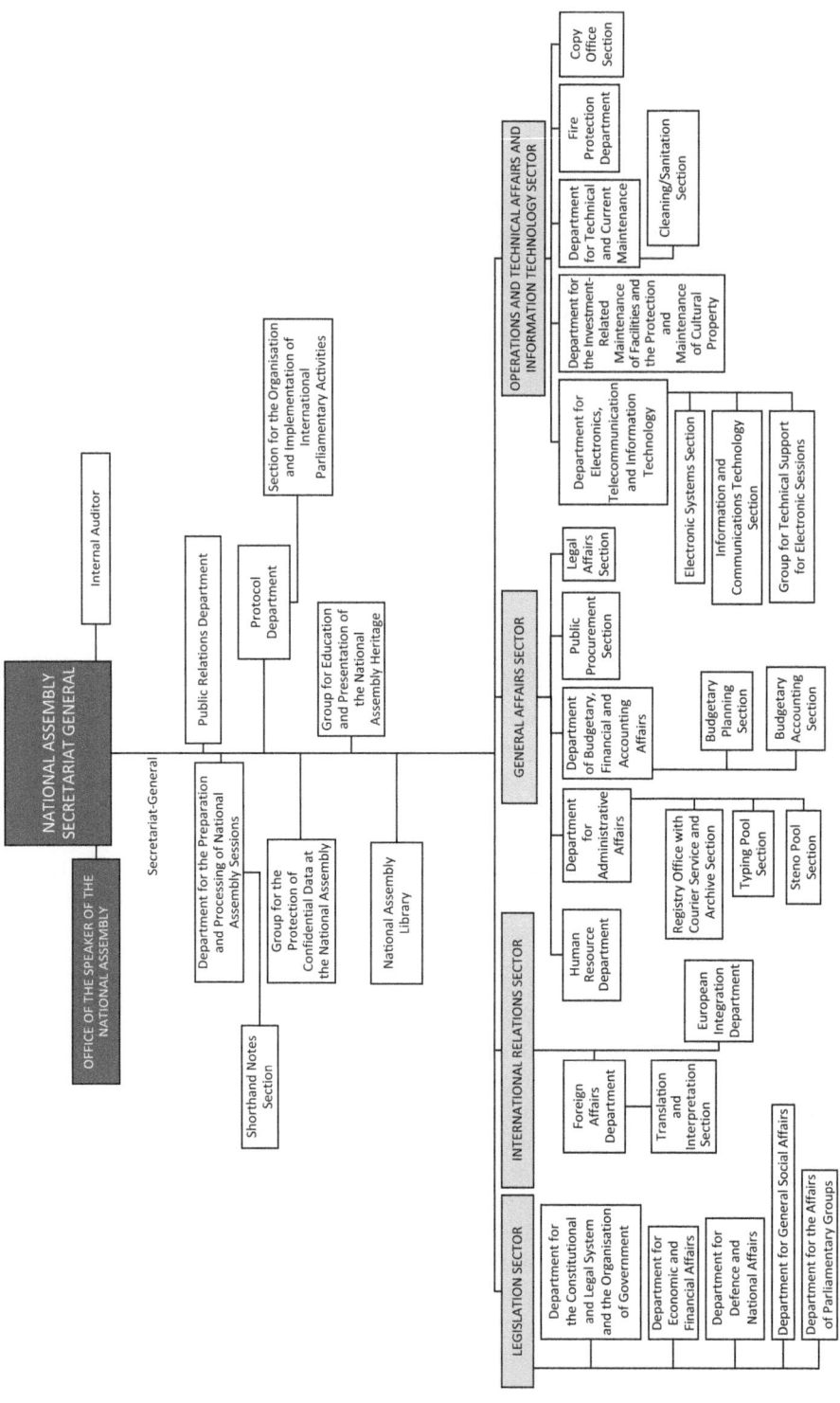

Finally, the administrative apparatus of the Serbian National Assembly has been described as "often the most competent and most operative part of parliamentary process" (Orlović 2012: 36). As such, a stronger and better resourced Service could gradually help to improve the substantive quality of legislation. Nonetheless, it appears acutely ill-equipped to address the widespread cultural deficiencies that continue to plague the Assembly's democratic functioning. The latter will require deeper social and economic reforms if they are to yield tangible political dividends.

Notes

1 Duties related to transportation, maintenance, servicing and garaging of vehicles and catering services are performed by the Directorate for Common Administrative Services of the State Institutions, which is external to the Assembly and is established by the Government.
2 After participating in the first, constitutive meeting of OSCE PA in 1991, due to the sanctions imposed on Serbia, the Assembly only resumed membership in 2001.
3 Its full name is the Sub-Committee for Monitoring the Epidemiological Situation due to the Presence of the Infectious Disease Covid-19.

References

Bieber, Florian et al., 'The Western Balkans in Times of the Global Pandemic', *BiEPAG (Balkans in Europe Policy Advisory Group) Policy Brief*, April 2020.

Djurbabić, Jovana, 'Transparentnost i otvorenost Narodne skupštine Republike Srbije [Transparency and Openness of the National Assembly of the Republic of Serbia]', in Slaviša Orlović (ed.), *Iskušenja Parlamentarizma [The Challenges of Parliamentarism]* (Friedrich Ebert Stiftung and the Centre for Democracy of the Faculty of Political Sciences of the University of Belgrade, 2013), 167–175.

European Commission, "Serbia 2020 Report' Accompanying the '2020 Communication on EU Enlargement Policy", SWD(2020) 352 final, 6 October 2020.

European Parliament, 'Resolution of 25 March 2021 on the 2019-2020 Commission Reports on Serbia, doc. no. P9_TA(2021)0115'.

European Western Balkans, 'MEPs Warn Várhelyi of Serious Situation in Serbia in Regard to Human Rights', 16 April 2020, available at https://europeanwesternbalkans.com/2020/04/16/meps-warn-varhelyi-of-serious-situation-in-serbia-in-regard-to-human-rights, accessed on 25 April 2021.

Gordon, Rebecca and Nic Cheeseman, 'Legislative Leadership in the Time of Covid-19', *WFD Report*, January 2021.

Krstić, Ivana and Marko Davinić, 'Serbia: Legal Response to Covid-19', in Jeff King and Octávio LM Ferraz et al. (eds), *The Oxford Compendium of National Legal Responses to Covid-19* (Oxford University Press, 2021), doi: 10.1093/law-occ19/e7.013.7.

Minevich, Mark, 'Serbia and Key International Sovereigns Lead with Data and AI to Become Vaccination Champions', *The Forbes*, 5 February 2021.

Orlović, Slaviša. 'Constitutional, Political and Institutional Framework of the National Assembly of the Republic of Serbia', in Slaviša Orlović (ed.), *Comparative Analysis of Democratic Performances of the Parliaments of Serbia, Bosnia and Herzegovina and Montenegro* (The Centre for Democracy of the Faculty of Political Sciences of the University of Belgrade, Sarajevo Open Centre, and the Faculty of Political Science of the University of Montenegro, 2012), 17–46.

Radojević, Ivan and Nevenka Stanković, 'The Parliamentary Response to Covid-19 and States of Emergency in the Western Balkans', *WFD Report*, July 2020.

'Serbia Is Outpacing Nearly Every Country in the EU at Vaccination', *The Economist*, 3 April 2021.

Slavujević, Zoran Dj, 'Javnost rada parlamenta kao sredstvo promocije partija i političara [The Publicity of Parliamentary Work as a Means of Promoting Parties and Politicians]', in Slaviša Orlović (ed.), *Iskušenja Parlamentarizma [The Challenges of Parliamentarism]* (Friedrich Ebert Stiftung and the Centre for Democracy of the Faculty of Political Sciences of the University of Belgrade, 2013), 61–69.

Tepavac, Tara, *'Narodna skupština Republike Srbije: hram ili paravan demokratije? [The National Assembly of the Republic of Serbia: The Temple or Smokescreen of Democracy?]'*, Working paper prepared for the conference on 'Civil Society for Accountable Governance' held on 4-5 February 2019 in Belgrade.

UNDP Serbia, 'Strategy of National Assembly for Building and Sustaining Public Engagement Using Social Media', May 2016.

Verrier, June, 'Benchmarking Parliamentary Administration: the United Kingdom, Canada, New Zealand and Australia', (2007) 22(1) *Australasian Parliamentary Review* 45–75.

43

SWITZERLAND'S PARLIAMENTARY ADMINISTRATION

Andreas Ladner

43.1 Characteristics of the Swiss Parliament

For a better understanding of the role and functioning of the parliamentary administration in Switzerland, it is vital to have a short glance at the Swiss political system (see also Linder/Muller 2017) and its parliament, which differs in several aspects from the parliaments in other countries.[1]

The Parliament was created in 1848 with the creation of Switzerland as a democratic, federalist nation-state. It consists of the National Council, in which the cantons are represented according to their population, and which today has 200 seats, and the Council of States, which was created following the US American model, and in which the 20 cantons are represented with 2 seats and the 6 former half-cantons with 1 seat, resulting in a total of 46 seats. The National Council is usually referred to as the council of the people (applying the principle of democracy with one person, one vote), whereas the Council of States is referred to as the federalist chamber (one canton, two seats) representing the interest of the cantons.

Swiss bicameralism can be considered strong, symmetrical, giving basically the same power and competences to each chamber, and incongruent, with the National Council elected in a PR-system following national legislation, and the members of the Council of States, elected mainly in a majority system based on cantonal rules. Both chambers together are called the Federal Assembly. They are located in the same building in Berne and hold their sessions during the same periods of the year.

The Swiss system of government is neither fully parliamentary nor fully presidential but rather constitutes a hybrid model. The parliament elects the government – the seven-member Federal Council – which remains in office for the entire legislative term. New elections for political reasons are not intended during this period even if the Federal Council does not manage to obtain a majority in parliament for its policies or loses a popular vote.

The seven members of the Federal Council represent the main parties in the National Assembly (multiparty government), yet these governing parties are not linked to each other by a coalition agreement. Each member of government heads a department, but important decisions are taken jointly. If the government needs to receive the support of the two houses of parliament for its policies and projects, it must agree on a bill that finds a majority in parliament (consensus democracy). These majorities may change depending on the bill (variable geometry). Accordingly, party frontlines in parliament change and it is not always the same parties confronting each other.

Elected members of parliament are generally honorary or part-time politicians ("Milizsystem"). The idea behind this is that politics should not be entrusted to a group of professional elites, but that those elected are also active in other areas of life and professions, bringing their knowledge and experience into the political process. However, the advantage of proximity to citizens and to concrete real-life problem situations is confronted with the risk of hidden lobbying or preferential treatment for one's own professional sector. As a consequence, elected members may no longer represent the interests of their voters. Nowadays, the "Milizsystem" also reaches its limits – at least at the national level – because of the increasing time and professional knowledge demanded by parliamentary work. In the 2020s, one is more inclined to consider the two houses as a semi-professional parliament. What remains, however, is a less than professional organization in which not only the elected members of parliament but also the political parties lack the resources required for the diligent scrutiny of legislative proposals and other initiatives.

43.2 Origin and Development of the Swiss Parliamentary Administration

The formation and development of parliamentary administration is remarkable for its steadily growing scope and the increasing independence from the government and the executive administration.

In its early days, in 1848, the Federal Chancellery also handled the Federal Assembly's chancery business. The ongoing increase in federal tasks and the concomitant expansion of the federal administration led to a situation in which the share of the Federal Chancellery's activities for the Federal Council grew ever larger and its function for the Federal Assembly became secondary (Graf 2002: 536). In the first half of the 20th century, the Secretariat of the Federal Assembly was created, which was later supplemented by other services.

With the revision of the Federal Act on the Organization of the Federal Chancellery of 1919, a secretary was assigned to the Federal Chancellery for the taking of minutes in the Councils and their commissions. In the National Council, this task was performed by two part-time secretaries whose main occupation was journalism, while in the Council of States, the vice chancellor remained responsible for it. In 1934, the taking of minutes in the National Council reverted to the Chancellor or one of his deputies. In the 1950s, the Secretariat of the Federal Assembly increasingly performed advisory functions for the Presidents of the Councils and the members of the Councils independently of the Federal Chancellor (Stengel 1977: 46 ff.).

Additionally, the Federal Assembly's had its own services formed outside the Federal Chancellery with the permanent secretaries of the Finance Committee and the Delegation of the Finance Committee. Although the Parliamentary services were technically subordinate to the Federal Assembly and its organs, they remained administratively assigned to the Federal Chancellery. It was not until the Federal Constitution of 1999 that the Parliamentary services were completely, also administratively, separated from the Federal Chancellery.

The problems of dependency and workload were taken up in the second half of the 20th century. In its message for a new Parliamentary Procedures Act, the Federal Council noted in 1960 that it was originally assumed that the chancery work of the Federal Assembly could be done by the Federal Chancellery in a quasi-sideline capacity. In the meantime, the workload had increased to such an extent that a permanent secretariat was sufficiently busy. The Federal Assembly was to have its own administrative apparatus. Hence, it was no longer to be dependent on the Federal Council and the Federal Chancellery. This plea was taken up in the total revision of the Parliamentary Procedures Act in 1962.

The direct subordination of the secretariat to the presidencies of the Council also served the idea of separation of powers. By anchoring the Secretariat in the law, it should be expressed that the Federal Assembly has its own administrative apparatus and is not dependent on the cooperation of the Federal Council and the administration dependent on it. The National Council and later the Council of States followed these considerations but set accents towards a strengthening of the secretariat of the Federal Assembly compared to the draft of the Federal Council despite its opposition: it was not defined as a mere "service branch of the Federal Chancellery", but with a deliberately more open formulation "within the Federal Chancellery"; the secretary was given the title "Secretary General", who not only receives his instructions from the presidents of both councils "in individual cases" but is also generally "subordinate" to them. This, first of all, concerned a professional or technical subordination and not an organizational or civil service subordination.

In the course of the revision of Parliamentary Procedure Act in 1966, a documentation service and a permanent Secretariat of the Control Committee (GPK) and, with Art. 49, the long-standing permanent Secretariat of the Finance Committee (FK) and the Finance Delegation (FinDel) was enshrined in law. More important than control was, at this stage, the right of the parliament to take its own decisions and to take over its own responsibilities (Graf 2014:538). The question of control became increasingly salient in the early 1970s. Following the Mirage affair, a political affair which, starting from cost overruns in a fighter procurement for the Swiss Air Force, had far-reaching consequences for Swiss defence policy, in 1972, the National Council Control Committee demanded a "parliamentary administration that is independent of the executive", that is a service that is answerable only to parliament itself.

The only remaining result out of this debate was a new Federal Decree on the Parliamentary services of 9.3.1972 integrating the former Federal Decree on the Secretariat on the Control Committee and the Documentation Service. New was the responsibility of the Secretary General for the election of staff, new was also the creation of a minute-taking service and a commission service (Art. 20: "for the permanent commissions not provided with their own secretariats and, as far as possible and necessary, for the non-permanent commissions").

The parliamentary reform of 1991 brought only minor changes to the legal basis, but a strong expansion of the staff of the Parliamentary services, especially as a result of the upgrading of the standing commissions to permanent status, each with their own secretariat, as well as the creation of a separate translation service. In the 1990s, the professionalization of the Parliamentary services was greatly advanced. A central role was played by former Federal Chancellor Annemarie Huber-Hotz, who, as the first Secretary General of the Federal Assembly from 1992 to 1999, strongly supported the reorganization of the Parliamentary services.

When the Federal Decree on the Parliamentary services (respectively the Ordinance of the Federal Assembly on the Parliamentary services) was adapted to the 2000 Federal Personnel Act, coming into force in 2002, the election of the Secretary General of the Federal Assembly was fixed to a term of office of four years without discussion or resistance.

Chapter 7 (Arts. 64–70) of the Parliamentary Act of 13.12.2002 did not bring any material changes compared to the partial revision of the Procedure Act of 22.12.1999 and did not give rise to any discussions in the Councils. A not insignificant formal innovation was that the organization of the Parliamentary services was no longer regulated in the ordinance itself but was delegated to the rules of procedures of the Parliamentary services, which are issued by the Secretary General and approved by the administrative delegation. With the minor amendment to the Parliamentary Administration Ordinance of 22.6.2007, the management structure in the Parliamentary services was slightly changed.[2]

The development of the parliamentary administration over the last 170 years was far from linear or straightforward but depended on political context and the personnel involved. Having started off as an additional task of the Federal Chancellery, it eventually became the administrative service of the parliament, underlining the commitment to a clear separation of powers in the Swiss political system.

43.3 Organization and Size

In general, in the Swiss bicameral system, each council has its own building and administration (like in France, Germany, Poland, India, Italy or the Russian Federation). However, there are various forms of collaboration between the administrations of bicameral parliaments, whether in the area of infrastructure, personnel and processes (Griglio and Lupo 2022). Switzerland (like Austria and Ireland) has the most tightly integrated administrative organization: both houses of parliament occupy the same building and have a single administration (Schwab 2017).

With the exception of a few functions directly related to the plenary sessions, all staff members work for the two chambers; for example, a secretary of a committee is responsible for the work of the committee in the National Council as well as for the one of the Council of States. He or she advises the members of parliament on procedural matters and assists the members in their work as legislators or scrutinizers. This privileged position in both Councils allows them to follow the entire course of a legislative project or a report and to contribute to the search for solutions (Schwab 2017).

This organization common to both chambers, with a Secretary General at its head, is quite atypical. Staff could theoretically find themselves in an awkward position when the chambers' bodies hold different views. In practice, conflicts of loyalty are rare because the staff of the Parliamentary services are aware of their commitment to the Federal Assembly as a whole rather than for a particular chamber. In keeping with their professional ethics, they strive to bring the views of the chambers closer together rather than fuelling any disagreements (Schwab 2013, 2017).

The Parliamentary services consist of the following four organizational units (see the organization chart in the annexe):

- the "Information" division is responsible for information, public relations, the website and the Official Bulletin;
- the "Commissions & Research" section consists of the Commission Secretariats and the Parliamentary Library;
- the "International Affairs & Languages" section is responsible for translations and administrative support for the parliamentary bodies active in the field of foreign policy;
- the "Infrastructure" section includes IT, security and the service responsible for the operation of the Parliamentary services themselves.

In addition, there are the two Secretariats of the Supervisory Committees, the central Secretariat, the Legal Service, Human Resources and Finance.

The Parliamentary services are headed by the Secretary General of the Federal Assembly. He or she is supported by a six-member management board. Since 1.7.2013, the Parliamentary services have been run by Philippe Schwab,[3] who chairs the management board in his capacity as Secretary General of the Federal Assembly. In addition to the Secretary General, the management board comprises:[4]

- the Deputy Secretary General and Secretary of the Council of States;
- the head of the Information Division;
- the head of the International Relations and Multilingualism Division;
- the head of the Infrastructure Division;
- the head of the Committees and Research Division;
- the head of Human Resources and Finance.

The Administrative Delegation supervises the Parliamentary services. It consists of three members elected by the Coordination Conference from the offices of each of the two Councils, as a rule from the presidium of the National Council and the Council of States.

Compared to other countries, the resources of the Parliamentary administration are rather limited (Vatter 2016: 279 quoting Z`graggen/Linder 2004). In the 1950s, the Secretariat of the Federal Assembly consisted of five persons. In 1976, the number increased to about 45 persons, twice as many as in 1971 and five times as many as in 1967 (Stengel 1977: 183f.). In 2019, there were about 300 people with 222 full-time equivalents working for the Parliamentary services and the expenses amounted to CHF 65 million.

Looking at the Parliamentary services only, however, can be misleading. More encompassing than Parliamentary services is the term Parliamentary Administration since it contains also functions which are provided by service of the administration on the behalf of the parliament (Graf 2002: 544). With the introduction of the term "parliamentary administration" in the Parliament Act, the corresponding committee of the National Council wanted to express that the Parliamentary services not only provide explicitly requested services, as their designation might suggest. Like the general federal administration and every modern administration, the Parliamentary services are not exclusively working in a delegated manner. They also have the task of independently and actively safeguarding and promoting the interests of the institution of Parliament and its organs. Consequently, like other administrations, they also play a policy-shaping role, albeit one that has to remain strictly neutral in terms of party politics.

A distinction can thus be made between the administrative *functions* of the Parliamentary services on the one hand and the *activities* of the Parliamentary services on the other, which are carried out on behalf of parliamentary bodies and therefore do not belong to the parliamentary administration but to parliament itself.

43.4 Tasks and Functions of the Parliament Services

The Parliamentary Service acts as the *interface* between the Federal Assembly on the one hand and the Federal Council, other authorities and the public on the other. It is meant to *protect and promote the interests and the image of the Federal Assembly* and its bodies. Additionally, it also *supports and assists the members of parliament*. This is not unimportant. When a new member of parliament takes up office in the Federal Assembly, she or he should become acquainted with how parliament works.

The Parliamentary services as the administrative office of Parliament assist the Federal Assembly in the fulfilment of its duties. More specifically, they *plan and organize the sessions*. The Swiss Parliament has four ordinary sessions of three weeks a year. These sessions apply for both chambers. The National Council very often has an additional session a year of three days, very often for particular questions and to cope with their workload. It is during these sessions when the work of the Federal Assembly becomes most visible. Debates are recorded in the Official Bulletin, which is produced while the sitting is in progress; individual speeches are available to read around an hour later at www.parlament.ch.

But before an item of business even makes it to the chamber for debate, it is first examined and discussed by the relevant committee. The *organization of the meetings of the different committees* is another important activity of the Parliamentary services. These meetings are also very important for the functioning of the parliament, since this is the place where the different bills and projects are debated and where the members of the different parties express their differences and try to find a proposal which is supported by the majority of the members of the committee and is finally accepted by the plenum. The meetings of the various committees are prepared in terms of content and organization by the respective committee secretariats.

To allow committee members to familiarize themselves with the wide range of topics and fields, they are *provided with documentation*, such as reports produced by federal offices, newspaper or journal articles and minutes from earlier meetings. Council members can also request personalized documentation packs and advice for more in-depth information or help prepare for visits at home and abroad.

They also have to *provide information online*. Council members can find most of the documentation they need on the intranet. Each member of the parliament receives a laptop, if requested, or at least the relevant codes to be able to log in to parliament's system. A team of IT staff and web specialists is responsible for the operation and maintenance of the entire IT infrastructure at the Parliamentary services and the secretariats of the parliamentary groups. The parliament website also has to be kept up to date so that the public can find out about items of business, members of parliament or events. During the sessions, debates are streamed live via internet. Furthermore, the services obtain and archive documents run the Parliamentary Library and provide documentation and IT support to members of parliament. Most outstanding here is the Curia Vista (https://www.parlament.ch/de/ratsbetrieb/curia-vista), the database of parliamentary proceedings which contains details of items of business (Federal Council dispatches, procedural requests, elections, petitions etc.) since the winter session 1995.

The parliament services also *prepare reports, minutes and transcripts of the dealings of parliament and its committees*. Quite important is also the production of *translations*, since the documents have to be available in the three working languages German, French and Italian. Translations occupy an important number of employees of the parliament services. Council members speak before parliament and in committee meetings in their own language. During sessions in the National Council, interpreters provide simultaneous translation of statements in the three official languages of German, French and Italian. Translations of most documents are also available.

They advise Assembly members, in particular the presidents of the two chambers and of the committees, *on matters of business and procedure*. This is not unimportant given the low degree of professionalization of the members of parliaments and the weak support they obtain from their parties and parliamentary groups.

And they inform the public about the Federal Assembly and its activities. Like many other parliaments, transparency has become quite important. Through its website (https://www.parlament.ch/de), *citizens and the media have direct access to a plethora of information*. A lot of information is published nowadays on the website of the Parliament (www.parlament.ch) and there is also alternative and more science-oriented information about roll call votes, and coalition behaviour on other privately provided websites (www.smartmonitor.ch). Meeting attendance, statistics about proposal of every MP and the cost she or he caused for the administration to respond to his or her queries are disclosed.

The public can follow the work of their representatives in parliament not only through the media or online but also in person from the viewing gallery. Council members receive individual visitors or groups in the Federal Palace, and visitors can find out about parliament by taking a guided tour. A large number of people from quite different walks of life pass through the doors of the Federal Palace: Council members, representatives of different interest groups and the media, civil servants and visitors.

An open house like this requires certain security measures and the presence of security staff. The building also has to be looked after. The activities that take centre stage would not be possible without all the work done behind the scenes. Work would soon grind to a halt if the wastepaper baskets were overflowing, if there was no heating in winter or if Council members weren't able to get a coffee (Schwaab 2017).

There have also been some quite important steps towards the provision of more information about the history of the parliament, the different instruments and the functioning to show its importance for the functioning of democracy and to make it accessible for civic education.

A very important field of information is the disclosure of the *members of parliaments' interest*, this even more since they generally also work in other fields, sometimes very closely related to national politics. On assuming office and at the start of every year thereafter, assembly members must inform the Parliamentary Service in writing about their professional activities, such as activities in management or on supervisory or advisory committees and similar bodies of Swiss and foreign businesses and public or private institutions and foundations, activities as a consultant or specialist advisor to federal agencies, permanent management or consultancy activities on behalf of Swiss or foreign interest groups, participation in federal committees or other federal bodies. The Parliamentary Service compiles a public register of members' interests, which is published online. This practice enables citizens to identify possible private activities likely to influence the activities of Assembly members. Assembly members are themselves responsible for the completeness of the disclosures in the register of interests. The offices therefore recommend in their annual letter on the subject that Assembly members disclose an interest in the event of any doubt. In the event of serious violations of the duty of disclosure, the relevant Council office may take disciplinary measures.

Another activity is to Maintain contacts outside and within the Federal Palace. The work performed by parliament does not only take place within the Federal Palace, but also there are numerous contacts with journalists and the public, as well as with foreign parliaments. Here too, the Parliamentary services provide Council members with the support they need. Press releases are drafted, media conferences are organized and arrangements are made for trips by Swiss delegations abroad and for visits by foreign delegations to Switzerland.

Switzerland not being a member of the European Union has to a lesser extent contacts with other European parliaments. Foreign politics are in the hands of the executive. There are, however, exchanges with other national parliaments and it in the Federal Assembly is a member of the Inter-Parliamentary Union (IPU), the international organization of national parliaments. Its primary purpose is to promote democratic governance, accountability and cooperation among its members; other initiatives include advancing gender parity among legislatures, empowering youth participation in politics and sustainable development.

An important instrument to receive the necessary information about the administration is the Parliamentary Control of the Administration (PCA), the evaluation service of the Federal Assembly. It conducts studies on behalf of the Control Committees (CC) on the legality, expediency and effectiveness of the activities of the federal authorities. When commissioned to do so, the PCA can also scrutinize the effectiveness of federal government measures on behalf of other parliamentary committees. A recent evaluation conducted by this service looked, for example, at the use of external experts in the Federal Administration, which has been more clearly regulated and has become more transparent in recent years. The statistical analyses applied in procurement controlling were considered generally appropriate; however, there are shortcomings in the in-depth monitoring process. The expert mandates are not recorded uniformly, and the controlling reports do not provide sufficient meaningful information.

A part from the guarantee of transparency and the provision of information and the support of the parliament in the decision-making process a final important function of the Parliamentary Service are all activities which allow the Parliament to fulfil the duty of parliamentary oversight independent from the executive in a professional way (vgl. Vatter 2016: 303).

The administration of the Federal Assembly on the contrary is not concerned with the drafting of bills of legislation. This takes place within the administration and in the different offices concerned together with the Federals of for Justice.

43.5 Current and Future Challenges

COVID-19 confronted the Parliamentary services with various additional problems to solve. These mainly concerned the functioning of the parliament and the provision of the information needed by the members of parliament. The more substantial reactions to the crisis were in the hands of other units of the administration.

Various measures had to be introduced to protect the members of parliaments (vaccination and hygiene measures), to maintain interactions between different actors, to regulate the entering of the parliamentary building and to guarantee the flow of information with respect to the political topics to be treated.

Most outstanding was the organization of two sessions of the parliament in a larger building in the city of Berne (BernExpo), which allowed for the recommended distance of the members of parliament. The service also had, of course, to organize itself differently to maintain its functioning (e.g. home office).

Apart from these additional challenges, the Parliamentary services and the parliamentary administration at the national level seem to meet the requirements they are confronted with. Discussions about the organization as well as about the organizational and administrative supervision are much more likely to take place at the lower political levels. However, this does not mean that the current organization will meet all the future demands.

One issue in the future will probably be the workload and the degree of professionalization. The burden of tasks that will fall on the "militia parliament" will certainly further grow and the parliamentarians will be dependent on additional support that will allow them to fulfil their tasks with a certain degree of independence.

The work of the parliamentary administration requires a good knowledge of political processes and politics, although one must be above party-political positions. The concordance and multiparty system entail that the search for political solutions accepted by a larger majority is paramount. Employees are not committed to a particular political line but rather have to demonstrate their loyalty to the institution.

Digitalization will also pose major challenges for the Parliamentary services. Obtaining information has become easier, but how can the relevant information be processed? Are there any possibilities to handle certain parliamentary processes in online procedures? The paperless parliament is only a first step.

In view of increasing interdependence and the advancing globalization of challenges, the Parliamentary services, as part of their proactive and creative activities, are also called upon to offer support services for the members of parliament, including a more international perspective.

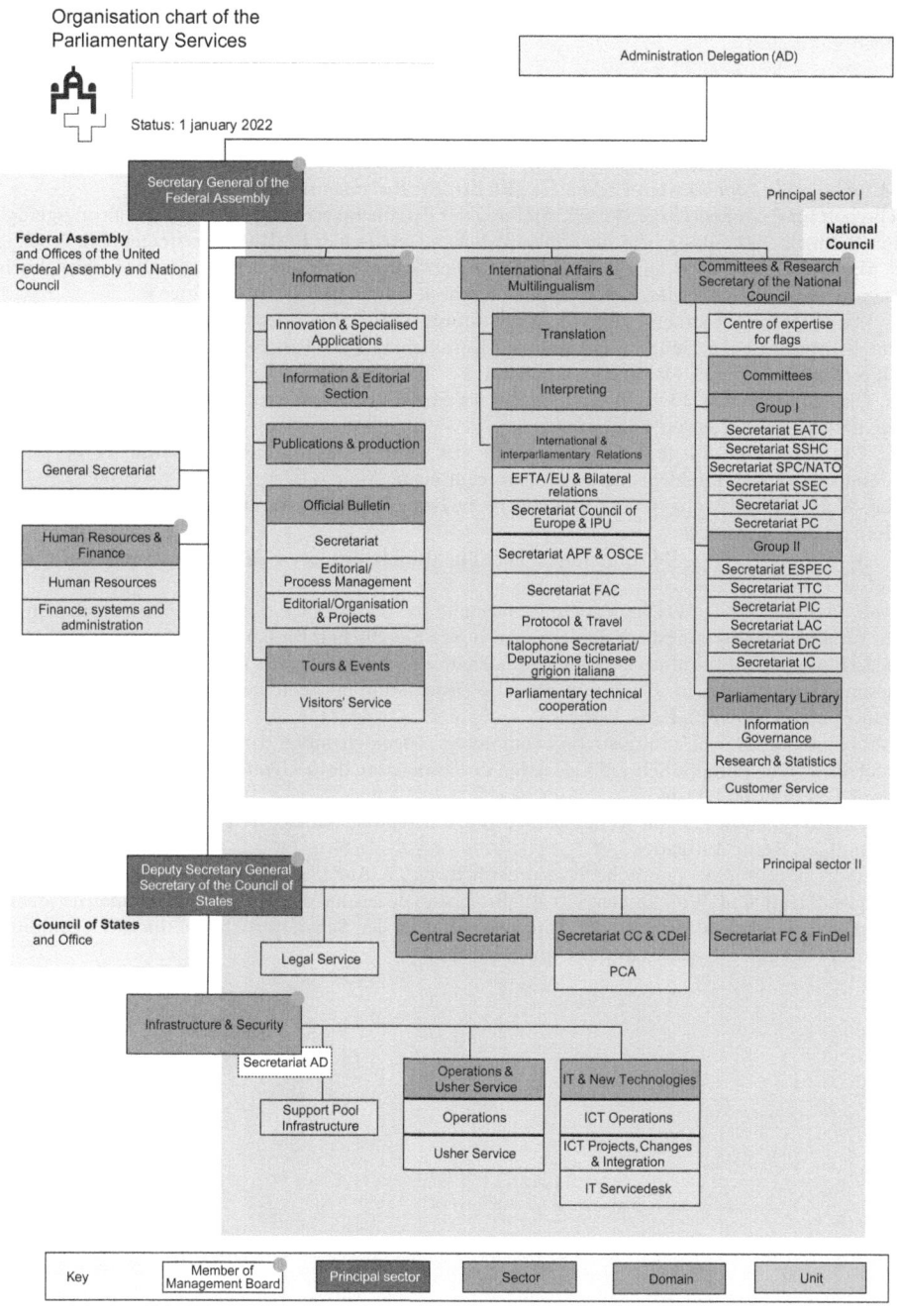

Notes

1 For more about the Swiss Parliament, see for example Schwab (2011), Lanz (2008) (2013), Graf (2014), Graf et al. (2014), Gesellschaft für Parlamentsfragen (2007) (2009), Vatter (2016: 271 ff.) or Linder/Muller (2017: 237 ff.).
2 https://www.fedlex.admin.ch/eli/cc/2003/510/en (1.4.2021).
3 Former Secretaries of the Parliamentary services were Annemarie Huber-Hotz (1992–1999), Mariangela Wallimann-Bornatico (1999–2008) and Christoph Lanz (2008–2013).
4 See https://www.parlament.ch/en/%C3%BCber-das-parlament/parliamentary-services/management-board (31.3.2021).

References

Gesellschaft für Parlamentsfragen (2007). Dienstleistungen für das Parlament, in: Parlament: Mitteilungsblatt der schweizerischen Gesellschaft für Parlamentsfragen. Nr. 1, 10. Jg.

Gesellschaft für Parlamentsfragen (2009). Stellung der Parlamentsverwaltungen im Verwaltungsgefüge, in: Parlament: Mitteilungsblatt der schweizerischen Gesellschaft für Parlamentsfragen. Nr. 2, 12. Jg.

Graf, Martin (2014). Art. 155, in: Ehrenzeller/Schindler/Schweizer/Vallender (Hrsg.), Die schweizerische Bundesverfassung, St. Galler Kommentar, Schulthess, Zürich/Basel/Genf, S. 2626 ff.

Graf, Martin, Theler, Cornelia und von Wyss, Moritz (2014). Parlamentsrecht und Parlamentspraxis der Schweizerischen Bundesversammlung. Kommentar zum Parlamentsgesetz (ParlG) vom 13. Dezember 2002. Basel, Helbing Lichtenhahn.

Lanz, Ch. (26 septembre 2008). A quoi servent les services parlementaires?, Rencontre des présidents des parlements cantonaux, Bâle.

Lanz, Ch. (4 octobre 2013). La confidentialité des séances de commission, Séminaire des vices-présidentes et vice-présidents des parlements cantonaux, Sion.

Linder, Wolf und Sean Muller (2017). Schweizerische Demokratie. Institutionen, Prozesse, Perspektiven, Bern: Haupt, 4. Auflage.

Sägesser, Thomas (1999). Bestimmungen über die Bundesbehörden der neuen Bundesverfassung. LeGes 1999/1, S. 11–49.

Schwab, Philippe (2011). Welche Vor- und Nachteile hat die Unabhängigkeit der Parlamentsdienste?, in: Parlament: Mitteilungsblatt der schweizerischen Gesellschaft für Parlamentsfragen. Nr. 2, 14. Jg.

Schwab, Philippe (2013). Administration parlementaire suisse: Partage des responsabilités en matière de gestion du personnel, in: Communication de l'association des secrétaires généraux des parlements francophones (ASGPF), Paris, France.

Schwab, Philippe (2017). L'administration conjointe des deux chambres dans les parlement bicaméraux, contribution de Philippe Schwab à la session de l'association des secrétaires généraux des parlements, Saint-Pétersbourg, Russie.

Stengel, Karl (1977) Die Parlamentsdienste im Bund. Entstehung, Arbeitsweise und verfassungsrechtliche Grundlage, Bern/Stuttgart.

Vatter, Adrian (2016). Das politische System der Schweiz, 2. Auflage, Baden-Baden: Nomos.

Z`graggen, Heidi und Wolf Linder (2004). Professionalisierung der Parlamente im internationalen Vergleich. Studie im Auftrag der Parlamentsdienste der Schweizerischen Bundesversammlung. Institut für Politikwissenschaft der Universität Bern.

44
TURKEY'S PARLIAMENTARY ADMINISTRATION

Damla Cihangir-Tetik and Selin Türkeş-Kılıç

44.1 Introduction

The Grand National Assembly of Turkey (GNAT) (*Türkiye Büyük Millet Meclisi, TBMM*) is a unique and important institution with a peculiar history of (d)evolution and (in)efficiency. While it had absolute political power during its initial phase, between 1920 and 1946 (Kalaycıoğlu, 2014; 2010; Soysal, 1969; Özbudun, 1992), its political power has been diminished gradually until today (Esen and Gümüşçü, 2018; Gönenç and Kontacı, 2019; Özsoy-Boyunsuz, 2016; Yılmaz, 2020) leading to an institutional paradox for the legislative. Its first name was the Grand National Assembly (GNA), founded in 1920 during the Turkish War of Independence. After the foundation of the Republic of Turkey in 1923, it officially became the GNAT. Since the 1982 Constitution, the GNAT is unicameral. With the 2017 constitutional referendum, the GNAT's legislative capacity has been narrowed due to the expansion of presidential power (Gençkaya, 2020).

Notwithstanding a limited number of studies on the GNAT's institutionalization with a focus on the deputies' turn-over rates and the content of its traditions and standing order (Gençkaya 2019; Kalaycıoğlu, 2014; 2010; 1990; Turan 2000; 2003), there is a gap in the literature on its administrative structure. This chapter aims to fill in this gap by analysing the GNAT's administration in the context of the democratization of Turkish politics. For this purpose, an account of the Parliament's historical evolution and administrative structure is followed by a critical analysis of its institutional mechanisms, external relations, and current challenges. The analysis is based on data collected from the GNAT's primary documents, the related laws and regulations as well as the existing literature. As such, the chapter discusses the role and limits of political developments on the evolution and functioning of the parliamentary administration and legislative-executive relations in Turkey. Further, it clarifies the institutional mechanisms that increase the possibility of partisanship and politicization in the parliamentary administration over time. Regarding its international dimension, we discuss the earlier contribution and current constraints of Turkey's European Union (EU) accession process on the Parliament's external relations. Finally, we argue that, albeit critical political changes and developments in the last two decades, the long-standing problems of the parliamentary administration rooted in its institutional mechanisms and relations with a strong executive continue to prevent its autonomy and contribution to democratic politics in Turkey.

44.2 Historical Evolution of the Parliament in Turkey

The historical evolution of the GNAT's administrative structure has been going hand in hand with Turkey's political developments and constitutional changes. Political representation and participation in Turkish politics have their roots in the 19th-century Ottoman Era. Following the official recognition of individuals as political actors for the first time by the 1839 *Tanzimat* (Reorganization) Reforms, the first Constitution was proclaimed on 23 December 1876, and a representative body was formed on 19 March 1877. As a part of constitutional monarchy, this bicameral parliament lacked legislative power since it could propose a bill only upon the Sultan's permission. Nevertheless, it drafted and accepted the first regulation on the bureaucratic administration of the Parliament (*Heyet-i Mebusân Nizamname-i Dâhilîsi*) on 13 May 1877. Sultan Abdülhamid II prorogued the first parliament indefinitely on 14 February 1878.

The second constitutional era came in July 1908 when the reformist members of the Committee of Union and Progress (*İttihat ve Terakki Cemiyeti*) revolted against the Sultan and reconvened the parliament by December 1908. The constitutional amendment of 8 August 1909, made ministers and the government accountable to the Parliament and limited the Sultan's power to dissolve the Parliament. The second regulation regarding the administration of the Ottoman Parliament, 'M*eclis-i Mebusân İdare-i Dâhiliye Nizamnamesi*', entered into force in 1916. However, the Parliament failed to provide the Empire's unity and represent diverse communities behind the principle of constitutional and representative government (Hale, 2012; Zürcher, 1993). After the defeat of the Ottomans by the Allied Powers in World War I, the British occupation forces officially terminated the second parliament in 1920.

The dissolution of the Ottoman Parliament provided the opportunity for the national resistance movement under the leadership of Mustafa Kemal Atatürk to create a provisional government in Ankara. Accordingly, the national parliament GNA was opened in Ankara on 23 April 1920. Although the 1916 regulation laid the basis of the GNA's administrative functioning, the GNA represents a clear-cut dissociation from the Ottoman rule and a step forward for establishing the Republic of Turkey.

Strikingly different from the Ottoman Parliament, the GNA became the only institution that constituted the legitimacy of the political power by transferring sovereignty from the sultanate to the nation. The GNA's ratification of the 1921 Constitution launched Turkey's governmental institutionalization. After the Lausanne Treaty, the GNA declared the country Republic on 29 October 1923, officially became GNAT, and established a parliamentary system in the 1924 Constitution. Regarding these, it is not only representing the notion of democracy, but it is the basic foundation of the Turkish national resistance movement as well (Kalaycıoğlu, 2014, 370–371; Kalaycıoğlu, 2010; Soysal, 1969; Özbudun, 1992).

The 1921 Constitution had empowered the GNA exceptionally during the War of Independence by granting executive, legislative, and judicial rights and making it the political power accomplishing all state affairs. Yet, the Government of GNA did not have a formal party system and presidential institution. Following the foundation of the Republic, the GNAT's extraordinary powers were normalized. Although the 1924 Constitution introduced the principle of the separation of powers, during the one-party (Republican People's Party-RPP/*CHP*) rule until 1946, legislative and executive powers were concentrated in the GNAT with party leader controlling both. Nevertheless, the GNAT prepared and accepted its first standing order on 27 May 1927, and made the first law (Law No. 2512 on 'the Organisation and Duties of the GNAT Officials') regarding its administrative structure on 14 June 1934.

The period from 1946 to 1960 is characterized by 'a multi-party regime of unchecked and uncontrolled dominance of the TGNA by a party majority, where the role and effectiveness of the opposition were minimal' (Kalaycıoğlu, 2010, 123). The predominant one-party rules between 1946 and 1950 by the RPP, between 1950 and 1960 by the Democrat Party (DP), lacked a checks and balances system. Among several legislative changes, one of the first legislative activities of the DP was to replace the existing law with Law No. 5509 on 'the Law on the Civil Servants Organisation of the GNAT' on 9 January 1950.

On 27 May 1960, military coup seized political power from DP. The 'National Unity Committee' formed by colonels added new regulations into Law No. 231 on 5 January 1961. A legacy of the constituent Assembly on the GNAT's administrative structure is the establishment of the Bureau of the Speaker that determines the units' duties and how they will be carried out. After the restoration of civilian rule, the 1961 Constitution restructured the GNAT as bicameral in order to check the excesses of the majorities in the Parliament of the previous era. The separation of powers was implemented for the first time with the introduction of various checks and balances mechanisms between the executive and the legislative. Independent public institutions such as the Senate, the Constitutional Court, and autonomous institutions were established in order to limit the absolute power of legislative majorities. While the new institutions failed to achieve democratic consolidation, another military intervention on 12 September 1980, suspended the GNAT's activities for three years.

The colonels drew up a new Constitution, which was accepted by 91.4% of the votes in the referendum held on 7 November 1982. The new Constitution abolished the Senate, limited the freedom of civil society organizations, introduced a new electoral law with a 10% threshold, and trimmed the powers of the Constitutional Court and autonomous institutions aiming to decrease the checks and balances over the executive. Thus, it curtailed the legislative power over a very powerful but two-headed executive, including a Prime Minister, his/her Cabinet on the one hand, and the President on the other. The new system established a Parliament liable to the executive and consequently institutionalized the arbitrariness of the executive (Kalaycıoğlu, 2014, p. 374). The 1982 Constitution has been amended 19 times until today. Law No. 5509 was replaced by Law No. 2919 on 'the Organization of the Secretary-General of the GNAT' on 13 October 1983.

While the new electoral system created several unstable coalition governments during the 1990s, it enabled Justice and Development Party (JDP/AKP) to come to power with only 34.28% of the votes of the November 2002 elections. Since then, the JDP has won all consecutive elections and been ruling Turkey under predominant one-party rule. In addition to thousands of laws changed and introduced over the last 20 years, the final version of Law No. 6253 on 'the Administrative Organisation of the GNAT Speaker's Office' entered into force on 18 December 2011. The new law enabled a less hierarchical administrative structure (The Grand National Assembly of Turkey [GNAT], 2021).

On 16 April 2017, Constitutional Referendum brought about the most striking change in the historical evolution of the Parliament as the executive presidentialism replaced the parliamentary system with 51.4% of the votes. Following a one-year *de facto* Presidential system, the amendment was officially implemented on 24 June 2018, when Recep Tayyip Erdoğan was elected by 52.59% of the votes as the first President of the Presidential executive system.

The new constitutional amendments have strengthened the executive tremendously, monopolized all executive powers in the hands of the President, whose constitutional audit and control by the legislature has become almost impossible and undermined the separation of powers that diminished the independence of the judiciary (Esen and Gümüşçü,

2018; Özsoy-Boyunsuz, 2016; Yılmaz, 2020). For instance, the new Constitution abolished 'interpellation', which was increasing the executive's responsibility to the Parliament. Additionally, while there is no precondition for the President to suspend the Parliament and call for the renewal of the elections now, the legislative needs the approval of the three-fifth of the Parliament to call for the renewal of the elections. This ambivalence increases the executive's power over the legislative (Gönenç and Kontacı, 2019).

The evolution of political participation and the legislative in Turkey has its roots in the Ottoman legacy. The first seeds of representative democracy in Turkey were planted for the first time by introducing the principle of national sovereignty during the establishment of the GNA 101 years ago. However, several drawbacks in democratization and the recent constitutional change have loosened the power of the legislative in Turkey and the role of its administration in supporting representative democracy. Keeping in mind the political developments and historical evolution of the legislature in Turkey, the GNAT's administrative structure, rules, and procedures, as well as its relations with other political actors, will be critically analysed in the next section.

44.3 Institutional Mechanisms of the GNAT

One of the measures to evaluate the degree of parliamentary administrations' autonomy from the executive is the existence of a separate administrative law from the civil service (IPU, 2020). Although the GNAT administrative staff are civil servants, the administrative structure, rules, procedures, and duties of the staff are determined by Law No. 6253 dated 1 December 2011, 'The Law on the Administrative Organization of the Assembly', instead of Civil Servants Law. Thus, the parliamentary administration seems independent from the executive. However, the concentration of power in the hands of the Speaker, who has been from the same political party during the last 20 years, has limited the administration's autonomy and increased the possibility for politicization and partisanship. Yet, the recent government system change from parliamentarism to presidentialism diminished the power of the legislative as well.

According to Law No. 6253 (2011), Article 3, the duties of the Administrative Organisation of the GNAT are:

a   providing all kinds of information together with administrative and technical support to the Plenary, the Bureau of the Speaker, committees, political party groups, and deputies;
b   by means of legislative experts, to inform committees by examining the bills and other legislative and supervisory documents, to assist in the preparation of the committee reports, and to make researches and examinations on the issues within the scopes of the committees;
c   preparing draft law proposals for deputies whenever they request for;
d   carrying out recording, analysing, and printing activities of the proceedings;
e   meeting all kinds of publication, documentation, and information needs of the committees and deputies;
f   maintaining coordination with the Presidency and other public institutions regarding the work of the GNAT.
g   carrying out the external relations of the GNAT and its Administration with international organizations and the work and processes related to international events;
h   carrying out the press and public relations services of the GNAT and announcing the activities of the GNAT through various means;

i   maintaining documentation and archive services;
j   fulfilling other duties assigned to the Administration of the GNAT by the Bureau of the Speaker and regulations.

44.3.1 Organizational Structure of the GNAT

The Speaker of the GNAT as the political leader of the Parliament is at the top of the administrative organization that consists of directorates primarily aiming to support the Bureau of the Speaker. The Bureau consists of 15 deputies in total, including the Speaker, 4 Vice-Speakers, 3 Quaestors, and 7 Secretaries, and ensures the proportionate representation of all political party groups. The Bureau, together with the Speaker, is responsible for the Parliament's overall administration.

The Directorate of Legal Affairs and the Department of Security, together with the Office of Private Secretary, is directly linked to the Bureau of the Speaker. Further, the Speaker appoints the Secretary-General whose role is now limited to preparing and applying the strategic plan and the budget of the administration (Law No. 6253 2011, Article 34). The Secretary-General and 4 Deputy Secretary-Generals are responsible for central service units, including 14 different directorates. There are specialized units, such as research, library, press and public relations, information technologies, and legal services under different directorates (see Figure 44.1).

From 2000 to 2020, the number of GNAT administrative staff increased by 52% (see Table 44.1). The main reasons for this increase are the arbitrariness of the employment of particularly the temporary staff and the 2018 government system change. After the abolishment of the Prime Ministry in 2019, 367 new staff from Prime Ministry were transferred to the Parliament. Besides, since the number of deputies was increased from 550 to 600, their advisors and secretaries registered as new staff. Although the number of staff increased tremendously over the last 20 years, the number of expert staff has still been insufficient, since there is a considerable amount of temporary staff, such as security staff, deputy advisors and secretaries, and staff working in political party groups (Bilgiç, 2020a) (see Table 44.2). Deputy advisors, secretaries, and staff working for political party groups usually change each term and that prevents the accumulation of legislative expertise and institutionalization. There is also plenty of support services staff, including cooks, waiters, drivers, gardeners, technicians, kindergarten teachers, and security guards, particularly working in the recreational facilities of the GNAT. Besides, until 2018, around a thousand of them were working in national palaces registered to the GNAT by then (NTV-MSNBC, 2000; Işık, 2009; Pakdil, 2009). Although these palaces have been registered to the Presidency by 2018, the total number of the GNAT staff has not decreased. Even the number of support services staff has increased. Finally, out of 6976 staff members, only 1984 (28%) of them are women (Çolak, 2020; Bilgiç, 2020a). Yet, there is no official gender equality policy in the parliamentary administration (IPU, 2021). Out of 70 senior executives, only 8 of them are women, and only 1 of them is the head of a directorate. Since its establishment, all speakers of the GNAT have also been male.

The conditions of appointment of the GNAT's administrative staff are regulated by Law No. 6253. According to Article 29, the Secretary-General, Deputy Secretary-Generals, Chief Advisors and Advisors to the Speaker, and the Head to the Bureau of the Speaker are appointed directly by the Speaker. Other public officer positions are established and opened upon the proposal of the Secretary-General by the Speaker. The Speaker can delegate his/her

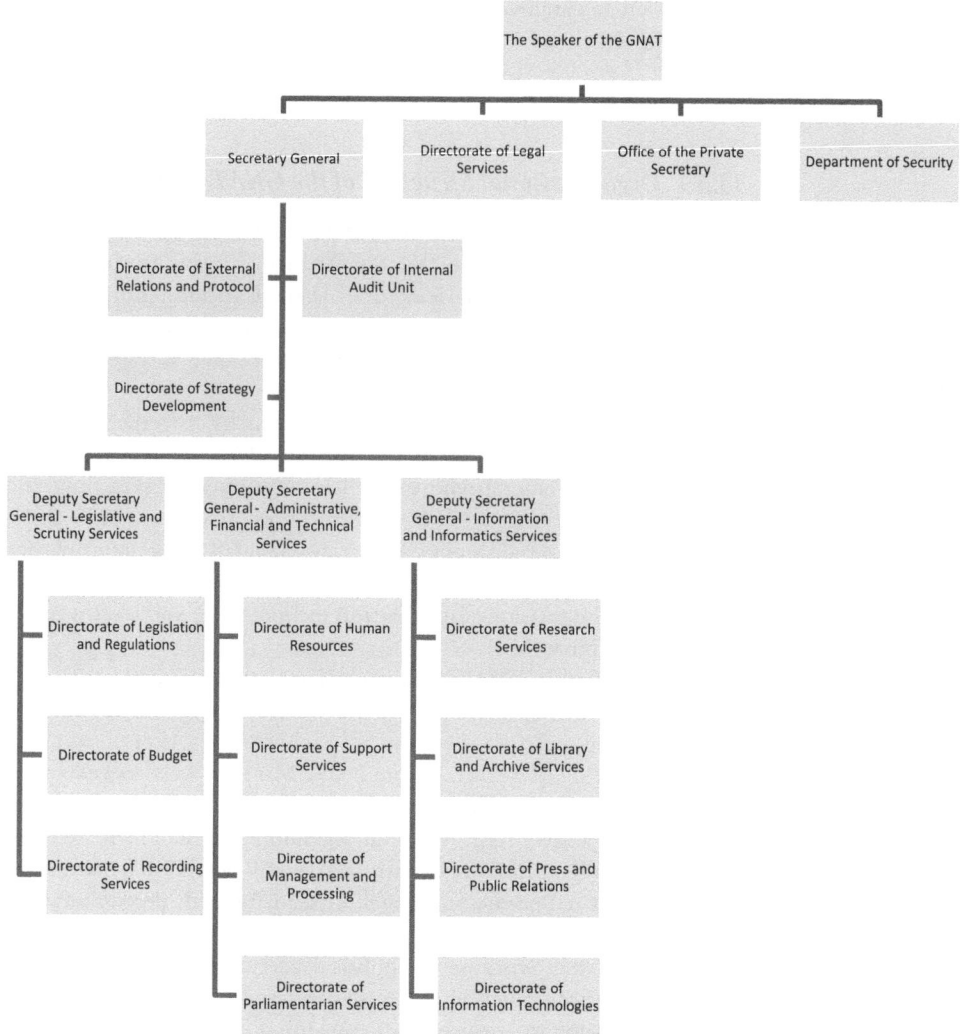

Figure 44.1 Organizational chart of the administrative structure of the GNAT

The GNAT, www.global.tbmm.gov.tr

authorities to the Secretary-General upon his/her request. Similarly, the Secretary-General and Deputy Secretary-Generals can also delegate their authorities, respectively, to Deputy Secretary-Generals and head of the directorates. Although these delegation opportunities seem to increase the degree of discretion at various organizational levels, their individual decision-making capacities are limited for two reasons: firstly, administrators do not prefer to

Table 44.1 Total number of the staff member of the GNAT (NTV-MSNBC, 2000; Pakdil, 2009; The Journal of the Committee on Planning and Budget, 2019; 2020)

Year	2000	2009	2019	2020
# staff member	4576	5040	6919	6976

Table 44.2 Total number of the staff member of the GNAT and their units by December 2020

Unit	# staff member
General Secretariat	172
Directorate of Legislation and Regulations	172
Directorate of Budget	30
Directorate of Recording Services	137
Directorate of Human Resources	67
Directorate of Support Services	2283
Directorate of Management and Processing	363
Directorate of Parliamentarian Services	226
Directorate of Research Services	60
Directorate of Library and Archive Services	92
Directorate of Press and Public Relations	301
Directorate of Information Technologies	107
Directorate of Legal Services	21
Directorate of External Relations and Protocol	101
Directorate of Strategy Development	86
Office of the Private Secretary	23
Directorate of Internal Audit Unit	7
Personnel of Political Party Groups and Deputies	1826
Personnel of Department of Security	902
Total	6976

Source: Bilgiç 2020a

delegate their authority in practice, and secondly, there is a high number of senior executives directly appointed by the Speaker.

The Deputy Secretary-General in charge of legislative and scrutiny services is assigned among the administrators who have served before or are still in office in the directorates of Laws and Resolutions or Budget Services or among the legislative experts. The head and deputy heads of the Directorate of Recording Services are appointed among the stenographers. However, there are no similar internal prerequisites for the appointments of the other central units' administrators. They can be appointed externally. This situation increases the possibility of politicization and arbitrariness of administrative careers. Secondly, it prevents the institutionalization of the GNAT's administrative structure by increasing the number of turn-overs among the administrators (Kalaycıoğlu, 2014; Turan, 2000) when a new Speaker and Bureau of the Speaker are elected. Except for those positions eligible for direct appointment prescribed by law, the officers to be appointed are selected through an examination. The special conditions, procedures, and principles regarding the examination and the contracted staff to be appointed are determined through a regulation issued by the Bureau of the Speaker (GNAT, 2021). Thus, these conditions, procedures, and principles are not permanent and well institutionalized. They can change just after the appointment of a new Speaker and Bureau members.

According to the law, opportunities for staff training and development are limited. Training opportunities are available only for legal experts and stenographers since they have to take a special examination and succeed before their appointments. If they fail in the examination, they are appointed as officers to other units. Opportunities for external consultancy are limited as well. Only the Speaker, political parties, and deputies are eligible to get external consultancy as contracted advisors. Although Article 30 of Law No. 6253 states that the Speaker can employ at most five advisors as contracted staff, according to the answer of the Bureau of the Speaker as a reply to the parliamentary question of one of the MPs of the main opposition party, Sezgin Tanrıkulu (2020a; 2020b), in December 2020, the current Speaker has 53 advisors (Bilgiç, 2020b), whose salaries and conditions are decided by the Bureau of the Speaker. The reply states that 'Advisors are employed to assist the Speaker in matters of importance and priority' (Bilgiç, 2020b). Opposition parties have severely criticized this issue as an example of squandering and clientelism in the GNAT's recruitment processes. Until 2011, each deputy employed only one advisor and a secretary (Yıldız, 2007). After then, they can employ at most three advisors. Political party groups can also employ contracted staff according to their needs for specific issues requiring legislative activities expertise. In that regard, each political party group can employ at most 10 advisors, 25 staff members, and additional staff, whose number should be at most 10% of the total number of their deputies.

However, '"Advisors" usually run errands for the deputy. Most are high school graduates and do not possess any particular skills' (Turan 2003, 170; Kalaycıoğlu, 2010). The term and definition of 'advisor' are not clear enough to avoid overlaps on the duties of the permanent staff and individual advisors of deputies and the Speaker. Yet, consultancy to deputies is not considered a profession, unlike its counterparts in European states and the United States of America. The content and efficiency of the work that advisors do cannot be considered 'legislative or political consultancy'. Kinship and paisan relations are argued to be more prominent than expertise for the employment of deputy advisors (Yıldız, 2007; Kalaycıoğlu, 2010). All public officials in Turkey can also be employed in the Parliament with the permission of their institutions on a contract basis. Even only these wide opportunities for the employment of contracted staff in the Parliament explain well the significant increase in the total number of the administrative staff of the GNAT during the last two decades.

While the permanent or temporary administrative staff carries out GNAT's central services, members of the committee secretariats are deputies. In their first meetings, the deputies assigned by their party groups as committee members elect the Chair, vice-Chair, rapporteur, and clerk of the committee by absolute majority voting (Standing Order of the GNAT, 1973, Article 24). Among the GNAT's administrative staff, legislative experts (*yasama uzmanları*) have heavy schedules with committee secretariats and members. Legislative experts are responsible for informing the committee regarding the bills – after examining them – preparing for committee negotiations, assisting for the preparation of committee reports, and conducting research and analysis on topics that fall into the committee's area of responsibility (Law No. 6253 2011, Article 6). However, existing limited literature on the Administration of the GNAT indicates that even though the total number of the administrative staff is impressive, the legislative experts, who conduct legislative services and support the legislative process and the staff in central units, including officers, secretaries, and administrators, who do research, conduct library and archive services, are understaffed (Turan, 2003; Kalaycıoğlu, 2010; Gençkaya, 2019). While the Directorate of Support Services has 2283 staff members, the Directorate of Legislation and Regulations has only 172, and the total staff number of research, library, and archive services are only 152 (see Table 44.2). These figures clearly show the Administrative Organisation's limited capacity in the functioning of the legislative, professionalization of specialized units such as library and legal services, and development of functional expertise in the GNAT.

One of the primary duties of the parliamentary administration is to assist the functioning of the committees. However, the legislative support of the administrative staff in the committees is limited since draft legislation is prepared particularly by the Presidency after the government system change in 2018. Secondly and importantly, as Turan mentions, 'the TGNA committees are not entities that represent accumulated expertise, as is the case in the United States. Accumulation of expertise from service on the same committee over time is not typical for several reasons. However, the rapid turn-over of deputies in the TGNA and the lack of continuity in committee assignments constitute sufficient explanation without analysing others. The committees do not have access to a staff of experts. Such expertise as may exist comes from that gained by committee members in their earlier professions. A systematic study of committees is lacking, but, as Kalaycıoğlu has observed, "the concern for expertise does not go above partisan considerations" (Turan 2003, 168; Turan, 2000; Kalaycıoğlu, 2010; Gençkaya, 2019). Yet, 'Individual advisers to legislators deal primarily with constituency problems and therefore are hindered in their attempts to address legislative-related activities' (Gençkaya 2019, 274). Thus, the contribution of the administrative staff to the legislative process and, consequently, the functioning of the representative democracy in Turkey are limited.

Among all interest groups, particularly with political parties, the administrative staff has a special relationship, since one of the duties of the administration is 'to provide the all available information, together with the administrative and technical support to the political party groups' (Law No. 6253, 2011, Article 3). Although its comprehensiveness is questionable, both human resources and technical needs of political party groups are met by the GNAT administration. The relationship of the Parliament with other interest groups, civil society organizations, media, and citizens is carried out by the Directorate of Media and Public Relations Services within the framework and demand of the Bureau of the Speaker. However, political parties and deputies maintain their relations with other interest groups, various civil society organizations, media organs, and citizens within the framework of their party policies and individually. Regarding the participation of the members of different civil society organizations and interest groups as 'experts' to the committee meetings, the Standing Order states that 'they can participate only by invitation of the committee and speak up if the Chair of the committee decides the necessity' (Standing Order of the GNAT, 1973, Articles 29–30). This shows the minimal role and participation of relevant stakeholders and interest groups officially in the functioning of the legislative.

44.3.2 External Relations of the GNAT

In the last two decades, GNAT's external relations activities increased tremendously. Turkey's soft-power policy prioritization in foreign policymaking boosted the GNAT's inter-institutional and inter-parliamentary relations (Öniş and Yılmaz, 2009; Oğuzlu, 2007). The GNAT has been represented in 12 different international parliamentary assemblies. Several joint parliamentary committees, unions, and friendship groups have been established with international organizations, national parliaments, and the European Parliament (EP). The number of inter-parliamentary friendship groups has increased from 29 in 1983 to 144 today, including 23 national parliaments of EU member states – excluding Cyprus, Greece, Luxembourg, and the Netherlands – and the United Kingdom (see Table 44.3). This has resulted in a significant rise in the number of mutual official visits of the Speaker and deputies as well as the inter-parliamentary meetings and projects that the Parliament both participates in and organizes. While the Directorate of External Relations and Protocol officers conduct the whole administrative and technical work of external relations, the decision-making process is carried out by the Speaker and the Bureau of the Speaker.

The EU-Turkey relations date back to 12 September 1963, when the Ankara Agreement was signed between the European Economic Community (EEC) and Turkey. The EU/EP and the GNAT relations are conducted through the EU Harmonization Committee and the

Table 44.3 Number of inter-parliamentary friendship groups of the GNAT

Legislative term	Years	# of Inter-parliamentary friendship groups
17	1983–1987	29
18	1987–1991	29
19	1991–1995	31
20	1995–1999	44
21	1999–2002	69
22	2002–2007	82
23	2007–2011	106
24	2011–2015	125
27	2018–Today	144

Source: The GNAT, www.global.tbmm.gov.tr

Turkey-European Union Joint Parliamentary Committee (JPC). The Turkey-EU JPC has been established pursuant to EP's decision on 14 May 1965, GNAT's decision on 22 June 1965, and the decision of Turkey-EEC Association Council on 27 July 1965. The primary duties of the Committee are to support Turkey's EU membership bid by discussing the issues related to Turkey's accession process and to improve relations between the GNAT and the EP. However, Committee members and their advisors try to prepare the contents of the meetings that prevent the sustainability and the accumulation of the knowledge and expertise among the administrative staff. Yet, meetings were cancelled four times, respectively, between 1980 and 1987, 1992 and 1995, 2015 and 2018, and since the latest one was held on 19-20 December 2018 in Ankara, until today.

Besides, the EU Harmonization Committee was established in 2003 to monitor developments regarding Turkey's accession process, negotiate and follow developments in the EU, and inform the Parliament about them. The committee is also responsible for carrying out relations with EU institutions, the parliaments of EU members and candidates, and EP the committees (The Grand National Assembly of Turkey [GNAT], 2021). However, the latest committee meeting was on 11 April 2018. Although Turkey-EU relations are frozen at the moment, Turkey's accession process has benefitted both the staff and deputies with several joint projects and exchange programmes conducted by the EU. 'Strengthening the Institutional Capacity of the GNAT' conducted between October 2007 and October 2008 and 'Parliamentary Exchange and Dialogue' conducted between January 2012 and January 2014 are among those projects. These projects enabled the training of a limited number of GNAT staff on the EU harmonization process, strengthening the role of the independent legislature, and developing relations with civil society. However, the current stalemate between Turkey and the EU locks in both parliaments to distrust, suspicion, securitization of migration issue and consequently privileged partnership discussions (Demirsu and Müftüler-Baç, 2019; Türkeş-Kılıç, 2019) that would prevent any positive dialogue between the GNAT and the EP in the near future.

44.3.3 Current Challenges

The GNAT has been meeting the requirements of current challenges such as ensuring security, transparency, and citizen engagement, digitalization, and combating against the COVID-19 at different levels. Relatively high number of security staff working in the Parliament shows that the maintenance of the institution's security is the priority, particularly since 15 July 2016 coup attempt, when an airstrike bombed the Parliament. However, this caused 'the securitization of the GNAT' that citizen engagement, public visits, and even some deputies' actions, such as protesting or organizing a press meeting, have been limited by the administration. Yet, the eruption of the COVID-19 pandemic has been adding fuel to the fire of securitization. Public visits have been cancelled due to the pandemic. Administrative staff has been working part-time or flexible since the emergence of COVID-19 in March 2020. However, measures taken against the spread of the COVID-19 and its budget have not been transparent enough. The information is not updated publicly and is gathered only from the Speaker's replies to the written questions regarding the COVID-19 cases and measures taken in the Parliament.

On the other hand, regarding transparency, all legislative and scrutiny documents, draft laws, laws, statutory decrees, minutes of the Plenary, parliamentary questions, inquiries, investigations, and their answers are accessible online. However, in 2020, out of 34,713 written questions, 11,792 of them could not be replied to by the Bureau of the Speaker and only 4299 of them were answered in time (The Journal of the Committee on Planning and Budget, 2020). The GNAT has an English website and several social media accounts as well. However, the contents of these social media accounts cover news and announcements about the administration, particularly the Speaker, rather than the details of legislative acts.

44.4 Conclusion

Controversially, the GNAT both has roots from the Imperial Ottoman Parliament and represents a clear-cut disassociation from it by introducing national sovereignty and political participation into Turkish politics in 1920. This makes it a unique and indispensable political institution of Turkey. However, critical political changes over time and finally recent government system change has situated the Parliament as a symbolic organ rather than an effective political institution regarding law-making and achieving checks and balances. Consequently, the parliamentary administration has inherited a tendency to politicization and partisanship fuelled by the 20-year-old single-party rule of the JDP. Nevertheless, the political power could not transform the institutional capacity of the parliamentary administration into an autonomously functioning legislative body that would contribute to the development of representative democracy in Turkey. As being the representative of the same political party since 2002, the Speaker has tremendous power over the administration's rules, duties, and functioning. Although the number of staff members has been increasing over the last two decades, the staff working in central units and doing the main legislative work is still understaffed, and there is no gender equality policy. Thus, the contribution of the administrative staff to the legislative process and, consequently, the functioning of the representative democracy in Turkey are limited. On the other hand, the GNAT has built multiple international ties with its counterparts worldwide and developed its relations with the EP due to Turkey's accession process since 1999, albeit the stalemate in its membership track.

Turkey's responses to current domestic and global challenges derived from the ongoing political unrest and economic crises inside the country, its deteriorated relations with the EU and the United States, and the COVID-19 pandemic that seem to be decisive for the future legislative-executive relations. Consequently, they would be crucial for the possibility of reform on the parliamentary administration to make it an autonomous body that would contribute to Turkey's further democratization in the near future. However, the historical evolution of the Parliament and political developments until today signify the complexity of such a reform.

References

Bilgiç, S. S. (2020a) *Reply to the written question No. 7/36779*. The Grand National Assembly of Turkey. Available at: https://www2.tbmm.gov.tr/d27/7/7-36779c.pdf (Accessed: December 12, 2020).

Bilgiç, S. S. (2020b) *Reply to the written question No. 7/36466*. The Grand National Assembly of Turkey. Available at: https://www2.tbmm.gov.tr/d27/7/7-36466c.pdf (Accessed: December 12, 2020).

Çolak, Y. (2020) 'Meclis çalışanlarının sadece %28'i kadın', *Birgün Newspaper* 14 December. Available at: https://www.birgun.net/haber/meclis-calisanlarinin-sadece-yuzde-28-i-kadin-326507 (Accessed: December 12, 2020).

Demirsu, İ. and Müftüler-Baç, M. (2019) 'The Turkish–EU Cooperation on the Refugee Crisis: The Turkish Perceptions in the Parliamentary Debates', in Raube K. Müftüler-Baç M. and Wouters J. (eds.) *Parliamentary Cooperation and Diplomacy in EU External Relations: An Essential Companion*. Cheltenham: Edward Elgar Publishing, pp. 251–268.

Esen, B. and Gümüşçü, Ş. (2018) 'The Perils of 'Turkish Presidentialism'', *Review of Middle East Studies*, 52(1), pp. 43–53. DOI: 10.1017/rms.2018.10

Gençkaya, Ö. F. (2019) 'The Grand National Assembly of Turkey: A Decline in Legislative Capacity', *Politics Spotlight*, April, pp. 273–274. DOI: 10.1017/S1049096518002287

Gençkaya, Ö. F. (2020) 'The Grand National Assembly of Turkey: A Decline in Legislative Capacity' in Khamelko I., Stapenhurst R. and Mezey M. L. (eds.) *Legislative Decline in the 21st Century: A Comparative Perspective*. New York and Oxon: Routledge, pp. 82–93.

Gönenç, L. and Kontacı, A. E. (2019) '2017 Tarihli Anayasa Değişikliği Sonrasında Yasama-Yürütme İlişkileri', *Türkiye Barolar Birliği (TBB) Dergisi*, 145(1), pp. 53–79.

Hale, W. (2012) *Turkish Foreign Policy since 1774*. New York: Routledge.

Inter-Parliamentary Union (IPU) (2020) *Comparative research paper on parliamentary administration*. Available at: https://www.ipu.org/resources/publications/reference/2020-09/comparative-research-paper-parliamentary-administration (Accessed: June 7, 2021).

Inter-Parliamentary Union (IPU) (2021) *Turkey*. Available at: https://data.ipu.org/content/turkey?chamber_id=13548 (Accessed: June 7, 2021).

Işık, A. (2009) *The written question No. 7/9632*, The Grand National Assembly of Turkey. Available at: https://www2.tbmm.gov.tr/d23/7/7-9632s.pdf (Accessed: December 12, 2020).

Kalaycıoğlu, E. (1990) 'Cyclical Breakdown, Redesign and Nascent Institutionalization: The Turkish Grand National Assembly', in Liebert U. and Cotta M. (eds.) *Parliament and Democratic Consolidation in Europe*. London: Pinter, pp. 184–222.

Kalaycıoğlu, E. (2010) 'The Turkish Grand National Assembly: New Challenges and Old Problems' in Kerslake C., Öktem K. and Robins P. (eds.) *Turkey's Engagement with Modernity*. London: Palgrave Macmillan, pp. 119–141.

Kalaycıoğlu, E. (2014) 'Siyasal Rejim Tasarımı ve Demokrasi', in Kalaycıoğlu E. and Sarıbay Y. (eds.) *Türk Siyasal Hayatı*. Ankara: Sentez Yayıncılık, pp. 423–449.

NTV-MSNBC (2020), 'Meclis'te kaç kişi nerede çalışıyor?', Archive, 4 December. Available at: http://arsiv.ntv.com.tr/news/48469.asp (Accessed: July 7, 2021).

Oğuzlu, T. (2007) 'Soft Power in Turkish Foreign Policy', *Australian Journal of International Affairs*, 61, pp. 81–97. DOI: 10.1080/10357710601142518

Öniş, Z. and Yılmaz Ş. (2009) 'Between Europeanization and Euro-Asianism: Foreign Policy Activism in Turkey During the AKP Era', *Turkish Studies*, 10(1), pp. 7–24. DOI: 10.1080/14683840802648562

Özbudun, E. (1992) *1921 Anayasası*, Ankara: Atatürk Kültür, Dil ve Tarih Yüksek Kurumu, Atatürk Araştırma Merkezi Yayınları.

Özsoy-Boyunsuz, Ş. (2016) 'The AKP's Proposal for a 'Turkish Type of Presidentialism' in Comparative Context', *Turkish Studies*, 17(1), pp. 68–90. DOI: 10.1080/14683849.2015.1135064

Pakdil, N. (2009) *Reply to the written question No. 7/9632*, The Grand National Assembly of Turkey. Available at: https://www2.tbmm.gov.tr/d23/7/7-9632c.pdf (Accessed: June 7, 2021).

Soysal, M. (1969) *Dinamik Anayasa Anlayışı: Anayasa Diyalektiği Üzerine bir Deneme*, Ankara: Ankara Üniversitesi Siyasal Bilgiler Fakültesi Yayını.

Tanrıkulu, S. M. (2020a) *The written question No. 7/36779*, The Grand National Assembly of Turkey, November 19. Available at: https://www2.tbmm.gov.tr/d27/7/7-36779s.pdf (Accessed: June 7, 2021).

Tanrıkulu, S. M. (2020b) *The written question No. 7/36466*, The Grand National Assembly of Turkey, November 13. Available at: https://www2.tbmm.gov.tr/d27/7/7-36466s.pdf (Accessed: June 7, 2021).

The Grand National Assembly of Turkey (GNAT) (2021). Available at: www.global.tbmm.gov.tr (Accessed: June 7, 2021).

The Journal of the Committee on Planning and Budget (2019), The Grand National Assembly of Turkey, November 7. Available at: https://www.sbb.gov.tr/wp-content/uploads/2020/02/07-Kasim-2019_PBK_Gorusmeler.pdf (Accessed: June 7, 2021).

The Journal of the Committee on Planning and Budget (2020), The Grand National Assembly of Turkey, October 28. Available at: https://www.tbmm.gov.tr/develop/owa/komisyon_tutanaklari.goruntule?pTutanakId=2588 (Accessed: June 7, 2021).

The Law No. 6253 (2011), 'The Law on the Administrative Organization of the Assembly', *Official Gazette No. 28146*, December 18. Available at: https://www.mevzuat.gov.tr/MevzuatMetin/1.5.6253.pdf (Accessed: June 7, 2021).

The Standing Order of the GNAT (1973), *Official Gazette No. 14506*, April 13. Available at: https://www.tbmm.gov.tr/docs/ictuzuk.pdf (Accessed: June 7, 2021).

Turan, İ. (2000) *Devlet Reformu: TBMM'nin Etkinliği*, İstanbul: TESEV Yayınları. Available at: https://www.tesev.org.tr/wp-content/uploads/rapor_TMBB_Etkinligi.pdf (Accessed: June 7, 2021).

Turan, İ. (2003) 'Volatility in Politics, Stability in Parliament: An Impossible Dream? The Turkish Grand National Assembly During the Last Two Decades', *The Journal of Legislative Studies*, 9(2), pp. 151–176. DOI: 10.1080/1357233032000250671

Türkeş-Kılıç, S. (2019) 'Justifying Privileged Partnership with Turkey: An Analysis of Debates in the European Parliament', *Turkish Studies*, (21)1, pp. 29–55. DOI:10.1080/14683849.2019.1565941

Yıldız, M. (2007) 'Türkiye'de Yasama İşlevi Açısından Milletvekili Danışmanlığı', *Yasama Dergisi*, 4 (1), pp. 100–114.

Yılmaz, Z. (2020) 'Erdoğan's Presidential Regime and Strategic Legalism: Turkish Democracy in the Twilight Zone', *Southeast European and Black Sea Studies*, 20(2), pp. 265–287. DOI: 10.1080/14683857.2020.1745418

Zürcher, E. J. (1993) *Modernleşen Türkiye'nin Tarihi*, İstanbul: İletişim Yayınları.

45
UNITED KINGDOM'S PARLIAMENTARY ADMINISTRATION

Alexandra Meakin, Ben Yong and Cristina Leston-Bandeira

45.1 Introduction

The UK Parliament is a unique legislature. Developed literally over centuries, rather than as a result of the establishment of a new regime or political system, this is an institution shaped by informal rules and practice, and the ad-hoc development of services and departments. As such, its parliamentary administration presents equally unique and sui generis characteristics. As this chapter will show, the parliamentary administration of the UK Parliament is characterized by a lack of clear hierarchy and leadership, and a fragmentation of services, committees and departments; all of which have developed on the basis of ad-hoc needs, often in response to specific crises, such as the 2009 expenses scandal or the 2018/2019 wave of bullying and harassment claims. We set out the chapter as follows: we start by providing a brief overview of the structural framework within which the parliamentary administration of the UK Parliament operates, then focus on its governance structures and how these have developed over time, and end with staff and their functions, and how they support parliamentarians' work.

45.2 The Structural Framework of Parliamentary Administration of the UK Parliament

The UK Parliament is bicameral. The House of Commons (the lower chamber) consists of 650 elected Members of Parliament and the House of Lords (the upper chamber) of approximately 820 peers, the vast number being appointed, but with a small rump of hereditary peers and bishops (numbering 92 and 26, respectively). The two Houses have therefore very different types of legitimacies and forms of working; whereas MPs undertake this as a full-time job, this only applies to a very few peers, the vast majority of whom have very active working lives outside Parliament. Likewise, the nature of the roles performed varies considerably between the two Houses, which affects not only the type of administrative support needed but also the way the Houses are governed. The administration of the UK Parliament is carried out by almost 4,000 permanent staff, such as those working in the tea-rooms, clerking in the Commons and Lords chambers or committee rooms, or maintaining the building.

Constitutionally, both Houses are financially autonomous from the executive. Both Houses determine their own budgets. In 2019/2020, the Commons administration had an annual budget of approximately £789 million; the Lords administration £215 million (House of Commons Administration, 2020; House of Lords Administration, 2020).[1] About 20 years earlier, in 2000, the figures had been £240 million for the Commons, £31 million for the Lords (House of Commons Commission, 2001; House of Lords Administration, 2001). These numbers are not easily comparable though: there have been shifts in accounting practice, and some costs have now been shifted elsewhere. Much of the increase, however, is due to the rising cost of infrastructure—in particular, the rising cost of maintaining the crumbling Palace of Westminster estate.

All that said, the financial stance of the executive may have an influential role on parliamentary finances. For instance, in 2010–2015, the Coalition government had a policy of fiscal austerity; in the same period, the Houses of Parliament also chose to find savings wherever possible, in line with other public services (e.g., House of Commons Commission, 2011).

Like the UK constitution, the administration of the two Houses of Parliament at Westminster has developed in a haphazard manner over a long period of time. For instance, it is only very recently that the governance of the Houses has begun to professionalize. The House of Commons Commission, the governing body for the administration of the lower House, was only established in 1978, despite the existence of the House of Commons for centuries. Until then, House of Commons administration had been "governed" by a commission which included the Speaker and ministers from the executive. This late professionalisation of the parliamentary administration at Westminster is partly because there wasn't much to administer. The parliamentary estate (initially, just the famous Palace of Westminster) was controlled by the executive for much of the 20th century. Full control of the Palace of Westminster only passed to the parliamentary authorities in 1992, and it was only at this point that the Houses gained corporate status (Yong, 2018). But it is also because parliamentarians have collectively focused their energies on partisan battles and have given little time to systematic reform. Where reform has taken place, it has been ad-hoc and incremental. Thus, the governance arrangements of the Houses and between the Houses remain hazy and unclear, with the organisation and professionalisation of staff developing only recently and unevenly in response to parliamentarians' needs.

45.3 Administrative Governance

Currently, each House has a relatively similar set of administrative arrangements. We can divide these arrangements into two: the *governance* of administration—the political control and oversight of administration—and then *staff organisation, roles and functions*. Dealing first with governance, at the apex of House administration is a political body: the Commission. This is chaired by the Speaker or Lords Speaker and consists of parliamentarians from key parties or groups, including the Leader of the House and their opposition counterpart, the Shadow Leader. The Leader of the House is a minister who represents government in Parliament, having significant powers over the scheduling and overall running of parliamentary business; the Shadow Leader is the MP from the official opposition covering that area (the official opposition being the largest opposition party). Since 2016, non-executive external members also sit as Commission members. The Commission is responsible for setting direction of the administration: the strategic priorities for services and the staffing and pay of House staff. It is worth noting that Commission members in both Houses do not have portfolios: decisions (if they are made at all) are made on a consensual basis by all members.

Supporting each House Commission is a set of "domestic committees"—so-called because they deal not with matters "external" to Parliament but rather cover particular areas of House administration, such as finance, services and audit. These committees consist of parliamentarians, who advise the Commission on the matters within their remit. Also below each Commission is an Executive Board or Management Board, which are each composed of non-partisan, permanent staff. This is usually chaired by the relevant Clerk, the most senior permanent official of the respective House and who in recent years has come to lead the House service or administration. The Board also consists of senior officials from key departments of the House service: library and research, chamber services, the committee office, finance and so on. The role of the Board is not only to provide advice upwards to the Commission but also to provide direction downwards to the respective House departments or operating units. Each House service has a number of functional departments—devoted to supporting the plenary chamber, committees, research services, security and so on.

The two organograms below (Figures 45.1 and 45.2) help explain House governance.

There have been a number of reviews of the governance and administration of each House. By and large, these reviews have focused more on administrative arrangements and organisation rather than governance and the appropriate degree of political oversight and control. Where reviews have touched upon governance arrangements, they have been highly critical: the Commissions in particular have been seen to be weak in providing oversight and direction (for a more detailed discussion, see Yong, 2018).

There are several reasons for this weakness. The first, already highlighted, is that change has come about in an ad-hoc rather than systematic fashion. Second, relationships, personalities and a lack of clear purpose have traditionally made the Commissions weak as governance bodies. The Commissions are structured to reduce government influence, but in practice power is relative and determined by relationships. Although non-executive external members now sit on the Commissions, the key players have always been politicians. As the Chair, the Speaker is perhaps the most powerful figure in the Commons Commission. They are usually the longest serving member of the Commission and set the Commission agenda, but they are limited by the requirement of impartiality. The Leader of the House can also be very powerful. As indicated above, they are *not* the leader of the reigning political party—they are the government minister responsible for organising government business in the House. The Leader's power comes from the government's usual majority in the Commons and their power to control the business of the House. Indeed, where long-term administrative and procedural change has come in the Commons, it has often been because the Leader of the House has been reform-minded (e.g., Norman St John-Stevas and Robin Cook). And, excepting the Speaker, the political members of the Commission rarely stay in post long—often as short as two years—and so their primary concern is with the partisan battle in the Chamber, rather than the institution. In short, no one seems fully in charge.

A similar state of affairs exists in the Lords. It has a larger Commission, because of the inclusion of a greater number of political groups and their representatives. Moreover, the Lords operate under a self-regulation principle, which presumes equality between peers; so, for example, contrary to the Speaker in the House of Commons, the Lord Speaker is not in fact the Presiding Officer and does not lead the development of debates in the Lords' plenary chamber. Instead, peers self-regulate their own participation in debates. At the same time, the Leader of the Lords is weaker than their Commons counterpart because no government has had a majority in the Lords for the last two decades. Finding consensus for administrative and organisational change within the House can be difficult.

Moreover, while domestic committees only advise, and do not order, their Commissions, there has been a long history of a lack of clarity about the committees' respective remits. Finally, it is worth noting that permanent officials in the administration have often been cautious in acting given the requirement of impartiality in an intensely political environment. The saying "officials advise, ministers decide" from Whitehall (the civil service branch supporting

House of Commons – Governance structure

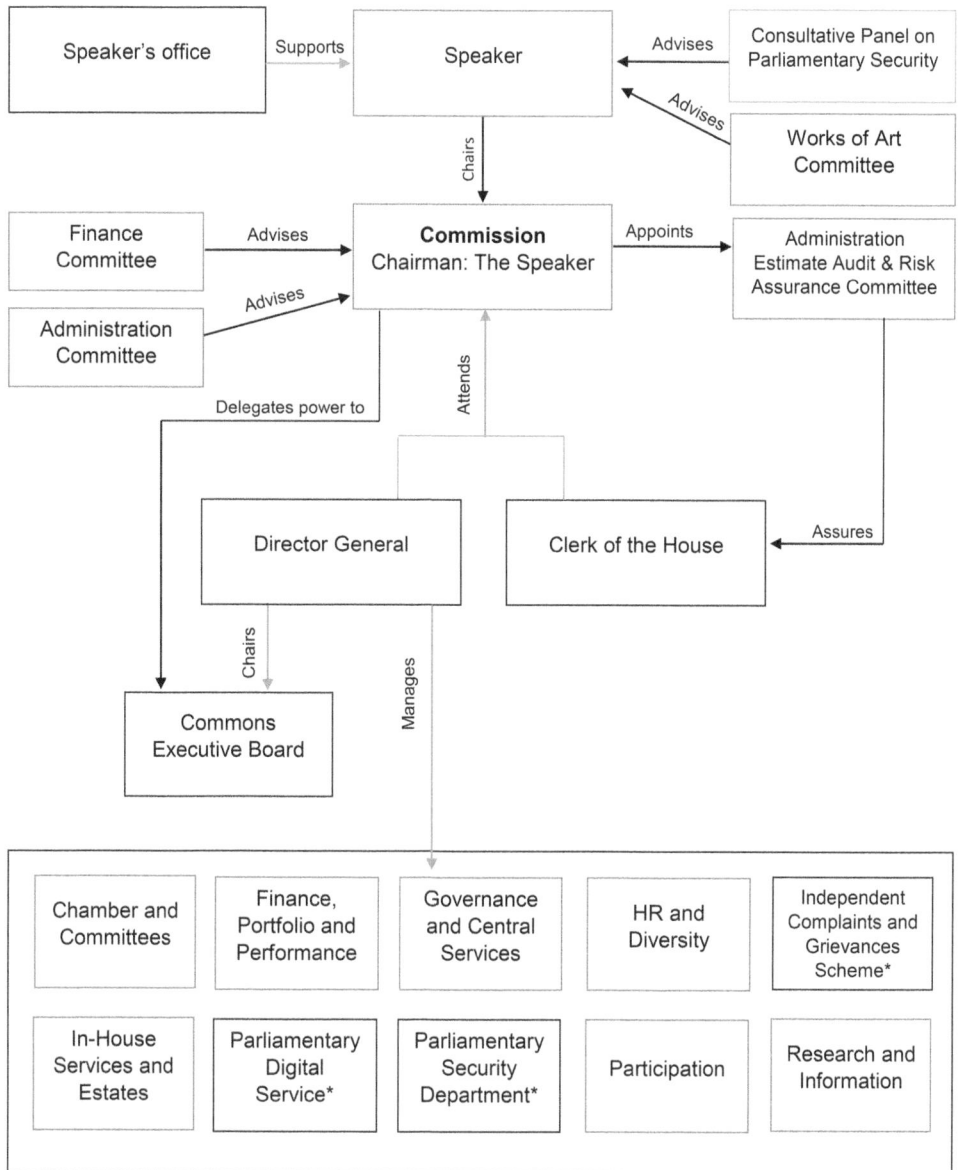

Figure 45.1 House of Commons—governance structure

the executive) applies with equal force in Westminster—perhaps with even stronger force, since (as we have seen) there is no obvious "minister" for officials to follow in either House.

All this—weak governance and the absence of clear leadership—has meant that systemic, long-term institutional problems have persisted without clear resolution, sometimes erupting into highly publicized controversies. The most well-publicized is the expenses scandal of 2009, in which a number of MPs in the House of Commons were exposed for having misused their expenses. This came about largely because of fragmented governance, and a failure

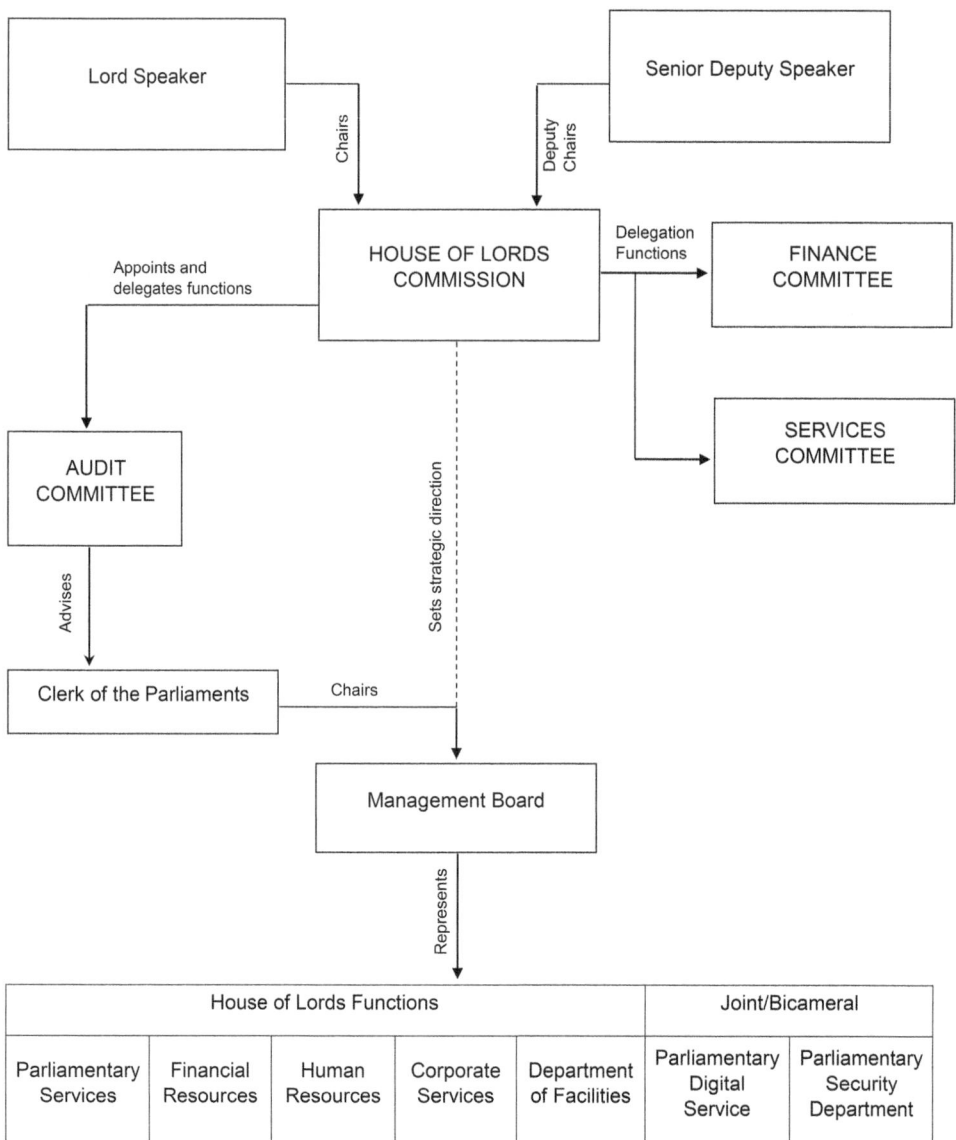

Figure 45.2 House of Lord—governance structure

on the part of successive administrations to take decisive action. But there have been other institutional problems: the controversy over the appointment of a new Clerk of the House (Meakin and Geddes, 2022); bullying and harassment of staff in both Houses (Cox, 2018; Ellenbogen, 2019; White, 2019); and the ongoing saga of the refurbishment of the crumbling Palace of Westminster, which is now a major health hazard (Meakin, 2021). These problems stem from two fundamental predicaments: a lack of clarity about who is in charge and the inability of those in charge to take decisive action. That said, in recent years, there have also been institutional successes in developing and strengthening services—particularly in terms of the development of public engagement services and digitalisation (Leston-Bandeira, 2016). Public engagement services, which include participatory mechanisms as well as broader services such as education, have expanded exponentially since the turn of the 21st century, in response to a perceived need to strengthen engagement with the public.

Historically, bicameral relations have also been limited due to the problems noted above. However, there are now both formal and informal meetings of the key bodies and actors from each House, in order to communicate, coordinate and negotiate. Bicameral relations have accelerated in recent years, partly because of austerity and partly because of capital development. As we see below, some services such as security, most of public engagement services, digital and maintenance of the parliamentary estate, are shared. So too, are some costs in a pre-determined ratio (usually with the Commons paying more—70:30 or 60:40). But both Houses remain keen to maintain their autonomy. A long-standing concern—particularly of the Lords—is that they do not lose out in any proposal to share resource.

45.4 Staff Organisation, Roles and Functions

This section sets out the structures and departments that make up the administration of the UK Parliament, discusses its objectives and character and considers how the administration may evolve in the future.

The bicameral nature of the institution means most of these staff are split between the two Houses: over 3,000 staff in the Commons and approximately 570 in Lords (House of Commons, 2020; House of Lords, 2020). The services have grown substantially in the past two decades: since 2001, the number of Commons staff has more than doubled (from 1377), and the size of the Lords staff has increased by over 50% (from 377) (House of Commons Library, 2016). Over this same period, there has also been a move towards unifying some cross-parliamentary services, following the passing of the Parliament (Joint Departments) Act 2007. IT services were the first to be managed jointly: through the Parliamentary Information and Communication Technology Department, renamed and remodelled as the Parliamentary Digital Service in 2015, following the Digital Democracy Commission set up by then Speaker John Bercow. Security, estates, procurement, the education service and the Archives are also shared between both Houses, although without designation as joint departments. Table 45.1 lists the different departments within the parliamentary administration in both Houses.

The structures show the wide-ranging variety of tasks carried out by the people who make up the administration of Parliament. Tasks range from ensuring parliamentary business can proceed smoothly and in line with procedural rules: staff clerk debates in the lower House's two plenary chambers (the Commons chamber and Westminster Hall) and in the chamber of the House of Lords, processes parliamentary questions, manages votes (divisions) and produces an edited verbatim record of proceedings (Hansard). Separate teams clerk select committee meetings, lead their inquiries and draft their reports, for committees in both Houses (and joint committees). Parliamentary staff also support the institution by helping the public engage with and feel part of their legislature through outreach and participation activities in Westminster and around the country. Archivists and heritage specialists manage the Parliamentary Archives and art collections. Parliamentary staff also keep the parliamentary buildings secure, clean and operational—a major undertaking given the age and condition of the Palace of Westminster, and the needs of a UNESCO World Heritage Site—and manage the corporate, commercial, administrative and financial services required for a multi-thousand workforce. The Parliamentary Digital Service staff provides Members and their staff with essential IT equipment and support,

Table 45.1 Departments within the parliamentary administration

Commons	Lords	Joint/shared services
Chamber and Participation Team	Parliamentary Services (Black Rod's Department, Committee Office, Journal Office, Legislation Office, Library, Hansard)	Parliamentary Digital Service (joint department)
Select Committee Team	Department of Facilities (Property and Office Services, Catering and Retail Services)	Parliamentary Security Department (hosted by the Commons)
Research and Information Services	Clerk of the Parliaments' Office	In-House Services and Estates (hosted by the Commons)
Governance and Strategic Business Resilience Team	Communications Team	Parliamentary Archives (hosted by the Lords)
Member Services	Human Resources Office	Parliamentary Procurement and Commercial Services (hosted by the Lords)
Interparliamentary Relations Office	Finance Department	

as well as building and maintaining key digital services and outputs, such as the website and other applications, such as the tool to submit questions to the government electronically; in addition to contributing to the development of the virtual and hybrid chambers during the coronavirus pandemic, alongside the Parliamentary Broadcasting Unit (part of the Chamber and Participation Team). Individual members in each House can also access advice on procedure from clerks, helping to ensure parliamentary questions and proposed amendments to legislation are in order. They can also use the services of the libraries of each House, which produce briefing papers on a vast range of policy areas, as well as on legislation and business scheduled for debate. The libraries also respond to queries directly for members and their staff provide a bespoke and impartial research and information service. The Interparliamentary Relations Office, based within the Commons, and Overseas Office in the Lords, manages relations with other parliaments and the delegations provided to inter-parliamentary assemblies.

As noted earlier, both Houses have undergone periodic reviews of their administrative structures, aiming to modernize and professionalize the administration: for example, the external review of the management of the House of Lords in January 2021 which found that the "organisational performance of the House of Lords lags that of many commercial, public sector and voluntary organisations" (House of Lords Commission, 2021, p 5). The general trend of reviews in the Commons since the 1974 Compton Review has been to unify the administration, moving away from a federal system of departments. These reviews have also considered the "bureaucratic" leadership of the institution. The House of Commons Service is led by the Clerk of the House, and the House of Lords Administration by the Clerk of the Parliaments. In addition to their roles as the chief procedural adviser to each House, the occupants of these posts also serve as the Accounting Officer and Corporate Officer for their House, under the Parliamentary Corporate Bodies Act 1992. The wide-ranging responsibilities of the Clerks' roles have led to questioning over whether any single occupant of each post can offer both procedural and management expertise. In 2014, this issue caused the recruitment of the Clerk of the House to be paused and then terminated, due to the concerns of MPs that the selected candidate, the Director of Parliamentary Services in the Australian Parliament, did not have the necessary procedural expertise (Meakin and Geddes, 2022). A select committee was established to consider the future of the post and recommended the establishment of a Director General post, with "responsibility for resource allocation and delivery across the House service", working as a leadership team with the Clerk (House of Commons Governance Committee, 2014, p60). The External Management Review of the Lords, mentioned above, recommended the creation of a Chief Operating Officer post, to "focus on the work outside the Chamber and Committees i.e., the management of the House as against the business of the House" (House of Lords Commission, 2021, p 7).

Developments in recent years have led to the establishment of departments or organisations which are technically independent of the House of Commons Service or House of Lords administration, but part of the wider governance of the institution. The Independent Complaints and Grievance Scheme was first established in July 2018 and became a fully independent bicameral team in December 2018. The major refurbishment of the parliamentary building—the Restoration and Renewal of the Palace of Westminster—has required the establishment of two organisations independent of the parliamentary administration: the Parliamentary Works Sponsor Body and its Delivery Authority.

A further part of the wider staffing of the institution—but independent of the administration of each House—are the researchers, secretaries and caseworkers serving the elected and non-elected parliamentarians in the Commons and Lords. These staff are employed directly by the MP or peer for whom they work, with approximately 3,200 staff for MPs (an increase of 75% since 2001) (House of Commons Library, 2016; IPSA, 2020). Typically, each MP has a team of about two to three members of staff, though some, particularly those with ministerial and/or party responsibilities, have much larger teams. MPs' staff are key in supporting the various roles performed by MPs. Although this division varies, most MPs have staff based in both Westminster and their constituencies. The salaries of MPs' staff are paid through allowances provided by the Independent Parliamentary Standards Authority (IPSA), with set job descriptions, salary scales and model contracts provided. Again, IPSA is another body independent from Parliament, which was set up following the expenses scandal in 2009.

Following the recommendation of Gemma White QC's independent report into the bullying and harassment of MPs' staff in 2019, that "there must be a fundamental shift away from regarding Members of Parliament as '650 small businesses' with near complete freedom to operate in relation to their staff", the House of Commons Commission has also established a Member Services team to act as an HR department for Members and their staff (House of Commons Commission, 2020; White Report, 2019, p 3). Arrangements for peers' staff in the Lords are far less formalized, however, with no set allowances for staffing or formal structures for supporting such staff (as highlighted by Lord Foulkes, HL Deb, 30 April 2019, c868). This means their figures on the number of staff are not provided, although there are nearly 600 people as receiving a staff pass for peers of the Lords (House of Lords Commission, 2020).[2] Where the staff of individual peers receive a salary for this work, this is paid by the individual member personally (and many have paid employment outside of Parliament).

The staff fulfilling the governance of the institution are classed as "crown servants", rather than civil servants, serving the legislature rather than the executive and crucially, are politically impartial. There are strict restrictions on political activity for members of staff in the House of Commons who advise or work directly with MPs, as set out below:

> The core tasks of the House of Commons Service include supporting the House and its committees and supporting individual Members (and their staff). Members are

entitled to expect that these services are provided with complete political impartiality and that briefing, and advice are not influenced by the personal political opinions of individual members of staff. Staff who advise Members must be, and appear to be, impartial. When the impartiality of such staff is compromised, not only may their ability to do their job be impaired, but the reputation of the House of Commons Service may also suffer.

(House of Commons, 2021, Chapter 18)

It is a permanent administration, serving successive parliaments. It is often permanent on an individual level also, with many clerks, in particular, spending their entire career within Westminster. This can pose a conflict inherent in the role: staff are in post to serve both the current cohort of parliamentarians and also the institution of Parliament itself (Crewe, 2017; Yong, Davies and Leston-Bandeira, 2019). The two aims can—and often do—conflict. Yong (2018, p 90) describes the "fundamental tension lying at the heart of the relationship between the political wing and the permanent House administration" as:

> the constitutional (and prudent) necessities for permanent staff to be *both* responsive *and* politically impartial. House staff must be responsive to each and every member, but balance this with their responsibility to the House as a corporate entity which exists across time.

A further example comes from the long-running saga over the need to repair the parliamentary building, the Palace of Westminster. As Corporate Officer, the Clerk of the House would be legally responsible under the Corporate Manslaughter and Corporate Homicide Act 2007 if a fire within the Palace were to prove fatal. Despite this responsibility, however, he has no power to force MPs or Lords to approve fire safety works and indeed was accused of being part of a conspiracy to force parliamentarians out of the building (as noted in HC Deb, 16 Jul 2020, c1750).

Even the House of Commons Twitter account reflects this essential tension, with staff banned from tweeting the results of divisions in the Chamber, after complaints from Conservative MPs (Hern, 2020). This row, although seemingly superficial, points to another tension for permanent parliamentary staff: striving to increase public engagement with Parliament, but having to do so on a non-partisan basis, while the institution operates primarily on a partisan basis. Prior and Leston-Bandeira (2022, p 71) have highlighted how the idea of a single "brand identity" is a "problematic concept for parliaments". This concept is of primary concern for staff: public engagement activities by the institution are primarily delivered by staff rather than parliamentarians (Judge and Leston-Bandeira, 2018).

45.5 Conclusion

The parliamentary administration of the UK Parliament reflects the sui generis characteristics and nature of this legislature, as an institution that has developed in a piecemeal fashion, often in response to specific crises, rather than in a strategic and systemic manner.

This starts with the relationship between its lower and upper chambers, the House of Commons and the House of Lords. These are in theory separate bodies, with the vast majority of their parliamentary administration operating independently according to the relevant House's rules and procedures. However, in practice an increasing number of services are shared. This is in great part due to both Houses being hosted within the same building, leading to the sharing of key services such as security, which has become all the more important over the last few decades in face of more tangible terrorism and other threats. Likewise, the need to address the repair, restoration and renovation of the main building itself, the Palace of Westminster, has made the need to work together all the more real. Besides this, newer services such as digitisation and some elements of public engagement such as education services have also been developed mainly as joint services, again in great part due to the sharing of physical resources. This increase in joint working has been concomitant with the development of more comparable roles and administration structures, such as the Speaker and Lord Speaker, or the Boards supporting the work of the Commissions.

However, this masks a much messier reality, which reflects the ad hoc way in which parliamentary administration has developed. As this chapter has shown, the UK Parliament is characterized by a relatively late professionalisation of its governance system, which has followed a considerable expansion of the needs to be met by parliamentary services over the past three decades. This expansion of needs results from the development not only of new functions for parliament such as public engagement, but also of a strengthened role in policymaking for Parliament (Cowley and Russell 2016) following a few key reforms of parliamentary business since the turn of the century. Although governance structures are now more clearly delineated, there remains a lack of overall leadership of parliamentary administrative services and functions. Amendments to structures and governance processes are often made in response to specific needs arising from crises, such as the latest bullying and harassment claims. There is also an inherent separation and tension between parliamentary and institutional duties of staff, along with the existence of 650 separate mini-businesses (MPs' offices) which remained out of reach from parliamentary administration oversight. Notwithstanding the very professional and efficient delivery of services by parliamentary administration of the UK Parliament, this is an institution supported on the basis of dispersed and often disjointed service processes. Still, recent reviews and reforms have begun to create a more unified parliamentary administration.

Notes

1 Note the budget of the Commons *includes* capital expenditure (e.g., cost and maintenance of infrastructure and the estate, but *excludes* the cost of members' salaries and staff, which is now paid out of a separate vote. That separate vote—the cost of members' expenses (which includes partisan staff employed by members in the Commons)—is currently an additional £226 million (Independent Parliamentary Standards Authority, 2020).
2 This figure is not limited to those providing research or secretarial assistance, including, for example, drivers for individual peers. This data is only provided since 2014, preventing historical comparison.

References

Cowley, P. and Russell, M. (2016) 'The Policy Power of the Westminster Parliament: the Parliamentary State' and the Empirical Evidence', *Governance*, 29(1), pp. 121–137.
Cox, L. (2018) *The Bullying and Harassment of House of Commons Staff: Independent Inquiry Report*. https://www.parliament.uk/globalassets/documents/conduct-in-parliament/dame-laura-cox-independent-inquiry-report.pdf Accessed on: 2 April 2021.
Crewe, E. (2017) 'Magi or Mandarins? Contemporary Clerkly Culture'. In Evans, P., (ed), *Essays on the History of Parliamentary Procedure*. Oxford; Portland: Hart, pp. 45–68.
Ellenbogen, E. (2019) *An Independent Inquiry into Bullying and Harassment in the House of Lords*. https://www.parliament.uk/globalassets/documents/lords-committees/house-of-lords-commission/2017-19/ellenbogen-report.pdf Accessed on: 2 April 2021.

Hern, A. (2020) 'Commons Twitter account banned from tweeting vote results,' *The Guardian*. 4 October 2020. Available at: https://www.theguardian.com/politics/2020/oct/04/commons-twitter-account-banned-from-tweeting-vote-results Accessed on: 28 February 2021.

House of Commons (2020) *Annual Report and Accounts 2020*. HC 580.

House of Commons (2021) *Staff Handbook*. Available at: https://www.parliament.uk/business/commons/governance-of-the-house-of-commons-/house-of-commons-staff-handbook/ Accessed on: 3 March 2021.

House of Commons Commission (2001) *Annual Report 2000–2001*. HC 155.

House of Commons Commission (2011) *Thirty-Third Report of the Commission, and Annual Report of the Administration Estimate Audit Committee: Financial Year 2010/11*. HC 1439 London: TSO.

House of Commons Commission (2020) *Minutes of Meeting of the House of Commons Commission 13 January*. Available at: https://old.parliament.uk/business/committees/committees-a-z/other-committees/house-of-commons-commission/news-parliament-2019-21/commission-decisions-13-january-2020/ Accessed on: 28 February 2021.

House of Commons Commission (2020) *Minutes of Meeting of the House of Commons Commission/MEC 9 November 2020* Available at: https://committees.parliament.uk/publications/3612/documents/44093/default/ Accessed on: 28 February 2021.

House of Commons Governance Committee (2014) *House of Commons Governance, Session 2014–15*. HC 692.

House of Commons Library (2016) *Research Briefing: Total Number of MPs, Peers and Staff 3 October 2016*. Available at: https://commonslibrary.parliament.uk/research-briefings/sn02411/ Accessed on: 9 March 2021.

House of Commons (2020) *Annual Report and Accounts 2020* HC 580. https://www.parliament.uk/globalassets/documents/commons-expenditure/admin-annual-accounts/administration_annual_report_and_accounts_2019_20.pdf

House of Lords (2020) *Annual Report and Resource Accounts 2019–20* HL 110. https://www.parliament.uk/globalassets/documents/hl-management-board/house-of-lords-annual-report-and-accounts-2019-20.pdf

House of Lords Administration (2001) *Annual Report and Accounts 2000–01*.

House of Lords Commission (2020) *Rules relating to Parliamentary passes for Members' Staff: follow-up report* 1st Report of Session 2019–21 HL 160.

House of Lords Commission (2021) *House of Lords External Management Review*. Available at: https://committees.parliament.uk/committee/362/house-of-lords-commission/news/138780/external-management-review/ Accessed on: 28 February 2021.

IPSA (Independent Parliamentary Standards Authority) (2020) *Freedom of Information Response: Request for Details on the Numbers of Staff Working for MPs* 11 June 2020 Available at: https://www.theipsa.org.uk/freedom-of-information/rfi0292992-4 Accessed on: 8 March 2021.

Judge, D. and Leston-Bandeira, C. (2018) 'The Institutional Representation of Parliament', *Political Studies*, 66(1), pp. 154–172.

Leston-Bandeira, C. (2016) 'Why Symbolic Representation Frames Parliamentary Public Engagement', *The British Journal of Politics and International Relations*, 18(2), pp. 498–516.

Meakin, A. (2021) 'Groundhog Day for Restoration and Renewal after the Strategic Review: There is still no alternative', *Hansard Society Blog*. https://www.hansardsociety.org.uk/blog/groundhog-day-for-restoration-and-renewal-after-the-strategic-review-still-no-alternative Accessed on: 30 April 2021.

Meakin, A. and Geddes, M. (2022) 'Explaining Change in Legislatures: Dilemmas of Managerial Reform in the UK House of Commons', *Political Studies*. Online First publication 70(1), pp. 216–235.

Prior, A. and Leston-Bandeira, C. (2022) 'Parliamentary Storytelling: A New Concept in Public Engagement with Parliaments', *The Journal of Legislative Studies*, 28(1), pp. 67–92. https://www.tandfonline.com/doi/full/10.1080/13572334.2020.1848081.

White, G. (2019) *Bullying and Harassment of MPs' Parliamentary Staff: Independent Inquiry Report*. HC 2206. https://www.parliament.uk/globalassets/documents/Conduct-in-Parliament/GWQC-Inquiry-Report-11-July-2019_.pdf Accessed on: 28 February 2021.

Yong, B. (2018) 'The Governance of Parliament'. In Horne, A. and Drewry, G. (eds) *Parliament and the Law* (second edition). Oxford: Hart Publishing, pp. 75–102.

Yong, B. Davies, G. and Leston-Bandeira, C. (2019) 'Tacticians, Stewards, and Professionals: The Politics of Publishing Select Committee Legal Advice', *Journal of Law and Society*, 46(3), pp. 367–395.

PART II.III

Worldwide

46
ARGENTINA'S PARLIAMENTARY ADMINISTRATION

María Paula Bertino[1]

46.1 Introduction – A Closer Look to the Argentinean Congress

As shown by Aleman (2013), the Argentinian Congress is the second most studied Parliament of Latin America, both in cross-national or case studies. A lot has been said about it, about their members and how they are selected, the laws they approve, the relationship between party, benches and representation. If it was a rubber seal, if it contributed to policy making, about how a Congress works in a politically fragmented presidential system, or how federalism affects the legislative branch. Ever since the third wave of democracy hit Argentina in 1983, the Congress has been in the spotlight. Mostly because some used to believe it didn't have any importance, and then because some others showed it had. But no one, so far, has asked (and properly answered) about the parliamentary administration in Argentina. This may be so because bureaucracy and politics are driven in parallel – but as we may see in this article this affirmation is not completely true – or because the very complex administrative structure of the Congress combines both formal institutions (mainly visible in the internal rulebooks of both the Lower and Upper Chamber) and informal practices (circumstantial political arrangements) that regulate the administrative parliamentary life.

In order to do so, this chapter will focus on the links that bond politics and administration in the Argentinean Congress and how they developed in the last 20 years. It will feature in the second section the most salient characteristics of the congress administrative organization, the legislators and the congress permanent staff, the size of the Congress Staff, the level of administrative autonomy of the five administrative structures of the Congress and the Congress against the Executive Branch. The third section of the chapter will focus on the political and bureaucratic organization in the Argentine Congress, describing the conformation of legislatives groups and commissions. It would look deeper into the rules for both chambers for the legislative labour organization. It will analyse the legislative process, looking forward to finding the way in which the administrative staff collaborates with the politicians in the generation of legislation, taking the budgetary commission as an example of the combined work of both the administrative and political staff, in the lower and upper chamber. The fourth section will concentrate on what goes beyond the law-making process for the administration of the Congress; analysing administrative staff unionism, parliamentary diplomacy and the Library, the Print and Health Insurance System (HIS) of the Congress, since the last three represent distinctive administrative structures within the Congress. It will concentrate mainly on the structures of the Chamber of Deputies but will also compare and contrast with the Senate.

The Argentinean Congress is a highly politicized organization. Not only because of the representation principle that leads to the origins of this institution, but because in its rules it is stated that the administrative organization will also be guided by a partisan principle. This chapter will show that the parliamentary administration in Argentina is leaded by the Speakers of the Chambers but greatly influenced by the Parliamentary Labour Union (*Asociación de Personal Legislativo* or *APL* for the Spanish acronym), and also that the Congress is an enormous and complex bureaucratic structure that includes – but is not limited to – the oversight of the legislative process.

46.2 Congress: Structure, Size and Autonomy

As a federal system, Argentina has a bicameral parliament, composed of two Chambers. The lower chamber is the Honourable Chamber of Deputies, representing the people of all the country, and the upper chamber is the Honourable Chamber of the Senate, representing the interest of the 23 Argentine provinces and the Autonomous City of Buenos Aires. Commonly known as *Diputados* and *Senado*, the constitutional text gives them both very similar legislative powers. There are 72 Senators – three for every district, two for the first electoral party and one for the second – with a six years term, elected by thirds every two years[2] and 257 representatives elected by half every two years.[3] Each Chamber has its own rulebook that sets the tone not only for the legislative process itself, but also of the administration within. This bicameral Legislature may be depicted as one with a divided parliamentary administration, although some of the bureaucratic structures seem to be joint in paper. This means that some administrative structures are only apparently bicameral, because in paper they serve both Chambers, but in practice they are ruled and governed by one Chamber, or even by their own administrative body.

The parliamentary administration of the Argentinean Congress is composed by five bureaucratic structures: the upper and lower chambers administration, the Congress Library, the Congress Print and the Congress HIS. Each of these structures has their own administrative staff. Even though both the lower and upper chamber are politically related, their bureaucratic structures are completely autonomous. Each of these bureaucratic bodies duplicates in almost every direction and programme within and works independently from each other. As for the Congress Library, the Congress Print and the Congress HIS, these bureaucratic structures emerged as assistant to the administration of the Congress as a whole, but in time the three of them developed an autonomy that allows them to bond with the citizens beyond the Congress and developed an administrative body of its own, as it will be explained in section four. It should be noted that these five administrative bodies are governed by the same law and share a budget and a Union and are considered for all purposes a part of the Argentine Congress Administration.

With more than 12,500 staff members, the parliamentary administration in Argentina is a very autonomous structure that not only operates in isolation of the executive branch but also differs between the structures, having different dynamics in the lower and upper chamber, and even a distinctive role for the three other autonomous structures.

46.2.1 Administrative Authorities and Staff

The position of Speaker (*Presidente*) of the lower chamber is given to a representative of the majoritarian – or first minority – party, while in the Senate this position is constitutionally assigned to the vice president of the nation, elected in the presidential formula in a different but concomitant election. The Speaker of each House is the most important authority – both politically and administratively – within each Chamber and, according to the rulebook of both the upper and the lower chamber, it has the control of the day-to-day administration. The bureau of political authorities is made up of three vice presidents for each chamber, also selected from the elected legislators[4] who are designated to fulfil the Speaker's functions should he/she be absent but have no say in the administration of the legislative body. The internal rules of both chambers established that, in order to execute this administrative authority, the Speakers have a staff of Secretaries who are in charge of "making the wheels turn". These are the Secretary General of the Presidency, the Administrative Secretary, the Operative Coordination Secretary and the Parliamentary Secretary.[5] These Secretaries are selected by the *presidente* of the chamber and for the Administrative, Operative Coordination and Parliamentary Secretaries the appointment is endorsed by the legislative body: according to the rules of procedure of each Chamber, these assignments must be given to members of the speakers party (Art. 43° of the internal rulebook of the lower chamber), often being former legislators who lost their seats. They fill a role that mixes both political and technical capacities and are in charge of handling everyday work, depending directly on the Chamber Speaker. The administrative authorities body of Secretaries is completed with one deputy head secretary for each Secretary.[6] And every Secretary has an organizational chart that divides the staff in directions and sub directions that vary in number depending on each of them.[7]

The Parliamentary Secretary supervises the legislative work, and everything that is related with the law-making process. From the start of the legislative process until the submission to the Senate or to the Executive of an approved bill, this office has to look after the well-functioning of the legislative sessions. This is the link that bonds politics and administration within the floor. This office looks after the submission to committee (although as it will be seen in the third section of this chapter, this is a highly partisan process that also involves the Parliamentary Labour Committee, whose role will be depicted in Section 46.3), the liaison with the executive branch and with the Senate, the file and dispatch of the bills, the stenographers direction, among other tasks. It also falls under its orbit the coordination of the parliamentary training institute (*Instituto de Capacitación Parlamentaria*). During a session, the Parliamentary Secretary tends to be seated beside the Speaker and acts as a Master of Ceremonies in the shadow.

The Administrative Secretary is also involved in the legislative process, since it falls under this office's responsibility to summon the legislators to a session, and to check the vote count. It also has the responsibility to handle the budget, security and human resources of the Chamber.[8] This may sound as a very operative function, but as depicted above, it is given to a partisan member of the majoritarian party, thus making their task a conjunction of partisan and technical capacities. It is also the space in which the union discusses most of its interest – mainly the hiring of staff, making it at last one of the most sensitive spaces in the organizational chart. In the Senate, it is usually given to a sort of chief of staff for the Senate presidency, having even the delegation of the signature of the Senate's presidency. In the lower chamber, the function emulates a sort of Treasury Secretary since the Secretary General assumes a more political role.

The Secretary General acts as the chief of staff to the President of the House. This role exists only in *Diputados*, not in the Senate, and was created in 1983, and was never included in the internal rulebook. It emerged from the necessity of the Speaker of the lower Chamber to counterbalance the power of the administrative secretary designated at the time, and it is appointed by the Speaker unilaterally via an internal resolution. This is, by far, the most powerful Secretary of the lower Chamber – like the Administrative Secretary is in the Senate. The Secretary General controls the signature of the Speaker and is the firewall between him/her and the legislators. Since it shares missions and functions with the Administrative Secretary, the tension between the two tends to be high and it requires the generation of a political equilibrium in order to reduce the conflict and manage to get the administration of the lower chamber in order.

At last, the Operative Coordination Secretary appears as a "consolation prize" for the second party in the Chamber. Although this Secretary is responsible for selected administrative tasks, this office doesn't get involved in the day-to-day administration. It is a space for the opposition to get some staff, to enforce political discussions, including offices allocations, and to negotiate some minor administrative discussion.[9]

46.2.2 Staff Organization and Unionism

The Argentinean Congress staff is normed by the 24,600 law[10] that establishes the rights and obligations of the parliamentary administration. It also states the existence of a parliamentary union (being *A.P.L.* the biggest organization within, followed by *Asociación de Trabajadores del Estado – ATE*.) and states the hierarchy of the parliamentary agents. Although this law does not regulate the actual functions of the Congress administration, it shapes the role of permanent and transitory staff. The transitory staff is designated by every legislator, responds politically to them, and can't aspire to an administrative career in the congress. Sometimes, transitory staff can be designated in a typically permanent office after their legislator has fulfilled the mandate and expect to build an administrative legislative career. For the permanent staff, the role of the union is central both for the recruitment and for the appointment to permanent positions within the parliamentary structure.

Parliamentary Staff is also divided between the maintenance staff (chofers, cleaning, kitchen staff and general services) and the administrative technical staff and is organized in 14 different levels of hierarchy that apply both to transitory and permanent agents.[11] On the whole, Deputies and Senate have over 10,000 people working as Parliamentary Staff to this day. A total of 5000 of them are the House, 5000 in the Senate. The other three bureaucratic structures (Library, Print and HIS) add another 2500 legislative agents.[12] Through the last 20 years, the size of the parliamentary administration has been growing unevenly between (and inside) the Congress. Every Chamber president shapes the role of the organizational charts beyond their missions and functions, by distributing budget and positions. These changes are made with the consent of the Union that uses its power of negotiation to pursue the transfer of temporary agents to permanent position and to have members moving up in the internal hierarchical ladder.[13]

46.2.3 Moving Up: From Temporary to Permanent Staff

Although the legislative group staff should be temporarily designated according to the 24,600 law, it's not unusual to find permanent staff designations in party groups. The party group staff is independent from the legislator individual staff, having the latter's professional path in the congress determined by the lengths of the representative in its chair. But the first ones can aspire to a lengthy professional career, especially if they are assisting a big party group, whose existence is guaranteed. The highly partisan bias of the Argentinean congress is also shown in this matter, since internal lines inside every party may shape the composition of the party group staff. But it's more likely in these cases to find transient agents that can aspire to a permanent nomination (commonly known as "*pase a planta*") that, in time, may shift their position to a legislator office and then move back to the party group when needed. Eventually, they can also be asked to move to a less partisan office, depending on the authorities of the Chamber, once they get the permanent position as congress agents.

The permanent position is, by law, for life. Once an agent is given the permanent condition, they can move to a higher category, from the 14th, the most basic and less paid, to the 1st. These categories do not imply responsibilities in themselves but they do state the salary of the agent, which is shaped by modules.[14] To scale up in the categories is another negotiation both with the Union and with the Chamber presidency, since the directive positions and subsequent ranks do get an extra payment. Although there is a sort of tenure track for the less partisan offices, the ones of Administrative Technical Staff, the chances of getting a higher position with more responsibilities are contingent on the vacancy of the position and are in most cases surrogate. The Union has great influence in the nomination to fulfil these vacancies, and although the petition of the move and of the category supposes a signature of an authority (of the Chamber or of the party group), the Union also promotes members and negotiates the lists of promotions. But in a whole, professionalization is not particularly sought, but rather something developed after having reached a position.

46.2.4 Autonomy of the Parliamentary Administration

The organizational charts of the five parliamentary structures (Deputies, Senate, Library, Print and HIS) have autonomy within the Congress. Although they are led by the same law, the mobility of an agent from one structure to another is almost as a move to the executive branch. And even though formally the Library's administrative authority is led by a special bicameral committee composed by legislators of both Chambers, and both the Print and the HIS are dependent from one of the two Chambers (the Print currently depends of the House and the HIS is under the Senate control), it is within their own bureaucratic structures that they define the day-to-day operations.

In sum, it is possible to see that the administration of the Argentinean Congress has five autonomous bureaucratic structures. The fact that every Chamber dictates its own rulebook and has its own organizational chart gives the idea that they are even autonomous between them. The operational decisions of any of the five bureaucratic structures are not influenced by the others, nor is the recruitment of the staff, but they are considered a whole because they are all framed under the same law, and all staff are considered congress personnel.

Although the rules are similar for both chambers, they differ in the number of permanent commissions and the structure of their organizational charts so much that one bill is entered twice (and is given two different names), because each chamber has its own *Mesa de Entradas* (the submission office where the bills are entered, named and then distributed), and there is no unanimous code book to classify the legislative initiatives. Beyond this example, it is also to be noted the duplication of many of the non-legislatives activities developed by the Congress, like the Museums (one for the lower chamber, one for the Senate), the agents formation institutes (one for each chamber) and even two different TV Channels (*SenadoTV* and

DiputadosTV) that work independently. The independence between the Chambers unfolds through highly autonomous functioning.

46.3 Political and Bureaucratical Organization of the Argentinean Congress: Legislative Groups and Commissions

The political dynamics of legislative labour has been largely studied. For the Argentinean case, Calvo (2014) describes the political process that is needed to get legislative success in a fragmented congress. The institutional gridlock derived from the institutional framework gives the Chair of each commission large political resources to get bills into the floor. Ferretti (2012) also shows that the political discussion over the authority designation in each commission is based on an institutional arrangement made in 1963 in the internal rulebook that states both the formation and importance of party groups and the existence of one of the most important commissions in both Chambers: The Parliamentary Labour Commission.

46.3.1 Party Groups and Legislators Offices: Assisting the Decision Makers

The 24,600 law states a value, in modules,[15] for every type of agent – no matter if it's permanent or temporary – and when a legislator enters the Chamber is given 2012 modules to hire their staff. This accounts for four consultants of the most basic category. The legislators individual staff may grow if they are Legislative Party Brokers[16] (Calvo and Tow, 2009): these consultants help the legislators in drafting legislative bills, assist them in carrying out the legislative tasks, follow committee work and conduct the legislator office. Since the Argentinean legislators tend to be amateurs (Jones, Saiegh et al, 2002), the selection of this staff is fundamental in shaping the efficiency of the legislator. Having the legislators a highly politicized role, this is one of the causes that leads to the necessity of a large number of staff that not only advises the legislators but also coordinates the numerous activities that take place beyond the, in itself, complex, legislative process, since more experienced consultants may help the legislator in getting her/his legislative initiatives to the floor. But in most cases, the legislators tend to use their modules to hire trusted staff.

The law-making assistance is given by two types of administrative technical staff: the Parliamentary Information Direction (PID) that depends on the Parliamentary Secretary and is a non-partisan direction providing advice and support services, and the legislator staff.[17] To consult the PID is optional for the legislator and its staff and usually not much practiced. Although it is a highly professionalized direction – one of the few that actually has tenure track assigned staff – politicians don't usually use their services. This tends to affect the quality of the bills. But the greatest difficulties a legislator has by hiring amateur staff has to do with the knowledge of the rulebook. Having a senior adviser in the offices gives a legislator the chance to advance a bill within the committee and also into the floor.[18]

Beyond the political staff, the legislative brokers (committee Chairs or rapporteur) can also count on the permanent technical staff who integrates the committee. These agents depend on the Parliamentary Secretary and are distributed by the Committee's Direction. They advise on the structure of a bill but are also in charge of setting the committee's meetings, entering the projects in the agenda – sometimes by making joint assignment of bills – and eventually, once the bill gets an opinion, send it to the Parliamentary Labour Committee to be included in the session's agenda.

46.3.2 The Legislative Process. Administrating the Legislative Process

Every bill that enters the Congress has to go a long way to become a law. This journey starts in the *Mesa de Entradas* of the Chamber where the project is sent. This office, depending on the Parliamentary Secretary, gives the project a name and a code and delivers it to the Speaker of the Chamber, who assigns it to the referent committee. The more committees it's turned, the lower are the chances it has to get to the floor. There are 46 standing committees in the lower chamber,[19] and when it comes to parliamentary staff, committees have a structure of one Committee secretary, one chief of committee and – depending on the importance and periodicity of meetings – a staff of base employees that look after the correct procedure of the process within the committee. Politics is made by the legislators and their political advisors. But a well-cultivated relation between the Committee Chair and the Committee Secretary may give these legislative brokers more weapons to delay or accelerate the approval of a bill.

As Calvo (2013) states, the bulk of legislative work at committee level is made by the political advisors of every legislator. By order of the committee authorities, the staff sets the meeting to discuss the agenda – the agenda setting of the committee is made by the committee Chair – and in order to improve the legislator's time, they set advisers meetings first, and once they come to an agreement, a committee meeting is called to dictate over the project.

To introduce the bill to the Parliamentary Labour Committee, the one that sets the agenda for the plenary sessions, implicates a few other steps. The approved project is sent to the Agenda Department, an office of the Parliamentary Secretary, that in time sends it to the Print, which comes back with a preview. The previews are sent back to the referent committee where the new version is checked, so that the project has no administrative errors, and once it is cleared, it goes to publication. Seven days later, the project can be introduced to the Parliamentary Labour Committee, integrated by the Party Group Chiefs, that will decide if it is included in the next session.

The Parliamentary Labour Committee has its own direction assigned in the organization chart and operates in a very different way compared to standing committees. Installed in the rulebook in 1963, this is the political space in which parties negotiate the sessions agenda. The administrative staff who integrates this committee has to elaborate the expected script of the session. Unlike the tasks of the rest of the committee staff, the parliamentary labour staff's tasks are much more related with the Parliamentary Secretary than any other direction on their chart, since they have to take care of formal issues of the agenda: from the order in the use of the word, to the definition of the projects that are to be treated and in which order they are presented. The agreed agenda is sent to Print and the agenda subdirection[20] delivers it to the legislators. After that, it reaches the session and it is put in discussion during the session. Once on the floor, the Administrative Secretary plays a key role in checking the legislators' assistance and voting. If a project gets approved, it is sent to the Senate, where it gets a new ID number, and the process of discussion and negotiation starts again.

46.3.3 Budget: The Law of Laws

Bonvecchi and Rodriguez (2004) describe in a very meticulous way the legislative process for the budgetary law that is meant to be approved every year. Known as "The Law of Laws", this bill is submitted by the Executive branch and then passed to the House and the Senate for approval. There is a special direction in charge of the budgetary committee in the House, depending on the Parliamentary Secretary that has the mission to assist the legislative commission, and linking with both the executive and the Senate. The Budget and Finance Committee, the largest committee in the House integrated by 48 legislators, has a say in every project that requires any kind of budgetary check.

The Direction that coordinates this committee is integrated by permanent staffers who have accessed the position by tenure and have the mission to assist the legislators in the process of overseeing the financial consistency of the projects. This particular prerogative differs from the technical advice of the other committees, since here the permanent staff is compelled to have a say in the political discussion. When it comes to the annual budget treatment, the formal and informal negotiations tend to override the influence of the committee permanent staff (Bonvecchi and Rodriguez, 2004), but the informal negotiations that include the Senators involvement in the definitive draft to be approved by the House, allows to reduce treatment time in the second Chamber.

46.4 What Goes beyond the Legislative Process

The Argentinean Congress supports multiple tasks that do not necessarily involve legislative production. As a matter of fact, bureaucratically speaking, there are five different units in the Congress that work independently from each other and three of them are not directly involved in the legislative process.[21] Although regulated by the same law, the Library, the Print and the HIS historically emerged from legislative needs and the first two have developed a link with citizenship.

The Congress Library was created in 1859 as an exclusive space for the Legislators to consult. By 1923, it was opened to the public. An administrative special bicameral committee presides it over, but its administrative authority is the General Coordinating Director, who is part of the permanent staff of the Congress. It has several programmes and directions, including a body of translators, a legislative references direction, a general references direction, and since it is also a public library has several public cultural programmes, as well as a mobile library and an open digital catalogue for consultation. It has its own building, and besides being a space for reference consultation for the legislators, it provides translation services for the legislators, as well as spaces for the non-legislative meetings the legislators may ask.[22]

The Congress Print opened in 1919, when the lower chamber acquired a printing machine for salary receipts. In time, it started to print the session diaries and increased their professionalization. Since it is considered a structure that provides services for both chambers, its political authorities pivot every four years from the Administrative Secretary from the lower chamber, to the Administrative Secretary from the upper chamber. Today is under the lower chamber administration. But the administrative authority depends on the Administrative Direction of the Print, a permanent staff position. It has top of the line equipment that allows it to have a commercial area. Beside assisting the Congress as a whole with the printing of the session diaries, schedules and official publications, they do commercial print jobs for various state areas, from electoral material to official publications, that give revenues to this specific structure.

As for the HIS, it was created in 1948 as an administrative organism of the Congress in charge of orienting, directing, administrating, distributing and ruling the health insurance plan for all the Congress Staff and the Legislators. It is co-administered between the Union and the Congress political authorities. As the Print, the political direction of the HIS also pivots every four years from the lower to the upper Chamber Administrative Secretary. Because the Argentine health system allows this type of organization to raise funds from a quota that is extracted from the salary (3% of the salary in Argentina is directed to the employee's social work) by 2016, the HIS had a budget equivalent to 14% of the total congress budget, derived from the contributions of its members. In 2016, an internal audit was conducted that led to an intervention to the HIS due to complaints of embezzlement and continues in this state.

46.4.1 Modernization and Transparency: A Linkage with the Citizenship

In 2015, the lower house presidency promoted the creation of the Modernization Direction, depending directly on the Presidency. This Direction pursues the open parliamentary programme and the open data programme. Even though it is linked with a modernization commission integrated by legislators, their work depends on the guidelines that the Chamber Presidency establishes. It was established as a way of being a linkage with the NGOs that also work for a more transparent Congress and collaborated with the implementation of the open data web page of the Congress that provides both legislation and human resources information to the public.

46.4.2 International Relations

Directly dependent on the Presidency of the lower house, there are a series of Directions whose role and scope is defined by whoever holds the said chair. Among them is the General Directorate of Parliamentary Diplomacy, International Cooperation and Culture. Its functions are to assist the Speaker in all matters concerning parliamentary diplomacy and international relations; in matters of international cooperation; official abroad missions and trips; the Parliamentary Friendship Groups; international organizations; the regional integration processes; and liaison with cults and religious entities. Given that, the implementation of these functions depends on the role that the Presidency of the Lower House wants to give it, its relevance within the parliamentary bureaucracy has varied. But in general, this office focuses on strengthening ties between parliamentary friendship groups, and the regulation of official missions and trips. It does not intervene in legislative processes in international matters nor does it advise the International Relations Committee.

46.4.3 COVID-19 and the Parliamentary Adaptation to the Digital Era

The COVID-19 crisis hit every aspect of life, including the adaptation of the parliamentary process to the social distancing era. The Argentinean Congress had to digitalize not only the administrative process – that already was transitioning to the digital – but also plenary and Committee sessions, since the legislators were not able to summon altogether on the floor. Once the political decision of remote sessions was made, the Congress staff was dedicated to the task of implementing the digital tools both of the plenary and of the committees, a task that was effective once the protocol was approved[23] and that mainly involved the implementation of tools for conducting remote sessions. The Congress Print and both the Senate and the House Administrative Secretary were key factors in working for the correct implementation of these digital tools. While the administrative circuits remained untouched, the way in which they reconfigured included the implementation of the Cisco Webex technology for remote sessions.

46.5 Conclusion

The Argentine Congress is a complex bureaucratic structure, divided in five units. Each of them has its own formal – but mostly informal – ways of work that are determined by the guidelines that their political bodies establish. Professionalization of the parliamentary administration is not a priority for these authorities, but in the last 15 years the power of the Union allowed congress staff to imprint an incipient tenure track inside the administration. However, the incentives to pursue professionalization collide with the highly partisan bias that the administrative nomination has. Less partisan units, like the Print or some direction within the Parliamentary Secretary in the House, have developed a more professional staff.

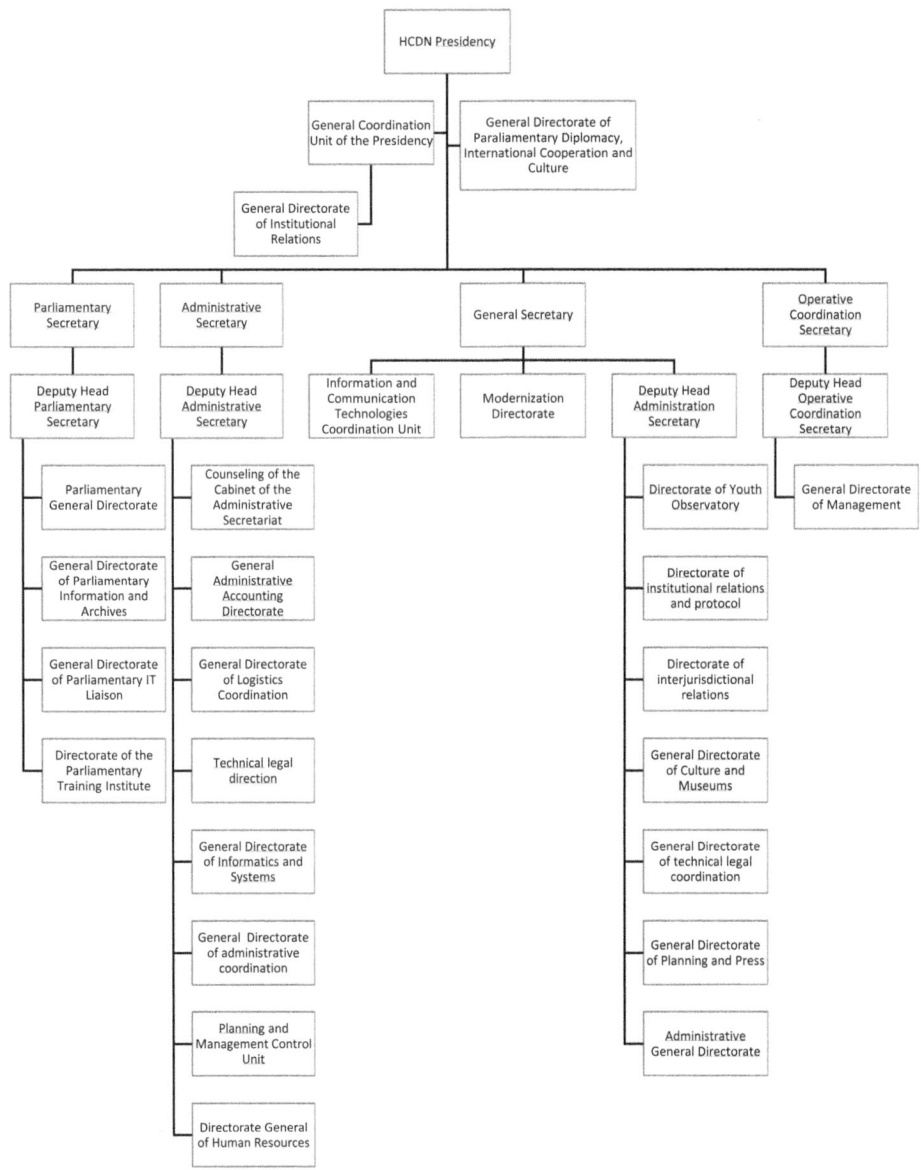

Source: Own elaboration based on www.diputados.gob.ar

Argentina's Parliamentary Administration

Organizational chart of the House of Deputies

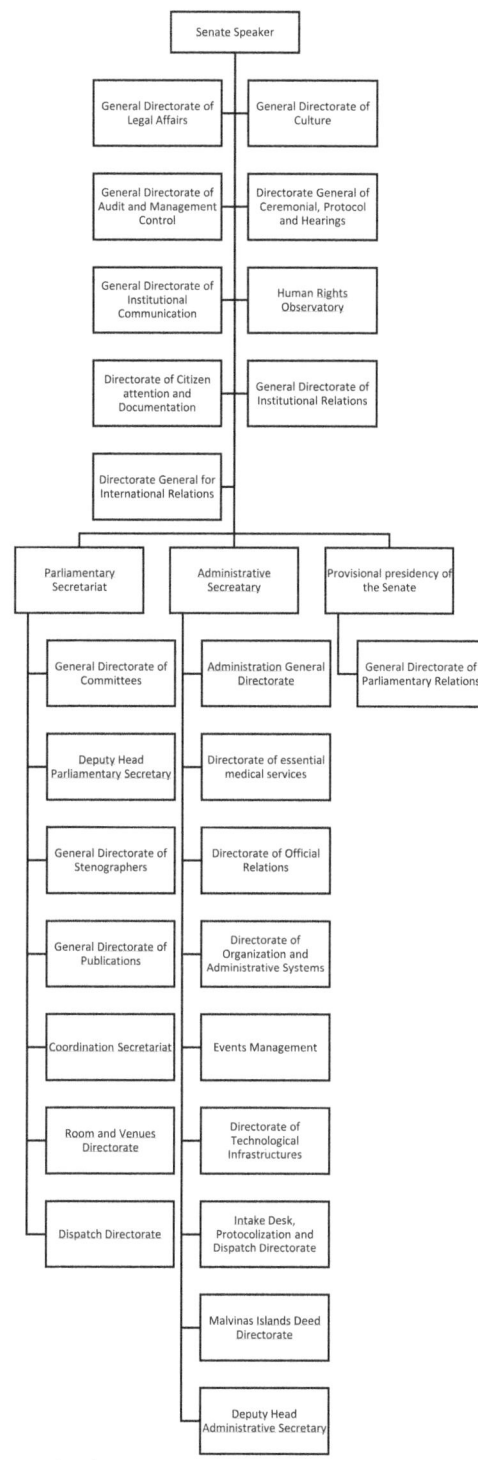

Source: Own elaboration based on www.senado.gob.ar

But the informal culture of preserving the temporary staff and promoting it to permanent – by moving them to a permanent position – remains strong.

The negotiation between the circumstantial political authorities of the Congress and the Union is key to understanding how the congress administration is built. The relationship between the Union and the Chamber speakers has allowed growth or reduction of the Staff but has not changed the perception that the position is not related to a function. Even though the Union has established a sense of belonging to the Congress staff, the personal pursuit of the individuals tends to be for a more paid category, but not necessarily with more responsibilities. Given that, this is possible by the 24,600 law – to get the higher category but not attached to a specific function – to modify this culture is a hard job.

But beyond this, the Argentinean congress administration, perhaps because of this sense of belonging provided by the Union, has accomplished a modernization, shifting from an opaque bureaucracy to a more transparent institution. Certainly this path is not near to be finished but definitely is being walked. And the more the bureaucratic maze is unveiled for the public, the easier it is to get out of it.

Notes

1. The author would like to thank Luciana Berman, Matias Antelo, Helio Rebot, former Administrative Secretary of the Senate, Francis Estada of the Commissions Direction in the House, Esteban Nanni, Subdirector of commissions of the House, and Gonzalo Herrera, Director of Operative Coordination of the Congress Print for their valuable contribution to this chapter.
2. Each midterm election, 8 of the 24 districts have a Senatorial election.
3. For each district, every two years half of the representatives are elected. In the smaller districts – the ones with only five representatives – each electoral year they select between two or three representatives, giving the election a definitive majoritarian bias, although the proportionality of the electoral formula. The constitution states that the representatives are selected in electoral districts constituted by the provinces and the Autonomous City of Buenos Aires, with a representative electoral principle in proportion to their population. The electoral law also states that no district should have less than five *Diputados*. This fact gives the representation in the first chamber an extra malapportionment and gives the small districts an overrepresentation against the big district like the province of Buenos Aires, that is under-represented in both Chambers. This gives the Congress a marked federal bias (Reynoso, 2004) that shows mostly in the way laws are negotiated. As Mustapic and Bonvecchi (2011) would say, here lies the inefficient secret of the Argentinean Congress. In a presidential system, the fact that the representatives in congress respond to a territorial constituency allows to establish a national executive/parochial legislative dynamic, as depicted by Molinelli (1991).
4. In the Senate, since the presidency of the Chamber is exercised by the Vice President of the Nation, a Provisional President of the Chamber and two Vice Presidents are selected from among the Senators. The provisional president of the Senate is the third in line of succession before a situation of vacancy of the executive power. See D'Abate (2016), Estrada (2002) and Pitt Villegas (2019).
5. The Senate has only three of this Secretaries (administrative, parliamentary and operative coordination). See Tchintian et al (2019).
6. Even though the Secretaries are given to party affiliates, the deputy secretaries tend to be assigned to professional parliamentary staff. For example, in the story of the House of Deputies, Marta Alicia Luchetta has been the parliamentary deputy Secretary for the last 15 years, assuming this role during the presidencies of different political parties.
7. In the lower Chamber, for example, the Parliamentary Secretary runs.
8. In the last ten years, both in Deputies and the Senate, they pursued the infrastructural renovation of the Legislative Palace, and this task was conducted by the Administrative Secretary of each Chamber.
9. It has to be noted that directly under the presidency of the House are a few other directions. This organizational chart allows the presidency of each Chamber to shape the scope of the role these directions have. In doing so, even with the missions and functions of these directions set by the

internal rulebook, it is found that every change of presidency of the chamber states a different role for the office in question. This may also be noted in the power and budget of each Secretary. Every President can strengthen or weaken the power of a Secretary by augmenting or reducing the number of staff under each secretary. This may be done necessarily with the consent of the legislative union.

10 This is the *Estatuto y Escalafón para el Personal del Congreso de la Nación (1995)* law that governs the five administrative bodies that make up the congressional bureaucracy. Also see www.apldigital.org ar.
11 The hierarchy of the categories of the law applies to the amount of salary that the agent will receive, not so much to the job responsibilities.
12 Most of them are located in the Congress Library.
13 Between 2001 and 2019, the Congress's salary budget grew from an 82 to a 91.3% (Sued, 2019), and the growth of the staff both permanent and transitory increased from 2005 and up, but mostly through the presidency of Amado Boudou in the Senate (2011–2015) and Julián Dominguez in the House (2011–2015), where the Senate grew a 112% – from 2713 employees to 5752 – and the House a 9.3% – from 5149 to 5625 employees. In the Senate, between 2015 and 2019, with Gabriela Michetti as Senate president, a reduction of staff was intended, via voluntarie retreats, reducing the staff by 12%.
14 A higher category does not imply higher responsibilities. An agent may have the higher categorie (a one, as they call it) but no direction or subdirection rank, just a plain advisor job.
15 A module is a unit used to give unanimity to the value of the salary, and its amount is agreed between the union and the political authorities of the Chambers. It is established in the 24,600 law. Each module is currently equivalent to 169 pesos.
16 Legislative party brokers are the political actors who administer the institutional and political resources that are distributed in the Chamber, Block Chiefs and Commission Chairs, as well as party leaders. They distribute budgetary resources, the ability to hire personnel, public exposure and the ability to exchange favours.
17 The Senate has developed the CALISEN, a tool to unify the criteria for the project production. See Grandio et al (2018).
18 There are many anecdotes in the Argentinean Congress of laws that have been passed by using shortcuts in the rulebook. Usually these anecdotes implicate senior legislators who are familiarized with the rulebook and know when, for example, call a privileged motion to treat a project on the floor, like the one used to approve parity in the electoral formulas.
19 In the lower chamber, permanent commissions are made up from 10 (Culture) to 48 (Budget and Finance) legislators. In the Senate, the rulebook states that every commission is integrated by 17 senators.
20 Until 2020, stenographers – one of the few directions in the Congress that actually fills the vacancies via tenure – play a key role in this process, since they have to type not only the sessions but also the commission's discussions. The digitalization of the stenographic version is made by the Print, who has had a constant process of modernization for the last 15 years.
21 Although the Print, as seen above, plays a role in the legislative process, that is not it's main activity within the Congress.
22 This may go from book presentations, to diplomatic meetings.
23 The political tension behind the definition of an effective protocol was high since it required the approval of all the party groups in both the lower and upper Chamber but it didn't involve the effectiveness of the Congress bureaucracy.

References

Alcántara Sáez, M., García Montero, M., & Sánchez López, F. (2005). *Funciones, Procedimientos y Escenarios: Un Análisis del Poder Legislativo en América Latina*. Ediciones Universidad de Salamanca.

Aleman, E. (2013). Latin American Legislative Politics: A Survey of Peer-Reviewed Publications in English. *Journal of Politics in Latin America*, 5(1), 15–36.

Alexander, D. A. (2020). The Committee Secretariat of the European Parliament: Administrative Mobility, Expertise and Keeping the Legislative Wheels Turning. *The Journal of Legislative Studies*. https://doi.org/10.1080/13572334.2020.1832389

Bonvecchi, A., & Rodriguez, J. (2004). *El papel del poder legislativo en el proceso presupuestario: la experiencia argentina*. División Desarrollo Económico (CEPAL – Naciones Unidas).

Bonvecchi, A., Cherny, N., & Cella, L. (2018). *Modernizar el Congreso. Propuestas para el Reglamento de la Cámara de Diputados*. Documento de Políticas Públicas/Recomendación N°200 CIPPEC.

Calvo, E. (2013). Representación Política, políticas públicas y estabilidad institucional en el Congreso argentino. In *¿Cuanto Importan las Instituciones? Gobierno, Estado y actores en la política argentina* (pp. 121–157). Carlos H. Acuña.

Calvo, E. (2014). *Legislator Success in Fragmented Congresses in Argentina. Plurality Cartels, Minority Presidents, and Lawmaking*. Cambridge: Cambridge University Press.

Calvo, E., & Sagarzazu, I. (2011). Legislator Success in Committee: Gatekeeping Authority and the Loss of Majority Control. *American Journal of Political Science*. DOI: 10.1111/j.1540-5907.2010.00476.x

Calvo, E., & Tow, A. (2009). Cajoneando el debate: El papel de los presidentes de las comisiones en la productividad del Congreso argentino. *Desarrollo Económico. Revista de Ciencias Sociales, 195*, 451–477.

Dirección de Asistencia Social del Congreso de la Nación. (2021). https://das.gob.ar/

Estrada, J. H. (2002). *Comentarios en torno al parlamento*. Prometeo.

Ferretti, N. (2012). Centralización y poder compartido: la creación de la Comisión de Labor Parlamentaria en la Cámara de Diputados de la Nación. In *Los Legisladores en el Congreso Argentino* (pp. 13–61). Ana María Mustapic, Alejandro Bonvecchi, Javier Zelaznik.

Grandío Buzaleh, M., Taibo, L., Martinez, F., & Da Cruz, J. (n.d.). *De la lógica partidaria a la profesión legislativa: El rol del asesor legislativo en el Senado de la Nación Argentina*. GICP – Carrera de Ciencia Política – UBA.

Honorable Cámara de Diputados de la Nación. (2021). https://www.diputados.gov.ar/

Honorable Cámara de Senadores de la Nación. (2021). https://www.senado.gob.ar/

Jones, M. P., Saiegh, S. Spiller, P. T., & Tommasi, M. (2002) Amateur legislators–professional politicians: The consequences of party-centered electoral rules in a federal system. *American Journal of Political Science, 46*(3), 656–669.

Llanos, M., & Mustapic, A. M. (2006). *El Control Parlamentario en Alemania, Argentina y Brasil*. HomoSapiens.

Molinelli, G. (1991). *Presidentes y congresos en Argentina. Mitos y Realidades*. Grupo Editor Latinoamericano.

Molinelli, G., Sin, G., & Palanza, V. (1999). *Congreso, Presidencia y Justicia en Argentina*. Temas Grupo Editorial.

Mustapic, A. M., & Bonvecchi, A. (2011). El Secreto Eficiente del presidencialismo argentino. In *Algo más que Presidentes: el papel del Poder Legislativo en América Latina* (pp. 305–338). Manuel AlcántaraSáez y Mercedes García Montero (editores), Algo más que Presidentes: el papel del Poder Legislativo en América Latina, Zaragoza: Fundación Manuel Giménez Abad de Estudios Parlamentarios y del Estado Autonómico.

Pitt Villegas, J. (2019). *Reglas del Reglamento de la Cámara de Senadores de la Nación Argentina*. Dunken.

Reynoso, D. (2004). Bicameralismo y sobre-representación en Argentina en perspectiva comparada. *Revista SAAP, 2*, 69–94.

Sued, G. (2019). *Los secretos del Congreso*. Ediciones B, Penguin Random House.

Tchintian, C., Goyburu, M. L., & Cella, L. (2019). *Reglamentos comparados de Cámaras de Diputados de América del Sur*. Documento de Trabajo N°18. CIPPEC.

47
AUSTRALIA'S PARLIAMENTARY ADMINISTRATION

Valerie Barrett

47.1 Introduction

This contribution deals only with Australia's national legislature, the bicameral Commonwealth Parliament, established on 1 January 1901 when the six states, previously separate British colonies, became a federation, the Commonwealth of Australia. The national legislature consists of two popularly elected chambers: the House of Representatives comprising single-member electorates determined on population, and the Senate consisting of the same number of senators from each state (regardless of state populations) elected by proportional representation.

The Commonwealth Parliament's administrative structure, established in the *Public Service Act 190*2, comprised the Department of the House of Representatives (DHR), the Department of the Senate (DOS), the Department of the Parliamentary Reporting Staff (DPRS), the Department of the Parliamentary Library (DPL) and the Joint House Committee which became a department in 1922 (JHD). That structure was unchanged until 2004 when DPRS, DPL and JHD merged into a new entity, the Department of Parliamentary Services (DPS). (A fourth department, the Parliamentary Budget Office [PBO] was established in 2012 but has no parliamentary administrative or management functions and is not considered here.)[1]

This account sets the historic context for the parliament's administration, citing factors and events which have influenced the current environment, including organizational structure and performance issues. It then discusses present functions, resourcing and governance, and concludes by highlighting some current and potential management challenges facing the parliament's administrators.[2]

47.2 Towards an Efficient Parliamentary Administration

A continuing concern relating to the parliament's effective administration is its financial dependence on executive government. Reid and Forrest noted this concern in their account of the parliament's evolution since federation in 1901—from "the modest group of

36 senators, 75 members and 53 officials who assembled in … Melbourne" after the official opening, to a large and complex organization, spread between four locations in the national capital (1989, p. 398).

Podger (in Adams 2002, p. 5) claimed the parliament's administrative structures were "based essentially on history and sometimes on chance, rather than a careful consideration of good management". Adams (2002) documented at least 20 attempts to restructure parliamentary departments from 1911, the main proponents being incumbent governments, central agencies and, only recently, the presiding officers. The main resistance came from presiding officers, clerks of the two chamber departments and their senior staff and, more latterly, senators, some backbench members of the House of Representatives and academics. Concerns were regularly raised about the diminution of the parliament at the hands of the executive and a weakening of the "separation of powers".[3] Russell (2000) identified two conditions which have contributed to the Senate's fierce guardianship of its own independence. One was the demand by the smaller states at federation for equal representation, resulting in a constitutional structure which sought to meld elements of the Westminster and US models. The other was the adoption in 1946 of proportional representation for Senate elections. Combined with compulsory voting, this has meant that incumbent governments since have rarely had majority control of the Senate.

In recent decades, significant exogenous factors have provided a new context for change. These include budgetary and performance expectations arising from the adoption of "new public management" principles in the 1980s (leading to a concentration on reducing costs and improving client service); the move to the new and much larger Parliament House in 1988; the *Parliamentary Service Act 1999* (which removed parliamentary staff from the wider public service); and perceived threats to parliament's physical security after 2001.

In 2004, the three service departments—JHD, DPRS and DPL—were amalgamated to create DPS. This followed a review in 2002 by the then Parliamentary Service Commissioner into aspects of parliamentary administration with the objectives of improving security and efficiency (Podger 2002). Although the bulk of funding for existing and new security measures was transferred to the new department, the two chamber departments were anxious that they should not lose influence and that the new department should not take resources from key legislative functions (Evans 2004).

The early years of DPS did not run smoothly. Key challenges included a budget reduction of $6m in 2004–05 in advance of projected savings from the amalgamation; operational costs rising disproportionately higher than compensatory funding[4]; and rapid turnover of senior staff resulting in loss of corporate knowledge and political awareness. Dissatisfaction with management mounted: of particular concern were critical reports of DPS's performance from inquiries by the Senate Finance and Public Administration Legislation Committee (SFPALC) from 2012 to 2021. The first raised deficiencies in leadership, strategic planning, security management, ICT, project and contract management, a poor employment culture and a lack of acceptance by presiding officers of administrative responsibility (Senate Finance and Public Administration Legislation Committee 2012). The second concluded that DPS was "deeply dysfunctional" and recommended greater oversight of DPS's funding and administration (Senate Finance and Public Administration Legislation Committee 2015). A related external review of DPS recommended whole-of-parliament strategic planning and funding; a governance body with external directors similar to those in the UK and other parliaments; targeted funding for key building functions; and organizational and nomenclature changes (Baxter 2015). The recommendations were not taken up.

In the third SFPALC inquiry, DPS management mounted a strong defence against many of the claims made about its performance. The Committee noted that systemic cultural issues were now being "appropriately investigated by other bodies" (p. 24) while acknowledging DPS's efforts to improve workplace culture, protect ICT security and continue improvements to overall security. Additional concerns were, however, raised by non-government senators on the committee (Senate Finance and Public Administration Legislation Committee 2021).[5]

The two chamber departments have also faced challenges since 2004. DHR annual reports noted the need to improve departmental culture, reduce barriers across the department, and ensure that its specialized working environment did not obscure its external view (2006, 2007). The 2010 general election, which resulted in the first minority government since 1940, led to procedural changes and reforms, including the establishment of the PBO in 2012 and a new Appropriations and Administration Committee to consider, inter alia, departmental funding.[6] The committee was able to secure supplementary funding to meet additional costs incurred as a result of the new parliamentary arrangements and came to be seen as an important conduit between members and departmental staff (Department of the House of Representatives 2012).

Continuing management themes for DHR in the 21st century have been dominated by its highly specialized focus, both internally and in its inter-parliamentary and outreach work with various parliamentary associations; strong emphasis on staff development, departmental leadership and services to members, resulting in high satisfaction rates on these counts; and an acknowledgement of the need for cooperative relations with other parliamentary departments. DHR's annual reports depict a well-supported department, providing high-quality services but with few complex management issues, at least until the Covid-19 pandemic.

Former Senate Clerk, Harry Evans, considered himself a "sceptical questioner" of the reorganization of parliamentary departments and considered the "demand for public sector departments to look and sound like private commercial corporations" as conceptually poor and institutionally inappropriate (Evans 2004, p. 5, 2005, p. 5). DOS continued to forcefully stake its claims for resources and vigorously defend the Senate's institutional role. The continued focus on financial independence was enhanced by consultation between the executive and the Senate President (Department of the Senate 2013) but years of efficiency dividends[7] and an unprecedented level of committee activity contributed to budget deterioration, requiring the Appropriations, Staffing and Security Committee to secure further supplementation (Department of the Senate 2017). DOS has been assertive in its relationships with the executive and other parliamentary departments to achieve its outcomes.

In part, the chamber departments have been "hollowed out" by the transfer of functions to DPS, allowing them to concentrate on core procedural activities. Neither has appeared to face strong internal criticism.

47.3 Parliamentary Administration Today: Functions, Resourcing and Governance Issues

More than 3500 people work in Parliament House when the two chambers meet, including a large media contingent. Not all staff are directly employed by the parliamentary departments; many work for external contractors, including cleaning and catering staff, under contracts managed by DPS. Staff of parliamentary departments are employed under the *Parliamentary Service Act 1999* on terms and conditions similar to those of public servants employed under the *Public Service Act 1999*. Staff working for Members, Senators and Ministers are employed by the Department of Finance (DOF) under the *Members of Parliament (Staff) Act 1984* (the *MOPS* Act).

Parliamentary departments are funded under annual *Appropriation (Parliamentary Departments) Acts*. There has been a small increase in reported staff numbers since the 2004 amalgamation (7 per cent) although the number of senior executives in DPS has increased by 64 per cent compared with its predecessor departments (from 11 to 18), a likely response to increasing management responsibilities, expanded functions and criticism of its performance. Figures 47.1 and 47.2 present the growth in staffing and financial resources for each department between 2004–05 and 2019–20.

The revenue figures reflect transfers of resources between departments after the amalgamation (principally for security and information technology costs), capital funding variations, and the ongoing government-imposed efficiency dividend. (Administered funding and available prior appropriations are excluded.) The increase in cash funding (44.5 per cent over the period) does not reflect real-term increases in costs, particularly for DPS which has faced additional performance challenges. From an efficiency perspective, the decrease in real funding might be welcomed; from an effectiveness perspective, the outcome is not clear.

In the face of continuing financial pressures, the departments continue to provide a range of diverse services.[8] The principal focus of the two chamber departments is providing procedural support to members and senators in both their chamber and committee roles while operating in accordance with the *Public Governance, Performance and Accountability Act 2013 (the PGPA Act)*. Clerks in both houses describe the overarching role of their departments as providing a secretariat to each house. Table 47.1 outlines the chamber departments' main functions.

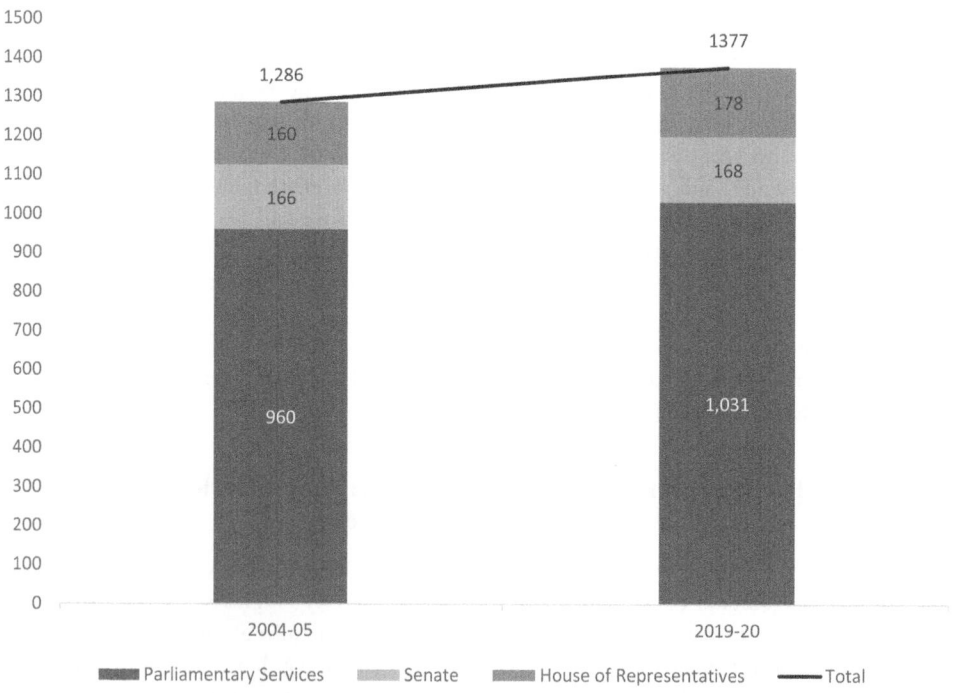

Figure 47.1 Parliamentary departments staffing growth: 2004–05 to 2019–20

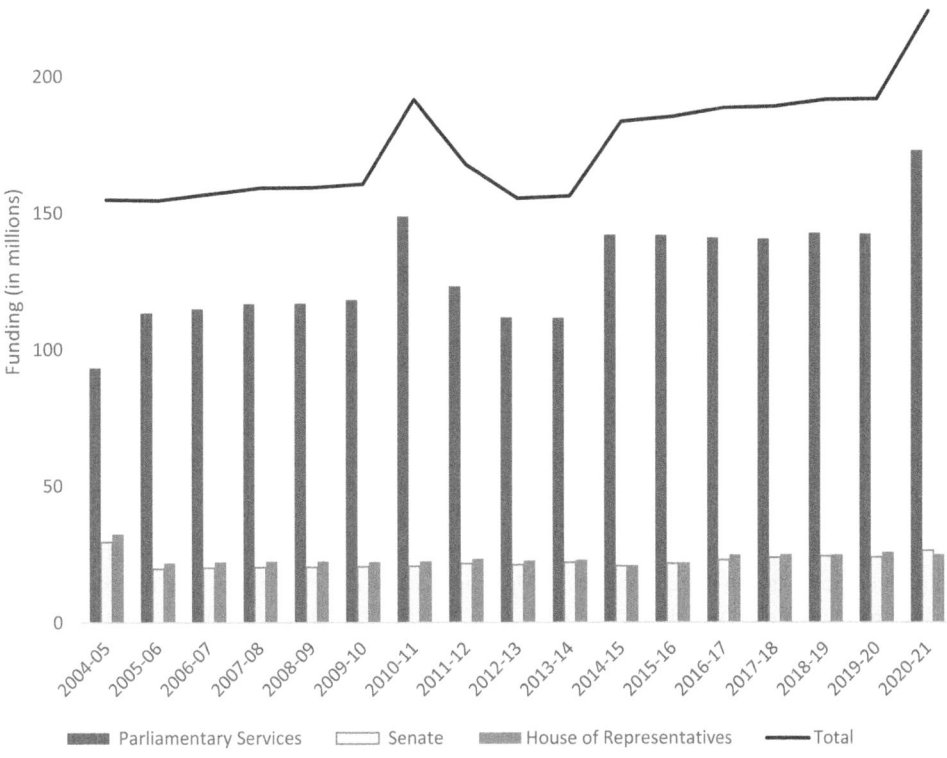

Figure 47.2 Parliamentary departments funding growth: 2004–05 to 2020–21

Table 47.1 Main functions of the chamber departments

Department of the House of Representatives	Department of the Senate
Procedure Office: procedural research, publications and services explaining the work of the House and its institutional role	Procedure Office: procedural support, legislative scrutiny and parliamentary information resources
Table Office: programming, procedural and legislative support to HoR chamber and Federation Chamber★	Table Office: procedural and secretariat support for the Senate
Committee Office: procedural, research, analytical, drafting and administrative support to committees	Committee Office: secretariat support for committees
International and Parliamentary Relations Office: inter-parliamentary relations and capacity-building	Parliamentary Education Office: resources for teachers and students
Community relations and awareness	Public information Office: information management, resources, ICT liaison
Serjeant-at-Arms' Office: members' and corporate support (accommodation, work health and safety, salaries and allowances); ceremonial, security and access	Black Rod's Office: corporate support for the department, administrative advice for senators

★ A secondary chamber to the House of Representatives used for debating non-contentious legislation, committee reports and constituency matters. It was established in 1993 as the Main Committee and renamed in 2004 (HOR Procedure Committee 1993).

The Clerks of the House and the Senate are appointed by their respective presiding officers for a single, non-renewable ten-year term. Under the *Parliamentary Service Act 1999*, their appointments can be terminated only by resolution of their respective houses and they are regarded as institutional guardians. As non-elected officials the clerks have limited capacity to influence procedural, rather than departmental, reform; however, they can and do work with members of their respective procedure committees.

Much of the parliament's business occurs in committees. Discussion about their work centres on the contribution they make to public policy through their roles in scrutiny, investigation and legislative appraisal, including the extent to which they facilitate public participation (Halligan *et al.* 2007). Evaluating committee effectiveness is complex; inherent political interests are a contributing factor (see Aldons 2001, Monk 2009). The Senate's scrutiny role is highly regarded publicly; however, for the Senate department, the capacity of independent or minority party senators to propose new inquiries with little notice leads to challenges, particularly financial (for which supplementary funding may be provided). While some outcomes from inquiries may contribute to effective policy-making, others might be considered "stapled together party policies" (Barrett 2019, p. 156). The house departments receive strong support in relation to their appropriations from members of their respective appropriations committees, particularly at periods of high workload, usually in the middle of Australia's three-year election cycle.

The Senate's capacity to scrutinize the performance of agencies, particularly through estimates committees, which examine budget proposals each year, extends to the parliament's administration but only in respect of DOS, DPS and the PBO. Senate scrutiny has had a significant effect on DPS operations but some senators have questioned the value of Senate inquiries in improving its performance (Senate Finance and Public Administration Legislation Committee 2021). Table 47.2 outlines the main functions of the Department of Parliamentary Services.

Table 47.2 Main functions of the Department of Parliamentary Services

Department of Parliamentary Services	
Protecting Parliament House's design integrity; special collections/art collections	Liaison with moral rights administrators, collaboration on design intent for capital works and maintenance/managing Parliament's art collection
Parliamentary Library	Research and library services
Information services	Business applications for parliamentary administration, public engagement; parliamentary network; cyber security services; broadcasting and Hansard
Finance and property services	Financial advice to DPS; maintenance, landscape, building information, furniture, strategic accommodation and asset management services; capital works projects
Corporate services	Human resources, legal and governance services; visitor, catering and events management services for the parliament, and the community
Security and communications	Operational and building security for parliament and visitors; internal and external communication and media inquiries

The DPS Secretary is appointed for up to five years (renewable) by both presiding officers following advice from the Parliamentary Service Commissioner and is accountable to both for all DPS services. Since 2004, there have been seven secretaries (including three acting) resulting in organizational and governance changes, high staff turnover and loss of continuity, which may have worsened, rather than improved, the performance issues noted earlier. Relationships with other parliamentary departments and between DPS and members and senators have at times been strained (Barrett 2019). Successive secretaries have pointed to difficulties in establishing an inclusive culture following the amalgamation of diverse parliamentary functions.

Recent years have seen greater collaboration between departments, including a parliamentary service strategic framework and initiatives such as a parliamentary digital strategy 2019–22 and a parliamentary service reconciliation action plan. Each department prepares a corporate plan as required by the *PGPA Act 2013*. Table 47.3 presents governance and oversight mechanisms in the Australian Parliament.

Table 47.3 Governance and oversight mechanisms in the Australian Parliament

Parliamentary department	Governance feature
Parliamentary Service Commissioner and Merit Protection Commissioner	Advise presiding officers on Parliamentary Service management policies and practices
Presiding officers and/or departmental heads	Advisory committees to presiding officers and parliamentary departments include the Joint House Committee, Security Management Board, Parliamentary ICT Advisory Board, Joint Standing Committee on the Parliamentary Library, Strategic ICT Group, Parliamentary Administration Advisory Group, quarterly meetings of departmental heads and service level agreements
Department of House of Representatives	Speaker of the House, as presiding officer; Clerk of the House, as accounting authority; Executive Management Committee and Audit Committee
	House of Representatives Standing Committee on Appropriations and Administration determines amounts for inclusion in appropriations bills and considers proposals for changes to the department's administration
	Standing Order 222A provides for committee to confer with Senate Committee on estimates of funding for DPS
Department of Senate	President of the Senate, as presiding officer; Clerk of the Senate, as accounting authority, Program Managers Group and Audit Committee.
	Senate Standing Committee on Appropriations, Staffing and Security determines amounts for inclusion in appropriations bills and can inquire into proposals for Senate estimates and variations to staffing structures and policies
	Standing Order 19 provides for committee to confer with House of Representatives committee on funding for information and communication technology services
Department of Parliamentary Services (DPS)	Presiding officers (jointly responsible), Secretary, Executive Committee and Audit Committee
	(See Senate Standing Order 19)
	(See House of Representatives Standing Order 222A)

Each house has its own oversight committee which advocates on behalf of its department, but there is no overarching governance body or commission responsible and accountable for parliamentary administration, similar to the House of Lords and House of Commons commissions in the UK Parliament, which include members of parliament, senior staff and external commissioners. Arguably, this has contributed to a lack of support for DPS and its services (Baxter 2015, Joint Committee of Public Accounts and Audit 2008, Senate Finance and Public Administration Legislation Committee 2020). The governance and senior executive structure is shown in Figure 47.3.

Parliamentary scholars in other jurisdictions have lamented the lack of a single authority to advocate for parliaments in an era when parliaments are subject to public dissatisfaction and negative media coverage (Judge and Leston-Bandeira 2018, Norton 2017). Norton observes that:

> Resources are devoted to educating people about the institution, but not necessarily to defending it from scandal and a constant barrage of criticism. There has tended to be what may be characterised as a 'tin hats' mentality, sheltering in the bunker and trying to escape the barrage of media missiles. Parliament lacks the confidence and the resources to mount an effective counter-offensive.
>
> Norton (2017)

The situation in Australia is exacerbated by the distributed nature of administrative and workplace accountability. Formal administrative engagement between the two Houses appears limited despite the mechanisms described above. Departmental staff employed under the *Parliamentary Service Act 1999* are bound by the Parliamentary Service Values and Code of Conduct, while staff working for members, senators and ministers are employed under the *MOPS Act*, which includes no such values or code.[9] The behaviour of members and senators is not governed by a code of conduct; complaints regarding bullying or harassment are generally left to the respective parties to determine (Barrett 2019). Ministers' offices are in the Ministerial Wing of Parliament House for which both DPS and DOF share responsibility. Ministers are subject to a code of conduct but its application is subjective. These features increase complexity and diminish the performance, reputation and accountability of the whole institution.

47.4 Negotiating Increasing Expectations of Parliamentary Administration

While management responsibilities burgeon and complexity increases, there appears to be a gap between expectations and outcomes, both from the parliament's internal clients and the public, creating an "expectations gap" between what politics—in this case parliament—should deliver and what it actually can deliver given current resources and context (Flinders and Kelso 2011). In the case of DPS, there may also be a "perceptions gap": even when the department meets service performance targets, its clients may fail to appreciate this.

Trust in government, often converging with perceptions of democracy and parliament,[10] is at a low ebb (Karp and Evans 2019, Stoker et al. 2018), fuelled in part by perceptions of policy failure. Public concern over workplace behaviour and culture within parliament has increased following bullying claims by female members of parliament (Barrett 2019), and more recently the reporting of an alleged sexual assault in a ministerial office by a ministerial staff member (Walker et al. 2021). Although accountability for the alleged incident seemed to fall within the jurisdiction of DOF, it led to questions about the actions of parliamentary

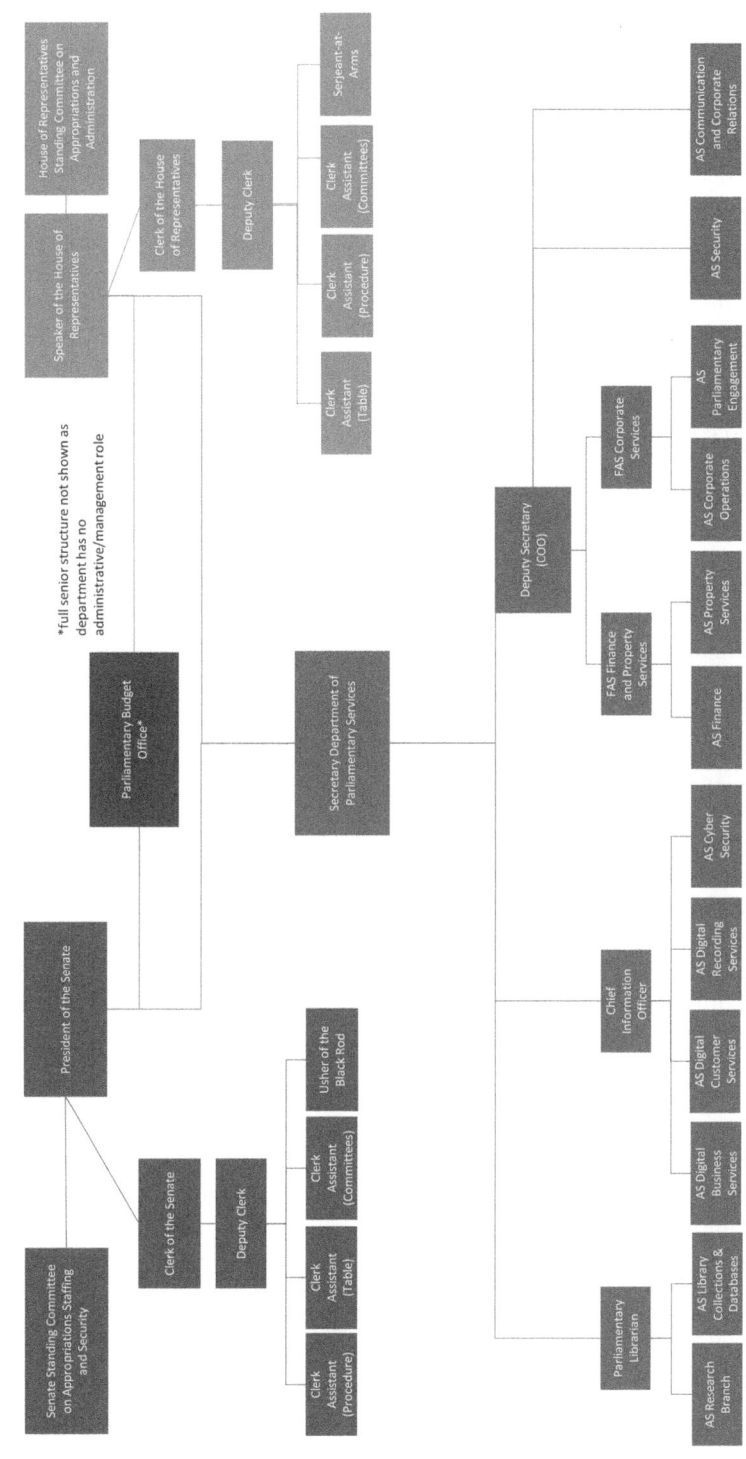

Figure 47.3 Parliament of Australia: governance and senior executive structure

security guards employed by DPS. In response to what was publicly regarded as a crisis, the government, in addition to its own internal inquiries, appointed the statutorily independent Sex Discrimination Commissioner, Kate Jenkins, to inquire into parliamentary workplace culture (Birmingham 2021a). Although this inquiry is primarily directed towards political staff employed under the *MOPS Act,* its terms of reference include all staff working in the parliament—bullying claims have also emerged in parliamentary departments (Maley and Curtis, 2021, Senate Finance and Public Administration Legislation Committee 2012, 2015). The fallout touches everyone with a role within parliament; public approbation does not necessarily take account of structural nuances. The recent incidents bear a strong resemblance to bullying and harassment issues raised in the UK Parliament, through the Cox and Ellenbogen reports (2018, 2019). Although the Jenkins inquiry is expected to report in November 2021, change is already afoot: the government has announced that a new Parliamentary Workplace Support Service (PWSS), including an independent complaints mechanism, will be available to staff and parliamentarians in Commonwealth parliamentary workplaces (Birmingham 2021b). This body will provide additional scrutiny; it remains to be seen how it will improve workplace culture.[11]

Returning to Norton's observations that, too often, parliaments rely on institutional education, what else is the parliament doing to enhance public trust and participation in parliamentary democracy and respond to exogenous threats? The *Strategic Framework: the Parliamentary Service* binds the three departments in common purpose to ensure that:

- the community can easily access and engage in the work of the Parliament and parliamentary committees;
- national, international and regional relationships are maintained with other parliaments, parliamentary bodies and organizations;
- Australian Parliament House (APH) is sustained as a workplace and national institution.

Limited resources already require the parliament to rely on external sources of funding to maintain its parliamentary strengthening activities (Department of the House of Representatives 2020) and greater collaboration with external organizations is also important, particularly when trying to reach the public at large. The Joint Standing Committee on the National Capital and External Territories (2019) expressed concern that Australia's national cultural institutions were not presenting a shared and consistent vision about Australian democracy, or clearly delineating programmes and activities (p. viii). It recommended student programmes be accessible to the general public and that educational support and visitor services across institutions be more closely aligned with the parliament.

Digitization has increasingly helped members, senators and parliamentary administrators connect with the public and made the work of parliament more efficient and accessible. The Covid-19 pandemic has highlighted the potential for radical innovation although the parliament's response has been conservative. Initially, sittings of both houses were suspended or severely limited, leading to wide concerns about parliament being bypassed[12]; the use of emergency powers by the executive; and the ad hoc administrative creation of a new and seemingly dominant "National Cabinet" comprising the Prime Minister and State and Territory Premiers and Chief Ministers (Daly 2020, Mills 2020, Twomey 2020). As the pandemic grew, the two houses responded with changes to standing orders and practical measures to allow for socially distanced parliamentary sittings. Members and senators unable to physically attend for divisions were "paired" with counterparts, with some publicly recording their voting intentions. Second and third waves of infection in Victoria and New South Wales also led to severe border restrictions and some members and senators (generally those whose health might be compromised by attending, or who were unable to fulfil quarantine requirements) have participated remotely.

Overwhelmingly, these measures were viewed as temporary; aside from committee proceedings, remote participation has been limited; remote voting has been dismissed; the Senate remains concerned about the restrictions placed on senators in carrying out their parliamentary duties; and there appears to be little appetite for a virtual parliament (House of Representatives Procedure Committee 2020, Senate Procedure Committee 2020a, 2020b).

47.5 Conclusion

The Australian Parliament, perhaps more than other public institutions, is highly exposed to criticism: from the public, the media, the parliamentarians it seeks to serve and even its own staff. It is unsurprising therefore that parliamentary administrators might prefer to stick with what they know, avoiding the risks of innovation and reform, particularly in the face of limited enthusiasm from members and senators.

Challenges facing the parliament include acquiring sufficient resources to meet increasing expectations (in common with all publicly funded organizations); building internal capacity; maintaining relevance in its relationship with the executive; gaining internal support for parliament-wide reform; and restoring public confidence. These challenges are more likely to be met if members and senators, their political staff and parliamentary staff can work collaboratively across parties and across the parliament, including with relevant external bodies and academics, to create wider public understanding of how parliament operates and facilitate greater participation and inclusion.

Efficiency and integrity are paramount; the public will not accept incompetent or unethical behaviour, so effective scrutiny is essential. But whatever the outcome of ongoing inquiries into workplace culture, scrutiny alone will not guarantee effective parliamentary administration. Much will depend, as Norton contends, on the capacity of its management by both elected members and officials. This will depend more than ever on inclusive and robust parliamentary governance, advocacy and support from members and senators, adequate resourcing and political will.

Notes

1. The PBO informs the parliament 'by providing independent and non-partisan analysis of the budget cycle, fiscal policy and the financial implications of proposals' *(Parliamentary Service Act 1999)*.
2. The parliament's website provides an excellent resource for further reading (www.aph.gov.au).
3. The concept of the 'separation of powers' as it is actually embedded in Australia's constitutional framework is at odds with the argument for greater parliamentary independence (Sloane 2014).
4. Although DPS was able to secure cash injections in 2011 and 2020 principally for security works.
5. The inquiry was overshadowed by a number of investigations into an alleged sexual assault in a ministerial office within Parliament House.
6. Other reforms related to private members' business, conduct of question time and the committee system. Proposals for a code of conduct for members and senators and a parliamentary integrity commissioner were not achieved (Parliamentary Library 2013).
7. Since 1987, Commonwealth entities (including the parliamentary departments) have been subject to an annual efficiency dividend (generally up to 1.5 per cent but with one off additions) that reduces operational budgets each year in anticipation of efficiencies being found.
8. For a full description of activities and performance outcomes, see each department's latest annual report.

9 Although see recommendations of the Joint Committee on Parliamentary Standards (2022).
10 In the UK, the Hansard Society conducts an annual survey of public satisfaction with parliament: in Australia, the Museum of Australian Democracy canvasses public satisfaction with how democracy works (Barrett 2019).
11 A new government elected in 2022 accepted all the recommendations in the Jenkins review of workplace culture, see Australian Human Rights Commission (2021).
12 The Senate established the Select Committee on Covid-19 to inquire into the government's pandemic response and "discharge the parliamentary oversight that Parliament itself was not able to carry out via regular means" (2020, p. 3). The Committee will report by June 2022.

References

Adams, J 2002, *Parliament: Master of Its Own Household?* Australian Public Service Commission, Canberra.

Aldons, M 2001, 'Performance indicators for the Parliament—sharp or blunt instruments of reform?', *Australasian Parliamentary Review*, vol. 16, no. 2, pp. 27–37.

Australian Human Rights Commission 2021, Set the standard: report on the independent review into Commonwealth parliamentary workplaces, Sydney.

Barrett, V 2019, *Parliamentary administration: what does it mean to manage a parliament effectively?* Doctoral dissertation, Australian National University.

Baxter, K 2015, *Review of the Department of Parliamentary Services*, Senate Finance and Public Administration Legislation Committee, Additional Estimates 2016-17 (February and March 2017), 'Answers to Questions on Notice', no. 111, 13 April 2017, viewed 25 May 2017, http://www.aph.gov.au/Parliamentary_Business/Senate_Estimates/fapactte/estimates/add1617/parliamentary/index.

Birmingham, S 2021a, *Independent review into Commonwealth parliamentary workplaces*, Minister for Finance Media Release, 5 March 2021, viewed 7 March 2021, https://www.financeminister.gov.au/media-release/2021/03/05/independent-review-commonwealth-parliamentary-workplaces.

―――― 2021b, *Launch of Parliamentary Workplace Support Service*, Minister for Finance Media Release, 23 September 2021, viewed 5 October 2021, https://www.financeminister.gov.au/media-release/2021/09/23/launch-parliamentary-workplace-support-service.

Cox, L 2018, *The bullying and harassment of House of Commons staff*, Independent inquiry report, 28 October 2018, viewed 28 November, 2018, https://www.parliament.uk/globalassets/documents/conduct-in-parliament/dame-laura-cox-independent-inquiry-report.pdf.

Daly, T 2020, 'In times of crisis, does Parliament really matter?', *Pursuit*, University of Melbourne, 10 August 2020, viewed 18 March 2020, https://pursuit.unimelb.edu.au/articles/in-times-of-crisis-does-parliament-really-matter.

Department of the House of Representatives 2006, *Annual report, 2005-06*, viewed 8 March 2018, http://webarchive.nla.gov.au/gov/20070831040247/http://www.aph.gov.au/house/pubs/ar05-06/index.htm.

―――― 2007, *Annual report, 2006-07*, viewed 8 March 2018, http://webarchive.nla.gov.au/gov/20080730014510/http://www.aph.gov.au/house/pubs/ar06-07/index.htm.

―――― 2012, *Annual report, 2011-12*, viewed 17 March 2021, https://www.aph.gov.au/About_Parliament/Parliamentary_Departments/Department_of_the_House_of_Representatives/Annual_Reports/2011-12_Annual_Report.

―――― 2020, *Annual report 2019-20*, viewed 18 March 2021, https://www.aph.gov.au/About_Parliament/Parliamentary_Departments/Department_of_the_House_of_Representatives/Annual_Reports.

Department of the Senate 2013, *Annual report 2012-13*, viewed 15 February 2018, https://www.aph.gov.au/About_Parliament/Parliamentary_Departments/Department_of_the_Senate/Annual_Reports/Annual_Report_2012-2013.

―――― 2017, *Annual report 2016-17*, viewed 26 April 2018, https://www.aph.gov.au/About_Parliament/Parliamentary_Departments/Department_of_the_Senate/Annual_Reports/Annual_Report_2016-2017.

Ellenbogen, N 2019, *An Independent inquiry into bullying and harassment in the House of Lords*, Report, 10 July 2019, viewed 19 July 2019, https://www.parliament.uk/documents/lords-committees/house-of-lords-commission/2017-19/ellenbogen-report.pdf.

Evans, H 2004, in *Department of the Senate annual report 2003-04, Clerk's review*, Canberra.
_____ 2005, in *Department of the Senate annual report 2004-05, Clerk's review*, Canberra.
Flinders, M & Kelso, A 2011, 'Mind the gap: political analysis, public expectations and the parliamentary decline thesis', *The British Journal of Politics and International Relations*, vol. 13, no. 2, pp. 249–268.
Halligan, J, Miller, R & Power, J 2007, *Parliament in the Twenty-First Century: Institutional Reform and Emerging Roles*, Melbourne University Press, Melbourne.
House of Representatives Standing Committee on Procedure 1993, *About time: bills, questions and working hours*, report of the inquiry into reform of the House of Representatives, October 1993, viewed 17 March 2021, https://www.aph.gov.au/parliamentary_business/committees/house_of_representatives_committees?url=reports/1993/1993_pp194.pdf.
_____ 2020, *The House must go on: report of the inquiry into the practices and procedures put in place by the House in response to the COVID-19 pandemic*, December 2020, viewed 18 March 2021, https://www.aph.gov.au/Parliamentary_Business/Committees/House/Procedure/ResponsetoCOVID-19/Report.
Joint Committee of Public Accounts and Audit 2008, *The efficiency dividend and small agencies: size does matter*, Report 413, December 2008, viewed 18 March 2021, https://www.aph.gov.au/parliamentary_business/committees/house_of_representatives_committees?url=jcpaa/efficdiv/report/fullreport.pdf.
Joint Select Committee on Parliamentary Standards 2022, *Final report*, November 2022, viewed 1 December 2022.
Joint Standing Committee on the National Capital and External Territories 2019, *Telling Australia's story—and why it's important: report on the inquiry into Australia's national institutions*, April 2019, Canberra.
Judge, D & Leston-Bandeira, C 2018, 'The institutional representation of parliament', *Political Studies*, vol. 66, no. 1, pp. 154–172.
Karp, D & Evans, M 2019, *Submission to the Legal and Constitutional Affairs References Committee inquiry into nationhood, national identity and democracy*, 30 September 2019, viewed 16 March 2021, https://www.democracy2025.gov.au/documents/Senate%20Constitutional%20Inquiry%20Democracy%202025%20Submission.pdf.
Maley, J & Curtis K, 2021, '"Suck it up": parliament staff claim bullying is rife and complaints ignored', *Sydney Morning Herald*, 17 February, viewed 20 February 2021, https://www.smh.com.au/politics/federal/suck-it-up-parliament-staff-claim-harassment-complaints-ignored-20210217-p57381.html.
Mills, S 2020, 'Parliament in a time of virus: representative democracy as a non-essential service', *Australasian Parliamentary Review*, vol. 34, no. 2, pp. 7–20.
Monk, D 2009, *In the Eye of the beholder? A framework for testing the effectiveness of parliamentary committees*, Parliamentary Studies Paper 10, Crawford School of Economics and Government, Australian National University, Canberra.
Norton, P 2017, 'Speaking for parliament', *Parliamentary Affairs*, vol. 70, no. 2, pp. 191–206.
Parliamentary Library 2013, *The Hung Parliament: procedural changes in the House of Representatives*, research paper, 22 November 2013, viewed 29 November 2018, https://parlinfo.aph.gov.au/parlInfo/download/library/prspub/2855740/upload_binary/2855740.pdf;fileType=application/pdf).
Podger, A 2002, *Review by the Parliamentary Service Commissioner of aspects of the administration of the Parliament: final report*, Canberra.
Reid, G S & Forrest, M 1989, *Australia's Commonwealth Parliament: 1901-1988 Ten Perspectives*, Melbourne University, Melbourne.
Russell, M 2000, *Reforming the House of Lords: Lessons from Overseas*, Oxford University Press, Oxford.
Senate Finance and Public Administration Legislation Committee 2012, *The performance of the Department of Parliamentary Services: final report*, 28 November 2012, Commonwealth of Australia, Canberra.
_____ 2015, *Department of Parliamentary Services: final report*, 17 September 2015, Commonwealth of Australia, Canberra.
_____ 2020, *Estimates*, 19 October 2020, viewed 14 March 2021, https://www.aph.gov.au/Parliamentary_Business/Committees/Senate/Finance_and_Public_Administration/Estimates_reports/Budget2021.
_____ 2021, *Operation and management of the Department of Parliamentary Services*, viewed 17 March 2021, https://www.aph.gov.au/Parliamentary_Business/Committees/Senate/Finance_and_Public_Administration/OperationofDPS.
Senate Procedure Committee 2020a, *Routine of business: remote participation in Senate proceedings*, First report of 2020, 21 August 2020, viewed 18 March 2021, https://www.aph.gov.au/Parliamentary_Business/Committees/Senate/Procedure/2020/Report.

_____ 2020b *Covid-19 and the Senate*, Second report of 2020, October 2020, viewed 18 March 2021, https://www.aph.gov.au/Parliamentary_Business/Committees/Senate/Procedure/2020/Report2.

Senate Select Committee on COVID-19, 2020, *First interim report*, viewed 6 October 2021, https://parlinfo.aph.gov.au/parlInfo/download/committees/reportsen/024513/toc_pdf/Firstinterimreport.pdf;fileType=application%2Fpdf.

Sloane, M 2014, 'The role of the separation of powers and the parliamentary budget setting processes', *Australasian Parliamentary Review*, vol. 29, no. 2, pp. 140–158.

Stoker, G, Evans, M & Halupka M 2018, Democracy 2025, *Trust and democracy in Australia: democratic decline and renewal*, Museum of Australian Democracy, University of Canberra, Institute for Governance and Policy Analysis, viewed 5 December 2018, https://www.democracy2025.gov.au/documents/Democracy2025-report1.pdf.

Twomey, A 2020, 'A virtual Australian parliament is possible—and may be needed—during the coronavirus pandemic', *The Conversation*, 25 March 2020, viewed 13 July 2020, https://theconversation.com/a-virtual-australian-parliament-is-possible-and-may-be-needed-during-the-coronavirus-pandemic-134540.

Walker, J, Chambers, G & McKenna, M 2021, 'Life's dream torn apart under glare of publicity', *Weekend Australian*, 20–21 February, p. 8.

48
BRAZIL'S PARLIAMENTARY ADMINISTRATION

Fabiano Santos and Fernando Saboia Vieira

48.1 Introduction

This chapter discusses the politics of parliamentary administration in Brazil. The Brazilian Parliament (*Congresso Nacional* or National Congress) is made up of two Houses: the lower House (*Câmara dos Deputados* or Chamber of Deputies) and the upper House (*Senado Federal* or Federal Senate), our focus here being on the former (*Câmara dos Deputados*). As in other Latin American countries, formally its design and functions are based on the one hand, on the Constitution of the United States and, on the other, on formal rules and details stemming from the Continental tradition, more specifically the Portuguese constitutional law. Hence, like the Mexican case described in this volume, the 1988 Brazilian Constitution follows the checks and balances model. However, in practice and throughout most of the end of the 20th century and the beginning of the new one, Brazilian politics has been characterized by a powerful executive branch, especially when and if the president decides to build majoritarian or super majoritarian coalitions with the main parties represented in the parliament. Besides the right to give and take ministerial positions, the Constitution also grants the presidency a considerable range of institutional tools, such as the right to initiate and veto, totally and partially, bills, as well as decree and huge budgetary powers (Raille, Pereira and Power, 2011).

With its origins remounting the 1900s, and despite periods of authoritarian and military rule (Skidmore, 1967, 1988; Baaklini, 1993), the history of the Brazilian Congress can be understood as a stop and go process towards a more institutionalized structure, meaning an institutional dynamics of ring-fencing vis-à-vis other political organizations. Institutionalization, thus, is seen here as a complex process through which a legislature acquires the ability to take better informed decisions concerning a nation's relevant policy agenda (Polsby, 1968, Krehbiel, 1990). In this sense, decisive steps in this direction eventually occurred after the country's transition to democracy and the crisis of the military rule from the mid-1970s to 1985, but only in a restricted manner. Like many other democratization trajectories in Latin America and Southern Europe during the 1980s, the breakdown of the authoritarian regime was a gradual process, featured by various tentative reforms, mutual concessions, and the sluggish liberation of party pluralism into the political system (O'Donnell, Schmitter and Whitehead, 1986; Mainwaring, 1986). These circumstances led to the mentioned stop and go process of institutional autonomy, in which increased leeway for exercising policy making, budgetary and oversight scope have coexisted with a rather powerful presidency (Figueiredo and Limongi, 1999).

Anyway, it is obvious that the *Congresso Nacional* advanced a lot in terms of its professional and institutional capacity. We can say that this dynamic has contributed to an increasing internal complexity, as well as an enhanced ability to respond to multiple demands coming from the outside world (Polsby, 1968). Likewise, it is reasonable to state that the Brazilian legislators comprise a rather professionalized political class as well as a set of highly resourceful actors (Almeida, 2018), counting on a well-developed internal administrative capacity (Squire, 2007). However, as with the Mexican case, the topic has been object only of scant academic concern and with this chapter, we will also try to start fulfilling the gap.

Both chambers of the *Congresso Nacional* have developed important administrative structures, processes, and staff. As we will see, parliamentary administration in Brazil consists of a complicated set of tasks and functions encompassing since more bureaucratic and parliamentary civil service as much as complex policy making advice and oversight activities. There are, in sum, niches of specialized knowledge that provide expert analyses and information services in favour of a more qualified intervention in the public debate and in the decision-making process. Thus, our argument in this chapter is that Brazilian displays a mixed model of parliamentary administration, featured by a stop and go process of institutionalization and professionalization of the two Houses that comprise the *Congresso Nacional*. That is, key attributes and roles of the administration adopted over the last three decades – including a dramatic growth of its organizational complexity, size, and functions – resulted from a layering development where in different incentives impacted upon the decisions about the administrative structure to be adopted.

We structure the chapter as follows: in Section 48.2, we describe the Brazilian basic institutional structure, its party system recent evolution as well as its model of legislative organization; in Section 48.3, we present the logic behind the recent adoption of informational features of parliamentary organization and, thus towards a more institutionalized legislature; Section 48.4 is dedicated to an overview of the basic traits of parliamentary administration of *Congresso*, with a special focus on the *Câmara*. In Section 48.5, we outline current challenges for parliamentary administration, and the last section concludes.

48.2 Institutional Structure, Party System, and Legislative Organization

The current democratic era in Brazil was set after the collapse of the authoritarian regime, which took place in the country from 1964 to 1985. Hence, the politics of parliamentary administration analysed in this chapter will be limited to the political system consolidated with the democratization process in the country from the late 1980s. The 1988 Constitution maintained the basic structure of the countries' political system in place since the end of the WWII, the new democracy in the country remaining presidential, with a bicameral legislature, with its lower house elected through proportional representation with open lists distributed among its 27 independent districts. These coincided with the borders of the states of the federal republic.

Considering the competition for seats in the *Câmara dos Deputados* between 1990 and 2014, the number of elected parties is increasing. More specifically: in 1990, 33 parties competed for a seat in the lower chamber, and 19 were successful (58.6 per cent); in 1994, there were 22 competing parties and 18 elected (81.8 per cent); in 1998, 18 out of 30 parties elected at least one legislator (60 per cent); in 2002, 19 out of 30 competing parties were elected

(63.4 per cent); in 2006, 21 out of 29 were successful in elections to the *Câmara dos Deputados* (72.41 per cent); in 2010, the number of parties with a seat increased – 22 out of 27 (81.5 per cent) – and reached the highest level in 2014: 28 out of 32 parties elected at least one deputy (87.5 per cent) (Santos, 2018). It is true, however, that the main parties that prevailed in Congress remained the same until the 2018 elections: *Partido dos Trabalhadores* (PT), *Partido Democrático Trabalhista* (PDT), and *Partido Socialista Brasileiro* (PSB) on the left and centre-left, and *Movimento Democrático Brasileiro* (MDB), *Partido da Social Democracia Brasileira* (PSDB), *Democratas* (DEM), and *Partido Progressistas* (PP) on the centre-right and right.

This relatively high number of parties makes it almost inevitable to form governments based on coalitions, similarly to parliamentary systems around the world, basically in Europe. As to the electoral arena, Brazilian parties are commonly characterized as being ideologically weak or little cohesive. However, it is they, through party leaders, who organize and coordinate legislative activities. This behaviour is somehow structurally induced, given that the institutions created in post-democratization Brazil has centralized the decision-making process inside the *Câmara*, gave party leaders powers to control roll calls taken on the floor, to define a bill proposal's timetable, and endowed the Executive with broad agenda-setting powers. Thus, the system is characterized by the predominance of the Executive, which is elected by a majority vote, and that has both an independent term and the prerogative to appoint ministers unilaterally. Conversely, there is an organized and reasonably disciplined set of legislative parties regarding plenary decisions and public policy decision-making process (Figueiredo and Limongi, 1999).

This does not mean that the literature has not identified strongly individualistic traits in the legislative behaviour of federal deputies.[1] Indicators such as opinion polls, legal production, budget process, and party discipline reveal at least two fundamental points. First, there is widespread recognition of the importance of building a personal reputation with voters. Thus, the task of political representation in Brazil is firmly anchored in the individual image of the politician. The second point, however, is that the space for legislators' individual action is exceedingly small in the legislature. It is noteworthy that the legislative activity, its organization, and the decision-making process are centralized in the parties' leaderships, particularly those who form the government's support coalition. In addition to that, there is also a consensus that the *Congresso Nacional* lacks, in its decision-making process, rules and procedures that encourage the development of legislators' expertise and training in policy formulation and implementation. In short, *Congresso* is yet to develop minimally efficient informational mechanisms in support of the analysis and decision-making process of relevant policies on the country's public agenda.

Given these contradictory vectors, to deal with the parliamentary organization in Brazil, we adopted an analytical approach which combines the functionalist tradition with the rational choice paradigm. This approach classifies the Brazilian Legislature as being in the transition from a reactive profile towards a transformative one. Being reactive,[2] it delegates the initiative of the most important legal proposals to the Executive, such as the definition of the agenda and the priorities regarding the plenary's timetable, who, later negotiates with party leaders, especially of those comprising the majoritarian coalition in the legislature. The power of oversight is, in general, widespread, although the internal complexity is not as well developed. This makes the Parliament, to some extent, dependent on information processed by agents outside the legislature, such as the bureaucracy at the executive-level, the Judiciary, or interest groups. Regarding their career, politicians do not prioritize the Legislature. They prefer, whenever possible, to compete, through an election or by appointment, for government positions at the national or local level.

Amorim Neto and Santos (2003) observed that from 1985 to 1999, in a sample of more than two thousand bills passed by congress, only 336 were legislator-led initiatives. In addition, it was found that, although they were relevant to groups and sectors of society, such bills did not affect the country's economic and social status quo, being rather specific on pertinent issues to the lives of ordinary people. The budgetary process, moreover, was controlled by the Executive branch and organized to favour the priorities set by the alliance of parties which dominate the government, with only marginal interventions from legislators (Figueiredo and Limongi, 2008). Although the internal complexity is increasing, as corroborated by the recent increase in the number of technical committees in the *Câmara dos Deputados* (i.e., from 16 to 20), it would still be insufficient to resist the Executive's information-producing machine. Finally, regarding the careers of lawmakers, several studies have shown that these are characterized by a "zigzag" profile, often having their priorities set at appointment positions in the local government (Samuels, 2003; Santos, 2003).

Recently, however, Freitas (2016) and Almeida (2018) found strong evidence, from different means, that the Brazilian national legislature has become an originator and a proactive agent in its policy decision-making process. This suggests caution when it comes to a definitive categorization regarding the power of passing successful bills or in a broader view of the political system. In addition, if we use Squire's classification (2007) on the professionalization of legislatures, it is easy to conclude that the Brazilian legislature is a highly professionalized institution, with a high level of advising services, high salaries compared to the national average income and almost uninterrupted annual operation. In this sense, we can say that the *Câmara* is evolving in the direction of a transformative profile, as it is predominating not only as to the origin of the approved measures but also in the implementation of government programs and on budgetary measures. A high internal complexity, which is expressed in the broad division of legislative work in standing committees (or *comissões permanentes* in Portuguese) and highly specialized technical committees, is the hallmark of this type of Parliament (Almeida, 2018).

In summary, Brazilian Legislative studies and the diverse perspectives that evaluate the role and behaviour of Parliament in contemporary democracy indicate that the Brazilian legislature is an institution in transition from a reactive to a transformative profile. Furthermore, it is organized and makes decisions through a combination of party and distributive elements, with decisive but decreasing influence from the Executive Branch. Our question now is what to expect from an institution with such characteristics when it comes to the politics of parliamentary administration. Before doing that, let's see how the informational element has been breaking inside both chambers of *Congresso*.

48.3 The Brazilian Model of Parliamentary Administration

A debate between two important figures of Brazilian public administration in the mid-1990s serves to enlighten aspects that are today essential to understanding the current administrative model of the Brazilian legislature.[3] On one side, one of the main advisors to the party leaders of the *Partido da Social Democracia Brasileira* (PSDB) in the *Senado Federal*, Antonio Carlos Pojo do Rego, denounced the "logical impossibility" underlying the institutional advisory structure of the Legislative Branch, particularly the *Câmara dos Deputados*. According to him, the model adopted, which is centralized in the Chamber's Bureau and ostensibly bureaucratic, is based on the existence of a neutral technical body at the service of the quality of the public policies under discussion in parliament. The logical impossibility would rest on the fact that this conception would be in contradiction with the eminently partisan role of an elected representative, to whom the staff is supposed to be accountable to in the first place. On the other side, Mozart Paiva Vianna, Secretary General of the Bureau of the *Câmara dos Deputados* for over 20 years, advocated this eventually victorious model, which is based on the idea that the contemporary demands inherent to the decision-making process require speedy and well-informed responses from parliament regarding a wide variety of topics. Furthermore, he argued that the political and partisan work of elected representatives and the advisory services of highly specialized civil servants were perfectly compatible. The victory of the model advocated by Vianna, in fact, resulted in the coexistence of an eminently partisan and political advisory body with an advisory body known in the *Câmara dos Deputados* as the Legislative Consultancy (CONLE), an essentially technical body whose members view themselves as experts and non-partisan. In this section, we argue that the evolution of such a type of advisory service, that is, the institutionalization of a consultancy service that views itself and acts as neutral, which can be understood through an informational logic applied to the legislative administration in Brazil.

The literature on the *Congresso* has ascertained the coexistence of distributive and partisan elements in the legislative behaviour of representatives in the current democratic period.[4] Recent analyses, however, have applied informational models to several aspects of the congressional dynamics in Brazil, with important theoretical and empirical results.[5] Such models are based on a situation in which a representative must choose a public policy p and the decision-making takes place in uncertain conditions. With each policy p, an outcome x is associated, both usually defined in a one-dimensional space. Legislators, however, do not know the exact relationship between p and x, but only that for each value of the former there is a probability distribution of values of the latter. By way of simplification, let us define the relationship between policies and their outcomes in an additive fashion, as $x = p + \omega$, where ω is a parameter, whose value is not known with certainty *a priori*.[6] From a substantive point of view, one can conceive ω as the expression of factors exogenous to the legislative decision.

The decisive and differential element of the informational approach is that the Legislative branch will under certain conditions obtain information about ω and thus reduce its uncertainty and the corresponding informational loss, "consulting" actors who hold information about the effects of the policy.[7] It is assumed that in the Brazilian political dynamics, two actors are key: The Executive and the Legislative's own system of standing committees, or simply a specialized committee. In general, the Executive is highly informed about ω, possessing more information than the committee and the median legislator. However, the point of interest is that the committee also has the means to collect relevant information, especially through its administrative organization. Thus, inspired by the informational approach, two key questions can be formulated about the role of legislative administrative model: (1) How is the *Câmara dos Deputados* structured to meet the challenge of collecting information other than that already embedded in Executive's messages? (2) How might legislators be able to alter the proposed policies and thus reduce uncertainty regarding the decision's expected outcomes?

Two meanings can be given to the concept of parliamentary administration. The first one refers to the administrative notion of carrying out activities through an organization. Such activities are vital for the routine functioning of an institution, helping it to achieve its ultimate goals. For analytical purposes, we must separate from this notion the support aimed at functions of an "intellectual nature", that is, the production of alternatives for the Legislative decision-making process.[8] In this last sense, the administrative structure refers to an institutional support that is endogenous, permanent and has a bearing both on the preparation and the processing of proposals and serves both individual representatives and the collective bodies of the *Câmara* such as committees, party leaderships and the Bureau's General

Secretariat (Paiva, 1995; Horta, 2011). A structure, in sum, derived from the logic of informational behaviour present in the Brazilian context.

So, our mixed model of parliamentary administration stems from this layering of partisan, individualistic and informational elements which have been impacted upon legislators' decision regarding how to structure the administration of the legislature.[9] In the description that follows, we will show that parliamentary parties and representatives as individuals both have a huge number of administrative resources and personnel under their control, however, it will also reveal that the *Câmara* counts with a powerful centralized machine, a feature consistent with the informational approach.

48.4 Key Aspects of the Organization of the Parliamentary Administration[10]

48.4.1 General Overview

The *Congresso Nacional* is composed of two houses: The *Câmara dos Deputados*, which has 513 representatives of the people chosen by a proportional electoral system, and the *Senado Federal*, composed of 81 senators, with 3 representatives from each unit of the Brazilian federation. The administrative structures of the two houses are separate and function independently but are quite similar in their organization and the services they provide. Each has a General Directorate, responsible for general administrative support, and a General Secretariat, responsible for technical and administrative support for activities more related to the functions of the members of *Congresso*, such as the presentation, processing and consideration of legislative matters and holding of meetings and sessions. In the following, we will mainly deal with the parliamentary administration of the *Câmara dos Deputados*.

In global terms, according to data from the *Câmara* webpage (www.camara.leg.br), at the beginning of 2021, the *Câmara dos Deputados*' functional staff included 13,900 civil servants, divided into three main categories:

1. Permanent employees, those who joined by taking a civil service examination, have tenure and are not linked to political parties – 2,742.
2. Commissioned employees, those who occupy freely appointed positions and are appointed by the leaders of the political bodies of the *Câmara* (members of the Bureau, leaders of the political bodies of the House, party leaders) – 1,787.
3. Freely appointed employees hired for the personal offices of the members of the *Câmara* – 9,376.

This overall contingent has decreased over the last decade from 15,069 in 2011 to the current 13,905. This decrease was mainly in permanent and parliamentary office staff, with the number of commissioned employees appointed to political bodies having grown from 1,319 to 1,787 over this period. The figures show a trend of growth of the decentralized, partisan parliamentary structure to the detriment of centralized, non-partisan bureaucracy.

48.4.2 Organizational Structure of the Administration

The *Câmara dos Deputados* makes the following support services central to legislative activity available to the Deputies: The General Secretariat of the Bureau; two Consultancies, one composed of specialists in the many areas of interest to the House and the other focusing exclusively on the budget and financial oversight of the Government; and a Document and Information Centre, which includes a library, research services, and document and legislation archives.

The committees have centralized support services at their disposal, as well as their own administrative and technical structures made up of both permanent and commissioned staff. In the parliamentary organization of the committees, an increase in the number of staff appointed by political parties is also noticeable. The legislative consultancies, although centralized, are structured internally to meet the requirements of the committees, appointing their staff to monitor meetings and prepare technical work requested by their members.

In quantitative terms, up to date data from the *Câmara*'s webpage (www.camara.leg.br) shows that on 03/17/2021, the distribution of employees in these bodies was the following:

1. Consultancies – 224 permanent employees.
2. Documentation centre – 155 permanent and 2 commissioned employees.
3. Committees – 230 permanent and 56 commissioned employees.
4. Party leaders – 295 permanent and 687 commissioned employees.
5. Offices of the members of the Bureau – 88 permanent and 92 commissioned employees.
6. General Secretariat of the Bureau – 119 permanent employees.

48.4.3 Assessment, Security, IT, and Presence of Specialized Units (e.g., Library, Research, Legal Service, and Risk)

The Câmara has three main specialized technical advisory bodies to support parliamentary activity: The Legislative Consultancy (Conle), the Budget and Financial Inspection Consultancy (Conof), and the Centre for Documentation and Information (Cedi). The Legislative Consultancy is a body made up of 175 specialist consultants in the many areas of interest to the *Câmara dos Deputados*. They are recruited by taking a civil service examination and many have master's and doctoral degrees (as of March 2021). The Conle is divided into four main areas: Law and Government; Economy and Addresses; Social Policies; and Sectoral Policies. This consultancy encompasses both the personal demands of parliamentarians and those of the committees, producing work to support all stages of the legislative process, from the production of bill proposals to their examination at the committee stage and final deliberation by the full house on the floor. Its approach is technical and non-partisan, although it may work with Deputies who are rapporteurs of bills in the committees and prepare opinions under their orientation.

In March 2021, the Budget and Financial Inspection Consultancy had 24 active consultants among its staff. This Consultancy provides technical support to parliamentarians on budgetary and financial matters, especially to the Mixed Budget Committee of the *Congresso*, responsible for examining and issuing opinions on budget laws submitted by the Executive Branch. Conof also provides advisory services for the monitoring and supervision of budget execution and the application of public resources.

The *Câmara dos Deputados*' Documentation and Information Centre is composed of approximately 150 permanent staff members and has a library, a publishing house, an archive centre, and research and information management services. The House Library has a general collection of approximately 200,000 books, as well as over 6,000 rare works. Its bibliographic and document research service is integrated with a computerized network of public libraries. The House Archive contains historical documents dating from the creation of the Brazilian parliament, with the 1823 Constituent Assembly of the Imperial Period, to the present day, as well as the entire collection of records of House sessions and legislative documents produced. Research services cater to parliamentarians and to House bodies and staff, as well as to researchers and the public. They include bibliographic and document research, legislation research, and general legislative information.

48.4.4 The Mechanisms in Place to Enable Professionalization and the Development of Functional Expertise

The House's permanent employees are recruited through civil service examinations. Commissioned employees and those who work in the parliamentary offices are hired by appointment of the leaders of the political bodies of the House, provided they meet the education and training requirements set forth in the internal rules of the House. Permanent employees occupy structured career posts, for which there are established education, training, and assessment requirements for progression to higher levels.

As to opportunities for staff training, the *Câmara dos Deputados* has a school of government, the Centre for Education, Training and Development (Cefor). This centre offers several of its own postgraduate diploma courses in areas of interest to the House, and a Legislative Branch Master's degree course, all of which are recognized by the Ministry of Education. It also has agreements with several Brazilian universities to train its employees. Cefor offers on-site and distance-learning courses for training and educating House employees, as well as programs and events for society, involving students, bodies, and professionals of several areas.

48.4.5 The Role of the Administration in the Context of Parliamentary Work

The bodies of the administrative structure of the *Câmara dos Deputados* dedicated to supporting parliamentary activity offer services to members and bodies of the House such as research, data and information gathering, preparation of studies and documents on legislative activity, and legal and technical consultancy in the many areas of parliamentary activity. They also prepare draft bills and opinions for Deputies who request them, as well as for the committees in which the themes and propositions are being dealt with. In addition, they provide services such as secretarial services; organizing and recording committee meetings and plenary sessions; receiving, processing, and forwarding legislative documents; and updating the computerized systems for recording, processing, and publicizing the work.

48.4.6 The Nature of Institutional Hierarchy

The Secretary General of the Bureau of the *Câmara dos Deputados*, like that of the *Senado Federal*, is appointed by the House Speaker from the permanent staff and remains in the position until they are replaced. The Secretary's General main attributes are to advise the Bureau, especially the Speaker, regarding the exercise of their legislative and constitutional duties. They are also responsible for coordinating and supervising the performance of the various bodies of the House's administrative structure involved in these tasks. The Secretary General oversees organizing, advising, monitoring, and recording Plenary sessions and Bureau meetings, as well as those of other collegiate bodies in which the Speaker participates. It is up to the body under their leadership to receive, register, and monitor the proposals presented to the House for examination, as well as other documents forwarded to it. To carry out their duties, the Secretary General has an administrative structure at their disposal that includes a legal-technical consultancy specialized in constitutional and routine legislative procedures.

The Secretary General of the Bureau reports directly to the Speaker of the House and acts under their direction. They are not subordinated to party leaders or committee chairs. Although their function is essentially to advise the Speaker, who is responsible for making decisions and conducting the legislative process, the Secretary General enjoys reasonable independence in legal and technical questions concerning the procedures and regulations, often acting as an arbiter in controversial issues. Generally, they do not act as a political advisor or as an advisor of any sort to the Speaker.

The *Câmara*'s organizational structure is quite hierarchical, with few degrees of autonomy given to the various departments in terms of allocation of personnel, material resources, and expenditures. However, the technical bodies that support the parliamentary activity have reasonable autonomy to produce the studies and opinions requested of them.

The *Câmara*'s permanent employees are hired through civil service examinations and their careers are not politicized, apart from some leadership positions in advisory and management bodies more closely related to parliamentary activity, such as the committee secretariats, the appointment to which depends on the consent of their political leaders. Commissioned and parliamentary office staff do not integrate careers and occupy single positions.

48.4.7 Managing Inter-institutional and External Relations

Although independent from each other, the *Câmara* and *Senado* administrations have in common some of the services rendered to the members of parliament, especially regarding matters that are considered in mixed committees or deliberated in joint sessions of the *Congresso Nacional*, such as budget laws and presidential vetoes. In the current legislature, which began in 2019, some of the electronic systems for legislative monitoring were integrated, allowing a digital transmission of documents between the two Houses.

The *Câmara dos Deputados* has constitutional and budgetary autonomy to hire its employees and organize its services. However, it is subject to the general management rules of the federal public administration regarding procedures for spending and hiring and its employees' work regime. The *Câmara*'s administration is subject to inspection by the Federal Accounting Court.

48.5 Current Challenges Facing the Parliamentary Administration

Today, the legislative process in the *Câmara dos Deputados* is fully electronic, both in terms of document production and of monitoring the processing of proposals and voting procedures. Plenary sessions and most committee meetings are also organized and conducted digitally, with online access available through the *Câmara*'s webpage.

The *Câmara dos Deputados* webpage – camara.leg.br – provides extensive data and information on parliamentary activity, including the deputies' presence and participation in committee meetings and plenary sessions, speeches, proposals, opinions, and votes in the deliberations; attendance and absences; and their offices' spending and expenses. It also offers information and tools for following proposals presented for examination, as well as data on House administration – staff and their salaries, budget expenses, etc. Citizens have access to several channels through which to participate on the webpage and the House's social media accounts.

Both the *Câmara dos Deputados* and the *Senado Federal* have adopted measures to make it possible to hold their sessions through remote channels during the Covid-19 pandemic. Most administrative and technical support services have been provided remotely. The two Houses also adopted special, faster procedural rules to enable a quick response to the legislative demands needed to address the crisis. These rules even made it possible to amend the Federal Constitution to guarantee budget resources.

The *Câmara dos Deputados* and *Senado* have their own autonomous security services, which are provided by their own staff, and resort only occasionally to external police forces.

48.6 Conclusion

The transition to democracy in Brazil, eventually established with the 1988 Federal Constitution's promulgation, represented both an opportunity and a great challenge for the *Congresso Nacional*. Not only it was an opportunity because as democracy advanced, legislators were increasingly empowered in their duties to make laws, oversee the government, and decide on budgetary issues. But it was also a challenge for they were increasingly pressure to reorganize and modernize the organization to meet both state and society's demands.

As demonstrated in this chapter, the organizational structure of Brazil's parliament has evolved significantly in recent decades, with a growing institutionalization, marked by the diversity and complexity of tasks, qualification of the staff of effective servers and use of modern technologies for the performance of legislative and administrative activities, to the point that the two Houses of the *Congresso Nacional* responded efficiently to the challenges imposed by the pandemic that has been plaguing the planet since the end of 2019, remaining in operation with processes of appreciation of fully electronic materials and virtual meetings.

This institutionalization has produced a hybrid model of parliamentary organization, with elements of centralization and decentralization, in line with the model of democracy inscribed in the current constitutional text.

On the one hand, the proportional open-list electoral system has induced a growing partisan fragmentation and stimulated, in the dispute for seats in parliament, especially in the *Câmara dos Deputados*, an individualistic behaviour of Members. As a result, congressmen have significant material, technical and personnel resources made available to them in their personal offices and in organs of the *Câmara* structure.

On the other hand, the individualistic and parochial behaviour of members of *Congresso* is contained by internal rules and institutions of parliament that concentrate decision-making powers and resources on leaders, supporters, whose caucuses count on support structures and staff of their free nomination in an amount proportional to their size.

Between these two aspects, one sees a significant informational element in the organization of the Brazilian parliament, represented in its structure by consulting and advisory and technical support bodies integrated by effective servants, recruited by public tender, who produce information, studies and assist in the preparation of documents and legislative activities without party affiliation.

This last aspect has been relevant to enable the *Congresso Nacional* to act less dependent on the Executive Power in the formulation of public policies, in addition to the supervision and control of the acts of the federal administration. However, this strengthening of parliament in the context of a system of government considered semi-parliamentary, called by political scientists as coalition presidentialism, also gives specific contours to the conflicts inherent in the separation of powers.

Administrative structure of the National Congress of Brazil

Notes

1 See Figueiredo and Limongi (1999); Carvalho (2003); Amorim Neto and Santos (2003).
2 This classification is used by Cox and Morgenstern (2002) to characterize the national legislatures of Latin America as a whole.
3 See Abreu and Dias (1995).
4 See Figueiredo and Limongi (1999); Pereira and Mueller (2000); Carvalho (2003); and Amorim Neto and Santos (2003).
5 See Santos and Almeida (2011) and Santos and Canello (2016).
6 The most usual assumption is that ω is the realization of a uniformly distributed random variable with support in [0, 1].
7 It is from this basic aspect that both the theoretical arsenal and the applications of the informational perspective have developed. Initially, Crawford and Sobel's (1982) model of the signaling game and cheap talk assumes that the uninformed decision maker – faced with a context of uncertainty – has the option to "listen" to the recommendation of an expert with potentially distinct preferences, creating an incentive structure for the production and sharing of information. Gilligan and Krehbiel (1987) promote a kind of application of the model to the U.S. Congress, while Krehbiel (1990) brings together several findings and reflections to further shape informational theory. More recent developments extend the standard cheap talk model to legislative games by allowing the decision maker to consult multiple advisors (Krishna and Morgan, 2001) and by endogenizing the production of information with variable costs (Beniers and Swank, 2004; Dur and Swank, 2005), sophisticating the incentive structure. The works of Santos and Almeida (2009, 2011) are non-formal adaptations of these theoretical indications to the context of the *Câmara dos Deputados*, combined with empirical efforts.
8 See Ribas and Silva (2011, p. 17).
9 For an application of the mixed model of parliamentary behaviour to the politics of parliamentary speech, with good empirical results, see Santos, Guarnieri and Salles (2021).
10 For the sources and references used in this section, see Appendix A.

References

Abreu, A. A.; DIAS, J. L. (1995), *O Futuro do Congresso Brasileiro*. Rio de Janeiro: FGV Editora.

Almeida, A. (2018), Governo Presidencial Condicionado: delegação e participação legislativa na Câmara dos Deputados. Tese de Doutorado. Programa de Pós-Graduação em Ciência Política do Instituto de Estudos Sociais e Políticos da Universidade do Estado do Rio de Janeiro (IESP-UERJ).

Amorim Neto, O.; Santos, F. (2003), "The Inefficient Secret Revised: Legislative Input and Output of Brazilian Deputies". *Legislative Studies Quarterly*, XXVII(4), pp. 449–479.

Azevedo, L. H. C. (2011), "Consultoria Legislativa e Assessoramento Institucional: 40 anos". *In:* Câmara dos Deputados (ed.), *40 anos de Consultoria Legislativa: Consultores Legislativos e Consultores de Orçamento*. Brasília: Edições Câmara, Centro de Documentação e Informação. Brasília.

Baaklini, A. (1993), *O Congresso e o Sistema Político no Brasil*. Rio de Janeiro, Paz e Terra.

Beniers, K.J.; SWANK, O. H. (2004), "On the Composition of Committees". *Journal of Law, Economics and Organization*, 20(2), pp. 353–378.

Carvalho, N. R. (2003), *E no início eram as bases: Geografia Política do Voto e Comportamento Legislativo no Brasil*. Rio de Janeiro, Revan.

Cox, G. W.; Morgenstern, S. (2002), "Epilogue: Latin America's Reactive and Proactive Presidents". *In:* Morgenstern, S.; Nacif, B. (eds.), *Legislative Politics in Latin America*. New York: Cambridge University Press.

Crawford, V. P.; Sobel, J. (1982), "Strategic Information Transmission". *Econometrica*, 50(6), pp. 1431–1451.

Dur, R.; Swank, O. H. (2005), "Producing and Manipulating Information". *The Economic Journal*, 115, pp. 185–199.

Figueiredo, A. C.; Limongi, F. (1999), *Executivo e Legislativo na Nova Ordem Constitucional*. Rio de Janeiro: Fundação Getulio Vargas Editora.

Figueiredo, A. C.; Limongi, F. (2008), *Política Orçamentária no Presidencialismo de Coalizão*. Rio de Janeiro: Editora da FGV.

Freitas, Andréa. (2016), *O Presidencialismo da Coalizão*. Rio de Janeiro: Konrad Adenauer Stiftung.

Gilligan, T. W.; Krehbiel, K. (1987), "Collective Decision-Making and Standing Committees: An Informational Rationale for Restrictive Amendment Procedures". *Journal of Law, Economics, and Organization*, 3, pp. 145–193.

Horta, A. B. (2011), "Breve Memória sobre o Assessoramento Legislativo na Câmara dos Deputados". *In*: Câmara dos Deputados (ed.), *40 anos de Consultoria Legislativa: Consultores Legislativos e Consultores de Orçamento*. Brasília: Edições Câmara, Centro de Documentação e Informação.

KrehbieL, K. (1990), *Information and Legislative Organization*. Ann Arbor: The University of Michigan Press.

Krishna, V.; Morgan, J. (2001), "A Model of Expertise". *Quarterly Journal of Economics*, 116(2), pp. 747–775.

Mainwaring, S. (1986), "The Transition to Democracy in Brazil". *Journal of Interamerican Studies and World Affairs*, 28(1), pp. 149–180.

O'Donnell, G.; Schmitter, P. C.; Whitehead, L. (1986), *Transitions from Authoritarian Rule: Latin America*. Baltimore and London: The Johns Hopkins University Press.

Paiva, M. V. (1995), "Assessoramento do Poder Legislativo, Experiência Pessoal e Profissional, Avaliação da Situação Brasileira". *In*: Abreu, A. A.; Dias, J. L. (eds.), *O Futuro do Congresso Brasileiro*. Rio de Janeiro: FGV Editora.

Pereira, C.; Mueller, B. (2000), "Uma Teoria da Preponderância do Poder Executivo: O Sistema de Comissões no Legislativo Brasileiro". *Revista Brasileira de Ciências Sociais*, 15(43), pp. 45–68.

Polsby, Nelson W. (1968), "The Institutionalization of the House of Representatives". *American Political Science Review*, 62(1), pp. 144–168.

Raille, E. D.; Pereira, C.; Power, T. J. (2011), "The executive toolbox: building legislative support in a multiparty presidential regime". *Political Research Quarterly*, 64(2), pp. 323–334.

Rego, A. C. P. (1995), "O Assessoramento do Congresso". *In*: Abreu, A. A.; Dias, J. L. (eds.), *O Futuro do Congresso Brasileiro*. Rio de Janeiro: FGV Editora.

Ribas, A. N.; Silva, P. V. (2011), "A Natureza do Assessoramento Legislativo". *In:* Câmara dos Deputados (ed.), *40 anos de Consultoria Legislativa: Consultores Legislativos e Consultores de Orçamento*. Brasília: Edições Câmara, Centro de Documentação e Informação.

Samuels, D. (2003), *Ambition, Federalism, and Legislative Politics in Brazil*. New York: Cambridge University Press.
Santos, F. 2003. *O Poder Legislativo no Presidencialismo de Coalizão*. Belo Horizonte: Editora da UFMG.
Santos, F.; Almeida, A. (2011), *Fundamentos Informacionais do Presidencialismo de Coalizão*. Curitiba: Appris.
Santos, F.; Canello, J. (2016), "Comissões Permanentes, Estrutura de Assessoramento e o Problema Informacional na Câmara dos Deputados". *Dados*, 59, pp. 980–1015.
Santos, F.; Guarnieri, F.; Salles, N. (2021), "Brazil: Legislative Debate under Coalition Presidentialism". *In:* Back, H.; Deus, M.; Fernandes, J. M. (eds.), *The Politics of Legislative Debate*. Oxford: Oxford University Press.
Santos, W. G. dos. (2018), *A Difusão Parlamentar do Sistema Partidário: exposição do caso brasileiro*. Rio de Janeiro: Editora da UFRJ.
Skidmore, T. E. (1967), *Politics in Brazil, 1930–1964: an experiment in Democracy*. Oxford: Oxford University Press.
Skidmore, T. E. (1988), *Politics of Military Rule in Brazil, 1964–1985*. Oxford: Oxford University Press.
Souza, C. de. (2011), "A Resolução n. 48, de 1993, e a Consolidação do Assessoramento Legislativo Institucional da Câmara dos Deputados". *In*: Câmara dos Deputados (ed.), *40 anos de Consultoria Legislativa: Consultores Legislativos e Consultores de Orçamento*. Brasília: Edições Câmara, Centro de Documentação e Informação.
Squire, P. (2007), "Measuring State Legislative Professionalism: The Squire Index Revisited". *State Politics and Policy Quarterly*, 7(2), pp. 211–227.

Appendix A

As to the sources and references used in Section 48.4:

1. Human Resources Board of Directors – Interview with Director Milton Pereira on the general composition of the Câmara, available on the Câmara dos Deputados website.
2. Secretariat General – interview with the Chief of Staff Leano Toguchi, data and information provided to the authors.
3. Legislative Consulting – CONLE – interview with servant Maria Fernanda Saback, report sent to the authors with information and data.
4. Documentation and Information Centre – Interview with Director André Freire, Management Report 2020, available on the Câmara dos Deputados website.
5. Budget Consulting – Interview with Consultant Graciano Mendes, data available on the Câmara dos Deputados website.
6. Training Centre – CEFOR – Interview and data provided by Director Juliana Werneck, Management Report 2020, available on the Câmara dos Deputados website.
7. Câmara dos Deputados Standing Orders.
8. Resolution 20, 1971, of the Câmara dos Deputados and its amendments.

49
CANADA'S PARLIAMENTARY ADMINISTRATION

Jonathan Malloy

49.1 Introduction

The Canadian Parliament has two chambers – the House of Commons and the Senate. (For brevity, this study will not address the third constitutional component of the Crown.) The House of Commons is directly elected by single-member plurality seats, as in the United Kingdom, with the prime minister and ministers holding Commons seats. The Senate is appointed, with terms lasting until age 75. Until 2016, Senate appointments were almost entirely supporters of the government party of the day. In 2016, a non-partisan independent appointment process was instituted and nearly all appointments since then have not had a party affiliation. This has created a new and still-evolving dynamic in the Senate with effects for its administration.

The administration of the Parliament of Canada is characterized by not only a high degree of professionalism but also silos and separate worlds. The House and the Senate operate as separate organizations along with jointly-run services and offices, most notably the Library of Parliament. And while parliamentary administrators are deeply non-politicized, this may lead to an overly deferential culture that is less able to stand up for the institution as a whole.

This can be linked to broader issues in the institution. The Canadian Parliament has long been seen as excessively partisan by Westminster standards, more so than its founding counterpart in Britain. Party voting levels are very high (Godbout 2020); government backbenchers are noticeably more docile than their British counterparts; and the Commons Speaker in particular is noticeably weaker than in the United Kingdom. There is a striking contrast between the skilled and discreet non-partisan professionalism of Canadian parliamentary administration and the very high politicization of Parliament as an overall institution. Increasingly, no one seems able or willing to stand up publicly for Parliament itself.

Canada has long had multi-party Parliaments but has only seen single-party government. About two-thirds have been majority governments where the governing party holds a majority of Commons seats; the remainder are minority governments where the governing party bargains informally with other parties for support. Canada has never seen a coalition government at the national level (excluding an unusual arrangement in 1917 that defies easy categorization). Only two parties have held power – the Liberals and the Conservatives – but other parties like the New Democrats and Bloc Québécois are typically important parliamentary players. To receive official recognition and resources in the 338 seat House, parties must hold at least 12 seats, and since the 1990s, the House of Commons has almost always had at least four 'recognized' parties – one governing and three in opposition.

Recognition in the smaller 105 seat Senate requires nine members, and the 2016 shift in Senate appointments has led to a complex set of groupings. Historically, all senators were members of either the Liberal or Conservative parties – appointed by those parties when in power – or sat as independents. While the Conservatives have largely continued as a cohesive party group, the Liberal Party disavowed its Senate caucus in 2014 as part of its new policy of independent appointments. The orphan group continued to operate as 'Senate Liberals' until 2019 when it became the Progressive Senate Group. The Canadian Senators Group forms another party-like entity. The largest grouping, the Independent Senators Group, expressly identifies only as a coordinating body and does not take policy stances. Meanwhile, government business in the Senate is conducted by an individual senator designated the Government Representative, supported by two other senators, who are all designated as 'non-affiliated' with any other party or group. Overall, the post-2016 Senate is remarkably fractured and fluid, posing challenges for cohesive administration.

49.2 Organizational Structure

The House of Commons and Senate operate as separate organizations with their own core administrative services such as finance and human resources, though a number of resources and services are administered through joint agreements. The Library of Parliament operates as a third distinct organization, though subservient to the first two. Some services are also administered in cooperation with the Government of Canada. For example, the extensive parliamentary language interpretation services are supplied through a memorandum of understanding with Public Services and Procurement Canada.

Parsing out similarities and differences between the core House and Senate organizations is difficult. Many aspects are subtle; surface differences may not be substantive differences, and vice versa. For example, both houses have a Law Clerk responsible for legal matters; however, the reporting relationship is different, as we see below. The Library of Parliament performs two main functions. One is research for parliamentarians, especially committees. The other is general parliamentary public relations, overseeing public outreach, educational programs, tours, etc.

At a high level, this fundamental structure of separate House and Senate organizations along with the subsidiary Library has remained the same since the Canadian Parliament was established in 1867, just as Parliament itself has retained the same basic structure. While obviously expanding in size, complexity, and professionalism, changes in parliamentary organization have been evolutionary – adding to the historic core structures rather than reorganizing them.

While in the past there may well have been a tendency to build up individual organizational silos, more recent years have seen collaborations to reduce historic gaps and inefficiencies. A striking past example of a gap is when the House and Senate each operated separate security services. The possible risks of this was pointed out in a 2012 audit (Auditor-General of Canada 2012) but was only addressed after a deadly 2014 incident when an armed attacker broke into the main Centre Block building, coming very close to the prime minister and many other MPs (McCarthy and Grant 2014). While the split jurisdiction may not have been the critical factor, the fallout from this incident subsequently led to a joint Parliamentary

Protection Service. protection service that is directed by the Speakers of both chambers but under the operational control of the Royal Canadian Mounted Police (Parliamentary Protective Service n.d.).

A final separate category of entities are the Officers of Parliament. These are difficult to classify; arms-length oversight organizations reporting directly to Parliament, but operating largely independently. As we will see in Section 49.7, tensions can surround these Officer entities.

Information and especially comparable data on staff levels for parliamentary administration is not easy to obtain publicly. Parliamentary employees are not part of the regular public service and thus are not included in government-wide staffing statistics. The House, Senate, and Library all issue separate annual reports and financial statements that lack a uniform format and report total salary expenses but not numbers of employees. This opaqueness may suggest not only a certain sensitivity to the costs and levels of parliamentary staffing, but also the sheer complexity of classifying the many types of employment arrangements and organizations and services operating at least partly under the parliamentary administrative umbrella. Overall, the mix of separate, joint, independent, and third-party relationships means the Parliament of Canada does not make for a simple organizational chart or set of statistics, even if it generally works well in practice.

49.3 Governance and Hierarchy

The House of Commons is overseen by a Board of Internal Economy. The Board is chaired by the Speaker of the House, with senior government and opposition members and additional MPs to achieve a balance between government and opposition members (House of Commons n.d.). Once a secretive institution, the Board now meets largely in public similar to a regular standing committee. The Clerk of the House serves as secretary to the Board and is the chief administrative officer of the permanent House of Commons bureaucracy.

The Speaker of the House is in the middle of this arrangement, but their exact authority is sometimes unclear. While the Clerk reports to the Speaker, the Speaker presides over, rather than controls, the Board of Internal Economy and thus can find themselves in an ambiguous position. The Canadian Speaker is generally a somewhat weak figure with less independent power than their British counterpart, particularly in determining the speaking order of MPs (Cooper 2017). However, in the dimension of governance, the Speaker provides a layer of insulation between the political actors and the non-partisan staff, further protecting the latter from politicization.

The Senate has a different structure. The Standing Committee on Internal Economy, Budgets, and Administration is the key oversight body (Senate of Canada n.d.b). However, administrative authority is more divided (Senate of Canada n.d.a). The Chief Corporate Services Officer, rather than the Clerk of the Senate, serves as secretary to the Standing Committee and holds responsibility for many administrative aspects of the institution, while the Clerk of the Senate serves as the Chief Legislative Services Officer. The Law Clerk is a third administrative official with an independent relationship with the Standing Committee. This trifecta is quite different from the clear primacy of the Clerk of the House of Commons.

Both the Senate and House Clerks are order-in-council appointments, meaning they are named by the government of the day, though the exact process may vary. For the House Clerk, this has historically not been a significant issue. However, the 2017 naming of the current Clerk, formerly the Clerk of the Senate, over the previous serving interim Clerk was controversial and was publicly questioned by two former Clerks (Mazereeuw

2017). This led to an unconventional divided vote in the Commons over the appointment, with the governing Liberal and New Democrats prevailing over the opposition of the Conservatives. This was a disturbing development for such a traditionally non-politicized office, though controversy appears to have dissipated, at least publicly.

It is an even more fraught story in the Senate, which has not had a permanent Clerk since 2015, cycling through four interim appointments as of this writing. Here, senators are willing to question publicly the prime minister's authority to appoint the Clerk, especially Conservative senators who have generally opposed the entire new independent appointment process for the Senate (Mazereeuw 2018a; Mazereeuw 2018b). We will not get into the full issue here, but it is logical to link ongoing changes and instability in the overall chamber to instability and ambiguity in its administrative hierarchy.

Both the Board of Internal Economy and Standing Committee on Internal Economy, Budgets, and Administration, including their composition, are established in law under *The Parliament of Canada Act*, though provisions are more detailed for the House Board than its Senate counterpart (*Parliament of Canada Act*). The Library of Parliament is clearly subordinate in its governance arrangements. Its chief executive officer, the Parliamentary Librarian, reports jointly to the House and Senate Speakers and is overseen by a Standing Joint Committee on the Library of Parliament comprising both House and Senate members (Library of Parliament).

Overall there is a bright and clear line between partisan and non-partisan actors in Canadian parliamentary governance arrangements. Ultimate authority is vested in political actors, while day-to-day administrative responsibility rests with professional administrators. However, recent developments and controversies in the appointment of Clerks for both chambers are concerning, hinting at a possible new politicization of roles previously seen as highly impartial.

49.4 Personnel

There is a similarly strict divide in Canada between political staff advisors to politicians and the non-partisan permanent staff of Parliament. All MPs and senators receive funds to hire personal office staff, typically two or three employees; House members also receive additional funds for constituency offices in their electoral districts (Wilson 2020a). Recognized parties receive additional funds to staff leadership offices and also a general caucus service office that theoretically works for all members of the parliamentary party group but primarily serves the party leader and central party objectives (Wilson 2020b). These political employees typically have strong party ties; their jobs depend on the electoral fortunes of their employers and they are hired, and fired, largely at the pleasure of the party or MP/senator.

In contrast, permanent parliamentary staff are generally career recruits with no party ties. Discretion and strict non-partisanship are extremely important values in this culture. Unlike the regular public service, which retains rights to engage in political and election activity outside of work, parliamentary staff are more restricted, partly by rules but perhaps even more by culture, from engaging in anything remotely partisan. Involvement with advocacy groups or other entities that might interact with parliamentary business is similarly restricted. While some of the above political staff do move into the regular public service as government employees, it is rare to see a political staff person transition to the permanent parliamentary staff, at least at professional levels. Thus, while they interact extensively, the two groups of political staff and parliamentary staff exist in highly separate employment worlds, and the boundaries are well understood by both sides.

As in other Westminster-model systems, professional procedural staff carry the title of 'clerk' (MacMinn and Vaive 1998). This professional designation ties them closely to counterparts in other jurisdictions, aligning them with a distinct class of highly professional, permanent parliamentary employees that typically spend their entire careers serving legislative institutions.

In modern times, the top Clerks in both houses have spent their entire careers in Parliament. While some 20th-century House Clerks were former MPs, such an arrangement would be inconceivable today. Transfers from provincial legislatures are rare, though Bev Koester (Clerk of the House from 1980 to 87) and Gordon Barnhart (Clerk of the Senate from 1989 to 94) were both former Clerks of the Legislative Assembly of Saskatchewan. In general, promotion in Parliament is internal, especially for the clerk ranks. There is somewhat greater interchange with the rest of the government public service for more administrative and technical roles, though hiring senior employees directly from outside the public service entirely is rare. There is however interchange between the House and Senate (and Library), again particularly for high fliers, though this is informal and episodic, not a systematic arrangement. For example, as noted in Section 49.3, the current Clerk of the House was formerly Clerk of the Senate; similarly, the current Parliamentary Librarian was previously a senior Senate clerk.

While political staff jobs are seen as stressful with no job security and not always desirable, permanent employment in Parliament is generally considered prestigious and desirable. The House prides itself on being listed as a nationally desirable employer in industry listings (House of Commons 2019: 37). However, the Senate appears to be a more unstable employer in recent years, as illustrated in the inability to maintain a permanent clerk (Mazereeuw 2018a).

49.5 The Role of the Administration in the Context of Parliamentary Work

Parliamentary staff play a variety of support roles for parliamentarians. This work is generally considered to be highly competent, but sometimes under-resourced and/or limited by the strict non-partisan nature of parliamentary staff. Parliamentary staff are responsible for a wide variety of operations supporting parliamentary business, similar to other legislatures.

Legislative drafting guidance is available and widely praised. Parliamentary staff are also readily available to answer procedural questions and offer advice on almost any technical or administrative subject. However, their strongly neutral nature can limit the scope of advice. While parliamentarians generally appreciate the unbiased and typically confidential nature of advice, some may feel frustrated that they cannot get more substantive and proactive advice from parliamentary staff. The competent but constrained role of parliamentary staff may mean that parliamentarians become overly dependent exclusively on party sources for more tactical and strategic guidance.

An example of this constraint is provided by Louise Cockram's research on orientation of new MPs in the House of Commons (Cockram 2020). Cockram finds that the House has devoted extensive effort to guiding new MPs in their jobs. However, the support is overwhelmingly administrative in character, with little guidance for 'how to *be* an MP.' Consequently, MPs appreciate but do not absorb much of their formal orientation and instead turn to fellow parliamentarians within their parties for substantive guidance. This not only creates cohesion and solidarity but also solidifies the role of parties as the dominant and guiding forces of parliamentary life.

Canadian parliamentary committees are competently but lightly resourced. Committees typically have one clerk assigned to them, possibly with some additional general administrative assistance, along with one or two research analysts from the Library of Parliament. Canadian House of Commons committees have long been seen as underperforming (Malloy 1996; Stilborn 2014), and one of the longstanding calls is for enhanced staff resources for committees. Yet it is not clear how additional resources would be used, other than in a politicized way, since Canadian committees are more likely to split along party lines than the British counterparts. It is thus unclear how non-partisan research staff would be able to effectively and fully serve a divided committee, especially given the typical presence of three separate opposition parties, each with their own agendas.

Canadian House committee membership is also heavily manipulated by parties; many MPs only stay with the same committee for about two years, with provisions for even more short-term substitutions, undermining long-term continuity among members. It is therefore not clear that staff under-resourcing is the main problem for committees, though presumably an increase would at least contribute positively to enhanced committee activity and institutional memory. Senate committees do have a greater reputation for substance and consensus, though actual evidence of this in the pre-2016 partisan arena is mixed (Lawlor and Crandall 2013). This may be changing under the increasingly independent-dominated chamber but it is too early to make a full assessment.

49.6 External Communications and Relations

Parliamentary administrators engage externally in many ways, but again in restricted capacities. Clerks interact with their counterparts in Canadian and international legislatures, but typically operating quite separately from the meetings and interactions of parliamentarians. One exception is the Canadian Council of Public Accounts Committees, which holds annual meetings involving both legislators and staff (Canadian Council of Public Accounts Committees n.d.); this mixing of the two worlds of parliamentarians and staff is relatively unusual. Parliamentary administrators are also involved in a variety of educational and study activities. One of the most longstanding is support for the Canadian Study of Parliament Group, an independent organization that receives substantive in-kind support from Parliament, particularly the House of Commons. However, compared to its same-name counterparts in the United Kingdom and Australasia, parliamentarians are less involved in the Canadian Group, further suggesting a bifurcated world in which political actors and parliamentary professionals operate in separate silos.

International activities are overseen by the Joint Interparliamentary Council which coordinates House and Senate international activities (Parliament of Canada, Joint Interparliamentary Council). Parliament formally supports, though generally only in a limited way, a number of international parliamentary associations and interparliamentary groups formally linked to other legislatures (or multilateral organizations, such as legislators from NATO countries), and these may involve both parliamentarians and parliamentary staff. This is distinct from a larger category of 'friendship groups,' typically sponsored by foreign governments, not legislatures. Recent years have seen an increase in both international 'friendship' groups as well as externally sponsored 'all-party groups' in Parliament dedicated to particular issues or industries. These receive little or no support from the parliamentary administration, though they may be supported through sponsoring MPs' offices. Paul Thomas finds these to be a growing but still relatively modest phenomenon in Canada, while in the United Kingdom they have proliferated and become increasingly embedded in parliamentary administration itself, and this trend may grow in Canada (Thomas 2016).

One area where Parliament has most upped its game in recent years is external communication. The House, Senate, and Library have made the most of digital tools to make increasing amounts of information accessible, including data downloadable for researchers, along with increased general information on aspects of parliamentary administration. Transparency has also increased in other ways, such as opening up the House Board of Internal Economy, as mentioned, and disclosure of parliamentarians' expenses.

The Senate is particularly noticeable for an enhanced public relations campaign of communications that emphasize the role and value of the Senate, including publishing a children's book (Tasker 2017). This responds both to the longstanding ambiguity surrounding this appointed institution as well as a series of expense scandals that greatly embarrassed the Senate. One senator was charged with breach of trust in a very high-profile case, but was acquitted, with the court accepting his argument that expense guidelines were so lax and unclear that his expenses, though seemingly egregious, were permissible (MacCharles 2016). This has led to considerable updating of rules and a much more proactive culture of disclosure.

49.7 The Officers of Parliament

As noted earlier, the Parliament of Canada has a series of arms-length 'watchdogs' reporting to it. While properly understood as parliamentary entities, they are difficult to classify. They include the Auditor-General of Canada, responsible for certifying government annual financial public accounts; the Information Commissioner and the Privacy Commissioner, responsible for overseeing issues in their respective areas, the Conflict-of-Interest and Ethics Commissioner, responsible for investigating violations by parliamentarians (Bergman and Macfarlane 2018), and others. These officials are appointed by either the House of Commons or Parliament as a whole (Barnes et al 2019) but operate quite independently, setting their own agendas and sometimes acquiring a high public profile of their own. They also have, to varying extents, working relationships with relevant parliamentary committees.

The relationship between Parliament and its Officers has always been somewhat contentious, with some observers seeing Officers as 'free agents accountable to no one' (Savoie 2008: 167) but others, including many parliamentarians, applauding their neutrality and expertise. They lack a common enabling framework, and at times there is even confusion about how many officials even qualify as independent Officers (Thomas 2003). A recent authoritative study by the Library of Parliament lists nine Officers (Barnes et al 2019) but excludes the Senate Ethics Officer, who performs functions similar to the House's Conflict-of-Interest and Ethics Commissioner, and who is identified as one of the nine. The exact number is less important than the larger point that even agreement on the number of Officers can be elusive.

Issues about the Officers as well as broader principles of parliamentary administration are particularly illustrated in the story of the first Parliamentary Budget Officer (PBO). The PBO was created in 2006 by the newly elected Conservative government and was intended to support MPs in researching and understanding government financial plans and forecasts; distinct from the Auditor General's retrospective focus. The Officer was administratively housed in the Library of Parliament, alongside the longstanding Parliamentary Information and Research Service that provided general research support for parliamentarians and committees, and the PBO reported to the Parliamentary Librarian.

However, the first appointed PBO, Kevin Page, quickly became publicly critical about government forecasts and spending. This alarmed the Librarian and many observers, including the Speakers of both the House and Senate, since the Research Service, like all aspects of parliamentary administration, was known for strict neutrality in its opinions (Ibbitson 2009). Page argued that his reporting relationship was unacceptable and his office needed to be fully independent, with the same status as an Officer of Parliament. Page was supported by some opposition MPs and the issue was not resolved before the expiry of Page's five-year term. Only in 2017 was the issue fully resolved, with legislation passed establishing the PBO as reporting directly to Parliament, equivalent to other Officers.

The PBO episode illustrates both the ambiguity surrounding Officers of Parliament as well as the strong culture of discretion among permanent parliamentary staff. Page's vision of a more outspoken role, even if driven by neutral expertise rather than partisanship, was simply incompatible within the framework of the Library of Parliament and traditional parliamentary staff culture. The issue was only resolved by upgrading the office into a fully independent status. While ending the conflict, the dispute reinforced the boundaries in which parliamentary staff operate, and the overriding value of discretion among regular parliamentary employees.

49.8 Response to COVID-19

Though the issue is ongoing as of this writing, brief mention can be made of the Canadian Parliament's response to the COVID-19 pandemic and how it again illustrates the bifurcation between the professional staff and political worlds. At the onset of the pandemic, many parliamentary employees shifted to working partly or entirely remotely, similar to most other Canadian employers. This transition was relatively smooth under the circumstances, at least publicly. However, both MPs and senators disagreed along party lines whether to move to hybrid or entirely remote sittings.

The opposition Conservatives were supportive of overall public health measures, unlike many right-wing parties internationally. But they were sceptical of remote arrangements as sufficient to hold the Liberal government to account, especially as the government failed to present a 2020 budget entirely. These partisan disputes masked more substantive technical concerns about how to actually support and administer remote sittings and arguably politicized implementation issues unnecessarily. After months of disagreement and short-term measures, each chamber reached agreements in the fall of 2020 on systems of hybrid sittings (Allen 2020). The relevance of our discussion is that while the regular parliamentary bureaucracy was able to adapt reasonably well and professionally to the crisis, the political actors could not agree – leading to confusion and uncertainty for the institution as a whole.

49.9 Conclusion

The Parliament of Canada enjoys a highly competent and non-partisan administration. It is complex organizationally but generally operates with a high level of collaboration and efficiency. Most staff spend their entire careers with Parliament and clerks enjoy a strong sense of elite professional status. While the Senate has seen turnover and instability, likely due to overall changes in the institution, and the most recent appointment of the House Clerk was contentious, overall there is a high degree of public and legislator confidence in the quality and impartiality of Canadian parliamentary administration.

This contrasts with the generally low regard for Parliament itself. Disdain for legislative institutions is hardly restricted to Canada, However, Canadians have long lamented the high dominance of political parties in all aspects of the House of Commons. Compared to the United Kingdom Parliament, Canadian MPs do seem to enjoy less opportunity to operate independently of party; and as noted, the Canadian House Speaker is weaker than their British counterpart. Unusually high turnover of MPs has long been seen as a problem for the Canadian House of Commons, eroding institutional memory and the supply of veteran parliamentarians, especially for committee work, and increasing MPs' dependence on parties for support and direction in all things (Franks 1987). In turn, the legitimacy of the unelected Senate has been a perpetual issue; the 2016 changes have diluted partisan control but created new dynamics that are still evolving and risk permanent instability.

Overall, there is a powerful sense of separate worlds in the Canadian Parliament, between the highly discreet, risk-averse permanent staff and nakedly partisan parliamentarians and their personal staff. Few or no one is in the middle, able to speak openly for the institution itself. Kevin Page, the outspoken PBO, was a rare exception of a nominally non-partisan figure willing to rock the boat, and he himself realized his position was not tenable except as a full independent Officer. The Officers of Parliament do enjoy legitimacy to speak out but focus on their individual areas of competence and not Parliament itself.

It would be foolish to discount or endanger the professional and neutral competence of Canadian parliamentary staff. Yet one can wish for a slightly more assertive culture along with a corresponding receptivity from parliamentarians to stand up for the institution regardless of partisanship. A slight merging of the worlds might not be a bad thing.

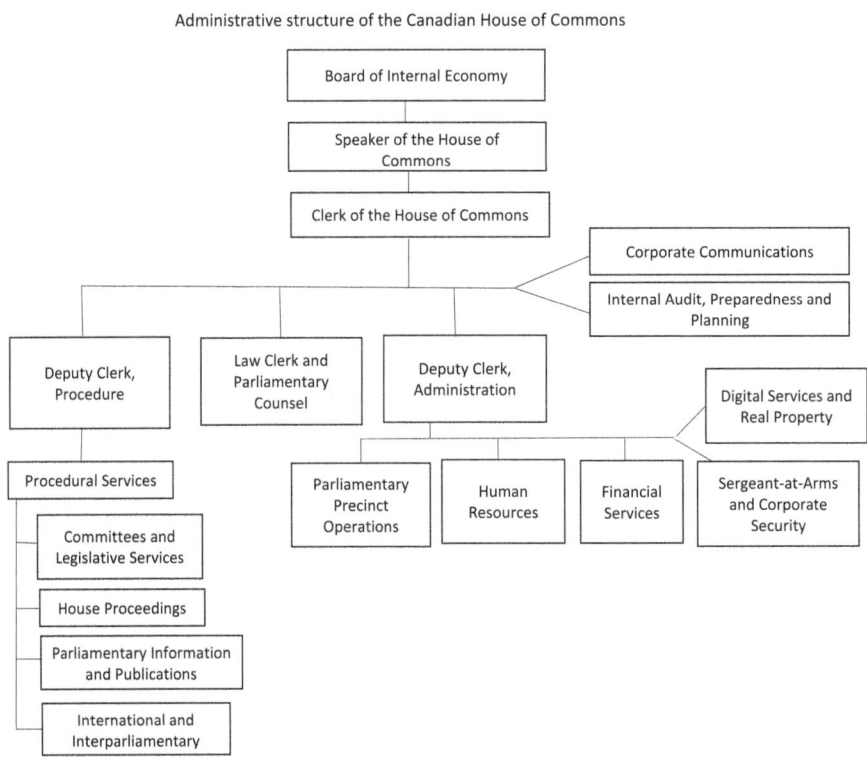

Administrative structure of the Canadian House of Commons

Information Classification: General

Source: https://www.ourcommons.ca/About/Administration/index-e.html

Administrative structure of the Canadian Senate

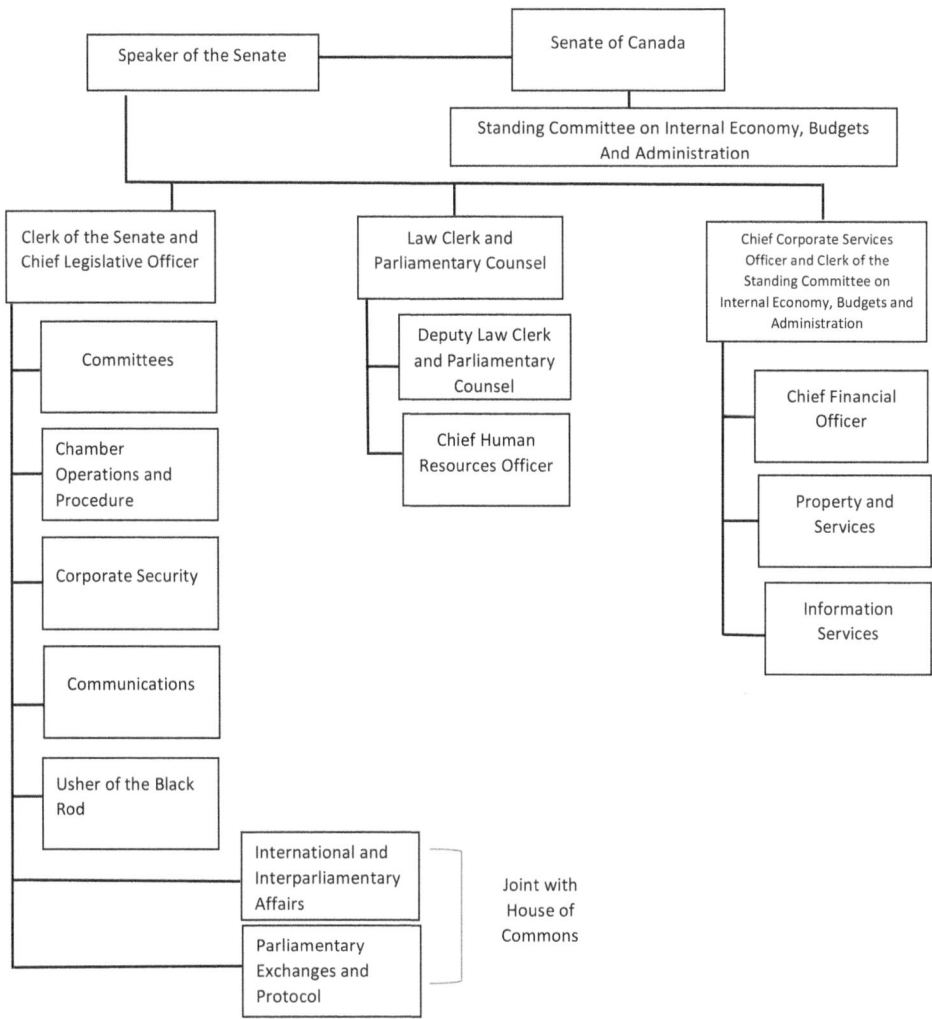

https://sencanada.ca/media/367470/sen-admin.structure_e.pdf

References

Allen, Samantha Wright (2020) "'Historic' effort to run two hybrid Chambers a balancing act" *The Hill Times*, November 18, 2020.

Auditor-General of Canada (2012) *Report of the Auditor General of Canada to the Board of Internal Economy of the House of Commons—Administration of the House of Commons of Canada* (Ottawa).

Barnes, Andre, Brousseau, Laurence, and Hurtubise-Loranger, Élise (2019) *Appointment of Officers of Parliament: Background Paper* (Ottawa: Library of Parliament).

Bergman, Gwyneth. and Macfarlane, Emmett. (2018) "The impact and role of officers of Parliament: Canada's conflict of interest and ethics commissioner" *Canadian Public Administration* 61: 5–25.

Canadian Council of Public Accounts Committees (n.d.) "About CCPAC" (Viewed July 29, 2021).

Cockram, Louise (2020) *From Candidate to Elected Member: Does Organized or Informal Institutional Learning Shape the Careers of MPs in Canada and the UK?* (Unpublished paper, Department of Political Science, Carleton University).

Cooper, Michael (2017) "How to Fix Question Period: Ideas for Reform" in *Turning Parliament Inside Out: Practical Ideas for Reforming Canada's Democracy* ed. Michael Chong, Scott Simms, and Kennedy Stewart (Vancouver: Douglas+McIntyre).

Franks, C.E.S. (1987) *The Parliament of Canada* (Toronto: University of Toronto Press).

Godbout, Jean-François (2020) *Lost on Division: Party Unity in the Canadian Parliament* (Toronto: University of Toronto Press).

House of Commons (2019) *Report to Canadians* (Ottawa: Parliament of Canada).

House of Commons (n.d.) "About the Board of Internal Economy" https://www.ourcommons.ca/Boie/en/about (Viewed July 29, 2021).

Ibbitson, John (2009) "The man who knows too much" *The Globe and Mail*, October 2.

Lawlor, Andrea and Crandall, Erin (2013) "Committee performance in the Senate of Canada: some sobering analysis for the chamber of 'sober second thought'" *Commonwealth & Comparative Politics* 51:4: 549–568.

Library of Parliament "About the Library" https://lop.parl.ca/sites/PublicWebsite/default/en_CA/About/Overview

MacCharles, Tonda (2016) "Mike Duffy cleared on all charges of defrauding the Senate" *The Toronto Star*, April 21, 2016.

MacMinn, E. George and Vaive, Robert (1998) "The office of clerk" *Canadian Parliamentary Review* 21:2 (Summer 1998); 28–32.

Malloy, Jonathan (1996) "Reconciling expectations and reality in House of Commons committees: the case of the 1989 GST inquiry" *Canadian Public Administration* 39:3: 314–335.

Mazereeuw, Peter (2017) "'Shocked,' 'profoundly disappointed': ex-clerks pan appointment process after Bosc passed over for House clerk" *The Hill Times*, June 21.

Mazereeuw, Peter (2018a) "'Our senior ranks have been fleeing the ship,' Senate administration still in flux, Liberal and Independent Senators push through temporary reorganization" *The Hill Times*, July 23.

Mazereeuw, Peter (2018b) "Senators split over new clerk, Sen. McCoy calls him 'prime minister's man' in the Red Chamber" *The Hill Times*, February 12.

McCarthy, Shawn and Grant, Kelly (2014) "Potential flaws in parliamentary security pointed out in 2012 report" *The Globe and Mail*, October 22.

Parliament of Canada Act (1985) https://laws-lois.justice.gc.ca/eng/acts/p-1/page-2.html#h-390060

Parliament of Canada (n.d) "Joint Interparliamentary Council" https://www.parl.ca/diplomacy/en/icci (Viewed July 29, 2021).

Parliamentary Protective Service (n.d.) "Creation of the Service" https://pps.parl.ca/the-service/ (Viewed July 29, 2021).

Savoie, Donald (2008) *Court Government and the Collapse of Accountability in Canada and the United Kingdom* (Toronto: University of Toronto Press).

Senate of Canada (n.d.a) "Administration and Support" https://sencanada.ca/en/about/administration-support (Viewed July 29, 2021).

Senate of Canada (n.d.b) "Standing Committee on Internal Economy, Budgets and Administration" https://sencanada.ca/en/committees/ciba/ (Viewed July 29, 2021).

Stilborn, Jack (2014) "The investigative study role of Canada's House Committees: expectations met?" *Journal of Legislative Studies* 20 10.1080/13572334.2014.890801

Tasker, John Paul (2017) "'Wise owls': Senate issues children's book to explain role of Red Chamber" *CBC News*, May 1.

Thomas, Paul G. (2003) "The past, present and future of officers of Parliament" *Canadian Public Administration* 46: 287–314.

Thomas, Paul E.J. (2016) *Across Enemy Lines: A Study of the All-Party Groups in the Parliaments of Canada, Ontario, Scotland and the United Kingdom* (Unpublished dissertation, Department of Political Science, University of Toronto).

Wilson, R. Paul (2020a) "The impact of the COVID-19 pandemic on Canadian parliamentary political staffers" *Canadian Parliamentary Review* 43:3 (Autumn).

Wilson, R.P. (2020b) "The work of Canadian political staffers in parliamentary caucus research offices" *Canadian Public Administration* 63: 498–521.

50
INDIA'S PARLIAMENTARY ADMINISTRATION

Milind Thakar

50.1 Introduction

India's polity has entered its eight decade and has until recently been considered one of the most stable and consolidated democracies in the developing world. Its political system is best described as a federal republic with a parliamentary style government. The political system has changed over time from a one-party dominance amidst a multiparty parliament where other parties were too minor to make a national or state impact, to two dominant parties in an increasingly competitive system, to a recent dominance by one national party albeit with greater competition from state and local parties. India opted for a bicameral legislature with the Rajya Sabha (Assembly of the States) representing the states and having limited powers and the Lok Sabha (Assembly of the People) being the main vehicle of legislation and representation in that its members represent the populace at a district level. While the Lok Sabha is dominant in legislation and policy-making, the Rajya Sabha has some delaying powers pertaining to passing legislation. The Lok Sabha is fixed at 552 potential seats under the Constitution of which currently 543 are active and contested with members directly elected by the rule of plurality from single-member districts. The Rajya Sabha is set at 250 and its members are nominated by state legislatures (as opposed to national) and one-third of its members face re-election every two years. This vast parliamentary body split into two is supported by an intricate parliamentary administration.

50.2 Key Aspects of the Organization of the Parliamentary Administration

The Lok Sabha is headed (structurally) by the Speaker, who is elected by incoming newly elected (or re-elected) Members of Parliament (hereafter MPs). The criteria for the Speaker are that the candidate should have familiarity with the functions of the Lok Sabha. If there is no opposition to a candidate then there is no need for a formal vote, otherwise members vote on respective candidates. Speakers need not be from the ruling party or even coalition, minor party members as well as those not in the government have functioned as Speakers. The Leader of the Opposition is the leader of the largest non-government party or coalition.

The Rajya Sabha is headed by the Chairman (the position is still referred to by the specific gendered status) of the body who is always the Vice President of India. However, day-to-day matters are usually taken care of by the Deputy Chairman who is elected by the members.

The Rajya Sabha also has a Leader of the House who is a Cabinet Minister (or Prime Minister if he/she is from this house), as well as a Leader of the Opposition who is the accepted leader of the largest non-government party.

50.2.1 Size of the Parliamentary Administration

The Lok Sabha and Rajya Sabha are each served by a secretariat headed by a Secretary General and Chairman, respectively. The sizes of these organizations reflect those of the chambers they serve with the Lok Sabha's staff at 3000 plus being roughly double of the Rajya Sabha's 1500. These bodies derive their source from the Indian constitution's Article 98(1) which states: "Each House of Parliament shall have a separate secretarial staff: provided that nothing in this clause shall be construed as preventing the creation of posts common to both Houses of the Parliament."

The staff of the two secretariats are recruited internally and not through the process of the Union Public Service Commission, which is responsible for recruitment and selection of officers and staff members of the national administration of India.

Fundamentally, both secretariats help in the administrative parts of the work of each chamber in parliament. They help draft legislation based on MPs recommendations, carry out corrections and changes as required after parliamentary debates, transcribe and translate parliamentary proceedings, and provide many other services which are described more fully below (Narmadeshwar Prasad, 2021).

50.2.2 Administrative Structure and Services of the Assembly

The origins of parliamentary administration lie in colonial times when a Legislative Assembly was allowed to convene with limited representation and advisory capacity to the British staffed executive of the Governor-General and was allowed an administrative department that fell under the purview of the Speaker. Upon independence in 1947, this body changed its name to the Central Legislature of Parliament and after 1954 to the specific two chambers Lok Sabha and the Rajya Sabha (the new names being Hindi rather than English). The Secretariat of Parliament dates its existence to this time as well (Kaul and Shakdher, 2016, 1126, and Achary, 2021). As mentioned above, these secretariats functioned under the purview of the Lok Sabha Speaker and the Chairperson of the Rajya Sabha, respectively.

It should be noted that the two parliamentary secretariats are not the same as the civil services of India. The latter are union (federal or national) services that comprise general or specialized civil servants who serve the executive branch in states or the national level. So, the Indian Administrative Service (national and state level general bureaucrats), the Indian Postal Service, the Indian Revenue Service, the Indian Customs and Exercise Services, and others are not the services that assist the Indian chambers of parliament. The staff of the secretariat is chosen differently and independently of the executive branch (Economic Times, 2021).

Over time, the structure of the secretariat has evolved to include the following services and departments: a Legislative, Financial, Executive and Administrative Service (hereafter LAFEAS), a Library, Reference, Research, Documentation and Information Service (hereafter LARRDIS), a Verbatim Interpretation Service, Simultaneous Interpretation Service, a Private Secretaries and Stenographers Service, a Printing and Publications Service, an Editorial and Translation Service, a Technical Department, a Parliament Security Service and Housekeeping Wing/Watch and Ward, Door Keeping and Sanitation Service in the Rajya Sabha, a Clerical Service/Drivers and Dispatch Riders Service in the Rajya Sabha, a Messenger Service, a Welfare Office (Lok Sabha alone), and an office devoted to SC/ST/PH employees (Scheduled Castes, Scheduled Tribes, and Physically Handicapped – all minorities in need of affirmative action – also only in the Lok Sabha) (Lok Sabha website).

Each Secretariat is headed by a Secretary General, and that position is comparable in rank to that of Cabinet Secretary – the highest position in the Indian Administrative Service, which consists of bureaucrats that serve the national (federal) and state governments. The current Secretary General of the Lok Sabha's Secretariat in 2021 is a former Chief Secretary of a state – the highest ranked bureaucrat at the state level (Indian Express, 2020) However, appointments to both secretariats are free of the Union Public Service Commission, the body that conducts exams for state and national level administrative positions, instead the appointments are made in house (Achary 2021).

Specifically, appointments to both secretariats are made through internal advertising and, interviews, and the process is not linked in any way to the recruitment of the civil servants and staff of the executive branches. Those (executive branch) staff are recruited separately by the above-mentioned Union Public Service Commission. In this way, the parliamentary secretariats procure staff through an independent system that in no way overlaps with the staff of the executive branch. "The competent authority for assessing the number of posts in various cadres, services, etc. and revision of scales of pay, allowances, etc. in the Secretariats be a Board of the Secretaries-General of the Lok Sabha and the Rajya Sabha who could, after consultation with the Ministry of Finance, make suitable recommendations to the Speaker/Chairman, as the case may be, from time to time. Accordingly, it is the Joint Recruitment Cell (JRC) that conducts recruitment examinations, interviews and draws up panels of selected candidates for recruitment in the Lok Sabha and the Rajya Sabha Secretariats" (Achary, 2010; Figure 50.1).

The above chart is actually that of the Lok Sabha. The Rajya Sabha has a similar breakdown by service/office except that the Housekeeping service is managed by a Watch and Ward, Door Keeping and Sanitation Service, and instead of a Clerical Service it has a Drivers and Dispatch Riders Service (Lok Sabha Secretariat Organization Chart, 2021; Rajya Sabha Organization).

Lok Sabha organization of senior officers by workload/Rajya Sabha has a similar though not identical chart.

Table 50.1 demonstrates the Lok Sabha's senior officers – Additional and Joint Secretaries are civil service ranks of upper middle to senior levels – and their responsibilities by committees and functions. The Rajya Sabha has a similar workload distributed amongst a corresponding hierarchy of functionaries.

50.2.3 The Mechanisms in Place to Enable Professionalization and the Development of Functional Expertise

50.2.3.1 Procedures for Recruitment, Training, and Promotion

The secretariats assumed their current form in 1954, after years of functioning as administrative assistants to the former colonial entity of India and its independent successor state. The

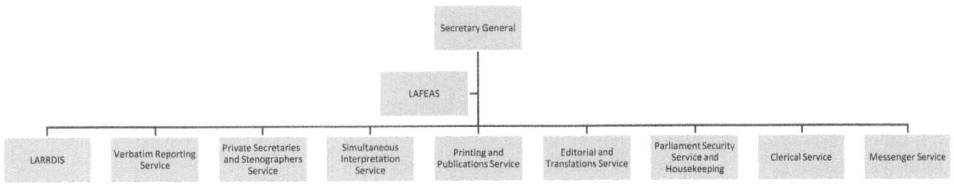

Figure 50.1 Lok Sabha and Rajya Sabha secretariat organization chart

Table 50.1 The Lok Sabha's senior officers

Secretary General	
Additional Secretary	(1) Committee on Defence, (2) Committee on Empowerment of Women, (3) R&I Division, (4) Members Reference Wing including Press Clipping Section, Documentation Section, (5) Parliament Library and related Sections/Units including Audio-Visual and Telecasting Unit, Microfilming Unit and Publication Unit.
Additional Secretary	(1) Conference Branch, (2) Committee on External Affairs.
Additional Secretary	(1) Members' Services Branch including House Committee, (2) Members' Salaries and Allowances Branch, (3) Digitization Unit, (4) Simultaneous Interpretation Service, (5) Committee on Petroleum and Natural Gas, (6) Welfare Branch.
Joint Secretary	(1) Committee on Agriculture, (2) Distribution Branch
Joint Secretary	(1) Administration Branch-I, (2) Administration Branch-II, (3) Confidential Cell, (4) Organization and Methods(O&M) Section, (5) Vigilance Unit, (6) Committee on Finance, (7) General Works Branch including Heritage Management, (8) Committee on Urban Development, (9) Director, ICPS.
Joint Secretary	(1) Committee on Public Undertakings, (2) Committee on Energy, (3) Committee on Subordinate Legislation, also functions as the Appellate Authority in the Lok Sabha Secretariat under RTI Act, 2005.
Joint Secretary	(1) Committee on Labour, (2) Committee on Petitions, (3) Public Accounts Committee.
Joint Secretary	(1) Committee on Social Justice and Empowerment, (2) Committee on Welfare of Other Backward Classes (OBCs).
Joint Secretary	(1) Recruitment Branch, (2) Committee on Food, Consumer Affairs and Public Distribution, (3) Question Branch, (4) Committee on Government Assurances, (5) Committee on Coal and Steel.
Joint Secretary	(1) Legislative Branch-I, (2) Legislative Branch-II, (3) Parliamentary Notice Office (PNO), (4) Table Office, (5) Privileges and Ethics Committee Branch, (6) Verbatim Reporting Service.
Joint Secretary	(1) Legislative Branch-I, (2) Legislative Branch-II, (3) Parliamentary Notice Office (PNO), (4) Table Office, (5) Privileges and Ethics Committee Branch, (6) Verbatim Reporting Service.
Joint Secretary	(1) Committee Branch-II, (2) Editorial and Translation Service, (3) Parliament Museum and Archives (PMA), (4) Stenographers' Pool, (5) Records Branch.
Joint Secretary	(1) Committee on MPLADS, (2) Committee on Rural Development, (3) Press and Public Relations Wing (PPR), (4) Committee on Welfare of Scheduled Castes and Scheduled Tribes (SCTC).
Joint Secretary	(1) Parliament Security Service, (2) JPC on Security in Parliament House Complex.
Joint Secretary	(1) Integrated Finance Unit, (2) Bills and Payment Branch, (3) Pay and Accounts Office, (4) Committee on Railways, (5) Parliamentary Research and Training Institute for Democracies (PRIDE), (6) Computer (HW&SW) Management Branch. And also discharge the functions of Financial Advisor of Lok Sabha Secretariat.
Joint Secretary	Conference Branch.
Joint Secretary	Members' Salaries and Allowances Branch.
Joint Secretary	(1) Committee on Information Technology, (2) Conference Branch.

need for autonomy from the executive branch and central civil services was maintained with no recourse or role for the Union Public Service Commission in recruitment of staff. Instead, the two chambers would constitute joint recruitment tests for direct recruitment of the secretariat staff. The rules, regulations, and mode of selection are determined by a Board that comprising the two Secretaries-General who submits its recommendations to the Speaker (Lok Sabha) and Chairman (Rajya Sabha) with some assistance from the Ministry of Finance (Kaul and Shakdher, 2016, 1133).

50.2.3.2 Opportunities for Staff Training and Development

Staff are trained by the PRIDE (Parliamentary Research and Training Institute for Democracies) office, formerly called the Bureau of Parliamentary Studies and Training. This office was set up in 1976 and was meant to train both MPs and secretariat (and state legislative) staff. Additionally, PRIDE also conducts training programmes for foreign visitors and staff. The aim of PRIDE is to "provide a thorough grounding to the participants in different disciplines of parliamentary work in order to improve their functional skills, widen their horizons and sharpen their perspectives through discussions and exchange of ideas and experiences."

This is done by offering foundation courses for new staff members as well as refresher courses for experienced staff. Courses target the following: staff dealing with Questions (parliamentary) and Legislative and Budgetary Processes, officers working in financial committees, Watch and Ward Officers, reporters, officers providing research, reference and information services, Hindi assistants, translators and editors, librarians, and Management Development Programmes for Middle Level Officers. Finally, PRIDE also organizes programmes for media personnel and civil service officers to understand the workings of the parliament (see PRIDE website).

50.2.4 Rules/Arrangements for Interaction with Stakeholders

The two parliamentary secretariats are required to be autonomous of the executive branch as well as the centralized civil services. Despite this, the presence of current or former civil service officers suggests that the autonomy may not be complete. However, structurally, the secretariats have budgets that are separate from that of the Union (central/federal) government and come from the Consolidated Fund which administers parliamentary needs (Kaul and Shakdher, 2016, 1135). It has already been stressed that the staff are selected through an independent process that is not reliant on government selection processes (For more, see Lok Sabha Secretariat Rules, 2021).

In recent times, interaction with the public has become significant after the passage of the Right to Information Act (hereafter RTI Act) which was enacted in 2005 to allow citizens to access information that was supposedly in the public domain, in an effort to allow transparency and accountability. While the act targeted government offices, ministries, and laws, its impact was also felt by the parliamentary secretariats. In response to this act, these bodies created an Information Cell to be directed by a Central Public Information Officer for receipt of requests for information from citizens. The cell forwards these requests to officials in the concerned units to be sent to the applicants. There is even an Appellate Authority set up with an officer senior in rank to the Central Public Information Officer to adjudicate in case of disputes arising with the Cell. If the information asked for is not pertinent to the secretariats, the request is forwarded to the concerned Ministry or Department of the Government of India (Shakdher and Kaul, 1134).

To enable citizens and external observers to view the workings of the parliamentary administration, a number of websites have been created in addition to the numerous publications brought out each year by the secretariats. These include the parliamentary websites of both houses (http://parliamentofindia.nic.in), which provide information on members, daily questions, debates with their text and synopses, all legislative bills and committees. The secretariats have their own websites that are linked to the above websites, as well as to the component Lok Sabha and Rajya Sabha websites, and include information about current officers, their workload, structures and organizations within the secretariats as well as notices, circulars, and announcements.

50.3 The Role of the Administration in the Context of Parliamentary Work

Representation of the people (and the states for the upper house Rajya Sabha), *legislation*, and *policy debates* are the main tasks of the two houses of parliament. The role of the parliamentary service is to facilitate these tasks with assistance to MPs. This is done by providing the following services: secretarial assistance and support to the effective functioning of the members, payment of salary, and other allowances to the members, providing amenities as admissible to members, servicing the various parliamentary committees, preparing research and reference material and bringing out various publications recruitment of staff and officials in the secretariat and attending to personnel matters such as training and promotion, and preparing and publishing records of daily proceedings in the two chambers and bringing out any other publications that might serve the members' needs.

a   Officials in the LAFEAS serve the Legislative wings as well as Parliamentary committees. The former is concerned with House business (Lok Sabha or Rajya Sabha) and works on business from the Parliamentary Notice Office, Table Office, Legislative Branch, and Questions Branch. The latter serves various Parliamentary committees such as the Public Accounts Committee, Estimates Committee, and the Committee on Public Undertakings. The Executive and Administrative parts of the service assist in matters such as Administration, Works and General Branch, Budget and Payment Branch, Pay and Accounts Office, Members' Salaries and Allowances, Members Services. Staff in the Committee Branches often provide secretarial work for different parliamentary committees, while the Protocol Branch carries out liaison work in terms of organizing meetings, conferences, or interacting with visiting Indian or foreign dignitaries.

b   LARDDIS or the Library Research Reference Documentation and Information Service is responsible for keeping MPs informed on any developments that are brought up in legislative debates. This includes numerous activities such as reference and research material for parliamentarians, background notes and information for parliamentarians (including when they are going abroad on visits). This branch of the secretariat is responsible for bringing out publications and material for dissemination to parliament as well as the wider public. This wing also includes the Media and Public Relations Office as well as the PRIDE office mentioned above.

c   The reporters of the Verbatim Reporting Service compile and provide daily reports of the parliamentary proceedings, or of training seminars and sessions organized by PRIDE.

d   Staff in the Private Secretaries and Stenographers Service provide dictation, transcription, typing, attending to phone calls and to visitors as well as keeping important records for the officials of the secretariat.

e   As evident the Printing and Publications Service provides proof reading, binding, and printing services to the secretariat.
f   The staff of the Simultaneous Interpretation Service do translations from Hindi to English (or vice versa) or into other regional languages of India of not just parliamentary proceedings but also of seminars, conferences, training sessions, as well as services for visiting international delegations.
g   Officials of the Parliament Security Service provide two important needs – the security of the Parliament Estate itself (the offices of the secretariats) and the included Housekeeping Wing undertakes sanitation and cleaning tasks of the premises. In the Rajya Sabha, these tasks are undertaken by the Watch and Ward, Door Keeping and Sanitation Service.
h   Officers in the Editorial and Translation Service translate edit and vet proceedings, debate, prepare synopses, and do the same for parliamentary committees. This service is divided into the following sub-branches – including Editorial Branch, Synopsis Branch, Rajbhasha Prabhag (Official Language Division – to promote use of Hindi language), Translation (Committee) Branch, Translation (Parliamentary Papers) Branch.
i   The Drivers and Dispatch Service in the Rajya Sabha are entrusted with ferrying MPs when needed as well as sending publications from the secretariat to be distributed.
j   The Clerical Service provides secretarial assistance in the Lok Sabha.
k   The Messenger Service provides attendants and messengers for both houses.

Source: Lok Sabha and Rajya Sabha Secretariat websites

A major component of the secretariats is their assistance to parliament with regard to the budget of the two houses. This budget draws its finances from the Consolidated Fund of India which is the most important of all government accounts. All expenditures of the government are met from this fund save a few exceptional expenses and must be approved of by parliament. The Budget Estimates of the secretariats, however, cannot be decided by parliament and therefore each chamber has a committee set up by the head – namely the Speaker (Lok Sabha) and Chairman (Rajya Sabha) to examine the budget requests of the secretariat concerned. It should be noted that such requests do not go to the Ministry of Finance since that is an executive branch body and on the rare occasion when it (MOF) has a suggestion to make regarding the budget of the secretariats it is submitted to the Speaker/Chairman for consideration and discussion (Kaul and Shakdher, 2016, 1134).

Finally, both houses have a TV channel dedicated to telecast uninterrupted live proceedings of the Lok Sabha and Rajya Sabha. Both houses had channels which were relatively recent additions with the Lok Sabha TV launched in 2006 and the Rajya Sabha TV launched in 2011.

As of September 15, 2021, the government announced that the two channels – Lok Sabha TV and Rajya Sabha TV would be merged into one entity Sansad (parliament) TV (The Hindu, 2021).

50.4 Managing Inter-Institutional and External Relations

The Indian parliament is dominated by its executive branch and this has been a longstanding issue. Consequently, the focus on relations with external bodies (outside India) is more within the government purview than with parliament. Unlike countries within Europe, where collaboration and cooperation with other EU member parliaments is necessary given the union, the Indian legislature exists in relative isolation. External visitors do come to observe parliamentary proceedings and such visits are organized by the secretariats. The secretariats prepare the visit with details of meetings, conferences, and seminars for the incoming delegation and submit this to the head of their chamber – Speaker or Chairman. Upon their approval, the visit is finalized.

International visits and training are also facilitated via the PRIDE (formerly Bureau of Parliamentary Studies and Training), which organizes annual orientation and training programmes. Such programmes are also offered to government officials, legislators at the state level, and media persons (See PRIDE).

50.5 Current and New Challenges Facing the Parliamentary Administration

India's parliamentary administration has faced two major challenges in recent times. The first is that of digitization. This includes the creation of websites for material hitherto published and distributed, as well as the computerization of the parliamentary library and much of its collection. The second challenge was of transparency, which was addressed by the RTI Act passed in 2005.

India's parliament made a start towards computerization in 1985 by setting up a computer centre to manage the Parliamentary Information System. Beginning as a database of subject references to parliamentary information, it grew to include full-text databases in web format that were displayed on the website. The library contents are now accessible online via a software package – LIBSYS – specific to parliamentary purposes. Catalogues, details about journals and articles, indexes to select books and articles, and a press clippings section are available to library users, who are mostly MPs (Kaul and Shakdher, 2016, 1141).

Parliament created a website (http://parliamentofindia.nic.in) in 1996 which contains information about members (state wise, party wise, gender information, and vacant seats) and includes contact information as well as biographical sketches. The site also has business of the house listed as well as question lists and texts of question and answers dating back to 1998. Text and synopses of daily debates, bills introduced in either house searchable by member/ministry/title, papers laid in either house, committees and their components and issues in both houses, forums in parliament, information about the secretariat (each one), and recruitment information for staff positions are all available in the main website and subsidiary Lok Sabha and Rajya Sabha sites. On balance, the Rajya Sabha website appears to be better organized particularly the section on the secretariat. Additionally, officers of the parliament such as the Speaker have a page, the Parliamentary Museum has a website, and PRIDE has a website as well (PRDIE, 2021). Computer facilities are provided to members at work and home and digitization/computerization is now well established within the Indian parliament (Kaul and Shakdher, 2016, 1142–4).

A demand for transparency in government and it is its associated institutions was increasingly voiced in the 1990s and in response the government enacted the RTI Act in 2005, through which citizens could access records, legislation, and documents that pertained to public matters. As indicated earlier, the parliamentary secretariats established a Central Public Information Officer and a process for the public to apply for and collect information and documents from the parliament. The process also includes an appellate authority that can adjudicate cases where information dissemination is contested.

50.6 Conclusion

India's parliamentary administration is well developed and specialized and serves the needs of its bicameral legislature well, if inconspicuously. While there is a wealth of information in books, periodicals, and websites on the composition, functioning, and politics of parliament, very little is published on the administration that supplies daily services for MPs and the broader agenda of the two houses. Apoliticization is a given since there is no need for staff to assume any political agenda, that is the province of the politicians who are served by the secretariat. The selection of serving civil service officials to the secretariats (even though by an independent process) does suggest the possibility of political colouring, however, given that the tasks carried out by the secretariat are mundane – recording, typing, reproducing, publishing, secretarial assistance – there does not appear to have been a need to politicize the administration. Where there is latitude to take decisions that have an impact on governance and policy formulation, such as in the civil services that staff the executive branches at both national and state levels, there is a high and acceptable level of politicization. Civil servants who are part of the executive bureaucracy and are involved in revenue collection, or law enforcement, or general administration, have much greater policy implementation power and consequently are pressurized more to fall in line with the ruling party diktat. This is usually not the case with the parliamentary secretariats whose staff, as noted above, perform uncontroversial tasks.

In an increasingly polarized environment in India between diametrically opposing visions of the major political forces, the parliamentary administration provides a much-needed apolitical service to the country and to democracy.

References

Achary, P.D.T. 2010. "Independence of Parliamentary Secretariat." P.101. Bangkok Session, March/April 2010, Association of Secretaries-General of Parliaments, Inter-Parliamanetary Union. https://www.asgp.co/past-meetings?page=18. Accessed Nov 3, 2021.

Achary, P.D.T. 2021. "Securing the Autonomy of House Secretariats, The Patel-Naidu way." in the Hindustan Times, Sep 14, 2021. https://www.hindustantimes.com/opinion/securing-the-independence-of-legislative-secretariats-the-patel-and-naidu-way-101631537849817.html. Accessed Sep 15, 2021.

ET (Economic Times). August 29, 2021. "The Men Who Shaped India's Parliamentary Secretariat." https://economictimes.indiatimes.com/news/india/the-men-who-shaped-independent-indias-parliamentary-secretariat/articleshow/85731494.cms. Accessed Sep 6, 2021.

Indian Express. November 30, 2020. "Senior IAS Officer Utpal Kumar Singh Appointed Secretary-General of Lok Sabha." https://indianexpress.com/article/india/senior-ias-officer-utpal-kumar-singh-appointed-as-secretary-general-of-lok-sabha-7074029/. Accessed Aug 22, 2021.

Kaul, M.N. and S.L. Shakdher (2016). *Practice and Procedure of Parliament*, 7th edition. Lok Sabha Secretariat.

Lok Sabha Secretariat Organization Chart. 2021. http://164.100.47.194/Loksabha/Secretariat/OfficersOfSecretariat.aspx. Accessed Sep 22, 2021.

Lok Sabha Secretariat Rules. 2021. http://164.100.47.194/Loksabha/Secretariat/Rules.aspx. Accessed Sep 16, 2021.

Prasad, Narmadeshwar. Director PARI and former Additional Director, Rajya Sabha Secretariat. Personal interview on Sep 14, 2021.

PRIDE (Parliamentary Research and Training Institute for Democracies). 2021. (https://pride.nic.in/). Accessed Aug 22, 2021.

Rajya Sabha Organization. 2021. https://rajyasabha.nic.in/rsnew/rssorgchart/showallrecord.aspx# Additional. Accessed Aug 22, 2021.

Rajya Sabha Secretariat. 2021. https://rajyasabha.nic.in/rsnew/rss_recruitment/rssecretariat.asp. Accessed Aug 22, 2021.

The Hindu. Sep 15, 2021. "Sansad TV launched; Modi calls it new voice of Parliament." https://www.thehindu.com/news/national/sansad-tv-launched-modi-calls-it-new-voice-of-parliament/article36483067.ece. Accessed Sep 22, 2021.

51
ISRAEL'S PARLIAMENTARY ADMINISTRATION

Susan Hattis Rolef[1]

Israel has a parliamentary regime. The first Knesset – Israel's single chamber parliament, which has 120 members – was first elected in February 1949.

51.1 The Structure of the Knesset Administration

51.1.1 Background

The current administrative structure of the Knesset is the direct result of the decision of the Knesset Speaker of the 17th Knesset (2006–2009), Dalia Itzik (Kadima), to appoint a Director General, who would take over all the non-parliamentary functions of the Knesset from the Secretary General, since both in quantitative and qualitative terms, the administrative workload had become too heavy for the Secretary General to bear alone.

The hierarchical administrative structure that one may see in Figure 51.1 is the direct result of this development.

51.2 The Top Figures in the Administration

51.2.1 The Speaker of the Knesset

The Speaker of the Knesset, who heads the hierarchical structure of the Knesset Administration, is elected from among the Knesset members by the Knesset Plenum at the beginning of each new Knesset for the duration of that Knesset, and he/she has up to nine deputies from the various parliamentary groups. With very few exceptions, the Speaker has been from the Prime Minister's party and worked in relative harmony with him.

The Speaker's job is defined in article 6 of the Knesset Rules of Procedure. Among his/her tasks: to run the affairs of the Knesset, represent it externally, uphold its dignity, preside over the sittings of the Knesset and run them, determine the results of votes, and in addition perform any task assigned to him/her by law. The Speaker is formally responsible for the administration of the Knesset and the Knesset Secretariate, including the preparation and implementation of the Knesset budget.

Israel's Parliamentary Administration

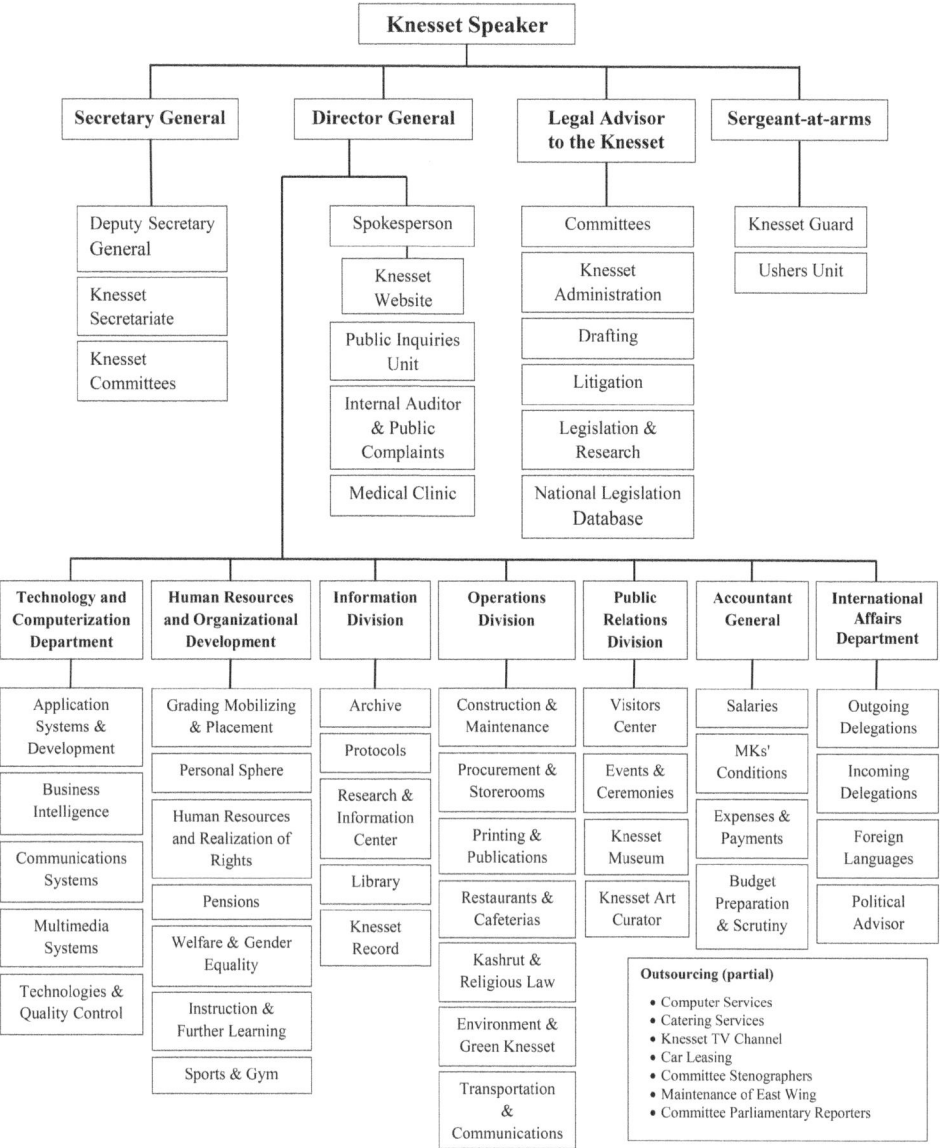

Figure 51.1 Knesset administration chart (2021)

The Speaker chairs the **Knesset Presidium**, which is a statutory body. According to article 10 of the Knesset Law (5754-1994), the members of the Presidium are the Speaker and his/her Deputies. Among those attending, the Presidium's weekly meetings (on Mondays) are also the four senior Knesset officials (see below), the Knesset Spokesperson, and the Deputy Government Secretary. In accordance with the Knesset Rules of Procedure, the Presidium is the body that approves the Knesset Agenda and decides which Private Members' Bills will be placed on the Knesset's agenda.

Under the Speaker, there are the four highest ranking officials in the Knesset: the **Secretary General**, the **Legal Advisor**, the **Sergeant-at-arms,** and the **Director General**.

51.2.2 The Secretary General of the Knesset

The Secretary General of the Knesset is appointed by the Speaker and his/her Deputies, in accordance with the Appointment of the Knesset Secretary General Law (5728-1968).

Since 2006, the Secretary General is in charge only of the parliamentary work of the Knesset which includes the preparation and organization of the sittings of the Plenum; giving advice to the Speaker and his/her Deputies on the Rules of Procedures, procedure and custom; and supervising the implementation of the Plenum's decisions. The Secretary General or his/her Deputy attends the Plenum when it is in session and manages the list of speakers.

The Secretary General is also responsible for the activities of the **Knesset Secretariat**, which coordinates the Knesset agenda with the Parliamentary Groups, the Committees, the Government Secretariat, and the Ministries. The Secretariat ensures that all the parliamentary items – motions of no-confidence, motions for the agenda, Questions to Ministers and to the Prime Minister, and bills – are circulated among all the required recipients, in the Plenum, Committees, and Ministries, in accordance with the decisions of the Speaker, the Presidium, and the Plenum; for following the parliamentary processes, and supervising them.

With regard to the Committees, the Secretary General is in charge of dealing with problems that might emerge in their work – both parliamentary and administrative.[2]

The Secretary General is a member of the Association of Secretary Generals of Parliaments.

51.2.3 The Legal Advisor to the Knesset

The position of the Legal Advisor was created in the early 1980s and became statutory in 2000, when provisions for his/her selection were introduced into the Knesset Law (5754-1994) (Horowitz & Bar-Siman-Tov, 2020). Article 17 of the Knesset Law states that the Legal Advisor to the Knesset shall provide legal advice to the Speaker of the Knesset, other position holders and its institutions on all matters related to law and order that are connected to their powers and roles; shall advise the Knesset Plenum and its Committees on all matters connected to legislation procedures and act to ensure their propriety; shall advise Knesset members on all matters connected to the Knesset that result from their membership in it; shall represent the Knesset in judicial instances and perform every other task assigned to him/her by any law or regulation. Articles 18–22 of the Knesset Law deal with the selection of the Legal Advisor by a Public Committee, headed by a retired Supreme Court Justice. The candidates must have the qualifications to serve as a Supreme Court Justice, and not to have been engaged in politics, or to have been a member of a political party in the previous five years. The Speaker, with the approval of the Knesset House Committee, appoints one of the candidates recommended by the Committee.

The Legal Advisor heads the Knesset's **Legal Department**. In the 1990s, the number of attorneys in the Knesset was a mere handful. Today, the Legal Department consists of 50–60 attorneys and interns, who are divided into several sections, including Committees (each Knesset Committee has a legal team), administration, representation in judicial instances, drafting legislation, and research.[3] The legal department has developed a Legislation Database, available on the Knesset website (in Hebrew) since 2015.

51.2.4 The Sergeant-at-Arms

In accordance with article 8 of the Knesset Building, its Compound, and the Knesset Guard Law (5728-1968), the Sergeant-at-arms is appointed by the Knesset Speaker, in consultations with his/her deputies, and with the approval of the Knesset House Committee. The

Sergeant-at-arms is in charge of maintaining the security and the order in the Knesset building and its compound, and of securing the confidential information at the Knesset's disposal. He is the commander of the Knesset Guard, and of the Ushers Unit.

The Knesset Guard is responsible for keeping the security and order in the Knesset building and its compound, to protect the Knesset's immunity, in addition to participating in official ceremonies within the Knesset compound, and certain state ceremonies outside the Knesset compound. Since 2003, the Knesset guard includes a unit for the protection of Knesset members, whose personal security is threatened.

The members of the Knesset Guard are employed in accordance with the employment conditions of the Israeli Police. Guards in the lower ranks are employed for up to five years.

Neither the police nor the general security units are allowed to enter the Knesset compound, except by invitation, or with the consent of the Knesset Speaker.

The current Secretary General and Knesset Legal Advisor were both Knesset employees before being appointed to their current positions, but some of their predecessors were selected from outside the Knesset.

51.2.5 The Director General

The position of the **Director General** was created in 2006. He (so far all the holders of the position were men) is a personal appointment of the Speaker and usually serves for as long as the Speaker who appointed him remains in office. The Knesset Finance Committee must approve the appointment.

The Director General is in charge of all the non-parliamentary administrative aspects of work in the Knesset: maintaining administrative order in the Knesset building, managing and supervising the Knesset employees, and being responsible for the operation of the logistical and administrative system. Amongst his specific responsibilities are the Knesset's budget and expenditure, the Knesset's contracts and tenders, and the management of the Knesset's human resources, and employment conditions of the Knesset's employees,[4] all of which he performs by means of the Divisions and Departments subject to him.

The Director General chairs the **Knesset Administration**, which is not a statutory body, and consists of himself, the heads of the Divisions and Departments, which are directly subject to him (see the Knesset Administration Chart). The other three senior officials in the Knesset also participate in the Administration's weekly meetings, on Sundays. The Knesset Administration is responsible for all the major administrative decisions taken by the Knesset, which are subsequently approved by the Speaker.[5] In the case of major construction projects in the Knesset, such as the current "Knesset 2040" project which will see a vast increase in the Knesset's built space by the year 2040, the Knesset Administration also serves as their Steering Committee, in which all the relevant administrative units and persons participate, and in which Knesset members might be invited to take part as well.

51.3 Developments in the Knesset Administration since the 1980s

Important changes in the Knesset administrative structure began in the 1980s, when the Legal Department (see above) and the Computerization Department were established.

The Computerization Department was established in 1981. In the course of the 1990s, Microsoft was introduced into the Knesset, and by the late 1990s, the Knesset started to develop its Microsoft based "*Sanhedrin*" parliamentary management system,[6] which integrates all elements of the Knesset's parliamentary activity in the Plenum and the Committees.

Sanhedrin, which is currently in its third version, was developed by the Knesset computer team, with the technical assistance of external experts. Today, around 20 of the computer personnel in the Knesset are Knesset employees and another 40 are employed by the company that provides the Knesset with outsourced computer services (Confortes, 2017).

In 1996, **the Knesset Website** was developed within the **Library**, with the assistance of the Computerization Department, and outside experts in the design of websites. In 2006, the Internet was detached from the library. In addition to current information about the work of the Knesset and Knesset members and notices, the Knesset website contains the full minutes of the Plenum and of the Committees (except those of the Foreign Affairs and Defence Committee) since the establishment of the Knesset in 1949.[7] A narrower level of information appears also in English, Arabic, and Russian. In mid-March 2021, the Knesset website was moved to the Spokesperson's office.

At the turn of the millennium, there was a second surge of change, initiated by the Knesset Speaker Avraham Burg (Labour Party, 1999–2003), who established two important new administrative units: the **Research and Information Centre**, and the **Commission for Future Generations**.

The Research and Information Centre was established in 2000. Today, the Centre, which includes a **Budget Control Department**, has a staff of 47, most of it made up of researchers with Master degrees or Doctorates in relevant fields, which provides the Knesset Committees, Knesset members, and Knesset administrative units with politically and professionally neutral studies and data, at their request. According to article 64 of the Knesset Law, the Research and Information Centre is entitled to demand from anybody subject to the State Comptroller's scrutiny, information, documents, and reports, but its sources of information are almost unlimited. The Centre is an observer in the European Centre for Parliamentary Research and Documentation (ECPRD) which is a source of invaluable comparative information. Most of the documents written in the Research and Information Centre appear on the Knesset website, and some are translated into English or Arabic.

The tasks of the Commission for Future Generations were to submit data and opinions on issues that are of special interest to future generations, with special emphasis on sustainable development, primarily in connection to bills submitted to the Knesset, relating to such issues. The Commission was active from 2001 to 2006 and was officially abolished in 2010, allegedly for financial reasons. Its functions were formally transferred to the Research and Information Centre (Lavi, 2021).

The Knesset International Affairs Department was opened in 1997. In 2004, it was upgraded, upon the appointment of a full time Political Advisor who is an Ambassador from the Foreign Ministry, borrowed by the Knesset for a term of several years. The advisor is responsible for advising the Speaker, the Knesset members, and the Knesset administration on foreign policy issues, and helping develop and maintaining the Knesset's relations with parliaments of other countries. The Department is responsible for incoming and outgoing delegations and individuals, and bilateral contacts with other parliaments. With regard to delegations of Knesset members going to participate in meetings of the various international organizations of which the Knesset is a member, associate, or observer,[8] and official visits abroad by Knesset employees, the department's staff is responsible for the logistics of the travel, and the preparation of background material. Frequently a member of the department, or another Knesset official accompanies the delegations. Official delegations receive security services from the Knesset Guard or state services.

The most significant change in the administrative structure of the Knesset, which followed the creation of the position of the Director General in June 2006, was to divide most of the various units in the Knesset into administrative divisions (see administration chart) even though some of them do not bear the official title of Division. Each division is headed by a senior official. Some of the divisions are based on departments that have existed in the Knesset, in one form or another, since the early days of the Knesset, while others reflect contemporary developments. The division heads are selected by means of tenders. Tenders in the public service are first held within the organization, and only if a suitable candidate is not found inside the organization are external tenders held. When he entered office, the Knesset's fourth Director General, Albert Sakharovich (2016–2020), tried to change the methods by which the division heads are selected, by introducing search committees, which he believed would raise the standard of the persons selected. However, his success in this was limited and short-lived, due to opposition within the Knesset by the unionized workers' committees, and concerns that the proposed method would result in the politicization of the appointments (Zerahia, 2016).

The most recent Knesset unit established, which was also dismantled several years later, was the **Knesset Parliamentary Oversight Coordination Unit** (*KATEF* in Hebrew), established in 2017 by Knesset Speaker Yuli Edelstein (the Likud, 2013–2020), to strengthen the Knesset's ability to oversee the executive branch – which has always been viewed as one of the weaker aspects in the Knesset's parliamentary work. The Unit's goal was to create a positive organizational culture in the relationship between the Knesset and the Government. However, following the election of Yariv Levin (the Likud) as Knesset Speaker in May 2020, and despite the fact that he had strongly supported the establishment of the unit, he decided to dismantle it, since in his opinion the unit did not function effectively and did not bring the expected results.[9] The functions of the Unit were transferred to the Research and Information Centre.

51.4 The Sovereignty of the Knesset

The sovereignty of the Knesset is laid down in Basic-Law: the Knesset.[10] According to article 18 of the law "The Knesset buildings shall be inviolable", while according to article 19 "The Knesset shall determine its procedures. In so far as the procedures have not been prescribed by law, the Knesset shall lay them down in rules of procedure".

The Knesset's "non-dependence" (*ii tlut* in Hebrew) on the executive branch manifests itself in several ways. Most significant is that the Knesset Administration is not subject to the Government supervisory apparatuses. Consequently, the Knesset's Accountant General, Legal Advisor, and head of the Human Resources Department are not subject to the Finance Ministry Accountant General, the Attorney General, and the Civil Service Commissioner, respectively, as government ministries are.[11]

Thus, the Ministry of Finance has no control over the Knesset's annual budget, which is put together independently of the State Budget by the **Knesset's Accountant General**, approved by a joint committee of the Knesset's Finance and the House Committees, and is then attached to the State Budget as an integral part of it. In addition, the Knesset is not subject to the laws that regulate the management of the state economy, nor the financial and economic rules of procedure of the Accountant General of the Ministry of Finance.[12]

In addition, the Knesset has full control over its administrative apparatus, and the powers that the Civil Service Commissioner exercises over civil servants in general, in the case of the Knesset, are bestowed upon the Knesset Speaker, or to anyone he appoints to this effect [Article 40 of the Civil Service Law (appointments) (5719-1958)]. Nevertheless, the Knesset Administration, and especially the **Human Resources Department**, have, over the years, generally followed the Civil Service Rules of Procedure (*Takshir* in Hebrew),[13] on a voluntary basis. *Inter alia,* the *Takshir* lays down the rules for the various forms of employment in the civil service, conditions of employment, and the rights and duties of civil servants (including strict limitations on their political activities).

Since the Knesset's acceptance of the *Takshir* is a voluntary and not a statutory act, the Knesset may decide on exceptions[14] and does so in accordance with normative procedures of proper rules of administration.[15] The Knesset acts similarly with regard to the Financial and Economic Rules of Procedure (*Takam* in Hebrew) of the Accountant General of the Ministry of Finance, especially with regard to tenders and contractual engagements.[16]

Another significant manifestation of the Knesset's non-dependence is the independence of the Knesset's Legal Advisor from the Attorney General. What this means is that the Legal Advisor can present legal positions with regard to bills or other legal issues, which differ from those of the Attorney General, on legal grounds. It should be noted, however, that the opinions of the Knesset Legal Advisor are not binding and do not necessarily prevail in the Knesset, or in the High Court of Justice, when issues concerning the Knesset are brought before it, and the Legal Advisor appears to present the Knesset's case.[17]

At a lower level of the administration, one may perceive of the Research and Information Centre (see above), as another manifestation of the Knesset's non-dependence on the executive branch. Until the establishment of the Centre in 2000, the Knesset was heavily dependent on government sources of information, and on requests from experts from outside the Knesset to prepare studies and reports for its use.

The Knesset is subject to the scrutiny of the State Comptroller, on the basis of article 9(2) in the State Comptroller Law (5718-1958), but only with regard to purely administrative issues and its financial management, and not to its parliamentary activities and deliberations. The State Comptroller occasionally includes chapters on the Knesset in his annual reports, and at least on two occasions prepared special reports about "Issues in the Knesset Administration" (in 2004, and 2015). In these reports, the State Comptroller has focused on administrative failings in such issues as the planning process and implementation of new projects in the Knesset, how external experts and consultants have been engaged, how certain administrative units in the Knesset have been managed, and failure to abide by the *Takshir* (see above).

It should also be noted that the Speaker is a political figure, usually from the ruling party, and that the Director General is his/her personal appointment. Nevertheless, it is only rarely that a Speaker and his/her Director General have been accused of acting in their administrative capacity in an inappropriate political manner, though this allegedly occurred on several occasions during the recent political crisis in Israel, that lasted from December 2018 to November 2022.[18]

51.5 The Knesset Employees

In 2020, the number of Knesset employees (excluding the Knesset Guard) was over 700 (Alon, 2020-I). In 2000, the number of employees had been 366.[19] Employment is usually in accordance with the *Takshir* (see above). Employees may be employed in official positions by means of tenders, temporary employment, or contracts. Temporary employees are all employed by means of contracts. This includes the temporary engagement of experts for special projects (Tables 51.1 and 51.2).

All employees in standard positions are encouraged to study for academic degrees in relevant subjects, and the Knesset participates in their tuition fees. In accordance with the

Table 51.1 Number of positions in the Knesset (excluding Knesset Guard) 2000–2019

	2000	2003	2005	2007	2009	2011	2013	2015	2017	2019
Standard Knesset positions				322	375	450	486	527	557	592
Temporary positions				65	57	36	58	60	60	60
Total number of positions	366★	430	412	387	432	486	544	587	617	652

Sources: Knesset Reports under Freedom of Information Law for 2007, 2009, 2011, 2013, 2015, 2017, 2019, and Special State Comptroller Report on Issues in the Knesset Administration for 2015. p. 49

★ Letter from the head of the Human Resources Department of the Knesset, to the Knesset Accountant General, dated August 10, 1999.

Table 51.2 Number of positions in the Knesset Guard 2003–2019

	2000	2007	2009	2011	2013	2015	2017	2019
Standard Guard positions		162	194	194	201	206	212	232
Temporary Positions		23	8	8	8	8	8	8
Total number of Guard positions	107★	185	202	202	209	214	220	240

Sources: Knesset Reports under Freedom of Information Law for 2007, 2009, 2011, 2013, 2015, 2017, 2019.

★ Information received from the human resources department of the Knesset Guard.

collective salary agreements, employees can also take annual 400 hour further-study courses approved by the Human Resources Department, for which they receive salary benefits. In the Human Resources Department, there is a section in charge of instruction and further learning, which also organizes special instruction for employees inside the Knesset.

The employees of the parliamentary groups, and the parliamentary assistants (who are called "parliamentary advisors") are not counted as Knesset employees. The parliamentary group employees are employed by the parliamentary groups, but their salaries are paid by the Knesset from party financing funds [based on the Party Financing Law (5733-1973)], and the salaries of the Parliamentary Advisors, who are employed by the Knesset members, are also paid by the Knesset, on the basis of the Decision on the Salary of the Knesset members (grants and payments), which is updated periodically. Other personnel employed in the Knesset but not considered Knesset employees are persons who receive their salaries from the companies that provide the Knesset with outsourced services, and external experts who are hired by the Knesset for specific projects.

51.6 Administrative Support for the Plenum and Committees

As mentioned above, both the Plenum and Committees are under the responsibility of the Secretary General. The Knesset Secretariat is responsible for all the preparations connected to the logistics of the parliamentary work of the Plenum. The various technical tasks in the Plenum are carried out by the relevant administrative units. In addition, the Protocols Department ensures that one of its parliamentary reporters (formerly stenographers) is always present during sittings in the Plenum. The unedited minutes of the speeches appear on the

Knesset website an hour or two after being delivered. The Knesset TV channel broadcasts all the plenary proceedings live.

As to the Knesset Committees, each Committee has a director and basic staff, in addition to a Legal Advisor and additional legal staff provided by the Knesset Legal Department, a spokesperson (since 2010) on behalf of the Knesset Spokesperson's Office, one to three specialist researchers provided by the Research and Information Centre, and a parliamentary reporter, who is in charge of recording the proceedings of meetings. Committee minutes are usually available on the Knesset website within three weeks.

Only the Foreign Affairs and Defence Committee has its own researchers, and in the past all its minutes were treated as confidential and not published. Since 2017, minutes of meetings that are not closed, started to be published, but they constitute a small percentage of the total.

51.7 Transparency and Citizen Engagement

The Knesset is subject to the Freedom of Information Law (5758-1998), and every year publishes an annual report about its activities in the previous year. Citizens may approach the Knesset with requests for information that is not confidential.

The Knesset website provides a very wide range of information concerning the Knesset's activities, and the Knesset TV channel broadcasts all Plenary proceedings, Committee proceedings are also available online. Citizens have access to Committee meetings if they are invited to participate in a particular meeting by the Committee, or if their request to participate in a meeting is approved by the Committee (Shapira, 2010).

The Knesset offers a variety of tours of the Knesset, which may include lectures and activities, to various population groups. A Visitor's Centre was established in 2011 and is expected to expand in the future.

Citizens can approach the Knesset through its Public Inquiries Section, founded in 2014, which is subject to the Director General. In 2017, the Section was provided with a Customer Relationship Management (CRM) system, which has greatly improved its work. Among the Knesset' parliamentary committees, there is a Special Committee for Public Petitions, whose members are Knesset members, which deals with petitions from the public and various organizations concerning citizens' rights and the services that the public receives from the government. Many citizens prefer to approach individual Knesset members directly for assistance.[20]

51.8 The Knesset's Relations with the Media

The Spokesperson's Office is responsible for all the contacts and interrelationships with the media. At the time of writing, the personnel of the Spokesperson's Office numbered 17. Over half of these are assigned to the various Knesset Committees. Spokespersons may be responsible for several committees and/or units. The Knesset website carries "Knesset news" and "Committee news", issued by the Spokesperson's Office and Committee spokespersons. The Spokesperson's Office places great importance on the credibility of the information it distributes. The Knesset Speaker and individual Knesset members have their own spokespersons.

Around 20 parliamentary correspondents, from both the written and electronic media have offices in the Knesset. Assigned reporters can move relatively freely throughout the building, where they can film, photograph, and interview. The Knesset restaurants and snack bars, and the corridors are out of bounds. Journalists may enter Knesset members' or administrative offices only with explicit permission from their occupants.

The Knesset TV channel broadcasts all Plenary sittings and Committee meetings in real time (with the exception of confidential meetings). In accordance with article 15b of the Knesset's TV Broadcasts Law (5764-2003), all the broadcasts prepared by the Knesset channel are available for free to everyone, including the commercial and public TV networks, unless otherwise prescribed.

Since the middle of March, 2021, the Knesset website is administratively attached to the Spokespersons' Office.

51.9 Dealing with the Coronavirus Pandemic

In February 2020, the Director General, appointed the Sergeant-at-arms, to head a team to deal with the issue of Covid-19 within the Knesset building and compound. His task was to do everything possible to ensure the orderly functioning of Knesset (Alon, 2020-2). Besides the Director General and the relevant administrative units subject to him, the Sergeant-at-arms worked closely with the Knesset Secretary General and Legal Department. The first decisions of the team were to cancel all visits and tours in the Knesset building, to limit the number of Knesset employees in the building, so that only a third of the employees continued to arrive, another part was told to work from home, while a third group was sent on leave without pay. As time went by all Ministers, Knesset members and employees who contracted the virus or who had been in close contact with a person who had contracted the virus were sent into home confinement.

Since the pandemic broke out a little before the third round of general elections in the space of a year, which took place on March 2, 2020, the first event that had to be taken care of was the opening ceremony of the 23th Knesset, on March 16, at which the 120 newly elected Knesset members declare their allegiance. Even though the Director General of the Ministry of Health had informed Knesset Speaker Yuli Edelstein (Likud) that the Corona regulations his Ministry had issued did not apply to the Knesset, which is sovereign to decide on its own proceedings, the Speaker decided to adopt the regulations, and during the opening ceremony no more than ten persons were present in the Plenum at any given moment of time – including the Speaker, Secretary General, basic administrative staff, and two to three Knesset members. Following the ceremony, the sitting arrangements in the Plenum were changed so that all 120 Knesset members could be present during sittings, seated in the Plenum itself, and the two galleries above – the important guests and media gallery, and the visitors' gallery – where all the required equipment was installed.

The fact that neither the Knesset Plenum nor its Committees have quorums requirements for holding their meetings, greatly facilitated the Knesset's work during the pandemic, as did the fact that Israel is a small country, and Jerusalem is easily accessible. (Bar-Siman-Tov, 2020.)

In general, separations were installed in committee rooms, and masks were made available for anyone who arrives without one. As time went by, and as Israel went into and out of lockdowns, the Director General updated the rules and regulations concerning the activity of the Knesset, especially with regard to the persons who may enter the Knesset building. All the rules and regulations were approved by the Speaker.[21]

By mid-June 2021, as the effects of the Covid pandemic were reduced, Israel returned to near normality, as did the work of the Knesset, at least in so far as the pandemic was concerned. In April 2022, the requirement to wear masks indoors, with few exceptions, was cancelled.

51.9.1 Postscript

Since the end of 2018, Israel has been going through a political crisis that so far (December 2022) has resulted in five rounds of elections since April 2019, several transition governments, one government in 2021 that survived for seven months, and another, formed in June 2021, which survived for just over a year, leading to a fifth round of elections on November 1, 2022 a new government was sworn in on December 29, 2022. It should be noted that despite the extreme political instability the Knesset administration has continued to function regularly and manage the administrative affairs of the Knesset smoothly. (For a description of the effect of the crisis on the work of the Knesset and its members since the end of 2018, see epilogue in Rolef, 2022.)

Notes

1. Unless otherwise mentioned, the information in this chapter comes from the Knesset website, provided by numerous Knesset employees, past and present, with whom I held lengthy conversations, or my own personal experience as a full-time or part-time Parliamentary Assistant or Knesset employee in the years 1977–2010.
2. Conversation with the former Secretary General of the Knesset, Yardena Meller-Horowitz, on March 2, 2021.
3. Conversation with former Knesset Legal Advisor, Attorney Eyal Yinon (2010–2020), on December 30, 2020.
4. Special Report of the Comptroller General on "Issues in the Administration of the Knesset", 2015, p. 47.
5. Conversation with former Director General of the Knesset, Albert Sakharovich (2016–2020), on January 28, 2021.
6. Conversation with the first director of the Knesset's Computerization Department, Arik Fischel, on February 17, 2021.
7. The documents from before the computer era were all scanned by the Knesset Archive.
8. The Inter-Parliamentary Union, The Euro-Mediterranean Parliamentary Assembly, the Parliamentary Assembly of the Mediterranean, the NATO (North Atlantic Treaty Organization) Parliamentary Assembly, the European Cuncil, the European Parliament, and the Organization for Security and Cooperation in Europe.
9. Conversation with Knesset Speaker Yariv Levin Yariv Levin (2020–2021), March 17, 2021.
10. Israel does not have a constitution. It has Basic Laws that deal with specific issues. Basic-Law: the Knesset was the first one to be enacted in 1958. Unlike ordinary laws, Basic Laws do not bear a date.
11. State Comptroller, 2015, p. 47.
12. Ibid.
13. The *Takshir* is a 983 page document, that in available online.
14. Attorney Eyal Yinon told the author on February 22, 2021, that the procedure he followed as Legal Advisor was to review requests for exceptions provided by the head of the Human Resources Department, and after approval to inform the Knesset Speaker and Director General of his decisions.
15. Both the State Comptroller and the Labour Courts have issued statements to this effect over the years.
16. Information received from the Knesset Legal Advisor for Administration.
17. For two such examples, see Horowitz and Bar-Siman-Tov op. cit. Chapter C.
18. See for example Azulai, 2021; Bar-Siman-Tov, 2020.
19. Knesset statistics speak of "positions" rather than "employees", since some employees hold part-time positions.
20. Since Israel's electoral system is not based on constituencies (electoral districts), citizens do not have an MK who they elected directly and therefore contact any MK, who seems to them suitable.
21. The information in the section on the Covid-19 pandemic is based on various documents that appeared on the Knesset website, and interviews with the previous Secretary General of the Knesset, Yardena Meller-Horowitz, on March 2, 2021, and the former Director General of the Knesset Albert Sakharovich, on January 28, 2021. See also Alon, 2020-1.

References

Alon, Gideon, 2020-1. "The Sergeant-at-arms: we never thought of such dimensions", *Yisrael Hayom*, April 6, 2020. (Heb)

Alon, Gideon, 2020-2. "The Knesset's Director General leaves: todays MKs seek jobs", *Yisrael Hayom*, June 29, 2020. (Heb)

Azulai, Moran, 2021. "Levin refused to announce when the vote on the new Government will take place: 'we shall convey later'", *Ynet*, June 7, 2021. (Heb)

Bar-Siman-Tov, Ittai, 2020. "Covid-19 Meets Politics: The Novel Coronavirus as a Novel Challenge for Legislators", *Theory and Practice of Legislation*, 8 (1–2): 11–48.

Confortes, Judah 2017. "The goal: full transparency of the Knesset work – by means of information systems", *People and Computers*, February 7, 2017. (Heb)

Horowitz, Keren and Ittai Bar-Siman-Tov, 2020. "The Knesset Legal Advisor and his position in the separation of powers in the legislative procedures", (Article to appear in *Iyunei Mishpat*). (Heb)

Lavi, Aharon Ariel, 2021. "The rise and fall of the Commission for Future Generations", *Hashilo'ah*, January 2021. (Heb)

Rolef, Susan Hattis, 2022. *Israel's Knesset Members: A Comparative Study of an Undefined Job*, Routledge, Taylor & Francis Group, London and New York.

Shapira, Assaf, 2010. "Citizens in the Knesset Committees", the Israel Democracy Institute, *Parlament* No. 66, September 15, 2010. (Heb)

State Comptroller, 2015. Special Report of the Comptroller General on "Issues in the Administration of the Knesset".

Zerahia, Zvi, 2016. "The Knesset Director General of the Knesset wishes to appoint senior officials in the House by means of a search committee rather than tenders", *TheMarker*, November 5, 2016. (Heb)

52
JAPAN'S PARLIAMENTARY ADMINISTRATION

Karol Żakowski

Japanese bureaucrats have been known as important players in decision-making process. Nevertheless, while much attention has been paid to examining the role played by the administrative staff of the ministries and the Cabinet Office, analyses of parliamentary administration in Japan have remained scarce. This chapter tries to fill this gap. It examines the structure, functions, and relations with politicians of bureaucratic institutions in the Kokkai.[1]

52.1 Organizational Structure of Parliamentary Administration in Japan

Due to bicameral structure of the Japanese Diet, each chamber of the parliament hosts independent administrative organs. The proceedings of the 248-member Sangiin[2] (Upper House) and the 465-member Shūgiin[3] (Lower House) are assisted by separate Secretariats (Jimukyoku) and Legislative Bureaus (Hōseikyoku). In addition, both chambers collectively supervise the National Diet Library (Kokuritsu Kokkai Toshokan).

The Secretariat of the Shūgiin is presided by secretary-general *(jimu sōchō)* and composed of 11 organs: Secretary Section (Hishoka), Proceedings Department (Gijibu), Committee Department (Iinbu), Records Department (Kirokubu), Police Department (Keimubu), General Affairs Department (Shomubu), Management Department (Kanribu), International Department (Kokusaibu), Parliamentary Museum (Kensei Kinenkan), Secretariat of the Constitution Review Committee (Kenpō Shinsakai Jimukyoku), as well as Secretariat of the Information Oversight Audit Committee (Jōhō Kanshi Shinsakai Jimukyoku). Two high-ranking officials are placed under secretary-general: deputy secretary-general *(jimu jichō)* as well as Research Bureau director-general *(chōsakyokuchō)* who supervises the work of the staff who prepares documents for the Chamber's standing and special committees (see Figure 52.1). The organizational structure of the Sangiin Secretariat is similar, except for the lack of the Parliamentary Museum and the Research Bureau, which is substituted with the Planning and Coordination Unit (Kikaku Chōsei Shitsu), Standing Committee Research Unit (Jōnin Iinkai Chōsa Shitsu), and Special Research Unit (Tokubetsu Chōsa Shitsu) (see Figure 52.2).

Between 2000 and 2021, the number of the Shūgiin Secretariat staff decreased from 1732 to 1620 and of the Sangiin Secretariat staff from 1276 to 1213 (see Figure 52.3). The

Figure 52.1 Organizational structure of the Shūgiin Secretariat

Source: Compiled by the author based on data from: The House of Representatives, Japan, no date.

downscaling of parliamentary administration was a result of rationalization of budget expenses implemented between 2005 and 2010. The reforms consisted in digitalization of stenography system that enabled closing of a shorthand training centre, employment of drivers by external companies, as well as liquidation of two parliamentary hotels for lawmakers from countryside regions. The downscaling of administration was consistent with the fact that also the number of Shūgiin members was reduced from 480 to 465 after amendments of voting system in 2013 and 2017. Decrease in the number of parliamentary administration staff contrasted with the strengthening of the institutional backing to the prime minister after establishment of the Cabinet Office (Naikakufu) in 2001. Opposite direction of the two reforms symbolized a relative empowerment of the government vis-à-vis the legislative branch.

In 1948, the Legislative Department was detached from the Shūgiin Secretariat, becoming the Shūgiin Legislative Bureau. The Bureau, presided by commissioner-general *(kyokuchō)*, is divided into 14 divisions gathered in six departments. While four divisions in the Legislative Planning and Coordination Department (Hōsei Kikaku Chōseibu) focus

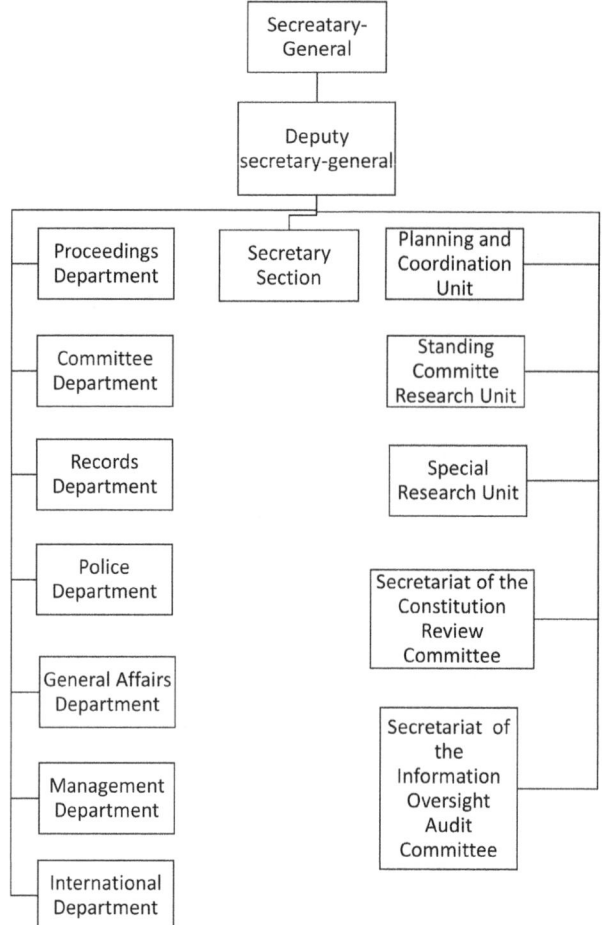

Figure 52.2 Organizational structure of the Sangiin Secretariat

Source: Compiled by the author based on data from: House of Councillors, The National Diet of Japan, no date.

on general issues, such as planning, coordination, fundamental legislation, and research, departments 1–5 handle the issues discussed in corresponding parliamentary committees, such as security, internal affairs and communications, judicial affairs, financial affairs, foreign affairs, economy, trade and industry, or health, labour and welfare. The Bureau employs 86 bureaucrats (Legislative Bureau of the House of Representatives, 2012). The Legislative Department of the Sangiin is almost a carbon copy of its counterpart in the Lower House.

Director-general of the National Diet Library is nominated by the speakers of both houses after authorization by the two chambers. Apart from the main building in Tokyo, the National Diet Library supervises Kansai-kan in Keihanna Science City as well as the International Library of Children's Literature in Ueno Park in Tokyo. The three facilities boast storage capacity of about 24 million volumes in addition to electronic resources. As of April 2021, the National Diet Library employed 893 persons excluding staff of 27 branch libraries in executive and judicial agencies of the government (National Diet Library, Japan, 2021a).

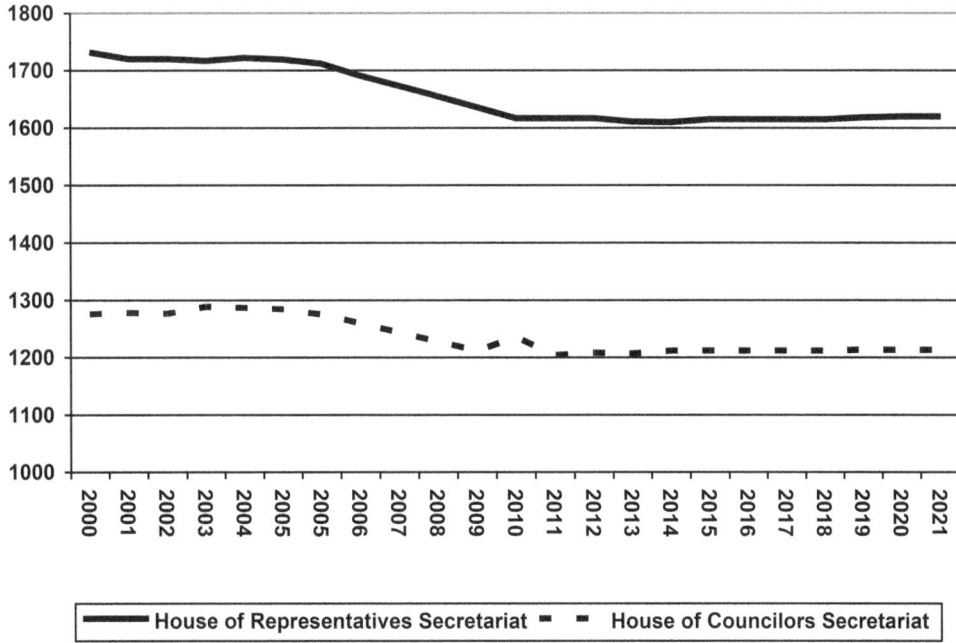

Figure 52.3 Number of staff of the Shūgiin and the Sangiin Secretariats
Source: Compiled by the author based on data from: National Diet of Japan, 2000-2021.

In addition to the Secretariats and the Legislative Bureaus of both houses and the National Diet Library, parliamentary bureaucrats serve in the secretariats of the Judge Impeachment Court (Saibankan Dangai Saibansho) and the Judge Indictment Committee (Saibankan Sotsui Iinkai) – two institutions established by the Diet to prosecute judges accused of crimes.

Central administration bureaucrats in Japan have been considered important veto players whose tendency to protect the status quo constituted a major obstacle against bold policy change by the government. Characterized by elitist self-esteem, sectionalism, collectivism, and life-time employment, they were often accused of steering ministerial affairs over the heads of their political superiors. Each ministry recruits staff from among fresh university graduates (in particular from the University of Tokyo) through entry exams organized on an annual basis. Once employed, bureaucrats usually remain in one ministry until retirement and can expect that their careers will proceed according to fixed stages. As a result, even when temporarily dispatched to the Cabinet Secretariat, they tend to place their loyalty in their home ministries rather than in the government as a whole (Shinoda, 2000, pp. 5–10; Iio, 2008, p. 39).

Similarly, the organs of parliamentary administration in both chambers organize separate entry exams and ensure stable employment. The Diet Staff Act excludes from recruitment those persons who had been sentenced to imprisonment or who had been demoted from public office due to disciplinary action within the previous two years (e-gov, 1947a). Career in the Shūgiin or the Sangiin Secretariats has not been considered as attractive as work in the most powerful and prestigious ministries, such as the Ministry of Finance, the Ministry of Economy, Trade and Industry, or the Ministry of Foreign Affairs. Still, the parliamentary administration staff has played an important role in ensuring legality and impartiality of Diet proceedings.

52.2 The Role of the Administration in the Context of Parliamentary Work in Japan

Parliamentary administration provides lawmakers with necessary data, assists them in drafting bill projects and in preparing interpellations, as well as supervises committee proceedings. Under the long Liberal Democratic Party (LDP) rule, it has also not been uncommon for parliamentary bureaucrats to assist ruling party officials in political bargaining with the opposition parties.

According to the Article 17 of the Diet Staff Act, parliamentary administration is to "perform their duties fairly, impartially, and sincerely, thus serving the entire nation" (e-gov, 1947a). Secretariats of both houses deal with a broad array of routine activities. They supervise Diet facilities, such as legislative offices, cafeteria, lodging buildings and means of transportation; care for security of lawmakers; provide secretaries to speakers and deputy speakers; manage domestic and offshore delegations of Diet members; gather data necessary for parliamentary work and disclose such information as legislators' asset reports; issue entry passes for external visitors; prepare minutes and television transmission of Diet proceedings; or count votes during committee meetings and plenary sessions. The most important duty of the Secretariat staff, however, is to assist MPs in the legislative process.

Lawmakers need to rely on parliamentary administration when drafting new bills as they lack sufficient staff under their direct jurisdiction. Until the 1990s, only two official secretaries could be employed in the legislative office of each MP. In reality, they were often stationed in the politician's electoral office and dealt with contacts with voters rather than policy matters. To redress this situation, an additional post of secretary in charge of policy-making was introduced in 1993. Nevertheless, the reform did not change much, because also the third staffer usually lacked expertise and time to focus on assisting his/her superior in drafting new bills (Shimizu, 2011, pp. 104–146).

According to Article 15 of the House Secretariat Law, the main responsibility of the Research Bureaus or Units in the Secretariats of both chambers is to conduct necessary examination of the matters proceeded by parliamentary committees (e-gov, 1947b). As indicated by Hirano (2020, p. 35), the parliamentary administration's role exceeds strictly technical functions. Its importance in decision-making process stems from the fact that many lawmakers only mechanically read documents prepared by the bureaucrats, and all speeches by speakers, deputy speakers, and committee chairs in both chambers are actually prepared by the Secretariat staff. Moreover, in case of any disturbance in the legislative process, politicians have to rely on expert knowledge of their staff who, based on rules of procedure and precedents, propose legally accepted solutions.

While performing their duties, parliamentary bureaucrats remain in close contact with the representatives of both ruling and opposition parties. In particular, they deal with party secretary-generals and chairpersons of the Diet Affairs Committees (Kokkai Taisaku Iinkai) – party organs established specifically to conduct backstage negotiations with other parties. Due to broad discretionary powers enjoyed by the speakers of both houses and parliamentary committee chairs, coupled with an unwritten tradition of seeking consensus with opposition parties, the government has little ways of controlling the legislative process after the submission of legislative bills to the Diet. The schedule of deliberations is established by the Steering Committees (Giin Un'ei Iinkai) of both chambers, which host the representatives of all parliamentary caucuses (Takenaka, 2013, pp. 146–149). Parliamentary bureaucrats not only provide administrative backing to these organs but also ensure that political bargaining between different parties does not violate the Constitution and Diet rules.

Under the Japanese consensual political culture, it was not uncommon for the Shūgiin Secretariat secretary-general to interfere whenever ruling party members tried to abuse their dominant position in the Diet. For instance, in 1967, Secretary-General Chino Torao expressed his opposition against Deputy Speaker Sonoda Sunao's and LDP Secretary-General Fukuda Takeo's plan to steamroll Health Insurance Special Bill through the Diet without heeding to the opposition parties' motions for providing more discussion time and changing voting method to registered voting. Under Chino's threat that he would step down from office if Diet regulations were broken, LDP leadership was forced to initiate time-consuming negotiations with the Japan Socialist Party, Democratic Socialist Party, and Kōmeitō (Hirano, 2020, pp. 58–79).

According to Article 20-2 of the Diet Staff Act, parliamentary bureaucrats cannot be involved in any political activities, receive donations or other benefits from political parties, run in elections for public offices, and "serve as officials of political parties or other political organizations, political advisers, or other members with similar roles" (e-gov, 1947a). Nevertheless, occasionally, high-ranking parliamentary bureaucrats assisted their political superiors in appeasing opposition parties. Such involvement in political bargaining between parliamentary caucuses stemmed from the fact that one of the responsibilities of the Secretariat was to ensure that bills were proceeded without obstruction by lawmakers through filibuster techniques, rostrum blockade, complete boycott of proceedings, or "cow's walk" – walking extremely slowly to put registered vote in a ballot box during plenary session. Hirano (2020, pp. 168–262) admits that when he was a parliamentary bureaucrat, he used to play a role of a mediator between the ruling party and the opposition parties. For example, in 1987, he prepared a plan of appeasing opposition politicians after Prime Minister Nakasone's failed attempt at passing a sales tax. His involvement in politics was so obvious that LDP Secretary-General Gotōda Masaharu complained that political bargaining was conducted by a non-legislator. Between 1990 and 1992, in turn, Hirano was instructed by LDP Secretary-General Ozawa Ichirō to hold backstage negotiations with opposition politicians on the passage of a revolutionary bill that authorized Japan's participation in the United Nations peacekeeping operations. According to Hirano, occasional performance of a role of a "puppeteer" *(kuroko)* by the Secretariat staff is in line with the spirit of parliamentarism.

Another role of parliamentary bureaucrats is to provide administrative backing to the committees established in the Diet to deal with important state matters. For example, the Secretariats of the Information Oversight Audit Committees were established in both houses in 2014, after the passage of a controversial Bill on Protection of Specially Designated Secrets that introduced severe penalties for disclosing information designated as "special secrets." The Committees were to assess whether information was classified correctly or not, but they could hardly perform their duty. As the members of the Committees gained access only to the list of "specially designated secrets," not to their contents, the government's control over classified information remained intact (Shindō, 2019, p. 132).

The main function of the Legislative Bureaus in both houses is to ensure that bill projects do not violate the Constitution. Theoretically, the power of judging constitutionality of all laws is vested in the Supreme Court. However, due to the fact that the Court has often declined clear judgement on highly political matters, it has been central administration bureaucrats who enjoyed much authority in interpreting the Constitution. In particular, the Cabinet Legislation Bureau (Naikaku Hōseikyoku) issued many "unified government interpretations" *(tōitsu kenkai)* that became the foundation of Japan's legal order (Samuels, 2004). Legislative Bureaus in both houses handled only those bill projects that were submitted by the lawmakers, which were usually less numerous than government-sponsored laws. Theoretically, 20 members of the Lower or 10 members of the Upper House have the right of legislative initiative, but they can use it only after having gained permission from their party leadership (Kōno, 2003, pp. 75–76).

Still, the Legislative Departments of both chambers occasionally ruled on important policy matters and enjoyed high authority within the Japanese parliamentary administration. For instance, in 1974, the Sangiin Legislative Department dissuaded conservative lawmakers from passing a bill on nationalization of Yasukuni – a Shinto shrine in central Tokyo where spirits of soldiers who had died for Japan were worshipped. As argued by parliamentary bureaucrats, not to violate the constitutional rule of separation of state and religion, the shrine would have to abandon all Shinto symbols and rituals, which was unacceptable to the priests and right-wing activists (Hirano, 2020, pp. 89–96).

As the only legal deposit library in Japan, the National Diet Library gathers all domestic publications, including maps, microfilms, CDs, and DVDs. It uses this vast collection not only to respond to requests from legislators on any national issues related to politics, society, economy, or science and technology, but also to conduct research and publish papers on any topics relevant to national politics. In addition, the Library maintains an index database of Japanese laws, regulations and bills, as well as a full-text database of the minutes of all committee meetings and plenary sessions available on the Internet (National Diet Library, Japan, 2018). Particularly active has been the Research and Legislative Reference Bureau (Chōsa oyobi Rippō Kōsa Kyoku), which holds an ambition to act as brains of the legislature. It has launched several research projects in cooperation with scholars and experts, which involved interviews, roundtable discussions, and field studies. For instance, it examined transformation of the British political system, analysed regionalism in Europe, translated several foreign constitutions into Japanese, and compared the science and technology policies of major countries (Hirose, 2014).

The work of parliamentary administration in Japan has not attracted as strong interest from scholars as the influence of ministerial bureaucrats on decision-making process. Nevertheless, the Shūgiin and Sangiin Secretariats have not only dealt with routine activities of both chambers but also played a control role against political abuse and even occasionally participated in backstage bargaining between the ruling and opposition parties. At the same time, the Legislative Departments have guarded the constitutional order, and the National Diet Library has provided documents and expertise that facilitated the legislative process.

52.3 Managing Inter-institutional and External Relations

In their work, parliamentary bureaucrats cooperate with their colleagues from the other Diet chamber, the executive branch, and foreign institutions. While parliamentary administration in Japan has been traditionally characterized by professionalism and high independence from political pressure, the government's control over the bureaucrats has significantly strengthened in recent years. At the same time, globalization has led to an increase in importance of parliamentary diplomacy.

All laws have to be passed by both houses of the Diet. While the legislative process may be initiated by any of the chambers, usually it has been the Shūgiin that started proceedings on a bill project. After deliberation on a law is ended, the speaker sends it through the Secretariat secretary-general to the speaker of the other chamber (The House of Representatives, Japan, 1947).

Administrative reforms that entered into force in 2001 empowered the prime minister and his/her direct entourage (so-called Kantei – the Prime Minister's Residence) against the other institutional players in the Japanese political system. When the Democratic Party of Japan came to power in 2009, it tried to completely isolate the bureaucrats from policymaking, which caused a temporary disturbance of relations between politicians and their administrative staff (Zakowski, 2015). Under the second cabinet of Prime Minister Abe Shinzō (2012–2020), the influence of the bureaucrats on decision-making process was weakened in a more systematic manner. In particular, in 2014, the government created the Cabinet Bureau of Personnel Affairs (Naikaku Jinji Kyoku), which enabled the Kantei to grasp control over nomination of all bureaucrats ranked department head and above. The reform weakened to some extent ministerial sectionalism, but it had some detrimental effects as well. As bureaucratic careers started depending on the loyalty towards the prime minister, central administration stopped performing its control role against political leaders (Zakowski, 2021, pp. 108–113). Although it is the speakers of both houses rather than the government that nominates parliamentary bureaucrats, also the Diet administration's independence from political pressure has been considerably weakened. Hirano (2020, pp. 34–97) deplored the fact that neither Shūgiin Secretariat nor Legislative Bureau voiced their objection against such controversial decisions by the Abe administration as reinterpretation of the Constitution to legalize collective self-defence in 2014 or refusal to hold extraordinary Diet session in 2017 despite a motion submitted by the opposition parties.

According to Article 41 of the Diet Staff Act, parliamentary bureaucrats can be dispatched to international organizations that Japan is a member of or to the institutions of foreign governments. During their stay abroad, they preserve their status of Diet staff without engaging in their ordinary duties (e-gov, 1947a). Parliamentary diplomacy has been usually conducted by parliamentary friendship leagues that gathered lawmakers interested in maintaining exchange with distinct countries. Dispatch of legislators abroad is managed by the International Departments of the Secretariats of both houses. Parliamentary staff not only prepares lawmakers' foreign delegations but also occasionally participates in visits to other countries. For instance, in 1990, a high-ranking bureaucrat from the Shūgiin Secretariat became a member of a supra-party delegation to France, UK, and West Germany that met with foreign politicians and academics in order to gain knowledge on different kinds of parliamentary systems. Its aim was to prepare ground for a comprehensive political and electoral reform in Japan after the end of the Cold War (Hirano, 2020, pp. 223–224).

The administrative reforms and globalization processes have led to intensification of inter-institutional and external relations maintained by parliamentary bureaucrats. In particular, empowerment of the prime minister has made parliamentary staff more prone to political pressure, thus weakening its control role against the ruling party.

52.4 Managing Current Challenges Facing the Parliamentary Administration in Japan

In recent years, parliamentary administration in Japan has faced the challenges of institutional downscaling and change of work patterns due to Covid-19 pandemic. Some of its problems have not been sufficiently addressed yet, such as the need to digitalize and modernize administrative work and voting methods in the Shūgiin as well as clarify the rules of management of documents.

The Covid-19 pandemic accelerated digitalization of parliamentary administration in Japan. According to the "National Diet Library Vision 2021–2025," the Library plans to convert more than one million materials to full-text data within five years in order to digitize all domestic publications. In addition, its aim is to convert no longer playable media into usable formats and create a search platform openly available not only to legislators, but also to the general public (National Diet Library, Japan, 2021b).

Another challenge facing parliamentary administration in Japan is to continue digitalization of administrative work and modernize voting methods in the Shūgiin. Digitalization of stenography system enabled budget cuts and downscaling of the Diet staff, but some of the fields of Diet's activities have not been sufficiently modernized yet. While electronic voting machines were introduced to the Upper House in 1998, the Lower House still relies on traditional methods: lack of objection, rising in places, and registered voting through name cards. The first two methods decrease transparency of the legislative process (data on individual votes is not recorded), and the last method creates room for abuses (e.g. "cow's walk"). Electronic voting machines would simplify and automate vote counting.

Parliamentary administration also needs to elaborate better rules of managing documents. The Public Records and Archives Management Act, enforced in 2011, stipulated the obligation of proper management of documents by public institutions. Nevertheless, regulations on writing, arrangement, and preservation of records by the Secretariats of both chambers remain unclear. Without a central archive, documents are stored in separate departments and divisions, without proper temperature and humidity control, which can cause their gradual deterioration. Moreover, while the Secretariat is obliged by law to prepare records of Diet's plenary sessions and committee meetings, no such obligation exists regarding Committee Board of Directors meetings. Lack of unified standards of management of documents leaves much space for discretionary decisions by the Diet staff, which weakens transparency of the legislative process (Ōkura, 2018, pp. 23–47).

Although the Covid-19 pandemic accelerated digitalization of administrative work, the Shūgiin has not introduced electronic voting machines yet, and the rules of managing documents in both chambers remain unclear. While the downscaling of the Diet staff has brought budget savings, it should be coupled with further institutional reforms towards greater simplicity and transparency of the legislative process.

52.5 Conclusions

The role of parliamentary administration in Japan often exceeded its main function of simply providing institutional assistance to lawmakers. The staff of the Secretariats of both houses has not only followed orders from their political superiors but also occasionally performed a control function vis-à-vis the ruling party. Secretariat secretary-general has a responsibility to guard Diet regulations, while Legislative Bureau commissioner-general is obliged to ensure that all bill projects submitted by lawmakers conform with the Constitution. They were able perform these functions thanks to high professionalism and relative impartiality of the Japanese bureaucratic system. Nevertheless, in recent years, the empowerment of the Kantei (the prime ministers and their direct entourage) has considerably weakened the Diet staff's ability to resist political pressure. In addition to institutional downscaling and the need to continue modernization and digitalization of administrative work, this tendency constitutes a major challenge for parliamentary bureaucrats.

Notes

1 National Diet of Japan.
2 House of Councillors.
3 House of Representatives.

References

e-gov (1947a). "Kokkai Shokuin Hō" [Diet Staff Act], https://elaws.e-gov.go.jp/document?law_unique_id=322AC0000000085_20190914_501AC0000000037 (accessed August 24, 2021).

e-gov (1947b). "Giin Jimukyoku Hō" [House Secretariat Law], https://elaws.e-gov.go.jp/document?lawid=322AC0000000083 (accessed August 13, 2021).

Hirano, Sadao (2020). *Shūgiin Jimukyoku. Kokkai no Shin'ōbu ni Kakusareta Saikyō Kikan* [Secretariat of the House of Representatives: The Strongest Institution Hidden in the Depths of the Diet]. Tokyo: Hakushūsha.

Hirose, Junko (2014). "Enhancing our Role as the 'Brains of the Legislature': Comprehensive and Interdisciplinary Research at the National Diet Library, Japan," IFLA Library and Research Services for Parliaments Section Preconference 2014, https://www.ifla.org/wp-content/uploads/2019/05/assets/services-for-parliaments/preconference/2014/hirose_japan_paper.pdf (accessed August 26, 2021).

House of Councillors, The National Diet of Japan (no date). "Sangiin no Aramshi. Soshiki-zu" (Summary of the House of Councillors. Organizational Chart), https://www.sangiin.go.jp/japanese/aramashi/jimu_sosikizu.html (accessed October 23, 2021).

Iio, Jun (2008). *Nihon no Tōchi Kōzō* [Structure of Government in Japan]. Tokyo: Chūō Kōron Shinsha.

Kōno, Tarō (2003). *Kōno Tarō no Kokkai Kōryaku Hon* [The Book about Capture of the Diet by Kōno Tarō]. Tokyo: Eiji Shuppan.

Legislative Bureau of the House of Representatives (2012). "Organisation of the Legislative Bureau of the House of Representatives," https://www.shugiin.go.jp/internet/itdb_annai.nsf/html/statics/housei/html/h-organisation.html (accessed August 17, 2021).

National Diet Library, Japan (2018). "Mission and Roles," https://www.ndl.go.jp/en/aboutus/missionandroles.html (accessed August 20, 2021).

National Diet Library, Japan (2021a). "Organization, Staff and Budget," https://www.ndl.go.jp/en/aboutus/outline/organization.html (accessed August 19, 2021).

National Diet Library, Japan (2021b). "National Diet Library, Vision 2021–2025: The Digital Shift at the National Diet Library," https://www.ndl.go.jp/en/aboutus/vision_ndl.html (accessed August 26, 2021).

National Diet of Japan (2000–2021). "Kokkai Kaigiroku Kensaku Shisutemu" [Diet Minutes Search System], https://kokkai.ndl.go.jp/#/ (accessed August 18, 2021).

Ōkura, Ayako (2018). "Sangiin Jimukyoku oyobi Shūgiin Jimukyoku ni okeru Gen'yō Bunsho no Kanri" [Record Management in the House of Representatives and the House of Councillors, the National Diet of Japan], *Rekōdo Manejimento*, No. 74.

Samuels, Richard J. (2004). "Politics, Security Policy, and Japan's Cabinet Legislation Bureau: Who Elected These Guys, Anyway?," JPRI Working Paper, No. 99, http://www.jpri.org/publications/workingpapers/wp99.html (accessed July 19, 2019).

Shimizu Katsuhiko (2011). *"Seiji Shudō" no Otoshiana* [Pitfall of "Politician-Led Government"]. Tokyo: Heibonsha.

Shindō, Muneyuki (2019). *Kanryōsei to Kōbunsho. Kaizan, Netsuzō, Sontaku no Haikei* [Bureaucratic System and Official Documents. Manipulation, Forgery, Sontaku]. Tokyo: Chikuma Shobō.

Shinoda, Tomohito (2000). *Leading Japan. The Role of the Prime Minister.* Westport: Praeger Publishers.

Takenaka, Harukata (2013). "Minshutō Seiken to Nihon no Giin Naikakusei" [DPJ Government and Japan's Parliamentary System], in Iio Jun (ed.) *Seiken Kōtai to Seitō Seiji. Rekishi no Naka no Nihon Seiji 6* [Alternation of Power and Party Politics. Japanese Politics in History 6]. Tokyo: Chūō Kōron Shinsha.

The House of Representatives, Japan (1947). "Shūgiin Kisoku" [Rules of the House of Representatives], June 28, https://www.shugiin.go.jp/internet/itdb_annai.nsf/html/statics/shiryo/dl-rules.htm#19 (accessed August 24, 2021).

The House of Representatives, Japan (no date). "Jimukyoku" (Secretariat), https://www.shugiin.go.jp/internet/itdb_annai.nsf/html/statics/kokkai/jimukyoku.htm (accessed August 13, 2021).

Zakowski, Karol (2015). *Decision-Making Reform in Japan: The DPJ's Failed Attempt at a Politician-Led Government*, London and New York: Routledge.

Zakowski, Karol (2021). *Gradual Institutional Change in Japan. Kantei Leadership under the Abe Administration*, London and New York: Routledge.

53
KOREA'S PARLIAMENTARY ADMINISTRATION

Youngah Guahk

53.1 Introduction

The Republic of Korea (hereafter Korea) is a relatively young democratic state which was established in 1948. After experiencing decades of authoritarian rule, Korea underwent a transition to democracy in 1987 with the creation of the Sixth Republic. The current political system of Korea is formed based on the constitutional revisions coming with this process of democratization (Heo & Roehrig 2010). The Korean political system is a presidential representative democracy in which the president – who is directly elected every five years – is both the head of state and the head of government.

The Korean political system establishes the separation of powers among the executive, legislature and judiciary branches. The National Assembly of the Republic of Korea is the unicameral legislature in this system. The composition of the 300 seats in the Korean National Assembly (hereafter KNA) is based on a mixed system of constituencies (253 seats) and a national proportional list (47 seats). The KNA has the power to propose and adopt on legislative bills, confirm the national budget for each fiscal year and conduct an annual inspection of the state administration in Korea (KNA no date).

As of 2021, there were 17 Standing Committees (Parliamentary Committees) in the KNA.[1] Each Standing Committee's responsibility is set out in the National Assembly Act (KLRI 1 2019). For example, the Legislation and Judiciary Standing Committee deals with matters under the jurisdiction of the Ministry of Justice, the Ministry of Government Legislation, the Board of Audit and Inspection as well as matters regarding the administrative affairs of the Constitutional Court, judicial administrative courts and military courts (Article 37 of National Assembly Act: KLRI 1 2019).

In general, legislative power in Korea is shared between the Assembly and the government. As a matter of fact, Korea is remarkable among representative democracies in that the majority of legislative initiatives originate from the legislature rather than the executive. For example, in the first year of the 21st KNA's term, between May 2020 and May 2021, the Korean government filed 2413 bills, while lawmakers filed 9093 bills (Citizen Participation Legislative Center 2021). In other words, in a period of less than 12 months, the 300 members of parliament filed more than 9000 bills, implying the degree to which elected members depend on the assistance of a capable parliamentary administration office.

53.2 The Organizational Structure of the KNA's Parliamentary Administration Offices

The KNA is supported by a number of offices as well as the staff assigned to the standing committees. With regard to the former, there are four organizational units supporting the KNA: the National Assembly Secretariat (hereafter Secretariat), the National Assembly Budget Office (NABO), the National Assembly Research Service (NARS) and the National Assembly Library (NAL). According to the organizational arrangement of the KNA, those four organizations are under the leadership of the Korean National Assembly Speaker, yet interestingly there is no hierarchy among these organizations which support the Assembly in various ways.

Each of the Standing Committees is assisted by a number of staff members. Under the Deputy Chiefs of Staff, they are on two folders, one is (head) specialists, who have a special knowledge of the committee jurisdiction so that they offer relevant services to the committee members. Specifically, the specialists conduct to review and report of the matters concerning legislative bills, budget bills and petitions (Article 9 of National Assembly Act: KLRI 1 2019). They also collect, investigate the materials and provide interpellation materials to the Standing Committee members (Kim & Ko 2013). There are also a number of public officials in the Standing Committee for the purpose of supporting the legislative activities.

It is important to point out that all of the Standing Committees' assisting staff members, specialists or the public officials are expected to maintain the political neutrality in performing their duties (Article 42.2 of National Assembly Act: KLRI 1 2019). Surely those staff members can continue to work at the committee where the head of Standing Committee can be switched from the liberal to conservative party member, based on the election result. The Deputy Chiefs of Staff of each Standing Committee are appointed by the KNA Speaker upon the recommendation of the Secretary General of the Secretariat (Article 42.3 of National Assembly Act: KLRI 1 2019).

The Deputy Chiefs of Staff coordinate the work on Standing Committees' reports, the collection of related materials, its investigations and studies, in connection with the scrutiny of bills, petitions, inspections and other matters under their jurisdiction. Furthermore, the Deputy Chiefs of Staff can demand the submission of materials necessary to carry out their duties from the administration, ministries and agencies. The request can be made in the name of the Committee chairperson with his or her permission (Article 42 of National Assembly Act: KLRI 1 2019).

The number of staff assigned to each Standing Committee varies there are, for example, 20 officials working for the Legislation and Judiciary Committee, 12 staff members for the Foreign Affairs and Unification Committee and just 6 civil servants for the National Defence Committee. This could be an indication of the relative importance of each standing committee or merely a reflection of the workload of the various committees' experiences in the past.

The assembly's Secretariat is the most long-standing organization, having been established together with the KNA from the beginning of the Republic of Korea in 1948. The National Assembly Secretariat supports its congressional activities, including the conduct of legislative and budget settlement reviews, and also handles its administrative affairs (Article 2 of National Assembly Act: KLRI 1 2019).

It is directed by a Secretary General who is appointed by the KNA Speaker with the approval of the majority members in a plenary session of the National Assembly after consultation with the representatives of the major political groups (Article 21 of National

Assembly Act: KLRI 1 2019). The Secretary General works under the supervision of the KNA Speaker, controls the affairs of the National Assembly and directs and supervises public officials working for the National Assembly Secretariat. The Secretary General is considered a political civil servant and receives a remuneration as a member of the cabinet, implying that this is a position comparable to the level of a minister (Article 4 of National Assembly Act: KLRI 1 2019).

Under the Secretary General, there are two Deputy Secretary Generals in charge of, respectively, Legislative Affairs legislative and Administrative Affairs (including such planning, budgeting, human resources, inter-parliamentary affairs, training, general services and public information). The Deputy Secretary Generals are also considered to be political officials, with a remuneration equivalent to that of a deputy minister (Article 5 of National Assembly Act: KLRI 1 2019).

The National Assembly Secretariat is responsible for several components, most importantly offering support for the parliamentary activities of the KNA. This includes assisting with the bill-related processes (budget and inspection and investigation of state administration, national policy appraisal etc.) and also assisting in the plenary sessions and Committee meetings. The National Assembly Secretariat is also involved in the broadcast and publicizes the proceedings of the KNA as well as supports the citizens' petitions. All these activities fall under the responsibility of the Deputy Secretary General for Legislative Affairs.

One should point out that the Legislative Counsel Office (LCO) is an important department in within the Division of Legislative Affairs of the National Assembly Secretariat. This office was created in 1989 as a legislation-supporting body to assist Assembly members' legislation activities. Over time, LCO office has been enlarged and as of 2021 includes ten divisions: Judicial, Administrative, Education-Science-ICT and Culture, Welfare and Gender Equality, Political Affairs and Environmental, Financial, Industry-Agriculture-Oceans and Fisheries, Land-Infrastructure and Transport, Legislative Research and Analysis (NAS no date).

Furthermore, the staff of the National Assembly Secretariat is tasked with training and educating public officials (Ahn et al 2004). The various training programmes covering legislative processes and the parliamentary system are intended for members and staff of local councils, school educators and the wider public. The National Assembly Secretariat also manages the security of the National Assembly buildings, provides welfare for its staff members and is responsible for the diplomatic activities of the KNA. The Deputy Secretary General for Administrative Affairs is managing the relevant offices of those activities (Article 2 of National Assembly Secretariat Act: KLRI 4 2018).

Lastly, there are a few offices which are directly supervised under the Secretary General. These are the Public Affairs (PA) Office and the Culture and Communication Office and Inspector General. Specially, the PA office is responsible for managing public relations, dealing with the press plan and supporting the media coverage of the Assembly. The Culture and Communication Office is handling the public promotion of the National Assembly's activities and policies through cultural events, manages a comprehensive plan for visits to the National Assembly and publishes the constitutional data (NAS no date).

Separate from the National Assembly Secretariat, all issues relating to the national budget are handled by the National Assembly Budget Office (NABO). This office was established in October 2003, as a fiscal scrutiny institution to support the activities of the legislative body (Article 22-2 of National Assembly Act: KLRI 1 2019). NABO focuses on research and analysis of budget bills, settlement of accounts, bills for fund operation and settlement of fund accounts. Furthermore, the office is analysing and assessing the costs of public projects and providing forecasting of macroeconomic trends. It ultimately aims to enhance the National Assembly's effectiveness in keeping the government in check and monitoring its use of public funds (NABO no date).

The National Assembly Research Service (NARS) was established on March 2007 as the research institution of the KNA (Article 22 of National Assembly Act; National Assembly Research Service Act: KLRI 1 2019; KLRI 3 2019). Broadly speaking, NARS supports lawmakers' legislative activities by conducting research and analysis on legislation and policy. NARS promises first, strict confidentiality regarding the research enquires and outcomes. This is an important issue due to the fact that it is still initial stage of the law-making process so the information may misuse among different interest groups. Second, non-partisanship, regardless of the lawmaker's political party affiliation, NARS will support and fulfil the lawmaker's request (NARS no date).

The National Assembly Library is established to administrate affairs concerning books and legislative materials of the KNA (Article 22 of National Assembly Act; National Assembly Library Act: KLRI 1 2019; KLRI 2 2016).

53.3 Professionalization and Staff Development

In South Korea, all public employment is guided by an open competition policy for recruitment and the relevant procedures and requirements are arranged through national laws. This also applies to the staff of the National Assembly. Public officials are ranked from level one, which is the equivalent of the ministerial level, and level nine that is a civil servant at the municipal bureau. Generally speaking, the public service levels five and above are considered to as high rank and only these can be promoted all the way up to level one (ministerial rank).

The Assembly has its separate public recruitment process, and the vacancies and the relevant information, such as exam procedures and methods, are published on their website (KNA n/d). Like those for other public positions, the Assembly open competition is also set in two different pillars, one for high ranks (level five) and one for low ranks (level eight and/or level nine). The low-rank public officials are selected by two rounds of selection procedure, compassed of a written test and a personal interview. Those lower rank officials may be promoted up to level five during their service. Level five public officials by contrast have to go through a three-round selection procedure containing two rounds of written exams followed by a personal interview. The officials, who have passed the national concours, are working in the Assembly and other branch organizations and can also be promoted and rotated within these organizations (State Public Officials Act: KLRI 5 2018).

There is also other type of vacancies, which are opened for a special position within the Assembly. For example, "(head) specialists" are recruited for the Parliamentary Committees, to provide special assistance based on their knowledge, past experiences and expertise. Those special positions are opened when it is necessary and involve an open competition like other public official's positions yet without the regular written exams. On the whole, the national law on the public officials' regulation determines the selection procedure, the rules of promotion and also the ethical behavioural codes (Code of Conduct of the National Assembly Official Act).

Due to the nature of their work, to assist the Assembly and the lawmakers, the National Assembly Secretariat and the other Assembly offices occasionally open a call for particular research projects. The research can be on various topics that are required information related to the drafting of a bill. The calls are open to the public and the selection result and the final research papers are also accessible to citizens (NAS no date).

53.4 The Role of the Administration in the Context of Parliamentary Work

The Legislative Counsel Office (LCO) offers substantive assistance to the motions and bills proposed by lawmakers. When an MP wants to advance a motion, he or she needs to file and application form with the office. The LCO division officials are going through the analysis of the purpose and contents of the bill and examine the relevant existing legislative policies. After that, the LCO prepares a preliminary draft and will consult with other external bodies such as government agencies, interest groups and relevant experts. The preliminary draft is reviewed and revised according to the bill drafting standards considering the object of the proposition, the relation with existing statues, the legality and the wording. Those reviews are done by several layers, by the LCO division officials, by the head of the divisions, the legislation counsels and finally the Director General of the LCO. After the review process, the LCO transfers the bill to the MP(s) (NAS no date).

In this regard, one of the critical concerns – discussed in more detail below – is the increasing workload of the LCO. In the 18th KNA, for example, lawmakers made applications for just over 7,000 motion bills to the LCO, and this number massively increased further to more than 20,000 bills in the 19th KNA (Jeong 2015: 110).

The Assembly is actively communicating with the citizens and has opened their parliamentary activities to the public through the traditional media. There is a public assembly broadcasting company which has been set up to meet the interests and rights of the public. The broadcast is on-air for 24 hours a day covering either parliamentary activity *live* and or presenting other reports on legislature procedures as well as cultural and arts programmes. The Assembly's broadcasting channel can be viewed on TV and on YouTube. The KNA is also actively seeking to engage with citizens via social media channels such as Facebook and Twitter. Furthermore, the Assembly Broadcasting company is also communicating with citizens on Assembly matters via an official blog and its Instagram, Kakao TV and KaKaoTalk (Korean equivalent of WhatsApp) channels (NATV no date).

53.5 Nature of Institutional Hierarchy in the Administration of the KNA

The Assembly's four support organizations discussed above all operate under the KNA Speaker's leadership, with no hierarchy among them. However, there are some differences among those organizations that are worth mentioning. First of all, the National Assembly Secretariat is the largest organization by the number of hired public officials and also consumes the highest portion of the annual budget among those bodies. Second, the heads of the various offices are not exactly of the same status in their respective positions. For example, the Secretary General of National Assembly Secretariat is equivalent to the minister level, whereas the Chiefs of NARS, NABO and NAL are equivalent to the vice-minister level. Third, reviewing the profiles of the heads of each organization, one can conclude that some of positions are closer to a political office rather than having a purely high-level public bureaucrat background.

The nature of the appointees to the position of Secretary General of the National Assembly Secretariat, in particular, is evidence of this. Since 1988, political practice has been to appoint as Secretary Generals former MPs, many of whom later again took up their mandate as assembly member after their term ended. For example, the 35th Secretary General Lee Choon Suak (appointed in 2021) had been an elected member of the 18th, 19th and 20th KNA.

Furthermore, it is noticeable that the term of Secretary Generals tends to be relatively short. Former Secretary General Kim Young-Choon, for example, resigned from the position only six months after his appointment, due to his candidacy for the mayoral bye-election in the city of Busan which was held in April 2021. Coincidentally, in this election he was standing against – and lost to – Park Heong-joon, who had previously also served as Secretary General from September 2014 to June 2016. Looking at these patterns, we can say that an appointment as Secretary General plays an uncertain role in political careers: while sometimes functioning like a stepping stone towards (or a placeholder until) another elected mandate, on other occasions, it is also the final office prior to retirement.

In addition, it is apparent that the appointed Secretary Generals come from same political party as the KNA Speaker, despite the fact that the Korean law prevents the political party affiliation of the Secretary General. The Korean State Public Officials Act states that "*No public official may participate in an organization of, or join in, any political party or other political organization*" (Article 65.1: KLRI 5 2018). However, the legal prohibition is being circumvented in that appointed as the Secretary General is suspending membership political party in order to satisfy the formal demand of political neutrality of public officials. Consequently, as the Busan mayoral by-election in April 2021 mentioned above shows, former Secretary Generals then re-join their previous political party once they end their term of office at the National Assembly Secretariat.

In assessing the practice of appointing career politicians to this position, one can arrive at a mixed picture: on the one hand, the role requires in-depth knowledge of the nature of the KNA's work, its procedures, working culture and legal processes, which is why a former career of being elected member of the Assembly may be helpful. On the other hand, however, the political appointments and the constant change of the leadership of the National Assembly Secretariat are bound to have a negative impact on the smooth running of the institute and the continuity of its work.

53.6 The Management of the KNA's External Relations

On the whole, the KNA is actively engaging and promoting inter-parliamentary cooperation and friendship with other parliaments. There is an open invitation to hold talks between parliamentary leaders, meet with Speakers of other parliaments abroad and also organize visits to industrial facilities and historical sites. The KNA Speaker and other delegation members of the KNA also infrequently visit other countries to conduct research and gather relevant information on the jurisdiction of their respective area. In the 20th Assembly, four inter-parliamentary councils were established with the US, China, Russia and the EU and 112 Parliamentary Friendship Groups were formed with other countries to exchange cooperation in politics, economics, society and culture. Lastly, the bilateral parliamentary cooperation protocol was signed between South Korea and China in 2006, since then the two parliaments are holding joint meetings on the regular basis (KNA no date).

The National Assembly Secretariat is offering administrative support for the Assembly members' diplomatic activities, including official visits of foreign dignitaries to the KNA, arranging talks with Korean parliamentary or governmental officials and visits to industrial facilities and/or historical sites. An official invitation is extended when parliament-level exchanges occur, Parliamentary Friendship Group meetings are held or visits are being proposed by the Ministry of Foreign Affairs (NAS no date).

53.7 Managing Current Challenges Facing the Parliamentary Administration Offices

In the early 2020s, the KNA is facing a number of challenges. In particular, attention should be focused on digitalization, the rising demand of transparency and citizen access and the rapidly increasing workload for the administration arising from the growing number of legislative proposals.

With regard to the first point, the approach adopted by the administration of the KNA is best understood in the context of the wider domestic developments in the country. South Korea has established itself over the past two decades as one of the leading worldwide countries regarding the digitalization of the public service. E-governance system has been introduced and applied throughout the governments since early 2000s. The Korean system has been well recognized and received several international awards for their efforts such as, for example, the UN Public Service Award in 2007 and the E-Challenge Award in 2008. In 2006, Korea's online tax system was recognized as one of the best practices of E-government system, according to OECD. Since 2010, Korea has been ranked consistently as the top country in the UN E-government survey, an index that combines three essential dimensions of E-governance: the provision of on-line services, telecommunication connectivity and human capacity (Beschel Jr, Kim, & Choi, 2016). South Korea was ranked first in the "Open, Useful, Reusable Government Data Index" (OUR data Index) in 2015 (OECD 2015). This index evaluates the level of availability and accessibility of government data through a national portal; also, the level of government support for the reuse of these data for creating public value.

Korea's E-government system progressed through four different stages starting from the 1980s. The digitization of national key databases, including citizen registration and vehicle registration, began in this first stage. In the second stage, the Korean government established a nationwide broadband network. The Korean E-government 1.0 was launched in 2003 included a home tax service and the public service available around the clock. This development continued, and in 2013, the E-government 3.0 initiative was launched which focused on big data for the creative economy and ICT-enabled growth and jobs. Korea's E-government system was initiated for two reasons; first, focus on achieving efficiency and transparency in government, and, second, it was national strategy to use technology to shift the economic paradigm from an industrial manufacturing economy to that of a knowledge-based economy and information society (ibid 2016: 5).

As the OECD has indicated, Korean public administration has been opening up and sharing government-owned data with the public while also encouraging communication and collaboration among government departments. This data is labelled "OPEN", containing all the relevant public information from various governments, ministries and agencies (OECD 2015). Furthermore, citizens can request a specific governmental document of public interests if it is not already publicly available. Such requests are made through a digital platform via the official government's website: www.open.go.kr. The request must receive a response from the central or local governments within 30 days. The authorities only have the right to deny such requests in cases when documents contain personal information, if the document could influence any future policy decision or if it might have negative implications for a particular individual or group. However, Korean governmental administrative records only have a lifespan of three, five or ten years, depending on the importance of the contents, and are destroyed after that period.

The KNA also follows the executive's open policy and releases all relevant parliamentary information and legal documents generated by the Assembly. Those documents are available digitally on Assembly website: https://open.assembly.go.kr. Citizens can also request other relevant information from the Assembly that should be public knowledge. For example, in January 2020, a request was made for the information of the number of female officials employed in the National Assembly Secretariat, and the data is now available to the public in the excel file or chart.

One of the critical challenges facing the National Assembly Secretariat is the exponentially increasing number of bill motions in the Assembly (Jeong 2015). As shown in Figure 53.1, the KNA bills statistics since 13th National Assembly indicate that there is significant increase in the number of bills introduced in the Assembly, from 1,439 bills for the period 1988–1992 it rose to more than 13 times that figure in the period 2012–2016. Considering the fact that the bill numbers indicate only formally introduced one, which means there should be larger number of bill applications to LCO.

In addition, there is also the problem of a large number of abolished bills due to the end of each Assembly term. In the 13th Assembly, the rate of abolished bill was 11.2%, which could be considered a relatively small number. However, this number increased to 17.8% for the 15th Assembly and to 25.9% for the 16th Assembly, and then further to 39.9% (17th Assembly), and 43.9% (18th Assembly) until reaching 53.6% for the 19th Assembly. It means that the time devoted to preparing the bills was effectively wasted and the work and time devoted by the Assembly staff was ultimately futile. This is by now a well-recognized trend, and a number of Korean scholars already expressed their concerns about this issue, indicating that this might require a change of practice or actual reform in order to make legislative work sustainable (Kim 2014; Jeong 2015).

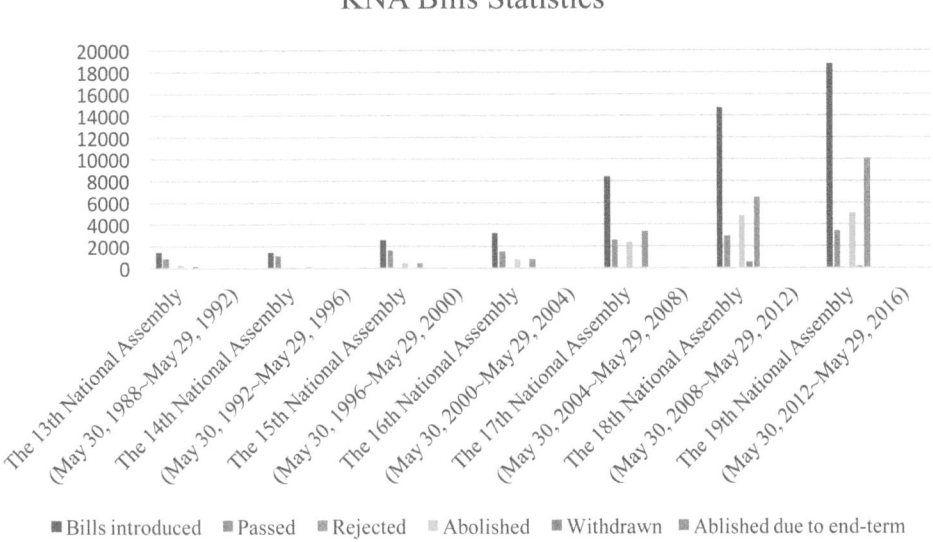

Figure 53.1 Korean Assembly bills statistics

Author created the figure based on the Assembly bills statistics information on KNA website

53.8 The Impact of COVID in KNA Since January 2020

From a global perspective, South Korea has dealt comparatively well with the COVID-19 pandemic. Initially, when the virus first appeared in neighbouring China, the Korean authorities acted quickly to prevent the spread. Experts observed that Korean policymakers had learnt lessons from MERS outbreak in 2015 and had since made numerous policy-reforms to boost the capacity of responding to a public health emergency. Thus, when the COVID virus broke out the in early 2020, key government bodies in South Korea, such as the President's Office, the Ministry for Health and Welfare, the Ministry of Foreign Affairs and the Korea Disease Control and Prevention Agency (KDCA), were able to respond promptly to the emerging crisis (Kim et al 2021).

By early 2022, there were in total just over 700.000 cases and 6,378 total deaths in South Korea (WHO no date) – a very low figure compared to other industrialized countries. Pursuing a "zero Covid policy", there was no country-wide lockdown in South Korean society between 20th January 2020 and 18th January, 2022. Instead, the central government introduced a social distancing policy comprising four different levels. In a nutshell, this policy limited the opening hours of business premises and the maximum number of people that could get together (KDCA no date).

In line with this zero Covid policy, and the success in minimizing the spread of the virus in the community, the Korean National Assembly (KNA) managed to continue more or less with "business as usual". Certainly, the usual COVID preventative measures were established: wearing the face mask in the premises at all times, setting up prevention shields between the seats in the Plenary and the Committee rooms and limiting the maximum number of participants in the various meetings. Overall, one can say that the KNA was operating in-person throughout the pandemic with these strict COVID prevention measures. Exceptions were made only twice due to visits to the Assembly premises by someone identified as positively infected. On these occasions, KNA buildings were partially closed for disinfection for 24 hours. Individual members of parliament also organized legislative debates and public hearings which were held online as well as the offline. In case of offline events, organizers followed the rule regarding the maximum capacity, and the online meetings were live-streamed via the KNA TV broadcast (NAON no date).

However, it is worth noting that in early 2022 the facilities for home office work were not checkedbeen fully established in the KPA offices. The KNA Speaker had encouraged the administrative staff to work remotely in August 2020. However, the IT system of KNA is not fully accessible externally due to national security provisions, some tasks had to be completed from the Assembly premises. This involves, for instance, the management of file for a joint motion bill (Choi 2020). This issue was eventually solved, and the Parliamentary Administration Office launched the VIVA-NA System Construction Project in October 2021, allowing the administrative staff to fully access the KNA IT system from the distance. This new system was expected to be fully functioning as of April 2022 (Bak 2021).

53.9 Conclusion

The discussion in this chapter has demonstrated that the KNA is supported by a well-organized structure composed of four major organizational units as well as the staff assigned to the 17 standing committees. Even if the KNA operates in the context of a presidential political system that gives priority to the role of the executive branch, the assembly has

Korea's Parliamentary Administration

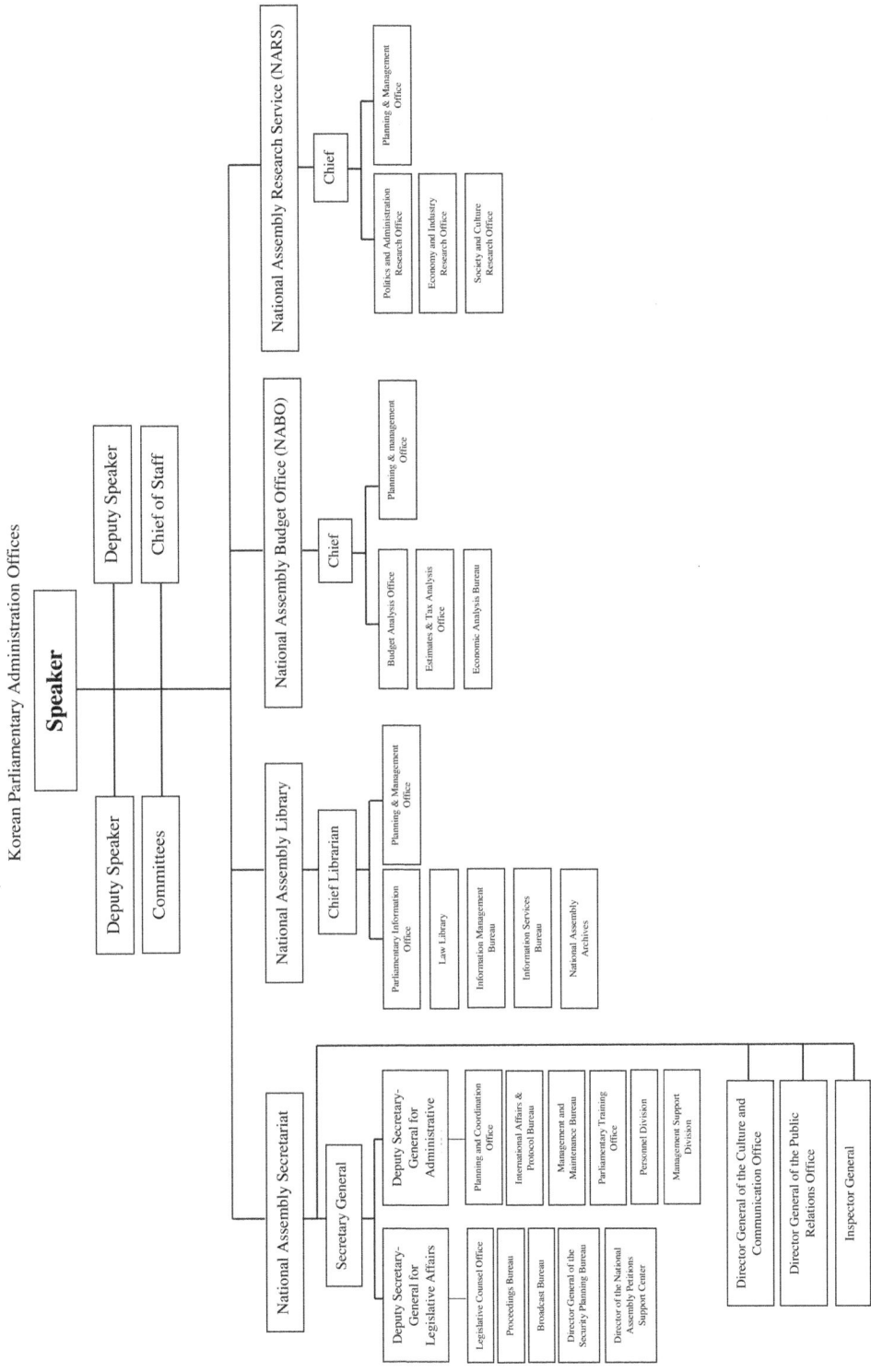

played an important role in the context of passing laws, adopting the national budget and scrutinizing the government – all tasks that require significant administrative report.

Consequently, the parliamentary administration offices have grown over time, in recognition of the greater number of tasks that it is responsible for, and above all the more important role that the national assembly has acquired in the period since democratization in the 1980s. However, as the previous section demonstrated, there are concerns that the rapidly increasing number of bill motions coming from individual members puts severe strains on the capacity of the administration. The fact that more than 50% of proposed bills were not ultimately voted upon is further evidence of a potentially unsustainable trend.

Finally, we observed that during the global pandemic, COVID-related issues were also well managed at the KNA administration, and that officials after some delays were enabled to carry out their duties remotely from home as of April 2022. However, the Assembly continued to function and facilitate meetings and the work of elected members throughout the pandemic, with comparatively little disruption compared to other advanced democracies.

Note

1 As of 2021, the KNA was composed of the following committees: House Steering, Legislation and Judiciary, National Policy, Strategy and Finance, Education, National Defense, Science-ICT-Broadcasting and Communications, Foreign Affairs and Unification, Public Administration and Security, Culture-Sports and Tourism, Agriculture-Food-Rural Affairs-Oceans and Fisheries, Trade-Industry-Energy-SMEs and Startups, Health and Welfare, Environment and Labor, Land-Infrastructure and Transport, Intelligence and Gender Equality and Family Committee.

References

Ahn, Hyung-Ki, Min, Jin, Kwon, Kyungdeuk & Yim, Dong-Wook (2004), "A Study on the Strategy to Improve Core Competencies of the Korea National Assembly Secretariat", Journal of Korean Society and Public Administration, No.15, Vol.1, pp.71–94.

Bak, Jun-gyu (November 2021), Newspaper Nailshinmun, "The National Assembly opens the 'digital age'… 'Telecommuting system' to be implemented next year *(Gughoe 'dijiteolsidae' yeonda … 'jaetaeggeunmusiseutem' naenyeon sihaeng)*, article published on 19/11/2021, last assessed on 19/01/2022, available at: http://m.naeil.com/m_news_view.php?id_art=405438

Beschel Jr, Robert, Kim, Soonhee & Choi, Changyong (2016), "Digital Government in Developing Countries: Reflections on the Korean Experience", Chapter one in edited book of Bringing Government into 21 Century – The Korean Digital Governance Experience, World Bank, NY.

Choi, Hyungchang (August 2020), Newspaper Segyeilbo, "Despite the recommendation to work from home… National Assembly system that cannot be 'at home *(Jaetaeggeunmu gwongo-edo… 'Jaetaeg' moshaneun gughoesiseutem)*', article published on 26/08/2020, last assessed on 19/01/2022, available at: http://m.segye.com/view/20200826521533

Citizen Participation Legislative Center (2021), *Legislative Progress Report*, available at https://opinion.lawmaking.go.kr/gcom/gcomMain

Heo, Ok & Roehrig, Terence (2010), South Korea Since 1980, Oxford University Press, New York.

Jeong, Kuk-won (2015), "An Efficient Support Organization for Increasing Legislations by the National Assembly", Public Law Journal, Vol. 2, pp. 109–134.

KDCA (no date), Korea Disease Control and Prevention Agency, "Overview of Social Distancing System - Key Points of the Revised Social Distancing Plan", last assessed on 19/01/2022, available at: http://ncov.mohw.go.kr/en/socdisBoardView.do?brdId=19&brdGubun=191&dataGubun=191&ncvContSeq=&contSeq=&board_id=

Kim, Dong Won & Ko, Myeon Chul (2013), "A Study on the Professionalism of Legislative Bureaucrats: The Case of Committee Staff Directors in the Standing Committees of the National Assembly", Journal of Korean Society and Public Administration, Vol. 24, No.1, pp. 29–50.

Kim, June-Ho et al (March 2021), "Emerging COVID-19 success story: South Korea learned the lessons of MERS", Exemplars in Global Health platform, last assessed on 19/01/2022, available at https://ourworldindata.org/covid-exemplar-south-korea

Kim, Tae Yoon (2014), "Legislative Branch and Regulatory Reform -About the Problems of Korean Regulatory Legislation Focusing on the Search for Institutional Improvement Plans- *(Ibbeobbuwa Gyujegaehyeog -Ulinala Gyujeibbeobui Munjejeome Daehan Jedojeog Gaeseonbanganui Mosaegeul Jungsimeulo-)*", Journal of Regulatory Studies, Vol. 23, September, pp. 69–114.

KLRI 1 (2019), Statutes of Republic of Korea, Korean Legislation Research Institute (KLRI), "National Assembly Act", Act No 16325, Last amended on 16/04/2019, last assessed on 01/04/2021, available at: https://elaw.klri.re.kr/eng_service/lawView.do?hseq=25732&lang=ENG

KLRI 2 (2016), Statutes of Republic of Korea, Korean Legislation Research Institute (KLRI), "National Assembly Library Act", Act No 14375, last amended on 16/12/2016, last assessed on 25/04/2021, available at: https://elaw.klri.re.kr/kor_service/lawView.do?hseq=40615&lang=ENG

KLRI 3 (2019), Statutes of Republic of Korea, Korean Legislation Research Institute (KLRI), "National Assembly Research Service Act", Act No 16327, Last amended 16/04/2019, last assessed on 25/04/2021, available at: https://elaw.klri.re.kr/eng_service/lawView.do?hseq=50740&lang=ENG

KLRI 4 (2018), Statutes of Republic of Korea, Korean Legislation Research Institute (KLRI), "National Assembly Secretariat Act", Act No. 15710, last amended on 12/06/2018, last assessed on 07/04/2021, available at: https://elaw.klri.re.kr/kor_service/lawView.do?hseq=48573&lang=ENG

KLRI 5 (2018), Statutes of Republic of Korea, Korean Legislation Research Institute (KLRI), "State Public Officials Act", Act No. 15857, last amended on 16/10/2018, last assessed on 28/04/2021, available at: https://elaw.klri.re.kr/kor_service/lawView.do?hseq=49778&lang=ENG

KNA (no date), National Assembly of the Republic of Korea, last assessed 15/04/2021, available at: https://korea.assembly.go.kr:447/int/org_06.jsp

NABO (no date), National Assembly Budget Office, last assessed on 28/04/2021, available at: https://korea.nabo.go.kr

NAON (no date), National Assembly News On, last assessed on 18/01/2022, available at: http://www.naon.go.kr/search/searchList/addIns.do?query=코비드

NARS (no date), National Assembly Research Service, last assessed on 28/04/2021, available at: https://www.nars.go.kr/eng/intro/researchServices.do

NAS (no date), National Assembly Secretariat of Republic of Korea, last assessed 15/04/2021, available at: https://korea.assembly.go.kr:447/secretary/

NATV (no date), National Assembly Television, last assessed on 25/04/2021, available at: https://www.natv.go.kr/natv/main.do

OECD (2015), Government at a Glance 2015, last assessed on 24/04/2021, available at: https://www.oecd.org/gov/Korea.pdf

WHO (no date), World Health Organization, WHO Coronavirus (COVID-19) Dashboard, last assessed on 19/01/2022, available at: https://covid19.who.int

54
MEXICO'S PARLIAMENTARY ADMINISTRATION

Fernando Nieto-Morales

54.1 Introduction

The Mexican Congress (formally the General Congress of the United Mexican States) is the country's national legislature. It comprises a lower chamber, the Chamber of Deputies *(Cámara de Diputados)*, and an upper chamber, the Senate of the Republic *(Senado de la República)*. As in other Latin American countries, the configuration and the constitutional role of Congress are based, on the one hand, on the Constitution of the United States and, on the other, a set of norms and principles from the Continental tradition, in particular, French constitutional law (Zamora and Cossío, 2006). Formally, the 1917 Mexican Constitution subscribes to the theory of the separation of powers. However, in practice and throughout most of the 20th century, Mexican politics were characterized by an authoritarian regime consisting of a powerful executive branch with low levels of accountability. Further, a dominant-party system exerted extensive control over the national legislature, the judicial system, and state and local governments (Ugalde, 2000; Loaeza, 2001).

Beginning in the 1990s, the Mexican Congress experienced an ongoing institutionalization in the sense of a movement towards differentiation and independence from other political actors and organizations (Judge, 2003). Institutionalization is crucial because it relates to performing functions with greater competence and independence (Puente Martínez, 2017). The institutionalization process of the Mexican Congress directly results from the country's transition to democracy and the crisis of the dominant-party system from the mid-1990s to 2018. Unlike other democratization trajectories, the breakdown of the authoritarian regime in Mexico was an incremental process marked by successive constitutional and electoral reforms, transactional concessions, and the paced introduction of political pluralism into the political system—mainly as a result of the fracture of local and national elites (Lujambio, 2000; Loaeza, 2001; Merino, 2003; Klesner, 2005). These circumstances gradually developed congressional autonomy, including increased leeway for exercising regulatory and oversight capacities. Thus, as Ugalde (2000) argued, studying the Mexican Congress was once considered an irrelevant undertaking; however, it is now fundamental for understanding the dynamics of present-day Mexican politics.

A crucial aspect of the institutionalization process of the Mexican Congress is the gradual acquisition and expansion of congressional capacity. This is related to increased adaptability, autonomy, and internal complexity and coherence of both chambers of Congress (cf. Huntington, 1996). There are indications that Mexican parliamentarians are becoming more professionalized and resourceful, thus making them more independent from the executive branch (Puente Martínez, 2018). Increased professionalization and empowerment relate to internal administrative capacities, including developing a parliamentary bureaucracy and supportive services and processes (see, e.g., Hix & Høyland, 2013). However, this aspect has received only marginal scholarly attention. Most studies on the Mexican Congress focus on the parliamentarians themselves, the political dynamics within legislative processes (such as budgeting), or the relation with other political and social institutions and organizations.

Nevertheless, both chambers of the Mexican Congress have developed particular administrative structures, processes, and staff. Generally speaking, parliamentary administration in Mexico consists of a secretariat and the parliamentary civil service. These perform most of the core administrative tasks and staff some specialized and supporting agencies with different levels of autonomy that provide expert analyses and information services.

The main argument of this chapter is that the current characteristics of the parliamentary administration are the product of the ongoing institutionalization of the Mexican Congress. That is, key attributes and roles of the administration that have developed over the last decade or so—including a dramatic growth of its organizational complexity, size, and functions—are, at least in part, the product of a process leading to the consolidation of autonomous legislative and oversight capacities of Congress. Accordingly, this chapter presents critical aspects of the administration of the Mexican Congress, its role in legislative processes, and some crucial challenges. Most of the chapter describes the structure and management of the secretariats, the parliamentary civil service, specialized agencies, and their roles in the functioning of the legislature. It should be noted that, as in other bicameral systems, differences exist between the administration of the lower and upper chambers in terms of both organization and management.

The chapter is organized as follows: The following section describes the organization of parliamentary administration of the Chamber of Deputies and the Senate of the Republic. Next, the role of administration in core legislative tasks and processes is described, followed by a section on the management of the bicameral relation. The subsequent section outlines current challenges for parliamentary administration, and the last section concludes with a general overview and reflection.

54.2 Critical Aspects of the Organization of Parliamentary Administration

The Conference for the Direction and Programming of Legislative Work (CDPLW) is the chief authority responsible for administering the lower chamber. It is a statutory governing body comprised the president of the Chamber of Deputies and the chairpersons of all political groups represented in the chamber. In the case of the Senate, all administrative departments, both executive and auxiliary, answer directly to the Presiding Board. Additionally, a Commission of Administration formed by up to 15 senators oversees the organization of the secretariats and supervises administrative programmes. The president and vice-presidents of the Senate are not allowed to participate in this commission. The CDPLW, the Presiding Board, and Commission of Administration of the Senate establish internal policies, issue general administrative guidelines, and formulate the annual budget proposal of their respective chamber.

Secretariats constitute the central part of the parliamentary administration in both the Chamber of Deputies and the Senate. The Secretariats are in charge of providing parliamentary services, as well as managing core administrative processes. In the case of the Chamber of Deputies, a single Secretary-General performs these functions. In the Senate, a Secretary-General of Parliamentary Services and a Secretary-General of Administrative Services divide these responsibilities. In both cases, however, the core functions of these bodies are similar. Parliamentary services generally consist in providing internal services to the chamber. This includes keeping the registry of accords and votes, managing the parliamentary archive, providing support during the chamber sessions, and providing legal and expert counsel to the president, the Board, and the members of the chamber (including parliamentary committees and commissions). Administrative services encompass human resources, material resources, financial management, technical and legal services, facility management, security, and medical assistance.

The Secretary-General is a public servant (although not necessarily a member of the parliamentary civil service) and the chief executive officer of the Chamber of Deputies. The CDPLW proposes her appointment, and a two-thirds majority of the chamber elects her. Her primary responsibilities are: to provide the necessary conditions for the chamber's sessions, participate as secretary of the CDPLW, supervise the secretariats of parliamentary services and financial and administrative services, supervise the implementation of all administrative policies, develop an annual administration programme, and advise and inform the CDPLW about the performance of all administrative units. In addition, the Secretary-General has overall responsibility for staffing and expenditure of the two secretariats (parliamentary services and financial and administrative services) and management and development of the parliamentary civil service through the Unit for Permanent Training and Education. In total, the administration of the Chamber of Deputies comprises just over 2,400 public servants (47% women in 2021), divided among administrative departments and specialized units. Specialized units of the Chamber of Deputies, such as congressional libraries and research centres, report directly to the Secretary-General (except for the Internal Comptroller Office, which is directly accountable to the CDPLW). Figure 54.1 shows the overall organizational chart of the chamber.

A simple majority elects both the Secretary-General of Parliamentary Services and the Secretary-General of Administrative Services for the Senate. They are public servants and may not be part of the Senate's parliamentary civil service. They answer to the Presiding Board of the Senate, which also proposes their appointment and removal. This is also the case for the heads of specialized units such as the Technical Unit for Gender Equality, the Belisario Dominguez Research Institute,[1] the Gilberto Bosques Centre for International Studies,[2] the Senate Comptroller, as well as the training, communications, and transparency units. The Secretary-General of Parliamentary Services is responsible for assisting the President and the Presiding Board during the sessions of the Senate, for documental and archive management, technical and legislative consultation, and assisting parliamentary commissions and committees. This Secretariat employs 120 public servants, most of whom belong to the parliamentary civil service of the Senate. The Secretary-General of Administrative Services manages administrative services, labour relations, material resources, and facility management. Additionally, she is responsible for the Senate Treasury. In total, 525 public servants work in this Secretariat. Specialized and autonomous units employ another 213 workers, although most are not tenured and do not necessarily belong to the parliamentary civil service. In these cases, appointments can be purely political. Figure 54.2 shows the organizational chart of the Senate.

Mexico's Parliamentary Administration

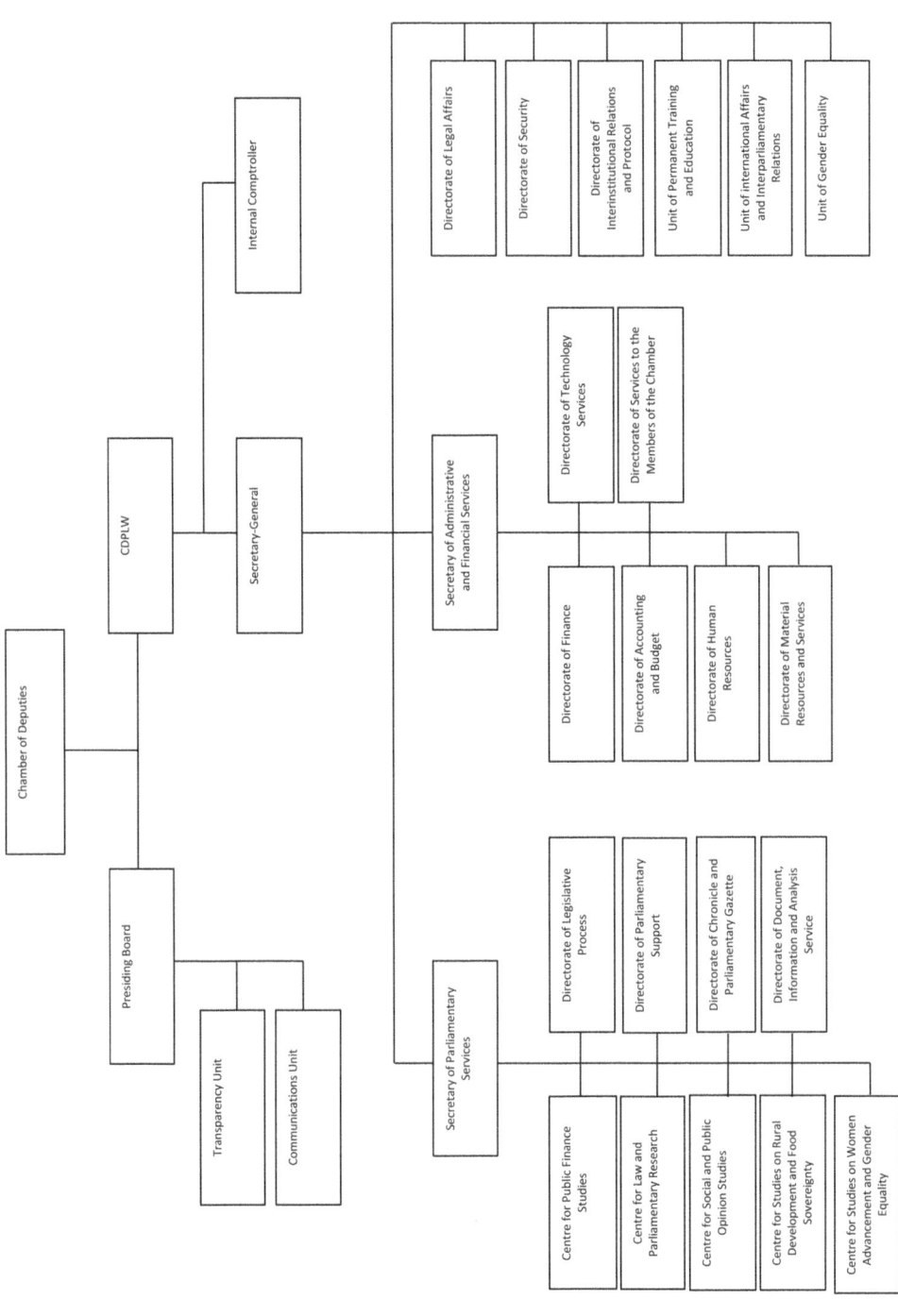

Figure 54.1 Organizational chart of the administration of the Mexican Chamber of Deputies

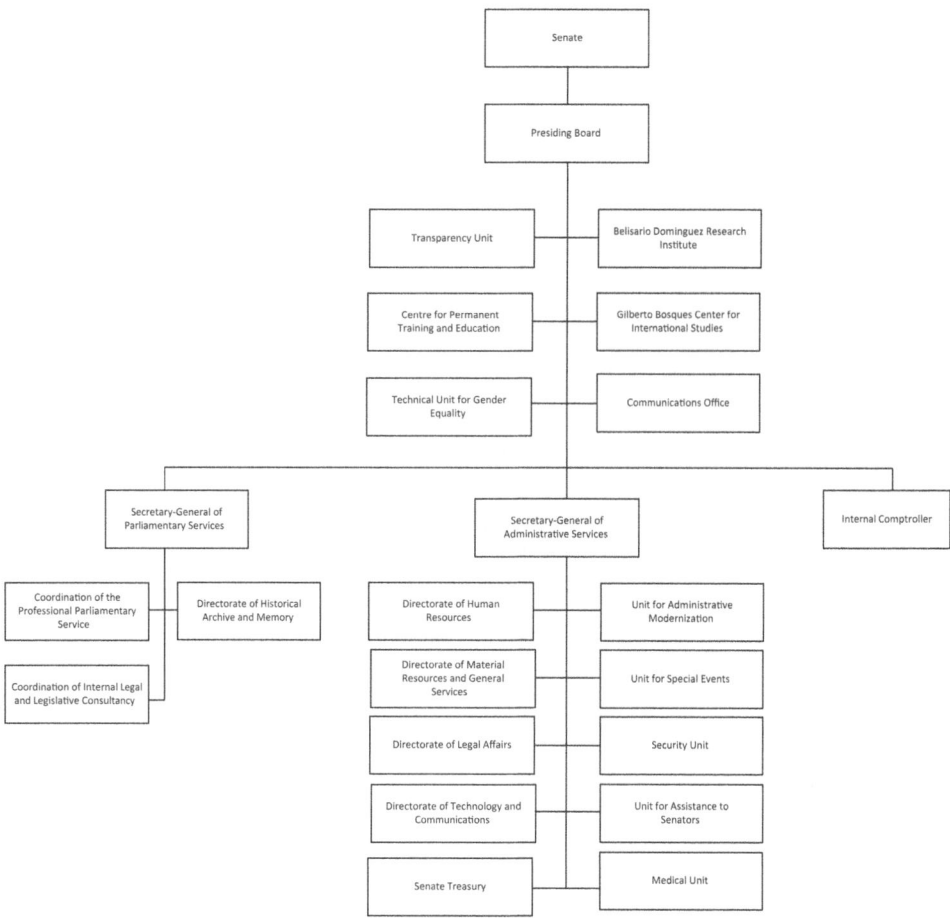

Figure 54.2 Organizational chart of the administration of the Mexican Senate

There are some critical differences between the administrative organization of the Chamber of Deputies and the Senate. First, the administration of the lower chamber is larger and more structurally complex (cf. Copeland & Patterson, 1994). It comprises more administrative departments and personnel, and the role played by the Secretary-General is more salient and autonomous from the Board. Second, whereas the administration of the Chamber of Deputies lays upon in a (single) secretariat overseen by a special commission, the administration of the Senate is primarily the responsibility of the Presiding Board. It directly oversees the secretariats (albeit with the intervention of the Commission of Administration). Third, there is a difference in the structural niche occupied by specialized and supportive agencies. In the lower chamber, most specialized units fall within the purview of the Secretary of Parliamentary Services and, thereby, of the Secretary-General. By contrast, in the Senate, most of these units are directly accountable to the Presiding Board and are formally independent of the secretariats. They may not necessarily be staffed with members of the parliamentary service, as they may also employ political appointees.

The current organizational structure of both chambers is the result of changes implemented mainly in the last 15 years, which coincide with the more active role played by Congress after democratization. Most significant reorganizations date from the mid-2010s. The general tendency of these changes has been to increase organizational size and complexity. The previous entailed creating new units and departments, expanding personnel, and increasing the proportion of positions reserved for the parliamentary civil service. For instance, a new General Administrative Manual for the Chamber of Deputies introduced in 2011 created several new departments and expanded the responsibilities and powers of the Secretary-General (e.g., by creating a unit for international and interparliamentary relations and a unit for gender equality). Furthermore, the professional parliamentary service administration was entrusted to a specialized department (Unit for Permanent Training and Education). A series of additional reorganizations led to an expansion of the administrative positions of about 24% in the last nine years.

Finally, the parliamentary civil service increasingly plays a significant role in the administration of both chambers of the Mexican Congress. Although formally established in 1999, the parliamentary civil service was largely overlooked, particularly in the lower chamber. In the Senate, the Statue for the Civil Service of the Senate of the Republic was adopted in 2002. A year later, the Unit for Permanent Training and Education began operations. The first civil service appointments of the Senate were issued in 2005. In the Chamber of Deputies, similar attempts were made in the early 2000s, but no actual procedures or organization existed for almost 20 years. On the initiative of the Secretary-General, changes in structure led to implementing the first civil service of the lower chamber in 2019.

Although there is no space here to go into the details of both services, it suffices to say that they share characteristics regarding recruitment, promotion, and opportunities for the training and development of civil servants. For both services, personnel recruitment uses examinations—either open to all applicants or limited to current employees who wish to join the service—and parliamentary civil servants must comply with permanent training and evaluation programmes. Also, they enjoy a specific scheme of promotions and incentives for good performance. In both chambers, members of the service work in both parliamentary services and administrative functions. The parliamentary service is explicitly divided into two branches in the lower chamber: one dedicated to parliamentary support and research and another dedicated to administration. Employees in the former branch provide parliamentarians and parliamentary bodies with expert advice and analyses on several sectors, including national and public security, social and economic development, legal counsel, international relations, and public finance.

54.3 The Role of Parliamentary Administration

The core function of the secretariats, the specialized units, and the parliamentary civil service is to assist parliamentary work. In doing so, parliamentary administrative bodies perform a wide-ranging set of tasks from, for instance, information and documental management, publishing services, infrastructure, facility management, assisting parliamentary groups, as well as managing and executing internal budgets. Some of these tasks are directly related to the decision-making processes of the legislature, such as assisting the governing bodies of Congress and providing expert and legal analyses to commissions and parliamentarians throughout the law-making process. More generally, administration activities can be divided into four groups: (a) counsel and assistance to the assembly and governing bodies, (b) counsel and assistance to parliamentary groups, (c) assistance to parliamentary commissions and committees, and (d) general administration of the chamber.

The first role of bodies that make up Congress Administration involves coordination and provision of parliamentary services before, during, and after sessions of Congress. This includes assisting and counselling the respective Board of each Chamber, statutory governing bodies (such as the Political Coordination Board[3] of each Chamber or the CDPLW in the Chamber of Deputies), as well as the Permanent Commission of Congress.[4] This coordination role entails several specific responsibilities. These include preparing and circulating documentation regarding the issues to be discussed during sessions, producing the Parliamentary Gazette, and collecting documentation to be included in the Diary of Debates. It also involves managing information and the registry of issues referred to the Board, governing bodies, and parliamentary commissions, including law proposals, technical opinions, accords, and decrees. Another essential function involves providing technical analysis and support during plenary debates, such as assisting in case of legal controversies, providing statistical information or evidence on an issue under discussion, or preparing reports on different legislative processes and products. Parliamentary administration is also in charge of receiving documentation and managing information from local congresses (e.g., during constitutional reforms) and handling interparliamentary and bicameral relations (see below). In both chambers of the Mexican Congress, congressional relations with the media are directly managed by the Board. However, the website of Congress and the management of the digital congressional repository are the secretariats' responsibilities.

The second role of parliamentary administrative bodies entails technical counsel and assistance to parliamentary groups. Eight political groups (and a small number of independent parliamentarians) were represented in the Chamber of Deputies and the Senate in 2020. Although each group has its specific administration and staff, it falls under the purview of parliamentary administration to provide information and documentation services to all political groups. Administration may also assist political groups with legal and expert analysis, particularly during law drafting and budget analysis. In addition, the parliamentary administration keeps permanent communication with the administrative liaisons from each political party. It is also in charge of checking and registering the legislative agendas presented by each party at the beginning of each legislative period.

Regarding assistance to parliamentary commissions and committees, the secretariats and specialized units such as research centres regularly aid in drafting laws, accords, and other legislative outputs (e.g., analysis of the national budget or the analysis of annual government report issued by the executive). Specific tasks in this role include internal consultancy services such as research, data, and impact analysis. The administration also prepares semi-annual reports of the work of the parliamentary commissions and committees. In addition, it assists in the organization of events, subcommittees, conferences, and congressional hearings. Finally, it also keeps and manages commissions' archives and provides material support to the secretaries of each commission and committee.

Finally, the last role of the secretariats is the general administration of the chamber. This comprises human and material resources management, accreditation and security services, financial services, procurement, accounting, and internal budgeting. The administration is also in charge of providing IT and communication services to all members and bodies of Congress. It also provides (usually through outsourcing) catering, cleaning, and medical services. Lastly, the parliamentary administration manages and maintains facilities, including the cataloguing, preservation, and promotion of the historical, artistic, and cultural heritage of the Mexican Congress.

54.4 Managing Bicameral Relations

As in other bicameral legislatures, both chambers of the Mexican Congress perform their legislative function interdependently. Both chambers participate in the legislative process, and neither may suspend sessions for more than three days without the consent of the other. Interdependence primarily concerns the federal law-making process, which is always carried out by both chambers. The only exceptions are cases in which the Constitution grants exclusive powers to either one of the chambers. For example, defining and auditing the national budget, appointing members of the Board of the National Electoral Institute, or ratifying the presidential appointment to the Secretary of Finance are exclusive functions of the Chamber of Deputies. The Senate exercises exclusive functions regarding foreign relations (e.g., ratification of treaties), suspension of government in any state of the Union, and the appointment of Supreme Court justices and the Attorney General.

Besides these specific powers (in which administration bodies of each chamber also participate by providing support and advice), the interdependence of both chambers of the legislature implies that managing bicameral relations is paramount. The secretariats are the organizations directly responsible for the day-to-day management of the relation between chambers. Naturally, this entails some tasks and coordination between secretariats. For instance, it is the responsibility of parliamentary administrations to organize joint or solemn sessions of Congress and assist during the sessions of the Permanent Commission. Another crucial aspect of the bicameral relation involves bicameral commissions. Currently, five such commissions exist: Bicameral Commission for Fiscal Discipline of the States and Municipalities, Commission for the Congressional Television Channel, Commission of Congressional Libraries, Bicameral Commission of National Security, and the Bicameral Commission for Peace-making and Reconciliation. Secretariats of both chambers assist these commissions by providing expert analysis and information inputs and material and logistical support.

54.5 Current Challenges

Administration of the Mexican Congress calls for a complex organization, a significant number of managerial and administrative processes, and a group of professional parliamentary civil servants capable of providing auxiliary and substantive services to the members and bodies of Congress. The movement towards increased administrative capacity is evident in the diversification of tasks and the expansive nature of reorganizations in both chambers. This can also be seen in the historical trend of budgetary resources. As seen in Figure 54.3, annual budgets experienced significant growth (in real terms) during the 2011–2018 period, particularly in the case of the Chamber of Deputies. Growth is directly related to the expansion of parliamentary administration, as the number of parliamentarians and their staff suffered no changes in the same period. This tendency stopped after the adoption and implementation of austerity measures after 2018 (see below). Nevertheless, increased complexity, differentiation, and resource endowments seem a testament to the institutionalization of the Mexican Congress.

Despite the previous, a series of significant challenges remain. First, one of the most significant tasks currently faced by parliamentary administration is providing digital services, including digital data security. This challenge became particularly salient during the 2020–2022 Covid-19 pandemic. The secretariats of both chambers were to guarantee that the legislative work would continue even when public health restrictions impeded sessions. This

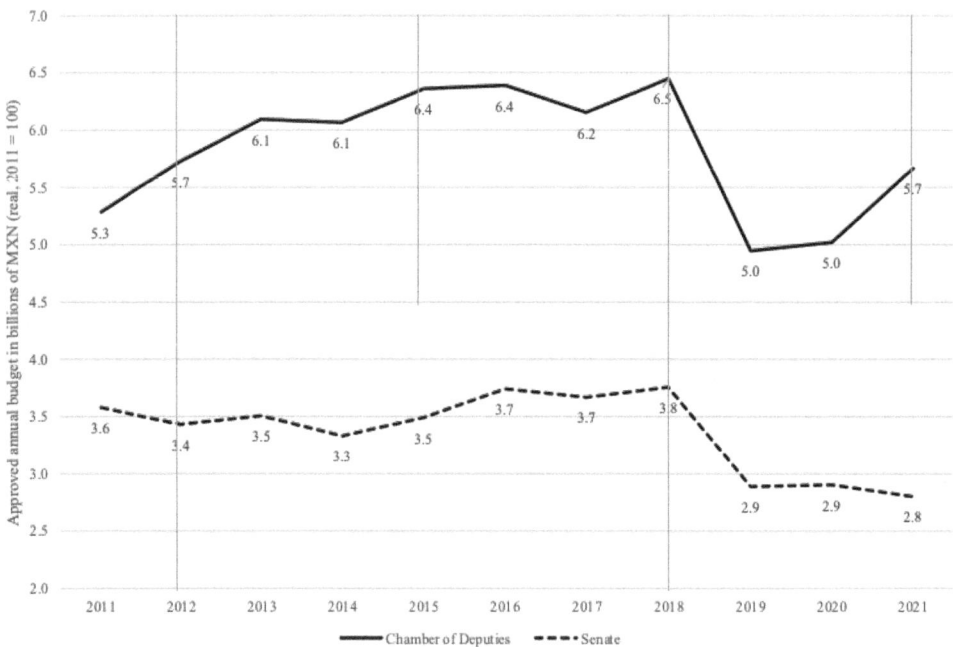

Figure 54.3 Annual budget of the Mexican Congress (2011–2021). NB. Vertical lines mark the beginning/end of legislative terms

implied significantly expanding and updating installed technology, as well as making it safer and more reliable.

The pandemic substantially disrupted a series of organizational routines and processes. For example, both chambers of Congress needed to figure out a way to maintain periodic parliamentary sessions with increasing social distancing restrictions. This meant providing "at distance" services for all parliamentarians and commissions. In addition, the administration asked a significant part of the staff to work from home. As a result, several administrative processes and services stopped or were delayed during significant periods throughout 2020 and 2021.

Moreover, the pandemic had significant effects on employees' health and well-being. Adverse effects were particularly notable among female employees, single parents, and temporary workers. Human resource departments of both chambers reported high levels of stress and dissatisfaction among staff, particularly during the summer and fall of 2020. Now that some restrictions have relaxed, the Mexican Congress administration, like other parliamentary administrations around the globe, faces a challenge to create a roadmap for new work patterns, including ways to improve work-life balance and more attention to overall employee well-being.

Another challenge is decreasing the widespread mistrust in Congress and a perception of low transparency and openness. Congress is one of the least trusted public institutions of Mexico. According to data from the National Statistics Institute of Mexico (INEGI), only 30% of the population has some or much trust in Congress, compared to 75% that trusts the Armed Forces or 52% that trusts the Federal Government (INEGI, 2019). Furthermore, mistrust in Congress is only surpassed by mistrust in political parties (INEGI, 2019). In order to partially address this issue, administrations of both chambers have implemented some actions within their purview to increase public accountability and openness. For instance, transparency websites were updated and expanded, and an open data initiative was adopted. Also, both chambers have expressed their willingness to increase collaboration with the National Anticorruption System and the National Transparency and Data Protection Institute.

The third set of challenges relates to human resources. First, much remains to be done to fully develop and institutionalize the parliamentary civil service in both chambers. As mentioned earlier, professionalization is a relatively new phenomenon, with personnel appointments and severances remaining at the discretionary powers of many areas. Nevertheless, the administrative bodies of both chambers seem committed to staff professionalization and the adoption of meritocratic personnel management, thus furthering the expansion of the parliamentary civil service. Second, although some efforts have been made (such as implementing sexual harassment prevention protocols), several challenges regarding equality and diversity remain. For instance, not all staff members receive training on gender equality or discrimination, and the implementation of diversity management is still pending.

A final set of challenges concerns overall resource management. For example, administrations of both chambers made commitments regarding sustainability and so-called green management. As a result, some actions have been implemented to reduce energy consumption and improve waste and water management. However, perhaps the main challenge in this regard relates to the recent implementation of austerity measures. After the 2018 election and the victory of current president López Obrador's political party, MORENA, the majority in both chambers of Congress implemented a programme of significant budget cuts. This has meant a substantial reduction in resources (cf. Figure 54.3), limiting possibilities and imposing restrictions on parliamentary administrative bodies. Although it is unknown whether austerity will remain a priority after the 2021 mid-term election, for now, it has undoubtedly demanded scrutiny, justification, and increased attention to how resources are being spent.

54.6 Conclusion

Parliamentary administrative bodies of both chambers of the Mexican Congress have experienced an ongoing organizational growth and development process, particularly in the last decade. Although recent austerity measures may have slowed down this process, changes reflect a general movement towards increased administrative capacity.

Many serious challenges remain for the administrators of the Mexican Congress, most notably, pressures for rapid digitalization, pandemic-related challenges, increased transparency, management of personnel diversity, and the implementation of austerity measures. However, the evidence does suggest that the Mexican legislature is becoming more institutionalized in the sense initially proposed by Polsby (1968). Both chambers have increased their internal complexity and have adopted more universalistic criteria for staffing administrative positions. No less relevant, the institutionalization of Congress and the formalization and expansion of administrative capacities may have increased the legislature's autonomy vis-à-vis other political organizations and actors over the last two decades (cf. Ugalde, 2000; Puente Martínez, 2017).

Besides the *external* effects of increased administrative capacity, it may also have important *internal* effects. For instance, increased specialization and professionalization of the secretariats could have direct and indirect effects on concrete legislative processes (e.g., law-making or oversight over the executive branch), and legislative outputs (e.g., legal reforms or interparliamentary ties) and their attributes (e.g., quality, number, robustness). Additionally, these factors may reduce the dependence of the parliamentary administration on parliamentarians and congressional bodies. Another possibility is increasing the number and capacity of specialized units, which could reflect an incipient form of horizontal specialization within Congress. Many of these relations remain understudied and, thus, constitute exciting avenues for future research.

Notes

1 The Belisario Dominguez Research Institute produces strategic research on national development and provides analysis services related to the legislative agenda of the Senate. It is also in charge of promoting civic culture and education.
2 This Centre focuses on producing actionable research on foreign policy and international relations. It also delivers expert and protocolary advice during international and interparliamentary events.
3 The Political Coordination Board is formed by the chairpersons of all political factions represented in the Chamber of Deputies or the Senate.
4 The Permanent Commission of Congress is the body that assumes legislative functions during the recesses between the ordinary periods of sessions of the General Congress.

References

Copeland, G. and Patterson, S. C. (1994) *Parliaments in the Modern World, Parliaments in the Modern World: Changing Institutions*. Ann Arbor: University of Michigan Press.
Hix, S. and Høyland, B. (2013) 'Empowerment of the European Parliament', *Annual Review of Political Science*, 16(1), pp. 171–189.
Huntington, S. P. (1996) *Political Order in Changing Societies*. New Haven, Connecticut: Yale University Press.
INEGI (2019) *Encuesta Nacional de Calidad e Impacto Gubernamental 2019*.
Judge, D. (2003) 'Legislative Institutionalization: A Bent Analytical Arrow?', *Government and Opposition*, 38(4), pp. 497–516.
Klesner, J. L. (2005) 'Electoral Competition and the New Party System in Mexico', *Latin American Politics & Society*, 47(2), pp. 103–142.
Loaeza, S. (2001) 'México: La rebelión de las elites', *Estudios Sociológicos*, 19(56), pp. 363–380.
Lujambio, A. (2000) *El poder compartido*. Mexico City: Oceano.
Merino, M. (2003) *La transición votada. Crítica a la interpretación del cambio político en México*. Mexico City: FCE.
Polsby, N. W. (1968) 'The Institutionalization of the U.S. House of Representatives', *American Political Science Review*, 62(1), pp. 144–168.
Puente Martínez, K. (2017) *Cómo se decide el gasto público en México. congreso y proceso presupuestario durante la democratización (1994–2016)*. Mexico City: Universidad Nacional Autonoma de Mexico.
Puente Martínez, K. (2018) 'Los congresos locales en México. Un modelo para evaluar su grado de institucionalización.', *Estudios Políticos*, 9(44), pp. 65–91.
Ugalde, L. C. (2000) *The Mexican Congress: Old Player, New Power*. Washington, DC: Center for Strategic and International Studies.
Zamora, S. and Cossío, J. R. (2006) 'Mexican Constitutionalism after Presidencialismo', *International Journal of Constitutional Law*, 4(2), pp. 411–437.

55
SOUTH AFRICA'S PARLIAMENTARY ADMINISTRATION

Timothy Paul Layman

55.1 Introduction

This chapter focuses on the parliamentary administration of the Parliament of the Republic of South Africa (RSA), which is the national legislature consisting of the National Assembly (NA) and the National Council of Provinces (NCOP). Thus, the Parliament of the RSA, with its two houses, has a single parliamentary services administration.

This chapter starts out with providing the historical context and background in terms of how the Parliament of the RSA has transformed over various epochs. This follows by dealing with the parliamentary administration and its organizational adjustments and challenges within changing environments, followed by appropriate recommendations as a way forward.

Since the beginning of the parliamentary system in South Africa in the 1800s, the parliament has undergone a series of gradual changes. It has become a hybrid system[1], but one still fundamentally based on the Westminster system[2]. This system developed in the United Kingdom and spread to many British colonies. Although British colonial rule effectively ended in South Africa in 1910, the Westminster parliamentary system did not. This model of politics continued throughout, with some changes in the 1960s and 1980s.

The history of the Parliament of the RSA has an impact on the model of government in place today, developing into a hybrid-parliamentary model. For the purposes of the evolution of South Africa's parliamentary system, its political history can be divided into two main periods, i.e. the first starting with the British occupation, continuing through the colonial and "apartheid"[3] years and ending in 1994; and the second being the democratic era post-1994. With the democratic era, there was further change, towards a more hybrid system, suitable to the new political dispensation. There are points of both similarity and contrast between the original Westminster parliamentary system and the current South African system.

55.2 Modern Constitutional Democracy with a Hybrid Bicameral Parliamentary System

Since the first South African democratic elections of 1994, and the adoption of the new Constitution in 1996, South Africa has been a constitutional democracy with three spheres of government, namely the executive, legislature and judiciary. These three spheres enshrine the doctrine of separation of powers with an executive President, a two-chamber (bicameral[4]) Parliament, Legislature, and an independent Judiciary signifying the rule of law (Monstad, 1999). Furthermore, the three tiers of government, namely national, provincial[5] (regional) and local, all have legislative and executive authority within their own areas of competence, and the arrangement is defined by the Constitution as "distinctive, interdependent and interrelated" (South African Government, 1996). Parliament is bound by the Constitution and can only act within the limits of the Constitution. In this regard, it differs from the Westminster system, in which Parliament, not the British Constitution, is supreme (Pypers, 2015).

The bicameral Parliament of the RSA consists of the NA and the NCOP, as well as the 9 Provincial Legislatures that have been established in terms of the RSA Constitution Act, No 108 of 1996 (South African Government, 1996). Together these 11 legislative institutions form part of the constitutional state (South African Legislative Sector. n.d.[6]). Some of the key features of South Africa's present parliamentary system continue to reflect the traditions of Westminster, but in other respects, it has departed from that precedent. Furthermore, in the early stages of reforming Parliament, there may also have been a preoccupation with the German model. However, one important difference between the Bundesrat[7] and the NCOP relates to its composition. While the Bundesrat consists of members of the state governments, South Africa's dispensation, in contrast, favours the provincial legislatures at the expense of the executive (Humphries and Meierhenrich, 1996).

Furthermore, "South Africa has a committee system endowed with various constitutional and parliamentary procedural powers to enforce […] oversight of the executive, initiation of legislation and scrutiny of government departments." (Calland, Emling and Jacobs, 1997).

55.3 The Role of the Parliamentary Administration

The single parliamentary service administration is headed by the secretary[8] to Parliament as the accounting officer. The parliamentary administration provides professional support services to the houses of Parliament, committees and individual Members of Parliament. This primarily takes the form of information and advisory products and services and facilities management services, which capacitate and enable Members of Parliament to fulfil their constitutional obligations.

The core business branch provides advisory and information services for the proceedings of the NA, the NCOP and their respective committees and joint committees. These services include procedural and legal advice; analyses, information and research services; language; content; secretarial; and legislative drafting services. It further provides public education, information and access to support public participation, and analyses, advice and content support for parliamentary international engagement. The branch consists of the following divisions: National Assembly Table; National Council of Provinces Table; Core Business Support; Knowledge and Information; and International Relations and Protocol.

The support services branch provides facilities and support services to Parliament, including institutional communication services; human resource management; information communication and technology services; institutional support services; and Members' facilities. The Branch consists of the following divisions: parliamentary communication services; human resources; information communication technology; Members' support services; and institutional support services.

A number of management and administration functions are co-located with the purpose of providing strategic leadership support; institutional policy; governance development programmes for Members; sector co-ordination; overall management and administration; internal audit; financial management; and the registrar of Members' interests. The group consists of the Office of the secretary to Parliament; Legislative Sector Support[9]; strategic management and governance; Finance Management Office; Internal Audit; and the Registrar of Members' Interests (Parliament Republic of South Africa, 2020a. Revised Annual Performance Plan).

The aforementioned explanation, as illustrated in Figure 55.1 represents the current macro structure, which may change as the outcome of the Organizational Re-alignment Process (ORP) dictates. This ORP started in 2017 is an institutional project that is geared at revisiting the current organizational design of the institution. At the time of publication, the design work is in progress, and implementation is tentatively planned to be concluded by the end of 2023.

55.4 Analysis of External and Internal Factors

The environmental analysis covers fundamental aspects of the economy, budget and finance, as well as facilities, human resources and professionalization. In addition, also elements regarding management and capacity building, including matters related to the Covid-19 pandemic, and Parliament's resolve to embrace the Fourth Industrial Revolution (4IR)/First Digital Revolution, together with the resultant speeding up of technological advances.

The poor global economic performance and the subsequent low growth forecast for South Africa is apparent. Such a forecast affects Parliament directly because of continued fiscal consolidation that limits nominal budget increases. Parliament may find that it can buy less with its allocations. It may have fewer resources to support the work of the legislature and its committees. In recent years, the budget allocation to Parliament, via the national appropriation, indicated a decreasing trend below the inflation rate (as illustrated in the line graph in Figure 55.2). Although this situation is applicable to the state as a whole, it has affected the work of Parliament in some areas.

Therefore, Parliament implemented cost containment measures and efficiency initiatives. The measures reduced operational costs and ensued difficulties in undertaking critical activities in the value chain of Parliament. The 2017/2018 to 2019/2020 financial years, in particular, saw further reductions in budget for operational expenditure, with budget pressures in almost all areas of work where remuneration and operating costs are increasing at a rate above the inflationary adjustment. This will require mitigation to ensure financial viability and sustainability levels.

Furthermore, reductions in budget led to an unsustainable wage bill and therefore necessitated a freeze in respect of some positions in the organizational structure. This freeze in posts is clearly illustrated in the bar graph of Figure 55.2. However, this did not resolve the problem as the high cost of compensation continued to put pressure on the institutional budget.

In addition, Parliament is dependent on the Department of Public Works for the provision of physical facilities. While there is a visible need for more space, this cannot be easily attained due to this dependency. Consequently, the parliamentary precinct is under serious strain, and facilities require renovation and modernization. In addition to these constraints,

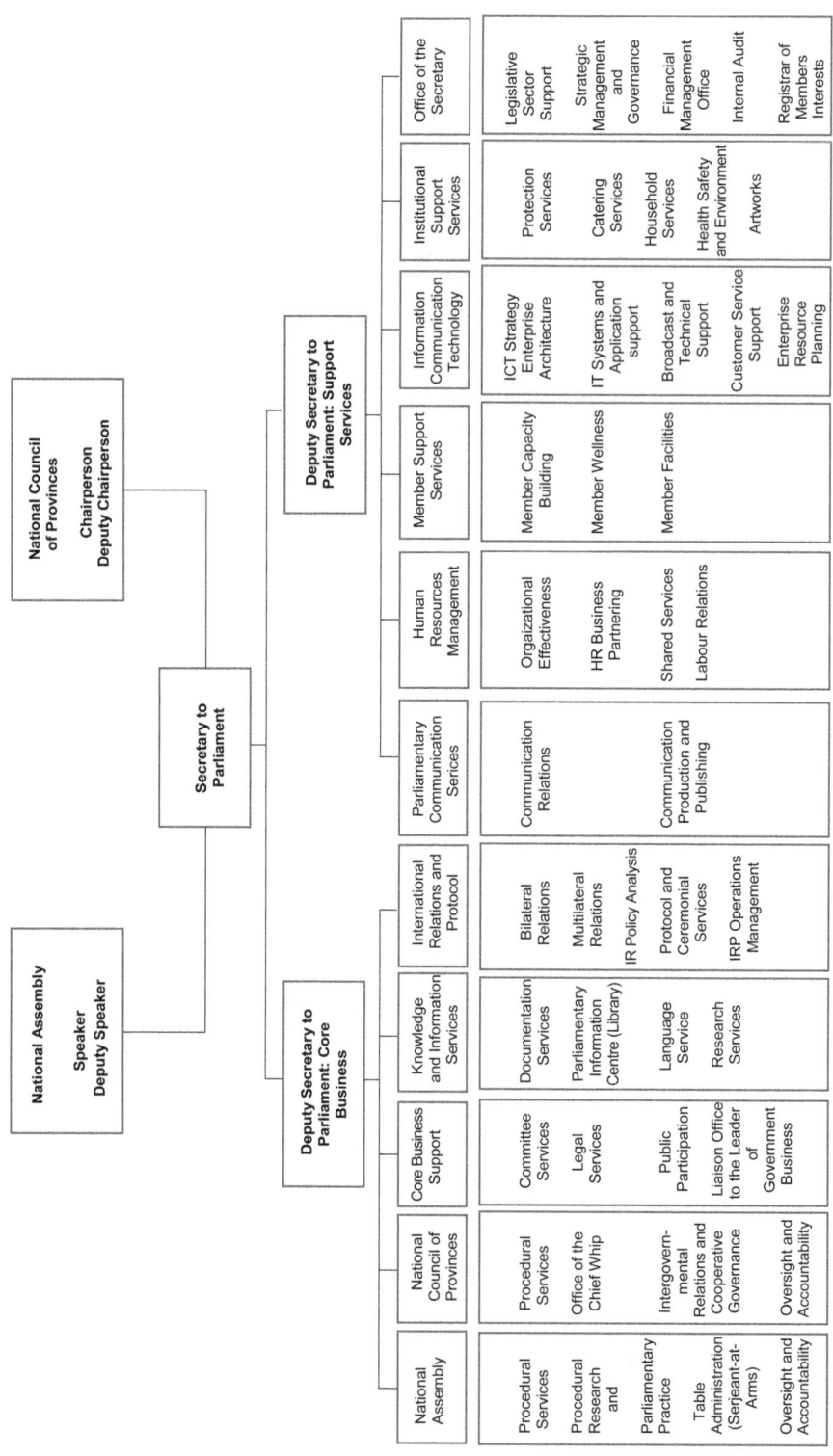

Figure 55.1 The current macro structure of the Parliamentary Administration of South Africa

Source: Parliament Republic of South Africa. n.d. Official Website

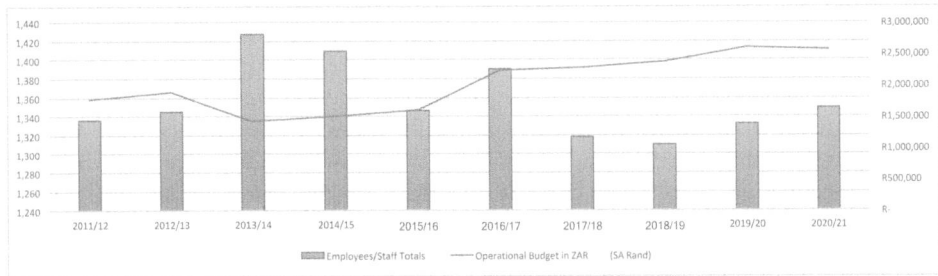

Figure 55.2 Parliamentary staffing and funding over a ten year period (Parliament Republic of South Africa, Annual Report, 2011 – 2020).

tragically Parliament experienced an unfortunate fire crisis in January 2022, which particularly engulfed the entire National Assembly Building with the chamber, committee rooms and several offices. The crisis adversely affected all matters, and alternative arrangements had to be made for various activities and events, including house sittings, committee meetings, public hearings and office space. Therefore, the rebuilding process is a serious resource and financial setback at a crucial time, and even including the effects of the war in Eastern Europe.

Parliament has a human resource workforce of about 1300 posts (illustrated in the bar graph, Figure 55.2), with access to diverse and specialized skills. Some capacity remains untapped, mostly due to structural challenges. Since 2001, the workforce in Parliament has changed dramatically. In 2001, 67% of the workforce was employed on the skilled and lower skilled levels, with only 31% in the highly skilled and professional levels. By 2019, more than 71% was employed on the highly skilled and professional levels.

The increase in the highly skilled and professional levels is due to Parliament's requirements for knowledge and information skills. It is estimated that by 2030 almost 80% of employees in Parliament will be knowledge workers – highly skilled and professional employees, including legal, procedural and content advisors, researchers and analysts, and various subject matter experts. This also means that the conditions of service and working environment will need to change to accommodate knowledge workers. A recent report on staff engagement levels indicated details that only 10% of staff are highly engaged, with 54% at risk of burnout, and that Parliament is paying a heavy cost for the disengagement. According to the report and ongoing enquiries and surveys on workplace culture, the main risk factors include inadequate communication, autocratic management style, inadequate job information and performance management, and inadequate growth and development opportunities. The report recommends that managers must be empowered with people and workplace management skills; apply a servant leadership approach; use coaching and communication skills; apply participatory management styles; promote job information; and use constructive performance management skills (Parliament Republic of South Africa, 2020b. Strategic Plan for Parliament).

Furthermore, there are continuous efforts to professionalize the parliamentary service administration of the RSA. In terms of capacity building and training for staff, various opportunities exist, i.e. learning management short courses are available on the online platform of parliament; various certificated functional programmes on parliamentary practice;

including certificated short executive courses, and graduate development programmes, which are formally structured, personally relevant and contextually based, in terms of development programmes. Funding for studies are available by means of bursaries. The Institution also has an approved Succession Planning Policy (Parliament Republic of South Africa, 2021b. Succession Planning and Graduate Development Programme).

The arrival of Covid-19 has considerably hastened the resolve of Parliament to embrace the Fourth Industrial Revolution (4IR)/First Digital Revolution. Parliament adopted technology as the main mechanism to resume the core business. "Despite its challenges, this digital migration has increased public participation for example. The majority of the meetings of committees, public hearings and plenaries of the houses of Parliament were broadcast and streamed live on social media channels and radio and this increased the level of public access and participation in the work of Parliament." (Masondo[10] as cited in Mputing, 2021). "The impact of the 'new normal' will require Parliament to continue to accelerate its digital journey. This will include systems that will enable Parliament to better track and monitor oversight activities." (Masondo as cited in Mputing, 2021). Parliament has fully adapted to operating within the COVID pandemic environment as the new normal. Furthermore, a hybrid form of working, a combination of physical face to face, and remote online work has been subject to policy development, and is continuously under review.

55.5 Conclusions and Recommendations

At the dawn of South Africa's relatively young democracy in 1994, the overwhelming priority was to build the new Parliament of the RSA's capacity to implement its new constitutional mandate. Naturally, the parliamentary service administration, like the state, had to undergo much needed transformation from representing and reflecting a privileged white minority to representing the black majority who have been oppressed and excluded. Therefore, it makes sense that the entire demographics of the South African population should be reflected if matters were to be fair.

Having a single parliamentary service not separated by the different houses and committees is beneficial in terms of reporting, conditions of service, and undergoing processes of reorganization and realignment. Incidentally, the parliamentary service has undergone several processes of restructuring in order to maximize capacity and enhance service delivery. However, this latest initiative is the most comprehensive approach where parliament and the country may also reap the benefits of a maturing democracy.

Moreover, similar to the public service and judiciary that has regulatory bodies such as the Public Service Commission,[11] and a Judicial Service Commission[12] respectively, it may be high time to introduce a Parliamentary or Legislative Service Commission[13] for the entire Legislative Sector (Parliament and the 9 Provincial Legislatures), just as in the case of the executive and judicial arm of state. The establishment of a Parliamentary and/or Legislatures' Service Commission will further professionalize the parliamentary service and provides an opportunity to finally set the administrative staff apart from the public service. This bodes well for the spirit of separation of powers espoused in the Constitution and assists in strengthening the service. This could be leveraged towards enhancing the effectiveness. The proposed Legislative Service Commission (LSC) can be brought about by an amendment to the Constitution or introducing an Act of Parliament. The LSC could be entitled to advise Parliament and provincial legislatures on any matters relating to legislative service and administration. It can also be tasked and empowered to, amongst others, investigate, monitor and evaluate the organization and administration of the parliamentary and legislative service. This mandate could also entail the evaluation of achievements or lack thereof of parliamentary/legislative programmes. It should also have an obligation to promote measures that would ensure effective and efficient performance within the legislative service and to promote values and principles of legislative administration as set out in the proposed legislation, throughout the legislative service with the appropriate values and principles (adapted from the Public Service Commission, RSA. n.d.) and (Office of the Chief Justice RSA. n.d.)

As a developing country and economy with many contending policy and budgetary priorities, the economic and financial difficulties facing the fiscus with the resultant parliamentary budgetary constraints, as indicated in Section 55.4, makes the situation all the more challenging. As much as the process of realignment, referred to in the last paragraph of Section 55.3, has as its objectives to enhance service delivery, product offering and improving support to bring about more efficiency, effectiveness, productivity and so forth, the parliamentary service is facing a very delicate balancing act in terms of the reorganization and realignment of resources, systems, staffing and services to where these may be most needed to ensure better service delivery and quality product development and offering.

The executive authority of parliament (as the head of the legislative arm of state) has started a process of consultations with the president (as the head of state, and the executive arm of state) together with national treasury in the form of the minister of finance, regarding budgetary allocations to parliament and the legislative sector as a whole. The major issue that has been discussed is the continuous underfunding and cuts to the budgetary allocation of parliament (also reflected in Section 55.4). These are ongoing discussions, and there remain contestations about the executive arm of state allocating increased funding to the legislative arm in order to oversee it, among others, also continuous shrinking budgeting allocations, and in principle the way in which allocations are made to parliament. As a result, the current funding situation of parliament is untenable and undesirable. In this regard, the consideration of international best practice together with "best [possible] fit[14]" approaches with the necessary creativity and innovation becomes of paramount importance. As a case in point, in some countries, separate allocations are made to parliaments before departmental allocations are made, and these have established Parliamentary Commissions to run all parliamentary processes, including planning and budgeting. The agreed principle is two per cent of the national allocation that the Parliament receives. South Africa and many African countries are nowhere near the target. This proposed increase should be done incrementally considering various factors such as the state of the economy as had been alluded to at the beginning of Section 55.4.

Furthermore, the possibility of Zero-Based Budgeting (ZBB) has been touted as a possible justified methodology by the South African government (including parliament), especially in the interest of alignment to strategy and performance plans. International experiences of ZBB include Nigeria in 2016, China in the 1990s, South Korea in the 1980s and the United States (US) in the 1970s. In all cases, countries faced challenges in implementing ZBB (Parliamentary Monitoring Group, 2020).

ZBB is also a budgeting process that allocates funding based on programme efficiency and necessity rather than budget history as opposed to traditional, incremental budgeting (Deloitte, 2021). This may be conducive to parliamentary organizational realignment of the parliamentary service in that ZBB further implies a reallocation of expenditure to match current priorities, and eliminating programmes that are no longer serving their intended purpose (National Treasury, Republic of South Africa. n.d.). It involves an in-depth examination of all the activities, as well as the need to review the budget system through regular monitoring and evaluation, as the operational expenditure from previous years may already include inefficiencies and wasteful amounts (Parliamentary Monitoring Group, 2020). For example, the following potentially cost-saving steps could be considered:

> Smart procurement by re-negotiating contracts of Information and Communication Technology (ICT) and other big cost drivers including financial lease agreements; Getting rid of duplicated and fragmented processes; Relooking at policies with financial implications; Getting rid of unnecessary bottlenecks without compromising the process; Seconding staff to assist in areas with work pressures. A major initiative to manage and reduce the wage bill have been mooted, which includes the possibility of a voluntary early retirement dispensation for Parliament. In the long term this could potentially lead to real cost saving.

However, it must also be understood and appreciated that ZBB is extremely time-consuming and takes real expertise to draw up a budget from scratch on an annual basis (Deloitte, 2021). If government were to implement ZBB successfully, complementary measures would be required including:

> Additional specialized training of personnel; Employment of additional specialized personnel; Budgeting for additional cost and time attached to ZBB; Appropriate cost-benefit analysis; Alignment of current monitoring and evaluation mechanisms to ZBB. *(Parliamentary Monitoring Group, 2020).*

Ultimately, the implementation of ZBB may not be easy, but it may be beneficial to shift the mind-set of budgeting according to priorities in order to embark on a different paradigm that is transformative and revolutionary. Finally, a crucial element of reorganization and that of realignment processes are constant Lekgotla[15] (consultative meetings and discussions), be it on budgetary matters and otherwise, but involving all stakeholders of the Parliament of the RSA.

Notes

1. A hybrid system refers to a combination or mixture of systems.
2. The Westminster system is a democratic parliamentary system of government modelled after that of Britain.
3. 'Apartheid' refers to a system of institutionalized racial segregation that existed in South Africa from 1948 until 1994.
4. In a two-chamber (bicameral) Parliament, legislation are made and passed by both houses. In the case of the South African Parliament, legislation should first pass through the National Assembly (NA), and then the National Council of Provinces (NCOP).
5. Provinces refer to particular regional geographical areas within a country.
6. The Legislative Sector of South Africa consists of the Parliament (National Assembly) and National Council of Provinces NCOP together with the 9 Provincial Legislatures.
7. The German Bundesrat (Federal Council) is a legislative body that represents the 16 federated states of Germany at the federal level. The Bundesrat participates in legislation, alongside the Bundestag consisting of directly elected representatives of Germany. Laws and all constitutional changes need the consent of both houses.
8. The Secretary to the Parliament of the Republic of South Africa is the Accounting Officer of the Parliament. Usually referred to as the Clerk of Parliament in the United Kingdom and Commonwealth tradition. This is the de facto Chief Executive Officer (CEO) of the institution.

9 The Legislative Sector Support (LSS) was set up to provide management, project, administrative and technical support to the structures of the South African Legislative Sector, which includes the National Parliament and 9 Provincial Legislatures. The purpose and scope of LSS includes programme and project management and implementation, as well as institutional and programme development and coordination, by supporting policy-making and structures, e.g. the Speakers' Forum of South Africa.
10 In the Parliament of RSA's Budget Vote of 2020/2021, the Chairperson of the National Council of Province (NCOP), Mr Amos Masondo, gave a broad overview of how the NCOP fared in the last financial year and what it seeks to amend in how it conducts its mandate. Mr Masondo reflected on the impact on Covid-19 and the budget cuts on the work of Parliament and Parliament's swift adjustment to such challenges.
11 The Public Service Commission (PSC) derives its mandate from sections 195 and 196 of the Constitution, 1996. The PSC is tasked and empowered to, amongst others, investigate, monitor and evaluate the organization and administration of the Public Service. This mandate also entails the evaluation of achievements, or lack thereof of Government programmes. The PSC also has an obligation to promote measures that would ensure effective and efficient performance within the Public Service and to promote values and principles of public administration as set out in the Constitution, throughout the Public Service [with the appropriate] values and principles.
12 The Judicial Service Commission (JSC) was established in terms of section 178 of the Constitution and consists of 23 members. In terms of section 178(5) of the Constitution, the JSC is entitled to advise the national government on any matters relating to the Judiciary or administration of justice. Additionally it performs the following functions:
 a Interviewing candidates for judicial posts and making recommendations for appointment to the bench and
 b Dealing with complaints brought against Judges.
 The first function is handled by the JSC as a whole and the second is handled by a smaller group of 13 commissioners. Complaints against Judges who contravene the Code of Judicial Conduct must first be reported to the JSC Secretariat in the Office of the Chief Justice. The Code of Judicial Conduct provides for ethical and professional standards required of every Judge.
13 The proposed Parliamentary and/or Legislature Commission is a regulatory body also found internationally.
14 From the Public Participation Framework of the South African Legislative Sector.
15 This is a Setswana word, one of the South African official languages, implying an important meeting of politicians or government officials in a consultative process pursuing a common goal. Especially a meeting that involves public officials.

References

Calland, R., Emling D. and Jacobs, S. (1997). *Extracts from PIMS Discussion Paper: The South African Parliamentary System in a Comparative Perspective*. Cape Town: IDASA.

Deloitte. (2021). Perspectives: Zero-Based Budgeting. [online] Available at: https://www2.deloitte.com/za/en/pages/operations/articles/gx-zero-based-budgeting.html [Accessed 15 June 2021].

Humphries, R. and Meierhenrich, J. (1996). South Africa's New Upper House: The National Council of Provinces. *Indicator SA*, Vol 13, No 4.

Monstad, T. (1999). *The New South African Parliament: An Evaluation of Parliament's Oversight Function of the Executive'*. Master of Social Science. University of Cape Town.

Mputing, A. (2021). *Parliament RSA Official Website*. [online] Available at: https://www.parliament.gov.za/news/advent-covid-19-has-hastened-parliaments-resolve-embrace-fourth-industrial-revolution-ncop-chairperson [Accessed 23 June 2021].

National Treasury, Republic of South Africa. (n.d.). A Framework for achieving spending efficiency in a fiscally constrained environment. [online] Available at: http://www.treasury.gov.za/publications/guidelines/Zero%20Based%20Budgeting%20Framework.pdf [Accessed 22 July 2021].

Office of the Chief Justice RSA, Judicial Service Commission. (n.d.) [online] Available at: http://www.psc.gov.za/about/mandates.asp [Accessed 6 February 2022].

Parliament Republic of South Africa. (2011). *Annual Report, 2010–2011*.

Parliament Republic of South Africa. (2012). *Annual Report, 2011–2012*.

Parliament Republic of South Africa. (2013). *Annual Report, 2012–2013*.
Parliament Republic of South Africa. (2014). *Annual Report, 2013–2014*.
Parliament Republic of South Africa. (2015). *Annual Report, 2014–2015*.
Parliament Republic of South Africa. (2016). *Annual Report, 2015–2016*.
Parliament Republic of South Africa. (2017). *Annual Report, 2016–2017*.
Parliament Republic of South Africa. (2018). *Annual Report, 2017–2018*.
Parliament Republic of South Africa. (2019). *Annual Report, 2018–2019*.
Parliament Republic of South Africa. (2020). *Annual Report, 2019–2020*.
Parliament Republic of South Africa. n.d. Official Website. [online] Available at: https://www.parliament.gov.za/organogram [Accessed 4 April 2022].
Parliament Republic of South Africa. (2020a). *Revised Annual Performance Plan 2020/21 to 2022/23*.
Parliament Republic of South Africa. (2020b). *Strategic Plan for Parliament 2019 to 2024*.
Parliament Republic of South Africa. (2021). *Succession Planning and Graduate Development Programme, 2021*.
Parliamentary Monitoring Group. (2020) Zero-Based Budgeting: Parliamentary Budget Office briefing. [online] Available at: https://pmg.org.za/committee-meeting/30912/ [Accessed 19 May 2021].
Public Service Commission Republic of South Africa South Africa. (n.d.) [online] Available at: https://www.judiciary.org.za/index.php/judicial-service-commission/about-the-jsc [Accessed 6 February 2022].
Pypers, E. (2015). South Africa's Parliamentary System: From Westminster to Hybrid? In: *South African Catholic Bishops' Conference*, Briefing Paper 380, Parliamentary Liaison Office, May 2015.
Selim, G. (1996). The Manager Monitored. In: L. Wilcocks, and I. Harrow, eds., *Rediscovering Public Service Management*. New York: McGraw-Hill Books.
South African Government. (1996). *The Constitution of the Republic of South Africa, 1996*.
South African Legislative Sector (SALS). (n.d.) *Official Website*. [online] Available at: https://sals.gov.za/history-and-context/ [Accessed 31 March 2021].
Tomkins, C.R. (1987). *Achieving Economy, Efficiency and Effectiveness in the Public Sector*. Great Britain: Institute of Chartered Accountants of Scotland.

56
TUNISIA'S PARLIAMENTARY ADMINISTRATION

Faten Sliti

56.1 Introduction

On 27 January 2014, Tunisia undertook a major reform of its political system when the National Constituent Assembly (NCA) adopted a new constitution. This constitutional change[1] reflected the common vision of the various components of Tunisian society and was based on a commitment to liberal democratic principles such as respect for civil rights, the separation of powers and decentralization.[2] The first elections under the new constitutional framework were held in October 2014, leading to the first meeting of the People's Representatives Assembly (PRA) – in December of the same year.

The new parliament was given a central role in the system of governance established by the constitution. Specifically, Parliament was to be responsible for ensuring that the constitutional framework would be fully implemented. Charged with the role of representing the Tunisian citizens, the PRA became the key place for political dialogue and for interaction among civil society organizations, citizens and the executive power.

Since its creation, the Tunisian Parliament underwent a transformation to become a significantly different institution from the one that began its work at the end of 2014 and a fortiori from the one that preceded it between 2011[3] and 2014, the National Constituent Assembly (NCA). The administration of the second PRA became more efficient and better structured following a restructuring. During this period, the institution significantly modernized and continued the capacity building of its elected members and officials. Since the beginning of 2015, we have observed a certain takeover of the administrative structures of the PRA and coordinated work aimed at establishing clear and functional work processes within the various departments, in parallel with general reflections aimed at conferring on the administration the means to assume its future administrative and financial autonomy[4], constitutionalized in 2014.

56.2 An Overview of the People's Representative Assembly

The PRA was created according to the constitution of 27 January 2014 and was granted powers that are broader than those that were approved under Tunisia's 1959 constitution. Before addressing the role of the administration, it will be useful to briefly review the main functions of the PRA.

DOI: 10.4324/9781003181521-61

According to Chapter 3 of the constitution, "The people are the holders of sovereignty and the source of the powers they exercise through their elected representatives or through a referendum".

Members of the PRA are elected in general, free, direct, secret, fair and transparent elections for a representative term that extends to five years.

The assembly holds regular sessions starting during the month of October of each year and ending during the month of July, with the possibility of holding an extraordinary session during the parliamentary holiday to consider a specific agenda.

According to its rules of procedures (ROP)[5], the PRA exercises three main functions: legislation, oversight and representation.

The legislative role of the assembly mainly consists in the following actions:

- studying and discussing draft constitutional, organic and regular laws presented by the government or the Presidency of the Republic and ratifying them.
- studying and discussing proposals for laws submitted by at least ten representatives, and approving them.

The PRA shall, by a two-thirds majority of its members, approve the amendment of the Constitution and by an absolute majority of its members on draft organic laws and by a majority of its members present on ordinary draft laws, provided that this majority is not less than one-third of the members of the Assembly, and article 65 of the Constitution defines the field of law.

The oversight function lies in monitoring government work and constitutional bodies and holding them accountable. The latter is divided into two types: political oversight and financial oversight. Political oversight is carried out through a set of mechanisms set by the constitution and ranges in strength from flexible instruments (such as directing written and oral questions and holding dialogue sessions with the government) to more severe mechanisms such as:

- expressing confidence in the government, or in one of its members, either through a single vote by an absolute majority of all members of the government or the task assigned to each member;
- voting by an absolute majority on a censure motion against the government, based on a justified request by at least one-third of members of parliament;
- voting by an absolute majority that the government continues its activities, at the request of the Head of Government or the President of the Republic;
- a justified list to exempt the president of the republic from serious breach of the constitution, and approved by the parliament by a majority of two-thirds.

The powers regarding financial oversight mainly consist of approval of the state budget[6] and the latest finance law[7] every year, and monitoring the constitutional bodies by discussing their annual reports.

The representative function carried out by the PRA concerns elections. According to the provisions of Chapter 6 of the Constitution[8], the PRA supervises the election of members of the various constitutional bodies and their compensation in case of vacancy. It may also discuss annually the various reports issued by these bodies and withdraw confidence from the councils of these bodies or from one or more of their members.

Finally, according to Chapter 5 of the Constitution related to the judicial authority, the PRA has the right to appoint four members of the Constitutional Court according to the election mechanism.

56.3 The Organizational Structures of the PRA

With reference to the ROP of the PRA of 2 February 2015, its main elements are as follows:

- President
- Bureau
- President's Symposium
- Committees
    - Legislative Committees
    - Special Committees
    - Committees of Inquiry
- Plenary

In order to better understand the nature of administrative support required by these organs, in the following, a brief explanation of their roles is provided.

The president of the PRA is the institution's legal representative, the head of its administration, in charge of the budget, supervising the smooth running of all its interests and ensuring the implementation of the provisions of the bylaw and the implementation of the decisions of the plenary session and the Bureau. He or she is assisted in the performance of their duties by two deputies.

The PRA's Bureau represents a key link in the parliamentary work due to the nature of the vital functions assigned to it in the internal system to organize the assembly's work, set its priorities, define its business calendar and take the necessary decisions for that by virtue of its balanced representation based on the principle of proportional representation. The Bureau consists of the president of the PRA in his capacity as the head of the Bureau, his two deputies and ten other members who are assistants to the president. The Bureau takes all its decisions by a majority of those present, provided that it is not less than one-third. In case of a tie, the president's vote is decisive. According to article 59 of ROP[9], the Bureau holds its meetings periodically every Thursday and whenever the need arises, at the invitation of its president or one-third of its members. The meetings are closed (to press and administrators) and only attended by the secretary general of the assembly and whoever is required to attend. The secretary general has the role to keep the minutes of the meetings initialled by the President. The President of the Assembly may, on an exceptional basis, invite any administrative staff whose contribution would be useful to discuss specific questions.

The President's Symposium is an advisory coordinating body that is chaired by the president of the PRA and that convenes upon an invitation from him or from one-third of its members compulsorily once every three months and whenever the need arises. In particular, the President's Symposium is responsible for submitting proposals related to the legislative and parliamentary work programme, the plenary sessions agenda, and responsible for examining the topics referred to it by the Speaker and his Bureau.

The committees of the PRA represent the solid core of legislative, oversight and representative work by virtue of the powers granted by the internal rules. The committees of the PRA are formed in accordance with the rule of proportional representation between the political groups which is announced at the beginning of each parliamentary session during a dedicated plenary meeting. The committees' sessions are normally held in public, but a committee may decide the confidentiality of its session by the majority of its members.

The PRA has 18 permanent committees: 9 legislative committees that undertake, in particular, the study of draft laws and proposals of laws presented to the Assembly before referring them to the plenary session and consider all issues referred to it. There are also nine special committees that deal with oversight issues, examine all issues falling within their competence and follow up all related files and issues.

In addition, the PRA may, upon the request of at least one-fourth of the members, establish non-permanent committees of inquiry. The PRA shall approve its creation by the majority of its attending members, provided that the number of the approvers is not less than one-fourth of the members. The PRA shall approve its creation by the majority of its members present, provided that the number is not less than the number of those who approve it is not less than one-third. The majority of the opposition members in every parliamentary year have the right to request the formation and presidency of an investigation committee.

The plenary session is considered the main legislative body, in which public debate takes place and decisions are taken in it by voting according to the quorum set by internal rules, and voting is by declaring approval, rejection or retention. The president or, if necessary, one of his deputies chairs the plenary session. He or she organizes the debate, maintains order, manages the voting process and announces any voting result.

The PRA holds its plenary sessions every Tuesday, unless the Bureau decides otherwise. Its actions are public, and the assembly may hold a closed session at the request of its president, the head of a political group, or at least seven members, or a member of the government, with the approval of three-fifths of the members.

56.4 The Organization of the Parliamentary Administration

The departments of the PRA administration are organized into units, directorates, general directorates and offices. Employees working within can be assigned one of the functional positions of the central administration according to the provisions of decree 2006 – 1245 of 24 April 2006 related to setting the system for assigning and exempting from job positions within the central administration[10]. The PRA's administration is involved in the declaration of principles and values in the public administration[11], just as the 2014 constitution had been set on serving the citizen, the public interest, neutrality, equality and continuity, and adopting the rules of transparency, integrity, efficiency and accountability.

Given how the nature of parliamentary administration has changed over time[12], Table 56.1 provides a brief summary of the key features in each historical period.

56.5 Recent Developments of the Organization of the Parliamentary Administration

The current Tunisian unicameral parliament, the PRA, does not publish a formal organization chart. The administration has several departments that were created to respond to concrete needs to support the parliamentary work but these structures (such as the international cooperation department, the parliamentary academy, the parliamentary resources and consultations center, or the government oversight unit) were created just through internal decisions. The last time there was a formal organizational chart[13]; it was during the national

Table 56.1 Evolution of the organization of the Tunisian administration

Period	Name of the institution	Key developments in the evolution of the parliamentary administration
1956–1961	National Constituent Assembly	**The first nucleus of the administration** • unavailability of an official administration • insuring the necessary work through an administrative core from the agents of other departments • two MPs were elected to oversee security and order within the assembly
1961	National Assembly (Majlis Al'Umma)	**The first formal establishment of the administration** • the general secretariat is created. It supports the whole parliamentary action • the special statute for parliamentary employees was enacted
1982	Chamber of deputies	**The creation of the administrative and financial structure** A central administration for administrative and financial affairs directly linked to the president of the chamber is created
1983	Chamber of deputies	**The creation of the Cabinet** the cabinet is the third structure created within the administrative apparatus. It was entrusted with the functions of general coordination, information and external relations
1989 and 1993	Chamber of deputies	**Horizontal and vertical development of administrative structures** a significant development of administrative units in line with the development of public administrative functions, specializations and professions
2007	Chamber of deputies	**The creation of the Parliamentary Research and Studies Bureau** the creation of a fourth structure concerned with the creation of knowledge content and concerned with developing intellectual support for parliamentary activity and optimal management of research and documentation work and information and communication technology
2012	National Constituent Assembly	**Functional organization and pooled competencies** Abandoning the hierarchical organization and adopting the system of functional groupings (Functional poles) appropriate to the nature of the parliamentary administration that is mainly based on consultation and visualization and is characterized by its high rate of supervision

constituent assembly in 2012 and did not accurately describe the actual estate of the administration after the 2014 reforms[14].

Having said that, we can observe that the PRA administration is divided into three main departments: the cabinet, the secretariat general and common services. Below are brief descriptions of the main tasks of each of these departments.

The cabinet has the following essential functions:

- informing the PRA's president about administrative departments' activities and communicating president's decisions upon that activities to all administrative structures
- coordinating between the departments of the PRA
- parliamentary protocol, international cooperation and external relations
- ensuring contacts with the Presidency of the Republic, the Presidency of the Government, official bodies and national organizations

Its substructures are:

- protocol department (added in 1993)
- external relations
- international cooperation department (created in 2015)
- media and communication unit
- Bureau of relations with citizen and with civil society
- administrative archives and documents management directorate (added in 1993)
- parliamentary academy (created in 2016 and added in 2020)
- parliamentary resources and consultations centre (created in 2019 and added in 2020)
- central order desk (resgistry)(internal and external mailing exchange office). The central order desk works on sending correspondences to the representatives, with their personal and electronic addresses, transfers draft laws, transfers the files of the plenary sessions prepared by the Plenary Sessions Department and, therefore, the representatives must inform the parliament at the beginning of the parliamentary term of the correspondence address, and then of any change that occurs to it.

The cabinet includes a significant number of civil servants (91 officials, nearly 20% of the total number of employers of the PRA administration).

The secretary general has the following essential functions:

- organizing plenary sessions and applying the ROP
- supporting the work of the committees in terms of advice, documentation and administrative follow-up
- preparing the official gazette for parliamentary deliberations
- follow up on the activities of public institutions
- managing and developing the parliament's library and documentation activity
- maintaining and organizing the legislative archives

It is organized in the following substructures:

- the coordination and follow-up affairs
- the plenary session Affairs
- the legislative path and the relationship with the executive authority

- the legislative committees
- official gazette of deliberations
- the services of the special committees and the follow-up and investigation committees
- the services of following up on the activities of public institutions
- the legislative archives

The role and tasks of advisors working for the general secretariat are:

- coordinating and organizing committee's work
- making researches and communicating on committee's activities
- help drafting and documentation reports
- logistic organization of committees' meetings includes providing information and documentation
- preparing studies and reports
- providing expertise and consultations to MPs on financial, legal and economic issues
- taking notes of committees' minutes
- writing and sending resumes on committees' meetings to the communication unit for publication on PRA's official website

The essential functions of the common services department are:

- managing the representatives' affairs
- ensuring services and providing necessary means for the proper functioning of parliamentary work, especially transportation, printing, and telecommunication
- ensuring security, and guests reception
- managing financial affairs, and supplies
- taking care of buildings, equipment, and outdoor spaces
- managing human resources (HR), promoting social work, and providing health care
- conceiving and following up the implementation of administrative reforms and development programs, competencies development
- information systems management
- setting modern communication and information technologies

The common services department has the following substructures:

- MPs affairs
- financial affairs
- human resources management
- administrative reform and competency development
- building and equipment technical affairs
- general services and reception
- governance and inspection
- information systems and digital services

In addition to these main departments, we also need to note the presence of a number of specialized units. Since 2011, the change in the political regime from presidential to parliamentary has influenced the functions of the parliament that have grown and have diversified. The administration has evolved to meet new parliamentary needs to exercise the functions of oversight, legislation, diplomacy and representation. It has also evolved to meet new priorities related to transparency, efficacy and openness. For this purpose, specialized units have been set up.

The "Governmental Action Monitoring Unit" is made of five staff (one general director, three executives and one administrator). The work of this Unit is to evaluate public policies and ensure their implementation in an effective manner. It monitors also written and oral questions, follow-up of MPs interventions on the meaning of article 118[15] of the ROP. The parliament performs the oversight function through mechanisms defined by the constitution and the ROP[16]:

- attending and following dialogue sessions with members of the government
- attending plenaries of granting or confidence withdrawal
- receiving and forwarding written and oral questions

The "Parliamentary Academy" was created at the initiative of the president of the PRA 1, and according to the recommendation of the Presidents' Symposium on 24 June 2016 and the decision of the Parliament's Bureau on 3 November 2016 in order to provide continuous support for parliamentary work by supporting and strengthening the competencies of the MPs, advisors and parliament's frameworks in the legislative, oversight, representative and diplomatic fields (short-term training).

The training activity, in addition to the short-term training courses organized according to the diagnosed needs, consists in organizing long-term annual courses that include various axes, such as monitoring government action, drafting legal texts, communication techniques, the English language and other specialized issues (according to the committees' need).

The "MPs Affairs Department", consisting of only four officials, deals exclusively with the affairs of MPs and it is mainly tasked with the following:

- managing all administrative MPs affairs
- undertaking travel procedures during both MPs and parliamentary staff missions abroad.
- following up the issues and files of MPs at the National Fund for Retirement and Social Security[17]
- managing the system of parliamentary assistantswhich implementation is in line with the requirements of article 37 of PRA's ROP of 2015. This article stipulates the necessity for the PRA to provide the necessary material and human resources for the MPs. Parliamentary assistants must have a master's degree in social sciences, economics or law.

The PRA also has a multidisciplinary library that covers all areas of knowledge. The "PRA Library" has its headquarter divided between the original building and the subsidiary building. It provides a set of services deirected primarily to MPs, to the parliament's frameworks and assistants, as well as external beneficiaries. These services include:

- Library and Documentary Research providing MPs with several ways to access information accurately and quickly.
- Ongoing Briefing, including preparing lists of the new holdings of the library available at the disposal of MPs.
- selective information search providing each MP periodically with information that falls within the scope of his or her legislative work

- responding to MPs' inquiries when they visit the library, or by phone or electronic communication, and the MP receives the answer about his or her inquiry on the same day
- electronic search of the databases produced by the library for books and articles selected from relevant periodicals, through the website of the PRA, the Internet or on the internal network of the PRA.
- document loan process allowing MPs to borrow books. As for periodicals, reports and legal magazines, they can review them in the reading room.

The "Plenary Sessions' Deliberations Unit" takes the minutes of the deliberations during the plenary sessions of the PRA and thereby preserves the legislative memory of the country. These minutes are considered an official document and a legal reference, not only for MPs but also for all researchers, as they are useful to understand the intention of the legislator and include what is going on in the PRA from the legislative side through the approval of ordinary or organic laws, ratification of agreements and treaties, and from the oversight side through holding dialogue sessions with members of government and asking oral or written questions. The unit ensures the preparation of the minutes of the plenary sessions by transferring the deliberations from an audio/video format (audio/video recordings) to a word format. The president of the PRA authorizes to print and publish the parliamentary deliberations.

The creation of the "Parliamentary Resources and Consultations Centre" falls within the context of the new dynamic within the PRA, which necessitated the search for new ways to support parliamentary work that takes into account the changes in the representative, legislative and oversight functions.

With the growing role of the parliamentary institution in building an emerging democracy and the consolidation of its pivotal position in the political system stemming from the constitution of 27 January 2014, various needs and requirements of MPs have emerged, requiring the provision of up-to-date and accurate information as a necessary resource to help decision-making and to enhance the quality of parliamentary debate regarding policies[18]. The establishment of the centre was based on the German experience.

Despite being understaffed, with only six researchers, the centre aims to strengthen the parliamentary function and representative work, by facilitating access to information for all MPs requesting it, and to ensure that the mediating role between the deputy and the various instances producing information, by providing MPs with suitable and objective answers to their inquiries from reliable and accurate sources.

The functions of the centre require that it be a horizontal structure with close relations with internal parliamentary structures that deal with information such as the library and the archives, in addition to linking partnership relations with various sources of information, and to provide MPs with impartial scientific information as soon as possible and according to an effective work methodology.

The department of "Information Systems and Digital Services" manages:

1. a website under the following address: www.arp.tn that enables users to:

   - access to all parliamentary activities
   - follow the discussion of draft laws or proposals, preparatory work for draft laws, approved texts and deliberations in plenary sessions
   - Know the MP, his party affiliation, his political group, the interventions and initiatives that he has undertaken, and his presence and votes in the plenary sessions and in committee meetings.

- access to the oversight function of the PRA from dialogue sessions with the government, oral and written questions, sessions of granting and withdrawing confidence from the government and interventions on the meaning of article 118.
- the video portal covers and broadcasts the various filmed legislative activities (plenary sessions, committee meetings, press conferences …) and the activities of the president.

2. a digital system, Societecivile.arp.tn, dedicated to the interaction between the legislative institution and civil society, which enables associations to contribute to the drafting of laws and provides a space for presenting legislative initiatives and questions to the government, provided that they are adopted by the MPs.
3. Mail.arp.tn is the electronic messaging system for communication between the administration and the MP and is used by the MP in all his electronic correspondences in his capacity as an MP.
4. A personal electronic voting card that enables the MP to initiate the voting process in a context of complete and certain transparency
5. the PRA's presence on a number of social media platforms:

   - YouTube channel broadcasting directly the work of the plenary sessions: https://www.youtube.com/c/Assembléedesreprésentantsdupeuple. This includes all the interventions of the representatives, divided according to the name of the intervening deputy, where he can view it and download it directly.
   - A Facebook page: https://www.facebook.com/Tunisie.arp?fref=ts
   - A Twitter account: https://twitter.com/ARPtn

In terms of HR management, we can say that the PRA does not have a real system for evaluating its staff. In short, ARP managers do not currently benefit from an effective personnel appraisal system, which deprives them of a powerful management tool. Thanks to the twinning project with the European assemblies (2016–2018), it was proposed to set up an "annual activity meeting" allowing a line manager and his collaborator to discuss the successes and difficulties encountered during the past year and to determine the objectives to be achieved during the coming year. It is also during this interview that wishes for mobility or training are gathered. This procedure was chosen by the HR manager because it can be implemented very quickly because it does not require any legislative[19] or regulatory change.

From now on, with the development of job descriptions, the definition of a training policy and the establishment of an annual activity meeting, the PRA benefits from high-performance tools to implement a modern and efficient human resources management policy at the service of MPs: a final step remains the validation of these documents prepared within the framework of the twinning project mentioned above.

56.6 Conclusion: A Parliamentary Administration in Need of Further Reform

Based on the previous discussion, a number of observations deserve to be raised.

First, as the last formal organization chart is dated on 6 November 2012, the present organizational structure has new and "informal" substructures. Parliamentary organization lacks in some part of it clarity and legibility as well as effective interdepartmental coordination.

Besides, as there is no written legal document describing the real organization of the administration, the organization of services is not known by all officials. It is therefore essential to establish a new organizational chart describing very precisely the "who does what" within the departments. This will allow more coordination and specific responsibility while avoiding personal and organizational conflicts.

Second, it should be noted that some regulatory departments could be created in order to reach higher performance. These include a structure responsible for "foresight department". Having to play an exemplary role, the parliament should also equip itself with an "ethics department". As the performance of the parliament has become central, care should also be taken to set up a structure responsible for "parliamentary performance assessment" as well as the implementation of development strategies for its effectiveness.

Third, there is a lack of organizational and human resources in addition to the poor distribution of the workload to properly carry out its missions. In fact, some departments have been created because of the importance of the missions entrusted to them but without having the human or financial resources to actually be able to constitute them. This is the case, for example, of the Inspection and Governance Directorate (or the parliamentary resources and consultations center) which only has one staff, the director. If the objective of good governance is essential, the fact of creating a directorate to fulfil this mission, including only one official could prove to be counterproductive. and other managers may think that the issues of good governance are not their concern. That is also the case of "the governmental action monitoring unit" that is responsible essentially for the management of written and oral questions, supporting the control function, should be enhanced by providing more human resources, more expertise and deeper trainings. This is the same case of the "office in charge of relations with citizens and civil society" that has only two officials despite the fact that the PRA has adopted a strategic vision based on openness to civil society and citizens.

It is also better to distribute among the officials (essentially committee advisors) the workload which can vary greatly depending on the circumstances and on committees (for example, we can't compare the workload of the advisor of a special committee which meets every Monday morning with the workload of the legislative committee of finance, planning and development, for example, which meets every day morning and afternoon). Likewise, regrouping archiving (administrative and legislative) within the same department would lead to more efficacy.

The parliamentary administration also lacks effective internal communication.

During 2014–2019 mandate, there was, within the secretariat general, a new experience of deputy general secretaries that were director generals charged, respectively, of committees and of plenary session organization. This experience didn't continue because of the lack clarity and effectiveness in their missions and because of the departure of the defender of this idea.

The Parliamentary Academy is, since 2020, directly attached to the cabinet. This academy plays a strategic role in relation to a certain number of cross-cutting issues, including in particular those of the research required for evaluations of public policies and the training of parliamentarians. It should be given more autonomy and neutrality in relation to the various political currents present within the Assembly.

The use of the concept of unit (instead of directorate or general directorate) is also problematic. Indeed, this denomination does not give a precise idea on the function and the rank of the person supposed to lead it.

Some structures seem to have the same functions[20], according to their names, and this led to tangles in some circumstances (for example: "external relations unit" and "international cooperation department" within the cabinet). Some others do the same function of staff training such as "the parliamentary academy" and "administrative reform and competency development unit". In fact, sharing a task by different directorates is a source of complexity and has led to various conflicts (three structures offering the same training to the same audience and proposing the same timing: "Human Resources Department", "parliamentary academy" and "administrative reform and competency development unit"). This has affected HR management because the training policy is a strategic tool for the HR department, and as the training resources are modest and in many cases involve international partnerships, they thus arise communication problems and possible synergies were lost.

In 2019, the frightening spread of the Covid-19 pandemic has affected the Tunisian parliament which carefully respected the rules laid down by the government[21] and especially the Ministry of Health. In March 2020, the Bureau took a number of concrete steps to address the new situation. This included the constitution of a crisis unit which remained in permanent session and also maintained a dialogue with government about the management of the pandemic. It included the members of the Bureau and the presidents of the parliamentary groups and the reduction of the number of employees present at the assembly (only staff whose presence is essential to directly support parliamentary work is physically present, a list is announced and revised periodically). Homeworking was encouraged while keeping all professional advantages. In some directorates, only the heads were present in the office. In the same vein, the number of parliamentary assistants present at the assembly was reduced to a maximum of one per group.

Additional measures were taken to allow the continuity of the work in plenary and limitation of the time of the general discussion (phase which precedes the discussion article by article of the bill). These measures included the prohibition of guests by MPs inside the assembly (instead an open space in the garden of the assembly was dedicated to MPS to receive citizens), special checks at the entry to the assembly, distancing also among MPs in the chamber and adopting a single voting mechanism (remote voting via a dedicated application).

In addition, the PRA faced an even greater challenge when on 25 July 2021 President Kaïs Saïed announced that he would suspend parliament and dismiss the head of government[22]. The announcement followed protests in some cities across the country which demanded among other things the "dissolution of Parliament". The President's announcement came at a time when Tunisia was facing a peak in the Covid pandemic, a difficult economic and social situation, and a deep political crisis due to the confrontation between the President and some parliamentary parties. Legally, the announcement was based on article 80 of the constitution[23], which allows this type of measure in the event of "imminent danger" while it does not allow the dissolution of parliament.

These developments also had serious impact on the parliamentary administration. Following the announcement of 25 July 2021, the secretary-general of the parliament in charge of financial and administration affairs informed the parliamentary staff that the majority is considered in an open holiday, with only staff from financial and administrative affairs department attending work at particular times to prepare required administrative documents for the employees and ensure the payment of wages.

Further reformsfollowed a referendum on a new constitution (in July 2022) and parliamentary elections (in 17 December 2022) which were announced by the President of the Republic in December 2021, together with the organization of electronic consultations through digital applications to directly poll citizens about the political and constitutional reforms they desire[24].

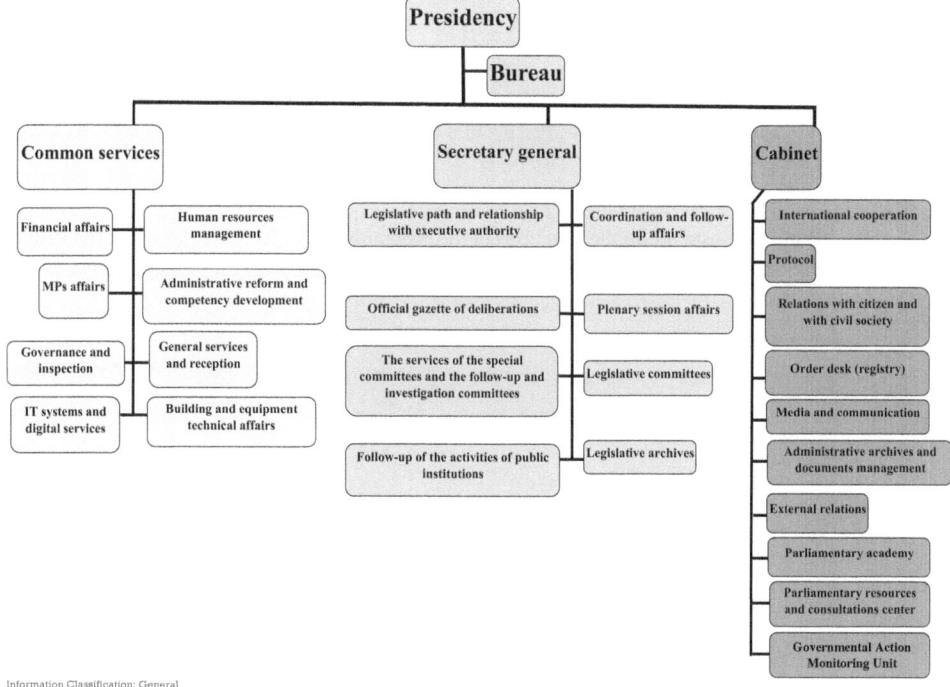

Administrative Structure (de facto) of the Tunisian People's Representatives Assembly

Notes

1. the constitution of 1 June 1959.
2. the constitution of 27 February 2014.
3. The constituent law n° 2011-6 dated. 16 December 2011, related to the temporary organization of the public authorities.
4. Law No. 2019-15 of 13 February 2019 on Organic Budget Law.
5. Rules of procedures (ROP) of the People's Representatives Assembly, of 2 February 2015.
6. State budget of 2021.
7. Law No. 2019-15 of 13 February 2019 on Organic Budget Law.
8. the constitution of 27 February 2014.
9. Rules of procedures (ROP) of the People's Representatives Assembly, of 2 February 2015.
10. Decree No. 2006 – 1245 of 24 April 2006, related to setting the system for assigning and exempting functional positions within central administration.
11. Draft of conduct code of parliamentary public officials.
12. See Table 56.1.
13. Decision dated 06 November 2012 regulating the administrative departments of the National Constituent Assembly.
14. See chart n° 1.
15. Article 118 – If a Member wishes to discuss an important or urgent matter, he must submit a written request stating the reason for his request. It is up to the chairman to give him the floor at the end of the plenary.
16. Rules of procedures (ROP) of the People's Representatives Assembly, of 2 February 2015.
17. Law No. 16 of 1985 of 8 March 1985, amended by the law No. 57 of 1997 of 28 July 1997 related to the organization of the retirement system for members of the House of Representatives.
18. IPU (2020) Comparative Study on Parliamentary Administration, 33p.

19 Law No. 1983 - 112 of 12 December 1983 organizing the general statute of state officials, of local groups and of public institutions of administrative character, and all texts that have revised or supplemented it, especially Decree-Law No. 2011-89 of 23 September 2011.
20 See chart n° 1.
21 State budget of 2021.
22 Presidential decree n° 2021-69 dated 26 July 2021 relating to the dismissal of the head of government and members of the government; Presidential decree n° 2021-80 dated 29 July 2021 regarding the suspension of the functions of the Assembly of the Representatives of the People.
23 The constitution of 27 February 2014.
24 Presidential decree n° 2021-109 dated 24 August 2021 regarding the extension of the exceptional measures relating to suspending the functions of the Assembly of the Representatives of the People. Presidential decree N° 2021-117 dated 22 September 2021 relating to exceptional measures.

57
THE UNITED STATES CONGRESSIONAL ADMINISTRATION

B. Guy Peters

Legislatures perform many functions for democratic political systems. They are representative bodies that permit the public to have some direct influence over government. They also perform a symbolic function by legitimating actions made by government in the name of the people. But the two most important functions of legislatures are making public policy and holding the executive accountable for its actions. Even though many of the rules that govern the economy and society are made by executive degrees or by bureaucracies (Kerwin and Furlong, 2018), the most important rules in democracies must be adopted by legislative bodies. Likewise, there are numerous institutions for accountability, but legislatures play a central role in democracies.

The Congress of the United States performs all the other functions of a legislature, but it is perhaps particularly well-equipped to make law, when compared to other legislative bodies. Nelson Polsby (1975) argued that there are two basic types of legislatures – arena and transformative. Arena legislatures are places for political theatre, rather than true law-making organizations. These assemblies are found readily in authoritarian regimes, but it has been argued for some time that legislatures in democratic countries also are losing their governing role to cabinets and prime ministers (Grosser, 1964; Poguntke and Webb, 2007). Many legislatures continue to debate policy, but the real formulation of that policy is conducted elsewhere. The Congress, however, has the capacity to make law and, when sufficiently unified, to overrule the president and his veto. It has the capacity to be one of the few remaining transformative legislatures in the world.

In the current political climate, however, that transformative role for Congress in law-making has become more questionable. The severe partisan gridlock and the use of procedural devices such as the filibuster have made it difficult for any significant legislation to be passed. President Biden's COVID relief bill could only be passed through the somewhat arcane reconciliation process in the Senate, and any subsequent legislation of any consequence during his presidency looks at best challenging (Reich and Kogan, 2021). Indeed, it is claimed that some newer members of Congress view their role more as media personalities than as legislators (Cillizza, 2021), one indication of an increasing arena style within the institution.

A number of factors contribute to the potential for Congress to be a transformative legislature. The Constitution clearly gives Congress law-making powers, and especially control over the budget. Congress is well organized, with an elaborate system of committees and sub-committees with investigative as well as legislative powers. But perhaps the factor that distinguishes Congress more from other legislatures is its large staff, and the amount of support which individual congressmen, the committees, and Congress as a whole have when they attempt to make law. If members of Congress want to make good law, they certainly have the staff support to facilitate their doing so. Even with those negative political factors affecting Congress, it appears that the availability of staff do make a difference for legislating and do influence the output of the legislature (Price, 2004). This chapter will focus on the role of Congress in making law, but the staffing available also is important for accountability.

Although not discussed in any detail here, it is worth noting that the state legislatures in most of the 50 states are also well staffed. State legislatures combined employ roughly 30,000 staff members. The staffs range from under 100 employees in Vermont to almost 3,000 in New York, and those numbers may not include all personal staffs for the legislators. The staffing obviously not only varies with the size of the state and the legislature but also reflects the level of professionalism in the legislature (Squire, 2007). But even compared to many national legislatures, larger state legislatures in the United States are well equipped with staff.

57.1 Staffing for the Two Houses of Congress

In 2021, the Congress of the United States directly employs roughly 20,000 people. It also has some influence over hiring several thousand other employees, such as the Capitol Police.[1] These employees range from highly skilled economists, lawyers, and scientists to clerks and lower level technicians. These numbers do not include ancillary organizations such as the Library of Congress,[2] or the National Botanical Gardens (for historical reasons controlled by Congress). Although small when compared to the executive branch bureaucracy, this is a very large staff when compared with other legislatures.

There are five major groups of staff serving Congress (see Table 57.1). The largest group are personal staffs of each Congressman and Senator. Then there are staffs for the committees in each house, as well as for several joint committees. The third group are the staffs for the leadership of the two houses, e.g. the majority and minority leaders and whips.

Table 57.1 Congressional staff members (1979–2015)

Individual Legislators (average)	House of Representative	16
	Senate	39
Each Committee[5] (average)	House of Representative	69
	Senate	37
Leadership and Officers	House of Representatives	529
	Senate	1093
Congress as a Whole	Congressional Research Service	616
	Congressional Budget Office	240
	Government Accountability Office	2,997
Approximate total		20,000

The fourth group are the various officers of each house, e.g. parliamentarians, doorkeepers, and clerks. Some of these posts are more ceremonial than functional but they are still part of the Congressional staff. The final group of staff are the employees of the three major support agencies that provide research and analysis to Congress.

Employment in Congressional staff positions is largely a patronage system (Panizza et al, 2019), as opposed to the merit-based system found in most of the executive branch.[3] Staff members are generally talented and well qualified, but the hiring process is based more on political loyalty and personal compatibility than on the formalized criteria characteristic of the Civil Service. Likewise, these staffers can be fired with ease. The personalization of hiring and firing is especially evident for personal staffs of Congressmen, while the three major supporting organizations have at least the rudiments of a personnel system.

Going along with the patronage basis of employment, although they are government employees, Congressional staff members are not members of the Civil Service. Indeed, except for some employees such as the Capitol Police, there is no fixed system of rewards. Each member of Congress receives an allowance for staff, with Senators from larger states receiving somewhat more than Senators from smaller states.[4] It is them up to the Congressmen and Senators to decide how to spend the money, and how to reward their staff members. Further, some members may supplement their allowances from Congress with money from other sources, such as donors or personal funds, and hire more people and/or pay somewhat higher salaries.

The market for legislative staffers tends to produce outcomes that are approximately ten per cent lower than the pay offered to career civil servants. For example, in 2019, the average maximum payment for staffers in the House of Representatives was $173,900 (Congressional Research Service, 2020). Salaries in the three supporting organizations for Congress are approximately the same, although the personnel systems in those have regular procedures for granting performance bonuses. In that same year, the top civil servants in the United States earned just over $190,000. In fairness, those top level civil are career employees who tend to have longer experience in government than most staffers. Given that many of the staff employees are lawyers, economists, and accountants, they may be able to earn more money outside government but choose public sector careers either because of their interest in public service, or because they hope to themselves have political careers.

57.1.1 The Staffs of Individual Members

As shown in Table 57.2, each member of the House of Representatives employees on average of 16 staff, and each Senator an average of 39 staff. Although members of Congress have substantial latitude to shape their staffs as they might see fit, in practice the staffs of most appear rather similar. There is generally a chief of staff responsible for running the office and serving as the connection between the member and the staff. The additional top figures are a legislative assistance and an administrative assistant. The first of these is responsible for working on legislation, both within the office and in liaison with other congressional and committee staffs, and the latter manages the day-to-day affairs, scheduling, etc. There will

Table 57.2 Staffing in the US congress, 2015

	Staff per member (app.)
House	31
Senate	46

almost certainly be a communications officer, as well as other staff members responsible for media affairs.

The above members of staff not work primarily in Washington, but members will also have staff members back in their constituencies – Senators tend to have multiple offices scattered around the state – responsible for maintaining the political connections with the voters, while the member is in Washington. One of the most common type of employees in the district offices are caseworkers who are responsible for managing complaints coming from citizens about their problems with various federal agencies, and trying to redress those grievances. Congressmen have always helped their re-election chances by serving their constituents in this manner (Fiorina, 1989) and with the decline of legislative activity these caseworkers may be even more important for the member.

The staff of the individual members are important politically and legislatively for the members. Most members of Congress "go home" on weekends to maintain their political connections, but their staff is there full time dealing with constituency business and with the media. Further, staff members are especially important for new members of Congress. After each election, there is some movement of staff members. There are retirements and defeats and the staffers left without a job will seek to catch on with a new member. The experience that the veteran staff member can bring to the office of a new member can be extremely valuable for their success, as they embark on a different type of career (Leal and Hess, 2004).

There is also evidence that legislative staff in general affect the performance and even the policy ideas of members of Congress. Careful selection of staff could improve the effectiveness of Representatives and Senators, simply because staff with experience had connections with other staffers and with other members that enabled better communication and collaboration. Further, staff with previous service in Congress tended to be able to shape the policy preferences of members.

The influence of experienced staffers on their members leads to another important point about the staff in Congress. Many of these staffers are careerists who will spend their working lives in Congress, in some position or another. Some may have progressive ambition and want to move up, whether to being a member of Congress themselves, or perhaps moving into a career position in the executive branch, but many will be content to remain as Congressional staffers. The longevity of many staff members in office, and the frequent contacts with other staffers, means that there is an important network of experienced individuals who can help make Congress work better than it might otherwise.

57.1.2 Committee Staffing

In addition to the staffs serving individual Congressmen, each of the committees in Congress has its own staff. For some committees with greater responsibilities, e.g. appropriations, that staff may be 100 or even more, while for smaller committees the staffing may be only around 40. Those staffs are divided into majority and minority staffs, with some staff being neutral (largely because of performing technical functions for the entire staff). There are always lawyers as members of the staff to advise on the legality of proposed legislation, as well as economists to provide an economic analysis of proposed legislation, with most members simply described as "professional staff".[6]

As was true for the staff of individual members, these committee staff have substantial influence over the legislation proposed by Congress. Most of the work off Congress is done in committees and subcommittees, and the content of any legislation that emerges will be influenced by staff work. In general, members of Congress have broad-brush ideas about policy but then rely on their own staffs and the staffs of committees to flesh out those ideas and produce workable legislation. The executive branch is also at work drafting legislation, as seen very clearly in the first days of the Biden administration, but in a transformative legislature such as Congress is meant to be a good deal of policy work must be done there, even if that work is only analysing and reshaping the proposals from the executive.

The committee staffs are important for the oversight function of Congress and well as the legislative function. The committees of Congress tend to mirror the structure of the executive branch, and committees find that they can not only perform effective oversight but also gain political visibility by holding hearings on real or perceived failures of executive agencies. The staff of the committee is important for preparing these hearings and assisting committee members in developing good questions that will have the maximum impact for both oversight and for visibility.

57.2 General Support Organizations for Congress

The third type of staff employment for Congress is in the three major support organizations that serve both houses, as well as serving both parties. At present, these are three of the small number of organizations that attempt to be bipartisan, and to provide expert advice to Congress, as well as to the interested members of the public. Most legislatures around the world have organizations that are analogous to at least two these organizations – the Congressional Research Service (CRS) and the Government Accountability Office – but the American versions tend to be somewhat more extensive than other organizations performing similar functions.

57.2.1 Government Accountability Office

The oldest of the three general support organizations for Congress is the Government Accountability Office (GAO), formerly the General Accounting Office. This was, and is, the organization that audits the government's books, but it now does much more. Over time, from at least the 1970s (Mosher, 1979), the GAO has become a policy analytic organization. It asks not only is the money spent by the executive branch being spent legally, but it also asks if it is being spent in the best manner possible. Almost every day, the GAO is issuing reports discussing how particular programmes could perform better, in addition to its continuing work as the auditor, and its continuing monitoring of high risk programmes.

Although its output is of interest to many people in the executive branch, and the private sector, the GAO serves Congress. Each of its analyses of policy, with the exception of on-going reviews of key policy areas, is at the request of a member of Congress or a committee. These reports not only facilitate writing better legislation, but perhaps more importantly they are means of Congress enforcing accountability. As already noted, that accountability goes beyond simple financial oversight and includes assessments of whether money is spent wisely and efficiently. Thus, the GAO is performing both accounting and policy analysis on behalf of Congress.

57.2.2 Congressional Research Service

The CRS is the second of the support organizations for Congress. As the name implies, this organization performs research for Congress to help make the laws passed by Congress better informed. The CRS is formally housed in the Library of Congress and was originally designed to be more of a public think tank about policy and government, rather than a service to Congress. Over time, however, Congress demanded more direct service and although most reports form the CRS are publicly available, the "client" is Congress.

Each year, the staff of the CRS turns out hundreds of reports on policy issues, as well as monitoring the institutions of the federal government. Some distinguished scholars have spent all, or some of their careers in CRS, and have had the latitude to write scholarly books and papers as well as serving the needs of Congress. Further, unlike the Government Accountability Office, the CRS has the capacity to choose more of its own subjects for research.

57.2.3 Congressional Budget Office

The Congressional Budget Office (CBO) was created as a result of the Congressional Budgeting and Impoundment Control Act of 1974. Although the Constitution gives the power of the purse to Congress, the executive branch had gained supremacy in this area. This dominance by the executive was at least in part a function of the president having the Office of Management and Budget and the Council of Economic Advisors to give him expert advice on the budget and the economic implications of the budget. Congress had some expertise located in the appropriations committees, and in the revenue committees[7], but was at a severe disadvantage when compared with the president.

Because of its bipartisan nature (see Binder, 2017), the CBO has been established a reputation for "honest numbers" and tends to be more accurate in its economic forecasts than the Council of Economic Advisors serving the president (see Joyce, 2011). Its work is primarily on the expenditure side of the budget and is supplemented by the work of the Joint Committee on Taxation on the revenue side. One of the important aspects of that work on expenditures is estimating the long-term costs of spending proposals, so that Congress can understand better the implications of any policy choices (see Congressional Budget Office, 2021).

57.3 Trends in Legislative Staffing

Although the basic facts of legislative staffing in the United States have been stable, there are several important trends that should be considered. The first is that some types of legislative staffing, while remaining much higher than in other countries, have been declining (see Table 57.3). Staffing for committees and for individual members of Congress has been declining, and in the case of personal staff declining significantly. Interestingly, although so much of the power in Congress, and especially in the Senate, has passed to the leadership, that staffing has also declined.

This chapter has emphasized the importance of staffers for the legislative work of Congress and its members. The assumption has been that the staff constitute a "bureaucracy for democracy" (Peters, forthcoming) that enables legislators to perform their central task better and more easily. There is some evidence, however, that increasing amounts of staff time are going to constituency service, to fund-raising, and to electoral politics, rather than to legislation (Furnas, 2018; Reynolds, 2019). Congressmen have always invested heavily in providing services to their constituents (Cain, Ferejohn and Fiorina 2013), and that activity seems to be a guaranteed political winner. That practice seems to have become more important, perhaps because Congress now does relatively less legislating, and sees even more clearly that taking policy stands alienates some voters as well as pleasing others.

Table 57.3 Congressional Staff Members 1979–2015

	1979	1985	1995	2001	2005	2010	2012	2015
House of Representatives								
Committee	2027	2146	1266	1201	1272	1454	1289	1164
Personal	7067	7528	7186	7209	6804	7012	6683	6030
Leadership	162	144	134	166	176	202	217	201
Officers	1487	1818	1327	892	490	332	312	308
Senate								
Committee	1410	1178	796	889	957	n.a.	973	951
Personal	3593	4097	4247	3994	3934	n.a.	3894	3917
Leadership	91	118	126	221	189	n.a.	171	173
Officers, etc.	828	976	994	950	1114	n.a.	922	846
Support Agencies								
GAO	5303	5042	4342	3155	3215	3350	2997	2989
CRS	847	860	746	722	700	679	616	609
CBO	204	222	214	228	235	254	240	235

That same tendency to focus on constituency service, rather than on making policy, has also been argued to be undermining at least one of the central institutions serving Congress. One former CRS analyst (Kosar, 2015) wrote that he resigned from the CRS because he was spending more and more of his time answering queries from constituents passed on to him by congressional offices rather than doing the policy research he thought he was hired to do. The downsizing of the staff of CRS, and the other central service organizations for Congress, reflects this general shift away from a focus on legislation, and on the institution of Congress, in favour or more individualistic pursuits. The emphasis on constituency service appears to demoralize the expert talent that is hired to work in the CRS.

Some of the decline in staffing in Congress may also represent that with the increasing digitalization of information gathering and processing, performing the research tasks that were important for staffers is now that much easier. And the increased polarization of politics in the United States has meant that information gathering can be easier simply because the sources consulted, and the ideas considered, are being narrowed. Democratic members of Congress will want one type of information and Republicans another, and although the central support organizations attempt to remain bipartisan, the individual staffs do not.

In addition to the decline in staffing numbers, average salaries for legislative staff have been declining slightly over the past several years (Congressional Research Service, 2020; Table 57.4). When considered in real terms, the decline in pay over the past two decades has been approximately 20 per cent. These numbers are based on limited samples of staff salaries, so may be influenced by changes in the seniority of the staffers involved. For example, average salaries tend to be lower after each election, when newer staff with less experience (and lower salaries) are hired. The general decline of salaries does, however, appear to

Table 57.4 Annual Maximum Pay for Selected Staff in House Member's Offices, 2001–2019

	Nominal $	Constant $ 2020
2001	$140,451	$204,258
2005	156,848	206,847
2010	168,411	198,919
2012	168,411	192,832
2020	173,900	173,900

Source: Congressional Research Service, Staff Pay Levels for Selected Positions in House Members' Offices, (Washington, DC: CRS, Report R44323).

reflect some devaluing of staff services This may reflect changing priorities of members of Congress, as well as the impact of technology such as social media that may make staff services less valuable. That said, salaries in the support organizations for Congress have been keeping their value better, in part because of more institutionalized personnel management systems.

57.4 Conclusion

The Congress of the United States has had the potential to be a truly transformative legislature. The Constitution gives it ample legislative powers, especially over the raising and spending of public money. As the discussion above has demonstrated, it has had ample staffing for individual Congressmen and Senators, for the committees in the two houses, and for the institution as a whole. With these resources, Congress should be able to make good public policy and defend its policy choices in any conflicts with the executive branch.

When we examine the current trends in the use of staff, and of legislating, the picture of an active and effective Congress does not emerge so clearly. The level of staffing for Congress is declining, as are the salaries paid to staff. The anecdotal evidence is that members of Congress now are more concerned with fund-raising and with creating a media presence than they are with the work of making law. This loss of interest in legislating may be explained in part by the difficulties in legislating in a Congress that is deeply divided politically and ideologically. Given that little real policymaking is likely, the members might as well work to perpetuate their own position in Congress, and become "influences" on social media.

This deinstitutionalization of Congress undermines the transformative nature of the institution. While still better supported than most legislatures, there is now less staff and some of it is demoralized by the declining interest in governance by many members of Congress. The Congress still has some capacity to be a transformative legislature, if it has the interest, but that interest is waning. The question then becomes whether it will also lose interest in exercising oversight and cede power to the executive and judicial branches.

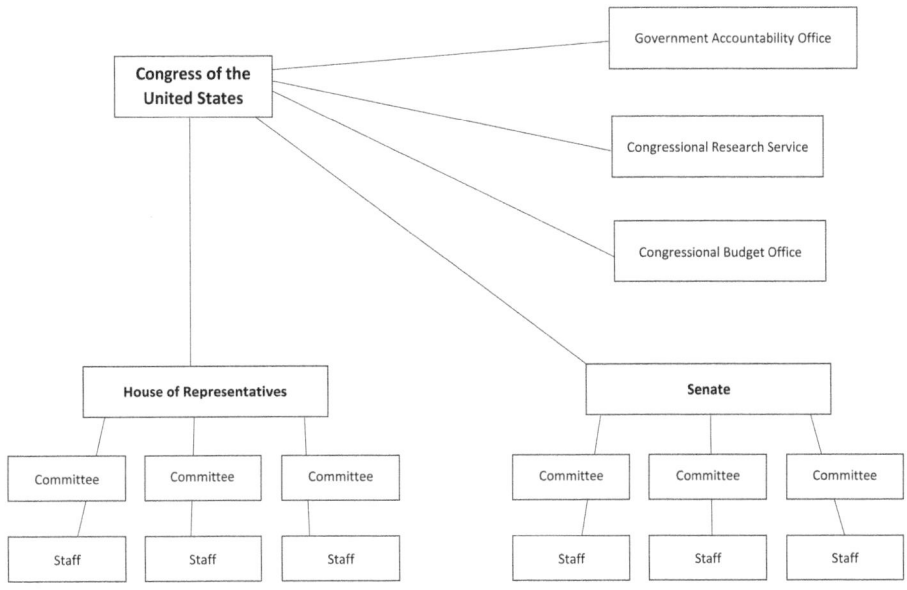

Administrative Structure of the Congress of the United States

Notes

1. This role became apparent during the January 6, 2021, invasion of the capitol when that small police force was overwhelmed by the insurrectionists.
2. The Congressional Research Service, to be discussed below, is technically a component of the Library of Congress and is included in this tabulation. The actual library staff, another 3,000 people, is not included.
3. The president can fill approximately 4,500 positions by appointment, but merit system employees are over 2 million.
4. Each member of the House receives close to $1 million per year for staff. Senators receive between $3 and 5 million (Congressional Research Service, 2018).
5. Average for standing committees. Select Committees, Special Committees usually lower levels of employment.
6. For listing on Senate committee staffing, see https://www.govinfo.gov/content/pkg/CDIR-2020-07-22/pdf/CDIR-2020-07-22-SENATECOMMITTEES.pdf
7. Ways and Means in the House and Finance in the Senate.

References

Cain, B., J. Ferejohn and M. Fiorina (2013) *The Personal Vote: Constituency Service and Electoral Independence* (Cambridge, MA: Harvard University Press).

Cillizza, C. (2021) Matt Gaetz Has Zero Interest in Being in Congress" *CNN Politics* March 30, https://www.cnn.com/2021/03/30/politics/matt-gaetz-congress-newsmax/index.html

Congressional Budget Office (2021) *Estimated Budgetary Effects of the American Rescue Plan 2021* (Washington, DC: CBO) https://www.cbo.gov/publication/57012.

Congressional Research Service (2018) *Congressional Salaries and Allowances In Brief* (Washington, DC: CRS), Report RL30064.

Congressional Research Service (2020) *Staff Pay Levels for Selected Positions in House Member Offices, 2001-19* (Washington, DC: Congressional Research Service).

Fiorina, M. (1989) *Congress: Keystone of the Washington Establishment*, 2nd ed. (New Haven, CT: Yale University Press).

Furnas, A. C. (2018) Legislative staff are spending an increasing amount of time on constituent services," *LegBranch*, April 11, https://www.legbranch.org/2018-4-11-legislative-staff-are-spending-an-increasing-amount-of-time-on-constituent-services/

Grosser, A. (1964) The Evolution of European Parliaments, *Daedalus* 93, 153–178.

Hertel-Fernandez, A., M. Mildenberger and L. C. Stokes (2019) Legislative Staff and Representation in Congress, *American Political Science Review* 113, 1–18.

Joyce, P. (2011) *The Congressional Budget Office: Honest Numbers, Power and Policymaking* (Washington, DC: Georgetown University Press).

Kerwin, C. M. and S. R, Furlong (2018) *Rulemaking: How Government Agencies Write Rules and Make Policy*, 5th ed. (Washington, DC: CQ Press).

Kosar, K. R. (2015) Why I quit the Congressional Research Service, Washington Monthly, January/February https://washingtonmonthly.com/magazine/janfeb-2015/why-i-quit-the-congressional-research-service/

Leal, D. L. and F. M. Hess (2004) Who Chooses Experience?: Examining the Use of Veteran Staff by House Freshmen, *Polity* 36, 651–664.

Mosher, F. C. (1979) *The GAO: The Quest for Accountability in American Government* (Boulder, CO: Westview Press).

Ornstein, N. J., T. E. Mann, M. J. Malbin, A. Rugg and R. Wakeman (2019) *Vital Statistics on Congress* (Washington, DC: Brookings Institution and American Enterprise Institute).

Panizza, F., B. Guy Peters and C. Ramos Larraburu (2019) "Roles, trusts and skills: A typology of patronage appointments" *Public Administration*, 97: 147–161.

Peters, B. G., (forthcoming) Bureaucracy for Democracy: Administration in Support of Democracy, Unpublished paper, University of Pittsburgh.

Poguntke, T. and P. Webb (2007) *Presidentialization of Politics: A Comparative Study of Modern Democracies* (Oxford; Oxford University Press).

Polsby, N. W. (1975) 'Legislatures', in F. I. Greenstein and N. W. Polsby (eds), *Handbook of Political Science*, vol. 5 (Reading, MA: Addison-Wesley).

Price, D. E. (2004) *The Congressional Experience*, 3rd ed. (Boulder, CO: Westview Press).

Reich, D. and R. Kogan (2021) Introduction to Budget "Reconciliation", (Washington, DC: Center for Budget and Policy Priorities) January 22, https://www.cbpp.org/sites/default/files/atoms/files/1-22-15bud.pdf

Reynolds, M. (2019) The Decline of Congressional Capacity, in T. M. Lapira, L. Drutman and K, R. Kosar, eds., *Congress Overwhelmed: The Decline of Congressional Capacity and Prospects for Reform* (Chicago, IL: University of Chicago Press).

Squire, P. (2007) Measuring State Legislative Professionalism: The Squire Index Revisited, *State Politics and Policy* 7, 211–227.

PART III

The Transnational Dimension of Parliamentary Administration

58
EUROPEAN PARLIAMENT'S ADMINISTRATION

Francis Jacobs and Alfredo De Feo

This entry covers five topics, the specificity of the European Parliament, key aspects of the organisation of its Administration, the latter's role in the context of Parliamentary work and how it manages both Inter-institutional and External Relations and a number of current challenges.

58.1 The Specificity of the European Parliament

The European Parliament is a very distinctive Parliament in many respects, in its large size, multinational and multilingual nature, its divided location in three different countries and its unusual and rapidly evolving institutional context.

Before detailing some of these specific characteristics, it should, however, be recalled that the formal competences of the EP are defined by the Treaties, and that these have progressively increased as a result of successive Treaties from the Single European Act up to Lisbon. It has thus evolved from being a mere consultative Assembly in 1957, to being a full co-legislator in almost all areas of activities of the EU, including the Budget. Beyond the formal competences attributed by the Treaties, the European Parliament has also been very active in enlarging its sphere of competences and influence in a pragmatic way through soft law.

58.1.1 An Exceptionally Large Parliament

The Lisbon Treaty provides for the European Parliament to have 751 members, which would make it the world's largest directly elected Parliament. Even after the departure of the UK, it still has 705 members, second only in size to the German Bundestag. It could again increase in numbers in the future, either in the case of further EU enlargement or if an additional transnational European constituency is also created.

The consequences of this large size are self-evident, with large buildings required to house the MEPs and an exceptionally large Parliament staff. Besides the permanent staff, the numbers of MEPs, political groups and parties all help to push up the overall numbers of staff.

58.1.2 A Multinational Parliament

The European Parliament is directly elected in 27 EU Member States and is thus one of only a handful of multinational parliamentary bodies. Of these, it is both the largest and the only one with real powers. Both its MEPs and staff come from many different countries, and this is reflected in a wide range of different parliamentary traditions and cultures which have also given rise to different elements of Parliament's rules and procedures.

58.1.3 A Multilingual Parliament

Having MEPs from 27 Member States also implies a large number of official and working languages, the most used in any Parliament in the world, with the right for all elected Members to speak their own language and the obligation to legislate in all languages of the Union being fundamental principles of the European Union.

If the principles are undisputed, there is often flexibility in their practical implementation, and the system that has been developed is often referred to as "controlled multilingualism", with some interpretation and translation only being provided on demand.

In spite of these pragmatic measures, direct linguistic services still amount to about 25% of the 5,400 permanent staff of the Parliament and account for a substantial portion of its administrative budget.

Linguistic constraints also have other practical effects on the workings of the Parliament, such as by slowing down the adoption of Parliament texts both in committee and then in plenary.

As regards the languages used by EP staff, French used to be the leading language within Parliament's administration but, especially after the enlargement in 2004, English has become increasingly dominant.

58.1.4 A Parliament with Several Places of Work

A further major constraint on EP organisation, and one now imposed by the Treaties, is its dispersion over three working places, with most EP permanent staff divided between Luxembourg and Brussels, political group staff and most EP committee meetings in Brussels and most plenaries in Strasbourg.

Parliament's staff had almost entirely been based in Luxembourg, but over time the Parliament's political group staff mainly moved to Brussels as well as a considerable part of the permanent secretariat, particularly those services most linked to committee work and to communications.

There are two sets of rigidities caused by the geographical dispersion of its staff, the political agreement which obliges the EP to maintain a minimum number of staff based in Luxembourg; and Parliament's policy to only transfer its staff on a voluntary basis, which has limited both the geographical and functional mobility of its staff. Although much less than in the past, there has also been a considerable financial and human cost in all the travel between the two working places. All this has been only partly mitigated by video conferences and other technological aids.

This dispersion has also seen the development of a different administrative culture in the two cities, often more political in Brussels due to the need to work closely with MEPs, and more administrative in Luxembourg where staff very often have little contact with members.

The European Parliament is also highly unusual, however, among parliamentary administrations in having small branch offices in each of the Member States and in Washington, DC and London as well as running training centres, museums and interactive visitor facilities.

The European Parliament holds 12 part sessions a year in Strasbourg, almost 500 km from the centre of its core activities. A small number of permanent staff are based in Strasbourg primarily for the maintenance of the buildings, and about 1,000 EP staff have to travel there to each plenary, along with Commissioners and their staff, Council Ministers, journalists, interest groups (IGs) as well as visitors. The human and financial (and environmental) costs of all this are significant, in spite of efforts to mitigate this by greatly reducing the number of physical documents transported.

Although MEPs are divided on the question, a majority within the Parliament have questioned the costs of all this travelling and contest the inability of the Parliament to have the freedom to choose its own organisation and working place. Modification of the legal status quo will be difficult, but this issue will continue to be raised in the future.

58.1.4.1 A Parliament Operating in a Rapidly Evolving Institutional Framework

The EP administration is distinctive in other respects as well. It has had to operate in a rapidly changing institutional framework, with its powers being steadily increased through European Union Treaty changes, Inter-Institutional Agreements and other mechanisms. It has thus had to constantly adapt its working methods to new powers and procedures to a much greater extent than most national parliaments.

The European Parliament has also operated in a separation of powers system more akin to that enjoyed by the US Congress than that facing all European national parliaments. It is elected every 5 years and cannot be dissolved by the EU Executive. On the other hand, it has no direct hold over the Council or European Council although it elects the European Commission and can also censure it. It also shares legislative and budgetary powers with the Council. The implications of all this are discussed in Section 58.4.

58.2 Key Aspects of the Organisation of the Parliamentary Administration

The European Parliament administration supports the work of the Members of the EP both logistically and in their parliamentary work.

58.2.1 Size and Structure of the Administration

The total number of staff (2021) within the EP administration is 5,400, which increases to 6,513 if contract agents, employed for specific tasks and a limited period of time, are also added to the total. Staff is divided within 12 Directorates Generals **although there is now a proposal to create a 13th one as well (see below). These DGs** basically serve five functional groups (see Table 58.1).

The fact that only 25% is devoted to active linguistic services is misleading, in that most of the other services also have a requirement for multilingualism. This is particularly true not only for the Communication Services, which have offices in 35 European cities, but also for plenary and committee services.

Table 58.1 Functional distribution of EP staff and contractual agents 2019

Staff supporting directly parliamentary work (plenary and committees secretariats)	1,153	18%
Staff supporting indirectly parliamentary work research service and communication	1,065	16%
Active linguistic services (translation and interpretation)	1,650	25%
Central services (personnel, buildings, finance, IT and security)	2,535	39%
Legal service	110	2%
Total	**6,513**	**100%**

Source: Own calculations on EP documents on Discharge 2019

58.2.2 Political Groups and Members Assistants

The EP Administration also has to work closely with the staff of political groups (1,135 persons in 2021) and with MEPs personal assistants (1,941 in 2021). The balance between these three categories (pillars) of staff has evolved considerably over time. During the first three decades of the directly elected Parliament, the EP administration was particularly influential over the political choices of the EP with MEPs and staff united in pursuing the reinforcement of EP competences. The Lisbon Treaty, however, reinforced the legislative role of the EP, which enhanced the role of individual MEPs and their personal assistants, and increased their influence on the decision-making process.

EP Committees' secretariats remain at the core of parliamentary activities, but a wider range of services are now offered to MEPs in their work as legislators.

58.2.3 Professionalisation and Recruitments

The provision of expertise to support MEPs and committees legislative work has been enhanced. An EP Research Service has been steadily built up and in 2019 has a staff of 294 to respond to requests not only from individual MEPs but also from EP bodies, political groups and citizens. The EPRS is also at the services of two other Institutions, the Committee of the Regions and the Economic and Social Committee. In addition, Parliamentary committees have also been allocated their own financial resources to purchase external expertise. These resources are managed by five Policy Departments, each of which serves a specific set of committees.

Enhancing legislative quality has been another key EP objective, and one that has been furthered by the creation of a dedicated service of lawyer-linguists who assist MEPs, committees and the plenary in the preparation of amendments in the final legislative stages.

Institutional Communication has been another area which has seen significant development in as discussed in Section 58.5.

The professionalisation of the EP Administration was accelerated in 2014, when the EP Secretary General launched a new "Strategic Execution Framework" which sought to move from a system based on rules to a culture more focused on results and on client satisfaction. The Strategic Execution Framework defines the EP's long-term goals as well as the strategy to accomplish them. This approach not only sets the objectives but also provides more accurate measurement of progress over time (key performance indicators), as well as establishing decentralised managerial structures for each project, in order to overcome existing silo structures and to strengthen matrix organisation.

The EP staff is recruited mainly by external competitions, organised by a central office (EPSO) serving all EU Institutions but also by internal competitions to upgrade Assistants to Administrators and to allow staff of the political groups to enter into the Administration. In the period from 2018 to 2020, about 75% of the 500 new staff was recruited centrally through EPSO.

A sensitive issue related to the EP Secretariat is that of the balance between its independence and the extent of politicisation. The culture of the EP Administration is to be independent from political appointments, and this has been true of most jobs within the Parliament. The staff policy of the Secretary General is, however, closely monitored by the political authority (the Bureau of the EP) which has increased the politicisation of the Secretariat, with a clear political influence on certain nominations, especially to the top jobs, and not just to that of Secretary General. An overall consensus on these top jobs is sought between the political groups, implying upward pressure on the number of such jobs available so that a majority of the groups can have their fair share. This was again shown in June 2022 when the then Secretary General announced his intention to retire in January 2023. Following this announcement, the EP Bureau took a decision to create a new Directorate-General for Parliamentary Democracy Partnerships, the structure and cost of which were not immediately clear.

Geographical balance between staff and gender equality are two other factors which influence EP recruitment policy.

The need for geographical balance is not a legal requirement for the EU institutions but instead a political and moral commitment, constantly present in the recruitment phase. Figure 58.1 below shows the relations between managers (blue line) and all staff (brown line) and the number of MEPs. The table below shows a varied situation: a high percentage for small countries among all staff and a relatively balanced situation concerning managers from the biggest countries.

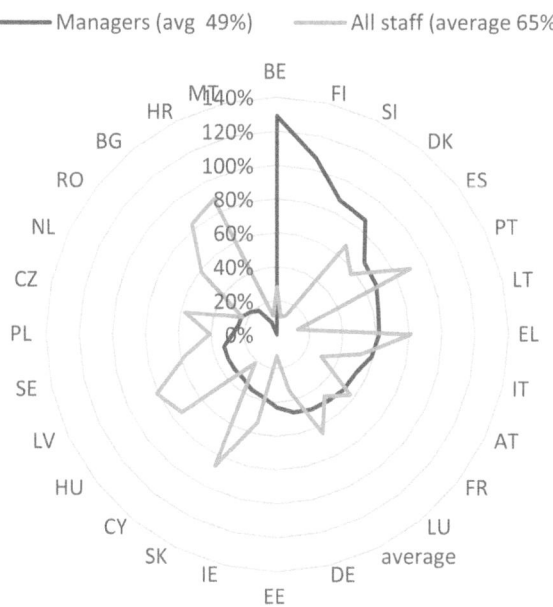

Figure 58.1 Ratios EP managers and all staff related to MEPs (in %)

Source: Own calculations on EP documents on Discharge 2019

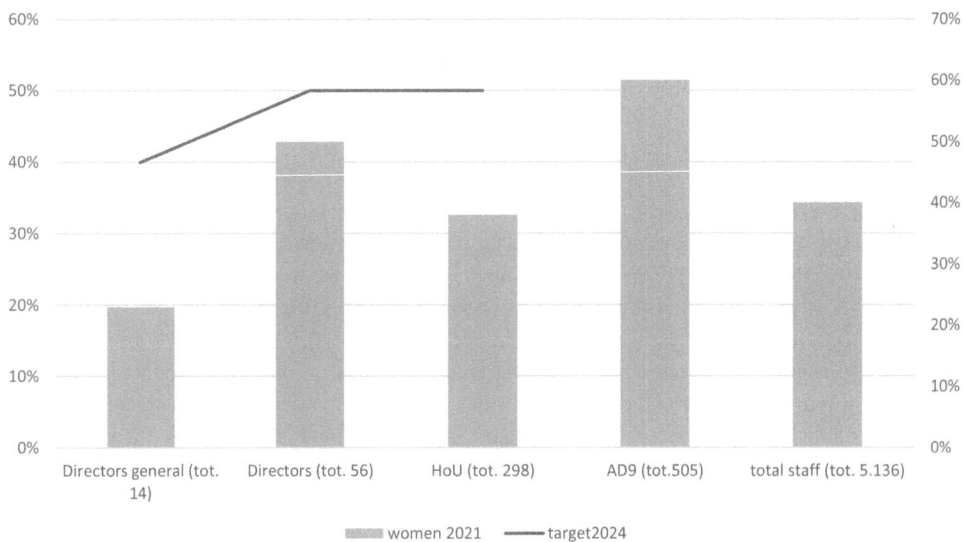

Figure 58.2 Gender equality in the EP 2021

Source: Own calculations on EP documents

The search for better gender balance has been particularly successful in the EP. The ambitious targets that were set for top managers (objective 2024) have been almost attained for Directors and are steadily progressing for Heads of Unit (HoUs) and Directors Generals. It is also interesting to note the high percentage of women who are in the AD9 grade, a requirement to attain top managers' positions (Figure 58.2).

To conclude, the EP Administration has successfully adapted over time to new challenges and has become more professional in offering the best possible services to the Institution, its MEPs and its Governing bodies. At the same time, its structures will need to be constantly re-examined, for example the functionality of its division into 12 Directorates General and Directorates, the logic of having expertise provided both by a separate Research Directorate-General and by Policy Departments within the Committees and the ongoing questions concerning the politicisation of the administration.

58.3 The Role of the Administration in the Context of Parliamentary Work

58.3.1 *The Nature of the Institutional Hierarchy*

The day-to-day work within the Administration is controlled by the Bureau, whereas overall political guidance is provided by the Conference of Presidents (CoP).

The Bureau of the Institution takes financial, organisational and administrative decisions on matters concerning the internal organisation of the EP secretariat and is composed by the President and 11 Vice-Presidents, each responsible for a sector of the administration.

The CoP consists of the President of the European Parliament and the chairs of the EP Political Groups, along with a representative of the non-attached members. The CoP provides direction for the political activities of the Parliament and supervises its agenda and future legislative planning. It is also the authority responsible for matters concerning relations with the other EU institutions and bodies, including national parliaments of Member States and all relations concerning non-member countries and non-Union institutions and organisations.

The President of the Parliament is elected for a two-and-a-half-year term of office at the beginning of, and half way through, the EP's 5-year cycle. In theory, his or her term of office can be renewed, but this has only occurred in the case of one EP President (Martin Schulz) since the first direct elections in 1979. The extent to which the President is a Speaker with limited powers or someone who can play a more active leadership role is not clearly defined in the EP Rules and depends to a considerable extent on the personality of the President.

The President chairs both the Bureau and the CoP and liaises with the Secretary General to prepare all important decisions concerning the two bodies. The President is backed up by his or her Cabinet or private office which may consist of outsiders or else officials from within the EP permanent staff or political groups. Tensions are possible between the President's office and the Secretary General but these are generally mitigated by the compromise culture of the Institution.

The CoP is supported on EP legislative work by the Conference of Committee Chairs (CCC), a body grouping all the Chairs of parliamentary committees. The CCC advises the CoP on the state of play of the different legislatives files in order to help prepare the plenary agenda. The CCC also brings to the attention of the CoP any conflicts of competence among committees as it is the CoP which is the body ultimately entrusted to decide which committee(s) should be in charge of a legislative file.

The Secretary General is appointed by the Bureau and is responsible for all decisions taken to it, in conjunction with the President of the Parliament. He or she can also have considerable influence on the shaping of those decisions, as shown by several of the EP's five Secretaries General since the first direct elections in 1979. At the time of his resignation, Klaus Welle, the longest serving SG, had worked with seven EP Presidents since taking office in 2009. The Secretary General is supported in all of his or her preparatory work by the 12 (and eventually 13) Directors General who were mentioned above.

58.3.2 The Politicisation of EP Role

The politicisation of the role of the EP has increased the influence on Parliamentary work of political groups and MEP Assistants, with this accentuated over time by a more rapid increase in their numbers, particularly in the case of Assistants. The role of the Administration appears, therefore, to be becoming more technical and more focused on the provision of background information for MEPs.

A final word on the relationship between the three categories of staff that were mentioned in Section 58.2, namely the EP Administration, the Secretariats of the Political Groups and the personal assistants to individual MEPs (whether accredited or local). There is no particular hierarchy among these three groups, as each has their own specific domain, but overlapping of responsibilities and conflicts of competence are not infrequent.

58.3.3 Support of the Administration for Parliamentary Committees

EP Committee and plenary work is backed up by many EP Services but, in particular, by the Directorates-General for Internal and External Policies (IPOL and EXPO) and the Directorate-General of the Presidency.

Their role reinforced by legislative co-decision, EP Committees have exceptionally large staffs by national parliamentary standards with over 20 permanent officials in the case of the larger committees and with the capacity to speak and/or write in several languages being an important factor.

In their various tasks, the committee staff have to interact closely with the political group staff (with three or more such staff following individual committees in the case of the larger political groups) as well as with MEPs personal assistants.

The formal hierarchy within each committee is provided by its Chair and four Vice-Chairs but in practice a vital role is also played by the Committee Coordinators, the spokespersons for each political group within a committee and who meet regularly along with the Committee Chair to decide on a committee's agenda and legislative priorities.

Another key task within a committee is carried out by "rapporteurs", the MEPs entrusted by a committee to draw up a specific legislative or non-legislative report for adoption in the committee and then in the plenary. In most cases, other political groups appoint "shadow rapporteurs" whose role has now also been codified in the EP Rules of Procedure and who increasingly form informal working groups under the leadership of the rapporteur.

An example of adaptation of committee working methods is when an EU legislative proposal overlaps the areas of competence of individual EP committees, where the possibility of associating several committees or even for Joint Committee reports and meetings is now provided for in the EP Rules of Procedure.

The ways in which background expertise can be mobilised by committees has also been adapted. For the most complex legislative files, a project team can now be put at the service of the rapporteur (and shadow rapporteurs). This is normally composed by a member of the committee secretariat, experts from the Research Service and Policy Departments and might also include staff in charge of communications, lawyer-linguists and the legal service as well as Members' assistants.

A further aspect which has been developed has been the enhancement of ex ante and ex post impact assessments, both to improve decision-making on EU legislation and to monitor its implementation.

58.4 Managing Inter-Institutional and External Relations

The "sui generis" EU Institutional Structure and the distinctive separation of powers system that was mentioned above means that the European Parliament is not in the same position as that of most other parliaments. Its relations with the other EU institutions are complex, as described below, but lead to the EP having much greater autonomy than most national parliaments from their own national executives. This is reflected in the work not just of the EP leadership but also that of EP "backbenchers" who have more independence than their national parliamentary counterparts, as well as on the work and structure of Parliament's Administration.

58.4.1 Inter-Institutional Relations

Inter-institutional relations among the European Parliament, European Commission and Council and European Council have become increasingly intense as the EP has grown in power.

In the early days, the EP was very much the weakest of the three main EU Institutions with a merely consultative role. There were few contacts with the Council and most developments of importance to the EP were first filtered through the Commission.

The EP's role has since evolved greatly, especially since the first direct elections in 1979, not just through formal Treaty changes but also through inter-institutional agreements and other soft law, which gradually expanded its own influence.

In less than 40 years, the EP has evolved from only having a modest budgetary power, covering around 30% of EU expenditure to becoming a co-legislator in most EU policies, including on the entire budget. It has also become more fully involved in the whole legislative cycle.

Relations with the other EU Institutions have consequently become ever closer. European Commissioners and their officials have long been present in the Parliament's committees and plenary sessions and the Commission has also made many explicit undertakings to the EP, notably in successive "Framework Agreements" negotiated with the Parliament (and frequently criticised by the Council) and in the political programmes put forward by new Presidents of the Commission.

Contacts with the Council, and, in particular, with Council Presidencies, are also now much greater than they were, in plenaries, in EP committees, in informal Council meetings and in many other fora.

These developments have had considerable implications for the European Parliament administration. EP staff have worked closely with MEPs to extend the powers of the Parliament and have acted as "sherpas" on inter-institutional relations. Moreover, the EP Administration has been proactive in adapting its structures to its new powers, such as when it pioneered a dedicated conciliation unit to handle the new legislative co-decision procedures.

EP committee staff have regular contact with the Commission and Council staffs in their areas of responsibility. Inter-Institutional Coordination Groups have been established to monitor progress on legislative procedures. New efforts are also being made to have better coordinated forward legislative planning among the EP, Council and Commission and also to promote better EU Regulation, through enhanced impact assessments and other means.

58.4.2 EP Parliamentary Diplomacy and Inter-Parliamentary Cooperation

The European Parliament has developed a dense network of inter-parliamentary contacts throughout the world and has also been proactive in parliamentary diplomacy in the promotion of human rights and of other EU policy objectives, such as in the field of climate change.

The European Parliament has created around 50 inter-parliamentary delegations. They vary greatly in size and have been created in a wide range of different contexts, such as delegations to parliamentary assemblies as well as many other delegations to individual countries or to groups of countries.

The European Parliament has sent a large number of ad hoc delegations to take part in both EU-led and international election observation activities.

The EP has sought to influence political debate and to engage in parliamentary diplomacy in a number of other contexts, participation of MEPs in EU delegations to international conferences, in the Transatlantic Legislative Dialogue and even bilateral initiatives with legislators in other countries (such as the Lange-Gibbons Code on Conduct on Multinational Cooperation drawn up by EU and US legislators in 1976). A more recent example has been on climate change where delegations of MEPs sought to convince counterparts in other countries, such as the Japanese Diet, in 2002, and the Russian Duma in 2004, to ratify the Kyoto Protocol.

A particular area of focus has been on promotion of Human Rights, notably, through urgency resolutions in practically every plenary session and through the established Sakharov Prize to human rights defenders around the world.

To back up the above activities, a separate Directorate-General for External Policies was set up in the 1980s, containing the EP Committees on Foreign Affairs, Development and International Trade as well as dedicated subcommittees on Security and Defence and on Human Rights. A Democracy Support and Election Coordination Group has been established. The EP offices in Washington, DC and in London are also active in EP parliamentary diplomacy, and the network is to be extended to cover ASEAN, the African Union and the United Nations – although some initiatives such as EP offices outside the EU and others considered non-essential to parliamentary core business, such as the House of European History have been subject to criticism, including by the other EU Institutions.

58.4.3 Relations with National Parliaments

Until 1979, all MEPs were nominated by their national parliaments. After direct elections, this was no longer the case and links with the national parliaments became much weaker, especially as the number of dual mandate MEPs continued to decline before being explicitly forbidden.

Since the 1990s, relations between the EP and national parliaments have again been enhanced, encouraged, in particular, by the greater role given to national parliaments in successive EU Treaties. There are now a large number of contact channels, such as conferences of parliamentary Speakers, and Joint Parliamentary and Committee meetings, of which the Conference of European Affairs Committees or COSAC is perhaps the best known.

The EP has established its own Directorate for Relations with National Parliaments and there is also a lot of technical cooperation at staff level, such as through the European Centre for Parliamentary Research and Documentation and through the Inter-parliamentary Information Exchange Platform or IPEX. For their part, the national parliaments have set up their own national parliamentary offices in Brussels which liaise on a permanent basis with the EP and its staff.

58.5 Managing Current Challenges Facing the Parliamentary Administration

This last section will present some specific features of the EP administration notably how it is handling digitalisation, security questions, relations with citizens and the impact of Covid-19 on parliamentary work.

58.5.1 Digitalisation of Parliamentary Work

The EP's Directorate-General for Innovation and Technological Support (DG ITEC) has played a crucial role in ensuring business continuity during the pandemic. As in other administrations, the modernisation of IT has encountered some resistance but over the long term has had a crucial impact on the simplification of procedures, the streamline of processes and financial savings for the institution.

The achievement of a "paperless Parliament" has been the most visible innovation and one which has represented a true revolution in the working methods of MEPs and staff. The aim of this project is to make all information and documents necessary to MEPs available anytime, anywhere, on any devices (desktops, tablets smartphones) and using any operating system (Windows, IOS and Android). Another IT tool has facilitated the making of budgetary and legislative amendments through dedicated applications. This has simplified the introduction of amendments not just for the end-users (MEPs) but also for the back office (translation and distribution) while still guaranteeing security and confidentiality.

The generalised use of tablets, which have become the primary working tool for MEPs, has facilitated the implementation of these innovations.

58.5.2 Transparency and Citizen Engagement

These have steadily become more important priorities for the European Parliament and for its Administration.

Before direct elections in 1979, European Parliament Committee meetings were closed to the public but they are now practically all open with only very limited exceptions. Access to the EP buildings has become more restricted because of growing security concerns but committee meetings are now web-streamed so that they can be followed by all those who are interested.

Other key aspects of transparency have included access to EP documents and regulation of the activities of IGs.

As regards the former, a register of documents has been established and there is a dedicated service within the EP Administration to handle public requests for documents.

The administration of the EP set up the first database to register IGs in the mid-1990s and in 2011 the Commission and Parliament created a Joint Register. Political agreement on a new Inter-institutional agreement also including the Council was adopted in December 2020 and is pending final approval. Each Institution would define the activities which only registered companies could perform (i.e. access to EP premises, participation in hearings).

An important form of interaction with citizens has been through the EP Petitions Committee and the handling of European Citizens Initiatives.

The EP Administration has also sought to be proactive in promoting awareness on the European Parliament among citizens, stakeholders and opinion leaders through communication and information campaigns and online channels and social media.

The EP thus has around 650 posts in its Communications Directorate-General (DG COMM), most of whom are in Brussels. Inter alia, they have developed a social media platform with over 1 million followers and which played an important role in the institutional campaign for the 2019 elections.

DG COMM is also the most decentralised part of the EP Administration with Liaison Offices in all of the 27 Member States (including two in all the largest Member States) as well as in London and Washington, DC. A key mission for all these offices is to "go local" and to communicate the work of the European Parliament in their own national languages and in a way best suited for their own national context.

Another important aspect of outreach to citizens (and one exceptionally developed by international parliamentary standards) is promotion of visits to the Parliament both centrally and locally, with more than 1.5 million visitors to EP premises in 2019.

A dedicated visitors facility, or "Parliamentarium", was first developed in Brussels. Interactive visitors' centres ("Europe Experiences") have now also been created in Strasbourg, and in other EP external offices, with the intention to provide them in all EU Member States by 2024. The European Parliament also runs the Museum of European History in Brussels and owns and promotes visits to Jean Monnet's house outside Paris.

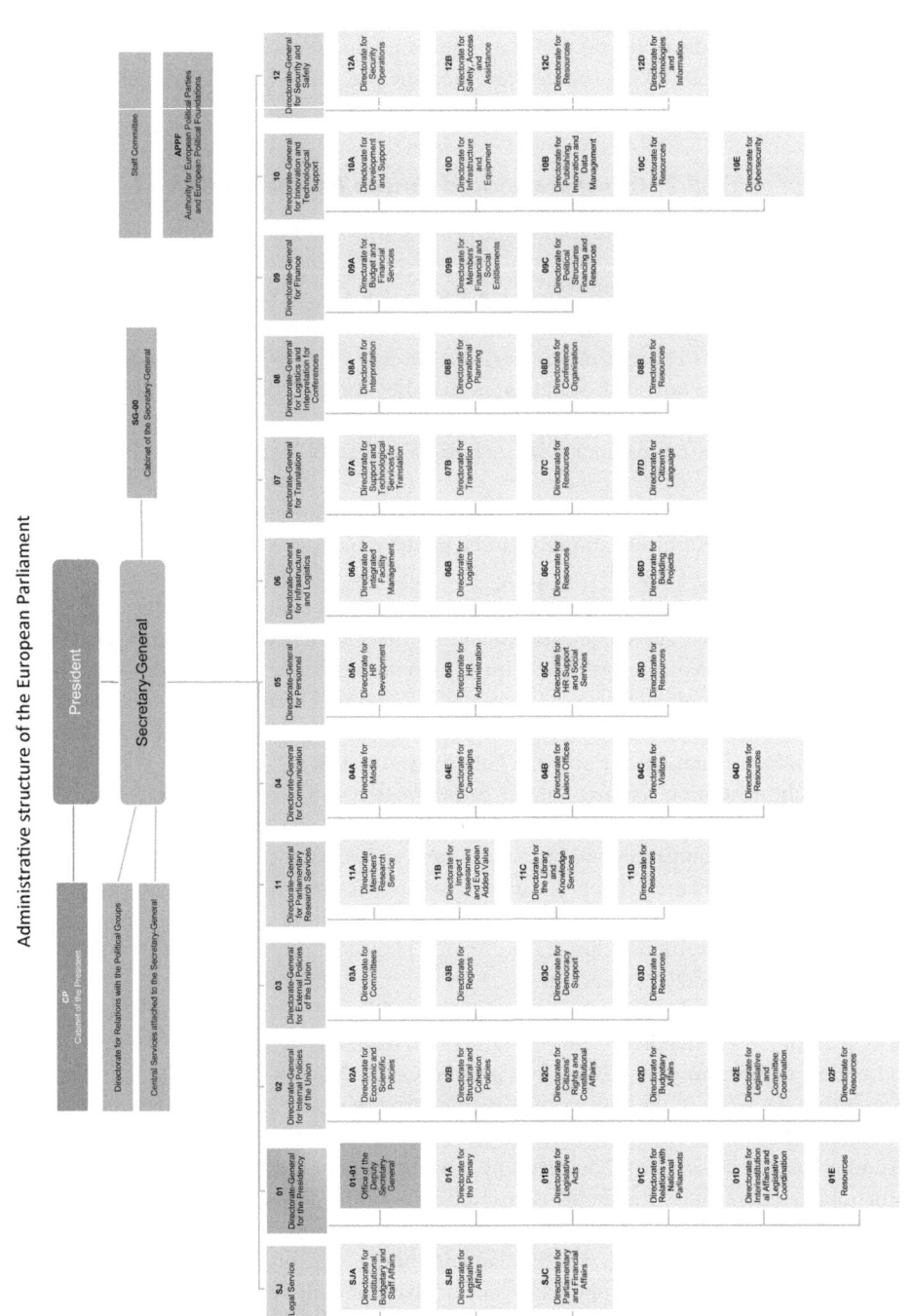

58.5.3 The Impact of Covid-19 Pandemic on Working Patterns

The EP is often defined as a travelling Parliament, as MEPs have to commute weekly from all part of Europe in order to meet. It has been particularly affected by the partial or total lockdowns.

Since the very beginning of the pandemic the EP leadership (its President and the heads of the political groups) took two crucial decisions, to permit 100% teleworking and to ensure business continuity. Modifications were made to the EP Rules of Procedure to allow remote participation and votes in committees and plenary meetings. The necessary technological adaptations were gradually put in place so that Committees and plenary could operate, with some limitations, in remote mode.

It is clear that no Parliament, by definition, can work indefinitely in remote mode. Arriving at the best compromises on complex political matters can only be reached through face-to-face debates, discussions and exchange of information, in particular, by means of informal conversations, preferably around a coffee or lunch. This is especially true for a Parliament that has no government to follow but needs to create separate majorities on each piece of legislation.

The (long) experience made during the pandemic, however, has opened up a wider debate on which positive features of the adaptation process might be retained when the EP reverts to "normal" procedures. How, for example, might the technological enhancement of MEPs and staff facilitate future EP activities and organisation, in such fields as hearings of experts, relations with National Parliaments, inter-parliamentary delegations and last but not least preparatory legislative work?

Moreover, in June 2021, a process of reflection was launched internally, through the creation of focus groups, in order to incorporate a new way of working based on the experience made during the pandemic, both at political and administrative level. EP working patterns are thus likely to continue to adapt to new situations in the future.

58.6 Final Considerations

Three main features have helped to shape the (short) story of the European Parliament: its specific characteristics, its evolving competences and its capacity to adapt. The European Parliament's reaction to the pandemic has provided a good illustration of these various features.

The European Parliament does its best to fulfil its "abnormal" role of a Parliament without a government. In particular, it has proved itself to be a worthy partner in the legislative process to the Member States sitting in the Council and has often helped to find the best compromises in order to permit the final adoption of European legislation.

In the future, the European Parliament might have an even more complete role, in particular if it is given greater responsibilities on such matters as European tax policy, and if and when qualified majority voting (QMV) becomes the normal modus operandi of the Council.

References

European Parliament Ascendant, Parliamentary Strategies of Self-Empowerment in the EU by Adrienne Héritier, Katharina L Meissner, Catherine Moury and Magnus G Schoeller, Palgrave 2019.
The European Parliament by Ariadna Ripoll Servent, Palgrave 2018.
The European Parliament by Richard Corbett, Francis Jacobs and Darren Neville, 9th edition, John Harper Publishing 2016.
The European Parliament in Times of EU Crisis, Dynamics and Transformations, edited by Olivier Costa, Palgrave Macmillan, 2019.

59
GLOBAL AND REGIONAL PERSPECTIVES ON TRANSNATIONAL PARLIAMENTARY ADMINISTRATIONS

Davor Jančić

59.1 Introduction

This chapter analyses the administrative dimension of international parliamentary institutions (IPIs) beyond Europe. It investigates the applicable legal framework and certain elements of political practice in order to determine their structure, roles and institutional characteristics. This is an important step towards a deeper understanding of the nature and operation of the broader, more encompassing phenomenon of parliamentary diplomacy. The present enquiry is theoretically intriguing because transnational administrative parliamentary arrangements are only remotely comparable to national and EU parliamentary administrations (Högenauer 2022; Jacobs and De Feo 2022). Learning about the administrative dimension of transnational parliamentary forums is therefore instructive, because it allows us to identify good and bad practices, determine the existence of deficits and shortcomings, consider their consequences, and reflect on ways to address them.

Transnational parliamentary networks are a common institutional feature of global and regional governance (Luciano 2021; Schimmelfennig et al. 2021; Cofelice 2018; Stavridis and Jančić 2017; Jančić 2015). IPIs with different setups, decision-making powers and functions have been established around the world. Most of them have more or less elaborate administrative apparatuses. For example, the Pan-African Parliament, a continent-wide IPI gathering 55 member states, has a Secretariat composed of a Secretary-General and two Deputy Secretaries-General, one in charge of legislative business and the other in charge of finance, administration and human resources. The ASEAN Inter-Parliamentary Assembly (AIPA), consisting of ten member parliaments, is assisted not only by a Secretariat composed of a Secretary-General, a Deputy Secretary-General and four directorates but also by a network of AIPA national secretariats. The MERCOSUR Parliament, instead, is headed by four secretaries – the Parliamentary Secretary, the Administrative Secretary, the Secretary for Institutional Relations and Social Communication, and the Secretary for International Relations and Integration–reflecting a 'deep-seated Mercosur tradition' that 'each country nominates one chief' (Malamud and Dri 2013: 230). This shows the variety and context-dependency of the institutional approaches to the administrative structuring of IPIs.

This chapter focuses on two case studies: the Inter-Parliamentary Union (IPU) and the East African Legislative Assembly (EALA). This selection was made in order to illustrate the different aspects of transnational parliamentary administrations and capture several institutional traits of IPIs: (a) territorial scope, with the IPU being a global one and the EALA a regional one; (b) nature and powers, with the IPU being an independent parliamentary association with no legislative powers and the EALA an international parliamentary organ performing legislative functions; and (c) size, with the IPU covering most parts of the globe and the EALA having only six member states. The differences among the case studies yield insights into the different needs and operative dynamics of administrations within IPIs. This chapter therefore provides a descriptive and exploratory account of these IPI administrations as a basis for more in-depth follow-on empirical studies.

The chapter is structured as follows. The next section discusses the findings and shortcomings of the existing literature and queries their applicability to transnational parliamentary administrations. The analysis then turns to the two case studies, presenting their administrations' institutional setup and their added value in terms of the support and services that they provide. The concluding section points to the positive and negative developments faced by transnational parliamentary administrations and ways in which they could be overcome.

59.2 Transnational Parliamentary Administrations in Context

The topic of parliamentary administrations has not been very extensively researched but has become an increasingly important strand of social science agendas. This is so because of the significant role that administrations play in enabling the elected, more distinctly political, echelons of parliamentary institutions to address the rising number of challenges ranging from the changing landscapes of democratic participation, differing levels of trust by the citizens, various information asymmetries across institutional and territorial spectrums, all the way to multifaceted global crises, tectonic shifts in power and the resulting claims to normative and discourse leadership. To place the idea of transnational parliamentary administration in the wider context, it is requisite to wed the literature on parliamentary administration with that on IPIs.

Apart from studies on the parliaments of some of the developed countries such as the US and Australia, a large segment of the existing literature on parliamentary administration is Euro-centric (Högenauer et al. 2016), which is understandable given the extent of institutional adaptations necessary to engage in the EU's multilevel system of governance and the need to ensure that appropriate capacities exist to enable parliaments to act effectively within the remit of their competences.

Within the European Parliament (EP), its sizeable administrative staff, divided into party group staff and secretariat staff (Alexander 2021; Coremans and Meissner 2018), help to address both partisan ideological concerns and the technical sectoral ones all the while exercising some policy-shaping tasks, such as providing background information, giving advice, drafting documents and facilitating compromise, including in the EU legislative processes (Neuhold and Dobbels 2015; Egeberg et al. 2013: 510; Romanyshyn and Neuhold 2013).

When it comes to the EU's national and regional parliaments, Europeanisation has generated bureaucratic and transnational growth, seen, on the one hand, in increased investment in administrative resources and technical expertise of the complex matters of EU policymaking, and, on the other, in the higher levels of transnational engagement with other parliaments and executive actors (Högenauer and Christiansen 2015; Christiansen et al. 2014). That these processes do not evolve at the expense of democratisation and that they do not prejudice the power of party political and partisan components of parliaments (Buzogány and Häsing 2017; Winzen 2014) is shown by empirical evidence from the parliaments of Sweden, Czechia and Romania, where parliamentary administrators have neither developed political preferences of their own nor influenced scrutiny outcomes (Strelkov 2015: 367). There is nevertheless some consensus that national parliaments can and do contribute to agenda shaping in EU affairs (Winzen 2014: 686), not least by allowing their administrations to preselect dossiers for scrutiny (Högenauer and Neuhold 2015: 348).

The importance of independent information provision by parliamentary administrators working as researchers is also evident from national parliamentary experiences across Europe (Jágr 2022; Fitsilis and Koutsogiannis 2017), as well as from the EP's own European Parliamentary Research Service. In parallel, a web of in-person networks and digital platforms for administrative interparliamentary cooperation have developed to foster the exchange of information, analyses and best practices, among which the European Centre for Parliamentary Research and Documentation (ECPRD), Interparliamentary EU Information Exchange (IPEX), the Secretariat of the Conference of Parliamentary Committees for Union Affairs of Parliaments of the European Union (COSAC), meetings of the Secretaries-General of the EU national parliaments and of the EP, and an informal network of national parliamentary representatives in Brussels (Fitsilis 2018; Pegan and Högenauer 2016; Buzogány 2013). The EU has also provided funding of €5 million for the period 2019–2021 for the Inter Pares project, aimed at the capacity building of parliamentarians and staff in EU partner countries.

These findings show that the services provided by parliamentary administrations in Europe are becoming essential to the functioning of representative democracy and that, paradoxically, in the European integration process 'representation is inextricably linked to bureaucratisation' (Högenauer et al. 2016: 139). Yet, while the European experience provides us with rich insights and lessons about the institutional mechanics of parliamentary administration, the premises on which they are based are not easily applicable to the wider transnational parliamentary arenas (Lupo 2016: 65). This is because outside the EU, the majority of regional integration organisations are not as advanced and developed as the EU, thereby denying them the usual channels for the fulfilment of parliamentary functions. Consequently, most of these organisations do not perform legislative but consultative roles. Their contribution to holding the executive actors to account is also far less tangible and is as a rule restricted to requests for information and submission of non-binding recommendations. Similarly, there are no or no clear party political affiliations given that most regional integration parliaments are not directly elected but remain appointed by the participating national parliaments. At an even more basic level, not all IPIs consist of delegations from liberal democracies, thus significantly diverging from the fundamental values inherent in EU interparliamentary cooperation. Much of the rationale for the evolution of parliamentary administrations that exist within the EU thus falls away. The question therefore arises of how administrative support and cooperation is envisaged within international and regional organisations beyond the idiosyncrasies of the EU.

The literature on parliamentary diplomacy in general and IPIs in particular has considerably grown in the last two decades with a number of studies specifically devoted to their institutionalisation and categorisation (Raube et al. 2019; Stavridis and Jančić 2017; Costa et al. 2013). These studies demonstrate that the key motive for establishing IPIs lies in strategic legitimation, whereby governments create weak parliamentary organs as a smokescreen of transnational democratic legitimacy, while eschewing the constraints that usually attach to national parliamentary processes (Schimmelfennig et al. 2021; Winzen and Rocabert 2021; Lenz et al. 2019; Rocabert et al. 2019).

However, rather than dismiss IPIs as inconsequential in terms of the formal powers they enjoy, it is important to enquire about the advantages they can generate for parliamentarians. In fact, virtually all parliamentary functions – be they legislative, controlling, communicative or representative – can be strengthened through action within IPIs. At the turn of the millennium, over 20 years ago, Slaughter observed that what she calls parliamentary networks are 'an increasingly effective forum for the resolution of international problems' and 'can have an influence' on domestic legislative initiatives, while promoting cross-fertilisation of policy ideas (Slaughter 2000: 219). IPIs can indeed enhance parliamentarians' access to information, particularly if they belong to opposition parties domestically, thus increasing their ability to exercise democratic control over the executive institutions (Lipps 2021; Habegger 2010). The transnational representation of domestic constituency interests is also empirically shown to be part of parliamentarians' motivation to participate in the work of IPIs (Malang 2019: 426). These benefits of parliamentary engagement within IPIs can furthermore multiply if claims are made within different IPIs devoted to the same region or the same subject matter (Jančić 2015).

However, even if the functions of IPIs are demonstrably different to those of national parliaments, they all feature similar internal administrative structures. They mostly follow the institutional blueprint of a dedicated secretariat or bureau (Cofelice and Stavridis 2014: 165; Kissling 2011; Habegger 2010: 192; Šabič 2008: 258). Their roles range from purely managerial tasks to those of a more political nature (Cofelice 2018: 62), which is why high-ranking administrative officers, like secretaries-general of IPIs, have been classed as norm entrepreneurs (Cofelice 2019: 9). The importance of well-staffed secretariats and permanent delegations within IPIs is well known as a way to address the difficulties in the latter's democratic functioning, which stem from insufficient access to information and poor publicity of IPIs' activities (Cutler 2013: 121; Kraft-Kasack 2008: 553). The following two sections shed light on the key administrative features of the IPU and the EALA to examine these claims in greater detail.

59.3 Global Level: Administration of the Inter-Parliamentary Union

The IPU is the world's first and most important international organisation of national parliaments. Created in 1889 to promote world peace (Albers 2012; Zarjevski 1989), it now performs a wide variety of tasks: (a) information sharing through dialogue, coordination and exchange of data and experiences; (b) capacity building aimed at parliamentary strengthening and development as cornerstones of well-functioning parliamentary democracies (Johnsson 1995); and (c) expression of views on international issues through the adoption of recommendations and parliamentary action at the national level. The IPU places particular emphasis on the protection and promotion of human rights worldwide, including notably gender equality and youth empowerment. As at December 2022, the IPU has 178 member parliaments out of the 193 member states of the United Nations, and 14 associate members, all of which are IPIs (including the EP).[1]

Other than the President, the Assembly, the Governing Council and the Executive Committee, the IPU has a Secretariat, headed by a Secretary-General. After an examination of candidatures by the Executive Committee, the Governing Council appoints the

Secretary-General for a period of four years, renewable twice, although the applicable recruitment procedures can be waived by the Governing Council on the proposal of the Executive Committee.[2] The Secretary-General may not be a member of any parliament and must work solely for the IPU. The role of the Secretary-General is not to serve MPs, but to work alongside the President and the Executive Committee in order to define and implement the IPU's strategic direction. Since the IPU's founding, there have only been eight Secretaries-General, of which two have won the Nobel Peace Prize: Christian Lange (Norway) in 1921 and Albert Gobat (Sweden) in 1902.

Under Article 28 of the Statutes of the IPU (adopted in 1976 and last amended in November 2020), the Secretariat's duties are to be the permanent headquarters of the IPU; keep records on IPU members and endeavour to foster new requests for affiliation; support and stimulate members' activities, including technical support for the harmonisation of these activities; prepare and distribute the questions to be considered at interparliamentary meetings; to provide for the execution of the decisions of the Governing Council and of the Assembly; prepare proposals for the five-year IPU Strategy, the annual work programme and budget for consideration by the Executive Committee; prepare policies and reports on transparency and accountability for consideration by the Executive Committee and approval by the Governing Council; collect and disseminate information on the structure and functioning of representative institutions; maintain relations between the IPU and other international organisations and ensure the IPU's representation at international conferences; and maintain the IPU's archives.

In various formats, the Secretary-General acts in advisory capacity at sessions and meetings of different IPU organs. In particular, the President of the IPU's twice-yearly Assembly and the Presidents of the four IPU Standing Committees – those on Peace and International Security, on Sustainable Development, on Democracy and Human Rights, and on United Nations Affairs – are assisted by the Secretary-General.[3] The said Presidents may invite the Secretary-General to advise or speak on any matter under consideration at a given meeting. The work of each standing committee is guided by an 18-member bureau. These bureaux are composed of three representatives of each of the IPU's six geopolitical groups, among whom the President and Vice-President of the committee in question. Unlike committee presidents, ordinary bureau members are supported in this role by their respective national parliament.[4] Additionally, the IPU Secretariat receives proposals from IPU members on items for discussion at a future Assembly; receives and distributes all documents, reports, draft resolutions and explanatory memorandums prepared by standing committees; provides simultaneous translation of committee and Assembly debates in English, French, Arabic and Spanish; and prepares summary records of meetings.

Depending on their size and needs, other IPU bodies enjoy similar administrative support from the Secretary-General and the Secretariat. Such support is provided to the non-standing committees, groups and forums established within the Governing Council: the Committee on the Human Rights of Parliamentarians (10 members), the Committee on Middle East Questions (12 members), the Committee to Promote Respect for International Humanitarian Law (12 members), the Group of Facilitators for Cyprus (3 members), the Advisory Group on Health (11 members and 2 special advisers),[5] the High-Level Advisory Group on Countering Terrorism and Violent Extremism (23 members), the Forum of Women Parliamentarians (33-member bureau), and the Forum of Young Parliamentarians (12-member board).

To perform their administrative functions, the Secretariat has some 40 staff members, who are based in the IPU Headquarters in Geneva and in the IPU's New York office, which was established after the IPU was granted permanent observer status in the UN in

November 2002. Organisationally, the Secretariat is divided into six units: Executive Office, Member Parliaments and External Relations, Programmes, Human Rights Programmes, Communications and IT, and Support Services. All staff are required to adhere to the Code of Conduct for Personnel and to the Fraud and Corruption Prevention and Control Policy, both adopted in September 2012. The IPU also organises yearly information seminars for senior parliamentary staff acting as secretaries of IPU groups within member parliaments. The goals are not only to share in-depth knowledge about the IPU but also to discuss ways to implement global parliamentary commitments and improve interparliamentary cooperation.

When it comes to the use of parliamentary expertise, the IPU is not only entitled to hire contractors but also provides parliaments across the world with advisory and consultancy services of its own, often on a pro bono basis. The latter are delivered by serving or retired MPs, parliamentary staff or subject specialists selected from a roster maintained by the IPU.

A further important administrative component of the IPU is the Association of Secretaries-General of Parliaments (ASGP), whose first meeting took place in Oslo on 16 August 1939. Under Article 29 of the Statutes of the IPU, the Association is a consultative body of the IPU and its Rules are approved by the IPU's Governing Council. Although the Association is administered autonomously, it is funded from the IPU's budget and through annual contributions by the Association's members, observers and associate members. Even so, the ASGP gathers secretaries-general regardless of their country's membership of the IPU. The key tasks of the Association are to facilitate personal contact between its members; cooperate with parliaments that request legal and technical assistance; study the law, practice and procedure of parliaments; propose measures for improving parliamentary working methods; and foster the cooperation between different parliamentary services. These tasks are conducted through general debates, member communications and presentations, questionnaires, and reports based on the results of these questionnaires. In doing so, the Association complements the work of IPU organs which are tasked with studying parliamentary institutions, with which it should closely consult and collaborate on preparing and implementing projects. The Association's members meet at the same time and place as the IPU Assembly sessions but may also meet otherwise. One such exceptional meeting took place in May 2021 to address the role and organisation of parliaments in a pandemic. The Association is governed and led by an 11-member Executive Committee (President, two Vice-Presidents and eight other members) and a Bureau (President, two Vice-Presidents, and two joint secretaries). It also publishes a review named Constitutional and Parliamentary Information, which collects the materials presented by ASGP members during its six-monthly meetings. This outlet is a valuable tool for exchanging information and ideas as well as for gaining insight into comparative parliamentary practices. Another important legacy of the ASGP was the adoption in Geneva in October 2013 of the Principles for the Recruitment and Career Management of Parliamentary Staff, which has informed subsequent studies of this matter by other organisations.

Furthermore, the IPU has since 1996 hosted a large global online database called Parline, which is a collaborative project of the IPU and national parliaments. Apart from being used by the OECD's annual 'Government at a Glance' report and by the UN Electoral Affairs Division, this database is used as an official source for the monitoring of the implementation of the UN Sustainable Development Goals on women in parliament (indicator 5.5.1(a)) and on decision-making positions in parliament (indicator 16.7.1(a)). Importantly for parliamentary administrations, it centralises information not only on elections, mandates, lawmaking, oversight and budget but also on working methods, administration and parliamentary bodies.

The information is provided and checked by Parline Correspondents, who are staff members within national parliaments, subject to ex post verification by IPU staff. To facilitate their exchanges, a network of Parline Correspondents was created in April 2019.

Recognising the transformative power of digital technologies and their positive contribution to enhancing parliamentary processes, the IPU launched the Centre for Innovation in Parliament at the World e-Conference in December 2018. This Centre focuses specifically on improving parliaments' digital and electronic tools in order to boost their openness, engagement with citizens, library and research services, document and records management, and presence on the internet and social media. In addition to a quarterly blog named Innovation Tracker, where MPs and parliamentary staff can share ideas and solutions for increasing their institutions' effectiveness, the Centre is divided into three horizontal hubs (ICT Governance, Open Data, Transparency) and four regional ones (Caribbean, East African, Hispanophone, Southern African, and Pacific).

Finally, for both parliamentarians and members of parliamentary administrations, the IPU's standard-setting role is crucial. This role, fulfilled with the help of experts and external organisations, consists of determining the benchmarks and criteria of good practice in the conduct of a wide array of parliamentary affairs. These are compiled and published as non-binding soft law instruments in the form of declarations, handbooks, common principles, toolkits, policy and guidance notes, and research papers.[6] Their utility is palpable. For instance, Anders Johnsson, who was the IPU Secretary-General from 1998 to 2014, identifies the IPU's Handbook on refugee protection from 2001 as a 'parliamentary bestseller', which has been widely translated and which continues to be used by many parliaments around the world (Jönsson and Johnsson 2018: 314). More recently, the IPU addressed the Covid-19 crisis, including by compiling worldwide parliamentary responses to the pandemic; formulating a practical Q&A on remote working tools and technology; issuing guidance and policy notes on the pandemic's impact on gender, human rights and green economic recovery; dedicating an issue of the Innovation Tracker to different national experiences of parliamentary adaptation to Covid-19; and organising various events on this matter.

59.4 Regional Level: Administration of the East African Legislative Assembly

At the regional level, we find a flourishing diversity of IPIs ranging from those that perform varying degrees of lawmaking functions to those serving purely as socialisation and information-sharing platforms.

A rare example of an IPI with legislative functions is the EALA, whose seat is in the East African Community (EAC) headquarters in Arusha, Tanzania. Although designated as the 'legislative organ' of the EAC,[7] the EALA's legislative power is limited in several ways. Procedurally, to become Acts of the Community, all bills require assent by all Heads of State of the EAC member states,[8] thereby giving each of them the right of individual veto (Jančić 2019: 210). Materially, no bill or amendment is admissible if the presiding officer finds that they would have negative financial implications for Community funds (e.g. the Development Fund or the Partnership Fund) through the imposition of a charge or provision for payment or withdrawal therefrom[9]; or, helpfully, if they would result in a derogation from human rights instruments to which a member state may be signatory.[10] Functionally, the Assembly as a rule only meets once a year,[11] thus restricting the opportunity for debate. Politically, two interrelated issues arise. On the one hand, because of sovereignty concerns, member states prefer making law through Treaty Protocols adopted by the member states rather than through

Acts of the Community adopted by parliamentarians gathered in the Assembly, which can result in frictions and litigation before the EAC Court of Justice (Ruhangisa 2017: 142 and 160). On the other hand, frictions can also result from conflicting legislative intentions and lack of coordination between the Council and the Assembly due to their concurrent right of legislative initiative (Gastorn 2015: 38).

In relation to its internal organisation, the EALA is headed by the Speaker, while the core of its substantive work is performed by sectoral committees.[12] In performing its tasks, the EALA is assisted by an administrative structure which is regulated by the Administration of the East African Legislative Assembly Act (adopted by EALA in 2011, assented to in 2012). This Act establishes an EALA Commission, composed of the Speaker, the Chairperson of the Council of Ministers (ex officio member) and two Assembly members from each member state. Commission members are elected by the Assembly for a period of two and a half years, after which they may be re-elected. The Commission is presided over by the Speaker, while the Clerk of the Assembly serves as the Commission Secretary. Having replaced the former House Business Committee, the Commission is the Assembly's governing body in charge of its strategic and policy direction. It manages and organises the business and programme of the Assembly, nominates committee members, and ensures the preparation of annual revenue and expenditure estimates. The Commission also makes recommendations to the Council of Ministers on staff rules and regulations and the appointment, terms and conditions of service, promotion and disciplinary control over the Clerk and other Assembly officers and staff. The terms and conditions of service are decided by the EAC Summit on the Council's recommendation. The Commission further ensures the financial management of the Community, the Assembly and the Assembly's committees by ensuring that the Community budget is debated and approved and that the Community's resources are adequately utilised. The Commission meets at least once every two months and submits bi-annual reports to the Assembly on its operation and activities.

The head of the EALA's administration is the Clerk. The Clerk's functions are to give expert advice to Assembly members on parliamentary procedure and practice, ensure the Assembly's bookkeeping and recordkeeping and be responsible for the efficient conduct of the business of the Commission and the Assembly.[13] The Clerk also has an important role in facilitating interparliamentary cooperation between the Assembly and the national parliaments of the EAC, owing to her/his Treaty obligation to transmit to these parliaments copies of records of all relevant Assembly debates along with Bills and Acts of the Community.[14]

In organisational terms, as at the end of November 2019, the EALA's administrative staff counted a total of 52 persons, of which 33 officers (20 employed at the professional level and 13 at the general level) and 19 short-term/temporary staff.[15] Staff are divided into two directorates – Legislative Services and Administrative Services – while the Office of the Clerk is further divided into seven departments: Legislative Business and Procedural Services; Hansard; Library, Information and Research Services; Finance and Administration; Serjeant-At-Arms; Public Relations Services; and ICT Services. Legislative support by EALA staff includes processing bills and motions and acting as secretaries to the standing and select committees of EALA. Additionally, in drafting private member's bills, which are at the root of the majority of EAC law, Assembly members are provided with reasonable professional assistance by the Counsel of the Community, who is the principal legal adviser of the EAC.[16]

Regarding the EALA's administrative evolution, it has in recent years experienced some staffing upgrades: not only does the Office of the Clerk now have two rather than one deputy clerk, but also some other positions are recruited at more senior and more professional levels than before.[17] However, this is outweighed by the acute general problem of understaffing. This is highlighted by the EALA's Strategic Plan for 2019–2024, the third such policy instrument to date. Beyond the more overarching issues of sovereignty delegation and funding, the EALA's administration is particularly affected by two challenges. The first challenge is the need to consolidate the Assembly's financial and administrative autonomy from the other organs of the Community because the former is currently dependent on the content and timeliness of the latter's policy decisions, thus decreasing the EALA's efficiency. As a corollary, the Assembly cannot decide and review its own administrative structure, appoint and exercise disciplinary control over its staff, determine the welfare and remuneration of its members and staff and oversee budget execution.[18] The second challenge is the need to ensure timely recruitment of well-qualified staff with the skills necessary to provide adequate administrative and technical support. This has become especially pronounced following the 2016 enlargement, when South Sudan joined the EAC and the Assembly membership increased from 52 to 62 members. The staffing problem is exacerbated by high staff turnover and delays in hiring their replacement. This is caused by EAC Staff Rules and Regulations, which mandate the employment of professional staff in a way that mirrors the term of office of Assembly members: they are employed on fixed-term contracts of five years, renewable once, and this 'continues to cripple the functioning of the Assembly'.[19] This is further coupled with weak mechanisms of internal control (e.g. internal audit, planning, monitoring and evaluation) and the lack of policies on the career progression, retention and remuneration of the EALA staff.[20] To address these issues, the Council of Ministers decided at its 33rd meeting in March 2016 to grant financial and administrative autonomy to the Assembly, although this is yet to materialise.[21]

A development of importance to the EALA's administration is the launch of the East African Parliamentary Institute in Nairobi, Kenya in March 2019. Its establishment as an institution of the Community was foreseen in the East African Parliament Institute Act (adopted in 2011, assented to in 2012). The Institute's key roles are to provide training to parliamentarians and staff on parliamentary procedures and practices in order to improve their knowledge, skills and capacity as lawmakers so as to increase their professionalism and develop closer linkages in the spirit of parliamentary democracy promotion. Although primarily aimed at parliamentarians, the Institute is also open to civil servants and representatives of the private sector and the civil society. Regarding the Institute's governance, the EALA Speaker serves as the Chairperson of the Institute's Board of Trustees, and the EALA Clerk as its Secretary. Building on this, the Assembly passed a resolution in 2015 calling for the establishment of the East African Parliamentary Centre for Peace and Security within the East African Parliament Institute.[22] However, the Institute itself is not yet fully operational and is hosted in the interim by the Centre for Parliamentary Studies and Training of the Parliament of Kenya. Moreover, the EALA has been running Inter-Parliamentary Relations Seminars, also known as Nanyuki seminars, which aim to strengthen the relationship between the Assembly and the Community's national parliaments through knowledge exchange.

For a regional integration project which has begun its path to a political confederation[23] and which ultimately aims to morph into a political federation, like the EAC does,[24] addressing the above shortcomings seems paramount to enable its Assembly fully to participate in this ambitious constitutional process.[25] Indeed, a report which the EALA Committee on Regional Affairs and Conflict Resolution adopted in late 2020 criticises the Council of Ministers for the lack of Assembly involvement in the process of formulating a Constitution for East Africa contrary to the principle of good governance laid down in Article 6 EAC Treaty.[26]

Some of the deficiencies identified above could be mitigated by implementing the recommendations of the EALA Strategic Plan for 2019–2024. The following suggested interventions seek to enhance the quality of the Assembly's legislative and oversight functions: developing tailor-made capacity enhancement programmes for Assembly members and staff; organising inductions for Assembly members on the Rules of Procedure; strengthening Assembly members' capacity to introduce bills, motions and petitions and scrutinise the budget and the Community's financial statements; facilitating committees' access to professional expertise; bolstering the Assembly's functional relationship with the East African Parliamentary Institute; and fostering parliamentary staff networks and staff exchange programmes with national and regional parliaments.[27]

Other challenges, such as the Covid-19 pandemic, have been addressed by the EALA by moving to online meetings and by taking a joint coordinated approach to contain the pandemic. The Assembly has also taken stock of some more specific aspects of the pandemic, such as its impact on women in cross-border trade within the Community, which inter alia drew on insights from the member states, the East African Women in Business Platform, and women entrepreneurs.[28]

Finally, although the EALA's experience of administrative parliamentary structuring may functionally be inapplicable to IPIs without legislative competences, the problems that it has encountered and the solutions that it has pursued in terms of resources and capacity building may contextually apply not only to IPIs around the globe but also to parliamentary institutions at national levels of governance.

59.5 Conclusion

While the existing literature has predominantly focused on European and some non-European parliamentary administrations, those of IPIs have been almost entirely off the scholarly radars. This is unsurprising given the low levels of formal influence that IPIs exercise, the absence of any or meaningful political party structures, and the predominant absence of direct electoral processes. However, this runs the risk of neglecting other parliamentary roles which are particularly salient in the transnational realm, such as those of capacity building, value mainstreaming, issue framing, moral advocacy, agenda setting and norm entrepreneurship. This chapter hence focused on two IPIs that combine at least some of these analytical ingredients.

The key general finding of this chapter is that transnational parliamentary administrations can and do support both non-traditional parliamentary functions and, where relevant, the more traditional ones. The above analysis of the legal frameworks and institutional arrangements indicates that, regardless of the structural and constitutional differences between IPIs and national parliaments, there is a pronounced need for parliamentarians to receive high-quality administrative support and assistance to enable them to fulfil their international agendas. The nature of support provided by transnational parliamentary administrations is primarily technical, evidence-based and expertise-oriented rather than political and ideological. Yet, although IPIs widely differ in terms of their administrative make-up and it is hard to draw inferences, several propositions can be advanced.

On the *positive side*, the IPIs' normative agendas realised through standard-setting and benchmarking provide helpful soft law parameters for the benefit of parliamentary administrations operating at the global, regional, national and sub-national levels of governance. These parameters establish voluntary ground rules, drawn from comparative analyses of legal and policy solutions, which administrators can implement in supporting and advising parliamentarians. Where IPIs exercise legislative or quasi-legislative functions (e.g. the adoption of model laws), their capacity-building agendas aimed at training and professional development of administrative staff stand out as beneficial to increasing the quality of these outputs. Periodic seminars (Fitsilis 2018: 51), induction sessions, technical assistance programmes (Beetham 2006: 176 et seq) and networking opportunities aimed at parliamentary administrators can all help to elevate their contribution to transnational governance processes. At the heart of achieving these goals is the creation of formal procedures, incentives and adequate platforms for practical engagement in interparliamentary learning. In this way, administrative staff can indirectly contribute to the more visible processes of reaching policy outcomes for IPIs and the participating states. The importance of this is evidenced by the findings of the second Global Parliamentary Report, published in 2017, which states that:

> Committee staff now are much more aware of international parliamentary best practice and are beginning to display more confidence in the provision of procedural, research, writing and advisory services, rather than just administrative support services.[29]

On the *negative side*, however, the chapter has shown that the good functioning of transnational administrative mechanisms can suffer from the executive capture of institutional processes and from their dependence on executive approvals, which, to varying degrees, pervades regional integration organisations. The lack of administrative parliamentary autonomy at the transnational level is aggravated by the lack of parliamentary interest for administrative structures at the national level in some countries. Evidence from the British and Australian parliaments, for example, demonstrates that, owing to their loyalty to political parties and constituents, most of their parliamentarians are 'disengaged' from parliamentary administrations and unconcerned about their institution's long-term ability to support them (Barrett 2019: 238). This stifling of administrations in IPIs can to some extent be alleviated by the proactive engagement of the leading administrative figures, such as the Secretary-General or the Clerk, with parliamentarians regardless of any institutional limitations. This informal activism serves as an important complement to the formal parliamentary administrative setups, especially within IPIs where resource allocation for administrative purposes is insufficient and uncertain.

Finally, even though administrative apparatuses of IPIs come in different shapes and sizes, they exhibit commonalities which merit their categorisation as transnational parliamentary administrations and which warrant further research into the more granular, empirical aspects of their operation.

Notes

1 It is noteworthy that, due to concerns over the non-democratic nature of some IPU members, the US withdrew from the IPU in 1997.
2 Rule 3 of the Secretariat of the Inter-Parliamentary Union.
3 Rule 35 of the Rules of the Assembly and Rule 41 of the Rules of the Standing Committees.
4 Rule 7(3) of the Standing Committees.
5 This Advisory Group is the only body within the IPU which includes technical partners with an advisory role. The Group's current partners are: UNAIDS, the Global Fund to Fight AIDS, Malaria and Tuberculosis, the World Health Organization and the Partnership for Maternal, Newborn and Child Health.

6 Examples include: Declaration on Criteria for Free and Fair Elections (1994); Universal Declaration on Democracy (1997); Parliament and Democracy in the Twenty-First Century: A Guide to Good Practice (2006); Common Principles for Support to Parliaments (2014); Guidelines for Parliamentary Research Services (2015); Evaluating the Gender Sensitivity of Parliaments: A Self-Assessment Toolkit (2016); Global Parliamentary Report (1st in 2012, 2nd in 2017); Good Practices in Nationality Laws for the Prevention and Reduction of Statelessness (2018); Comparative Research Paper on Parliamentary Administration (2020); Social Media Guide for Parliaments and Parliamentarians (2021); Handbook for Parliamentarians on Nutrition and Food Systems (2021).
7 Article 49(1) EAC Treaty.
8 Article 63(4) EAC Treaty.
9 Article 59(2) EAC Treaty.
10 Rule 63 of the Rules of Procedure of EALA of 2015.
11 Article 55(2) EAC Treaty.
12 Article 80 of the Rules of Procedure of EALA of 2015 foresees six committees: (a) Accounts; (b) Legal, Rules and Privileges; (c) Communication, Trade and Investment; (d) Agriculture, Tourism, and Natural Resources; (e) Regional Affairs and Conflict Resolution; and (f) General Purpose.
13 Article 12 of the Administration of the East African Legislative Assembly Act.
14 Article 65 EAC Treaty.
15 EALA, Strategic Plan (2019–2014), at 9.
16 Article 64(2)–(3) of the Rules of Procedure of EALA of 2015.
17 EALA, 'EALA hails Messrs Kenneth Madete & Alex Obatre Lumumba', 6 December 2019, available at https://www.eala.org/index.php/media/view/eala-hails-messrs-kenneth-madete-alex-obatre-lumumba, accessed on 16 May 2021.
18 EALA, Strategic Plan (2019–2014), at 18.
19 EALA, Strategic Plan (2019–2014), at 17.
20 EALA, Strategic Plan (2019–2014), at 21.
21 EALA, Strategic Plan (2019–2014), at 18 and 35.
22 EALA, Resolution no. EALA/RES/3/2/2015 of 28 January 2015.
23 Joint Communiqué of the 18th Ordinary Summit of the Heads of State of the EAC, 20 May 2017, point 9. This meeting adopted political confederation as a transitional model on the path towards an East African political federation and directed the Council of Ministers to form a team of constitutional experts to draft a Constitution for the Political Confederation. The drafting process, which began with first consultations in Burundi in January 2020, is underway at the time of writing.
24 Article 5(2) EAC Treaty.
25 EALA, 'Towards Political Federation in the East African Community–Achievements and Challenges', 2013, at 43.
26 EALA, Committee on Regional Affairs and Conflict Resolution, 'Report on the Progress Made by the Community Towards Achieving the East African Community Confederation Constitution and the EAC Elections Observer Missions', 29 November to 3 December 2020, at 13.
27 Strategic Objective 6 of the EALA Strategic Plan (2019–2014), at 42.
28 EALA, Committee on General Purpose, 'Report on the Oversight Activity to Assess the Impact of Covid-19 Pandemic on Women in Cross Border Trade in the EAC', 25–28 February 2021.
29 IPU and UNDP, 'Global Parliamentary Report 2017–Parliamentary Oversight: Parliament's Power to Hold Government to Account', 2017, at 41.

References

Albers, Martin. 'Between the Crisis of Democracy and World Parliament: The Development of the Inter-Parliamentary Union in the 1920s', (2012) 7(2) *Journal of Global History* 189–209.

Alexander, David A. 'The Committee Secretariat of the European Parliament: Administrative Mobility, Expertise and Keeping the Legislative Wheels Turning, (2021) 27(2) *Journal of Legislative Studies* 227–245.

Barrett, Val. *Parliamentary Administration: What Does It Mean to Manage a Parliament Effectively?* (PhD thesis at the Australian National University 2019).

Beetham, David. *Parliament and Democracy in the Twenty-First Century: A Guide to Good Practice* (IPU 2006).

Buzogány, Aron. 'Learning from the Best: Interparliamentary Networks and the Parliamentary Scrutiny of EU Decision-Making', in Ben Crum and John Erik Fossum (eds), *Practices of Interparliamentary Coordination in International Politics: The European Union and Beyond* (ECPR Press 2013) 17–32.

Buzogány, Aron and Jens Häsing. 'Spokes in the Wheel. European Affairs and the Parliamentary Administration of German *Landtage*', (2017) 23(2) *Journal of Legislative Studies* 200–220.

Christiansen, Thomas et al. 'National Parliaments in the Post-Lisbon European Union: Bureaucratization rather than Democratization', (2014) 12(2) *Comparative European Politics* 121–140.

Cofelice, Andrea. *Parliamentary Institutions in Regional and International Governance: Functions and Powers* (Routledge 2018).

Cofelice, Andrea. 'Ideas, Beliefs and Norms: What Role for International Parliamentary Institutions?', *Centro Studi sul Federalismo*, December 2019.

Cofelice, Andrea and Stelios Stavridis. 'The European Parliament as an International Parliamentary Institution (IPI)', (2014) 19(2) *European Foreign Affairs Review* 145–178.

Coremans, Evelyn and Katharina L. Meissner. 'Putting Power into Practice: Administrative and Political Capacity Building in the European Parliament's Committee for International Trade', (2018) 96(3) *Public Administration* 561–577.

Costa, Olivier et al. (eds). *Parliamentary Dimensions of Regionalization and Globalization: The Role of Inter-Parliamentary Institutions* (Palgrave Macmillan 2013).

Cutler, Robert. 'International Parliamentary Institutions as Organizations', (2013) 4(1) *Journal of International Organizations Studies* 104–126.

Egeberg, Morten et al. 'Parliament Staff: Unpacking the Behaviour of Officials in the European Parliament', (2013) 20(4) *Journal of European Public Policy* 495–514.

Fitsilis, Fotios. 'Inter-Parliamentary Cooperation and Its Administrators', in Elena Griglio and Stelios Stavridis (eds), Special Issue on 'Joint Scrutiny of EU Policies: The Contribution of Interparliamentary Cooperation', (2018) 10(3) *Perspectives on Federalism* 28–55.

Fitsilis, Fotios and Alexandros Koutsogiannis. 'Strengthening the Capacity of Parliaments through Development of Parliamentary Research Services', *Working paper presented at the 13th Workshop of Parliamentary Scholars and Parliamentarians, Oxfordshire, 29-30 July 2017*.

Gastorn, Kennedy. 'The Inevitable Reforms of the Legislative Competencies of the East African Legislative Assembly', (2015) 48(1) *Verfassung und Recht in Übersee/Law and Politics in Africa, Asia and Latin America* 28–48.

Habegger, Beat. 'Democratic Accountability of International Organizations: Parliamentary Control within the Council of Europe and the OSCE and the Prospects for the United Nations', (2010) 45(2) *Cooperation and Conflict* 186–204.

Högenauer, Anna-Lena. 'National Parliamentary Administrations in the European Union: The Process of Europeanisation', in Thomas Christiansen et al. (eds), *The Routledge Handbook of Parliamentary Administrations* (Routledge 2023), forthcoming.

Högenauer, Anna-Lena and Christine Neuhold. 'National Parliaments after Lisbon: Administrations on the Rise?', (2015) 38(2) *West European Politics* 335–354.

Högenauer, Anna-Lena and Thomas Christiansen. 'Parliamentary Administrations in the Scrutiny of EU Decision-Making', in Claudia Hefftler et al. (eds), *The Palgrave Handbook of National Parliaments and the European Union* (Palgrave Macmillan 2015) 116–132.

Högenauer, Anna-Lena et al. *Parliamentary Administrations in the European Union* (Palgrave Macmillan 2016).

Jacobs, Francis and Alfredo de Feo. "European Parliament", in Thomas Christiansen et al. (eds), *The Routledge Handbook of Parliamentary Administrations* (Routledge 2023), forthcoming.

Jágr, David. 'Parliamentary Research Services as Expert Resource of Lawmakers: The Czech Way', (2022) 28(1) *Journal of Legislative Studies* 93–121.

Jančić, Davor. 'Transnational Parliamentarism and Global Governance: The New Practice of Democracy', in Elaine Fahey (ed), *The Actors of Postnational Rule-Making: Contemporary Challenges of European and International Law* (Routledge 2015) 113–132.

Jančić, Davor. 'Regional Parliaments and African Economic Integration', (2019) 30(1) *European Journal of International Law* 199–228.

Johnsson, Anders B. 'The Inter-Parliamentary Union and the Promotion of Representative Institutions', (1995) 1(4) *Journal of Legislative Studies* 104–111.

Jönsson, Christer and Anders Johnsson. 'Parliaments in Global Governance', (2018) 24(3) *Global Governance: A Review of Multilateralism and International Organizations* 309–320.

Kissling, Claudia. *The Legal and Political Status of International Parliamentary Institutions (Background Paper #4)* (Committee for a Democratic UN 2011).

Kraft-Kasack, Christiane. 'Transnational Parliamentary Assemblies: A Remedy for the Democratic Deficit of International Governance?, (2008) 31(3) *West European Politics* 534–557.

Lenz, Tobias et al. 'Legitimacy and the Cognitive Sources of International Institutional Change: The Case of Regional Parliamentarization', (2019) 63(4) *International Studies Quarterly* 1094–1107.

Lipps, Jana. 'Intertwined Parliamentary Arenas: Why Parliamentarians Attend International Parliamentary Institutions', (2021) 27(2) *European Journal of International Relations* 501–520.

Luciano, Bruno Theodoro. *Parliamentary Agency and Regional Integration in Europe and Beyond: The Logic of Regional Parliaments* (Routledge 2021).

Lupo, Nicola. 'The Role of International Parliamentary Cooperation: Political Tourism or Added Value for Intergovernmental Relations?', in Wilhelm Hofmeister and Jan Melissen (eds), *Rethinking International Institutions: Diplomacy and Impact on Emerging World Order* (Konrad Adenauer Stiftung and Clingendael 2016) 53–66.

Malamud, Andrés and Clarissa Dri. 'Spillover Effects and Supranational Parliaments: The Case of Mercosur', (2013) 19(2) *Journal of Iberian and Latin American Research* 224–238.

Malang, Thomas. 'Why National Parliamentarians Join International Organizations', (2019) 14(3) *The Review of International Organisations* 407–430.

Neuhold, Christine and Mathias Dobbels. 'Paper Keepers or Policy Shapers? The Conditions under Which EP Officials Impact on the EU Policy Process', (2015) 13(5) *Comparative European Politics* 577–595.

Pegan, Andreja and Anna-Lena Högenauer. 'The Role of Parliamentary Administrations in Interparliamentary Cooperation', in Nicola Lupo and Cristina Fasone (eds), *Interparliamentary Cooperation in the Composite European Constitution* (Hart Publishing 2016) 147–164.

Raube, Kolja et al. (eds). *Parliamentary Cooperation and Diplomacy in EU External Relations: An Essential Companion* (Edward Elgar 2019).

Rocabert, Jofre et al. 'The Rise of International Parliamentary Institutions: Purpose and Legitimation', (2019) 14(4) *The Review of International Organizations* 607–631.

Romanyshyn, Iulian and Christine Neuhold. 'The European Parliament's Administration: Between Neutral and Politicised Competence', in Christine Neuhold et al. (eds), *Civil Servants and Politics: A Delicate Balance* (Springer 2013) 205–228.

Ruhangisa, John Eudes. 'The Scope, Nature and Effect of EAC Law', in Emmanuel Ugirashebuja et al. (eds), *East African Community Law: Institutional, Substantive and Comparative EU Aspects* (Brill Publishing 2017) 139–160.

Šabič, Zlatko. 'Building Democratic and Responsible Global Governance: The Role of International Parliamentary Institutions', (2008) 61(2) *Parliamentary Affairs* 255–271.

Schimmelfennig, Frank et al. *The Rise of International Parliaments: Strategic Legitimation in International Organizations* (Oxford University Press 2021).

Slaughter, Anne-Marie. 'Government Networks: The Heart of the Liberal Democratic Order', in Gregory H. Fox and Brad R. Roth (eds), *Democratic Governance and International Law* (Cambridge University Press 2000) 199–236.

Stavridis, Stelios and Davor Jančić (eds). *Parliamentary Diplomacy in European and Global Governance* (Brill Publishing 2017).

Strelkov, Alexander. 'Who Controls National EU Scrutiny? Parliamentary Party Groups, Committees and Administrations', (2015) 38(2) *West European Politics* 355–374.

Winzen, Thomas. 'Bureaucracy and Democracy: Intra-Parliamentary Delegation in European Union Affairs', (2014) 36(7) *Journal of European Integration* 677–695.

Winzen, Thomas and Jofre Rocabert. 'Citizen-Centred or State-Centred? The Representational Design of International Parliamentary Institutions', (2021) 47(1) *Review of International Studies* 128–153.

Zarjevski, Yefime. *The People Have the Floor: History of the Inter-Parliamentary Union* (Dartmouth Publishing 1989).

INDEX

Abe, Shinzo 663
Act 40, 44, 46–49, 61, 67, 69, 71, 118, 159, 163–168, 172, 177, 199, 210, 223, 228, 285, 291–293, 296–297, 304, 356, 358–360, 363, 381, 383–384, 387–389, 404, 413–421, 424, 447, 449–450, 452, 454, 457, 488, 498, 501, 516, 534, 537–540, 548–549, 551, 575–578, 598–600, 603–604, 606–607, 627, 634, 638–639, 642, 659–661, 663–669, 671, 677, 690, 694, 718, 725, 744–746, 749
Ad hoc development 570
administrative capacity 12, 75, 77, 81, 83, 85, 99, 170–171, 256, 328, 405, 473, 523, 612, 650, 685, 687
administrative services 46, 53–66, 71, 165, 244, 246–247, 389, 433, 464, 477, 479, 482, 512, 534, 545, 579, 625, 680, 745
administrative staff 4, 7, 24, 61, 93, 106, 147, 163, 166, 168, 181, 215, 237, 349, 360, 362–363, 375, 391, 393, 410, 431, 439, 463–466, 468–469, 473, 484–485, 487, 512, 525, 527, 560–561, 564–567, 583–584, 589, 653, 656, 663, 674, 694, 701, 739, 745, 748
administrative structure 9, 14–15, 19, 22, 30, 32–34, 38–39, 41, 43, 45, 47–49, 51–56, 68–69, 72, 123, 132, 163, 200, 226, 247, 312, 314, 360, 435, 463–464, 466–467, 543, 557–560, 562–563, 576, 583–584, 597–598, 612, 615–616, 618–619, 636, 644, 647–648, 679, 699, 703–704, 741, 745–746, 748
administrative support 1, 4, 21–22, 30–33, 54, 90, 100, 141, 211, 217, 269–270, 272, 278, 302, 365–367, 372–375, 394, 396–397, 472–473, 482, 512, 537, 550, 570, 601, 616, 651, 671, 701, 740, 742, 747–748
advice 1, 42–43, 45, 58, 64, 68–69, 75, 78–79, 81, 83, 85, 90–92, 98, 104, 127, 145–146, 155, 157, 193, 204, 216, 219, 228, 231, 256, 259, 263, 265, 271, 291, 294–296, 298–299, 301, 323, 325, 346, 359–360, 372–374, 381, 394, 405, 419, 436–439, 442, 489, 493–494, 524–525, 537, 539, 552, 572, 576, 578, 580, 588, 590, 601–603, 612, 628, 646, 683, 685, 688, 690, 704, 717–718, 739, 745
Advisor 12, 15, 25, 29, 31, 44, 50, 69, 81, 85, 92, 141, 157–158, 168–169, 176, 180–181, 183, 188–189, 198, 216, 224, 228–231, 248–250, 270–272, 274, 277, 285, 294, 301–302, 318, 332, 336, 339, 359, 370, 372, 374–375, 378, 387, 392, 393, 402, 407, 422, 438–439, 466, 472–473, 479, 481, 485, 488–489, 500, 514–515, 526–527, 529, 540, 545, 548, 553, 561, 563–564, 566, 589, 595, 603, 614–615, 617, 619–621, 627, 636, 638, 645–652, 654–655, 690, 693, 701, 705–706, 709, 718, 742–743, 748
African Union (AU) 734
Akoma Ntoso 112
Albania 7, 40, 42–44, 98, 275, 398, 463–475, 513
Althingi 8, 487–498
amendment 31, 35, 63, 107–109, 111, 114, 127, 146, 157, 160, 170, 172, 192–193, 196, 205, 215, 229, 241, 244, 249–252, 260–261, 284, 288–289, 296, 301, 310, 312, 314, 317, 321, 327, 339–340, 350, 367, 372, 375, 382–383, 397, 414, 416, 418–420, 424, 428, 451, 459, 469, 483, 489, 493–494, 503, 514–516, 519, 522, 536–537, 550, 558–559, 576, 579, 622–623, 657, 694, 700, 728, 735, 744
annual workforce 448
Anti-Corruption Agency 538
Argentinean Congress 8, 583–584, 586–588, 590–591, 594–595
artificial intelligence 105–106, 116, 118, 353, 362

Assemblée nationale 36, 41, 44–45, 133, 243–254
Assembly 3, 6–7, 13, 25–26, 28, 31–32, 34, 39–40, 42–46, 55, 60, 63, 67–69, 71, 76, 90, 94, 101–102, 106, 123, 125, 128, 163–174, 176, 185, 215, 218, 222, 246, 248, 253, 275, 278–279, 281–287, 289–290, 298, 302, 308–310, 312–313, 320, 327–328, 348–361, 391, 403–404, 407, 409, 421, 433, 435, 463–478, 484–485, 506, 511–521, 534–543, 545–554, 568–569, 618, 628, 635–636, 654, 666–671, 673–674, 676–677, 683, 689–690, 693, 696, 699–704, 709–712, 725, 738–739, 741–750
Assembly of North Macedonia 511, 515, 519–520
assistants (to MPs) 15, 41, 45, 83, 86, 90, 106–109, 140, 157, 166, 168, 179, 204, 216, 224, 228, 234, 237–240, 249, 251, 256, 259, 307, 321, 324, 332, 402, 409, 414, 417, 420, 439, 440, 470, 500, 517, 526, 637, 639, 651, 701, 706, 710, 728–729, 731–732
Association of Secretaries-General of Parliaments 92, 643, 743
Atatürk, Mustafa Kemal 558, 568
Athenian democracy 268
Audit Committee 291, 295, 580, 603, 656, 661
Austerity 77, 321, 366, 426, 571, 575, 685, 687
autodichia 306, 309, 317
automation 109, 367–368, 371
autonomy 5, 7–9, 12–14, 20–29, 31, 33–34, 38–43, 48, 52–55, 66, 68–70, 122, 124, 140–141, 145, 155, 167, 196, 222, 230–231, 243, 247–248, 253, 274, 279, 282, 302, 306–310, 317, 324, 348, 384, 391, 394, 404, 407, 426, 432, 435–436, 440–441, 443, 455, 473, 476, 501, 504–505, 557, 560, 575, 583–584, 587, 612, 619, 639, 643, 678–679, 687, 699, 709, 732, 746, 748

Belgium 7, 12, 40, 42, 44, 50, 56, 64–65, 72–73, 79–80, 85, 152–153, 155, 157–161, 402
Benchmarks 55, 89, 96, 102, 109, 744
Bicameralism 38, 52–53, 64, 70, 72–74, 307, 309, 314, 317–318, 403, 435, 477, 547, 596
bicameral Committees 54, 64, 308
bicameral relations 575, 684–685
bicameral system 4, 50, 52–55, 63–65, 67–70, 72, 255, 277, 306, 308, 318, 376, 444, 446, 550, 679
bicephalic structure 58, 244
Bill 12, 27–28, 30, 32, 36, 50, 65, 107, 111, 124–126, 133, 145, 147, 157, 190, 192–193, 212, 214–216, 219, 223, 228–229, 249, 251–252, 260–262, 272–273, 278, 284, 286, 288, 290, 294–296, 301–302, 305, 309–312, 331, 336, 339–340, 359, 366–367, 375, 381–383, 385, 397, 403–404, 409–410, 438–439, 442–443, 450–452, 455–456, 488–489, 494, 496, 498–499, 527, 529–530, 536–537, 539, 547, 552, 554, 558, 560, 564, 585, 587–589, 603, 609, 611, 613–614, 617–618, 638, 640, 642, 645–646, 648, 650, 660–662, 664, 666–670, 673–674, 676, 691, 696, 710, 713, 744–745, 747
Bills Office 295–295, 301
black-box decision 112
Board of Administration 43–44, 49, 395, 398, 402
Bosnia and Herzegovina 98, 476–477, 479, 481, 483, 485–486, 545
Brazil 5–7, 9, 11–14, 21, 23–24, 28, 36–37, 42–44, 55, 57, 65, 74, 115, 117, 127, 611–623
British-Irish Parliamentary Assembly (BIPA) 302
Broadcasting Unit 298, 301, 576
Budget 3, 7–8, 13, 15, 20–29, 31–37, 46–47, 57, 63, 66, 78, 88–90, 92, 97, 102, 106, 109, 122, 124, 130, 139, 140–146, 148, 150–152, 154, 164–165, 168, 170, 173, 177, 188–190, 192–193, 196, 198, 203, 212–213, 220–223, 227–228, 230–231, 234, 236, 247, 249, 255, 258–259, 262, 269–270, 271, 273, 278, 282–283, 285–286, 288–289, 291–292, 294, 298, 301–302, 304, 309, 311–312, 320–321, 323, 331, 333–334, 343, 358–360, 366–368, 373, 384, 386–388, 390, 394–398, 402–403, 407–408, 413–414, 417, 422–424, 438–443, 448, 451–459, 464, 466–473, 475, 477–478, 489, 499–500, 503–504, 512, 514–516, 519, 521, 526, 536–537, 539, 561–563, 567, 569–570, 579, 583–586, 589–590, 595, 597–599, 602, 607, 609–614, 617, 619–620, 623, 626–627, 630–631, 634, 639–641, 644, 647–649, 657, 664–668, 670, 676–677, 679, 683–687, 691, 695–698, 701, 711–712, 714, 718, 721–722, 725–727, 733, 735, 742–743, 745–747
Budget Council of the Assembly 512, 515
Budget Lekgotla (Business Meeting) 396
Budget of the Assembleia da República 398
budgetary power 3, 15, 31, 152, 611, 727, 733
Bundesrat 25, 43, 58, 63–64, 68, 139, 151, 255–256, 258–267, 690, 696
Bundestag 2, 11, 25, 28, 31, 37, 40, 43, 49, 58, 63, 77–78, 81, 83, 87, 92, 98–99, 103, 123–125, 133–134, 244, 255–258, 260–267, 346, 696, 725
Bureau 8–9, 40–41, 44–46, 69, 154–155, 244, 248, 251, 253, 271, 307–309, 313, 325, 347–348, 378, 381–387, 396, 404–406, 408–409, 436–440, 464, 466, 468, 471, 500, 559–561, 563–565, 585, 614–619, 639, 656–664, 669–670, 701–702, 704, 706, 710, 729–731, 741–743
Bureau for Research 385
Bureau of Finance 384
Bureaucracy 7, 16, 31, 33, 37, 39–40, 42, 46, 54, 60, 67–68, 71, 73, 87, 91, 237, 306, 308, 435, 438, 583, 591, 594–595, 613, 616, 626, 631, 643, 679, 714, 718, 722, 751
business process re-engineering 112, 119

Index

Cabinet 19, 21, 48, 168, 231, 233, 237, 239, 243, 248, 326, 328–329, 348, 403, 405–407, 409, 412, 434, 440, 443, 472, 500, 512, 516–517, 534, 559, 606, 636–637, 656–657, 659, 661, 663, 665, 668, 703–704, 709, 713, 731
Cabinet Bureau of Personnel Affairs (Japan) 663
capacity building 98–99, 103, 265, 421, 484, 513, 601, 691, 693, 699, 740–741, 747–748, 750
Catering Facilities 300
Cathaoirleach 291, 295
Ceann Comhairle 291–292, 295, 302
Central Fund 291, 302
central services 166, 200, 256, 336, 368, 448, 564, 728
Centre for Innovation in Parliament 96, 117, 744
Centre for Parliamentary Studies and Training of the Parliament of Kenya 746
Centre for Research, Transparency and Accountability 536
Chairman's Council 163, 166–167
Chamber of Deputies 2, 15–16, 24, 26, 28, 32, 35, 44–46, 49, 59, 71, 123, 125, 126, 129, 199–201, 202, 205, 210, 305, 344, 345, 353–354, 405, 407, 584, 611, 618, 678–685, 688, 703
Chancellery of Riigikogu 222, 225
Chancellery of the Sejm 60, 378–379, 381–390
Chancellery of the Senate 60, 378, 380, 382, 384, 388–389
Chief of the Chancellery 43, 378, 384, 386–388
Citizen engagement 10, 111, 196, 275, 303, 399, 443, 456, 566, 652, 735
citizen participation 242, 341, 400, 502, 666, 676
Citizens 5, 9–10, 14, 106–111, 117–118, 121–122, 128, 130, 132, 139, 147, 150, 159–161, 165, 170, 177, 180, 184, 188, 190, 194–195, 204–205, 215, 217, 229, 236, 242, 250–253, 256, 258, 275, 279, 303, 306, 325–327, 340–341, 352–353, 385, 388, 394, 397, 399–402, 406, 408, 418, 430, 443, 456, 473, 476–477, 481, 483, 499, 504–505, 511–512, 519, 521, 535–538, 543, 548, 552–553, 565, 584, 590–591, 619, 639–640, 642, 652, 654–655, 668–670, 672–673, 699, 709–710, 716, 728, 734–735, 739, 744
Citizens Service 147, 177, 184
civil servants 7, 26–30, 33–34, 39–40, 48, 67, 69, 71, 81, 106, 109, 140, 143, 153, 176–177, 179–185, 188, 198, 227, 230, 233–235, 237, 239–240, 258, 265, 292–293, 332, 334, 337, 349–350, 388, 398, 402, 405–406, 408–410, 415–418, 420, 422, 430–432, 437–439, 443, 449, 452–453, 463–464, 466, 468, 471, 473, 475, 478, 481–482, 484, 485, 488, 500–501, 505, 510, 534, 538, 553, 559–560, 577, 615–616, 636–637, 643, 649, 667, 683, 685, 704, 715, 746, 751
Civil Servants Act 117, 182, 534, 538
Civil Service 8, 13, 21, 23–24, 26, 29, 33, 39, 41, 48, 59, 67, 176–177, 179–182, 184, 188–189, 193, 196, 198, 271, 293, 300, 321, 337, 349, 351, 354, 404–406, 409, 413–418, 424, 454, 468, 481, 486, 549, 560, 572, 612, 616–619, 636–637, 639, 643, 649, 679–680, 683, 687, 715
Civil Service Code 271, 293
Clerk of Dáil Éireann 291–292, 295, 301
Clerk of Seanad Éireann 295
Clerk of the Dáil 292
Clerk of the House 45, 47, 49, 356, 360, 363, 574, 576, 578, 603, 626, 628
Clerk of the Parliaments 45, 47, 576
Clerk of the Seanad 292
Clerks 9, 30, 31, 44, 50, 62, 65, 234–235, 243–244, 249–253, 263, 265, 351, 359–360, 368, 371–372, 437–439, 442–443, 445–446, 576, 578, 598, 600, 602, 626–629, 631, 634, 714–715
code of conduct 418, 443, 469, 604, 607, 669, 743
Collegium of the President of the Parliament 499
Commemorative events 147
Commission 8, 23–24, 34–35, 44, 46–47, 49, 58, 69, 71, 76–77, 81, 84–85, 94, 103, 115, 118, 122, 129, 146, 158, 180, 200–201, 203, 210, 217, 222, 227, 234–235, 248, 256, 264, 274, 284, 291–293, 295, 297–299, 301–305, 317–318, 324, 327, 329, 336, 339–340, 343, 346, 353, 373–375, 385, 392, 399, 405, 422, 429, 441, 452, 455, 466, 473–474, 477, 479, 481–482, 485, 502–503, 510, 534, 538, 542–543, 545, 548–550, 553, 556, 571–572, 575–577, 579–580, 583, 587–588, 590–591, 594–595, 598, 603–604, 606–609, 616–619, 630, 633, 636–637, 639, 648–649, 655, 657, 664, 679–680, 682–686, 688, 694–695, 697–698, 727, 732–733, 735, 745
Commission for Public Service Appointments (CPSA) 293
committee initiatives 451, 458
Committee of Public Accounts (PAC) 305, 604
Committee on Budgetary Oversight 294, 301
Committee on Parliamentary Privileges and Oversight 291, 295–296
Committee on Public Petitions 302
committee reports 108, 215, 296, 383, 419–420, 450–451, 456, 489, 494, 527, 560, 564, 601, 732
Committee secretariats 63, 144, 166, 189, 226, 235, 237, 246, 258, 261, 263–264, 336, 339, 340, 343, 345, 347, 350, 372, 382, 386, 417–418, 420, 422, 449–450, 452, 454–455, 458, 552, 564, 619
Committee secretaries 215–218, 233, 235, 237, 240, 419, 479, 524, 527–528
Committee secretary 212, 216–217, 235, 479, 589
Committee Stage 260, 301–302, 617

Index

Commonwealth Parliamentary Assembly 361
Communication 5, 8, 12, 77, 94, 96, 105–111, 133, 141, 144, 146–147, 150, 159–160, 164, 169–170, 184, 189–190, 192–195, 200, 206, 220, 223, 227, 229, 234–236, 240, 246, 256, 258–259, 271–273, 275, 281–282, 292, 294, 297–298, 300, 303–304, 314, 321, 325, 328–329, 340, 360, 368, 373, 394, 399–400, 423, 443, 448, 450, 456, 469, 472, 479, 482, 503–504, 512, 514, 518, 525–526, 528, 531, 535–537, 542, 545, 556, 575–576, 602–603, 629–630, 658, 668, 672, 676. 680, 684, 690–691, 693, 696, 703–710, 716, 726–728, 732, 735, 738, 743, 749
Complexity 39, 52, 55, 63, 70, 106, 109, 112, 121, 126, 177, 196, 204, 219, 253, 334, 397, 432, 458, 477–478, 517, 567, 604, 612–614, 620, 625–626, 679, 683, 685, 687, 710
Comptroller and Auditor General (C&AG) 305
Conference of Leaders 396–398
Conference of Parliamentary Committee Chairs 396
Conference of Parliamentary Committees for Union Affairs (COSAC) 83, 314, 740
Confidentiality 42, 125–126, 219, 394, 669, 702, 735
Conflict of interest 166, 469, 538, 630, 633
Congress 1–2, 5, 7–8, 13, 20–23, 28–34, 40, 43, 47, 54, 69, 75, 97, 108, 123, 126, 265, 311, 328, 435–436, 438, 583–584, 586–592, 594, 611, 613–614, 678–679, 682–688, 713–721, 727
Congress Library 123, 584, 590, 595
Congress Print 584, 590–591, 594
Congress Staff 123, 584, 590, 595
Constitution 1–4, 7, 20, 37, 40, 48, 53, 60, 67, 71, 83, 103, 108, 123, 140–141, 152–153, 155, 163, 166, 169, 171–173, 176, 185, 187, 193, 198, 233–234, 241, 243, 259, 268–269, 274, 277, 296, 301, 306–308, 310, 312, 318, 320, 353, 355, 356, 363, 378, 387, 389, 391, 397, 403–404, 412, 425–426, 428, 435–436, 438, 440, 445, 447, 453–454, 456–457, 463, 470, 475–477, 484, 486–487, 498–499, 510–512, 514, 521–523, 534, 542, 548, 557–560, 571, 594, 611–612, 620, 635–636, 654, 656, 660–664, 678, 685, 690, 694, 697–702, 706–707, 710–712, 714, 718, 720, 746, 749, 751
Constitution of the Republic of Croatia 185
Constitution of the Republic of South Africa, Act No 108 of 1996 698
Constitutional Amendment 35, 146, 196, 314, 327, 558–559
Constitutional Court 121, 155, 163, 172–174, 186, 283, 306, 309, 311, 356, 439, 446, 542, 559, 66, 701
Constitutional Democracy 15, 67, 690
Constitutional Mandate 68, 694

Constitutional Reform 3, 64–65, 176, 182, 238, 243, 309, 314, 318, 684, 710
control 7–8, 15, 30, 34, 37, 40, 42, 49, 61, 66, 69, 75.76, 84, 87, 106, 119, 132, 145, 165, 167–168, 171–172, 174, 182, 211–212, 218–221, 223, 227, 235, 243, 246–247, 249, 251–252, 255, 262, 264, 272–273, 276, 278–279, 283–285, 291, 312, 328, 332, 334, 339, 344, 354, 356, 361, 372–374, 376, 383, 389, 394, 396, 401, 416, 423, 435, 445, 457, 459, 471–473, 478, 483, 507, 525–528, 532–533, 537, 539, 549, 553, 559, 571–572, 585–587, 596, 598, 613, 616, 620, 626, 632, 648–649, 661–664, 668, 674, 676, 678, 709, 714, 718, 741, 743, 745–746, 750–751
coronavirus pandemic 496, 576, 610, 653
Correspondence and Information Bureau 385
Corruption Prevention Act 538
COSAC 84, 93, 184, 264–265, 297, 314, 351, 399, 438, 734, 740
Council of Parliamentary Factions 324
Council of States 67, 547–551
Council Presidency 146, 182, 263, 265, 507
COVID-19 77–78, 95, 108–119, 128, 131, 145, 160–162, 171–172, 174, 176, 183, 194–196, 207, 212, 219–221, 229, 230, 240, 266, 269, 272, 276–277, 279–280, 299–300, 303, 305, 314, 326–329, 340, 352, 355, 358, 362, 375, 388, 399, 401–402, 422, 428, 433, 443, 446, 456, 470, 475, 484–486, 495, 508, 511, 519, 522, 532, 542–543, 545, 554, 566–567, 591, 599, 606, 608–610, 620, 631, 634, 653–655, 663–664, 674, 677, 685, 691, 694, 697, 710, 734, 737, 744, 747, 749
Croatian Parliament 84–85, 176–178, 182, 186
Czech Republic 43–45, 55, 58, 125, 199, 201, 207, 210

Dáil Éireann 291–292, 295–296, 298, 301, 305
Debates Office 297, 301
debt crisis 31, 193, 196, 269, 276
Democracy Workshop 147
Denmark 12, 42–44, 46, 79–81, 211, 213, 215, 217, 219, 221, 402, 522, 533
Department for International Cooperation 518
Department of Public Expenditure and Reform 293
Departments 41, 47, 55–56, 58, 61, 66, 71, 86, 98, 143–144, 153, 155, 157, 160, 164–165, 182, 185, 199–202, 204, 206, 208, 220, 222–224, 230, 256, 258, 283–284, 287, 296, 302, 308, 310–313, 334, 336–337, 357, 368, 394–395, 405, 408, 417–418, 420–422, 429, 466, 468, 479, 481–482, 489–490, 512, 517, 524, 526, 535–536, 570–572, 575–577, 598–603, 606–608, 619, 636, 647, 649, 657–658, 662–664, 672, 679–680, 683, 686, 690, 699, 702–705, 709, 711, 728, 730, 732, 745

Deputy Chief of the Chancellery 378
Deputy Secretary General 144, 155, 179, 181, 212, 220, 224, 258–259, 261, 308, 347, 352, 430, 489, 535, 551, 561–563, 656, 668, 738
Deputy SG 46, 500
development 4–5, 7, 9–10, 12, 30, 34, 37, 50, 52, 54, 70, 76, 85, 89–90, 93–105, 107, 109, 111–113, 116, 122–123, 127–130, 133–134, 139–140, 142–144, 148, 166, 171, 176, 179, 185, 190, 201, 203, 210, 212–213, 215, 219–220, 223–224, 230–231, 240, 242, 248–249, 253, 259, 263, 268–269, 271, 275–276, 278, 282, 288, 292, 298–300, 311, 318, 320–321, 325, 329, 334, 336–337, 339, 341–343, 345, 351, 356, 358, 366, 370–371, 389, 392, 399, 401, 414, 416, 420, 423, 426, 428, 432, 454, 466, 468–469, 472–473, 477–478, 481–484, 489, 492, 495, 501–502, 505, 508, 510–511, 513–514, 516–518, 522–523, 525, 528, 532, 537–538, 540, 542, 548, 550, 553, 557–560, 563–564, 566–567, 570, 572, 575–577, 579, 599, 612–613, 618, 621, 627, 637–640, 647–649, 669, 672, 680, 683, 687–688, 691, 693–695, 697–698, 702–703, 705, 708–710, 726, 728, 732–734, 739, 741–744, 746, 748–750
Diet Affairs Committee 660
digital communication 94, 111, 275
digital marketing 111, 275
digital media 105, 115–116, 118, 120, 159, 273, 279, 531
digital parliament 11, 96, 106, 110–112, 116, 118, 276, 279, 303, 399, 443–444, 456
digital Parliament Programme 303
digital Transformation 11, 105, 112, 115–118, 269, 275, 292, 294, 303, 443
digitalization 105, 113, 347, 361, 542, 575, 734
diplomatic advisor 271, 274
Directorates-General 153, 258, 270, 731
disruptive technologies 105, 112
dissemination of information 190, 194, 495
Distrust 113, 430, 566
Division (Vote) 12, 31, 42, 49, 55, 69–71, 122, 152, 155, 157, 177, 185, 200, 237, 239, 246, 256, 258–259, 261–263, 265, 278, 292–294, 344, 346–347, 352–353, 357, 366–368, 370, 378, 394, 396, 419–421, 423, 428–430, 448, 456–457, 477, 499, 550–551, 575, 577–578, 595, 606, 614, 634, 638, 641, 647, 649, 657, 664, 668, 670, 690, 730, 743
draft/drafting 12, 14, 23, 25, 27–28, 46, 63, 75–77, 79–85, 85–86, 92, 94, 96, 101, 105, 107–108, 111, 113, 122, 126–127, 141, 145–147, 154, 157–158, 164, 167, 169–172, 179–181, 190, 192–194, 196, 198, 215, 222–223, 227–229, 235, 244, 249–250, 260–263, 272–273, 284, 288, 290, 294–296, 301, 303, 305, 309–312, 318, 320, 324–327, 329, 331, 336, 338–340, 350–351, 358–359, 361, 363, 372, 375, 378, 382–385, 390, 395, 397, 404, 416–417, 419–421, 424, 428–430, 433, 438, 442, 449–450, 452, 466, 469–471, 479, 481–484, 489, 493–499, 503–504, 515–516, 519–521, 524, 535–537, 539–540, 549, 553–554, 558, 560, 564, 567, 575, 588, 590, 601, 618, 628, 636, 646, 660, 669–670, 684, 690, 700, 702, 704–708, 711, 717, 739, 742, 745, 749

e-democracy 109–110, 213–215, 229
e-governance 213–215, 229, 672
e-Parliament 96–97, 102–103, 105, 114, 118, 508, 512, 538
Early Warning Mechanism 76, 158, 162, 318, 358, 361, 399
Early Warning System 76, 94, 104, 162, 171, 263–264, 269, 313, 358, 361, 375, 455, 472
East African Legislative Assembly Act 745, 749
East African Parliamentary Centre for Peace and Security 746
East African Women in Business Platform 747
economic and fiscal politics 503
ECPRD 2, 14–15, 39, 41, 50, 79, 86, 93–94, 101, 124, 130, 133–134, 182, 265, 275, 303, 384, 402, 428, 506–507, 648, 740
educational material 304, 386, 495, 536
Eduskunta 25, 233–242
Efficiency 5, 12, 16, 106, 109, 111, 115, 169, 172, 196, 231, 347, 389, 404, 455, 468, 543, 557, 564, 588, 598–600, 607, 609, 631, 672, 691, 695, 697–698, 702, 746
Electronic Document Information System (ELDIS) 326
electronic petitions 110
emerging technologies 112, 116, 118
Employment statistics 415
EP parliamentary diplomacy 733–734
Equality Diversity and Inclusion Unit 300
Erdoğan, Recep Tayyip 559, 569
Estimates 291, 299, 301, 360, 602–603, 608–609, 640–641, 745
Estonia 12, 42–43, 79–80, 222–224, 226–227, 229–232, 328–329
ethnic groups 476–477, 481
EU affairs 15, 63, 68, 75–87, 144, 146, 150, 158, 171, 183, 200, 204, 206, 230, 255–256, 261–266, 287, 313, 351, 354, 358, 361, 374–375, 381, 384, 399, 437, 451, 453, 455, 740
EU Affairs Committee 262–263, 314, 382, 384, 451
EU Co-ordination Unit 303
EU integration clause 171
EU National Parliament Representative 297

European affairs 76–77, 84, 86, 93, 125, 148, 177, 179–184, 190, 192, 200, 212, 217–218, 230, 246, 256, 259, 262–263, 274, 286, 328, 343, 346, 353, 358–359, 361, 374, 404, 414, 420–421, 423, 525, 734, 750

European Centre for Parliamentary Research and Documentation 41, 75, 93, 124, 133, 148, 265, 275, 384, 420, 533, 648, 734, 740

European Commission 76–77, 81, 85, 94, 103, 115, 118, 129, 146, 158, 264, 297, 392, 399, 474, 502, 510, 543, 545, 727, 732–733

European Parliament 2–3, 6, 9, 11, 13–16, 21, 23, 31, 34–37, 39–41, 43–45, 48–50, 73, 75–76, 89, 93, 100, 102–103, 117–119, 123–125, 133, 141, 146, 150, 173, 185, 199, 211, 221, 229, 235, 247, 255, 264–265, 277, 287, 297, 303, 314, 331, 374, 376, 383–384, 399, 455, 472, 484, 518, 540, 545, 563, 565, 569, 595, 654, 688, 722, 725–727, 729–733, 735, 737, 739–740, 747, 749–751

European Union Affairs 87, 226, 261–262, 303, 378, 383, 398, 455

European Union integration 472, 482, 484

Europeanization 3, 75–78, 81, 83–87, 231, 329, 353, 404, 437, 568

Events Team 298

Executive: Executive Arm of State; Executive Board/Management Board; executive centralism; executive legislative relations 20, 30, 403, 523

expert advice 323, 525, 683, 717–718, 745

expert assistance 381, 438, 502–503, 525, 527

expert support 139–140, 145, 381, 430–431, 455, 504

Explanatory Memorandum 367, 372, 442, 742

extended Presidency 179

external experts 31, 182, 236, 239, 422, 466, 554, 648, 650–651

external members of committees 184

Facilities Management Unit 299–301

Federal 12, 24–26, 40, 42, 47–48, 56, 63, 67–68, 71, 99, 129, 139–141, 143–148, 152–153, 158–159, 161, 255, 260–262, 265–266, 547–554, 576, 584, 594, 596, 609, 611–614, 616, 618–620, 635–637, 639, 685–686, 696, 716, 718

Federal Assembly 40, 42, 68, 71, 547–554

Federal Chancellery 67, 140, 145, 548–550

Federal Council 24, 67, 139–140, 144–146, 148, 547–549, 551–552, 751

Federal Parliament 48, 56, 148, 152, 159, 161

Finance Committee 78, 229, 259, 291, 295, 301, 548–549, 590, 647

Finance Unit 299, 301, 638

Financial independence 7, 513–515, 520, 599

Financial resources/ the budget of the lower chamber 28, 238, 309, 332–333, 367, 373, 395, 404, 407, 438, 440, 442, 600, 709, 728

Finland 8, 21–23, 25, 29, 31, 33, 37, 42–45, 49, 79–81, 99, 116, 233, 235, 237, 239, 241–242, 402

Fiscal Council 22, 35, 124, 133, 312, 318

Folketing 211–212, 214–219, 221

Foreign and European Affairs Committee (Malta) 358–359, 361

friendship groups 183, 265, 274, 298, 398, 484, 506, 536, 540–541, 565–566, 591, 629, 671

Funding (of parties / party groups) 7, 140, 151, 220, 223, 238, 256, 307, 366–367, 431, 468, 598–603, 606, 693–695, 740, 746

funding growth 601

general management 492, 495, 619

General Secretary 201–202, 212, 238–239, 281, 347–348, 353, 428

generalist profile 250

Global Parliamentary Report 748–749

Governance 3, 7–8, 15–16, 35, 50, 54–55, 60–61, 67–70, 89, 91–96, 103–105, 109, 112, 115, 119, 176, 213–215, 229, 265, 275–276, 279–280, 291–292, 295, 299, 314, 333, 357–358, 395, 412, 433–434, 443, 525, 546, 553, 570–574, 576–577, 579–580, 597–600, 602–605, 607, 610, 626–627, 643, 672, 676, 691, 699, 705, 709, 720, 738–739, 744, 746–748, 750–751

governing parliament 40, 268, 277–278, 392, 402, 501

government 1–2, 6, 10, 13–14, 16, 19–31, 33–37, 39–40, 44–45, 53, 63, 66–67, 69, 71, 76, 79–80, 85, 87–88, 92, 97, 99, 105, 107, 118–119, 121–122, 125, 132–134, 141, 143, 145, 148, 152, 157–161, 170–172, 174–177, 182–184, 187, 192–193, 198, 205, 211–212, 215–217, 219–220, 223, 228–231, 233, 235–239, 244, 249, 251–252, 255–256, 259–263, 265–266, 271, 276, 279, 283, 291, 293–294, 296, 299, 301–302, 305–307, 309–312, 318, 321, 325–327, 331, 333–334, 336, 340, 344, 347–350, 352–355, 357–358, 360–363, 366, 370–373, 375, 391, 396–398, 401–403, 407, 411, 414, 416, 418, 420–422, 425, 429, 435–437, 440, 443, 447–448, 450–452, 454–456, 458, 472, 484, 488–489, 491–492, 494, 498–499, 512–516, 523, 525–528, 531–532, 537, 539, 542–543, 545, 547–548, 554, 558–561, 564, 567, 571–572, 576, 597–600, 604, 606, 608–609, 613–614, 617–618, 620, 624–631, 634–639, 641–642, 645–646, 649–650, 652, 654–655, 657–663, 665–666, 669–670, 672, 674, 676–678, 684–686, 688–690, 695–698, 700, 702, 704, 706–708, 710, 712–715, 717–718, 722, 737, 741, 743, 749, 751

Government Bills 36, 192–193, 284, 296, 301, 305, 450–451, 455–456, 494

government system change 560–561, 564, 567

governmental employees 176–177, 182
Grand National Assembly of Turkey (GNAT) 275, 557, 559, 566, 568–569
Guided tours 10, 236, 400, 456, 495, 525

Hearings (committees) 108, 212, 216, 219, 227, 235, 237, 249–251, 261, 264, 284, 314, 339, 386, 397, 451, 458, 469, 479, 499, 525, 527–528, 532, 536, 674, 684, 693–694, 717, 735, 737
Hellenic Parliament 48, 50, 118–119, 133, 268–280
Hierarchy 3, 6, 8, 47, 55, 166, 179, 184, 200, 224, 234, 271, 273, 324, 334, 347, 357, 369–370, 386, 413, 422, 436, 452–453, 471–472, 478–479, 504–505, 570, 586, 595, 618, 626–627, 637, 667, 670, 730–732
horizontal communication 482
House Business Committee 360, 745
House Commission 571
House of Commons 16, 19, 27, 45, 47–49, 51, 123, 128, 133, 244, 570–573, 575–580, 604, 608, 624–626, 628–634
House of Counties 176, 182
House of Lords 27, 45, 47, 49, 66, 570–571, 575–580, 604, 608–609
House of Representatives 16, 24, 28, 30, 32, 36, 44–46, 56, 59, 73, 98, 112, 119, 152–162, 187–190, 192–196, 198, 355–357, 364–367, 369, 477, 597–599, 601, 603, 606–609, 622, 657–658, 662, 664–665, 688, 711, 714–715, 719
HR Recruitment Unit 299
HR Systems and Change Unit 300
HR Unit for Members 300
HR Unit for Staff 299
Hrvatski sabor (Sabor) 176–177, 179–186
Human Resources Management 348, 502, 517, 705, 708
human rights 95, 258, 309, 317–318, 343, 475–476, 525, 542, 545, 608, 733–734, 741–744
Hungary 6–7, 42–44, 79–80, 281, 283, 285, 287, 289–290, 411

Iceland 8, 487, 489, 491, 493–495, 497–498
ICT infrastructure 155, 272, 514, 520
impact assessment 76, 107, 124–126, 130, 145, 169, 236, 261, 272, 302, 312, 317, 325, 329, 340, 396, 452, 503, 539, 732–733
impacts of Covid 19 674, 734, 737
impartiality 6, 8, 27, 33, 42, 144, 189, 307–308, 317, 348, 378, 393, 492–493, 496, 505, 572, 578, 631, 659, 664
incongruent 547
independence 6–9, 11, 21–22, 35, 38–39, 41–42, 49, 55, 66, 85, 99, 122, 125, 144–145, 165, 170–171, 176, 181, 184, 188, 196, 222, 227, 237, 243, 253, 268, 270, 283, 306, 312, 317, 320, 331–332, 341, 347–348, 355–356, 362, 391, 393, 414, 429, 436, 438, 473, 500, 507, 511–516, 520, 523, 538, 538, 554, 557–559, 588, 598–599, 607, 619, 636, 643, 650, 662–663, 678, 721, 729
induction programme 420, 422, 494
information 2, 4, 11–12, 22, 30–32, 34, 41, 49–51, 54, 64, 68, 75–76, 80, 84–85, 87, 93–95, 106–110, 112, 115–127, 129–130, 132–134, 141, 144–148, 164–165, 168–169, 173, 177, 182, 184, 186, 190, 194, 198, 200, 205–207, 210–212, 215–220, 224, 228–230, 232, 234–237, 239–241, 246, 250–252, 256, 258–260, 262–267, 271–273, 275, 278, 282, 284, 287, 289, 292–293, 297–298, 300, 304, 308, 311, 318, 321, 325–326, 328, 340–341, 346, 351, 353–354, 357, 360, 362–363, 365, 368, 371–376, 381–387, 393–394, 397, 399–402, 408, 419–424, 430, 433, 442–443, 449, 456–458, 464–467, 469–470, 478–479, 481–484, 488–489, 492, 494–496, 498, 503–504, 506–507, 511–513, 518–519, 525–527, 531, 535–537, 539–540, 542–543, 550–554, 560–561, 563, 565, 567, 575–576, 580, 588, 591, 600–603, 612–623, 626, 630, 636, 638–640, 642, 647–652, 654–656, 660–661, 668–669, 671–673, 679, 683–685, 690–691, 693, 696, 703, 705–707, 719, 731, 734–735, 737, 739–745
Information and Communication Technologies 272, 394, 399, 423
Information Centre of the Sejm 386
Information service 34, 146–147, 200, 212, 236, 282, 287, 298, 300, 357, 381, 576, 602, 612, 636, 639–640, 679, 690
Information systems 64, 115, 118–119, 341, 394, 423, 470, 525, 655, 705, 707
Innovation 5, 94–97, 106, 109–110, 115, 117, 130–131, 148, 275–276, 314, 328, 337, 341, 356, 358, 361, 443, 508, 549, 606–607, 695, 734–735, 744
Innovation Tracker 744
institutional hierarchy 166, 273, 347, 369, 386, 452–453, 471, 504, 618, 670, 730
institutional memory 39, 43, 112, 126, 176, 185, 269, 332, 492, 629, 632
Institutionalisation 330, 740
Inter Parliamentary relations 298, 302, 374, 437, 565, 601, 746
inter-institutional cooperation 106, 116, 274–275, 421
Inter-institutional relations 167, 171, 205, 302, 312, 351, 454–455, 732–733
Inter-Parliamentary Conference on Stability, Economic Coordination and Governance in the EU 314

Inter-parliamentary cooperation 36, 103, 148, 171, 269, 272, 274–276, 278, 302, 312, 378, 383, 437, 506, 671, 733, 750
Inter-parliamentary friendship groups 484, 565–566
Inter-parliamentary institutions 235, 750
Inter-parliamentary Relations and Travel Unit 298, 302
Inter-parliamentary Union 10, 39–40, 43, 50, 52, 55, 72, 89, 95, 102–103, 105, 124, 134, 158, 218, 230, 264, 276, 298, 421, 443, 454, 484, 501, 510, 541, 553, 568, 654, 739, 741, 748–751
Inter-Parliamentary Union Assembly (IPU) 298
Intergovernmental Relations 751
international affairs 125, 134, 144, 148, 182–183, 185, 235–236, 238, 246, 274, 357, 382–384, 437, 494, 550, 568, 648
International Affairs Bureau 382–383
international co-operation 98–492
international engagement 92, 690
international parliamentary institutions 92, 97, 103, 274, 540–541, 738, 750–751
international secretariat 212, 217–218
international work 219, 493
Internet portal 398–401
Internship program 143, 165
Interoperability 105–107, 111–112, 118, 276
Interpellations 285, 309, 419, 450, 456, 469, 660
IPEX 10, 93–94, 206, 264–265, 275, 384, 507, 734

job requirements 504–505
Joint Law Portal 326
Joint Parliamentary Scrutiny Groups (JPSGs) 265, 297
joint service (bicameralism) 49, 56–62, 65–66, 68, 70, 477–479, 481–482, 485, 579
Journal of Laws 381, 383
Journal of the Assembleia da República 397–398, 402
Journal Office 295–296, 301, 576
Journalists 5, 108–109, 130, 159, 165, 190, 215, 229, 252, 273, 278, 289, 386, 400–401, 456, 504, 535, 553, 653, 727
Judiciary 274, 309, 353, 412, 436, 445, 537, 559, 613, 666–667, 676, 690, 694, 697–698
Justice and Development Party (JDP) 559

Knesset 25, 29, 31, 34, 49, 644–655 see Knesset Legal Advisor
Knesset Administration 644, 645, 647–651, 654
Knesset Director General 655
Knesset Guard 646–648, 650–651
Knesset Legal Advisor 647, 650, 654–655
Knesset Presidium 645
Knesset Rules of Procedure 644–645
Knesset Secretariat 644, 646, 651

Knesset Speaker 644, 646–649, 652–654
Knowledge Management 346
Kokkai 656, 660, 665
Korean National Assembly 13, 28, 666–667, 674
Korean National Assembly Budget Office 667–668
Korean National Assembly Research Service 667, 669
Korean National Assembly Secretariat 667–671, 673
Korean National Assembly TV 674

Labour Act 177
labour contract 166, 177
Language training 203
Law on Administrative Servants 512, 516–517, 521
Law on Assembly 512, 514–518, 520–521
Lawmaking 15, 275, 306, 326, 352, 442, 496, 676, 713, 743–744
LCO - Legislative Counsel Office 668, 670
Legal and Personnel Bureau 385
legal framework 48, 139, 177, 193, 261, 473, 487, 505, 543, 738, 747
legal informatics 105, 110–112, 116, 276, 280
legal service 80, 85, 112, 177, 179, 212, 215–217, 220, 300, 324, 336, 346, 358, 381, 383, 419, 423, 428–429, 466–467, 469, 471, 524, 550, 561, 563–564, 617, 680, 728, 732
legislative activity 117, 162, 165, 168, 250, 383, 401, 472, 535, 613, 616, 618, 716
Legislative advisors 50, 318
Legislative Arm of State 695
Legislative Assistance 150, 383, 715
Legislative Bureau 14, 46, 381–383, 385, 656–659, 661, 663–665, 676
Legislative Committee 16, 180, 383, 701–702, 705, 709
Legislative expert 560–561, 563–564
legislative procedure 3, 31, 46, 147, 159, 162, 193, 249, 251–253, 261, 284, 288, 318, 396–397, 400, 403, 410, 437, 439, 444, 536, 538, 619, 655, 733
legislative process 12, 16, 21, 31, 80, 139–140, 144, 157, 169–171, 190, 205, 252, 255–256, 258, 260, 274, 284, 311, 318, 340, 372, 381, 383, 389, 405, 419–421, 429, 442, 473, 483, 507, 512, 543, 564–565, 567, 583–585, 588–591, 595, 617, 619, 660, 662, 664, 668, 679, 684–685, 687, 737, 739
Legislative Sector Support (LSS) 69, 691, 697
legislative services 32, 46–47, 63, 244, 246–247, 249, 251, 419, 464, 564, 626, 745
length of service 488, 491
Letrado, Cortes Generales 49, 69, 436–439, 441, 445
level of activity 522, 527–528, 531–532

liaison office 69, 84, 86, 93, 256, 262–263, 374, 698, 735
Liberal Democratic Party (Japan) 660
Liberal State 308
Library 24, 27, 47, 56–58, 65, 85, 94, 96, 103, 106, 108, 115, 117, 123–124, 128, 130, 133–134, 144–145, 152, 157, 164–165, 169, 177, 182, 190, 194, 200, 212, 214–215, 224, 236, 241, 246, 249, 258–259, 270–272, 278–279, 282, 285, 287–288, 293, 298, 301–302, 304–305, 310, 317, 324, 336, 359, 378, 381, 384, 394, 400–402, 417, 420–421, 423–424, 449, 466–467, 481, 483, 492, 500, 512, 518, 523, 525, 535, 539, 550, 552, 561, 563–564, 572, 575–577, 580, 584, 586–587, 590, 595, 597, 602–603, 607, 609, 617, 624–631, 633–634, 636, 638, 640, 642, 648, 656, 658–659, 662–663, 665, 667, 669, 677, 704, 706–707, 714, 717, 721, 744–745
Library and Research Service (L&RS) 94, 96, 298, 301–302, 304–305, 665, 744
Lisbon Treaty 75–76, 87, 183, 269, 279, 376, 725, 728
Lobby registry 235
Lobbying Act 293, 386, 538

Majoritarianism 307, 363
Malta 6, 12, 79–80, 355–364
Management Board 47, 144, 292, 295, 489–490, 492, 496, 550, 572, 580, 603
management by gender 490
management challenges 597
management positions 143–144, 491
Mandate, Ethics and Submissions Commission (MESC) 327
mandating 217
media 5, 9, 12, 28, 69, 88, 96, 100–103, 105–106, 110–112, 115–118, 120, 126, 129–131, 143, 145, 147, 151, 159, 170, 172–173, 184, 190, 198, 201, 204, 221, 223, 227, 229–230, 235–236, 238–240, 246, 252, 258–261, 273, 275, 279, 282, 286, 297–298, 303, 325–326, 329, 331, 334, 340, 358, 360, 363, 365, 373, 386, 398–402, 407, 409, 411, 423, 443, 450, 456, 469–470, 483, 504, 507, 525, 531, 535, 539, 542–543, 546, 552–553, 565, 567, 599, 602, 604, 607–608, 615, 619, 639–640, 642, 652–653, 661, 663, 668, 670, 684, 694, 704, 707–708, 713, 716, 720, 729, 735, 744, 749
Members of Parliament 4, 39, 45, 57, 80, 90, 98, 106, 117–118, 151, 187–188, 211–212, 217–219, 233, 255, 268, 321, 345, 357, 365, 391, 413, 417, 440, 442, 476, 483, 485, 495, 505, 510–511, 537, 548, 550–551, 555, 570, 577, 600, 604, 619, 635, 666, 674, 690, 700, 744
Memorandum of Understanding 68, 118, 271, 279, 519, 625

Mexico 6–7, 9, 21, 23, 26, 28, 32, 37, 42, 44, 59, 678–679, 681, 683, 685–688
Minister for Public Expenditure and Reform 291, 293
Mixed model 612, 616, 621
Model Parliament 288
Monday Morning Meeting 84
MP and party audits 270–271, 273, 277
MPs 4–8, 10–16, 21–22, 24–34, 40–41, 49–50, 52–54, 63, 68, 70, 72, 78, 80–83, 85–86, 88, 90, 98, 105–108, 111, 114, 116–117, 119–120, 123, 126–127, 131, 134, 141–142, 144–145, 148, 153–155, 157–158, 160, 163–166, 168–170, 172–173, 176–177, 179–182, 184–185, 199, 202–206, 211–212, 214–220, 223–224, 226–229, 231, 233–240, 242, 244, 246, 249–253, 255–256, 258, 262, 266, 268, 270, 272–273, 277–278, 281–282, 284–285, 287–288, 307, 309–311, 314, 317–318, 321, 323–328, 331–336, 339–341, 345–349, 352–353, 355–356, 358, 360–363, 365–369, 371–375, 382–383, 385, 387–388, 391, 397, 399–401, 403–404, 408–414, 417, 419–423, 426, 428–433, 439–440, 442–444, 447, 449–450, 452, 455–458, 463, 464–467, 469–473, 475, 481, 483–484, 499–500, 503–506, 508, 511–513, 515, 517–529, 531–532, 535–540, 542–543, 564, 570, 573, 576–580, 625–632, 634–636, 639–643, 660, 670, 703, 705–708, 710, 742–744
MPs assistants 41, 237–239, 417
MPs Groups 499
MPs 4, 39, 45, 57, 80, 90, 98, 106, 117–118, 151, 187–189, 211–212, 217–219, 233, 255, 268, 321, 345, 357, 365, 391, 413, 417, 440, 442, 476, 483, 485, 495, 505, 510–511, 537, 548, 550–555, 570, 577, 600, 604, 619, 635, 666, 674, 690, 700, 744; *see also* Members of Parliament
multi-layered 153, 161
multilingualism 551, 726–727
Multinational: multinational character; 34, 152–153, 725–726, 733
MyVoice (Manabalss.lv) 327, 329–330

Nanyuki seminars 746
Narodna skupština 534, 546
National Assembly 3, 7, 13, 25–26, 28, 31–32, 45, 69, 123, 125, 163–174, 275, 278–279, 281–287, 289–290, 421, 433, 477–478, 534, 537–541, 543, 545–547, 557, 559, 566, 568–569, 666–671, 673–674, 676–677, 689, 690, 693, 696, 703
National Assembly Act 534, 537–540, 666–669, 677
National Congress 57, 611
National Constituent Assembly (NCA) 699, 703

National Council 24, 26, 56, 67–69, 71, 126, 139–141, 143–148, 413–424, 433, 467, 512, 518, 547–552, 689, 690, 696–697
National Council of Provinces 67, 69, 689–690, 696–697
National Diet Library (Japan) 656, 658–659, 662–663, 665
national legislature 36, 41, 87, 176, 233, 254, 267, 328, 597, 614, 621, 629, 678, 689, 714
national sovereignty 435, 476, 560, 567
National Treasury 26, 695, 697
network of parliamentary representatives 87, 265, 267, 376
neutral/neutrality 7–9, 13, 41, 49, 185, 188–189, 196, 253, 324, 392–393, 418, 443, 630–631, 667, 671
NGOs 184, 250, 341, 503, 510, 591
Nobel Peace Prize 742
North / South Inter-Parliamentary Association (NSIPA) 302

Office of the Attorney General 305
Office of the Commission and Secretary General (OCSG) 295, 301
Office of the National Assembly 281
Office of the Parliamentary Legal Advisers (OPLA) 174–175
Official Report 297, 525
Oireachtas Library 298
Oireachtas Student Placement Programme 304
Oireachtas TV 298, 303
Oireachtas Work Learning (OWL) Programme 304
Ombudsman 356, 441, 525
One Stop Shop 300, 525
online platforms 110
open competition 40, 44, 292–293, 321, 468, 488, 491, 505, 669
open data 12, 97, 109–110, 112, 251–253, 399, 591, 687, 744
Open Parliament project 536
Order Paper 295–297
Orders of Reference 296
organigram 357
organization 2–3, 5–8, 10–16, 21–22, 31–32, 34, 38–39, 42, 47–49, 52–55, 57–61, 63, 65–72, 76, 79, 81, 83, 86, 88–90, 93–99, 103, 118–119, 122, 124–125, 127–128, 140–143, 145, 148, 153–155, 158–161, 163, 166–170, 173–174, 176–178, 181–185, 187–188, 190, 194–195, 198–201, 203, 206–207, 210, 212–213, 216, 227–230, 233, 235, 237–240, 242, 244–250, 252–253, 256, 258–259, 261, 263, 265–266, 269–270, 272, 275–276, 278–279, 281–284, 287, 292, 294, 296, 298–300, 306–307, 313–314, 317, 321, 325–326, 328, 332–335, 337, 340–342, 365–368, 371–375, 378–382, 384–388, 390–391, 394–395, 398–399, 404, 407–408, 413–415, 417–424, 426–432, 434, 436–437, 447, 453–455, 463, 468–469, 471–473, 477–480, 482–485, 488–490, 496–497, 499–500, 502, 505–506, 508, 511–526, 534–543, 548–550, 552–554, 558–562, 565, 569, 583–591, 594, 597–599, 603, 606–607, 611–613, 615–617, 619–620, 622, 624–626, 629, 631, 634–638, 640, 643, 646, 648–649, 652, 654, 656–658, 661, 663, 665, 667, 669–671, 674, 676–687, 689, 691, 694–697, 699, 701–705, 708–711, 713–715, 717, 719–720, 748, 750–751
organizational structure 5, 15, 59–60, 259, 270, 282–283, 333–335, 365, 368, 378, 395, 413–414, 422–424, 436, 473, 478, 488, 497, 517, 520, 542, 561, 597, 616, 619–620, 625, 656–658, 667, 682, 691, 701, 708
organizational chart 63, 174, 178, 200, 212–213, 294, 379–380, 395, 407–408, 427, 441, 490, 524, 562, 585–587, 594, 626, 665, 680–682, 702, 709
organizational department 206, 419, 423, 519
organizational rules 199–201, 203, 206, 210, 378, 381, 384, 419, 424
organizational units 142, 177, 182, 321, 378, 387, 417–418, 422, 479, 482, 485, 489, 512, 516–517, 550, 667, 674
organogram 188, 276, 369, 376, 572, 698
OSCE 218, 265, 313, 361, 472–473, 475, 484, 502, 506, 538, 541, 545, 750
outreach activities 275, 278, 478
Oversight 7, 20, 31, 34, 36, 61, 72, 88, 92, 94, 97, 105, 107, 113, 116–118, 130, 152, 219, 255–256, 273, 291, 294–296, 301, 307–308, 310–312, 318, 328, 336, 403, 413, 419–421, 439, 499–500, 503, 512, 519–520, 525–526, 543, 554, 571–572, 579, 584, 598, 603–604, 608, 612–613, 617, 626, 649, 656, 661, 678–679, 687, 690, 694, 697, 700–702, 706–708, 717, 720, 743, 747, 749

ParLex 288, 290
Parliament Channel 166, 397–398, 400
Parliament Guard 378, 381
Parliament of Malta 355–359, 361, 363–364
Parliament of South Africa 13, 26, 29, 61
Parliament TV 360, 362, 641
parliamentary academy 702, 704, 706, 709–710
parliamentary activity 5, 12, 52, 54, 113, 160, 172–173, 212, 249, 308, 394, 400, 404, 406, 408, 437, 443, 469–473, 617–619, 647, 670, 703
Parliamentary Assembly of Bosnia and Herzegovina 476–477
Parliamentary Assembly of the Council of Europe 94, 185, 218, 298, 313, 361, 484, 506, 541

Parliamentary Assembly of the Council of
  Europe (PACE) 484, 541
Parliamentary Assembly of the Mediterranean
  313, 361, 541, 654
Parliamentary Assembly of the Organization for
  Security and Co-operation in Europe 185, 484
Parliamentary Assembly of the Union for the
  Mediterranean 218, 361
parliamentary autonomy 29, 39, 140, 167,
  436, 748
parliamentary bodies 22, 32, 34, 90, 96–97, 122,
  126–127, 132, 141, 351, 436, 438, 482, 489,
  506, 550–551, 606, 683, 726, 743
parliamentary budget 22, 32–33, 89, 102, 124,
  141, 143, 145, 148, 164, 168, 269, 271, 273,
  292, 294, 298, 301, 304, 312, 368, 373,
  440, 468, 470, 500, 519, 521, 597, 610, 630,
  695, 698
parliamentary Budget Office 22, 32–33, 35, 89,
  102, 124, 143, 145, 148, 271, 292, 294, 298,
  301, 304, 312, 500, 519, 521, 597, 630, 698
parliamentary bureaucracy 31, 33, 39, 42, 46, 60,
  67, 237, 591, 631, 679
parliamentary civil service 13, 26, 28, 59, 404,
  406, 409, 612, 679–680, 683, 687
parliamentary committees 37, 83, 123, 126,
  163, 166–169, 189–193, 195, 212, 227–229,
  235, 242, 265, 272, 277, 284, 313–314,
  324–326, 358, 365, 368, 371–375, 382–383,
  393, 396–298, 404–405, 415, 419–423, 442,
  447, 455, 459, 466–467, 469–470, 472, 507,
  527, 533–534, 537, 554, 565, 609, 628, 630,
  640–641, 652, 658, 660, 666, 669, 680, 728,
  731, 740
parliamentary constituency offices 538
parliamentary control 87, 119, 145, 165, 167–168,
  171–172, 218–221, 223, 264, 272, 278, 339,
  354, 376, 553, 750
parliamentary cooperation 3, 5, 34, 36, 75, 83,
  103, 148, 165, 171, 182–183, 230, 256, 264,
  269, 272, 274–276, 278, 302, 312–314, 318,
  378, 383, 399, 423, 427, 454, 472, 483, 499,
  505–506, 536, 568, 671, 733, 740, 743, 745,
  750–751
parliamentary departments 598–601, 603,
  606–608
parliamentary development assistance 420
parliamentary diplomacy 4, 5, 10, 16, 88–95, 97,
  99, 101, 103–105, 111, 116, 148, 171, 194–195,
  274, 279, 302, 313, 383, 398, 421, 437, 454,
  472, 506, 512–513, 536, 540, 584, 591,
  662–663, 733–734, 738, 740, 751
parliamentary Education Officer 304
parliamentary groups 6, 24, 44, 49, 116–117, 126,
  130, 141, 143–146, 148, 163–164, 166–168,
  170, 230, 237–238, 250, 273, 286, 307, 310,
  321, 339, 393, 396, 402, 405–406, 417–420,
  423–424, 440, 442, 463–464, 468, 471–472,
  483, 512, 514–515, 518, 534, 536–537, 542,
  552, 629, 644, 646, 651, 683–684, 710
parliamentary institute 58, 65, 123, 125–126,
  200, 204, 417, 420–424, 500, 512, 518,
  520–521, 746–747
parliamentary leadership 269, 419, 526
parliamentary library 56, 65, 106, 117, 124,
  145, 164, 169, 200, 310, 336, 417, 420–421,
  423–424, 550, 552, 597, 602–603, 607,
  609, 642
parliamentary Network on Digital Security 542
Parliamentary networks 92, 173, 218, 275, 738,
  741, 750
Parliamentary Office 34, 93, 234–237, 239–241,
  288, 472, 616, 618–619, 734
Parliamentary party groups 87, 140, 185, 211,
  219–220, 428, 431, 439, 487, 489, 492–494,
  522, 524–526, 532, 751
parliamentary public official 285, 711
parliamentary Question (PQ) 122, 212, 215–216,
  221, 251, 275–276, 296–297, 359, 362, 499,
  530, 564, 567, 575–576
parliamentary research 15, 41, 75, 84–85, 93–95,
  103, 122–124, 133–134, 148, 158, 265, 275,
  278–279, 298, 325, 372, 375, 384, 420–421,
  442, 466–467, 473, 535, 638–639, 643, 648,
  703, 734, 740, 749–750
parliamentary research service 84, 103, 122–124,
  134, 278, 298, 384, 420–421, 740, 749–750
parliamentary resolutions 458
parliamentary secretary 46, 212, 220, 585,
  588–589, 592, 594, 738
parliamentary service 12, 15, 40, 42, 44–46, 49,
  56, 66–67, 69, 71, 256–258, 259–260, 293,
  295, 328, 355–356, 358, 360–361, 363, 387,
  389, 393–395, 399, 401, 404, 466, 471–472,
  489, 499–506, 508, 510, 513, 515, 548–556,
  575–577, 579, 597–599, 602–604, 606–609,
  640, 680, 682–684, 689–690, 693–695, 743
parliamentary Service Act 40, 44, 69, 71, 356,
  358, 360, 363, 501, 551, 598–599, 602,
  604, 607
parliamentary services 15, 42, 45–46, 56, 66–67,
  69, 293, 295, 328, 356, 393–395, 399, 401,
  405, 466, 471–472, 548–556, 575–577, 579,
  597, 602–603, 608–609, 680, 682–684,
  689, 743
parliamentary staff 5–8, 10–12, 16, 20–22,
  24–28, 33, 40, 49, 68, 71, 75, 86, 96, 98,
  130, 180, 282, 298, 302, 309, 311, 359–360,
  362, 375, 385–391, 393, 397–398, 401–402,
  404–405, 407–410, 414, 418, 421, 437, 441,
  453, 468, 470–473, 484–485, 495, 499, 503,
  505–507, 510, 575, 578, 580, 586, 589, 594,
  598, 607, 626–629, 631–632, 663, 693, 706,
  710, 743–744, 747

parliamentary Support Program (PSP) 97, 518
parliamentary television 271, 401
parliamentary term 176, 180–181, 338, 367, 375, 488, 492, 704
parliamentary transparency 275, 507
parliamentary work 3, 4, 12, 75, 88–89, 96, 105–106, 109, 111–114, 123, 130, 141, 155, 166–167, 171, 176, 184, 190, 204, 215, 219, 249, 268, 270, 272–273, 275–276, 293, 325–326, 339, 346, 356, 365, 369, 371, 373, 381, 384, 388, 394–396, 398–399, 419, 442, 450, 469, 481, 494, 496, 503, 526, 545, 548, 577, 606, 608, 618, 628, 639–640, 646, 649, 651, 660, 670, 683, 701–702, 705–707, 710, 725, 727–728, 730–731, 734, 743
parliamentary workforce 270
Parline 96, 158, 501, 504, 743–744
ParlTech 105, 110, 112, 115–118
Party Brokers 588, 595
Party group secretariats 239, 447, 449, 522, 524–527, 529, 531–532
Party groups 13–14, 24–25, 28, 83, 86–87, 106, 140, 143, 185, 211, 219–220, 233–234, 236–240, 332, 334, 336, 366–367, 371, 373, 428, 431, 439, 449, 457, 487, 489–494, 522, 524–527, 529, 532, 560–561, 563–565, 386, 388, 395, 629, 634, 751
party loyalists 406
patronage 6–7, 13, 28, 332, 405–407, 410, 715
Pensions Unit 300
People's Representatives Assembly (PRA) 699, 711
performance 8–9, 35, 39, 72, 89, 91, 96, 99, 133, 159, 174–175, 177, 194, 223, 246, 259, 282, 285, 291–292, 295, 299, 302, 321, 334–335, 339, 384, 386–387, 389, 392–393, 416, 418–419, 430, 505, 507, 514, 518, 538–539, 545, 576, 597–600, 602–604, 607–609, 618, 620, 634, 661, 680, 683, 691, 693, 695, 697–698, 701, 708–709, 715–716, 728
personal assistance to MPs 526
personnel costs 408
plenary session 44, 46, 61, 68, 165, 168, 172, 177, 179, 181–182, 184, 190, 195–196, 229, 235–236, 246, 258, 261–262, 273, 278, 283–284, 288, 326, 339, 347–348, 353, 371, 378, 382–383, 405, 408, 419, 422–423, 428, 430, 443, 466–468, 470, 482, 506, 542, 550, 589, 618–619, 660–662, 664, 667–668, 701–702, 704, 707–709, 733
policy 8–10, 16, 22, 24, 32, 36, 41, 50, 73, 76–77, 80–81, 84, 86, 91, 93, 102–104, 109–111, 113, 117–119, 125–126, 128, 132–133, 144–145, 153, 155, 157, 171, 173–174, 183, 185, 194, 204–205, 212, 217, 219, 221, 226–231, 233, 235, 238–240, 242, 259, 266, 274, 279, 281, 287, 293–294, 296, 298, 301–302, 305, 307, 314, 321, 324–325, 327–328, 336, 356, 363, 366, 372–373, 376, 384, 388, 390, 393, 408, 420, 429–430, 434–435, 441–442, 451–452, 459, 477, 489, 492–493, 496, 503, 519, 523, 525–526, 533, 543, 545, 549–551, 561, 565, 567–568, 571, 576, 579, 583, 602, 604, 607, 610–615, 623, 625, 635, 640, 643, 648, 659–660, 662–663, 665, 668–669, 672–674, 676, 688, 691, 694–695, 697, 708. 710, 713, 716–720, 722, 726, 728–730, 732–733, 737, 739, 741, 743–748, 750–751
policy advice 296
Political appointees/ Contract-based personnel 227, 405–406, 409–410, 682
political culture 53, 171, 543, 661
political Dialogue 76–77, 79, 86, 264, 452
political group 7–8, 13, 24
political independence 184, 243
political influence 9, 163, 166, 324, 336, 404, 473, 481, 485, 729
political interference 348, 415, 422, 491
political posts 273
political staff 30, 41, 83, 86, 143, 177, 215, 299–300, 361, 464, 468, 487–488, 490–493, 583, 588, 606–607, 627–628, 634
political-administrative relations 153, 161
politically impartial 429, 437, 577–578
Politicization 7, 9, 42, 143, 335, 410, 454, 505, 557, 560, 563, 567, 624, 626–627, 643, 649
power-sharing 476
Pre-Committee Stage Scrutiny 301–302
Pre-Legislative Scrutiny 50, 301, 311, 318
Preselection 81, 85, 263
Presidency 47, 100, 146, 179, 182–183, 212, 215, 244–245, 249, 251–252, 263, 365, 313–314, 337, 351, 356, 362, 399, 415, 468, 507, 560–561, 564, 585, 587, 591, 594–595, 611–612, 700, 702, 704, 713, 731
President 2, 4, 6, 11, 13, 15, 19–24, 26–37, 41–48, 50, 53, 55–57, 68, 71–73, 92, 100–102, 122, 124–125, 140–141, 143–144, 146–148, 154–155, 157–159, 167, 169–170, 200–202, 233, 243–244, 246–248, 250, 253–254, 256, 258–259, 264–266, 268, 270–271, 273–274, 277–278, 281, 296, 309–310, 313–314, 317–318, 327, 331, 346, 353, 355, 358, 383, 391, 394–396, 398, 402–405, 407–408, 411–412, 416, 425–426, 428–431, 434, 454, 464, 466, 471–472, 499–500, 503–505, 507, 512–515, 518–521, 524, 542, 544, 546–547, 549, 552, 556–560, 586, 594–595, 596, 599, 603, 611, 622, 635, 666, 679–680, 687, 690, 695, 700–708, 710, 713, 718, 721, 730–731, 733, 737, 741–743
President of the *Assembleia da República* 393
President of the Assembly 472, 512–515, 517–521, 701
Presidential executive system 559

Presiding Officers 44, 284, 598, 602–603
Presidium 8, 43–44, 212, 258–259, 320–321, 324–326, 328, 369–370, 372–373, 377, 381, 387, 453, 524, 551, 645–646
Presidium of the Sejm 387
Press Office 48, 177, 184, 273, 275, 289, 297, 301, 304, 308, 360
Principal Officer 292–293, 295
Print Facility 300
Private Members' Bill (PMB) 192–193, 301, 529–530, 645
procedural support 81, 145, 193, 296, 600–601
Procurement Unit 299
Professional development 321, 345, 371, 482, 492, 495, 502, 516–518, 538, 748
professional Parliamentary Staff/Officials 594
Professionalization 143–145, 148, 166, 173, 210, 271, 337, 370, 404, 410, 418, 478, 501, 538, 549, 552, 554, 564, 587, 590–591, 612, 614, 618, 637, 669, 679, 687, 691
proportional representation (electoral system) 403, 413, 463, 476–477, 540, 597–598, 612, 701
Provincial Legislatures 29, 36, 61, 67, 628, 690, 694, 696–697
public administration 1, 15–16, 23–26, 28–29, 36, 40, 43, 72–73, 91, 105, 143, 163, 173, 234, 248, 253, 271–272, 276, 279, 283, 285, 287–288, 350, 353, 388, 405, 410, 438, 442–443, 468, 475, 510, 520, 523, 528, 537, 598–599, 602, 604, 606, 608–609, 614, 619, 633–634, 672, 676, 697, 702, 722, 750
public announcement 481, 502
Public Appointments Service (PAS) 293
public competition 13, 24–29, 33, 40, 248, 307, 309, 409, 468, 481–482, 501
public consultations 252–253, 397, 469
public engagement 96, 119, 292, 341, 546, 575, 578–579
public oversight 503
public Participation 430, 469, 602, 690, 694, 697
public relations 1, 8, 68, 139, 165, 168, 170, 224, 226–227, 229, 258–259, 270, 272, 274, 278, 282, 286, 288, 297, 345, 394, 430, 467, 479, 481–483, 500, 503, 525–526, 535, 539, 550, 560–561, 563, 565, 625, 630, 638, 640, 668, 745
publicity 32, 91, 173, 231, 503, 536, 538–539, 545, 610, 741

Quaestors 47, 164–165, 169, 307, 309, 561
Questions Office 295–296, 301
Questions Paper 296

Rajya Sabha 635–637, 639–643
Rannóg an Aistriúcháin 297, 301
Records Management Unit 298

recruitment 7, 13–14, 21–29, 33, 40–41, 49, 68, 71, 153, 155, 165–166, 177, 201, 210, 214, 224, 250, 253, 271, 293, 299, 307, 309, 321, 333–334, 337, 348–350, 358, 361, 370–371, 392, 394, 401–402, 407, 409, 412, 438, 454, 464, 468, 481, 489, 491, 495, 501, 505, 510, 525, 564, 576, 586–587, 636–640, 642–643, 659, 669, 683, 728–729, 742–743, 746
recruitment policy 41, 729
recruitment process 26, 28–29, 40, 293, 337, 481, 491, 501, 505, 510, 514, 669
reforming the parliamentary staff 405
Relations between EP permanent staff, political groups and MEP assistants NO
relationships 4, 8, 41–42, 70, 89, 93, 95, 119, 124, 194, 216–217, 292–293, 312, 370, 444, 572, 599, 603, 606, 626, 630, 652
remuneration 106, 177, 184, 189, 285, 349, 388, 392, 398, 417, 489, 510, 668, 691, 746
reorganization 201, 246, 263, 367–368, 372, 375, 426, 490, 549, 558, 599, 634, 683, 685, 694–696
Report Stage 301
Representatives' House 176
Republic of Cyprus 187, 190, 193–194, 198
Republic of South Africa (RSA) 67, 689, 691–698
Republican People's Party (RPP) 558
Research Analyst 358–359, 361, 363, 629
research and analytical papers 503
research department 31, 157, 224, 287, 310–312, 359, 421, 482–483, 658
research section 263, 429, 433–434, 550
research service 22, 30–31, 33–34, 64–65, 68, 80, 84–85, 94, 96, 103, 111, 115, 122–126, 129, 133–134, 144, 236–237, 256, 258, 278, 287, 293–294, 297–298, 301–302, 304–305, 311, 384, 420–421, 449, 452–453, 492, 495, 525, 563, 572, 617–618, 630–631, 665, 667, 669, 677, 690, 714–715, 717, 719–722, 728, 732, 740, 744–745, 749–750
research unit 64, 76, 81, 124, 324, 336, 339, 442, 656
Right To Information (RTI) 470, 639
Riigikogu 222–232
Rule as Code 110, 113, 116–117
Rule of Law 10, 101, 276, 419, 475, 690
Rulebook for Internal Organization 512–513, 518
Rules of Procedure 34, 43–44, 55, 59, 64, 70–71, 76, 140–141, 145, 160, 199, 210, 212, 216, 228, 234, 240–241, 244, 247, 261, 266, 277, 281–282, 284, 306–309, 311–314, 317, 320, 329, 349, 355, 368, 371, 383, 386–387, 389, 394, 397, 413–414, 416, 418–422, 424, 426, 428–429, 434, 436, 438, 440–442, 466, 468–471, 474, 478, 481, 483–484, 491, 499, 504, 508, 510, 512, 514, 518–519, 521,

Index

524, 534–535, 539–540, 549, 585, 644–646, 649–650, 660, 700, 711, 732, 737, 747, 749
Rulings of the Chair 296
Rules of Procedure of the Assembly 468–470, 474, 512, 521

Saeima 320–321, 323–329
Saeima Administration 320–21, 324
safe and secure parliament 515
Salaries Section 299
School Parliament 495
Scientific Service 47–48, 270–273, 346, 350
scrutiny 20, 31, 34, 75–77, 79, 81, 84–85, 106, 111, 116, 122, 130, 153, 157, 183, 192–193, 204, 218, 249, 255–256, 258, 263, 265, 272, 294, 297, 301–303, 311, 313–314, 321, 339, 343, 351, 361, 366, 372–375, 398, 421, 437, 503, 525, 548, 563, 567, 602, 606–607, 648, 650, 667–668, 687, 690, 740
Seanad Éireann 291, 295, 298, 305
Seanad Office 69, 295, 301
secondment 248–249, 265, 409
secretariat 8, 31, 41–43, 45–48, 63, 67, 81, 96, 115, 123, 141, 144–145, 155, 157–158, 165–166, 177, 179–183, 189, 193, 200, 212, 214–218, 222, 224, 226–227, 234–235, 237–240, 244, 246–247, 249–250, 252, 256, 258, 260–261, 263–265, 274, 281–284, 287, 289, 295–296, 298, 301–303, 310, 336, 339–340, 345–347, 350, 357, 360, 368, 372, 378, 382–383, 386, 399, 417–418, 420–422, 428–429, 436–438, 440, 447–455, 458, 466, 470–472, 477–479, 481–482, 484–485, 487–496, 503, 506, 522, 524–527, 529, 531–532, 534–535, 539, 542, 548–552, 564, 600, 616–617, 619, 636–637, 639–643, 644, 646, 651, 656–657, 659–664, 667–671, 673, 679–680, 682–685, 687, 697, 704–705, 709, 726, 728–732, 738–743
secretariats of the committees and the commission 503
Secretary General 8–9, 38, 43, 46, 53, 55, 68–69, 92, 143–1144, 155, 157, 163, 165, 167–168, 177, 179, 181, 184, 188–189, 199–200, 212, 224, 234, 237, 240, 244, 247, 256, 258, 261, 270, 273, 275, 291–293, 295, 297, 301, 308, 310, 320–321, 328, 332, 334–335, 341, 347–348, 351, 368–371, 373–374, 393, 395, 399, 404–407, 414, 417–420, 422, 425, 428–430, 432, 437, 439, 442, 447, 452, 454, 463, 468, 470–472, 487–489, 491, 500, 512–518, 520, 524, 526, 535–539, 549–551, 559, 561–563, 585–586, 615, 618–619, 636–637, 644–647, 651, 653, 656, 660–662, 664, 667–668, 670–671, 680, 682–683, 701, 704, 710, 728–729, 731, 738, 741–742, 744, 748
Secretary General of Riigikogu 224

sectoral committee 75, 77, 79–81, 83–86, 262–63, 351, 374, 420, 536, 745
Security 5, 8, 10–12, 46–47, 64, 66, 84, 95, 114, 117, 141, 143–144, 148, 155, 159, 165, 177, 182–183, 188, 201, 206–207, 214–215, 227, 234–235, 244, 247, 249, 258, 265–266, 270, 275, 281, 287–288, 294, 298, 300, 311, 313–314, 321, 328, 336, 342–343, 345–346, 357–358, 367–368, 381, 394–395, 401, 420, 432, 441, 447–449, 457–458, 466, 484, 495, 501, 513, 515, 524–526, 532, 535, 538, 542, 550, 553, 561, 566–567, 572, 575, 579, 585, 598–600, 606, 617, 620, 625, 628, 636, 641, 647–648, 658, 660, 668, 674, 680, 683–685, 705, 734–735, 742, 746
Sejm Committees' Bureau 382, 386
Sejm Library 378, 381, 386
semantic web 105, 112, 115–16
Senate 9, 30, 32, 40, 43–47, 64–65, 69, 81, 83–184, 90–92, 97, 125, 152–153, 157, 159, 199–200, 202, 205, 268, 306–313, 350, 365–368, 370–371, 373–374, 378, 381–384, 386, 388–389, 403, 407, 435–436, 438, 559, 584–587, 589–591, 597–599, 602, 604, 606–607, 611, 624–632, 678–680, 682–685, 713, 718
Senator 200, 244, 291, 308, 625, 627, 630, 714–715
Separation of power 11, 21, 115, 187–188, 193, 247–248, 253, 268, 522, 549–550, 558–559, 598, 620, 666, 678, 690, 694, 699, 727, 732
Shūgiin 656–657, 659, 661–664
Shūgiin Secretariat 656–657, 661, 663
Single Transferable Vote 355
Slovenia 44, 142, 425–426, 428–429, 431–432
Služba 534
social media 5, 12, 96, 110–112, 130, 145, 147, 159, 184, 229, 236, 239, 275, 298, 303, 325–326, 329, 360, 365, 373, 398, 400, 456, 470, 525, 531, 542, 567, 619, 670, 694, 708, 720, 735, 744
social platforms 504
socialization and mentorship 538
soft law 274, 725, 732, 744, 747
South African Legislative Sector (SALS) 67, 690
South African Parliament 696
Spain 6–7, 21–23, 28–29, 31–32, 40–41, 44, 66–67, 69–70, 435, 438, 442–443
Speaker 4, 8, 38, 41–48, 53, 55, 68–69, 94–95, 100–101, 124, 147–148, 153, 177, 179, 181–182, 188–189, 194, 212, 216–217, 222, 230, 234–235, 270, 273, 275, 281–284, 289, 291, 297, 302, 307–313, 320–321, 328, 333–34, 341, 347–348, 355–360, 362–363, 368–371, 373–374, 381–386, 388, 393–396, 398, 404–407, 417–419, 422, 436–437, 440, 442–443, 447, 450, 452–454, 458, 471–472, 477–479, 481–483, 488–489, 491, 493, 507,

534–536, 538, 540, 542, 559–561, 563–565, 567, 571–572, 575, 579, 584–586, 589, 591, 594, 618–619, 624, 626–627, 631–632, 635–637, 639, 641–642, 644–650, 652–653, 658, 660–663, 667–668, 670–671, 674, 701, 731, 734, 745–746
Speakers' Forum of South Africa (SFSA) 69, 697
Speakers' Committee 488–489, 491, 493
speaking parliament 171
Specialization 5, 123, 132, 171, 231, 250, 410, 687–688
staff Education Commission 538
staff recruitment 7, 40, 201, 392, 401, 489, 491, 495
staff resources 69, 522, 526–528, 531–532, 629
staff Service 176–77, 179–185
staff size 448
staff structure 464
staff turnover 182–83, 185, 603, 746
staffing 13–14, 41, 83, 86, 177, 179–180, 201, 204, 213, 291, 357, 388, 442, 464, 517, 571, 577, 599, 626, 680, 687, 695, 714, 716, 718–720, 745–746
standard-setting 744, 747
Standing committees 5, 21–22, 30–31, 33, 47, 95, 123, 126, 158, 167, 180, 192, 212, 217–219, 226, 258, 273, 286, 308–311, 323, 332, 336, 339–340, 356, 382, 396, 437, 466, 494, 524, 526–527, 530, 589, 614–615, 666–667, 674, 742
standing orders 48, 69, 177, 180–181, 188, 271–275, 291, 293, 295–297, 301–302, 348, 356–357, 404–405, 407, 487–488, 491, 493, 606
standing parliamentary delegations 484
state budget 32, 189, 227, 269, 273, 309, 312, 321, 387, 397–398, 403, 407, 413, 456, 464, 468, 470–471, 539, 649
State of emergency 172, 350, 353, 401, 403, 542
State subsidy 220
Statute governing parliamentary staff 40, 392
Statutory Instruments 297
Storting's (central) administration 524
Strategic Plan 2021–2023 514
strategic planning 271–272, 321, 598
Sub-Committee on Covid-19 542
Sub-Committee on the Information Society and Digitalisation 542
Superintendent's Section 300–301
supportive role 153, 158, 161
symmetric 63, 65, 477
Syntagma 268

Teachta Dála (TD) 291
technical note 396
technology 11–12, 96, 105–106, 108–116, 141, 144, 160, 182, 194–195, 224, 229, 235, 276, 292, 294, 300, 303, 308, 311, 321, 328–329, 355, 361–362, 381, 382, 394, 443, 470, 482, 492, 495–496, 512, 537, 575, 591, 600, 662, 672, 686, 691, 694, 696, 720, 744
teleconferencing 276
temporary contractual employment 182
Top-Level Appointments Committee 292
topical issue 298, 420
training 81, 98–99, 109, 112, 115, 126, 143, 146, 165–166, 177, 203, 226, 229, 234, 249, 271, 276, 285, 298–299, 337, 345, 350, 358, 370, 385, 393–394, 398, 405, 426, 428, 432, 438–439, 454, 458, 468, 473, 484, 516, 518, 525, 531, 538, 563, 566, 585, 613, 618, 639–642, 657, 668, 680, 683, 687, 693, 696, 706, 708–710, 727, 746, 748
Training and Development Unit 299
transition 7, 11, 48, 98, 115, 128, 131, 159, 251, 276, 281, 303, 309, 352, 414, 425, 435, 439, 450, 507, 591, 611, 613–614, 620, 627, 631, 654, 666, 678
transparency 5, 8–10, 12, 14, 32, 92, 97, 106, 110–111, 125, 131, 144, 159, 196, 202, 206, 215, 251, 275, 304, 326, 337, 340, 360, 362, 382, 397, 433, 443, 456, 464, 466, 469–470, 473, 479, 502–503, 507, 514, 518, 520, 536, 543, 552, 554, 566–567, 591, 630, 639, 642, 652, 664, 672, 680, 686–687, 702, 706, 708, 735, 742, 744
transparency openness 502–03, 507
Treaty of Lisbon 76, 86, 93–94, 398
trust 42, 111, 159–160, 215, 237, 342, 360, 363, 370, 393, 409, 489, 493, 495, 503, 604, 606, 630, 686, 739
Turkey 6, 8–9, 194, 275, 507, 557–60, 564–67
Turkey-EU Joint Parliamentary Committee (JPC) 566
turnover rate 491–492

understaffed 28, 328, 564, 567, 707
UNDP 97–100, 502, 538, 542
UNICEF 502, 538, 540
Unification 65, 306, 308–09, 667
United Nations 90, 95–97, 99, 128, 287, 538, 540, 661, 734, 741–742
United Nations Sustainable Development Goals (SDGs) 96, 129, 743

vacancies 177, 259, 351, 370, 406, 464, 468, 482, 491, 501, 514, 587, 669
vellums 296
vertical communication 482
videoconferencing 114
vision 47, 160, 304, 342, 606, 631, 663, 669, 709
voting applications 114
voting system 114, 164–165, 285, 339, 381, 657

Web Team 298
WebTV 399
Welfare State 308, 533
Western Balkans 134, 433, 484, 506, 542–543, 545
Westminster 29, 37, 97, 113, 124, 355–356, 363, 500, 519, 538, 571, 573–575, 577–579, 598, 624, 628, 689–690, 696, 698
WFD 113, 120, 500, 502, 519, 521, 538, 542–543, 545
Whitehall 355, 572

Women 95–96, 101, 127, 168, 173, 234, 259, 490–491, 500, 502, 512, 520, 561, 638, 680, 730, 742–743, 747, 749
Women MPs 520
Work in the public interest 415–417
Work pressure 63, 365–366, 372, 375, 696
working bodies 413, 422, 428–430, 481, 499, 501–504, 508, 512, 519–520, 534–536, 538
workplace culture 599, 606–608, 693

youth parliament 194, 196, 236, 275, 400